COMMENTARIES

UPON

INTERNATIONAL LAW.

BY

ROBERT PHILLIMORE,

ADVOCATE TO HER MAJESTY IN HER OFFICE OF ADMIRALTY,
JUDGE OF THE CINQUE PORTS.

"Wars are no massacres or confusions, but the highest trials of Right."
BACON, *Certain Observations upon a Libel, &c.*, 1592.

"Lex est . . . . . Communis Reipublicæ Sponsio."—*Dig.* l. i. t. iii. § 1.

VOL. III.

PHILADELPHIA:
T. & J. W. JOHNSON & CO.,
LAW BOOKSELLERS AND PUBLISHERS,
NO. 535 CHESTNUT STREET.
1857.

PREFACE.

THIS volume completes the system of *Public* International Law, and fills up the outline sketched out in the first volume of this work.(*a*)

I. Since the publication of the last (the second) volume, great events have happened in the history of the Community of States. Some of these are noticed in the following pages; others belong to the subjects which have been already treated of in the preceding volumes. It is proposed to draw the attention of the Reader to these events in the following imperfect sketch:—

II. *Turkey* has been formally, and in a manner to place the question beyond all doubt, admitted, by the Treaty of Paris,(*b*) into the family of States(*c*) which are bound, not only, as all States are, by the principles of PUBLIC INTERNATIONAL LAW, but by those usages and customs which constitute what may be considered the Positive Law of Christian Communities. The object of the new Treaty of Paris is to secure, "through effectual and *reciprocal guarantees, the independence and integrity of the Ottoman Empire."(*d*) This result is the subject of a [*iv]
common Guarantee.(*e*) The Plenipotentiaries declare that "the Sublime Porte is admitted to participate in the advantages of the Public Law and system (*concert*) of Europe.(*f*) This proposition must receive, as to PRIVATE INTERNATIONAL LAW, some obvious limitation from the very nature of Mohammedanism: though it be true that this religion is professed by a comparatively small number of the subjects of European Turkey; but the proposition holds good as to PUBLIC INTERNATIONAL LAW; and the fact which it affirms marks an important epoch in the History of the Progress of International Jurisprudence. For if Turkey has acquired the Rights, she has also subjected herself to the Duties of a civilized Community. How long this new condition of thing, so utterly

(*a*) The reader is referred upon this point to the concluding pages of the present volume.

(*b*) This Treaty is printed in the Appendix to this volume.

(*c*) Vide ante, Vol. I. pp. 113-17, as to the effect of the Treaty of Adrianople in 1829, and of usage upon this point.

(*d*) Preamble.

(*e*) Article vii.

(*f*) Art. vii. of the Treaty of Paris, 30 March, 1856.

at variance with the former traditions and habits of Christendom, may endure, is a speculation without the province of this work. It is to be remarked, however, even in this place, that this condition is the more complicated because the same Treaty which recognizes this quasi-Christian *status*(g) of the Turkish Empire, contains the following most singular provision, which might almost seem intended at once to recognize and to prohibit the Right of INTERVENTION by the Powers of Christendom on behalf of their co-religionists:—

"His Imperial Majesty the Sultan having, in his constant solicitude
[*v] for the welfare of his subjects, issued a *firman which, while ameliorating their condition without distinction of religion or of race, records his generous intentions towards the Christian population of his empire, and wishing to give a further proof of his sentiments in that respect, has resolved to communicate to the Contracting Parties the said firman, emanating spontaneously from his Sovereign Will.

"The Contracting Powers recognize the high value of this communication. It is clearly understood that it cannot, in any case, give to the said Powers the right to interfere, either collectively or separately, in the relations of His Majesty the Sultan with his subjects, nor in the international administration of his Empire."(h)

The *Principalities of Moldavia and Wallachia* are placed under the *Suzeraineté* of the Porte, and the *Guarantee* of the Protecting powers, but without "any *separate* right of interfering in their internal affairs."

III. Another event of great International importance, which has happened since the publication of the former parts of this work, is the recent CONCORDAT entered into between the Austrian Empire and the Pope.

It will be seen, from a comparison of this Ecclesiastical Treaty with former instruments *ejusdem generis* entered into between these two Powers, and mentioned in the last part of the preceding volume, how wide and grave a departure Austria has sanctioned, both from the traditions of her own previous policy, and from the International usages of other States. The recent Spanish CONCORDAT preserves in express language the ancient rights of the Crown.

[*vi] *IV. *The Black Sea*(k) is neutralized: its waters and its ports, thrown open to the mercantile marine of every nation, are formally and in perpetuity interdicted to the flag of war, either of the Powers possessing its coasts, or of any other Power.(l) Russia and Turkey are allowed to keep light vessels for the service of the coasts, and each of the Contracting Powers have the right to station at all times two light vessels at the mouths of the Danube.(m)

V. The opening of the great *River St. Lawrence* justifies the opinion expressed in the first volume of this work(n) respecting the expediency

(g) The Sultan has even received from the Queen of England the essentially Christian Order of the Garter.

(h) Article ix.

(k) Vol. I. p. 216.

(l) Article xi. of the Treaty of Paris, 1856.

(m) Articles xiv., xix.

(n) Vol. I. pp. 181, 182.

of allowing to the whole world the benefit of this great channel of traffic. The free navigation of the Danube, secured by the recent Treaty of Paris,(*o*) places this magnificent stream under the same Public Law of Europe to which other European rivers, flowing through the territories of different States, have been subjected by the Treaty of Vienna.(*p*) Certain provisions also with respect to the freer navigation of the *Po* have been the subject of Treaty(*q*) between Austria, Parma, and Modena.

VI. The recent Treaty with *Honduras* will, it may be hoped, cover any defects which were alleged to have existed in the *Clayton-Bulwer Treaty* with respect to a free passage over the Inter-oceanic Isthmus of America, the beneficial consequences of which to the future intercourse of States are yet to be developed by the marvels *of Electricity and Steam. A Treaty concluded at London (December 23rd, 1856,) between England and the United States, of North America, appears to settle the much vexed question relating to the territory of the *Mosquito Indians*, the *Republics* of *Nicaragua* and *Costa Rica*, and the condition of the Porte of *Greytown* or *San Juan*. By this Treaty, England and the United States of North America agree to propose certain arrangements to the Republics of Nicaragua and Costa Rica, which there can be no reasonable doubt will be accepted. [*vii]

VII. The decision of the Judge of the High Court of Admiralty and Prize upon the International *status* of *the Ionian Islands* furnishes the first recorded instance of a formal adjudication by an English Court of International Law upon a subject of this character. Indeed, the peculiarity both of the Public and of the International *status* of this Septinsular Republic(*r*) presented a case *primæ impressionis*. The judgment was not appealed from. It rests, therefore, upon the authority of the Court which delivered it.

VIII. The doctrines of GUARANTEE and INTERVENTION(*s*) have received additional recognition and confirmation from the practice of the European States.

With respect to GUARANTEE, the case of *Turkey* has been already mentioned. Moreover, the liberties of that important member of the Scandinavian Society of States, *Sweden*, were formally *guaranteed* by England and France during the recent war with Russia.

The succession to the throne of *Denmark* has also become the subject of European guarantee.

*With respect to INTERVENTION, *Greece* has afforded an instance in which this exceptional right, the offspring of necessity, has been exercised both by France and England, as it should seem (but the case is not quite clear) upon two grounds: (1.) That the sending of foreign troops to Greece was necessitated by the unneutral conduct of the Government of that country towards Russia, the enemy of France and England; (2.) and also that this course was justified by the open, notorious, and admitted insecurity of life and property to French and [*viii]

(*o*) Articles xv., xix.

(*p*) Vol. I. Part III. Ch. V.

(*q*) De Cussy and De M. Tr. t. vi. p. 293.

(*r*) Vide ante, Vol. I. p. 94.

(*s*) Vide Vol. I. Pt. IV. Ch. I.

English subjects commorant or resident in Greece. It should also be added, that Greece does not appear to have formally protested against, or seriously objected to—probably on account of the undeniable inefficiency of her own internal police—the temporary introduction of these foreign troops into her territory.

With respect to the Balance of Power in the North, the Treaty between France, England, and Sweden of the 21st of November, 1855, is *expressly* founded on the principle of preserving it.

With respect to *Naples*, it appears that remonstrance having been addressed to the King of that State, upon the injustice practised towards political offenders, upon the general mal-administration of justice in that country, and upon the danger thereby accruing to the Italian peninsula especially, and generally to the peace of Europe, and such remonstrance having been rejected by the King, that England and France have withdrawn, in order to mark their condemnation of his *internal* policy, their ambassadors from his dominions. Such a proceeding it was certainly competent to them to take, according to the principles laid down in the second volume of this work respecting ambassadors.(*t*) It furnishes, [*ix] nevertheless, the strongest *example of *passive intervention*, so to speak, in the strictly internal affairs of a Foreign State which the world has yet seen. The facts, however, relating to the whole transaction, are as yet but imperfectly and inauthentically known. It is a curious illustration of the extent to which the doctrine of *Religious Intervention*(*u*) may be carried, that, according to some reports, the Persians justified their assault upon Herat on the plea that they *intervened* to protect their co-religionists of the Semitic Faith.(*x*)

The origin and causes of the War between England and Persia have not yet been fully stated on competent authority. The War between England and China has recently undergone a full and elaborate discussion in both Houses of Parliament. The House of Lords approved, the House of Commons condemned, the war. The portions of this memorable debate which will chiefly interest the International Lawyer are those which relate to the criteria by which the *national character of a merchant vessel* is to be ascertained, and to the distinction between *Reprisals* and *War*.

The Annexation of the Kingdom of Oude to the British dominions depends for its justification upon the right application of the doctrines laid down in the first volume respecting the Rights of Acquisition(*y*) and of Intervention,(*z*) partly also on the Law of Treaties discussed in the second volume.(*a*)

[*x] *IX. The Convention (proposed 14th October, 1854, confirmed 18th of October, 1855) of Nagaski, between England and Japan, is not an unimportant extension of International relations to a part of the globe from which they have been hitherto practically excluded. By

(*t*) Vide Vol. II. p. 148.
(*u*) Vide ante, Vol. I. p. 470.
(*x*) The Times, November 8, 1856.
(*y*) Vol. I. Part III. Ch. XII.
(*z*) Vol. I. Part IV. Ch. I.
(*a*) See also remarks as to the binding character of International Law between Christian and Heathen civilized States, Vol. I. pp. 22-6.

that Convention, certain ports are open for certain purposes to British ships, and the jurisdiction of British authorities over British subjects in Japanese ports is retained: and *ships of war*, in the necessary performance of their duties, have a general right to enter all the ports of Japan; but, unless compelled by necessity, they, like the merchant ships, are confined to certain ports named in the Convention.(*b*)

X. The CONDUCT, and still more the CONCLUSION, of the recent War must always be memorable to the historian or the expounder of International Law.

In the *former* Great Britain waived,(*c*) in the *latter* she abandoned, one of the most certain and highly valued Belligerent Rights, namely, the right of confiscating enemies' goods found on board neutral vessels.(*d*)

The mode of abandoning this right was little less remarkable than the abandonment itself. The abandonment of that Right was not formally incorporated in the provisions of a treaty, but was stated in a *Declaration* accompanying the *Treaty*, with the objects of which, however, it had no natural connection.

This anomalous Declaration, whatever may be its binding effect, was signed by most of the European States, but not by the State the most interested, and—next *to Great Britain—the best acquainted with the subject—the United States of North America. On the contrary, but a few months afterwards,(*e*) this State formally declined—as it was perfectly competent to her to do—to sanction the general principle of abandoning *Privateering*,—that is, of carrying on war by the aid of the individual exertions of the Subject as well as of the Government,—unless, indeed, the same Powers would agree to a Treaty securing the free navigation of the sea to *all* merchant vessels whatsoever. [*xi]

This is not the place in which the expediency of the abandonment of this great maritime Right of the Belligerent can be fully discussed; but, it may be observed, that a defence which has been put forth, namely, that nations are defeated by fleets and armies, and not by attacks upon their commerce, does not appear either very well founded in history or well supported by reason.

It is obvious that the food and the means which procure the food of your enemy are as valuable to him, to say the least, as his weapons or his ships. It is no less obvious that wars are always shortened, and frequently ended, by the privations of the Subjects of the Belligerent. These privations of the Subjects, the inquiries which they sharpen, and the demands which they beget, are the natural correctives of the ambition and passion of Rulers.

It is, moreover, surely plain, that the Neutral who is the carrier of the commerce of the Belligerent, enables him to convert his commercial into his military marine, and greatly to increase and strengthen the latter.

Nor is it a light objection that a state of things is produced, in which

(*b*) Correspondence respecting the late negotiations with Japan, laid before Parliament, 1856.

(*c*) Vide pp. 292, 293, and Pt. IX. Ch. X. of this volume.

(*d*) Vide p. 294 of this volume.

(*e*) August, 1856.

[*xii] the Governments of States are at war *while their subjects are at peace. Lately, indeed, it has been suggested at public meetings, that the commerce of Belligerents should continue to be carried on in War as in Peace; that being the condition on which the United States of North America offer to abandon the right of *Privateering.* Let it, however, be remembered, that to redress a present injury, to take security against a future transgression, are the only legitimate causes of war: and that in such cases, "toto certatum est corpore regni." The continuance of commercial intercourse between the subjects of the offended and the offending nations is, as a matter of *Public* Law, utterly destructive of the first notion of allegiance on the part of subjects to their respective sovereigns: and as a matter of International Law, the proposition that the will of the subject is, so far as other States are concerned, bound up in the will of his government, is a proposition of the most vital importance to the due administration of International Law, and to the peace of the world. After all, the question is whether the tendency of these exemptions is not to prolong hostilities, to protract the horrors of war: are they not, in truth, devices for making war perpetual rather than real mitigations of its attendant calamities?

"If we were to go to war with the United States of North America it would not much matter, we could carry on our trade all the same," was the language of a merchant to the author when this fundamental change in the principles of Public and International Law was proposed. Such a remark bore true testimony to the fact that, by this fundamental change, one great check imposed by Providence upon the hasty beginning of this terrible scourge is removed; and the same observation applies, [*xiii] with at least equal force, to its continuance. How many *wars have been, in fact, ended by the sufferings which their duration inflicted upon the subjects of the Belligerents? or rather, who, looking back into history, can fix a probable period of termination to many wars kindled by the passions of Nations or of their Governors, if the commerce of the Belligerents had remained unaffected? or if the famous, but perhaps legendary, precedent of the two Dutch admirals—who, commanding antagonist fleets, sold powder to each other, and, most commercially, contributed to their own destruction—had been generally followed?

XI. The important International questions of the Sound Dues levied by the Crown of Denmark, have been the subject of several State Papers, and are now under the consideration of the Governments of all civilized States.(*f*)

Those who are interested in the progress of International Justice, may look with satisfaction upon the general state of feeling and usage throughout the civilized world upon the much vexed question of Foreign Enlistment.(*g*) There is no International subject perhaps in which, during the last thirty years, so decided an improvement has taken place. The

(*f*) Vol. I. pp. 201, 217.
See Papers and Report of Committee laid before Parliament on this subject in 1856.

(*g*) See this volume, p. 209, &c., and Vol. I. pp. 397, 398, Appendix, pp. 504-14.

axiom that to enlist foreign soldiers without the consent of their Governments is a grave breach of the Right of States, is now, it may be reasonably hoped, firmly incorporated into the Code of International Law.

XII. The writer of these pages is anxious to acknowledge [*xiv] *the service which he has derived from the works of his own countrymen and from those of the United States of North America in the compilation of this volume. To the works of Ward, of Manning, of Wheaton, and Story,(*h*) he is under great obligations. To various writers on the European continent, and especially to the learned Pfeiffer, his acknowledgments are also due. He also desires to draw attention to the Spanish works of Abreu and Pando, particularly of the latter, with the contents of which he became acquainted, for the first time, during the preparation of the present volume for the press. An excellent essay by Mr. Hurd, an American jurist, on "Topics of Jurisprudence connected with Conditions of Freedom and Bondage," a sketch by M. van Hogendorp, a Dutch jurist, of the Dutch School of Jurisprudence founded by Grotius, some pamphlets on Maritime International Law, by Professor Wurm of Hamburg, and a new edition of Wheaton's "Elements of International Law" by Mr. Lawrence, a new edition by M. Demangeat of the "Droit International Privé" by M. Fœlix, must be hailed as valuable recent accessions to the library of the International Jurist.

(*h*) I have acknowledged, p. 518, note (*k*), the kindness of Dr. Pratt, which has enabled me to incorporate a great part of his useful edition of "Story on Prize" into the present volume.

CONTENTS.

PART IX.

The pages referred to are those between brackets [ ].

PART X.

CHAPTER I.

CHAPTER II.

CHAPTER III.

CHAPTER IV.

PART XI.

PART XII.

LIST OF AUTHORITIES

REFERRED TO IN THIS VOLUME.

BEING ADDITIONAL TO THOSE REFERRED TO IN THE FORMER VOLUMES.

A.

Abreu y Bertodano (Joseph Antonio de), Coleccion de los Tratados de Paz, Allianza, Neutralidad, &c. (De Felix Joseph de), Tratado Juridico Politico sobre Presas de Mar, &c.
Acton's Admiralty Reports.
Acts and Papers, a Collection of, brought forward in the Years 1780-1, (London, 1801; published by Hatchard).
Admiralty Digest.
Adolphus's History of England.
Ærodius, Rerum Judicatarum Pandectae.
Afflictis (Matthaus de), Decisiones Neapolitanæ Antiquæ et Novae.
Almon's Debates in Parliament.
Armed Neutrality, Secret History of (1792); a Translation of a former inaccurate Edition of Goertz's Work.
Arrêt du Conseil d'Etat.
Atkyns's Reports.
Azuni, Droit Maritime de l'Europe.

B.

Bacon's (Lord) Certain Observations on a Libel published in 1592.
" " Essays, Of Unity in Religion.
" " " Of a Holy War.
Baldus (de Perusio), Consilia.
Barbeyrac's Translation of Puffendorf.
Beavan's Reports.
Beawes, Lex Mercatoria.
Binney's Reports (American).
Blackstone's (Henry) Reports.
Bouvier's (American) Law Dictionary.
Bowyer's Public Law.
British and Foreign State Papers.
Brooke's Abridgment.
Brown's Civil and Admiralty Law
Brown's Parliamentary Cases.
Brumleger, Diss. de Occupatione Bellica.
Buckingham's (Duke of) Memoirs of the Court and Cabinets of George III.
Bulstrode's Reports.

C.

Carthew's Reports.
Chalmer's Collection of Treaties.
Cicero, Epist. ad Familiares.
" De Republica.
" Epist. ad Atticum.
" Epist. ad Brutum.
" Epist. ad Familiares.
Clerk's Praxis.
Cocceius, De Postliminio in Pace et Amnestia. Grotius Illustratus.
Code de Commerce (par A. Sautayra).
Code des Prises (ed. 1784).
Collectanea Maritima (Robinson's).
Congress (American) Documents.
Considerations respecting the Marriage of the Duke of Montpensier with reference to the Treaty of Utrecht, &c. (London: Ridgway, 1847).
Conversations-Lexikon.
Courtenay's Life of Temple.
Cowper's Reports.
Coxe's Life of Marlborough.
Croke's (Dr.) Answer to Professor Schlegel.
Croke's Reports, (temp. Elizabeth.)
Cromwell, Histoire de (by Villemain).
Curtis's Reports (American).

D.

Deane (Dr.), Effect of War upon the Trade and Property of Neutral and Maritime Capture and Prize (London, 1854).
Debrett's State Papers.
Decius (Philip), Consilia.
Demosthenes, Phil. (320.)
De Pistoye et Duverdy. *See* Pistoye (De), &c.
Diaries and Correspondence of James Horris, first Earl of Malmesbury (London, 1844).
Digest (Admiralty).
D'Hauterive et De Cussy, Recueil des Traités et de Navigation de la France.
Dohm, Materialien für die Statistik.
Du Ponceau's Translation (American) of Bynkershoek.
Duverdy. *See* Pistoye (De.)
Dyer's Reports.

E.

Ecclesiastical and Admiralty Reports (Spinks's.)
Emérigon, Traité des Assurances.
Espinasse's Reports.

F.

Fortescue's Reports.
Foster (Sir Michael,) Discourse of High Treason.
Fox (Charles James,) Memorials and Correspondence of (edited by Lord John Russell. London, 1853.)

G.

Galiani, De' Doveri de' Principi Neutrali verso i Guerregianti, e di questi verso i Naturali.
Goertz, Mémoire sur la Neutralité armée Maritime.

Grenville (Lord,) Speech of, on the Subject of Contraband (January, 1801.) Published by Cobbett, Pall Mall.
" " Speech on the subject of Privateering (November, 1801.) Published 1802.
Grotius Illustratus. *See* Cocceius.
Guertede, Œuvres du R. de P.
Guichard, Code des Prises.

H.

Hall's Law (Americ.) Journal.
Hare's Reports.
Hautefeuille, Des Droits et des Devoirs des Nations Neutres en Temps de Guerre Maritime.
Heineccius, De Navibus ob Vecturam vetitarum Mercium Commissis.
Henning, Sammlung der Staatsschriften.
Histoire de Cromwell (by Villemaine.)
Horne's Translation of De Martens's Essai concernant les Armateurs, les Prises, et surtout les Reprises. A Gœttingue, 1795 (London, 1801.)
Hotman, Quæst. Illustr.
Hübner, De la Saisie des Bâtimens Neutres.

J.

Jefferson's Correspondence.
Journals of Congress (American.)

K.

Klint, Historia Fed. Belg.

L.

Lampredi, Del Commercio dei Popoli Neutrali in Tempo di Guerra.
Lauterbach, Colleg. Pandect.
Lawrence's Edition of Wheaton's Elements.
Lee, on Captures.
Lee Guidon.
Lehrbuch (Hugo) des Heutigen Römischen Rechts.
Lindh, Ny Lag. Samling, Första Häftet innehåltende de Trya förste Balkarne af 1734 års Lag.
Letters in the State Paper Office.
Liverpool's (Lord) Treatise on the Conduct of Great Britain respecting Neutral Nation, (written in 1758, published in 1801.)
Lucas's Reports.
Lutwyche's Reports.

M.

Mackintosh (Sir James,) Life of.
Mahon's History of England.
Manning and Ryland's Reports.
Marriott's Formulary.
——— Case of the Dutch Ships considered by.
Marshall, on Insurances. (Americ.)
" Reports.
Martens (G. F. Von,) Ueber die Erneuerung der Verträge in den Friedenschlüssen der Europäischen Mächte.
Martens (De,) Essai sur les Armateurs.
" Hist. des Armateurs (546.)
Mémoire sur la Neutralité armée Maritime, par M le Comte de Goertz, Prussian Minister of State.

Memoirs of the Court and Cabinets of George III., by the Duke of Buckingham.
Memorials and Correspondence of Charles James Fox (edited by Lord John Russell. London, 1853.)
Menochius.
Moniteur, The (French Newspaper.)
Moore's Common Pleas Reports.
Moore and Payne's Reports.

N.

Newspapers :—
The Times.
" Morning Chronicle.
" Moniteur (French).
" Remembrancer.
Noodt, De Pactis.

O.

Ordonnance de la Marine.
Ordonnances (of France).
" (of Denmark).
" (of the Hanse Towns).
" (of Holland).
" (of Sweden).
Owen's Reports.

P.

Pando (Don José Maria de) Elementos del Derecho Internacional obra póstuma.
Papers, Correspondence respecting M. Pacifico's Claims, presented to the House of Commons, Aug. 7, 1851.
" Correspondence relative to the Neutrality of Denmark, Sweden, and Norway, presented to both Houses of Parliament, 1854.
Papers, Correspondence relating to the Marriage of the Queen and Infanta of Spain (presented to Parliament, 1847).
" Protocol of Warsaw, and Correspondence relative to the Danish Succession; Return to an Address of the House of Commons, dated 18th February, 1856.
Paponius, Recueil d'Arrêts notables des Cours Souveraines de France.
Parker's Reports.
Parliamentary Papers. *See* Papers.
" History of England.
Pfeiffer, Das Recht der Kriegseroberung in Beziehung auf Staatscapitalien.
" in Wiefern sind Regierungshandlungen eines Zwischenherrschers für den rechtmässigen Regenten nach dessen Rückkehr verbindlich, 1819.
Phillimore (Dr. Joseph), Letters on the orders in Council respecting Neutrals (published in 1812).
" Reflexions on the Nature and Extent of the Licence Trade (1812).
Pistoye (De) et Duverdy, Traité des Prises Maritimes, dans lequel on a réfondu en partie le Traité du Valin, en l'appropriant à la Législation nouvelle (Paris, 1855).
Ponceau's (Du) Translation of Bynkershoek. (Americ.)
Pothier, Traité du Droit de Propriété.
Pratt's (Dr.) Story on Prize Courts.
Preussisches Landrecht.
Pritchard's Admiralty Digest.
Prize Act (British), 17 & 18 Vict. c. 18.
Prize Court and Court of Appeal Reports (Spinks's).

R.

Rastel's Entries.
Raymond's (Lord) Reports.
Recueil von Placaarten.
Recueil van Zeezaken.
Reid's Essay on the Powers of the Human Mind.
Remembrancer, The (Newspaper).
Reports. *See* List of.
Robinson's Collectanea Maritima.
Rotteck and Welcker's Staats-Lexikon.
Rousseau, Contrat Social.
Russell and Mylne's Reports.

S.

Salkeld's Reports.
Schweikart's Napoleon und die Churheissischen Capitalschuldner (Königsberg, 1833).
Search (Tucker's), Light of Nature.
Shower's Parliamentary Cases.
Skinner's Reports.
Sparks's Life of Washington.
Spinks's Ecclesiastical and Admiralty Reports.
" Prize Court and Court of Appeal Cases.
State Papers.
" (American), published by order of Congress, 1795.
Statutes at Large of the United States.
Statutes (English). *See* List of.
Steck (De), Essais sur divers Sujets de Polit.
Stewart's Reports (American).
Story's (Judge) Life and Letters.
" Commentaries on Equity.
" Jurisprudence.
" Prize Law, by Dr. Pratt.
Stypmannus, Ad jus marit. Anseat.
Sulpicius (Lord Grenville), Letters of.

T.

Tindal's History.
Titius, in Observat. ad Lauterbach, Observat. 1438.
Treaties of the United States.
Tucker's Light of Nature. (*See* Search.)

V.

Valin, Traité des Prises.
Villemain, Historie de Cromwell.

W.

Ward, Treatise on the relative Rights and Duties of Belligerent Powers.
" Enquiry into the Manner in which the different Wars in Europe have commenced during the last two Centuries, &c.
" On Contraband.
Webster's (American) Works.
Wellington (Duke of,) Despatches of.
Westphaliens, Monumenta inedita.
Wheaton, (American,) on the Right of Search.
" An Enquiry into the Validity of the British Claim to a Right of Visi-

tation and Search of American Vessels suspected to be engaged in the African Slave Trade (London, 1842.)
Wheaton On Captures.
Whitelock's Memorials.
Woodeson's Lectures.
Würm (Professor,) Die Politik der Seemächte und der Fortschritt des Völkerrechts (Hamburg, August, 1855.)

Z.

Zachariah, Ueber die Verpflichtung zur Aufrichtshaltung der Regierung des Königreichs Westphalen. (Heidelberg, 1817.)
Zouch, Admiralty Jurisdiction.
Zuarius, De Usu Maris.

LIST OF REPORTS.

ENGLISH.

A.

Acton's (Admiralty).
Atkyns's.

B.

Barnewall and Alderson's.
" and Cresswell's.
Beavan's.
Bingham's.
" (New Cases).
Blackstone's (Henry).
" (William).
Bosanquet and Puller's.
Brown's Parliamentary Cases.
Bulstrode's.
Burrows's.

C.

Campbell's.
Carthew's.
Clarke and Finnelly's.
Coke's.
Common Law and Equity.
Cowper's.
Croke's.

D.

Denison's Crown Cases.
Dodson's (Admiralty).
Douglas's.
Durnford and East's.
Dyer's.

E.

East's.
Ecclesiastical & Admiralty (Spinks's).
Edwards's (Admiralty).
Espinasse's.

F.

Fortescue's.

H.

Haggard's (Ecclesiastical).
" (Consistory).
Hare's.
Hay and Marriott's (Admiralty).

K.

Knapp's (Privy Council).

L.

Lucas's.
Lutwyche's.

M.

Manning and Ryland's.
Marshall's.
Maule and Selwyn.
Modern.
Moore's (Common Pleas).
" (Privy Council).
Moore and Payne's.

O.

Owen's.

P.

Parker's.
Prize Court and Court of Appeal Cases (Spinks's).

R.

Raymond's (Lord).
Robinson's (Admiralty).
Russel and Mylne's.

S.

Salkeld's.
Shower's Parliamentary Cases.
Skinner's.
Spinks's (Ecclesiastical and Admiralty).
" (Cases in Prize Court and Court of Appeal).

T.

Taunton's.

V.

Vesey's.
Vesey and Beame's.

AMERICAN.

B.

Bay's.
Bee's.
Binney's.

C.

Cranch's.
Curtis's.

D.

Dallas's.

G.

Gallison's.

H.

Hall's Law Journal.

J.

Johnson's.

M.

Massachusetts'.

P.

Peters's United States.

S.

Stewart's.

W.

Wheaton's.

LIST OF CASES

CITED IN THIS VOLUME.

The pages referred to are those between brackets [ ].

IN THE ENGLISH COURTS.

E.

F.

G.

M.

N.

W.

Y.

Z.

AMERICAN

A.

B.

C.

FRENCH.

ADDENDA.

The following decisions by the Judicial Committee of the Privy Council, in matters of Prize Law, were delivered after the other contents of this volume had been printed.

They are of importance, inasmuch as they may be considered as modifying in favour of the Neutral certain propositions of Prize Law formerly maintained by the English Prize Courts.

Judgment of the Judicial Committee of the Privy council on the Appeal of Sorenson v. *Our Sovereign Lady the Queen* (the Ariel,) *from the High Court of Admiralty of England (Prize,) delivered March* 21, 1857.

Present: Chancellor of the Duchy of Cornwall, Sir Edward Ryan, Sir John Patteson, the Dean of the Arches.

The first question in this case relates to the national character of the claimant, Mr. Sorenson, Jun. It was strongly contended on the part of the captors that he could not be properly considered to be a Dane. The circumstances under which he took a counting-house at Altona, with a lodging at Hamburgh, are undoubtedly peculiar; and the precise time when he went thither, and of consequence the exact length of time that he had continued there when the war between this country and Russia broke out, are not fully ascertained. Their lordships, however, looking at the general law on this subject, and particularly adverting to the case of the Conferenzrath, 6 Rob. 362, entirely agree with the learned Judge of the Admiralty, that Mr. Sorenson, Jun., has succeeded in establishing his claim to a Danish national character.

The next and important question is whether Mr. Sorenson, Jun., was the owner, and sole owner, of the ship Ariel at the time of the capture. Now this question turns upon two points—

First, was there a real bonâ fide sale absolutely to Mr. Sorenson, Jun., of the Ariel, without collusion or fraud?

Secondly, did any interest in the ship remain in the seller at the time of the capture?

[*xlvi] *The ship Ariel is one of several vessels alleged to belong to the claimant, which were seized in British ports some time after the breaking out of the war, the Ariel being seized at Belfast on her return from America with a cargo, on the 2nd of December, 1854. This case is distinguishable from the others, as to which there is not any appeal at present before their lordships, but which have been so alluded to in the argument that it is impossible wholly to exclude the mention of them. The distinction between them is in regard to the precise terms of the original sale to Mr. Sorenson, Jun., and is such that their lordships might perhaps determine this case on that distinction, without coming to any positive decision as to the general question which applies to them all. But, upon consideration, their lordships have thought it right to state their opinion upon that general question.

The facts appear to be, that the Ariel was a Russian ship, and before the breaking out of the war belonged to a Russian subject, Mr. Eckhoff, as administrator of Mr. Hagedorn, who had been for some time Consul for the Netherlands at Libau, and also a merchant and shipowner there, and died in April, 1853. Some stress was laid on this in the argument, it being contended that Mr. Eckhoff was bound to sell the Ariel for the benefit of the estate of Mr. Hagedorn, who was not a native of Russia, but had only a mercantile domicile in Russia during his life and residence there, and, having died before any contemplation of war, never was or could be, by any possible construction, an enemy of this country, nor could his property, after his death, be considered as Russian property. The doctrine of *utile tempus* for a foreigner residing in a country, between which country and another a war breaks out, to remove himself and his property from that country to his own, was supposed to apply. But that doctrine applies only to cases where there is a bonâ fide intention to remove. There is no evidence whatever of any intention on the part of Mr. Eckhoff, the administrator, to remove Mr. Hagedorn's property to the Netherlands, and the doctrine of *utile tempus* appears to be wholly inapplicable. The most that can be made of the representative character of Mr. Eckhoff is to place him in the same position as Mr. Hagedorn himself would have been had he been still alive. Now Mr. Hagedorn had unquestionably a mercantile domicile at Libau, in Russia, and, had he been living, and become the seller of the Ariel, instead of Mr. Eckhoff, he and his ship must, according to all authorities, have been considered Russian. Another of the ships seized, namely, the John, belonged to another Russian subject, Mr. Gamper; and another, the Industrie, to a Mr. Rode; and the rest of the ships belonged to Mr. Sorenson, Senior (the father of the claimant,) who had for many years been the Danish Consul at Libau, and was also a merchant and shipowner, there, and therefore clearly a Russian subject, so far as relates to these ships.

The Russian Ambassador left England on the 8th of February, 1854.

At that time the claimant was carrying, and had, for about two years, carried on, the business of an agent in England. On the 22nd [*xlvii] *of February, 1854, he was summoned to Hamburgh by his father by a telegraphic message. They met at Hamburgh, and it was then arranged that the claimant should leave England and establish himself at Altona, and become a Danish subject with a view to purchase his father's ships, and some others, and trade with them on his own account. He had not sufficient means of his own to pay for such ships, but he was told that the speculation would, probably, be very advantageous, even to the extent of 100 per cent., and arrangements were made between him and his father to enable him to carry it out, and he accordingly returned to England and disposed of his concerns there, and came to Altona to become a Danish subject. He purchased his father's vessels, and also the John, and the Industrie, and the Ariel (the ship in question.) The Ariel was sold to him by his father under a power of attorney given by Mr. Eckhoff to the father for that purpose, he (Mr. Eckhoff) being personally unacquainted with the claimant, on the 6th of March, 1854.

The British declaration of war, issued on the 29th March.

These dates seem of themselves to show that the sale was made in contemplation of war, and *imminente bello* in a popular sense; but the evidence in the case goes further, and shows conclusively that the Russian shipowners at Libau, feeling that the war was at hand, and that they could not employ their ships under the Russian flag, determined, on consultation, to sell their vessels, even at considerably reduced prices, to neutrals, rather than keep them unemployed in Russian ports. It is argued that war cannot be said to be imminent unless there be an embargo, or some similar act of the country about to be belligerent, and cases are cited in which such circumstances have occurred, but none of those cases go the length of laying down any positive rule as the necessity of such circumstances. Their lordships are of opinion that there is abundant proof that the sale was made *imminente bello*, and in contemplation of it. Still, if the sale was absolute and bonâ fide, there is no rule of international law, as laid down by the courts of this country, which makes it illegal. Such a bonâ fide sale made even *flagrante bello* would be legal, much more *imminente bello*. The ship Ariel was in port at the time of the sale, therefore the cases as to the illegality of sales *in transitu* do not apply. Was, then, the sale of this ship absolute and bonâ fide?

Assuredly the time of the sale, the circumstance of the claimant making himself a neutral for the express purpose of buying this and the other ships, and his inability to pay the whole price, all tend to throw suspicion upon the sale, and to make it incumbent on the court to look closely into the history of the transaction, it being obviously the intention of all parties to place the ship, by such sale, out of the reach of capture by the belligerent. If there had been facts leading to a well-founded conclusion that a secret understanding existed between the seller and the claimant that the ship should be restored to the seller in the event of no war breaking out, or in the event of a speedy peace, or that the ship should be employed by the claimant under the direction [*xlviii] *and for the benefit of the seller, the court would be bound to hold the sale to be collusive and void, and to condemn the ship as Russian property. But no such facts are even surmised in this case.

It appears by the evidence of Mr. Eckhoff himself (Appendix, p. 31,) that Mr. Sorenson, the father, informed him that he should advise his son to purchase the Ariel if Mr. Eckhoff did not require all the purchase money at the time of the sale and transfer, inasmuch as his son would not have sufficient money to pay for all the vessels he intended offering him for sale, and that he therefore intended to sell his ships to his son, to accept a portion of the purchase money at the time of sale, and to allow his son to pay him the remainder of the purchase money out of the earnings of the vessels.

Mr. Eckhoff, goes on to say, that by reason of what Mr. Sorenson, the father, had so communicated to him, he agreed to sell the Ariel to the claimant under the following stipulation or condition, namely, that the amount of the purchase money should be, 10,000 silver roubles, that 3,333 silver roubles and 33 copecks, or say one-third of the purchase money, should be paid in cash at the time of effecting the sale or transfer of the Ariel: that a similar sum or instalment of one-third of the purchase money should be paid in six months after the sale and transfer, and the remaining one-third in nine months. He adds, that had it not been for the very high character and well-known honour and integrity of Mr. Sorenson, the father, he would not have agreed to sell the Ariel to the son except for ready cash, inasmuch as he was then, and still was, personally unknown to the son.

It is argued that Mr. Eckhoff does not in terms deny that he agreed to be paid the remaining two-thirds of the purchase money out of the earnings of the Ariel, and therefore it must be inferred that he did so agree, and accepted the same terms as the father did on the sale of his vessels. Their lordships are of opinion that the drawing such an inference would be putting an unfair construction on Mr. Eckhoff's affidavit, especially as it is plain that he looked to Mr. Sorenson (the father) to carry him through the transaction, and being personally unknown to the son (the claimant) would be very unlikely to enter into any engagement with him as to the earnings of the ship. Afterwards, indeed, when upon the death of Mr. Sorenson, the father, in May, 1854, Mr. Eckhoff became somewhat anxious about the price of the ship, he did by his agent procure the claimant's acceptances, falling due at six and nine months from the sale and transfer of the Ariel, and a promise from the claimant that the earnings of the Ariel should be applied to the liquidation of those acceptances, being the best security he could get. It appears that they were so applied, and that a small sum, only about 90*l.*, remained due when the Ariel was seized in December, 1854. This subsequent arrangement is the circumstance above alluded to, in which this case is perhaps distinguishable from the cases of the other ships, as to which the appropriation of the earnings formed part of the original contract.

It was urged further, that the bill of sale of the Ariel is untrue, [*xlix] *because it states the whole purchase money to be paid. Their lordships are of opinion that there is no weight in this objection. In all conveyances of freehold or leasehold estates the purchase money is always mentioned to have been fully paid, and yet there may be a collateral instrument, showing that nothing has been paid, or the whole or part of the money left upon mortgage of the estate. A bill of sale of a ship is a conveyance of a similar nature, and open to the same considerations; the object is to enable the purchaser to become the absolute owner.

After the sale and transfer of the Ariel, it appears to have been employed under the sole control of the claimant, without any interference on the part of the seller (Mr. Eckhoff,) in voyages to England and Ireland and America, with a crew composed indeed of Russians, except the master and mate, who were Danes, but not with Russian cargoes. Under these circumstances the learned judge in the court below says:—"I am inclined to hold the present sale (speaking of that of the Baltica, one of the father's ships) was bonâ fide." By which their lordships understand him to mean that the sale was real, intended to pass the property in the ship to the claimant, without any engagement to restore it under any circumstance, and without fraud or collusion.

In this opinion their lordships fully concur.

But, then, the second point above stated remains. Did any interest in the ship remain in the seller at the time of capture? And this is a point more difficult of solution. The decision of the learned judge that some interest did remain in the seller rests almost entirely on the language used by Lord Stowell in the case of the Sechs Geschwistern, 4 Rob. 100, for with the exception of that one all the other cases proceed on the ground of *mala fides* and collusion.

Lord Stowell there says:—

"The rule which this country has been content to apply is, that property so transferred (this is, by purchase from an enemy) must be bonâ fide and absolutely transferred; that there must be a sale divesting the enemy of all further interest in it; and that anything tending to continue his interest vitiates a contract of this description altogether.

Applying that rule to the case then before him, Lord Stowell condemned the ship, and rightly so; because there were covenants in that case which preserved and retained the interest of the enemy-seller, and for restitution at the end of the war. It was a conditional, not an absolute sale. Lord Stowell concludes his judgment in these words: "Is there in this any sign of a bonâ fide transfer? Is not the hand of the French vendor still on the vessel? Looking to the control which the French Government and the vendor still retain over this property, it is impossible for me to hold that all the interest of the enemy is completely divested." In the present case there is a total absence of any such covenant or condition. The utmost that can be said is, that there is an engagement on the part of the buyer to apply the earnings of the ship to the payment of part of the price.

*The mere non-payment of a part of the price cannot of itself be sufficient to leave an interest in the ship in the seller. That [*1] is distinctly stated by Lord Stowell in the Marianna, 6 Rob. 26.

"That objection can have little weight, since it is a matter solely for the consideration of the person who sells to judge what mode of payment he will adopt. He may consent to take a bill of exchange, or he may rely on the promissory note of the purchaser, which may come in payment for a considerable time, or may never be paid. The court will not look to such contingencies. It will be sufficient that a legal transfer has been made, and that the mode of payment, whatever it is, has been accepted."

Here, however, there is more than mere non-payment of part of the price; there is an engagement to pay it out of the earnings, and that is contended to create an interest in and lien on the freight, and, through the freight, on the ship.

We must observe here that even supposing that the facts of this case were sufficient to show that the vendor had a lien on the freight for the purchase-money unpaid, it by no means follows that he had a lien on the ship. The ship and the freight are quite distinct—the ship may belong to one person and the freight to another; and that not only for a single voyage, but, as a security for a debt, for future voyages, provided that the contract and assignment be not such as to seperate the freight and earnings of the ship for ever from the ship itself so that they could not be re-united, but only to separate them for the temporary purpose of securing a debt, and operating only upon that separation of title till that debt should be paid. The law on this subject was distinctly laid down, as stated above, by Lord Eldon, in the case of the ship Warre, which is to be found in the notes to 8 Price, 269. The same doctrine was held in 3 Beavan, 342, Stevenson v. Dowson; in 1 Hare, 549, Langton v. Horton; in 1 Bingh. New Rep. 697, Leslie and others v. Guthrie; and in other cases.

There are no means by which, according to the contract with respect to the earnings stated in this case, the ship could in any manner be affected, either in the Admiralty, the Courts of Common Law, or the Court of Chancery. It may be doubtful, considering the loose terms of the contract, and that it was made between foreigners, whether the Court of Chancery would interfere by appointing a receiver of the freight, if the ship arrived in England and the owner had not applied the earnings towards payment of the purchase-money. But, as between English subjects, if the court interfered, it would not be in pursuance of the contract, but by reason of breach of contract. It was said in argument that by the law, either of Russia or Denmark, some lien might be created on the ship, but that is a matter of foreign law, and therefore a fact to be proved by those who rely upon it, and no proof was offered. The difficulty, or rather the impossibility, of obtaining a satisfactory result by such inquiries appears to have been one of the reasons why Lord Stowell, in the case of the Tobago, to which we are about to allude more at length, refused to enter into them at all.

[*li] *Supposing, however, that a lien on the freight, or even on the ship, in favour of the vendor, who is to be considered as an enemy, did exist, would that lien render the ship in the possession of the neutral owner liable to be captured? That such a lien on an enemy's ship would not be sufficient to found a claim by a neutral in a Court of Prize is clear. It was so held by Lord Stowell in the case of the Tobago, 5 Rob. 218, which was the case of a British subject claiming in respect of a bottomry bond on a French enemy's ship which had been captured, and again in the case of the Marianna, 6 Rob. 24. That was the case of a lien on the freight and cargo of a ship, which was sold by an American

neutral to a Spanish enemy, and the lien was in respect of part of the purchase money remaining unpaid. It is true that in 1 Spinks's Admiralty Cases, 24, the Christine, the court said that the doctrine in the Marianna did not apply to cases when the bona fides of the sale was disputed, in which proof of actual payment is always essential; and no doubt that upon a question of bona fides such proof would be most important, and even essential. But the question of bona fides, in this case, has been already disposed of; their lordships are now considering the only point as to an interest remaining in the bonâ fide seller. The same doctrine as in the Tobago and the Marianna is laid down by the Supreme Court of the United States of America, in the Frances (Irvin's claim,) 8 Cranch's Rep. 417, and in San José, 2 Gallison's Rep. 283; and other cases.

Indeed, it was not disputed at the bar that such is the law of prize as regards a claimant in respect of a lien. But the converse of the proposition was contended not to be true, and that although the lien of a neutral on an enemy's ship or its freight is not sufficient to found a claim, yet the lien of an enemy on a neutral ship or its freight is sufficient to show an interest in the enemy, of which the belligerent captor is entitled to avail himself, and to defeat the neutral's claim; that a lien on an enemy's ship which would not be recognized in favour of a neutral, would be recognized against a neutral for the purpose of condemnation, if the lien be in favour of an enemy. Their lordships asked, and asked in vain, for some authority which went to establish that distinction. No such authority was produced, but their lordships were referred again to the language of Lord Stowell, in the case of the Sechs Geschwistern, which, as has been already observed, was a question as to the right of property, not of lien. Their lordships have been unable to find any authority for the alleged distinction, and, on the contrary, they are of opinion that the cases of the Tobago and of the Frances (Irvin's claim,) already cited, are plainly against the distinction. In the Tobago, the counsel for the captors argued: "Suppose a bond of this nature given upon a neutral ship, and to a person now become an enemy, could a proceeding of prize be instituted against the neutral ship, or any part of it, as the property of the enemy? Certainly not." The counsel for the claimants argued, "With regard to the case put of an enemy's interest of this description on a neutral ship, the distinction is obvious, that this interest is a thing *accessorial only to the ship; and that it might well consist with the principles of justice, that the accessory [*lii] might be restored though the ship was condemned, at the same time that it would not be reasonable or just to seize the ship itself on account of such an accessorial interest which an enemy might possess in it." Lord Stowell, in giving judgment, says: "Can the court recognize bonds of this kind as titles of property, so as to give persons a right to stand in judgment and demand restitution of such interests in a Court of Prize? The total silence of those who had argued for the claimant as to any precedents for this demand, strongly shows that it has not been the practice of the court to consider such bonds as property entitled to its protection, and I think I may venture to say that there has been no such instance.

The person advancing money on bonds of this nature acquires by that act no property in the vessel; he acquires the *jus ad rem*, but not the *jus in re*, until it has been converted and appropriated by the final process of a court of justice. The property of the vessel continues in the former proprietor, who has given a right of action against it, but nothing more. If there is no change of property, there can be no change of national character." And further, "The captor has no access whatever to the original private understanding of the parties in forming such contracts; and it is therefore unfit that he should be affected by them. His rights of capture act upon the property without regard to secret liens possessed by third parties; *in like manner his rights operate on no such liens where the property itself is protected from capture.* Indeed, it would be almost impossible for the captor to discover such liens in the possession of the enemy upon property belonging to a neutral; the consequence, therefore, of allowing generally the privilege here claimed would be that the captor would be subject to the disadvantage of having neutral liens set up to defeat his claims upon hostile property, *whilst he could never entitle himself to any advantge from hostile liens upon neutral property.*" It is difficult to conceive stronger language than this to show that the distinction now attempted to be set up is wholly without foundation. The observations of the same learned judge in the Marianna are substantially to the same effect. Both these cases, it is to be observed, were decided subsequently to that of the Sechs Geschwistern. The language of the court in the Frances (Irvin's claim,) 8 Cranch's Rep. 419, is equally strong: "In cases of liens created by the mere private contract of individuals depending upon the different laws of different countries, the difficulties which an examination of such claims would impose upon the captors, and even upon the Prize Courts, in deciding upon them, and the door which such a doctrine would open to collusion between the enemy, owners of the property, and neutral claimants, have excluded such cases from the consideration of those courts." Then, after referring to the cases of the Tobago and the Marianna, it is added, "From this it appears that the doctrine of the Prize Courts upon this subject works against, as well as in favour of, captors." Their lordships have [*liii] come to the conclusion that the supposed distinction does not exist, *and that liens, whether in favour of a neutral on an enemy's ship, or in favour of an enemy on a neutral ship, are equally to be disregarded in a Court of Prize.

One other argument was pressed, arising from the number of vessels bought by the claimant, and the magnitude of the transaction was insisted on; and the case of the Rendsberg, 4 Rob, 121., was particularly adverted to. That case was such, that Lord Stowell held it to amount to an adhering to and assisting the enemy, and it was of a very peculiar character. Their lordships are unable to see why, if the transfer of one ship was legal, under the circumstances which have here occurred, if it had stood alone, such transfer should be rendered illegal because six other ships were purchased, under similar circumstances, at the same time; unless, indeed, as affording ground to believe that all the purchases were fraudulent and collusive.

In effect, the whole case resolves itself into a question of bona fides, and that being once established, their lordships feel obliged to come to the conclusion that the Ariel was the bonâ fide property of the claimant alone, and that no interest remained in the seller, Mr. Eckhoff.

They must, therefore, humbly advise her majesty that the decision of the court below ought to be reversed, and the proceeds of the ship restored to the claimant; however, without costs and damages, not only because further proof was ordered and gone into, but also on account of the particular circumstances of the case.

Judgment of the Judicial Committee of the Privy Council on the Appeals of Cremidi v. *Powell and Dyke (Cargo ex "Gerasimo"), and likewise Cremidi* v. *Parker and Dyke (Cargo ex "Aspasia"), and of Cremidi* v. *Parker and Dyke (Ship "Achilles"), from the High Court of Admiralty of England (Prize,) delivered March* 24, 1857.

Present: Chancellor of the Duchy of Cornwall, Sir Edward Ryan, Sir John Patteson, the Dean of the Arches.

This is an appeal from a decree of the High Court of Admiralty dated 8th August, 1856, condemning the cargo of the ship Gerasimo as lawful prize.

At the time of her capture this ship was bound to Trieste with a cargo of Indian corn, which she had taken on board at Galatz. She was sailing under Wallachian colours, and on the 19th July, 1854, during the prosecution of her voyage was captured as she was coming out of the Sulina mouth of the Danube, by her majesty's ship Vesuvius, under the command of Captain Powell.

*It was the duty of the captors, as soon as possible, to send their prize to some convenient port in her majesty's dominions for adjudication, to procure the examination in preparatory of the principal officers of the vessel, and to deposit in the Admiralty Court, upon oath, all papers found on board the vessel, in order that speedy justice might be done, and that the property, if illegally seized, might be restored, with as little delay as possible, to the owners. [*liv]

None of these steps were taken; the vessel and her cargo were sent to Constantinople, and detained there, together with the crew, till (after a delay, as to the cargo, of nearly three months, and as to the ship, of nearly eight months,) the vessel was released upon security, and the cargo sold at Constantinople.

The captors appear after this to have taken no steps whatever in the matter until they were stimulated to action by the claimants of the cargo.

On the 21st June, 1855, a claim was brought into the Admiralty Court by M. Cremidi, in which he claimed the cargo on behalf of Epaminondas Pana and Co., who are merchants at Galatz, and on their behalf demanded restitution with costs and damages, and at the same time he sued out a monition requiring the captors to proceed to adjudication.

The captors proceeded accordingly, and on the 14th November, 1855, the case was heard upon the claim.

There was an absence of the usual evidence in such cases; there was no examination of the witnesses in preparatory; no affidavit verifying the ship's papers made *recente facto*, but an affidavit sworn by Captain Powell, on the 30th August, 1855, more than twelve months after the seizure, verifying certain papers as being all the papers which were found on board the vessel, and none of which related to the cargo.

The captors, however, produced an affidavit by a gentleman of the name of Young, who stated that he was the agent in England of the captors, and that he had received a letter from Captain Powell, dated in the month of May, 1855, informing him that the cargoes of this and other ships sent to Constantinople had been sold at that place, with the consent of the owners thereof, and the proceeds deposited in the hands of an agent.

There was also a certificate by Mr. Nicholson, who had been sent out (under what circumstances it does not appear) as a Commissioner appointed by the Court of Admiralty to take evidence on the subject at Constantinople, and Mr. Nicholson thereby certified that he had been informed that the master and the whole of the crew of the Gerasimo had long since quitted her, and could not anywhere be found.

The only evidence of property on the part of the claimant was the affidavit of Cremidi, who stated his belief that E. Pana and Co., subjects of the Ionian Islands, were the owners, and that no enemy had any interest in it.

Neither the affidavit nor the claim stated anything as to the place of residence of E. Pana and Co.

[*lv] *The learned judge, therefore, made an order, dated November 14, 1855, by which he admitted the claim of Cremidi for the cargo, but directed further proof to be given by the claimant as to the property thereof, and also allowed both parties to bring in further proof as to the non-examination of witnesses in preparatory, and as to whether there was any agreement as to the sale of the cargo, such further proof to be given without prejudice to the question of costs and damages.

The cause was heard on further proof in July and August, 1856, when the learned judge was of opinion that the claimant was to be considered as an enemy of the British Crown at the time of the seizure, and that he had, therefore, no *persona standi* in the court. The grounds of the decision are thus stated in the report of the judgment printed at the end of the respondent's case. After referring to two documents brought in by the claimant upon further proof, the learned judge expresses himself in these terms:—

"It appears, therefore, that the claimant was a merchant, resident at Galatz at the time of the shipment, and that, being so, the next question is, what national character the law impresses upon him. Galatz is in Moldavia; Moldavia was in possession of the Russians; and, so long as any territory is in possession of the enemy, I apprehend that the law declares that all the inhabitants thereof, and all the persons resident therein and carrying on trade, are to be considered as enemies with respect to that trade. The claimant is erroneously described as an Ionian subject, he being resident at Galatz, and undoubtedly he is not entitled to that character for the purposes of trade. Had the truth been stated in the first instance, I should have disposed of the case at once."

Upon this ground the learned judge felt himself under the necessity of condemning the cargo, but he added, "that he should have experienced very great difficulty in coming to the conclusion that the claimant had proved his property in the cargo claimed, even if he was entitled to any *persona standi* in the court."

Upon the present appeal the first question is, whether the appellant, in regard to this claim, is to be considered as an alien enemy; and for this purpose it will be necessary to examine carefully both the principles of law which are to govern the case, and the nature of the possession which the Russians held of Moldavia at the time of this shipment.

Upon the general principles of law applicable to this subject there can be no dispute. The national character of a trader is to be decided for the purposes of the trade by the national character of the place in which it is carried on. If a war breaks out, a foreign merchant carrying on trade in a belligerent country has a reasonabe time allowed him for transferring himself and his property to another country. If he does not avail himself of the opportunity, he is to be treated, for the purposes of the trade, as a subject of the Power under whose dominion he carries it on, and, of course, as an enemy of those with whom that Power is at war. Nothing can be more just than this principle; but *the whole foundation of it is, that the country in which the merchant trades is enemy's [*lvi] country.

Now the question is, what are the circumstances necessary to convert friendly or neutral territory into enemy's territory. For this purpose, is it sufficient that the territory in question should be occupied by a hostile force, and subjected, during its occupation, to the control of the hostile Power, so far as such Power may think fit to exercise control; or, is it necessary that, either by cession or conquest, or some other means, it should, either permanently or temporarily, be incorporated with, and form part of, the dominions of the invader at the time when the question of national character arises?

It appears to their lordships that the first proposition cannot be maintained. It is impossible for any judge, however able and learned, to have always present to his mind all the nice distinctions by which general rules are restricted; and their lordships are inclined to think that, if the authorities which were cited and so ably commented upon at this bar had been laid before Dr. Lushington, he would, perhaps, have qualified in some degree the doctrine attributed to him in the report to which we have referred.

With respect to the meaning of the term "dominions of the enemy," and what is necessary to constitute dominion, Lord Stowell has in several cases expressed his opinion. In the case of The Fama, 5 Rob. 114, he lays it down that in order to complete the right of property, there must be both right to the thing and possession of it; both *jus ad rem*, and *jus in re*. "This," he observes, "is the general law of property, and applies, I conceive, no less to the right of territory than to other rights. Even in newly discovered countries when a title is meant to be established for the first time, some act of possession is usually done, and proclaimed as a notification of the fact. In transfer, surely, when the former rights of others are to be superseded and extinguished, it cannot be less necessary that such a change should be indicated by some public acts, that all who are deeply interested in the event as the inhabitants of such settlements may be informed under whose dominion and under what law they are to live."

The importance of this doctrine will appear when the facts with respect to the occupation of the Principalities come to be examined.

That the national character of a place is not changed by the mere circumstance that it is in the possession and under the control of a hostile force, is a principle held to be of such importance that it was acted upon by the Lords of Appeal in 1808, in the St. Domingo cases of The Dart and Happy Couple, when the rule operated with extreme hardship.

In the case of The Manilla (1 Edw. 3), Lord Stowell gives the following account of those decisions :—

"Several parts of the island had been in the actual possession of insurgent negroes, who had detached them, as far as actual occupancy could do, from the mother country of France and its authority, and maintained within those parts, at least, an independent government of [*lvii] *their own. And although this new power had not been directly and formally recognized by any express treaty, the British Government had shown a favourable disposition towards it on the ground of its common opposition to France, and seemed to tolerate an intercourse that carried with it a pacific and even friendly complexion. It was contended therefore that St. Domingo could not be considered as a colony of the enemy. The Court of Appeal, however, decided, though after long deliberation, and with much expressed reluctance, that nothing had been declared or done by the British Government that could authorize a British tribunal to consider this island generally, or part of it (notwithstanding a power hostile to France, had established itself within it to that degree of force, and with that kind of allowance from some other States) as being other than still a colony, or part of a colony of the enemy. There can be no doubt that the strict principle of that decision was correct."

On the other hand, when places in a friendly country have been seized by and are in possession of the enemy, the same doctrine has been held.

While Spain was in the occupation of France, and at war with Great Britain, the Spanish insurrection broke out, and the British Government issued a proclamation that all hostilities against Spain should immediately cease. Great part of Spain, however, was still occupied by the French troops, and, amongst other, the port of St. Andero.

A ship called the Santa Anna was captured on a voyage, as it was alleged, to St. Andero, and Lord Stowell observed :—

"Under these public declarations of the State, establishing this general peace and amity, I do not know that it would be in the power of the court to condemn Spanish property, though belonging to persons resident in those parts of Spain which are at the present moment under French control, except under circumstances which would justify the confiscation of neutral property."

The same principle has been acted upon in the Courts of Common Law.

In the case of Donaldson v. Thompson, 1 Campb. N. P. R. 429, the Russian troops were in possession of Corfu and the other Ionian Islands, though the form of a Republic was preserved, and it was contended that the islands must be considered as substantially part of the territory of the Russian Empire if the Russian power was there dominant, and the supreme authority was in the Russian Commander; or, if not, that the Republic must be considered as a co-belligerent with Russia against the Porte, since the Emperor of Russia derived the same advantages, in a military point of view, from this occupation of the islands as if he had seized it hostilely, or the Ionion Republic had been his ally in the war he was carrying on.

Both these propositions, however, were repudiated by Lord Ellenborough, and afterwards, on a motion to set aside the verdict, by the Court of King's Bench, Lord Ellenborough observing, "Will any one contend that a Government which is obliged to yield in any quarter to *superior force, becomes a co-belligerent with the power to which it yields? It may as well be contended that neutral and belligerent mean the same thing." [*lviii]

The same doctrine was afterwards laid down by the Court of King's Bench, in the case of Hagedorn v. Bell, 1 Maule & Sel. 450, in the case of a trade carried on with Hambugh, which had been for several years, and at the time was, in the military occupation of the French.

The distinction between hostile occupation and possession clothed with a legal right by cession or conquest, or confirmed by length of time, is recognised by Lord Stowell in the case of The Boletta, 1 Edw. 171.

A question there arose whether certain property belonging to merchants at Zante which had been captured by a British privateer, was to be considered as French or as Russian; that question depending upon the national character of Zante at the time of the capture.

Lord Stowell observes:—

"On the part of the crown it has been contended, that the possession taken by the French was of a forcible and temporary nature, and that such a possession does not change the national character of the country until it is confirmed by a formal cession or by a long lapse of time. That may be true, when possession has been taken by force of arms and by violence; but this is not an occupation of that nature. France and Russia had settled their differences by the peace of Tilsit, and the two countries being at peace with each other, it must be understood to have been a voluntary surrender of the territory on the part of Russia."

On this ground he held the territory to have become French territory, remarking, in a subsequent passage of his judgment, "that this was a cession by treaty, and not a hostile occupation by force of arms, liable to be lost the next day."

These authorities, with the other cases cited at the bar, seem to establish the proposition that the mere possession of a territory by an enemy's force does not of itself necessarily convert the territory so occupied into hostile territory, or its inhabitants into enemies.

It is necessary now to inquire, what was the nature of the possession of Moldavia held by the Russians, at the time when the shipment in question was made?

The political position of the Provinces of Moldavia and Wallachia is very anomalous. They are classed by Wheaton, in his "Elements of International Law," 6th Ed. 48, amongst semi-sovereign States. By the Convention of Ackermann in 1826 between Russia and Turkey, it was provided that the government of those Provinces should be administered by Hospodars chosen from amongst the native Boyars, and they were to enjoy their authority for the term of seven years. By the Treaty of Adrianople between the same Powers in 1829, and by a separate act annexed to that Treaty with respect to the provinces of Moldavia and Wallachia, it was provided that the Hospodars, instead of being elected for a term of seven years only, should in future hold *their dignities for life, and that they should freely administer the internal affairs of those Provinces in concert with their respective Divans. It was further provided that they should pay a fixed tribute to the Porte in lieu of certain charges to which they were previously subject, and be free from all other exactions. The inhabitants were to enjoy full liberty of commerce for the productions of their soil and their industry, without any restriction, except such as the Hospodars, in concert with their respective divans, should establish. They were to be at liberty freely to navigate the Danube with their own vessels, furnished with passports by their Government: and it was provided that the Pruth, which bounds one side of Moldavia, should continue to be the limit of the two empires of Russia and Turkey.

[*lix]

This independent administration was enjoyed by the two provinces at the time when the differences arose between Russia and Turkey in the year 1853. Their government was administered by the Hospodar of each province, with the assistance of a council: they had a national flag, and a Charge d'Affaires resident at Constantinople.

The Sultan having refused compliance with demands made upon him by Russia, the emperor gave orders that his troops should enter the Danubian Principalities, and on the 26th June, 1853, he issued a manifesto, declaring, in the following terms, the grounds upon which, and the purposes for which, this step was taken:—

"Having exhausted all the means of persuasion, and all the means of obtaining in a friendly manner the satisfaction due to our just reclamations, we have deemed it indispensable to order our troops to enter the Danubian Principalities, to show the Porte how far its obstinacy may lead it. Nevertheless, even now it is not our intention to commence war. By the occupation of the Principalities we wish to have in our hands a pledge which will guarantee to us in every respect the re-establishment of our rights.

"We do not seek conquests. Russia does not need them. We demand satisfaction for a legitimate right openly infringed."

On the 2nd and 3rd days of July, 1853, the Russian troops, under Prince Gortchakoff, crossed the Pruth and entered Moldavia; and upon that occasion the prince issued a proclamation to the inhabitants of Moldavia and Wallachia, in which he declared—

"We come amongst you neither with projects of conquest, nor with the intention of modifying the institutions under which you live, or the political position which solemn treaties have guaranteed to you."

The proclamation then stated that the occupation was only provisional, and that on the day on which the emperor should obtain the reparation due to him, and guarantees for the future, the Russian troops should return within the frontiers of Russia; and it concluded with exhorting the inhabitants to engage with security in their agricultural labours and commercial speculations, and to be obedient to the laws under which they lived, and to the established authorities.

The Russian Government informed the Hospodars that their relations with the Porte must be broken off, and that all action on the part of *the sovereign power must for a time cease; that the fixed tribute which they were accustomed to pay to the Porte must be stopped. [*lx] But the Hospodars were not removed from office; they continued, with the assistance of the adminstrative council, to conduct the affairs of the government, and the Wallachian flag continued to be used. When war afterwards was declared between Russia and Turkey, the two Hospodars were recalled by the Porte, and directed to leave the government in the hands of a provisional council of boyars. A Russian commissary was appointed to conduct the government in their stead, but nothing was said or done by the Russian Government to change the nature of the occupation, or to indicate any intention of converting into a conquest what had been originally announced as a provisional and temporary measure. On the contrary, when General Budberg was appointed commissary, the Russian Government avoided giving him the title of governor, as being one which was calculated to give rise to misapprehension as to the emperor's intentions, which remained those of not incorporating the provinces.—(Sir G. H. Seymour to Lord Clarendon, Nov. 5, 1853.)

The occupation, however, such as it was, led to a declaration of war by the Porte, in October, 1853, and, in that war, England and France engaged as allies of the sultan in the following spring. Austria and Prussia, though not actively engaged as belligerents, were not less opposed to the occupation of the Principalities, and negotiations were entered into by both those powers with Russia, for the purpose of securing the immediate evacuation of the provinces by the Russian troops.

The Russian Minister, in his answer to the demands of Austria on the $\frac{17}{29}$th June, 1854, stated that from the moment when the Porte declared war against Russia, the occupation of the Principalities, whatever might have been its original character, had been for Russia only a military position, the maintenance or abandonment of which was entirely a matter connected with strategical considerations. The answer then contained the following passage:—

"Our august Master still wishes, as he has always wished, peace. He has no desire—we have repeated it, and we repeat it once more—either to prolong indefinitely the occupation of the Principalities, or to establish himself there in a permanent manner, or to incorporate them with his dominions, still less to overthrow the Ottoman Government."

On the 8th August, 1854, Prince Gortchakoff announced that the Emperor of Russia had ordered the complete evacuation of the two Principalities, and soon afterwards the Russian troops retired across the Pruth.

It seems impossible to hold that, by means of an occupation so taken, so continued, and so terminated, Moldavia ever became part of the dominions of Russia, and its inhabitants subjects of Russia, and therefore enemies of those with whom Russia was at war? The utmost to which the occupation could be held to amount was a temporary suspension of the suzeraineté of the Porte, and a temporary assumption of that [*lxi] *suzeraineté by Russia; but the national character of the country remained unaltered, and any intention to alter it was disclaimed by Russia. At what period, then, could foreigners dwelling there be said to have that notice of a change in the dominion and in the laws under which they were to live, to which Lord Stowell refers in the case of the Fama? At what period were they under the obligation of changing their domicile in it, under the penalty, if they omitted to do so, of being treated as enemies of Great Britain?

Moldavia and Wallachia were not treated by the Porte as enemies, and it would be singular if these countries, though not held to be enemies, by Turkey, should be held to be enemies of the allies of Turkey. That the Wallachian flag was recognised, both by the Russian and Turkish authorities, sufficiently appears from the documents before the court; and their lordships have ascertained, by communication with the Foreign Office, the other facts above stated; and, further, that no act was ever done by the British Government to change the national character of the provinces in relation to Great Britain; and without some such act the occupation by the Russians, under the circumstances stated, could not produce such an effect.

Being of opinion, therefore, that the claimant has a *persona standi* in the court, we have now to consider the effect of the evidence upon further proof.

The only evidence offered, on further proof, by the claimant (if, indeed, it is to be treated as evidence,) consisted of the production of two documents; a bill of lading, and an account, to both of which Dr. Lushington refers in his judgment, as showing that the claimant of the property is to be considered as a Moldavian, for the purposes of this case.

The bill of lading is not verified by any affidavit: it purports to bear date at Galatz, on the 30th June, 1854, and to be signed by Caralambo S. Pana, the master of the Wallachian brig Gerasimo, and to acknowledge the shipment at Galatz, by Messrs. Epaminondas Pana and Co., for account and risk of whomsoever it may concern, of 838 chilos of maize of Moldavia, of good quality, dry, sifted, and in good condition, consigned, at Trieste or Venice, to the order of Signor Antonio de Ralli.

The account is what is termed a *pro forma* account, and purports to be signed by Ralli, at Trieste. His signature is attested by two witnesses, and the signature both of Ralli and the witnesses is attested by a Notary Public, whose official character of a Notary, and whose signature, are attested by the British Vice-Consul at Trieste.

This document is headed :—

"Messrs. Pana and Co., Galatz.

"*Pro forma* account of cargo of Indian corn, on board the Wallachian brig Gerasimo, Pana."

It purports to state, in the first place, what would have been the *gross proceeds of the cargo at Trieste on the 20th November, 1854; and it then contains an account of the charges which would have attended the sale, including commission. [*lxii]

It seems, therefore, that this account was made out as between Pana and Co., as the shippers, and Ralli as consignee and agent for the sale.

Though these documents were produced only on the further proof, the account of Ralli had been made out long before, with a view, probably, to the proceedings then in contemplation; for it appears to have been made on the 17th April, 1855, and signed and witnessed before the Notary on the 19th of that month. This was before any question of property had been raised, and it therefore does not, except incidentally, show the right of property.

On the part of the captors, evidence was produced as to the other two points, viz., the omission to examine witnesses in preparatory, and the sale.

The material evidence upon both these points is given in the affidavit of M. La Fontaine, made at Constantinople on the 16th February, 1856, in which he says that, since 20th August, he has acted as prize agent for the British squadron in the Black Sea; that the Gerasimo "was brought to Constantinople on the ——— day of August (not naming the day;) that at such time the exigencies of the service totally precluded the possibility of sending the said ship down to Malta for adjudication; that later in the year, when it was proposed to send her down to Malta for adjudication, she, owing to the unseaworthy state of the said ship, and the difficulty at that time of sending a sufficient prize-crew to navigate her to Malta, was detained at Constantinople by the admiral superintendent there."

He then proceeds to state matters relating to the sale, and concludes in these words—

"And the deponent further made oath, that, as there is no Vice-Admiralty Court, and no standing commissioner at Constantinople, it was impossible to get any of the said crew examined there; and that after they had been detained for a considerable time on board her, they were allowed to leave her without being examined; and the said vessel was delivered up, and her cargo sold, in pursuance of the above arrangements."

This is the only evidence by which it is attempted to justify the non-examination of witnesses in preparatory.

With respect to the sale of the cargo, he says (Appendix 8 :) That as both the ship and her cargo were deteriorating in value, deponent, in his quality of agent and representative of the British squadron, by virtue of the authority given him as aforesaid, entered into an arrangement with Captain C. Pana for himself, and as lawful representative of the said vessel and her cargo, respecting them. That the conditions of the arrangement so entered into were reduced into writing, and duly executed by the deponent and by the said C. Pana; and he then states that certain documents, which he numbers, are the papers so executed, and are all the documents relating to the said arrangement.

[*lxiii] *Now their lordships regret to observe that, on reference to those documents, it appears that the account given of the transaction by M. La Fontaine's affidavit, is entirely inaccurate in the most important particulars.

This gentleman swears that the arrangement which he made with C. Pana was made with him as lawful representative of the cargo, as well as of the ship; and that under that arrangement, the cargo, as well as the ship, was sold. If that statement had been true, it would have been of the utmost importance; for, not only would it have materially affected the evidence of the claimant's right of property, but it would have amounted to a waiver of his demand for costs and damages.

But, on reference to the agreement itself (Appendix 14,) it appears that it has no reference whatever to the cargo. It is made by C. Pana, not as representing the cargo, nor as having any right whatever over it, but solely as the lawful attorney of the owner of the said ship. The agreement is confined to the ship and freight. At the time when it was made, viz., on the 31st March, 1855, the cargo had been actually sold by M. La Fontaine himself, under the circumstances to be now stated.

There is great confusion in the dates assigned to the documents, partly, perhaps, from misprints, and partly from the difference between the new style and the old not always being observed; as far as we have been able to collect the order of proceedings, it was as follows. With respect to the material facts there is no doubt.

Signor Paspali was the owner of the vessel. Spiridione Pana was the agent of E. Pana and Co., the shippers of the cargo. Mr. Hanson, a banker of Constantinople, at first acted as agent for the captors, and soon afterwards M. La Fontaine succeeded to that office. At one period both seem to have been acting.

Paspali and the captors claimed freight for the cargo, and called upon Pana and Co., or Spiridione Pana, as the agent, to pay it. This he refused to do, or to consent to terms which Hanson, on behalf of the captors, desired to impose as the conditions of an arrangement. Under these circumstances Paspali and the captor's agent were desirous that the cargo should be sold, being first valued, and in the month of September, 1854, Paspali presented a petition to the Chargé d'Affaires of the Wallachian Principality at Constantinople, praying that, in accord with the

Britannic Chancery, surveyors might be appointed to verify the condition of the cargo. The petition states that M. La Fontaine assents to this application.

This petition was communicated by the directors of the Wallachian Chancery to what is termed the Royal Britannic Chancery, which seems to mean the consulate-general of her majesty, with a request that it would be pleased to name a surveyor for the purpose of deciding, amongst other things, whether the Indian corn on board the Gerasimo ought to be discharged.

Hereupon, Spiridione Pana, on the 6th October, 1854, addressed to the British Consul-General a statement in which, after alluding to an *earlier petition of Paspali, and an answer which he had put in [*lxiv] to it, he observes (Appendix 11,) that Paspali had presented a second petition, in which he continued to hold him (S. Pana,) in the capacity in which he acts, responsible for the payment of the freight claimed, because he had not consented to take out the cargo existing on board under the conditions imposed on him by Mr. Hanson.

The statement concludes in these words:—

"In reply to the above adverse petition it is sufficient for the undersigned to refer Signor D. Paspali to the reply given to him by the Act of the 15th of September last. And in order that Signor D. Paspali may no longer have reason to consider the undersigned as being an impediment to the delivery and sale of the cargo, he declares that he is not opposed to the appointment of the survey demanded, nor to the sale of the cargo; but he does not take any trouble in the matter, nor to assume any responsibility towards any person whomsoever, still less towards Signor D. Paspali, for the freight claimed; and provided from the survey it should appear that the cargo ought to be sold, the undersigned will not refuse to be present at the sale in the same manner as the other consignees will be present who are in the same position as the undersigned; his preceding protestations, however, remaining still in all and singular their items in full vigour, and without any prejudice to the rights and actions of the shippers against whomsoever it may concern, or any responsibility of the undersigned in the capacity in which he acts towards Signor Paspali for the freight claimed in the event that the proceeds of the cargo should not be sufficient to cover it."

He prays that a copy of this paper may be communicated to Paspali and to Mr. Hanson, in the capacity in which he acts.

Neither the first petition of Paspali, nor the answer to it by Spiridione Pana, are amongst the papers in the Appendix.

In consequence of these proceedings the Wallachian and British authorities appointed surveyors, who, on the 17th October, 1854, made a report (Appendix 12,) in which they stated that they had betaken themselves to the vessel in the company of M. La Fontaine, assisted by the public broker, Lazzaro de Nicolini, and there, in the presence of the captain, had examined the cargo, which they found in a state of serious heat; that the odour it sent forth, and the commencement of rot, induced them unanimously to advise the sale of the cargo, for account of whom it may concern, in order to prevent the total deterioration thereof.

On the same day the cargo was sold by M. La Fontaine, as the royal British navy agent, to Messrs. Charnaud, exactly as it may be found on board the Gerasimo, that is to say, rotten, wetted, damaged, or with any other defect, at the price of 15¾ piastres for every chilo.

This sale seems to have been made without the knowledge of E. Pana and Co., or S. Pana, their agent, for, on the 6th November, 1854, he presented a petition to the British consulate, stating that he was authorised by E. Pana and Co., the proprietors of the cargo, to sell it, and [*lxv] receive the proceeds, and praying that he might be at *liberty to do so, depositing the proceeds in the hands of the Royal Britannic Chancery until it should be definitely settled as to the fate of the said cargo, he being ready to tender valid security for the due deposit of the price obtained.

Nothing further appears upon the evidence or documents, but it is obvious that some further arrangement was made, for it was agreed between the counsel at the bar that the proceeds of the cargo had been paid over to Pana and Co., or their agent, on security being given to answer the amount in case of condemnation.

The question for their lordships to decide is, what is the effect of this evidence with reference to the three points: the property; the sale; and the omission to examine witnesses; and upon none of these points are they able to find any serious doubt.

At Constantinople, where the facts were probably known, and, at all events, were capable of easy proof, no doubt was ever suggested as to the fact of Pana and Co. being owners of the cargo through the whole of the long proceedings which led to the sale. They were dealt with, both by the captors and the shipowner, as the proprietors; they were called upon in that character to pay the freight; they were called upon in that character to consent to the sale; they were called upon in that character to be responsible for the amount in case of condemnation; and can it be argued that they are only to be treated as owners in case of condemnation, and not in case of restitution? At the hearing of the claim none of these facts appeared. At the hearing on further proof, the view taken of the case by the learned judge made it unnecessary to investigate them. The affidavit of La Fontaine was calculated to mislead anybody who had not carefully examined the documents to which it refers; the inaccuracies in it were not pointed out at this bar, and were, probably, therefore not brought to the notice of Dr. Lushington. When the documents are examined, it appears to their lordships that no fair doubt as to the property can be raised by the captors. Indeed, the respondent's own case on their lordship's table states that the cargo was sold with the consent of S. Pana, the agent of the proprietor of the cargo. Can a doubt be suggested whether the principals for whom S. Pana was agent were E. Pana and Co., of Galatz? As to the sale, the evidence clearly shows that it took place under circumstances which cannot in the least prejudice the right of the owners to relief.

Then as to the excuse for the non-examination of the witnesses, there is literally none whatever. What is the value of a statement by M. la Fontaine of what the exigencies of the public service would or would not permit? What knowledge has he upon the subject, even if what appears in this case was calculated to induce the court to place entire confidence on his accuracy? But, if the exigencies of the public service did not permit the sending these vessels either to England or to Malta, are the claimants to suffer? Is it their fault that there was no commission for the examination of witnesses at Constantinople; *that crews could not be spared to send the vessel to Malta? Is it consistent with [*lxvi] justice that the crews should be kept prisoners, and the ship and cargo detained, without the least authority, at Constantinople; that the captain should take no steps whatever for more than twelve months to proceed to adjudication; that the claimants should lose all the advantage of having the examination of their own witnesses; and that for all these wrongs they should be entitled to no remedy?

It was strongly insisted by the Appellants that the penalty on the captors for omitting to comply with the rules of the Admiralty Court, if unaccounted for or not sufficiently explained, was a forfeiture of all their rights, and restitution to the claimants, with costs and damages; and many authorities were cited which were supposed to warrant that proposition.

It is not, in their lordships' view, necessary to adopt in this case so severe a rule, and they think it will be more satisfactory to examine the grounds on which it is attempted to justify the seizure, and on which condemnation is required.

The ground now suggested is, that the Gerasimo was guilty of a breach of blockade in coming out of the Danube when the mouths of that river were in a state of notified blockade. It is singular that if this were the ground of capture, no notice whatever of the blockade should have been contained in the affidavit originally prepared for Captain Powell to swear when the seizure was made, and the facts recent; that notice of it should be introduced for the first time in the affidavit made by him on the 30th of August, 1856; and that even in that late affidavit it is not stated that breach of blockade was the cause of seizure.

There is no doubt, however, that breach of blockade, whether it was the cause of seizure or not, may be used as ground of condemnation, if the circumstances of the case bring it within the law.

What, then, were the circumstances? In the summer of 1854 the Russian forces in the Turkish territories were straitened for provisions. The allied fleets desired to prevent the importation of provisions up the Danube, and with that view the two admirals in command of the English and French fleets issued a proclamation, dated June 2d, 1854, in which they declared to all whom it might concern, that they had established an effective blockade of the Danube, in order to stop all transport of provisions to the Russian armies; they declared that this blockade included all those mouths of the Danube which communicate with the Black Sea, and they apprised all vessels of every nation that they will not be able to enter the river till further orders—("qu'ils ne pourront entrer dans ce fleuve jusqu'à nouvel ordre.")

On the 26th of June the Russians forbade all export of cereals after the 2nd of July. Any exportation of cereals, therefore, was in furtherance of the objects of the allies, and to the prejudice of the Russians. Could a Moldavian merchant imagine, if he had heard of this blockade, that [*lxvii] he was to be liable to capture by the allies for exporting provisions, *when the whole purpose of the blockade was declared to be to prevent their import?

But, by the rules of law, a ship which has entered a blockaded port before the blockade is entitled to come out again; and if she has a cargo taken on board before notice of the blockade, she is entitled to bring it out. The blockade of a port is primâ facie notice of the existence of the blockade to all who are within it, because the inhabitants who see the blockading ships off their coast cannot be well ignorant of the blockade. But this was no blockade of the port of Galatz, but a blockade of the mouths of the Danube, Galatz lying on its banks up the river, at a distance of 150 miles from its mouth.

In this case the ship had entered the river before the blockade; the cargo was taken on board on the 30th of June; and the ship must have sailed on or before the 2nd of July; otherwise she would have been detained by the Russians. If she had no notice of the blockade, she was, on that general ground, entitled to bring out her cargo; if she had notice, she never could suppose that, according to the notification, she could be liable to capture; but if the case had been open to any suspicion, though, in fact, there is none, no weight could be given to such suspicions, when the claimant has been deprived, by the wrongful act of the captors, of the opportunity of affording the explanations which the rules of law were intended to secure to him.

Of the law applicable to the case, as it appears to their lordships, they cannot express their opinion better than in the language used by Dr. Lushington, in the beginning of his judgment on the hearing before him:

"On the part of the claimant, a very long argument was addressed to the court, impugning the conduct of the captors, and charging them with having improperly brought the vessel to Constantinople. It has been further stated that there being no means of examining witnesses at Constantinople, great unnecessary delay had occurred, and that the captors were responsible for such delay and all the consequences. The court is not disposed to deny the truth and justice of the principle contended for; on the contrary, I am clearly of opinion, that if a delay in bringing to adjudication, and the non-examination of witnesses, arose, though it may be almost impossible for the government of the belligerent nation to prevent such occurrence, still that the neutral ought to be indemnified if injustice has been done him. The captor in the first instance, though he may be perfectly blameless, is responsible to the neutral, and he must look to his own government for redress, if he has been compelled to make good any injury sustained by a neutral, in consequence of his fulfilling the commands which he, the captor, dares not disobey. In many cases the captains of some of Her Majesty's cruisers may have a discretion to release at once, but this may not be so in case of a blockade, when special orders may have been given to capture and detain."

In this statement of the principles of law, their lordships cordially *concur. What claim the captor may have upon her majesty's government, it is not their duty to judge, nor have they any means of forming an opinion. But as regards the claimant, his conduct appears to be without any excuse, and their lordships have no hesitation in advising restitution of the cargo, with costs and damages against the captor. [*lxviii]

CARGO EX "ASPASIA."

Cremidi v. Parker and Dyke.

As regards the claimant, this case differs, in no material particular, from that which has just been decided, and the same decree must be pronounced. As between the captor and the crown there may be a very material distinction, as the death of Captain Parker, in the service of his country, within a few days after the capture, relieves him from personal blame, in respect to the gross irregularities which have since taken place.

THE SHIP "ACHILLES."

Cremidi v. Parker and Dyke.

This case differs from the two which have just been disposed of, in this circumstance, that the claimant's right of property is not sufficiently established. The claim is made on behalf of Paolo Focca, as the sole owner; but the ship's papers do not establish the title, but, on the contrary, throw some doubt upon it, and the agreement made with the captain on behalf of the owners does not show who the owners are.

Considering, however, the hardships imposed on the claimants by the course pursued by the captors, their lordships will admit the claimants to further proof as to the property. The other facts are sufficiently clear, and they will not order further proof as to them.

COMMENTARIES

UPON

INTERNATIONAL LAW.

PART THE NINTH.

CHAPTER I.

INTERNATIONAL RIGHT OF ACTION.(a)

I. We have hitherto considered States in their *normal*, that is, their *pacific* relations to each other. We have inquired into the origin and character of their reciprocal *Rights* and *Obligations*. We have now to consider the *abnormal* state of things which ensues upon a disturbance of these normal relations, when these Rights have been invaded and these Obligations not fulfilled.

In the case of individuals, a redress for this infringement of Right and neglect of Obligation is provided for in every system of National or Municipal Law. In these systems the individual is furnished with a *Right of Action*, and the regulation of this Right, in all its various shapes, forms the subject of a *Code of Procedure;* whether there be, as in the case of most Continental States, such a Code made by express enactment part of a general Code of Law, or whether, as in England, such a Code *practically* exists in *usage and judicial precedent amended and amplified by positive statute. [*2]

In the system of International Law, this Civil Right of Action becomes of necessity an appeal to arms,(b) for war is the terrible litigation of States.

By what rules this International Right of Action(c) is governed, both

(a) *Litis Contestatio.* (b) Vide ante, vol. i. pp. 10-12.

(c) Heffters most correctly entitles the second book of his clever work "Das Völkerrecht im Zustande des Unfriedens, oder *die Actionenrechte der Staaten.*"

with respect to the *principals* in the suit and to the *bystanders*, we shall presently consider at length.

II. But as we approach these awful confines, we must remember that it is the bounden and most sacred duty of every State, to exhaust every legal means of redress,(*d*) before it has recourse to the dreadful necessity of war. These means are, as we have already seen,(*e*) classed under two heads, viz :—

1. Measures taken *viâ amicabili.*
2. Measures taken *viâ facta,* which nevertheless fall short of war.

III. Measures taken *viâ amicabili*, are, 1. Negotiation; 2. Arbitration.

With respect to *Negotiation*—it is, of course, the principal object of Embassies,(*f*) the nature and privileges of which have been so fully discussed, to adjust international differences before they ripen into war.

With respect to *Arbitration*,(*g*) this mode of adjustment must be considered both with reference to the *Parties* and to the *Arbitrator;* as much with reference to the latter as to the former.

[*3] *First, as to the *Parties*. It cannot be laid down as a general and unqualified proposition that it is the duty of States to adopt this mode of trial. There may, under the circumstances, be no third State willing, or qualified in all respects, for so arduous and invidious a task. Moreover, a State may feel that the contested Right is one of vital importance, and one which she is not justified in submitting to the decision of any Arbiter or Arbiters.

We know from history that Congresses of crowned heads have not always proved themselves to be impartial or competent tribunals of International Law,(*h*) and the circumstances which justify the *Intervention* of Foreign States, both when invited and when uninvited by the contending parties, have been already under our consideration.(*i*)

Secondly, with respect to the *Arbitrator*. It should be observed that if any arbitrator be appointed, the terms of the appointment will of course limit his authority, and if his award exceed or be inconsistent with those limits it will be altogether null.(*k*)

(*d*) Wolff, *Jus Gentium*, c. v., *De Modo componendi Controversias Gentium*. Zouch, Pars ii. l. s. 3, p. 54.

(*e*) Vide ante, vol. i. p. 11.

(*f*) Vol. ii. pp. 124-234.

(*g*) See an excellent chapter upon the subject, considered as a question of general jurisprudence, in Voet, at Pandect., l. iv. t. viii., *De Receptis qui Arbitrium receperunt, ut Sententiam dicant.*

(*h*) Vide ante, vol. i. pp. 456-7.

(*i*) Vol. i. pt. iv. c. i., on Intervention.

(*k*) "Uti ex adverso cavendum quoque arbitro est, ne compromissi fines egrediatur, ac alia dirimat, quàm quæ ipsius arbitrio commissa sunt, aut alio modo quàm quo compromissum est. Generaliter enim sciendum, omnem de officio arbitri ac potestate tractatum ex ipso compromisso sumendum esse; nec aliud ei licere, quàm quod ibi, ut efficere possit, cautum est. Non ergo quodlibet statuere poterit, nec in re quâlibet, sed de quâ re compromissum, et quatenus compromissum est, et, compromisso generaliter concepto, de his solis judicare rebus et rationibus et controversiis, quæ ab initio fuerunt inter eos, qui compromiserunt, non quæ postea supervenerunt."—Voet, ib. l. iii. t. viii.

For the powers and duties of the *Recuperatores* under the early Roman Law, see vol. i. Append., pp. 492-3.

For the power of the Pope as International Arbitrator, see vol. i. Preface, p. ix. p. 82; vol. ii. pp. 327-8.

As to the authority of General Councils in this matter, see vol. ii. pp. 313-18. Of Universities, ib., p. 318.

Otherwise, the *Jus inter gentes* is well expressed in the opinion of Ulpian, as it stands incorporated in the Roman Law;—"Si se subjiciant alicui jurisdictioni, et consentiant, *inter consentientes cujusvis judicis, qui tribunali præest, vel aliam jurisdictionem habet, est jurisdictio."(*l*) The Arbitrator cannot be compelled, unless, indeed, a clause to this effect has been inserted in the International Covenant, to continue the exercise of his functions.(*m*) Nor can he alter his decision when it has once been formally delivered;(*n*) for, where this has been done, he is *functus officio*. If there be an uneven number of Arbitrators, the opinion of the majority(*o*) would, according to the *Reason of the Thing*, and the *Jus commune* of Nations, be conclusive. If one of the Arbitrators were maliciously to absent himself, it might be competent for the others to proceed; but if one were dead, the Arbitration would be dissolved, unless provision had been made for the contingency in the original covenant.(*p*) Nor, if there be two Arbiters, and they differ in opinion, can they call in, without the consent of both parties, a third person as umpire (*superarbitrum*.)(*q*) [*4]

*The sentence, once given, is binding upon the parties whose own act has created the jurisdiction over them. The extreme case may indeed be supposed, of a sentence bearing upon its face glaring partiality, and attended with circumstances of such evident injustice as to be null. "Nec tamen" (Voet observes) "executioni danda erit, si per sordes, aut per manifestam gratiam vel inimicitiam probetur lata." But for such exceptions no rules can be safely laid down.(*r*) [*5]

IV. It is a duty, according to Hubner,(*s*) the great champion of Neutrality, incumbent upon Neutrals to use every means in their power

(*l*) Dig. v. t. i. 1.

(*m*) "Præterea cogendus non fuit arbiter, si pœna compromisso non fuisset inserta."—Voet, ib., l. iv. t. viii.

(*n*) "Sententiæ secundùm requisita superiùs commemorata latæ effectus est, quod nec ab arbitris mutari possit, etsi errorem allegantibus; quippe quorum officium absolutione vel condemnatione finitum est."—Ibid.

(*o*) "Quod si plures arbitri electi dissentiant in ferendâ sententiâ id quod majori parti placuerit, ratum erit."—Ibid.

(*p*) "Quia tamen illa absoluta arbitrorum omnium præsentiæ necessitas non rarò malitiis atque calumniis posset ansam præbere, dùm aliquando unus aut gratiâ aut odio aut sordibus corruptus sui copiam non faceret; atque ità quæstiones malitiosâ absentiâ diutiùs protelarentur ac manerent indecisæ; commodè cautum fuit jure Canonico, ut si legitimè omnes citati fuerint, nec justum allegaverint impedimentum quò minùs adessent, liceat duobus præsentibus, absente tertio, perindè ad negotii commissi examen accedere, illudque suâ dirimere sententiâ, ac si tertius legitimè vocatus ipsis præsens fuisset. Aliter quàm statuendum foret, si unus ex arbitris fato functus sit: morte enim tali compromissum dissolvi verius est; nisi superstitibus reliquis in casum mortalitatis tributum sit alterius in mortui locum cooptandi jus."—Ibid.

(*q*) "Sed vix est, ut hæc aliter admiseris, quàm si compromittentes, non ignaros tertium assumi, patientiam præbuisse atque ità tacitè consensum accommodâsse constet: nam si ob dissensum arbitrorum malint à compromisso resilire, utì id leges ipsis permittunt, ideòque testationibus denunciaverint ambo, vel alteruter, ne tertius assumeretur, aut assumptus sententiam diceret, non animadverto, cur efficax foret quod ab eo, quem *superarbitrum* vulgò appellant, fuisset definitum, cùm nunquam in eum consensisse dici queant: nullus verò satis idoneus arbiter sine partium voluntate possit censeri."—Voet, ib.

(*r*) Ib. s. 24.

(*s*) De la Saisie des Bâtimens Neutres, t. i. pt. i. c. ii. s. 11.

to procure the re-establishment of peace; and, of course, as much their duty to prevent, if possible, the breaking out of war. Galiani(*t*) is of a different opinion. The part of mediator, he thinks, may be accepted; but its acceptance is not obligatory by National or International Law. Future neutrality might be, he says, compromised, and the spite of one of the belligerents attracted by it. In short, that justice does not require, and prudence forbids an accepting, much more a seeking, of the office of mediator.

It is impossible to lay down any certain rule upon a subject which must be greatly affected by the circumstances of each case as it arises. But it may be allowed to express a preference for the manlier and more Christian principle of Hubner, to the low, and probably after all unsafe, expediency of Galiani. Much, however, must depend upon the subject of dispute, upon the character of the disputants, and upon the [*6] *position and authority of the State which tenders its good offices.

V. Lastly, it must be remembered that, as in the litigation of individuals, if one of the parties refuse to submit to the award of the Arbitrator, a compulsory process is put in motion against him; so, in the litigation of States, if the decision of the umpire State be resisted by the plaintiff or defendant State, war must be resorted to, in order to compel the obedience of the recusant to the decree; though the umpire cannot be compelled, even under these circumstances, to become a belligerent.

VI. There remains a question of much importance:—May a State be compelled to make peace by THIRD Powers? The question applies to two hypotheses, not immaterially different. For the State may have accepted an Arbitration, and the award, which must, of course, be presumed to have been fairly conducted, may have been given against her; or the State may not be under this self-imposed obligation, and may have altogether refused Arbitration.

In both cases the general principles of International Law answer the question in the negative, though with less confidence in the former than in the latter hypothesis.

Bynkershoek(*u*) says, that it is as unjust to compel a State to make peace, as to compel it to make war. Such compulsion, he observes, was used by England, Sweden, and Holland, who bound themselves by Treaty, on the 23rd January, 1668, to *force* the Spaniards and the French, who were at war with each other, to make peace upon certain conditions; and thus these two nations were *compelled* to make peace. Before this event, on the 21st May, 1659, the French, English, and Dutch *compelled* Sweden to make peace with Denmark, and thereby prevented the total ruin of the latter country.

[*7] The pretext, as Bynkershoek calls it, for these interferences *on the part of third Powers, was the general welfare of Europe. In the former case the undue aggrandizement of France, in the latter, the undue aggrandizement of Sweden, was prevented.

(*t*) Galiani, De' Doveri de' Principi Neutrali, verso i Guerregianti, e di questi verso i Neutrali, c. ix. 162.

(*u*) Quæstiones J. P., c. xxv.-xxx.

Bynkershoek, however, says, that under the pretence of preserving peace, these forcible interventions violated International justice. His words are remarkable:—

"His injuriis prætexitur studium conservandæ pacis, quod et ipsum prætexitur injuriis longè adhuc majoribus, quæ potissimùm ab aliquot retrò annis invaluerunt, quum nempe Principes mutuis Pactis de aliorum Principum Regnis et Ditionibus ex animi sententiâ statuunt, atque si de re suâ statuerent. Has injurias peperit, et adhuc parit *Ratio*, quam vocant, *Status*,(*x*) quam ipse definio, *Mostrum horrendum, informe, ingens, cui lumen ademptum.* Huic monstro si semel cedas, semelque tibi indulgeas, aliena non alio loco habere, quam tua, jam frustra est omnis Disputatio de Jure Gentium et Publico."(*y*)

The sincerity of the motives of the interfering Powers may be always questioned; and it is clear that for this, as well as for other and weightier reasons, such compulsory interference is liable to the gravest objections, as infringing upon the sacred principle of *national independence.* Whether, however, and how far, and when the necessities of *preventive Self-defence*, also a sacred national right, may justify such a course, has been treated of at length in the Chapter of INTERVENTION, in a former part of this work.(*z*)

VII. If Negotiation and Arbitration fail, there remain certain measures to be taken *viâ facti*, which yet fall short of open war. There are certain means of redress which, though *tinged with a hostile character, and though often but the train which awaits only a spark to be [*8] kindled into the full blaze of open war, are, nevertheless, not in themselves inconsistent with the maintenance of peace.

(*a*) We have already seen that the class of acts which militate against kindness, courtesy, generosity, or gratitude, are not those for which the Law, either in the case of the Individual or the State, can afford a definite relief or a positive redress.

We have, however, also seen that, in the case of States, the confines of COMITY and RIGHT are ofen separated by a very fine, and sometimes a scarcely perceptible, line of demarcation. These are cases in which long *usage* has given a colour to the axiom, *mos pro lege*;(*b*) and where the abrupt withdrawal of liberties and facilities, originally the fruit of indulgence and concession, without due premonition to the parties interested, is clearly a tortious and illegal act, for which reparation may, if necessary, be exacted by force. A concession of Comity, secured by Treaty, stands, of course,—until suspended or destroyed by open war between the two States,—upon the footing of clear and positive Right. But, as a general rule, violations of COMITY are clearly not the subjects of a just or necessary war. Their redress, if remonstrance have failed, is to be sought in a corresponding reciprocity of practice upon the part of the injured State towards the Government and the inhabitants of the

(*x*) Bynkershoek's horror of the *Reason of State* is again vigorously expressed in the tenth chapter of the second book of the Q. J. P., where he calls it, "*bellua illa multorum capitum.*" Vide ante, vol. i. pp. 154-8.

(*y*) Q. J. P., l. i. c. xxv. s. 10.

(*z*) Vol. i. Pt. iv. c. i.

(*a*) Vide ante, vol. i. pp. 12, 13. Schmalz, p. 214.

(*b*) Vide ante, vol. i. pp. 160-1.

injuring State; for here, on the threshold of the terrible code of war, as indeed throughout the whole system of International Jurisprudence, we are met by this cardinal maxim, viz., that the opinions and feelings of the individual citizen are, so far as foreign States are concerned, bound up in the declarations and acts of the Government of his country.

[*9] *The *jus iniquum*(c) of one State is to be encountered by the *retorsio legis et juris* of another.(d)

"*Quod quisque in alterum statuerit, ut ipse eodem jure utatur,*" is the maxim of jurisprudence applicable to this case. In other words, *Retorsion* is the remedy for these departures from *Comity*. How and in what manner the *Retorsion* shall be effected,—whether by withdrawing reciprocal, analogous, or other privileges from the subjects of the offending State,—is a matter not of International, but of Public Law.(e)

[*10]

*CHAPTER II.

REPRISALS.

VIII. RETORSION, we have seen, is a vindication of offended COMITY.(a) But even an injury done to the *Rights, stricti juris*, of a State, may be vindicated by the employment of a kind of *force*, which nevertheless falls short of war, and the use of which is, and has always been held to be, compatible with the maintenance of general pacific relations. Such a vindication may be sought and obtained through the medium of *Reprisals.* "Observa," Bynkershoek says, "Repressaliis locum non esse nisi in pace."(b)

IX. It must be remembered, that as the *Rights* of a State partly respect the collective capacity of the State, its Government or its Representative, partly the individuals of which it is composed, so a State may be injured in two ways,—either *directly*, by a violation of the Right affecting its collective capacity, or *indirectly*(c) by a violation of the Right of the individual to whom it owes protection, in return for his allegiance.

For it is to be borne in mind that individuals have committed the defence of themselves to the State of which they are members, and, having done so, they are not entitled to redress their own injuries, or, to use a common but expressive phrase, "to take the law into their own hands." The principle of law which forbids this course is thus laid down in the Digest: "Non est singulis concedendum, quod per magistratum publicè possit fieri, ne occasio sit majoris tumultûs *faciendi."(d) This [*11] important doctrine is enforced by a judgment of Lord Stowell,

(c) For the distinction between *jus iniquum* and *injustitia* vide post.
(d) Klüber, s. 234, n. d.
"Die Retorsion ist eine Reaction gegen eine Iniquität (*jus iniquum*), die Repressalien gegen eine Ungerecttigkeit (*Injustitia*)."—Heffters, s. 111, note.
(e) Vide ante, vol. i. p. 13.
(a) Heffters, s. 110. (b) Bynk. ubi supr. (c) Klüber, 231.
(d) Dig. Z. t. xvii. s. 176.

in which he says, "It is a wild conceit, that wherever force is used, it may be lawfully resisted. A lawful force cannot be lawfully resisted. The only case where it can be so is in the state of war and conflict between two countries, where one party has a perfect right to attack by force, and the other an equal right to resist by force. But, in the relative situation of two countries at peace with each other, no such conflicting rights can possibly co-exist."(*e*)

And it is also to be observed that *force* is substituted for *law*, whenever redress is sought otherwise than *judicially*, (including under this term, in International Law, remonstrance by Governments, (even though no injury be inflicted upon person or property. It is well said in the Roman Law, "Tu vim putas esse solum si homines vulnerentur; vis est tunc, quoties quis id, quod deberi sibi putat, non *per judicem* reposcit."(*f*)

X. (*g*) It most commonly happens that *Reprisals* are resorted [*12]
*to for the purpose of redressing injuries inflicted upon the Right of Individuals.

As we are now drawing very near to the borders of actual war,(*h*) and are discussing a redress which is to be enforced *viâ facti*,(*i*) it is expedient to consider what kind of injuries inflicted upon *individuals* justify a recourse to Reprisals. With respect to injuries upon *States*, in their *collective capacity*, it may be laid down as acknowledged law, that Reprisals, according to the modern understanding of International Law, cannot, and ought not to be, granted. *General Reprisals*, that is, a general permission accorded to the subjects of one State to seize the goods and attack the lives of the subjects of another, do, in fact, constitute a state of war, and are yet considered to be without the pale of the rules of law applicable to war.

De Witt was quite correct in saying that he could discover no distinction between *General Reprisals* and open War. The two are now, by the practice of nations, synonymous.(*k*) In the present war, an Order

(*e*) The Maria, 1 Robinson, Adm. Rep., pp. 360-1. The Marianna Flora, 11 Wheaton's (Amer.) Rep. 56.

(*f*) Dig. iv. ii. 13.

(*g*) Grotius, 1, iii. c. ii., Quomodo Jure Gentium bona subditorum pro debito Imperantium obligentur: ubi de Repressaliis, ss. 4, 5, 6, 7. Wolff, Jus Gentium, c. v. ss. 589-606. Bynkershoek, Q. J. P., c. xxiv. See, too, notes to Mr. Du Ponceau's (American) translation. (Philadelphia, 1810.) Ib. De For. Leg., c. xxii. Vattel, l. ii. c. xviii. ss. 342-354. Valin, Ordonnance de la Marine, 1, iii. t. x., Des Lettres de Marque, ou de Représailles. De Martens, l. viii. c. ii. 260. Zouch, p. 120, on Repræsaliæ sint licitæ. Sir L. Jenkins, ii. pp. 718, 721-2, 759, 763, 778. Wheaton, Elem., i. 4me P[tie] ch. ii. Manning, L. of N., c. iii. Kent, Comm. i. pp. 56-8.

"Alia executionis violentæ species est ἐνεχυρασμὸς sive *pignoratio inter populos diversos* quod *jus repressalium* vocant recentiores jurisconsulti, Saxones et Angli *Withernamium* (probably from *wiedernehmen*, to retake), et Galli etiam, ubi à rege impetrari id solet, *literas Marcæ*."—Grot. ib. iv.

"*Repressalium* nomen servo, quia nullum aliud magis aptum occurrit quod rem ipsam significat: alii utuntur voce *pignorationis* alii *clarigationis*, sed neutram convenire satis est manifestum; operam ludunt qui rem, apud Romanos incognitam, Latino vocabulo conantur exprimere."—Bynk. ib.

(*h*) "Postquam autem Repressaliæ involvêre et hæc, et secuta mox bella," &c.—Bynk., ib.

(*i*) Vide ante, vol. i. p. 11.

(*k*) Jefferson appears to have contemplated a recourse to *General Reprisals*, but as a *form of open war*, against the "Continental System," "because on a repeal of

of the English Council issued on the 29th of March, 1854, in these terms:—"Her majesty having determined to afford *active assistance* to her ally, his highness the Sultan of the Ottoman Empire, for the protection of his dominions against the encroachments and unprovoked aggression of his imperial majesty the Emperor of all the Russias, her majesty is therefore pleased, by and with the advice of her Privy Council, to order,
[*13] and *it is hereby ordered, that *General Reprisals* be granted against the *ships*, *vessels*, and *goods* of the Emperor of all the Russias, and of his *subjects*, or *others inhabiting*(l) *within* any of his countries, territories, or dominions, so that her majesty's fleets and ships shall and may lawfully seize all ships, vessels, and goods," &c.(m)

XI. What are the causes which justify *Special Reprisals?*—"locum autem habet, ut aiunt jurisconsulti, ubi jus denegatur."(n)

An *injury* committed upon one of his subjects, for which justice has been *plainly denied*, or *unreasonably delayed*,(o) warrants a Sovereign in issuing *Letters of Marque or Reprisal*, which may either constitute the *commission of a privateer*,(p) or the Reprisals may be committed to a King's ship, as in the recent case of Reprisal granted by England against Naples.

[*14] *The *injury* may be of an *active* kind, *i. e.*, accompanied with actual force and violence, or it may be of a *passive* kind, *i. e.*, withholding, or refusing to pay a debt justly due, for which the creditor has not been able to obtain justice in the Courts of Law of the debtor's country.

their edicts by the belligerents, a revocation of the letters of marque would restore peace without the delay, difficulties, and ceremonies of a Treaty."—Jefferson, Correspondence, vol. iv. p. 119, cited by Manning, p. 116.

(l) Vide post. (m) See Appendix to this volume. (n) Grot. ib. l. iii. iv.

(o) Vattel, l. ii. c. xviii. s. 343. "Ne repressaliæ concedantur nisi palam denegatâ justitiâ.—Bynk., ib.

"Nor do I know of any Treaty, either ancient or modern, wherein provision is made for this case; but it requires a legal process, first in the Law Courts, then an appeal or supplication to the Prince or Supreme Power, before such a denial of justice can be stood upon, as is to be repaired by Letters of Marque or Reprisals." —Life of Sir L. Jenkins, vol. ii. p. 759, et vide ib. pp. 718, 721, 722, 759, 772.

"Alors en cas de refus sans cause légitime, ou *des délais trop affectés* un Roi manqueroit à sa gloire et à la justice qu'il doit à ses sujets, s'il ne leur accordoit pas des Lettres de Représailles sous prétexte que la guerre peut s'ensuivre."—Valin, ubi supr. 419.

"The provisions as to Reprisals in the famous French Ordonnance of 1681, are little more than a modernised reproduction of those in the Guidon de la Mer on the same subject. In this collection of the maritime usages of the 15th and 16th centuries it is said: "Lettres de Marque ou Représailles se concèdent par le Roy, Potentats, ou Seigneurs Soverains en leurs terres; quand hors le fait de la guerre, les sujets de diverses obeyssances ont pillé, ravagé les uns sur les autres, et que par voye de justice ordinaire, droit n'est rendu aux intéressez, ou que par *temporisation* ou *délais*, justice leur est desiniée."—C. x. art. i., cited Ortolan, Dipl. de la Mer, i. 389.

(p) Vide ante, vol. i. pp. 393-406. Klüber, 234. n. c.

"Dans les principes du Droit des Gens, pour légitimer l,éxercice des Représailles, *il n'est nullement nécessaire que le Prince contre qui ce remède est employé, ni ses sujets, aient usé de violence*, ou aient fait quelque saisie ou autre entreprise irrégulière sur les biens de l'autre, ou de ses sujets; il suffit qu'il y ait déni de justice, ou réfus de paiement d'une dette légitime, que cette dette soit due par le Souverain lui-même ou par ses sujets."—Valin, ubi supr. p. 414.

XII. Reprisals may be of a (1) *Negative*, or of a (2) *Positive*(q) character. *Negative*, when the State of the injured subject refuses to fulfil some *obligation, stricti juris*, like the payment of a debt. We have seen what the conduct of England has been with respect to the Russo-Dutch Loan;(r) and we shall presently be led to consider, in the order of this work, the case of the Silesian Loan. *Positive*, when the State of the injured subject seizes upon the goods or persons of the State of the injuring subject.

XIII. Letters of Reprisal are not to be granted without a *full knowledge of the causes*(s) which justify them. Moreover, it must be *res minimè dubia* in which justice has been denied; and it must have been absolutely denied by all the tribunals of the country before which the cause could be brought, and also by the Sovereign in the last resort.

An erroneous sentence conscientiously given by free judges, unbiassed and unintimidated by any extra-judicial authority, affords no just ground for Reprisals, and the presumption *of law is clearly in favour of the decision of lawfully-constituted judges.(t) It is otherwise [*15] when, as Grotious says, *"planè contra jus judicatum sit."* Justice administered partially, and in a different manner to the foreigner than to the subject, or with a denial or omission of any of the incidents essential for ascertaining the truth, would be in fact *injustice*, and would warrant Reprisals.

Grotius approves of that doctrine of the Roman Law,(u) which maintained that an unjust sentence did not extinguish a just debt, even among subjects. The difference, he observes, between subjects and foreigners is, that the former must submit to the authority of the law, even when it is the instrument of injustice; but the latter are under no such obligation, but may by force compel the execution of justice on their behalf.(x)

It has been said that the *res* must be *minimè dubia* for which Reprisals are granted: it may be added, that the *res* must not be in itself *minima*.(y)

(q) Klüber, 234, n. c. (r) Vol. ii. pp. 101-7.

(s) "Cum plenâ causæ cognitione."—Bynk., ib.

"The Law of Nations, founded upon practice, equity, convenience, and the reason of the thing, and confirmed by long usage, does not allow of Reprisals, except in cases of violent injuries, directed or supported by the State, and justice absolutely denied by all the tribunals and afterwards by the Prince."—Letter from the Duke of Newcastle to the King of Prussia, 1753. Vide ante, vol. i. pp. 14, 15.

(t) "In dubiâ re præsumptio est pro his qui ad judicia publicè electi sunt."—Grotius, l. iii. c. ii. s. v. § 1.

"Where the judges are left free, and give sentence according to their conscience, though it should be erroneous, that would be no ground for Reprisals. Upon doubtful questions, different men think and judge differently; and all a friend can desire is, that justice should be as impartially administered to him as it is to the subjects of the Prince, in whose Courts the matter is tried."—Letter of the Duke of Newcastle, ubi supr.

(u) "Verus debitor, licet absolutus sit, naturâ tamen debitor manet," is the doctrine contained in Dig. xii. 6, 60-1. . . . et cum per injuriam judicis domino rem quæ debitoris non fuisset abstulisset creditor quasi obligatam sibi, et quæreretur, an soluto debito, restitui eam debet debitori, Scævolæ restituendam probavit."—Dig. xx. 5-12-1.

(x) "Exteri autum jus habent cogendi."—Grot., l. iii. c. ii. s. v.

(y) "Les Représailles étant une espèce d'acte d'hostilité ou du moins *le prélude*

[*16] It is a maxim of jurisprudence *even more applicable to International than to Municipal Law, that *de minimis*(z) *non curat lex.*

XIV. Reprisals, therefore, are a means of redress, to which recourse may only be had in case of an absolute denial of justice. But in order that a rash and hasty complaint of such denial may not be made, Bynkershoek(a) observes, that different nations have made special provisions by Treaty upon this subject; so that Reprisals in such cases are not to be granted except *sub modo.* Thus by the 24th Article of the Treaty between England and Holland, of the 5th of April, 1654,(b) three months are to elapse after application for redress before Reprisals are granted. This stipulation was renewed by the 31st Article of the Treaty between the same nations, of the 31st of July, 1667. By the 17th Article of the Treaty between France and Holland, 27th of April, 1669, four months are to elapse after the application for redress before Reprisals are granted.

The same period is prescribed by the Treaty of Ryswick (Article 9,) and by the Treaty of Utrecht (Article 16,) 11th of April, 1713, between France and England; and by the third Article of the Commercial Treaty, concluded on the same day, between the same parties. The same period is prescribed by the famous Commercial Treaty of Versailles, 1789, between France and England, (Article 3.) In fact, the obligation to allow a *tempus idoneum*(c) to elapse before Reprisals are granted, may now be considered, still more reasonably than in the time of Valin, "le droit commun des nations."(d)

[*17] XV. This matter of Reprisal has been the subject of municipal *regulation in different countries. In France it is provided for the celebrated *Ordonnance de la Marine*(e) of 1681:

"Article I.

"Ceux de nos sujets dont les vaisseaux ou autres effets auront été pris ou arrêtés hors le fait de la guerre, par les sujets des autres Etats, seront tenus, avant que d'avoir recours à nos Lettres de Représailles, de faire informer de la détention de leurs effets pardevant le plus prochain Juge de l'Amirauté du lieu de leur descente, et d'en faire faire l'estimation

de la guerre, il est clair que personne ne sauroit légitimement user de ce droit, qu'au nom et par l'autorité du Souverain, qui, avant que d'en accorder la permission, doit bien examiner si l'intérêt public permet de se porter à cette extrémité. Il faut aussi que le sujet pour lequel on use de Représailles soit bien clair, et la chose dont il s'agit de grande conséquence."—Valin, ubi supr., citing Puffendorf, l. viii. c. vi. s. 13.

(z) Silius Italicus, thus praises Fabius:

"Cautâ speculator mente futuri
Nec lætus *dubiis parvisque* lacessere Martem."

Grotius (l. ii. c. xxiii. 6,) adopts the view of S. Italicus.

(a) "Ne quis autem temerè de justiciâ denegatâ conqueratur variis Gentium pactis prospectum est. Unde non nisi sub modo Repressaliarum usus placuit in," &c.—Bynk., ubi supr.

(b) For similar provisions in earlier Treaties, see Manning, p. 108.

(c) Grot., l. iii. c. ii. s. v.

(d) "De sorte qu'en cette partie, c'est le droit commun des nations."—Valin, ubi supr. 420.

(e) Vide ante, vol. i. p. 51.

par experts nommés d'office, entre les mains desquels ils mettront les charte-parties, connoissemens, et autres pièces justificatives de l'état et qualité du vaisseau et de son chargement.

"Article II.

"Sur l'information faite, et le procès-verbal justificatif de la valeur des effets pris et retenus, pourront nos sujets se retirer pardevers nous, pour obtenir nos Lettres de Représailles, qui ne leur seront néanmoins accordées qu'après avoir fait faire par nos ambassadeurs les instances, en la forme et dans le temps porté par les Traités faits avec les Etats et Princes dont les sujets auront faits les déprédations.

"Article III.

"Les Lettres de Représailles *feront mention de la valeur* des effets retenus ou enlevés, porteront *permission d'arrêter et saiser* ceux des sujets de l'Etat qui aura refusé de faire restituer les choses retenues, *et régleront* le temps pendant lequel elles seront valables.

"Article IV.

"Les impétrans des Lettres des Représailles seront tenus de les faire enrégistrer au greffe de l'Amirauté du lieu où ils feront leur armement, et de donner caution *jusqu'à concurrence de moitié de la valeur des effets déprédes* pardevant les officiers du même siége.

"Article V. [18]

"Les prises faites en mer en vertu de nos Lettres de Représailles, seront amenées, instruites et jugées en la même forme et manière que celles qui auront été faites sur nos ennemis.

"Article VI.

"*Si la prise est déclarée bonne, la vente en sera faite pardevant le Juge de l'Amirauté, et le prix en sera délivré au impétrans* sur et tant moins, ou jusqu'à concurrence de la somme pour laquelle les lettres auront été accordées; et le surplus demeurera déposé au greffe pour être restitué à qui il appartiendra.

"Article VII.

"Les impétrans seront tenus, en recevant leurs deniers, d'endosser les Lettres de Représailles des sommes qu'ils auront reçues, et d'en donner bonne et valable décharge, qui sera déposée au greffe de l'Amirauté, pour demeurer jointe à la procédure.

"Article VIII.

"Si l'exposé des lettres ne se trouve pas véritable, les impétrans seront comdamnés aux dommages et intérêts des propriétaires des effets saisis, et à la restitution du quadruple des sommes qu'ils auront reçues."(*f*)

(*f*) Valin, Ordonnance de la Marine, l. iii. t. x. Des Représailles, pp. 416-25.

In England Reprisals were once the subject of an act of parliament. A statute passed in the reign of Henry V.,(*g*) which, after reciting that the king had received the complaints of his subjects respecting the injuries they had sustained by truce-breakers and enemies, enacts that, "The king willing, as well in this case as in other, to take order for the
[*19] indemnity *of his liege people and faithful subjects, hath declared in this present parliament, that of all attempts made by his enemies upon any of his faithful liege people, against the tenor of any truce taken before this time, wherein is no express mention made, that all Marques and Reprisals shall cease, the same our sovereign lord the king will grant Marque in due form to all them that feel themselves in this case grieved, and our said lord the king will do the like to all his liege people that feel them grieved against the tenor of any truce, which betwixt him and any of his enemies shall be newly taken hereafter. And to the greater comfort of his faithful liege people, to the intent that they may the more readily, and without long delay, have remedy in this case, the same our lord the king will, that if he or they that feel them grieved against the tenor and form of such truce within the realm of England, out of the said marches of Scotland, or upon the sea, or in the parties beyond the sea, shall complain to the keeper of the Privy Seal, which for the time shall be, who after such complaint heard and perceived, thereof shall make to the party complainant (if he the same require) letters of request under the Privy Seal in a due form. And if, after such request made, the party required do not make, within a convenient time, due restitution or satisfaction to the party grieved, then the Chancellor of England, for the time being, shall cause to be made to such party grieved (if he that demand) Letters of Marque under the Great Seal, in a due form."(*h*)

But the learned editor of Blackstone, Mr. Serjeant Stephen, observes that "this manner of granting Letters of Marque has long been disused, and the term itself is now somewhat differently applied. If during war a subject should take an enemy's ship without commission from the king, the prize would, by the effect of the prerogative, become a droit
[*20] of Admiralty, and would belong not to the *captor but the crown. Therefore, to encourage merchants and others to fit out privateers or armed ships in time of war, the Lords of the Admiralty have been empowered by various Acts of Parliament, and sometimes by proclamation of the king in council, to grant commissions to the owners of such ships, and the prizes captured by them have been directed to be divided between such owners and the captains and crews. These commissions are ordinarily denominated Letters of Marque; and it is in that sense alone that the term now usually occurs."(*i*)

(*g*) Shakspere puts the word into the mouth of Hotspur, after he has heard the praises of the future Henry V.:

"I am on fire
To hear this rich *reprisal* is so nigh,
And yet not ours."—Henry IV., act iv. sc. i.

(*h*) 4 Henry V., c. vii.

(*i*) Stephen's Blackstone's Comm. vol. ii. p. 516.

Lord Chief Justice Hale, in his Pleas of the crown, says:—"We may observe in the wars we have had with foreign countries, that they have been of two kinds, viz., special and general. Special kinds of war are that which we usually call *Marque* or Reprisal, and these again of two kinds: 1. Particular, granted to some particular persons upon particular occasions to right themselves, for which *vide* statute 4 Hen. V. cap. 7; but this is not the proper place to treat touching it. 2. General *Marque* or Reprisal, which, though it hath the effect of a war, yet it is not a regular war, and it differs in these two instances: 1. Regularly, it is not lawful for any person by aggression to take the ship or goods of the adverse party, unless he hath a commission from the king, the admiral, or those that are specially appointed thereunto. 2. It doth not make the two nations in a perfect state of hostility between them, though they mutually take one from another, as enemies, and many times in process of time these General Reprisals grow into a very formed war: and this was the condition of the war between us and the Dutch, 22nd February anno 1664, the first beginning whereof was by that Act of Council which instituted only a kind of universal Reprisal, and there were particular reasons of State for it; but in process of time it grew into a very war, and that without any war solemnly denounced; and therefore, by the *statute of 17 Car. II. chap. 5, Doleman and others, that were in Holland, were declared to have traitorously [*21] adhered to the king's enemies, and were attainted of treason, unless they rendered themselves by a day certain, and all others that served the States of the United Provinces during the continuance of the war, soldiers or seamen, by sea or land, and not returning by a time certain, were attainted of treason; and this had all the effects of war and hostility: the goods of the English taken by the Dutch, and brought *intra præsidia*, the property was wholly changed, and, though retaken again, should not be restored again to the first owner, according as in captures by enemies, 7 E. IV. 14, 22 E. III. 16, and so it was practised during that war."(*k*)

XVI. A question arises at whose instance are Letters of Reprisal to be granted?—must the grantee be a natural-born subject?

Valin(*l*) says that they may be granted to *naturalized* as well as to *natural* subjects.

Bynkershoek speaks of these Letters being granted "ob injuriam *suis subditis* illatam,"(*m*) but he probably did not intend to limit the meaning of the term *subditi* to natural-born subjects. The reason of the thing would seem to include all *bonâ fide domiciled* inhabitants. Though in countries which require, as France does, certain specific formalities to be complied with before a legal domicil can be established, Reprisals would probably be confined to those who were *de jure* as well as *de facto* domiciled. Naturalized subjects would certainly be entitled to them, except—and the exception applies to domiciled and naturalized inhabitants—in one case, namely, where the goods which were to be seized as

(*k*) Hale's Pleas of the Crown, vol. i. pp. 162-3.

(*l*) Ubi supr.

(*m*) Ubi supr.

Reprisals appertained to the subjects or territory of the *original* country of the person entrusted with the Letters of Marque.

[*22] It is not, however, probable that in these days Letters of *Marque or Reprisal would be granted to private individuals, however unquestionably legal such a commission might be.

XVII. Whatever may be the correct opinion with respect to the legality and propriety of issuing Reprisals at the request of any *bonâ fide* permanent inhabitant of the territory, there can be no reasonable doubt of the illegality as well as the impropriety of granting them on behalf of *foreigners* or of a *third* party.

Such a proceeding directly violates the independence of States; it sets up, as Vattel(*n*) justly observes, one nation as a judge over two other nations; and, in truth, none of the arguments used to justify Reprisals on behalf of subjects, are applicable in the case of foreigners. In 1664, England granted Reprisals on behalf of the Knights of Malta against Holland, but Holland asserted, with irrefragable reason, that it was a breach of International Law to issue Reprisals for an affair in which the nation issuing them had no concern; and it appears that England eventually admitted the justice of the Dutch remonstrance.

It is true that Bynkershoek, speaking of this very transaction, in his treatise *De foro legatorum*,(*o*) intimates an opinion that such Reprisals are lawful; but the opinion is clearly at variance with the higher authority of the *Reason of the Thing*,(*p*) (an authority he most highly esteemed,) and with his own opinion in the *Quæstiones Juris Publici*.(*q*)

XVIII. In whom does International Law vest the power of granting Letters of Reprisal? In the Sovereign authority(*r*) alone. Such a power exceeds the competence of subordinate magistrates: though it seems that at one time the Parliament of France exercised it, as did the cities of the Netherlands, when they waged separate wars.

[*23] *The constitution of the North American United States lodges this power in the President and Congress.(*s*)

XIX. What are the subjects of Reprisals? Strictly speaking, they affect the *persons* (ἀνδροληψία)(*t*) as well as the *goods* of the subjects of the subjects of the Government against which they are granted.(*x*)

In modern times, however, they have been chiefly confined to *goods;* and here it is to be observed, that, *jure gentium*, all the subjects of the injuring Government are liable to Reprisals, whether they be native or domiciled,(*y*) but not those who are travellers or passing guests.(*z*)

(*n*) L. ii. c. xviii. s. 343. (*o*) Cap. xxii.

(*p*) Vide ante, vol. i. pp. 15-29, c. iv.

(*q*) "Ob vim et injuriam antea *suis subditis* illatam."—C. xxiv.

(*r*) "Repressalias concedere solius Principis esse videtur, egreditur emim ea res legitimam magistratûs potestatem, et sic nunc ubique servatur."—Bynk., ubi supr.

(*s*) Vide ante, vol. i. p. 139. (*t*) Grot., ib. l. iii. iii.

(*x*) "Denegatam igitur justitiam *Repressaliæ* solent excipere, eos enim accepimus pro *licentiâ, à principe concessâ, occupandi aliorum personas bonaque* ob vim et injuriam antea suis subditis illatam, et negatam de eo facinore justitiam."—Bynk., ubi supr.

(*y*) Vide post, terms of the recent Order in Council, 1854: "*Subjects* or others *inhabiting* within any of his countries," &c.

(*z*) "Jure Gentium subjacent pignorationi omnes subditi injuriam facientis, qui

Ambassadors of course are excepted, with their property, from whatever country and to whatever country they be sent, for the limitation of Grotius to those "non ad hostes" "nostros missi" is, *pace tanti vari*, wholly inadmissible.

The ownership of goods so taken is, according to International Law, *ipso facto* acquired to this extent, namely, so far as is necessary to satisfy the original debt which caused, and the expenses incurred by the Reprisals; the residue is to be returned to the Government of the subjects against whom Reprisals have been put in force.(*a*)

It is scarcely necessary to add, that if persons are seized, not only their life, but their good treatment, must be a matter *of primary care to all States—*Christianis præsertim*(*b*)—as Grotius reminds us. [*24]

It is to be hoped, however, that the Reprisal of *persons* has fallen, with other unnecessary and unchristian severities, into desuetude; and, certainly, to seize *travellers* by way of Reprisal, is a breach of the *tacit faith* pledged to them by the State, when they were allowed to enter her borders.(*c*)

The capture of the enemy's soldiers in open war is obviously defensible upon a very different principle.

XX. According to the 5th article of the French Ordonnance on this subject, ships and goods taken at sea under Letters of Reprisal, are, as we have seen, to be adjudicated upon, like prizes taken in open war, in the Courts of Admiralty.

This would not be the case in England without a special commission from the crown. The English Prize Court is only called into existence by *war*—which, as has been shown, *Reprisals* alone do not necessarily constitute.

XXI. It remains to consider what has been the *practice* of nations with respect to the exercise of this right of Reprisals in some memorable instances.

When France was ruled by Cardinal Mazarin, during the minority of Louis XIV., and England was under the vigorous despotism of Cromwell, an English merchant-vessel was illegally seized and confiscated on the coast of France. The owner of the vessel, a Quaker, complained to Cromwell, who gave him a letter of which he was to be the bearer to Mazarin, told him to wait three days for an answer, which answer must be the restitution of the ship and cargo. "Tell the Cardinal," said Cromwell, "that you have orders from me not to wait longer than three days." The Quaker went, and returned reporting the failure of his mission to Cromwell. Without any further diplomatic communication, that vigorous ruler despatched* two ships of war to make prize of French vessels in the Channel. They accomplished their task; Crom- [*25]

tales sunt ex causâ permanente, sive indigenæ, sive advenæ: non qui transeundi aut moræ exiguæ causâ alicubi sunt."—Grot., l. iii. c. ii. s. 7.

(*a*) "Jure Gentium ipso facto dominium rerum captarum acquiritur ad summam debiti et sumptuum, ita ut residuum reddi debeat."—Grot., ib.

"L'appliquer à son profit jusqu'à concurrence de ce qui lui est dû, avec dommage et intérêts."—Vattel, l. ii. c. xviii. s. 342.

(*b*) Grot. ib., vi.

(*c*) Vide ante, vol. i. pp. 12, 233, 355-9.

well sold the prizes, paid, out of the proceeds, to the Quaker the value of his loss, and then apprised the French Ambassador that the residue was at his service.

"Cette insolente *justice*," says Mr. Villemain in his Biography of Cromwell, "n'excita ni reclamation ni guerre;" but in truth it was an act of substantial *justice*, and *insolent* only because *the forms* of previous diplomatic remonstrances, certainly a great defect, had been omitted.(*d*)

XXII. In 1752, the King of Prussia, by way of *negative* Reprisals, stopped the payment of a loan to England, the obligation to discharge which had been incurred at the time when he acquired the Duchies of Silesia from the Empress of Austria, the Duchies being at that time mortgaged for payment of the loan, and the King of Prussia having moreover bound himself by the 7th article of the Treaty of Breslau(*e*) (11th June, 1742,) to pay off the mortgage.

This act of the King of Prussia called forth the memorable(*f*) reply of the English jurists, which has been so often referred to in this work. This reply is referred to by Vattel, as containing a just and masterly exposition of this branch of International Law. It proved by irresistible argument—

1. That the King of Prussia had sustained no injury.
2. That *this kind* of Reprisal was contrary to International Law.

[*26] "The King of Prussia," they said, "has engaged his *royal word to pay the Silesian debt to private men. It is negotiable, and many parts have been assigned to the subjects of other Powers.

"*It will not be easy to find an instance where a prince has thought fit to make Reprisals upon a debt due from himself to private men.* There is a confidence that this will not be done; a private man lends money to a prince upon the faith of an engagement of honour, because a prince cannot be compelled, like other men, in an adverse way by a Court of Justice. So scrupulously did England, France, and Spain adhere to this public faith, that, even during the war, they suffered no inquiry to be made whether any part of the public debts was due to subjects of the enemy, though it is certain many English had money in the French funds, and many French had money in ours."(*h*)

How sincerely and consistently England has adhered to the rule which she here laid down, has been already shown in the discussion on the Russo-Dutch Loan.(*k*)

In 1778,(*i*) Louis XVI. granted Letters of Reprisal against England

(*d*) Histoire de Cromwell, t. ii. l. x. pp. 236-7, cited by M. Ortolan, Dipl. de la Mer, i. 393-4.

(*e*) "Sa Majesté le Roi de Prusse se charge du seul payement de la somme hypothéquée sur la Silésie aux marchands Anglais selon le contrat signé à Londres, le 7me de Janvier, 1734-5."

(*f*) Pronounced by Vattel "un excellent morçeau de droit des gens," l. ii. c. vii. s. 84. n., and by Montesquieu, "une réponse sans réplique."—Lettres Persannes, l. xlv. Vide ante, vol. i. Pref. pp. xxiii.-iv. pp. 14-15.

(*g*) Vide post.

(*h*) Vide ante, vol. ii. pp. 101-7.

(*i*) Ortolan, Dipl. de la Mer, i. 395-456.

"Tendant ladite requête, pour les causes y contenues, à ce qu'il nous plaise leur accorder nos Lettres de Représailles *sur les biens* des sujets du Roi d'Angleterre,

to two Bordeaux merchants, from whom the English had taken eleven vessels, upon the ground that they were carrying munitions and succour to the revolted colonies of North America.

The ambassadors, however, at this time had been mutually recalled, and the letters state this fact as a reason why amicable remonstrances could not be *continued.*(*k*)

XXIII. In the year 1840, the British Government issued Reprisals against the Kingdom of the Two Sicilies.

*The history of this proceeding was as follows:—

By a Treaty concluded in 1816, between the two kingdoms, [*27] certain commercial advantages were secured to England, and it was stipulated that the Neapolitan Government should grant to no other State mercantile privileges disadvantageous to these interests; the spirit of the Treaty was to place the commercial intercourse between the two countries on the most favourable footing for both. In the month of June, 1838, the King of Naples granted to a company of private individuals, some of whom were natives of France, and others of different countries, a monopoly of all the sulphur produced and worked in Sicily. This was a most valuable article of commerce, and the monopoly threw the whole trade into the hands of a few favoured persons. Great Britain considered the grant of this monopoly a direct infraction of the stipulations of the Treaty of 1816. She accordingly remonstrated vigorously through the British Chargé d'Affaires at the Court of Naples; and in July, 1839, the king promised that the monopoly should be abolished, and cease on or before the 1st of January, 1840. It however continued, and in February of 1840, the English Secretary of Foreign Affairs, Lord Palmerston, called on the Neapolitan Government immediately to terminate the monopoly, and to grant full indemnity for all losses sustained by British subjects since its commencement.

The king professed to comply, and Prince Cassaro, the Minister for Foreign Affairs, wrote an official note to the British Chargé d'Affaires, stating that the monopoly should be abolished, and that His Neapolitan Majesty acted thus in deference to England. A few days afterwards, the British Minister, who had been absent in England for some time, returned to Naples, with full powers and instructions from Lord Palmerston to insist that the sulphur monopoly should be forthwith put an end to. He notified this to the Government; and after the delay of a few days, it was announced to him that the king in council had determined not to consent to the demands of Great Britain, and did *not [*28] consider the sulphur contract a violation of the Treaty of 1816. Prince Cassaro, however, considering his honour pledged by the note which he had written officially to the British Chargé d'Affaires, refused to sign the communication to the British Minister, and gave in his resignation to the king, who accepted it, and sent him into exile at Foggia, a small town about a hundred miles from Naples. The British Govern-

jusqu'à concurrence de la valeur des dits onze navires pris, et de leur chargements, sauf les dommages-intérêts, et frais d'exécution."—Ib., 456.

(*k*) Vide ante, vol. ii. ch. iv. RECOGNITION.

ment immediately prepared to enforce its demands, by sending orders to the admiral who commanded the fleet in the Mediterranean, to hold himself in readiness to commence active hostilities against the Neapolitan flag. This monopoly caused such a decline in the British trade in sulphur, that although previously it was of the average value of 35,000*l.* per annum, it became, after the grant to the company, too small for a return to be made by the customs. The increase in cost was above 200 per cent. On the 17th of April, the British ships-of-war in the vicinity of Naples commenced hostilities, and captured a number of Neapolitan vessels; and an embargo was laid on all vessels in the ports of Malta that bore the Sicilian flag. At first the king made preparations to resist, but he was finally induced to accept the proposed mediation of France in adjusting the quarrel, on the principle that the monopoly should be dissolved, and an indemnity given to the contractors. And early in May amicable relations between the Court of Naples and the British legation recommenced.(*l*)

In 1847,(*m*) a motion was made in the House of Commons, the object of which was to induce the Government to give redress to the British holders of unpaid Spanish bonds, by issuing Reprisals against Spain. The Secretary for Foreign Affairs (Lord Palmerston) resisted the motion [*29] solely on the *grounds of *expediency* and *public policy*, but admitted that it was justified by the principles of International Law, and gave no vague intimation that, if the British holders continued to receive no redress from Spain, the time would come when it would be *politic* as well as *just* to compel by measures of force the payment of this debt.

The last instance of a recourse to Reprisals by England took place in 1850. In that year the British Government made six demands upon the Government of Greece for reparation and redress for alleged injuries inflicted upon British subjects. The demand, which, not being conceded, led to the issue of the Reprisals, was that of Don Pacifico, whose claim was thus stated by the English Foreign Secretary:—"M. Pacifico is a native of Gibraltar, and therefore a British subject. His claim is for the value of property and effects belonging to him which were destroyed in April, 1847, when a riotous mob, aided by Greek soldiers and gendarmes, broke into and plundered his house at Athens in open day. The amount claimed by her majesty's Government for M. Pacifico on account of his personal sufferings and those of his family is 500*l.* A detailed account of the amount of his losses was sent in to the Greek Government by Sir Edmund Lyons, in 1847."(*n*)

Now the real question of International Law at issue in this case was, whether the state of the Greek tribunals was such, as to warrant the English Foreign Minister in insisting upon M. Pacifico's demand being satisfied by the Greek Government, before that person had exhausted the legal remedies which, it must be *presumed*, are afforded by the ordinary

(*l*) Annual Register (1840), vol. lxxxii pp. 209-10, from which this account is taken.

(*m*) 6th July. Vide ante, vol. ii. pp. 9-12.

(*n*) Annual Register (1850), vol. xcii. p. 281.

legal tribunals of every civilized State. That M. Pacifico had not applied to the Greek Courts of Law for redress appears to be an admitted fact; and the most eminent lawyers in Athens advised the Greek Government upon this point in the following manner:—

*"In regard to the affair of Signor D. Pacifico, it appears from the documents which the Council of Ministers has been pleased [*30] to communicate to us, that the authorities charged with the investigation, used every effort both to stop the consummation of the deplorable act already begun before their arrival, and also to deliver the authors of it into the hands of justice.

"These efforts did not, as it appears, fully succeed, for reasons independent of the will of those authorities and of the Greek Government; but according to the Greek legislation and to that of other European nations, as also according to the principles that regulate their International Relations, and which the Government of Great Britain also invoked in its favour in the difference that arose betwixt it and Prussia in the year 1752,(o) quoted *in extenso* in the second volume of the Causes Célèbres du Droit des Gens, by Martens, pages 1–88; according to these principles, we say that Signor Pacifico ought to have instituted before the civil tribunals of Greece an action for damages against those whom he might have considered the authors of this culpable action; and the success of this suit was the more certain, inasmuch as Signor Pacifico affirms that, among the authors of the crime, committed in open day, there were persons known to him and to many other witnesses of the act; and such an action, instituted in time, and supported with regard to the amount of the indemnity claimed, by solid proofs, would certainly have succeeded; and in this way the complaints of Signor Pacifico would not have been made."(p)

The British Government continued to press, and the Greek Government to refuse, the claim. The British Government then proceeded to enforce it *viâ facti;* and first the English Admiral in the Greek waters received orders to prevent any vessels belonging to the Greek Government from putting to sea, and one which had put to sea was compelled to return. *Upon this the Greek Minister put forth the following dignified and temperate protest—"I have received the note [*31] you did me the honour to write to me yesterday. It is impossible for me to convey to you the feelings with which it has been read by the King of Greece, and by his Government. The whole nation will partake them. Greece is weak, sir, and she did not expect that such blows would be aimed at her by a Government which she reckoned, with equal pride and confidence, among her benefactors. In the presence of a force like that which awaits your instructions, His Majesty's Government can only oppose its rights, and a solemn protest against acts of hostility done in profound peace, and which, without reference to other interests of the highest order, are violations, in the supreme degree, of its dignity and its independence. In this painful conjuncture, certain of the support of the Greek people and of the sympathies of the civilized world, the King

(o) Vide ante, p. 25. (p) Ib., pp. 283-4.

of Greece and his Government await with sorrow, but without weakness, the end of the trials which, by order of the Government of Her Britannic Majesty, you may still inflict upon them."(*q*)

The next step of the British admiral was to lay an embargo on all Greek merchant-vessels, and to capture and detain all that he found upon the seas.

The French Government tendered its good offices for the adjustment of these claims; and although the Greek Government was compelled to accept unconditionally the terms imposed by England, the French mediation was practically accepted.

Three commissioners were appointed to examine into M. Pacifico's claims, and that person having demanded 21,295*l.* 1*s.* 4*d.*, they awarded to him 150*l.*(*r*)

The case at the time excited, from a variety of reasons, a great sensation both in England and on the Continent.

[*32] A vote in the House of Peers censured, by a majority of *37,(*s*) the act of the British Foreign Ministers. In the House of Commons the issue was in some degree changed, the whole foreign policy of the British Minister was brought under consideration, and was sanctioned by a majority of 46,(*t*) after a debate remarkable for animation and eloquence, and for the brilliant defence of the Minister himself. His answer to the charge of issuing Reprisals before the Courts of Law of the country had been applied to and had denied justice,—the real point of International Law in M. Pacifico's case,—was, that the state of the courts rendered it a mockery to expect justice at their hands. Upon the evidence as to the accuracy or inaccuracy of this position, the historian will condemn or absolve this act of issuing Reprisals.

But the International Jurist is bound to say that the evidence at present produced does not appear to be of that overwhelming character which alone could warrant an exception from the well-known and valuable rule of International Law upon questions of this description.(*u*)

It should also be mentioned that Russia addressed a strong remonstrance to the British Government, in consequence of these proceedings

(*q*) Ann. Reg., vol. xcii. p. 286.

(*r*) See Correspondence respecting M. Pacifico's Claims, presented to the House of Commons August 7, 1851.

(*s*) Contents :—

Present	113	
Proxies	56	
	169	
Non-Contents :—		
Present	77	
Proxies	55	
	132	
Majority against Govt.		37

(*t*)

Ayes	310
Noes	264
Majority in favour of Govt.	46

(*u*) Hansard's Parl. Deb. for 1850. Annual Register, vol. xcii. c. iii. pp. 57-88, 281-94.

against Greece, which she ended in these words :—"It remains, indeed, to be seen whether Great Britain, abusing the advantages which are afforded her by *her immense maritime superiority, intends, henceforward to pursue an isolated policy, without caring for those engagements which bind her to the other Cabinets,—whether she intends to disengage herself from every obligation as well as from all community of action, and to authorize all great Powers on every fitting opportunity, to recognise towards the weak no other rule but their own will, no other right but their own physical strength."(*x*) [*33]

No country has better understood both the theory and practice of Reprisals than the United States of North America.

In 1834, President Jackson, in his speech, thus expressed himself on the subject of Reprisals against France :—

"It is my conviction that the United States ought to insist on a prompt execution of the Treaty, and, in case it be refused or longer delayed, take redress into their own hands. After the delay on the part of France of a quarter of a century in acknowledging these claims by treaty, it is not to be tolerated that another quarter of a century is to be wasted in negotiating about the payment. The laws of nations provide a remedy for such occasions. It is a well-settled principle of the International Code, that where one nation owes another a liquidated debt, which it refuses or neglects to pay, the aggrieved party may seize on the property belonging to the other, its citizens, or subjects, sufficient to pay the debt, without giving just cause of war. This remedy has been repeatedly resorted to, and recently by France herself towards Portugal, under circumstances less questionable. The time at which resort should be had to this or any other mode of address, is a point to be decided by Congress. If an appropriation shall not be made by the French Chambers at their next session, it may justly be concluded, that the Government of France has finally determined to disregard its own solemn undertaking, *and refused to pay an acknowledged debt. In that event every day's delay on our part will be a stain upon our national honour, as well as a denial of justice to our injured citizens. Prompt measures, when the refusal of France shall be complete, will not only be most honourable and just, but will have the best effect upon our national character. Since France, in violation of the pledges given through her Minister here, has delayed her final action so long that her decision will not probably be known in time to be communicated to this Congress, I recommend that a law be passed, authorizing Reprisals upon French property, in case provisions shall not be made for the payment of tho debt at the approaching session of the French Chambers. Such a measure ought not to be considered by France as a menace. Her pride and power are too well known to expect any thing from her fears, and preclude the necessity of a declaration that nothing partaking of the character of intimidation is intended by us. She ought to look upon it as the evidence only of an inflexible determination on the part of the United States to insist on their rights. That Government, by doing only [*34]

(*x*) Annual Register, vol. xcii. p. 294.

what it has itself acknowledged to be just, will be able to spare the United States the necessity of taking redress into their own hands, and save the property of French citizens from that seizure and sequestration which American citizens so long endured without retaliation or redress. If she should continue to refuse that act of acknowledged justice, and, in violation of the Law of Nations, make Reprisals on our part the occasion of hostilities against the United States, she would but add violence to injustice, and could not fail to expose herself to the just censure of civilized nations, and the retributive judgments of heaven."(y)

One of the grounds of the recent *War*, not *Reprisals*, between the
[*35] N. A. United States and Mexico was the non-payment *of debts due from the Government of that country to the subjects of the United States.

XXIV. These observations on Reprisals may not unfitly be closed in the words of Bynkershoek(z).

"Sic *manente pace*, ipsius Principis est judicium de jure vel injuriâ querelæ, et sic Princeps qui judicavit litem suam facit. Utile sanè est ejusmodi pactis Repressaliarum usum restringere, in totum enim tollere, eorum, qui non uni Principi subsunt, improbitas non patitur."

[*36]

*CHAPTER III.

EMBARGO.

XXIV. There is a mode of redress known to International Law which stands, as it were, midway between Reprisals and War, and which is known by the name of Embargo.

Embargo is an act of the State,(a) done in contemplation of hostilities, a *retorsio facti*, a seizure or rather a sequestration of property belonging to the Government or the individual members of the State which is the alleged wrong-doer. It may or may not be accompanied by a seizure of the persons to whom the goods belong. In maritime Embargoes the persons and goods are usually seized.(b)

The character and effect of such *sequestration* is thus described by Lord Stowell:(c)—

Upon property so detained the declaration of war is said to have a retroactive effect, and to render it liable to be considered as the property of enemies taken in time of war. The property is seized provisionally,—

(y) Annual Register (1834), vol. lxxvi. pp. 360-1.
(z) Q. J. P., l. i. c. xxiv.
(a) The Theresa Bonita, 4 Rob. Adm. Rep. 431.
(b) So Lord Stowell, discussing the claim of the master of an *embargoed* but subsequently restored vessel to freight, observes: "In the situation in which the two countries stood, the master had no right to make his demand against any subject of this country, *being himself under detention as well as the vessel, on whose behalf this demand arises*."—Ib. 241.
(c) The Bædes Lust, 5 Ib. 245-6.

an act hostile enough in the mere execution, but equivocal as to its effects, and liable to be varied by subsequent events, and by the conduct of the Government, the property of whose subjects is so detained. This first seizure is equivocal, and if the matter in dispute terminates in reconciliation, the seizure *is converted into a mere Civil Embargo, so terminated. This would be the retroactive effect of that course [*37] of circumstances. On the contrary, if the transactions end in hostility, the retroactive effect is directly the other way. It impresses a hostile character upon the original seizure. It is declared to be Embargo; it is no longer an equivocal act, subject to two interpretations; there is a declaration of the *animus*, by which it was done, that it was done *hostili animo*, and is to be considered a hostile measure *ab initio*. The property taken is liable to be used as the property of persons trespassers *ab initio*, and guilty of injuries which they have refused to redeem by any amicable alteration of their measures.

This is the necessary course, if no particular compact intervenes for the restitution of such property taken before a formal declaration of hostilities."(*d*)

XXVI. There is another kind of Embargo which is a matter of English Public Law,— namely, the Civil Embargo.

The established law in England is, that the sovereign may prohibit any of his subjects from leaving the realm; a proclamation, therefore, forbidding this, in general, for three weeks, by laying an Embargo upon all shipping in time of war will be equally binding as an Act of Parliament, because founded upon a prior law.(*e*)

These *Civil* Embargoes are founded upon a particular and urgent necessity of state,—upon the maxim, in fact, *salus populi suprema lex*,—yet the proclamations by which they are laid may be illegal, as contradicting an established law. This was the case respecting the Embargo to prevent the exportation of corn in 1766, such exportation being allowed by law at the time; and therefore the preamble to the stat. 7 Geo. 3, c. 7, for indemnifying all persons advising or acting under the order of Council, laying an Embargo on all ships laden *with corn or flour, during the recess of Parliament, in 1766, says, "which order could not [*38] be justified by law, but was so much for the service of the public, and so necessary for the safety and preservation of his majesty's subjects, that it ought to be justified by Act of Parliament." This Embargo, as was allowed, saved the people from famine; yet it was declared illegal by the above act of the legislature; and the proprietors of the embargoed ships and cargoes were accordingly indemnified by Government.(*f*)

The leading case upon this subject is that of Sir Josiah Child v. Sands,(*g*) in which it was finally agreed by the judges that the king

(*d*) See, too, as the possible *retroactive* effect of a Declaration of War. The Herstelder (1 Rob. Adm. Rep. 117-18).

(*e*) Stephen's (Blackstone's) Com. vol. ii. p. 528.

(*f*) Beawes, Lex Mercatoria, vol. i. p. 393. Chapter Of Embargoes or Restraints of Princes.

(*g*) This case will be found referred to in the books as follows:—In Skinner's Reports, p. 91, Sandys and the East India Company; and p. 334, Sands v. Child

might lay Embargoes, but then it must be *pro bono publico*, and not for the private advantage of a particular trader or company.

The crown, of course, has not this power of imposing a Civil Embargo in foreign ports, though possibly it might have power to do so in the ports of any ally.

The distinction between the Civil and the Belligerent (so to speak) Embargo, is explained in a judgment given by Lord Stowell, in the matter of the Dutch ships detained in port, at the Cape of Good Hope, before declaration of hostilities against Holland, claimed as *droits* of Admiralty, condemned to the Crown, *jure coronæ.*

"On the breaking out, I cannot say of war, but of that ambiguous situation into which the irregular conduct of France had put different countries, by dissolving the connection between the governors and the governed, it was found necessary, when Holland became exposed to the invasion of the French arms, to detain by the strong hand of [*39] *power a number of Dutch ships in the ports of this kingdom. At the same time, conciliating language was used to the proprietors, and promises were held out to all such as should voluntarily come in, that their property should be restored to them. It is notorious also, that on the declaration of hostilites that ensued, these seizures were enforced, with a retrospective operation, on all who had not complied with the terms; and were not considered as mere Civil Embargoes, but as acts of forcible possession, on which the property so seized was finally condemned as prize to the Crown. Now, unless very strong and solid distinctions can be pointed out between this case, and those which have pursued this course, I see no reason why this should not journey in the same track. Two or three distinctions have been taken. In the first place, it is said, that the detention in the ports of England was a mere Civil Embargo, and that an Embargo of that nature could not extend to foreign ports, where the Crown of England has no jurisdiction. In the first place, it is not necessary, that the Embargo should be exactly of the same nature, in order to vest the rights of the Crown: for any mode of forcible occupancy or detainer prior to hostilities is sufficient for the purpose; and, secondly, the nature of the Embargo in the ports of this kingdom is not very accurately described, when it is termed a mere Civil Embargo; for it was a detention by actual force applied to them. The ships were generally taken possession of by an armed power; it was not the mere hand of the custom house that was laid upon them, in the civil mode of forbidding an egress, but it was a restraint and compulsion, acting by the terror and use of force. The Embargo at the Cape was likewise an Embargo of force; and the very argument that it could not be a Civil Embargo, because this Government had no right to lay on a Civil Embargo in a foreign port, proves that it was an Embargo of force; though, if it was at all necessary that it should partake of anything like a civil authority, it must be remembered that the Stadtholder's name and authority *is likewise employed; but it is notorious, that some [*40] ships of war that attempted forcibly to escape, were forcibly

& Lynch. In 4 Modern Reports, 176 (Case 70), Sands v. Child. In 1 Salkeld's Reports, 31, tit. Admiralty, (Case 2), Sir Josiah Child v. Smith.

detained: that is enough to show its nature, if it were at all necessary.(*h*)

XXVII. As a belligerent Embargo is a species of Reprisal, the observations already made with respect to Reprisals by confiscation of *public* debts are applicable to Embargo.(*i*)

With respect to the operation of Reprisal and Embargo upon *private* debts, this delicate and difficult question will be considered hereafter, when the effect of war upon all property falls under discussion. For if the Embargo does not end in war, the private debts are, it may be almost certainly said, at the most only suspended, and not confiscated. Whether the same limited and temporary effect may not also, under the modern practice of nations, be predicated of an Embargo which does end in war, and especially with respect to what is due from *third* parties to the wrong-doer or the open enemy, will be the subject of future consideration.

XXVIII. In a great number of Treaties concluded between the Maritime and Continental Powers, provision is made for the contingency of a war, and a certain time allowed for the withdrawal of goods and persons.(*k*) In the present war England allowed the enemy from the 29th of March to 10th of May, for this purpose. It is well known that Magna [*41] *Charta(*l*) contains a provision that at the commencement of a war the enemy's merchants shall be kept and treated as our own merchants are treated in the country of the enemy.

XXIX. (*m*) There is yet another measure partaking also of a belligerent

(*h*) The Gertruyda, 2 Rob. Adm. Rep. 219-21. (*i*) Vide ante, pp. 25-6.

(*k*) E. g., Art. II. of Treaty between France and England, Sept. 26, 1786.

Art. XLV. of Treaty between France and Russia, Jan. 11, 1787.

E. g., also, the recent Treaties of 1852, (1) between England and the Republic of Peru, (2) of the Equator, (3) of Paraguay, (4) the Sandwich Islands.

1. Art. XII., six months.
2. Art. XI., no time specified; protection as long as good behaviour lasts.
3. Art. XIII., the same.
4. Art. XIV., a year for those who wish to depart; otherwise, protection to last as long as good behaviour.—Ann. Reg., vol. xcv.

(*l*) "Art. XLI.—Omnes mercatores, &c. Et si sint de terra contra nos gwerrina, et si tales inveniantur in terra nostra in principio gwerre, attachiantur sine dampno corporum et rerum, donec sciatur à nobis, vel Capitali Justiciario, nostro quomodo mercatores terre nostre tractentur qui tunc inveniantur in terra contra nos gwerrina, et si nostri salvi sint, alii salvi sintin terra nostra."

The Statute of Staples, 27 Edw. III., c. xvii., enacted that foreign merchants, residing in England when war commenced between their Princes and the King of England, were to have convenient warning of forty days, by proclamation, to depart the realm with their goods; and if they could not do it within that time, by reason of accident, they were to have forty more days to pass with their merchandizes, and with liberty in the meantime to sell the same.

(*m*) Des Droits et des Devoirs des Nations Neutres en Temps de Guerre Maritime, par L. B. Hautefeuille (Paris, 1849), t. iv. tit. xiv. pp. 433-52.

It is much to be lamented that a work indicating so much pains, care, and reading, should be disfigured throughout by the blindest prejudice.

The author's violent and unreasoning hatred of England, may be estimated from the following assertions:—

1. England has invariably disregarded International Law, unless it happened to be in her favour.—I. pp. 296-7.
2. She has never been sincerely anxious to suppress slavery; her real object, since 1815, has been to destroy the Antilles.—I. p. 161.
3. She is now, under the transparent plea of encouraging the immigration of her labourers, continuing slavery under another name.—I. p. 162.

character, though exercised, strictly speaking, in time of peace, called by the French *le droit d'Angarie.* It is an act of the State, by which foreign as well as private domestic vessels which happen to be within the jurisdiction of *the State, are seized upon, and compelled to [*42] transport soldiers, amunition, or other instruments of war; in other words, to become parties against their will to carrying on direct hostilities against a Power with whom they are at peace. The owners of these vessels receive payment of freight beforehand. Such a measure is not without the sanction of practice and usage, and the approbation of many good writers upon International Law;(*n*) but if the reason of the thing and the paramount principle of national independence be duly considered, it can only be excused, and perhaps scarcely then justified, by that clear and overwhelming necessity which would compel an individual to seize his neighbour's horse or weapon to defend his own life. At all events, justice demands that the owners of such goods and vessels be indemnified for all damages caused by the interruption of their lawful gains, and for the possible destruction of the things themselves, though so high an authority as M. Massé(*o*) says that usage has not hitherto gone that length.

[*43] It is worse than idle to speak or write in a depreciating *tone, as some modern writers do, of the value and influence of *usage*(*p*)

4. The King of Prussia (despite the author's countrymen, Vattel and Montesquieu, and every writer of any repute,) in refusing to pay the Silesian loan, acted in accordance with the principles of International Law.

More need not, though much more might be said, to show how the prejudices of this author disqualify him from performing the *semi-judicial* functions of a writer upon International Law.

That he should be quite certain that England would never waive her right of commissioning *Privateers*, which she has recently waived (I. p. 342), and that her maritime strength depends upon her *Navigation Laws*, (I. p. 277), which, to her great advantage, she has recently abolished,—these are circumstances which, perhaps, do not so much affect the *judicial* character of the author.

(*n*) " . . . Angariarum onus etiam exteros afficit, quod quotidiana confirmat praxis. Vinnius ad Peckium *de navib. non excus.* Stypmannus, *ad jus marit.* Anseat."—Pt. v. c. i. n°. 23.

Loccenius, De Jure Marit., l. i. c. v. s. 3.

Azuni, Droit Maritime de l' Europe, t. i. c. iii. art. 5.

Massé, Droit Commercial, t. i. l. ii. tit. i. c. 2, s. 7. Sect. 5, s'exprime en ces termes: "Les belligérants tout en respectant d'ailleurs la neutralité, la soumettent quelquefois à certaines exigences qui, sans lui porter atteinte, entravent momentanément la liberté des neutres. C'est ce qui a lieu lorsqu'un Etat belligérant met en réquisition les bâtiments neutres qui se trouvent dans les ports et rades de sa domination et les oblige à transporter, moyennant salaire, des armes, des troupes, des munitions: on donne à cette réquisition le nom d'angarie."

These authorities are cited by M. Hautefeuille, concerning whose work see note (*m*) in the last page.

(*o*) "Observons, au surplus, que les prestations imposées aux navires atteints par l'angarie ne sont pas gratuites, et que les armateurs doivent recevoir la salaire du service forcé qu'ils ont rendu. . . . Il serait juste aussi,' dit-il, 'de les indemniser en outre des dommages qu'ils ont pu souffrir par suite de l'interruption de leur voyage, ou de leurs expéditions; mais l'usage ne paraît pas aller jusque-là."—Massé, t. i. l. ii. tit. i. c. ii. s. 2, § 5, n°. 324.

(*p*) Vide ante, vol. i. c. v.

"Probatur autem *hoc jus gentium* (here used for *jus inter gentes*) fori modo quo jus non scriptum civile *usu continuo*, et testimonia peritorum. Est enim hoc jus, ut rectè notat Dio Chrysostomus, εὕρημα βίου καὶ χρόνου repertum temporis et *usûs*,

in all international affairs. Not only is it a law to which both contending parties may be held to have assented, but its notoriety operates as a notice and warning to foreigners that in certain contingencies certain consequences will follow within a certain jurisdiction. It is optional with them to place themselves or not within that jurisdiction; but when the contingency does arise, and the consequence does follow, *ignorantia juris*(q) is morally and legally a bad plea,—an argument which, in truth, answers much shallow declamation upon this and similar subjects.

XXX. We have been considering this *droit d'Angarie* solely with respect to *neutrals*. So far as subjects are concerned, it is a question of Public, and not International Law; so far as *allies* are concerned, they cannot reasonably complain if they meet with the same treatment as subjects.

XXXI. It may perhaps be thought that these remarks have trespassed upon that part of this work which treats of open war, but it does not necessarily follow that war ensues upon the first exercise of this right, and the *droit d'Angarie* is always classed with Reprisals and Embargo by writers upon International Law.

Blockade is an essentialy *belligerent* right, both as regards the parties immediately concerned in it, and as regards neutral States, and will therefore be examined hereafter.

*XXXII. *Special Reprisals*, long continued, must end in *General Reprisals*, that is, in war.(r) [*44]

It must not, however, be supposed that Reprisals are always a necessary prelude to war; they are a gentler means of redress in cases in which they can be employed, but Vattel(s) says, with justice, that there are cases in which Reprisals would be reprehensible, though a declaration of war would be justifiable. If the dispute arise not from an act of violence or an inqury, but from a contested right, then, after pacific measures have been established, and the right is such that it must be maintained, *War* must follow: to issue *Reprisals* in such a case is to carry on war in disguise, in fact, and not in name, and has a tendency to weaken public faith and to confuse the distinct international relations of war and peace, and thereby to disturb the mutual obligations of States.

XXXIII. No person who has read the three chapters in the Second Book of Grotius's noble work, can fail to be struck with the piety, the wisdom, and the learning of this truly great man.(t)

These Chapters are:

1. *De causis injustis* (XXII.)
2. *De causis dubiis* (XXIII.)
3. *Monita de non temerè etiam ex justis causis suscipiendo bello* (XXIV.)

atque in eam rem maximum nobis usum præbent illustres annalium conditores."—Grot., l. i. c. i. xiv. 2.

(q) Vide post.

(r) "Repressalien gegenseitig fortgesetzt gehen in Kreig über."—Schmalz, 216.

(s) L. ii. c. xviii. s. 289.

(t) "Juris Gentium Princeps Magister Grotius is magni operis."

The considerations which they contain naturally precede the chapters on the principles and rules of law which govern the conduct of war.

It is true that these chapters are chiefly of an *admonitory* character, [*45] and that they contain less of instituted rule than other *parts of the work. They are, to a certain extent, sermons, written in the universal language of Christendom, for the guidance of Christian States; they are valuable from the truth of the sermon, and from the authority of the preacher. Grotius was not merely a profound jurist of the closet, or a learned divine, though the author of one of the best works on divinity, but one who had learned in the hard school of practical life, in the management of international affairs of high import, in the terrible teaching of public and civil wars, the justice, and therefore the expediency of the doctrines, which, as the mature fruit of his well-disciplined and well-cultivated mind, he in these chapters promulgated to the world. It is in the true spirit of a Christian statesman that he tells us: "Non est inter artificia bellum, imo res est tam horrenda, ut eam nisi summa necessitas, aut vera caritas honestam efficere nequeat."(*u*) But before he arrives at this conclusion, he has impressed upon us the following, among other reflections. It may happen in many controversies that on both sides probable arguments may be adduced, and in matters of light moment the decision may be innocently taken either way. The same cannot be predicted of a decision in matter of grave moment.(*x*) In the instance of inflicting capital punishment, for example. But war is of the gravest moment, because in it the innocent as well as the guilty must suffer. If there be doubt, therefore, the rule of reason and morality enjoins the maintenance of peace,—and here we are reminded of the profound wisdom and majestic language of Bacon :—

"As the cause of a war ought to be just, so the justice of that cause ought to be evident, not obscure, not scrupulous. For by the consent of all laws, in capital cases, the evidence must be full and clear; and if so, where one man's life is in question, what say we to a war which is ever the sentence of death upon many."(*y*)

[*46] *Try, then, says Grotius,(*z*) the three methods of avoiding war, which are open to you.

1. Conference (*Colloquium.*)
2. Arbitration or compromise (*Compromissum.*)
3. Casting lots (*Per Sortem.*)

The two former methods have been considered; the third, though Solomon said "The lot causeth contentions to cease, and parteth between the mighty,"(*a*) is neither feasible nor rational in the present state of independent societies. The *single combat*, which Grotius considers to bear a close affinity to the lot, is open to the same objections. If, indeed, there were *two* Princes so absolutely despotic as to make war without

"ὁ μεγας:" vide Bynkershoek, passim.

Mr. Whewell's recent edition has laid all admirers of Grotius—indeed all who wish well to jurisprudence and civilization—under great obligations to him.

(*u*) Grot., l. ii. c. xxv.-ix. 3.

(*x*) Ib., l. ii. c. xxiii.-v.

(*y*) Lord Bacon, Of a Holy War.

(*z*) Grot., ib., vi.

(*a*) Proverbs, xviii. 18.

the consent of their subjects, such a mode of terminating their differences might be far from undesirable in the opinion of the rest of the world.

Although, *in causâ dubiâ*, both parties are bound to seek for a compromise by which war may be avoided, nevertheless *melior est possidentis conditio*, both by Natural and Roman Law; therefore the State which makes the claim is more bound to seek for the compromise or arbitration than the State which is in possession.(*b*)

But when neither party is in possession, or both are equally so,(*c*) and the right is doubtful, then there should be a division of the matter in question, and the State which refuses it is guilty of much injustice; for

> "Such peace is of the nature of a conquest,
> For then both parties nobly are subdued,
> And neither party loser."(*d*)

Grotius(*e*) further reminds us that it is the doctrine and duty *of a Christian to give up rights rather than cause the shedding of blood; at all events it is a reason for not prosecuting them by a means so necessarily injurious to others as war. [*47]

But here it must be remembered that, as a matter of fact, States,(*f*) though justly considered as moral persons, are not Individuals, and that a Christian individual may be bound to give up a right, which a Christian State, acting for the collective good, may be bound to maintain. And Grotius(*g*) himself points out, in the very next chapter, that it may be the duty of a State to make war not only on behalf of subjects, but also on behalf of allies, and on behalf of friends, to whom we have not promised assistance, nay, on behalf of all who are injured (*imo et pro hominibus quibusvis*,) on account of the bond of our common humanity.(*i*) Yet what a wide door for the oppression of national liberties might be opened under this last plea.

XXXIV. A careful examination of the whole subject will lead us to the following *affirmative* and *negative* conclusions.

XXXV. *Affirmatively* we may conclude that war may be justly waged upon two grounds:—

1. For the prevention of wrongs.
2. For the redress of wrongs.

These wrongs may arise from the breach, or non-fulfilment of a Treaty, which founds a clear *obligation* arising from positive contract (*obligatio ex contractu;*) or they may arise(*k*) from an infringement of a custom, or disregard of a legal presumption, *that a certain usage, well established by International Practice, would be followed upon [*48]

(*b*) Grot., ib., xi. (*c*) Ib., xii.
(*d*) Shakespere, Hen. IV., pt. ii. act iv. sec. 2. (*e*) Grot., c. xxiv.
(*f*) Vide ante, vol. i. pp. 1, 5, 6. (*g*) Grot., c. xxx.
(*h*) Vide ante, vol. i. pp. 441-2.
(*i*) "The blood of man should never be shed but to redeem the blood of man. It is well shed for our family, for our friends, for our God, for our country, for our kind. The rest is vanity, the rest is crime."—Letters on a Regicide Peace, Burke, v. viii. 165.

It is, perhaps, still better stated by Livy: "Justum bellum, quibus necessarium; et pia arma, quibus, nulla, nisi in armis, relinquitur spes."—L. ix. c. i.
(*k*) Heffters, ss. 100-1.

certain occasions, such conduct founds an *obligation* upon an implied or *quasi contract* (*obligatio ex quasi contractu.*)

For instance, it has been shown that the reception of foreigners(*l*) generally, and of Ambassadors and Consuls,(*m*) as foreigners clothed with particular privileges, is a matter which it is within the abstract competence of each State to accord or refuse, or accord under certain previously specified conditions. But that by the admission of foreigners, without any such prohibition or limitation, the State contracts a tacit obligation to treat them according to general international custom and usage; and a contrary conduct is an injury which gives the Government of the foreigners a claim for redress.

XXXVI. The Roman Law classed among *obligations* the consequences of the commission of an offence (*obligationes ex delicto;*) it thereby recognised the important truth that *crimes* might subject the *criminal* to the double obligation of undergoing punishment at the hands of the State,(*n*) and of making reparation to the individual.

It enumerated four offences (*delicta*) from which these obligations (*obligationes*) flowed:—

1. Robbery (*furtum.*)
2. Robbery with violence (*rapina.*)
3. Damage accompanied by injury (*damnum injuriâ datum.*)
4. Injury to character (*injuria seu contumelia.*)

XXXVII. The members of the society of States cannot indeed be guilty of *crime* in the sense in which that term is used in Municipal or [*49] Private Law, nor can they be subjected *to *punishment*(*o*) inflicted by other States. But one State may suffer from another, either in its corporate capacity or in the person of its individual subjects, injuries and wrongs arising from the *delicta* which have been mentioned.

For a State has, as we have seen, both Moral and Physical Rights of INDEPENDENCE and EQUALITY, which may be so injured by these *delicta*, as to entitle, perhaps as to oblige it to seek, through war, the "highest tribunal of right:"—

1. A Security against injury *threatened;*
2. A Reparation for injury *done;*
3. A Reinstatement of its *character* within the bounds of that social and moral estimation, which it had previously enjoyed within the society of States, and of which the *contumely* of the aggressor had deprived it.

In other words, one State may lawfully make war upon another which has menaced or violated those General Rights which have been discussed in the former volumes of this work.

It may also lawfully make war to protect and assist an ally which has suffered the like injuries, or, indeed, a Third State, which is not *formally* an ally, in the strict sense of the word, but on terms of amity with it, and a member of the great community of States.(*p*)

(*l*) Vol. i. s. 209; vol. ii. pp. 151-156. (*m*) Ib., vol. ii. p. 235.

(*n*) Crimen: or indeed, at the hands of the individual, *privatum delictum.*

(*o*) Vol. i. c. i. s. 11.

(*p*) "Imo tanto honestiùs est alienas injurias quam suas vindicare, quanto in suis magis metuendum est ne quis doloris sui sensu aut modum excedat, aut certè animum inficiat."—Grot., l. ii. c. xx. ss. 40-1.

XXXVIII. The Roman Law classed under the head of *quasi-delicta* those injuries which arose not from *malicious intention*, like the aforesaid *delicta*, but from *culpable imprudence*. And the conduct of a State which allowed, through indifference or gross remissness, its subjects to invade the rights of another State, would fall under the principle of this law. If, indeed, the State permitted, or connived at the offence, and sheltered the offender, it would be just as much an aggressor as if the *invasion had been made by the regular military forces of the kingdom.(*q*) [*50]

Blackstone observes,(*r*) that "offences against this law are principally incident to whole States or nations; in which case recourse can only be had to war, which is an appeal to the God of Hosts, to punish such infractions of public faith as are committed by one independent people against another; neither State having any superior jurisdiction to resort to upon earth for justice. But, where the individuals of any State violate this general law, it is then the interest, as well as the duty of the Government, under which they live, to animadvert upon them with a becoming severity, that the peace of the world may be maintained. For, in vain would nations, in their collective capacity, observe these universal rules if private subjects were at liberty to break them at their own discretion, and involve the two States in a war. It is, therefore, incumbent upon the nation injured, first, to demand satisfaction and justice to be done on the offender by the State to which he belongs; and, if that is refused or neglected, the Sovereign then avows himself an accomplice or abettor of his subjects' crime, and draws upon his community the calamities of foreign wars."

The case of Mr. M'Leod fell exactly under the principle of International and Public Law, which is here most correctly laid down. It grew out of the case of the *Caroline*, which has been already adverted to in a former part of this work;(*s*) but it is necessary to notice it again in this place.

During the disturbances in Upper Canada, in the winter of 1837, a steamboat called the *Caroline*, belonging to an American owner, had been actively engaged in conveying arms and stores from the American side of the river to the Canadian rebels, who were in possession of Navy Island, and had been boarded in the night time by a party of Canadian loyalists, while she was lying within the jurisdiction of the territory of *New York, set on fire, sent down the stream, precipitated over the Falls of Niagara, and dashed to pieces. An American citizen, named Durfee, was killed in the affray, and several others were wounded. In the month of January, 1841, a British subject, domiciled in Canada, named Alexander M'Leod, was suddenly arrested while engaged on some business within the territory of the State of New York, and thrown into prison by the authorities, on the charge of having been concerned in the destruction of the *Caroline*, and the alleged murder of Durfee. A correspondence immediately ensued between the British [*51]

(*q*) Vide ante, vol. i. pp. 227-232.
(*r*) Comm., vol. iv. c. v. p. 67.
(*s*) Vol. i. p. 228.

ambassador, Mr. Fox, and Mr. Forsyth, the American Minister of Foreign Affairs. Mr. Fox called upon the Government of the United States to take prompt and effectual steps for the liberation of Mr. M'Leod.

"It is well known," said Mr. Fox, "that the destruction of the steamboat Caroline was a public act of persons in her majesty's service, obeying the orders of their superior authorities. The act, therefore, according to the usages of nations, can only be the subject of discussion between the two National Governments. It cannot justly be made the ground of legal proceedings in the United States against the individuals concerned, who were bound to obey the authorities appointed by their own Government." Mr. Forsyth, in his reply, after stating the anxious desire of his Government to maintain amicable relations between the United States and England, said :—

"It is then with unfeigned regret, that the President finds himself unable to recognize the validity of a demand, a compliance with which you deem so material to the preservation of the good understanding which has been hitherto manifested between the two countries.

"The jurisdiction of the several estates which constitute the Union is, within its appropriate sphere, perfectly independent of the Federal Government. The offence with which M'Leod is charged was committed within the territory, and against the laws and citizens, of the State of New York, and is one that comes clearly within the competency [*52] *of her tribunals. It does not, therefore, present an occasion where, under the constitution and laws of the Union, the interposition called for would be proper, for which a warrant can be found in the powers with which the Federal Executive is invested. Nor would the circumstances to which you have referred, or the reasons you have urged, justify the exertion of such a power, if it existed."

"Mr. Fox, in reply to the Note of Mr. Forsyth, dated December 26th, in which the application for the relief of M'Leod is refused, regrets this refusal, and intimates that it, and the ill-treatment of M'Leod, will lead to the most grave and serious consequences. He states again, that the attack on the Caroline was made in pursuance of orders from the colonial authorities, and he says that the Caroline was a piratical vessel,(*t*) and was but nominally within the jurisdiction of the United States. The authorities of New York had been unable to maintain their jurisdiction at the place where the Caroline was attacked, or even to prevent the pirates from carrying off from that place the cannon belonging to the State. He was not authorized to state what were the views of Her Majesty's Government on this subject, but he took this occasion to place his own opinion on record.

"Mr. Forsyth expresses his belief that Mr. Fox would not entertain this opinion if he had seen the whole evidence on the subject, which was carefully collected by the United States, and communicated to the British Government. He has no more to say to Mr. Fox on the matter, and awaits the result of the demand upon Great Britain for reparation."(*u*)

(*t*) Vide ante, vol. i. c. xx.

(*u*) This account is taken from the Annual Register (1841), vol. lxxxiii. p. 310.

M'Leod was, in the month of May, removed by *habeas corpus* from Lockport to New York, in the custody of the Sheriff of Niagara County. Previously to this, the following Note dated the 12th of March, 1841, was sent by Mr. Fox to Mr. Webster, the new American Foreign Secretary:—

*"Her Majesty's Government have had under consideration the subject of the arrest and imprisonment of Alexander M'Leod, [*53] on a pretended charge of arson and murder; and I am directed to make known to the Government of the United States, that the British Government entirely approved of the course pursued by him. I am instructed to demand formally, and in the name of the British Government, the immediate release of Alexander M'Leod, for the reason that the transaction was of a public character, planned and executed by persons duly authorized by the Colonial Government to take such measures as might be necessary for protecting the property and lives of her majesty's subjects; and being therefore an act of public duty, they cannot be held responsible to the laws and tribunals of any foreign country."(*x*)

The British Government having thus formally adopted the act of their public officer, it is clear that, according to International Law, the individual ought to have been instantly set free, and redress sought against his Government; such Mr. Webster, himself no mean jurist, well knew to be the law, and accordingly he answered,

"The Government of the United States entertains no doubt that, after this avowal of the transaction as a public transaction, authorized and undertaken by the British authorities, individuals concerned in it ought not, by the principles of public law and the general usage of civilized States, to be holden personally responsible in the ordinary tribunals of law for their participation in it; and the President presumes that it can hardly be necessary to say that the American people, not distrustful of their ability to redress public wrongs by public means, cannot desire the punishment of individuals when the act complained of is declared to have been an act of the Government itself."(*y*)

Nevertheless, the complicated nature of the Federal System *of the North American United States presented in this instance [*54] a great obstacle to the due discharge of their international obligations; for the State of New York claimed a distinct jurisdiction, on account of the violation of its territory and the alleged murder of one of its citizens when the Caroline was destroyed; and in defiance of the clear and sound principle of International Law, which has been mentioned, the Supreme Court of New York delivered its judgment, overruling the plea that M'Leod acted under the orders of the British Government and was therefore irresponsible.

The consequence of the decision was, that M'Leod was left in the custody of the Sheriff, to take his trial for murder and arson at Utica at the next Assizes.

It is clear, however, that Mr. Webster's correct opinion upon the law remained unshaken, for he informed the Attorney-General of the Union,

(*x*) Annual Register (1841), vol. lxxxiii. p. 316. (*y*) Ibid.

that the case, if brought ultimately before the last Court of Appeal, would there be dealt with as a question of International Law.

The trial took place at Utica, in the State of New York, on the 4th of October, and the jury returned a verdict of Not Guilty upon *the facts*, and so this affair terminated; but the consequences of any other decision might have involved the two countries in war. And the whole proceeding demonstrates the truth of the opinion given by the American Attorney-General, that the Federal System, with respect to the discharge of international obligations, is "crippled" and "imperfect."(z)

XXXIX. A State, like an individual, accused of having inflicted wrong upon another, may shape its defence against the charge with reference to the *facts* or to the *law*.

XL. It may *deny*, or it may plead *ignorance* of the *fact*. With respect to the *denial*, it must always be a question of evidence, both as to the wrong itself, and as to the wrong-doer.(a)

[*55] *With respect to *ignorance of fact*, a State may certainly allege that it was not aware of the act of its subjects; but then it must allege this fact *credibly*, as an individual must not only swear, but swear credibly, in order to exculpate himself. For instance, a State would plead idly that it was ignorant of the act of its naval or military forces, or of its accredited public servant.

"It is a wild conceit," said Lord Stowell, sitting in the tribunal of International Law, "that any Court of Justice is bound by mere swearing; it is *swearing credibly* that is to conclude its judgment. If the papers, though formal and regularly attested by a foreign Government on board a ship, say one thing, and the facts another, the court must determine according to the common rules of evidence to which preponderance is due.(b) The circumstances of a case may be such as to make it utterly incredible, although there are confident attestations in support of it; and when judgment is to be passed upon the act of a State, it must proceed, as in the case of an individual, upon the ordinary principles on which the probity and fairness of transaction is examined in the general practice of mankind."(c)

Moreover, when a State can and does plead this credible ignorance, it is bound to repair the injury or punish the *individual* offender, as the case may require; unless, indeed, the injured State, as in the case of a *private* offender it may sometimes lawfully do, has executed justice for himself.

XLI. With respect to the plea of *ignorance of the law*, we are fur-

(z) Vide ante, vol. i. p. 143, note *q*.

(a) The passage usually cited, "Juris ignorantia non prodest adquirere volentibus, suum vero petentibus non nocet," Dig. xxii. t. vi. 7, cannot be properly understood without applying to it those limitations which other parts of the law on the same subject furnish. It probably means no more than to assert the distinction between *error of fact* and *error of law*.

See Savigny, R. R., iii. 348, who has thrown a flood of light upon the difficulties arising from apparently contradictory passages in the Roman Law upon this subject.

(b) The Odin, 1 Rob. Adm. Rep. 252.

(c) The Argo, ib. 159. The Juno, 2 Rob. Adm. Rep. 118. The Neptunus, ib. 111-112.

nished with some valuable maxims of written reason *from the Roman Law(*d*) upon this important *thesis* of jurisprudence, "*de jurist et facti ignorantiâ.*" [*56] The ignorance may relate to a (1) *civil* or (2) a *criminal* subject; but a cardinal maxim with respect to both, and one as applicable to States as individuals, is, that the excuse of *ignorance of the law*, whether it relate to a *civil* or a *criminal* act, can under no circumstances be understood of other than *positive instituted law*, and never of the *law of nature*,(*e*) of which nobody can be ignorant.

XLII. With respect to *civil* subjects, the general rule of jurisprudence, founded upon the Roman Law, is that *ignorance of an error in law* may not, but *an error of fact* may avail to annul a covenant. A person of the best ability may be ignorant of *facts*, but nobody is excused from knowing the *law*, and therefore persons, although ignorant, are subject to it. Some jurists have indeed thought, that in certain matters of covenant, the plea of *ignorance of the law* might be of avail. For instance, when the ignorance was such, that it was the *only cause* of a covenant, whereby a person bound himself under an obligation, to which he would not otherwise have been liable. But even this exception would not, in their opinion, avail to preserve the *erring* or *ignorant* person from suffering loss, though it might avail to preserve him from being deprived of a right which he did not know belonged to him; and if the *ignorance* or *error* was *not* the *sole* cause of the covenant, it could not be annulled. And again, they say, the rights of *third* parties must be considered; for *if, by *ignorance* or *error* of law, a person has injured himself but the injury can not be repaired without [*57] hurting the right of a third person, the injury can not be repaired.

XLIII. With respect to the plea of *ignorance* or *error of law* alleged to cover the commission of a *crime* (*delictum*,) the general rule is clear, that such a plea is inadmissible. The rule is, indeed, subject to certain exceptions; for it must be remembered, that there are two classes of *delicta*.

1. Those, of which the overt act carries with it evidence of the evil intent of the wrong-doer,—acts of *fraud* and *violence* (*dolus, culpa.*)

2. Those, of which the overt act is compatible with a good intent, or the absence of any bad intent, and with *ignorance* that the act is *criminal;* so that the essence of a *delictum* is wanting. Here, however, a distinction must be carefully observed. *Ignorance* of the *nature* of the punishment, or of the *particular law* which inflicts the punishment, does not bring the *delictum* within the shelter of a legal excuse. It must be ignorance that the act is a *delictum*, and a *delictum jure civili*. But, as

(*d*) The reader is referred to the following among other authorities:—
Dig., xxii. t. vi. c. i. t. xviii. Domat, Tr. des Lois, Prél. ix., P. I. l. i. t. xviii. s. 1. Savigny, R. R., iii., Ab. 115, Bey. viii., "Irrthum und Unwissenheit." Story's Commentaries on Equity Jurisprudence, vol. i. c. v., "Mistake." D'Aguesseau, Dissertation sur l'Erreur de Droit, t. v. p. 468.

(*e*) "Veniâ Edicti non petitâ, Patronum, seu Patronam, eorumque parentes et liberos, hæredes insuper etsi extranei sint à libertis seu liberis eorum non debere in jus vocari jus certissimum est: nec in eâ re *rusticitatis* venia prebeatur, cum *naturali ratione* honor hujusmodi personis debeatur."—C., l. ii. t. ii. *Rusticitas* here means rude, unletterred, *ignorance of law*. Domat, ubi supr.

has been said, ignorance that the act is a *delictum jure gentium* is an inadmissible plea. It was upon this principle that the Danish ship, the Neutralität, was condemned (in spite of its name) in the last war. It was carrying the contraband article of *tar* from a foreign port, knowing it to be contraband. "This ship," Lord Stowell said, "goes to a foreign port, to effect that which she is prohibited from doing, even for the produce of her own country: in this respect, throwing off the character of a Danish ship, by violating the Treaties of her country; and all this is done with the full privity of the asserted owner, who is the person entering into the charter-party. In such a case as the present, the known ground on which the relaxation was introduced, the supposition that freights of noxious or doubtful articles might be taken without the personal knowledge of the owner, entirely fails; and the active guilt of the parties is aggravated by the circumstances of its being a criminal traffic [*58] in foreign *commodities, and in breach of explicit and special obligations. The confiscation of a ship so engaged will leave the general rule still untouched, that the carriage of contraband works a forfeiture of freight and expenses, but not of the ship."(*f*)

XLIV. Ignorance that an act is a *delictum Jure Civili*, is illustrated by the instance of a person who *ignorantly* appropriates a thing, the property of another, but which he believes to be his own. Such a person is not guilty of robbery, and the thing is not *res furtiva,* nor is he liable for casualties, or, according to the Roman Law, for intermediate profits.

But a person who takes from another *by force* that which is his own, cannot be heard to plead *ignorance of the law*, which forbids an individual to redress himself by violence, and commands him to have recourse to the established tribunals of the country; and although such an *offender* could not be punished as a robber, the Roman Emperors decreed that he should forfeit the possession of the property which he had so regained.(*g*)

XLV. We have already seen how important this doctrine is in its application to questions of an international character, and that it is as unlawful for the public representative of a State to resist by force the lawful authority of another State, with which his country is at peace, as for a citizen to take by violence the property that is his own without having recourse to the aid of municipal law.(*h*)

Another striking illustration is afforded by the Roman Law, in the case of a lawsuit to recover an inheritance (*hereditatis petitio,*) or a particular thing (*rei vindicatio.*) [*59] In *this case the actual possessor was in a very different condition, accordingly as his possession had been originally *bonæ* or *malæ fidei*. To the former, the *ignorantia juris* was an available plea; to the latter, it was wholly unavailable. No one can be holden to be ignorant of the law applicable to a dishonest

(*f*) The Neutralität, 3 Rob. Adm. Rep. 296.

(*g*) "Sed ne, dum talia excogitantur, inveniatur via, per quam raptores impunè suam exerceant avaritiam: meliùs Divalibus Constitutionibus pro hâc parte prospectum est, ut nemini liceat *vi rapere vel rem, mobilem vel se moventem, licet suam eandem rem existimet* sed si quis contra statuta Principium fecerit, *rei quidem suæ dominio cadere,*" &c.—Inst., l. iv. t. ii. 1. The rule was also applied to immovables.

(*h*) Vide ante, p. 11. The Maria, 1 Rob. Adm. Rep. 360-1.

possession, or to the consequences of it,—his possession is undistinguishable from that of a robber (*prædo.*) But of the former, the law said justly, "*non puto hunc esse prædonem, qui dolo caret, quamvis in jure erret.*"(*i*)

So, in the case of the Betsy,(*k*) Lord Stowell said, "The principal points for our consideration are, whether the possession of the original captors was, in its commencement, a legal, *bonæ fidei* possession? and, secondly, whether such a possession, being just in its commencement, became afterwards, by any subsequent conduct of the captors, tortious and illegal? For on both these points the law is clear, 'that a *bonæ fidei* possessor is not responsible for casualties; but that he may, by subsequent misconduct, forfeit the protection of his fair title, and render himself liable to be considered as a trespasser from the beginning.' This is the law, not of this court only, but of all courts, and one of the first principles of universal jurisprudence."

XLVI. But, besides these particular instances which have been cited, frequent and important applications of these rules of general jurisprudence respecting *ignorance of fact* and *law*, have, it will be seen, taken place in international questions respecting *Capture*,(*l*) *Contraband*, and *Blockade*, in time of war.(*m*) The whole doctrine of the Law of Blockade, with respect to the guilty knowledge or innocent ignorance of those who have, howsoever, violated it, will be found to be built upon the general principles of law which we have been considering.

*The case of the Adams,(*n*) an American ship condemned for breach of the Revenue Laws, was decided, though in fact an international question, by the *Instance*, that is, the municipal side, so to speak, of the High Court of Admiralty; but it furnishes an application of the general principles of law which have been discussed. In that case Lord Stowell observed, that the *misericordia* of the court had been appealed to on account of the *probable ignorance* of a foreign captain, coming in not acquainted with the law, and misled by the governor, the extent of whose authority he could not accurately define. But the learned judge considered it to be an obvious answer to this plea, that whoever trades with a country, be he a foreigner or not, is bound to know the laws of the country with which he trades, *as far as they concerned his own acts*, be the nature and extent of those laws what they may: and so indispensable is the principle of law, that even if he trades under the advice of a skilful practitioner of the law, and that advice should prove erroneous, it would not protect him from forfeiture; and so if he trade under an authority which is insufficient, it will not protect him, because he is as much bound to know the extent of that authority, relatively to himself in that act of trading, as he is to know any other circumstance that is required to constitute the legality of the act. [*60]

The law, it must be confessed, is here laid down with some severity, though it would be difficult to impugn its accuracy. But, in the same case, Lord Stowell exempted from confiscation a certain article, the pro-

(*i*) Dig., v. t. iii. 25-6 (*k*) 1 Rob. Adm. Rep. 95.
(*l*) The Mentor, Ib. 183; The John, 2 Dodson's Adm. Rep. 339-40.
(*m*) Vide post. (*n*) Edwards's Adm. Rep., vii. pp. 309-10-11.

hibition of which could not have been known to the American, upon the ground that, with respect to that article, there was an *invincibe ignorance*, which must excuse the importer of it. Nor has any judge been [*61] more indulgent, in applying the doctrine of *necessity*,(o) as *an excuse for an international offence. The Law of Cases of Necessity, he observes, is not likely to be furnished with precise rules Necessity creates the law,—it supersedes rules; and whatever is *reasonable* and *just* in such cases is likewise *legal*. It is not to be considered as a matter of surprise, therefore, if much instituted rule is not to be found on the subject.(p) A clear necessity is a sufficient justification for every thing that is done *fairly* and with *good faith* under it.(q) It has been well remarked, that it is not the private opinion of the judge upon the policy of the law, national or international, which ought to guide his judgment. He must follow where the law leads, in a general, unbending course. But the law itself, and the administration of it, must yield to that to which every thing else must bend—necessity. The law, in its most positive and peremptory injunctions, is understood to disclaim, as it does in its general aphorisms, all intention of compelling men to perform impossibilities; and the administration of the law must adopt that general exception in the consideration of all particular cases. In the performance of that duty, it has three points to which its attention must be directed. In the first place, it must see that the nature of the necessity pleaded be such as the law itself would respect; for there may be a necessity which it would not. A necessity created by a man's own act, with a fair previous knowledge of the consequences that would follow, and under circumstances which he had then a power of controlling, is of that nature. Secondly, that the party so placed used all practicable endeavours to surmount the difficulties which had already formed that necessity, and which, on a fair trial, he had found insurmountable; not, indeed, the endeavours which a man of the acutest understanding might use, but such as might reasonably be expected from a fair degree of discretion and an ordinary knowledge of business. Thirdly, that all [*62] this *should appear by distinct and unsuspected testimony; for the positive injunctions of the law, if proved to be violated, can give way to nothing but the clearest proof of the necessity that compelled the violation.(r)

When it is so proved, a Court of Justice should strain hard to give, even in the administration of the most unbending laws, the benefit of those maxims in which the common sense and feelings of mankind have always acquiesced.(s) But there is a manifest distinction between cases of *physical necessity*, and cases of *ignorance*. For instance, a ship may be compelled by a storm, which is *vis major*, to put into an interdicted port; the master may *protest*, as the nautical phrase is, against the wind

(o) See Puffendorf, Droit de la N. et des Gens (Barbeyrac,) l. ii. c. vi. "Du Droit et des Privilegés de la Nécessité." Grotius, l. ii. c. ii.; vi. 2; l. iii. c. i. 11; l. iii. c. xvii. 1; l. iii. c. xi. 4.

(p) The Gratitudine, 3 Rob. Adm. Rep. 266-7.

(q) The Cristiansberg, 6 Ib. 378. (r) The Generous, 2 Dod. Adm. Rep. 323-4.

(s) The Adonis, 7 Edw. Adm. Rep. 307.

and the waves, but he cannot bring his action,—there is no person against whom he can have his remedy. But it is otherwise where a party is imposed upon by false appearances, for he has then a remedy against the person by whom he has been deceived.(*t*)

XLVII. Another maxim of Roman and general jurisprudence upon this subject, with respect to individuals, is in some degree also applicable to the mutual intercourse of States,—the maxim that all laws ought to be so intelligible, and so promulgated, as to allow no reasonable plea of ignorance.(*u*)

This requisite is very clearly stated by our own Blackstone(*x*) in his observations upon Municipal Law, which he defines as a rule of civil conduct, *prescribed* by the supreme power of the State. It must be *prescribed,* he says, "Because a bare resolution, confined in the breast of the legislator, without manifesting itself by some external sign, can never be properly a law. It is requisite that this resolution be *notified [*63]
to the people who are to obey it. But the manner in which this notification is to be made, is matter of very great indifference. It may be notified by universal tradition and long practice, which supposes a previous publication, and is the case of the common law of England. It may be notified, *vivâ voce,* by officers appointed for that purpose, as is done with regard to proclamations, and such acts of parliament as are appointed to be publicly read in churches and other assemblies. It may, lastly, be notified by writing, printing, or the like; which is the general course taken with all our acts of parliament. Yet, whatever way is made use of, it is incumbent on the promulgators to do it in the most public and perspicuous manner; not like Caligula, who (according to Dio Cassius) wrote his laws in a very small character, and hung them up on high pillars, the more effectually to ensnare the people. There is, still a more unreasonable method than this, which is called making of laws *ex post facto;* when after an action (indifferent in itself) is committed, the legislator then, for the first time, declares it to have been a crime, and inflicts a punishment upon the person who has committed it. Here it is impossible that the party could foresee that an action, innocent when it was done, should be afterwards converted to guilt by a subsequent law: he had, therefore, no cause to abstain from it; and all punishment for not abstaining must, of consequence, be cruel and unjust. All laws should be therefore made to commence *in futuro,* and be notified before their commencement; which is implied in the term *'prescribed.'* But when this rule is in the usual manner notified, or prescribed, it is then the subject's business to be thoroughly acquainted therewith; for if ignorance of what he *might* know were admitted as a legitimate excuse, the laws would be of no effect, but might always be eluded with impunity."(*y*)

With respect to the general principles of International *Law, [*64]
they are sufficiently promulgated by the dictates of Public

(*t*) The Beaver, 1 Dod. Adm. Rep. 159.

(*u*) "Leges sacratissimæ quæ constringunt hominum vitas intelligi ab omnibus debent ut universo præscripto eorum manifestiùs cognito vel inhabita declinent vel permissa sectentur," &c.—Cod., l. i. t. xiv. 9. Domat, ubi supra, Prél. ix.

(*x*) Comm. vol. i. (Introd. s. 2,) pp. 45-6.

(*y*) Blackstone's Comm. vol. i. p. 45.

Morality, by Custom, by Practice, and by the Reason of the Thing, so far as States, in their *corporate character*, are affected by them. But, with respect to the *Individual subjects* of States, and the operation upon them of belligerent rights which spring out of the *abnormal*(*z*) state of war, and especially with reference to the notification of the particular right of blockade, the doctrine laid down by Blackstone will be found, when the subject comes under discussion, to be extremely applicable.

XLVIII. We have now discussed the causes which *affirmatively* justify war, and the pleas which it is competent to a State to allege either in bar or in mitigation of hostilities. It remains to consider briefly the *negative* side of the question, and to mention the causes which, however often they may have led to this terrible calamity, do *not justify* war.(*a*)

It appears, then, that it is not lawful to make war for the purpose of hindering that aggrandizement of a nation which arises out of the condition of its laws, its liberties, its agriculture, its manufactures, its commerce, or any other source of domestic internal prosperity.

It is not lawful to make war for the purpose of compelling a nation to adopt a particular form of government, or even to vindicate the true religion from the insults of idolatry, or to propagate a particular religion —not even that of our blessed Lord,(*b*)—or, as Grotius observes, to bring
[*65] about the fulfilment *of prophecy; the instrument of which fulfilment may perhaps be the criminal acts of individuals or States.(*c*)

Lastly, if the reasoning be sound and the proposition correct which have been advanced in the early part of this work,(*d*) it is not lawful to make war for the *punishment*(*e*) of a nation.

The early *fecial* practice of Rome conveys, amid all the pedantic minuteness of its forms, a lesson upon the scrupulous mnnner in which

(*z*) Vide ante, p. 1.

(*a*) "Quæ autem sint causæ injustæ cognosci aliquatenus potest ex justis causis quas hactenus explicavimus. Rectum enim obliqui est index. Sed perspicuitatis causâ summa genera annotabimus."—Grotius, l. ii. c. xxii. 4.

(*b*) "Perduxit nos ad delicta quæ in Deum committuntur, quæritur enim an ad ea vindicanda bellum suscipi potest . . . Potior ratio pro sententiâ negante justa esse bella talia, hæc est, quando Deus sufficiat vindicandis quæ in se committuntur." —Grot., l. ii. c. xx. s. 44.

"Concerning the means of procuring unity, men must beware that, in the procuring or muniting of religious unity, they do not dissolve or deface the laws of charity and of human society. There be two swords amongst Christians, the spiritual and the temporal: and both have their due office and place in the maintenance of religion: but we may not take up the *third sword*, which is Mahomet's sword, or like unto it, that is, to propagate religion by wars, or by sanguinary prosecutions to force consciences, except it be in cases of overt scandal, blasphemy, or intermixture of practice against the State."—Bacon's Essays, of Unity in Religion.

"The overt scandal,', and "blasphemy," are not, if the doctrine in the text be correct, among the just causes of war.

(*c*) Grot., l. ii. c. xxii. s. 15.

(*d*) Vol. i. c. i. s. 11.

(*e*) Grotius: the c. xx. of l. ii. is "De Pœnis." It begins, "Supra cum de causis ex quibus bella suscipiuntur agere cœpimus, facta diximus duplici modo considerare, aut ut reparari possunt, aut ut puniri. Priorem partem jam absolvimus. Superest posterior quæ est de pœnis: quæ res eò diligentiùs tractanda est nobis, quod origo ejus et natura, minus intellecta, multis errationibus causam dedit." Ib., c. xxi., is "De Pœnarum Communicatione."

International Justice should be prosecuted, which ought to sink deep into the hearts of Christian Governments. Grotius reminds us,(*f*) that upon the same principle as the Romans consulted the *Collegium Feciale*, the early Christian Emperors rarely made war without consulting the bishops, in order that, if religion interposed any impediment, they might be made aware of it; and among the most striking speeches in Shakspere, is the adjuration of Henry V. to the Archbishop of Canterbury, to speak boldly his opinion as to the lawfulness of the intended war against France; as the verses contain an admirable admonition upon the terrible wickedness of an unjust war, it *may perhaps be allowed to relieve the necessary dryness of a legal discussion, and to close this chapter by their citation: [*66]

"And God forbid, my dear and faithful lord,
That ye should fashion, bow, or wrest your reading,
Or nicely charge your understanding soul
With opening titles miscreate, whose right
Suits not in native colours with the truth.
For God doth know how many now in health
Shall drop their blood in approbation
Of what your reverence shall incite us to.
Therefore, take heed how you impawn our person,
How you awake the sleeping sword of war;
We charge you, in the name of God, take heed:
For never two such kingdoms did contend
Without much fall of blood; whose guiltless drops
Are every one a woe, a sore complaint
'Gainst him whose wrongs give edge unto the swords
That make such waste in brief mortality.
Under this conjuration speak, my lord,
And we will hear, note, and believe in heart
That what you speak is in your conscience washed,
As pure as sin from baptism."(*g*)

---

*CHAPTER IV. [*67]

WAR.

XLIX. The necessity of War, and the laws relating to it, are a consequence of the depraved nature of societies, just as the necessity of the criminal law of a society is a consequence of the depraved nature of the individual.(*a*)

(*b*) War is the exercise of the international right of action, to which, from the nature of the thing and the absence of any common superior tribunal, nations are compelled to have recourse, in order to assert and vindicate their rights.

(*f*) L. ii. c. xxiii. s. 4.

(*g*) Henry V. act i. sec. 1.

(*a*) Hooker, Eccles. Pol., b. i. s. 10.

(*b*) The student of Grotius will perhaps find that he will obtain the most consecutive view of the great master's opinion upon the whole subject of War by reading the whole of l. i. and l. ii. c. i. to end of s. 17, then leaping to l. ii. c. xx. s. 38, and from thence reading on to the end of c. v. of l. iii.

A War ought, therefore, to combine the following characteristics:—

1. It must be declared or waged by the public authority of the State, and carried on through the agency of those who have been duly commissioned for that purpose by that authority. A War between private individuals who are members of a society cannot exist. The use of force in such a case is a trespass or violation of Municipal Law, and punishable as such, and not War. "Neque, quod singulorum hominum est, rectè dixeris privatum bellum, quia privatum nihil est, nisi ratione publici, quod, ubi civitas non est, nullum est."(c) According to an early
[*68] but very sound definition offered by **Albericus Géntilis*, the precursor of Grotius, "Bellum est publicorum armorum justa contentio."(d)

2. It must have the reparation of injury, the re-establishment of right, the restoration of order into the mutual relations of States, and security against future derangement of these relations, for its object and end.

3. The means, therefore, through which this terrible process is to be executed, must be in strict conformity with this end.

War is not to be considered as an indulgence of blind passions, but as an act of deliberate reason, and, as Lord Bacon says, "no massacre or confusion, but the highest trial of right."(e)

L. This international right of action has become from long usage, implying general consent, from the reason of the thing, from Christian principles, and partly, no doubt, from the peculiar institution of chivalry, well furnished with rules and maxims for its conduct. It is regulated by a code as precise and as well understood as that which governs the intercourse of States in their pacific relations to each other.

The great principle upon which all these rules are framed, is that of, on the one hand, compelling the enemy to do justice as speedily as possible, and, on the other hand, of abstaining from the infliction of all injuries both upon the subjects of the enemy, and upon the Government and subjects of third Powers which do not, certainly and clearly, tend to the accomplishment of this object.

(f)Wanton devastation of the enemy's territory, wanton cruelty exer-
[*69] cised towards his subjects, are, therefore, according *to the principles and practice of Christian nations, unjustifiable and illegal.

Nevertheless, it is to be remembered, that as the will of the subject is bound up in that of his Government, it may well be that the consequences of the conduct of his rulers may be attended with injury both to the person and property of the subject, and that the enemy is justified in striking through them at the Government from which he has received a wrong, and for which redress has been denied.

It is, in fact, in many cases, only through the privations and distresses

(c) Bynkershoek, Q. J. P., l. i. c. i. (d) De Jure Belli, lib. i. cap. ii.

(e) Vide ante, vol. i. p. 11.

(f) "Le droit des gens est naturellement fondé sur ce principe, que les diverses nations doivent dans la paix le plus de bien, et dans la guerre le moins de mal qu'il est possible, sans nuire à leurs véritables intérêts."—Montesquieu, De l'Esprit des Lois, l. i. c. iii. Blackstone's Comm., b. iv. c. v.

of the subject that his Government will be induced to put an end to the War by according the justice demanded.

Nevertheless, as War is the conflict of *societies*, that is, of corporate bodies recognising and governed by law in all their actions, War must be and is, as has been stated, carried on with reference to rules and principles of law governing that particular mode of social action; and if this were true in the time of Cicero, who said that in the beginning, the continuing, and the ending of War, justice and faith were largely interested,(*g*) surely it is not less true since the introduction and profession of Christianity; and if the Romans have justly merited our praise for those *Fecial*(*h*) institutions by which they sought to invest War with the character and formalities of civil justice, it would be disgraceful to Christian Governments if they assented to the doctrine that in War the furies are to be let loose, and each party is to be at liberty to do that which seems good in his own eye. It is the more necessary to protest against such a doctrine as, from particular causes, such as the desire to maintain a particular theory, it has received some colour of sanction from the writings of eminent men.

Thus Mr. Hume, arguing "that public utility is the sole origin of justice, and that reflections on the beneficial consequences *of this virtue are the sole foundation of its merit,"(*i*) supports his [*70] proposition by a reference to public War: "What is it," says he, "but a suspension of justice among the warring parties?—the laws of War which then succeed to those of equity and justice, are rules calculated for the advantage and utility of that particular state in which men are now placed." Mr. Hume has been well answered by one of his countrymen and a brother philosopher: "I answer," says Professor Reid,(*k*) "when war is undertaken for self-defence or for reparation of intolerable injuries, justice authorizes it. The laws of War which have been described by many judicious moralists are all drawn from the fountain of justice and equity; and everything contrary to justice is contrary to the laws of War. That justice which prescribes one rule of conduct to a master, another to a servant, one to a parent, another to a child, prescribes also one rule of conduct towards a friend, and another towards an enemy. I do not understand what Mr. Hume means by the *advantage* and *utility* of a state of War, for which he says the laws of War are calculated, and succeed to those of justice and equity. I know no laws of War that are not calculated for justice and equity."(*l*)

Bynkershoek, rioting in the exercise of his vigorous but somewhat coarse intellect, expresses his opinion that everything is lawful against an enemy *as such*. "You make war," he says, "because you think that

(*g*) "Sequitur enim de jure belli: in quo et suscipiendo et gerendo et deponendo *jus* ut plurimum valet et *fides*."—De Leg., l. ii. c. xiv.

(*h*) "Horumque ut publici interpretes essent lege sanximus."—Ib

(*i*) Hume's Essays, Of Justice, vol. ii. pt. i. p. 217.

(*k*) Reid's Essays on the Powers of the Human Mind, vol. iii. p. 435, Essay V., "Of Justice."

(*l*) Mr. Hume argues, consistently, that when a criminal is punished, there "is a suspension of the ordinary rules of justice," and that it is *suitable* that there should be such a suspension.

your enemy, on account of the injury which he has done to you, has deserved the destruction of himself and his subjects; and that being your object, what does it matter how you attain it? You may therefore kill [*71] him when he is unarmed, or hire an assassin *to do so,(*m*) poison him, or make a slave of him. A judge," he says, "who orders a convicted criminal to be slain by the axe of the executioner, though he be in chains and unarmed, is not, on that account, called *unjust*. If he were to loosen the bonds of the criminal and put a weapon into his hands, there would be a trial of courage and fortune, and not a punishment of a wrong-doer."

This illustration appears, by the incorrectness of its analogy, to furnish an answer to the doctrine which it is adduced to support.

In the case of the criminal, there is no doubt that he is a wrong-doer, and that his execution has been lawfully ordered by a competent authority.(*n*) But in the case of contending nations, it may, and we must hope generally does, happen that both parties believe that right is on their side. "Atque hinc," says Grotius, "passim recepta est sententia, subditos quod attinet, dari *bellum utrimque justum*, id est injustitiâ vacans, quò illud pertinet."(*o*) But as States acknowledge no common tribunal upon earth, they are constrained, as the civilians say, *litem suam facere*, or, according to the common English phrase, "to take the law [*72] into their own hands," and *to consider success in the strife as the decision of God in their favour.

To say that this is often a mistaken presumption, to object that this method of obtaining justice is unsatisfactory, uncertain, and attended with cruel injury to the innocent, is but to complain that we live in a world in which evil and good are mixed together, and which has the blemishes of imperfection;(*p*) but this absence of a common tribunal, this want of a competent International Judge, this consequent necessity of war, does furnish in its admitted imperfection, as a mode of judicial procedure, a very good reason to all societies, and especially to all Christian societies, why a broad distinction should be made between the criminal convicted by the judge, and the enemy conquered by the enemy,—

(*m*) Dixi, *per vim*. Non per vim *justam*, omnis enim vis in bello justa est, si me audias, et ideo justa, cum liceat hostem opprimere, etiam inermem, cum liceat veneno, cum liceat *percussore immisso*, et igne factitio, quem tu habeas, et ille forte non habet; denique cum liceat, ut uno verbo dicam, quomodocunque libuerit."—Bynkershock, Q. J. P., l. i. c. l. I am sorry to see that the words *percussore immisso* are incorrectly rendered *missile weapons*, in the generally useful translation of Mr. Du Ponceau. (Philadelphia, 1810.)

(*n*) "Quod inter duos populos de jure belli pronuntiare velle periculosum fuerat aliis populis, qui eâ ratione bello alieno implicarentur, sicut Massilienses in causâ Cæsaris et Pompeji dicebant, neque sui judicii neque suarum esse virium discernere utra pars justiorem haberet causam: deinde, quod etiam in bello justo vix satis cognosci potest ex indiciis externis, quis justus sit se tuendi, sua recuperandi, aut pœnas exigendi modus, ita ut omnino præstiterit hæc religioni bellantium exigenda relinquere, quam ad aliena arbitria vocare."—Grotius, l. iii. c. iii. 4.

(*o*) L. ii. c. xxvi. s. 4, p. 3.

(*p*) "As to War, if it be the means of wrong and violence, it is the sole means of justice among nations: nothing can banish it from the world. They who say otherwise, intending to impose upon us, do not impose upon themselves. But it is one of the greatest objects of human wisdom to mitigate those evils which we are unable to remove."—Burke, Letters on â Regicide Peace, viii. 181.

why it is not lawful to treat the honest warrior and the guilty murderer in one and the same manner; and if this be so, reason, morality, and religion, alike commend to the understanding and the conscience of nations, that cardinal principle of the law of war, to which reference has been already made, and by which it is decided "that everything is *not* lawful against an enemy," but only those things which are essential to the vigorous prosecution and speedy termination of the war.(*q*)

The truth is that here again we may apply a remark made in an early part of this treatise with respect to the distinction between Right and Comity, namely, that the practice and *usage of nations was perpetually transplanting the concessions of Comity into the domain [*73] of Right;(*r*) and so it has fared with the law of War since the time when Bynkershoek lived. As to mere historical precedents in such a matter, we are reminded of Bynkershoek's own indignant but just attack upon one who defended the fraudulent evasion of treaties. "Sed quia eam rem rationibus tueri non potest unicè tuetur scelerum exemplis."(*s*)

Those harsh and barbarous practices, that pushing of an extreme principle to its most odious extreme, has ceased to be among the legal usages of War. An abstinence from them, which Bynkershoek would have ascribed to the dictates of magnanimity (*animo magnitudo*) and not to the obligations of right (*justitia,*) is now enjoined by the recognized rule of warfare of civilized States. To put to death the unarmed and unresisting prisoner, to poison the enemy, to sell the captive into slavery,(*t*) to employ the arm of the assassin, are practices which the voice of Christendom has both reprobated and rendered illegal; for instance, Bynkershoek says, that when the Roman Consuls wrote to King Pyrrhus "*nobis non placet pretio aut prœmio, aut dolis pugnare,*" and apprised him that an offer to poison him had been made to them, they did an act of extraordinary generosity; but during the last war with France, the British Government sent notice to the First Consul of a similar offer which had been made to them, and not to have done so would have been unworthy of any Christian State.

With respect to the use of fraud or stratagem, while it cannot be contended that such an instrument of War is illegal, the doctrine of Bynkershoek that every species of deceit, except perfidy, is lawful, is too broad a proposition; for instance, Prize Courts have held that though sailing under false *colours does not, firing under them does subject the vessel to the penaties of the illegal act. [*74]

Perfidy is clearly illegal, and for the reason assigned by this author, namely, that the parties to the promise or stipulation, are, so far as that is concerned, divested of the character of enemies.

(*q*) I cite with pleasure the language of Bodinus, far sounder upon this point than Bynkershoek, however inferior to him as a jurist in other respects:—"At qui bello injusto captivos servare humanitatis esse putant, consimiliter faciunt, ut latrones, ac piratæ, qui se vitam dedisse jactant, quibus non ademerunt."—De Repub., l. i. p. 34. (Parisiis: ed. 1586.)

(*r*) Vol. i. pp. 160-1.

(*s*) Quæst. Jur. Pub., l. ii. c. ix.

(*t*) "Of being taken by the insolent foe,
And sold to slavery."—Othello, act i. sc. iii.

[*75] *CHAPTER V.(*a*)

WAR—DECLARATION UNNECESSARY.

LI. THE precise date which marks the beginning of the War is, on account of the change which is then effected in the duties and obligations both of belligerent and neutral States, a subject of very great importance.

Some International Jurists dwell upon the distinction between a War which is *solemnly*, and a War which is *not solemnly* proclaimed.

Albericus Gentilis, Grotius, Puffendorff, Huberus, Zouch, are of opinion that every War should be preceded by a solemn declaration; though Gentilis and Zouch think that it may be dispensed with in certain cases; and it certainly would appear that Valin and Emerigon considered hostilities not preceded by such a declaration as little, if at all,
[*76] removed from acts of *piracy. On the other hand, Bynkershoek, Heineccius, and most modern publicists, hold that no such solemn declaration is necessary; and any person who has read the chapter of Bynkershoek on the subject, will perceive that his view is sustained both by the reason of the thing and by the practice of nations.

In the case of the Nayade, decided in the English Prize Court, property was claimed by a person professing to be a subject of Portugal, and with respect to the capture, it was argued, that there was nothing to show that Portugal was at that time at war with France; that if the Government of Portugal submitted to suffer injury and indignity rather than give a pretext to the rapacious ambition of France by declaring War, merchants resident within that country were entitled to the benefit of a state of peace.

"Lord Stowell said in his judgment,—"It may be necessary to consider, in the first place, the situation in which Portugal then stood. The relation which that country has borne towards France, at different periods, has been extremely ambiguous. At first there was a wish on the part of Portugal not to consider herself as being at war with France; and if a submissive conduct, and a disposition not to resent injuries, could have afforded protection against the violence of France, she might have escaped. But it is equally notorious, that all these concessions were made without success, and proved utterly inefficacious to prevent Portugal from being implicated in War with France.

"In cases of this kind, it is by no means necessary that both countries should declare War. Whatever might be the prostration and submissive

(*a*) Grotius, l. iii. c. iii., "De Bello Justo sive Solenni Jure Gentium, ubi de Indicatione." Bynkershoek, Q. J. P., l. i. c. ii., "Ut Bellum sit legitimum, Indictionem Belli non videri necessariam." Heinecc., El., II. s. 198. Vattel, l. iii. c. iv. Klüber, s. 2, p. 238. Hautefeuille, Des Droits et des Devoirs des Nations Neutres, l. i. t. iii. s. 2, p. 1. Rutherforth, Inst., B. ii. c. ix. ss. 10, 15. Wheaton, Elém., t. i. c. i. ss. 6, 7, 8.

Ward, An Enquiry into the Manner in which the different Wars in Europe have commenced during the last two Centuries; to which are added the Authorities upon the Nature of a Modern Declaration (pub. 1805), a treatise full of information on this subject. Wildman, Int. Law, B. ii. pp. 5-8.

demeanour on one side, if France was unwilling to accept that submission, and persisted in attacking Portugal, it was sufficient; and it cannot be doubted by any body who has attended to the common state of public affairs, that Portugal was considered as engaged in War with France. Without adverting to particular instances, it is notorious and evident from this very *case, that there was a French commissary stationed at Lisbon for the regulation of French prisoners. At the time of this transaction, Portugal must, indubitably, be taken to have been at war with France."(b) [*77]

And in a later case (1813,) in which a question arose with respect to the neutrality of Sweden, at the time of the seizure of American ships in Swedish waters, Lord Stowell said, "After this, a declaration of War was issued by the Government of Sweden; but it is said that the two countries were not, in reality, in a state of War, because the declaration was *unilateral* only. I am, however, perfectly clear that it was not the less a War on that account, for War may exist without a declaration on either side. It is so laid down by the best writers on the Law of Nations. A declaration of War by one country only is not, as has been represented, a mere challenge, to be accepted or refused at pleasure by the other. It proves the existence of actual hostilities on one side at least, and puts the other party also into a state of War, though he may, perhaps, think proper to act on the defensive only."(c)

LII. The argument derived from the *practice* of nations, has received, as will be seen, strong confirmation from the precedents which have happened since the period when Bynkershoek wrote. We pass by, therefore, the continued conflicts between Queen Elizabeth and Philip II., which preceded the invasion of the Spanish Armada without any declaration, and, indeed, without any acknowledgment of War, only remarking, by the way, that no such declaration heralded the invasion of the Armada itself. But we must observe that the great Gustavus, without any declaration, invaded the dominions of the Emperor of Germany, and that he gave, as a reason for so doing, the assistance which the Emperor had afforded to his (Gustavus's) enemy, the King of Poland.

*It is to be remembered that this assistance had been rendered nearly a year before the invasion of Germany. [*78]

Loccenius observes upon this conduct of Gustavus in a remarkable manner:—"Cæsari vero indicere bellum, rex non necessarium esse putavit, quum vim sibi ab eo prius haud denuntiatis armis, illatam arcere, natura ipsa permitteret; et hoc ipso satis denuntiatum bellum a se esse crederet."(d)

We pass by, too, the celebrated Wars between the English and the Dutch in the seventeenth century, carried on, as Bynkershoek well knew, without any previous declaration.

It is worthy of remark, however, that Prince Rupert, in his narrative laid before Parliament (November, 1664,) says, that he considers certain violent acts on the part of the Dutch Admiral, as a denunciation of War against him.

(b) 4 Rob. Adm. Rep. 253. (c) The Eliza Ann, 1 Dod. Adm. Rep. 247.
(d) L. viii. p. 567.

LIII. In the war (1688) which ensued upon the League of Augsburg, Louis XIV. marched to the Rhine, invested all, and captured some, of the fortresses of the Palatinate before the publication of his manifesto of War.

The great War of the Spanish Succession was carried on for many months without any declaration.

The bloody battle of Chiari was fought on the 1st September, 1701—the formal declaration on the part of the Emperor was published on the 15th of May, 1702, and that of the King of France during the month of July in the same year.

LIV. After the Treaty of Utrecht, in 1718, England, resolving to prevent the invasion of Sicily by Spain, gave instructions to the Commander of her Mediterranean fleet to repair to Spain and apprize the King that England would not allow any further violation of the Treaties by which he was bound; and that if the invasion was not abandoned, England would oppose Spain with all her power.

Byng, the English Admiral, repaired to Cadiz, and sent his despatches to Stanhope, the English Ambassador at Madrid.

[*79] *Spain was governed at that time by the profligate adventurer Alberoni, who, after a few hours' consideration of the English demand, wrote a passionate answer to the effect that Byng might execute his orders; and the consequence was the entire destruction of the Spanish fleet at Passaro, on the 11th August, 1718.

Here we have an instance in which all the requirements of International Law are satisfied without any formal declaration of War, and in which the necessity of any such declaration would, by the intervening delay, have enabled Spain to destroy the ally whom the English fleet was sent to protect.

The Spanish Ambassador, Monteleone, at the British Court, and Alberoni, filled Europe with remonstrances against an act, which they stigmatised as being "contrary to the Law of Nations, and a breach of solemn Treaties;" and their language was echoed by some of the opposition to Government in Parliament; and on this side are to be ranged the authorities derived from the names of Walpole, Cowper, and Bathurst. But Sir Joseph Jekyll, though not a friend to the Government, expressed a sounder opinion upon the law of the case, when he said that "he was fully convinced, that if there was any injustice, it was on the side of the King of Spain; and that the conduct of His Majesty and his ministers was entirely agreeable to the Law of Nations, and the rules of justice and equity." Mr. Ward (who gives a very spirited account of the whole transaction) observes, that "his (Sir. J. Jekyll's) conduct and opinion were by far the most rational. No one denies, as a general, unexplained proposition, that it is unjust to attack, without declaration, or pending an *amicable* negotiation. No one, on the other hand, can deny that there may be specific circumstances, which may take the matter out of the general rule. In concluding the account of this remarkable case, we must observe, that by the fifth article of the Treaty of Madrid, June 13th, 1721, it was agreed that all the ships taken in the battle of Passaro, or their values, should be restored. That Treaty stipulated the mutual restitution of all goods, *merchandizes, money, and *ships* [*80] taken since the commencement of the War, *whether before or after the declaration;* that is, of all things, when or wheresoever taken. Hence the third article states, that Spain will restore everything, or its value, that had been seized in Europe, or in the West Indies, *by virtue of the orders in the month of September*, 1718. This was the epoch of hostilities on the part of Spain."(*e*)

LV. It was the sad destiny of Spain to fall under the misgovernment of Ripperda, after she had escaped from that of Alberoni. The mysterious Treaty of Vienna, in 1726, was almost the first act of the new minister, and led to a fresh embroilment. Ripperda soon made shipwreck of his fortunes in the storm which he had raised; and eventually, as we have seen, fled for refuge to the English Ambassador at Madrid.(*f*) From this refuge he was forcibly taken; the English Ambassador resented the act as a violation of ambassadorial privileges, and while sharp remonstrances were passing between the two Courts, an English fleet arrived in the Spanish waters. The Admiral obtained permission, on the faith of the existing peace, to enter Santona; the Spanish Minister, however, immediately wrote to the English Ambassador, desiring him to declare, "without any equivocation," what were the true intentions of the British Admiral. "The king," said he, "expects you to reply by the return of the messenger; and if your excellency does not immediately answer *categorically and without equivocation*, his majesty will take such measures, and give such orders, as suit his royal service."

"The import of these words," Mr. Ward observes, "is always understood as *a conditional declaration of War*."(*g*)

The English Ambassador replied, that he must communicate with his own Sovereign; and an answer was returned *from England [*81] containing a list of grievances, and complaining that no reparation had been offered for the insult to the ambassador. In the meantime, the ill-fated and ill-used Hosier sailed with another fleet to the West Indies, and prevented the sailing of the galleons from Portobello to Spain. It is difficult to distinguish such conduct from open War; but it was not till six months afterwards that the Spanish Ambassador at London delivered in a memorial to the Duke of Newcastle, in which he announced, that the longer continuance of the squadron in the West Indies would be a continuance of voluntary hostilities, authorised by his Britannic Majesty. "*As such,*" said the ambassador, "*the King, my master, does already, and will look upon them;* he thinks himself justified to repel these injuries and *hostilities* with all the power that God hath put into his hands; and he has a right to require the stipulated succours from his allies: he would be glad to cultivate peace, but he neither can nor will hearken any more to any complaint, while His Britannic Majesty shall be, with arms in hand, in the dominions of Spain, as he effectually is, while his squadron is continued in the West Indies."(*h*)

The King of England, in his speech to parliament, on the 17th of January, 1727, stated that he considered this language to be "little short

(*e*) Ward, pp. 22-3. (*f*) Vide ante, vol. ii. p. 210. (*g*) Ward, ib., pp. 24-5.
(*h*) Ward, ib., pp. 26-7. Historical Register, 1727.

of a *declaration* of War." Nevertheless, the squadron of Hosier was not withdrawn, and the British ministry did not conceive that the state of war had begun. Spain, however, making no further *declaration*, immediately entered upon the siege of Gibraltar; protesting, indeed, that she did so to preserve the tranquillity of Europe. The lives of many soldiers were lost, but England never declared war; though, six weeks after the trenches had been opened at Gibraltar, she issued letters of reprisal. Walpole, however, was at the helm in England, and on the 15th of May, in the same year, made the king observe, in his speech to parliament, [*82] *that, though the attack of Gibraltar put the views of Spain out of doubt, the love of peace had hitherto prevailed with him to *suspend*, in some measure, his resentment; and, *instead of having immediate recourse to arms*, to concur with France and Holland in making overtures of accommodation, which would demonstrate to whose ambition the calamities of war were to be imputed, *if these just and reasonable propositions were rejected.*(*k*)

No war was declared. Walpole continued to negotiate, until the preliminaries of peace were signed at Vienna, in the end of May, 1727.(*l*)

LVI. The famous war between England and Spain, which grew out of the story of the *guardas costas*, and the "fable of Captain Jenkins' years,"(*m*) was formally declared, though something not unlike open hostility had previously taken place. This war was arrested, for a very short time, by the Convention del Sardo, on the 17th of January, 1739. But, inasmuch as the sore subject of the Right of Search, as well as the demand of Spain for payment of a disputed debt by the South Sea Company, were left unsettled points, the flames of war were soon kindled again, but first came fresh negotiations, during which an English fleet made a demonstration in the Mediterranean; and the Spanish Minister observed, *that his master looked upon the peace as at an end;* that there was no dependence upon the Court of London while the squadron was on the coast; and that if they did not yield the right of search, *there was no occasion for further discussion.*(*n*)

Negotiation, however, continued: and an *ultimatum* was sent to Spain, requiring her to abandon the right of search. She evaded an answer, [*83] and *general*(*o*) letters of marque and *reprisal were issued by England on the 10th of July. Nevertheless, the ministers of both Courts remained.

France offered mediation; and, in the midst of hostile captures, negotiation was continued.

The English Ambassador at Madrid offered to revoke the letters, upon condition that justice was done to this country; but the King of Spain replied, with justice, that general reprisals were War, which he wonld repel with all his power. Spanish reprisals had issued on the 20th of July; but it was not till two months after the English letters of reprisal, that the ambassadors left the courts to which they were accredited; and,

(*k*) Ward, ib., pp. 27-8.
(*l*) Tindal, xix. 591. (*m*) Burke, vol. viii. p. 149, Letters on a Regicide Peace.
(*n*) Ib., xx. 419. Ward, p. 29. (*o*) Vide ante, p. 12.

as an *answer* to the Spanish manifesto, War was *formally declared* by England on the 19th of October.

LVII. In this War between England and Spain, France after a short time intervened as a principal; for with this War became mixed up another, which arose out of the disputed succession to the inheritance of the House of Austria upon the death of Charles VI. It is, however, a most singular circumstance, that before France openly intervened as a principal, the battle of Dettingen (1743) was fought between French and English troops, the latter commanded by their king in person, not only without any *declaration* of War, but while the ambassadors of both countries were still resident at the respective courts. After this battle, France entered into a secret Treaty with Spain, and at the same time assembled an army and fleet at Brest and Dunkirk, in order to assist the Pretender in a descent upon England, whose son was said to have been present in person at one of these two places. A naval action had taken place in the Mediterranean, between the English fleet on the one side and the Spanish and French fleets on the other; and it was not till after these hostilities by sea and land had been waged, that the English Ambassador—for, most strange to say, one was still resident at the Court of France—remonstrated on the 7th of February, 1747, and demanded the dismissal of the Pretender *by virtue of Treaties.* He was answered, on the 14th, by Amelot, the French Minister, that *when the King of England should give satisfaction* *for the breach of those very Treaties*, the King of France would explain himself upon the subject of the demand.(*p*) [*84]

Vattel says,(*q*) that in the last Treaty of Aix-la-Chapelle, that is to say, the Treaty of 1748, between France and Spain on the one side, and England on the other, it was agreed that all the prizes taken before the declaration of War should be restored. Now this statement is one of extraordinary inaccuracy; for, in the first place, there is no mention of declaration at all in the article; in the second place, though the article does fix a time, *after* which all prizes shall be restored, it says nothing about a time *before* which they shall be pronounced illegal; and in proof of this assertion the article is here given at length:—

"*Art.* IV. All the prisoners made on the one side and the other, as well by sea as by land, and the hostages required or given during the War, and to this day, shall be restored, without ransom, in six weeks at latest, to be reckoned from the exchange of the ratification of the present Treaty; and it shall be immediately proceeded upon after that exchange: and all the ships of war, as well as merchant vessels, that shall have been taken *since* the expiration of the terms agreed upon for the cessation of hostilities at sea, shall be, in like manner, faithfully restored, with all their equipages and cargoes; and sureties shall be given on all sides for payment of the debts which the prisoners or hostages may have contracted in the States where they have been detained, until their full discharge."(*r*)

(*p*) See this declaration, and the counter one of England, in Tindal's Hist., vol. ix. pp. 28-32. Ward, ib., p. 31. Mahon, Hist. of England, vol. iii. p. 267.

(*q*) L. iii. c. iv. s. 56.

(*r*) Chalmer's Collect. of Treaties, vol. i. pp. 428-9.

The mistake of Vattel is far too important to be passed by without notice and correction, in a treatise on International Law; for it is justly observed by Mr. Ward, that, before the formal *declaration* was made of [*85] that War, which was terminated* by the peace of Aix-la-Chapelle, eight months of bloody hostility had subsisted, the battle of Dettingen had been fought between France and England, as auxiliaries, and the fight of Toulon had taken place as principals; and it is therefore manifest that if the prizes taken *before the declaration* had been placed upon a different footing from those which were made afterwards, there would be room for the inference, not only that Vattel thought a declaration *exclusively* necessary, but that France, England, and Spain agreed with him in the opinion. It should be observed, also, that there is nothing in the preliminary Treaty, 19th April, 1748, which could have misled(*s*) Vattel in this matter.

LVIII. The Seven Years' War furnishes us with two more precedents upon this subject:—

1. The War between France and England, which was kindled by the disputes about the limits of their possessions in Canada, and which may be said to have begun in 1754, was not preceded by any declaration of War. On the 15th of March, 1755, the king announced to parliament that he had sent a fleet to protect our American possessions against the French, and the English Admiral had *instructions to fight the French fleet whenever he should meet them;* and these instructions were communicated to the French Ambassador, resident at our court, who replied, that his master would consider the first gun that was fired as a *declaration* of War. The English Admiral, shortly afterwards, took two ships [*86] of the French, off the coast of Newfoundland. *In the mean while open War had been carried on in America; a large number of French merchantmen, and one 74-gun ship, fell into the hands of the English; yet we find that on the 21st of December, 1755, the French Minister sent a Memorial to the English Secretary of Foreign Affairs complaining of the attack of the English Admiral and the cruisers in *Europe*, and offering to negotiate with respect to *America*, but demanding, as a preliminary, the restoration of all prizes which he said had been piratically taken. The Spanish Minister also protested, with respect to these prizes, upon the same ground.

Mr. Fox, the English Minister, replied, that nothing had been done until after the aggressions of the French upon the English in Canada; and he justly repudiated, as altogether untenable, the position which France endeavoured for the first time to establish, that a War in America was to be distinguished from a War in Europe, and, therefore, that the

(*s*) Mr. Ward observes, that what perhaps led Vattel into the mistake "was the frequent recurrence in the Treaty of the phrase, 'every thing shall be re-established on the footing they were on *before the War;*' and in particular, the second article, by which all 'effects, dignities, enclesiastical benefices, honours, and revenues, enjoyed at the *commencement of the War*, shall be restored, notwithstanding all dispossessions, seizures, or *confiscations* occasioned by the said War.' Vattel uses the word *prizes*, which generally means ships. But no ships were to be restored by name; nor could any that had been confiscated by the Admiralty have been restored at all, the right having passed out of the crown and vested in the captors."—Ward, ib., p. 68, note.

captures in Europe made before *declaration* were illegal. Mr. Fox also justly rested the attack by the English Admiral *on the law of self-defence,* and pointed out the situation where the captures were made, as evidence that they were taken in *an hostile enterprise;* and Mr. Ward correctly observes, "he would have done well to have added, what alone must have closed the subject, that a declaration had, in effect, been made to the Ambassador of France, who had accepted the challenge, and knew all its consequences."(*t*)

A regular declaration of War does not appear to have been made by France before the 15th of May, 1756; then ensued five years of one of the most memorable wars which England has ever carried on.

In 1761, a negotiation called, from the names of those who conducted it, the Negotiation of Stanley and Bussy, was set on foot.(*u*)

"By Article XI. of the first Memorial, presented by *France, it was demanded, that captures *before* the declaration, *except king's ships*, should be restored, or a recompense made, because taken *contrary to the Law of Nations.*"(*v*) [*87]

And here it may be remarked, that the exception proposed in favour of merchantmen, as contrasted with King's ships, is wholly at variance with one of the most fundamental rules of International Law, namely, that the will of the subject is bound up in the will of his Government.(*x*)

The answer to this demand was perfectly sound in point of reason and justice, and was no doubt framed with the advice of the eminent civilians who were at that time the advisers of the crown.

"The demand of restitution of captures before the War cannot be admitted, for it is not founded upon any particular convention, nor yet resulting from the Law of Nations; for the right of hostilities does not result from a formal declaration of War, but from the hostilities which the aggressor first offered."(*y*)

The soundness of the law and the justness of the reasoning appear to have been eventually admitted by the enemy himself; for though this answer was dictated while the genius and energy of Chatham presided over the British Councils, yet even at the Peace of Paris in 1763, when they had been exchanged for the narrow-minded pedantry of Lord Bute, the restoration of these prizes was not mentioned with respect to the claims of France, but with respect to Spain, who had subsequently become a party to the War,(*z*) the XVI. Article contained the following provisions:—

"The decision of the prizes made, in time of peace, by the subjects of Great Britain, on the Spaniards, shall be referred to the Courts of Justice of the Admiralty of Great *Britain, conformably to the rules established among all nations, so that the validity of the said prizes, between the British and Spanish nations, shall be decided [*88]

(*t*) Ward, ib., p. 37. (*u*) Mahon, vol. iii. pp. 346-7.
(*v*) Ann. Reg. (1761), vol. v. p. 260. (*x*) Vide ante, p. 8.
(*y*) Ann. Reg. vol. iv. art. x. "Of Answer," p. 263.
(*z*) Lord Chatham, as is well known, resigned in 1761, because the Cabinet would not declare War against Spain, of whose hostile intentions they then had abundant evidence.

and judged according to the Law of Nations, and according to Treaties, in the Courts of Justice of the nation who shall have made the capture."(*a*)

LIX. (2.) The second precedent which is furnished by the Seven Years' War, grows out of the conduct of the King of Prussia in his invasion of the territories of Austria and Saxony, without any previous declaration of War. His conduct with respect to the King of Saxony is so mixed up with flagrant and indefensible perfidy, that it affords little instruction upon the legal question as to the practice of nations in beginning a War, without any previous declaration. But with respect to Austria the case is different. A very clear account of this transaction is thus given by Mr. Ward :—

"On an inspection of the different diplomatic pieces, published by each party, the King of Prussia's cause for War seems to have been this. After the peace of Dresden, in 1745, the Cabinet of Vienna taking a hostile disposition on his part, as a sort of basis, revived and new-modelled a partition Treaty with Saxony, by which, in case of War, and on the supposition of conquests, their different shares of the King's dominions were settled in due precision. A secret Convention was afterwards made with Russia, by which any quarrel between her and the Court of Berlin was to be considered as the common cause of all the Three Courts. To this Convention the partition Treaty with Saxony was held to be applicable; and though it was not executed by the King of Poland, it was only in the fear that Prussia might discover it, and instantly make it a cause for War. It was, however, agreed, that he should be *considered* as a party, as much as if had actually signed. In pursuance of this alliance, attempts were made by Austria to bring on a War between the Czarina [*89] and Prussia, in order that she might *interfere without seeming to be the aggressor. This had nearly succeeded in 1755, and was only delayed from the want of magazines in Livonia, where an army of 70,000 men was ordered to be prepared, for the purpose of making actual War in the succeeding year.

"Such seems to have been the plan resolved upon by the three Courts, whose designs, with copies of all the Treaties and instructions were regularly communicated by a Saxon secretary to the King. It may be supposed that so vigilant a character was not indifferent to his situation. He kept an eye on Livonia, where, finding the Russians had begun to assemble, he marched an army into Pomerania. The Austrians, also beginning to march troops into Bohemia, he was resolved at once to bring the point to a decision. But though fully prepared, he wished to avoid a War if possible, and therefore demanded of the Court of Vienna a frank explanation of its views. The Empress, by the *previous* advice of Kaunitz, resolved to elude the demand by an answer neither sinister nor favourable. She therefore replied, that in the violent crisis of Europe, it was her duty to take measures for her security and that of her allies. This was settled (according to Kaunitz's own account to Fleming, the Saxon minister,) with a view to force the King of Prussia to become the aggressor, which account was also communicated to Berlin. The King

(*a*) Art. xvi., Chalmers's Collect. of Treaties, vol. i. p. 477.

yet made another effort, and offered to disarm, if the Empress would engage not to attack him for two years. To this was required a categorical answer; but proceeding upon the same principle, the Empress only returned, that the countries being at peace, no such caution was requisite. Upon this evasion, coupled with a knowledge of the motives upon which it was concerted, the king signified to the Court of Vienna, that he should consider the answer as a declaration of War;(*b*) and *his armies, without further form, or waiting for the departure of his Ambassador, instantly commenced hostilities."(*c*) [*90]

LX. To the conduct of France in forming an alliance (in 1788) with the revolted North American colonists of Great Britain, attention has been already drawn in an early part of this volume,(*d*) and it has been said, perhaps without sufficient precision of language, and in too popular a manner, that this conduct "was immediately followed by a declaration of War on the part of Great Britain against France."

It would have been more correct to say that it was followed by the withdrawal of the English Ambassador, and the communication of a message from the Crown to Parliament, as follows:—"His Majesty, having been informed by order of the French King, that a Treaty of Amity and Commerce has been signed between the Court of France and certain persons employed by his majesty's revolted subjects in North America, has judged it necessary to direct that a copy of the declaration delivered by the French Ambassador to Lord Viscount Weymouth, be laid before the House of Commons; and, at the same time, to acquaint them, that his majesty has thought proper, in consequence of this offensive communication on the part of the Court of France, to send orders to his Ambassador to withdraw from that Court.

"His majesty is persuaded, that the justice and good faith of his conduct towards foreign Powers, and the sincerity of his wishes to preserve the tranquillity of Europe, will be acknowledged by all the world; and his majesty trusts that he shall not stand responsible for the disturbance of that tranquillity, if he should find himself called upon to resent so unprovoked and so unjust an aggression on the honour of his Crown, and the essential interest of his kingdoms, contrary to the most solemn assurances, subversive of the *Law of Nations, and injurious to the rights of every Sovereign Power in Europe."(*e*) [*91]

A doubtful state of things ensued, fluctuating between Peace and War; for in spite of the remonstrance of some of the wisest statesmen of Great Britain,(*f*)—a remonstrance which subsequent events well justified,—the French Mediterranean fleet was allowed to proceed to America, where it arrived in July, 1778; there engagements took place between the English and French ships, though no declaration of war was then *known* to have been issued. In the meanwhile the channel fleet of

(*b*) Œuvres du R. de P. Guertede, Sept. Ans. i. 46. See also, for all the documents, Mém. Raisonnée, &c., avec les Pièces Justificatives (published by the Court of Berlin.)

(*c*) Ward, pp. 40-1. (*d*) Vide ante, p. 18.

(*e*) Ann. Reg. (1778), vol. xxi. p. 290.

(*f*) Almon's Debates in Parliament, vol. viii. pp. 292, 304; vol. x. p. 100.

England, under admiral Keppel, came into collision with the naval forces of France.

The English admiral's situation (observes the writer(*g*) of the History of England in the Annual Register of 1779)(*h*) was nice and difficult. War had not been declared, nor even reprisals ordered. It was, however, necessary to stop these frigates, as well in order to obtain intelligence as to prevent intelligence being conveyed. Indeed it seemed a matter of indispensable necessity not to miss the opportunity of acquiring some knowledge of the state, situation, and views of the enemy. But that fluctuation of counsels, which, as has been stated, seemed to prevail at that time, joined to the peculiar circumstances of the admiral's political situation, rendered any strong measure exceedingly hazardous. He might have been disavowed, and a war with France might be charged to his rashness, or to the views and principles of his party. In this dilemma, the admiral determined to pursue that line of conduct which he deemed right, and to abide the consequences. The subsequent behaviour of the French frigates seemed calculated to afford a justification for any measure of violence which he could have adopted; and the celebrated action
[*92] between La Belle Poule and the Arethusa, and *the capture of the Licorne,(*i*) took place off Brest on the 17th June, 1788; and then "the French king made use of the engagement with the Belle Poule, and the taking of the other frigates, as the ostensible ground for issuing out orders for reprisal on the ships of Great Britain; and the ordinance for the distribution of prizes, which, as we have already observed, had been passed a considerable time before, although hitherto kept dormant, was now immediately published. Similar measures were likewise pursued in England, as soon as the account of these transactions was received. Thus nothing of War was wanting between the two nations, excepting merely its name, or rather the formality of the proclamation."(*k*)

The French king complained that the Law of Nations had been violated, because there had been no declaration of war previously to the naval actions which we have mentioned. Now it is remarkable that the French king wrote to his admiral on June 5th, before a shot had been fired, to

(*g*) Probably Mr. Burke. (*h*) P. 58.

(*i*) Mr. Ward thus abridges the account given in the Annual Register: "The latter (the Belle Poule) was pursued out of sight of the fleet by the Arethusa frigate, and refusing to return to speak with the English Admiral, an action of great gallantry and desperation was fought on the very coast of France, by favour of which the *Belle Poule* escaped, after losing, by her own account, ninety-nine men in killed and wounded. The *Licorne*, was brought under the admiral's stern in the night, her captain treated with every sort of civility, and orders were issued that he should be attended without the least molestation till the morning. When that arrived, a shot being fired across his way, to keep him steady in his course, he poured his broadside into the *America*, at the very moment when her commander, Lord Longford, was speaking to him on the gunwale, in the most friendly terms, and instantly struck his colours. The *Pallas*, another French frigate, which hove in sight, was detained, in consequence of the hostility and bad conduct of the *Licorne*, but many merchantmen were allowed to pass unmolested; and the admiral then learning the immense superiority of the enemy's force, returned into port."—Ward, p. 46. Ann. Reg. (1779,) vol. xxii. pp. 59-60.

(*k*) Ann Reg. (1779), vol. xxii. p. 63.

express a hope that the enemy would grant the same immunity to his *fisheries, which he then promised to those of the English. But [*93] never, in truth, was a more groundless complaint published to the world.

France had *declared* War when she announced her Treaty with the rebellious subjects—for such at that time they were—of Great Britain, when she sent her fleet to America with orders which could not fail to lead to open hostilities; she declared War when she recalled her ambassador, and no one cognizant of the principles of International Law can seriously doubt that it was perfectly competent to England, upon the announcement of that Treaty and the withdrawal of her ambassador, to have immediately commenced open hostilities, or to have adopted the preventive measure of embargo. It was simply a question of discretion on the part of England as to the moment at which she would choose to order the first cannon to be fired,—a discretion which the timidity and bad judgment of her counsellors caused her to exercise in the manner least injurious to her enemy.

LXI. The War of the French Revolution was not preceded by any formal declaration between England and France. On the 31st of December, 1792, Lord Grenville wrote to M. Chauvelin: "If France is really desirous of maintaining friendship and peace with England, she must show herself disposed to renounce her views of aggression and aggrandisement, and to confine herself within her own territory, without insulting other governments, without disturbing their tranquillity, without violating their rights."(*l*)

To this the French Executive replied: "If her (England's) explanations are yet insufficient, and if we are yet obliged to hear a haughty language,—if hostile preparations are yet continued in the English ports, after having exhausted every means to preserve peace,—we will prepare for War, with a sense of the justice of our cause, and of our efforts *to avoid this extremity. We will fight the English, whom we [*94] esteem, with regret, but without fear."(*m*)

The English ambassador was withdrawn, and the French ambassador dismissed; and after all these proceedings there can be no doubt that the vote of War by the National Assembly of France, and the seizure of English property, was perfectly justifiable *in point of form.*

LXII. Mr. Ward observes, that in the short war with the northern confederacy in 1801, after much discussion and mutual embargoes, Sir Hyde Parker, at the mouth of the cannon, acquainted the Commandant of Cronenberg, that he should consider the first gun that was fired as a declaration of War.

LXIII. In the War of 1812, between the North American United States and England, hostilities were immediately begun on the part of the United States as soon as the Act of Congress was passed, without waiting to communicate to the English Government any notice of their intentions.(*n*)

LXIV. The War into which we are now plunged was preceded by

(*l*) Ann. Reg. (1793,) vol. xxxv. p. 118.

(*m*) Ann. Reg. (1793,) vol. xxxv. p. 122.

(*n*) 1 Kent's Comm. 54.

every possible formality, and, as we have seen, with an unexampled leniency towards the goods and persons of the subjects of the enemy.

The instances which have been adduced are sufficient in point of number and magnitude, to show that so far as the practice of nations is concerned, a *precedent declaration* of War is not *ex debito justitiæ inter Gentes.*

LXV. We have now examined, upon this question of the necessity of a *formal declaration* of War, two of the acknowledged sources of International Law, namely, *the Authority of Jurists*, and *the Practice of Nations;* and if we consider *the Reason of the Thing*,(*o*) another and principal source of this jurisprudence, it will be found to support the view which has been taken in the foregoing pages. For what does *the reason of the thing* require as a preliminary to [*95] *actual war? Not that the party compelled to seek redress should afford his enemy, the wrong-doer, an opportunity of strengthening himself in his injustice;(*p*) and even, taking the other supposition, that both parties conceived themselves to be fully in the right, no analogy of private jurisprudence suggests that the one party should concede to the other any advantage in the law suit, whether it be that of evading the tribunal or of mending his case; the truth is, that good faith and the general interests of the Society of States require that when one member of it is about to exchange friendly for belligerent relations with another, he should not do so until fair and reasonable notice of his intentions has been communicated, "*et quidem* (to adopt the words of Grotius) ita decretum publicè ut ejus rei significatio ab alterâ partium alteri facta sit."(*q*)

The channel of communication is, after all, of little importance, whether it be through a demand accompanied by a direct intimation that upon its refusal recourse would be had to War; or whether that intimation may be indirectly suggested by the nature of the demand itself, and the surrounding circumstances of the case, among which circumstances considerable weight must be ascribed to the withdrawal of the ambassador.(*r*)

(*o*) Vide ante, vol. i. c. iii.

(*p*) And so Vattel, who is sometimes cited as an authority for the necessity of the *declaration*, observes:—"Le droit des gens n'impose point l'obligation de déclarer la guerre pour laisser à l'ennemi le temps de se préparer à une injuste défensive. Il est donc permis de faire sa déclaration seulement lorsque l'on est arrivé sur la portière avec une armée, et même après que l'on est entré dans les terres de l'ennemi, et que l'on y a occupé un poste avantageux, toutefois avant que de commettre aucune hostilité. Car de cette manière, on pourvoit à sa propre sûreté, et on atteint également le but de la déclaration de guerre, qui est de donner encore à un injuste adversaire le moyen de rentrer sérieusement en luimême, et d'éviter les horreurs de la guerre, en faisant justice. Le généreux Henry IV. en usa de cette manière envers Charles-Emmanuel, duc de Savoie, qui avait lassé sa patience par des négociations vaines et frauduleuses."—L. iii. c. iv. s. 60.

(*q*) L. iii. 3-5.

(*r*) De Rayneval insists on the necessity of a declaration, but he says: "Quant à la forme des déclarations de guerre, elle a varié: l'essentiel est qu'elles soient connues, ou *censées connues*, par l'ennemi avant les hostilités. Elle doit être notifiée aux puissances neutres."—Instit. de la Nature et des Gens, t. ii. l. iii. c. ii. s. 2.

[*96] *And this is, after all, the conclusion to which a careful investigation of all the passages upon the subject in Grotius(*s*) and Vattel would lead us; for we must always distinguish between the necessity of a *declaration* of War, previous to the commencement of hostilities, and the necessity of some *public proclamation* or *manifesto*, accompanying hostilities when commenced; such a manifesto might perhaps well satisfy the *indictio* or the *denuntiatio* of Grotius, but at all events it is imperative, upon two grounds: first, in order that the other members of the society of States may be apprized of the reasons which have necessitated a recourse to War, that is, to a state of things which must greatly affect their rights and their duties, "*Interpellatio* requiritur quâ constet alio modo fieri fieri nequire ut nostrum aut nobis debitum consequamur;" and, secondly, in order that the subjects of the belligerents may be duly acquainted with an event which brings with it new obligations on their part towards their Government, "exterum jure gentium *ad effectus illos peculiares* omnibus casibus requiritur *denuntiatio*, non utrimque sed, ab *alterâ partium." Barbeyrac conceives [*97] that Grotius intends by these words "the right of appropriating what is captured from the enemy," which right, as he truly observes, cannot, as a matter of *International* Law, be affected by the fact of a declaration. And here must be repeated an observation made in an earlier part of this work, with respect to one great advantage to the general commonwealth of nations which flows from these manifestoes, namely, that they frequently contain, not only expositions of the causes which have led to this result, but also a defence of the conduct of the Government, founded upon a reference to the principals of International Law, whether in declaring an offensive or a defensive War. These public documents furnish, at all events, decisive evidence against any State which afterwards departs from the principles which it has thus deliberately and solemnly invoked; and in every case they clearly recognize the *fact*, that a system of law does exist, which *ought* to regulate and control the international relations of every State.(*t*)

It should be observed, before this subject be dismissed, that, according to Vattel,(*u*) the War might *lawfully* commence *immediately* after

(*s*) Grotius says: "Ut bellum *solenne* sit ex jure gentium *duo* requiruntur; primùm ut geratur utrimque auctore eo, qui summam potestatem habeat in civitate; deinde ut *ritus quidem adsint* de quibus agemus *in suo loco*."—L. i. 3-4. And yet *in suo loco*, he describes no particular ceremonial, and expressly rejects the notion of their being any necessity for observing the ceremonies of the *Fecial Law*, or, indeed, for a *bellum solenne* at all, which, indeed, had fallen in desuetude long before the passages were inserted in the Digest. Grotius goes on to say: "Sed ut justum hoc significatu non sufficit inter summas utrimque potestates geri, sed oportet, ut audivimus, ut et publicè decretum sit et quidem ita decretum, ut ejus rei sigificatio ab alterâ partium alteri facta sit, unde promulgata prœlis dixit Ennius."—L. iii. 3-5.

He then cites Cicero, as saying, "Nullum bellum esse justum nisi quod *aut rebus repetitis*, *aut denuntiatum* ante sit et indictum." This is exactly the doctrine in the text: War must be after satisfaction demanded—*rebus repetitis*. And Grotius says that when the War is waged to repel aggression or to repel an actual offender, "nulla requiritur denuntiatio."—L. iii. c. 3, 6.

(*t*) Vide ante, vol. i. p. 50.

(*u*) "Comme il est possible que la crainte présente de nos armes fasse impression

[*98] the *declaration*,—a concession which reduces *the supposed necessity of it to a practical absurdity. If a State may march an army to the frontiers of a State, declare War, and enter the borders of the State the next minute, no one object of a *declaration* is attained which is not equally attained by a promulgation at home, or by any other means of giving notice of hostile intentions: and here Bynkershoek's(*v*) question must be answered, "quid enim *a vi* distat *negata petitio?*" The refusal sufficiently puts the refusing State upon its guard.

LXVI. It remains to notice the doctrine of the *Public* Law of England upon this question.

Lord Chief Justice Hale, after speaking of the ceremonies attendant on a *Solemn Law*, observes, "whether these handsome methods be observed or not, yet if *de facto* there be a War between princes, they and their subjects are in a state of hostility, and they are in the condition of enemies (hostes) to each other; but now for the most part these ancient solemnities are antiquated."(*w*)

The learned judge goes on to say that "a general War is of two kinds: *bellum solemniter denuntiatum*, or *bellum non solemniter denuntiatum.* The former sort of War is when War is solemnly declared or proclaimed by our king against another prince or State; thus after the pacification between the king and the Dutch at *Breda*, upon new injuries done to us by the Dutch, the king by his printed declaration, 1671, declared War against them; and this is the most formal solemnity of a War that is now in use.

"A War that is *non solemniter denuntiatum* is, when two nations slip suddenly into a War without any solemnity; and this ordinarily happeneth among us. The first *Dutch* War was a real War, and yet it began barely upon general letters of *marque.* Again, if a foreign prince invades our coast, or sets upon the king's navy at sea, hereupon, a real, [*99] though not a solemn War, may, and hath formerly arisen, and *therefore, to prove a nation to be in enmity to England, or to prove a person to be an *alien enemy*, there is no necessity of showing any War proclaimed, but it may be averred, and so put upon trial by the country, whether there was a War or not; and therefore p. 31 Eliz. in Justice Owen's Reports,(*x*) in an action of debt, the defendant pleaded

sur l'esprit de notre adversaire, et l'oblige à nous rendre justice, nous devons encore ce ménagement à l'humanité, et surtout au sang et au repos des sujets, de déclarer à cette nation injuste, ou à son conducteur, que nous allons enfin recourir au dernier remède, et employer la force ouverte pour le mettre à la raison. C'est ce qu'on appelle *déclarer la guerre.*"—L. iii. c. iv. s. 51.

And to this he adds, in a subsequent passage: "Il faut que la déclaration de guerre soit connue de celui à qui elle s'adresse. C'est tout ce qu'exige le droit des gens naturel. Cependant, ci la coutume y a introduit quelques formalités, les nations qui, en adoptant la coutume, ont donné à ces formalités, *un consentement tacite*, sont obligées de les observer, tant qu'elles n'y ont pas renoncé publiquement. Autrefois les puissances de l'Europe envoyaient des hérauts ou des ambassadeurs pour déclarer la guerre; aujourd'hui on se contente de la faire publier dans la capitale, dans les principales villes, ou sur la frontière; on répand des manifestes, et la communication, devenue si prompte et si facile depuis l'établissement des postes, en porte bientôt la nouvelle de tous côtés."—L. iii. c. iv. s. 55.

(*v*) Ubi suprà. (*w*) Hale's Pleas of the Crown, vol. i. p. 162.

(*x*) Owen, 45.

that the plaintiff was an *alien*, born in Gaunt under the obedience of the King of Spain, enemy of the queen, the plea was ruled good, though he showed not that any War was proclaimed between the two realms; and according is the pleading, 7 E. 4, 13. Rastel's Entries, Trespass per Alien.(*y*)

"And in very deed there was a state of War between the Crowns of England and Spain, and the Spaniards were actual enemies, especially after the attempt of invasion in 88, by the Spanish Armada, and yet there was no War declared or proclaimed between the two crowns, as appears by Camden, sub anno 31,(*z*) ibidem, p. 404, et ibidem, p. 466;(*a*) so that a state of War may be between two kingdoms without any proclamation or indication thereof, or other matter of record to prove it.

And therefore in the case in question touching treason, it shall upon the trial be inquired by the jury, whether the person, to whom the party indicated adhered, were an enemy or not, and, in order to that whether there were a War between the King of England and that other Prince whereunto the party adheres. This is purely a question of fact, and triable by the jury, and accordingly is the book 19 E. 4, 6; and the reason is plain, because it may fall out, that though there were a league between the King of England and a foreign Prince, yet the War may be begun by the foreign Prince. Again, suppose we, that the King of England and *the King of France be in league, and no breach thereof between the two Kings, yet if a subject born of the King [*100] of France makes War upon the King of England, a subject of the King of England adhering to him is a traitor within this law, and yet the Frenchman that made the War is not a traitor but an enemy, and shall be dealt with as an enemy by martial law, if taken; this was the case ot the Duke of Norfolk adhering to the Lord Herise, a subject of the King of Scots, in amity with Queen Elizabeth, that made an actual invasion upon England without the King's commission:(*b*) so that an enemy extends further than a King or State in enmity, namely, an alien coming into England in hostility."(*c*)

Mr. Justice Blackstone, after commenting upon the rule of the Roman Law,(*d*) which distinguishes *enemies* from *robbers*, and upon the reasoning of Grotious with respect to a declaration of War, goes on to say, "So that, in order to make a War completely effectual, it is necessary with us in England that it be publicly declared and duly proclaimed by

(*y*) Rastel's Ent., pp. 605, d., 252, b.

(*z*) Viz. 1588.

(*a*) Sub anno 1592.

(*b*) M. 13 & 14 Elizabeth, Co. P. C., p. 11. Camden's Elizabeth, sub anno 1571, and also 1572, in principio. 14 Elizabeth, p. 175, and the case of Perkin Warbeck, a Frenchman, 7 Coke's Reports. Calvin's case, 6 Dyer's Reports, p. 145, n. (*a*). Sherlys's case, 7 Coke. Calvin's case, ib. 6, n. (*a*).

(*c*) Hale, pp. 163-4.

(*d*) "Hostes sunt, quibus bellum publicè populus Romanus decrevit, vel ipsi populo Romano; ceteri latrunculi vel prædones appellantur. Et ideo qui a latronibus captus est, servus latronum non est, nec postliminium illi necessarium est. Ab hostibus autem captus, ut puta a Germanis et Parthis, et servus est hostium, et postliminio statum pristinum recuperat."—Dig., xlix. t. xv. s. 24.

"Hostes hi sunt, qui nobis, aut quibus nos publicè bellum decrevimus; cæteri latrones aut prædones sunt.—Ib., L. t. xvi. s. 118.

the sovereign's authority; and then all parts of both the contending nations, from the highest to the lowest, are bound by it."(*e*)

[*101] *The English Courts have holden that they will take judicial notice that a War exists between this country and a foreign State, such War having been recognized in different Acts of Parliament; and, therefore, that an allegation to this effect need not be proved.(*f*)

The English Courts have also holden that the public acts of Government, and acts by the king in his political capacity, are commonly announced in the Gazette, published by the authority of the crown; and of such acts the Gazette is admitted in Courts of Justice to be good evidence. A proclamation for reprisals, published in the Gazette, is evidence of an existing War. Proclamations for a public peace, or for the performance of a quarantine, and any acts done by or to the king in his regal character, may be proved in this manner; and upon the same principle, articles of War, purporting to be printed by the king's printer, are allowed to be evidence of such articles.(*g*)

In the case of the Nayade, which has been already cited,(*h*) Lord Stowell decided that War might exist, so far as the rights of a third State were concerned, between two other States without any formal declaration; the point is perhaps not so clear when the question is between two States, one of which only has declared War, and of which declaration the other State has taken no public cognizance. This is a question rather of Public than International Law, but it should be mentioned that in a subsequent case in 1812, in which a question arose about the capture of a Swedish vessel by a British ship, Lord Stowell observed—"The point on which the captors rely for condemnation in the present case is, the legal incapacity of the claimants in their real character to carry on the trade in which they had engaged. What was the relative situation of British and Swedish subjects at the time when this [*102] capture took place? Sweden had *issued a declaration of War against this country, but that had not been echoed by any counter-declaration on the part of Great Britain; neither had the British Government caused any notification to be made to its own subjects respecting the fact of the Swedish proclamation. It might, perhaps, be a question of some nicety, to determine how far this unilateral declaration, not acted upon or even notified to them by the Government of their own country, would affect the right of British subjects to carry on their accustomed intercourse with the ports of Sweden."(*i*)

[*103]

*CHAPTER VI.

HOW WAR AFFECTS THE RELATIONS OF ALL STATES.

LXVII. WAR effects a change in the mutual relations of all States;

(*e*) Commentaries on the Laws of England, b. i. c. vii. s. 3.
(*f*) Rex v. Roberts & others, 1 Campbell's Reports, 399.
(*g*) Russell on Crimes, vol. ii. p. 805. (*h*) Vide ante, 76.
(*i*) The Success, 1 Dodson's Adm. Rep. 133.

more immediately and directly in the relations of the belligerents and their allies, but mediately and indirectly in the relations of States which take no part in the contest.

War, of necessity, brings with it new rights to the belligerent and new obligation to the neutral. It is not, as it is sometimes inaccurately expressed, that there ensues a *collision* between the *rights* of the two parties, because a collision of rights is, accurately speaking, impossible, but that the rights of the neutral were always subject to the contingency of being affected and modified by War; for "every duty is a limitation of some power."(*a*) And as war is a lawful mode of obtaining redress and adjusting differences between independent States, and as this end requires that compulsory means of destruction and distress should be inflicted upon the persons and property of the enemy,(*b*) no neutral State has a right, for the sake of private advantage, to prevent these compulsory means from producing their effects.

It matters not whether the war be called *offensive* on the one side, and *defensive* on the other. It may happen that the nominally offensive is the really defensive war,—that the *first blow has been struck by way of defence to ward off a menaced and anticipated blow,— [*104] nor does it matter upon which element, earth or water, the war be carried on,—the rules and principles of War, the rights of belligerents and the duties of the neutral are the same, whether the war be called offensive or defensive, and whether it be carried on by sea or by land.

In the case, indeed, of an ally, bound to assist when his friend is attacked, but not always when he attacks, the *casus fœderis* may, as will be seen hereafter, be affected by the fact, whether the war be offensive or defensive on the part of the friend. But as, owing partly to the fact of the establishment of International Courts of *Prize*, and the fact of the non-establishment of similar Courts of *Booty*,(*c*) and partly to the reason of the thing, arising from the character of warfare by sea, it has happened that the *maritime* intercourse of nations during war has been subject to a code of more detail and more precision than the intercourse by land, it will therefore be convenient to consider the questions relating to belligerent rights *at sea*, apart and distinct from those *on land*, though the principle of public policy and public law are, as Lord Stowell observed, "just as weighty upon the one element as the other."(*d*)

LXVIII. We must now proceed to consider the effect of War upon—

1. The property and persons of the subjects of the belligerent State.
2. The property and persons of the subjects of the ally.
3. The property and persons of the subjects of the enemy.
4. The property and persons of the subjects of the neutrals.

LXIX. First, as to the effect of War upon the property and persons of the subjects of the belligerent.

The cardinal maxim of law, which meets us on the threshold, and which

(*a*) Burke, Appeal from the New to the Old Whigs, Burke's Works, vol. ix. p. 202.

(*b*) "Neque enim bellum gerere, quicquam aliud est, quam id, quod quis sibi deberi existimat, manu extorquere ab invito et renitente Principe vel Populo."—Bynk., Q. J. P., l. i. c. iv.

(*c*) Vide post.

(*d*) The Hoop, 1 Rob. Adm. Rep. 217.

[*105] most materially affects the whole question, is this, *that the will of the subject is bound up in that of his Government, or of the government of the country in which he is domiciled, as to matters of trade,(e) so far as Public and International Law are concerned with the question.(f) The leading case on this subject is the Hoop,(g) which contains a review of the law of all countries on this important subject. Lord Stowell supports his opinion, that by the Law of England all trading with the public enemy is interdicted, by the following argument:—

"In my opinion, there exists such a general rule in the maritime jurisprudence of this country, by which all trading with the public enemy, unless with the permission of the sovereign, is interdicted. It is not a principle peculiar to the maritime law of this country; it is laid down by Bynkershoek as an universal principle of law—*Ex naturâ belli commercia inter hostes cessare non est dubitandum. Quamvis nulla specialis sit commerciorum prohibitio, ipso tamen jure belli commercia esse vetita, ipsæ indictiones bellorum satis declarant,* &c. He proceeds to observe, that the interests of trade, and the necessity of obtaining certain commodities, have sometimes so far overpowered this rule, that different species of traffic have been permitted *prout e re suâ, subditorumque suorum esse censent principes.* But it is in all cases the act and permission of the sovereign. Wherever that is permitted, it is a suspension of the state of war *quoad hoc.* It is, as he expresses it, *pro parte sic bellum, pro parte pax inter subditos utriusque principis.* It appears from these passages to have been the law of Holland; Valin, l. iii. tit. 6, art. 3, states it to have been the law of France, whether the trade was attempted to be carried on in national or in neutral vessels: it will appear, from a case which I shall have occasion to mention (the
[*106] Fortuna,) *to have been the law of Spain; and it may, I think, without rashness, be affirmed to have been a general principle of law in most of the countries of Europe.

"By the law and constitution of this country, the sovereign alone has the power of declaring war and peace—he, alone, therefore, who has the power of entirely removing the state of war, has the power of removing it in part, by permitting, where he sees proper, that commercial intercourse which is a partial suspension of the war. There may be occasions on which such an intercourse may be highly expedient. But it is not for individuals to determine on the expediency of such occasions on their own notions of commerce, and of commerce merely, and possibly on grounds of private advantage not very reconcilable with the general interest of the State. It is for the State alone, on more enlarged views of policy, and of all circumstances that may be connected with such an intercourse, to determine when it shall be permitted, and under what regulations. In my opinion, no principle ought to be held more sacred than that this intercourse cannot subsist on any other footing than that

(e) The Indian Chief, 5 Ib. 19. "A criminal transaction on the common principle, that it is illegal in any person *owing an allegiance, though temporary,* to trade with the public enemy."

(f) The Santa Cruz, 1 Ib. 61.

(g) The Hoop, 1 Ib. 198.

of the direct permission of the State. Who can be insensible to the consequences that might follow, if every person in time of war had a right to carry on a commercial intercourse with the enemy, and, under colour of that, had the means of carrying on any other species of intercourse he might think fit? The inconvenience to the public might be extreme; and where is the inconvenience, on the other side, that the merchant should be compelled in such a situation of the two countries to carry on his trade between them (if necessary) under the eye and control of the government charged with the care of the public safety.

"Another principle of law, of a less politic nature, but equally general in its reception and direct in its application, forbids this sort of communication as fundamentally inconsistent with the relation at that time existing between the two countries; and that is, the total inability to sustain any contract by an appeal to the tribunals of the one *country [*107] on the part of the subjects of the other. In the law of almost every country, the character of alien enemy carries with it a disability to sue, or to sustain in the language of the civilians *a persona standi in judicio.* The peculiar law of our own country applies this principle with great rigour. The same principle is received in our courts of the Law of Nations; they are so far *British* courts, that no man can sue therein who is a subject of the enemy, unless under particular circumstances that *pro hâc vice* discharge him from the character of an enemy; such as his coming under a flag of truce, a cartel, a pass, or some other act of public authority that puts him in the king's peace *pro hâc vice.* But otherwise he is totally *exlex;* even in the case of ransoms which were contracts, but contracts arising *ex jure belli,* and tolerated as such, the enemy was not permitted to sue in his own proper person for the payment of the ransom bill; but the payment was enforced by an action brought by the imprisoned hostage in the courts of his own country, for the recovery of his freedom. A State in which contracts cannot be enforced, cannot be a State of legal commerce. If the parties who are to contract have no right to compel the performance of the contract, nor even to appear in a Court of Justice for that purpose, can there be a stronger proof that the law imposes a legal inability to contract?—to such transactions it gives no sanction; they have no legal existence; and the whole of such commerce is attempted without its protection and against its authority. Bynkershoek expresses himself with great force upon this argument in his first book, chapter 7, where he lays down that the legality of commerce and the mutual use of Courts of Justice are inseparable: he says, that cases of commerce are undistinguishable from cases of any other species in this respect—*Si hosti semel permittas actiones exercere, difficile est distinguere ex quâ causâ oriantur, nec potui animadvertere illam distinctionem unquam usu fuisse servatam.*

"Upon these and similar grounds it has been the *established [*108] rule of the law of this court, confirmed by the judgment of the Supreme Court, that a trading with the enemy, except under a royal license, subjects the property to confiscation:—and the most eminent persons of the law sitting in the Supreme Courts have uniformly sustained such judgments."

An uniform current of English precedents is cited as supporting this opinion. The highest authority of the N. A. United States confirms this judgment of Lord Stowell. "No principle," says Mr. Justice Story, "of national or municipal law is better settled than that all contracts with an enemy, made during War, are utterly void. This principle has grown hoary under the reverend respect of centuries, and cannot now be shaken without uprooting the very foundations of national law."(*h*)

No rule of law is in fact better established by the universal usage of the community of States. This rule of interdiction in no degree arises from the commerce being carried on by sea, the principles of public policy and public law equally forbid commercial intercourse by land; and when an enemy existed in the other part of the island of Great Britain, such intercourse was deemed equally criminal in the jurisprudence of our country.(*i*)

When the belligerent maritime rights and the question of licenses come under consideration, we shall see with what strictness this rule has been applied during the last War to cases, in which supplies have been brought to a British colony during its temporary subjection to the enemy, and to cartel ships.

In the present War it has pleased the Crown of England both to waive [*109] a great portion of her belligerent rights respecting *neutral States, and also, with respect to her own subjects, to allow, with certain exceptions relating to Contraband of War and Blockade, that her subjects shall and may, during and notwithstanding the present hostilities with Russia, freely trade with all ports and places, wheresoever situate, which shall not be in a state of blockade, save and except that no British vessel shall, under any circumstances whatsoever, either under or by virtue of this order or otherwise, be permitted or empowered to enter or communicate with any port or place which shall belong to or be in the possession or occupation of her majesty's enemies.(*k*)

LXX. Every State has a right to call home its subjects who are in a foreign country, when their presence is deemed necessary by the Government for the defence of their country.

Every State has a right to forbid its subjects to serve the enemy against their country, and to punish them in case of disobedience. The same principle applies to prohibit all communication or correspondence, and, as we have seen, all commerce with the enemy. It is simply a question of policy and expediency whether, and with what degree of vigour, the right shall be enforced. But *all* contracts with the enemy are null and void,—even the insurance of an enemy's property is illegal, upon the ground of its being a species of intercourse with the enemy; for the same reason bills of exchange drawn by the subject of one belligerent

(*h*) Brown v. United States, 8 Cranch's (Amer.) Rep. 136. See also 1 Kent's Comm. 66-7. The Rapid, 8 Cranch's (Amer.) Rep. 155. Griswold v. Waddington, 15 Johnson's (Amer.) Rep. 57. 16 Ib., p. 438, s. c. Scholefield v. Eichelber, 7 Peters's United States (Amer.) Rep. 586.

(*i*) Mason v. Gist, 1 Durnford & East's Rep. 85. Potts v. Bell, 8 Ib. 548.

(*k*) Order in Council, dated 15th April, 1854. But even under this Order it is not lawful for the enemy to sell his ship in the ports of this country. The Odessa, Admiralty Prize Court (Dr. Lushington,) April 12th, 1855.

upon the subject of the other belligerent, are illegal and void. The remission of funds in money, or bills, to subjects of the enemy, the purchase of bills, or the deposit of funds in the enemy's country, are unlawful, because they tend to improve the resources and strengthen the hands of the enemy.(*l*) In fine, every communication with the State, however circuitous, is prohibited, unless it be sanctioned by the special authority of the Government.

*LXXI. It has been holden by the Law of England that if a man be adherent to the king's enemies in his realm, that is, [*110] the subjects of foreign Powers with whom the king is at open War, giving to them aid and comfort in the realm or elsewhere, he is guilty of treason. This must be proved by some overt act, as by giving them intelligence,(*m*) by sending them provisions, by selling them arms, by treacherously surrendering them a fortress or the like.(*n*)

The 11 & 12 William III. c. 7, and 18 George II. c. 30, relate to piracy committed under an enemy's commission.

Upon an indictment on the 18 George II. c. 30, a question was made whether *adhering to the king's enemies*, by hostilely cruising in their ships, could be tried as *piracy* under the usual commission granted by virtue of the statute 28 Henry VIII. c. 15. The 18 George II. recites that doubts had arisen whether subjects entering into the service of the king's enemies, on board privateers and other ships, having commissions from France and Spain, and having by such adherence been guilty of high treason, could be deemed guilty of felony within the intent of the 11 & 12 William III. c. 7, and be triable by the Court of Admiralty appointed by virtue of the said Act; and then enacts that persons who shall commit hostilities upon the sea, &c., against his majesty's subjects by virtue or under colour of any commission from any of his majesty's enemies, or shall be *any otherwise adherent* to his majesty's enemies upon the sea, &c., may be tried as *pirates*, felons, or robbers, in the said Court of Admiralty in the same manner as persons guilty of piracy, felony, and robbery, are by the said Act directed to be tried: but it does not say that they shall be deemed *pirates*, &c., as in the 11 & 12 William III. c. 7. The prisoner having been convicted, the question was reserved for consideration of the judges; and it was agreed by eight who were present,(*o*) *that the prisoner had been well tried under the commission. For that taking the 11 & 12 William III. and 18 George [*111] II. together, and the doubt raised in the latter, and also its enactment that in the instances therein mentioned, and also in case of any other adhering to the king's enemies, the parties might be tried as pirates by the Court of Admiralty according to that statute, it was substantially declaring that they should be *deemed pirates;* and that it was a just csnstruction in their favour to allow them to be tried *as such* by a jury.(*p*)

(*l*) 1 Kent's Comm. p. 69.

(*m*) Dr. Hensy's case, 1 Burrow's Rep. 650. R. v. Stone, 6 Durnford & East's Rep. 527.

(*n*) 3 Inst., x. Stephen's (Blackstone's) Comm., vol. iv. p. 192.

(*o*) Lord Loughborough, Lord C. B. Skynner, Gould, J.; Willes, J.; Ashurst, J.; Eyre, B.; Perryn, B.; and Heath, J.; who met Nov. 11, 1782.

(*p*) Evan's case, MS., Gould, J., 1 East, P. C., c. xvii. s. 5, pp. 798, 799.

The offence of serving foreign States is restrained and punished, as has been shown in an earlier part of this work,(*q*) by 59 Geo. III. c 69, generally known by the name of the "Foreign Enlistment Act;" but notwithstanding the provisions of this Act, it has been ruled by the judges that a British subject, who, in the service of a foreign State *at peace* with Great Britain, captures a *British* vessel which is lawfully condemned as prize for breaking blockade, is not liable to an action at the suit of the owner of the vessel.(*r*)

Since the breaking out of the present War between England and Russia, a statute has been passed, viz., on the 12th of August, 1852, "to render any dealing with securities issued during the present War between Russia and England by the Russian Government a misdemeanor."(*s*)

The statute recites "that it is expedient to prevent as much as possible the Russian Government from raising funds for the purpose of prosecuting the War which it at present carries on against this country," and enacts as follows:—

[*112] *"I. If, during the continuance of hostilities between Her Majesty and the Emperor of Russia, any person within her majesty's dominions, or any British subject in any foreign country, shall wilfully or knowingly take, acquire, become possessed of, or interested in any stocks, funds, scrip, bonds, debentures, or securities for money which, since the 29th day of March, 1854, have or hath been, or which, during the continuance of hostilities as aforesaid, shall be, created, entered into, or secured by or in the name of the Government of Russia, or any person or persons on its behalf, every person so taking, acquiring, becoming possessed of, or interested in any such stocks, funds, scrip, bonds, or debentures as aforesaid shall be guilty of a misdemeanor, and in Scotland of an offence punishable with fine or imprisonment: Provided always, that the provisions of this Act shall not extend to or include the case of any such person or subject claiming an interest in the estate or effects of any deceased person, or the case of any such person or subject taking the estate or effects of his debtor in execution, or the case of any such person or subject claiming in any country to be interested under any bankruptcy, insolvency, sequestration, cessio bonorum, or disposition of property in trust for creditors, but that in every such case the British subject may take and receive any stocks, funds, scrip, bond, or debentures, or any share, legacy, dividend, debt, or sum of money due or belonging to him, which may arise from or be produced by the sale or proceeds of any such stocks, funds, scrip, bonds, or debentures as aforesaid; and provided also, that nothing herein contained shall be construed to include the Government notes which are used as a circulating medium in the Russian dominions.

The third section of the 18 Geo. II. c. xxx., provides that this act shall not prevent any offender who shall not be tried according thereto from being tried for high treason within this realm according to the stat. 28 Hen. VIII. c. xv. Russell on Crimes, vol. i. p. 98.

(*q*) Vide ante, vol. i. p. 397, and p. 594, App.

(*r*) Dobree & Others v. Napier & Another, 2 Bingham (N. C.) Rep. 781.

(*s*) 17 & 18 Vict. c. cxxiii.

"II. All offences against this Act committed beyond the limits of the United Kingdom may be inquired of, tried, determined, and dealt with as if the same had been respectively committed within the body of the county of Middlesex.

*"III. Nothing herein contained shall have the effect of reducing to a misdemeanor any such offence which if this Act had [*113] not been passed would amount to the crime of high treason, or be deemed in any manner to alter or affect the law, relating to high treason; but no person indicted for a misdemeanor under this Act shall be entitled to an acquittal on the ground that the acts proved against him amount in law to the crime of high treason."(*t*)

LXXII. Prohibitory laws, whether they be civil or criminal, may follow the subject wherever he goes.(*u*)

According to the law of England, treasons committed by subjects of the British Crown, out of the realm, may be tried in the Queen's Bench;(*x*) and, by the law of the same country, if the crown send a writ to any subject when abroad, commanding his return, and the subject disobey, it is a high contempt of the royal prerogative, for which the offender's lands may be seized till he return; and then he is liable to fine and imprisonment.(*y*) And this doctrine is not one peculiar to England, but appertains to the general public jurisprudence of all civilized States.(*z*)

LXXIII. There is little, if any difference, in the effect of War upon allies and upon belligerents; for allies, to adopt *the accurate [*114] expression of Bynkershoek,(*a*) form one State (*unam constituunt civitatem*) with the confederate belligerent.

This principle, duly considered and applied, furnishes a solution for all questions relating to the position, the duties, and the rights of an ally.

Thus, for instance, the doctrine that all commerce and communication is interdicted with the enemy is enforced, not only against the subjects of the belligerent, but also against those of the ally, upon the supposition that the rule was founded on a strong and universal principle which allied States in War had a right to notice and apply mutually to each other's subjects.(*b*)

So the subject who returns to the allies of his sovereign is entitled to the Rights of *Postliminium,* because he is considered as having returned to his own country.(*c*)

(*t*) The Act concludes with this section: "VI. On any indictment for a misdemeanor under this Act the costs of the prosecution shall be allowed as directed by the several Acts, seventh George the Fourth, chapter sixty-four, and fourteenth and fifteenth Victoria, chapter fifty-five; and all the provisions of the said Acts empowering Courts to order payment of costs and expenses, and compensation for trouble and loss of time, in the cases of the misdemeanors in the said Acts mentioned, shall extend and be applicable to indictments for misdemeanor under this Act."

(*u*) Bowyer's Public Law, pp. 180, 181. Sussex Peerage Case, 11 Clark & Finelly's Reports. Suarez, De Legibus, l. iii. c. xxxii.

(*x*) 26 Henry VIII., c. xiii. 35 Ib., c. ii. 5 & 6 Edward VI., c. xi.

(*y*) Blackstone's Comment., b. i. c. vii. pp. 265, 266. Hawkins, Pleas of the Crown, 22.

(*z*) Voet, Ad Pandectas, l. i. t. iv. part. ii. De Statutis, s. 9.

(*a*) Quæstiones Juris Publici, l. 1, c. ix.

(*b*) Ib., l. 1, c. xv.

(*c*) The Hoop, 1 Rob. Adm. Rep. 217.

So a prize may be lawfully condemned in the port of, or by the tribunal of an ally;(*d*) though if the port were neutral, this would be perhaps(*e*) unlawful, with reference to the locality of the vessel, and certainly unlawful with respect to the tribunal, if that were neutral.(*f*)

LXXIV. We have now to consider the *effect of War* upon the *person* and *property* of the *enemy*.

[*115] *The first question which arises upon this branch of the subject is,—who is an enemy? And here some distinction must be made between *person* and *property*.

The character of an enemy appears to be indelibly impressed upon the *person*, according to the Municipal Law of England and the North American United States, by the allegiance which springs from *the place of birth*, or origin,(*g*) and also from the *the place of domicil*, when that domicil has been *formally acquired*, at the instance of the individual, under the authority of the State. It is for the individual, who has so acted, to take good heed that he be not taken in arms, either against the country of his origin, or against the country of his formal adoption; for the Government of each country will be entitled to treat him as a traitor.

With respect to *property*, a hostile character appears to be impressed upon it, principally in two ways, viz:—

1. By reason of the domicil of the owner;
2. By reason of the traffic of the owner.

LXXV. We have seen that the enemy has no *persona standi in judicio* in the country of the adverse belligerent.(*h*)

It may happen, indeed, that the enemy resides in the country of the adverse belligerent under a *safe conduct* from the sovereign, which *pro tanto* relieves him from the disability incident to his character, or he may be permitted by a special license to sue or be sued: these are exceptions,—but as a rule, he is in the enemy's country *exlex*.

When hostilities have begun, the person of the enemy is, strictly
[*116] speaking, liable to seizure, and his property(*i*) to *confiscation. The Romans(*k*) exercised this *summum jus*, in the harshest

(*d*) Bynk., Q. J. P., c. xv. Hughes v. Cornelius, Carthew's Rep. 32. The Christopher, 2 Rob. 209. Oddy v. Bovill, 2 East, 473.

(*e*) The Henrick and Maria, 4 Rob. 43. The Comet, 5 Rob. 285. La Purissima Conception, 6 Ib. 45. The Constant Mary, note to the Kierlighett, 3 Ib. 97. Tremoulin v. Sands, Carthew's Rep. 423. The Nostra Signora de los Angelos, 3 Rob. 287.

(*f*) The Flad Oyen, 1 Rob. 140. Havelock v. Rockwood, 8 Durn. & East, 268. Donaldson v. Thompson, 1 Campbell, 429. Smith v. Surridge, 4 Esp. 25. The Kierlighett, 3 Rob. 99. The Cosmopolite, 3 Ib. 333.

(*g*) Vide ante, vol. i. pp. 345-6-7.

(*h*) The Hoop, 1 Rob. Adm. Rep. 201. Bynk., Q. J. P., l. i. c. vii. Grot., l. iii. c. iv. De Jure interficiendi hostes in Bello solenni, et aliâ vi in corpus.

(*i*) With respect to the *goods* or *property* of an enemy, see Grotius, l. iii. c. ii. s. 2. Ib., c. vi. s. 2: "Cæterum jure gentium non tantum is qui ex justâ causâ bellum gerit, sed et quivis, in bello solenni, et sine fine modoque, dominus sit eorum qua hosti eripit, eo sensu nimirùm, ut a gentibus omnibus et ipse et qui ab eo titulum habent in possessione rerum talium tuendi sint; quod dominium quoad effectus externos licet appellare." Ib., c. vii. pp. 3-4; c. xiii. pp.1-2. Puff., De Jure Nat. et Gent., l. viii. c. vi. p. 23. Bynk., Q. J. P., l. i. c. vii. Vattel, l. iii. c. viii. s. 77.

(*k*) "In bello postliminium est, in pace autem his, qui bello capti erant, de

manner, upon the persons of those who, at the breaking out of the War, happened to be in their territory; but this practice has happily become obsolete.

Louis XIV.,(*l*) though his subjects produced excellent works during his reign upon International Law, was not himself the most scrupulous observer of the precepts of that science;—yet even he, by an Edict, in January, 1666, in which he declared War against and interdicted all commerce with England, declared also, by a subsequent Edict, that his first Edict affected only those English who should be found thereafter on *high seas*, or who should act the part of an enemy on the French territory, but not against those private individuals who had established their domicil in France; and that with respect to those enemies who were residing in France, but had not obtained the *jus subditorum*,(*m*) they were to depart, whithersoever they listed, before the lapse of three months.

This permission, however, Bynkershoek says, is to be ascribed solely to generosity and kindness (*humanitati*,) because, according to this author, the enemy has at all *times, and under all circumstances, [*117] an absolute power of life and death over his enemy,—an opinion which has already been combated in a former chapter of this volume. Bynkershoek indeed admits, that, even in his time, there were so many Treaties in which a reasonable time for withdrawal was made a matter of stipulation, "*Si subito bellum exarsisset*" (to borrow the language of the Digest,) that this *summum jus* was very rarely, if ever, put in force against those who were innocently abiding in the country of the enemy. Since the age of Bynkershoek, liberal provisions of this kind have been constantly inserted in Treaties between States, both of the New(*n*) and of the Old World; they have become, Mr. Chancellor Kent(*o*) observes, "an established *formula* in commercial Treaties."

Eminent jurists have considered these stipulations to be rather affirmations of the *jus commune* of nations, than as introductory of any novel principle; and among these jurists may be mentioned Grotius,(*p*) Emerigon,(*q*) and Vattel.(*r*) They argue that the foreigners entered the country under the sanction of public faith; that the Government which permitted them to enter did, by so doing, *tacitly contract* that they should be protected during their sojourn, and not prevented, unless by

quibus nihil in pactis erat comprehensum, quod ideo placuisse Servius scribit, quia spem revertendi civibus in virtute bellicâ magis quam in pace Romani esse voluerunt: *Item in pace qui pervenerunt ad alteros si bellum subito exarsissit, eorum servi efficiuntur, apud quos jam hostes suo facto deprehenduntur:* quibus jus postliminii."—Dig. xlix. t. xv. s. 12.

(*l*) Bynk., Q. J. P., l. i. c. iii.

(*m*) Bynkershoek renders this into Dutch, *ongenatur aliseert rynde* (*who were not naturalized*). It would appear, however, that they were a class put in opposition to those who were *domiciled.*

(*n*) Treaty between the N. A. United States and Columbia, ratified at Washington, May 27, 1825. Between the N. A. United States and Venezuela, May, 1836. Between the N. A. United States and Chili, May, 1832, art. xxiii., *permanent* protection guaranteed to foreigners who choose to remain.

(*o*) Comment., vol. i. p. 56. (*p*) L. iii. c. iv. p. 7. (*q*) L. i. p. 567.

(*r*) L. iii. c. iv. s. 63. See also Azuni, pt. ii. c. iv. art. ii. s. 7.

some personal act of misconduct, from their return.(s) They ought, therefore, to be allowed a reasonable time to retire with their moveable property, and after that time has elapsed, unless, indeed, their detention has been caused by illness, or some invincible necessity, to be treated as disarmed enemies.

[*118] *LXXVI. The effect of War upon the property of enemies generally, is a subject which requires a twofold consideration, namely:—as to

1. The property of enemies within the territory of the enemy.
2. The property of an enemy without the territory of their enemy.

It is with the former of these considerations that we are at present concerned.

LXXVII. It has not unfrequently been a provision in Treaties that foreign subjects should be permitted to remain and continue their employment or business,—so long, of course, as it was innocently conducted.

A Treaty of commerce between the North American United States and the Republic of Chili, which was made in May, 1832,(t) is an example of such a permanent protection being afforded to foreigners. It has, indeed, not unfrequently happened that this permission has been embodied in the very declaration of War,—several instances are to be found in former declarations by Great Britain,—and it is the opinion of a great English lawyer,(u) that when this permission is so announced, aliens are thereby enabled to acquire personal chattels, and to maintain actions for the recovery of personal rights, in as ample a manner as alien friends.

LXXVIII. The same humane and humanising permission has been made the subject of the municipal laws of many countries.

In England it was one of the provisions of *Magna Charta*, that merchants belonging to the country of the enemy, found in England at the breaking out of a War should be attached "without harm of body or goods," till the king or his chief justiciary be informed how our merchants are treated in the country with which we are at war; and if ours be secure in that country they shall be secure in ours. This equitable maxim does not appear to have been peculiar to England, but [*119] *to have been adopted by other northern nations; for instance, the rule, "*quam legem exteri nobis posuêre, eandem illis ponemus*," prevailed among the Swedes and Goths.(x) But it is extraordinary that such a provision should have been inserted in a federal act between the English monarch and his own subjects; "il est beau," Montesquieu observes, "que la nation Angloise ait fait de cela une de ces articles de sa liberté."(y)

This remarkable provision was sustained by a decision of the English judges in the time of Henry VIII., to the effect that if a Frenchman

(s) Vide ante, vol. i. p. 355. (t) Art. xxiii., 1 Kent's Comm. 56.

(u) Sir Michael Foster, Discourse of High Treason, pp. 185-6.

(x) Black. Comm., book i. c. vii., citing Stiernhook, De Jure Sueton, l. iii. c. iv.

(y) De l'Esprit des Lois, l. xx. c. xiv. Ib., c. vii.: "C'est le peuple du monde qui a le mieux su se prévaloir à la fois de ces trois grandes choses: la religion, le commerce, et la liberté."

came to England before the war, neither his person nor his goods should be seized.(z) But this provision is confined to the effects of alien merchants *domiciled* within the realm before the beginning of the war. The Statute of Staples, 27 Edward III. c. 17, carries the liberality of this provision still further, for by it foreign merchants *residing* in England when war broke out, were to have convenient warning of forty days by proclamation to depart the realm with their goods; and if by reason of accident they should be prevented from doing so, they were allowed forty days more to pass with their merchandise, with liberty to sell the same. Nevertheless, it has been, until the recent War, the uniform custom of Great Britain to seize as prizes all vessels and cargoes of her enemies found afloat in her ports at the commencement of war. Her practice in the matter of embargoes has been already mentioned. In the articles respecting the *Droits of Admiralty* in 1665, there is a very formal recognition of the rights of the crown to all cargoes and vessels seized before hostilities.(a)

*LXXIX. Spain, by a decree of February, 1829, made Cadiz a free port, and declared that, in the event of war, foreigners who [*120] had established themselves there for the purposes of commerce, should be allowed a proper time to withdraw, and that their property should not be subject to sequestration or reprisals.(b)

LXXX. Charles V. of France, by an Ordinance dated about a century after the English *Magna Charta*, decreed that foreign merchants resident in France at the time of a declaration of war with their country, should have nothing to fear, but be allowed to depart freely with their effects.(c)

LXXXI. The United States of North America, by an Act of their Congress, on the 6th of July, 1798,(d) authorized the President, in case of war, to direct the conduct to be observed towards subjects of the hostile nation, being aliens and within the United States, and in what cases, and upon what security, their residence should be permitted; and it declared, in reference to those who were to depart, that they should be allowed such reasonable time as might be consistent with the public safety, and according to the dictates of humanity and national hospitality, for the recovery, disposal, and removal of their goods and effects, and for their departure. Nevertheless, the Supreme Court of the United States(e) has,

(z) Brooke's Abridg., tit. "Property," pl. 38. Jenkins, Centenaries, 201, case 22. 1 Kent's Comm. 57-58.

(a) The Rebecca, 1 Rob. Adm. Rep. 227. Ib., p. 230, n. (a).

(b) 1 Kent's Comm. 56, n.

(c) Ib., I. p. 59, citing Henault, Abrég. Chron., l. i. p. 338.

(d) Ib., c. lxxiii., ubi supr.

(e) The cargo of the ship Emulous, 1 Gallison's (Amer.) Rep. 563. Judge Story held that the Declaration of War imported *a right* to confiscate enemies' property found within the country at the commencement of the War, and that the *Executive, without* the authority of *Congress*, might exercise this right. This case was decided in the *Circuit Court*, and appealed from the Supreme Court, under the title of Browne v. The United States. In that Court it was held that the confiscation required a legislative Act of Congress. In the Supreme Court, however, Judge Story said that his opinion was unchanged, and was shared by another judge. The two Courts differed upon a question of Constitutional and Public Law; upon the question of International Law they were agreed.

[*121] in a very elaborate and important decision, declared that no *doubt can now be entertained respecting the right of every Government to take the persons and confiscate the property of the enemy wherever found; that the mitigations of this rigid rule, which the humane and wise policy of modern times has introduced into modern practice, may more or less affect the exercise of this right, but cannot impair the right itself. That right, the American judges say, remains undiminished, and when the sovereign authority shall choose to bring it into operation, the judicial department must give effect to its will. Mr. Chancellor Kent remarks that, "though this decision established the rights contrary to much of modern authority and practice, yet a great point was gained over the rigour and violence of the ancient doctrine, by making the exercise of the right to depend upon a special Act of Congress."(*f*)

LXXXII. The legal incapacities and disabilities imposed by a state of war, both upon the alien *individual* enemy and the alien *corporation* of the enemy, underwent a profound discussion in the case, The Society for the Propagation of the Gospel, &c. v. Wheeler, in which Mr. Justice Story delivered the judgment.(*g*)

"The defence (he observed) of alien enemy is by no means favoured in the law;(*h*) and some modern cases have gone a great way in discountenancing it,—further, indeed, than seems consistent with the general rules of pleading. In Casseres v. Bell,(*i*) the court held, that the plea of alien enemy must not only aver such hostile character, but also set forth every fact that negatives the plaintiff's right to sue; and this decision is expressly put upon the mere ground of authority. On a careful examination, however, of the cases cited, it will not be found that they support the doctrine. In Derrier v. Arnaud,(*k*) the original record [*122] *of which, Lord Kenyon says, had been examined, the plea negatived every presumption that could arise in favour of the plaintiff's right to sue. But the case did not turn at all upon that point, but simply on the question, whether *oriundus,* in the plea, was equivalent to *natus,* and upon examining precedents, the court held the plea good; and, as no such objection was made, it seems difficult to admit, that a mere averment of the additional facts was adjudged necessary, when upon the judgment of the court it stands purely indifferent. In Openheimer v. Levy,(*l*) to an action of *assumpsit,* the defendant pleaded *alien nee,* without saying saying alien enemy, and the court held, that, as an alien friend may maintain a personal action, and in order to abate the writ, the plaintiff should be shown to be an alien enemy, which is not to be presumed, nor the contrary necessary to be replied, therefore the plea was bad; and so the law had before that time been held.(*m*) The case, therefore, steers wide of the doctrine contended for. In Wells

(*f*) Comm., I. p. 59.

(*g*) 2 Gallison's (Amer.) Rep., Judgment of Story, J., October Term, 1814, p. 127.

(*h*) See Stephens on Pleading, p. 67, (ed. 1824.)

(*i*) 8 Dunford & East's Rep. 166.

(*k*) 4 Modern Rep. 405.

(*l*) 2 Strange's Rep., p. 1082.

(*m*) Dyer's Rep., p. 2.

v. Williams(*n*) to debt upon a bond by an executor, the defendant pleaded that the plaintiff was an alien enemy, and came into England without a safe conduct. The plaintiff replied, that at the time of making the bond he was, and yet is, in England, by the license, and under the protection of the king; and upon demurrer the court held, not that the plea was bad, but that the replication was good; and the court resolved, that if the defendant came there before the war, there was no need of a safe conduct; and if he came since the war, and continued without molestation, it should be intended that he came by a license, and his right to sue was consequent upon his protection. In this case, also, the objection did not arise; for the only question seemed to be, whether *a residence by the licence, and under the protection of the king, would entitle the party to sue without having a safe conduct; and the court held that it would. And this is but an affirmance of the doctrine of the year-books.(*o*) [*123]

"These are all the authorities upon which Casseres v. Bell professes to have been decided. On the other hand, in Sylvester's case(*p*) (which was not cited,) where the plea was *alien enemy*, on demurrer, the court held it good; and that, if the party were entitled under a general or special protection of the king, he ought to reply that fact. And so were the pleadings in George v. Powell.(*q*) And there are several other precedents, in which the plea does not negative the facts, which might enable an alien enemy to sue.(*r*)

"The case of Clark v. Morey(*s*) pushes the doctrine further, and asserts that an alien enemy who comes and resides within the North American United States without a *safe conduct or license* from the Government (for so is the averment in the plea,) is at all events entitled to sue, until ordered away by the president; and this too, although the party is not known by the Government to have his residence there. The English authorities have always required an express safe conduct or an implied license; and Poulton v. Dobree(*t*) decides, that a license is not to be implied from mere residence, unless sanctioned by the Government after the commencement of hostilities.

"It is certainly true that, as to individuals, their right to sue in the courts of a belligerent, or to hold or enforce civil rights, depends not on their birth and native allegiance, but on the character which they hold at the time when these rights are sought to be enforced. A neutral, or *a citizen of the United States, who is domiciled in the enemy's country, not only in respect to his property, but also as to his capacity to sue is deemed as much an alien enemy as a person actually born under the allegiance and residing within the dominions of the hostile nation. This, indeed, has long been settled as the general law of nations, and enforced in the tribunals of prize; and has been latterly recognized and confirmed in the Municipal Courts of other nations.(*u*) And the [*124]

(*n*) Lord Raymond's Rep. p. 282. S. C. Lutwyche's Rep. p. 311. Salkeld, 46.
(*o*) 32 Henry VI., 23, (*b*). (*p*) 7 Modern Rep. 150.
(*q*) Fortescue's Rep. p. 221. (*r*) 9 Edward IV., 7. Croke's Elizabeth, p. 142.
(*s*) 10 Johnson's (Amer.) Rep. 69. (*t*) 2 Campbell's Rep. 163.
(*u*) Omealy v. Wilson, 1 Campbell's Rep. 482. McConnell v. Hector, 3 Bosanquet & Puller, 113.

same principle has been applied to a house of trade established in a hostile country, although the parties might happen to have a neutral domicil; the property of the house being, for such purpose, considered as affected with the hostile character of the country in which it is employed.(*x*)

LXXXIII. "In this respect" (the learned judge continued) "a corporation authorized by its charter to carry on a trade, and established in the hostile country, such as the East India Company, would undoubtedly be held, as to its property, within the same rule, even admitting its members possessed a neutral domicil. In general, an aggregate corporation is not in law deemed to have any commorancy, although the corporators have;(*y*) yet there are exceptions to this principle, and where a corporation is established in a foreign country by a foreign government, it is undoubtedly an alien corporation, be its members what they may; and if the country become hostile, it may, for some purposes at least, be clothed with the same character.

"If the reason of the rule of the disability of an alien enemy be, as is sometimes supposed, that the party may not recover effects, which, by
[*125] being carried hence may *enrich his country, that reason applies as well to the case of a corporation as of an individual in the hostile country. If the reason be, as Lord Chief Justice Eyre, in Sparrenburg v. Bamatine,(*z*) asserts it to be, that a man professing himself hostile to our country, and in a state of war with it, cannot be heard, if he sue for the benefit and protection of our laws, in the courts of our country, that reason is not less significant in the case of a foreign corporation, than of a foreign individual, taking advantage of the protection, resources, and benefits of the enemy's country. In point of law, they stand upon the same footing."

The learned judge afterwards proceeded as follows:—

"Let us now advert to the second objection, which is, that the members of the corporation are all alien enemies. In the writ, it is expressly alleged, that all the members are *aliens* and *subjects* of the King of the United Kingdom of Great Britain and Ireland. It does not, however, hence necessarily follow that they are *alien enemies*. This averment in the writ was proper, if not indeed indispensable, in order to sustain the jurisdiction of this court; for the corporation, as such, might perhaps have no authority whatsoever to maintain an action here, under the limited jurisdiction confided by the constitution of the United States to their own courts. But in the character of its members as *aliens*, we have incontestable authority to enforce the corporate rights; and it has been solemnly settled by the Supreme Court, that, for this purpose, the court will go behind the corporate name, and see who are the parties really interested.(*a*) And if, for this purpose, the court will ascertain who the corporators are, it seems to follow, that the character of the corporators may be averred, not only to sustain, but also to bar, an action

(*x*) The Vigilantia (and the cases therein cited), 1 Rob. Adm. Rep. 1. The Indiana, 2 Gallison's (Amer.) Rep. 267.

(*y*) Inhabitants of Lincoln County v. Prince, 2 Massachusetts Amer. Rep. 544.

(*z*) 1 Bosanquet & Puller's Rep., p. 163.

(*a*) Bank of United States v. Deveaux, 5 Cranch's (Amer.) Rep. 61.

brought in the name of the corporation. It might therefore have been pleaded in this case, even if the corporation had been *established in a neutral country, that all its members were alien enemies; and [*126] upon such a plea, with proper averments, it would have deserved great consideration, whether it was not, *pendente bello*, an effectual bar. Where the corporation is established in the enemy's country, the plea would *á fortiori* apply. But although the corporation itself, and the members also, may be liable to the imputation of being alien enemies, yet that character does not necessarily or unavoidably attach to either. For aught that appears upon the face of the record, every member of the corporation may be now domiciled in the United States, under the safe conduct or license of Government. In such a predicament, it is clear that, though aliens, they would not be enemies, but might sue and be sued in our courts.(*b*) And in respect to the corporation itself, although established in Great Britain, it may have the safe conduct or license of the Government of the United States for its property and the maintenance of its corporate rights. It is clearly competent for the Government, under the general rights of War, to grant letters of protection, and thereby to suspend the hostile character of any person; and when he has such protection, wherever he may be domiciled, he is to be considered, *quoad hoc*, a neutral.(*c*)

"Nor is there, in this respect, any difference between a corporation and an individual. And it would be highly injurious to humanity, as well as public policy, if institutions established in a foreign country for religious, literary, or charitable purposes, might not, during war, obtain protection and patronage for their laudable exertions to soften private misery and diffuse private virtue. To support the motion in arrest of judgment, it is necessary for the court to negative every presumption that could arise of a safe *conduct or license, either to the members or to the corporation itself. This cannot be done in the [*127] present case consistently with the principles of law. The suit was commenced in a time of peace, and every presumption, which can, ought to be made, to support it. It is sufficient, however, that by possibility the demandants, in their corporate capacity, and the capacity of their members, may have a *persona standi in judicio*, to entitle them to judgment.

"There is another consideration also, which may properly weigh in this case. The suit was commenced during peace, and on the declaration of War it was competent for the tendants to plead the hostile alienage of the demandants, if it existed, in bar to the further prosecution of the suit, in the nature of a plea *puis darrein continuance*, as it was pleaded in Le Bret v. Papillon.(*d*) They did not so plead, and thereby have affirmed the ability of the demandants to prosecute the suit to judgment. Upon this ground, where the disability of alien enemy occurred before judgment, and on a *scire facias* on the judgment the disability was pleaded, the plea has been held bad.(*e*)

(*b*) Bynk., Q. J. P., c. xxv. s. 8. Wells v. Williams, 1 Lord Raymond's Rep. 282.

(*c*) Bynk., Q. J. P., c. vii. Usparicha v. Noble, 13 East's Rep. 332.

(*d*) 4 East's Rep. 502. (*e*) West v. Sutton, 2 Lord Raymond's Rep. 853.

"Upon the whole the motion in arrest of judgment must be overruled."

The same doctrine, namely, that the plea of alien enemy is one which the court will not favour, has been holden by the English Courts of Common Law.(*f*) Nevertheless, under the relaxation of belligerent rights introduced by the Orders in Council of the existing War (1854-5,) the English Prize Court has holden that the affidavit of the claimant, being an enemy, must state matter showing that he has a *persona standi in judico;*—such a *persona* will not be presumed, but must be proved.(*g*)

[*128] *LXXXIV. The national character of corporations, as well as of individuals, frequently undergoes discussion in Treaties of Peace which award compensation for losses unjustly sustained before or during War.

It has been held in England, by the high authority of the judicial Committee of the Privy Council, that a *Corporation of British Subjects* in a foreign country, under the control of a foreign Government, must be considered as a *Foreign Corporation,* and is not therefore entitled to claim compensation for the loss of its property, under a Treaty giving the right of doing so to *British* Subjects.(*h*)

LXXXV. *Domicil* is, to a certain extent, another test of an enemy. This circumstance imposes a hostile character upon the *property,* though not necessarily upon the *person,* of the domiciled individual.

The question has been much considered in the Prize Courts of England and the North American United States. They have acted upon the principle laid down by Bynkershoek,(*i*) and it is now a well-established rule, that every person is to be considered as belonging to that country where he has his domicil, whatever may be his native or adopted country.(*k*)

(*f*) Schepeler v. Durant, 2 Common Law & Equity Reports (Finlason,) 729.

(*g*) Eccles. & Adm. Rep. (Spinks,) The Troiga, vol. i. pp. 342-3.

(*h*) Long v. Commissioners for Claims on France, 2 Knapp's Privy Council Rep. 51. Daniel v. Commissioners for Claims on France, ib., p. 23.

(*i*) "Hostium nomine an et amici nostri intelligantur, qui victi apud hostes sunt, urbe eorum forte occupatâ, dubitari posset? Nou putat Petrinus Bellus, De Re Militari, Pt. II. tit. ii. n. 5; et nihil definit Zouchœus, De Jure Fecial., Pt. II. s. viii. q. 4. Ego putarem, etiam eos intelligendos esse, *certè quod ad bona,* quæ sub hostium imperio habent, atque adeo ea bona jure belli probe rectè a nobis occupari, si hostes antea ab amicis occupaverint. Quæcunque hostium sunt rectè capimus, ea autem bona pars sunt Imperii hostilis, quæque ita hosti prodesse, nobis nocere possunt."—Bynk., Q. J. P., l. i. c. iii., *in fine.*

(*k*) The Vigilantia, 1 Rob. Adm. Rep. 1. The Endraught, 1 Ib. 19. The Sarah Christina, 1 Ib. 237. The Indian Chief, 3 Ib. 23. The President, 5 Ib. 277. The Neptune, 6 Ib. 403. The Venus, 9 Cranch, (Amer.) Rep. 253. The Frances, Gillespie's claim, 1 Gallis. (Amer.) Rep. 614. The Mary and Susan, Richardson's claim: McConnel v. Hector, 3 Bosanquet & Puller's Rep. 113.

"On n'aura aucun égard aux passe-ports accordés par les princes neutres ou alliés, tant aux propriétaires qu'aux maîtres des navires sujets des Etats ennemis, s'ils n'ont été naturalisés, et n'ont transféré leur domicile dans les Etats des dits princes avant la déclaration de la présente guerre.

"Ne pourront pareillement les dits propriétaires et maîtres des navires ou sujets des Etats ennemis, qui auront obtenu les dits lettres de naturalité, jouir de leur effet si, depuis qu'elle ont été obtenues, ils sont retournés dans les Etats ennemis your y continuer leur commerce."—Réglement du 21 Octobre, 1744, art. xi. décr. xxvi., Juillet, 1788. art. vi.

*Thus the masters and crews of ships are deemed to possess the national character of the ships to which they belong during the time of their employment;(*l*) and even if a person goes into a belligerent country originally for temporary purposes, he will not preserve his neutral character, if he remain there several years, paying taxes, &c.(*m*) And a neutral Consul, resident and treating in a belligerent country, is, as to his mercantile character, deemed a belligerent of that country;(*n*) and the same rule applies to the subject of one belligerent country resident in the country of its enemy and carrying on trade there;(*o*) but the character acquired by mere domicil ceases upon removal from the country.(*p*) The native character easily reverts, and it requires fewer circumstances to constitute domicil in the case of a native, than to impress the national character on one who is originally of another *country;(*q*) and in his favour, a party is deemed to have changed his domicil, and his native character reverts, as soon as he puts himself *in itinere* to return to his native country *animo revertendi*.(*r*) [*129] [*130]

In general, a neutral merchant trading in the ordinary manner with a belligerent country, does not, by the mere accident of his having a stationed agent there, contract the character of the enemy.(*s*) But it is otherwise if he be not engaged in trade upon the ordinary footing of a neutral merchant, but as a privileged trader of the enemy, for then he is in effect carrying on a hostile trade.(*t*) And the same remark applies if his agent carry on a trade, which is not clearly neutral, from the hostile country;(*u*) if a person be a partner in a house of trade in an enemy's country, he is, as to the concerns and trade of that house, deemed an enemy, and his share is liable to confiscation as such, notwithstanding his own residence is in a neutral country, for the domicil of the house is considered in this respect as the domicil of the partners.(*x*) But if he has a house of trade in a neutral country, he has not the benefit of the same principle; for if his own personal residence be in the hostile country, his share in the property of the neutral house is liable to condemnation. A man may have commercial concerns in *two* countries, and if he acts as a *merchant of *both* he is liable to be considered as a subject of both, with regard to the transactions respectively originating in both countries; but shipments made by an enemy's house on account and risk, *bona fide and exclusively*, of a neutral partner or a neutral house are not subject to confiscation as prize of War.(*y*) How- [*131]

(*l*) The Endraught, 1 Rob. Adm. Rep. xxii. The Bernon, 1 Ib. 102. The Embden, 1 Ib. 17. The Frederick, 5 Ib. 8. The Ann, 1 Dodson, 221.
(*m*) The Harmony, 2 Rob. 332. The Embden, 1 Ib. 17.
(*n*) The Indian Chief, 3 Ib. 22. The Josephine, 4 Ib. 25.
(*o*) The Citto, 3 Ib. 38. M'Connel v. Hector, 3 Bos. & Pull. 113.
(*p*) The Indian Chief, 3 Rob. 12. (*q*) La Virginie, 5 Rob. 98.
(*r*) The Indian Chief, 3 Ib. 12. The St. Lawrence, 1 Gall. (Amer.) 467.
(*s*) The Anna Catharina, 4 Rob. 119. The Rendsborg, Ib. 139.
(*t*) The Anna Catharina, Ib. 119. (*u*) Ibid.
(*x*) The Vigilantia, 1 Ib. 1, 14, 19. The Susa, 2 Ib. 255. The Indiana, 3 Ib. 44. The Portland, Ib. The Vriendschap, 4 Ib. 166. The Jonge Klassina, 5 Ib. 297, The Antonia Johanna, 1 Wheaton (Amer.,) 159. The St. Joze Indiana, 2 Gall. (Amer.) 268.
(*y*) The St. Joze Indiana, 2 Gall. (Amer.) 268, 274-289, 290, 291. The Frances, 1 Ib. 618. S. C., 8 Cranch (Amer.,) 348.

ever, if a neutral be engaged, *in peace*, in a house of trade in the enemy's country, his property so engaged in the house is not, at the commencement of War, confiscated; but if he continues in the house after the knowledge of the War, it is liable, as above stated, to confiscation.(*z*) It is a settled principle, that traffic alone, independent of residence, will, in some cases, confer a hostile character on the individual;(*a*) and if a neutral be engaged in the enemy's navigation, it not only affects the peculiar vessel in which he is employed, but all other vessels belonging to him that have no distinct national character impressed upon them.(*b*)

LXXXVI. But in considering who are enemies, it is to be observed that a declaration of War does not *per se* recall subjects home.

"It has been further argued,"—Mr. Justice Story said in a case in which he delivered judgment—"that a declaration of War is, in effect, a command to the citizens of the belligerent country abroad at the time, to return home, and that the law allows a reasonable time and way to to effect it.

"I am not aware of any principle of public law, which obliges every absent citizen to return to his country, on the breaking out of a War; nor has any authority been produced which countenances the position. It may be admitted, that the sovereign power of the country has a right [*132] *to require the services of all its citizens, in time of War, and for this purpose may recall them home under penalties for disobedience. But until the sovereign power has promulgated such command, the citizens of the country have a perfect right to pursue their ordinary business and trade in and with all other countries, except that of the enemy. Upon any other supposition, all foreign commerce would, during War, be suspended; for if it were the duty of absent citizens to return, it would, upon the same principle, be the duty of those at home to remain there. As to citizens in the hostile country, the declaration of War imports a suspension of all further commerce with such country and obliges them to return, unless they would be involved in all the consequences of the hostile character. If they wish to return, they must do it in a manner which does not violate the laws; and their property cannot be removed with safety from the enemy's country, unless under the sanction of their own Government.

"But even if the position were generally true, that is contended for, the law would never deem that a reasonable mode of conveying property home, which involved it in a noxious trade with the public enemy. That can never be held to be a reasonable mode of returning a ship to the United States, which involves her in a traffic forbidden by the laws. However, I am well satisfied, that the position cannot be maintained in any extent adequate to the purpose for which it has been introduced."(*c*)

LXXXVII. The right of confiscating the *debts* of the enemy is a corollary to the right of confiscating his property.

(*z*) The Vigilantia, 1 Rob. 1, 14, 15. The Susa, 2 Ib. 251, 255.
(*a*) Ibid. The Vriendschap, 4 Ib. 166. (*b*) Ibid.
(*c*) The brig Joseph, Judgment of Story, J., October Term, 1813, 1 Gall. (Amer.) 551-2.

The strict right,(*d*)—the *summun jus*—by the Reason of the Thing, and by the opinion of every eminent jurist, remains unquestioned. "I take upon me to say," (observes Mr. *Justice Story,) "that no jurist of reputation can be found who has denied the right of confiscation of enemies' debts."(*e*) [*133]

Bynknershoek, writing in 1737, observes: Sed profecto videtur esse jus commune, ut et *actiones* publicentur, ex eâdem nempe ratione quâ corporalia quælibet—*actiones* utique sive *credita* non minus Jure Gentium sunt in dominio nostro, quam alia bona, eccur igitur in his jus belli sequamur, in illis non sequamur? et cum nihil succurrat, quod distinctioni idoneæ locum præbere possit, etiam sola ratio jus commune defendit."(*f*)

The article of the English *Magna Charta,* already referred to,(*g*) does not protect the property or the *debts* of foreign enemies *without* the realm. And it appears to be the ancient and well established rule of the English Common Law, as laid down in the old *Year Books,* and confirmed by the judgment of the Court of Exchequer,(*h*) that all debts, all, what are technically and barbarously called, *choses in action,* belonging to an enemy are forfeitable to the crown; albeit this power is, as Lord Alvanley, the Master of the Rolls, observed, very rarely executed.(*i*)

This doctrine has been confirmed by the judgment of the Supreme Court in the United States of North America,(*k*) in which, as Dr. Story says, it was explicitly asserted by some, reluctantly admitted by some, but denied by none of the judges.(*l*)

One, however, of the English(*m*) Common Law Tribunals has arrived at a different conclusion, and pronounced that, *according to modern International Law, the confiscation of *private* debts is illegal and invalid. The case in which this law was laid down, and the subject generally, will be considered when the effect of the restoration of peace upon the possessors of property is discussed. [*134]

LXXXVIII. So much as to the *strict right;* but the rigour of this right has been mitigated by the humane and wise practice of nations, for nearly a century and a half, which has forborne from the seizure of debts and credits, and has been accompanied by a principle, which has obtained universally,(*n*) of allowing rights to debts and actions to *revive* with the

(*d*) Dig., l. xli. t. i. s. 51: "Transfugam jure belli recipimus. Et quæ res hostiles apud nos sunt non publicæ sed occupantium fiunt." Dig., l. xlix. t. xv.

(*e*) Brown v. The United States, 8 Cranch, (Amer.) (March 1, 1814,) 140.

(*f*) Q. J. P., l. i. c. vii.

(*g*) Vide ante, p. 116.

(*h*) Attorney-General v. Weeden, Parker's Rep., p. 267, citing Maynard's Edw. II. Hale, Pleas of the Crown, I. p. 95.

(*i*) Furtado v. Rodgers, 3 Bos. & Pull. 191.

(*k*) Ware v. Hylton, 3 Dallas, (Amer.) 199.

(*l*) Brown v. The United States, 8 Cranch, (Amer.) 143.

(*m*) Wolffe v. Oxholm, 6 Maule & Selwyn, 92.

(*n*) So much so, that Vattel says: "Aujourd'hui l'avantage et la sûreté du commerce ont engagé tous les souverains de l'Europe à se relâcher de cette rigueur. Et dès que cet usage est généralement reçu, celui qui y donnerait atteinte blesserait la foi publique; car les étrangers n'ont confié à ses sujets, que dans la ferme persuasion que l'usage général serait observé." He has before asserted, however, and not very consistently, that the War gives the same right over our enemies' debt "qu'elle peut nous donner sur les autres biens." Azuni follows in the same track, pt. ii. c. iv. art. ii. s. 7.

restoration of peace. We have already considered, in the preceding chapter on *Embargo*,(*o*) the manner in which this extreme Right has been mitigated in practice; the memorable case of the Silesian(*p*) Loan in 1752, did not, Dr. Story observes,(*q*) in the slightest degree intimate that International Law prohibited a sovereign from confiscating debts due to his enemies, even where the debts were due from the nation, though it contained a very able statement of the injustice in that particular case; and this memorial admitted that when Sovereigns or States borrowed money from foreigners, it was very commonly expressed in the contract that it should not be seized as reprisals or in case of War; various other Treaties have subsequently been entered into containing a similar stipulation.(*r*)

[*135] *LXXXIX. We have been considering the question of *private debts*. The subject of debts due from the State, in its corporate capacity, to individuals,—money invested in the Public Funds and the like,—has been already discussed. The opinion of Vattel upon this point is thus emphatically expressed: "L'Etat ne touche pas même aux sommes qu'il doit aux ennemis; partout, les fonds confiés au public sont exempts de confiscation et de saisie, en cas de guerre." Emerigon(*s*) and Martens(*t*) are of the same opinion. Indeed, it is one which now may happily be said to have no gainsayers.

XC. With respect to *immoveable property*,—lands or houses of the enemy,—the general rule of civilized States appears to be, that this kind of property is never confiscated, upon the principle, that the sovereign, by permitting the proprietors to purchase and possess such property, has incorporated them amongst his subjects. In cases, however, where the income of the estate would otherwise be sent out of the country to augment the resources either of the private or public wealth of the enemy, it may be sequestrated during the pendency of the War, without any breach of international usage.(*u*)

We shall have occasion hereafter to consider the protection usually [*136] afforded by an invading or conquering State to the **landed* property of foreigners in the invaded or conquered territory.(*x*)

XCI. Before this subject of enemies'(*y*) property be dismissed, it should be observed, that if it have been *wrongfully* seized before the War, it must be resorted. In the Report of the English Law Officers (1753,) in answer to the Prussian Memorial, it was stated that French

(*o*) Vide ante, p. 36, c. iii. (*p*) Ib., p. 25.

(*q*) Brown v. The United States, 8 Cranch, (Amer.,) 142.

(*r*) E. g., Treaty between N. A. United States and England, 1794, art. x. Between N. A. United States and Holland, 8th October, 1782, art. xviii. Between N. A. United States and France, 1778, art. xx. Between N. A. United States and Prussia, 11th July, 1799, art. xxiii. Between N. A. United States and Morocco, 1787, art. xxiv. In this Treaty the confiscation of the debts of individuals was said to be "unjust and impolitic." Between the N. A. United States and Columbia, 1825. Between the N. A. United States and Chili, 1832. Between the N. A. United States and Venezuela, 1836. Between the N. A. United States and the Peru-Bolivian Treaty, 1838.

(*s*) Des Assur., t. i. p. 567. (*t*) Vol. iii. c. ii. s. 5.

(*u*) Bynk., Q. J. P., l i. c. vii. *in initio*. Vattel, l. iii. c. v. s. 76.

(*x*) Grot., l. iii. c. vi. s. 5. Heffters, s. 133. (*y*) 1 Comment. 65.

ships taken before the War of 1741, were restored by the Admiralty Court, both during the heat of the conflict and afterwards, to the French owners.

Such property may not be confiscated, because, but for the wrong done, it would not have been within the territory of the belligerents. Mr. Chancellor Kent cites the Santa Cruz(*z*) as an instance that in England *such* property is subject to the rules of vindictive retaliation. But this seems to be a mistake. Lord Stowell is not speaking of property *wrongfully* taken, but of property *lawfully* seized by Embargo, when he says, "at the breaking out of War it is the constant practice of this country to condemn property seized before the War, if the enemy condemns, and to restore if the enemy restores."

The restoration in these cases is not matter of *right*, but of *expediency*. The English Law-officers, in the Memorial which has been just mentioned, were speaking of restoration in cases where *wrong* had been done.

---

*CHAPTER VII. [*137]

WAR—WHO MAY MAKE.

XCII. It is important to consider the doctrine of International Law, both with respect to those who may be actually engaged in warlike operations, and to those who may possess themselves of the enemy's property. This is, however, quite strictly speaking, a question of Public rather than of International Law. A declaration of War, as Vattel remarks, which enjoins the *subjects at large* to attack the enemy's subjects, implies a *general order*.(*a*) If the unauthorized subject carry on War, or make captures, it may be an offence against the sovereignty of his own nation, but it is not a violation of International Law.(*b*) It is true that the sovereign's order which commands acts of hostilities, and gives a right to commit them, is usually a *particular order*,(*c*) that is, an order to *certain persons*, and that such an order greatly conduces to the mitigation of the evils inseparable from War; but there are many conceivable cases in which a sovereign may appeal to *all* his subjects to protect their country.(*d*) Certainly the sovereign may commission whomsoever he pleases to carry on the War, both by land and sea. Maritime volunteers or *Privateers*(*e*) will be considered hereafter; but it must be remembered here that they carry *Letters of Marque*.

The legal position that no subject can lawfully commit hostilities, or capture property of an enemy, when his sovereign has either expressly or constructively prohibited it, is unquestionable.(*f*) *But it appears to be equally unquestionable that the sovereign may [*138]

(*z*) 1 Rob. Adm. Rep. 64.

(*a*) "At the same time usage does require a lawful commission for the exercise of hostilities."—Martens, l. viii. c. iii. s. 2.

(*b*) Vattel, l. iii. c. xv. ss. 224-28.

(*c*) Ib., s. 224.

(*d*) Ib., s. 228.

(*e*) Et vide ante, vol. i. p. 393.

(*f*) Brown v. The United States, 8 Cranch, (Amer.,) 133. (Story.)

retroactively ratify and validate the unauthorized act of his subject. In fact, the subject seizes at his peril, and it is for the sovereign to decide in the last resort whether he will ratify or repudiate the act.(*g*) It is another unquestionable proposition that all captures in War enure to the sovereign, and can become private property only though his grant.(*h*) But this doctrine has not prevented the English Prize Courts from holding that a subject may seize hostile property for the use of the Crown, wherever it is found: it will be in the discretion of the Crown to ratify the capture by proceeding to condemnation; but to the Prize Court it is quite indifferent whether the capture was originally authorized or subsequently sanctioned by the Crown. This principle is illustrated by various decisions of the Prize Courts in cases of capture by non-commissioned vessels, by commanders on foreign stations anterior to the War, by private individuals in port or on the coasts, and by naval commanders on shore, or unauthorized expeditions;(*i*) and in cases where private captors have sought to obtain a condemnation of their captures to themselves, it has been the practice of the Prize Court, on failure of their title, to decree condemnation to the Crown or the Admiralty, as the circumstances
[*139] required.(*k*) "Nor," *says Mr. Justice Story, in a judgment which really exhausts the argument and learning which belong to this subject, "can I consider these principles of the British Courts a departure from the Law of Nations."(*l*) And he proceeds to show that Puffendorf and Vattel are improperly cited as authorities for the position, that private subjects who seize enemies' property are to be considered as Pirates;(*m*) and that Puffendorf,(*n*) Vattel,(*o*) Grotius,(*p*) and Bynkershoek,(*q*) when carefully and thoroughly examined, fully sustain the law administered in the Prize Courts of Great Britain; and he adds the remarkable words, "If the principles of British Prize Law go further, I am free to say that I consider them *as the law of this country.*"

So Mr. Chancellor Kent observes in his Commentaries, that "there is scarcely a decision of the Prize Courts on any general question of public usage which has not received the express approbation and sanction of our national courts."(*r*)

XCIII. We have seen under what circumstances the property of Foreign Corporations may be subject to Belligerent Rights; it remains

(*g*) Thorshaven, 1 Edwards's Rep. 102.

(*h*) The Elsebe, 5 Rob. 173. The Maria Françoise, 6 Rob. 282; 11 East's Rep. 619. Brown v. The United States, 8 Cranch, (Amer.,) 131.

(*i*) The Aquila, 1 Rob. 37. The Twee Gesuster, 2 Ib. 284, n. The Rebeckah, 1 Ib. 227. The Gertruyda, 2 Ib. 211. The Mariamne, 5 Ib. 11. The Charlotte, Ib. 282. The Richmond, 5 Ib. 325. Thorshaven, 1 Edward, 102. Hale, in Hargrave's Law Treatises, c. xxviii. 245.

(*k*) The Walsingham Packet, 2 Rob. 77. The Etrusco, 4 Ib., p. 262, note, and see cases just cited.

(*l*) Brown v. United States, Cranch, (Amer.,) 132.

(*m*) Ib. 132, 134.

(*n*) L. viii. c. vi. p. 21.

(*o*) L. iii. c. xv. ss. 22-328.

(*p*) L. iii. c. vi. ss. 2, 10, 12.

(*q*) Q. J. P., cc. iii. xviii. xx. "Looking to the general scope of his arguments (id., cc. iii. iv. xvi. xvii.,) I think it might not unfairly be argued that, independent of particular edicts, the subjects of hostile nations might lawfully seize each other's property wherever found."—Story, ubi supr., p. 134.

(*r*) Part. i. l. iii. p. 70.

to observe that Corporations may also, under certain circumstances, exercise these Rights. Thus, wars have been carried on *out of Europe* by Companies or Societies, but these wars have been waged under the direct or implied authority of the sovereign. The right of waging them is a consequence of the power granted by the State to those *companies over particular territories.(*s*) It has so happened that this [*140] power has been only granted with respect to possessions *out* of Europe, but there does not appear to be any absolute necessity that it should be so limited.

The East India Companies, as has been already observed,(*t*) present the most remarkable illustration of the enjoyment of this authority by corporate bodies. But though they have made war and peace in their own name, it is clear that they have done so as delegates of their sovereign; and it may be observed, that the sovereign regulates the distribution of the *Booty* captured in time of war by the East India troops.(*u*)

XCIV. With respect to the instruments by which the work of destruction and devastation may be carried on, but little can be said by the International Jurist, and that little must be chiefly of a negative character.

The means of carrying on war are either (1) secret or (2) open.

With respect to *secret* means, those of poison, of assassination, of treachery, are proscribed by Christian and civilized Heathen nations. It was a noble reply of the Roman Senate, even in the days of its corruption, to the offer of a barbarous ally to destroy their enemy by poison:—"Si patrandæ neci veneum mitteretur—non fraude neque occultè, sed palam et armatum, populum Romanum suos ulcisci."(*x*)

Memorable also is the language of our own Lord Bacon upon the same subject:—"It were," he says, "just and honourable for princes, being in wars together, that however they prosecute their quarrels and debates by arms and acts of hostility; yea, though the wars be such as they pretend, the utter ruin and overthrow of the forces and states one of *another, yet they so limit their passions as they preserve two [*141] things sacred and inviolable,—that is, the life and good name each of other.

"For the wars are no massacres and confusions; *but they are the highest trials of right*, when princes and States, that acknowledge no superior upon earth, shall put themselves upon the justice of God for the deciding of their controversies by such success as it shall please Him to give on either side. And as in the process of particular pleas between private men, all things ought to be ordered by the rules of civil laws, so in the proceedings of the war nothing ought to be done against the Law of Nations or the Law of Honour; which laws have ever pronounced these two sorts of men, the one conspirators against the persons of princes, the other libellers against their good fame, to be such enemies of common society as are not to be cherished,—no, not by enemies.

(*s*) Martens, l. viii. c. iii. s. 2. (*t*) Vol. i. s. 122.

(*u*) Case of the Army of the Deccan, 2 Knapp's Privy Council Rep. 103. The question related to booty captured in the Pindaree and Mahratta War, 1817-18. Vide post as to this case and *booty* generally.

(*x*) Tacit. Annal., l. ii. c. lxxxviii.

"For in the examples of times which were less corrupted, we find that when, in the greatest heats and extremities of wars, there have been made offers of murderous and traitorous attempts against the person of a prince to the enemy, they have been not only rejected, but also revealed; and in like manner, when dishonourable mention shall have been made of a prince before an enemy prince by some that have thought therein to please his humour, he has shown himself, contrariwise, utterly distasted therewith, and been ready to contest for the honour of an enemy."(*y*)

Nevertheless, stratagems by land and sea are not held to violate the laws of War. Thus, the ambush, the disguise of uniform, the false flag are allowable, though it is held that before a naval action be begun the true flag should be hoisted.

[*142] With respect to open means, the employment of savages(*z*) *and cannibals, the well-known subject of Chatham's vehement censure, the use of poisoned weapons, the wanton devastation of territory, the slaughter and ill-usage of the unarmed and unoffending men, much more of women and children, are universally reprobated.(*a*)

Yet the use of every instrument of *open* destruction (though the non-use of particular kinds of shot has sometimes been the subject of treaties,) the cutting off the resources of the enemy, by stopping the supplies of water, or by devastating the adjacent territory, are certainly legitimate means of harrassing the foe.

XCV. Something must be said with respect to the belligerent's right over the person of (1) the enemy and (2) of the prisoner.(*b*)

In the middle ages, when the most gross and cruel treatment of prisoners prevailed, the Western(*c*) and the Eastern Churches contributed, as we have seen, all the mitigation in their power to the exercise of their hostilities; and the Third Council of Lateran (A. D. 1179) forbad Christians to make or to purchase *slaves*,—a principle which the Eastern Church also enforced about eighty years afterwards (A. D. 1260.)

[*143] *1. As to the enemy before he is a prisoner.(*d*) Soldiers are not of the unoffending and unarmed class referred to in the last paragraph,—to wound and to kill, to be wounded and to be killed, is a large part of their terrible though necessary vocation in this imperfect

(*y*) Lord Bacon, Certain Observations upon a Libel published this present year, 1592, vol. v. p. 384. (Ed. B. Montagu.)

(*z*) "But who is the man that has dared to authorise and associate to our arms the tomahawk and scalping-knife of the savage? To call into civil alliance the wild and inhuman savage of the woods; to delegate to the merciless Indian the defence of disputed rights; and to wage the horrors of his barbarous War against our brethen? These enormities cry aloud for redress and punishment, and, unless done away with, will leave an indelible stain on the national honour." —Speech of Lord Chatham, in Adolphus's Hist. of England, vol. ii. p. 485.

(*a*) In the War now waged by England, France, and Turkey, against Russia (1854) in the Crimea, the English General refused to abstain from firing upon a particular quarter of Sebastopol, said to be inhabited by women and children, but offered them a free passage beyond the lines of the army.

(*b*) Martens, l. viii. c. iii. Vattel, l. iii. c. viii. passim.

(*c*) De Sagittar., l. x. c. i. De Treugâ et Pace, l. x. c. ii. Pütter, Beitr., pp. 69, 86.

(*d*) Vattel, l. iii. c. viii. passim.

and unquiet world. But when, whether by surrender or by capture, they are manifestly without the will or the power to resist, their injury or destruction is brutal, sinful, and indefensible.(*e*) The conqueror is obliged, by the laws of just War, to spare those who lay down their arms, who ask for quarter, or who lie wounded and helpless,—to put such to death is to commit murder. And those who commit it ought to die by the hand of the hangman, and not of the soldier. It is said that exceptions to this generally admitted rule are furnished by cases in which the preservation of the life of the enemy is inconsistent with your own safety, in which the cruelty of the enemy justifies and necessitates retaliation, in which the crime of the enemy before he becomes defenceless, warrants you in taking his life.

2. As to the enemy after he is a prisoner. Is Henry V. to be condemned, when, after the battle of Agincourt was over, being suddenly attacked by a body of armed peasants, he ordered his numerous prisoners to be put to death, lest the scanty remains of his victorious army should be annihilated? Was Anson justifiable, when, after the capture of the Acapulco galleon, finding that his crew was outnumbered by his prisoners, he consigned the latter to the horrors and dreadful suffering of incarceration in the hold?

These are instances "at which morality is perplexed, reason is staggered, and from which affrighted nature recoils."(*f*) At least, it may be said, that the clearest evidence of the absolute necessity of self-preservation is required to palliate them. The *prisoner who has yielded under conditions, cannot be injured so long as he [*144] fulfils his part of the condition. The prisoner who has made no such condition may be subject to all necessary restraint, proportioned, of course, to his readiness to submit or his intention to escape.

But surely the brave, the wise, and the humane will join in preferring the conduct of Charles XII., when, after the battle of Narva, he disarmed and set at liberty the prisoners who encumbered him, to that conduct of his adversary, who after the battle of Pultowa, sent the prisoners, whose prowess he had experienced and dreaded, into the wilds of Siberia.

The selling(*g*) prisoners as slaves, is, as Vattel observes, a disgrace to humanity, happily banished from Christendom.(*h*) Prisoners are ex-

(*e*) "Weder in dem einem noch anderen Falle kann nach Rechtsregeln dem Gefangen noch das Leben gefangen werden; *denn jede erlaubte Gewalt endigt* wenn der Gegner widerstandloss geworden ist, und berechtiget bloss zu weiteren Sicherungsmitteln."—Heffters, s. 127. Vide ante, p. 73.

(*f*) Burke's Works, vol. iv. p. 127.

(*g*) —— "of being taken by the insolent foe,
And sold to slavery, and my redemption thence."—Oth., act 1, sc. 3.

Vide ante, vol. i. c. xvii. pp. 317-18, SLAVERY AND THE SLAVE TRADE, and ib. the opinion of Grotius and Bynkershoek.

(*h*) "Le droit de guerre, disent les jurisconsultes Romains, permet de tuer les prisonniers; en les rendant esclaves, on leur fait grâce de la vie. Nous répondons, avec Brusseau, que 'la guerre n'est point une relation d'homme à homme, mais une relation d'Etat à Etat, dans laquelle les particuliers ne sont ennemis qu'accidentellement, non point comme hommes, ni même comme citoyens, mais comme soldats. La fin de la guerre étant la destruction de l'Etat ennemi, on a droit d'en tuer les défenseurs tant qu'ils ont les armes à la main; mais sitôt qu'ils les posent

changed in War, are dismissed on their parole, under promise not to carry arms for a certain time, or during the continuance of the War. A commander may make engagements with the enemy to this effect, but such engagements must have their limits; he cannot undertake that his troops shall never bear arms again against the enemy, though he may engage that they shall not do so during the existing War, because the enemy may so long detain them in captivity.(*i*)

The ransom of prisoners is a practice now much discountenanced, but [*145] which cannot be said to be unlawful. If prisoners *are not released during the War, their freedom should always form one of the conditions of the peace which terminates it.

XCVI. The following classes of persons have no claim to the treatment of prisoners of War:(*k*)—

1. Bands of marauders, acting without the authority of the sovereign or the order of the military commander,—a class which of course does not include volunteer corps, which have been permitted to attach themselves to the army, and which act under the command of the general of the army.
2. Deserters captured among the enemy's troops.
3. Spies, even if they belong to the regular army.

The most melancholy and affecting instance in modern times of the severity with which this class of persons is treated, is afforded by the well-known history of Major André, of which some further mention will be made hereafter.

[*146]

*CHAPTER VIII.

INTERCOURSE BETWEEN ENEMIES DURING WAR.

XCVII. That enemies, during the fiercest raging of War, must keep their word and fulfil their plighted faith, is an undeniable maxim of all civilized States; without the religious observance of these obligations, proposals of peace could never be entered upon, and the horrors of War would be perpetual.(*a*) This word may be pledged, and this faith plighted by implication as well as by express promise. Every belligerent acts upon the presumption that the usages of civilized War will be observed.

Hence, Flags of Truce, Cartels for the exchange of prisoners, Passes, Safe Conducts, are holden sacred by all States.(*b*)

They are among the "*belli commercia*,"(*c*) which whoever violates deserves to be treated as a pirate.

et se rendent, cessant d'être ennemis, ils redeviennent simplement hommes, et l'on n'a plus de droit sur leur vie.'"—Rousseau, Contrat Social, l. i. p. 4.

(*i*) Vattel, ubi supr.

(*k*) Heffters, s. 126.

(*a*) "Inter hostes quæ conveniunt fide aut expressâ aut tacitâ constant."—Grot., l. iii. c. xx. s. 1, *et vide passim*, cc. xxi.-xxiv.

(*b*) Vattel, l. iii. c. xvii. (*c*) Virg. Æn., l. x. 532.

XCVIII. Some of these usages appear to deserve a fuller consideration. A *Safe Conduct*,(*d*) or *Passport*, is a privilege which ensures safety to those who hold it while passing or repassing from one place to another, or while occupied in the performance of some act specified in, and permitted by the *instrument. Such an instrument must emanate from the supreme authority upon the spot, that is from the officer in command, to whom the sovereign has for these and other purposes delegated his power, either by express commission or as the natural consequences of other powers. [*147]

XCIX. The *safe conduct* for the *person* cannot be transferred from one man to another; the abuses which might flow from such a permission are manifest. But the *safe conduct* for *goods* admits of their being removed by some person other than their owner, unless there be some specific objection against the person employed.

The extent of the *safe conduct* must of course be limited by the extent of the command of the grantor; it would not necessarily be limited by territorial boundary, but would, unless otherwise limited, follow the grantee wherever the forces or troops of the grantor are.

C. The grantor of the safe conduct tacitly pledges himself both to protect the grantee and to punish any person subject to his command who may violate it. A safe conduct, strictly construed, does not include more than one person and his reasonable baggage, unless the terms of the instrument expressly admit more.

CI. If a safe conduct be granted for a *limited time*, its virtue expires with the expiration of this time; but if the grantee has been prevented by sickness, or some cause over which he has no control, from returning within the time, the spirit of the promise of security conveyed in the instrument protects him. The case, as Vattel remarks,(*e*) is different from that of an enemy coming into a country during a truce: to him no particular promise has been made; he has, at his own peril, taken advantage of a *general* liberty allowed by the suspension of hostilities; all that has been promised to him is forbearance from hostilities during a certain period; it may be a matter of importance to his enemy that at the expiration *of that period, the War should in all respects freely take its course. [*148]

The safe conduct is granted by the public authorities, therefore the grantor in fact never dies; it does not expire with the death of the particular officer who happened to subscribe it.(*f*) If the safe conduct contains any such limitation as *for such time as we shall think fit*, it is of course revocable at the discretion of the grantor;(*g*) but even without such limitation it can hardly be said to be, *under all circumstances*, irrevocable; circumstances subsequent to the granting of it may render its revocation imperative, but it must be so revoked that the grantee be allowed time and liberty to depart in safety, though a very urgent and

(*d*) Jus commeandi extra inducias (Grot., l. iii. c. xxi. s. 14.) Sauvegarde. Salva guardia. Schutz-oder Salvegardenvertrag. Literæ liberi commeatûs. Passeport, Sauf conduit.

(*e*) L. iii. c. xvii. p. 274. (*f*) Grot., l. iii. c. xxi. s. 20.

(*g*) Ib., s. 22. Vattel, l. iii. c. xvii. p. 275.

supervening necessity may possibly authorize his temporary detention. But a safe conduct is not to be converted into a snare, the safety of the bearer is at all hazards to be secured.(*h*)

CII. *Safe conducts* are privileges, and therefore, if any doubt arise as to their construction, should be interpreted by the general rules applicable to such grants.

But inasmuch as the right of safe passage conveyed by the instrument of safe conduct is neither hurtful to a third person nor onerous to the grantor, it should always receive a liberal construction, and the instrument, whatever the language of it may be, must be so interpreted as to avoid the consequence of a manifest injustice or absurdity.(*i*) Thus, for instance, a *safe conduct* granted to soldiers and sailors *generally* must be construed to extend to all officers of the army and the fleet. So a permission "to depart freely," must be holden to continue till the grantee arrives in a place of safety. The privilege is, in fact, always to be so construed, as not to be useless to the grantee. But the grantee allowed [*149] to depart, is not *necessarily allowed to return, and he who is allowed to come is allowed to do so once, and not oftener, unless there be some words relating to time which give rise to a reasonable conjecture that such was the intention of the grantor. If permission be given for other persons to accompany the grantee, describing them by some general name, such as *companions*, this must be construed to exclude those whose case is, to borrow the expression of Grotius, *more odious* than that of the grantee himself; such, for instance, as deserters, refugees, pirates, or robbers. If the instrument speaks of companions, *belonging to a certain nation*, the expression operates to exclude all companions who do not belong to that nation.(*k*)

CIII. The occasions upon which (1) the extreme rights of War have been pressed with the greatest severity, and (2) upon which barbarities inconsistent with the Laws of War have been practised, will chiefly be found to have been those arising during a War which was in its origin of a *civil* or *revolutionary* character. The latter proposition is illustrated by the conduct even of the French, who are usually as remarkable for their chivalry as for their valour. At the beginning of the Wars of the first French Revolution, the French General announced his intention of giving no quarter to English prisoners. The English did not retaliate, and the Laws of War upon this subject were soon restored.

CIV. Of the truth of the former proposition the War between England and her revolted American colonies affords various melancholy examples upon both sides; but two have been specially recorded by history. They are remarkable for the affecting character of their incidents, and for their having been sanctioned by the authority of the brave and virtuous Washton. They are the examples of André and Asgill.

[*150] *In the year 1776, Lee, an American general, while advancing to join the commander-in-chief, quitted his camp before Morris-

(*h*) Vattel, l. iii. c. xvii. p. 276.

(*i*) Vide ante, vol. ii. c. viii. p. 79. INTERPRETATION OF TREATIES.

(*k*) Grot., l. iii. c. xxi. *De fide manente bello, ubi de induciis, commeatu, captivorum redemtione,—præsertim*, ss. 14-22.

town, and went upon a reconnoitering expedition. He was surprised by a detachment of English light horse, under Colonel Harcourt, and conveyed to New York. This exploit caused no less joy in the British, than regret in the American army. No officer of equal rank being in captivity among the Americans, General Washington offered six field officers in exchange; but received for reply, that General Lee, being a deserter from the British service, could not be considered as a prisoner of war. It was ineffectually alleged, on the other side, that he had resigned his commission before the commencement of hostilities; no arguments or offers could procure his release; he was confined, and vigilantly guarded. General Washington declared that he would not exchange certain Hessian field-officers, or a Lieutenant-Colonel Campbell, unless Lee were recognised as a prisoner of war; and the English commander, fearing that if Lee were sent to England the Hessian officers would be closely confined, and that thereby much discontent would arise, detained Lee in America. The proceedings of Congress warranted these apprehensions. They rescinded a kind of cartel for the exchange of captives, deprived of their parole several British officers, and declared that the treatment experienced by Lee should form the model of their conduct towards prisoners.(*l*)

CV. The case of Captain Asgill was as follows:—In 1782, after the capitulation of Lord Cornwallis, many loyalists urged Sir Henry Clinton to threaten vengeance for injuries inflicted on those who had joined the royal standard; but he declined issuing a proclamation, and was deterred by the advice of the principal refugees, from establishing the civil government, which would have permitted the trial of captive continentals as rebels. While he was engaged in *projects of defence, and while commissioners, appointed by him and General Washington, were [*151] negotiating for an exchange of prisoners, one Joshua Huddy, a captain in the service of Congress, was taken by a party of loyalists, and after being conveyed to several prisons, and confined some days, delivered, with two others, by a written order from the Board, to a Captain Lippencott, for the ostensible purpose of being exchanged; but Huddy was hung on a tree, with a label on his breast, denoting that his fate was a retaliation for that of one White, an associator.

Sir Henry Clinton, highly resenting this disgraceful outrage on humanity, and insult on himself as commander, arrested Lippencott, and with the concurrence of a council of war, ordered him to be tried for murder. But the Americans were not appeased by this act of justice. The inhabitants of Monmouth county urgently entreated General Washington, as the person in whom was lodged the sole power of avenging their wrongs, to bring a British officer of the same rank as Huddy to a similar end.

Acting with great promptitude on this requisition, the American commander wrote to the British commander, "I *demand* that the guilty Captain Lippencott, or the officer who commanded at the execution of Huddy, *must* be given up; or, if that officer was of inferior rank to him, so many of the perpetrators as will, according to the tariff of exchange,

(*l*) Adolphus, History of England, vol. ii. p. 380.

be equivalent. In failure of it, I shall hold myself justified, in the eyes of God and man, for the measures to which I shall resort."

Clinton expressed surprise and displeasure at this imperious language. He had taken, he said, due measures for bringing the delinquents to justice; but would not consent to adopt and extend barbarity, by sacrificing innocence, under the notion of preventing guilt; and added that, if violations of humanity could be justified by example, those committed by General Washington's party exceeded, and probably gave rise to that in question. The board of loyalists, corroborating this assertion, stated
[*152] circumstances relating to the execution of Huddy, *in which, though Lippencott had exceeded his authority and their orders, he had merely adopted the precedent shown by the Americans in the case of White. They also recited many instances in which cruelty towards the loyalists had only been restrained by retaliation.

It should be observed that the letter of Washington had been accompanied with depositions to show that Huddy was not concerned in the murder of White; but, on the other hand, there was produced Huddy's own confession of his activity in murdering associated loyalists.

Unmoved by these representations, Washington seized as deserters Messrs. Hatfield and Badgely, though protected by a flag of truce. To an application for their liberation, he answered, that deserters, or persons whom crime rendered amenable to the civil laws, could not be protected, even under a flag.

Subsequently to this act, General Washington wrote to the English General Robertson, the temporary successor of Sir Henry Clinton, that he adhered to the resolutions which he had expressed to the latter officer. Orders had been given to designate a British officer for retaliation; the time and place were fixed, but still he hoped that the result of a court-martial would prevent this dreadful alternative. This proceeding was resorted to, but was not attended with the effect which the Americans desired. The prisoner, at first pleaded that he was not subject to martial law, and by common law could not be tried in New York for an offence alleged to have been committed in another State—that of New Jersey. This objection, being submitted to the consideration of the Chief Justice and the Attorney-General, was overruled; the trial proceeded; but as it appeared from the evidence that Lippencott acted under the orders of a board which he was bound to obey, he was acquitted. And now the barbarous edict of retaliation was about to be enforced. The officers, who had been surrendered at York Town, and whose persons ought to have been sacred under the terms of the capitulation, were directed to
[*153] cast lots, to determine who should be the expiatory victim. *It fell on Captain Asgill, son of Sir Charles Asgill, who was only in his nineteenth year; and against this inhuman sacrifice entreaty and argument were, with the American General, equally unavailing. To close at once this painful and disgraceful narrative, it is to be added that the innocence and amiable qualities of the young officer, and the anguish and the pathetic supplications of his family, which produced no effect on Washington, found their way to the heart of the French queen. Influenced by the prayers and tears of the captive's mother, she interposed

her powerful mediation; and, with the aid of M. de Vergennes, and through him of M. de la Luzerne, the plenipotentiary of Louis, obtained from Congress an order for Asgill's discharge.(*m*)

CVI. The case of Major André was on this wise. The American General Arnold, an officer of great abilities, had determined to leave the American and join the royalist forces. In July, 1779, he had been appointed by Washington to the important post of West Point, on the North River. Here he opened a negotiation with the English General, Sir Henry Clinton, for the surrender of West Point and the adjacent posts. When the project was ripe for execution, Major André, Adjutant-General of the British army, an officer in whose prudence and address Sir Henry Clinton reposed the greatest confidence, and who had chiefly conducted the correspondence between him and General Arnold, was commissioned to adjust the final arrangement. He was conveyed from the Vulture sloop by night, in a boat despatched by Arnold, landed on neutral ground, and held a conference with him till the approach of day. The American General, fearful of discovery, advised Major André not to return on board the Vulture, but conveyed him to a place of concealment *within the American lines, where he remained till night. [*154] During the day the sloop had shifted her position, and the boatmen refusing to convey André on board, he was compelled to attempt reaching New York by land; and, by the direction of Arnold, changed his regimentals for a plain suit, and received a passport under the name of John Anderson. Protected by the passport, he had already passed the lines, and conceived himself free from danger, when a patrol of three men sprang from a wood and seized his horse. In a moment of surprise, the unfortunate André inquired of the soldiers "whence they came?" and to their answer, "from below," replied, "and so am I;" avowing himself to be a British officer. He discovered his error too late; the captors searched him, and finding several papers concealed in various parts of his dress, carried him before their commander. During his examination before the American colonel of militia, Major André continued his assumed name of John Anderson, and contrived to obtain the transmission of a letter to Arnold, who escaped to the British head-quarters. The captive had now no further occasion for disguise: he wrote to General Washington a full and frank statement of the circumstances which occasioned his being within the American lines, exculpating himself from the imputation of being a spy, and demanding, "whatever might be his fate, a decent treatment."

Washington referred the case to a board of fourteen general officers, all Americans except La Fayette and the Baron de Steuben, before whom André was compelled to appear. The facts alleged against him were chiefly drawn from his own letters, and supported by his own answers to interrogatories unfairly administered; while he was, by situation, precluded from the advantage of adducing explanatory testimony.

(*m*) Adolphus, History of England, vol. iii. pp. 383-386. Remembrancer, vol. xiv. p. 155, et seq. Ann. Reg. (1783,) Appendix to the Chronicle. Spark's Life of Washington, vol. i. p. 378. Letters in the State Paper Office.

The board reported that, agreeably to the law and usage of nations, he ought to suffer death as a spy.

From the moment of his capture, no exertions were spared to avert his fate. Colonel Robinson, commander of the loyal Americans, and Sir
[*155] Henry Clinton wrote to General Washington, *affirming that he had been sent to confer, under a flag of truce. Arnold certified the same fact, and further insisted that every subsequent proceeding had been sanctioned by his authority, which he had a right to exercise according to his discretion. These letters were produced before the board of officers; but a previous question was artfully put to the captive, who, in answer, is said to have denied that he had come on shore with a flag of truce.

After promulgation of the sentence, Sir Henry Clinton sent a deputation to state such facts as could not be disclosed to the board. General Washington would not receive them, but appointed General Greene, president of the court which condemned Major André, to meet General Robertson,—the person who accompanied him not being permitted to land. In this conference Robertson urged reasons of humanity and policy, and especially the hazard which many Americans would incur in case of retaliation, and the previous moderation of Sir Henry Clinton, who, on several occasions, had shown the most humane attention to General Washington's intercession in favour of avowed spies, and had still in his power many delinquents. General Robertson offered to prove, by unexceptionable testimony that André went on shore in a boat bearing a flag of truce, with the knowledge and under the protection of Arnold, who was commander of the district; and he strongly urged the injustice of considering Major Andre as a spy, merely on the foundation of an improper phrase in a letter to General Washington. None of these arguments or proposals had the desired effect; and an offer to exchange, for the intended victim, any prisoner whom the Americans should select, was equally disregarded. General Robertson then proposed a reference to disinterested foreigners, acquainted with the Laws of War and of Nations; but this proposition was not complied with. A letter written by Arnold, repeating his explanations of Andre's situation, and threatening retaliation if the sentence against him was executed, produced, as might be expected, no good effect; every sentiment of humanity and
[*156] policy was absorbed in the *base desire of revenge: General Washington justified the decision of the board.

Major André, during his examination, studiously avoided every disclosure which might affect the interests or character of those with whom he had been engaged. He received the sentence without alarm or dejection, acknowledged the politeness with which he had been treated during his captivity, and only solicited the sad privilege of dying by the musket, like a soldier, and not by the cord, like a felon.

This request was cruelly denied; but his courage surmounted even this terrible and unexpected trial.(*n*) The manner of his execution was scarcely justifiable by the sternest rules of International Law; it was one

(*n*) His monument is in Westminster Abbey.

of the few acts which can be cited as discreditable to the great hero, Washington, and, like the case of Asgill, was the fruit of the proverbial bitterness of a civil war.

CVII. The Civil War which immediately followed upon the outbreak of the first revolution carried the ferocity of the civil contest into the International War which sprung from it; but for a short period only. Regular military discipline soon conferred upon the French army that reputation for humanity which it has subsequently so well deserved, and the reputation for courage it has never lost.

But the contrast between the conduct of that army with respect to prisoners in 1794 and in 1810, is very striking, and illustrates the remark respecting the effects of civil war upon belligerent practice.

In 1794, the Duke of York, Commander-in-Chief of the British army in Holland, put forth a proclamation to the following effect:—

"The National Convention has just passed a decree that their soldiers shall give no quarter to the British or Hanoverian troops. His Royal Highness anticipates the indignation and horror which has naturally arisen in the minds of the brave troops whom he addresses upon receiving *this information. He desires, however, to remind them that [*157] mercy to the vanquished is the brightest gem in the soldier's character, and exhorts them not to suffer their resentment to lead them into any precipitate act of cruelty on their part, which may sully the reputation they have acquired in the world. In all the wars which from the earliest times have existed between the English and French nations, they have been accustomed to consider each other in the light of generous as well as brave enemies, while the Hanoverians, the allies of the former, have shared for above a century in this mutual esteem. Humanity and kindness have at all times taken place the instant that opposition ceased, and the same cloak has been frequently seen covering those who were wounded, friends and enemies, while indiscriminately conveyed to hospitals of the conquerors. The British and Hanoverian armies will not believe that the French nation, even under their present infatuation, can so far forget their character as soldiers as to pay any attention to a decree as injurious to themselves as it is disgraceful to their Government; and, therefore, His Royal Highness trusts that the soldiers of both nations will confine their sentiments of abhorrence to the National Convention alone, persuaded that they will be joined in them by every Frenchman who possesses a spark of honour or one principle of a soldier."(*o*)

What a contrast to this state of things is exhibited in the despatches of the Duke of Wellington during the Peninsular War. Take, for instance, the following despatch:—

Celorico, August 8, 1810.

"To the Right Hon. H. Wellesley,

"Since I have commanded the troops in this country, I have always treated the French officers and soldiers who have been made prisoners with the utmost humanity and attention; and in numerous instances I have saved their lives. The only motive which I have had for this con-

(*o*) Proclamation, May 30, Ann. Reg., 1794, State Papers, p. 169.

[*158] duct has been that they might treat our officers and soldiers well *who might fall into their hands; and I must do the French the justice to say that they have been universally well treated, and in recent instances the wounded prisoners of the British army have been taken care of before the wounded of the French army."(*p*)

CVIII. During the present war waged by France and England against Russia, complaints have been preferred by the former Powers that the wounded English and French were, while lying helpless on the field of battle, put to death by the Russian soldiers. It is lamentable to add, that this charge was palliated, and not wholly denied by the Russian authorities. The palliation consisted in an averment that the Russians had been exasperated by the spoliation of a Russian church by English soldiers previous to the battle.(*q*)

CIX. The conventions which take place during war respecting prisoners are those which relate to (1) their ransom or (2) their exchange.

Formerly, the right to exact *Ransom* belonged to the individual captor; the practice so often met with in Homer and Virgil, prevailed in the middle ages of Christianity, and is even referred to as existing by Vattel.(*r*) The custom of demanding *Ransom* is now nearly extinct among civilized nations, but if exacted at all, it would now, according to the better usage, be exacted by the State, and not by the individual conqueror or captor,—except, indeed, in cases of maritime capture, among those nations which permit their subjects to take ransom for captured ships. This practice has been for some time disallowed by the Law of England.

This branch of the question will be discussed with the other subjects of Maritime International Law.

But there are certain general maxims on the subject of Ransom which [*159] may be mentioned in this place. In the *middle and early ages, a person who had acquired a right to demand a ransom from his prisoner, might transfer that right to a third person. The price of the ransom was usually proportioned to the military rank, and not to the wealth of the prisoner; the agreement once made as to the price was held to be a perfect contract between the captor and the prisoner, and one which could not be rescinded unless the prisoner had fraudulently disguised his rank.

Vattel has no doubt that if a prisoner, who has been set at liberty, dies before his ransom be paid, the obligation to discharge it descends to his heirs. The same authority holds that if a prisoner be rescued before he has received his liberty, though he may have agreed for the price of his ransom, he is released from all obligation to pay it.

If a prisoner be released upon condition of procuring the release of another, and that other dies before his liberty has been obtained, it is said that the survivor ought to return to his prison. It is certain, however, that if a hostage be given in order to procure the liberty of a prisoner, and the prisoner die, the hostage should be set free; but if the

(*p*) The Despatches of the Duke of Wellington, vol. iv. p. 212.
(*q*) Lord John Russell's Speech in the House of Commons, December, 1854.
(*r*) L. iii. c. xvii. ss. 278-286.

hostage die, the prisoner is not thereby restored to his liberty. If however, one prisoner has been substituted for another, the death of one releases the other.(*s*)

CX. (*t*) In general, all contracts in favour of alien enemies are, in Great Britain, void, both at law and in equity,(*u*) unless the enemy shall have come into this country *sub salvo conductu*, or live here by the king's license.(*x*) And a bill *drawn abroad by an alien enemy on a British subject here, and indorsed, during War, to a British subject *voluntarily* resident in the hostile country, cannot be enforced by the latter after peace has been restored, because it was illegal in its concoction.(*y*) But upon the principle laid down by Vattel, it was decided that where two British subjects were declared *prisoners* in France, and one of them drew a bill in favour of the other on a third British subject, resident in England, and such payee indorsed the same, in France, to an alien enemy, that the transaction was legal, that the alien's right of action was only *suspended* during the War, and that, on the return of peace, he might recover the amount from the acceptor; for, otherwise, it was said, such persons would sustain great privations during their detention: and, for the same reason, it has been holden to be no objection to an action on such bill, that it is brought as to part in trust for an alien enemy.(*z*) [*160]

The Law of the North American United States is thus stated by Mr. Chancellor Kent:(*a*)—"The effect of a ransom is equivalent to a safe conduct granted by the authority of the State to which the captor belongs, and it binds the commanders of other cruisers to respect the safe conduct thus given; and under the implied obligation of the Treaty of Alliance, it binds equally the cruisers of the allies of the captor's country.(*b*) From the very nature of the connection between allies, their compacts with the common enemy must bind each other, when they tend to accomplish the objects of the alliance. If they did not, the ally would reap all the fruits of the compact, without being subject to the terms and conditions of it; and the enemy with whom the *agreement was made would be exposed, in regard to the ally, to all the disadvantages of it, without participating in the stipulated benefits. Such an inequality of obligation is contrary to every principle of reason and justice.(*c*) [*161]

"The safe conduct implied in a ransom bill, requires that the vessel

(*s*) Vattel, ubi supr.

(*t*) Vattel, l. iii. c. xvi. s. 264; and see note to this section in Chitty's translation of Vattel. Kent, Comment., i. p. 104.

(*u*) Williamson v. Patterson, 7 Taunton's Rep., p. 439. 1 J. B. Moore, 333, S. C. 2 Vesey & Beames, p. 332. Vide ante, p. 321, n. (*a*)

(*x*) Cowper, p. 163. 6 Durnford & East, p. 23. 2 Vesey & Beames, p. 332.

(*y*) Williamson v. Patterson, 7 Taunton, p. 439. M'Connell v. Hector, 3 Bosanquet & Puller, p. 113. Roberts v. Hardy & others, 3 Maule & Selwyn, p. 533.

(*z*) Antoine v. Moorshead, 6 Taunton, pp. 237, 447. 1 Marshall, p. 558, S. C. Danberg v. Moorshead, 5 Taunton, p. 332, C.

(*a*) Kent, Comm., vol. i. p. 112.

(*b*) Miller v. The Resolution, 2 Dallas, (Amer.) p. 15.

(*c*) Miller v. Miller, 2 Dallas, (Amer.) p. 15. Pothier, Traité du Droit de Propriété N°. 134.

should be found within the course prescribed, and within the time limited by the contract, unless forced out of her course by stress of weather, or unavoidable necessity.(*d*) If the vessel ransomed perishes by a peril of the sea, before arrival in port, the ransom is, nevertheless, due, for the captor has not insured the prize against the perils of the sea, but only against recapture by cruisers of his own nation, or of the allies of his country. If there should be a stipulation in the ransom contract, that the ransom should not be due if the vessel was lost by sea perils, the provision ought to be limited to total losses by shipwreck, and not to mere stranding, which might lead to frauds, in order to save the cargo at the expense of the ship."(*e*)

CXI. Closely connected with the subject of Ransom is that species of convention which has for its object the release of prisoners, and which is usually designated by the name of Cartel. The English Prize Courts have given some valuable and well-considered decisions upon this subject. They have holden that the privileges and immunities of Cartel Ships are of a very sacred nature, and are to be received with great respect, from their obvious tendency to mitigate the miseries of War, and to facilitate the return of peace.(*f*) It is to be observed that the actual existence of War is not necessary to give effect to contracts for the employment of vessels as Cartel Ships. It is sufficient if they [*162] *are entered into prospectively, and in expectation of approaching War.(*g*)

As the privilege of a Cartel is allowed for the mutual exchange of prisoners of war, the employment of such vessels is confined to belligerents.(*h*) But these vessels are, on general principles, to be protected in their office *eundo et redeundo*, both in carrying prisoners and returning from that service.(*i*)

It has not been the habit of Courts of International Law to scrutinize with severity the formal papers of these privileged conveyances; they have always been satisfied with substantial evidence of the bonâ fide character of their employment.(*k*)

The privileges of Cartel are not confined to the object of negotiating the ransom of prisoners; they attach where the vessel is employed in execution of a Treaty of Peace, conformably to orders of Government, and for the purpose of carrying the stipulations of the Treaty into effect.(*l*)

It has been holden that a Cartel Ship appointed in time of peace, but in contemplation of War, by an officer in the East India Company, and subsequently confirmed by officers of the Crown, and employed in carrying into effect the stipulation of a Treaty, but captured on hostilities supervening, is entitled to the privileges of that character, and restitution has been decreed accordingly.(*m*)

CXII. But Cartel Ships are not allowed to abuse their privilege; the

(*d*) Ib., Nos. 134-5. (*e*) Ib., No. 138. (*f*) The Carolina, 6 Rob. p. 336.
(*g*) The Carolina, 6 Rob. p. 336. (*h*) The Rose in Bloom, 1 Dodson, p. 60.
(*i*) The Daifjie, 3 Rob. p. 141. (*k*) La Gloire, 5 ib. p. 192. The Caroline, 6 ib. p. 337. The Daifjie, 3 ib. p. 139.
(*l*) The Carolina, 6 ib. p. 338. (*m*) Ib. p. 336.

sacred character which is the cause of it must be religiously maintained, and their employment must be wholly unconnected with commercial or other objects. Therefore Cartel Ships have no right to trade or take in a *cargo; and the doing so subjects, strictly speaking, the vessel,(*n*) and always the cargo, to confiscation.(*o*) [*163]

But it has been holden that a Cartel appointed in time of peace, but in contemplation of War, and which, in accordance with the stipulations of the Cartel contract, took on board a cargo at an intermediate port after the breaking out of hostilities, had not forfeited her privileges of a Cartel thereby; and restitution of a ship and cargo was accordingly decreed, save as to some few articles subsequently taken on board, and as to which no proof of property was adduced.(*p*)

A ship going to be employed as a Cartel Ship is not protected *by mere intention* on her way from one port to another of her own country, for the purpose of taking on herself the character when she arrives at the latter port. If such a necessity occurs, it is proper to apply to the Commissary of Prisoners in the enemy's country for a *pass.*(*q*)

Lastly, it is to be remembered that persons put on board a Cartel Ship with their own consent by the Government of the enemy, to be carried to their own country, are bound to do no act of hostility. Therefore a capture made by such persons of a vessel of their own country from the enemy, is not a recapture in contemplation of law; it gives them no title to salvage, and confers on the former owner no title to claim the vessel; and property so recovered has been decreed to be given up to the disposal of the Crown.(*r*)

CXIII. Belligerent States(*s*) sometimes enter into *General *Conventions*, either at the beginning or during the course of the War, respecting the mode in which their necessary intercourse during War shall be carried on. The subjects of these General Conventions are usually conditions to be observed respecting the exchange and redemption of prisoners, passports, safe conducts, flags of truce, and other matters of the like kinds. Sometimes, also, agreements to abstain from certain modes of injuring each other, and also with respect to the levying contributions on the invaded territory. The duration of these Conventions is usually limited to the War, or to a certain number of years. [*164]

CXIV. But besides these *General*, there are usually *Particular* Conventions, which arise *pendente bello*,—these may be divided into two principal classes:—

1. Truces, including partial suspensions of hostilities.
2. Capitulations (*pacta deditionis*,) by virtue of which a particular

(*n*) The Venus, 4. Rob. p. 355.

(*o*) Tin plates for canister-shot put on board a Cartel Ship by a British manufacturer at Dover were condemned as *droits* of Admiralty. La Rosine, 2 Rob. p. 372.

(*p*) The Carolina, 6 Rob. p. 337.

(*q*) The Daifjie, 3 Rob. p. 143.

(*r*) The Mary, 5 Rob. p. 200.

(*s*) Grot., l. iii. c. xxi. *De fide manente bello, ubi de induciis, commeatu, captivorum redemptione.* Ib. c. xxii. *De fide minorum potestatum in bello.* Vattel, l. iii. c. xvi. Martens, l. viii. c. iv. 1 Kent, Comm., Lecture viii.

body of troops, or a particular town or territory, submits, under certain conditions, to the enemy.

CXV. The usual and recognized mode of proposing a *Truce* is to hoist, if it be the case of a besieged town, a *white flag*, or otherwise to send a messenger with one.

In the case of the Besieged town, after the besiegers have responded to the signal, hostilities cease till the parley be over. In the case of sending a message, the bearer of the white flag is inviolable by all but savages. It should be mentioned, that when a ship hoists a white flag it is a recognized signal of surrender.

CXVI. (*t*) "*Publica conventio est* (said Ulpian) *quæ fit per pacem (aut)*(*u*) *quoties inter se duces belli quædam paciscuntur.*"

Every general or commander is invested with the power of sanctioning a *Truce*, or cessation of arms, for a short period and a particular [*165] purpose;(*x*) such as that a town, if not relieved *within a few months, shall surrender, cessation of warfare to bury the dead, and similar purposes; a Truce for a long period and for a general object is a Peace, and requires the ratification of the sovereign. But the authority of the sovereign, and the national honour and faith, are pledged to the observance of Truces and suspensions of arms concluded by his generals. A Truce is binding from the moment that it is solemnly proclaimed and duly notified. It is then a law binding on the subjects of both parties: but it must be known; for a law that could not have been known, imposes no obligation. Therefore subjects are not to blame who make captures or prizes after the Truce, if circumstances have prevented them from being warned of it; but their sovereign is bound to make restitution of the property so taken, though not to make indemnification for actual losses sustained, if it has been impossible to notify the Truce to the officer, naval or military, who, in ignorance of it, made the capture.(*y*) In order to obviate these difficulties, it is usual, both with

(*t*) Dig., l. ii. t. xiv. p. 5. De Pactis.

(*u*) Compare Noodt, De Pactis, c. vii., with Barbeyrac's note on Grot., l. iii. c. xx. i.

(*x*) "Inducias dare ducum est, nec summorum tantum sed et minorum, iis nempe quos oppugnant aut obsessos tenent, et se suasque copias quod attinet; nam alios duces pares non obligant."—Grot., l. iii. c. xxii. p. 8. Thus Mr. Grenville writes, in April, 1800, to his brother, Lord Buckingham:—"You will have seen by the last French papers, which contain the Egyptian Convention, and Kleber's account of it, that our Christian knight (Sir Sydney Smith) is a better soldier than politician; yet although I entirely dislike and disapprove the countenance which he has given to this Convention, as he has taken upon himself to give it his sanction in the quality of a British commanding officer, we must, I fear, respect that character, however prejudicial to our wishes and interests."—Memoirs of the Court and Cabinets of George III., by the Duke of Buckingham, vol. iii. p. 57.

(*y*) Grot., l. iii. c. xxi. s. 5. "Illud obiter dicam, inducias et siquid est simile ipsos contrahentes statim obligare ex quo contractus absolutus est: at subditos utrimque obligari incipere ubi induciæ acceperunt forman legis, cui inest exterior quædam publicatio: quâ factâ statim quidem incipit habere vim obligandi subditos. Sed ea vis, si publicatio uno tantùm loco facta sit, non per omnem ditionem eodem momento se exserit, sed per tempus sufficiens ad perferendam ad singula loca notitiam. Quare si quid interea a subditis contra inducias factum sit, ipsi a pœnis immunes sunt, neque tamen eo minùs contrahentes damnum resarcire debebunt."

respect to *Truces* and *Treaties of Peace*, to assign different periods, according to *the differences of situations and distance, for the cessation of hostilities. [*166]

With respect to the interpretation of the terms used in *Covenants of Truce* the same principles and rules are applicable as those, which have been already laid down for the interpretation of *Treaties*.(z)

CXVII. (a) We have now to consider the effect of a *Truce* upon the parties to it, or what is allowed or forbidden to be done during its continuance. This subject is treated by Grotius and Vattel with great fulness of detail. The general principle, however, laid down by Grotius embraces nearly the whole question: "illiciti enim sunt omnes actus bellici, sive in personas sive in res; id est quicquid vi fit adversus hostem: id enim omne per induciarum tempus sit contrà jus gentium."(b)

An important distinction exists between what a belligerent may do at home and in his own territories, and what he may do in the place to which the cessation of hostilities relates. He may do *at home*, unless, of course, there be a specific condition to the contrary, whatever he might do in time of peace; he may repair fortifications, levy soldiers, assemble an army, or take any other step of a similar kind. He has a right to do these things in time of peace, and the Truce, therefore, does not tie up his hands.

But he may do none of these things in the place to which the cessation of hostilities relates; because he may not take advantage of this cessation to do, without danger to himself, what is injurious to the enemy, and what but for the Truce he could not have done except with danger to himself. Therefore, on the one side to continue the works of a siege, or on the other to repair the breaches made in the fortifications by the artillery of the besiegers, to introduce succours and reinforcements, to do any act of the like kind, is the conduct of *gross and shameless perfidy, and reprobated by the practice and conscience of every civilized State. [*167]

CXVIII. Vattel makes a distinction in applying the principles just laid down to a suspension of hostilities for the express purpose of burying the dead. He thinks that the implied contract in this case is, that the firing is to cease in order that each party may carry off their dead, and that it is unlawful to carry on any works which the firing, if it had not been intermitted, would have impeded; but he thinks that it is lawful to introduce a reinforcement, during this cessation, into some quarter remote from the point of attack, and which the firing would not have reached; that the vigilance of the besiegers ought not to lulled by a special armistice of this kind, and that the armistice itself does not enable the besieged to bring in the reinforcement. Upon the truth or falsehood of this last assertion, it would seem that the lawfulness of this act must depend. Where it cannot be truly predicated, the act is clearly perfidious. Nor can it be denied that strict good faith, and the general

(z) Vide post, vol. ii. c. viii. p. 79.
(a) Grot., l. iii. c xxi. ss. 6-9, et c. xxii. Vattel, l. iii. c. xvi. ss. 245-258.
(b) Ubi supr. s. 6.

interests of belligerents, would be best promoted by an abstinence from every equivocal act of this nature.

Vattel himself admits, that if an army were to avail itself of such a suspension of hostilities in order to extricate itself from a disadvantageous position by marching off unmolested in sight of the enemy, it would be a flagrant violation of the compact; but he thinks if they silently filed off in the rear, and thus reached a safer position, there would be no breach of faith. It is, however, surely impossible to justify the morality of this doctrine, the tendency of which is to infuse that suspicion and distrust into the mind of the belligerent which leads in practice to the worst horrors of war.

CXIX. It is a clear violation of this compact to receive offers of submission or adherence from rebellious towns, provinces, or subjects during the suspension, and of course a still greater violation to induce them to revolt from their sovereign. During this suspension enemies may, unless specially forbidden, pass and repass into each other's territories; but the [*168] right of *postliminium* cannot take effect during *a truce, for that right is founded only on a state of war, and the truce suspends all acts of war and leaves everything in its existing state; and even prisoners do not *then* recover their former condition.

The question of the necessity of a declaration of war previously to the commencement of hostilities has been already considered;(c) but it is universally admitted, that after the expiration of a truce hostilities may be renewed without any declaration of war.

CXX. It is lawful, in time of Truce, to take possession of what is *really* derelict, that is, what has been left, without any intention of being resumed by those to whom it belonged; but not what merely happens to be unguarded, whether the custody was removed before or after the truce, because the ownership (*dominium*) remaining, causes the possession of another to be unjust. Therefore, Grotius says, Belisarius was without excuse, when, in time of truce with the Goths, he seized two of their places which happened to be denuded of their garrisons.(d)

CXXI. If the conditions of the truce be broken by one belligerent, there is no doubt the other may immediately return to war, and without a declaration (*sine indicatione,*) unless, indeed, it happen that it has been agreed that a certain penalty shall be paid by the violator of the truce; then, if that penalty be paid, there is no right of going to war, "ideo enim pœna solvitur; ut cætera salva maneant."(e) The acts of a private person cannot be holden to break the truce, unless they be *ordered* or *ratified* by public authority. And such order or ratification will be legally presumed, unless the private offenders be punished or surrendered, and unless the thing seized be restored, (f) or compensation tendered for it.

CXXII. 2. We have next to consider the subject of Capitulations [*169] (*pacta deditionis,*) by virtue of which a particular *body of troops, a particular town or territory, submits under certain conditions to the enemy.

(c) Vide ante, pp. 75-93.

(d) Grot., l. iii. c. xxi. s. 10.

(e) Ib., s. 12.

(f) Ib., s. 13.

The rules which ought to govern the construction of these instruments of International Law have been considered in a former volume of this work; but it may be added here that this construction of the articles of a truce or capitulation, and the decision as to who are entitled to the benefit of it, and the manner in which it is to be executed, belongs at the time to the conqueror. If he misconstrue or break the articles, he is guilty of a violation of International Law, for which reparation must be given, or enforced, according to the modes prescribed by International Jurisprudence; but which, according to English law, cannot be the ground of an action in a Municipal Court.(*g*)

CXXIII. The opinions of a jurist so accurate, profound, and accomplished as the late Sir James Mackintosh, are extremely valuable upon all questions of International Law; and though opinions delivered in Parliament are liable to some deductions from their weight as legal propositions, on account of the excitement of debate, and of the party to which the speaker belongs, yet it will rarely be found that upon questions of Public or International Law, Sir James Mackintosh was swayed by other considerations than those arising from a thorough mastery and an enlightened application of the acknowledged authorities upon the subject.

"To establish the breach of faith, I must first ask, What did Lord William Bentinck promise as commander-in-chief of his majesty's troops in Italy, by his Proclamations of the 14th March and 26th April, 1814? The first is addressed to the people of Italy. It offers them the assistance of Great Britain to rescue them from the iron yoke of Bonaparte. It holds out the example of Spain, enabled, by the aid of Great Britain, to rescue 'her independence,'—of the neighbouring Sicily, 'which hastens to resume her ancient *splendour among the independent nations. . . . Holland is about to obtain the same object. . . . [*170] Warriors of Italy, you are invited to vindicate your own rights, and to be free! Italy, by our united efforts, shall become what she was in her most prosperous periods, and what Spain now is!'"

"Now, sir, I do contend that all the powers of human ingenuity cannot give two senses to this Proclamation: I defy the wit of man to explain it away. Whether Lord William Bentinck had the power to promise is an after question; what he did promise can be no question at all. He promised the aid of England to obtain Italian independence. He promised to assist the Italians in throwing off a yoke,—in escaping from thraldom,—in establishing liberty,—in asserting rights,—in obtaining independence. Every term of emancipation known in human language is exhausted to impress his purpose on the heart of Italy."

And, pursuing his arguments upon the just interpretation of the language of Lord William Bentinck, this eloquent jurist asked—

"Are the references to Spain, to Sicily, and to Holland, mere frauds on the Italians,—'words full of sound and fury signifying nothing?' If not, can they mean less than this,—that those countries of Italy which were independent before the war, shall be independent again? These

(*g*) So successfully contended by Sir E. Sugden, arguendo in Elphinstone v. Bedreechund, 1 Knapp's Privy Council Rep., p. 340.

words, therefore, were at least addressed to the Genoese;—suppose them to be limited as to any other Italians;—suppose the Lombards, or, at that time, the Neapolitans, to be tacitly excluded. Addressed to the Genoese, they either had no meaning, or they meant their ancient independence."(*h*)

"In short, sir," continued Sir James Mackintosh, "I am rather fearful that I shall be thought to have overlaboured a point so extremely clear. But if I have dwelt too long upon this Proclamation, and examined it too minutely, it [*171] *is not because I think it difficult, but because I consider it is decisive of the whole question. If Lord William Bentinck in that Proclamation bestowed on the people of Genoa their place among nations, and the government of their forefathers, it must have been because he deemed himself authorized to make that establishment by the repeated instructions of the British government, and by the avowed principles and solemn acts of the Allied Powers, and because he felt bound to make it by his own Proclamation of the 14th March, combined with the acts done by the Genoese nation, in consequence of that Proclamation. I think I have proved that he did so,—that he believed himself to have done so, and that the people of Genoa believed it likewise.

"Perhaps, however, if Lord William Bentinck had mistaken his instructions, and had acted without authority, he might have been disavowed, and his acts might have been annulled. I doubt whether, in such a case, any disavowal would have been sufficient. Wherever another people, in consequence of the acts of our agent, whom they had good reason to trust, have done acts which they cannot recall, I do not conceive the possibility of a just disavowal of such an agent's acts. Where one party has innocently and reasonably advanced too far to recede, justice cuts off the other also from retreat. But, at all events, the disavowal, to be effectual, must have been prompt, clear, and public."(*i*)

CXXIV. This reasoning, however just and unanswerable, did not prevail; neither the principles of international justice, nor the ancient renown of this once illustrious republic, preserved it from being a victim to that false and unrighteous policy which measures States by their square miles, and by numbers told by the head, and which transfers the lesser to the greater kingdom without considering the consent of the former as in any way necessary to the validity of the act.(*k*)

[*172] *CXXV. The great case of the ships taken at Genoa(*l*) arose on a demand made by the merchants of Genoa, for the sum of 17,000*l*., said to have been exacted by Lord Keith, as a commutation for ships seized in the harbour of Genoa, and left behind, at the evacuation of that place, by the British and Austrian forces. After a memorial had been presented to his majesty in council, the claimants were advised, that the proper mode of proceeding would be to apply to the Court of Admi-

(*h*) Sir James Mackintosh's Works, vol. iii. p. 324. Speech on Annexation of Genoa to the Kingdom of Sardinia.

(*i*) Sir James Mackintosh's Works, vol. iii. p. 336.

(*k*) Ann. Reg., vol. lvi. (1814,) p. 85.

(*l*) 4 Rob., p. 388.

ralty, for a motion on Lord Keith to proceed to adjudication. In this form the question now came forward.

The judgment of Lord Stowell was as follows:—

"This cause arises out of the seizure of Genoa in June, 1800. It now comes on in the naked shape of the admission of the claim on the behalf of the *inhabitants* of Genoa, at that time undoubtedly in a state of hostility with this country. There is no suggestion in the claim that any other persons are aggrieved than merchants of Genoa, who were decidedly *enemies;* unless it can be shown that they had been taken into the protection of this country, and that the seizure was made after the time when they had so become entitled to protection under the capitulation. Undoubtedly, if the seizure was made *after* that time, it would be to be considered, not as the exercise of any rights of war, but as mere lawless rapine and plunder. The question therefore appears to me to respect entirely the time of seizure. If it is shown to have been before the convention, it will be in exercise of the rights of war; if after, it will be liable to the description, that I have given of it, of illegal plunder and violence. On this fact the different parties give different representations. Lord Keith describes it to have passed *before* the convention; whilst the claimants state it to have been *after* the capitulation, and in violation of the faith of the parties that entered into it.

"In the first place, it may not be improper to consider the circumstances under which the seizure was made. All *Genoese *property* was subject to condemnation, unquestionably. There is [*173] nothing to raise a doubt upon this point. As to other property, I conceive that the commander-in-chief had a right to proceed with respect to *that* also, on a presumption that it was subject to condemnation, as belonging to persons of Genoa, leaving it to the owners to show that it was neutral property—or, since blockade had been imposed upon the port of Genoa for a considerable time, that the particular vessel which was the subject of each claim, and the goods on board had not violated the blockade. The next thing to be considered is the capitulation, in which two articles are principally relied on, as decisive of this question. The eighth article, which grants permission to the inhabitants 'to withdraw themselves, their money, merchandizes, movables, or effects, by sea or land,' —that is, as I understand it, *to withdraw by sea or land.* And the ninth article, which stipulates for the freedom of trade. Now, on the construction of these articles, it has been contended, that it was the intention of the parties to exempt the shipping from seizure; and if the court was to abstract itself from the consideration of what has usually been understood and done, the terms are perhaps large enough to admit this interpretation, although it is an acknowledged rule, that *ships* themselves, being property of a peculiar species, do not necessarily pass under such a description. It is impossible not to refer to the practice of commanders of other fortunate expeditions, by whom a broad distinction has usually been taken between property afloat and property on land. In many capitulations this distinction is expressed; and when it is *not* expressed, the terms of the convention must admit some qualification from the usual practice, which, in late wars, has almost invariably been observed.

"That a naval commander should mean to exempt property afloat, would form a particular instance, and such an exception from the general rule, that it is impossible not to attend to this consideration, in judging of the credit to be given to the representation on one side, or on the
[*174] other. *But the question is, what was the interpretation which the convention had received in the understanding of the parties —that is, of the contracting parties? I do not mean of the merchants of Genoa, but of the French generals on the one side, and the Austrian generals and English admiral on the other. If it was the intention of these parties, that the shipping should not be exempted, it will be of little consequence whether the merchants of Genoa were apprised of it or not; since they are concluded by the act of those who held the government over them at the time, and are to be reputed capable of binding them by their acts.

"If we give credit to Lord Keith's positive declaration, the shipping was not exempted. He states, 'that the proposal *was* made, but that it was rejected, and expunged with his own hand.' It is said, that this refusal might apply only to ships of war, to which it would have been highly proper for him to refuse any exemption; and that this account does not negative the supposition of an exemption being granted to merchant ships. Lord Keith certainly does not so consider it. He makes no distinction; and what weighs materially with me is, that no such proposal seems to have been offered on the part of the French generals. On their part, no such distinction is proposed; and therefore it is, I think, to be inferred, that Lord Keith's declaration, 'that he would not suffer the ships to be included in the protection,' must have referred to merchant ships.

"Then what followed! I have already said that the commander had a right to make a seizure of all ships in port, for the purpose of confiscating all such as were Genoese property, and of affording to others their just rights. It is stated by Lord Keith that he was proceeding to inventorize and examine the circumstances of the particular ships. A more legal or cautious mode of proceeding could not have been adopted; and if the seizors were so employed, it is the strongest evidence to convince me that they were doing it, with an intention of exercising the rights of capture over them, and for the purpose of bringing to legal adjudication
[*175] *such as should appear liable to condemnation. But it is said, that the ninth article grants 'the freedom of trade,' and that it would be nugatory to grant *that*, and at the same time to seize their shipping. To this observation I can only say, that nugatory as such a clause might be, it is in every day's practice, to seize all property afloat, and yet to allow a general freedom of trade, exclusive of such particular seizure. It is admitted that Lord Keith executed the capitulation in all other respects with perfect good faith, and it is said, that he continued to give passports. If it could have been shown, that any passports had been obtained for *ships*, it might have been material as affording a practical interpretation, but no such averment is advanced in the affidavit which

has been made to introduce the claim. That no such application was made for the removal of ships is, I think, a strong circumstance to show that Lord Keith's hand was upon them from the beginning.

"Finally, after the unfortunate and never enough to be lamented battle of Marengo, Lord Keith could no longer continue his examination. To carry all the ships away was impossible—yet *he had a right to take away the value of all*, as having a right to the possession; and if he was not able to retain the body and substance, he had a right to secure the value in any manner that he could. The sum first demanded was 500,000*l.* sterling, as an equivalent *for all ships* in the port. Remonstrances were made on the part of the Genoese; and, in my opinion, naturally enough. For in what respect were the merchants of Genoa obliged to contribute for the ships of all the other States of Italy. Even with regard to their own, if they had considered that species of property as protected by the Capitulation, they might have said—No, take the ships, we are protected by the terms of the Capitulation; we will apply to the justice of your country; we will not ransom them. I do not see, therefore, any thing like that duress or compulsion, which has been insinuated; much less were they necessitated to advance money for other ships. If they ransomed for other *persons, they must [*176] seek compensation from them. They do not *claim* for any persons but themselves; yet they now hold out, that they were under the necessity of ransoming both for themselves and for others.

"The contract is, I think, by no means to be represented as an involuntary contract; and when 17,000*l.* was accepted as a compensation for what was admitted to be of the value of 500,000*l.*, I cannot but think that that sum can amount to but a small part of what must have been justly subject to condemnation. If the case had been what the claimants state it to be, it might have been proved long ago; it must have been known to the Austrian and French Generals what were the true intentions of the contracting parties. During the interval of peace it was easy for the claimants to have obtained their testimony, and to have produced *them* to prove 'that *they* never intended to confiscate property afloat, and that this is a violent and perverse exposition of Lord Keith.' If such persons had given testimony to this effect, it would have been received with great attention. Instead of such evidence, we hear nothing after an interval of three years, but a bare claim on behalf of persons who, after having had the benefit of the convention, come now to complain for others, as well as for themselves. Under all the circumstances of the case, I think it is a capitulation very much for the benefit of the parties claiming, and one which ought to be supported.

"The next question is, to whom is this property to be condemned? Capitulations are certainly of the nature of ransoms, but admitting of very favourable distinctions. Ransoms have been forbidden, as subject to great abuse, being, in the common acceptation, contracts entered into at sea, by individual captors, and very liable to be abused, to the great inconvenience of neutral trade. But *even ransoms*, under *circumstances of necessity, are still allowed.* Capitulations, in their nature, can scarcely become liable to the same objection; they being contracts between the

[*177] commander and the conquered State; on the contrary, they *have always been favourably supported, and it is of great importance to the general interests of the captured that they should be sustained.

"I am not aware, however, that the Prize Act authorizes me to condemn *to the captors* in such a case as the present. The act gives them *ships, goods, &c., afloat.* This is a sum of money, which is not exactly of that description of things, though, in some measure it may be taken as the representation of them. It is to be recollected also, that this was a transaction in which the Austrian army was co-operating; and that there are considerations of a public tendency, which make it highly important that Capitulations of this nature should be confirmed by his majesty. On this view of the question, it will be more expedient, on all accounts, that the condemnation should pass to the Crown. As to the effect of the Capitulation, I decide that question upon the merits, and without the slightest hesitation."

CXXV. It has been holden by the English Prize Court that vessels used as *Privateers,* though not at the time of capture in actual employment as such, are not within the terms of a Capitulation protecting *private property* generally.(*m*)

It has been also holden, by the same authority, that *public property* ceded by Capitulation, but not taken possession of by the *captors,* and afterwards seized by a privateer, belongs to the Crown and not to the *privateer.*(*n*)

The case in which this doctrine was laid down is well worthy of attentive consideration, inasmuch as it throws great light upon the principles of International Law, both as they relate to *Capitulation,* and also as they relate to the effect of the *act of a commander done upon his own responsibility, and without specific instructions from his sovereign.*

[*178] It appeared in this case of Thorshaven and its Dependencies(*o*) *that Captain Baugh, of H. M.'s ship Clio, had attacked the Castle of Thorshaven, in the island of Stromoe, on the 16th May, 1808, and obtained possession of the place under a Capitulation, consisting of three articles, by which it was stipulated that the castle and batteries should be given up, that the garrison should not serve against His Britannic Majesty during the term of one year, that all private property should be respected, and that all government property should be at the disposal of the captors. Part of the public property was carried on board the Clio, and Captain Baugh sailed soon afterwards, without leaving any of his own people upon the island, but entrusted the charge of it, together with the custody of the remainder of the public property, to the Danish municipal officers. About a fortnight after this, Gilpin, the commander of the Salamine, landed with a part of his crew, with the intention of storming the fort, but upon being informed of the Capitulation, he re-embarked and put to sea. Having, however, in the course of his cruise, obtained intelligence that some merchandize and moneys

(*m*) Dash and Others, 1 Edwards, p. 271.
(*n*) Thorshaven and its Dependencies, ib., p. 102.
(*o*) Edwards's (Adm.) Rep., p. 102.

belonging to the King of Denmark had not been delivered up under the Capitulation, he returned and took possession of the property in question.

In this case Lord Stowell gave the following judgment:—

(*p*) "This is a proceeding of a very singular nature, arising from the capture of this Danish island by one of His Majesty's ships of war, and a subsequent seizure of certain property found there by a commissioned privateer. The particular circumstances of the transaction are stated in an act on petition. On the part of the Crown it is alleged, 'that Thomas Baugh, esquire, commander of His Majesty's ship Clio, whilst cruising with the said ship off the Faro Islands, received intelligence that some enemy's vessel were lying in Thorshaven, in the island of Stromoe, one of the Faro *Islands; that the said island being a place of considerable strength, as well as of advantage to the enemy from its [*179] situation, the said Captain Baugh conceived it a duty incumbent on him to capture the said island, if possible, and, accordingly, on the 15th of May, 1808, having arrived off the island, he anchored the Clio within half-gunshot of Thorshaven Castle, when the Danish governor consented to a surrender of the Island. That articles of Capitulation were entered into, by which it was provided, that the castle and batteries, together with all the arms, ammunition, and warlike stores, should be delivered up to the British force; that the garrison should march out with the honours of War, and engage not to serve in any capacity against His Britannic Majesty, during the term of one year; that all private property should be respected; and that all Government property should be at the disposal of the captors.' The right, therefore, of the privateer to capture and proceed against this property is denied by the Crown, on the ground that it was protected under this Capitulation; but it is contended on the part of the privateer, that the Capitulation was not a valid proceeding, because it originated wholly in the mind of the commander of the Clio, and was not the result of any instructions communicated to him from Government. Now there are instances innumerable in which it has been held by this court, that an officer not immediately under the eye of Government, may originate such expeditions, subject to a responsibility; and that Government in the present instance has approved of what was done, is demonstrated by this circumstance, that the Crown is here standing upon the act of Captain Baugh, and claiming an interest under it. It is, therefore, as much an authorized Capitulation, as if Captain Baugh had gone out under special directions to make the capture. If the Government had disavowed and disclaimed the whole proceeding, and had said, we do not think this remote island a proper object of the public force, there might have been room for the objection; but looking to what has actually been the conduct of Government, it must *be considered as giving its sanction to the whole transaction. [*180] The object of Captain Baugh, as it is stated in the act, was not merely to reduce the fortress, but to capture the island, and the Capitulation which was entered into between him and the governor who had the chief command, was not made in their own names, but in those of their respective sovereigns. Now what is this but a public convention?—it is a

(*p*) Edwards's (Adm.) Rep., pp. 107-114.

Treaty bearing the stamp and impress of public authority, between persons acting in the names, and as the representatives of the Governments to which they belong. In the first article it is stipulated, 'that the castle, with all the arms and ammunition, shall be delivered up:' in other words, that all the means by which the Danish Government could keep a forcible possession of the island, shall be put into the hands of the British. The next is, 'that the garrison shall not serve against His Majesty for one year;' and the third article, which is the most pertinent to the present inquiry, provides that 'all private property shall be respected.' By which I understand, not merely the property of persons belonging to the garrison, but of all the individuals under its protection: for the surrender of the fortress was in fact, and in all reasonable understanding, the surrender of the island, and it was so acted upon. The same article then goes on to say, that 'all public property shall be at the disposal of the captors,' referring undoubtedly to the public character in which they profess to treat, and not to the assumption of any right to dispose of it on their own private account. It is merely, that it shall pass into the possession of the captors, for the purpose of being brought to adjudication, subject to the legal considerations applying to such property under our own internal regulations. It has been argued much at length, upon the effect of such a Capitulation, that it does not convey the sovereignty; but though it may not operate to the direct conveyance of the sovereignty, which is usually left to be determined by Treaties of peace, it transfers a present possession to the capturing power, subject
[*181] to the future events of War and *Treaties; it is part of its present possession, and perhaps part of its ultimate jurisdiction. It appears that when possession of the island was taken, the British colours were hoisted on the castle; now can there be a more direct assertion of British jurisdiction, or a more entire divesting of Danish authority than this? It is not clear whether the English flag was still flying at the time of the second capture. When Captain Baugh quitted the island, which was in a few days after the capture, he did not leave any of his own people to keep possession, but entrusted it, together with some public stores and treasure, to the charge of the Danish municipal officers, whom he commissioned to act provisionally; having accepted that trust, if they removed the British flag, it was a breach of duty on their part, which will not deprive the British Government of the rights acquired by the Capitulation. Captain Baugh left the island it is true, but how did he leave it? He did not relinquish it on the part of Great Britain, but, as is not unusual, deputed the former magistracy to maintain the public tranquillity under a new authority. It is said to be hardly credible, that Captain Baugh would have left this treasure behind if it had come to his knowledge, when there could be no difficulty in bringing it off. What may have been his views in suffering it to remain, is not stated, but if it is necessary to suggest a reason founded on public convenience, I think that suggestion might easily be furnished from the obvious policy to be observed in reference to a newly-constituted Government in a remote and newly acquired possession. The act then states, 'that since the said surrender or capitulation, the said property

has been illegally taken possession of by Baron Hompesch, and others, concerned in the Salamine privateer; which treasure and other public property was and is within the true intent and meaning of Government property, as specified in the third article of the Capitulation, and that if any part of the property taken was private property, it is protected from 'capture and confiscation under the said third article.' *Now what was the condition of this island under the Capitulation? [*182] I conceive that nothing can be more clear, than that if the Capitulation was not disavowed by the British Government, it was binding upon the respective parties: it was a stipulation operating on the Danes to give up all public property, and on the British to respect all private property. Suppose that the English Government, without disavowing the Capitulation, had sent a force the next day to take possession of the private property in the island, could there have been a more outrageous breach of public faith? On the other hand, what was the obligation on the part of the Danes?—they were bound to give up all public property, and if any was kept back, as it is alleged on the part of the privateer that this was, it was kept back in fraud of the British Government, in whom it already vested by compact, and being fraudulently withheld, it did not become again the property of the Danes. By the Capitulation the English Government became legally entitled to the whole of the public property, and this seems to be admitted in the act on petition, for it is there stated, 'that the ship Salamine having arrived at Thorshaven, the said Thomas Gilpin, the captain of the privateer, and part of his crew, immediately landed, in order to storm and take possession of the fort, but found that it had been about a fortnight before partly destroyed by His Majesty's ship Clio: that the Clio had quitted the said town without having left any part of her crew, after having taken on board such of the public stores and property as were found in the said town and delivered up to the said Thomas Baugh as government property under the articles of Capitulation, the purport of which Capitulation was communicated to the said Thomas Gilpin: that in consequence thereof, and in full persuasion that all public property had been given up to the said Thomas Baugh, he, the said Thomas Gilpin, his officers and crew, the following day reëmbarked and went to sea.' The act then goes on to state, that 'having been afterwards informed that *certain goods and moneys belonging to the king of Denmark had been kept back, the said Thomas Gilpin returned [*183] and took possession of the property in question.' Here, then, is a distinct admission that the Capitulation operated, and was intended to operate, upon the whole of the public property; but, say they, some of the public property was not delivered up! Whether it was fraudulently withheld, or whether it was left there for the purposes of Government, or the convenience of the captor, does not appear; but supposing that it was surreptitiously detained, what was the duty of the privateer? Certainly, upon making the discovery, the only proper course was to take possession of the property as salvor for the Crown, and to notify the circumstance. To say, that in this short period of time, the Capitulation and all its consequences were gone by, while the inhabitants claimed protection under it, and while this qualified possession of the island still continued, is contrary to all reason. If private individuals had at that period a right to shelter their property under the Capitulation, the British Government had also a title to all public property under the same Capitulation. It is clear, that if the property was fraudulently withheld, it ought to have been taken possession of for the Crown of Great Britain, and the private captors ought not to have attempted to appropriate it to themselves by setting up a title of their own. It is hardly necessary for me to enter into the other topics which have been thrown out in the argument; but as they have been touched upon, I will just state my opinion upon one point, which is, that the commissions of privateers do not extend to the capture of private property upon land; that is a right which is not granted even to the king's ships. The words of the third section of the Prize Act extend only to the capture by any of his majesty's ships 'of any fortress upon the land, or any arms, ammunition, stores of war, goods, merchandise, and treasure belonging to the State, or to any public trading company of the enemies of the Crown of Great Britain [*184] upon the *land.' Here, then, the interests of the king's cruisers are expressly limited with respect to the property in which the captors can acquire any interest of their own, the State still reserving to itself all private property, in order that no temptation might be held out for unauthorized expeditions against the subjects of the enemy on land. With regard to private ships of war, the Lords of the Admiralty are empowered, by the ninth section, to issue letters of marque to the commanders of any such ships or vessels—for what purpose? Why, 'for the attacking and taking any place or fortress upon the land, or any ship or vessel, arms, ammunition, stores of war, goods or merchandise, belonging to, or possessed by any of his majesty's enemies,'—where?—'in any sea, creek, river, or haven.' I perfectly well recollect that it was the intention of those who brought this Bill into Parliament, that Privateers should not be allowed to make depredations upon the coast of the enemy for the purpose of plundering individuals, for which reason they were restricted to fortified places and fortresses, and to property water-borne; and, therefore, although I am not sufficiently informed as to the precise nature of this property, yet taking it to be private property and not within the reach of the Capitulation, it is that in which the privateer has acquired no legal interest under her commission. I cannot dismiss this subject, without at the same time observing upon the conduct of the persons concerned in this privateer, in terms of some disapprobation. When they found this public property, which under the Capitulation enured to the benefit of the Crown of Great Britain, it was their duty to have given notice to the Crown Officers of the fraud which had been practised, limiting their own expectations to the interest which they would derive as salvors for the Crown. The only witness brought forward to speak of the circumstances of the capture, and the nature of the property, is Baron Hompesch, a realising witness, who was rated on board this privateer as chaplain; no one person has been produced who from his own knowledge can speak to the nature *of the property. [*185] Upon any supposition, I am of opinion that the privateer has no interest, and I shall therefore condemn the public property to the Crown conformably to the terms of the Capitulation, and reserve the consideration of the private property till it is claimed."

CXXVI. After the general reverses that befel the arms of France in the spring of 1814, and the consequent withdrawal of her troops from Italy, Lord William Bentinck was instructed to occupy the territories of the Republic of Genoa, "without committing his Court or the Allies with respect to their ultimate disposition."(*q*) Of the proclamation which he issued upon the occasion of carrying these orders into effect, dated March 14th, Lord Castlereagh had himself observed, that "an expression or two, taken separately, might create an impression that his views of Italian liberation went to the form of the Government, as well as to the expulsion of the French. On the success of the military movement, the General reported that he had, 'in consequence of the unanimous desire of the Genoese to return to their ancient state,' proclaimed the old form of government."

It was the object of Sir James Mackintosh, in his motion and admirable speech(*r*) on the Annexation of Genoa to the Kingdom of Sardinia, to show that this "unanimous desire" had been unjustly thwarted, and that these expectations, fairly raised by Lord William Bentinck's proclamation, had been wrongfully disappointed by the final territorial settlement of the Allies at Paris.(*s*)

CXXVII. When we arrive at the description of Maritime International Law in time of War, the constitution, authority, functions, and mode of procedure of the Prize Court will be found worthy of close attention and careful investigation. *It will be seen that by this tribunal International justice is wisely, carefully, and honestly dispensed; [*186] and it is matter of reasonable surprise that such a jurisdiction should have been strictly confined to *sea-prize*,(*t*) and without power of cognizance over *land-booty*, except in cases where the two, owing to the co-operation of the army and fleet, had been blended together.(*u*) It is not surprising that in great maritime kingdoms the jurisdiction of the Admiral's Court should have thrown into the shade the tribunal of the General. But that the latter should have left such faint traces of its origin and mode of procedure, and should so soon have fallen into desuetude, is a very remarkable fact in the history of jurisprudence.

The features of this *curia militaris* in England are perspicuously stated in the following learned and curious note of Mr. Knapp, appended to his report of the great case of the Army of the Deccan, argued before the Privy Council in 1833.

"It is probable, notwithstanding the dicta of Lord Mansfield in Lindo v. Rodney,(*x*) that 'there is no instance in history or law, ancient or modern, of any question ever having existed respecting Booty taken in

(*q*) See Ann. Reg., vol. lvi. (1814,) pp. 32-84.

(*r*) Delivered in the House of Commons on 27th April, 1815.—Mackintosh's Works, vol. iii. p. 311.

(*s*) For the papers referred to see Hans. Parl. Deb., vol. xxx. p. 387, and for the resolutions moved, Ib. p. 932.

(*t*) How far the powers of this Court have been extended by 3 & 4 Vict. c. 65, will be seen hereafter.

(*u*) The Ships taken at Genoa, 4 Rob., p. 388.

(*x*) Douglas's Reports, 592.

a continental land-war before any legal judicature in this kingdom,' that in very early times causes respecting it were determined in the Court of Chivalry held before the Constable and Marshal. In the MS. Treatise of Lord Hale, De Prærogativâ Regis, cap. 12, s. 3, fol. 191, he says, 'In matters civil, for which there is no remedy by the common law, the military jurisdiction continues as well after the War as during the time of it; for that part of the jurisdiction of the Constable and Marshal stands still, notwithstanding the War determines as concerning right of prisoners and Booty, military contracts, ensigns, &c.'

[*187] *"The only direct instance of the exercise of this jurisdiction which the reporter has been able to find, is one mentioned in a MS. Treatise of Lord Hale, in Lincoln's Inn Library, which is headed, 'Upon certain petitions of late exhibited in the Court of Chivalry, there have been raised divers questions of law,' and afterwards proceeds to discuss the power of that Court to fine and imprison, and give costs and damages in an action commenced there for opprobrious words, and whether the Earl Marshal alone might in that, and in such like cases, hold pleas. In page 33, of this manuscript, amongst the precedents cited to prove that this Court might give damages, there is the following passage: 'About the 17th year of Richard II, in a cause depending in the Court of Chivalry between John Haulce and John Rosque, concerning certain goods taken from a captain of a castle beyond the seas, the plaintiff in the libel demanded costs and damages according to the custom of the Court of Chivalry.' There are, however, many instances on record of its exercising a jurisdiction in the analogous cases of disputes respecting the right to or ransom of prisoners, whom their captors were, by the usual custom of those times, allowed to ransom for their own benefit. Thus in Edward III.'s reign, there were special commissions to Guido de Brien and Richard de Stafford, in the place of the Constable of England, who was then a minor, to hear, together with Edward de Mortimar, the Marshal, two cases respecting the right to prisoners; Rot. Pat. 48 Edw. III., *in dorso* p. 2, m. 10, mentioned in an an anonymous treatise in Hearne's Curious Discourses, vol. ii. p. 150; and in the 2nd Henry IV., there was a commission to delegates to hear an appeal from the Court of Chivalry held before the Constable and the Marshal respecting the custody of a hostage and for the ransom for the Count of Denia (8 Rym. Fœd., 211,) in which case there was subsequently a commission to co-delegates (Ibid. 423;) and in the same volume of Rymer, p. 292, there is a commission, in 4th Henry IV., to judges appointed to determine the rights of
[*188] persons claiming the *prisoners taken at the battle of Humbledon Hill, in the room of the judges of the Court of Chivalry, the Earl of Westmorland, the Constable, and the Earl of Northumberland, the Marshal. The reason of this appointment is stated to have been because these peers were absent in the Marches of Scotland, and interested in the cases; and the issuing of it probably was one of the principal causes of their rebellion in the course of the same year. Since the time of Henry VIII., when the office of Constable of England ceased, the jurisdiction of the Court of Chivalry was frequently disputed, on the ground that it could not be held before the Earl Marshal alone; and it seems to have

confined itself wholly to questions of pedigrees, escutcheons, pennons, and coat-armour, with occasionally a few actions for slanderous words, as to which, however, its jurisdiction was expressly denied by the King's Bench, on an application for a prohibition in the case of Chambers v. Jennings.(*y*) In the same case it was decided, that it could neither fine nor imprison; and it was determined in the House of Lords, in Oldis v. Donmille,(*z*) that it had no power to prevent persons who were not heralds from painting escutcheons and marshalling funerals. After these decisions the Court appears to have fallen into desuetude. The last case tried in it was Sir Henry Blunt's case, in 1737.(*a*) The best account of it is to be found in the various discourses concerning the antiquity and offices of the Constable and Earl Marshal of England; and the defence of the jurisdiction of the Earl Marshal's Court in the vacancy of a Constable, by Dr. Plott, which are printed in the second volume of Hearne's Curious Discourses by eminent Antiquaries."(*b*)

The Court of the Constable and Marshal was limited by the Statute of the 13 Richard II., chapter 2, to a contract touching "deeds of arms and War without the realm, and things that touch War within the realm, which cannot be determined by the Common Law as [*189] touching prisoners, prize, &c.; and in these proceedings the customs and laws of War ought to direct their judgment."(*c*)

CXXVIII. The maxim "*bello parta cedunt reipublicæ*,(*d*) is recognised by all civilized States. In England all acquisitions of War belong to the Sovereign, who represents the commonwealth. The Sovereign is the fountain of Booty and Prize.

The law upon this subject has been laid down by Lord Stowell and by Lord Chancellor Brougham,(*e*) in a manner which leaves nothing to desire; the opinion of both these eminent men is given in the following extract from the judgment of Lord Brougham:—

"That Prize is clearly and distinctly the property of the Crown, that the Sovereign in this country, the executive Government in all countries, in whom is vested the power of levying the forces of the State, and of making War and Peace, is alone possessed of all property in Prize, is a principle not to be disputed. It is equally incontestable that the Crown possesses this property *pleno jure*, absolutely and wholly without control; that it may deal with it entirely at its pleasure, may keep it for its own use, may abandon or restore it to the enemy, or, finally, may distribute in whole or in part among the persons instrumental in its capture, making that distribution according to whatever scheme, and under whatever regulations and conditions it sees fit. It is equally clear, and it follows from the two former propositions, that the title of a party claiming Prize, must needs in all cases be the act of the Crown, by which the royal pleasure to grant the Prize shall have been signified to the subject. Whether, where that act has once been completed, and it distinctly

(*y*) 7 Mod., p. 127. (*z*) Show Parl. Cas. p. 58. (*a*) 1 Atkyns, p. 296.
(*b*) 2 Knapp's P. C. Rep., pp. 149-151. (*c*) Cap. 12, f. 186.
(*d*) Bynk., Q. J. P.
(*e*) See also the decision of Lord Eldon in Nicholl *v.* Goodall, 10 Vesey's Rep. p. 156.

[*190] appears that the Crown was *minded to part with the property finally and irrevocably; whether, even in that case, the same paramount and transcendant power of the Crown might not enure to the effect of preserving to his majesty the right of modifying, or altogether revoking the grant, is a question which has never yet arisen, and which, when it does arise, will be found never to have been determined in the negative. But this, at all events, is clear, that when the Crown, by an act of grace and bounty, parts, for certain purposes, and subject to certain modifications, with the property in Prize, it by that act plainly signifies its intention that the Prize shall continue subject to the power of the Crown, as it was before the act was done.

"This latter proposition is capable of illustration from a variety of sources, which were but slightly adverted to in the argument; for whether we refer to the decisions of venerable judges, to the precedents furnished by prize-proclamations, or to the more venerable authority of the letter of the statutes, from all these it will be found that, in stating the absolute nature of the principle, I have not strained, but have rather fallen short of the truth.

"The doctrine has been frequently recognized in cases where the question has arisen subsequently to the capture, and before condemnation; but the same principle was afterwards extended in the case of the Elsebe,(*f*) at the cock-pit, in which, after final adjudication in the court below, but pending an appeal, and before the final decision of the appeal, the Crown thought proper, for reasons of state and public policy, to restore the Prize at the expense of the captors. In other words it was there determined, and that too upon a solemn and most able argument, and by a Judge the most learned and eminent of his time, the present Lord Stowell, that when the Crown saw fit to restore the capture, the captors, who had run the risk and suffered the loss, who had moreover, borne the charge [*191] of bringing the Prize into *port, and the further costs of proceeding in the Admiralty to adjudication, and had even undergone additional expenses in contesting their claim upon appeal, were altogether without a remedy. 'It is admitted,' says Lord Stowell—in language which it would be vain to praise or to attempt to imitate—'it is admitted on the part of the captors whose interests have been argued with great force (and not the less effective, surely, for the extreme decorum with which that force has been tempered,) that their claim rests wholly on the Order of Council, the Proclamation, and the Prize act. It is not, as it cannot be, denied, that independent of these instruments, the whole subject-matter is in the hands of the Crown, as well in point of interest as in point of authority. Prize is altogether a creature of the Crown. No man has, or can have any interest, but what he takes as the mere gift of the Crown; beyond the extent of that gift he has nothing. This is the principle of law on the subject, and founded on the wisest reasons. The right of making War and Peace is exclusively in the Crown. The acquisitions of War belong to the Crown, and the disposal of these acquisitions may be of the utmost importance for the purposes both of War

(*f*) 5 Rob., p. 173.

and Peace. This is no peculiar doctrine of our Constitution; it is universally received as a necessary principle of public jurisprudence by all writers on the subject, "*Bello parta cedunt reipublicæ.*'"(g) Upon that principle, accordingly, and holding that right not to be devested by the proclamation, and Order in Council, and the Prize Act, Lord Stowell decided, that up to the period of final adjudication the Crown can restore the Prize, without thinking of consulting, or taking the consent of the captor, who at his peril, and at the expense of his own blood and treasure won that Prize from the enemy."(h)

CXXIX. The mode by which the Crown usually exercises its jurisdiction over Booty, is to refer the claims of those *who petition for a share in the distribution of it to the Lords of the Treasury; [*192] who usually submit a recommendation to the Crown that a grant may be made of the Booty to trustees, to be appointed by the Crown for the purpose of ascertaining and collecting the Booty, and for preparing a distribution thereof conformably to certain principles which the Lords lay down as fitting to govern the whole case; and this scheme, so prepared by the trustees, the Lords submit to the Crown for its final approbation and sanction under the Royal sign-manual warrant.(i)

Though the Lords usually consider that they have no authority to interfere with the exercise of the discretion of the trustees, it has sometimes happened that a memorial has been presented by a particular claimant to the Crown in Council, and that the Privy Council, as in the case of the Army of the Deccan, have advised the Crown to allow the Lords of the Treasury to hear counsel upon points arising between the claimants and the trustees, as to what shall, or shall not be cosidered legal Booty. But, in the same case, the Privy Council determined that they would not exercise jurisdiction as a Court of Appeal from the decisions of the Lords Commissioners of the Treasury, as to grants by the Crown of property accruing to it by virtue of its prerogative.(k)

CXXX. It should also be observed that according to the English Law, which is in this respect in accordance with the principles of general law and public jurisprudence, no action can be maintained in a Court of *Municipal* Law against the captor of Booty or Prize.(l) If an English naval commander seizes property as belonging to the enemy, which turns out *clearly to be British property, he forfeits his Prize in the Court of Admiralty, and that Court awards the return of it to [*193] the party from whom it was taken; but the case of Le Caux v. Eden(m) decided the question that no British subject can maintain an action against the captor. The Court of Admiralty is the proper tribunal for

(g) 5 Robinson, p. 581.

(h) Alexander v. The Duke of Wellington, 2 Russell & Mylne's Rep., p. 54. This case grew out of the booty captured by the army of the Deccan in the war carried on by the Marquis of Hastings, Governor-General of India, against the Pindarees and Mahratta Princes, in 1817.

(i) The Army of the Deccan, 2 Knapp's P. C. Rep., p. 106.

(k) In the present war (1855) the distribution both of Prize and Booty captured by the allied forces of France and England has been the subject of specific convention between these two Powers.

(l) Sir James Scarlett (Att.-Gen.), arguendo in Elphinstone v. Bedreechund, 1 Knapp, p. 357, (A. D. 1830.)

(m) Douglas's Rep., p. 573.

the trial of questions of Prize or no Prize, and it exercises this jurisdiction as a Court of Prize under a commission from the Crown; and if that Court make an unsatisfactory determination, the appeal lies to the Crown in Council, for the Crown reserves the ultimate right to decide on such questions by its own authority, and does not commit its determination to any Municipal Court of Justice. In like manner, Booty taken under the colour of military authority, falls under the same rule. If property be taken by an officer under the supposition that it is the property of an enemy, whether of a State or of an individual, which ought to be confiscated, no Municipal Court(*n*) can judge of the propriety or impropriety of the seizure; it can be judged of only by an authority delegated by the Crown.

CXXXI. The English Privy Council gave a solemn decision to this effect, by the mouth of a very distinguished judge, Lord Tenterden, in the year 1830. The cause which called forth this important decision, was an appeal from a judgment of the Supreme Court of Bombay, which their lordships reversed.

The substance of the case was as follows:—The members of a provisional government of a recently-conquered province seized the property of a native who had not been allowed to benefit by the articles of the capitulation of a fortress of which he was governor, but who had been permitted to reside under military surveillance in his own house, in the city, in which the seizure was made, and which was made at a distance from the scene of actual hostilities.

[*194] In the Court of Bombay the representatives of the governor *had brought a civil action for damages against the seizors, and had succeeded in recovering a certain sum of money awarded as damages. The circumstances which appear to have principally influenced the decision of this court were, first, that at the time of the seizure the city in which it was made had been for some months previously in the undisturbed possession of the provisional government; and secondly, that courts of justice under the authority of that government were sitting in the city for the administration of justice. But in the Appellate Court Lord Tenterden said:—

"We think the proper character of the transaction was that of hostile seizure, made, if not *flagrante*, yet, *nondum cessante bello*, regard being had both to the time, the place, and the person, and consequently that the Municipal Court had no jurisdiction to adjudge upon the subject; but that if anything had been done amiss, recourse could only be had to the government for redress. We shall therefore recommend it to his majesty to reverse the judgment."(*o*)

CXXXII. In the case which has just been mentioned, a distinction was taken by the Court of Bombay between the *public* and the *private* property of the Prince (the *Peishwa.*) The Privy Council in the case of the Advocate-General of Bombay v. Amerchund, declared that distinction to be unfounded. In that case the Advocate-General of Bombay

(*n*) Le Caux v. Eden, Daug. Rep., p. 592.
(*o*) Elphinstone v. Bedreechund, 1 Knapp's Priv. Coun. Rep., pp. 360-1.

filed an information against Amerchund, who was a banker at Poonah, to recover, on behalf of the crown, a large sum of money, which had been deposited with him by the Peishwa previously to the conquest of that city by the British troops. The court below gave a verdict and judgment against the crown. The Advocate-General appealed from that judgment, and the case was argued before the Privy Council on the 28th March, 1829. The ground of defence taken by the respondent's counsel, independently of some technical *objections to the information and general arguments on the evidence, was, that part [*195] of the money was the private property (Khasgheet) of the Peishwa, and not belonging to or used by him for public purposes; and that, not having been seized by the Government during the war, it could not be recovered after the termination of it.(*p*) The Privy Council reversed the judgment of the court at Bombay. In the course of the argument, Lord Tenterden asked: "What is the distinction between the public and private property of an absolute sovereign? You mean by public property, generally speaking, the property of the State; but in the property of an absolute sovereign who may dispose of every thing, at any time, and in any way he pleases, is there any distinction?" And in delivering the judgment of their lordships, he also observed: "Another point made, which applies itself only to a part of the information, is, that the property was not proved to have been the public property of the Peishwa. Upon that point I have already intimated my opinion, and I have the concurrence of the other Lords of the Council with me in it, that when you are speaking of the property of an absolute sovereign there is no pretence for drawing a distinction, the whole of it belongs to him as sovereign, and he may dispose of it for his public or private purposes in whatever manner he may think proper."(*q*) In this case it was strongly argued that the Privy Council had no original jurisdiction in the matter, and that they could not exercise jurisdiction as a Court of Appeal from the decisions of the Lords Commissioners of the Treasury, as to grants by the *crown of property accruing to it by virtue of its prerogative.(*r*) [*196]

CXXXIII. The tribunal of trustees recommended by the Lords of the Treasury appears to be open to many objections, some of which are well stated by Lord Stowell, in the case of the Buenos Ayres.(*s*) "It has been usual (he says) of late to introduce a clause in the grant, appointing certain officers of elevated rank, who have themselves been concerned in the capture, to act as trustees for the division of the property which may be captured, and as arbitrators of any disputed claims that may arise; and their decision is considered as binding and final, unless it

(*p*) In support of these propositions, they cited Puffendorff, book viii. c. vi. ss. 22, 23, and the Attorney-General v. Weeden and Shooles, Parker, p. 267. The Solicitor-General and Serjeant Bosanquet for the appellants, cited *e contra* Bynk., Quæst. Jur. Pub., l. i. c. iv: "Ecquando res hostium mobiles et præsertim naves fiunt capientium;" and c. vii: "Hostium actiones et credita quæ apud nos inveniuntur an exorto bello recte publicentur."

(*q*) Elphinstone v. Bedreechund, 2 Knapp's Priv. Coun. Rep., p. 329, n.

(*r*) Elphinstone v. Bedreechund, 2 Knapp's Priv. Coun. Rep., p. 159.

(*s*) 1 Dodson, p. 29.

should be reversed by an order from the king. It is not for me to say how far this is a convenient mode of proceeding; it seems at least liable to suspicions of error, and even perhaps of some partiality. It must be intended that the decisions should be made in conformity to known and fixed principles of law; and these principles of law are contained in the decisions of this court, and the Court of Appeal, with which it is almost impossible that the trustees should be personally and accurately acquainted. In what way these principles of law are to travel to the minds of these gentlemen, unassisted with legal advice, or how they are to steer their way through the difficulties which may occur, it is not easy to say. Their determinations must, of necessity, sometimes occasion dissatisfaction to the parties interested, to whom no right of Appeal is given. His majesty has indeed preserved the right of control; and may, if he pleases, *ex mero motu*, or upon petition from any of the individuals interested, take the matter into his consideration, but he is not bound so to do."

In this case of the Buenos Ayres, the crown made a grant to trustees of the booty; and they drew up a scheme, a petition against which was [*197] presented to the king in council: it *was received and referred to a committee, and in consequence of their report, it was referred for adjudication to the High Court of Admiralty.

In the cases of Seringapatam(*t*) and Toulon original jurisdiction appears to have been exercised by the Privy Council, without any reference to the Court of Admiralty.(*u*)

And by a statute passed in 1833, intituled, "An Act for the better Administration of Justice in his majesty's Privy Council," it is enacted,(*x*) "that it shall be lawful for his majesty to refer to the said Judicial Committee for hearing or consideration any such other matters whatsoever as his majesty shall think fit, and such committee shall thereupon hear or consider the same, and shall advise his majesty thereon in manner aforesaid."

CXXXIV. By a statute passed in 1840, "to Improve the Practice and extend the Jurisdiction of the High Court of Admiralty," it is enacted,(*y*) "that the said High Court of Admiralty shall have jurisdiction to decide all matters and questions concerning Booty of War, or the distribution thereof, which it shall please her majesty, her heirs and successors, by the advice of her and their Privy Council, to refer to the judgment of the said court; and in all matters so referred the court shall proceed as in case of Prize of War, and the judgment of the court therein shall he binding upon all parties concerned."

CXXXV. The mention of Seringapatam naturally leads us to the consideration of the peculiar *status* of the English East India Company with respect to the distribution of Booty, inasmuch as that extraordinary and anomalous corporation has an *army* of its own which co-operates with that of the crown.

[*198] After the capture of Seringpatam by General (afterwards *Lord) Harris, Lord Mornington,(*z*) the Governor-General directed the

(*t*) Vide post. (*u*) The Army of the Deccan, 2 Knapp, p. 152 and n. †.
(*x*) 3 & 4 Will. IV., c. 41, s. 4. (*y*) 3 & 4 Vict. c. 65, s. 22.
(*z*) Better known as Marquis of Wellesley.

Secretary to write to General Harris an exposition of the law and practice of the East India Company upon this subject in the following letter :—

" *To Lieutenant-General Harris, Commander-in-Chief, &c., &c., &c.*

"Fort St. George, June 2nd, 1799.

"SIR,

"The Right Honourable the Governor-General in Council having considered your report upon the ordnance, ammunition, military stores, treasure, and jewels, taken in the Fort of Seringapatam, directs me to acquaint you that his Lordship in Council has resolved to order an immediate distribution of the treasure and jewels which have fallen into your hands. At the same time that the Governor-General in Council communicates this resolution to you, his Lordship thinks it expedient to impress upon your attention the principles of the Law of Nations, by which all property conquered from an enemy becomes the property of the State, and by which all idea of positive right in the captors to property in a fort taken by assault is exploded. In conformity to these principles, the king has been pleased to grant to the Company, by letters patent, bearing date January 14th, 1758, the right of all booty and plunder which shall be taken by their troops alone, reserving in express terms his royal prerogative of distribution in such manner and proportions as he shall think fit, in all cases in which the royal forces may have cooperated with those of the Company.

"Although the orders of the Court of Directors, prescribing the mode of carrying those letters patent into execution, expressly prohibit their governments in India from disposing of the 'whole plunder and booty which shall be taken in wars, hostilities, or expeditions, by the Company's forces;' and although his majesty, by the letters *patent themselves, has reserved to himself in express terms his 'pre- [*199] rogative royal to distribute the said plunder and booty in such manner and proportion as he shall think fit,' in all cases in which his own troops may have been employed; yet, having no doubt that the gracious bounty of his majesty, and the liberality of the Court of Directors, will be proportioned to the important services of the gallant army under your command, his Lordship has no hesitation in charging himself with the responsibility of anticipating the royal sanction, and the determination of the Court of Directors. In adopting this decision, his Lordship trusts that he will manifest to the army an unequivocal proof of the gratitude which he feels for the continued exertion of their matchless bravery and discipline, by the prompt distribution of a reward, which their decisive success has enabled him to bestow. In their letter of the 8th March, 1758, the Honourable Court of Directors have ordered that, 'in land operations all cannon, ammunition, and military stores of all kinds, are not to come into the division, but are to belong to the Company.' Upon a further consideration, therefore, of this positive injunction, as well as of the principles of the Law of Nations applied to the right of booty, plunder, and conquest, and to the expenses incurred by the Company for the support of the present war, the Right Honourable the Governor-General in Council directs me to inform you of his Lordship's intention to reserve all ordnance, ammunition and military stores (including grain,) for the ultimate decision of his majesty, on such application as shall be made to him by the Honourable the Court of Directors.

"It will accordingly be necessary that a proper board of officers should be selected and appointed for the purpose of valuing, and of taking an exact inventory of, all that part of the captured property which is included under the denomination of ordnance, ammunition, and military stores of all kinds, for transmission to the Honourable Court of Directors. In ordering the distribution of the treasure and jewels, the Governor-
[*200] General in Council directs you *to be guided by the established usages, which have been observed in the British service in all cases of a similar nature; and to take upon yourself the decision of all points whatever, referable to this distribution, without further communication to his Lordship in Council. The proportion of prize-money to be allotted to the contingent of his Highness the Nizam, is to be determined by the number of his highness's troops actually employed in the field with the army before Seringapatam at the time of taking that place.

"The British subsidiary force, serving with the contingent of his Highness the Nizam, will, of course, be included in the Company's army, and receive its proportion of prize-money according to the distribution made to the rest of the British forces. As it is probable that Meer Allum Bahadur may not be inclined to dispense with the right of his sovereign over that part of the captured property which may be allotted to his Highness the Nizam, the Governor-General in Council directs you to consult him upon this point, and to give orders for the appropriation of the Nizam's share, in such a manner as shall be most agreeable to Meer Allum.

"I have the honour to inclose a general order by Government, which the Governor-General in Council directs you to publish to the army, in order that the distribution of the prize-money may be immediately announced to them.

"I have the honour to be,
"Sir,
"Your most obedient humble servant,
"J. WEBBE,
"Secretary to Government."(a)

[*201]

*CHAPTER IX.

NEUTRALS AND NEUTRALITY.

CXXXVI. WE have next to consider the effect of War upon the

(a) Life and Services of General Lord Harris, by the Right Hon. S. R. Lushington, pp. 374-8. Nevertheless, Lord Harris appears to have sustained a most unjust and vexatious law-suit instigated by the East India Company, both in Chancery and before the Privy Council, upon the subject of this booty.—See cc. xxi. and xxvi. of his Life.

Rights and Duties of those who are not engaged in it—that is, of *Neutrals.*(*a*)

It is of the greatest importance to the well-being of the Society of States, that the relations of Neutrality should be respected, and preserved uninjured within those just limits which the reason of the thing, embellished by the wisdom of jurists, and fortified by the usage of nations, prescribes to it.

The relation of Neutrality will be found to consist in two principal circumstances:—

1. Entire abstinence from any participation in the War.
2. Impartiality of conduct towards both Belligerents.

Klüber says, tersely and happily, "A Neutral state is neither judge nor party."(*b*)

This *abstinence* and this *impartiality* must be combined in the character of a bonâ fide Neutral.

*CXXXVII. The *Neutral* is justly and happily designated by the Latin expression *in bello medius.* It is of the essence of his character that he so retain this central position, as to incline to neither belligerent. He has no *jus bellicum* himself; but he is entitled to the continuance of his ordinary *jus pacis*, with, as will presently be seen, certain curtailments and modifications which flow from the altered state of the general relations of all countries in time of War. He must do nothing by which the condition of either belligerent may be bettered or strengthened—*quo validior fiat.* [*202]

It is for him perpetually to recollect, and practically to act upon the maxim, "*hostem esse qui faciat quod hosti placet.*"(*c*) But it is not necessary that he should make any public declaration of Neutrality; the legal presumption is that his pacific status will continue unless he declare the contrary. The Neutral has nothing to do with the justice or injustice of the War, and the error of Grotius in this respect, though copied by Vattel, is rightly corrected by Bynkershoek,(*d*) and subsequent writers.

CXXXVIII. Some jurists(*e*) have divided alliances into *perfect* and *imperfect*, or *absolute* and *qualified;* but such a distinction can scarcely be said to be supported by the reason of the thing. It may be that a State, which is not a belligerent, may have bound itself, by stipulations *previous to the war*, to furnish certain limited succours to one of the

(*a*) Grotius, l. iii. c. xvii. *De his, qui in bello medii sunt.* It is a short and meagre chapter, with no allusion to the questions of *maritime* neutral law. He gives his reason for this brevity in the first section:—"Supervacuum videri posset, agere nos de his qui extra bellum sunt positi, quando in hos satis constet nullum esse jus bellicum. Sed quia occasione belli multa in eos, finitimos præsertim, patrari solent prætexta necessitate, repetendum hic breviter quod diximus alibi, necessitatem ut jus aliquod det in rem alienam, summam esse debere: requiri præterea ut ipso domino par necessitas non subsit: etiam ubi de necessitate constat, non ultra sumendum quam exigit. Id est, si custodia sufficiat non sumendum usum, si usus, non sumendum abusum: si abusu sit opus, restituendum tamen rei pretium."

(*b*) "Ein neutraler Staat ist weder Richter noch Partei."—Klüber, s. 284.

(*c*) Borrowed by Grotius from Agathias, Grot., l. iii. c. xvii. iii. 2.

(*d*) Q. J. P., l. i. c. ix.

(*e*) Klüber, s. 281.

belligerents; but it is idle to contend that either this previous stipulation, or the limited character of the succour can take away the *hostile* and *partial* character of such an action.(*f*) "If I am neutral," says
[*203] Bynkershoek,(*g*) "*alteri non possum prodesse *ut alteri noceam*," —and all jurists have agreed that Livy's(*h*) admonition, *bello se non interponant*, is a sound exposition of Neutral duty. To send succours is to co-operate *pro tanto* with the belligerent to whom they are sent. What does it matter to the other belligerent under what obligation contracted by a third Power his enemy is strengthened and heartened against him? Upon this principle of International Law, England and the North American United States have enacted the statutes commonly called the Foreign Enlistment Acts, the consideration of which has been partially anticipated in an earlier part of this work.(*i*)

It has often happened, no doubt, that political circumstances have caused such conduct on the part of a State, not actually belligerent, to be overlooked by the injured State; but we are not here speaking of expediency, but of right.(*k*)

In all probability, the peculiarity of position which Switzerland enjoys, the fact that she is hemmed in on all sides by States who have a direct interest in maintaining her Neutrality, has been the cause why that Neutrality has been unquestioned, while that European States have recruited their armies from the population of her Cantons. If she had been a commercial and maritime State, as M. Massé most justly observes, a very different rule would have been applied to this singular state of things. She has lately, to her great credit, passed regulations prohibiting her citizens from enlisting in foreign service.(*l*)

CXXXIX. There are acts of minor partiality, which, when they are the result of convictions previous to the breaking out of the War, it would be pedantically rigid to consider as violations of Neutrality,—for instance, the allowing prizes captured by one belligerent to be brought into the Neutral port,(*m*) especially, in compliance with the provisions
[*204] of a *Treaty made antecedently to the War, could scarcely be considered as a violation of Neutrality. "Thus" (Mr. Wheaton observes)(*n*) "by the Treaty of amity and commerce of 1778, between the United States and France, the latter secured to herself two special privileges in the American ports;—1. Admission for her privateers, with their prizes, to the exclusion of her enemies. 2. Admission for

(*f*) Massé, Le Droit Commercial dans ses Rapports avec le Droit des Gens et le Droit Civil, l. ii. t. i. c. ii. s. 2. But Vattel holds that an ally may furnish succour due from him and remain neutral.—L. iii. c. vi. 101; c. vii. s. 105.

(*g*) Ubi supr.

(*h*) L. xxxv. c. xlviii.

(*i*) Vide ante, vol. i. pp. 397-594. App.

(*k*) Martens, s. 304.

(*l*) Massé, ubi supr., s. 173.

(*m*) "Ist die Neutralität eine unvollkommene, so sind ihre Gsenzen der strengsten Auslegung unterworfen. Es kann auch, wenn durch vorausgegangene Verträge einem Kriegsführenden Theile gewisse vortheilhafte Zugeständnisse gemacht sind, der hierdurch benachtheiligten Partei das Recht nicht abgesprochene werden, diese Vergünstigungen durch Reactionen zu paralysiren, wenn nicht darauf von ihm verzichtet ist.. Keinesweges kann er aber präcise von dem Neutralen dieselbe Vergünstigung als ein Recht fordern."—Heffters, s. 146.

(*n*) Elements of International Law, vol. ii. p. 134.

her public ships of war, in case of urgent necessity, to refresh, victual, repair, &c.; but not exclusively of other nations at war with her. Under these stipulations, the United States not being expressly bound to exclude the public ships of the enemies of France, granted an asylum to British vessels and those of other Powers at war with her. Great Britain and Holland still complained of the exclusive privileges allowed to France in respect to her privateers and prizes, whilst France herself was not satisfied with the interpretation of the Treaty by which the public ships of her enemies were admitted into the American ports. To the former it was answered by the American Government that they enjoyed a perfect equality, qualified only by the exclusive admission of the privateers and prizes of France, which was the effect of a Treaty made long before, for valuable considerations, not with a view to circumstances such as had occurred in the War of the French Revolution, nor against any nation in particular, but against all in general, and which might therefore be observed without giving just offence to any.(*o*)

*"On the other hand, the Minister of France asserted the right [*205] of arming and equipping vessels of war, and of enlisting men within the Neutral territory of the United States. Examining this question under the Law of Nations, and the general usage of mankind, the American Government produced proofs from the most enlightened and approved writers on the subject, that a Neutral Nation must, in respect to the War, observe an exact impartiality towards the belligerent parties; that favours to the one, to the prejudice of the other, would import a fraudulent Neutrality of which no nation could be the dupe; that no succour ought to be given to either, unless stipulated by Treaty, in men, arms, or anything else directly serving for War; that the right of raising troops being one of the rights of sovereignty, and consequently appertaining exclusively to the nation itself, no foreign Power can levy men within the territory without its consent; that, finally the Treaty of 1778, making it unlawful for the enemies of France to arm in the United States, could not be construed affirmatively into a permission to the French to arm in those ports, the Treaty being express as to the prohibition, but silent as to the permission."(*p*)

CXL. The question whether the furnishing of auxiliary troops, in compliance with the provisions of a Treaty made previously to the War, is not incompatible with the character of Neutrality, was discussed in 1788, in a Declaration and Counter-Declaration, between Denmark and Sweden.

The Declaration of Denmark was as follows:—

"His Danish Majesty has ordered the undersigned to declare, that although he complies with the Treaty between the Courts of Petersburg and Copenhagen, in furnishing the former with the number of ships and troops stipulated by several Treaties, and particularly that of 1781, he

(*o*) Mr. Jefferson's Letter to Mr. Hammond and Mr. Van Berckel, Sept. 9, 1793.—Waite's State (American) Papers, vol. i. pp. 169-172.

(*p*) Mr. Jefferson's Letter to Mr. G. Morris, Aug. 16, 1793.—Waite's State Papers, vol. i. p. 140. Wheaton's Elements of International Law, vol. ii. p. 134.

[*206] yet *considers himself in perfect amity and peace with His Swedish Majesty; which friendship shall not be interrupted, although the Swedish arms should prove victorious, either in repulsing, defeating, or taking prisoners, the Danish troops now in the Swedish territories, acting as Russian auxiliaries, under Russian flags. Nor does he conceive that His Swedish Majesty has the least ground to complain, so long as the Danish ships and troops now acting against Sweden do not exceed the number stipulated by Treaty; and it is his earnest desire that all friendly and commercial intercourse between the two nations, and the good understanding between the Courts of Stockholm and Copenhagen, remain inviolably as heretofore.

"(Signed) COUNT DE BERNSTORF.

"Delivered to the Baron de Sprengtporten, His Swedish Majesty's Minister Plenipotentiary at the Court of Copenhagen.

"Sept. 23, 1788."

The Counter-declaration of Sweden was as follows:—

"The declaratory note delivered by the Count Bernstorf to the undersigned, in which his Danish Majesty conceives that his Swedish Majesty cannot have any ground of complaint, as long as the Danish ships and troops merely act as auxiliaries to Russia, is a doctrine which His Swedish Majesty cannot altogether reconcile with the Law of Nations and rights of Sovereigns, and against which His Majesty has ordered the undersigned to protest.

"Nevertheless, to prevent an effusion of blood between the subjects of the two kingdoms, and particularly at the moment when a negotiation has begun to restore perfect peace and tranquillity in the North of Europe, which affords a pleasing prospect of a general peace, His Swedish Majesty from motives of a love of peace, waives entering into a speculative discussion, whether or not there is a cause or ground of complaint on his side, and rests perfectly satisfied with the assurances contained in [*207] His Danish *Majesty's declaration, that His Danish Majesty has no hostile views against Sweden, and that the friendly and commercial intercourse between the subjects of both kingdoms, and the good understanding between the two Courts, shall remain uninterrupted.

"His Swedish Majesty puts the strongest faith and utmost confidence in what Mr. Elliot, Envoy Extraordinary and Minister Plenipotentiary of His Britannic Majesty, has represented to him on this important occasion.

"His Majesty, therefore, to prevent the horrors of War, and the calamities impending the two nations, anxious to behold peace and union restored between them, embraces with satisfaction His Danish Majesty's declararation, and particularly as it will facilitate the negotiation for a general peace, which is happily begun through the mediation of Great Britain, France, Holland and Prussia, and the good success of which is the greatest object of His Majesty's ambition, and which His Majesty has fully declared to the aforesaid Mr. Elliot, provided the defeating of the Russian auxiliaries is not considered as hostilities against his Danish Majesty, agreeable to the declaration delivered by Count Bernstorf.

"(Signed) BARON DE SPRENGTPORTEN.

"Dated, Stockholm, Oct. 6, 1788, and delivered to the Count Bernstorf, at Copenhagen."(q)

CXLI. At the beginning of the War now waged by England, France, and Sardinia, against Russia, the doctrine of Neutrality was carefully laid down by Sweden and Denmark in the following terms:—

"The system which His Majesty the King of Sweden and Norway intends to follow, and steadfastly to adopt, is that of a strict Neutrality, founded on good faith, impartiality, and an equal respect for the rights of all the Powers. This Neutrality, according to the identic views of the two *Courts, would impose on the Government of His Majesty the King of Sweden and Norway, the following obligations, and would assure to him the following advantages:— [*208]

"1. To abstain, during the conflict which may occur, from all participation, direct or indirect, in favour of one of the contending parties to the detriment of the other.

"2. To admit in the ports of Sweden and Norway the ships of war and of commerce of the belligerent parties, the Government reserving always to itself the power of denying to the first the entrance into the following fortified ports; that is to say: that of Stockholm, within the fortress of Waxholm; of Christiana, within the fort of Kaholm; the interior basin of the Norwegian military station at Horten; the ports of Karlsten and of Carlscrona, within the fortifications; and the port of Slito, in the Island of Gottland, within the batteries erected at Encholm.

"The sanitary and police regulations which circumstances have rendered or may render necessary, must naturally be observed and respected. Privateers will not be admitted in the ports, nor tolerated in the roads of the States of His Majesty the King of Sweden and Norway.

"3. To accord to vessels of the belligerent Powers the facility of supplying themselves in the ports of the United Kingdoms with all the provisions and stores of which they may stand in need, with the exception of the articles looked upon as contraband of War.

"4. To exclude from the ports of Sweden and Norway, except in cases of proved distress, the entrance, the condemnatian, and the sale of every prize; and finally,

"5. To enjoy, in the commercial relations of the United Kingdoms with the countries at war, all security and all facilities for Swedish and Norwegian vessels as well as for their cargoes, with the obligation, at all times, for such vessels to conform to the regulations generally established and recognized for special cases of declared and effective blockade.

"Such are the general principles of the Neutrality adopted by His Majesty the King of Sweden and Norway in the event *of a War breaking out in Europe. The King flatters himself that they will be acknowledged as in conformity with the Law of Nations, and that the true and faithful observance of them will place His Majesty in a position to cultivate with the Powers, his friends and allies, the rela- [*209]

(q) Annual Register (1788,) vol. xxx. pp. 292-3.

tions which, for the good of his people, he earnestly wishes to preserve from all interruption."(*r*)

The king of Denmark has sent a precisely similar statement to the Court of St. James.

CXLII. We now arrive at the discussion of an important and much vexed question which grows out of this branch of our subject, namely, the right of a Neutral State to *permit the enlistment of troops* for the purposes of any belligerent to take place within its borders.(*s*)

CXLIII. International Jurists are in the habit of drawing an important distinction between auxiliary troops furnished by a third Power in consequence of a Treaty, which existed previously to the War, binding it to assist the belligerent, and auxiliary troops furnished without any such obligation.

They have considered that, in the former case, only the *troops* so sent are to be considered as enemies, and not the *country* which sends them.

The right of a third Power to allow levies of troops to be made within its territories for the purpose of assisting exclusively one belligerent, has been said to be lawful when such permission has been the subject of a Treaty antecedent to the breaking out of the War.

[*210] There remains, however, the grave question, which has *been already discussed, whether a State has any right to stipulate in time of Peace, that, when the time of War arrives, it will do the act of a Belligerent and yet claim the immunity of a Neutral.

During the Middle Ages the practice of employing mercenary troops was common. *Companies,* as they were called, of freebooters were formed under some adventurous captain, and sold their services, without regard to the cause, to any belligerent that paid for them,—not unfrequently to both in succession during the continuance of the same War. And at a later period, not only did English troops serve against the Spaniards during the revolt of the Netherlands, but six thousand Scotchmen fought under the standard of the Marquis of Hamilton in the thirty years' War of Germany, in which contest England was neutral.

By the Treaty of Munster in 1648, it was stipulated that neither of the contracting parties should furnish arms, money, soldiers, provisions, refuge, or means of passage to the enemies of the other; but, nevertheless, a right was reserved to the individual States, who were members of the Empire, to serve as mercenaries according to the constitutions of the empire.(*t*)

On the other hand, many Treaties may be found in the fifteenth and sixteenth centuries, in which it is expressly stipulated that the Govern-

(*r*) Correspondence relative to the Neutrality of Denmark and Sweeden and Norway. Presented to both Houses of Parliament by command of Her Majesty, 1854.

(*s*) Bynk., Q. J. P., c. xxii. *An liceat militem conducere in amicæ gentis populo.* Wolff, Jus Gent., ss. 753-8. Vattel, l. iii. c. ii. s. 15. Statute of 59 Geo. III., c. lxix. 1 Kent's Comm., p. 122. Ward's law of Nations, ii. p. 291. Of Auxiliary Treaties. Manning's Law of Nations, pp. 170-81.

(*t*) Dumont, Corps Dipl., l. vi. i. p. 451. Manning, p. 174.

ments of the States who are the contracting parties, shall not permit their subjects to enlist against each other.(*u*)

CXLIV. It appears, as has been already observed, upon all sound principles of International Jurisprudence to be incompetent to a State, to contract in time of Peace obligations to assist another State in time of War by furnishing troops or ships, however limited their number, and when so furnishing them to claim the character of a Neutral; but whatever course a Belligerent may or ought to adopt with respect to a State claiming to be Neutral, while, under the obligations of a Treaty contracted previously to the War, it *furnishes this limited aid, and no more, to the other Belligerent, the proposition that without [*211] such special Treaty a State may remain Neutral while it accords to one and refuses to the other Belligerent permission to levy troops within its dominions, is a proposition not warranted by any principle or practice of International Law, and which, whatever may have formerly been urged in its favour, is now generally and wisely repudiated.(*x*) The opinion of Vattel has been already canvassed; the private opinion of Bynkershoek inclines to allow *generally* levies in a *Neutral* country, but he admits that it was a question which had long agitated, and, when he wrote, still agitated Christendom. But the chapter in the *Quæstiones Juris Publici* of this great jurist(*y*) appears to contain, either directly expressed, or by certain inference, two important propositions of International, and one of Public Law, upon this subject.

The propositions of International Law are:

1. That to enlist soldiers(*z*) within the Neutral territory, without the consent of the Government of the Neutral State, is a clear and gross violation of International Law.

2. That on the principle that the Neutral is bound to consider both belligerents as equally in the right, the permission to levy troops must be accorded equally to both.(*a*)

3. The proposition of Public Law is that the Governments *of his own country had, by repeated ordinances, declared that the [*212] enlisting troops within the Dutch territories without their consent was illegal.

CXLV. It behoves all States both to make and to enforce such or

(*u*) Manning, ib., refers to a great many Treaties of this kind.

(*x*) Heffters, 147.

(*y*) Bynk., Q. J. P., l. i. c. xxii. He treats the question partly with reference to Public, partly with reference to International Naw; it is with the latter that we are principally concerned in this chapter.

(*z*) All jurists agree in this proposition. Thus Wolff: "Quoniam nemini *in alieno territorio militem* conscribere licet *invito superiore; si quis legere audet jus gentis violat, ac ideo injuriam eidem facit*, cumque injuria hæc crimen sit a peregrino commissum, peregrini autem in territorio alieno delinquentes juxta leges loci puniendi sint, *si peregrinus in territorio alieno invito superiore militem legere audet, deprehensus puniri potest.*"—Wolff, Jus Gent., s. 754.

(*a*) Constat enim . . . utriusque amico *et hanc et illam partem* oportere *justam* videri." So he says you may sell implements of war to *both*:—"Idque in instrumentis bellicis, comparandis vulgò servamus, ut ut enim ea ad utrumque amicum non rectè vehamus, sine fraude tamen vendimus utrique amico, quamvis invicem hosti, et quamvis sciamus, alterum contra alterum his in bello esse usurum."—Bynk., ubi supr.

similar ordinances. The peace of their own dominions and the general peace of the world may greatly depend upon it.

The subject, so far as it concerns England and the United States of North America, has been already partially discussed in a former volume of this work.(*b*)

CXLVI. The history of the English Law(*c*) upon this matter of *Foreign Enlistment*, shows, since the reign of James I., an increasing severity in the measures of the Government.

The Statute of the Third of James I., chapter four, made it felony for any person whatever to go out of the realm, to serve any foreign Prince, without having first taken the oath of allegiance before his departure. It was felony also for any gentleman, or person of higher degree, or for one who had borne any office in the army, to go out of the realm to serve such foreign Prince or State, without previously entering into a bond with two sureties, not to be reconciled to the See of Rome, or enter into any conspiracy against his natural Sovereign. And further it was enacted by statute 9 Geo. II. c. 30, enforced by statute 29 Geo. II. c. 17, if any subject of Great Britain shall enlist himself, or if any person shall procure him to be enlisted in any foreign service, or detain or embark him for that purpose, without license under the king's sign-manual, he shall be guilty of felony without benefit of clergy; but if the person, so enlisted or enticed, shall discover his seducer within fifteen days, so as he may be apprehended and convicted of the same, he shall be indemnified. It was moreover, by statute 29 Geo. II. c. 17, enacted that to serve under the French King, as a military officer, shall be felony without benefit of clergy; and to enter into the Scotch brigade, in the Dutch service,
[*213] *without previously taking the oaths of allegiance and abjuration, shall be a forfeiture of 500*l*.(*d*)

The present *Foreign Enlistment Bill* was introduced in the month of May, 1819, by the Attorney-General, into the House of Commons.(*e*) Its passage through the House of Commons was marked by debates in which speeches of unusual ability were made both for and against the measure.

The great opponent of the measure was Sir James Mackintosh; his arguments were, however, mainly directed against the tendency of the measure to assist the King of Spain, and to injure the Spanish American Colonists in the War for independence which was then being waged between them and the mother-country; and that therefore, under these circumstances, it was *practically* a departure from the policy of Neutrality between the two belligerents. He also cited a variety of precedents from English History, to show that Foreign Enlistment had been often

(*b*) Vol. i. pp. 397-8. Appendix, pp. 504-14, contains *in extenso* the Foreign Enlistment Act, 59 Geo. III. c. 69.

(*c*) Blackstone's Commentaries, vol. iv. c. vii. s. 3.

(*d*) Blackstone's Commentaries, vol. iv. c. vii. s. 3.

(*e*) Hansard's Parl. Deb., vol. xl. Debate in the House of Commons, pp. 362-74. Ib. pp., 867-907. Ib., pp. 1084-1125. Ib., p. 1232, Speech of Sir W. Scott, Lord Stowell. Ib., p. 1273, Speech of Dr. Phillimore (the only two civilians who spoke in the debate.) Ib., Debate in the House of Lords, pp. 1377-1416. A division took place on the second reading: ayes, 155; noes, 142.

permitted in this country, and not objected to by other nations, and he dwelt upon the great advantages which Great Britain would derive from the emancipation of the Spanish Colonies.

Mr. Canning replied to what he justly called "the splendid impediment" which the eloquence of this speech had opposed to the passing of the measure. The speeches of Mr. Canning, it should be observed, both on this and on another occasion, are marked by the calm wisdom of a statesman, and by a distinct knowledge of the principles of International Law applicable to this important subject. Mr. Canning contended, that by the Treaty of 1814, England was bound to more than "a *nominal Neutrality" between Spain and her revolted Colonies; [*214] and that no prospect of advantage to be derived from the independence of these Colonies ought to induce England to depart from her duty and policy of Neutrality. Mr. Canning then replied to the argument of precedent used by Sir James Mackintosh.

"The honourable and learned gentleman," Mr. Canning said, "had cited many instances from history, in which the subjects of this country had been not only permitted, but encouraged, by the Government to enter into the service of foreign States, and had sometimes even been thereby brought into the field to combat with each other. The fact was indisputable; but the honourable and learned gentleman was not to be told that in respect to military service and enterprize a great change had taken place in the tone, and temper, and state of Europe since the times of Elizabeth and James I. In those times there was a general thirst for military glory pervading all Europe. The profession of arms, instead of being a duty and task imposed upon the people, was a proud and honourable profession. Since those times a most material alteration had taken place; but it was not the policy of governments, but the temper of the people, which had undergone the change. Formerly a spirit of adventurous enterprize was cherished and sanctioned, which would not now be deemed justifiable. The usages of modern Europe did not recognize such proceedings as those adverted to by the honourable and learned gentleman. It surely could not be forgotten that in 1794 this country complained of various breaches of Neutrality (though much inferior in degree to those now under consideration,) committed on the part of subjects of the United States of America. What was the conduct of that nation in consequence? Did it resent the complaint as an infringement of its independence? Did it refuse to take such steps as would insure the immediate observance of Neutrality? Neither. In 1795, immediately after the application from the British Government, the Legislature of the United States passed an act prohibiting, under *heavy penalties, the engagement of American citizens in the armies of [*215] any belligerent Power. Was that the only instance of the kind? It was but last year that the United States passed an act, by which the act of 1795 was confirmed in every respect, again prohibiting the engagement of their citizens in the service of any foreign Power; and pointing distinctly to the service of Spain, or the South American provinces."(*f*)

(*f*) Mr. Canning's Speeches, vol. iv. pp. 152-3. Foreign Enlistment Bill, (June 10, 1819.)

Mr. Canning then argued the question of International Law, demonstrating that to permit Foreign Enlistment was incompatible with the character of Neutrality in the country which permitted it.

"Did," Mr. Canning said, "the honourable and learned gentleman not think that the allowing of armaments to be fitted out in this country against a foreign Power was a just cause of War? He knew well indeed that, from the exhaustion of Spain, we were perfectly secure from hostility in that quarter. That consideration, however, afforded a complete reply to the taunt that had been thrown out against Ministers, that they allowed themselves to be dictated to by Spain. But it was precisely because Spain was weak—because her resentment could be attended with no practical inconvenience—that they were desirous to discharge the duties of Neutrality towards her the more scrupulously. The maxim of 'Do unto others as you would they should do unto you,' was as applicable to politics as to morals. Did the honourable and learned gentleman recollect the celebrated *Mémoire Justificatif*, which was understood to have been drawn up for the Government of the day by Mr. Gibbon, previous to the War with France, during our contest with the American Colonies? The language of that document was such, that if it were to appear for the first time at the present moment, it might be considered as the memorial of the Spanish Ambassador, addressed to the Govern-
[*216] ment of this country. In that paper *it was stated, that agents from our American Colonies had endeavoured to penetrate into, and settle in the different States in Europe, but that it was only in France they found an asylum, hopes, and assistance. That the French merchants furnished America, not only with useful and necessary merchandize, but even with saltpetre, gunpowder, ammunition, arms, and artillery; and loudly declared that they were assured not merely of impunity, but even of the protection and favour of the Ministers of the Court of Versailles. The marks of these facts, which could be considered only as manifest breaches of the faith of Treaties, multiplied continually, and the diligence of the King's Ambassador to communicate his complaints and proofs to the Court of Versailles, did not leave them the shameful and humiliating resource of appearing ignorant of what was carried on and daily repeated in the very heart of the country."(*g*)

CXLVII. In the month of April, 1823, Lord Althorpe moved the repeal of the Foreign Enlistment Bill, and again a debate ensued, which was made memorable by the eloquence of Mr. Canning, who resisted the motion.(*h*)

"I do not now," he said, "pretend to argue in favour of a system of *Neutrality;* but it being declared that we intend to remain neutral, I call upon the House to abide by that declaration so long as it shall remain unaltered.

"No matter what ulterior course we may be inclined to adopt—no matter whether, at some ulterior period, the honour and the interests of

(*g*) Canning's Speeches, vol. iv. pp. 155-6.

(*h*) Hansard's Parl. Deb., N. S., vol. viii. (1823.) Petition against the bill, p. 230; Debate on Lord Althorpe's Motion, pp. 1019-59. The ayes were 110; the noes, 216.

this country may force us into a War, still, while we declare ourselves neutral, let us avoid passing the strict line of demarcation.

"When War comes, if come it must, let us enter into it with all the spirit and energy which become us as a great *and independent nation. That period, however, I do not wish to anticipate, much less desire to hasten. [*217]

"If a War must come, let it come in the shape of satisfaction to be demanded for injuries, of rights to be asserted, of interests to be protected, of Treaties to be fulfilled. But, in God's name, let it not come on in the paltry, pettyfogging way of fitting out ships in our harbours to cruise for gain.

"At all events, let the country disdain to be sneaked into a War. Let us abide by our *Neutrality* as long as we mean to adhere to it; and, by so doing, we shall, in the event of any necessity for abandoning that system, be the better able to enter with effect upon any other course which the policy of the country may require."(*i*)

Mr. Canning also referred to the excellent example of true Neutrality which the Government of Mr. Jefferson, the President of the N. A. United States, had shown to the world.

"If I wished," Mr. Canning said, "for a guide in a system of Neutrality, I should take that laid down by America in the days of the presidency of Washington and the secretaryship of Jefferson. In 1793 complaints were made to the American Government that French ships were allowed to fit out and arm in American ports for the purpose of attacking British vessels, in direct opposition to the laws of Neutrality. Immediately upon this representation, the American Government held that such a fitting out was contrary to the laws of Neutrality; and orders were issued prohibiting the arming of any French vessels in American ports. At New York a French vessel fitting out, was seized, delivered over to the tribunals, and condemned. Upon that occasion the American Government held that such fitting out of French ships in American ports for the purpose of cruising against English vessels, was incompatible with the sovereignty of the United States, and tended *to interrupt the peace and good understanding which subsisted between that country and Great Britain." [*218]

"Here, Sir, (he added,) I contend, is the principle upon which we ought to act."(*k*)

CXLVIII. In fact the maxim adverted to in a former volume of this work(*l*) is sound, viz., that a State is *primâ facie* responsible for whatever is done within its jurisdiction, for it must be *presumed* to be capable of preventing or punishing offences committed within its boundaries. A body politic is therefore responsible for the acts of individuals which are acts of actual or meditated hostility towards a nation, with which the Government of these subjects professes to maintain relations of friendship or Neutrality.(*m*)

(*i*) Canning's Speeches, vol. v. pp. 51-2.

(*k*) Canning's Speeches, vol. v. pp. 50-1. Speech against Repeal of the Foreign Enlistment Bill (April, 1823.)

(*l*) Vol. i. c. x., Self Preservation.

(*m*) Grot. l. ii. c. 21, s. 2. Puffend. l. i. c. 5, s. ult.

"Culpâ caret, qui scit, sed prohibere non potest,"(*n*) is the doctrine of the Roman Law; but such an avowal, actual or constructive on the part of the unintentionally injuring State, justifies the injured State in exercising, if it can, that jurisdiction by foreign force which ought to be, but cannot be, exercised by domestic law.

CXLIX. The British Foreign Enlistment Act gave a power to the Crown, by Order in Council, to relax its provisions.

In 1835, Great Britain signed the Treaty of the Quadruple Alliance,(*o*) in favour of Queen Isabella of Spain, when a Civil War raged in that country. Soon after the signature of this Treaty, an Order in Council exempted British subjects who might engage in the service of Isabella from the penalties of the Foreign Enlistment Act. A Spanish Legion was formed of British soldiers, and commanded by a most distinguished British officer, Sir De Lacy Evans.

[*219] *A debate on the policy of this relaxation took place in the House of Commons, in June, 1835, upon a motion made by Lord Mahon, as to the *expediency* of this relaxation;(*p*) but the *competency* of the Crown to make such relaxation was not disputed.

CL. Nevertheless, Vattel's native predilections carry him so far, that, in his eagerness to defend the practice of Switzerland, he declares, that not only when there is a Treaty anterior to the War binding a State to afford succour to another, but when there is none, that a *custom* of the country may justify a *Neutral* in supplying *one* belligerent with troops: "Lors donc qu'un peuple *est dans l'usage pour occuper et pour exercer ses sujets*, de permettre des levées de troupes en faveur de la puissance à qui il veut bien les confier, l'ennemi de cette puissance ne peut traiter ses permissions d'hostilités, à moins qu'elles ne soient données pour envahir ses Etats, ou pour la défense d'une cause odieuse et manifestement injuste. *Il ne peut même pretendre de droit qu'on lui en accorde autant; parce que ce peuple peut avoir des raisons de le refuser, qui n'ont pas lieu à l'égard du parti contraire; et c'est à lui de voir ce qui lui convient.*"

The writer proceeds to instance the Swiss as having always acted upon these *Neutral* principles of affording aid to *one* and refusing it to *another* belligerent; and observes that no State has made war upon them in consequence; and he adds, a limitation which renders transparent the feebleness of the proposition of International Law, which his love for Switzerland makes him strive against justice and reason to establish: "Il faut avouer (he says,) cependant, que si *ces levées étaient considérables*, si elles faisaient la principale force de mon ennemi, trandis que, sans alléguer de raisons solides, on m'en refuserait absolument, j'aurais tout [*220] lieu de regarder ce peuple comme ligué avec mon ennemi; et en ce cas, *le soin de ma propre sûreté m'autoriserait à le traiter comme tel."(*r*)

There is no test of Neutrality to which this proposition of Vattel can be submitted without demonstrating its futility. Try it by the law of

(*n*) Dig. l. l. t. 17, s. 50.
(*o*) Great Britain, France, Spain, and Portugal. See Wheaton's Hist., pp. 523-38.
(*p*) Hansard's Parl. Deb. (3rd Series,) vol. xxviii. (1835,) pp. 1133-1180.
(*q*) Vattel, l. iii. c. vii. s. 110. (*r*) Vattel, l. iii. c. vii. s. 110.

natural justice, by the reason of the thing, by the acknowledged definitions of Neutrality, it will prove to be untenable.(s)

It is not pretended that the *partially-treated* belligerent might not intercept the passage of these mercenaries, after they had left their *neutral* countries, and put them to the sword, or sink the ship which was conveying them: and by what law of common justice or common sense is he to wait till the danger is at his door before he encounters it? Why is he to allow the cockatrice to be hatched to his destruction, if he can break the egg and secure himself from the peril? Why is he to allow his *neutral friend* to send his troops and arms to his *enemy*, because, forsooth, it has been the habit of this Neutral so *to occupy and exercise* his forces? May a maritime State, without a breach of Neutrality, send a fleet to one belligerent, and allege that it is her habit to keep her sailors in exercise? But he may do so, Vattel says, if the Neutral espouses *an odious or manifestly unjust cause*, or *if the levies be considerable.* And who is to judge whether these justifications exist? The puerility of the argument is such that it really only requires to be stated in order to be refuted.

The Right on the part of the State so hostilely treated to deal with the State which so treats her in every respect as an enemy, is clear; whether she will exercise it or no, is a mere question of expediency.

Vattel found no such doctrine as that which he lays down in his Master Wolff, but the contrary.

"Qui neutrarum partium sunt (Wolff says,) ea præstare utrique belligerantium parti debent, quæ jure gentium debentur extra bellum, nisi expressè de quibusdam aliter conventum, quæ respectum ad bellum habere possunt."

*And again: "Qui neutrarum partium sunt, eorum respectu bellum non est, ipsi vero utrique belligerantium amici sunt. Quæ igitur extra bellum, seu pacis tempore, gentibus præstantur a gente, ea etiam præstanda sunt utrique belligerantium parti. Quod uni præstatur, id præstandum quoque alteri est, si eodem indiget. Potest autem conveniri, ut etiam quædam præstentur, quæ respectum quendam ad bellum habent, vel ut non præstentur, quæ quidem per se ad bellum minimè faciunt, propter casum vero emergentem respectum quendam ad idem habere possunt, et tunc illa utrique præstanda, hæc utrique deneganda sunt."(t) [*221]

This passage enunciates both the principles which have been mentioned(u) as indispensable to neutrality, viz,—1st, Abstinence from the war; 2nd, Impartiality between the belligerents. A nation which furnishes aid, whether of men or money, to both belligerents may be *impartial*, but certainly is not *neutral.* With respect to muniments of war, M. Massé, wisely says, there should be not an impartiality of action but of inaction.(x)

CLI. The principles which have been laid down prohibit the Neutral from assisting a belligerent by money, in the shape of a loan, or in any other form, as much as by arms; and so it has been solemnly decided by the English Courts of Justice in the case of Demetrius De Wütz v.

(s) Vide ante, vol. i. p. 64.
(t) Wolff, Jus Gent., s. 683.
(u) Vide ante, p. 201.
(x) Massé, Droit Commercial, t. i. p. 199.

Hendricks. This case was tried, A. D. 1824, before Lord Chief Justice Best(*y*) at Guildhall. It appeared that the plaintiff had proposed to raise money by way of loan, to espouse the cause of the Greeks against the government of the Porte; that he stated publicly that he was authorized to do so, and in consequence, applied to the defendant, a stock-broker, to [*222] negotiate the loan, who required certain securities to be left *with him for that purpose; that the plaintiff accordingly lodged with him a power of attorney, which, he stated, was signed and executed abroad by the *Exarch of Ravenna*, authorizing him, the plaintiff, to raise money for the Greek cause; he also requested the defendant to procure certain scrip receipts to be engraved, which he accordingly did, and which were afterwards stamped at the Stamp Office, as such receipts. The defendant suspecting the accuracy of the plaintiff's statement or authority, the intended loan failed, and no money was raised by him. The plaintiff then claimed the power of attorney, and engraved scrip receipts from the defendant, which he refused to deliver up, until the engraver's bill, and the other expenses, had been paid. On their amount being tendered, the defendant claimed a commission for scrip on part of the loan, which the plaintiff also offered to pay, provided the defendant would transfer the scrip to him, on which he claimed such commission; but none was in fact ever raised, as the projected loan fell to the ground in the first instance. The plaintiff having again formally demanded the above documents from the defendant, who refused to deliver them up, he commenced the present action.

For the defendant, it was submitted, that the whole of the transaction was a fraud on the part of the plaintiff, as he had no authority to negotiate the loan in question. And his lordship being of opinion that a resident in this country could not enter into an engagement to raise money by way of loan, to assist subjects of a foreign State, so as to enable them to prosecute a war against a government in alliance with our own, without the license of the crown, the jury accordingly found a verdict for the defendant.(*z*)

Afterwards, a *rule nisi* was applied for to set aside the verdict of the jury; that is to say, the points of *law* were again argued before Judges of the Court of Common Pleas.

[*223] Lord Chief Justice Best then said:—" I am of opinion, *that the whole of the transaction on which the plaintiff rested his claim to recover the articles in question from the defendant, was bottomed in fraud,—the jury so found at the trial,—and I am perfectly satisfied with their verdict. I then thought that it was contrary to the Law of Nations, for persons residing in this country, to enter into engagements to raise money, by way of loan, for the purpose of supporting subjects of a foreign State in arms against a government in alliance with our own, and that no right of action could arise out of such a transaction; and I consequently suggested a nonsuit; but as it was not insisted on by the defendant's counsel, I allowed the cause to proceed. A case in circumstances precisely similar to the present, except that a different

(*y*) Afterwards Lord Wynford.
(*z*) Moore's Common Pleas Reports, vol. ix. p. 586.

loan was proposed to be raised, was lately decided in the Court of Chancery, in which the Lord Chancellor entertained the same opinion as myself, and in which he is stated to have said, that English Courts of Justice will not take notice of, or afford any assistance to persons who set about raising loans for subjects of the King of Spain, to enable them to prosecute a war against that sovereign; or, at all events, that such loans could not be raised without the license of the crown."(*a*) The other judges concurred in this opinion.

Vattel, indeed, as he justified the Neutral in allowing levies under certain circumstances, consistently maintains that the previous *custom* of a nation to lend her money justifies her in time of war in lending it to a belligerent: "Il en est de même de l'argent qu'une nation *aurait coutume* de prêter à usure;"(*b*) and he is so far right that the loan of levies and money falls pretty much under the same principle: he proceeds to assert, that if a neutral power lends money to one belligerent, and refuse it to another, there is no breach of neutrality; because he may lend it to one on the ground of confidence in his financial condition, which he *may not feel with respect to the rival power. If, indeed, he says, it appear that the neutral does not lend his money for the purpose of getting good interest for it, but for the purpose of attacking a belligerent, then he loses his character of neutrality; and so if the troops were furnished to an enemy at the expense of the neutral, or the money lent without interest, the neutrality disappears. [*224]

But is not all this a manifest frittering away of the important duties of the neutral? Is it to be supposed that any but the weakest belligerent would permit a power, calling itself impartial, to supply his enemy, whom perhaps he would otherwise have vanquished, with the means of recruiting his sinking energies and restoring his decaying powers, whether those means be the succour of troops or the succour of money? If it be the act, not of a neutral, but of an enemy—

> "to *advise* how War may, best upheld,
> Move by her two main nerves, iron and gold,
> In all her equipage."(*c*)

It is, of course, still more the act of an enemy to *furnish* either of these nerves.

CLII. The *territory* and the *waters* of the Neutral are sacred and inviolable by both belligerents,(*d*) because they are neutral; but the character, and the protection incident to it, cease when the Neutral allows a right of passage (*jus transitus*) to one belligerent which he withholds from the other. It is clear that this passage must be refused or accorded to both.

*It is said by some jurists, that the *jus transitus innoxii* cannot, under proper precautions and conditions, be lawfully refused. [*225]

(*a*) Moore's Common Pleas Reports, vol. ix. p. 587.
(*b*) Vattel, l. iii. c. vii. s. 110.
(*c*) Milton's Sonnet to Sir Henry Vane the Younger.
(*d*) Grot., l. ii. c. ii. s. 13. Bynk., l. i. c. viii. Wolff, Jus Gent., s. 687. Vattel, l. iii. c. vii. ss. 119-31. Martens, ss. 310, 311. Heffters, s. 147, n. (1). Wheaton, Elém., l. xi. s. 8. Manning, pp. 182-86. The Twee Gibroeders, 3 Robinson, p. 353.

Wolff maintains this proposition, but with it, the important corollary that the Neutral is the only competent judge whether the *transitus* be or be not *innoxious.* But the opinion itself does not seem well founded. The neutral has a right to judge whether such permission may be likely to be fraught in any way with present or future mischief to himself. Cases of extreme necessity may be put, and are suggested by Vattel; but no safe rule of law is to be derived from the consideration of a state of things in which the operation of the law is, by the very hypothesis, suspended. The rule is plain and clear; justice and the reason of the thing are entirely in favour of the absolute right of the Neutral to decide the question for himself. The notion of the *imperfect* right of the belligerent is the offspring of indifferent metaphysics and bad law.

CLIII. In the alliance between France and Switzerland, in 1452, it was stipulated that the Swiss should not allow passage through their territories to the enemies of France;(*d*) and this article was inserted in a great number of subsequent treaties between the same powers; the last instance being in the treaty of 1803.(*e*) In 1512, Louis XII. and the King of Navarre agreed to allow no passage to the enemies of the other party. In consequence, when the King of Arragon and Castile demanded passage, he was refused; and using this as a pretext for hostilities, he overran Navarre.(*f*) By the Treaty of Munster, in 1648, the German princes were to be allowed passage through each other's dominions; but passage is otherwise expressly forbidden by the same treaty.(*g*) The [*226] clause that neither *party shall allow passage to the enemies of the other, is inserted in a great many subsequent treaties; and, whenever the integrity of a neutral territory was violated by the passage of troops, it was invariably considered as an unjustifiable aggression.(*h*) In 1792, Russia and Austria agreed that they would *conjointly request* passage for their troops through the territories of third parties.(*i*) And, in 1798, Russia and the King of Naples agreed that they would *request* the Emperor and the Porte to allow the passage of certain troops.(*k*) During the numerous wars which grew out of the French Revolution, it became a constant object of French diplomacy to obtain this privilege for the French armies, which was done in a great variety of treaties; see, for instance, that with Prussia in 1796 (for the county of Le Mark;)(*l*) and, in the same year, those with Sardinia, Parma, the Pope, Wirtemberg, Baden, and Bavaria;(*m*) and, in 1800, the treaties with the Princes of Isemberg, Hesse Homburg, Wied, and Nassau.(*n*) And, by the Confederation of the Rhine in 1806, passage was to be allowed to the troops of any of the members, but was to be refused to any who were not members of the Confederation.(*o*)

(*d*) Dumont, Corps Dipl., l. iii. c. i. s. 193.
(*e*) De Martens, Rec. de Tr. Suppl. l. iii. s. 570.
(*f*) Dumont, Corps Dipl., l. iv. c. i. s. 148. (*g*) Ibid., l. vi. c. i. ss. 451, 459.
(*h*) Coxe's Life of Marlborough, vol. iii. p. 112. Moser, Versuch X. i. 218, 238, et seq.
(*i*) De Martens, Rec. l. v. s. 349. (*k*) Ib., l. iii. s. 525. (*l*) Ib., s. 57.
(*m*) Ib., ss. 215, 226, 240, 265, 277, 294. (*n*) Ib., l. vii. ss. 113, 116, 118, 121.
(*o*) Ib., Suppl. l. iv. ss. 385, 389, 392, 394, 397, 482, 484. Manning, Law of Nations, pp. 185, 186, to which I am indebted for this summary.

CLIV. It has been said that the territory and waters of the Neutral are inviolable, and that no hostility can be exercised therein. Bynkershoek,(*p*) indeed, suggests that a *belligerent who has begun an attack upon another belligerent without the neutral territory or water, may so far trench upon the inviolability thereof, as, *dum fervet opus*, to continue the chase and complete the capture. But the opinion is not admissible. The great principle of the inviolability of neutral territory, so long as a strict Neutrality is maintained, must not be impaired by any exceptional cases of this kind.(*q*) [*227]

CLV. It is indeed true that Lord Stowell has said, in a particular case, that he was disposed so far to agree with Bynkershoek, that if a vessel, having refused to submit to visitation and search, fled within neutral territory to some uninhabited place, like the little mud islets at the mouth of the Mississippi, and the belligerent cruiser there, without injury or annoyance to any person, should quietly take possession of his prey, that he would not stretch the point so far, as, on that account only, to hold the capture illegal.(*r*) But, even in this case, the neutral State itself would have a clear right, if it chose to intervene, to insist on a restitution of the property. The sound doctrine is thus stated by Lord Stowell: "that when the fact (of neutral territory) is established, it overrules every other consideration. The capture is done away: the property must be restored, notwithstanding that it may actually belong to the enemy."(*s*)

CLVI. This portion of the subject would be left imperfect, without some further observations upon the question of vessels captured within neutral limits: though, in making them, the intention before expressed of reserving for a separate exposition all that appertains to Maritime or Prize Law may appear to be in some degree departed from.

*CLVII. It is laid down by jurists(*t*) that with respect to the captured property of its own subjects, brought within the limit of its own territory, a neutral State may so far exercise jurisdiction as to restore such property, where of course the capture has not been warranted by the conduct of the neutral owner or his agent. The jurisdiction is conceded, according to Valin, to the neutral state, as a compensation for the asylum granted to the captor and his prize.(*u*) [*228]

The courts of the North American United States have decided that foreign ships which have offended against the laws of the United States, within their jurisdiction, may be pursued, and seized upon the ocean, and rightfully brought into the ports of the United States for adjudication.(*x*)

(*p*) Q. J. P., c. viii. Bynkershoek says that he has never seen this opinion mentioned either in the writings of jurists or maintained by any European nation except the Dutch. But Mr. Chancellor Kent observes (vol. i. p. 119,) that Casaregis, and some other jurists mentioned by Azuni, held a similar doctrine. Kent adds his own authority to that of D'Abreu, Valin, Emerigon, Vattel, Azuni, and others, in support of the doctrine in the text.

(*q*) Vattel, l. iii. c. vii. s. 132. Emerigon, Tr. des Ass., i. 449.

(*r*) The Anna, 5 Rob., p. 365. Vide ante, vol. i. c. viii.

(*s*) The Vrow Anna Catharina, 5 Rob., p. 15. (*t*) Kent's Comm., i. 121.

(*u*) Valin, Comm., t. ii. p. 274.

(*x*) The Marianna Flora, 11 Wheaton, (Amer.,) p. 42.

The law relating to enemy's property in neutral vessels, and to neutral property in enemy's vessels will be discussed in a later chapter of this work.

CLVIII. Though a Neutral may, in the case which has been mentioned, be entitled to demand restitution of the belligerent's capture; yet he has no right to inquire into the validity of a capture, except in cases in which the neutral jurisdiction has been violated. In such cases only, the neutral power will, in spite of a sentence of condemnation in the court of the belligerent, restore the property if it be found within its jurisdiction, and in the hands of the offender.(*y*)

It belongs, however, exclusively to the neutral government to raise the objection to a title, founded upon a capture, made within the neutral territory. So far as the adverse belligerent is concerned, he has no right to complain if the case be duly tried before a competent court.(*z*)

The government of the owner of the captured property, may indeed [*229] call the Neutral to account, for permitting a *fraudulent, unworthy, or unnecessary violation of its jurisdiction, and such permission may, according to the circumstances, convert the Neutral into a belligerent.

CLIX. The civil war in Portugal, in the years 1828–9, gave rise to a very important question respecting the duties of a Neutral State pending such contest.

In 1827, Don Pedro, having retained to himself the empire of the Brazils, formally renounced the throne of Portugal in favour of his daughter Donna Maria, having delegated to his brother Don Miguel the office of Regency of the kingdom, with the intention that he should marry his niece.

Donna Maria II. was recognized by Great Britain and the other great Powers of Europe as the legitimate Sovereign of Portugal. Don Pedro imagined that he had adopted the most efficacious expedient for reconciling the parties of the Constitutionalists and the Absolutists which divided Portugal, and also that he had secured to that country the enjoyment of those free institutions which he had recently bestowed upon it.

Don Miguel, however, after a very short period, violated all his engagements, placed himself at the head of the Absolutists, procured himself to be proclaimed king in 1828, proscribed the Constitutionalists, and plunged the country into the horrors of a most barbarous civil war. The Constitutionalists were at first defeated in the struggle.

The King of Spain, though at first, in common with the other European Powers, he had withdrawn his ambassador from the court of the usurper, in a short time re-established with him relations of amity.

The other sovereigns of Europe still kept aloof from any communication with the usurper—from any act which might be considered a recognition of this title. The Portuguese refugees, and the ministers of Don Pedro, insisted that they ought to do more, and drive him from his throne by positive interference. These applications were addressed

(*y*) The Arrogante Barcelones, 7 Wheaton, (Amer.,) p. 496. La Amistad de Rues., 5 Ib., p. 390.

(*z*) The Etrusco, 3 Rob., p. 162, n.

particularly to the British Ministry. The Marquis of Barbacena, the Brazilian envoy, presented an official note to Lord Aberdeen, detailing the Treaties that regulated the *relations between Britain and Portugal; exposing the lawless course of Don Miguel's aggressions; and concluding that Miguel's proceeding, crowned by his assumption of the style and state of king, formed an attack upon the rights of the true Sovereign of Portugal, Donna Maria, which Britain, by her Treaties with that country, was bound to lend her aid in repelling. Lord Aberdeen, in answer, admitted to their fullest extent the obligations created by these Treaties; but he maintained that they did not countenance the demand now made of an armed interference, on the part of Britain, to remedy the consequences of an internal revolution. "It is assumed," he said, "that the usurpation of the throne of Portugal by the Infant Don Miguel has given to Her Most Faithful Majesty the right of demanding from this country effectual succours for the recovery of her crown and kingdom. But in the whole series of Treaties there is no express stipulation which can warrant this pretension, neither is such an obligation implied by their general tenor and spirit. It is either for the purpose of resisting successful rebellion, or of deciding by force a doubtful question of succession, that Great Britain is now called upon to act. But it is impossible to imagine that any independent State could ever intend thus to commit the control and direction of its internal affairs to the hands of another Power. For, doubtless, if His Britannic Majesty be under the necessity of furnishing effectual succours, in the event of any internal revolt or dissension in Portugal, it would become a duty, and, indeed it would be essential, to take care that no such case should exist, if it could be prevented. Hence a constant and minute interference in the affairs of Portugal would be indispensable; for his majesty could never consent to hold his fleets and armies at the disposal of a King of Portugal, without exercising those due precautions, and that superintendence, which would assure him that his forces would not be employed in averting the effects of misgovernment, folly, or caprice. Is this a condition in *which any State, professing to be independent, could endure to exist?(a) The truth is, that the whole spirit of the Treaties, as well as their history, shows, that the principle of the guarantee given by England is the protection of Portugal from foreign interference."

[*230]

[*231]

The British Government refused, therefore, to interfere in this domestic quarrel; and, holding that it was not entitled to make any distinction between the claimants of the Portuguese Crown, in so far as their respective pretensions were supported only by domestic force, considered itself bound to observe, in regard to all military operations, a strict Neutrality. A great number of Portuguese refugees, most of them military men, had arrived in England, taking up their residence principally in Portsmouth, Falmouth, and the neighbourhood. As it was believed that they were meditating to fit out some expedition from these ports against Don Miguel, the British Government, holding that to permit this would be

(a) Vide ante, vol. i. pp. 434, 441-2, 457; vol. ii. pp. 76-7.

a breach of Neutrality, informed the Brazilian Minister, that it would not allow such designs to be carried on in British harbours, and that, for security's sake, the refugees must remove farther from the coast. The envoy then stated that those troops were about to be conveyed to Brazil; and accordingly four vessels, having on board 652 officers and men, under the command of General Count Saldanha, who had been the constitutional Minister of War, sailed from Plymouth. The British Government suspected that the true design was to land these troops at Terceira, although the ostensible destination was Brazil. Notice was given to them before they sailed, that any such attempt would be resisted, and a small force of armed vessels, under the command of Captain Walpole of the Ranger, was dispatched beforehand to Terceira, to enforce the prohibition. His instructions were to cruise off the island, to inform the Portuguese, if they appeared, that he had authority to prevent their [*232] landing; *"and, should they persist, notwithstanding such warning, in hovering about, or in making any efforts to effect a landing, you are then to use force to drive them away from that neighbourhood, and keep sight of them until you shall be convinced, by the course they may steer, and the distance they may have proceeded, that they have no intention of returning to the Western Islands, or to proceed to Madeira."

The expedition of Count Saldanha appeared off Terceira on the 16th of January, and was discovered by Captain Walpole standing right in for Port Praya. He fired two shots, to bring them to, but they continued their course. The vessel, on board of which was Saldanha, although now within point blank range of the Ranger's guns, seemed determined to push in at all hazards. To prevent him from effecting his object, Captain Walpole was under the necessity of firing a shot at the vessel, which killed one man and wounded another. The vessel then lay to, and to a note from Captain Walpole, inquiring what was their object in coming thither, Saldanha answered, "My object in appearing here is to fulfil the orders of Her Majesty the Queen of Portugal, and which prescribe me to conduct, unarmed, without any hostile appearance, to the isle of Terceira, the men that are on board the four vessels in sight, which island has never ceased to obey and acknowledge, as its legitimate Sovereign, Her Faithful Majesty Donna Maria II. As a faithful subject and soldier, I think it unnecessary to assure you that I am determined to fulfil my duty at all peril." Captain Walpole replied, that he too had instructions to obey, and an imperious duty to perform; that both of them prevented him from allowing the Count, or any part of his force, to land, either at Terceira, or on any of the Western Islands or the Azores, or even to continue in that neighbourhood; that, therefore, unless the Count immediately quitted the vicinity of the islands, he should be obliged, and was determined, to use force to [*233] compel him to do so. Saldanha then declared that *he considered himself, and his men, as being, in these circumstances, Captain Walpole's prisoners; that they would follow his vessel wherever he chose to take them, but must have a written order to that effect, and be supplied with water and provisions. Captain Walpole simply answered, that they were at liberty to go to England, to France, or wheresoever they chose, provided only they quitted the islands. Saldanha still insisted that he should be told whether or not he was considered a prisoner of war: if he was, he would follow; if he was not, he would pursue his course, and endeavour, at every risk, to fulfil his instructions: "Only force shall prevent me from executing the orders of my Queen." Captain Walpole's reply still was, "Go where you choose, but don't stay here: if you persist in hovering about these islands, it is my duty and firm determination to carry those measures you are already in possession of into full effect. I therefore trust you will see the wisdom of quitting this neighbourhood." The Portuguese vessels then made sail for the westward, accompanied by the British ships. They continued together till the 24th of January, when Captain Walpole, having sent a note to Count Saldanha, resquesting to know whether it was his intention to proceed to England, as the captain, who was himself to return to Terceira, wished to forward despatches to Government, Count Saldanha returned the following answer: "Sir,—I am astonished at your question. What, Sir? you came to Terceira to make us prisoners; you have escorted us these eight days; you have prevented me fulfilling my orders; you have endangered the lives of so many faithful subjects of the most ancient allies of your sovereign; you have made us consume our scanty provisions; you have positively obliged me not to separate my vessels; you have used over me the discretion of a conquror, and, at the end of all this, you ask me where I am going! I do not know, Sir, where to; the only thing I know is, that I am going wherever you lead us, according to my positive assertions in every one of my official *letters." [*234] Captain Walpole answered: "Sir,—I am both surprised and confounded at the contents of your letter just received, after my repeatedly declaring to you in my correspondence that you were at liberty to pursue your own course and discretion. I have now to inform you, that your conduct has determined me to escort you no farther." The captain accordingly, having now brought them within five hundred miles of Scilly, and seeing them still pursuing a channel course, parted company, and returned to his station at Terceira, leaving them to go wheresoever they might think good. In February he stopped another vessel, with about forty Portuguese officers and men, entering Port Praya, which had likewise sailed from London, and, having supplied her with water and provisions, sent her off from the islands. Count Saldanha, and his squadron, instead of returning to England, proceeded to Brest.(*a*)

It is to be observed that Terceira alone of the Islands of the Azores, had not fallen into the possession of Miguel, but had remained faithful to the Queen of Portugal.

The act of the British Government produced a great excitement in England, and very animated debates in Parliament, in which the principles of International Law were laid down with great precision, and discussed with no ordinary ability.

The Government defended the instructions given to Captain Walpole,

(*a*) Annual Register for 1829, vol. lxxi. p. 186, from which this account is taken.

upon the ground that the refugees had fitted out a warlike armament in a British port: that the armament having been equipped under the disguise of a destination to Brazil, had not been prevented from sailing, as it otherwise would have been, out of the port of Plymouth; and that they were therefore bound, by the duties of Neutrality, to prevent by force an armament so equipped from disembarking, even in the harbour of the Queen of Portugal's dominions. The Government was supported [*235] by a majority *in both Houses of Parliament; but in the protest of the House of Lords, and in the resolutions of the House of Commons, the true principles of International Law are to be found.

CLX. The protest of the House of Lords is as follows:(b)—

"PROTEST—TERCEIRA.

"Because the forcible detention or interruption of the subjects of a belligerent State, upon the high seas, or within the legitimate jurisdiction of either of the Belligerents, by a Neutral, constitutes a direct breach of Neutrality, and is an obvious violation of the Law of Nations. And such an act of aggression, illegal and unjust at all times against a people with whom the interfering Power is not actually at war, assumed in this instance a yet more odious and ungenerous aspect, inasmuch as it was exercised against the unarmed subjects of a defenceless and friendly Sovereign, whose elevation and right to the Crown of Portugal had been earnestly recommended and openly recognized by his majesty, and whose actual residence in Great Britain, bespeaking confidence in the friendship and protection of the king, entitled both her and her subjects to especial favour and countenance, even if considerations of policy precluded his majesty's Government from enforcing her just pretensions by arms,

"VASSALL HOLLAND.	COWPER.
SOMERHILL.	MELBOURNE.
CARLISLE.	SEAFORD.
GRANVILLE.	KING.
WM. FREDERICK.	CALTHORPE.
RADNOR.	CARNARVON."(c)

[*236] *The Resolutions moved in the House of Commons were:(d)—

"That prior to the 12th of December, 1828, her majesty the Queen Donna Maria II., had been recognized by his majesty, and the other great Powers of Europe, to be legitimate Queen of Portugal; and that at the period above-named, the said Queen was residing in this country, and had been received by his majesty with the accustomed honours of her royal rank.

(b) Lord Clanricarde brought forward the resolutions in the House of Lords. The numbers on the division were: content present, 21; proxies, 10; total, 31. Non-content present, 61; proxies, 65; total, 126. Majority, 95.—Hansard's Parl. Deb. (N. S.,) vol. xxiii. pp. 738-81. Some Resolutions moved in March 23, 1830, by the Marquis of Clanricarde, in the House of Lords.

(c) Hansard's Parl. Deb. (1830,) vol. xxiii. pp. 780, 781.

(d) "The resolutions were moved in the House of Commons by Mr. Grant, and supported in a very elaborate and able speech by Dr. Phillimore. On the division the numbers were,—for the motion, 78; against it, 191. Majority, 113."—Hansard's Parl. Deb. (N. S.) vol. xxiv. pp. 126-214, (April 28, 1830.) Debates in the House of Commons on the Resolutions moved by Mr. Grant.

"That on the said 12th of December, the Island of Terceira, part of the dominions of the Queen of Portugal, was governed by authorities, civil and military, in allegiance to her majesty.

"That on the said 12th of December, instructions were given by the Lords Commissioners of the Admiralty, stating that a considerable number of Portuguese soldiers, and other foreigners, were about to sail in transports from Plymouth to Falmouth, and it is supposed they intend making an attack on Terceira, or other of the Western Isles; and his majesty having been pleased to command that a naval force should be immediately dispatched to interrupt any such attempt, you are hereby required and directed to take the ship and sloop named in the margin under your command, and to proceed with all practical expedition to Terceira; and having ascertained that you have succeeded in reaching that island before the transports alluded to, you will remain yourself at Angra or Praira, or cruising close to the island in the most advisable position for intercepting any vessels arriving off it; and you will detach the other ships as you shall deem best for preventing the aforesaid force from reaching any of the other islands.

*"That on the arrival of the naval force sent to Terceira, in pursuance of these instructions, the commanding officer found [*237] that island in possession of, and governed by, the authorities above-mentioned.

"That in the beginning of January, 1829, a number of Portuguese subjects or soldiers of her said majesty, voluntarily left this country, with a view of repairing to the said island, and that their departure and destination were known to his majesty's Government; that they appear to have embarked and sailed in unarmed merchant ships, to have been unaccompanied by any naval force, and themselves without any arms or ammunition of War.

"That these unarmed merchant ships and passengers were prevented by his majesty's naval forces, sent for the purpose, from entering the harbour of Porto Praira; and that after they had been fired into, and blood had been spilled, they were compelled, under the threat of the further use of force, again to proceed to sea, and warned to quit the neighbourhood of Terceira, and the rest of the Azores, but that they might proceed wherever else they might think proper.

"That the use of force in intercepting these unarmed vessels, and preventing them anchoring and landing their passengers in the harbour of Porto Praira, was a violation of the Sovereignty of the State to which the island of Terceira belonged; and that the further interference to compel those merchant ships or transports to quit the neighbourhood of the Azores was an assumption of jurisdiction upon the high seas, neither justified by the necessity of the case, nor sanctioned by the general Law of Nations."(*e*)

(*e*) Hansard's Parl. Deb. (1830,) vol. xxiv. pp. 126, 127.

[*238] *CHAPTER X.

THE RIGHTS AND DUTIES OF THE NEUTRAL.—1. WITH RESPECT TO COVERING ENEMY'S GOODS.

CLXI. THERE is no more unquestionable proposition of International Law, than the proposition that neutral States are entitled to carry on, *upon their own account*, a trade *with* a Belligerent.(*a*)

Once only has Great Britain attempted to enforce a contrary doctrine; viz., by the Treaty of Whitehall, contracted in 1689,(*b*) with Holland. An endeavour was then made by these two States to prevent *all* commerce with France.

Great Britain and Holland, by this act, were guilty of a grievous violation of International Law. They repented of it, however; and, to borrow the language of Vattel, who justly censures them, "les deux puissances maritimes, reconnoisant que les plaintes des deux couronnes (that is, of Denmark and Sweden) étoient bien fondées, leur firent justice."(*c*)

It is true, indeed, that upon two other occasions, besides the one just mentioned, Great Britain has been a party to measures, which had for [*239] their object, in one instance, to *prevent the Neutral from carrying on trade *generally*, and, in another instance, carrying on a *particular* trade, *on his own account*, with a Belligerent. Her conduct upon these two occasions does not appear to the writer of these pages to be defensible. It is to be observed, however, that Great Britain, upon both these occasions, rested, however erroneously, her defence upon a highly *exceptional* state of things, warranting, as she alleged, a temporary departure from what she admitted to be the general rules of law.

On one of these two occasions, Orders in Council were issued, and defended as being *retaliatory* to the Berlin and Milan Decrees. On the other occasion, a demand was made by Great Britain, in concert with Russia and Prussia, upon Denmark and Sweden, in 1793, to abstain from commerce in grain and provisions with revolutionary France.

The conduct of Great Britain upon these two occasions will presently be examined and discussed, when the Belligerent right of Blockade and the doctrine of Contraband come under consideration.

CLXII. The question whether Neutral States may extend the limits of their trade, during war, not *with*, but *on account of* a Belligerent, is of a wholly different character. This question really is, may the Neutral be carrier for one Belligerent, and thereby necessarily relieve him from

(*a*) Hübner (c. i. s. 1,) seems to think that it has been contended that Belligerents have claimed a right *to prevent Neutrals from trading with their adversaries*. This is a mistatement or a mistake.

(*b*) August 12.

(*c*) L. iii. s. 112, condemned by Lord Liverpool. Treatise on the Conduct of Great Britain, &c., p. 116, (vide post,) and in Letter on the Orders in Council, pp. 20, 1, by Phillimore, (1812.)

the pressure of the attack of the other Belligerent? The answer of General International Law, apart from specific Treaties, is clearly in the negative, whether that response be derived from reason, usage, or authority—whether from one or all of these "*dijudicationum fontes.*"(*d*)

Before we proceed to examine the evidence derived from these sources, it should be observed that this proposition, which, it has been just remarked, is negatived by the voice of International Law, practically resolves itself into two positions, viz:—

*1. That the ships of the Ally or Neutral may lawfully carry the goods of the Enemy, and that such goods will not be subject to capture or confiscation by a belligerent ship,—or in other words, that *free ships make free goods.* [*240]

2. That it is competent to Neutrals (*bello mediis*)—the essence of whose character is to assist neither Belligerent—to carry on, in time of war, a particular trade restrained, in time of peace, exclusively to the subjects of one Belligerent, and from which, in time of peace, they are rigorously prohibited by that Belligerent, but which that Belligerent now opens to them, because, under the pressure of his enemy's attack, he is no longer able to carry it on himself. Such trade, so closed in peace, and so opened in war, being,—

(α) The coasting; or,

(β) The colonial trade of the Belligerent.

CLXIII. First, as to the doctrine expressed in the *cantilena—free ships make free goods.* (Vaisseau franc, cargaison franche; frey Schiff, frey Gutt; verfallen Schiff, verfallen Gutt.) And here it will be expedient to borrow the language of the "Discourse on the Conduct of the Government of Great Britain towards Neutral Nations," written by Mr. Jenkinson in 1758, and deliberately republished by him when Earl of Liverpool, after the lapse of forty-three years, in 1801. This treatise has never been answered, and in reason and expression it is admirable; and it embodies the opinions of some of the ablest writers upon International Jurisprudence.

"But it will be asked," the author says, "from whence then arises the right which governments always enjoy of protecting the property of the enemy within the precincts of their own country? It is a consequence of the right of dominion: unless, therefore, their dominion extends over the ocean, the right of protection cannot there take place. Dominion gives a right of enacting laws, of establishing new jurisdictions, and of making all (whether its own subjects or those of other countries) submit to these who come within the pale of its power. Here, then, the trial which the *Law of Nations gives, is, as it were, superseded, and any proceedings upon it would of course be unjust; but as soon as you are out of the verge of this particular jurisdiction, the laws thereof, and the privileges which attend them, cease at once, and the general laws of nations again have their force. Here the property even of an ally hath no other protection than what these laws allowed it; being joined, therefore, to the goods of an enemy, it cannot [*241]

(*d*) Vide ante, vol. i. p. 14.

communicate its protection to these, since the same law which gives security to the first, allows you to seize and destroy the latter. These reasonings are exemplified by a common fact;—within the precincts of the dominion of any Government you are not at liberty to search the ships of any country: but is not this liberty universally and immemorially practised over all on the main sea? And wherefore is this search made, but that, according to the Law of Nations, all are here answerable for what they may convey?

"There is something analogous to this in most Civil Governments. Few countries are without some places which enjoy a right of protection from the general laws of the State, such as palaces, houses of religion, and the like; and this right generally arises from some pretence to an exclusive jurisdiction. As long, therefore, as any particular property remains within the verge of these, however justly it may be the object of the law, it is not subject to the power of it. But suppose it conveyed from hence into the public roads, beyond the precincts of this particular palace or convent, the protection it received would vanish at once, and the general laws of the community would fully then have force upon it. Thus the protection which governments can give within their dominions extends not to the sea; the ocean is the public road of the universe, the law of which is the Law of Nations, and all that pass thereon are subject to it without either privilege or exemption.

[*242] *"If this manner of reasoning should not clearly establish my point, I can appeal, in support of it, to the ablest writers on public law, who will be found to have decided the question in my favour.

"And, first, I will produce the testimony of that learned native of Delft, who wrote so nobly on the freedom of navigation to serve his ungrateful country. In one of the passages which are now before me, it is remarkable how much he labours to give the greatest extent to the rights of commerce, and yet, with all his laudable bias to this favourite point, he is clearly of opinion that the ship of a neutral nation cannot protect the property of an enemy; he manifestly implies,(*k*) that the vessels even of allies are subject to condemnation, on account of the enemy's property with which they are laden, when it appears that this property was put on board them with the consent of the owners of the vessels, but not otherwise. His words are, 'neque amicorum naves in prædam veniunt ob res hostiles, nisi ex consensu id factum sit dominorum navis;' and, producing several authorities in confirmation of this opinion, he afterwards adds, 'Alioqui res ipsæ solæ in prædam veniunt;' but if the enemy's property should be found laden on board a neutral vessel, without the connivance of the owner, in such a case, 'that property alone is lawful prize.' And speaking again, in another place, on this point, he says that if the wrong done me by my enemy is manifestly unjust, and that any one by affording him succours should encourage him in his enmity against me, 'jam non tantum civiliter tenebitur de damno, sed et criminaliter, ut IS, qui judici imminenti reum manifestum

(*k*) Grotius, De Jure Belli et Pacis, l. iii. c. vi. s. 6, in notis.

eximit.'(l) A fine and animated manner of expression, which shows how clear the opinion of this great author was upon the question.

"To the testimony of Grotius, I shall add that of Bynkershoek, a native also of Holland, and whose sentiments in *point of maritime jurisprudence Barbeyrac often prefers even to those of the [*243] former: and what makes his opinion at this time of great importance is, that he wrote principally for the use of the Courts and States of the United Provinces, and generally confirms what he advances by their judgments and resolutions. He speaks expressly in favour of my point. 'Ratione consultâ,'(m) says he, 'non sum qui videam, cur non liceret capere res hostiles, quamvis in navi amicâ repertas, id enim capio, quod hostium est, quodque jure belli victori cedit.' Upon attending to all the reasons which occur to me on this point, I cannot discover why it should not be lawful to take the property of an enemy, though found on board the ship of a friend; for I take that only which belongs to the enemy, and which, by the rules of War, is always ceded 'to the captor.' He then assigns his reason also for his opinion, that, as it is lawful to stop on the ocean any vessel, though she carries the colours of a neutral nation, and to examine, by her papers, to whom she really belongs, and, in case she appear to be the property of an enemy, to seize her as lawful prize, so he can see no cause why this rule should not extend to the effects which any ship may have on board; and if the goods of an enemy should be there concealed, why they also by the right of War should not be taken and condemned: he even declares it to be his opinion, that the owner of the neutral vessel should in such a case lose the price of the freight; a severity which the English Courts of Admiralty never practise, where some particular circumstance doth not require it.

"I shall add to these, the opinion of Albericus Gentilis,(n) esteemed the ablest writer on national jurisprudence, till Grotius bore the palm from him; and his fame in this respect was so great, that Philip III. of Spain appointed *him perpetual advocate for his subjects in all causes which they might have depending in the Courts of Eng- [*244] land. This author states a case where the Tuscans had taken the effects of the Turks, at that time their enemies, which they found on board some English ships; and he determines that the Turkish goods are legal prize, but that the captor must pay the freight to the English. 'Transeunt res,'(o) says he, 'cum suâ causâ, victor succedit in locum victi, tenetur Etruscus pro toto naulo.' The property of the enemy passeth to the captor, but all its consequences attend it; the goods justly belong to him, but he must pay to the freighter all which the enemy would have paid, to whose right he hath in every respect succeeded.

"To enter particularly into the sentiments of any more writers on this subject, would be equally tedious and unnecessary; it will be sufficient to mention the names alone of such others as are in favour of the

(l) Ibid., c. i. s. 4.
(m) Bynkershoek, Q. J. P., l. i. c. xiv.
(n) Vide ante, vol. i. pref. p. xxvi.
(o) Albericus Gentilis, De Advocatione Hispanica, c. xxviii.

question. Among these, I find Heineccius,(*p*) no less famed for his knowledge of laws, than for his learning in what are the best expositors of laws, the antiquities of Governments; Zouch,(*q*) who for many years presided in the Court of Admiralty of this kingdom; Voet,(*r*) Zuarius,(*s*) and Loccenius,(*t*) all of them writers of reputation, and whose opinions are universally relied on by all who treat on public jurisprudence."(*u*)

CLXIV. To the authority of Albericus Gentilis, Grotius, Zouch, [*245] Bynkershoek, Heineccius, Zuarius, Voet, and Loccenius,(*x*) *cited in this extract, may be added that of the Consolato del Mare, the earliest in point of date, but of admitted influence with all commercial nations; of Valin, Emerigon, Lord Stowell, Lord Grenville, and of the greatest statesmen and judges of the North American United States, honestly, and to their eternal credit, delivering their sentence upon this most important subject of International Practice and Law.(*y*) In opposition to this illustrious catalogue is to be set, before the nineteenth century, the works of Hübner(*z*) and Schlegel, avowedly written at a particular juncture and for a particular purpose.(*a*) The extraordinary inaccuracy of the citations of Hübner are incontrovertibly established by Ward.(*b*) Schlegel was overthrown by Croke;(*c*) and M. de Hautefeuille, the most recent champion of what are called neutral rights, admits that, with the exception of Hübner, *all the jurists* who have held this opinion that free ships make free goods, belong to the *nineteenth* century. To the catalogue of *negative* proofs should be added the work often referred to in these volumes, of the Abbé Mably. A portion of this work is dedicated to "Conventions Générales touchant la Navigation et le Commerce;" and herein he discusses the maritime rights and [*246] duties of States in great detail, and especially *notices the rule that the goods of friends shall partake of the character of the ship which covers them, and that both are condemnable in the Prize Court; but he is altogether silent as to the maxim "Free ships Free

(*p*) Heineccius de Navibus ob Vecturam vetitarum Mercium commissis, c. ii. s. 9.

(*q*) Zouch, de Judicio inter Gentes, pars. 2, s. 8, c. vi. Zouch wrote in 1650.

(*r*) Voet, De Jure Militari, c. v., n. 21.

(*s*) Zuarius, De Usu Maris, consil. xi. n. 6.

(*t*) Loccenius, De Jure Maritimo, l. ii. c. iv. n. 11. Loccenius wrote in 1651.

(*u*) Cabinet Library of scarce and celebrated Tracts (On the Conduct of the Government of Great Britain,) vol. i. p. 37.

(*x*) Mr. Manning justly remarks (Law of Nations, p. 219,) that a civilian in the service of Spain (Albericus Gentilis,) a Dutch jurist, resident in France (Grotius,) an English Judge of Admiralty (Zouch,) and a Swedish professor of jurisprudence (Loccenius,) combine to establish the law as declared in the Consolato del Mare. Vide ante, vol. i. p. 60, for the effect of such concurrent opinions.

(*y*) "If the principles of the British Prize Law go further, I am free to say, that I consider them as the law of this country."—8 Cranch's (American) Reports, p. 155. Brown v. United States, per Justice Story.

(*z*) Hübner published his work, Abhandlung von der Neutralität in Kriegszeiten, or De la Saisie des Bâtimens Neutres, ou du Droit qui ont les Nations belligérantes d'arrêter les Navires des Peuples amis, in 1759, at La Hogue.

(*a*) Vide ante, vol. i. p. 59, as to the value of the works of international jurists, with respect to whom this remark is not applicable.

(*b*) Ward, Treatise on the relative Rights, &c., pp. 48-59.

(*c*) See Remarks on Mr. Schlegel's Work upon the Visitation of Neutral Vessels under Convoy, by Dr. Croke. London, 1801.

goods" having been established by natural right, usage, or treaty.(*d*) There remain two more jurists deserving of mention upon this point, and who flourished previously to the nineteenth century,—Moser and Lampredi. Moser was Counsellor of State in Denmark, and one of the parties to the first armed Neutrality; in the first year of it, 1780,(*e*) he published the tenth volume of his essays on International Law, which contains his remarks upon neutral rights and duties. He was a writer who belonged to the school which expounded International Jurisprudence chiefly according to positive law, that is, according to usage and treaty.

His bias was of course in favour of the new doctrine of the armed neutrality. Nevertheless, his exposition of the law(*f*) is, that the property of one belligerent found by another belligerent in the ships or land-carriage of a Neutral is lawful prize to the captor, though the ship or carriage ought to be restored, and with payment of freight, to the Neutral.

Lampredi was a professor of jurisprudence at Pisa, and it was his interest to enlarge the privileges of Neutrals. He was, moreover, as he tells us, anxious that the great European nations should agree amongst themselves to establish the principle that "free ships make free goods." But he altogether repudiates the proposition that any such principle is a part of International Law; and he examines, and rejects as both illogical and historically untrue, the positions of Hübner.(*g*) The doctrine of later writers such as De *Martens and Klüber, is simply a repetition of the positions in Hübner, without any additional authority of reason or practice. [*247]

CLXV. The principles of International Law(*h*) upon this subject which have been incorporated into the Private Law of France, are to be found in the following sources:—

The *édits* of 1543, 1584, 1639, 1650.

The law as contained in the *Ordonnance de la Marine* of 1681.

The *réglement* of the 26th July, 1778.

The law of the 29th Nivôse, an VI.

The *arrêt consulaire* of the 29th Frimaire, an VIII.

The *déclaration* of the Emperor Napoleon the Third, of the 29th March, 1854.

CLXVI. By the *édit* of 1543 (Francis I.,) followed in this respect by those of 1584, of 1639, of 1650, it was decreed that *enemies' goods* found on board *neutral ships*, enured to the condemnation not only of

(*d*) Droit Publ. de l'Europe, tom. ii. pp. 459-488. Ward, 147.

(*e*) See an excellent notice of him in Manning, p. 239.

(*f*) Versuch, Band. xx. Kap. ii. §§ 33-34.

(*g*) "Non è vero che una truppa di uomini che navigano in alto mare, vale a dire in territorio non sottoposto alla giurisdizione di alcuno, debba riputarsi territorio di quella nazione di cui essi inalberano la bandiera; ed Hübner lo asserisce gratuitamente, e senza la minima prova."—Ed. Firenze, 1788, p. 159, c. xi.

(*h*) Ordonnance de la Marine et Traité des Prises par Valin. Traité des Prises Maritimes, dans lequel on a réfondu en partie le Traité du Valin, en l'appropriant à la Législation nouvelle, par MM. A. de Pistoye et Ch. Duverdy (Paris, 1855,) T. i. tit. vi. c. ii. Manning, Book III. ch. vi. Orders in Council on Trade during War, Art. vi.

the *goods* but of the *ship*—a severity equally unwarranted by practice or reason, and unknown to the *Consolato del Mare*, but which remained substantially engrafted in French jurisprudence till 1744. De Witt strove in vain (1658,) to procure the abrogation of this unjust decree. At the Peace of Nimeguen (1678,) the French pretended to concede to the Dutch the doctrine that "free ships make free goods;" but it was only pretence, for in 1681, two maxims of the severest kind, unknown to and unpractised by British courts, were distinctly(*i*) laid down in [*248] *the famous *Ordonnance de la Marine*, namely, the maxims (1.) that the enemy's goods confiscated the neutral ship; and (2.) that the Neutral's goods were seizable on board the enemy's ship. The *Conseil des Prises* never failed practically and judicially to enforce these maxims, and even during a period when France had made several treaties, in which the new doctrine, that the ship covered the cargo, was recognized. Nor was this all. In 1704 a Royal Ordonnance decreed: "S'il se trouvait sur des vaisseaux neutres des effets appartenants aux ennemis de Sa Majesté, *les vaisseaux et tout le chargement* seront de bonne prise." It was not till 1744 that an *ordonnance* provided that enemies' goods should be seizable on board neutral ships, but that the ship should be restored. On the 26th of July, 1778, that is, at the time when the new doctrine was most injurious to Great Britain in the war with her revolted American colonies, a *Réglement* appeared, by the first article of which privateers were forbidden to stop, or to bring into any of the ports of France, the ships of neutral powers: "Quand même ils sorteraient des ports ennemis, ou qu'ils y seraient destinés.(*k*)

Though this *réglement* did not in express terms inculcate the doctrine, *free ships make free goods*, it was interpreted to this effect by the author of the *édits*, and, what is far more important, it was so *judicially* interpreted by the *Conseil des Prises.* The law of the 29th Nivôse of the year VI. of the Republic abrogated this law, fixing the character of the ship by the character of the cargo; but the law of 1778 was restored by the Decree of the 29th of Frimaire, an VIII. of the Republic: and it is said by French writers of authority to have been the law of France at the breaking out of the present war.

[*249] CLXVII. This assertion rests of course upon the hypothesis *that the Berlin(*l*) and Milan(*m*) Decrees, and the other acts of wrongful might under the Empire of Napoleon the First, were exceptional and temporary, and in truth, for so it is tacitly admitted, indefensible. Such they unquestionably were. No jurist, no statesman will ever again defend the legality of what was at the time called the "Continental System."(*n*) Napoleon, by a false averment of fact and law, declared

(*i*) Tous navires qui se trouveront chargés d'effets appartenants à nos ennemis, et les marchandises de nos alliés qui se trouveront dans un navire ennemi, seront pareillement de bonne prise."—Art. vii.

(*k*) De Pist. et Duverdy, t. i. p. 344.

(*l*) 21st November, 1806.

(*m*) 17th December, 1807.

(*n*) Manning, p. 333. De Martens, V. Suppl. pp. 439-442. Edinburgh Review, Nos. V., XXI., XXIII., XXXVIII.

A Letter addressed to a Member of the House of Commons, on the Subject of the Notice given by Mr. Brougham, for a Motion respecting the Orders in Council

the British Islands to be in a state of blockade, and interdicted all intercourse with them on the part of neutral States. Here was a gross and shameless violation of International Law injuriously affecting two parties :—First, the Neutral; secondly, the Belligerent. In this position of affairs, what was the *duty* and what was the *right* of the Neutral? Clearly he had the *right* either of becoming a belligerent, or of resisting by force of arms the execution of an iniquitous decree. But if he submitted to it, and thereby practically assisted the execution of it, was he guilty of a breach of *duty* towards the other belligerents?

It may be difficult to answer this question abstractedly in the negative; but it must be remembered that this is not an abstract question, but, on the contrary, one clothed with circumstances, and that the true consideration is, with respect to each neutral State, whether the submission on his part was really the result of bitter necessity, making him, against his will, an accomplice of the wrong-doer, or whether, by any reasonable sacrifice or hazard, such an evil might have been averted.

*The British Government had recourse to retaliatory measures, which they sought to justify by alleging the acquiescence of [*250] neutrals in the illegal measures of Napoleon.

These retaliatory measures consisted of *Orders in Council*,(*n*) by which all places in France, in the countries of her allies, or of any other State which had submitted to Napoleon's restrictions, were to be considered as blockaded by British forces, and subjected to the restrictions and penalties of blockade.(*o*)

In these orders the British Government, in their turn, enunciated a proposition, false in fact, and bad in law.

It may be some palliation that the measure was retaliatory, but it is not, according to the rules of eternal right and justice, a defence. The truth is, that France was the first wrong-doer—Great Britain the second. These French Decrees and English Orders in Council will be the subject of some further discussion when the law of blockade comes under our consideration.

But before, even for the present, we leave this subject, the conduct of one great neutral State at this period deserves our best attention. The United States of North America passed, but not till the 1st of March, 1809,(*p*) what was called a "Non-intercourse Act;" by this act all friendly intercourse of American subjects with France and Great Britain was prohibited, so long as the new restrictive measures of these kingdoms remained in force.

It is to be lamented that this act was not passed earlier, when the first wrong was done by France; but even with this deduction from its merit,

and the License Trade, by Joseph Phillimore, LL.D., &c. (second edition, April, 1812.) Reflections on the Nature and Extent of the License Trade, by the same author. (Third edition, 1812.)

(*n*) Principal Orders, 7th January, 1807; 11th November, 1807. Annual Register for 1807, pp. 236-333. See also Debates in Parliament of this year.

(*o*) Manning, c. x., a very carefnl and accurate sketch of "the Continental System."

(*p*) In December, 1807, an embargo was laid on all shipping in American ports, and all vessels except ships of war were forbidden to leave the United States.

[*251] it ranks high in the history *of nations. It conveyed a just and dignified rebuke both to France and England, and it was worthy of the country which has contributed such valuable materials to the edifice of International Law.

CLXVIII. It may be well to notice in this place the opinion of a great English jurist upon the old French Ordonnances, which have been now under our consideration.

It was upon a question arising out of a warrant of neutrality in a policy of insurance, alleged to be falsified by a sentence of a French Court of Admiralty, grounded on the ordinances of France, that Sir W. Grant said: "These ordinances have been misunderstood; sometimes by the French Courts of Admiralty themselves, and sometimes by the courts in this country. Those in France considered these ordinances as making the law, and as binding on neutrals, and have, therefore, sometimes declared, in the same breath, that the property was neutral, and yet that it was liable to condemnation: whereas, all that was meant by these ordinances was, to lay down rules of decision conformable to what the lawyers and statesmen of the country understood to be the just principles of maritime law. When Louis XIV. published his famous ordinance of 1681, nobody thought that he was undertaking to legislate for Europe, merely because he collected together, and reduced into the shape of an ordinance, the principles of the marine law as then understood and received in France. I say, as understood in *France*, for although the Law of Nations ought to be the same in every country, yet, as the tribunals which administer that law are wholly independent of each other, it is impossible that some differences should not take place in the manner of interpreting and administering it in the different countries which acknowledge its authority. Whatever may have been since attempted, it was not, at the period now referred to, supposed that one State could make or alter the Law of Nations; but it was judged convenient to declare certain *principles of* [*252] *decision*, partly for the purpose of giving a uniform rule to their own courts, and partly for the *purpose of apprizing neutrals what that rule was. And it was truly observed at the bar, in the course of the argument, that it has been matter of complaint against us (how justly is another consideration,) that we have no code by which neutrals may learn how they may protect themselves against capture and condemnation. Now, this court, in this case, seems to us to have well and properly understood the effect of their own ordinances. They have not taken them as positive laws binding upon neutrals, but they refer to them as establishing *legitimate presumptions*, from which they are warranted to draw the conclusion which it is necessary for them to arrive at, before they are entitled to pronounce a sentence of condemnation."(*r*)

CLXIX. To return to the subject of neutral ships and enemy's goods. The authority of the North American United States—always great upon all questions of Public and International Law, and surely not the less so when speaking in opposition to their private interests—is also strongly in favour of the ancient Law of Nations upon this subject.

(*r*) Marshall on Insurances, 426. Wheaton's (Amer.) Reports, vol. v. p. 53, App.

At the breaking out of the war of the first French Revolution, the President of the North American United States thus honestly and courageously replied to the French Government:—

"I believe it cannot be doubted, but that by the general Law of Nations, the goods of a friend found in a vessel of an enemy are free; and the goods of an enemy found in the vessel of a friend are lawful prize. Upon this principle, I presume, the British armed vessels have taken the property of French citizens found in our vessels, in the cause above mentioned, and I confess I should be at a loss on what principle to reclaim it. It is true that sundry nations, desirous of avoiding the inconveniences of having their vessels stopped at sea, ransacked, carried into port, and *detained under pretence of having enemy's goods on board, have, in many instances, introduced by their *special Treaties* another principle between them, that enemy bottoms shall make enemy goods, and friendly bottoms friendly goods; a principle much less embarrassing to commerce, and equal to all parties in point of gain and loss; but this is altogether the effect of particular treaty, controlling, in special cases, the general principle of the Law of Nations, and therefore taking effect between such nations only as have so agreed to control it. England has generally determined to adhere to the rigorous principle, having in no instance, as far as I can recollect, agreed to the modification of letting the property of the goods follow that of the vessel, except in the single one of her treaty with France. We have adopted this modification in our treaties with France, the United Netherlands, and Prussia, and therefore, *as to them*, our vessels cover the goods of their enemies, and we lose our goods when in the vessels of their enemies. With England, Spain, Portugal, and Austria, we have no treaties, therefore we have nothing to oppose to their acting according to the general Law of Nations, that enemies goods are lawful prize, though found in the bottoms of a friend."(*s*) [*253]

CLXX. Again we find the same authority enforcing this doctrine in the following language:—"Another source of complaint with Mr. Genet has been, that the English take French goods out of American vessels, which, he says, is against the Law of Nations, and ought to be prevented by us. On the contrary, we suppose it to have been long an established principle of the Law of Nations, that the goods of a friend are free in an enemy's vessel, and an enemy's goods lawful prize in the vessel of a friend. The inconvenience of this principle, which subjects merchant vessels to *be stopped at sea, searched, ransacked, led out of their course, has induced several nations latterly to stipulate against it by Treaty, and to substitute another in its stead, that free bottoms shall make free goods, and enemy bottoms enemy goods; a rule equal to the other in point of loss and gain, but less oppressive to commerce. As far as it has been introduced, it depends on the Treaties stipulating it, and forms exceptions in special cases to the general operation of the Law of Nations. We have introduced it into our treaties [*254]

(*s*) Extract of a letter from Mr. Jefferson, Secretary of State in America, to Mr. Genet, Minister Plenipotentiary of France, dated Philadelphia, July 24, 1793. See State Papers, published by order of Congress in 1795, p. 71.

with France, Holland, and Prussia, and the French goods found by the latter nations in American bottoms are not made prize of. It is our wish to establish it with other nations. But this requires their consent also, as a work of time, and in the meanwhile they have a right to act on the general principle, without giving to us or to France cause of complaint."(t)

CLXXI. The two distinct propositions, that enemy's goods found on board a neutral ship may lawfully be seized as prize of war, and that the goods of a Neutral found on board of an enemy's vessel are to be restored, have also been explicitly incorporated into the jurisprudence of the United States, and declared by the Supreme Court to be founded on the Law of Nations. The rule, as it was observed by the Court, rested on the simple and intelligible principle, that War gave a full right to capture the goods of an enemy, but gave no right to capture the goods of a friend. The neutral flag constituted no protection to enemy's property, and the belligerent flag communicated no hostile character to neutral property. The character of the property depended upon the fact of ownership, and not upon the character of the vehicle in which it was found. Nations, indeed, had changed this simple and natural principle [*255] of public law, by conventions between themselves, *in whole or in part, as they believed it to be for their interest; but the one proposition, that free ships should make free goods, did not necessarily imply the converse proposition, that enemy's ships should make enemy's goods. If a Treaty established the one proposition, and was silent as to the other, the other stood precisely as if there had been no stipulation, and upon the ancient rule. The stipulation that neutral bottoms should make neutral goods, was a concession made by the Belligerent to the Neutral, and it gave to the neutral flag a capacity not given to it by the Law of Nations. On the other hand, the stipulation subjecting neutral property found in the vessel of an enemy to condemnation as prize of war, was a concession made by the Neutral to the Belligerent, and took from the Neutral a privilege which he possessed under the Law of Nations; but neither reason nor practice rendered the two concessions so indissoluble, that the one could not exist without the other.(u)

This position is indeed supported by the fact, that whenever, during the period now under discussion, the maxim, "free ships make free goods" was admitted in treaties, it was always accompanied by the reversal of the other provision of the Consolato, that neutral property on board enemy's ships was free.

CLXXII. Mr. Chancellor Kent, in his Commentaries, written long

(t) Extract of a letter from Mr. Jefferson, Secretary of State in America, to Mr. Morris, Minister Plenipotentiary of the United States, with the Republic of France, dated Philadelphia, 16th August, 1793. See State Papers, published by order of Congress in 1795, p. 82.

(u) The Nereide, 9 Cranch's (Amer.) Rep., pp. 388-395, 418. And so it was holden by Lord Stowell, in the case of the Cygnet, 2 Dodson's Ad. Rep., p. 299, that stipulation by Treaty "that free ships should make free goods," does not warrant such a certain conclusion, "that enemies' ships should make enemies' goods," as to induce the Court to decree salvage for the recapture of property, otherwise neutral, on board British ships. See also Ward, p. 145. Kent's Comm., vol. i. pp. 128-9.

after the great European War, which arose out of the French Revolution, observes: "Neutral ships do not afford protection to enemy's property, and it may be seized if found on board of a neutral vessel, beyond the limits of the neutral jurisdiction. This is," says this great *authority, "a clear and well-settled principle of the Law of Nations."(x) [*256]

And again, he observes, "During the whole course of the wars growing out of the French Revolution, the Government of the United States admitted the English rule to be valid, as the true and settled doctrine of International Law; and that enemy's property was liable to seizure on board of neutral ships, and to be confiscated as prize of war.(y) It has, however, been very usual in commercial treaties, to stipulate that free ships should make free goods, contraband of war always excepted; but such stipulations are to be considered as resting on conventional law merely, and as exceptions to the operation of the general rule, which every nation, not a party to the stipulation, is at perfect liberty to exact or surrender."

And again: "It has been the desire of our government to obtain the recognition of the fundamental principles consecrated by the Treaty with Prussia in 1785, relative to the perfect equality and reciprocity of commercial rights between nations; the abolition of private war upon the ocean, and the enlargement of the privileges of neutral commerce. The rule of public law, that the property of an enemy is liable to capture in the vessel of a friend, is now declared, on the part of our Government, to have no foundation in *natural right, and that the usage rests entirely on force. Though, the high seas are a general jurisdiction, common to all, yet each nation has a special jurisdiction over its own vessels; and all the maritime nations of modern Europe have, at times, acceded to the principle, that the property of an enemy should be protected in the vessel of a friend. No neutral nation, it is said, is bound to submit to the usage; and the Neutral may have yielded at one time to the usage, without sacrificing the right to vindicate by force the security of the neutral flag at another. The neutral right to cover enemy's property is conceded to be subject to this qualification—that a belligerent nation may justly refuse to Neutrals the benefit of this principle, unless it be conceded also by the enemy of the Belligerent to the same neutral flag.(a) [*257]

"But whatever may be the utility or reasonableness of the neutral claim under such a qualification, I should apprehend the belligerent right to be no longer an open question; and that the authority and usage on

(x) Mr. Chancellor Kent cites:—Grotius, l. iii. c. vi. s. 6. Heineccius De Nav. ob. Vect., c. ii. s. 9. Bynkershoek, Q. J. P., c. xiv. Loccennius, De Jure Mar. et Nav., B. II. c. iv. s. 2. Molloy, De Jure Maritimo, B. I. c. i. s. 18. Lampredi, ss. 10-11. Vattel, B. III. c. vii. s. 115. Answer to the Prussian Memorial, 1753.—Vide ante. Consulat de la Mer, par. 1012, 1013. Boucher, tom. ii. cc. 273-276, s. 1004.

(y) Mr. Jefferson's Letter to Mr. Genet, July 24, 1793. Mr. Pickering's Letter to Mr. Pinckney, January 16, 1797. Letter of Messrs. Pinckney, Marshall, and Gerry to the French Government, January 27, 1798.

(a) A Letter of Mr. Adams, Secretary of State, to Mr. Anderson, 27th May, 1823. President's Message to the Senate of 26th December, 1825, and to the House of Representatives, March 15, 1826.

which that right rests in Europe, and the long, explicit, and authoritative admission of it by this country, have concluded us from making it a subject of controversy; and that we are bound, in truth and justice, to submit to its regular exercise in every case, and with every belligerent power who does not freely renounce it."(b)

CLXXIII. We must now pass from the examination of the opinions of jurists and statesmen to a consideration of the Conventional or Positive Law of Nations; and this subject admits of the following divisions:—

[*258] 1. The Treaties from 1643 to the Treaty of Utretcht, 1713.
*2. From 1713 to 1780.
3. The first armed Neutrality in 1780.
4. The Treaties from 1780 to 1800.
5. The second armed Neutrality in 1800.
6. The Treaties from 1800 to 1854.
7. The war against Russia in 1854.

CLXXIV. We start in 1642, as Mr. Ward remarks,(c) with the fact, [*259] that for 400 years, no one treaty(d) between *Christian Powers had been made in derogation of the doctrine of the *Consolato del Mare*, while many treaties had been made in confirmation of it; and the doctrine had been even extended by the ordinances of particular nations

(b) Kent's Comm., vol. i. pp. 124, 126, 130. The best authorities upon the *history* of the origin and growth of the two propositions, that free ships make free goods, and enemy's ships enemy's goods, and of the armed Neutralities of 1780 and 1800, are to be found in the following authorities:—

1. Ward's Treatise on the Relative Rights and Duties of Belligerent and Neutral Powers. London, 1801.
2. Manning's Law of Nations.
3. Wheaton's History.
4. Wheaton's Elements.
5. Annual Register, vol. xxiii. (1780.)
6. State Papers, p. 345, &c., vol. xliii. (1801.)
7. History of Europe, ch. v. p. 76, &c.
8. State Papers, p. 234, &c.
9. Letters of Sulpicius (Lord Grenville) to the Editor of the Porcupine.
10. Dr. Croke's Answer to Professor Schlegel.
11. Diaries and Correspondence of James Harris, First Earl of Malmesbury. London, 1844.
12. Memorials and Correspondence of Charles James Fox, edited by Lord John Russell. London, 1853.
13. Die Politik der Seemächte und der Fortschritt des Völkerrechts, August 11, 1855 (Hamburg,) by Professor Würm.
14. Mémoire sur la Neutralité armée maritime. Par M. le comte de Goertz, ministre d'Etat de S. M. Prussienne, et son ministre à la diète de l'Empire. Paris, 1805.
15. Kent's Commentaries, vol. i. Lecture vi.
16. Secret History of the armed Neutrality, 1792. A translation of a former inaccurate edition of Goertz's work.
17, A collection of public Acts and Papers relating to the Principles of armed Neutrality, brought forward in the Years 1780, 1781. London, 1801. (Hatchard.)
18. Dohm, Materialen für die Statistik, Band iv.
19. Henning, Sammlung der Staatsschriften, Band xi.

(c) Pp. 126-7. See Manning, pp. 244-8, for the Conventions preceding 1642.

(d) A Treaty between France and the Porte, in 1604, stipulated that French property found on board the ships of the enemies of the Porte, should be restored to the owner; and that goods belonging to the enemies of the Porte, laden on French Vessels, should not be liable to seizure.—Dumont, vol. ii. p. 40.

to a degree of unjust severity. In 1642, therefore, the law of the *Consolato* was the acknowledged International Law of Europe.

CLXXV. The Treaty which, if its language alone were considered, might be deemed the first which introduced between Christian Powers the principle of free ships free goods, is the Treaty of Paris between France and Holland in 1646.

But eight years afterwards, when the interpretation of it was disputed, De Witt found, to his amazement, that the French construed this treaty as containing only a relaxation of the severe French *ordonnance* of 1584 (to which indeed the treaty referred,) and as only restoring things to the condition in which they were before the *ordonnance*, viz., that enemies' goods found on board a neutral ship, should not entail the confiscation of the ship and of the remainder of the cargo.(*e*)

The language of the third article of a treaty between France and the Hanse Towns in 1655, is identical with the language in the treaty just named. It must therefore receive a similar construction.

De Witt's own opinion as to the rights of Neutrals is clearly shown in the *placaart* published by Holland, 1652, in the approaching war against England. Not only are Dutch subjects fordidden to carry neutral property to enemies' ports, but neutral vessels found near the coasts of England, or of her colonies, though on their way to a neutral port, are to be condemned by the Dutch Prize Court if laden "en partie ou entièrement de quelque munition de guerre *ou de bouche*."(*f*)

*The Treaty of Upsal, between Cromwell and Christina (11th of April, 1654,) was remarkable, among other reasons, for having [*260] been negotiated under the auspices of Oxenstiern and Whitelock. It recognized the rights of commerce and of neutral independence to the fullest extent; but it contained this clause:—"Lest such free navigation should be prejudicial to the confederate that is at war, and *lest hostile goods and wares should be concealed under the disguise of friendship*, and for removing all *suspicion and fraud*, passports and certificates shall be provided."(*g*)

CLXXVI. A variety of treaties between commercial nations, and especially between England and the Northern Powers, occupy the next eight or nine years, *all* containing general stipulations about the freedom of commerce, *none* containing the maxim of free ships, free goods.(*h*)

One of these treaties was contracted between England and Holland in 1662;(*i*) and the absence of any assertion of the maxim is remarkable, for it appears that in December, 1654, the Dutch had made an earnest attempt to procure its assertion from Cromwell,(*k*) offering, in order to obtain it, to yield a right of neutrality, which, according to the best authorities, is founded on the law of nature; viz., the right that the goods

(*e*) Ward, 130.

(*f*) Vide post as to the contraband character of provisions, Ward, 133.

(*g*) Chalmer's Treaties, vol. i. pp. 25, 26. Ward, 134.

(*h*) The Treaties between (1.) Cromwell and the Dutch, 1654; (2.) Cromwell and France, 1655; (3.) Denmark and Sweden, 1658, and (4.) another, 1660; (5.) Sweden and Moscow, 1661; (6) England and Prussia, 1661; (7.) England and Denmark, 1661; and (8.) England and Holland, 1662. Vide post.

(*i*) Ward, 135.

(*k*) Thurloe, xxxiii.

of friends taken on board the ships of enemies should be restored. Cromwell refused the offer, and the treaty of England and Holland in 1654(*l*) was made upon the old rule, though each of the contracting parties had stipulated for the new principle in their treaties with other Powers.

[*261] *It was with an offer to concede this ancient acknowledged neutral right, that the Dutch proceeded to negotiate for the introduction of the new principle with Spain in 1650, Portugal in 1661, France in 1662.(*m*)

[*262] CLXXVII. It was in 1650(*n*) that the maxim of the flag *covering the cargo became, for the first time, the subject of the provisions of a Treaty between Christian Powers.

By the 13th and 14th articles of a Treaty concluded in that year between Holland and Spain, it is provided that the goods of the Enemy on board the Neutral shall be free, but it is *at the same time* provided that the goods of the Neutral found on board the Enemy shall be confiscated.(*o*) The two rights are thus set one against the other. The Dutch obtained the same terms from Portugal(*p*) in 1661, and from France in 1662. Mr. Ward shows how clearly and precisely the right

(*l*) Dumont, viii. 11-74. (*m*) Ward, 135.

(*n*) It is to the Dutch that must be ascribed, not only the introduction of the principle, "that free ships shall make free goods," in the first Treaty in which this was recognized between two Christian Powers, but their steadfastness of purpose in negotiating for this privilege was the occasion of its ever having been at all generally stipulated in Treaties between European Powers. The carrying trade, one great source of their commercial wealth and maritime importance, evidently had its security incalculably augmented, and its value proportionably heightened, by an arrangement which allowed the Dutch, when neutral, to carry on the commerce of all States at war, at a time when war was the rule, and peace the exception among the States of Europe. De Witt made the attainment of this privilege the constant aim of his negotiations in France and England. But he never thought of claiming this principle as a right; his whole aim was to obtain it as a privilege; and his negotiators endeavoured to procure this stipulation, by offering, in return, invariably, that the goods of Neutrals found on board the ships of enemies should be lawful prize to the captors."—Manning's Law of Nations, pp. 250-1.

Treaties in which it is stipulated that Free Ships make Free Goods, from 1650 to 1713, inclusive:—

(1.) Spain and Holland, (arts. xiii.-xiv.) 1650.
(2.) England and Portugal, (first English Treaty) 1654.—Dumont, vi. 11-84.
(3.) France and Spain, (Treaty of the Pyrenees) art. xix., 1659.—Schmauss, I. 690. Renewed at Aix-la-Chapelle, 1668.
(4.) Holland becomes a party to this Treaty in 1661.—Dumont, vi. 11-346.
(5.) Denmark and France, 1662.
(6.) France and Holland, 1662 (art. xxv.)
(7.) England and Spain, 1667.
(8.) Sweden and Holland, 1667.
(9.) England and Holland, 1667 (at Breda.) Renewed 1668.—Dumont, vii. 1, 49.
(10.) England and Holland, 1674 (art. viii.)—Schmauss, I. 979.
(11.) Sweden and Holland, 1675.—Dumont, vii. 1, 317.
(12.) France and England, 1677 (art. viii.)—Dumont, vii. 1, 329.
(13.) France and Holland, 1678 (art. xxii.) Treaty of Nimèguen.—Dumont, vii. 1, 359.
(14.) Sweden and Holland, 1679.—Dumont, vii. 1, 440.
(15.) Treaties between England and Holland in 1689.—Dumont, vii. 11, 236.
(16.) France and Holland, 1697 (art. xvii.,) at Ryswick.—Dumont, vii. 11, 389.
(17.) Treaties of Utrecht, 1713-1714. Dumont, viii. 1, 348-349, 379-380, 409.

(*o*) Manning, 248. Dumont, vi. 1, 571. (*p*) Vide ante.

of the Belligerent is set against the right of the Neutral by citing the 24th article of the Treaty of the 6th of August, 1661:—"Bona quælibet ac merces, sive ad dictos regem ordinesque spectabunt sive ad utrumvis populum, si navibus alterutri parti inimicis hostibusque creditæ ac in iis deprehensæ fuerint, non minus quam naves ipsæ in prædam cedant, ac fisco occupantium addicantur: merces vero ac res quæcunque ad partes utriuslibet hostem pertinentes, regis ordinumque jam dictorum aut utriuscunque populi navibus impositæ, in eas fisco nil juris esto, adeoque nec detineantur, nec possessoribus intervertantur."

This article is almost literally translated in the thirty-fifth article of the Treaty with France in April, 1662; and here we find the first introduction(*q*) of the maxim, "Free ships, free goods."

*CLXXVIII. Between the date of the last Treaty in 1662 and the year 1715, there appears to be eleven(*r*) Treaties contracted by seven States, in which the same or similar terms were employed;(*s*) and during the whole period from 1642 to the Treaty of Utrecht, 1713,(*t*) there appears to be about seventeen Treaties in which this stipulation is inserted. [*263]

CLXXIX. It was in 1654 that England made a Treaty with Portugal, in which, for the first time, England agreed that the flag should cover the cargo; but in the same Treaty it was stipulated that the goods of either party should be lawful prize if found on board the enemies of the other.(*u*)

CLXXX. There are some very important observations which apply *generally* to all the Treaties, in which, during this period, the new rule was introduced.

1st. In these Treaties the maxim is acknowledged on *particular* occasions between *particular* States, not unfrequently inserted by a State in one Treaty, and omitted by it in another made almost contemporaneously with different States.(*x*)

(*q*) Full *twenty* years (Mr. Ward observes) *after* the commencement assigned to it by Schlegel and Busch.—Ward, 136.

(*r*) Twelve, therefore, inclusive of the Treaty of 1662.

(*s*) Ward, 140.

(*t*) England and France (art. xvii.) Treaty of Utrecht, 1713. "And as it is now stipulated, concerning ships and goods, that free ships shall also give a freedom to goods, and that everything shall be deemed to be free and exempt which shall be found on board the ships belonging to the subjects of either of the confederates, although the whole lading, or any part thereof, should appertain to the enemies of either of their majesties, contraband goods being always excepted, on the discovery whereof, matters shall be managed according to the sense of the subsequent articles; it is also agreed, in like manner, that the same liberty be extended to persons who are on board a free ship, with this effect, that although they be enemies to both, or to either party, they are not to be taken out of that free ship, unless they are soldiers, and in actual service of the enemies."—Chalmer's Collect. of Treaties, vol. i. p. 402.

(*u*) Dumont, vi. 11, 84. The new maxim continued to be the subject of stipulations between England and Portugal till 1842, when it was abandoned, and *the old principle restored.*

(*x*) E. g. England and Portugal, in 1654, not *inserted*, and for the first time England and Holland, same year, *omitted*, and the Treaty of England and Sweden the next year, 1655, contains express provisions negativing the maxim. "Indeed," Mr. Manning truly says, "in pursuing this investigation chronologically, nothing can be more obvious than that nothing like a general principle was established by the Treaties of the seventeenth century."—Law of Nations, p. 250. Thus, again,

[*264] *2ndly. The maxim is never propounded or acknowledged as one of International law, as one of universal obligation, and therefore binding upon the community of States.(*y*)

3rdly. The maxim is during this period universally found in connection with the converse maxim that "enemies' ships make enemies' goods."

4thly. The internal and municipal regulations of one of the principal maritime countries, viz., France,(*z*) are directly at variance with the recognition of this maxim; such regulations being promulgated as *universally* applicable *after* Treaties recognizing the maxim in question had been entered into by France with *particular* States.

Thus while by her Treaties of 1655 with England and the Hanse Towns, with Spain in 1659, with England in 1677, France stipulated for the maxim that "the neutral flag covers the cargo" (*que le navire libre rend libre la cargaison,*) in the month of August, 1681, France [*265] put forth her justly famous *"*Ordonnance de la Marine*," in which not only is the opposite doctrine precisely and firmly established, but the harsher principle that the enemy's property found on board the neutral ship entails the condemnation both of the ship and the *neutral* or *friendly* cargo. An *arrêt du conseil* of the 26th October, 1692, orders this *ordonnance* to be rigorously executed. In 1704, a *réglement du roi* carried the principle yet farther. And, lastly, in 1744, a new *réglement* re-enacted and reinforced all the severities of the French law upon this subject.

CLXXXI. It has been said that the very diversity of the stipulation into which the same countries have entered upon this same subject, demonstrates the character of the stipulation, viz., that of a particular compact binding particular parties, not that of a general rule obligatory upon all. But there is also strong *negative* proof upon this point, and that of two kinds.

First, the proof derived from commercial Treaties containing different or contrary conditions, which appear to be, during the period from 1642 to 1715, seven in number.(*a*)

Holland and France, 1662, (art. xx.) maxim introduced. Holland and England, same year, not mentioned.

(*y*) The two propositions have, however, been judicially held to be distinct and independent of each other. The Cygnet, 2 Dodson's Adm. Rep., p. 299. The Nereide, 9 Cranch's (Amer.) Rep., p. 338, confirming the opinions of Lord Liverpool. Discourse on Neutral Nations, p. 20, and Mr. Ward, pp. 145-6.

(*z*) I had occasion to observe, in a former note, that M. de Hautefeuille is strongly prejudiced against England. It is fair to say, that in his endeavour to establish that *free ships free goods*, is a primitive law of nations, he does not spare France: "La France, je le dis avec peine, mais je dois le dire, a dépassée toutes les autres nations dans cette voie. Protectrice ardente et éclairée des droits des peuples dans les artes diplomatiques, elle maintient et promulgue des loix intérieures qui anéantissent ces droits dans leur parties les plus essentielles, et emploie la force brutale pour faire aux peuples neutres et indépendants l'application de ces loix iniques et étrangères."—Des Droits et des Devoirs des Nations Neutres, t. iii. p. 261.

(*a*) Ward, 127. France and Courland, 1643. Duke of C. prohibited from carrying any merchandize to enemies of France. Otherwise perfect freedom of commerce. Placaart, by De Witt, in war against England (1632.) Treaty of Upsal between England and Sweden, 11th April, 1654. Dumont, t. vi. pt. ii. p. 80.

"Lest such free navigation," says the article, "should be prejudicial to the con-

Secondly, the proof derived from commercial Treaties which are altogether silent as to the maxim, though their object and *character would require its enunciation if it were to be relied upon. These appear to be, speaking of the same interval, between thirty and forty in number.(*b*) [*266]

*CLXXXII. The interval between the Treaty of Utrecht and the first Armed Neutrality,(*c*) (1713-1780) does not show any material change in the progress or decline of the new maxim. [*267]

It appears to have been sometimes the subject of stipulation, but more frequently passed over silently in the commercial Treaties of this period. And this estimate proceeds upon the basis, that all Treaties, though containing no new reference to the particular maxim, but being confirmatory of former Treaties in which it has been mentioned, are to be counted as new Treaties upon the subject.

Mr. Ward, after a careful and elaborate analysis, reckons the number of the Treaties in which the observance of the principle is stipulated for, to amount to twenty; that is, however, by including all the Treaties which *confirm*(*d*) the Treaties of Utrecht, and also by reckoning each contract between any two parties at a *general* Treaty as a *separate* Treaty of itself;(*e*) and he computes the number in which no notice of the principle is taken, to be not less than thirty-four.

And then he proceeds to state this summary of the whole numerical argument—that is to say, the argument derivable from the number of Treaties which have contained the stipulation that "free ships make free goods," in the long interval between 1642 and 1780:(*f*)—"And thus,"

federate that is at war, *and lest hostile goods and wares should be concealed under the disguise of friendship*, and for removing all suspicion and fraud, passports and certificates shall be provided."—Chalmer's Treaties, vol. i. pp. 25-26. Confirmed by Treaties of 1656 between Cromwell and Gustavus.—Dumont, ib., p. 125. Treaty of 1661. Denmark and France, November, 1645. France and Holland, 1646 (as explained by Ward, 128-132.) England and Denmark, 1670 (art. xx.)

(*b*) Mr Ward enumerates:—Denmark and Holland, 1645. Denmark and Sweden, 1658. The same, 1660. Spain and Hanse Towns, 1647. Cromwell and Holland, 1654. Cromwell and Spain, 1655. Sweden and Moscow, 1661. England and Prussia, 1661. England and Sweden, 1661. England and Denmark, 1661. England and Holland, 1662. Sweden and France in 1661, 1662, 1663. Denmark and Holland, 1666. England and Denmark (at Breda,) 1669. England and Spain, (at Breda,) 1666 and 1670. England and Savoy, 1668. England and Sweden, 1666. The same, 1674. France and Sweden, 1672. Sweden and Holland (at Nimèguen.) Spain and Holland (at Brussels, before Nimèguen.) England and the Porte, 1675. England, Sweden, and Holland, 1700. Holland and Denmark, 1701. Dutch Treaties with Barbary States. Tripoli, 1703. Tunis, 1708. Portugal and Spain, 1701. England and Portugal, 1703. England and Dantzic, 1706. Between the same parties, at Utrecht, 1713. Algiers, 1712. Utrecht in 1713, and in the second Treaty of Utrecht, 1714, between England and Spain. The new Treaties Between 1715 and 1780, containing the maxim "Free ships make free goods:"—Russia and Holland, 1715 (arts. v. ix.)—Dumont, t. viii. pp. 470-1. Spain and Austria (Treaty of Vienna, 1725) (arts. viii.-x.)—Dumont, t. viii. p. 479. Prussia and Sweden, 1762. —De Martens, Rec., t. i. p. 39. France and Holland, 1778, (arts. xiv.-xxiii.—De Martens, t. ii. pp. 594-597.

(*c*) Ward, 148.

(*d*) E. g. Treaty of Aix-la Chapelle, 1748. Treaty of Paris, 1763.

(*e*) Ward, 150.

(*f*) I do not pledge myself to an exact agreement as to the numbers; but the

he says, "according to this enumeration, not less than thirty-four Treaties passed between the various maritime States, from the year 1715 to 1780, which take no notice of the principle before us; and these, in addition to thirty-one which were formed between 1642 and 1715, the epoch whence Schlegel, on the authority of Busch,(*g*) commences the series of
[*268] contrary *conventions, make in all no less than sixty-five. Seven are to be added, which, as we see, were actually adverse. And the maxim is, therefore, either positively denied, or totally unnoticed, by as many as seventy-two. Granting, then, what is not improbable (calculating upon the ground which has here been pursued,) that there are thirty-five Treaties favourable to the principle, what is to become of the proof that it forms so considerable a majority as, of necessity, to make the rule for all countries not bound? The power of thus binding them, our principles have wholly denied, into whatever proportion, on the one side or the other, the Treaties may be divided. But it seems not a little extraordinary, that so new a paradox should be started as law with such fragile foundations, even as to the fact."(*h*)

CLXXXIII. There are two Treaties contracted during this period, the provisions of which require especial attention.

First. The Treaty between France and Hamburg in 1769.

Secondly. The Treaty between France and Mecklenburg in 1779.

The Treaty between France and Hamburg of 1769,(*i*) contains the following provisions: Art. XIV. "Comme il est nécessaire que les bourgeois et habitans de la dite vilie sachent en quoi consiste la liberté de leur commerce et navigation, en temps de guerre, et qu'ils ayent une connoissance parfaite des risques qu'ils courront en faisant un commerce illicite et défendu, il a éte arrêté, que la confiscation aura lieu dans les cas suivans:

1. "Lorsque des effets, marchandises et denrées appartenants aux bourgeois et habitans de la dite ville, se trouveront chargés dans un navire ennemi, quand même ils ne seroient pas de contrebande.

2. "Lorsque des effets et marchandises de contrebande, ci-après
[*269] désignés, se trouveront chargés dans un navire de *la dite ville, et que leur destination sera d'être portés aux pays et places des ennemis de la courronne.

3. "Lorsque des effets, marchandises et denrées, appartenants aux ennemis du Roi, et servants à l'équipement, approvisionnement, ou sustentation de leurs troupes, ou de leurs auxiliaries, se trouveront chargés dans un navire de la dite ville. Pour ce qui regarde le navire même, et le reste du chargement, la décision se trouve à l'Article XVII. du présent Traité."

* * * * * *

Art. XVII. The next article, it will be seen, contains a mitigation of

inaccuracy, *if any*, is so slight as to be immaterial, and to leave the argument from the relative numbers unaffected.

(*g*) Vide ante, p. 262, note (*q*) as to the value of such authority.

(*h*) Ward, p. 152.

(*i*) Treaty between France and Hamburg, 1769.—De Martens, Rec. de Tr. t. i. p. 634.

the peculiar severity of the French law:—"Les marchandises de contrebande et les denrées de la qualité spécifiée par les articles précédens, et dans les cas y expliqués, ainsi que tous les effets, denrées et marchandises généralement quelconques, appartenantes aux ennemis du Roi, qui se trouveront sur les navires de la dite ville, seront confisquées; mais le navire, ni le reste du chargemont, ne seront pas sujets à confiscation."

CLXXXIV. The Treaty between France and Mecklenburg Schwerin, of September, 1799,(*k*) contains the following provisions:—Art. XI. "S'il survenoit une guerre entre le Roi et quelques Puissances autres que l'Empereur et l'Empire d'Allemagne, ce qu'à Dieu ne plaise, les vaisseaux de Sa. Maj. et ceux de ses sujets, armés en guerre ou autrement, ne pourront empêcher, arrêter ni retenir les navires de Mecklenbourg sous quelque prétexte que ce soit, quand même ils iroient dans les villes, ports, hâvres et autres lieux dépendans des Puissances ennemies de Sa Maj., si ce n'est dans les cas ci-après expliqués. Et pour prévenir, autant qu'il sera possible, tout commerce illicite en temps de guerre, le Sérénissime Duc s'engage, dans le cas d'une rupture entre la France et quelque Puissance autre que *l'Empereur et l'Empire d'Allemagne, de ne pas permettre, sous quelque prétexte que ce soit, que les sujets de S. A. Sérénissime fournissent aux ennemis du Roi aucunes armes, munitions de guerre, ni marchandises de contrebande ci-après désignées." [*270]

Art. XII. "Comme il est nécessaire que les sujets du Sérénissime Duc de Mecklenbourg sachent en quoi consiste la liberté de leur commerce et navigation en temps de guerre, et qu'ils ayent une connoissance parfaite des risques qu'ils courront en faisant commerce illicite et défendu, il a été arrêté que la confiscation aura lieu dans les cas suivans, savoir:—

1. "Lorsque des effets, marchandises, et denrées appartenans aux dits sujets Mecklenbourgeois, se trouveront chargés dans un navire ennemi, quand même ils no seroient pas de contrebande.

2. "Lorsque les effets et marchandises de contrebande, ci-après désignés, se trouveront chargés dans un navire du dit Duché, et que leur destination sera d'être portés aux pays et places des ennemis de la couronne.

3. "Lorsque des effets, marchandises, et denrées appartenans aux ennemis du Roi, et servant à l'equipement, approvisionnement ou sustentation de leurs troupes ou de leurs auxiliaries, se trouveront chargés dans un navire Mecklenbourgeois. Pour ce qui regarde le navire même et le reste du chargement, la décision se trouve à l'Art. XV. du présent Traité.

* * * * * * * *

Art. XXI. "Les vaisseaux Mecklenbourgeois sur lesquels il se trouvera des marchandises appartenantes aux ennemis de S. M., ne pourront être retenus, amenés, ni confisqués, non plus que le reste de leur cargaison; mais seulement les marchandises et denrées de la qualité de celles spé-

(*k*) Treaty of Commerce between France and Mechlenburg Schwerin, dated 18th September, 1779.—De Martens, Rec. de Tr., t. ii. p. 709.

cifiées par l'Art. XV., appartenantes aux ennemis de la France, seront confisquées, de même que les marchandises de contrebande. S. M. dérogeant à cet égard à tous usages et ordonnances à ce contraires, [*271] *même à celles des années 1536, 1584, et 1681, qui portent que la robe ennemie confisque la marchandise et le vaisseau ami. Bien entendu que si la partie du chargement qui se trouvera sujette à confiscation étoit si considerable, qu'elle ne pût être chargée sur le navire François, il sera permis en ce cas au capitaine du vaisseau François, de conduire le navire Mecklenbourgeois dans le plus proche port de France, pour être les denrées et marchandises sujettes à confiscation déchargées sans retardement, après quoi le navire de Mecklenburg avec le reste de sa cargaison, sera relâché et mis en pleine liberte."

CLXXXV. Whatever, therefore, may be the correct opinion upon the *abstract question*, the *historical facts* which have been set forth render it impossible to deny, as far as we have hitherto gone, first, that the maxim "free ships make free goods," was *never* part of *general* International Law; and, secondly, that, of all nations, France had, in her *general* policy, enforced the opposite doctrine with the greatest severity, and had even added to it the supposed converse proposition that "enemies' ships make enemies' goods." This severity appears to have been confined to France and Spain.(*l*)

The practice of the International tribunals, the Prize Courts of England, has invariably maintained a doctrine opposed to the severities of the French and Spanish law, and, therefore, when in 1640 France attempted to justify her confiscation of English neutral vessels by alleging a similar practice on the part of England, it was replied by the best civilian of the age, Sir Henry Martin, "that which is alleged by the French to be practised in our Courts of Admiralty, is absolutely denied; and neither the law nor the practice hath ever been here to confiscate the goods of friends for having enemies' goods among them: we are so far from doing any such act of injustice, that, when in time *of war we have met with any such prizes, the freight hath always [*272] been paid by the taker for those enemies' goods that he took, and those that belonged to friends were duly restored to them."(*m*)

On the 16th of August, 1689, a treaty between England and Holland contained stipulations introducing the French law on this subject in the war against France; here, as in the later war against French aggression, we find the evil and unjustifiable principle of meeting by retaliation the violations of Internation Law committed by the enemy, a principle which, however just towards him, is certainly unjust towards the Neutral. The morality of the state and the individual is the same in this as in other respects: the injured party, whether it be a state or an individual, must not relieve itself from the act of the wrongdoer at the expense of a third and innocent party.(*n*)

CLXXXVI. The year 1780 opens a new chapter in the history of the intercourse of nations,—

(*l*) Valin, Ord. de la Marine, l. iii. t. ix. art. vii.

(*m*) Lord Liverpool's Discourse, p. 24. Vide ante, account of this work.

(*n*) Vide ante, vol. i. ch. xxxiv. p. 36.

"Longa est injuria, longæ
"Ambages, sed summa sequar fastigia rerum."(o)

In 1780, an accident brought into the field an unexpected and remarkable champion of the new doctrine—a then semi-barbarous Power of gigantic dimensions, touching at one extremity the farthest bounds of civilization, but gradually developing at the other extremity forces and resources in the European hemisphere which made her opinion weigh heavily in the scale into which it was thrown. The vast empire of Russia was governed at this time by Catherine II. Under her auspices arose the first of the associations known in history by the name of *the Two Armed Neutralities.*

It is rather the province of the historian than of the jurist to trace the origin and lay bare the causes of this event. But it must be observed that the memoir of Count *Goertz,(p) the diary of Lord Malmesbury, the records of De Flassan,(q) and of Von Dohm,(r) establish, beyond the possibility of a reasonable doubt, three things respecting it. [*273] First, that it was the result of a cabinet intrigue (which meant nothing less than the welfare of nations,) availing itself of an accident.(s) Secondly, that originally the Empress had fully adopted and meant to carry into effect the principles of International Law contended for by England. Thirdly, that to the last she never clearly understood what she had done, or why she had given offence to Great Britain.(t) Count Panin was Chancellor of the Empire; Prince Potemkin the reigning favourite of the Empress. England, in her war with her Colonies, France and Spain, sought aid in an alliance with Russia. Potemkin favoured, Panin opposed it. The seizure of two Russian ships by Spain at this time incensed the Empress; Potemkin availed himself of her wrath to induce her to order the equipment of a fleet, destined to co-operate with England against Spain, if redress were denied. Panin discovered both that the fleet was ordered, and its destination. He saw in these facts, however, the opportunity *of crushing his rival, and he seized it with great adroitness. [*274] He applauded the determination of the Empress, but artfully suggested that an occasion now presented itself to her of appearing in the magnificent character of the lawgiver of the seas,

(o) Æn. I. 341-2.

(p) Mémoire sur la Neutralité armée, p. 104.

(q) Hist. Gén. et Raisonée de la Dipl. Française, t. vii. p. 266.

(r) Denkwürdigkeiten meiner Zeit, Band II. 100.

(s) L'Impératrice Marie Thérèse, s'extasiant sur le rare bonheur de Cathérine, tint au Baron de Breteuil un discours qui confirme ce que rapporte le Baron de Goertz. "Il n'y a pas," lui dit elle, à l'occasion de la neutralité armée, "il n'y a pas jusqu'à ses vues les plus mal combinées, qui ne tournent à son profit et à sa gloire; car vous savez sans doute que la déclaration qu'elle vient de faire pour sa neutralité maritime, avait d'abord été arrêtée dans les termes les plus favorables à l'Angleterre. Cet ouvrage avait été fait par la seule influence de M. le Prince Potemkin, et à l'insu de M. le Comte de Panin; et cette déclaration, inspirée par l'Angleterre, était au moment de paraître, lorsque M. de Panin, qui en a été instruit, a trouvé moyen de la faire entièrement changer, et de la tourner absolument en votre faveur."—De Flassan, t. vii. p. 272, note (1).

(t) Professor Wurm (the author of so many well-known tracts on maritime law) tells us that Catherine said to Lord Malmesbury (18th December, 1783,) "Mais quel mal vous fait cette *neutralité* armée, ou plutôt, *nullité* armée?"—Die Politik der Seemächte, p. 314. (Hamburg, 1855.)

and the protectress of Neutrals, and at the same time of avenging the injury to herself. The flattery was so specious and so well applied, that the Empress placed herself in the hands of her wily and successful courtier. Panin drew up a manifesto of neutral rights, and the Empress communicated it to France, Spain, and England.

Seldom has a more important event grown from a more despicable origin. It is not, perhaps, with any unnatural reluctance, that we hear in these days that Europe acquired for the first time, towards the end of the last century, an acquaintance with the true doctrines of International Justice, from a quarrel between the unprincipled courtiers of a vain profligate woman, whom the inscrutable decrees of Providence had permitted to be the absolute sovereign of an half-civilized empire.

CLXXXVII. The propositions of the new Russian International Code, were as follows :(*u*)—

I. That neutral ships might freely trade from port to port, and upon the coasts of nations at war.

II. That the property of the subjects of belligerent Powers should be free on board neutral ships, excepting goods that were contraband.

III. That with regard to contraband goods, the Empress bound herself by what was contained in the Arts. X. and XI.(*x*) of her treaty with Great Britain, extending these obligations to all belligerent Powers.

[*275] *IV. That to determine what characterises a blockaded port, this term shall be confined to places where there is an evident danger in entering, from the arrangements of the Power which is attacking, with vessels stationary and sufficiently close.

V. That these principles shall serve for a rule in the proceedings and judgments on the legality of prizes.

CLXXXVIII. France, Spain, Holland, Denmark, Sweden, the two latter in direct violation of the faith of treaties, gave in their adherence to Russia. At a later period, Prussia and the Emperor of Germany joined the league. Still later, Portugal and the Two Sicilies acceded to the Russian confederacy.

CLXXXIX. As to France, we have seen what were the provisions of her treaty *seven months* before she joined the Russian League.

As to Spain, in the year 1780, *one month* before her accession, she had issued the severest ordinances against neutrals, ordering the seizure of vessels which carried enemies' *goods* or provisions.(*y*)

To Denmark and Sweden, Great Britain replied by a vain appeal to the faith of Treaties. Yet how did the matter stand between England and Denmark ?(*z*)

In 1670, a solemn treaty of commerce was concluded between Eng-

(*u*) De Martens, Rec.. iii. p. 158. Actes relatifs à la Neutralité armée.

(*x*) "L'Article XI. du Traité de 1766 désigne les seuls objets suivans comme étant de contrebande :—'les canons, mortiers, armes à feu, pistolets, bombes, grénades, boulets, balles, fusils, pierres à feu, mêches, poudre, salpêtre, soufre, cuirasses, piques, épés, ceinturons, poches à cartouche, selles et brides, au-delà de ce qui est nécessaire pour la provision du vaisseau.'"—De Flassan, vii. p. 273, (note 1.)

(*y*) De Martens, iv. 268. Ward, 163.

(*z*) Ward, 155, whose concise and clear statement I have transplanted into my text.

land and Denmark, the third article of which contained the definition of contraband; but in which, however, the words, "other necessaries for the use of war," were thought too indefinite. To remedy this, a convention was made to put the matter out of doubt, by an article to be substituted in the place of the other; by which contraband was declared to include the very subjects so often disputed,—ship-timber, tar, pitch, rosin, sheet-copper, hemp, sails, and cordage. This was signed on the 4th July, 1780. On the *8th was signed that declaration of the [*276] Armed Neutrality, which had long been concerting between its original members; and in which the King of Denmark declares, that he understands nothing under contraband, except the articles specified in the third article of the treaty of 1670.

CXC. To Russia, Great Britain made answer as to the *general* law, that "his majesty hath acted towards friendly and neutral Powers according to their own procedure respecting Great Britain, and conformably to the clearest principles generally acknowledged as the Law of Nations, being the only law between powers where no treaties subsist, and agreeably to the tenor of his different engagements with other powers, whose engagements have altered this primitive law, by mutual stipulations proportioned to the will and convenience of the contracting parties." She added, "that precise orders had been given respecting the flag and commerce of Russia, according to the laws of nations and the tenor of our treaty of commerce; that it was to be presumed that no irregularity would happen, but that otherwise redress would be afforded by our Courts of Admiralty, judging according to the Laws of Nations, in so equitable a manner, that her imperial majesty shall be perfectly satisfied, and acknowledge a like spirit of justice which she herself possesses."(*a*)

CXCI. But the most remarkable fact connected with the Armed Neutrality of 1780, remains to be stated, namely, that *every one* of the powers composing this hallowed league for the maintenance of International Justice upon the principles of the Russian edict, departed from the obligation which they had contracted as *Neutrals* as soon as they became *Belligerents*, and returned without shame or hesitation to the practice of the ancient law.

In the meantime it must be borne in mind that though this Russian convention professed to contain an exposition of the principles of universal justice, it took care to provide *that its stipulations should be [*277] binding only during the present war; it held out, indeed, the prospect of future arrangements in time of peace, and Sweden was particularly anxious to propose a congress in which the question should be finally settled. We shall see what course she pursued a few years afterwards.

CXCII. The dispute between Great Britain and the Russian League, was not arranged when the war was ended. But the Treaty of Versailles, 1783, between Great Britain, France, and Spain, confirmed the Treaty of Utrecht, and therefore between these contracting powers established the principle of "free ships free goods."

The treaty between Prussia and the United States of North America, 1785, stipulates that enemies' goods shall be free on board friends' ships,

(*a*) Annual Reg. for 1780. (115.)

but *not* that friends' goods shall be seizable on board enemies' ships.(*b*) France and Holland renewed in 1785 the articles of the Treaty of Utrecht,(*c*) which stipulated that *free ships make free goods*, and *enemies' ships enemies' goods*. In the same year, Austria and Russia(*d*) renewed the provisions of the Armed Neutrality on this subject.

In the great commercial treaty of 26th September, 1786, negotiated by Mr. Eden, under the auspices of Mr. Pitt, with France, Great Britain engaged that "free ships should make free goods, and enemies' ships enemies' goods."(*e*)

In the debate which took place in Parliament upon the preliminaries of this treaty, it was objected that they contained a recognition by Great Britain of the doctrines of the Armed Neutrality. To this it was answered that the provisions of this treaty were only intended to apply to a case, in itself improbable, that either of the contracting parties should be engaged in a maritime war, whilst the other should remain
[*278] *neutral, and that these provisions were not intended to furnish a general rule to be observed towards other nations.(*f*)

This authoritative interpretation of the treaty is remarkable and important, and appears to have been entirely overlooked by those(*g*) who have cited the treaty as evidence that Great Britain intended to introduce the general principle of *free ships free goods*, into the International Code of Maritime Law.

CXCIII. The United States of North America, the new Power which had firmly established itself before the Treaty of Versailles was made in 1783, and which carried the doctrines of International Law into a new hemisphere, incorporated the two maxims, *free ships free goods*, and *enemies' ships enemies' goods*, into her treaties with Holland in 1782, with Sweden in 1783, and with Prussia in 1785.(*h*)

CXCIV. The benevolent and philosophical Franklin introduced into this last-mentioned treaty various stipulations, having for their object to mitigate the necessary horrors of war, abolishing privateering, protecting fishermen and unfortified cities, and providing for the good treatment of prisoners.(*i*) The interval between the two Armed Neutralities is still more remarkable for the appearance of two celebrated works on the rights and duties of Neutrals by two Italian jurists, Galiani and Lampredi. Galiani was, as he tells us, ordered to write his book as fast as possible, to defend the conduct of the King of the Two Sicilies in adhering to the Russian League. He published his work at Naples in 1782.(*k*) In 1788, Lampredi published his work at Florence.(*l*) He expressed his

(*b*) De Martens, iv. 42. (*c*) Ib., 68. (*d*) Ib., 76.

(*e*) Arts. XX., XXIX. Chalmers, vol. i. pp. 530-536.

(*f*) Parliamentary History of England, vol, xxvi. p. 563.

(*g*) Edinburgh Review for July, 1854, p. 214.

(*h*) Elliot's (American) Diplomatic Code, I., pp. 134-168, 334.

(*i*) Wheaton's Hist., p. 308. Vide ante, p. 8, sec. iv.

(*k*) Dei Doveri dei Principi neutrali verso i Principi guerregianti, e di questi verso i Principi neutrali. Napoli, 4to., 1782.

(*l*) Del Commercio dei Popoli neutrali in Tempo di Guerra. Firenze. He had previously published Juris Publici Universalis, sive Juris Naturæ et Gentium Theoremata. Liburni, vol. iii., 1776-8. Mr. Wheaton considers him to be a much abler writer than Galiani.—Wheaton's Hist., 310.

conclusion, founded upon *very learned premises, that there was no comparison between the relative importance of the rights of [*279] the Belligerent and of the Neutral, assuming them to be in collision upon the question of enemies goods on board neutral ships. For what, after all (he says,) is the injury sustained by the Neutral from the capture of his vessel laden with enemies' goods, if his vessel be restored, and he, as the treaties and usage of nations require, be paid his freight? Merely the delay and the possible loss of a return voyage. On the other hand, if the right of the Belligerent be forgone, the fatal consequence may ensue that the entire commerce of the enemy may be carried on under the neutral flag, and thus escape from capture, to the great injury of the Belligerent, the main object of whose maritime warfare is to destroy the commercial resources and revenues of his enemy, the sinews of his naval power.

CXCV. It has been said(*m*) that *all* the members of the Armed Neutrality abandoned, upon the very next opportunity of their becoming *Belligerents*, the creed which they had sought to enforce by arms when *Neutrals*. The forward zeal of Sweden in favour of this creed has been noticed. Let us now, having careful reference to dates, look at the conduct of those States.

The Armed Neutrality was in 1780. The Peace of Versailles was in 1783. The next war, in which Sweden was a *Belligerent*, happened in 1788: it was a war against Russia. Her first act was absolutely to renounce the principle of free ships free goods, which she had contended for so furiously as a *Neutral*. "It would be too gross an affront" (Mr. Ward observes) "to her justice to suppose that she has two lines of conduct,—one as Neutral, the other as Belligerent: we *will therefore rather suppose that she saw the errors into which the [*280] aspiring genius of Russia, or her own impulses, heightened, perhaps, by the incidental injuries inseparable from war, had betrayed her; and that she thought, as her Treaties bade her think, that the principle before us could only be matter of convention."(*n*)

Such was the conduct of *Sweden*, practically affirming that this supposed right of the Neutral was inconsistent with the clear right of the Belligerent. As to *Denmark*, we have seen that in the year of the Armed Neutrality, 1780, she signed a Treaty against the principle, *free ships make free goods*, on the 4th of July, and in favour of it on the 8th. By the Convention of 1794, *Denmark* and *Sweden renewed* the *renunciation* of the maxim, *free ships make free goods*, which they had made in their Treaties about one hundred years before. These Treaties had never been abrogated, and by this convention these States declared that they claimed no advantages other than those which were clearly founded upon their respective Treaties with the different Powers at war. *Denmark*, moreover, especially confirmed her ancient Treaty, referring, in her instructions to her merchants,(*o*) to her Treaty of 1670 with England, in which it was stipulated that there should be a certificate amongst the ship's papers to prove *that the cargo belonged to a neutral*

(*m*) Vide ante, p. 275. (*n*) Ward, pp. 164-5. (*o*) Feb. 22, 1793.

Power, and ordered her magistrates in 1793 to deliver such necessary certificates.

But what did the author of the League(*p*) itself do? Why, on the 8th of February, 1793, Russia herself declared that her Treaty with France of 1786, in which the *two* principles which have been so much discussed were contained, were no longer obligatory until the restoration of order in France.(*q*) She went much farther, however, and renewed in the same year her Treaty with England of 1766, the stipulations of [*281] *which were, that neutral commerce should be carried on "according to the principles and rules of the Law of Nations generally recognized."(*r*)

Nor did she even stop here, but on the same day entered into another Treaty with Great Britain, by which the two Powers engaged to prevent Neutrals "from giving, on this occasion of common concern to every civilized State, any protection whatever, directly or indirectly, in consequence of their Neutrality, to the commerce or property of the French on the sea or in the ports of France."(*s*)

In the very same year, Great Britain concluded Treaties containing articles to the same effect with Spain,(*t*) with Russia,(*u*) and with Austria.(*x*)

France, the most important member of the Russian League, was not the last to throw overboard the doctrines for the propagation of which it was established.

On the 9th of May, 1793,(*y*) a decree of the National Convention declared that enemies' good on board neutral vessels were good prize; that the vessels were to be released, and freight paid to the captors on the 21st of March, 1797.(*z*)

The Executive Directory issued a similar decree.

CXCVI. So much for the fruits of the first Armed Neutrality. The soundness of the principle, and the faith of the engagements, were wafted, with the first breath of war, to those winds which bore the fleets and privateers of the *Neutral* League, now become *Belligerent*, to execute not the new but the ancient maritime International Law.

"Atque îdem venti vela fidemque ferunt."(*a*)

[*282] *CXCVII. The conduct of the United States of North America with respect to this subject, deserves especial notice. This nation had been the cause of that war during the course of which appeared the first Armed Neutrality. It was at least her apparent interest to sanction the new law. Still more was she animated to do so by her resentment towards Great Britain and by gratitude to France; but her conduct with respect to this matter has been, under the most trying circumstances, marked not only by perfect consistency, but by preference for duty and right over interest and the expediency of the moment.

The Treaty of the United States with France in 1780 was founded

(*p*) Manning, p. 272. (*q*) De Martens, v. 382. (*r*) De Martens, 432.
(*s*) Ib., v. 440. (*t*) Ib., 447. (*u*) Ib., 485. (*x*) Ib. 489.
(*y*) Ib., 382. (*z*) Ib., 393. (*a*) Ovid, Ev. vii.

upon the stipulations of 1778, by which this Power, as far as her own predilections and private wishes were concerned, was at all times ready to abide.

In her Treaty with England of 1795,(*b*) these predilections and wishes, which had found their legitimate issue in particular conventions, were abandoned, and their place was taken by the ancient general law. By the seventeenth article of this Treaty, the United States agreed that enemies' property on board her vessels should be confiscated, the ship and the remainder of the cargo being allowed to depart without hindrance; but that, on just suspicion, the vessels themselves might be detained and carried into the nearest port for the purpose of examining and adjudicating upon them.

CXCVIII. It was of course perfectly competent to this Power to make these two different Treaties with different States, and, to her enduring honour, she adhered to both under circumstances of some difficulty.

In 1798, France promulgated(*c*) a new doctrine to the United States, viz., that as this Power was bound to treat France as the *most favoured* nation, it was also bound not to allow French property on board American ships to be seized by British cruisers, while they prevented the seizure of *British property in the same situation by the French. [*283] This demand was refused, and France threatened war in consequence. It is most truly said by Mr. Ward,(*d*) that the answers of the United States to France were models of dignified and convincing argument.

"Before the Treaty with Great Britain" (it is represented in one of these notes,) "the Treaty with France existed. It follows, then, that the rights of England being neither diminished nor increased by compact, remained perfectly in their natural state, which is to seize enemies' property wherever found; and this is the received and allowed practice of all nations, where no Treaty has intervened." A *new Law of Nations*, it is pretended, was introduced by the Armed Neutrality; but who were the parties, and what was their object? "The compact was in its own nature confined, with respect to object and duration. *It did not purport to change, nor could it change permanently and universally the rights of nations not becoming parties to it.* The desire of establishing universally the principle, that neutral bottoms shall make neutral goods, is perhaps felt by no nation on earth more strongly than by the United States. Perhaps no nation is more deeply interested in its establishment; but the wish to establish a principle is essentially different from a determination that it is already established. The interests of the United States could not fail to produce the wish; their duty forbids them to indulge it, when decided on a mere right."(*e*)

"The complaints of the French," said another note of the American Minister to his President,(*f*) "had reference, amongst other things, to the abandonment by the Americans of their neutral rights, *in not main-*

(*b*) De Martens, v. 672. (*c*) Ward, 167. (*d*) Ward, 167.
(*e*) Ib., 168, citing Collection of Acts, 198, &c.
(*f*) Mr. Pinkney to General Washington.

taining the pretended principles of the modern Law of Nations, that [*284] free ships make *free goods; *and that timber and naval stores are not contraband of war.*

"The necessity, however, for the strong and express stipulations of the Armed Neutrality itself by all the various Powers which joined it, showed" (as the note went on to state) "that those maxims were not in themselves law, but merely the stipulations of compact; that, by the real law, belligerents had a right to seize the property of enemies on board the ships of friends; that Treaties alone could oblige them to renounce it; and that America, therefore, could not be accused of partiality to Great Britain, *because she did not compel her to renounce it.*"(*g*)

CXCIX. In the year 1795, the United States made a Treaty with Spain, including a stipulation the reverse of that contained in their Treaty with England in the same year. In the Spanish Treaty it is stipulated, that cargoes in neutral ships shall be free, no distinction being made as to who are the proprietors of the merchandises.(*h*)

In 1799, the United States entered into a Treaty with Prussia, by the 12th article of which they declared, that as experience showed that the maxim, free ships make free goods, had not been respected in any of the wars since 1785, Prussia and the United States should, in a future time of peace, either separately between themselves, or jointly with other Powers, concert measures for the future condition of neutral commerce in time of war; meanwhile, these two Powers agree that their ships shall conduct themselves as favourably towards the merchant vessels of the Neutrals as the cause of the war then existing might permit, observing the general rules of International Law.(*i*)

But in the next year, 1800, the old French doctrine of free ships free [*285] goods, enemy's ships enemy's goods, was *incorporated into a Treaty between France and the United States.(*k*)

During the war which commenced between the United States and Great Britain in 1812, the Prize Court of the former uniformly enforced the generally acknowledged rule of International Law, that enemies' goods in neutral vessels are liable to capture and confiscation, except as to such Powers with whom the American Government had stipulated, by subsisting Treaties, the contrary rule, that free ships should make free goods.(*l*)

CC. In the Treaty of Commerce of 1797, between Russia and England, the article which relates to neutral commerce(*m*) is silent on the question, and therefore the old law remained unchanged.

In the next year (1798,) Russia entered into a Treaty with Portugal, in which it was stipulated, that *free ships shall make free goods,* but also that *neutral goods in an enemy's ship should be confiscated.*(*n*)

CCI. The first Armed Neutrality(*o*) took its rise, as we have seen, in the ignoble rivalship of contending courtiers, and the vanity of a disso-

(*g*) State Papers, 5, 281, 286.
(*h*) Art. XV. De Martens, vi. 154.
(*i*) Ib., vi. 676.
(*k*) De Martens, vii. 103.—Arts. XIV., XV.
(*l*) Wheaton's Elem., p. 580.—Ed. Lawrence, 1855.
(*m*) Art. X., Ib., 362.
(*n*) Art. XXIV., Ib., 550.
(*o*) Manning, p. 274.

lute empress of Russia. The second Armed Neutrality had not a more distinguished origin; it was the offspring of a mad emperor of the same kingdom.

The question of *Convoy* is connected with the *Right of Search*, and the discussion of it belongs to a subsequent chapter; but it should be mentioned here, as having excited some irritation in the Danish and Swedish Courts against England; this, however, had been allayed by the mission of Lord Whitworth, the English Ambassador to Copenhagen.

At this juncture the Russian Emperor Paul claimed, without [*286] *a shadow of reason,(*p*) the island of Malta, which had been recently ceded to the English. He had become Grand Master of the once celebrated order of the knights in that island, and his attachment to this imaginary distinction was supposed to be one of the subjects on which his continually increasing insanity manifested itself. The refusal of England to surrender this island exasperated Paul, and, with an open contempt of the stipulations of an existing Treaty,(*q*) he laid an embargo on all British property within his dominions, and with a semi-Asiatic notion of justice, ordered one British vessel to be burned because another had escaped from harm.(*r*)

The next step of Russia was characteristic; it was to renew the abandoned Armed Neutrality, as if for the purpose of demonstrating how little the League had ever been concerned with general international justice, and how obviously it had always been intended to injure one particular State. Sweden,(*s*) Denmark,(*t*) and Prussia(*u*) joined the revived confederacy, which contained the old stipulations, with this important addition:—

"That the declaration of the officers who shall command the ship of war, or ships of war, of the King or Emperor, which shall be convoying one or more merchant ships, that the convoy has no contraband goods on board, shall be sufficient; and that no search of his ship, or the other ships of the convoy, shall be permitted. And the better to insure respect to those principles, and the stipulations founded upon them, which their disinterested wishes to preserve the imprescriptible rights of neutral nations have suggested, *the high contracting parties, to [*287] prove their sincerity and justice, will give the strictest orders to their captains, as well of their ships of war as of their merchant ships, to load no part of their ships, or secretly to have on board any articles, which, by virtue of the present convention, may be considered as contraband; and, for the more completely carrying into execution this command, they will respectively take care to give directions to their Courts of Admiralty to publish it, whenever they shall think it necessary; and to this end, the regulation which shall contain this prohibition, under the several penalties, shall be printed at the end of the present Act, that no one may plead ignorance."

(*p*) He alleged the Treaty of 1798, which was a Treaty of subsidy, in which no clause affords a pretext for the demand.—De Martens, vi. 557.

(*q*) The 12th Article provided, that, in the event of the breaking out of war, the goods and persons of neither country should be detained or confiscated.

(*r*) De Martens, vii. 155. (*s*) Ibid. (*t*) Ib., 181. (*u*) Ib., 188.

This attempt, happily, like the rest of the treaty, abortive, to introduce a new positive law upon *contraband*, does not require further discussion in this place.(*x*)

By other articles of the treaty, mutual assistance is promised in case of attack.(*y*)

CCII. The second Russian League was destined to enjoy even a shorter existence than the first. Great Britain began her war upon this new confederacy against her by an attack upon Denmark. Nelson's immortal victory at Copenhagen was followed by another event of great importance at the time, and which demonstrated in what *personal* feeling the new League had originated. There is no despotism so unlimited, none so absolute and unquestionable, according to the positive law or usage of the country over which it is set, as not to find some check in the necessities and feelings of mankind.

The tyranny of Tiberius and Robespierre(*z*) became at last unendurable to the poor as well as the rich, and then ensued, by violent means, their [*288] death. The ferocious acts of the *Emperor Paul, and the well-founded belief that they sprang, in a great measure at least, from a disordered brain, brought about at this critical period a similar result; not, however, from the combination of the humble and great, but from the aristocracy alone. Paul suddenly disappeared from the stage on which he was acting so terrible a part. He was assassinated, and, as it is generally, and certainly not without good warrant, believed, in accordance with the deliberate resolution of the notables of his Court. The act has indeed been defended as a necessary measure of self-defence, no other remedy being supplied for such an emergency by the constitution of Russia. We are only concerned in this work with the result, which was very remarkable. Alexander, the successor to Paul, immediately concluded a treaty with England, which adjusted the dispute. By this treaty, in June, 1801, certain concessions were made by England respecting *Convoy*, and it was stipulated that goods embarked in neutral ships should be free, *except* contraband *and the property of enemies.* Thus was the old rule re-established between Russia and England, and to this treaty both Sweden and Denmark acceded.(*a*)

CCIII. Among the most remarkable works upon International Jurisprudence which the crisis of the second Armed Neutrality produced, were the *Letters of Sulpicius*, by Lord Grenville, and a *Speech*, afterwards published by the same distinguished statesman upon the treaty between England and Russia in 1801.

In the *Letters*, Lord Grenville—who had but recently resigned the office of Foreign Secretaryship, which he had filled for many years—

(*x*) Vide post. (*y*) De Martens, vii. 172.

(*z*) "Sed periit postquam cerdonibus esse timendus
Cœperat, hoc nocuit Lamiarum cæde recenti."—Juv. Sat.

(*a*) De Martens, vii. 260-281, contains the *three* Treaties. Russia had only *a few days before* made a Treaty with Sweden, embodyiug the articles of the Armed Neutrality, March, 1801 (De Martens, vii. 329,) so that, in one and the same week, Russia embodied the two opposite principles in her Treaties with the same nation; and it has been gravely argued that the Treaties constitute the International Law on this subject!—Manning, 278.

maintained, with perfect knowledge of the subject, much erudition, great vigour of logic, and manly *eloquence, the ancient doctrines of International Law against those of the Armed Neutrality. [*289]

In the *Speech*,(*b*) he declared that dangerous concessions with respect to the coasting and colonial trade, to contraband of war and blockade, had been made by Great Britain. These subjects remain to be considered. With respect, however, to enemy's goods on board neutral ships, Lord Grenville admitted that it was fully recognized by the second section of the third article of the Convention, which implied an abandonment of the opposite principle of *free ships free goods*, on the part of the Northern Powers.(*c*)

CCIV. The period between the breaking up of the second Armed Neutrality and the breaking out of the present war (1801-1854), need not occupy us long.

Russia, after the peace of Tilsit, readopted for the moment, and avowedly in order to please Napoleon, the principles of the Armed Neutrality.

But in August, 1809, with a whimsical novelty of inconsistency, the Czar issued an ukase,(*d*) declaring "That ships laden in part with goods of the manufacture or produce of hostile countries shall be stopped, and such merchandize confiscated, and sold by auction for the profit of the Crown. *And if the merchandize aforesaid comprise more than half the cargo, not only the cargo, but also the ship shall be confiscated.*"(*e*) And in 1812, when he made peace with *England, it was stipulated that the political and commercial relations of the two Powers should be the subject of a future arrangement.(*f*) [*290]

CCV. The last observation brings us to what may be called the argument from the *silence of subsequent treaties*, and especially of that which closed the long war of the French Revolution.

At the Treaty of Amiens, in 1802, neither was the subject of this discussion, the claim of *free ships free goods*, mentioned, nor were former Treaties relating to it renewed.

The same may be predicated of the Treaties of Paris and Vienna, 1814-1815.

It may not be difficult to maintain that the *territorial arrangements* which have formed the subject of great cardinal Treaties,(*g*) such as those of Westphalia, Utrecht, Paris, Versailles, and Vienna, remain

(*b*) The argument was sound; but as subsequent Treaties upon the same subject have been contracted between England and Russia, the concessions have no present operation or effect.

(*c*) Vide ante, vol. i. p. 45, where this remarkable speech is referred to upon the important question of *permanent* alterations of *general* International Law being introduced into a Treaty. Mr. Wheaton (Hist., pp. 408-420,) gives very copious extracts from this speech, and remarks with truth upon "the very lame and inconclusive replies made by the other speakers," in the debate in the House of Lords.—Parliamentary History of England, vol. xxxvi. pp. 200-255.

(*d*) Art. XI. De Martens, Suppl., v. 485. Manning, 279.

(*e*) In 1810, 31st December, another ukase relaxed the rigour of the Continental System, and greatly irritated Napoleon.

(*f*) De Martens, N. R., t. iii. p. 226.

(*g*) Vide ante, vol. i. p. 47. Wheaton's Elem. (ed. Lawrence, 1855,) p. 513.

unchanged whether their provisions be specifically renewed or not, in later Treaties, except in so far as they are derogated from by subsequent conventions. But it will be morally impossible to contend with success that provisions respecting a particular subject, forming an exception to the general law, which have not been renewed in later Treaties naturally connected with the subject, can be holden, either by the usage of nations or by the reason of the thing, to be any longer in force.

CCVI. Up to the period of the present war, Great Britain has not renewed any of the few Treaties by which she formerly engaged herself to maintain the principle that "free ships make free goods;" but, on the contrary, she has withdrawn from her most ancient and favoured ally, Portugal, the privilege which on this subject she had once accorded to her. This privilege was abrogated by the Treaty of 19th February, 1810;(h) and [*291] in the Treaty between the two countries, *namely, that of July 13, 1842, it is expressly stipulated that the reciprocal liberty of commerce and navigation stipulated for in the present Treaty shall not be extended to contraband of war, nor *to objects belonging to the enemies of either party*; and it is hereby notified, that the *license hitherto allowed by former Treaties to the ships of both countries to transport any objects of merchandize belonging to the enemies of either country is henceforth abandoned and renounced.*"(i)

During the whole of this century, therefore, up to the period of the present war, England has either incorporated into her Treaties, as with Russia in 1801, and Portugal in 1842, a positive negation of the doctrine that free ships do make free goods, or has preserved an entire silence upon the subject, and therefore, according to the soundest principles of International Jurisprudence, has reserved to herself all the rights accruing to her from the *general* law.

CCVII. Since the Treaty of Vienna, various Treaties have been contracted between the European and the South American States, and between the different States themselves on the American Continent.(k)

The United States of North America, in their earliest negotiation with the different States of South America, proposed the establishment of the principle of *free ships make free goods* between all the Powers on that continent. In practice, however, the United States of North America have introduced this very important and significant qualification, namely, that the new rule is to be understood "as applying to those Powers only [*292] who recognize this principle; *but* if *either of the two contracting parties shall be at war with a third, and the other neutral, the flag of the Neutral shall *cover the property of enemies whose Government acknowledges the same principle, and not of others.*"

This extract is from a Treaty between the North American United

(h) Art. XXVI.

(i) Art. XIII. De Martens, N. R., t. iii. p. 327. In Oliver Cromwell's Treaty with Portugal, June 10, 1654, art. xxiii., it was said, "Omnia autem hostium alterutrius bona mercesve in naves partis alterutrius eorumve populi aut subditorum impositæ intactæ sint."—Dumont, Corps Diplom., t. vi. pt. 2, p. 84. This provision was continually renewed with Portugal till 1842.

(k) United States' Statutes at Large, vol. viii. pp. 262, 312, 328, 393, 437, 472, 490.

States and the Republic of Columbia;(*k*) but the restriction, which had been previously incorporated into the Treaty of 1819, between Spain and the North American United States, has been subsequently inserted, in most if not all the Treaties between the North American United States and the States of South America,(*l*) and indeed between the North American United States and the European States with the exception of England. It is remarkable, that though the subject was matter of discussion between these two Governments, the important Treaty of Washington was concluded August 8, 1842, without any reference to it.(*m*)

CCVIII. France, in her Treaty with Texas, revived her old doctrine, *enemy's ships enemy's goods*, though she conceded that *free ships made free goods*.(*n*) This is a fact well worthy of observation at the present time.

CCIX. At the breaking out of the present European war (1855,) England found herself in close alliance, offensive and defensive, with France. They were to wage war together, both by *sea* and land. It was therefore supposed to be necessary that there should be an agreement between them as to the question,(*o*) which has been so long under our consideration, *of the exercise of belligerent rights towards Neutrals. The result was a compromise. France abandoned [*293] her doctrine, that *enemy's ships made enemy's goods*. England agreed to allow, during her alliance with France in the present war, the doctrine that *free ships made free goods*. But she scrupulously and expressly declared that in so doing she "*waived a part of the belligerent rights appertaining to her by the Law of Nations*." It will be seen, therefore, from the principles already laid down in this work,(*p*) as well as from the reason of the thing,(*q*) that England has retained unimpaired her belligerent right upon this important subject.(*r*) In the communications which have passed on this subject between England and the North

(*k*) Art. XII. of Treaty, October 3, 1824.

(*l*) Wheaton's Elm., pp. 530-1-2-3. (Ed. Lawrence, 1855.) De Martens, N. R., vi. pp. 826, 991. Ib., Nouveau Suppl. t. ii. p. 412. 4th September, 1816, with Sweden, art. xii.—De Martens, N. R., iv. p. 258. Ibid., July 4, 1827.—De Martens, N. R. vii. p. 278. With Prussia, May 1, 1828, (art. xii.) vii. 615.

(*m*) Wheaton's Hist., pp. 669-739.

(*n*) De Martens, N. R., xvi. p. 988.

(*o*) Upon other points, it will be seen hereafter, considerable differences still remain.

(*p*) Vide ante, as to the effects of protests, vol. i. pp. 308-9.

(*q*) Vide ante, vol. i.

(*r*) A debate upon this subject took place in the House of Commons on the 4th of July, 1854, (motion of Mr. George Phillimore.) The House was remarkably thin from the commencement of the debate, and was *counted out*, forty members not being present after a few speeches. The conduct of the Government was defended by only one minister, and whose office (that of Chief Commissioner of Public Works) had no connection with the matter discussed. The Ministerial leader of the House of Commons was absent; the Foreign Office was not represented. The First Lord of the Admiralty was present, and did not speak, but signified, in the usual parliamentary manner, his approval of the statement, that England had only *waived for the present* her unquestionable belligerent right. This was not denied by the minister who did speak, and who in fact rested his case upon this ground; though in the course of his oration, he seemed to intimate his *private opinion*, in favour of the doctrine that *free ships make free goods*.

American United States, the minister of the latter country observed in his reply, "Nowithstanding the sincere gratification which Her Majesty's declaration has given to the President, it would have been enhanced if the rule alluded to had been announced as one which would be observed, *not only in the present*, but in every future war in which Great Britain shall be a party."(*s*)

[*294] *The Declaration is as follows:—

"Her Majesty the Queen of the United Kingdom of Great Britain and Ireland, having been compelled to take up arms in support of an ally, is desirous of rendering the war as little onerous as possible to the Powers with whom she remains at peace.

"To preserve the commerce of Neutrals from all unnecessary obstruction, Her Majesty is willing, for the present, *to waive a part of the belligerent rights appertaining to her by the Law of Nations.*

"It is impossible for Her Majesty to forego the exercise of her right of seizing articles contraband of war, and of preventing Neutrals from bearing the enemy's despatches; and she must maintain the right of a belligerent to prevent Neutrals from breaking any effective blockade which may be established with an adequate force against the enemy's forts, harbours, or coasts.

"But Her Majesty *will waive the right* of seizing enemy's property laden on board a neutral vessel, unless it be contraband of war.

"It is not Her Majesty's intention to claim the confiscation of neutral property, not being contraband of war, found on board enemies' ships; and Her Majesty further declares, that being anxious to lessen as much as possible the evils of war, and to restrict its operations to the regularly organized forces of the country, it is not her *present intention* to issue letters of marque for the commissioning of privateers."(*t*)

A declaration of Her Majesty, dated the 15th of April, 1854, further extended the privilege upon this subject, already accorded to Neutrals. "It is this day ordered, by and with the advice of her Privy Council, that all vessels under a neutral or friendly flag, being neutral or friendly [*295] property, shall be permitted to import into any port or place in Her *Majesty's dominions all goods and merchandize whatsoever, to whomsoever the same may belong; and to export from any port or place in Her Majesty's dominions to any port not blockaded, any cargo or goods, not being contraband of war, or not requiring a special permission, to whomsoever the same may belong.

"And her majesty is further pleased, by and with the advice of her Privy Council, to order, and it is hereby further ordered, that, save and except only as aforesaid, all the subjects of her majesty, and the subjects or citizens of any neutral or friendly State, shall and may, during and notwithstanding the present hostilities with Russia, freely trade with all ports and places, wheresoever situate, which shall not be in a state of blockade, save and except that no British vessel shall, under any circum-

(*s*) Wheaton's Elm. (ed. Lawrence,) p. 539, note. In 1823 and 1826-7 vain attempts were make to adjust this question between England and N. A. United States, ib., p. 535.

(*t*) Westminster, March 28, 1854.

stances whatsoever, either under or by virtue of this order or otherwise, be permitted or empowered to enter or communicate with any port or place which shall belong to or be in the possession or occupation of her majesty's enemies."

CCX. As the end of all war is peace, the expediency of abandoning or retaining a belligerent right ought to be chiefly ascertained by the tendency of the exercise of that right to delay or to hasten the return of peace; judged by this criterion, it may, to say the least, reasonably be doubted whether the waiver of the belligerent right under discussion has been an encouraging or successful experiment. The trade of Russia has been carried on during the present war, with comparatively small injury to her, by Prussia; the ports of the two countries, owing to the close neighbourhood and easy inland transit by railway between them, have been practically identical; thereby the pressure of the belligerent force has been materially weakened, the continuance of the horrors and evils of war much prolonged, and the return of the normal state of peace greatly delayed, not to mention the inducement to Neutrality which her increased commerce has offered to Prussia at a period when it was the professed object of the allies to form a general league of the *great European Powers against Russia as the one aggressor, [*296] and the great facility which has been afforded to the carriage of *contraband.*

CCXI. There are some miscellaneous points which should be noticed before we pass from the present subject: they relate to the decisions of International Tribunals with respect to the ships and goods of nations with whom Treaties authorizing the new maxim subsist.

It has been decided in the Prize Courts both of Great Britain and the United States of North America,(*x*) that the privilege of the neutral flag to protect enemy's property, whether the result of Treaty stipulations, or municipal ordinances, however comprehensive may be the terms in which it may be expressed, cannot be interpreted to extend to the fraudulent use of that flag to cover enemy's property in the ship as well as the cargo.(*y*)

The Treaty of 1654, between England and Portugal, embodied the two maxims of *enemy's ships enemy's goods,* and *free ships free goods.* But it was decided by Lord Stowell that the clause in the article which condemns the goods of either nation found on board the ships of the enemy of the other contracting party could not be fairly applied to the case of property *shipped before the contemplation of war.* "It did not follow," Lord Stowell observed, "that because *Spanish* property put on board a *Portuguese* ship would be protected in the event of the interruption of war, therefore *Portuguese* property on board a *Spanish* ship should become instantly confiscable on the breaking out of hostilities with Spain; that in one case the conduct of the parties would not have been different if the event of hostilities had been known. The cargo was entitled to the protection of the ship generally by this stipulation of the

(*x*) Wheaton's Elm. (ed. Lawrence, 1855,) p. 531.

(*y*) The Cittade de Lisboa, Robinson's Adm. Rep., vi. p. 358. The Estern, Dallas's (Amer.) Rep., vol. ii. p. 34.

Treaty, even if shipped in open war; and *à fortiori*, if shipped under [*297] *circumstances still more favourable to the Neutrality of the transaction. In the other case, there might be reason to suppose that the Treaty referred only to goods shipped on board an enemy's vessel in an avowed hostile character; and that the neutral merchant would have acted differently, if he had been apprised of the character of the vessel at the time when the goods were put on board."(*z*)

[*298]

*CHAPTER XI.

COLONIAL AND COASTING TRADE.—RULE OF 1756.

CCXII. It has been stated that it is perfectly competent to a Neutral to carry on a general trade with either belligerent; but we now approach the discussion of a question,(*a*) which at one time much agitated both Europe and America, which recent alterations, both in the colonial system and the navigation laws of many countries, especially of England,(*b*) have stripped in great measure, of its former importance, but which cannot, nevertheless, be passed by, because it is impossible to say what may be the future policy of nations with respect to the coasting trade, and also because the principle which lies at the root of the question demands a statement and examination in a work of this description.

This question, generally stated, is, whether it be lawful for a Neutral to carry on in time of war, with a Belligerent, a trade which he is not allowed to carry on in time of peace.

CCXIII. The practical shapes in which this abstract question became embodied, were:—

[*299] *1. The carrying on by the Neutral of the trade between the belligerent mother country and the colonies.

2. The carrying on the coasting trade of the Belligerent—such trade being confined in time of war to the Belligerent's subjects.

3. The carrying on the trade by a Neutral from a port in his own country to a port of the colony of the Belligerent.

4. The carrying on by a Neutral of a trade between the ports of the Belligerent, but with a cargo from the Neutral's own country.

It is necessary to bear in mind the distinction between these separate propositions: because while the two former have obtained, under the title of the Rule of the War of 1756, the approbation of the best authorities in England and America, the two latter propositions have been

(*z*) The Marianna, 6 Robinson's Adm. Rep., p. 28.

(*a*) Lee on Captures (1803,) first published 1759, p. 131. Manning, chap. v. Wheaton's (Amer.) Reports, vol. i., App., note 3, on the Rule of the War, 1756. Wheaton's Elements (ed. Lawrence,) p. 572. Judge Story's Life, vol. i. pp. 287-288. (London, 1851.)

(*b*) During the present war, the Rule of 1756 is superseded by the Order in Council of the 15th of April, 1854, allowing Neutrals to trade to all ports and places, wheresoever situated, that are not in a state of blockade.

powerfully attacked by the United States of North America, as being vicious corruptions of a sound principle of International Law.

CCXIV. It is not a matter worthy of much controversy, whether or no the Rule of 1756 was ever practically enforced before that year. It is unquestionable that its practical enforcement then first attracted general notice. But it is a matter well worthy of consideration whether the rule, whensoever practically enforced, was or was not founded upon a sound principle of International Law, upon a just view of the mutual relations of Neutral and Belligerent.

CCXV. Judge Story and Mr. Wheaton(*c*) give a faithful sketch of the circumstances which accompanied its introduction in 1756. They say with truth, that—

"The rule commonly called the Rule of 1756,(*d*) acquired *this denomination, from its having been first judicially applied by the [*300] Courts of Prize in the war of that period. The French (then at war with Great Britain,) finding the trade with their colonies almost entirely cut off by the maritime superiority of the British, relaxed their monopoly of that trade, and allowed the Dutch (then neutral) to carry on the trade between the mother country and her colonies, under special licenses or passes, granted to Dutch ships for this special purpose, excluding, at the same time, all other Neutrals from the same trade. Many Dutch vessels, so employed, were captured by the British cruisers, and, together with their cargoes, were condemned by the Prize Courts, upon the just and true principle, that by such employment they were, in effect, incorporated into the French navigation, having adopted the character and trade of the enemy, and identified themselves with his interests and purposes. They were, in the opinion of these courts, to be considered like transports in the enemy's service, and hence liable to capture and condemnation, upon the same principle as property condemned by way of penalty for resistance to search, for breach of blockade, for carrying military persons or despatches, or as contraband of war. In all these cases the property is considered, *pro hâc vice*, as enemy's property, as so completely identified with his interests as to acquire a hostile character. So, where a Neutral is engaged in a trade which is exclusively confined to the subjects of a country, in peace and in war, and is interdicted to all others, and cannot be avowedly carried on in the name of a foreigner, such a trade is considered so entirely national, that it must follow the hostile situation of the country.(*e*)

CCXVI. The Rule of the War of 1757,(*f*) or of the Seven Years' War, was intermitted during the war between Great *Britain and her American colonies; but on the ground that, a short time [*301]

(*c*) I mention *both*, because it will be seen from Judge Story's Life (vol. i. p. 288,) that both were concerned in the composition.

(*d*) For judicial opinions on this rule, see—Berens v. Rucker, 1 William Blackstone's Reports, p. 314, (published 1781); opinion of Lord Mansfield. Brymer v. Atkins, 1 Henry Blackstone's Reports, 191, (published 1791); Lord Loughborough's opinion.

(*e*) 1 Wheaton's Rep., p. 506; App., note 3. Story's Life, vol. i. p. 288.

(*f*) See the case of the Dutch ships considered by James Marriott, LLD. (published 1759; fourth edition, 1778.) London. 4 Robinson's Adm. Rep., App. A.

before the breaking out of hostilities, France had declared that she had abandoned the principle of monopoly, and meant, as a permanent regulation, to admit neutral merchants to trade with her colonies in the West Indies. It was considered by the British Prize Court of Appeal in 1801, that this conduct of France at the particular juncture of the American War had manifestly been adopted for the sake of avoiding the application of the principle which she clearly understood to be warranted by International Law.(*g*)

In the war of 1793, the first set of instructions to British cruisers were certainly framed, not on the exception of the American War, but upon the antecedent practice.(*h*)

But it is clear, from the judgments of the Admiralty Court—both the very early decisions of Lord Stowell, and the last of his immediate predecessor—that at first the Rule of 1756 was slowly and mildly restored to its supremacy.(*i*) At the same time the principle upon which it was founded was vindicated in various judgments delivered by Lord Stowell in a manner which it is easier to cavil at than to refute.

CCXVII. It is the usual practice of the Prize Court (acting on a rule in the *Consolato del Mare,*) to give freight to the neutral carrier of enemies' goods that are seized. In a case in which a Neutral had been captured for carrying on the coasting trade of the enemy, it was contended before Lord Stowell, that the freight was not due to the proprietors of this vessel; that she was a Danish ship, employed in the transmission of Spanish goods from one Spanish port to another, and so carrying on the coasting trade of that *country. "In Great Britain," the learned [*302] Judge observed, "it had long been the system, that the coasting trade should only be carried on by our own navigation. That in all the rage of novel experiment that had dictated the commercial regulations of France in its new condition, this policy had been held sacred. It had been enacted by a decree, 21st of September, 1793, that no goods, the growth or manufacture of France, should be carried from one French port to another, in foreign ships, under pain of confiscation.(*k*) The same policy had directed the commercial system of other European countries; in the ordinary state of affairs, no indulgence was generally permitted to the ships of most other countries to carry on the coasting trade; that, therefore, the *onus probandi* at least lay on that side, and always made it necessary to be shown by the claimants that such trade was not a mere indulgence and a temporary relaxation of the coasting system of

(*g*) 4 Robinson's Adm. Rep., p. xi. App.

(*h*) Order in Council, November, 6, 1793.
" " " January 8, 1794.
" " " January 25, 1798.
" " " Finally merged in the retaliatory Orders in Council of 1806-7.

(*i*) The Welwaart, 1 Robinson's Adm. Rep., p. 124. The Speculation, 2 Robinson's Adm. Rep., p. 293.

(*k*) "Les bâtimens étrangers ne pourront transporter d'un port Francais, à un autre port Français, aucunes denrées, productions, ou marchandises des cru, produit, ou manufactures de France, colonies ou possessions de France, sous les peines portées par l'article 3 Loi, contenant l'acte de navigation, 21st Septembre, 1793 (i. e., confiscation des bâtimens et cargaison, et de 3000 liv. d'amende,") &c.

the State in question, but that it was a common and ordinary trade, open to the ships of any country whatever. . . . As to the *coasting* trade (supposing it to be a trade not usually opened to foreign vessels,) can there be described a more effective accommodation that can be given to an enemy during a war, than to undertake it for him during his own disability? Is it nothing that the commoditities of an extensive empire are conveyed from the parts where they grow and are manufactured, to other parts where they are wanted for use? It is said that this is not importing anything new into the country, and it certainly is not; but has it not all the effects of such an importation? Suppose that the French navy had a decided ascendant, and had cut off all British communication between the northern *and southern parts of this island, and that [*303] Neutrals interposed to bring the coals of the North for the supply of the manufactures and for the necessities of domestic life in this metropolis; is it possible to describe a more direct and a more effectual opposition to the success of French hostility, short of an actual military assistance in the war?"(*l*)

CCXVIII. As to trading with the *colonies* of the enemy, Lord Stowell observed, that it was as an indubitable right of the belligerent to possess himself of such places, as of any other possession of his enemy. This was his common right; but he had the certain means of carrying such a right into effect, if he had a decided superiority at sea. Such colonies were dependent for their existence, as colonies, on foreign supplies. If they could not be supplied and defended, they must fall to the belligerent, of course; and if the belligerent chooses to apply his means to such an object, what right has a third party, perfectly neutral, to step in and prevent the execution? No existing interest of his is affected by it; he can have no right to apply to his own use the beneficial consequences of the mere act of the belligerent, and to say,—"True it is, you have, by force of arms, forced such places out of the exclusive possession of the enemy, but I will share the benefit of the conquest, and, by sharing its benefits, prevent its progress. You have in effect, and by lawful means, turned the enemy out of the possession which he had exclusively maintained against the whole world, and with whom we have never presumed to interfere; but we will interpose to prevent his absolute surrender, by the means of that very opening which the prevalence of your arms alone has effected. Supplies shall be sent, and their products shall be exported. You have lawfully destroyed his monoply, but you shall not be permitted to possess it yourself. We insist to share the fruits of your victories; and your blood and treasure have been expended, not for your own interest, but for the common benefit of others." It could not, upon these *grounds, be contended to be a right of Neutrals [*304] to intrude into a commerce which had been uniformly shut against them, and which is now forced open merely by the pressure of war; for when the enemy, under an entire inability to supply his colonies and to export their products, affects to open them to Neutrals, it is not his will but his necessity that changes his system. That change is the

(*l*) The Emanuel, Robinson's Adm. Rep., vol. i. pp. 297, 301.

direct and unavoidable consequence of the compulsion of war—it is a measure not of French Councils, but of British force.

Upon these and other grounds it was that an instruction issued at an early period of the last war with France, for the purpose of preventing the communication of Neutrals with the colonies of the enemy; it was intended to be carried into effect on the same footing on which the prohibition had been legally enforced in the war of 1756. Upon further inquiry, it turned out that one favoured nation, the Americans, had in times of peace been permitted, by special convention, to exercise a certain very limited commerce with those colonies of the French, and it consisted with justice that that case should be specially provided for; but no justice required that the provision should extend beyond the necessities of that case. Whatever went beyond that, was not given to the demands of strict justice, but was matter of relaxation and concession.(*m*)

As to the argument that variations are made in the commercial systems of every country, in wars and on account of wars, by means of which Neutrals are admitted and invited into different kinds of trade, from which they stand usually excluded; and if so, that no one belligerent country has a right to interfere with Neutrals for acting under variations of a like kind, made for similar reasons in the commercial policy of its enemy; it is answered, that certainly if this proposition could be maintained without any limitation, viz., that wherever any variation whatever is made during a war, and on account of the state of war, the party
[*305] *who makes it binds himself in all the variations to which the necessities of the enemy can compel him, the whole colonial trade of the enemy is legalized, and the instructions which are directed against any part, are equally unjust and impertinent. The opening of free ports is not necessarily a measure arising from the demands of war; it is frequently a peace measure in the colonial system of every country. There are others which more directly arise out of the necessities of war. The admission of foreigners into the merchant service, as well as into the military service of this country, the permission given to vessels to import commodities not the growth, produce, and manufacture of the country to which they belong, and other relaxations of municipal law, and other regulations founded thereon, these, it is true, take place in war, and arise out of a state of war; but then they do not *arise out of the predominance of the enemy's force, or out of any necessity resulting therefrom, and that is the true foundation of the principle.* It is not every convenience, or even every necessity, arising out of a state of war, but that necessity which arises out of the impossibility of otherwise providing against the urgency of distress inflicted by the hand of a superior enemy, than can be admitted to produce such an effect. Thus, in time of war, every country admits foreigners into its general service; every country obtains, by the means of neutral vessels, those products of the enemy's country which it cannot possibly receive, either by means of his navigation or its own. These are ordinary measures to which every country has resort in every war, whether prosperous or adverse. They

(*m*) The Immanuel, 2 Robinson's Adm. Rep., pp. 200-1.

arise, it is true, out of a state of war, but *are totally independent of its events*, and have, therefore, no common origin with these compelled relaxations of the colonial monopoly. These are acts of distress, signals of defeat and depression: they are no better than partial surrenders to the force of the enemy, for the mere purpose of preventing a total dispossession."(*n*)

*It was upon these grounds that Lord Stowell vindicated the principle of the Rule of 1756. [*306]

CCXIX. With respect to the penalty inflicted on the Neutral for a violation of this Rule, it should be observed, that in an early case(*o*) brought before the British Prize Court, the cargo was condemned, but the ship was restored, though without freight; in a subsequent case,(*p*) the ship was restored in the Admiralty Court; but in a later case, in which there was an appeal to the Lords, the ship, as well as the cargo, were condemned, on the ground of the illegality of the trade between the mother country and the colony.(*q*)

CCXX. The complaint of the United States(*r*) of North America, between whom and Great Britain this question was a fruitful source of contention, was directed partly against the Rule itself, and partly against the enlarged sphere of the Rule, accorded to it by the decisions of the Prize Court.

CCXXI. With respect to the Rule itself, the United States, in their diplomatic intercourse, constantly and earnestly protested against its legality, and insisted that it was an attempt to establish "a new principle of the Law of Nations," and one which subverted "many other principles of great importance, which have heretofore been held sacred among nations." They insisted that Neutrals were of right entitled "to trade, with the exception of blockades and contrabands, to and between all ports of the enemy, and in all articles, although the trade should not have been opened to them in time of peace."(*s*) It was considered to be the right of every independent Power to treat, in time of peace, with every other nation, for leave of trade with its colonies, and to enter into any trade, whether new or old, that was not *of itself illegal, and a violation of Neutrality. One State had nothing [*307] to do with the circumstances or motives which induced another nation to open her ports. The trade must have a direct reference to the hostile efforts of the Belligerents, like dealing in contraband, in order to render it breach of Neutrality.

Nevertheless, the Rule of 1756, especially in respect to colonial trade, has been defended, as well as attacked, by Jurists and Judges of great authority in the United States of North America. Mr. Chancellor Kent is of opinion that the principle of the Rule may very fairly be considered as one unsettled and doubtful, and open to future and vexed discussion. He remarks that the Chief Justice of the United States, in the case of

(*n*) The Immanuel, 2 Robinson's Adm. Rep., pp. 203-4.
(*o*) The Immanuel, 2 Robinson's Adm. Rep., p. 198.
(*p*) The Minerva (in 1801,) 3 Robinson's Adm. Rep., pp. 232.
(*q*) The Jonge Thomas (in 1801,) ib., p. 233.
(*r*) Wheaton's (Amer.) Reports, vol. i., App., p. 531.
(*s*) Mr. Munroe's Letter to Lord Mulgrave, of September 23, 1805, and Mr. Madison's Letter to Messrs. Munroe and Pinckney, dated May 17, 1806.

the *Commercen*,(*t*) alluded to the Rule, but purposely avoided expressing any opinion on the correctness of the principle; and the Chancellor winds up his observations by saying:—

"It is very possible, that if the United States should attain that elevation of maritime power and influence which their rapid growth and great rescources seem to indicate, and which shall prove sufficient to render it expedient for her maritime enemy (if any such enemy shall ever exist,) to open all his domestic trade to enterprising Neutrals, we might be induced to feel, more sensibly than we have hitherto done, the weight of the arguments of the foreign Jurists in favour of the policy and equity of the Rule."(*u*)

The opinion of Judge Story, it will be seen, is strongly in favour of the legality of the principle of the Rule of 1756, though opposed to the extension of it.(*x*)

[*308] Vattel's opinion(*y*) is clear and decided, that so long as Neutrals *only *continue their customary trade*, they exercise a right which they are not bound to sacrifice to the Belligerent. Hübner, the neutral champion at all risks,(*z*) in dealing with this question, gives a strange proof of his partiality to his clients. "Neutrals," he says, "have a right to trade in war as in peace."—Bien entendu qu'ils ne sortent point de leur caractère; qu'ils ne trafiquent avec les nations belligérantes que *comme en temps de paix*." But there is a difficulty, he adds, about the colonial trade of the Belligerent: true, it is notoriously closed to the Neutral in time of peace; true it is only open to him in war, and "à cause de la guerre;" nevertheless (he whimsically adds,) "je ne vois pas pourquoi les sociétés souveraines, qui sont neutres, devroint se refuser *un bénéfice considerable qui se présente*." A very honest, if not a very creditable avowal of the Rule which, in his opinion, should guide the consciences of neutral Governments.(*a*)

The(*b*) French *Réglement*, both of July, 1704, and of October, 1744, enforced, in the severest manner, the principle contained in the Rule of 1756.

CCXXII. But little, if any, light upon the question is thrown from the examination of Treaties. Independent States have pursued no con-

(*t*) 1 Wheaton's Reports, p. 396.

(*u*) Kent's Com., vol. i. pp. 90-92.

(*x*) Vide infra, p. 309.

(*y*) L. iii. c. vii. s. 3. (The words are remarkable.) "Mais si elles ne font que suivre *tout uniment* à leur commerce, elles ne se déclarent point par-là contre mes intérêts; elles exercent un droit que rien ne les oblige de me sacrifier."

(*z*) "M. Hübner, dans son Traite de la Saisie des Bâtimens Neutres, t. i. pt. ii. c. 2, ss. 5, et suiv., depuis la page 207, jusqu'à la 226, fait plus, car il entreprend de prouver fort sérieusement que le pavillon neutre couvre toute la cargaison, quoiqu'elle appartienne à l'ennemi, ou qu'elle soit chargée pour son compte, de manière qu'il n'en excepte que les effets de contrabande. Mais *cet auteur est absolument décidé pour les Neutres et semble n'avoir écrit que pour plaidre leur cause.* Il pose d'abord ses principes, qu'il donne pour constants; puis il en tire les conséquences qui lui conviennent. Cette méthode est fort commode. On commencera par lui demander sur quoi il établit que les marchandises ennemies sont exemptes de saisies sur un bâtiment neutre? Au surplus, par nos loix, cette saisie est autorisée; nous devons nous y tenir."—Valin, Traité des Prises, c. v. s. 5, § 5.

(*a*) De la Saisie des Bâtimens Neutres, tom. i. chap. iv. sec. 6. Manning, p. 200.

(*b*) Valin, Ord. de la Marine, t. ii. pp. 248-251.

sistent course upon this subject. It *appears,(c) that in 1674, the English being Neutrals, and the Dutch Belligerents, the latter contended that the English Treaty with them, by which it was stipulated that the ship covered the cargo, did not authorize England to carry on a trade between one enemy's port and another. Sir William Temple, however, maintained that the Treaty justified this kind of trading, and in this position the Dutch finally acquiesced.(*d*) Since that time, several Treaties have included provisions on this question, some permitting and some disallowing such traffic. Thus, in 1675, the year after the negotiation just mentioned, a Treaty between England and Holland declared that such trade between enemies' ports was allowable to the subjects of the contracting parties, whether the said ports belonged to the same Sovereign or to two different Sovereigns.(*e*) The same stipulation occurs in the Treaty between Holland and Spain in 1676(*f*) and 1679.(*g*) The trade is allowed in the Treaties of Utrecht, between France and England, and between France and Holland;(*h*) and in the Treaty between Holland and Russia, in 1715;(*i*) in the Treaty between Spain and the Empire, in 1725.(*k*) In several more recent Treaties, such trade is allowed to either contracting party; for instance, in the Treaty between France and the North American United States, in 1778;(*l*) in that between Sweden and the North American United States, in 1783;(*m*) in that between Great Britain and France, in 1786;(*n*) and in that between Spain *and the North American United States, in 1795.(*o*) On the other hand, such trade is declared unlawful in the Treaty between England and Denmark in 1691;(*p*) in the Treaty between Prussia and Sweden, in 1762;(*q*) and in the Treaty between Great Britain and Russia, in 1801.(*r*) [*309] [*310]

CCXXIII. But it was not only of the *principle* of the Rule itself, but of the *extension* given to it by judicial decisions, that the North American United States complained.

This remark brings us to the two latter of the four propositions which have been mentioned,(*s*) namely, (3.) the carrying on by a Neutral of a trade from a port in his own country to a port of the colony of the Belligerent. (4.) The carrying on by a Neutral of a trade between the ports of the Belligerent, but with a cargo from the Neutral's own country.

CCXXIV. The North American United States(*t*) complained that the decisions of the British Prize Courts and the instructions of the British Government had, either upon the principle of affecting the *return voyage* of a neutral vessel so engaged with the penalty, or upon the principle of the *continuity* of the voyage, upon one or other of these two assump-

(*c*) Manning, pp. 198-9, to whom I am indebted for the following remarks in this paragraph.
(*d*) Courtenay's Life of Temple, vol. i. pp. 433-434.
(*e*) Dumont, Corps Dipl., VII. i. p. 319. (*f*) Ib., p. 325.
(*g*) Ib., p. 439. (*h*) Ib., VIII. i. pp. 348-380. (*i*) Ib., p. 469.
(*k*) Ib., VIII. ii. p. 115. (*l*) De Martens, Rec., II. p. 598.
(*m*) Ib., III. p. 568. (*n*) Ib., IV. p. 168.
(*o*) De Martens, Rec., VI., p. 156. (*p*) Dumont, t. vii. c. ii. p. 295.
(*q*) Ib., I. p. 39. (*r*) Ib., VII. p. 272. (*s*) Vide ante, p. 299.
(*t*) Wheaton's (Amer.) Rep., vol. i. p. 531, App.

tions, so applied the Rule of 1756, as to cut off the exportation of the produce of the enemy's colonies from neutral countries, into which it had been imported, unless the produce had become incorporated into the general stock of national commodities, according to certain rules prescribed to break the continuity of the voyage, and which rules they denounced as fluctuating(u) and uncertain.

CCXXV. The writer of these pages is inclined to accept the opinion [*311] of Judge Story, as being on the whole a *judicial result of the evidence both as to fact, and the law respecting the decisions of the British Prize Courts upon this rather delicate subject. That most accomplished and learned American Jurist and Judge, writing to Mr. Wheaton in 1816, observes:—"My own private opinion certainly is, that the coasting trade of a nation, in its strict character, is so exclusively a national trade, that Neutrals can never be permitted to engage in it during war, without being affected with the penalty of confiscation. The British have unjustly extended the doctrine to cases, where a Neutral has traded between ports of the enemy, with a cargo taken in at a neutral country. I am as clearly satisfied that the colonial trade between the mother country and the colony, where that trade is thrown open merely in war, is liable in most instances to the same penalty. But the British have extended this doctrine to all intercourse with the colony, even from or to a neutral country, and herein it seems to me they have abused the rule. This at present appears to me to be the proper limits of the rule, as to the colonial and coasting trade; and the Rule of 1756 (as it was at that time applied,) seems to me well founded; but its late extension is reprehensible."(x)

Those who defer on the whole, as the writer of these pages does, to this opinion, may yet observe, that the instructions of the crown, and the decisions of the British Prize Court, allowed to Neutrals considerable relaxations from that strict rule which prohibited all intercourse between the Neutral and the colony of the belligerent.

Soon after the commencement of the war, which broke out in 1793, the first set of instructions issued by England, were framed, not on the exception already referred to, of the American war, but on the antecedent practice, and directed cruisers "to bring in for lawful adjudication, all [*312] vessels laden with goods, the produce of any colony of France, or *carrying provisions or supplies for the use of any such colony." The relaxations that have since been adopted, have originated chiefly in the change that has taken place, in the trade of that part of the world, since the establishment of an independent government on the continent of America. In consequence of that event, American vessels had been admitted to trade in some articles, and on certain conditions, with the colonies both of this country and of France. Such a permission had become a part of the general commercial arrangements, as the ordinary state of their trade in time of peace. The commerce of America was, therefore, abridged by the foregoing instructions, and debarred of the

(u) Upon the point of *continuity*, see—The Maria, 5 Robinson's Adm. Rep., p. 365. The William, ib., p. 385.

(x) Life and Letters of Joseph Story, vol. i. p. 287.

right generally ascribed to neutral trade in time of war, that it might be continued, with peculiar exceptions, on the basis of its ordinary establishment. In consequence of representations made by the United States Government to this effect, new instructions to our cruisers were issued, 8th January, 1794, apparently designed to exempt North American ships trading between their own country and the colonies of France. The directions were, "to bring in all vessels laden with goods, the produce of the French West India Islands, and coming directly from any port of the said Islands to any port in Europe."(*y*)

(*y*) 4 Robinson's Adm. Rep., App. A., p. iii. See also the Providentia, 2 Rob. Adm. Rep., p. 142. The Immanuel, ib., p. 197. The Margaretha Magdalena, ib., p. 138.

A neutral American ship, captured on a voyage from an enemy colony to a neutral island, both in the West Indies, though not the port of the proprietors of the ship or cargo, was restored. The Hector and the Sally (before the Lords of Appeal,) 4 Robinson's Adm. Rep., App. A., pp. 14, 15, and note.

The leading cases in the British Prize Court upon the subject of this chapter are well classified by Mr. Pritchard in his Analytical Digest of Admiralty Cases. London, 1847.

(1.) Colonial Trade generally:—The Calypso, 2 Robinson's Adm. Rep., p. 154. The Phœnix, 3 Ib., p. 186. The Star, Ib., p. 193, n. The Rose, 2 Ib., p. 206. *The Immanuel, 2 Robinson's Adm. Rep., p. 205. The New Adventurer, and also the Oxolen (before the Lords of Appeal,) 4 ib., App. A., p. 4, n. The Minerva, 3 ib., p. 229. The Anna Dorothea, ib., p. 229, n. The Jonge, 3 ib., p. 332, n. The Whilelmina (before the Lords of Appeal,) 4 ib., Appendix A., p. 4, and note, pp. 12-13. [*313]

(2.) Of the relations therein allowed by Great Britain: (*a*) Generally:—The Providentia, 2 Robinson's Adm. Rep., p. 142. The Immanuel, ib., p. 197. The Margaretha Magdalena, ib., p. 138. The Hector and the Sally (before the Lords of Appeal,) 4 ib., Appendix A., pp. 14, 15, and note. The Lucy, ib., p. 14. The Charlotte (before the Lords of Appeal,) ib., p. 13. The Conferenzrath, 6 Ib., p. 362. (*b*) As dependent on the question of the continuity of the voyage:—The Polly, 2 Robinson's Adm. Rep. p. 361. The Immanuel, ib., p. 197. The Mercury (before the Lords of Appeal,) 4 ib., Appendix A., p. 6. The Eagle, ib. The Maria, 5 ib., p. 365. The William, ib., p. 385. The John, 1 Acton's Rep., p. 39. The Star, 3 Robinson's Adm. Rep., p. 193, n.

(3.) Of the principles applicable to, as to settlements in the East Indies:—The Juliana, 4 Robinson's Adm. Rep., p. 328. The Patapsco, 1 Acton's Adm. Rep., p. 270. The Rebecca, 2 Ib., p. 119.

(4.) Under extraordinary and privileged contracts with the parent State:—The Anna Catharina, 4 Robinson's Adm. Rep., p. 107. The Rendsborg, ib., p. 121.

Coasting Trade:—The Emanuel, 1 Robinson's Adm. Rep., p. 302. The Speculation, 2 ib., p. 293. The Welvaart, 1 ib., p. 124. The Johannah Tholen, 6 ib., p. 72. The Ebenezer, ib., p. 252. The Schooner Sophie, ib., p. 251, n. *The Thomyris, Edward's Adm. Rep., p. 17. The Two Brothers, 2 Acton's Adm. Rep., p. 38. The Cora, ib., p. 44. The Yonge Jan, and other ships, 6 Robinson's Adm. Rep., p. 42, n. [*314]

Fishing Trade:—The Ospray, cited in the Vigilantia, 1 Robinson's Adm. Rep., p. 14. The Young Jacob and Johanna, ib., pp. 20-1. The Susa, 2 ib., p. 251.

Other cases:—The William and Grace, and cases therein cited, Hay and Marriott, p. 76. The Belle Sauvage, cited in the Friendship, ib., p. 79. The Sally, ib., p. 83. The Friendship, ib., p. 78. The Commerce, ib., p. 80. The Rebecca, ib., p. 197. The Jeane Isabelle, ib., p. 186. The Maria, 6 Robinson's Adm. Rep., p. 201. The Charlotte Sophia, ib., p. 204, n. The Lisette, ib., p. 394. The Mercurius, Edward's Adm. Rep., p. 53, and the Minna, therein cited.

Exemptions, under Treaties, from the penalties of:—

(1.) Where allowed, et contra. The Ringende Jacob, 1 Robinson's Adm. Rep., p. 89. The Catherina Joanna, 6 ib., p. 42, n.

Practice in cases of:—Vreede, 5 Robinson's Adm. Rep., p. 231.

[*315] *PART THE TENTH.

CHAPTER I.

CONTRABAND.

CCXXVI. It cannot be too emphatically declared that it is the unquestionable right of the Neutral to carry on a general trade with the Belligerents.

In their war with Spain, in 1599, the Dutch put forth an unlawful notification (*placaart*) to the world, whereby, as their historian Grotius says, "per edictum vetant *populus quoscunque* ullus commeatus *resve alias* in Hispaniam ferre; si qui secus faxint, ut hostibus faventes vice hostium futuros."(*a*) And, as we have seen in the last chapter, a most unjust attempt of a similar character was made by the allied forces of the English and the Dutch during the war waged by the English King William the Third against Louis the Fourteenth; and, as we have also seen, the clause in the Treaty of Whitehall(*b*) of August 12, 1689, which incorporated this vicious principle, was shortly afterwards annulled; the injustice of the principle was acknowledged, and the claim founded on it abandoned.

The French *Ordonnance* of 1704, containing a similar principle, was not justified, but in some degree at least palliated, by the fact of its being retaliatory to this unlawful Treaty.

[*316] *"It cannot, I think," says Lord Liverpool, "be doubted, that, according to those principles of natural equity which constitute the Law of Nations, the people of every country must always have a right to trade in general to the ports of any State, though it may happen to be engaged in war with another, provided it be with their own merchandise, or on their own account; and that, under this pretence, they do not attempt to screen from one party the effects of the other; and, on condition also that they carry not to either of them any implements of war or whatever else, according to the nature of their respective situations or the circumstances of the case, may be necessary to them for their defence. As clear as this point may be, it has sufficiently appeared, by the facts deduced above, that, amid the irregularities of war, the rules of equity, in this respect, were not always enough regarded; and that many governments in time of war have often most licentiously disturbed, and sometimes prohibited *totally*, the commerce of neutral nations with their enemies."(*c*)

(*a*) Grot., Hist., l. viii.

(*b*) It is remarkable (as Lord Liverpool, in his Essay on the Conduct of Great Britan, observes) that Puffendorf, who owed everything to the Northern Crowns, thought this Convention justifiable.—See Puffendorf's Letter in J. Groningii, Bibliotheca Universalis.

(*c*) Lord Liverpool, On the Conduct of the Government of Great Britain in respect to Neutral Nations, pp. 56-7.

Such was the attempt made by Russia,(*d*) thirty-five years after Lord Liverpool's treatise was published, to coerce the other Scandinavian Powers(*e*) into an abstinence from all *commerce with France. This attempt was a clear and indefensible violation of International [*317] Law,(*f*) the true doctrine of which is laid down by Lord Liverpool in the passage which has been just cited, and which is also judicially stated by Lord Stowell in the case of the *Wilhelmina*.

"The Dane (he observes) has a perfect right, in time of profound peace, to trade between Holland and France to the utmost advantage he can make of such a navigation; and there is no ground upon which any of its advantages can be withheld from him in time of war."(*g*)

Again, in a case decided a few months afterwards, it was promulgated, by the same authority, that "upon the breaking out of a war, it is the right of Neutrals to carry on their accustomed trade, with an exception of the particular cases of a trade to blockaded places, or in contraband articles (in both which cases their property is liable to be condemned,) and of their ships being liable to visitation and search; in which case, however, they are entitled to freight and expenses. I do not mean to say that, in the accidents of a war, the property of Neutrals may not be variously entangled and endangered. In the nature of human connections, *it is hardly possible that inconveniences of this kind should be altogether avoided. Some Neutrals will be unjustly [*318] engaged in covering the goods of the enemy, and others will be unjustly suspected of doing it. The inconveniences are more than fully balanced by the enlargement of their commerce. The trade of the Belligerents is usually interrupted in a great degree, and falls, in the same degree, into

(*d*) The language of part of the English note to Denmark would appear to lay England open to the same charge; but the whole note, as well as the fact, show that she only insisted upon the abstinence on the part of Denmark from a commerce in *provisions* with France, the justice or injustice of which will be considered bye and bye.—See Instructions to Cruisers, De Martens, Tr., V. p. 596, (1793.)

(*e*) "The usurpers of the government in France, after having subverted all order, after having embrued their murderous hands in the blood of their king, have declared themselves, by a solemn decree, the friends and protectors of all those who should commit the same horrors and excesses against their own Government in other States; and they have not only promised them succours and every assistance, but even attacked, by force of arms, most of the adjacent Powers.

"By so doing, they put themselves into an immediate state of war with all the Powers of Europe; and from that period, Neutrality could only take place when prudence prescribed, to conceal the resolution prescribed by the general interest. But this motive exists no longer, since the most formidable Powers have joined in league to make theirs one common cause against the enemy of the safety and prosperity of nations. If there be any whose situation does not allow such strong and decisive efforts as the other Powers have recourse to, it is but justice that they should join the common cause by other means which are wholly in their power, and especially by breaking off all commerce and intercourse with the perturbators of public rest."—Annual Reg., (1793,) vol. xxxv. pp. 175-6.

(*f*) See the Instructions of Russia iu 1793.—Collection of Acts and Papers, &c., p. 149. Ward's Treatise on the Relative Rights of Belligerent and Neutral, p. 169. He characterises them truly as "a gross and flagrant invasion on the part of Russia, of the independent Sovereignty of Denmark, and justly commends the Danish Minister's (Bernstoff) reply.

(*g*) The Wilhelmina, note to the Rebecca, 2 Robinson's Adm. Rep., p. 102. (July 3, 1799.)

the lap of Neutrals. But, without reference to accidents of the one kind or other, the general rule is, that the Neutral has a right to carry on, in time of war, his accustomed trade to the utmost extent of which that accustomed trade is capable."(*h*)

CCXXVII. In the last chapter we considered the lawfulness of one of the limitations by which the general liberty of the Neutral to trade with the enemy had been curtailed; and the question whether he was by the right of the Belligerent confined to his *customary* trade, and excluded from that which was only opened to him by the distress of one Belligerent arising from the pressure and success of the other Belligerent's force. It was shown that the lawfulness of this limitation in any shape was a question of much controversy; the same remark cannot be predicated of the subject of the present chapter.

The most ardent and partial supporters of neutral rights and privileges have admitted that it is not competent to a Neutral to trade with *Contraband* goods to a belligerent. The controversy has in this case arisen chiefly upon the following points, viz.:—

I. What is Contraband?

II. What is the penalty attaching to the Neutral for carrying it to the enemy?

CCXXVII. These questions(*i*) require a full discussion under the following heads:—

[*319] 1. *The carrying of unquestionable Munitions of War, military or naval, in their perfected and completed state.

2. The permitting the sale of such articles to a Belligerent within the territory of the Neutral.

3. The carrying of a material of a kind which does not certainly indicate whether their destination be for belligerent or ordinary commercial purposes. Articles *ancipitis vel promiscui usûs*, especially of *commeatus*, provisions and money.

4. The doctrine of Pre-emption.

5. The carrying of military persons in the employ of a Belligerent, or being in any way engaged in his transport service.

(*h*) The Immanuel, 2 ib., p. 198.

(*i*) One of the earliest legislative prohibitions on the subject of Contraband is probably of the Emperor Marcian, to his subjects:—"Nemo alienigenis barbaris cujuscunque gentis ad hanc urbem sacratissimam sub legationis specie vel sub quocunque alio colore venientibus aut in diversis aliis civitatibus vel locis loricas, scuta et arcus, sagittas et spathas et gladios vel alterius cujuscunque generis arma audeat venumdare: nulla prorsus iisdem tela, nihil penitus ferri, vel facti jam vel adhuc infecti, ab aliquo distrahatur. Perniciosum namque Romano imperio et proditioni proximum est, barbaros, quos indigere convenit, telis eos ut validiores reddantur instruere," &c.—Cod. iv. t. xli. 2.

The Canon Law forbade the exportation of arms to the Infidel—a prohibition which, just now, (1855,) it would be rather awkward to enforce:—"Ita quorundam animos occupavit sæva cupiditâs, ut, qui gloriantur nomine Christiano, Saracenis arma, ferrum, et ligamina deferant galearum," &c.; all such *excommunicandi.*—Decret., l. v. t. vi. c. 6.

See also a similar prohibition and punishment, Extrav. Comm., l. v. t. ii. As to the International authority of the Pope, vide ante, vol. ii. p. 327.

"Contrabannum—merces *banno* interdicta, Italis *contrabbando*, Gall. *contrebande*. Charta, anno 1445, tom. iii. Cod. Ital. Diplom. col. 1756, item quod non permittant committentes Contrabanna, dicti salis vel aliarum rerum. . . . . in dictis locis tutè et securè permanere."—Du Cange, Gloss. (ed. Carpenterius,) Parisils, 1842.

6. The carrying of the despatches of a Belligerent.
7. The penalty of carrying Contraband.
8. The principal Treaties upon the subject of Contraband.

*CCXXIX. 1st. With respect to the carrying of unquestionable munitions, military or naval, of war, in their perfect and [*320] complete state.

The general International Law upon this subject is founded upon the clearest principles of justice and reason.

"That person (said the great Athenian orator,) whoever he be, who prepares and provides the means of my destruction, he *makes war* upon me, though he have never cast a javelin or drawn a bow against me."(*k*)

"If (said Lord Grenville) I have wrested my enemy's sword from his hands, the bystander who furnishes him with a fresh weapon can have no pretence to be considered as a Neutral in the contest."(*l*)

No armed Neutrality(*m*) has as yet denied this position; indeed, upon this very ground, they have hitherto excepted in their Conventions those warlike stores which they have thought proper to designate as Contraband, from that general freedom which they otherwise maintain to be the right of neutral commerce.

No Hübner, no professed advocate of neutral claims, has as yet maintained a contrary proposition, however logically inevitable such a conclusion might appear, upon investigation, *to be from the premises [*321] usually adduced in favour of the maxim that Free Ships make Free Goods.

But with regard to furnishing arms and munitions of war, the opinion of Grotius meets with no gainsayers: "Verum est dictum (he says).... in hostium esse partibus qui ad bellum necessaria hosti administrat."(*n*)

CCXXX. 2ndly. As to the permitting the sale of such munitions to a Belligerent within the territory of the Neutral.

If the fountains of International justice have been correctly pointed out in a former volume of this work,(*o*) and it be the true character of a Neutral to abstain from every act which may better or worsen the condition of a Belligerent,(*p*) the unlawfulness of any such sale is a necessary conclusion from these premises.

For what does it matter, *where* the Neutral supplies one Belligerent with the means of attacking another? How does the question of locality,

(*k*) "... *ὁ γὰρ οἷς ἂν ἐγὼ ληφθείην ταῦτα πράττων ἢ κατασκευαζόμενος οὗτος ἐμοὶ πολεμεῖ, καὶ μήπω βάλλῃ μηδὲ τοξεύῃ.*"—Demosth. Phil.

(*l*) Letters of Sulpicius, p. 26.

(*m*) "Il est considéré, de l'aveu de toutes les nations de l'Europe, comme contraire à la neutralité, de permettre à nos sujets de transporter vers les ports de l'une ou des deux puissances belligérantes de certaines marchandises qu'on désigne sous le nom de *contrebande de guerre*."—De Martens, Précis du Droit des Gens, l. viii. c. vii. s. 318.

"Man hat ihnen dieselbe (i. e. Kriegscontrebande,) an und für sich niemals contestirt; nur gegen eine zu weite Ausdehnung ist gekämpft worden; was man aber selbst als Befügniss ausübt, kann man dem andern gleichstehenden nicht verweigern. Wenn dennoch einzelne Publicisten ein internationales gemeinsames Recht der Kriegscontrebande geleugnet, oder es nur von ausdrücklichen Vertragsbewilligungen abhängig erklärt haben, so muss dieses als der historischen Wahrheit widersprechend verworfen werden."—Heffters, § 158.

(*n*) L. iii. c. 1. v. 1. (*o*) Vol. i. c. 3. (*p*) Vide ante, p. 202.

according to the principles of eternal justice and the reason of the thing, affect the advantage to one Belligerent or the injury to the other accruing from this act of the alleged Neutral? Is the cannon or the sword, or the recruit who is to use them,(*q*) the less dangerous to the Belligerent because they were purchased, or he was enlisted, within the limits of neutral territory? Surely not. Surely the *locus in quo* is wholly beside the mark,—except, indeed, that the actual conveyance of the weapon or the soldier may evidence a bitterer and more decided partiality, a more unquestionable and active participation in the war.

CCXXXI. One of the principal champions of the doctrine which we [*322] are combatting is Lampredi;(*r*) but he reasons from *the very erroneous assumption, that the transport of contraband is only forbidden by treaties, and the usage derived from them, and that as treaties are silent with respect to the sale of contraband at home, such sale is not forbidden. From these false premises a false conclusion naturally flows.

CCXXXII. Bynkershoek,(*s*) however, entertains a different opinion; he says it is a *common and admitted practice* (*vulgo servamus*) that warlike implements, though they may not be carried, may be lawfully sold by Neutrals in their own country to either Belligerent, though it be well known that they intend to use them in war against each other.

It is remarkable that on this *assumption*, for it is not a deduction from reasoning, he builds his analogical argument that it is lawful for a Neutral to permit the enlistment [*323] *of troops in his country by a Belligerent: where is the difference, he pertinently asks, in principle between the two?—and it is in defending the legality of the foreign enlistment that he introduces incidentally the legality of the sale of contraband in the Neutral's own country.(*t*)

(*q*) Thus Bynkershoek argues:—"*Quod juris est* in instrumentis bellicis *idem* essé puto in militibus apud amicum populum comparandis, nisi in pace convenerit, ne vel uni vel alteri id facere licuerit."—L. i. c. 22, Q. J. P.

(*r*) Pt. i. s. 6. Martens doubtfully follows Lampredi's authority. See note *a*, to s. 318, of l. viii. c. vii. Azuni (Droit Marit., t. ii. p. 88,) also follows in Lampredi's wake.

Heineccius speaks doubtfully. After enumerating articles considered as Contraband in various Treaties, he says:—"Quamvis enim alter populus *forsan* suo jure utatur dum talia hosti alterius subministrat; nec minus tamen jure suo utitur, qui se adversus illos defendit, qui hostem reddere potentiorem non dubitant."—De Navibus ob Vect. Merc. vetit., Cap. I. s. xiv.

(*s*) "Si igitur subditi nostri, quorum ope in bello non indigemus, quibusque, ut civitatem mutent, nulla lex obstat, militarem operam recte exhibeant Principi amico, cur Princeps ille amicus hanc non recte conducat in amicæ gentis populo? Ubi locare licet, licet et conducere. Cur æque integrum non esset in imperio amici populi militem conducere, quam quasque emptiones venditiones, locationes conductiones celebrare, ceteraque commercia exercere? Neque obest, si forte, qui milites conducit, iis utatur adversus ejus, in cujus Imperio conduxit, amicos, cum quibus ei bellum est, constat enim, quod ad primam speciem, utriusque amico et hanc et illam partem oportere justam videri. Idque in instrumentis bellicis comparandis *vulgo servamus*, utut enim ea ad utrumque amicum non recte vehamus, sine fraude tamen vendimus utrique amico quamvis invicem hosti, et quamvis sciamus, alterum contra alterum his in bello esse usurum. Quod ad secundam speciem attinet, oportet sane præsentem Reipublicæ statum intueri, nec tantum prospicere in futurum, neque enim Principi amico interdicimus apud nos comparare pulverem bellicum, arma militum, et reliqua, quorum in bello usus est."—Bynkershoek, Q. J. P., l. i. c. 22.

(*t*) Vide ante, p. 217, and p. 321, n. q.

The answer seems to be that there is no difference in principle between the two permissions,—that both are, on one and the same principle, inconsistent with the duties of neutrality.

CCXXXIII. This remark, with respect to the identity of principle upon which the two permissions or prohibitions are found, is important, both in its general character, and also with especial reference to the doctrine of the North American United States upon both subjects. For it is remarkable that while the *foreign enlistment* is strenuously prohibited, as inconsistent with neutrality, by the United States, *the sale of contraband goods*, however, at home, and the *carriage* of them subject to the liability of seizure, are as strenuously insisted upon as being consistent with neutrality. "There is nothing" (their Supreme Court says, by the mouth of Mr. Justice Story,) "in our laws, or in the Law of Nations, that forbids our citizens from sending armed vessels, as well as munitions of war, to foreign ports for sale. It is a commercial adventure which no nation is bound to prohibit; and which only exposes the persons engaged in it to the penalty of confiscation."(*u*) The authority of Story is, and always will be, of the greatest weight; and it is not without sincere diffidence in his own opinion, though with a profound conviction of the inconsistency of the position laid down by this very learned Judge, with the general duties of neutrality, that the writer of these pages ventures to express his dissent from it. With respect to the bearing of municipal law upon this subject of International Law, the language of M. Portalis, no mean authority, is applicable: "Le droit ne nâit pas des réglemens, mais les réglemens doivent naître du droit."(*x*) [*324]

Belgium,(*y*) bound by the very charter of her national existence to a perpetual neutrality, might allow Russia, during the present war, to purchase any amount of ammunition and military stores without any infraction of neutrality, provided that she did not herself transport these articles to St. Petersburg, and provided, of course, that she allowed the same liberty of purchase to the allied Belligerents. But on what principle of reason or justice might she sell arms on *land* and preserve her neutrality, but the moment she transports them by *sea*, is she to be holden to have forfeited her neutrality?—or what is to be said if she sell and transport arms to one Belligerent, and only sell them from lack of transport, or any other cause, to the other Belligerent?—or if it be alleged that she has furnished arms of better quality, or of a different description to one than the other?—or why, if she may furnish arms, may she not also furnish men? It is clear that in either case there is an intermingling in the affairs of the Belligerents inconsistent with the *abstinence*, if not with that *impartiality*, which is essential to the character of the neutral.(*z*)

(*u*) The Santissima Trinidad, 7 Wheaton's (American) Reports, p. 340.

(*x*) Case of La Statira, cited Merlin, Rep., t. xiii. p. 108, ("Prise Maritime.")

(*y*) Vide ante, vol. i. p. 104.

(*z*) Galiani, c. ix. s. 4, refutes Lampredi; but the reader will find a very good chapter on the subject in M. de Hauteville's Work, t. ii. tit. viii. s. 3.

I cannot, however, understand why M. de H. thinks that he has made a great discovery, in deriving this, as well as other portions of Neutral Law, from the *Duty of the Neutral*, and not from the *Rights of the Belligerent;* there is, accurately speaking, no conflict between the two; in fact, the Duty of the Neutral springs from the right of the Belligerent.—Vide ante, p. 403.

The opinion which has been expressed as to the *unneutral* conduct of allowing the sale of contraband *at home*, coincides with that of the recent compilers and expounders of Valin: these learned persons say, "Il faut reconnaître que cette opinion est plus juste que la précédente, qui permet [*325] aux *Neutres de vendre des armes et des munitions aux Belligérants qui en feront le transport par terre, et qui ne le prohibe par mer que parce qu'il peut être empêché par les croisures; il faut reconnaître, en conséquence, que le transport et la vente des armes et munitions constituent une violation de la Neutralité, car c'est une immixtion à la guerre."(a)

CCXXXIV. Thirdly, the carrying of *materials* of a kind which does not certainly indicate whether their destination be for belligerent or ordinary commercial purposes—*res ancipitis vel promiscui usûs.*

Here we enter upon debateable ground:—

France adopts, as her existing law, the 11th Article of the Ordonnance de la Marine,(b) according to which, "Les armes, poudres, boulets, et autres munitions de guerre, même les chevaux et équipages, qui seront transportés pour le service de nos ennemis, seront confisqués en quelque vaisseau qu'ils soient trouvés, et à quelque personne qu'ils appartiennent, soit de nos sujets ou alliés."(c)

In the first place, it is to be observed, that, upon the subject of the present question, the Allied Powers,(d) England and France, are, according to the opinion of the modern rebuilders(e) of Valin's famous work, diametrically at variance with each other.

But in construing the language of this article, in itself, perhaps, sufficiently wide, France, according to this high authority already cited, considers herself under an obligation, springing from the variety and multiplicity of her Treaties upon the subject, to consider as Contraband [*326] only such *merchandize as has the form of an instrument which may directly subserve the purposes of war, "*ayant la forme d'un instrument pouvant servir directement à l'usage de la guerre.*"(e)

It would appear, therefore, that if all the *apparatus* of one of the most destructive engines of war were found on board a neutral ship in

(a) Traité des Prises Mar., par MM. De Pistoye et Duverdy, t. i. pp. 394-5.

(b) Vide ante, vol. i. p. 51.

(c) Nouveau Comment. sur l'Ordonnance, &c., t. ii. p. 264. (d) 1856.

(e) MM. de Pistoye et Duverdy, t. i. p. 405. "Mais ce qu'il y a de plus grave, c'est la diversité de la doctrine Anglaise et Française: elle tient les Neutres dans l'incertitude. Peuvent ils transporter des objets de *matériel naval?* Oui, s'ils interrogent la législation Française; non, s'ils interrogent la loi Anglaise." Nevertheless there is a Treaty between France and Denmark, 1742, which speaks a different language, vide post.

(e) MM. de Pistoye et Duverdy, t. i. p. 405. This was conceded by England in her Treaty with France of 1787, art. xxiii. The Treaty is not now in force.

In 1807, the Conseil des Prises decided, in the case of the Il Volante, "En effet, les bois de construction ne sont déclarés contrebande de guerre par aucun réglement Français encore subsistant, ni par aucun traité particulier."—Merlin Rep., c. xiii. p. 94. ("Prise Maritime.")

"Ainsi nous n'admettons pas que l'on puisse ranger, selon les besoins du moment, parmi les objets de contrebande de guerre à d'autres marchandises que celles qui sont dénominées dans l'art. xi. de l'Ordonnance de la Marine, et dans les traités diplomatiques signées par la France."—De Pist. et Duv., t. i. pp. 403-4.

detached pieces, and in an unfinished state, it might, according to the French interpretation, of International Law, be carried with impunity by the Neutral to the Belligerent. The Spanish Tribunals interpret the law of Contraband in the same manner as the French.(*f*)

CCXXXV. On the other hand, Grotius(*g*) divides the possible subject-matter of neutral transport into three heads:—

1. Things which can only be used in war—as arms.

2. Things which have no use in war, but which minister only to the pleasures of men.

3. Things which are capable of being used in war, but also in peace, "*quœ et in bello et extra bellum usum habent,*"—as money, provisions, ships, and the materials for ships.

Respecting the two former classes, there can be no question, namely, that the first do, and the second do not constitute Contraband.

As to the third class, as to things *ancipitis usûs*, they must *receive their construction by reference to the character and condition of the war. With his usual wisdom, he says, "*distinguendus erit belli status.*" If, Grotius says, I cannot defend myself without intercepting what the Neutral sends to the enemy, the necessity of the case gives me the right to do so, but it must be under the obligation of future restitution, "*nisi causa alia accedat.*" The illustrations used by Grotius in support of his position would seem to confine its application to beseiged or blockaded places; but the proposition itself, and the general reasoning upon it, are applicable to all articles *ancipitis usûs*, carried to the enemy, whatever may be his condition at the time. [*327]

CCXXXVI. Bynkershoek(*h*) justly rejects the opinion of Grotius, so far as it relates to any distinction to be made between the justice and injustice of a war, and he denies, with less reason, the distinction of Grotius with respect to the necessity of the Belligerent justifying his seizure of neutral goods under the obligation of restitution.

Bynkershoek infers, from a review of the jurisprudence of the tribunals of his own country, that contraband articles are such as are proper for war (*materia per se bello apta,*) and this irrespective of the consideration, whether or not their use extends beyond the occasion of war (*extra bellum.*)(*i*) Most implements of war have a use, he observes, in peace. In his time a sword was worn for the ornament, as well as used for the punishment of the criminal. Gunpowder is employed for amusement, and on occasions of public festivity, and yet, he observes, there can be no doubt that swords and gunpowder are Contraband.

The proposed test, therefore, of the possible use *extra bellum* of articles is inapplicable.

He proceeds to remark, that the examination of Treaties generally(*k*)

(*f*) D. Felix Joseph de Abreu y Bertodano, Tratado Juridico, Politico sobre Presas de Mar, y calidades que deben concurrir para hacerse legitimamente el Corso. Sm. 4to. Cadiz (1746) pt. i. c. 10, p. 136.

(*g*) L. iii. c. i. s. 5.

(*h*) Q. J. P., c. x.

(*i*) "Quæ uti sunt, bello apta esse possunt, *nec quicquam interesse an et extra bellum usum præbeant.*"—Ib.

(*k*) Vide post.

[*328] upon this subject would lead us to the conclusion, *that every thing is called Contraband which is of use to Belligerents in making war; whether they be warlike instruments, or materials *per se*, fit to be used in war.(*l*) Having made this admission, he enters upon the question, whether *the materials* themselves, out of which Contraband Goods are formed (*materia ex quâ quid bello aptari possit*) are themselves Contraband? and, not very consistently, avers that *reason* and *precedents* incline him to dissent from the opinion of Zouch,(*m*) who holds that such materials are Contraband. The *reason* appears to be, that inasmuch as there is scarcely any kind of material out of which something, at least, for war might not be fabricated, the interdiction of such materials would, he thinks, be a total prohibition of commerce, and it might be as well so expressed and understood.

Of the *precedent* which he relies upon, two Treaties between the Swedes and Dutch,(*n*) and one between the English and Dutch(*o*) alone are cited; quite insufficient, as nobody was better aware than Bynkershoek, to constitute the semblance of a general custom.

Indeed, in the very next sentence, we find him stating that it sometimes happens that *materials for building ships* *are interdicted [*329] if the enemy is in great need of them and cannot well carry on the war without them. Accordingly, he adds, that these materials were prohibited by edicts of the Dutch States General against the Portuguese in 1657, against the English in 1652, and against the French in 1639.

These precedents, the same in number as those relied on for the contrary opinion, he pronounces to be exceptions which confirm the general rule.

He then considers whether *scabbards* are Contraband. Bellus reports a decision of military judges condemning them as such, but expressing his private opinion the other way. Bynkershoek agrees with the military judges, because scabbards, although *promiscui usûs*, are instruments prepared for war. "Without scabbards," he says, "there would not be swords; without swords, there would not be war." Upon *sword-hilts* he passes the same judgment, and also upon *holsters*, *saddles*, and *belts*; unless, indeed, they should be in so small a quantity as to negative the presumption that they were designed for war. Here the reader will

(*l*) "Quæ uti hostibus suggeruntur, bella gerentibus inserviunt, sive instrumenta bellica sint, *sive materia per se bello apta.*"

(*m*) De Jure Feciali, pars. 2, s. 8, qu. 8. "Cum prohibitum est ne arma, aut naves ad hostes deferantur, quæritur, an si quis ferrum, ex quo arma, vel tabulas aut ligna, ex quibus naves construuntur, deferat, an incidant in commissum? Dubitari potest, quia à composito ad materiam non bene arguitur, et Statutum, vel Edictum pœnale non est extendendum. E contra statuitur quod ubi est eadem ratio prohibitionis materiæ, et speciei, idem jus in utraque intelligendum maxime ad præcavendum fraudem."

(*n*) November 26, 1675, art. iv. October 12, 1679, art. xvi.

(*o*) December 1, 1674, art. iv.

M. de Hauteville is in error when he says of Bynkershoek's disquisition on Contraband. "Sa discussion est appuyée sur *les traités qui, à ses yeux, forment la loi internationale*, et sur l'usage" (t. ii. p. 353); as, indeed, his own citation shows:— "Jus gentium in hanc rem non aliunde licet discere quam ex *ratione* et usu . . . . . usus intelligitur ex perpetua quodammodo paciscendi edicendique consuetudine."

observe the principle of considering the circumstances of each case is directly admitted—a principle which, it will be seen, has been fully adopted by the English and North American Tribunals. As to *saltpetre,* he says more doubt may be entertained, it not being *per se* an article fit for war; and yet he admits it is included in the catalogues of contraband articles on which he has been relying for evidence of custom, being sometimes mentioned with, sometimes without, the addition of gunpowder; that is to say, when gunpowder is omitted, saltpetre is used in lieu of it; and when both are mentioned, they are considered as synonymous. Bynkershoek here adopts that course, for the adoption of which, he is in the habit of reproaching Zouch; that is to say, he expresses no opinion of his own, but leaving his reader, after a statement on both sides, to infer what it may be from the course of his argument—a course which it may often be not only the most modest, but the wisest, the nature of the subject being remembered, for a writer upon International Law to adopt.

*CCXXXVII. Bynkershoek, therefore, as well as Grotius, though they furnish us with some valuable general principles, [*330] can hardly be said to solve the vexed question as to the power of deciding by *enumeration* the different articles which may compose the class of Contraband.

Yet Bynkershoek lived in a century(*p*) when the subject had undergone much more investigation than it had received in the time of Grotius. Bynkershoek was a jurist not less remarkable for his vigour and independence of mind, than for his accurate and profound erudition. He had filled the office of Judge in a country whose commerce was deeply interested in the settlement of the question of Contraband. The result of his investigation into the subject, are two general rules with regard to the articles which constitute Contraband:—

1. "Nequicquam interesse an et extra bellum usum præbeant."

2. That Contraband includes all things capable of use in war. "Sive instrumenta bellica sint, sive materia per se bello apta."

It is not an unfair inference, from the generality of these expressions, that the specification of what is "materia per se bello apta" must always in some measure depend upon the particular circumstances of each war, and upon the changes which science may have wrought in the adaptation of ingredients, formerly serviceable only for pacific purposes, to the uses of war.(*q*)

Such, it will be seen, has been the doctrine, carefully guarded indeed and restrained, which has been acted upon by the International Tribunals of England and the United States of North America.

CCXXXVIII. Such, too, is the doctrince of Heineccius himself, perhaps the principal writer upon this subject, and to *whom [*331] Bynkershoek refers in terms of high commendation.(*r*) It will

(*p*) Vide ante, vol. i. Preface, p. xiv. (*q*) Vide post, p. 359.

(*r*) Q. J. P., c. xiv. in fine.

Heineccius says, in the passage referred to by Bynkershoek, "Ad hostes vero quas merces deferre nefas habeatur, pluribus inter gentes conventionibus est explanatum. Exstant eam in rem *Tractatus Hispaniæ Regis* cum Belgis, Regis

be seen from the following extract from one of the writings of Heineccius, though not the one referred to by Bynkershoek, that the particular circumstances and state of the war are of paramount consideration in determining the question of Contraband.

"Magnum sanè aliquando momentum, in bellis habent etiam res minimi momenti, si hostis laboret inopiâ; nec rerum istarum aliunde copia sit. Sæpe urbes munitissimæ ob herbæ istius combustibilis, vel vini adusti inopiam fecerunt, et famem facilius tolerare militem præsidiarium quam rerum illarum desiderium. Quis ergo negat; tum cives, tum exteros male mereri de Republicâ, qui talia suppeditant hostibus nostris, sine quibus facilè adigi ad deditionem potuissent. Adeo verum est, belli temporibus, commercia non modo inter hostes cessare, verum etiam amicis et neutrarum partium gentibus non promiscuè permitti negotiationem cum hostibus (nisi sibi hæ securitatem à Belligerante utroque stipulantur.) Quum enim hosti in hostem infinitum omnia liceant quæ ad debellandum illum *sunt necessaria, licebit sanè et gentem [*332] amicam impedire quo minus hosti res quibus validior instructiorque ad bellum gerendum fiat advehere possit."(*s*)

CCXXXIX. Zouch(*t*) argues the question upon first principles. On the one hand, he says, it may be contended that the law of Contraband, being of a penal character, is not to be extended beyond its strict meaning, and the argument from the prohibition of a composite thing to the prohibition of the elements of which it is compounded is illogical. On the other hand, it consists with sound reasoning to say, that where the reason for the prohibition of both is applicable, the law is equally applicable to both ("*ubi est eadem ratio prohibitionis, materiæ et speciei, idem jus in utrâque censendum est,*") especially when the object is to prevent fraud; and therefore it was that in the Roman Law(*u*) the famous *Senatûs Consultum Macedonianum*, when it forbad loans of money to a minor, forbad also the loan of things for which money could be procured, *cum contractus fraudem sapit.*" So it is according to the "*jus commune,*" that when *weapons made of iron* are pronounced to be

Galliæ cum civitatibus Hanseaticis, ejusdem cum Batavis, *Anglorum* cum Polonis et Suecis, aliique hujus generis complures, in quibus mercibus vetitis accenseri animadvertimus omnia arma ignivomo, eorumque adparatus, qualia sunt tormenta, bombardæ, mortaria, betardæ, bombi, granatæ, circuli picei, tormentorum sustentacula, furcæ, balthei, pulvis nitratus, restes igni capiendo idoneæ, sal nitrum, globi, item hastæ, gladii, galeæ, cassides, loricæ, bipennes, spicula, equi, ephippia, aliaque instrumenta bellica. Quin et triticum, hordeum, avena, legumina, sal, vinum, oleum, vela, restes, et si qua alia ad adparatum nauticum pertinent. . . . . Ceterum sunt quædam, de quibus inter gentes aliquando disceptatum est, an mercibus vetitis sint accensenda. Sic de vaginis aliquando dubitatum. . . . . Vaginis non minus opus est hosti, quam gladiis; et quamvis vaginis non vulneret aut stragem edat; inutiles tamen essent ipsi gladii futuri, nisi vaginæ eos a pluvia et rubigine tuerentur. Eadem ergo ratio, quæ vela, restes nauticas, frumenta, prohiberi suasit, ipsis etiam vaginis facile poterit accommodari."—De Navib. ob Vect. Merc. vetit. Comm. xiv.

(*s*) Heineccius, De Jur. Princ. circ. Com., s. 12.

(*t*) Juris et Judic. Fecial Quæst., pars. 2, s. 8. "Utrum prohibitâ speciè ne ad hostes deferatur, materiam ex quâ conficetur species, intercipere liceat."

(*u*) How far this Law supplies analogical reasoning in questions of International Jurisprudence, see vol. i. pp. 31-36.

Contraband, the *iron* of which they are to be made should fall under the same *ban*.

CCXL. *Loccenius*,(*x*) it will be seen, comprehends *provisions* generally in his class of Contraband.

Vattel, who was not at all disposed to widen the sphere of Contraband, uses language which intimates the impossibility, in his opinion, of exact specification upon the subject.

"Les choses (he says) qui sont d'un usage *particulier* pour la guerre, et dont on empêche le transport chez l'ennemi, s'appellent marchandises de Contrebande. Telles sont les armes, les munitions de guerre, *les bois, et tout ce qui *sert à la construction et à l'armement des vaisseaux de guerre, les chevaux, et les vivres mêmes en certaines occasions où l'on espère de reduire l'ennemi par la faim.*"(*y*) [*333]

CCXLI. Nothing can be more unscientific or unsatisfactory than the reasoning by which Hübner(*z*) arrives at the conclusion that things *ancipitis usûs*, of which he gives a long catalogue, are not to be deemed Contraband unless they are being conveyed to blockaded ports. He attempts to make a "*fixation de la Contrebanda de guerre au premier et au second chef.*"

"*Contrebande au premier chef*" includes the class of goods useful only for war, and some of those *ancipitis usûs*, but only when supplied to besieged or blockaded places. "*Contrebande au second chef*" includes articles of both classes which are furnished to one Belligerent and refused to another. So that (as Mr. Ward(*a*) justly observes,) the conclusion of Hûbner's argument is, that none of the things contained in his long catalogue can ever become Contraband at all, so long as the Neutral is content to furnish *both* Belligerents with them *at the same time*.

In that catalogue there is scarcely an article which has not at one time or other been declared Contraband by the Treaties of all European nations. But it is manifest that the right of the Belligerent to prohibit the carriage of Contraband, and the duty of the Neutral to abstain from it, depends upon the noxious and nocent property of the article, not upon the partiality or impartiality of the Neutral to grant them to one and refuse them to another Belligerent. The speculation of Hübner has neither reason nor usage to recommend it.

CCXLII. The attempt to enumerate the articles of Contraband has been, with the exception of Hübner, rarely if ever made by International Jurists. They have been compelled, by the nature of the subject, to employ *comprehensive terms and general rules, both including and excluding many things which open a wide field for discussion; that is, of course, with respect to articles *ancipitis usûs*; for with respect to those of *immediate and exclusive use* for war, there can be but little dispute. Certainly some of the positions to be found respecting articles of *double use*, are so wide and flexible in their terms as to leave few things without their possible scope, and to justify the retort of the Swedish Ambassador(*b*) in 1655 to Cromwell, that inasmuch as *cloth* was [*334]

(*x*) De Jure Marit., l. i. c. iv. n. 5, p. 41.

(*y*) Vattel, Droit des Gens, tom. iii. c. vii. s. 112.

(*z*) Ib., p. 180.

(*a*) P. 244.

(*b*) Whitelock's Memorials, p. 635.

necessary in war for the troops, that staple of English commerce might be classed as Contraband, which he supposed would not be exactly agreeable to the English authorities.

Assuredly it will be found, as the result of an historical examination of the Treaties(c) upon this subject, that articles of an unchanged and unchangeable nature in themselves, have at different times, and under various circumstances, been variously regarded in their relation to the question of Contraband.

CCXLIII. It would seem, therefore, that *circumstances* must be taken into consideration; that reason and justice demand that the *state of the war*, as well as *the character* and *destination of the cargo*, should influence the decision whether articles of a *double use* be Contraband or not; that the observation of Grotius, "*distinguendus belli status*," is founded on theory and practice; that the doctrine, which Continental Jurists have of late years been in the habit of designating by the name of Contraband *per accidens*, and which will be seen to be in substance maintained by England and the United States of North America, is neither unjust nor unreasonable.

CCXLIV. It is not, however, to be inferred from what has been said, that the distinction between that species of Contraband, which is unquestionably *bellici usûs*, and that which is *ancipitis usûs*, is practically nugatory and of no avail. On the contrary, it will be seen that the most important practical *distinction subsists between them, namely, [*335] a distinction between the *penal consequences*(d) which the carriage of them entails upon the carrier.

It will be seen, too, that upon this part of the subject, namely, the penal consequences of carrying articles *ancipitis usûs*, that the circumstance of such articles being or not being of the natural growth, or of the manufacture of the country of the carrier, has been attended with very important consequences.

CCXLV. We now enter upon what may fairly be termed *nobilissima Juris Gentium quæstio;* viz.—Whether ever, and, if ever, under what circumstances, *Provisions* are Contraband?

On the 9th of May, 1793, the National Convention of France decreed that neutral vessels laden with provisions, destined to an enemy's port, should be arrested and carried into France; and one of the earliest acts of England, in that war,(e) was to detain *all* neutral vessels going to France and laden with corn, meal, or flour.(f)

CCXLVI. The Foreign Office of Great Britain was presided over, at that time, by a statesman(g) who had deeply studied the science of International Law, and who afterwards, on various occasions, but especially in the *Letters of Sulpicius* and the *Speech on the Convention with Russia*,(h) manifested to the world how completely he had mastered the subject of his labours.

(c) Vide ante, vol. i. pp. 45-7; vol. ii. pp. 55-6, as to the effect of Treaties upon general International Law.

(d) Heffters, s. 160.
(e) Instructions of 8th June, 1793.
(f) Vide post, p. 343.
(g) Lord Grenville.
(h) November 13, 1801.

In 1793, Great Britain addressed, through her minister at Copenhagen, the following :—

"*Declaratory Memorial to the Court of Denmark, respecting its Navigation during the War with France.*(*i*)

"No one can be mistaken, how much the circumstances *of the present war differ from those upon which the Law of Nations, [*336] introduced among the Powers of Europe, and its usual customs, are founded. It can be as little denied, that this difference must have an important and essential influence upon the exercise of the privileges which belong to the neutral Powers, by virtue of the universal Law of Nations, or by separate Treaties.

"At present there exists no Government in France which is acknowledged either by the belligerent Powers or even by those who still adhere to Neutrality. The Court of Denmark has no Minister at Paris; and since the tragical end of His late Most Christian Majesty, it has received none from France. This Court has taken care not to acknowledge the existence of a legitimate authority in France; and indeed there exists none in that country; and although special causes have prevented this Court from entering into the war, yet it cannot consider France as a Power with whom it would find it possible to preserve the former Treaties of Amity and Neutrality.

"If, therefore, in usual cases, a neutral Power continues to carry on commerce with two nations engaged in war with each other, and in friendship with the said neutral Power, the path of negotiations ever open, as well as the acknowledged usages of all the jurisdictions in Europe, constantly offer to the said neutral Power means of ascertaining whether or not the Neutrality kept by one of those nations is also observed by the other in the like manner; the said neutral Power may ascertain whether that Neutrality is not misused by one of those Powers to the prejudice of the other, and the impartial friendship thereby violated,—a friendship to which both nations have an equal claim; and if, by unforeseen circumstances, the usual mode of exercising the neutral commercial privileges should become especially and more detrimental to one of those Powers than the other, the injured Power might, by friendly representations, render valid this principle with the latter, and renounce without difficulty a right which ceases to be any longer consistent with that Neutrality.

*"None of these circumstances is admissible in the present case. Denmark, while she preserves all her neutral privileges [*337] of commerce with regard to England,—privileges which are secured to her in the usual cases by the universal Law of Nations and her separate Treaties,—she can, in no respect, be assured of the observance thereof in France, where that Neutrality, has already been and is still daily violated,—where His Danish Majesty has no Minister to enforce his rights and the rights of his subjects,—where His Danish Majesty acknowledges

(*i*) Annual Register, (1793,) vol. xxxv. p. 176. German translation in De Martens, Rec., v. 569; French translation in Koch, Hist. des Tr., ii. 119, (ed. Bruxelles, 1837.)

no lawful authority, and where there are indeed no other laws nor tribunals except the will of a licentious populace.

"His Danish Majesty will also find it impossible to treat with France in an amicable manner, and as a Neutral Power, respecting the means of introducing those measures of precaution, upon the observance of which the other Belligerent Powers have so great a right to insist, in order that the prerogotive neutral commerce, especially the corn and grain trade, be not abused at a time when so many circumstances, perfectly new, have acceded. It is a fact of universal notoriety, that the corn-trade of France with foreign countries is no longer a mere private trade, but that, contrary to all custom, it remains almost entirely in the hands of the pretended Executive Council, and of the different municipalities. It can, therefore, no longer be considered as a mere combination of private speculations, of which the individuals of other nations partake, but as a business immediately carried on by the above-mentioned pretended Government which has declared war against us.

"It is equally notorious, that at the present moment, one of the most essential expedients to compel those who have declared war against us to equitable terms of peace, consists in their being prevented by importation to prevent that want, which is a necessary consequence of what they have done, in order to arm the whole labouring class of the people of France against the other Governments and the general tranquillity of Europe. [*338] It is a principle allowed *by all the writers upon the public right, that importation may be prevented, if there are hopes that by so doing one can conquer an enemy, and especially so, if the want of that enemy has been occasioned by those measures which they took to injure us; and it is incontrovertible that this case, quite new in its kind, cannot be judged by the principles and rules which were only made for wars carried on according to the customs introduced among the Sovereigns of Europe.

"It is further to be observed, that His Danish Majesty, if he gives reception in his ports to French privateers with their prizes, cannot secure to himself that security which is requisite, according to the laws of nations, for the validity of their letters of marque, and for the regularity of their conduct. The Courts of Justice cannot, without involving themselves in a manifest contradiction, acknowledge the legality of any patent or letter of marque that is derived from a Government which his majesty does not acknowedge to be sovereign. On account of this non-acknowledgment, prizes can neither be condemned, nor British subjects and British property be retained, in the ports belonging to a friendly Power, whose protection they are entitled to claim, without a direct violation of the Treaties; and it is, above all, impossible to apply, in this case, the usual laws of an impartial Neutrality, since there is no acknowledged authority in France which can give to privateers the proper instructions respecting their conduct, and to which a Neutral Power might apply to bring them to punishment, whenever they deviate from those instructions, on the non-observance of which they are not to be considered as legal privateers, but only as pirates.

"(Signed) HAILES."

CCXLVII. This memorial produced a reply from Denmark, which the ability and courage of Count Bernstorf, the Prime Minister of that country, has rendered one of the most admirable state papers, and one of the soundest expositions *of the general principles of International Law, which any age or country can boast. [*339]

The Counter Declaration of the Court of Denmark, in reply to the Memorial delivered by the British Minister, was as follows :(*l*)—

"The Law of Nations is unalterable. Its principles do not depend on circumstances. An enemy engaged in war, can exercise vengeance upon those who forget these principles, but in this case, and without violating the rigid law, a reciprocity of injuries may take place; but a Neutral Power, which lives in peace, cannot admit of, nor acknowledge, a compensation arising from such a reciprocity; it can only defend itself by its impartiality and by its Treaties. It is not pardonable for it to renounce its rights in favour of any Belligerent Power. The basis of its rights is the universal and public law, which knows no distinctions; *it is neither a party nor a judge.* The Treaties of Neutrals do not give privileges and favours. All their Treaties are *perfecti juris;* they are mutual obligations. That would be a contract, the very nature of which would be changed, if any of the contracting parties might at pleasure suppress, interpret, or restrain its provisions. In this manner, all Treaties would in general become impracticable, because they would be useless. Equality, good-will, security would suffer alike, and oppression would be the more unjust, because it was preceded by an infringement of a sacred contract, the advantages of which had been enjoyed, but which was only acknowledged as binding so long as interest did not oppose it.

"Denmark does not attempt to justify the present government of France in its nature and origin; but she will not give her judgment on the past, and her Neutrality will not *permit her to express her whole mind on this subject. We only confine ourselves to lamenting the disasters which have befallen that country, and, on its account, all Europe; and to wishing to see them brought to a speedy termination. But the present question does not relate to the approval of the form of Government in France, or to its recognition, which we have always refused. The nation is there, and the authority which it acknowledges is that to which application is made in cases concerning single individuals. The commercial connections subsist likewise in the same manner as they did between England and France, as long as the latter chose to preserve peace. The nation has not ceased to acknowledge her Treaties with us; at least, she conforms herself agreeable to those Treaties.(*m*) As she appeals to them, so do we appeal to them, and frequently with good success, both for ourselves, and in favour of those subjects of the Belligerent Powers who commit their effects to the protection of our flag. In cases of refusal and delay, we have frequently [*340]

(*l*) Annual Register, (1793,) vol. xxxv. p. 180, contains a *most imperfect and most untrustworthy* translation. I have carefully and largely corrected it in the text, by reference to the German version in De Martens, v. 577, and to the French version in Koch, Hist. des Tr., ii. 122. (ed. Bruxelles, 1837.)

(*m*) Vide post, p. 344.

been obliged to hear, often and reluctantly, that France is justified in Reprisals, because the nations at war with her show so little regard for their Treaties with us; and thus the neutral flag becomes the victim of errors which it may not have committed. The path of justice still continues open in France. The Consuls and the Mandataries of private individuals are heard. No one is prevented from applying to the Tribunals of commerce. This is sufficient in ordinary cases. No fresh negotiations are required for the maintenance of existing Treaties. No negotiators are necessary; there are judges, and this is sufficient."

The Danish Minister then refers to a passage in the English statement, and continues :(*n*)—

[*341] "These considerations are already weakened by the observation, *that our grievances are frequently heard in France, and that there is no impossibility(*nn*) of getting them redressed. The municipalities, to whom application must be made, are certainly not alike equitable; the sentences of the Tribunals of Commerce are not founded upon uniform principles; the resource of an appeal to a central authority is wanting; and these circumstances occasion at times grievous acts of injustice. In this respect none are greater sufferers than the Neutral Powers; and it would be very inequitable that they should be punished for it, and especially by those Powers who cry aloud against these unjust proceedings, and yet justify them by their own imitation."

The Danish Minister refers to the English note,(*o*) and continues :—

"A negotiation between a Neutral and a Belligerent Power, which would have for its object that the latter should not make use of Neutrality to the detriment of the former, cannot be thought of. A Neutral Power fulfils all its duties if it never recedes from the strictest impartiality, and from the acknowledged sense of its Treaties. As to those cases in which the Neutrality happens to prove more advantageous to one of the Belligerent Powers than to the other, such cases are foreign to the question of Neutrality, and do not affect it. This depends on local situations and circumstances of the moment, and does not remain alike. The detriments and advantages are compensated and balanced by time. All that which does not absolutely depend on a Neutral Power, ought to have no influence upon its Neutrality; otherwise a partial, and frequently but momentary, interest would become the interpreter and judge of existing Treaties."

[*342] *Reference is then made to the English note,(*p*) and the Danish Minister continues :—

"The distinction between private speculations and those made by the Government and the municipalities, seems to us to be as new as it is totally unknown to us. As this case has not happened, it would be superfluous to discuss the question, whether a contract between a Neu-

(*n*) Vide antè, p. 336.—"If therefore," &c., to "consistent with that Neutrality."

(*nn*) Translated "*possibility*" in Annual Register, vol. xxxv. p. 181.

(*o*) Vide antè, p. 337.—"None of these circumstances," &c., to "a licentious populace."

(*p*) Vide antè, p. 337.—"His Danish Majesty will also find," &c., to "declared war against us."

tral Government and a Belligerent Power, respecting supplies of provisions for armies, garrisons, towns, or of ships of war, can violate a Treaty in which no such exception has been mentioned.

"The only question here is respecting speculations which might be made by private individuals,—respecting the sale of products quite harmless in their nature, the disposal of which is not less important to the vendor than the possession of them is to the purchaser,—respecting the use of the ships of the nation which must chiefly seek her subsistence in navigation and the corn-trade. Nor is the question here about ports of war, but about ports of commerce: and if it be lawful to reduce by famine blockaded harbours, it would not be quite so just to accumulate the misery upon so many others, where it befalls the innocent, and may even reach provinces in France which have not deserved this increase of wretchedness, either on the part of England or on that of her allies."

Reference is again made to the English note,(q) and the Danish State Paper continues:—

"The distress, which is a consequence of the failure of provisions, is not something unusual, which might only take place in the present moment, or which might be occasioned by the circumstances which constitute the difference so often alleged between the present and former wars. France is almost constantly obliged to make imports from [*343] *abroad.—Africa, Italy, America, furnish her with much more corn than the Baltic. In the year 1709, France was exposed to more terrible famine than she is now; and yet England would not then avail herself of her present argument. On the contrary, when, soon after, Frederick IV., King of Denmark, on account of his war with Sweden, which, like France, required almost constantly importations from abroad, believed that he might adopt the principle that exportation can be lawfully prevented if one Belligerent has hopes to conquer another by so doing, and intended to apply, with regard to a whole country, this principle, which is only considered as valid with regard to blockaded ports, all the Powers remonstrated, especially Great Britain, and unanimously declared this doctrine to be new and inadmissible; so that the King was convinced, and desisted from it. A war can certainly differ from others with regard to its occasion, tendency, necessity, justice or injustice. This may be a most important question for the Belligerent Powers. It can, and must have influence upon the peace, upon the indemnification and other accessory circumstances. But all this is absolutely of no concern to the Neutral Powers. They will unquestionably interest themselves for those on whose side justice seems to be; but they have no right to give way to this sentiment. *Where a Neutrality is not quite perfect, it ceases to be Neutrality.*"

Reference is again made to the English note,(r) and the Danish State Paper continues:—

"The ships bearing the British flag, like those which bear that of the

(q) Vide antè, p. 337.—"It is equally notorious," &c., to "the Sovereigns of Europe," p. 338.

(r) Vide antè, p. 338.—"It is further to be observed," &c., to end of English note.

allies of England, find in all the harbours of his majesty every possible safety, assistance and protection; but those cannot be reckoned among their number which have been captured by their enemies. The French [*344] privateers cannot be considered as pirates by the Neutral *Powers, for England herself does not consider and treat them as such. In England, the prisoners, are deemed to be prisoners of war; they are exchanged; and negotiations have even been entered into for this purpose. The usual laws of war are there observed in all respects; and by this rule alone we ought to go. The tricoloured flag was acknowledged in Denmark at a period when it was acknowledged everywhere else. Every alteration, in this respect, would be impossible, without involving ourselves into a war which we have not deserved.

"The admittance of privateers in Norway is a consequence of this Neutrality, which knows no distinction. This has been the usage in all the maritime wars which ever afflicted Europe. All the nations in their turn have availed themselves of and desired it. The nature of the country allows no general prohibition. It would only bring us into dilemmas, because we could not abide by it in a remote country, where there are coasts of immense extent, numberless harbours and anchoring places, and only a small number of inhabitants. The prohibition would therefore be illusory, and even dangerous, because the French, in virtue of their decrees, would then destroy the ships which they would no longer hope to put in a state of safety. The subject is otherwise of small importance; and the means against it are numerous, and easily to be applied.

"(Signed) A. P. Von Bernstorf."

CCXLVIII. To assert that *Provisions* going to an *unblockaded* port can *never* be Contraband, is surely too large a proposition. Provisions may be of more value to the Belligerent than the most acknowledged Contraband of fabricated arms and prepared munitions of war.

To assert that the circumstances which make provisions Contraband must be of a special and exceptional nature, is a proposition concerning which there can be no reasonable doubt. The authority of Vattel,(*s*) as [*345] we have seen, is in *favour of the doctrine that provisions may be Contraband. Pothier,(*t*) on the other hand, maintains an exactly opposite doctrine. Whatever may be the authority derivable from the stipulations of *Treaties*, it will be found upon both sides of the question.

In estimating the conduct of Great Britain and Denmark upon this occasion, the jurist must rather consider whether the facts were such as

(*s*) L. 3, c. vii. s. 103.

(*t*) "A l'égard des munitions de bouches que les sujets des Puissances neutres nous envoient, elles ne sont point censées de contrebande, ni par conséquent sujettes à confiscation, sauf dans un seul cas, qui est lorsqu'elles sont envoyées à une place assiégée ou bloquée."—Traité du Droit de Propriété, pt. i. c. ii. ss. 2, 104.

So Valin (l. iii. t. ix. art. xi.) admits that Loccenius considers them Contraband, but says, "Par nos lois, et le droit commun, elle (la prohibition) n'a lieu en cette partie que par rapport aux places assiégées."

to bring the exportation of corn to France within the exceptional state of things in which provisions become, generally, contraband.

The principal facts appear to be,—

1. The critical state of France under the pressure of internal disorganization and belligerent force.

2. That the grain was purchased by the Government of France, and was taken out of the category of ordinary commercial speculation. Though very considerable weight is due to the latter of these positions, it nevertheless appears to the writer of these pages, that upon the *facts*, the reply of Denmark is well founded, and that the claim of England was not warranted by International Law.(*u*) There is, however, one important inaccuracy in Count Bernstorf's reply. He speaks of the observation of treaties by France towards Denmark; now France, by a treaty in the year 1749, with Denmark, had excepted grain from the category of contraband, yet we have seen that on the 9th of May, 1793, France, though the treaty of 1749 was in full force, issued the decree(*x*) that grain should be seized and brought in for preëmption. *This happened about two months *before* the statement as to the observation of treaties by France in the Danish memorial. [*346]

Nevertheless, it is true that the priority of misconduct on the part of France towards a Neutral did not justify a retaliatory misconduct on the part of England.

It was not only by Denmark that this claim on the part of England was at the outset resisted, but by the United States of North America. They contended that corn, flour, and meal, *being the produce of the soil and labour of the country*, were not contraband of war, unless carried to a place actually invested.(*y*) America argued, also, that the case stated by Great Britain of a well-founded expectation of reducing the enemy by famine, did not in *fact* exist, inasmuch as provisions were cheaper in France than in England.

The Treaty of Commerce with England, in 1794, provided that whatever materials served directly to the building and equipment of vessels, with the exception of unwrought iron and fir planks, should be considered contraband, and liable to confiscation; but the treaty left the question of provisions open and unsettled, and neither Power was understood to have relinquished the construction of the Law of Nations which it had asserted. The treaty admitted that provisions were not generally contraband, but might become so according to the existing Law of Nations, in certain cases, and those cases were not defined.

It was only stipulated, by way of relaxation of the penalty of the law, that whenever provisions were contraband, the captors or their Government, should pay to the owners the full value of the articles, together with the freight, and a reasonable profit. The Government of the United States has repeatedly admitted, that as far as that treaty enumerated

(*u*) Mr. Ward defends the conduct of Great Britain, pp. 182, 215, 223, 224, 227. On Contraband.

(*x*) Vide antè, p. 334.

(*y*) Mr. Jefferson's Letter to Mr. Pinckney, September 7th, 1793, and Mr. Randolph's Letter to Mr. Hammond, May 1st, 1794.

[*347] contraband articles, it was declaratory of the Law of *Nations, and that the treaty conceded nothing on the subject of contraband.(z)

CCXLIX. By the 7th article of the above-mentioned treaty it was also stipulated that a mixed commission should decide upon the claims of American citizens by reason of irregular or illegal captures and condemnations of war-vessels and other property under the authority of the British Government.

An occasion for putting in force the provisions of this stipulation soon arose.

The British instruction of June, 1793, had been revoked previous to the signature of this treaty; but before its notification, the British Government issued in April, 1795, an Order in Council, instructing its cruisers to stop and detain all vessels laden wholly or in part with corn, flour, meal, and other articles of provisions, and bound to any port in France, and to send them to such ports as might be most convenient, in order that such corn, &c., might be purchased on behalf of Government.

This last order was subsequently revoked, and the question of its legality became the subject of discussion before the mixed commission, constituted under the treaty. The Order in Council was justified upon two grounds:—

1. That it was made when there was a prospect of reducing the enemy to terms by famine, and that, in such a state of things, provisions bound to the ports of the enemy became so far contraband, as to justify Great Britain in seizing them upon the terms of paying the invoice price, with a reasonable mercantile profit thereon, together with freight and demurrage.

[*348] 2. That the order was justified by *necessity;* the British *nation being at that time threatened with a scarcity of the articles directed to be seized.

The first of these positions was rested not only upon the general Law of Nations, but upon the article of the treaty between Great Britain and America.(a)

As evidence of the general International Law, the authority of Vattel(b) and of Grotius(c) was relied upon; but, in the opinion of the Commission, unsuccessfully; partly on account of the want of precision in Vattel, and on account of the context in Grotius, confining, as it was conceived, the penalty of carrying provisions to besieged or blockaded places; and partly, also, with reference to the commentaries of Rutherforth (d)and Bynkershoek,(e) as establishing a contrary position. With regard to the 18th article of the treaty of 1794, it was conceived, that it left the question of contraband where it found it.

(z) Mr. Pickering's Letter to Mr. Munroe, September 12th, 1795. His Letter to Mr. Pinckney, January 16th, 1797. Instructions from the Secretary of State to the American Minister to France, July 15th, 1797. Kent's Comm., vol. i. pp. 140-1.

(a) Wheaton's Elem. of International Law, (Lawrence,) pp. 555-6.

(b) Droit des Gens, l. iii. c. vii. s. 112. (c) Grotius, l. iii. c. i. s. 5.

(d) Rutherforth's Inst., vol. ii. b. ii. c. ix. s. 19.

(e) Bynkershoek, Q. J. P. l. i. c. ix.

As to the second ground upon which the Order in Council was justified—*necessity*—Great Britain being, as alleged at the time of issuing it, threatened with a scarcity of those articles directed to be seized, it was answered that it would not be denied that extreme necessity might justify such a measure. It was only important to ascertain whether that necessity then existed, and upon what terms the right it communicated might be exercised.

Grotius, and the other text-writers on the subject, concurred in stating that the necessity must be real and pressing; and that even then it does not confer a right of appropriating the goods of others, until all other practicable means of relief have been tried and found inadequate. It was not to be doubted that there were other practicable means of averting the calamity apprehended by Great Britain. The *offer of an advantageous market in the different ports of the kingdom, was [*349] an obvious expedient for drawing into them the produce of other nations. Merchants do not require to be forced into a profitable commerce; they will send their cargoes where interest invites; and if this inducement is held out to them in time, it will always produce the effect intended. But so long as Great Britain offered less for the necessaries of life than could have been obtained from her enemy, was it not to be expected that neutral vessels should seek the ports of that enemy, and pass by her own? Could it be said that under the mere apprehension (not under the actual experience) of scarcity, she was authorized to have recourse to the forcible means of seizing provisions belonging to Neutrals, without attempting those means of supply which were consistent with the rights of others, and which were not incompatible with her exigency? After this order had been issued and carried into execution, the British Government did what it should have done before; it offered a bounty upon the importation of the articles of which it was in want. The consequence was, that Neutrals came with these articles, until at length the market was found to be overstocked. The same arrangement, had it been made at an earlier period, would have rendered wholly useless the Order of 1795.

Upon these grounds, a full indemnification was allowed by the Commissioners, under the 7th Article of the Treaty of 1794, to the owners of the vessels and cargoes seized under the Orders in Council, as well for the loss of a market as for the other consequences of their detention.(*f*)

CCL. On the other hand, the Executive Government of the United States of North America has frequently conceded, that the materials for the building, equipment and armament of ships of war, as timber and naval stores, are Contraband.(*g*)

*Questions of Contraband generally were much discussed during the continuance of the Neutrality of the North American [*350] United States in the war which broke out in 1793, and the United States

(*f*) Wheaton's Elem. of International Law (Lawrence,) pp. 560, 561.

(*g*) Mr. Randolph's Letter to M. Adot, July 6th, 1795. Mr. Pickering's Letter to Mr. Pinckney, January 16th, 1797. Letter of Messrs. Pinckney, Marshall, and Gerry to the French Minister, January 27th, 1798.

professed to be governed by the modern usage of nations on this point.(*h*)

CCLI. We now arrive at the consideration of the treatment which this subject of things *ancipitis vel promiscui usû* has undergone in the Prize Courts of Great Britain and North America. "I am aware," Lord Stowell says, "of the favourable positions laid down upon this matter by Wolffius and Vattel, and other writers of the Continent, although Vattel(*i*) *expressly admits* that *provisions* may, under circumstances, be treated as Contraband; and I take the modern established rule to be this, that generally they are not Contraband, but may become so under circumstances arising out of the particular situation of the war, or the conditions of the parties engaged in it. The Court must, therefore, look to the circumstances under which this supply was sent.

CCLII. "Among the circumstances which tend to preserve provisions from being liable to be treated as Contraband, one is, that they are of the growth of the country which exports them. In the present case, they are the *product of another country*, and that a hostile country; and the claimant has not only gone out of his way for the supply of the enemy, but he has assisted the enemy's ally in the war by taking off his surplus commodities.

CCLIII. "Another circumstance to which some indulgence, by the practice of nations, is shown is, when the articles are in their *native and unmanufactured state*. Thus iron is treated with indulgence, though [*351] anchors and other *instruments, fabricated out of it, are directly Contraband. Hemp is more favourably considered than cordage; and wheat is not considered as so noxious a commodity as any of the final preparations of it for human use. In the present case, the article falls under this unfavourable consideration, being a manufacture prepared for immediate use.

CCLIV. "But the most *important distinction* is, whether the articles were intended for the ordinary use of life, or even for mercantile ship's use; or whether they were going with a highly probable destination to military use!(*k*) Of the matter of fact on which the distinction is to be applied, the nature and quality of the port to which the articles were going is not an irrational test; if the port is a general commercial port, it shall be understood that the articles were going for civil use, although occasionally a frigate, or other ships of war, may be constructed in that port. *Contra*, if the great predominant character of a port be that of a port of naval military equipment, it shall be intended that the articles were going for military use, although merchant ships resort to the same place, and although it is possible that the articles might have been applied to civil consumption; for it being impossible to ascertain the final use of an article, *ancipitis usûs*, it is not an injurious rule which deduces both ways the final use from the immediate destination; and the

(*h*) President's Proclamation of Neutrality, April 22nd, 1793. Kent's Comm., vol. i. pp. 139-40.

(*i*) Vattel, l. iii. c. vii. s. 112.

(*k*) This doctrine is confirmed by Maisonnaire v. Keating, 2 Gallison's Amer. Rep., p. 325.

presumption of a hostile use, founded on its destination to a military port, is very much inflamed, if at the time when the articles were going, a considerable armament was notoriously preparing, to which a supply of those articles would be eminently useful."(*l*)

CCLV. The doctrine laid down in the foregoing extracts from the judgment of Lord Stowell, was, Mr. Chancellor *Kent(*m*) observes, "fully adopted by the Supreme Court of the United States, when [*352] we come to know and feel the value of Belligerents' rights, by becoming a party to a maritime war." The Chancellor goes on to observe that, "in the case of the Commercen the Supreme Court observed, as Lord Stowell had done, that by the modern Law of Nations, provisions were not generally Contraband, but they might become so on account of the particular situation of the war, or on account of their destination; that if they were destined for the ordinary use of life in the enemy's country, they were not Contraband; but that it was otherwise if destined for the army or navy of the enemy, or for his ports of military or naval equipment."

"But it is argued" (Mr. Justice Story says in the Commercen) "that the doctrine of Contraband cannot apply to the present case, because the destination was to a neutral country; and it is certainly true that goods destined for the use of a neutral country can never be deemed Contraband, whatever may be their character, or however well adapted to warlike purposes. But if such goods are destined for the direct and avowed use of the enemy's army or navy, we should be glad to see an authority which countenances this exemption from forfeiture, even though the property of a Neutral. Suppose, in time of war, a British fleet were lying in a neutral port, would it be lawful for a Neutral to carry provisions or munitions of war thither, avowedly for the exclusive supply of such fleet?—would it not be a direct interposition in the war, and an essential aid to the enemy in his hostile preparations? In such a case, the goods, even if belonging to a Neutral, would have had the taint of Contraband in its most offensive character, on account of its destination; and the mere interposition of a neutral port would not protect them from forfeiture."(*n*) And in a later part of the same judgment *he says: "It is in vain to contend that the direct effort of the [*353] voyage was not to aid the British hostilities against the United States. It might enable the enemy, indirectly, to operate with more vigour and promptitude against us, and increase his disposable force. But it is not the effect of the particular transaction that the law regards, it is the general tendency of such transactions to assist the military operations of the enemy, and the temptations which it presents to deviate from a strict Neutrality. Nor do we perceive how the destination to a neutral port can vary the application of this rule; it is only doing that indirectly which is prohibited in direct courses. Would it be contended that a Neutral might lawfully transport provisions for the British fleet and army while it lay at Bordeaux preparing for an expedition to the United

(*l*) The Jonge Margaretha, 1 Rob., pp. 194-5.
(*m*) Commentaries, vol. i. p. 143.
(*n*) The Commercen, 1 Wheaton, (Amer.) Rep., p. 387.

States? Would it be contended that he might lawfully supply a British fleet stationed on our coast? We presume that two opinions could not be entertained on such questions; and yet, though the cases put are strong, we do not know that the assistance is more material than might be supplied under cover of a neutral destination like the present."(*o*)

CCLVI. Upon the principles laid down in the foregoing judgments of Lord Stowell and Mr. Justice Story, *cheeses* fit for naval use, and going to a port of naval equipment, have been condemned as Contraband.(*p*)

Biscuits have shared the same fate, especially when going from one enemy's port to another.(*q*) *Wines* are not generally and *per se* Contraband, but when taken on their way to supply an armament of the enemy are condemned.(*r*)

CCLVII. In 1797, a dispute arose between the United States of [*354] North America and Spain as to this question of **naval stores.* America had, by Treaty with Spain, covenanted to exclude, and, by Treaty with England, to include them in the catalogue of Contraband.

Spain protested against this as a failure in the duty of reciprocity. The Government of the United States, however, after having demonstrated that this reciprocity could only be shown when Spain was at peace and the United States at war, proceeded to defend the stipulation with England upon the ground of its conformity with the principles of International Law. "Ship timber and naval stores" (the American Secretary wrote) "are by the Law of Nations contraband of war. . . . . . Permit me to say, that our engagement with Great Britain ought to be no matter of surprise to the Catholic King; because His Majesty has seen, during the whole course of the American war, how steadily Great Britain persisted, in opposition to the demands of all the maritime Powers, to maintain her claims under the Law of Nations, to capture enemy's property, and timber, and naval stores, as Contraband in neutral ships. Could His Catholic Majesty, therefore, expect that Great Britain would relinquish her legal rights to a nation (the United States) which abounded in materials for building and equipping ships?"(*s*)

CCLVIII. We have seen, from the foregoing judgment, under what circumstances naval stores and materials for ship-building are holden confiscable by the English and North American Prize Courts. With respect to any aid to be obtained from an investigation of Treaties towards the elucidation of this subject, not only can no general inference be derived from their examination, but, on the contrary, it will appear that the same States have declared naval materials to be Contraband in one Treaty, and not Contraband in another.(*t*)

[*355] *CCLIX. The principles on which the French Prize Courts act, may be gathered from the following decision of the Conseil des Prises in 1807. The subject was the capture of the Austrian ship

(*o*) The Commercen, 1 Wheaton's (Amer.) Rep., p. 392.

(*p*) The Zelden Rust, 6 Robinson's Adm. Rep., p. 93. The Frau Margaretha, Ib., p. 92. The Jonge Margaretha, 1 Rob., p. 193.

(*q*) The Ranger, 6 Rob., p. 125. (*r*) The Edward, 4 Rob., p. 68.

(*s*) Debrett's State Papers, p. 380. Ward on Contraband, p. 254.

(*t*) Manning, pp. 287-9.

Il Volante, by he French privateer, l'Etoile de Bonaparte. The Court said:—

"Attendu qu'il est constant par les pièces de bord que le navire et le chargement sont propriétés neutres; que le port de Messine, pour lequel l'expédition était destinée, malgré l'autorité que peuvent y exercer les Anglais, n'est point soumis au blocus, qui, aux termes du décret du 21 Novembre, 1806 (rapporté ci-après, No. 7,) a lieu pour les ports et les Iles Britanniques; et que les sucres, suivant le manifeste et le connaissement, proviennent de Lisbonne, et ont été raffinés par la compagnie de Trieste et de Fiume;

"Attendu que le moyen déduit de la qualité des bois composant la majeure partie de la cargaison, et sur lequel les capteurs ont le plus insisté, ne peut être accueilli, si l'on considère que, loin qu'il soit démontré que ces bois appartiennent exclusivement à la construction des bâtimens de guerre, comme l'ont pensé les experts qui ont opéré, hors la présence des parties intéressées, le contraire semble résulter, tant de la teneur du procés-verbal de visite qu'ils ont irréguliérement dressé, que de la dimension des planches et de leur nombre comparé avec la capacité du navire;

"Qu'au reste, et en abordant la question de Contrebande élevée par le corsaire, il est facile de se convaincre que la solution lui en est contraire. En effet, *les bois de construction* ne sont déclarés contrebande de guerre par aucun réglement Français encore subsistant, ni par aucun traité particulier. C'est faute d'avoir lu le Traité de 1742, conclue entre la France et le Danemarc, qu'on a dit qu'il comprenait sous cette dénomination le bois de construction. Si, par l'arrêté du directoire, du 12 Ventôse de l'an V., ils ont été rangés parmi les objets prohibés, ce n'a été que relativement aux Américains, qui avaient souffert, par leur Traité de 1794 avec les Anglais, que ces objets fussent regardés comme de Contrebande; et la disposition de cet *arrêté est de droit annulée par la convention du 8 Vendémiaire de l'an IX., passée entre la France et les [*356] Etats-Unis d'Amérique, qui, en spécifiant tous les articles de Contrebande, n'y a point compris les bois de construction. Lors même que l'on aurait pu soutenir avec quelque fondement que la prohibition contenue dans le arrête du 12 Ventôse de l'an V., eût été applicable â tous les Neutres, elle se trouverait implicitement rapportée par l'arrêté du 29 Frimaire de l'an VIII., qui, à l'égard de la navigation des Neutres, a rétabli les dispositions du réglement du 26 Juillet, 1778, dont l'art. 15, ordonne l'exécution de l'ordonnance de la marine de 1681, laquelle, dans l'énumération des objets de contrebande de guerre, ne place point les bois de construction; d'où il faut conclure que la destination pour un port ennemi des planches chargées sur le navire Il Volante, quel qu'en dût être l'emploi, ne les a point rendues confiscables, et que tout au plus elle serait susceptible, avec les autres circonstances de la prise, d'exempter les capteurs des dommages et intérêts;

"Le conseil décide que la prise faite par le corsaire Français, l'Etoile de Bonaparte, du navire Autrichien Il Volante, est invalide; en faite pleine et entière main-levée au profit des propriétaires; en conséquence, ordonne que le dit navire, ensemble les marchandises de son chargement, seront remis avec les pièces de bord, à la disposition du capitaine Natali Hort; à quoi faire, tous gardiens, séquestres et dépositaires seront contraints par toutes voies, même par corps, quoi faisant déchargés. Sur la demande en dommage-intérêts, met les parties hors de cause."(u.)

CCLX. It is to be observed, however, that France in her Treaty with [*357] Denmark of 1742, which has been *subsequently confirmed by her Convention of 1842, has comprised in the category of Contraband, tar, pitch, rosin, sail-cloth, hemp, cordage, masts, and timber for purposes of war (*bois de construction.*)

CCLXI. Sail-cloth,(x) masts, anchors,(y) *tar*,(z) and *pitch* going to the enemy's use, are liable, under the modern Law of Nations to be seized as Contraband in their own nature, and without respect to the character of the port to which they are destined. In 1750, the Judges of the British Court of Appeal in matters of prize, declared pitch and tar, the produce of Sweden, on board a French ship bound to a French port, to be Contraband, and subject to confiscation. In the more modern understanding of this matter, however, goods of this nature being the produce of Sweden, the actual property of Swedes, and conveyed by their own navigation, have been deemed, in British Courts of Prize, subject only to the milder rights of *Pre-occupancy* and *Pre-emption*;(a) and it may be said that though pitch and tar are now generally Contraband in a maritime war, the rule is so far relaxed as to allow the carrying of these articles when they are the produce of the claimant's country.(b) This [*358] *relaxation is understood with a condition that it may be brought in, not for confiscation but for *Pre-emption:* to entitle the party to the benefit of this rule, however, a perfect bona fides is required.(c) On the other hand, the carrying of pitch and tar to a legal port, with an intention of selling them there, and, if not, of carrying them on to an enemy's port for sale, is illegal, and the intention of so doing being proved, and that the ulterior destination was concealed, the vessel, being the property of the same owners, is liable to condemnation.(d) But tar

(u) Merlin, Répertoire de Jurisprudence, vol. xiii. p. 94. Such too it appears is the present law:—"Peuvent-ils (les Neutres) transporter des objets de matériel naval? *Oui*, s'ils interrogent la législation Française; *non*, s'ils interrogent la loi Anglaise."—De Pist. et Duverdy, t. 1. p. 405. (Paris, 1855.)

(x) The Neptunus, 3 Rob. Adm. Rep. p. 108.

(y) The Staat Embden, 1 Rob. Adm. Rep. p. 29. The Charlotte, 5 Rob. Adm. Rep. p. 314.

(z) Dans la guerre de 1700, le *goudron* y fut compris, parceque les ennemis le déclarèrent de Contrebande, excepté celui qui étoit trouvé sur les vaisseaux Suédois, parceque c'est une production de leur cru . . . le *goudron* a aussi été déclaré de Contrebande, avec la *poix*, *résine*, *les voiles*, *chanvres*, et cordages, les mâts et *bois de construction* pour les navires. Ainsi en cette partie il n'y auroit à plaindre de la conduite des Anglais, sans leur contravention aux Traités particuliers, car *de droit ces choses sont de Contrebande aujourd'hui, et depuis le* commencement de ce siècle, ce qui n'étoit pas autrefois néanmoins."—Valin, Ord. de la Mar., t. ii. l. iii. art. xi. Vattel includes amongst Contraband "*les bois, et tout ce qui sert* à la construction et à l'armement de vaisseaux de guerre," &c., l. iii. c. vii. p. 112, in fine. Vide ante, vol. i. p. 41, remarks on this passage from Valin.

(a) The Maria, 1 Rob. Adm. Rep., p. 372. This is the famous case of the Swedish convoy.

(b) The Sarah Christina, ib. p. 241.

(c) The Sarah Christina, 1 Rob. Adm. Rep., p. 241.

(d) The Richmond, 5 Ib., p. 336.

and pitch which are neither the produce of the exporting country nor protected by Treaty, are Contraband.(*e*)

CCLXII. The British Order in Council of July, 1807, permitting to Sweden the liberty of trade with the common enemy in innocent articles only, was holden under the circumstances to imply a prohibition as to naval stores. A cargo, therefore, on board a Swedish ship, and consisting of pitch and tar, being naval stores, was holden to be of the nature of Contraband, in such a sense as to preclude their falling under the description of innocent articles. The cargo was accordingly condemned, but the ship and innocent articles of cargo were decreed to be restored under the above Order of Council, though in opposition to the general law.(*f*)

Pitch and tar bona fide intended for the *ship's use* which carries them, are not Contraband. The bona fides is a question to be determined by all the circumstances of the case, among which the *quantity* is a very material ingredient.(*g*)

*CCLXIII. With respect to *hemp* fitted for naval use,(*h*) the relaxation of the strict rule also prevailed during the last war, [*359] and when the produce and property of the exporting country, it was not confiscated,(*i*) though liable to seizure and pre-emption by the Belligerent. The burden of proof that it is such produce and property lies upon the claimant.(*k*)

Brimstone may or may not be contraband, according to the circumstances of the case.(*l*)

Copper in a state fit for sheathing(*m*) has been condemned.

Cargoes of *barks*, *fir planks*, *battens*, and *fire-wood*, are articles which, if destined for a port of naval equipment, *and pronounced by competent shipwrights to be fit for ship-building, will be con- [*360]

(*e*) The Twee Juffrowen, 4 Ib., p. 242.

(*f*) The Neptunus, 6 Ib., 403.

(*g*) The Richmond, 5 Rob., p. 334. Pitch and tar, the property of a Swedish merchant, and the produce of Sweden, taken on board a Swedish ship on a voyage from a Swedish to a Dutch port, were holden not to be Contraband, and restitution ordered, but captors' expenses of taking the depositions allowed. The Christina Maria, 4 Rob., p. 166. In a similar case, restitution having passed on the original evidence, and the cargo having been purchased by Government, the expenses of the claimant and captor were decreed to be paid by Government. The Resolution, ibid., note. A cargo of tar taken going from a port of the country of which it could not be the produce, condemned. The Jonge Tobias, 1 Rob. p. 329. Pitch and tar going on a concealed destination to the enemy's port, the ship and cargo were both condemned, the master being a part owner. The Richmond, 5 Rob., p. 325. A Swedish ship laden with tar, pitch, and deals, sailing under instructions to take British convoy for Lisbon, in case the master should not be able to obtain a purchaser at Copenhagen for the ship and cargo, but afterwards detected entering a Dutch enemy's port: holden by the Lords of Appeal (affirming the decision of High Court of Admiralty,) liable to condemnation with her cargo, notwithstanding the protest of the master, alleging the impossibity of obtaining convoy, and that the deviation was occasioned by his apprehension of capture by French cruisers, the suspicions circumstances in the case being held to remove all favourable construction usually applied with respect to the general trade of Sweden in such articles. The Charlotte, 1 Acton's Rep., p. 201.

(*h*) Other hemp is not seizable. The Gute Gesellschaft Michael, 4 Rob. Adm. Rep. p. 95. The Evert, ib., p. 354.

(*i*) The Apollo, 4 Rob. Adm. Rep., p. 158.

(*k*) The Evert, ib. p. 354.

(*l*) The Ship Carpenter, 2 Acton's (Appeals) Reports, p. 11, in which case it was holden not to be Contraband.

(*m*) The Charlotte, 5 Rob. Adm. Rep., p. 275.

demned(z) in the English Prize Courts. But in all these cases the destination of the cargo is the main circumstance.

CCLXIV. It will be obvious, from the principles which have been laid down, that the sale of a *ship for purposes of war* is the sale of the most noxious article of war. The sale by a Neutral of *any* ship to a Belligerent, is a very suspicious act in the opinion of the English and North American Prize Courts, and one which the French Prize Courts refuse to recognize; but to sell a ship for hostile use is to supply a Belligerent with a most powerful instrument of mischief—of contraband ready made up in its most malignant form.(a) Upon this principle, a vessel, which being in every respect fitted for a ship of war, was sent on her first voyage to a belligerent port, with instructions to her master to sell her, or to take goods on freight, but with an intimation that the owners would prefer selling to freighting, as she was not adapted to purposes of freight, was condemned.(b) But a ship of ambiguous use, and previously employed for purposes of trade, with a destination to be sold under circumstances not indicating a hostile use of her, was restored.(c)

CCLXV. From what has been already said with respect to the duties of Neutrals, it will be seen that, in the opinion of the writer of these pages, unwrought metals and coined *money*(d) may, regard being had to its destination, be well considered as contraband.(e)

[*361] **Horses* and their equipage are mentioned as contraband by the *Ordonnance de la Marine*, and this, Mr. Chancellor Kent says, "is doubtless the general rule."(f) They are mentioned as contraband in a great variety of treaties between various States,(g) to which, however, Russia appears to be an exception, for she has not included horses in her treaties respecting contraband.(h)

CCLXVI. In accordance with the construction of contraband upon which she has always acted, Great Britain during the present war, has, by an Order of Council,(i) "ordered and directed that, from and after the date hereof, all arms, ammunition, and gunpowder, military and naval stores, and the following articles, being articles we have judged capable of being converted into, or made useful in increasing the quantity of military or naval stores; that is to say, marine engines, screw propellers, paddle-wheels, cylinders, cranks, shafts, boilers, tubes for

(z) The Endrought, 1 Rob. Adm. Rep., p. 25. In the Neptunus, 3 Rob., p. 108, tallow and sail-cloth going to Amsterdam; former restored, latter condemned. In the Nostra Signora de Begona, 5 Rob., p. 98, resin going to a port *purely mercantile*, restored.

(a) The Richmond, 5 Rob. Adm. Rep., p. 331.

(b) The Brutus, Appendix I., ib.

(c) The Fanny, ib., note.

(d) For the Treaties in which they are so considered, see Manning, pp. 285-6; Ward, p. 231.

(e) Vide antè, p. 224.

(f) Commentaries, i. 136. "Parceque cela a beaucoup *d'analogie* avec les munitions de guerre." Valin, l. iii. t. ix. art xi; so the principle of *Contraband by analogy* is admitted.

(g) As late as 1825, in a Treaty between the United States of North America and Colombia.

(h) Manning, pp. 284-5.

(i) Order in Council, dated 18th February, 1854. See, too, Speech of Sir James Graham, (First Lord of the Admiralty,) 29th June, 1854, Hansard, Parl. Deb.

boilers, boiler-plates, fire-bars, and every article, or any other component part of an engine or boiler, or any article whatsoever which is, can, or may become, applicable for the manufacture of marine machinery, shall be and the same are hereby prohibited either to be exported from the United Kingdom, or carried coastwise."(*k*)

It is clear, too, that upon the principles which have been laid down, *coal* may, under the particular circumstances of the case, regard being had to its quantity and destination, become liable to seizure.(*l*)

*CCLXVII. Fourthly. We have now to consider the doctrine of Pre-emption as applied to cases of Contraband. [*362]

Before the Treaty of Munster, or about the middle of the seventeenth century, the custom of Pre-emption(*n*) by the Belligerent of the property of the subjects of another State, which was thus prevented from reaching its original destination, had a much wider operation than has been in more modern times allowed to it.

All cargoes without distinction were then subjected to Pre-emption, and various Treaties ackowledge and regulate, or prohibit, the exercise of this belligerent right;(*o*) and even as late as 1810, a Treaty between England and Portugal, after stipulating that military and naval stores seized by Portugal are to be paid for at the price fixed by the proprietors, adds, that if the Portuguese Government takes possession of any cargo whatever, or of any part of a cargo, with the intention of purchasing it, or otherwise, they are to be liable for the damage which the goods may sustain while under the custody of the Portuguese officers.(*p*)

CCLXVIII. But according to general modern usage, the doctrine of Pre-emption(*q*) rests upon the distinction between *articles which are Contraband *universally*, and those which, being *ambigui usûs*, are Contraband under only the particular circumstances of the case. [*363] The carrying of the former class alone is *punishable*, and entails the penalty of *confiscation* either of ship or cargo, or both.(*r*)

The latter class are subject to the milder belligerent right of Pre-emp-

(*k*) The like prohibitions were extended to the Island of Malta by Order in Council, dated 15th April, 1854.

(*l*) Ortolan, Dipl. de la Mer, t. ii. l. iii. ch. vi. p. 206, (second edition.) In this the author retracts his former opinion that coal might be Contraband.

(*n*) According to Grotius, (note to the words "publicæ significationes fieri") the true meaning of the French Ordonnance of 1584, art. lxix. subjected Contraband not to confiscation but pre-emption.

(*o*) Manning, p. 313, e. g. Denmark and Spain, 1641.—VI. Dumont, i. 210. England and Portugal, 1642, ib., 239. Denmark and Holland, 1645, ib., 313. Spain and Holland, 1648. Treaty of Munster, ib., p. 431. England and Holland, 1654, ib. ii. p. 76. England and Portugal, 1654, ib., p. 83.

(*p*) De Martens, Suppl., t. vii. p. 207.

(*q*) The right of Pre-emption (Mr. Ward says) is rather a waiver of a greater right than a right itself. It is an indulgence to the Neutral rather than a privilege of the Belligerent, and can only be called a right, because the Belligerent in fact may pretend to something more.—Of Contraband, p. 196.

(*r*) Heffters seems to have well understood this distinction. He speaks of horses, materials, provisions, money:—"Es kann daher den Kriegführenden nur gestattet sein, thatsächlich gegen die Neutralen oder der neutralen Handel einzuschreiten, wenn jenen Artikeln eine Bestimmung für die feindliche Staatsgewalt und deren Kriegsmacht mit zureichenden Gründen beizumessen steht." They do not fall under the category, "unerlaubten strafbaren Handel," § 160.

tion, which is considered as a fair compromise between the right of the Belligerent to seize, and the claim of the Neutral to export his *native commodities*, though immediately subservient to the purposes of hostility.(*s*)

CCLXIX. According to the practice of the British Prize Court, a profit of ten *per cent.* has been usually allowed to the proprietor of the goods seized for the purposes of Pre-emption. This practice is recognized in the Treaty between Great Britain and the United States of North America of the 19th November, 1794, which stipulates, that a full value of all articles seized, together with a reasonable mercantile profit thereon, together with the freight, shall be paid by the captors or their Government;(*t*) and in the Treaty between Great Britain and Sweden in 1803 it is stipulated that there shall be paid a profit of ten *per cent.* on the price of the merchandize, valued at the option of the proprietors, either in England or Sweden, with an indemnity for the freight and the expenses of detention.(*u*)

[*364] CCLXX. The case of The Haabet(*x*) may be considered *as containing the best enumeration of the principles which govern the decision of the British Courts of International Law upon this subject.

"This was a case arising on an objection to a report of the registrar and merchants respecting the allowance of insurance as part of the price of a cargo of wheat, going from Altona to Cadiz, but seized and brought into this country, and bought by Government. The demand of the claimant, Mr. Peschie, of Copenhagen, had been disallowed in the report, on the ground that the insurance had not actually been made." It was upon this state of facts that Lord Stowell said;—"'This is a question on a report of the registrar and merchants respecting an allowance of insurance on a cargo of corn, seized and brought into this country. The cargo was decreed to be restored, and the registrar and merchants were directed to make a report on the value due to the claimant; such reports are in their nature partly legal and partly mercantile; it is a report proceeding from persons qualified, in both these respects, to form a sound judgment on the subject before them; one of them being, from his connection with Courts of Justice, supposed capable of forming his own opinion, and of assisting his associates on all questions of law, in the first instance, subject to the inspection and correction of the court, whilst the other part of this domestic forum, as I may call it, consists of persons acquainted with trade, and exercising their judgment on matters relative to commerce. It is from the report of a commission so constituted, that the question is now brought before the court on a subject partly legal and partly mercantile.

"'The question is, whether there is any reasonable ground for me to pronounce that the registrar and merchants have disallowed a just

(*s*) The Sarah Christina, 1 Rob. Adm. Rep., p. 241.

(*t*) De Martens, v. p. 674. (*u*) Ib., Suppl., iii. p. 526.

(*x*) 2 Robinson's Adm. Rep., pp. 174-185. As to other cases on the same subject, see—The Maria Magdalena, Hay & Marriott's Adm. Rep., p. 250. The Vryheid, ib., p. 188. The Vrow Antoinette, Hay & Marriott's Adm. Rep., p. 142; also cases mentioned, ib., pp. 148, 169, 176, 217, 246, 267, 270, 272, 287, as to the purchase of mixed goods, i. e., some Contraband, some not.

demand, in disallowing a charge of insurance *which had not been made. It has been argued that this charge ought to have [*365] been allowed, because it is usually so allowed in the dealings of merchants with each other; I am not clear that this is a necessary consequence, for it is surely no certain rule that in *all cases* where a cargo is taken *jure belli*, but for the mere purpose of Pre-emption, that it is to receive a price calculated exactly in the same manner, and amounting precisely to the same value, as it would have done, if it had arrived at its port of destination in the ordinary course of trade.

" 'The right of taking possession of cargoes of this description, *Commeatus* or *Provisions*, going to the enemy's ports, is no peculiar claim of this country; it belongs generally to belligerent nations; the ancient practice of Europe, or at least of several maritime States of Europe, was to confiscate them entirely; a century has not elapsed since this claim has been asserted by some of them. A more mitigated practice has prevailed in later times of holding such cargoes subject only to a right of Pre-emption, that is, to a right of purchase upon a reasonable compensation, to the individual whose property is thus diverted. I have never understood that, on the side of the Belligerent, this claim goes beyond the case of cargoes avowedly bound to the enemy's ports, or suspected, on just grounds, to have a concealed destination of that kind; or that, on the side of the Neutral, the same exact compensation is to be expected, which he might have demanded from the enemy in his own port; the enemy may be distressed by famine, and may be driven by his necessities to pay a famine price for the commodity if it gets there; it does not follow that acting upon my rights of war in intercepting such supplies, I am under the obligation to pay that price of distress. It is a mitigated exercise of war on which my purchase is made, and no rule has established that such a purchase shall be regulated exactly upon the same terms of profit which would have followed the adventure if no such exercise of war had intervened; it is a reasonable indemnification *and a fair profit on the commodity that is due, reference being [*366] had to the original price actually paid by the exporter, and the expenses which he has incurred. As to what is to be deemed a reasonable indemnification and profit, I hope and trust that this country will never be found backward in giving a liberal interpretation to these terms; but certainly the capturing nation does not always take these cargoes on the same terms, on which an enemy would be content to purchase them; much less are cases of this kind to be considered as cases of costs and damages, in which all loss of possible profit is to be laid upon unjust captors; for these are not unjust captures, but authorized exercises of the rights of war.

" 'Two or three considerations have been urged, which may, with all propriety, be dismissed; one is, that it was undertood between the King's Government and the parties that this charge should be allowed. Certainly if it were made out by any credible proof, that the faith of Government had been in the slightest manner pledged to such an understanding, there is no principle which this Court would hold more sacred, than that the faith of Government should be held inviolate in transactions of this kind; but no sort of proof is offered of this, and the fact has in no way come to my knowledge. It is said, likewise, that in the cases of this kind which occurred last war, and which were then settled by the Navy Board, the charge of insurance was allowed, but the policy of insurance was never called for. How this practice came to prevail there, whether under a notion that the insurances had been really made whenever they were charged, whether under any order of Government, or how otherwise, I am not informed; the persons who had to settle those accounts were not mercantile men, and might be led by the charge to suppose, that it had actually been incurred. Under whatever circumstances such a practice grew up, if it did obtain, it is no binding rule upon the registrar and merchants here; it might be simple mistake, and at best it is no deciding authority.

[*367] *" 'I have already said, that the expected payment at the port of delivery, is not the necessary measure of compensation at the port of the Belligerent. It is not so with reference to any constituent of price; with respect to insurance, considered as such, it would be peculiarly improper: it is reasonably to be charged at the port of delivery, although it has never been paid, because the merchant has stood his own risk, and has purchased the insurance at the expense of his own danger. But is that the case where the voyage has been interrupted almost in its commencement, where the cargo has been carried into a neighbouring port? In the present case the voyage was from Altona to Cadiz, from the north to the south of Europe, and the cargo is seized upon its entrance into the British Channel very soon after quitting its port. Most of the cargoes have a similar destination, and are taken under similar circumstances. What pretence is there to say, that all risks of the voyage have been incurred?—the utmost that could be claimed is an insurance *pro ratâ itineris peracti*, amounting to a very small proportion of the whole, hardly deserving a particular consideration. As to what is said, that in the case of capture of ships you allow the full freight of the whole voyage, that allowance is made on another account; you take the ship in that case on account, not of itself, but of its cargo; you interrupt its occupation, which was legal and innocent, and it is therefore not unjust to allow it the benefit of its original contract, which you alone have prevented from being carried into execution. Very different is the consideration of risk, respecting a cargo, which has never been incurred, and of a payment which is due only, on the event of that risk having been actually incurred—no contract subsisting, and the cargo being, in its own nature, liable to this species of interception.

" 'Upon the whole, I see no sufficient reason to pronounce that the registrar and merchants have adopted a wrong measure of value in disallowing the charge of insurance; they have allowed what, upon their

[*368] own experience, they *pronounce to be a reasonable indemnification and profit, and I do not understand that the sufficiency of this indemnification and profit is impeached on any other ground than that an insurance would have been added in the ordinary course of a mercantile account, if the cargo had reached its intended destination. Being of opinion that the ordinary terms of a mercantile account, to be

settled on the completion of the voyage, do not furnish (all circumstances being duly weighed) the necessary or just measure of value to be applied in transactions of this kind, I do not find myself enabled to sustain the objection.' "

CCLXXI. Fifthly. An exception from the foregoing rule is furnished by the case of Ambassadors sending dispatches from the neutral country in which they are resident, for the purpose of preserving the relations of amity between that State and their own Government. It is indeed competent to a Belligerent to stop the Ambassador of his enemy on his passage; but when he has arrived, and has taken upon himself the functions of his office, and has been admitted into his representative character, he is entitled to peculiar privileges, as set apart for the protection of the relations of amity and peace, in maintaining which all nations are, in some degree interested. With respect to this question, the convenience of the neutral State is also to be considered; for its interests may require that the intercourse of correspondence with the enemy's country should not be altogether interdicted; it would be almost tantamount to preventing the residence of an Ambassador in a neutral State, if he were debarred from the means of communicating with his own.

Despatches found on board a neutral ship, containing communications from a hostile Government to their Consul resident in a neutral country, are not *generally speaking*, of the nature of Contraband.(*a*)

The legal *presumption* is that the communication has reference to the commercial relations of the Belligerent and the *Neutral, and if they were interdicted, the functions of the official persons charged with the maintenance of these relations would altogether cease. It is to be remembered, that the functions of the Consul relate to the joint commerce in which the neutral as well as the Belligerent is engaged.(*b*) [*369]

CCLXXII. Sixthly. As to carrying of military persons in the employ of a Belligerent, or being in any way engaged in his transport service.

It has been most solemnly decided by the Tribunals of International Law, both in England and the United States of North America, that these are acts of hostility on the part of the Neutral which subject the vehicle in which the persons are conveyed to confiscation at the hands of the Belligerent.(*c*)

It may be difficult to define what is the number of military persons the conveyance of whom may subject the neutral ship to this penalty; but, in truth, the number alone is an insignificant circumstance in the considerations on which the principle of Law is built; since fewer persons of high quality and character may be of more importance than a much greater number of persons of lower conditions: to send out one general may be a more noxious act than the conveyance of a whole regiment.(*d*)

It has been justly holden that a ship so employed cannot escape confiscation by alleging that she acted under duress and violence. If an act

(*a*) The Caroline, 6 Ib., p. 468.

(*b*) The Madison, Edwards's Adm. Rep., p. 224.

(*c*) The Caroline, 4 Rob. Adm. Rep. p. 256. The Friendship, 6 Ib., p. 420. The Orozembo, ib. p. 430. The Commercen, 1 Wheaton's (Amer.) Rep. 391.

(*d*) The Orozembo, 4 Rob. Adm. Rep., pp. 453-4.

of force, exercised by one Belligerent Power on a neutral ship or person, were to be deemed as sufficient justification for any act done by him contrary to the known duties of a neutral character, the rights of the Belligerent and the rules of International Law would be easily evaded [*370] and set at naught. The Neutral *must look to his own Government for redress against the Government which has coerced him. Moreover, the penal liability of the ship so employed is not extinguished until the vessel has shaken off the belligerent character which her occupation has impressed upon her. So long as she continues under the command of the enemy she remains liable to capture and condemnation.(*d*)

CCLXXIII. Official communications from an official person on the public affairs of the belligerent Government,(*e*) are such *despatches* as impress a hostile character upon the carriers of them.

The mischievous consequences of such a service cannot be estimated, and extend far beyond the effect of any Contraband that can be conveyed, for it is manifest that by the carriage of such despatches the most important operations of a Belligerent may be forwarded or obstructed.

In general cases of Contraband, the quantity of the article carried may be a material circumstance, but the smallest despatch may suffice to turn the fortunes of war in favour of a particular Belligerent.(*f*)

CCLXXIV. The penalty is confiscation of the ship(*g*) which conveys the despatches, and, *ob continentiam delicti*, of the cargo,(*h*) if both belong to the same master.

It is indeed competent to those entrusted with the care of the ship, on board of which such despatches are found, to discharge themselves from the imputation of being concerned in the knowledge and management of the transaction.(*i*) But the presumption is strong against the ignorance [*371] of the master of the ship, and when he has knowingly taken on *board a packet or letter addressed to a public officer of a belligerent Government, the plea of the insignificance of communication, and its want of connection with the political objects of the war, will not avail him, nor, except perhaps in an extreme case of imposition practised upon him, will the plea of ignorance of the *contents* of the despatches avail him; his redress must be sought against the person whose agent or carrier he was.(*k*)

With respect to such a case as might exempt the carrier of despatches from the usual penalty it is to be observed that where the commencement of the voyage is in a neutral country, and is to terminate at a neutral port, or at a port to which, though not neutral, an open trade is allowed, in such a case there is less to excite the vigilance of the master, and,

(*d*) The Caroline, 4 Rob. Adm. Rep., pp. 259-261.

(*e*) The Caroline, 6 Ib., p. 465.

(*f*) The Atalanta, ib. 440, is a leading case on the subject, in which all the premises which lead to the conclusion expressed in the text are fully set forth.

(*g*) The Caroline, ib., p. 461, note. (*h*) The Atalanta, ib. p. 460.

(*i*) Ib., p. 445. The Rapid, Edwards's Adm. Rep., 228.

(*k*) The Hope, cited in the Atalanta, 6 Robinson, p. 457. The same case cited in note to the Caroline, 6 Rob., pp. 461, 462. The Rapid, Edwards's Adm. Rep., pp. 228-229.

therefore, it may be proper to make some allowance for any imposition which may be practised upon him. But when a neutral master receives papers on board in a hostile port, he receives them at his own hazard, and cannot be heard to avow his ignorance of a fact with which, by due inquiry, he might have made himself acquainted.

CCLXXV. Seventhly. We have to consider the penalty of carrying Contraband.

By the ancient Law of Nations, the carrying of Contraband worked in all cases a forfeiture of the vehicle which carried it.

According to the mitigated rule of modern practice, the ship is not generally condemned, but *freight* and *expenses* only are forfeited.(*l*)

*The exceptional cases, in which the severity of the ancient law is still applied, are— [*372]

1. Cases in which there are circumstances of aggravation.
2. Cases in which the Contraband belongs to the owner of the ship.(*m*)

CCLXXVI. 1. Among the circumstances of aggravation, are to be mentioned:—

α. A false destination, which, with Contraband on board, subjects both ship and cargo to condemnation.(*n*)

β. The carriage of Contraband, with the privity of the owner, and in violation of a Treaty.(*o*)

γ. A concealment of Contraband in the outward cargo, which has been holden to render the ship, on her return, subject to condemnation; and the misconduct of the supercargo—the agent of the owner—has been holden to affect the owner's interest.(*p*)

δ. A private vessel has been forfeited by the contraband traffic of an officer placed in command by the Board of Admiralty.(*q*)

2. In cases in which the ship belongs to the owner of the Contraband, condemnation always follows. If the owner of the Contraband own a share only in the vessel, his share will be condemned: and this effect will be produced by the contraband articles, though unclaimed, if they appear by the evidence to belong to such part-owner.(*r*) [*373]

CCLXXVII. With respect to the effect of Contraband upon the rest of the cargo, it is to be observed that the penalty of Contraband extends to all the property of the same owner involved in the same unlawful transaction.(*s*) And therefore, if the same owner possess articles which are and which are not Contraband, all will be alike condemned. To

(*l*) Bynkershoek, Q. J. P., l. i. c. x. The Ringende Jacob, 1 Rob. Adm. Rep., p. 90. The Sarah Christina, ib., p. 242. The Jonge Jacobus Baceman, ib., p. 243. The Mercurius, ib. p. 288. The Emanuel, ib., p. 296. The Jonge Tobias, ib., p. 329. The Wilhelmina, note to the Rebecca, 2 Rob. Adm. Rep., p. 101. The Franklin, 3 Ib., p. 217. The Neutralität, ib., p. 295. The Atlas, ib., p. 304, n.

(*m*) The Mercurius, note, 1 Rob. Adm. Rep., p. 288. The Jonge Tobias, ib., p. 329. The Franklin, 3 Rob., p. 217. The Ringende Jacob, 1 Rob., p. 91. The Neutralität, 3 Rob., p. 295.

(*n*) The Franklin, 3 Rob., p. 217. The Ranger, 6 Rob., p. 125. The Edward, 4 Rob., p. 68.

(*o*) The Neutralität, 3 Rob., p. 295. (*p*) The Baltic, 1 Acton, p. 25.

(*q*) Blewitt v. Hill, 13 East's Reports, p. 13.

(*r*) The Floreat Commercium, 3 Rob., p. 178. The Franklin, ib., p. 217.

(*s*) The Sarah Christina, 1 Rob., p. 242. The Neptunus, 6 Rob., p. 409.

escape from the *contagion* of Contraband, the innocent articles must be the propety of a different owner.(*t*) "Sed omnino distinguendum putem," Bynkershoek says, "an licitæ et illicitæ merces ad eundem dominum pertineant an ad diversos, si ad eundem omnes rectè publicabuntur, ob continentiam delicti."(*u*)

In a case, however, in which the ship was condemned for carrying the particular Contraband of *despatches,* the penalty was not extended to the cargo, though the property of the same owner, it being shown that he was ignorant of the shipment, and it not being shown that the master had been appointed agent for the cargo.(*x*)

CCLXXVIII. A neutral ship cannot claim exemption from the penalty of carrying Contraband because there exists between her and the country of her seizors a Treaty that Free Ships make Free Goods,(*y*) or because a permission has been given to her to trade with the enemy in innocent articles.(*z*)

A British subject, resident and domiciled abroad, may engage in trade with the enemy; but nevertheless, the duty of allegiance so far travels with him as to restrain him from [*374] *trafficking with the enemy in articles of a contraband nature.(*a*)

CCLXXIX. Eighthly. It now remains to make some observations with respect to the Treaties—more especially, and in detail, those which affect England—upon this subject.

It should be premised that Treaties respecting Contraband are framed for cases in which one party is in a state of Neutrality, and not where both are connected in hostilities against one common enemy. They cannot, therefore, extend to the trade of either country, at a time when both countries are associated in war, and are bound to contribute their whole force and energy against the common enemy. In that case, questions of Contraband are not to be determined by the provisions of Treaties relating to a state of Neutrality on the part of one of the contracting parties, but by the rules provided by the common Law of Nations.

CCLXXX. The first armed Neutrality, 1780, declared(*b*) that the parties to it "shall only acknowledge to be contraband commodities those which are included and mentioned as such in the Treaties now subsisting between their respective Courts and the one or the other of the belligerent Powers."

(*t*) The Staadt Embden, 1 Rob. Adm. Rep., p. 28.

(*u*) Bynk., Q. J. P., l. i. c. 12.

(*x*) The Susan. The Hope. Notes to the Caroline, 6 Rob., pp. 462-3.

(*y*) The Asia, cited in Index to 6 Rob., p. 483.

(*z*) The Eleonora Wilhelmina, 6 Rob., p. 331.

(*a*) The Neptunus, 6 Rob., p. 409. See, too, Holland v. Hall, 1 Barnewall & Alderson's Reports, p. 53. "Where A. agreed to sell to B. one-third share of a ship, which was then to be employed on a joint adventure, in the exportation of military stores to South America, contrary to an Order in Council then in force; it was holden, that (the agreement being entire, and containing on the face of it an illegal stipulation) it lay on the party seeking to enforce the same, to show that means had been used to obtain a license, or that the illegal purpose had been abandoned, and that, in failure thereof, A. could not recover for the share of the ship." The Eleonora Wilhelmina, 6 Rob., p. 331. The Neptunus, 6 Rob. p. 403.

(*b*) Article 2.

The second armed Neutrality, 1800, acknowledged only "cannons, mortars, firearms, balls, flintstones,(c) *matches, gunpowder, saltpetre, sulphur, helmets, pikes, swords, hangers, cartridge-boxes, saddles and bridles, with the exception of such a quantity of the above-mentioned articles as may be necessary for the defence of their ships and crews."(d) [*375]

By the Treaty between England and Russia of 1797 and of 1801, it was agreed not to consider as Contraband the merchandise of the produce, growth, or manufacture of the countries at war which should have been acquired by the subjects of the Neutral Power, and should be transported for their account.(e)

The following articles only were acknowledged as Contraband:—cannons, mortars, firearms, pistols, bombs, grenades, balls, bullets, firelocks, flints, matches, gunpowder, saltpetre, sulphur, cuirasses, pikes, swords, swordbelts, knapsacks, saddles, bridles, with the same reservation as in the other Treaties as to the use and defence of the ship and crew.(f)

The 8th article provided that "these stipulations shall be regarded as permanent, and shall serve for a constant rule to the contracting Powers in matters of commerce and navigation."

In consequence of this article, Lord Grenville expressed, in a masterly speech, in which he reviewed the whole Treaty, his apprehension that England might be holden to have enunciated a general and universally binding principle of International Law upon this subject.(g) This Treaty is not now in force.

CCLXXXI. We now proceed to mention the provisions upon this subject which are now in force between Great Britain and other Powers.

*Between England and Denmark. [*376]

By the explanatory article of the Treaty with Denmark of 1780, "the two contracting Sovereigns reciprocally engage, for themselves and their successors, not to furnish to the enemies of either party in time of war any succour, neither soldiers nor vessels, nor any effects and merchandise called Contraband; and in like manner to prohibit their subjects from so doing, and to punish severely, and as destroyers of the peace, those who should dare to act contrary to their prohibitions in this respect; but in order to leave no doubt upon what is to be understood by the term Contraband, it is agreed that this denomination is meant only to comprehend arms, as well firearms as other kinds, with their furniture, as cannon, muskets, mortars, petards, bombs, grenades, carcasses, saucisses, carriages for cannon, musket-rests, bandoleers, gunpowder, matches, saltpetre, balls, pikes, swords, helmets, cuirasses, halberts, lances, javelins, horses, saddles, pistol-holsters, belts, and generally all other warlike implements, also ship-timber, tar, pitch, and resin, sheet copper, sails, hemp, and cordage,

(c) Would anybody contend that *copper caps* are not now Contraband?

(d) Article 2. (e) Ibid. (f) Article 3.

(g) Pp. 55-60, of Speech published by Cobbett, 18 Pall Mall, London, January, 1801. Vide ante, vol. i. (of this work,) pp. 44-5, upon this point.

and generally whatever immediately serves for the equipment of vessels; unwrought iron and deal planks, however, excepted.

"But it is expressly declared that this kind of contraband merchandise shall by no means comprehend fish and flesh, fresh or salted, wheat, flour, corn or other grain, vegetables, oil, wine, and generally whatever serves for the nourishment and support of life, so that all these articles may always be sold and transported like other merchandise, even to places in the possession of an enemy of the two Crowns, provided that such places are neither besieged nor blockaded.

"And their Majesties being desirous that this article, as it is actually settled, should hold precisely the place of that for which it is substituted, so that it shall have the same effect and validity as if it were inserted word for word in the said Treaty, and that it should be considered as [*377] *authentic and obligatory as the Treaty itself, they have agreed that it should be so declared and decreed by a declaration signed by the Minister for Foreign Affairs," &c.(*h*)

And by Article XIII. of Treaty of Kiel, in 1814, "All the ancient Treaties of peace and commerce between the former Sovereigns of England and Denmark are hereby renewed in their full extent, so far as they are not contradictory to the stipulations of the present Treaty."(*i*)

Between England and Sweden (1812.)

"The relations of friendship and commerce between the two kingdoms shall be re-established upon the footing on which they stood on the 1st day of January, 1791, and all the Treaties and conventions subsisting between the two countries at that epoch, shall be regarded as renewed and confirmed, and they are by the present Treaty renewed and confirmed accordingly."(*k*)

Between England and Sweden (1691.)

"Although in the preceding articles of this present Treaty, it be forbidden to either confederate to yield any aid or assistance to the enemies of the other, yet it is not to be so understood, as if either confederate, having no war with the enemies of the other, might not sail to or traffic with the said enemies, notwithstanding that the other confederate be in actual war with them. But it is only provided, that no goods, called goods of Contraband, and particularly, that no money, provisions, weapons, firearms, [*378] *with their appurtenances, fire-balls, gunpowder, match, bullets, spear-heads, swords, lances, pikes, halberts, ordnance, mortar-pieces, petards, grenadoes, rests, bandoleers, saltpetre, pistols, small shot, pots, head-pieces, backs and breasts, or such kind of armour; soldiers, horses, all furniture necessary for horses, holsters, belts,

(*h*) Declaration signed at Copenhagen, 4th July, 1780, explanatory of the 3rd Article of the Treaty of 1670. Hertslet's Treaties, vol. i. p. 203.

(*i*) Treaty of Peace between Great Britain and Denmark, signed at Kiel, 14th Jan., 1814.—Hertslet's Treaties, i. p. 233.

(*k*) Treaty between Great Britain and Sweden, signed at Orebro, 18th July, 1812.—Hertslet's Treaties, vol. ii. p. 335.

and whatsoever warlike instruments, as also, that no ships of war or convoys be furnished to the enemy, without peril, in case they be taken, of being adjudged lawful prize without hope of restitution. And neither of the confederates shall suffer any of his subjects to give aid, sell or lend ships, or be any way useful to the enemies or rebels of the other to his prejudice or deteriment; but it shall be lawful for either confederate, his people and subjects, to have commerce with the enemies of the other, and to carry to them all kind of merchandize, not before excepted, without any let or hindrance, unless it be into such ports and places as are besieged by the other, and in such case, it shall be lawful for them to sell their commodities to the besiegers, or otherwise to betake themselves to any other port which is not besieged."(*l*)

Between England and Russia.

"The relations of friendship and commerce between the two countries shall be re-established on both sides, upon the footing of the most favoured nations."(*m*)

Between England and Portugal.

"Under the name of Contraband, or prohibited articles, shall be comprehended not only arms, cannon, harquebusses, mortars, petards, bombs, grenades, saucisses, carcasses, *carriages for cannon, musket-rests, bandoleers, gunpowder, match, saltpetre, ball, pikes, swords, [*379] head-pieces, helmets, cuirasses, halberts, javelins, holsters, belts, horses and their harness, but generally all other articles that may have been specified as Contraband in any former Treaties concluded by Great Britain or by Portugal with other Powers. But goods which have not been wrought into the form of warlike instruments, or which cannot become such, shall not be computed Contraband, much less such as have been already wrought and made up for other purposes, all which shall be deemed not Contraband, and may be freely carried by the subjects of both Sovereigns, even to places belonging to an enemy, excepting only such places as are besieged, blockaded, or invested by sea or land."(*n*)

Between England and Brazil.

"In order to regulate what is in future to be deemed Contraband of War, it is agreed that under the said denomination shall be comprised all arms and implements serving for the purposes of war, by land or by sea, such as cannon, muskets, pistols, mortars, petards, bombs, grenadoes, carcasses, saucisses, carriages for cannon, musket-rests, bandoleers, gunpowder, match, saltpetre, balls, pikes, swords, head-pieces, cuirasses, hal-

(*l*) Treaty between Great Britain and Sweden, concluded at Whitehall, 1691.—Hertslet's Treaties, vol. ii. p. 328.

(*m*) Treaty of Peace between Great Britain and Russia, signed at Orebro, 18th July, 1812.—Hertslet's Treaties, vol. ii. p. 125.

(*n*) Treaty of Commerce and Navigation between Great Britain and Portugal, signed at Rio de Janeiro, (art. xxviii.) 19th February, 1810.—Hertslet's Treaties, vol. ii. p. 59.

berts, lances, javelins, horse-furniture, holsters, belts, and, generally, all other implements of war; as also timber for ship-building, tar or resin, copper in sheets, sails, hemp and cordage, and generally, whatsoever may serve directly to the equipment of vessels of war, unwrought iron and fir planks excepted; and all the above articles are hereby declared to be just [*380] *objects of confiscation, whenever they are attempted to be carried to an enemy."(*o*)

CCLXXXII. Among the later Treaties upon this subject, in which England is not concerned, should be noticed the Treaties between the States of North and South America, namely, the Treaty with Columbia,(*p*) 3rd December, 1824; with Chili,(*q*) 16th May, 1832, (Art. XIV.); with Central America,(*r*) 5th December, 1825; with the Mexican States, 5th April, 1831,(*s*) (Art. XVI.); with Venezuela,(*t*) 20th January, 1836, (Art. XVII.)

The Treaty between France and Brazil,(*u*) 28th January, 1826, (Art. XXI.); with Texas,(*x*) 25th September, 1839, (Art VI.)

In the Treaty between Prussia and Brazil,(*y*) 5th July, 1827; with Mexico,(*z*) 18th February, 1831, (Art. XI.)

The Treaty between the Hanse Towns and Venezuela,(*a*) 27th May, 1837, (Art. XVI.)

[*381] *In these Treaties, Contraband appears to be confined to weapons and munitions of war.

CCLXXXIII. The Prussian Government has incorporated into its Code of Municipal Law, an article prohibiting the carriage by its subjects to any other nation, of Contraband, consisting of munitions of war, or of articles forbidden by Treaties of the nations to whom it is carried.(*b*)

CCLXXXIV. In the following Treaties are specified articles which shall and which shall not be considered as Contraband between the contracting parties.

1662. Treaty between Denmark and France.

1669. Treaty between Denmark and Great Britain.

(*o*) Treaty of Amity and Commerce between His Majesty and the Emperor of Brazil, signed at Rio de Janeiro, 17th Aug., 1827.—Hertslet's Treaties, vol. iv. p. 43. The reader is also referred to the ample catalogue of Treaties between all Powers, and at various times, in vol. ix. of the Traité de Commerce of MM. Hauterive and De Cussy, title "Contrebande de Guerre," p. 228, &c.; and vol. i. of the successor to this work, by MM. De Cussy and De Martens.—Index Explicatif, tit. Contrebande.

(*p*) De Martens, N. R., t. vi. p. 831. (*q*) Ib., t. x. p. 334.

(*r*) Ib., t. xi. p. 442. (*s*) Ib., t. xiii. p. 544.

(*t*) Ib. Nouv. Suppl. t. ii. p. 415. (*u*) De Martens, N. R., t. vi. p. 874.

(*x*) Ib., t. xiii. p. 988. (*y*) Ib., t. vii. p. 274. (*z*) Ib., t. xii. p. 544.

(*a*) Ib., t. xvi. p. 242. Heffters, § 160, refers to the above Treaties. Mr. Lawrence, in his recent edition of Wheaton's Elements, observes:—"The United States of North America have only made one Treaty in which they have *not* confined Contraband to arms and munitions of war: viz., the Treaty of 1794 with England." —Wheaton's El., ed. Lawrence, p. 563, note. (United States' Statutes at Large, vol. viii.)

(*b*) "Verbotene Waaren sind grobes Geschütz und die dazu gehörende Ammunition, Granaten, Bajonnette, Flinten, Karabiner, Pistolen, Kugeln, Flintensteine, Lunten, Pulver, Salpeter, Schwefel, Piken, Säbel, Degen, Sättel, Hauptgestelle, Zelte, und was sonst durch besondere Verträge zwischen den verscheidenen Nationen einzunehmen verboten ist."—Preussisches Landrecht, B. ii. § 2034, p. 416.

1674. Treaty between Spain and Holland.
1713. Treaty between France and Great Britain.
1739. Treaty between France and Holland.
1742. Treaty between France and Denmark.
1766. Treaty between Great Britain and Russia.
1778. Treaty between France and the United States.
1780. Treaty between Denmark and Great Britain.
1786. Treaty between France and Great Britain.
1787. Treaty between France and Russia.
1794. Treaty between the United States and Great Britain.
1798. Treaty between Portugal and Russia.
1800. Treaty between Denmark and Russia.
1800. Treaty between France and the United States.
1803. Treaty between Great Britain and Sweden.
1810. Treaty between Great Britain and Portugal.
1818. Treaty between Denmark and Prussia.
1826. Treaty between France and Brazil.
1827. Treaty between Brazil and Denmark.

---

*CHAPTER II. [*382]

BLOCKADE.

CCLXXXV. Another limitation of the rights incident to the Neutral during peace, is imposed upon him by the right of the Belligerent during war; viz., it is the right of the Belligerent to prohibit the commerce of the Neutral with all besieged and blockaded places, and the duty of the Neutral scrupulously to abstain from all intercourse with them.

Among the rights of Belligerents there is none more clear and incontrovertible, or more just and necessary in the application, than that which gives rise to the Law of Blockade.(*a*)

CCLXXXVI. It is proposed to consider this important belligerent right under the following general heads:—

1. For what purpose a Blockade may be constituted.
2. Who may constitute a Blockade.
3. What constitutes the Blockade.
4. What maintains or continues a Blockade.
5. What vitiates a Blockade.
6. How a Blockade, having been discontinued or abandoned may be resumed.
7. How a breach of Blockade is caused, and the consequences of it.
8. Berlin and Milan Decrees. Orders in council of 1809. North American United States' Non-Intercourse Act.

*CCLXXXVII. (1.) *For what purpose a Blockade may be constituted.* [*383]

(*a*) Kent's Comm., vol. i. p. 145.

A blockade imposed for the purpose of obtaining a commercial monopoly, for the private advantage of the State which lays on such Blockade, is illegal and void on the very principle on which it is founded; but particular licences granted to individuals will not vitiate a Blockade.(*b*) The object of a Blockade is to prevent *exports* as well as *imports*, and to cut off *all communication of commerce* with the blockaded place.(*c*)

CCLXXXVIII. (2.) *Who may constitute a Blockade.*

A declaration of Blockade is a high act of Sovereign Power: it is a right of a very severe nature, operating lawfully, but often harshly, upon Neutrals, and therefore not to be aggravated or extended by construction.(*d*)

Nevertheless, a Blockade is not one of those acts of sovereignty which cannot be delegated.(*e*) The reason of the thing prescribes that a commander must carry with him such a portion of sovereign authority delegated to him, as may be necessary to provide for the exigencies of the service on which he is employed. On stations in Europe where Government is almost always at hand to superintend and direct the course of operations, under which it may be expedient that particular hostilities should be carried on, it may be different. But in distant parts of the world a commander must be held to carry with him sufficient authority to act, as well against the commerce of the enemy as against the enemy himself, for the more immediate purpose of reduction.(*f*) And if a commander so circumstanced did not originally possess this authority, [*384] and it should appear that he had acted irregularly, *and without orders, this is an affair between him and his Government, and the Blockade would hardly be impeachable by the Neutral on that ground; certainly not if that Government, by its subsequent conduct, had adopted his act: this would, on the principle *ratihabitio mandato æquiparatur*, retrospectively legitimate what had been done by their officer.(*g*)

It follows from what has been already observed respecting the authority and power of the East India Company,(*h*) that it must be fully competent to the Governor-General of India to order a Blockade. This power of the delegate of the Crown is incident to a state of war, and arises from the necessity of the case; for in civil cases it is holden that the royal confirmation of the act of a delegate exceeding the terms of his express authority, cannot, as a general rule, be inferred from acquiescence.(*i*)

CCLXXXIX. (3.) *What constitutes a Blockade.*

For this object two circumstances must combine:—

(α.) A proper notification of the Blockade *de jure*.

(β.) A sufficient force to maintain it *de facto*.(*k*)

A blockade may be of different descriptions; a mere maritime Block-

(*b*) The Fox and others, 1 Edwards, p. 320, ad Rep.

(*c*) The Frederick Molke, 1 Rob., p. 87.

(*d*) The Henrick and Maria, 1 Robinson's Ad. Rep., p. 148. The Juffrow Maria Schrœder, 3 Ib., p. 154.

(*e*) Vide ante, vol. ii. p. 141.

(*f*) The Rolla, 6 Rob., p. 366.

(*g*) The Rolla, 6 Rob., p. 366.

(*h*) Vide ante, pp. 197-200.

(*i*) Cameron v. Kyte, 3 Knapp's Privy Council Reports, p. 342.

(*k*) The Betsey, 1 Rob., p. 93. The Frederick Molke, ib., p. 86. The Nancy, 1 Acton, p. 57.

ade, or a Blockade by sea and land.(*l*) The latter description requires a complete investment by land as by sea.

CCXC. The proper *notification* may be conveyed either by—

(1.) The *simple fact* itself—that is, by the presence of the blockading force—accompanied by the declaration of an officer of the fleet; for public notifications between Governments are only meant for information of individuals, and *if the individual be personally informed, that purpose is still better obtained than by a public declaration.(*m*) [*385]

(2.) Or by a *formal declaration*, accompanied or followed by the *fact*. In the former case, when the fact ceases (otherwise, indeed, than by accident or the shifting of the wind,) there is immediately an end of the Blockade; but where the fact is accompanied by a public notification from the Government of a belligerent country to neutral Governments, *primâ facie*, the Blockade must be supposed to exist till it has been publicly repealed. It is the duty of a belligerent country, which has made the notification of Blockade, to notify in the same way, and immediately, the discontinuance of it. To suffer the fact to cease, and to apply the notification again, at a distant time, would be a fraud on neutral nations. It cannot, indeed, be said that a blockade of this sort may not in any possible case expire *de facto*, but such conduct is not hastily to be presumed against any nation. And, till such a case is clearly made out, it is the duty of the Prize Court to hold that a Blockade by notification is *primâ facie*, to be presumed to continue till the notification is revoked.(*n*)

A master of a vessel cannot be heard to aver that he was ignorant of such a notification of Blockade as has been mentioned; that is to say, he cannot be heard to say so in the Court of the Belligerent who is sustaining the Blockade: whether and how he may claim compensation on account of real ignorance from his own Government, is purely a question of public and constitutional law.(*o*)

CCXCI. All that is necessary to make a notification effectual and valid is, that it shall be communicated in a credible manner, because though one mode may be more formal than another, yet any communication which brings it to the *knowledge of the party, in a way which could leave no doubt in his mind as to the authenticity of the information, would be that which ought to govern his conduct, and will be binding upon him. The usual mode of communicating such intelligence is to the neutral State and not to the hostile Government, and when the more regular form is practicable, it ought to be observed; but if it be not practicable, the notification may be otherwise effected. The question in such cases will always be—Was it communicated in a credible manner?(*p*) [*386]

CCXCII. If the commander has effectually notified the Blockade, the regularity or irregularity of his conduct towards his own Government is a matter for which he is answerable to that Government, and not to

(*l*) The Stert, 4 Rob., p. 66. (*m*) The Mercurius, 1 Rob., p. 82.
(*n*) The Neptunus, Kuyp, 1 Rob., pp. 171-2.
(*o*) The Neptunus, Hempel, 2 Rob., p. 110. The Weelvaart Van Pillaw, ib., p. 130.
(*p*) The Rolla, 6 Rob., pp. 368-9

other States; and as has been seen,(*q*) it is not open to the individual subjects of other countries to dispute the validity of the Blockade on that account.(*r*)

CCXCIII. A Blockade *de facto* should be effected by stationing a number of ships, and forming as it were an arch of circumvallation round the mouth of the prohibited port, where, if the arch fails in any one part, the Blockade itself fails altogether.(*s*) This is the general safe definition of a Blockade. Nevertheless, it has been holden, that blockading ships are at libety to take a prize if it comes in their way, but not to chase to a distance, because that would in effect be a desertion of the duty imposed upon them, and would amount to a breaking up of the Blockade.(*t*)

CCXCIV. 4. *What maintains or continues a Blockade.*

A Blockade is to be considered as legally existing, although the winds occasionally blow off the invading squadron. It effects an accidental [*387] change to which every Blockade *is incident, but it does not *suspend*, much less *break*, the Blockade.(*u*) It is most satisfactory to be able to state, that upon this, as indeed upon every other point of Blockade, the decisions of the Courts of the North American United States are in perfect harmony.(*x*)

But this principle is not extended to the case of a blockading squadron driven off, by a superior force; under such circumstances a neutral Power is not obliged to presume the continuance of a Blockade, not to act upon a supposition that the Blockade would be resumed by any other competent force.(*y*)

The Neutral is not bound to foresee or to conjecture that this Blockade will be resumed; and therefore, if it is to be renewed, it must proceed *de novo* by the usual course, and without reference to the former state of facts by which it has been so effectually interrupted;(*z*) and the presumption, if the fact be dubious, as to the resumption of such Blockade, is in favour of the Neutral.(*a*)

The question as to the adequacy of the force to maintain the Blockade, is always, to a certain degree, one of fact and evidence, but the opinion, as to this point, of the commander on the particular station, must always have great, and perhaps predominant weight with the Court; and against that opinion in favour of the adequacy of the force, the fact that some part of it was employed in *chasing* vessels will have no effect.(*b*)

But a Blockade which has been previously vigorously maintained by [*388] a *number of ships*, cannot be continued by the *occasional appearance of a ship in the offing. Thus, in a leading case upon the question of the breach of the Blockade of Martinique, in the year 1804, Sir W. Grant said: "That to constitute a Blockade, the intention to shut up the port should not only be generally made known to vessels

(*q*) Antè, p. 383.
(*r*) Ib., p. 368.
(*s*) The Arthur, 1 Dodson, p. 423.
(*t*) The La Melanee, 2 Dodson, p. 130.
(*u*) The Columbia, 1 Rob., p. 156. The Frederick Molke, 1 Rob., p. 86. The Juffrow Maria Schrœder, 3 Rob. p. 148. The Hoffnung, 6 Rob., p. 116.
(*x*) 2 Johnson's (Amer.) Cases, p. 187. 7 Johnson's (Amer.) Cases, p. 38.
(*y*) The Hoffnung, 6 Rob., p. 116.
(*z*) Ib., p. 117.
(*a*) The Triheten, 6 Rob., p. 67.
(*b*) The Nancy. The Eagle, 1 Acton's Rep., pp. 64, 65.

navigating the seas in the vicinity, but that it was the duty of the blockaders to maintain such a force as would be of itself sufficient to enforce the Blockade. This could only be effected by keeping a number of vessels on the different stations, so communicating with each other as to be able to intercept all vessels attempting to enter the ports of the island. In the present instance, no such measures had been resorted to, and this neglect necessarily led neutral vessels to believe these ports might be entered without incurring any risk. The periodical appearance of a vessel of war in the offing, could not be supposed a continuation of a Blockade, which the correspondence mentioned had described to have been previously maintained by a number of vessels, and with such unparalleled rigour, that no vessel whatever had been able to enter the island during its continuance. Their Lordships were therefore pleased to order that the ship should be restored, the proof of property being sufficient, but directed further proof as to the cargo claimed for the American citizens mentioned."(*b*)

CCXCV. 5. *What Vitiates a Blockade.*

If a Blockade be so irregularly maintained by the blockading force, that some ships are suffered to go in and others to come out, the effect must be to deceive merchants, and such irregularity will vitiate the effect of a formal notification. Because a Blockade is an uniform exclusion of *all* vessels not privileged by law, and if *some* are permitted to pass, others have a right to infer that the Blockade is raised; and the Court would hold that merchants generally were justified in treating the Blockade as taken off, in a case in which some *ships were allowed to enter or come out, from motives of civility or other considerations.(*c*) [*389]

But licences to particular persons do not vitiate a Blockade.(*d*)

CCXCVI. 6. *How a Blockade, having been discontinued or abandoned, may be resumed.*

When a Blockade has been raised by the appearance of a superior force, there is an entire defeasance of that Blockade and of its operation. It must be renewed by *notification* before foreign nations can be affected with an obligation of observing it as a Blockade of *that species* still existing. The mere appearance of another squadron is not sufficient for that purpose, but the same measures are necessary to constitute a recommencement as were required for the original imposition of the Blockade; foreign merchants are not bound to act upon any presumption that a Blockade of which there has been such a defeasance will be *de facto* resumed.(*e*)

There is, however, a distinction to be taken according to the excellent judgment of Sir William Grant, between a Blockade *recommenced* and a Blockade *de novo:* the latter is a question depending upon the evidence as to the notoriety of the circumstances which constitute the actual Blockade.(*f*)

(*b*) The Nancy, 1 Acton's Reports, p. 58. (*c*) The Rolla, 6 Rob., p. 372.
(*d*) The Fox and others, 1 Edwards, p. 321. (*e*) The Hoffnung, 6 Rob. p. 120.
(*f*) The Hare. 1 Acton's Reports of Cases before the High Court of Appeal, p. 261.

CCXCVII. 7. That part of the subject which relates to *Breaches of Blockade*, admits of the following arrangement:—

1. Breaches generally.
2. Breaches owing to alleged ignorance.
3. Breaches by Ingress.
4. Breaches by Egress.

CCXCVIII. 1. *As to Breaches generally.*

[*390] It is important to observe, that there is no analogy between *violations of the law, caused by carrying Contraband, and by breaches of Blockade.

In the former case, the offence is deposited with the cargo; in the latter it may be continued and renewed in the subsequent conduct of the ship.

The absence of the analogy arises from the more extended object of the law of Blockade as compared with that of the law of Contraband. The object of the latter is to prevent import only, the object is to prevent both import and export.(*g*)

To sail with an intention of evading a Blockade, is, according to the Prize Law laid down by the English Courts, a beginning to execute that intention, and an overt act constituting the offence. From that moment the Blockade is fraudulently invaded.(*h*)

But a Blockade of a port is not violated by shipments forwarded by *inland* navigation from that port to an unblockaded port, as is well illustrated in the following case of the Stert. Lord Stowell said:—

"This is a question arising out of the Blockade of Amsterdam, respecting goods put on board in a port of the Texel, for the very purpose of being sent to London, without any interruption of the voyage, but conveyed out of Holland to Embden by the means of the canal navigation, as I understand it. The question is, whether this is to be considered as a breach of the Blockade? A Blockade may be of different descriptions. The Blockade of Amsterdam, which was imposed on the part of this country, was, from the nature of our situation, a mere maritime Blockade, effected by force operating only at sea. As far as that force could be applied, it was indubitably, a good and legal Blockade; but as to an [*391] interior navigation, how is it a *Blockade at all? Where is the blockading Power? Let us suppose the case of the Blockade of Havre. Can it be said that, by the maritime Blockade of the Seine, the interior access to Havre is blockaded, so as that goods belonging to a neutral subject, sent from Paris to Havre, could be held subject to confiscation by virtue of the Blockade? It is argued that, if this course of trade is allowed, the object of the Blockade, which is to distress the trade of Holland, will be defeated. If that is the consequence, all that can be said is, that it is an unavoidable consequence. It must be imputed to the nature of the thing, which will not admit of an effectual remedy of this species. This Court cannot, on that ground, take upon itself to say that a legal Blockade exists, where no actual Blockade can be applied.

(*g*) The Frederick Molke, 1 Rob., p. 87.
(*h*) The Columbia, 1 Rob., p. 156. The Frederick Molke, ib., p. 86. The Hoffnung, 6 Rob., pp. 112, 117.

In the very notion of a complete Blockade, it is included, that the besieging force can apply its power to every point of the blockaded State. If it cannot, it is no Blockade of that quarter where its power cannot be brought to bear; and, where such a partial Blockade is undertaken, it must be presumed that this is no more than what was foreseen by the blockading State, which nevertheless, thought proper to impose it to the extent in which it was practicable. The commerce, though partially open, is still subjected to a pressure of difficulties and inconvenience. To cut off the power of immediate export and import from the ports of Holland, is, of itself, no insignificant operation, although it may not be possible to exclude them from the benefit of an inland communication. If the Blockade be rendered imperfect by this construction, it must be ascribed to the physical impossibility of the measure, by which the extent of its legal pretensions is unavoidably limited.

"In laying down this rule, as applicable to the present case, I proceed upon the supposition that this was a real inland navigation, and not a navigation over the Watt, the character of which might be subject to a different signification. Conceiving this to be a cargo which had gone to *Embden on a neutral account, by an internal canal navigation, where no Blockade existed, I shall hold it free of all consequences of Blockade, allowing the captors their necessary expenses upon the particular facts of the case."(i) [*392]

A Blockade may be broken by the *obstinacy* as well as by the *fraud* of the master; if he chooses to say that he must go, and will go to the blockaded port in defiance of notice, his owners must take the consequence.(k)

There may be circumstances arising out of the particular *object* of the Blockade itself, which entitle the breakers of it to an indulgent consideration. Thus, during the last war, the Blockade of the *Elbe* was not imposed with the intention of injuring the Blockade of *Hamburg*, but of harassing the enemy in the interior,—it was directed principally against that enemy, and it was incidentally only, and by unavoidable consequences, that the trade of the neutral neighbourhood was made subject to it. It was successfully contended that the novelty and peculiarity of the case would, under circumstances that admitted of any latitude of interpretation, entitle merchants to every indulgent consideration that could be applied to their case; though not to the extent of introducing in their favour different *principles* of the General Law of Blockade.(l)

CCXCIX. There is no subject of Maritime or International Law upon which the Jurists of all nations are so unanimous and precise in their opinions, as upon the Right and Law of Blockade.(m) Authorities

(i) The Stert, 4 Rob., p. 65. (k) The Henrick and Maria, 1 Rob., p. 147.

(l) The Spes and the Irene, 5 Rob., p. 79.

(m) "In tertio illo genere usus ancipitis, distinguendus erit belli status. Nam si tueri me non possum nisi quæ mittuntur intercipiam, necessitas, ut alibi exposuimus, jus dabit, sed sub onere restitutionis, nisi causa alia accedat. *Quod si juris mei executionem rerum subvectio impedierit; idque scire potuerit qui advexit, ut si oppidum obsessum tenebam, si portus clausos, et jam deditio aut pax exspectabatur, tenebitur ille mihi de damno culpâ dato, ut qui debitorem carceri exemit; aut fugam ejus in meam fraudem instruxit;* et ad damni dati modum res quoque ejus capi, et

[*393] might be easily accumulated *upon this point; but it is sufficient to say, that the decisions of the tribunals in the matters of Blockade have never been denied to be in accordance with reason, practice, [*394] and the judgments of the best writers. To these decisions, *therefore, reference will be almost exclusively made in the following pages. It will be seen that there is no act by which a Neutral more clearly and deservedly forfeits the immunities of his national character than by the violation of the Belligerent's Blockade.

CCC. 2. We have now to consider *breaches of Blockade owing to alleged ignorance.*

And first it must be observed, that *ignorance* of the law(*n*) is an inadmissible plea in the instance of Blockade, as in other cases, and may not be pleaded by any civilized State, Christian(*o*) or Infidel. *Ignorance of the fact,* however, may be, and often has been, successfully pleaded as a defence against the penalties incident to the breach of a Blockade.

This question as to ignorance of the fact is bound up with the question

dominium earum debiti consequendi causâ quæri poterit. Si damnum nondum dederit sed dare voluerit, ejus erit rerum retentione eum cogere ut de futuro caveat obsidibus pignoribus, aut alio modo. Quod si præterea evidentissima sit hostis mei in me injustitia, et ille eum in bello iniquissimo confirmet, jam non tantum civiliter tenebitur de damno, sed et criminaliter, *ut is qui judici imminenti reum manifestum eximit:* atque eo nomine licebit in eum statuere quod delicto convenit, secundum ea quæ de pœnis diximus; quare intra eum modum etiam spoliari poterit."—Grotius, l. iii. c. 1, s. v. § 3.

"Scilicet commercii intercludendi ergo Ordines Generales portus Flandriæ navibus bellicis obsederant, adeoque omnes quorumcunque naves, eo destinatas, indeque exeuentes, publicabant, quemadmodum ex ratione et gentium usu Urbibus obsessis nihil quicquam licet advehere, vel ex his evehere. Atque inde dicebat Admiralitas, ut et Ordines decreverunt, idem quoque juris esse in navibus, quæ antea nobis ereptæ et deinde venditæ erant, cum, obsessis portubus, etiam amicorum naves liceat intercipere. Quod ita verum est, si capiantur itinere nondum absoluto, dum navarchæ versantur in re illicita, absolutum autem iter non intelligi, nisi hæ naves proprium emptoris vel amicum portum subierint. Id vero, neque aliud Ordines Generales complexi sunt illo Decreto 26 Jun. 1630, ex quo ad eam, de qua nunc disputo, quæstionem recte argumentaberis, si et anno 1666, Angliam, Scotiam, Hiberniam, et omnia illa, quæ in Asia, Africa et America habebant Angli, classibus suis obsessa habuerint Ordines Generales. Relatum quidem est, eosdem Ordines anno 1652, quod ad Anglos, tale quid jactitasse, omnibus sic interdicto cum Anglis commercio, (Aitzema, l. xxxii. pp. 774, 777,) sed quo jure jactitarint, nunc non quæro, contentus monere, eosdem Ordines anno 1663, Hispanis, cum hi Lysitaniam obsessam habere videri vellent, id ipsum negasse, quod contra Anglos antea sibi arrogaverant, sic enim proditum est in Annalibus."—(Apud eundem, l. xliii. p. 858.) Bynkershoek, Q. J. P., l. i. c. iv.

"Jusqu'ici nous avons parlé du commerce des peuples neutres avec les états de l'ennemi en général. Il est un cas particulier où les droits de la guerre s'étendent plus loin. Tout commerce est absolument défendu avec une ville assiégée. Quand je tiens une place assiégée, ou seulement bloquée, je suis en droit d'empêcher que personne n'y entre, et de traiter en ennemi quiconque entreprend d'y entrer sans ma permission, ou d'y porter, quoi que ce soit: car il s'oppose à mon entreprise, il peut contribuer à la faire échouer, et par là me faire tomber dans tous les maux d'une guerre malheureuse. Le roi Démétrius fit pendre le maître et le pilote d'un vaisseau qui portait des vivres à Athènes, lorsqu'il était sur le point de prendre cette ville par famine. (Plutarchus in Demetrius.) Dans la longue et sanglante guerre que les Provinces-Unies ont soutenue contre l'Espagne pour recouvrer leur liberté, elles ne voulurent point souffrir que les Anglais portassent des marchandises à Dunkerque, devant laquelle elles avient une flotte."—Vattel, l. iii. c. vii. s. 117.

(*n*) Vide antè, p. 394. (*o*) The Hurtige Hane, 3 Rob., p. 326.

of *notice*. It has been holden, that where vessels sail without a knowledge of the Blockade, a notice is necessary, but if they can be affected with the knowledge of the fact, a warning is not required.(*p*)

A Blockade may commence *de facto*, by a blockading force giving notice on the spot to those who come from a distance, and who may therefore be ignorant of the fact. Vessels *going in* are in that case entitled to a notice before they can be justly liable to the consequences of breaking a Blockade, but it is quite otherwise with vessels *coming out* of the port, which is the object of the Blockade; there no notice is necessary. After the Blockade has existed *de facto* for any length of time, it is impossible for those within to be ignorant of the forcible suspension of their commerce; the notoriety of the *thing supersedes the necessity of particular notice to each ship.(*q*) [*395]

Ignorance may perhaps be successfully urged when knowledge of the Blockade is to be inferred from general notoriety alone, but such an argument will not avail when it is proved that the master of the ship was personally aware of the fact.(*r*)

The plea of ignorance is however not taken away by partial and imperfect information or notice, and, therefore, in a case where notice had been given to a merchant that there was a general Blockade of the coast of Holland—which was untrue in fact—that notice was holden not to be available, by *limitation*, to a Blockade of Amsterdam only, though such Blockade did actually exist. Such a notice took from the Neutral all power of election as to what other port of Holland he should go, when he found the port of his destination under blockade. A commander of a ship has no right to reduce a Neutral to this kind of distress, and for contravening *such a notice* he is not subject to condemnation.(*s*)

CCCI. With respect to this plea of *ignorance of the facts*, it must be remembered that the breach of Blockade is one of the simplest and most universal operations of war.(*t*) The leading principles applicable to the infinite variety of circumstances which may occur, are these:—

α. That where there has been a formal notification of the Blockade, a reasonable time must be allowed for it to take effect.(*u*)

β. That where there has been no formal notification, the knowledge of the party must be proved.

*That after a certain time, it lies *primâ facie* upon the party to show that he was not apprised of the fact of the Blockade.(*x*) [*396]

What that period of time should be, must always chiefly depend upon the circumstances of each case; but in cases relating to the *agency* of persons in an enemy's country during a Blockade, it has been judicially holden that something more than the mere strict principle of law is necessary in order to bind *employers* by their acts.(*y*) There must

(*p*) The Columbia, 1 Rob., p. 156. (*q*) The Vrow Judith, 1 Rob. p. 152.
(*r*) The Tutela, 6 Rob., p. 181. (*s*) The Henrick and Maria, 1 Rob., p. 149.
(*t*) The Hurtige Hane, 3 Rob., p. 326
(*u*) The Ringende Jacob, 1 Rob., p. 91. The Adelaide, 3 Rob., p. 284. The Jonge Petronella, 2 Rob., p. 131. The Betsey, 1. Rob., p. 334.
(*x*) The Betsey, 1 Rob., p. 332. The Adelaide Rose, note to the Neptunus, 2 Rob., p. 111. The Calypso, 2 Rob., p. 298.
(*y*) The Neptunus, 3 Rob., p. 173.

be time allowed to give the principal an opportunity of countermanding.(*z*)

CCCII. 3. *Breaches of Blockade by the ingress* or by the *intended ingress* of ships, is the next division of the subject.

It is altogether unlawful for a neutral ship to *enter* a blockaded port at all, even in ballast,(*a*) and for the purpose of bringing away the property of neutral merchants deposited there before the Blockade.

The legal presumption arising from entering a blockaded port will be, that the ship went in for the fraudulent purpose of delivering her cargo. And her coming out again without having delivered her cargo, will not of itself oust that presumption and remove the illegality as some unexpected change of circumstances may have altered her intention.(*b*)

Such being the clear law with respect to *entering* a blockaded port, we have next to consider the penalty of *approaching* to such a port.

[*397] And upon this (as upon other points connected with this *subject,) it is necessary to bear in mind the distinction between a blockade *de facto* and a Blockade by *notification.*(*c*)

An approach for the purpose of inquiry in the former case may be justifiable, and quite unjustifiable in the latter. But in either case a neutral ship may not innocently drop anchor, or continue in a situation in which it will be in her power to break the Blockade with impunity whenever she pleases. She may not approach close up to the Blockaded port, so as to be enabled to slip in without obstruction, when an opportunity presents itself. It has been deemed no unfair rule of evidence to hold, as a presumption *de jure,* that she goes there with an intention of breaking the Blockade; and if such inference should operate with severity in particular cases, where the parties are innocent in their intentions, it is a severity necessarily connected with the rules of evidence, and essential to the effectual exercise of the rules of war.(*d*)

Upon the same principle, a vessel is not permitted, under the plea of obtaining a pilot, or any similar pretext, to approach so near to a blockaded port as to place itself within the effectual protection of the shore.(*e*)

CCCIII. It may be that the distance of the country of the Neutral from the locality of the Blockade, or of the country of the blockading Power, justifies *inquiry* near the situation of the Blockade. Such an equitable and temperate rule was applied by Lord Stowell, during the last war, to ships coming from the American Continent.(*f*) It must be remembered,

(*z*) The Adelaide, ib., p. 285. Mr. Pritchard's Analytical Digest of Cases decided in the High Court of Admiralty, (London, 1847,) has greatly facilitated the labours of all subsequent compilers of Maritime and International Law. I am anxious to take this opportunity of acknowledging the advantage which I have derived from it.

(*a*) The Comet, 1 Edwards, p. 32. (*b*) The Charlotta, ib., p. 252.

(*c*) The Neptunus, 2 Rob., p. 110.

(*d*) The Neutralität, 6 Rob., p. 35. The Gute Erwartung, ib., p. 182. The Arthur, 1 Edwards, p. 202. Radcliff v. Union Insurance Company, 7 Johnson's (Amer.) Rep., p. 47. Fitzsimmons v. Newport Insurance Company, 4 Cranch's (Amer.) Rep., p. 185.

(*e*) The Charlotte Christina, 6 Rob., p. 103. The Neutralität, ib., p. 35.

(*f*) The Betsey, 1 Rob., p. 334.

however, that the Atlantic was not then, as now, *traversed in twelve or fourteen days from the European shores, or India made [*398] acquainted with intelligence of European affairs in less than six weeks. The principle, indeed, remains the same, but the application of it during the present war will of course be materially affected by the marvellous agencies of steam and electricity,(*g*) unknown to our forefathers.

CCCIV. But it has never been held legal, under any circumstances, that the inquiry should be made at the very mouth of the river or estuary blockaded, from the blockading vessels themselves. Nor is the ship to be released from condemnation because the master was ordered by his owners to make his inquiries at such places.(*h*)

Such inquiries should be made in the ports that lie in the way, and which furnish opportunities for inquiry without furnishing opportunities for fraud.(*i*)

The inquiry is to be made in a safe and permitted place, and in a safe and permitted manner.

It is possible, indeed, that innocency of intention may be established, even when directions have been given to the master to inquire at the mouth of the blockaded port. But the circumstances must be very peculiar.(*k*)

CCCV. We have been considering blockaded *ports*, but *the *adjacent waters* may be so connected with the ports as to render [*399] the approach to, and navigation in them by Neutrals, an act of equal guilt with the approach to the ports. And therefore approximation to the blockaded port, so as to expose the blockader's forces to the batteries on the coast, cannot be permitted under the pretext of taking a pilot for a neighbouring port.(*l*)

CCCVI. Nor will this approach be successfully veiled by a general allegation that the approaching ship was only in *the roads* adjacent to the port. The law upon this point is thus stated by Lord Stowell:—

"This is the case of a ship taken on a professed destination to Embden; but the fact is, she was seized in Ostend Roads. Every witness uses the same expression, 'Ostend Roads;' and I understand the situation of the vessel to have been at no great distance from that port. The term 'roads,' undoubtedly, is not a word of very definite meaning; there may be roads

(*g*) The analogy of the following case is applicable to this subject:—"A bottomry bond was granted in New York by the master of a ship, to obtain money for necessary repairs, the owner whereof was residing at St. John's, New Brunswick. A communication by electric telegraph existed between the two cities. The bondholder had previously acted as the general agent of the owner, and no intimation of the transaction was made by the master to the owner until after the execution of the bond. Held, upon appeal (reversing the sentence of the Admiralty Court,) that the master having the means of communication with the owner, no such absolute necessity existed as to authorise him to pledge the ship without communication with the owner, and the bond declared void."—The Oriental, 7 Moore's Privy Council Reports, p. 398.

(*h*) The Spes, 5 Rob., p. 76.

(*i*) The Betsey, 1 Rob., p, 334. The Posten, note to the Betsey, ib., p. 335. The Little William, 1 Acton's Rep., p. 151. Dr. Arnold, arguendo.

(*k*) The Little William, 1 Acton's Rep., p. 161, was such a case.

(*l*) The Charlotte Christine, 6 Rob., p. 101. The Gute Erwartung, ib., p. 182. The Neutralität, ib., p. 30. The Arthur, Edwards, p. 202.

which have no immediate connection with any particular port, as the Downs; other roads are so connected with particular ports as almost to form part of them; and these two descriptions of roads may be subject to very different considerations. If a ship comes into the Downs, which is the common passage and highway to the German Ocean, and to different parts of Europe, it would not be at all just to infer from the mere coming there that she is necessarily coming to a British port. But if the roads are of the other species, there is then reason to conclude that a ship comes there with a view to some communication with that particular port.

"From the description given of the roads of Ostend, they are, I think, to be taken as being of the latter species. The ship was lying within a [*400] sand, and within the protection of *the batteries, and in a place, as I conceive, where ships of large burden are usually unlivered by lighters, as the most commodious method of delivering their cargoes at Ostend. If I am correct in that view, a ship going there must be considered as in the port of Ostend; since, for the purpose of enforcing a Blockade, it is not necessary to restrict the meaning of the word port to the limits of the particular local port regulations, which may not extend beyond the pier-head. A Belligerent is not bound to that restricted sense of the word. If the situation of the vessel is within the protection of the batteries, and in a place which vessels usually frequent for the purpose of unlivery, and from which importation into Ostend can safely be effected, and is not unusually effected, it would not unreasonably be held to be a part of that port."(*m*)

CCCVII. The ordinances of the American Congress of 1781, seem to have conceded this point to the extent of the English rule, for they made it lawful to take and condemn all vessels, of all nations, "destined to any such port," without saying anything of notice or proximity.(*n*)

CCCVIII. We have now to consider the legal effect of the *intention* of the master, or the *destination* of his ship.

A Dutch ordinance, of which Bynkershoek(*o*) approves, declared, in 1630, that vessels bound to the blockaded ports of Flanders were liable to confiscation, though found at a distance from these ports, unless they had voluntarily altered the voyage before coming in sight of the port.

It has been said(*p*) that the English Prize Courts have holden, that to sail for a blockaded port, knowing it to be such, is in itself an attempt, and an act sufficient to charge the party making it with a breach of the Blockade, without reference to the distance between the port of departure [*401] and the *blockaded port, or to the extent of the voyage performed when the vessel was arrested.(*q*)

The Courts of the North American United States, doubted at one time(*r*) whether they should recognize the legality of this doctrine to

(*m*) The Neutralität, 6 Rob., p. 34.
(*n*) Journals of Congress, vol. vii. p. 186. Kent's Comm., p. 153.
(*o*) Q. J. P., l. i. c. xi.
(*p*) Vide ante, p. 390.
(*q*) The Columbia, 1 Rob., p. 156. The Vrow Johanna, 2 Rob., p. 109. The Abby, 5 Rob., p. 256.
(*r*) Fitzsimmons v. Newport Insurance Company, 4 Cranch (Amer.) Rep., p. 199.

its full extent; but after mature consideration, they fully concurred in it,(s) aided by the high authority of Dr. Story.(t)

The offence continues, although, at the moment of capture, the vessel be, by stress of weather, driven in a direction from the port, for the hostile intention still remains unchanged.(u)

CCCIX. There is this distinction between a Blockade *de facto* and a Blockade by *notification*, that in the latter the act of sailing to a blockaded port is sufficient to constitute the offence, but in a Blockade existing *de facto* only, no presumption arises as to the continuance; and the ignorance of the party may be admitted as an excuse for sailing on a doubtful and provisional destination.(x)

CCCX. The mere sailing to a port which is blockaded, without an intention of breaking the Blockade, is not an offence against International Law, although the Blockade should be in force when the ship arrives at the port. A ship may lawfully sail(y) with the intention of inquiring if the Blockade be continued or not.(z)

*CCCXI. A *concealed* illegal destination is generally holden to furnish proof of real intention to break the Blockade :(a) and [*402] the presumption is fortified by the deviation of the ship from the course which her *alleged* destination would lead her to pursue.

In order to establish such deviations, assessors of nautical skill, called in England Trinity Masters, are sometimes invoked to aid the decisions of the Court.(b)

But if there be fair reason to infer that it was the intention of the ship to inquire at the port whether the Blockade continued or not, she ought not to be condemned because her papers do not disclose, in explicit terms, the place at which the inquiry was to have been made.(c)

CCCXII. 4. *Breaches of Blockade by egress* is the next subdivision of this subject; and first, it is to be observed, that a ship coming out of a blockaded place is, in all cases, in the first instance, liable to seizure; and in order to obtain a release, the claimant must give very satisfactory proof of the innocency of his intention.(d)

CCCXIII. Nevertheless, there are certain cases in which, according to well-established law, egress is permitted. Among these *exceptions* are the following:—

1. A ship that has entered *previously* to the Blockade, may retire in *ballast*.(e)

2. She may also take out a cargo put on board before a Blockade.(f)

(s) Yeaton v. Fry. It was a question as to the forfeiture of a policy of insurance. Marshall, C. J., said:—"Sailing from Tobago to Curraçoa, knowing Curraçoa to be blockaded, would have incurred this risk, but sailing for that port without such knowledge, did not incur it."—5 Cranch (Amer.) Rep., p. 343.

(t) The Nereide, 9 Cranch, (Amer.) pp. 440, 446. (u) Ibid.

(x) The Neptunus, 2 Rob., p. 110.

(y) Medeiros v. Hill, 8 Bingham's Reports, p. 231.

(z) Naylor v. Taylor, 4 Manning and Ryland's Rep., p. 526. S. C. 9 Barnewell & Cresswell's Rep., p. 718. Dalgleish v. Hodgson, 5 Moore & Payne, 407. S. C. 7 Bingham, p. 495.

(a) The James Cook, 1 Edwards, p. 261. (b) The Mentor, 1 Edwards, p. 207.

(c) The Dispatch, 1 Acton, p. 163. (d) The Frederick Molke, 1 Rob., p. 88.

(e) The Juno, 2 Rob., p. 119. (f) Ibid.

In this case the time of shipment is a most material fact.(*g*) But it must be a cargo *bonâ fide* purchased and delivered *before* the Beginning of the Blockade: to take on board a cargo *after* the Blockade has begun, is a [*403] fraudulent *violation of it;(*h*) and the permission to go out with a cargo laden before the Blockade, is confined to cases in which there has been a delivery of the goods *on board* the ship, or in lighters, and is not extended to shipment in *warehouses*.(*i*)

But it has been holden that if a Neutral has sent in goods before the Blockade, which are found unsaleable, or are otherwise *bonâ fide* withdrawn by the owner, they may come out without being subject to condemnation;(*k*) and it has also been holden that a neutral *ship* coming out of a blockaded port, in consequence of a rumour that hostilities were likely to take place between the enemy and the country to which the vessel belongs, is not liable to condemnation, though laden with a cargo, *where the regulations of the enemy would not permit a departure in ballast;* and in such a case as this the *cargo* was condemned, though put on board against the will of the master.(*l*)

It is not illegal for the Neutral to acquire by transfer or otherwise a vessel from another Neutral in a blockaded port, if the acquisition be in no manner connected with the commerce of that port; and where a ship so transferred, had come out in ballast, she was restored on payment of captor's expenses.(*m*)

But the permission is not pushed beyond this extent, and where a vessel was sold in a blockaded port by a Neutral, who had himself purchased of the enemy since the outbreak of hostilities, the request to obtain further proof was refused, and the ship condemned.(*n*)

[*404] *Among the cases of *exception* may be also mentioned that of a neutral vessel not stopped by any ship of the blockading squadron, but afterwards by a ship not employed upon that service. In a case of this description, it would seem, partly on the ground that the peculiar public duty of stopping the vessel was not cast upon the ship which stopped her, partly on the ground of the evidence of the remissness of the Blockade furnished by the escape of the vessel, not only was the vessel not condemned, but the captor was not allowed his expenses.(*o*)

Another case of *exception* is furnished by the instance of a ship employed by the Minister of a neutral State, resident in the country of the blockaded port, for the exclusive purpose of conveying home distressed marines belonging to that neutral country.(*p*) The purpose must be exclusively such as has been described, unless indeed there be

(*g*) The Betsy, 1 Rob., p. 93.

(*h*) The Vrow Judith, 1 Rob., p. 152. The Neptunus, ib., p. 171. The Juno, 2 Rob., p. 119.

(*i*) The Rolla, 6 Rob., p. 371.

(*k*) The Potsdam, 4 Rob., p. 89. The Juffrow Maria Schrœder, ib., note.

(*l*) The Drie Vrienden, 1 Dodson's Adm. Rep., p. 269.

(*m*) The Potsdam, 4 Rob., p. 89. The Vigilantia, 6 Rob., p. 124, affirms the same proposition, but rather more doubtfully.

(*n*) The Vigilantia, 6 Rob., p. 124.

(*o*) The Christina Margaretha, 6 Rob., p. 63.

(*p*) The Rose in Bloom, 1 Dodson, p. 58.

so trifling a cargo on board as to bring it within the scope of the maxim, *de minimis non curat lex.*(*q*)

CCCXIV. The carriage of goods through the medium of the *interior communication* from a blockaded port to a neutral port, is no breach of a purely *maritime Blockade*, and goods so transmitted cannot be seized on their passage from the neutral port to a lawful port, by reason of their having so, as they certainly have, defeated the object of the Blockade. It is included in the very notion, as has been already stated, of a legal Blockade, that the besieging force can apply its power to every point of the blockaded State. If it cannot, it is no Blockade of that quarter where its power cannot be brought to bear. The nature of a merely *maritime* Blockade must always expose it to the possibility of the partial defeat of its intention and operation ;(*r*) and upon *this principle, goods sent from blockaded Amsterdam to unblockaded Rotter- [*405] dam and neutral Embden, were not allowed, during the last war to be seized for breach of Blockade.

CCCXV. But it has been judicially decided that a cargo which had been brought *through the mouth of a blockaded river*, for the purpose of being shipped for exportation, was subject to be considered as taken upon a *continued* voyage, and as liable to all the same principles that are applied to a direct voyage, of which the terminus *à quo* and the terminus *ad quem*, are precisely the same as those of the more circuitous destination, and that ship and cargo were accordingly liable, under the general law to condemnation.(*s*)

CCCXVI. It remains to state the penal consequences of a breach of Blockade.

1. To the ship.
2. To the cargo.

CCCXVII. First, as to the ship, the penal consequence is confiscation.(*t*)

Lord Stowell says: "It is unnecessary for me to observe, if a ship that has broken a Blockade is taken in any part of the same voyage, she is taken *in delicto*, and subject to confiscation. The offence is not terminated until she reaches the end of the voyage."(*u*)

This is deemed reasonable, because no other opportunity is afforded to the belligerent force to vindicate the law.(*x*)

*In cases of Contraband, the return voyage has not usually been deemed connected with the outward, and the offence was depo- [*406] sited with the offending subject; but in distant voyages, with contraband

(*q*) The Rose in Bloom, 1 Dobson, p. 57.

(*r*) The Stert, 4 Rob., p. 67. The Ocean, 3 Rob., p. 297. The Maria, 6 Rob., p. 201. The Lisette, ib., p. 394. The Julia, 1 Dodson, p. 169, note. The Jonge Pieter, 4 Rob., p. 79.

(*s*) The Maria, 6 Rob., p. 201. The Charlotte Sophia, ib., p. 204, note. The Lisette, ib., p. 394.

(*t*) 1 Kent's Comm. p. 152. The Mercurius, 1 Rob., p. 83.

(*u*) The Welvaart van Pillaw, 2 Rob., p. 128. The Juffrow Maria Shrœder, 3 Rob., p. 153.

(*x*) The Welvaart van Pillaw, 2 Rob., p. 128. The Juffrow Maria Schrœder, 3 Rob., p. 147.

and false papers, the rule is different; the fraud contaminates the return cargo, and subjects it to condemnation, as being one entire transaction.(*y*)

But though the offence thus incurred remains during the voyage, it is subject to the condition of the continuance of the Blockade, the raising which does away with the offence.(*z*)

Where a vessel has been purchased in a blockaded port, that alone is an illegal act, and it is immaterial out of what funds the purchase is made, nor can she be said not to be taken *in delicto* when, on a voyage to the country of the purchaser, she has been driven to an intermediate port by stress of weather.(*a*)

CCCXVIII. Secondly, as to the cargo.

It is a general rule that ship and cargo are both confiscated for a breach of Blockade;(*b*) but here an important distinction must be taken, viz., whether the owners of the *cargo* are, or are not, identical with the owners of the *ship*.

If *they are*, the confiscation of the one follows upon the confiscation of the other; but if *they are not*, then the cargo is not confiscated, unless, before the goods were shipped, the owners of them were, or ought to have been, apprized of the existence of the Blockade, or unless it be shown that, under the circumstances, the act of the master personally binds them.(*c*)

[*407] *And it should seem, though the point is perhaps not quite clear, that in those cases in which the owners of the ship and cargo are divers persons, that the burden of proving the(*d*) guilt of the cargo lies upon the claimant.

For though the master is certainly the agent of the owners of the *vessel*, and can bind by his contract or his misconduct, yet he is not the agent of the owners of the *cargo*, unless expressly so constituted by them. Possibly cargoes of a *contraband* character might justify greater severity, though it will be seen that even in such cases the *innocent* parts of the cargo belonging to *other* owners have been held not to be infected(*e*)—a rule which seems to furnish an analogy for the lenient one laid down respecting the owners of cargoes in cases of breach of Blockade.

In cases of *insurance* and *revenue*, a severer law is enforced; but the act of the master is held to affect the cargo in the former case by virtue of an express contract which governs the whole case, and in the latter instance it proceeds from positive laws, and the necessary strictness of all fiscal regulations.(*f*)

In the year 1808, Lord Stowell reviewed and confirmed the principles

(*y*) The Rosalie and Betty, 2 Rob., p. 343. The Nancy, 3 Ib., p. 122. Carrington v. The Merchants' Insurance Company, 8 Peters's (Amer.) Rep., p. 495.

(*z*) The Lisette, 6 Rob., p. 387.

(*a*) The General Hamilton, 6 Rob., p. 61.

(*b*) The Comet, Edwards, p. 32.

(*c*) The Columbia, 1 Rob., p. 154. The Vrow Judith, ib., p. 150. The Imina, 3 Rob., p. 169. The Rosalie and Betty, 2 Rob., pp. 343, 351. The Alexander, 4 Rob., p. 93. The Elsebe, 5 Rob., p. 173. Story on Prize Courts, by Pratt, p. 72.

(*d*) Vide antè, p. 55, for discussion of the law belonging to *ignorantia juris et facti*.

(*e*) The Staadt Embden, 1 Rob., p. 30.

(*f*) The Mercurius, 1 Rob., pp. 85, 86.

of law applicable to this subject of the complicity of the owner of the cargo with the act of the master of the ship in the case of *Exchange*.

"It has been suggested," he said, "that though the ship was going to a French port, it might not be for the purpose of delivering her cargo there; but there is no rule which has been more clearly established in principle, than that the port of destination, being an interdicted port, is the port of delivery of the cargo. It is impossible to relax that principle: *if it were once admitted that a ship may enter an interdicted port to supply herself with water, or on any other pretence, a [*408] door would be open to all sorts of frauds, without the possibility of preventing them. The Court applied the principle when it was first led to the consideration of cases of Blockade, and there is none to which it has more inflexibly adhered. I am therefore to take the question with this condition, that the ship was going to a *French* port for the purpose of delivering her cargo, and I really know of no cases, except those which have been cited, where the owner of the cargo has been relieved from the penalty attaching to the ship. The cases cited, which are familiar to us all, were cases of a supervening illegality, where it was shown that the owner of the cargo stood clear of any possible intention of fraud, and *that* by proofs found on board at the time of capture, and not supplied afterwards. For instance, where orders had been given for goods prior to the existence of Blockade, and it appeared that there was not time for countermanding the shipment afterwards, the Court has held the owner of the cargo not responsible for the act of the enemy's shipper, who might have an interest in sending off the goods in direct opposition to the interest of his principal. And the same indulgence has been exercised where there was no knowledge of the Blockade till after the ship had sailed, and the master, after receiving the information, obstinately persisted in going on to the port of his original destination."(*g*)

CCCXIX. In cases of Blockade, the deviation into the blockaded port is presumed to be in the service of the cargo, and therefore, the owner is bound by the presumption, unless where there is no notice of the Blockade at the time the ship sailed.(*h*) And if the master, at the time of sailing put his *ship under convoy, whose instructions he is presumed to know, the act is illegal, and binds both the ship [*409] and cargo.(*i*) It is not considered like the case of an unforeseen emergency happening to a ship at sea, where the fact itself proves the owners to be ignorant and innocent, and where the Court has held, that being proved innocent by the very circumstances of the case, the owners of the cargo should not be bound by the mere principle of law, which imposes on the employer a responsibility for the acts of his agent. On the contrary, it is a matter done *antecedently to the voyage*, and must, therefore, be presumed to be done on communication with the owners, and with their consent; the effect of this presumption is such, that it cannot be permitted to be averred against, inasmuch as all the evidence must come from the suspected parties themselves, without affording a possibility of

(*g*) The Exchange, Edwards's Admiralty Reports, pp. 42, 43.
(*h*) The Alexander, 4 Rob., p. 93. The Shepherdess, 5 Rob., p. 262.
(*i*) The Elsebe, 5 Rob., p. 173.

meeting it, however prepared. The Court, therefore, applies the strict principle of law, and holds, as it does in blockade cases of that description, that the master must be taken to be the authorized agent of the cargo; and that if he has exceeded his authority, it is *barratry*,(k) for which he is personally answerable, and for which the owner must look to him for indemnification.(l) Whether a like principle ought not to be applied to the owner of the cargo, in cases where the ship originally sails on the voyage under an enemy's license, has not been decided. The point was made in the Supreme Court of the United States in a recent case; but inasmuch as knowledge was brought home to the actual agent of the owners of the cargo, it became unnecessary to decide the more general principle.(m)

[*410] CCCXX. There is a material difference in the application *of the law in the case of *commissioned* captors upon the high seas, and of non-commissioned captors who seize, in the execution of their duty as internal police, vessels in ports or harbours of the *captors' country*.

In the first place, Prize Courts would be unwilling to extend the *ex post facto* defence, which has been mentioned, to non-commissioned captors.(n) In the next place, the non-commissioned captor can rarely if ever be *inops consilii:* his Sovereign is bound to furnish him with the means of obtaining legal advice, whenever the emergency arises. He is not compelled by wind or weather, or any *vis major*, or any overwhelming necessity, to act according to his unaided discretion, upon the spur of the moment; but it is often the bounden duty of the commissioned captor so to act: and it is therefore with reason and justice, that Prize Courts usually award costs and damages to the captor, when they decree restitution of the vessel which he has seized. And it has been said, by high authority, that in all cases during the last war, except the *Acteon*, it was the endeavour of the English Prize Court so far to relieve the honest captor; and that the *Acteon*, though the circumstances caused the captor to be condemned in costs and damages, did, in its general bearing, confirm the rule which has been stated.(o) And even where the Court has decided that there has been probable ground for seizure, it has sometimes decreed a *simple restitution* of the ship without costs to the seizors, who were revenue officers, acting under the authority of the Lords of the Admiralty.(p)

[*411] *CCCXXI. 8. The last division of the subject relates to *The Orders in Council.*

(k) "A fraudulent act of the master or mariners, committed contrary to their duty as such, to the prejudice of the owners of the ship."—Bouvier's Law Dictionary, vol. i. p. 159.

(l) Ib., and p. 175.

(m) The Hiram, 1 Wheaton, (Amer.) p. 440. Story on the Prize Courts, by F. T. Pratt, D. C. L., pp. 72, 73.

(n) The Elise, (Dr. Lushington,) November, 1854. Eccles. and Adm. Rep. (Spink's,) vol. ii. p. 38. S. C. Reports of Cases in Adm. Prize Court and Court of Appeal, vol. i. pt. 1, p. 90.

(o) Ibid.

(p) The Caroline, June 12, 1855. Ib., vol. i. pt. 11, p. 252. The law of Blockade underwent a minute examination in a judgment of the judicial committee during the present war, but no new principle appears to have been promulgated. The Franciska and the Johanna Maria, Reports of Cases in the Admiralty Prize Court and Court of Appeal, vol. i. pt. 2, p. 287.

In one of the leading cases on this subject, Lord Stowell said:—

"It is matter of universal notoriety, that the French Ruler published, in November, 1806, a Decree dated at Berlin (from whence it usually takes its title,) by which he declared the British Isles to be in a state of Blockade; that the British Government, in January and November, 1807, published Orders of Blockade; the former prohibiting the trade of Neutrals *between* ports from which the British flag was excluded, the latter imposing a total Blockade of those ports. *These Orders were intended and professed to be retaliatory against France; without reference to that character they have not, and would not, have been defended; but in that character they have been justly, in my apprehension, deemed reconcileable with those rules of natural justice by which the international communication of independant States is usually governed.* On the 26th, of December following, the French Government issued an edict, dated Milan (from whence it is commonly denominated,) by which a still stronger pressure was imposed upon British commerce and British maritime warfare. On the 26th of April, 1809, the retaliatory measure on the part of Great Britain, dated November, 1807, was restricted to the extent of its local operation. . . . .

"The United States, in March, 1809, passed a Non-intercourse Act, directed against both countries, but accompanied with a legislative declaration that it should cease to operate against either Belligerent which should repeal their respective Orders of Blockade."(*q*)

The French Decree of *Berlin*, in 1806, was as follows:—

Art. 1. "Les Iles Britanniques sont déclarées en état de blocus.

2. "Tout commerce et toute correspondance avec elles est défendu."

*4. "Tout magasin, marchandise, ou propriété, quoi qu'elle soit, qui appartienne à un Anglais est de bonne prise. [*412]

5. "Le commerce des marchandises Anglaises est défendu, tous les produits d'industrie Anglaise et de ses colonies sont de bonne prise.

7. "Aucun vaisseau qui vient directement d'Angleterre, ou de ses colonies, ne pourra entrer dans des ports Français, ou qui sont sous la puissance Française.

8. "Tout vaisseau qui, par une fausse déclaration, se conduira contre ces dispositions, sera confisque."(*r*)

The French Decree of *Milan*, in 1807, contained a further outrage, of the same kind, upon International Law. It is not necessary to state it at length.(*s*)

The Orders in Council were as follows:—

At the Court of the Queen's Palace, January 7, 1807.
Present:
The King's Most Excellent Majesty in Council.

"Whereas the French Government has issued certain Orders, which, in violation of the usages of war, purport to prohibit the commerce of all neutral nations with his majesty's dominions, and also to prevent such nations from trading with any other country in any articles the growth,

(*q*) The Snipe and others, Edwards's Admiralty Reports, pp. 381-2.
(*r*) Moniteur, 1806, No. 339. (*s*) De Martens, V., Suppl., pp. 439-442.

produce, or manufacture of his majesty's dominions; and whereas the said Government has also taken upon itself to declare all his majesty's dominions to be in a state of Blockade, at a time when the fleets of France and her allies are themselves confined within their own ports by the superior valour and discipline of the British navy; and whereas such attempts on the part of the enemy would give to his majesty an unquestionable right of retaliation, and would warrant his majesty in enforcing the same prohibition of all commerce with France, which that Power [*413] vainly hopes to effect against the commerce of his *majesty's subjects, a prohibition which the superiority of his majesty's naval forces might enable him to support, by actually investing the ports and coasts of the enemy with numerous squadrons and cruisers, so as to make the entrance or approach thereto manifestly dangerous; and whereas his majesty, though unwilling to follow the example of his enemies, by proceeding to an extremity so distressing to all nations not engaged in the war, and carrying on their accustomed trade, yet feels himself bound, by a due regard to the just defence of the rights and interests of his people, not to suffer such measures to be taken by the enemy, without taking some steps on his part to restrain this violence, and to retort upon them the evils of their own injustice; his majesty is thereupon pleased, by and with the advice of his Privy Council, to order, and it is hereby ordered, that no vessel shall be permitted to trade from one port to another, both which ports shall belong to, or be in the possession of France or her allies, or shall be so far under their control as that British vessels may not freely trade thereat; and the commanders of his majesty's ships of war and privateers shall be, and are hereby instructed to warn every neutral vessel coming from any such port, and destined to another such port, to discontinue her voyage, and not to proceed to any such port; and any vessel, after, being so warned, or any vessel coming from any such port, after a reasonable time shall have been afforded for receiving information of this his majesty's orders, which shall be found proceeding to another such port, shall be captured and brought in, and, together with her cargo shall be condemned as lawful prize. And His Majesty's Principal Secretaries of State, the Lords Commissioners of the Admiralty, and the Judges of the High Court of Admiralty, and Courts of Vice-Admiralty, are to take the necessary measures herein as to them shall respectively appertain.

"W. FAWKENER."(*t*)

[*414] *At the Court of the Queen's Palace, the 24th of May, 1809.

Present:

The King's Most Excellent Majesty in Council.

"Whereas his majesty was pleased, by his Order in Council of the 26th of April last, to declare certain ports and places of the countries which have been lately styled the kingdom of Holland, to be subject to the restrictions incident to a strict and rigorous Blockade, as continued from his majesty's former Order of the 11th of November, 1807; and whereas advices have been received of a certain Provisional Agreement,

(*t*) Annual Register, 1807, vol. xlix. pp. 671-2.

entered into by His Majesty's Envoy Extraordinary and Minister Plenipotentiary in America with the Government of the United States, whereby it is understood that His Majesty's Orders in Council of the 7th of January, and of the 11th of November, 1807, shall be withdrawn so far as respects the United States, on the 10th of June next.

"And whereas, although the said Provisional Agreement is not such as was authorized by his majesty's instructions, or such as his majesty can approve, it may already have happened, or may happen, that persons being citizens of the said United States may be led, by a reliance on the said Provisional Agreement, to engage in trade with and to the said ports and places of Holland, contrary to, and in violation of the restrictions imposed by the said Orders of the 7th of January, and of the 11th of November, 1807, as altered by the Order of the 26th of April last; his majesty, in order to prevent any inconveniences that may ensue from the circumstance above recited, is pleased, by and with the advice of his Privy Council, to order, and it is hereby ordered, that the said several Orders shall be suspended, so far as is necessary for the protection of vessels of the said United States, so sailing under the faith of the said Provisional Agreement, viz: That after the 9th day of June next, no vessel of the United States, which shall have cleared out between the 19th of April last and the 20th of July ensuing, for any of the ports of Holland aforesaid *from any port of the United States, shall be molested or interrupted in her voyage by the commanders of his majesty's ships or privateers. [*415]

"And it is further ordered, that no vessels of the United States which shall have cleared out from any port of America previous to the 20th of July next, for any other permitted port, and shall, during her voyage, have changed her destination, in consequence of information of the said Provisional Agreement, and shall be proceeding to any of the ports of Holland aforesaid, shall be molested or interrupted by the commanders of any of His Majesty's ships or privateers, unless such vessel shall have been informed of this Order on her voyage, and shall have been warned not to proceed to any of the ports of Holland aforesaid, and shall, notwithstanding such warning, be found attempting to proceed to any such port.

"And it is further ordered, that after the said 9th day of June next, no vessel of the said United States which shall have cleared out, or be destined to any of the ports of Holland from any other port or place not subject to the restrictions of the said Order of the 26th of April last, after notice of such Provisional Agreement as aforesaid, shall be molested or interrupted in her voyage by the commanders of His Majesty's ships or privateers, provided such vessel shall have so cleared out previous to actual notice of this Order at such place of clearance, or in default of proof of actual notice previous to the like periods of time after the date of this Order, as are fixed for constructive notice of His Majesty's Order of the 11th of November, 1807, by the Orders of the 25th of November, 1807, and of the 18th of May, 1808, at certain places and latitudes therein mentioned, unless such vessel shall have been informed of this Order on her voyage, and warned by any of His Majesty's ships or privateers not to proceed to any port of Holland, and shall notwithstanding such warning, attempt to proceed to any such port.

[*416] "And His Majesty is pleased further to order, and it is *hereby ordered, that the said several Orders of the 7th of January and 11th of November, 1807, as altered by the said Order of the 26th of April last, shall also be suspended, so far as is necessary for the protection of vessels of the said United States which shall clear out to any ports not declared to be under the restriction of Blockade from any port of Holland between the 9th day of June and the 1st day of July next: Provided always, that nothing that is contained in the present Order shall extend, or be construed to extend, to protect any vessels or their cargoes that may be liable to condemnation or detention for any other cause than the violation of the aforesaid Orders of the 7th of January and the 11th of November, 1807, as altered by the said Order of the 26th of April last.

"Provided also, that nothing in this Order contained shall extend, or be construed to extend, to protect any vessel which shall attempt to enter any port actually blockaded by any of His Majesty's ships of war.

"And the Right Honourable the Lords Commissioners of His Majesty's Treasury, His Majesty's Principal Secretaries of State, the Lords Commissioners of the Admiralty, and the Judge of the High Court of Admiralty, and the Judges of the Court of Vice-Admiralty, are to give the necessary directions herein as to them may respectively appertain.

"STEPHEN COTTRELL."(u)

The only defence of these Orders by Lord Stowell is, it has been seen, that they were *retaliatory*. Why this defence appears to the writer of these pages unsatisfactory and insufficient, has been already stated.(x) The *Decrees* and the *Orders* violated International Law.

[*417]

*CHAPTER III.

RIGHT OF VISIT AND SEARCH.

CCCXXII. THE next limitation of the general rights of the Neutral is that which flows from his duty to submit to the Rights of *Visit and Search* on the part of the Belligerent.(a)

This important subject will, perhaps, be most conveniently discussed by considering:—

1. When the Right of Visit and Search may be exercised.
2. Where it may be exercised.
3. By what kind of force.

(u) Annual Register, 1809, vol. li. pp. 763-5. (x) Vide antè, pp. 248-51.

(a) "According to every known principle of reason, the establishment of any rule of law necessarily implies that the party interested in its observance shall have some means of ascertaining the fact of its violation."—Letters of Sulpicius (IV.) (Lord Grenville.)

4. How it must be exercised.

5. Upon what kind of property.

6. What are the consequences to the Neutral of offering resistance, with or without Convoy, to the exercise of this belligerent right.

7. A reference to the principal Treaties which have affirmed, modified, or taken away, between the contracting parties, this right.

CCCXXIII. First, as to *when* this Right may be exercised. Even in time of peace it is not lawful for a vessel to sail upon the *high seas* without any papers on board indicating the nation to which she belongs. Pirates, *hostes humani generis*, always seizable by everybody, and justiciable everywhere, sail the seas in time of peace. The lawful merchant, on this as well as other accounts, is bound by the general principles of International Law to be furnished with documents *proving her nationality and her identity.(*b*) This appears to be an uncon- [*418] troverted axiom of International Jurisprudence; nevertheless, it is evident that two important consequences flow from it.

1. That a vessel may, under extraordinary circumstances of grave suspicion, be *visited* in time of peace upon the *high seas;* for how otherwise could it be ascertained whether or no she carried the proper papers on board? Or for what purpose, if she may not be visited, is she to carry them?(*c*)

2. It follows that the *high seas* are not, as is sometimes contended, a place in which no inquiry whatever, under any circumstances, can be exercised by the ships of one State into those of another; though the maintenance of this extreme proposition is necessary to sustain the maxim already so much discussed, that "free ships make free goods."

CCCXXIV. It is quite true that the Right of *Visit and Search* is a strictly belligerent right.(*d*) But the Right of Visit in time of peace, for the *purpose of ascertaining the nationality of a vessel*, is a part, indeed, but a very small part, of the belligerent Right of Visit and Search.

When Bynkershoek argues for the Right of *Search* in time of war, he points out the necessity of it in these words, "Velim animadvertas, eatenus utique licitum esse amicam navem sistere, ut non ex *fallaci forte aplustri*, sed ex ipsis instrumentis in navi repertis constet, navem amicam esse."(*e*)

*Surely this reasoning applies to the right of ascertaining the national character of a suspected pirate in time of peace; and it [*419]

(*b*) "Un des principes du droit des gens est, que tout navire doit être muni de pièces de bord, qui permettent de constater son identité, et de reconnaître sa nationalité. Tout navire neutre qui, *en temps de paix*, navigue armé sans pièces de bord, s'expose à être traité comme pirate."—De Pistoye et Duverdy, Traité des Prises, t. i. p. 416.

(*c*) "Nous avons dit que le pavillon avait cessé d'être une marque certaine de la nationalite des navires; que tous, marchands et de guerres, ils se permettaient d'arborer des couleurs mensongères."—De Hautefeuille, t. iii. p. 438.

(*d*) Le Louis, 2 Dodson's Adm. Rep., p. 210. La Jeune Eugénie, 2 Mason's (Amer.) Rep., p. 409, and cited in the Antelope, 10 Wheaton's (Amer.) Rep., p. 66.

(*e*) Q. J. P., c. xiv. She must at least have a register on board, though that may be sufficient.—1 Paine's (Amer.) Rep., p. 594, 1 Kent's Comment., p. 161. (158.) n. (c.)

may be added, that it appears to have been so considered by no less a jurist than Mr. Chancellor Kent.(*f*)

CCCXXV. Whatever may be the correct opinion with respect to the Right of Visit in time of peace, the right, in time of war, to *visit*, to *search*, and to *detain* for search, is a belligerent right, which cannot be drawn into question;(*g*) it is a right which a Belligerent may exercise over every vessel, not being a ship of war, or, as it is sometimes called, a public vessel, that he meets with on the ocean.(*h*) This right is so rooted in the law and practice of nations, that great institutional writers rather refer to it as acknowledged than vindicate its existence.(*i*)

This right of mitigated Visit in time of peace, is sometimes delicately described as the *Right of Approach*. It is called by the French, *droit d'enquête du pavillon*, as distinguished from the *droit de visite ou de recherche*;(*k*) and it is said that this *nationality of the flag* may be ascertained by signals and hailing, and that even when there is a suspicion [*420] of piracy, all proceedings beyond the exchange of *hailing and signals, must be taken at the risk of the man-of-war(*l*) who visits. Whether these limitations be just or not, it is unquestionable that the *Visit*, for the purpose of ascertaining the nationality of the vessel, must be exercised without the Right of *Search*, which is exclusively incident to a Belligerent.

CCCXXVI. A serious controversy at one time took place between the United States of North America and Great Britain, on account of a claim put forth by the latter Power to detain vessels suspected of being engaged in the Slave Trade,(*m*) in order to ascertain the nation to which they belonged. The claim was thus expressed by Lord Aberdeen, the then Secretary for Foreign Affairs:—

"In certain latitudes, and for a particular object, the vessels referred to are visited, *not as American*, but either as British vessels engaged in an unlawful traffic, and carrying the flag of the United States for a criminal purpose, or as belonging to States which have by Treaty ceded to Great Britain the Right of Search, and which right it is attempted to defeat by fraudulently bearing the protecting flag of the Union; or finally, they are visited as piratical outlaws, possessing no claim to any flag or nationality whatever.

"Here, it will be seen, are three classes of cases enumerated, in which the right of Visitation and Search (for such we have shown it to be)

(*f*) 1 Commentaries, n. 6, to p. 153

(*g*) Merlin, Rép. t. xiii. p. 115. Le Louis, 2 Dodson's Adm. Rep., p. 244. The Anna Maria, 2 Wheaton's (Amer.) Rep., p. 332.

(*h*) "Im Uebrigen kann selbst die Maxime, 'Frei Schiff frei Gut,' das recht der Neutralen nicht ausschliessen, da wenigstens immer eine Nachfrage und Nachsuchung nach Contrebande, desgleichen nach der Nationalität des Schiffes, vergönnt werden muss."—Heffters, p. 296, § 178.

(*i*) Bynkershoek, Q. J. P., l. i. c. xiv. Valin, Ordonn., l. iii. t. ix. art. xii. Vattel, l. iii. c. vii. s. 114. De Martens, viii. c. 7, s. 321. Kent, Comm., i. pp. 153-4-5. Heffters, p. 294, s. 167.

(*k*) Ortolan, Dipl. de la Mer, p. 242.

(*l*) Ib., and note (*a*) by Mr. Lawrence to his edition of Wheaton's Elem., p. 187.

(*m*) Vide antè, vol. i. c. xvii., for an account of the Treaties authorizing in time of peace the capture of vessels belonging to certain States engaged in this detestable traffic.

may be exercised under the British claim. The first class is that of *British vessels* engaged in an unlawful traffic, and seeking to screen their offence under the American flag. The second consists of *vessels belonging to other States*, which have by Treaty ceded to Great Britain the Right of Visitation and Search, and which right is attempted to be defeated by fraudulently *bearing the protecting flag of the United States. The third comprises *piratical outlaws*, possessing no rightful claim to any flag or national character whatsoever."(*n*) [*421]

All these positions were strongly contested by the North American United States. It was said to be impossible to distinguish this *right of ascertaining the national character of the vessel* from *the belligerent right of Visitation :* further, that Visitation without Search would be nugatory, and that though the naval officer who visted might be ordered, and might be bound to release the vessel the moment that her national character was ascertained, yet it would always depend upon his judgment whether or no the vessel did or did not belong to any of the three classes mentioned above. That it might be necessary to bring her into the Admiralty Court for a decision upon the point, and that thus, in time of peace, rights exclusively appertaining to war would be frequently exercised. That as to indemnification by costs and damages, first, the obtaining them was uncertain; and, secondly, they would probably be inadequate.

That as to piratical outlaws, the Supreme Court of the United States had holden, that their character must be ascertained by other means than Visitation and Search; that, in fact, pirates were no longer formidable, and that piracy was rare.

It can scarcely be denied that this argument, whatever may be thought of those which preceded it, was extremely weak. And it is difficult to see why the penalty of costs and damages should not operate as a sufficient check upon the possible abuse incident to the inquiry of ascertaining the national character of the suspected vessel.(*o*)

*It is the language of the Prize Court of the North American United States that, "Upon the ocean, in time of peace, all possess an entire equality. It is the common highway of all, appropriated to the use of all; and no one can vindicate to himself a superior or exclusive prerogative there. Every ship sails there with the unquestionable right of pursuing her own lawful business without interruption; but, [*422]

(*n*) Wheaton on the Right of Search, pp. 153-4.

(*o*) Ibid. The Antelope, 10 Wheaton's (Amer.) Rep., p. 66. The dispute was closed by the Treaty of Washington of 1842. "The parties mutually stipulate that each shall prepare, equip, and maintain in service on the coast of Africa a sufficient and adequate squadron, or naval force of vessels, of suitable numbers and descriptions, to carry in all not less than eighty guns, to enforce, separately and respectively, the laws, rights, and obligations of each of the two countries for the suppression of the Slave Trade; the said squadrons to be independent of each other, but the two Governments stipulating nevertheless to give such orders to the officers commanding their respective forces as shall enable them most effectually to act in concert and co-operation, upon mutual consultation, as exigencies may arise, for the attainment of the true object of this article; copies of all such orders to be communicated by each Government to the other respectively." —Treaty between Great Britain and the United States, dated Washington, 9th Aug., 1842; Hertslet's Treaties, vol. iii. p. 853.

whatever may be that business, she is bound to pursue it in such a manner as not to violate the rights of others. The general maxim in such cases is, *sic utere tuo, ut non alienum lædas.*

"It has been argued, that no ship has a right to approach another at sea, and that every ship has a right to draw round her a line of jurisdiction, within which no other is at liberty to intrude. In short, that she may appropriate so much of the ocean as she may deem necessary for her protection, and prevent any nearer approach.

"This doctrine appears to us novel, and is not supported by any authority. It goes to establish upon the ocean a territorial jurisdiction, like that which is claimed by all nations within cannon-shot of their shores, in virtue of their general sovereignty. But the latter right is founded upon the principle of sovereign and permanent appropriation, and has never been successfully asserted beyond it. Every vessel undoubtedly has a right to the use of so much of the ocean as she occupies, and as is essential to her own movements. Beyond this, no exclusive right has
[*423] ever yet been recognized, and we see no reason for admitting *its existence. Merchant ships are in the constant habit of approaching each other on the ocean, either to relieve their own distress, to procure information, or to ascertain the character of strangers; and hitherto there has never been supposed in such conduct any breach of the customary observances, or of the strictest principles of the Law of Nations. In respect to ships of war sailing, as in the present case, under the authority of their Government, to arrest pirates and other public offenders, there is no reason why they may not approach any vessels descried at sea, for the purpose of ascertaining their real characters. Such a right seems indispensable for the fair and discreet exercise of their authority; and the use of it cannot be justly deemed indicative of any design to insult or injure those they approach, or to impede them in their lawful commerce. On the other hand, it is as clear, that no ship is, under any such circumstances, bound to lie by or wait the approach of any other ship. She is at full liberty to pursue her voyage in her own way, and to use all necessary precautions to avoid any suspected sinister enterprise, or hostile attack. She has a right to consult her own safety; but, at the same time, she must take care not to violate the rights of others. She may use any precautions dictated by the prudence or fears of her officers, either as to delay, or the progress or course of her vogage; but she is not at liberty to inflict injuries upon other innocent parties, simply because of conjectural dangers. These principles seem to us the natural result of the common duties and rights of nations navigating the ocean in time of peace. Such a state of things carries with it very different obligations and responsibilities from those which belong to public war, and is not to be confounded with it."(*p*)

The law is perhaps as clearly stated as the nature of the case will admit by Mr. Chancellor Kent,(*q*) when he says, "The *inter-visitation*
[*424] of ships at sea is a branch of the law *of self-defence, and is, in point of fact, practised by the public vessels of all nations, in-

(*p*) The Marianna Flora, 11 Wheaton's (Amer.) Rep., pp. 42-4.
(*q*) 1 Comment., p. 154, (153,) note (6).

cluding those of the United States, when the piratical character of a vessel is suspected. The Right of Visit is conceded for the sole purpose of ascertaining the real national character of the vessel sailing under suspicious circumstances, and is wholly distinct from the Right of Search. It has been termed by the Supreme Court of the United States *the right of approach* for that purpose;(*q*) and it is considered to be well warranted by the principles of public law and the usage of nations."(*r*)

CCCXXVII. Secondly as to *where* this right may be exercised.

This may be considered *affirmatively* and *negatively*.(*s*) Affirmatively it may be exercised, 1st, in the Belligerent's own waters; 2ndly, in those of his enemy, and thirdly, upon the high seas. Negatively, it may not be exercised in the ports, harbours, or territorial waters of a Neutral.

The law as to this subject has been already dwelt upon at length in a former part of this work.(*t*)

CCCXXVIII. A delicate question sometimes arises as to the right and duty of a Neutral State with respect to prizes made by Belligerents in violation of Neutrality. The Prize Courts of the United States of North America appear to have laid down sound rules of International Law upon this subject. They rightly hold, that whenever a capture is made by a Belligerent in violation of Neutrality, if the prize come voluntarily within the jurisdiction of the Neutral, it should be restored to its original owner. But this jurisdiction in such cases does not extend beyond the authority to decree restitution of the specific property, with the costs and expenses incurred by the judicial proceeding. The Neutral, it is rightly said by the *North American Courts, must entirely disclaim any right to inflict damages; and it is no part [*425] of the duty of a neutral nation to interpose, upon the mere footing of the Law of Nations, to settle all the rights and wrongs which may grow out of a capture between Belligerents. Strictly speaking, there can be no such thing as a marine tort between the Belligerents. Each has an undoubted right to exercise all the rights of war against the other; and it cannot be a matter of *judicial* complaint, that they exercised with severity, even if the parties do go beyond those rules which the customary laws of war justify. At least, they have never been deemed to be within the cognizance of the prize tribunals of neutral nations. The captors are amenable to their own Government exclusively for any excess or irregularity in their proceedings; and a neutral nation ought no otherwise to interfere, than to prevent captors from obtaining any unjust advantage by a violation of neutral jurisdiction. Neutral nations may, indeed, inflict pecuniary or other penalties on the parties for any such violation; but this must be professedly in vindication of its own rights, and not by way of compensation to the captured. When called upon by either of the Belligerents to act in such cases, all that justice seems to require is, that the neutral nation should fairly execute its own laws, and give no asylum to the property unjustly captured. It is bound, therefore, to restore the property if found within its own ports; but beyond this it

(*q*) The Marianna Flora, 11 Wheaton's (Amer.) Rep., vol. i. p. 43.
(*r*) Bynkershoek, Q. J. P., l. i. c. cxiv.
(*s*) Merlin, Rép., t. xiii. p. 111.
(*t*) Vide ante, vol. i. cc. vi. vii.

is not obliged to interpose between the Belligerents. If, indeed, it were otherwise, there would be no end to the difficulties and embarrassments of neutral prize tribunals. They would be compelled to decide in every variety of shape upon marine trespasses, *in rem* and *in personam*, between Belligerents, without possessing adequate means of ascertaining the real facts, or of compelling the attendance of foreign witnesses; and thus they would draw within their jurisdiction almost every incident of prize. Such a course of things would necessarily create irritations and [*426] animosities, and very soon embark neutral nations in *all the controversies and hostilities of the conflicting parties. Considerations of public policy, therefore, confirm the Law of Nations on this subject.(*u*)

CCCXXIX. The Courts of the North American United States allow that the property may be condemned in the Courts of the captor while lying in a neutral country; but still they rightly hold that it can only be so adjudicated upon while the possession of the captor remains: but if it be divested, either in fact or by operation of law, that possession is gone which can alone sustain the jurisdiction. And it is to be observed, that *à fortiori*, where the property is already in the custody of a neutral tribunal, and the title in these is *sub judice*, no other foreign Court can by any adjudication of its own, rightfully take away, forestall, or defeat the jurisdiction of this neutral tribunal.(*x*)

This would be to exercise, or to attempt to exercise, a sovereign authority over the Court having possession of the thing, and it would be to take from an independent State the right of vindicating its own justice, and of fulfilling its own obligations as a Neutral.

The United States have therefore restored prizes made by armed vessels, which in making them have violated the Neutrality of the United States, when these prizes have been brought into their ports.(*y*) They have even restored a prize, so taken in violation of their Neutrality, when it has been claimed by the *original wrong-doer*, though it may have come back to his possession after a regular condemnation as prize; nevertheless, it is not to be supposed that a regular condemnation would not be considered by them as protecting the title of a *third person*, being a *bonâ fide* purchaser, without notice of the original defect.(*z*) Lawful [*427] captors may, by a violation of the municipal regulations of *the State within whose limits their prize is brought, work a forfeiture of it.(*a*)

In these doctrines a severe but a just conception of the duties and rights of Neutrality appears to be embodied.

CCCXXX. Thirdly, by what kinds of force this Right may be exercised.

(*u*) La Amistad de Rues, 5 Wheaton's (Amer.) Rep., p. 385.
(*x*) The Santissima Trinidad, 7 Wheaton's (Amer.) Rep., p. 355.
(*y*) The Gran Para, 7 Wheaton's (Amer.) Rep., p. 471.
(*z*) The Arrogante Barcelones, ib., p. 496.
(*a*) The Josefa Segunda, 5 Wheaton's (Amer.) Rep., p. 338. Bynk., Q. J. P., l. xv., in fine. Such was the doctrine of the Courts of Holland, from which Bynkershoek himself dissented.

First, it must be exercised by an armed force, not by a merchant-vessel.

Secondly, it must be exercised by a vessel commissioned by the authority of the State to which she belongs.

Such vessels are of two kinds:—

1. The regular navy—the public ships of the State.

2. Private vessels commissioned for the purposes of the particular war, or, as they are generally called, *privateers.* The subject of privateers has been dealt with in a former volume of this work.(*b*) The power of granting commissions and the consequences of exercising belligerent rights without them, have been especially considered. To these former remarks it should be added, that it would not seem to be just to condemn a person acting with good faith under an illegal commission as guilty of piracy.(*c*)

In the present war, England and France have as yet waived their unquestionable right of commissioning privateers. Russia has maintained a silence upon this subject. It is true that great abuses were perpetrated by privateers: it is untrue, as will presently be seen, that they altogether escaped punishment in the Prize Courts. However, in the present war, the Queen of England has declared that "it is not her *present intention* to issue letters of marque for the commissioning of privateers."(*d*)

*CCCXXXI. Fourthly, *how* this Right must be exercised.

It is a principle which governs the whole subject, that this [*428] Right of Visit and Search must be conducted with as much regard to the rights and safety of the vessel detained as is consistent with a thorough examination of her character and voyage.

All that is necessary to this object is lawful, all that transcends it is unlawful.(*e*)

Whatever may be the injury that casually results to an individual from the act of another, while pursuing the reasonable exercise of an established right, it is his misfortune. The law pronounces it *damnum absque injuriâ,* and the individual from whose act it proceeds is liable neither at law, nor in the forum of conscience. The principal right

(*b*) Vol. i. p. 393.

(*c*) United States v. Klintock, 5 Wheaton's (Amer.) Rep., p. 149. The subject is here glanced at, but no judicial opinion expressed.

(*d*) Order in Council of 28th March, 1854. Speaking of privateers, Lord Grenville said, "The maxims of the British Naval Code do not depend on the fluctuating circumstances of occasional interest. They are fixed and permanent, drawn either from the immutable principles of natural law, or from the long-established usage of civilized societies; and whoever will turn from the fleeting dreams of modern speculation, to the immortal works of the great masters of this science, will easily convince himself that no practice can be more consonant to reason and justice than that of carrying on public war in some degree by individual exertions. Nor, although it be true that occasional irregularities may prevail, ought this country to renounce an important right, merely because we hear some exaggerated statements of rapine and violence committed by those who exercise it. Such assertions are made with great facility, because it is almost always impossible to disprove them, unless the Neutral would pursue his complaint in those Courts which are constantly open for his redress."—Speech of Lord Grenville in the House of Lords, Nov. 13, 1801, on the Motion for an Address, &c., (published 1802,) pp. 94-5.

(*e*) The Anna Maria, 2 Wheaton's (Amer.) Rep., p. 332. The Eleanor, ib., p. 358.

necessarily carries with it also all the means essential to its exercise. A vessel must be pursued in order to be detained for examination. And if in the pursuit she has been in any way injured, *e. g.*, dismasted, upset, stranded, or even run on shore, and lost, it would be an unfortunate case, but the pursuing vessel would be acquitted.

[*429] CCCXXXII. The mode of summoning the Neutral to undergo *Visitation is by the firing of a cannon-shot on the part of the Belligerent. The distance at which this shall be fired has often been the subject of particular convention, but the name given to it is usually that which is borrowed from the French, viz., *semonce, coup d'assurance*;(*f*) though it has also been called by Jurists who use the English tongue, the *affirming gun*. This subject and the general question of damage done to the Neutral in consequence of his neglecting to obey the summons of the Belligerent was much considered by the Judges of the North American United States in the case of the Marianna Flora.

"We are not disposed (the American Judge said) to admit that there exists any such universal rule or obligation of *an affirming gun*, as has been suggested at the bar. It may be the law of the maritime States of the European Continent already alluded to, founded in their own usages or positive regulations, but it does not hence follow that it is binding upon all other nations. It was admitted, at the argument, that the English practice is otherwise; and, surely, as a maritime Power, England deserves to be listened to with as much respect, on such a point, as any other nation. It was justly inferred, that the practice of America is conformable to that of England; and the absence of any counter proof on the record is almost of itself decisive. Such, however, as the practice is, even among the continental nations of Europe, it is a practice adopted with reference to a state of war rather than peace. It may be a useful [*430] precaution to prevent conflicts between *Neutrals, and allies, and Belligerents, and even between armed ships of the same nation. But the very necessity of the precaution in time of war arises from circumstances which do not ordinarily occur in time of general peace. Assuming, therefore, that the ceremony might be salutary and proper in periods of war, and suitable to its exigencies, it by no means follows that it is justly to be insisted on at the peril of costs and damages in peace. In any view, therefore, we do not think this omission can avail the claimants.

"Again; it is argued that there is a general obligation upon armed ships, in exercising the Right of Visitation and Search, to keep at a distance, out of cannon-shot, and to demean themselves in such a manner as not to endanger Neutrals. And this objection, it is added, has been

(*f*) Heffters, s. 169. "Lorsque deux vaisseaux de guerre se rencontrent à la haute mer, sous quelque pavillon qu'ils aient navigué jusqu'à ce moment, celui des deux qui désire connaître réellement la nationalité de l'autre, arbore ses vraies couleurs, et tire un coup de canon, soit à poudre, soit à boulet perdu. L'autre bâtiment doit répondre de la même manière, c'est-à-dire, hisser son pavillon, et tirer également un coup de canon à boulet perdu ou à poudre. Ce coup de canon, appelé *coup d'assurance*, est la parole d'honneur donnée par le commandant, par l'état-major tout entier, que le pavillon qui flotte sur leurs têtes est bien celui de la nation propriétaire du bâtiment."—Hautefeuille, t. iii. pp. 438-9.

specially provided for, and enforced by the stipulations of many of our own Treaties with foreign Powers. It might be a decisive answer to this argument, that here no Right of Visitation and Search was attempted to be exercised. Lieutenant Stockton did not claim to be a Belligerent entitled to search Neutrals on the ocean. His commission was for other objects. He did not approach or subdue the Marianna Flora, in order to compel her to submit to his search, but with other motives. He took possession of her, not because she resisted the Right of Search, but because she attacked him in a hostile manner, without any reasonable cause or provocation.

"Doubtless, the obligation of Treaties is to be observed with entire good faith and scrupulous care. But, stipulations in Treaties having sole reference to the exercise of the rights of Belligerents in time of war, cannot upon any reasonable principles of construction, be applied to govern cases exclusively of another nature, and belonging to a state of peace. Another consideration, quite sufficient to establish that such stipulations cannot be applied in aid of the present case, is, that whatever may be our duties to other nations, we have no such Treaty subsisting with Portugal. It will scarcely be pretended that we are bound to *Portugal by stipulations, to which she is no party, and by which she incurs no correspondent obligation. [*431]

"Upon the whole, we are of opinion, that the conduct of Lieutenant Stockton, in approaching, and ultimately in subduing the Marianna Flora, was entirely justifiable. The first wrong was done by her, and his own subsequent acts were a just defence and vindication of the rights and honour of his country,(*g*) in any Court of International Justice."(*h*)

In the foregoing sentences the language of the North American Prize Courts has been adopted. It is in perfect harmony with the doctrine of the British Courts of International Law:—"The right (Lord Stowell observes) of visiting and searching merchant-ships upon the high seas, whatever be the ships, whatever be the cargoes, whatever be the destinations, is an incontestible right of the lawfully commissioned cruisers of a belligerent nation—be the ships, the cargoes, and the destinations what they may—because, till they are visited and searched, it does not appear what the ships, or the cargoes, or the destinations are; and it is for the purpose of ascertaining these points that the necessity of this Right of Visitation and Search exists. This right is so clear in principle, that no man can deny it who admits the legality of maritime capture; because if you are not at liberty to ascertain by sufficient inquiry whether there is property that can legally be captured, it is impossible to capture. Even those who contend that free ships make free goods, must admit the exercise of this right at least for the purpose of ascertaining whether the ships are free ships or not. The right is as clear in practice as in theory; for practice is uniform and universal upon the subject. The many European Treaties which refer to this right, refer to it as pre-existing, and merely regulate the exercise of it. *All writers upon the Law of Nations unanimously acknowledge it, without the [*432]

(*g*) The Marianna Flora, 11 Wheaton's (Amer.) Rep. pp. 48-50.
(*h*) The Eleanor, 2 Wheaton's (Amer.) Rep., p. 258.

exception even of Hübner. The right must unquestionably be exercised with as little of personal harshness and of vexation in the mode as possible; but, soften it as much as you can, it is still a right of force, though of lawful force—something in the nature of civil process where force is employed, but a lawful force, which cannot lawfully be resisted."(*i*)

CCCXXXIII. But a very different principle applies to cases of *wilful misconduct* on the part of seizors.

If a neutral ship be destroyed by a captor, either wantonly or under an alleged necessity, in which she herself was not directly involved, the captor, or his Government, is responsible for the spoliation. The gravest importance of such an act to the public service of the captor's own State will not justify its commission. The Neutral is entitled to full restitution in value.(*k*) Severe damages ought to be inflicted upon those captors who have behaved with cruelty towards the captured crew, and also for negligence in the care of Prize property,(*l*) *e. g.*, for refusing to receive such nautical assistance as would in all probability have prevented the happening of damages which have actually accrued to the ship.(*m*) The captor who takes his prize, without necessity, to an inconvenient port for adjudication, may be justly mulcted in demurrage, [*433] costs, and damages, as the exigency of the case may require;(*n*) and *a similar principle governs cases in which the captor has shown an unnecessary delay in proceeding.(*o*) Captors who have made a justifiable seizure may forfeit their title by subsequent misconduct.(*p*)

CCCXXXIV. Fifthly. Upon what kind of property this right may be exercised?

It may be exercised upon the merchant or private ships of all Neutral States, but not upon their ships of war or public vessels.

An universal and long-established *usage* of nations, growing, perhaps, originally out of *comity*, but long ago transplanted into the domain of right,(*q*) exempts all such vessels from the belligerent right of Visit and Search. The same usage would no doubt, upon the other element, exempt all military equipage, and all such as belonged to the executive of a State from detention and spoliation by belligerent armies.

CCCXXXV. A question arises in time of war, often rife with international quarrels of the bitterest kind, viz. as to the right of a Belligerent to search *all* vessels, public and private, suspected of harbouring deserters from the navy and army of the Belligerent.

The Government of the United States of North America admits the Right of Visitation and Search by belligerent men-of-war of their pri-

(*i*) The Maria, 1 Robinson, p. 361.

(*k*) The Felicity, 2 Dodson's Adm. Rep., p. 381.

(*l*) The Maria and the Vrow Johanna, 4 Rob., p. 348. The Concordia, 2 Rob., p. 102. The St. Juan Baptista, and La Purissima Conception, 5 Rob., p. 33. The Eleanor, 2 Wheaton's (Amer.) Rep., p. 359.

(*m*) Die Fire Damer, 5 Robinson's Adm. Rep., p. 357. The St. Juan Baptista and La Purissima Conception, ib., p. 33. Der Mohr, 4 Rob., p. 314.

(*n*) The Anna, 5 Rob., p. 385. The Wilhelmsberg, ib., p. 143. The Principe Athælante, Edwards, p. 70 The Catherina Elizabeth, 1 Acton, p. 309.

(*o*) The Eliza, 1 Acton's Rep. p. 336. The Zee Star, 4 Rob., p. 71.

(*p*) The Speculation, 2 Robinson's Adm. Rep., p. 296, vide antè.

(*q*) Vide antè, vol. i. p. 161, for some remarks on this subject.

vate merchant vessels, for enemy's property, articles contraband of war, or men in the land or naval service of the enemy; but it does not understand the Law of Nations to authorize, and does not admit the Right of Search for subjects or seamen. England, on the other hand, has asserted the right to look for her subjects on the high seas, into whatever service they may embark. The claim of England to the Right of Search, on the high seas, of neutral vessels, for deserters and other persons liable to *military and naval service, has been a question of animated discussion between her and the United States of North America. [*434] It was one principal cause of the war of 1812 between these States, and remains unsettled to this day; in the discussions in 1842, between Lord Ashburton and Mr. Webster, relative to the boundary line of the State of Maine, the American Minister incidentally discussed the subject;(*r*) but no conclusion was arrived at. It appears clear to the writer of these pages, that in the present state of International Law, this Right of Search *ought* to be confined in its exercise to merchant vessels.

CCCXXXVI. Sixthly, what are the consequences which flow from a resistance, on the part of the Neutral, to the exercise of this belligerent right? This resistance may be exercised (1,) either by the ship herself, or (2,) by an armed vessel or vessels accompanying her by way of escort or *convoy*.

CCCXXXVII. It is admirably said by Lord Stowell, that it is a wild conceit, that wherever force is used, it may be lawfully resisted: a lawful force cannot lawfully be resisted. The only case where it can be so is in the state of war and conflict between two countries, where one party has a perfect right to attack by force, and the other has an equally perfect right to repel by force; but in the relative situation of two countries at peace with each other, no such conflicting rights can possibly co-exist.(*s*)

It is upon these principles that International Law universally, by its accredited voice, inflicts the penalty of confiscation upon the neutral merchantman or private vessel which resists the Belligerent's Right of Search.

CCCXXXVIII. It remains to be considered whether the *fact that the *private* is accompanied, or, according to the usual phrase, [*435] *convoyed*, by a *public* vessel, makes any, and, if any, what difference in the application of this principle.

Upon this subject it seems best to use the language of Lord Stowell, in one of his most careful and best reasoned judgments:—

"That the penalty for the violent contravention of this right is the confiscation of the property so withheld from Visitation and Search. For the proof of this I need only refer to Vattel, one of the most correct and certainly not the least indulgent of modern professors of public law.

(*r*) Kent's Comm., vol. i. p. 157, (note.) An Inquiry into the Validity of the British Claim to a Right of Visitation and Search of American Vessels suspected to be engaged in the African Slave Trade, by Mr. Wheaton. London, 1842. Webster's Works, vol. v. p. 142, vol. vi. p. 329, cited by Mr. Lawrence in his edition of Wheaton's Elem., note to p. 188.

(*s*) The Maria, 1 Robinson's Adm. Rep., p. 36.

In Book III. c. 7, sect. 114, he expresses himself thus: 'On ne peut empêcher le transport des effets de contrebande, si l'on ne visite pas les vaisseaux neutres que l'on rencontre en mer. On est donc en droit de les visiter. Quelques nations puissantes ont refusé en différents tems de se soumettre à cette visite; *aujourd'hui un vaisseau neutre, qui refuseroit de souffrir la visite, se feroit condamner par cela seul, comme étant de bonne prise.*' Vattel is here to be considered not as a lawyer merely delivering an opinion, but as a witness asserting the fact—the fact that such is the existing practice of modern Europe. And to be sure, the only marvel in the case is, that he should mention it as a law merely modern, when it is remembered that it is a principle, not only of the Civil Law (on which great part of the Law of Nations is founded,) but of the private jurisprudence of most countries in Europe,—that a contumacious refusal to submit to fair inquiry infers all the penalties of convicted guilt. Conformably to this principle we find in the celebrated French Ordinance of 1681, now in force, Article 12, '*That every vessel shall be good prize in case of resistance and combat;* and Valin, in his smaller Commentary, p. 81, says expressly, that although the expression is in the conjunctive, yet that the *resistance alone is sufficient.*(*t*) He [*436] refers *to the Spanish Ordinance 1718, evidently copied from it, in which it is expressed in the disjunctive, '*in case of resistance or combat.*' And recent instances are at hand and within view, in which it appears that *Spain* continues to act upon this principle. The first time in which it occurs to my notice on the inquiries I have been able to make in the institutes of our own country respecting matters of this nature, excepting what occurs in the Black Book of the Admiralty,(*u*) is in the Order of Council, 1664, Article 12,(*x*) which directs, 'That

(*t*) "In some of the Treaties of France, this article is expressly inserted in the disjunctive. Treaty between France and the Duchy of Mecklenburg, art. 18, an. 1779. De Marten's Tr., vol. ii. p, 40, also between France and Hamburgh, an. 1769."

(*u*) "B. 7. Item se aucune nef ou vessel de la ditte flotte a congie et pouvoir de l'admiral de passer hors de la flotte entour aucun message ou autre besongne, s'ilz encontrent ou trouvent aucuns vesseaulx estranges sur la mer ou en ports des ennemys, adonques ceulx de nostre flotte doivent demander des maistres et gouverneurs de telz vesseaulx estrangers dont ilz sont et eulx bien examiner de leur charge ensemblement avecques leurs muniments et endentures, et s'il est trouve aucune chose de suspicion en telz vesseaulx que les biens sont aux ennemys, qui sont trouvez dedens les dits vesseaulx avec leurs maistres et gouverneurs ensemblement avecques les biens dedens icelle estants sauvement seront amenees devant l'admiral, et illecques s'il est trouve qu'ilz sont loyaulx marchants et amys sans suspicion de colerer, les biens seront a eulx redelivrees sans eulx rien dommager, autrement seront pris avec leurs biens et raensonnez comme la loy de mer veult et demande.

"B. 8. Se aucunes de noz nefs ou vesseaulx encontrent sur la mer ou en ports aucuns autres vesseaulx, qui facent rebelletees ou defense encontre ceulx de noz nefs ou vesseaulx, adoncques bien lise a nox gents les autres comme ennemys assaillir et par forte mayn les prendre et amener entièrement, comme ilz les ont gaignez, devant l'admiral sans eulx piller ou endommager, illecques de prendre ce que loy et coustume de mer veult et demande," &c.

(*x*) "During the struggle for naval superiority, which took place between the maritime states of Europe, about the middle of the seventeenth century, the pretension of resisting search by the protection of convoy, was put forward with much caution, and apparently for the first time, by Christina Queen of Sweden, when any ship, met withal by *the Royal Navy or other ship commissionated, shall fight or make resistance, the said ship and [*437]

Aug. 16, 1653. Art. 4th, 'They shall in all possible ways decline that they, or any of those that belong to them be searched. For seeing they are only sent to prevent all inconvenience and clandestine dealings, it is expected that they may be believed, and suffered to pass and proceed on their course unmolested, with all such things as are under their care.'—It was restrained to neutral ports.—Art. 6th, 'And more especially, for certain reasons, it is our command, that our own men-of-war *do chiefly, and in the beginning*, steer their course to such *ports as are neutral*, in the English and Dutch war, till we give any farther directions on that account. However, without any hindrance to our own subjects, that intend to carry on their own free trade to England and Holland *without* convoy.'—Thurloe's State Papers, vol. i. p. 424.

"In 1655 it was taken up by Holland: 'They have a design to hinder the Protector all visitation and search; and this by very strong and sufficient convoy; and by this means they will draw all trade to themselves and their ships.'—Ibid., vol. iv. p. 203.

"In May 1656 there happened an actual rencounter on this subject, between a fleet of merchantmen from Cadiz, (Spain being then at war with England,) under the convoy of de Ruyter, with seven men-of-war, and the commodore of some English frigates. 'Antwerp.—We have certain news of the arrival of de Ruyter in Zealand from Cadiz, from whence he brought stores of plate, mostly belonging to merchants of this city; he was met withal at sea by some English frigates, but finding themselves too weak they let him go.'—Ibid., vol. iv. p. 740. See also the particular account of what passed, given by a Dutch officer to the States General; 'That upon de Ruyter declaring that there was not anything on board belonging to the King of Spain, they parted. Ibid., vol. iv. p. 730. It appears, however, that the arrival occasioned great triumph in Holland and Flanders, and that the fleet was deeply laden with silver for the king of Spain, aud the service of his armies in Flanders. 'De Ruyter brought in his own ship, and others in his fleet, the sum of 20,000,000 (perhaps rials) of gold and silver, the greatest part for the king of Spain's use and the merchants of Brabant and Flanders.'—Ibid., vol. iv. pp. 732, 748. The 12th article of the Eng. Ord. of 1664 might perhaps be pointed against these pretensions.

"In another letter in the same collection, 21st Sept. 1657, from Nieuport, the Dutch ambassador in England,—we find the subject of convoy was strongly pressed at that time, and resisted on the part of this country: 'respecting secret articles,' concerning the visitation of ships which are convoyed under the flag of the state. I acquainted their Lordships, that of old all kings and states had made a difference between particular ships sailing upon their risques and adventures and between ships of the state and those which pass the sea under their flag and protection. That their high and mighty lords were of an opinion that it does strengthen the security of this state, that the ships of the state and officers should be responsible, as it were, for the ships sailing under their convoy; and that which I had proposed in my last memorandum concerning the same on behalf of their high and mighty lords was no new thing, but that plan had been most commonly proposed on all the treaties since the year 1851, in that manner that without regulating the same according to the said articles, the troubles at sea, whereof I had so often complained, could not be removed and prevented, and I alleged several examples. Upon which now one then the other of the said three lords* replied, and did very much insist, that it could not consist with their security; that they could not nor *ought* to trust so much to particular captains at sea; that it would be an introduction and encouragement to disaffected persons to assist the enemy, and urged especially that in no former treaties any such articles were found, and that their high and mighty lords had no reason to desire now any such novelty. I said that the practice on this side in regard of searching and visiting ships without difference was a new thing, and that the inhabitants of the United Netherlands, feeling the trouble and inconveniency of it, had reason to insist that it may be rectified by a good regulation.—Vol. vi. p. 511. See also, for the former conference, vol. v. p. 663.

"It appears that so many objections had arisen on the treaty proposed on the

* Thurloe, Wolsely, Jones.

[*438] goods shall be adjudged *lawful prize.'—A similar article occurs in the Proclamation of 1672. I am aware, that in those orders [*439] and proclamation are to be found some articles not very *consistent with the Law of Nations as understood now, or indeed at that time; for they are expressly censured by Lord Clarendon.(*y*) But the article I refer to is not of those he reprehends; and it is observable that Sir Robert Wiseman, then the King's Advocate General, who reported upon the articles in 1673, and expresses a disapprobation of some of them as harsh and novel, does not mark this article with any observation of censure. I am therefore warranted in saying, that it was the rule, and the undisputed rule, of the British Admiralty. I will not say that that rule may not have been broken in upon in some instances by considerations of comity or of policy, by which it may be fit that the administration of this species of Law should be tempered in the hands of those tribunals which have a right to entertain and apply them; for no man can deny that a state may recede from its extreme rights, and that its supreme councils are authorized to determine in what cases it may be fit to do so, the particular captor having in no case any other right and title than what the State itself would possess under the same facts of capture. But I stand with confidence upon all fair principles of reason,—upon the distinct authority of Vattel,—upon the Institutes of other great maritime countries, as well as those of our own country,—when I venture to lay it down, that by the Law of Nations, as now understood, a deliberate and continued resistance to Search, on the part of a neutral vessel to a lawful cruiser, is followed by the legal consequence of confiscation."(*z*)

CCCXXXIX. It should, however, be stated that this penalty of confiscation for resistance to Visitation and Search cannot be inflicted in cases where the neutral vessel had no reasonable grounds to be satisfied of the existence of the war—for it is this existence which founds the duties of Neutrality.(*a*)

part of Holland, that it was found necessary to form an entirely new project.—Vol. v. pp. 523, 558.

"In a subsequent letter from the Hague, 30th Nov. 1657, it appears that the treaty broke off on this difference: 'Le Sieur Nieuport n'est pas encore ici arrivé, mais il escrit aussi d'avoir prins son congé. Il est fort croyable qu'il ne sera guère content d'avoir faillé à achever le traiteé de la marine; néanmoins je m'imagine que la Hollande à present ne seroit pas fort marry de ne l'avoir pas achevé, pour ne se pas oster la liberté de visiter des mêmes en cette guerre contre Portugal.'—Thurloe's St. Pap., vol. vi. p. 622.

"On the subject of search generally, without *any expressed reference* to convoy, there is this letter from Cromwell to General Montagu: 'The secretary hath communicated to us your letter of the 28th, by which you acquaint him with the directions you have given for the searching of a Flushing and other Dutch ships, which (as you are informed) have bullion and other goods aboard them belonging to the Spaniard, the declared enemy of this state. There is no question to be made, but what you have directed therein is agreeable both to the laws of nations and the particular treaties which are between this commonwealth and the United provinces, and therefore we desire you to continue the said direction, and to require the captains to be careful in doing their duty therein.—Hampton Court, 30th August, 1657.'"

(*y*) Lord Clarendon's Life, p. 242.

(*z*) The Maria, 1 Robinson's Adm. Rep., pp. 363-9.

(*a*) The St. Juan Baptista, 5 Robinson's Adm. Rep. p. 33.

*Nor will the forcible resistance of the master of an enemy merchant vessel enure to the condemnation of neutral property [*440] laden on board of it. The attempt of the enemy master to save or rescue his vessel from the captor is the hostile act of a hostile person, and a perfectly legitimate attempt.(b)

CCCXL. On the other hand, if a neutral master attempt a rescue, or to withdraw himself from Search, he is guilty of a breach of duty; and if he effect this breach by a recurrence to force, the penal consequence will reach the property of his owner, and the whole property entrusted to his care. In such a case ship and cargo will be condemned.(c)

CCCXLI. What if a Neutral put his property on board an armed ship, which he must presume will be defended against the enemy?

According to the opinion of Lord Stowell and Justice Story—and he is a bold jurist who opposes their combined opinion—a Neutral who so acts betrays an intention to resist Visitation and Search, which he could not do by putting his property on board a merchantman—and so far he adheres to the Belligerent—he withdraws himself from the protection of Neutrality, and adopts another mode of defence: he relies on an enemy's force for protection, and he must for the time be considered as an enemy.(d)

"If," says Mr. Justice Story, "for a moment it could be admitted that a Neutral might lawfully ship goods in a non-armed ship of an enemy, or might charter such a ship, and navigate her with a neutral crew, these admissions would fall far short of succouring the claimant. He must successfully contend for broader doctrines, for doctrines which in my humble judgment are of infinitely more dangerous tendency than any which Schlegel and Hübner, the champions of Neutrality, have yet advanced into the field *of maritime controversy. I cannot bring my mind to believe that a neutral can charter an armed [*441] enemy ship, and victual and man her with an enemy crew (for though furnished directly by the owner, they are in effect paid and supported by the charterer,) with the avowed knowledge and necessary intent that she should resist every enemy; that he can take on board hostile shipments on freight, commissions, and profits; that he can stipulate expressly for the benefit and use of enemy convoy, and navigate during the voyage under its guns and protection; that he can be the entire projector and conductor of the voyage, and co-operate in all the plans of the owner to render resistance to Search secure and effectual; and that yet, notwithstanding all this conduct, by the Law of Nations he may shelter his property from confiscation, and claim the privileges of an inoffensive Neutral. On the contrary, it seems to me that such conduct is utterly irreconcilable with the good faith of a friend, and unites all the qualities of a most odious hostility. It wears the habiliments of Neutrality only when the sword and the armour of an enemy become useless for defence. If it be, as it undoubtedly is, a violation of Neutrality to engage in the transport-service of the enemy, or to carry his despatches even on a

(b) The Catherina Elizabeth, 5 Rob. Adm. Rep., p. 232.
(c) The Franklin, 2 Acton's Rep., p. 106.
(d) The Fanny, 1 Dodson's Adm. Rep., p. 443.

neutral voyage, how much more so must it be to enlist all our own interests in his service, and hire his arms and his crew in order to prevent the exercise of those rights which, as Neutrals, we are bound to submit to. The doctrine is founded in most perfect justice, that those who adhere to an enemy connection shall share the fate of an enemy."(*e*)

It is true, however, that the Court was composed of four Judges, of whom Mr. Justice Story was one only, and that the other three dissented from his opinion, and, in a subsequent case adhered to this dissent.(*f*)

[*442] *So far, therefore, as the Prize Law of the United States of North America is concerned, it is competent to a Neutral to put goods on board an armed enemy's ship.

But with respect to International Law, this case is different. Mr. Justice Story adhered to his opinion;(*g*) and looking to his subsequent and daily increasing reputation, it is hardly too much to say that his agreement with such an authority as Lord Stowell upon a question of this kind, does constitute a balance in favour of the proposition which these great men have deliberately sanctioned in most elaborate judgments.

CCCXLII. Seventhly. We have to notice some of the principal Treaties which have affirmed, modified, or taken away, between the contracting parties, this Right.

The leading Treaty(*h*) which affirms and incorporates the Common Law of nations upon the subject, is the famous Treaty of the Pyrenees between France and Spain. By the 17th article of this Treaty it is stipulated as follows:—

"Les navires d'Espagne, pour éviter tout désordre, n'approcheront pas de plus près les Français que de la portée du canon, et pourront envoyer leur petite barque ou chaloupe à bord des navires Français, et [*443] faire entrer dedans deux ou *trois hommes seulment, à qui seront montrés les passeports par le maître du navire Français, par lesquels il puisse apparoir, non-seulement de la charge, mais aussi du lieu de sa demeure et résidence, et du nom tant du maître ou patron que due navire même, afin que, par ces deux moyens, on puisse connaître

(*e*) The Nereide, 9 Cranch's (Amer.) Rep., p. 454.

(*f*) In the case of the Atalanta, Chief Justice Marshall said: "On the first question the case does not essentially differ from that of the Nereide. It is unnecessary to repeat the reasoning on which that case was decided; the opinion then given by the three judges is retained by them. The principle of the Law of Nations, that the goods of a friend are safe in the bottom of an enemy, may be, and probably will be, changed, or so impaired as to leave no object to which it is applicable; but so long as the principle shall be acknowledged, this Court must reject constructions which render it totally inoperative."—3 Wheaton's (Amer.) Rep., p. 415.

(*g*) "I have been latterly engaged in drawing up my dissenting opinion in the case of the 'Nereide,' (9 Cranch's Reports, p. 449.) I have now completed it; and never in my whole life was I more entirely satisfied that the Court were wrong in their judgment."—Life of Story, vol. i. p. 256.

"Errare mehercule malo cum Platone."

(*h*) It is to be remarked that all treaties which have been concerned with this subject have admitted the exercise of this right in time of war.—De Hautefeuille, t. 3, p. 450. Heffters, 169.

s'il porte des marchandises de contrebande, et qu'il appraisse suffisamment tant de la qualité dudit navire que de son maître ou patron; auxquels passeports et lettres de mer, se décret donnera entière foi et créance."(*i*)

CCCXLIII. The matter of Convoy was made the subject both of the Treaty of the Armed Neutrality of 1800, and of the Treaty between England and Russia in 1801. The provisions respecting each appear in the following parallel columns:—

1800.

"Art. V. That the declaration of the officer who shall command the ship of war, or ships of war, of the king or emperor, which shall be convoying one or more merchant ships, that the convoy has no contraband goods on board, shall be sufficient, and that no search of his ship, or the other ships of the convoy, shall be permitted; and the better to ensure respect to those principles, and the stipulations founded upon them, which their disinterested wishes to preserve the prescriptible rights of neutral nations have suggested, the high contracting parties, to prove their sincerity and justice, will give the strictest orders to their captains, as well of their ships of war as of their merchant ships, to load no part of their *ships, or secretly to have on board any articles which, by virtue of the present convention, may be considered as contraband; and for the more completely carrying into execution this command, they will respectively take care to give directions to their Courts of Admiralty to publish it whenever they shall think it necessary; and to this end the regulation which shall contain this prohibition, under the several penalties, shall be printed at the end of the present Act, that no one may plead ignorance.(*k*)

1801.

"Art. IV. The two high contracting parties, wishing also to prevent all subjects of dissention in future, by limiting the right of search of merchant ships going under convoy to those cases only in which the belligerent power might experience a real prejudice by the abuse of the neutral flag, have agreed:—

"1. That the right of searching merchant ships belonging to the subjects of one of the contracting powers, and navigating under convoy of a ship of war of the same power, shall only be exercised by ships of war of the belligerent party, and shall never extend to letters of marque, privateers, or other vessels, which do not belong to the royal or imperial fleet of their majesties, but which their subjects shall have fitted out for war. [*444]

"2. That the proprietors of all merchant ships belonging to the subjects of one of the contracting sovereigns, which shall be destined to sail under convoy of a ship of war, shall be required, before they receive their sailing orders, to produce to the commander of the convoy their passports and certificates, or sea letters, in the form annexed to the present treaty.

"3. That when such ship of war, having under convoy merchant ships, shall be met with by a ship or ships of war of the other contracting party, who shall then be in a state of war, in order to avoid all disorder, they shall keep out of cannon-shot, unless the state of the sea, or the place of meeting, render a nearer approach necessary; and the commander of the ship of the belligerent power shall send a boat on board the convoy, where they shall proceed reciprocally to the verification of the papers and certificates that are to prove, on one part, that the ship of war is authorized to take under its escort such or such merchant ships of its nation, laden with such a cargo and for such a port; on the other part, that the ship

(*i*) Dumont, Corps Diplom., t. vi. 2 part. p. 264.

(*k*) See Appendix to Speech of Lord Grenville in the House of Lords, Nov. 13, 1801, (pub. 1802.)

1801.

of war of the belligerent party belongs to the royal or imperial fleet of their majesties.

[*445] "4. This verification made, no *search shall take place if the papers are found in form, and if there exists no good motive for suspicion. In the contrary case, the commander of the neutral ship of war (being duly required thereto by the commander of the ship or ships of war of the belligerent power) is to bring to, and detain his convoy during the time necessary for the search of the ships which compose it; and he shall have the faculty of naming and delegating one or more officers to assist at the search of the said ships, which shall be done in his presence on board each merchant ship, conjointly with one or more officers appointed by the commander of the ship of the belligerent party.

"5. If it happen that the commander of the ship or ships of war of the belligerent power having examined the papers found on board, and having interrogated the master and crew of the ship, shall see just and sufficient reason to detain the merchant ship, in order to proceed to an ulterior search, he shall notify such intention to the commander of the convoy, who shall have the power to order an officer to remain on board the ship thus detained, and to assist at the examination of the cause of her detention. The merchant ship shall be carried immediately to the nearest and most convenient port belonging to the belligerent power, and the ulterior search shall be carried on with all possible diligence.

[*446] *"Art. V. It is in like manner agreed, that if any merchant ship thus convoyed should be detained without just and sufficient cause, the commander of the ship or ships of war of the belligerent power shall not only be bound to make to the owners of the ship and of the cargo a full and perfect compensation for all the losses, expenses, damages, and costs occasioned by such a detention, but shall, moreover, undergo an ulterior punishment for every act of violence or other fault which he may have committed, according as the nature of the case may require. On the other hand, the convoying ship shall not be permitted, under any pretext whatsoever, to resist by force the detention of the merchant ship or ships by the ship or ships of war of the belligerent power; an obligation which the commander of a ship of war with convoy

is not bound to observe towards letters of marque and privateers."(l)

CCCXLIV. The following Treaties will be found to be among the most important of those which relate to the subject of Visitation and Search in time of War:—

Austria and Spain, 1725.
" and Morocco, 1805.
" and Russia, 1785.
Columbia and the United States of North America, 1824.
" and Holland, 1829.
*Denmark and The Two Sicilies, 1742. [*447]
" and France, 1663 and 1742.
" (confirmed by that of 1842.)
" and Great Britain, 1669.
" and Prussia, 1818.
" and Russia, 1782 and 1800.
" and Tripoli, 1752.
" and Tunis, 1751.
The Two Sicilies and Holland, 1753.
" and the Ottoman Porte, 1740.
" and Russia, 1787.
" and Sweden, 1742.
" and Tripoli, 1741 and 1816.
" and Tunis, 1816.
Spain and The United States, 1795.
" and France, 1659.
" and Holland, 1648 and 1650
" and The Ottoman Porte, 1782.
" and Portugal, 1668.
" and Tripoli, 1784.
" and Tunis, 1791.
The United States and Central America, (federation of,) 1825.
" and France, 1778 and 1800.
France and Great Britain, 1632, 1677, 1713, and 1786.
" and Morocco, 1682 and 1767.
" and Mecklenburg-Schwerin, 1779.
" and Holland, 1646, 1662, 1678, 1697, 1713, and 1739.
" and The Ottoman Porte, 1535.
" and Russia, 1787.
" and Tunis, 1604.
" and Sweden, 1672.
Great Britain and Holland, 1667.
" and Morocco, 1721, 1750, 1760, and 1801.
" and Ottoman Porte, 1675.
" and Portugal, 1642.
*" and Russia, 1766, 1797, and 1801. [*448]

(l) See Appendix to Speech of Lord Grenville in the House of Lords, Nov. 13, 1801. (Pub. 1802.)

Great Britain and Sweden, 1664, 1802, and 1803. (This last Treaty authorizes the exercise of a right of preëmption of 10 per cent.)
" and Tripoli, 1662, 1716, and 1751.
" and Tunis, 1662, 1686, and 1751.
Holland and Morocco, 1683 and 1782.
" and Sweden, 1781.
" and Tripoli, 1703 and 1728.
" and Tunis, 1662, 1704, 1708, and 1713.(*m*)

The Treaties which have conferred the right of Visitation and Search, in time of peace, upon the ships of certain States in certain latitudes and under certain conditions, for the purpose of extirpating the Slave Trade, have been mentioned in a former volume of this work.(*n*)

[*449] *CHAPTER IV.

THE RIGHT OF CAPTURE.—THE DUTY OF THE CAPTOR.

CCCXLV. The Right of Capture and the Duty of the Captor are, of course, not dependent upon the element on which they happen to be exercised. For instance, the rules of International Law with respect to the circumstances which are necessary to constitute an actual Capture, the exact time when the contest is at an end, the enemy's property actually acquired, *jure victoriæ*, by the conqueror, the recognized signs of surrender, and other questions of the like kind, are equally incident to all war, whether waged by sea or by land.

But with respect to the Rights and Duties incident to Capture, as with respect to the tribunal which adjudicates upon them,(*a*) they have, in *maritime* affairs, been moulded, by the reason of the thing and by usage, into a regular system of established practice, which has not yet been attained in matters connected with military operations by land.(*b*)

It is with the consideration of the law as applied to the Rights and Duties springing from *Maritime* Capture, that this chapter will be principally occupied.

CCCXLVI. This subject of Maritime Capture(*c*) presents for solution the following questions:—

1. What may be captured?
2. What constitutes Capture?
3. Where may Capture be made?

(*m*) De Martens et De Cussy, Rec. de Tr. et Conv., vol. i. pp. 46, 47, index explicatif. See also, Rec. des Traités de Commerce et de Navigation de la France, par M. le Compte D'Hauterive et M. le Chevalier F. de Cussy, t. ix. pp. 350—358, tit. Neutralité.

(*n*) Vol. i. chap. xvii.

(*a*) Vide antè, p. 104. (*b*) Ibid.

(*c*) Effect of War upon the Trade and Property of Neutral and Maritime Capture and Prize, by J. P. Deane, D. C. L. London, 1854.

*4. To whose benefit does the Capture enure? [*450]

5. When does it so enure?

6. What must be done by the Captor after Capture? and to what Ports may the captured property be taken?

7. In the Courts of what country must it be adjudicated upon?

8. Where must the captured property be at the time of condemnation?

9. The forfeiture by misconduct, of the Captor's title to Prize?

CCCXLVII. 1. *What may be captured?*

This question has already been answered in the foregoing chapters. The summary of the details discussed in these chapters is, that all property belonging to the enemy found afloat upon the high seas, and all property so afloat of Subjects or Neutrals conducting themselves as Belligerents may be lawfully captured.(*d*)

The limitations and mitigations by which this abstract principle of International justice has been curtailed and softened must be sought for in the preceding pages of this volume.

CCCXLVIII. 2. *What constitutes Capture?*

An act of taking possession is not indispensably necessary to a Capture: an obedience to the summons of a hostile attack or hostile force, though none of the enemy's crew be on board, is sufficient.(*e*) The attack on an enemy's ship *and the compelling her to run into the port of an ally amounts to legal capture.(*f*) [*451]

But if one party take a vessel and afterwards abandon her, and then another take the same vessel, the last seizor is in law the only Captor.(*g*) But the inability of the prize master to secure the captured vessel against a rescue, should one be attempted, his inability to bring in the vessel without the aid of the hands belonging to her, is, in reason, no proof of abandonment. If the circumstances of the captured vessel be such as to do away all apprehension of rescue, and inspire confidence that the crew will bring her into port, the property of the Captor may be retained as well by a prize master alone, as by a considerable detachment from his crew."(*h*)

The real surrender (*deditio*) of a vessel is to be dated from the time of striking the colours.(*i*) Restitution after a first seizure does not bar a second by another seizor, though, if *judicially recorded*, it would bar the first seizor; but *otherwise* a second seizure by the same seizor is lawful, though it is made under peril of costs and damages.(*k*)

(*d*) See Mr. Justice Story's judgment in the Julia, 8 Cranch's (Amer.) Rep., p. 189. "By fiction, or rather by intendment of law, all property condemned is the property of enemies, that is, of persons so to be considered in the particular transaction."—The Elsebe, 5 Rob. Adm. Rep. p. 176.

(*e*) La Esperanza, 1 Haggard's Adm. Rep., p. 91. The Edward and Mary, 3 Rob. Adm. Rep., p. 305. The Hercules, 2 Dodson's Adm. Rep. p. 363. The Resolution, 6 Rob., p. 13. The William and Mary, 4 Rob., p. 386.

(*f*) La Esperanza, 1 Haggard's Adm. Rep., p. 91.

(*g*) The Diligentia, 1 Dodson's Adm. Rep., p. 405. The Polly and the Margueritte, note to the John and Jane, 4 Rob., p. 217. The Lucretia, 1 Hay and Marriott's Adm. Rep., p. 227.

(*h*) The Alexander, 8 Cranch's (Amer.) Rep., p. 180.

(*i*) The Rebeckah, 1 Rob., p. 233.

(*k*) The Mercurius, 1 Rob. p. 80. The Woodbridge 1 Haggard, p. 74.

CCCXLIX. 3. *Where may Capture be made?*

It has been already shown in preceding portions(*l*) of this work, that it is not competent to a belligerent to exercise any Rights of War within the territorial jurisdiction of a Neutral State,(*m*) and that this jurisdic-[*452] tion extends not only *within ports, headlands, and bays, but to a recognized distance at sea from the shore itself. Thus Captures made by armed vessels stationed in a river of a Neutral Power, or in the mouth of his river, or in his harbours, for the purpose of exercising the rights of War from that river or harbour, are invalid; and where a belligerent ship, lying within neutral territory, made a Capture with her boats sent out of the neutral territory, the Capture was also held to be invalid; for though the hostile force employed was applied to the captured vessel lying out of the territory, yet no such use of a neutal territory for the purpose of War is to be permitted.(*n*)

CCCL. All Captures, therefore, made by Belligerents within these limits are, at the request of the *Government of the Neutral State*,(*o*) pronounced by Courts of International Law to be invalid.

But here two important observations must be made. First, that the request for restitution must be made by some person clothed with authority [*453] to represent his Government *in negotiations with foreign States, and not by a merely public agent, such as a Consul, whose authority extends only to commercial matters. Secondly, *as between enemies*, a Capture made within Neutral waters is deemed, to all intents and purposes, rightful; it is only by the Neutral Sovereign that its legal validity can be called in question; and as to him, and him only, is it to be considered void. The enemy has no right whatsoever; and if the Neutral Sovereign omits or declines to interpose a claim, the property is condemnable, *jure belli*, to the Captors. "This," says Mr. Justice Story, is the clear result of the authorities; and the doctrine rests on well-established principles of public Law."(*p*)

CCCLI. This restitution as Mr. Wheaton observes,(*q*) is generally made

(*l*) Vol. i. chap. iv. viii.

(*m*) "Jure Belli adversus hostem duntaxat utimur in nostro, hostis, aut nullius territorio. In nostro si hostem deprehendamus, nihil utique prohibet, quominus, si sine libero commeatu ad nos pervenerit, hostiliter eum excipiamus. Ipsum hostis territorium ingredi, et ibi prædam agere, ratio belli permittit. In medio mari, utpote nullius territorio, id ipsum licet. Sed in territorio utriusque amici cui hostem agit, agit et adversus principem, qui ibi imperat, et omnem vim, a quocunque factam, legibus coercet."—Bynkershoek, Q. J. P., l. i. c. viii.

(*n*) The Twee Gebroeders, 3 Robinson, p. 162, (leading English case.) The Anna, 5 ib., p. 373. The Vrow Anna Catharina, ib., p. 15. See the arguments of counsel in the Topaz, 2 Acton's Adm. Rep., p. 20.

(*o*) Merlin Rep., t. xiii. pp. 111-114. Prise Maritime, § iv., *en quels lieux peut être exercé le droit de prise maritime.* See the report of two cases:—

1. La Christiana Colbiornsen, restored, as being within neutral territory.

2. Le Daniel Frederick, condemned as having been à plus d'une *double* portée du canon from the neutral coast at the time of capture. In this case the Procureur-général (Collet Descotils) said: "Le conseil, sait qu'après de longs débats entre les publicistes sur l'entendue que l'on devait donner à la franchise de la mer territoriale, cette éntendue a été définitivement fixée par le droit commun à la portée du canon du rivage."—Ib., p. 113.

(*p*) The Anne, 3 Wheaton's (Amer.) Rep., p. 447.

(*q*) Wheaton's Elements of International Law, (Lawrence,) p. 495.

through the agency of the Courts of Admiralty and Maritime Jurisdiction. Traces of the exercise of such a jurisdiction are found in the writings of Sir Leoline Jenkins.(*r*) In a letter to the King in Council, dated October 11, 1675, relating to a French privateer seized at Harwich with her prize (a Hamburg vessel bound to London,) Sir Leoline states several questions arising in the case; among which was, "Whether this Hamburger, being taken within one of your Majesty's chambers, and being bound for one of your ports, ought not to be set free by your Majesty's authority, notwithstanding he were (if taken upon the high seas out of those chambers) a lawful prize. I do humbly conceive he ought to be set free, upon a full and clear proof that he was within one of the King's chambers at the time of the seizure, which he, in his first memorial, sets forth to have been eight leagues at sea, over against Harwich. King James (of blessed memory) his direction, by proclamation, March 2, 1604, being, that all *officers and subjects, by sea and land, shall rescue and succour all merchants and others as shall [*454] fall within the danger of such as shall await the coasts, in so near places to the hindrance of trade outward and homeward; and all foreign ships, when they are within the King's chambers, being understood to be within the places intended in those directions, must be in safety and indemnity, or else, when they are suprised, must be restored to it, otherwise they have not the protection worthy of your Majesty, and of the ancient reputation of those places. But this being a point not lately settled by any determination, that I know of (in case where the King's chambers precisely, and under that name, come in question,) is of that importance as to deserve your Majesty's declaration and assertion of that right of the Crown by an Act of State in Council, your Majesty's coasts being now so much infested with foreign men-of-war, that there will be frequent use of such a decision."(*s*)

CCCLII. In 1793, the North American United States, remaining Neutral, thought it necessary to define the extent of the distance from their coast within which they claimed jurisdiction; and Mr. Wheaton remarks that Washington, then President, gave instructions to the executive officers to consider it as restrained, for the present, to the distance of one sea league, or three geographical miles, from the sea shores. This distance it was supposed, could admit of no opposition, being recognized by treaties between the United States and some of the Powers with whom they were connected in commercial intercourse, and not being more extensive than was claimed by any of them on their own coasts. As to the bays and rivers, they had always been considered as portions of the territory, both under the Laws of the former Colonial Government and of the present Union, and their immunity from belligerent operations was sanctioned by *the general Law and Usage of nations. The 25th article of the Treaty of 1794 between Great Britain and the [*455] United States, stipulated that "neither of the said parties shall permit the ships or goods belonging to the citizens or subjects of the other to be

(*r*) Judge of the English High Court of Admiralty in the reign of Charles II. and James II.—Vide antè, vol. i. preface, pp. xxx. xxxi. xxxii.

(*s*) Life and Works of Sir L. Jenkins, vol. ii. p. 780.

taken within cannon-shot of the coast, nor in any of the bays, ports or rivers of their territories, by ships of war, or others having commissions from any Prince, Republic, or State whatever. But in case it should so happen, the party whose territorial rights shall thus have been violated, shall use his utmost endeavours to obtain from the offending party full and ample satisfaction for the vessel or vessels so taken, whether the same be vessels of war or merchant vessels." Previously to this treaty with Great Britain, the United States were bound by treaties with three of the belligerent nations (France, Prussia, and Holland,) to protect and defend, "by all the means in their "power," the vessels and effects of those nations in their ports or waters, or on the seas near their shores, and to recover and restore the same to the right owner when taken from them. But they were not bound to make compensation if *all the means in their power was used*, and failed in their effect. Though they had, when the war commenced, no similar treaty with Great Britain, it was the President's opinion that they should apply to that nation the same rule which, under, this article, was to govern the others above mentioned; and even extend it to captures made on the high seas, and brought into the American ports, if made by vessels which had been armed within them. In the constitutional arrangement of the different authorities of the American Federal Union, doubts were at first entertained whether it belonged to the executive government, or the judiciary department, to perform the duty of inquiring into Captures made within the Neutral territory, or by armed vessels originally equipped, or the force of which had been augumented within the same, and of making restitution to the injured party. But it has been long since settled that this duty [*456] *appropriately belongs to the federal tribunals, acting as Courts of Admiralty and Maritime Jurisdiction.(*t*)

CCCLIII. It has been judicially determined by the Prize Courts of the North American United States, that this peculiar jurisdiction to inquire into the validity of Captures made in violation of the neutral immunity, will be exercised only for the purpose of restoring the specific property when voluntarily brought within the territory, and does not extend to the infliction of vindictive damages, as in ordinary cases of maritime injuries. And it seems to be doubtful whether this jurisdiction will be exercised where the property has been once carried *infra præsidia* of the captor's country, and there regularly condemned in a competent Court of Prize. However this may be in cases where the property has come into the hands of a *bonâ fide* purchaser, without notice of the unlawfulness of the Capture, it has been determined that the Neutral Court of Admiralty will restore it to the original owner where it is found in the hands of the captor himself, claiming under the sentence of condemnation. But the illegal equipment will not affect the

(*t*) Wheaton's Elements of International Law, (Lawrence,) pp. 496-97. Mr. Wheaton cites the following authorities in support of the doctrines in the text:—Mr. Jefferson's Letter to M. Genet, Nov. 8, 1793. Waite's State Papers, vol. i. p. 195. Opinion of the Attorney-General on the capture of the British ship Grange, May 14, 1793. Ibid, vol. i. p. 75. Mr. Jefferson's Letter to Mr. Hammond, Sept. 5, 1793. Waite's State Papers, vol. i. p. 165. Wheaton's (Amer.) Reports, vol. iv. p. 65, note *a*.

validity of a Capture, made after the cruise to which the outfit had been applied is actually terminated.(*u*)

*CCCLIV. An exception to the general rule of the immunity of Neutral territory has been attempted to be raised in the case [*457] of a vessel met on the *high seas* and pursued thereon, but which, *during the chase*, enters the Neutral limits. Bynkershoek expresses his *private* opinion that in such a case the continuance, "*dum fervet opus*," of the pursuit and Capture within the Neutral jurisdiction is lawful.(*x*)

"True it is," Lord Stowell says, "that that great man (Bynkershoek) does intimate an opinion of his own to that effect; but with many qualifications, and, as an opinion, which he did not find to have been adopted by any other writers. I confess I should have been inclined to have gone along with him to this extent, that if a cruiser, which had before acted in a manner entirely unexceptionable, and free from all violation of territory, had summoned a vessel to submit to Examination and Search, and that vessel had fled to such places as these, entirely uninhabited, and the cruiser had, without injury or annoyance to any party whatever, quietly taken possession of his prey, it would be stretching the point too hardly against the captor to say that on this account only it should be held an illegal capture. If nothing objectionable had appeared in the conduct of the captors before, the mere following to such a place as this is, would, I think, not invalidate a seizure otherwise just and lawful."(*y*)

CCCLV. It seems, indeed, as Mr. Chancellor Kent observes, that Casaregis, and several other foreign jurists mentioned by Azuni, held a similar doctrine. But D'Abreu, Valin, Emerigon, Vattel, Azuni, and others, maintain the *sounder doctrine, that when the flying enemy has entered neutral territory, he is placed immediately [*458] under the protection of the neutral power. The same broad principle that would tolerate a forcible entrance upon neutral ground of waters, in pursuit of the foe, would lead the pursuer into the heart of a commercial port.

To the writer of these pages it certainly appears a much safer and juster construction of International Law, altogether to reject the private opinion of Bynkershoek, which he admits to be at variance with usage and authority, and to preserve strictly, under all circumstances, the sacred immunity of the neutral territory, and to say, with Mr. Chancellor Kent, that "there is no exception to the rule, that every voluntary entrance into neutral territory, with hostile purposes, is absolutely unlawful."(*z*)

(*u*) La Amistad de Rues, 5 Wheaton's (Amer.) Rep., p. 385. La Nereyda, 8 Ib., p. 108. The Fanny, 9 Ib., p. 658. The Arrogante Barcelones, 7 Ib., p. 519. The Santissima Trinidad, Ib., p. 283. Wheaton's Elements of Internation Law, (Lawrence,) p. 497.

(*x*) Bynk., Q. J. P., l. i. c. viii.: "An hostem liceat aggredi vel persequi in amici territorio vel portu." Sed aliud est vim inchoare, aliud *calente negotio*, vi instare. Scilicet novum non est, valere quid etiamsi in eam causam deductum sit unde incipere non possit. Uno verbo: territorium communis amici valet ad prohibendam vim, quæ ibi inchoatur, non valet ad inhibendam, quæ extra territorium inchoatur, *dum fervet opus*, in ipso territorio continuatur."

(*y*) The Anna, 5 Robinson's Adm. Rep., p. 385, d.

(*z*) 1 Kent's Comm., (120,) p. 125. Vattel, l. iii. c. vii. s. 133. 1 Emerigon, Traité des Ass., p. 449. Azuni, vol. ii. p. 223. It was observed by the American Secretary of State, (Mr. Webster,) in the diplomatic correspondence between him

CCCLVI. By a Treaty between England and the United Provinces, in 1654, if the ships of either party were taken by an enemy in the port of the other, being Neutral, the latter engaged to pursue and oblige the captor to restore his prize. A similar engagement was made by the Treaty of 1669, between England and Denmark, with the clause that such pursuit was to be at the expense of the captured ship.(*a*)

4. *To whose benefit does the Capture enure?*

The right to all captures vests primarily in the Sovereign. When the [*459] benefit of a capture enures to the benefit of an *individual, it is in consequence of a grant of the State of which he is a subject. Some States, indeed, like Portugal, seem, during the last war, to have reserved the property for the use and benefit of the State; others, as Great Britain, grant out the property to its captors. The original right is in all cases in the State.

If two States join their forces for a common capture, one of which has granted out its interest to captors and the other has not, the only effect which the difference of practice, in dealing with the booty, will have, is that the proportion of the value will pass to the captor in one instance, and will remain to the State in the other, if that State chooses to assert its rights against the pretensions of its own captors.(*b*)

The general practice, indeed, of States(*c*) is to distribute the proceeds of the capture when duly condemned as prize among the captors.

[*460] *But the general principles of public jurisprudence is that "bello parta cedunt Reipublicæ." The distribution of the proceeds of prizes, therefore, depends upon the regulations of each State, and unless the local law has otherwise provided, the prize vests in the Sovereign;(*d*) and it has been decided by the English Prize Court, that

and the British Minister (Lord Ashburton) relative to the case of the steamboat Caroline, on the Canadian border, and seemingly admitted by Lord Ashburton, that to justify a hostile entrance upon neutral territory, there must exist a necessity of self-defence, instant, overwhelming, leaving no choice of means, and no moment for deliberation.

(*a*) Dumont, Corps Dipl., VI. i. p. 129, and vi. ii. p. 76.

(*b*) The ships taken at Genoa, 4 Rob., p. 403.

(*c*) The French Guiana, 2 Dodson's Adm. Rep., p. 157.

The present Prize Act, (17 Vict. c. 18,) in accordance with many precedents, begins as follows, "Whereas her Majesty, by her Order in Council, dated the 29th day of March, in the year 1854, was pleased to order that general reprisals be granted against the ships, vessels, and goods of the Emperor of All the Russias, his subjects, and others inhabiting within any of his countries, territories, or dominions, so that her Majesty's fleets and ships shall and may lawfully seize all ships, vessels, and goods belonging to the Emperor of All the Russias, or his subjects, or others inhabiting within any of his territories, countries or dominions, and bring the same to judgment in such Courts of Admiralty within her Majesty's dominions, possessions, or colonies, as shall be duly commissioned to take cognizance thereof: and whereas her Majesty hath of her royal munificence been graciously pleased, by her proclamation bearing the same date, to declare her intention to give the benefit of all prizes taken during the present war to the captors thereof, being in her Majesty's service (save as therein excepted.) Now, for the encouragement of the officers and crews of her Majesty's ships and vessels of war, and for inducing all British seamen, who may be in any foreign service, to return into this kingdom, aud become serviceable to her Majesty; and for the more effectually securing and extending the trade of her Majesty's subjects: be it enacted," &c.

(*d*) "At de his quæ actu bellico capit alia est ratio. Ibi enim singuli reipub-

the power of the Crown to direct, before adjudication and against the will of the captors, the release of property seized as prize, is not taken away by any grant of prize conferred in the Order of Council, the Proclamation, or the Prize Act, these being the instruments which in England regulate the distribution of the proceeds of captures.(*e*)

It requires but little reflection to see how necessary the preservation of such a power must be to the Government of any State in its relations with foreign States.

CCCXLVII. 5. *When does it so enure?*

Strictly speaking, and as regards the belligerents only, the title passes and is vested when the capture is complete; and that is complete when the *deditio* has taken place, or when the battle is over and the *spes recuperandi* is gone.(*f*)

*Grotius(*g*) and other writers who have followed in his track, the Marine Ordinances of certain countries, *e. g.*, those of France and of the North American United States, make twenty-four hours' quiet possession the test of title by capture. Bynkershoek maintains that a firm possession at any time vests the property in the captor; and that there can be no doubt but that the ownership of captured property brought *infra præsidia* is vested in the captors. [*461]

Voet argues strongly that it vests immediately upon capture.(*h*) This is clearly the opinion which is warranted by the *reason of the thing*.(*i*) It is not, however, to be regretted that by the modern *usage* of States, neither the twenty-four hours, nor the bringing the prize *infra præsidia*, is sufficient to change the property of a captured vessel.

licæ personam sustinent, ejusque vice funguntur, ac proinde per eos populus, si lex civilis aliud non statuat, ut possessionem ita et dominium nanciscitur, et id in quos vult transfert."—Grotius, l. iii. c. vi. s. 14.

"Naturellement ce butin n'appartient pas moins que les conquêtes au souverain qui fait la guerre, car lui seul a des prétentions à la charge de l'ennemi, qui l'autorisent à s'emparer de ses biens et à se les approprier. Ses soldats, et mêmes les auxiliaires, ne sont que des instruments dans sa main pour faire valoir son droit. Il les entretient et les soudoie; tout ce qu'ils font, ils le font en son nom et pour lui. S'ils ne sont pas pas associés dans la guerre, elle ne se fait point pour eux; ils n'ont pas plus de droit au butin qu'aux conquêtes. Mais le souverain peut faire aux troupes telle part qu'il lui plaît du butin."—Vattel, l. iii. c. ix. s. 164.

(*e*) The Elsebe, (the leading case) 5 Rob. p. 173. (*f*) 1 Kent's Comm., p. 101.

(*g*) L. iii. c. 9, s. 16. "Eæ vero res quæ intra præsidia perductæ nondum sunt, quanquam ab hostibus occupatæ, ideo postliminii non egent quia dominum nondum mutarunt ex gentium jure. This doctrine is taken from the Roman Law. See—Dig. lxix. tit xv. De Captivis et de Postliminio, &c. Ib., s. v. § 1: "In bello cum hi, qui nobis hostes sunt, aliquem ex nostris ceperunt, *et intra præsidia sua perduxerunt*." See, too, analogies furnished by—Dig., xli. t. i.: "De acquirendo rerum domino," s. 44. Dig. x. t. ii.: "Familiæ erciscundæ," s. 8. On the other hand—Dig. xli. t. ii.: "De acquirendâ vel amittendâ possessione." Ib., s. 1. § 1: "Item bello capta . . . ejus fiunt, qui primus possessionem eorum nactus est."

(*h*) Comm. ad Pandectas, t. iv. (ed 1829, Constantiis) p. 644, lib. xlix. tit xv. iii.

(*i*) "By some writers (Lord Stowell says) possession alone has been deemed sufficient; but that rule, however agreeable to notions of natural occupancy, is defective in practical convenience; and therefore a middle doctrine has generally prevailed, under which it has been held, that something of a secure and definite possession is required to establish and complete the property in prize; that it should be in the possession of the captor twenty-four hours, or that it should be brought *infrà præsidia*." The Henrick and Maria, 4 Robinson, p. 46, De Martens, Précis du Dr. des G., l. iii. c. vii. s. 322. Lampredi, s. 13. The Henrick and Maria, 4 Robinson, p. 55.

[*462] International Law now requires that a judicial tribunal *should exercise, according to the known laws and approved practice of nations, a scrutiny into the circumstances of the capture, and that a regular sentence of condemnation should be pronounced by a court of competent jurisdiction; that is, as will presently be seen, a Court belonging to the sovereign of the Captor; documentary evidence of this fact must be produced in support of any title on behalf of any person other than the original owner.

CCCLVIII. This proposition of International Law was firmly incorporated into the Common Law of England by a decision of Lord Mansfield in 1758.(*k*)

The case which gave rise to this result related, indeed, to a question of *insurance.* The judgment decided that an insured ship *being taken*, the insured may demand as for a total loss, and abandon to the insurer.

It was agreed by all the Judges, that whether by the capture in question the property was or was not transferred to the enemy by International Law, was immaterial *as between the insurers and the insured.*

That question, it was truly said, could only arise in two cases:

1. Between the owner and a Neutral who had *purchased* from the enemy.

2. Between the owner and a *recaptor.*

Nevertheless this eminent jurist and judge proceeded to consider this question and expressed himself as follows:—

"If the ship taken by an enemy *escapes* from the enemy, or is *retaken*, or if the owner *redeems* (ransoms) the capture, his property is thereby *revested*, which property in the ship taken was, by the Law of Nations, obtained by the captor.

[*463] "The general proposition of writers upon this subject is, *that '*quæ ab hostibus capiuntur, statim capientium fiunt*,' which is to be understood 'when the *battle* is over.' Indeed, nothing can be said to be taken till the battle is over, and the battle is not over till all immediate pursuit has ceased, and all hope of recovery is gone. This is the definition of a capture, referred to by our Prize Act, 29 Geo. II. c. 34, of a ship taken by the enemy. And, accordingly, Voet in his Commentary upon the Pandects, lib. xlix. tit. xv. vol. ii. p. 1155, and many authors he refers to, maintain with great strength, '*per solam occupationem dominium prædæ hostibus acquiri.*'

"One argument used to prove it is, 'that the instant the captor has got *possession*, no friend, no fellow-soldier or ally, can take it from him, because it would be a *violation of his property.*'

"But other writers and States have drawn other lines by arbitrary rules, and partly from *policy*, to prevent too easy dispositions to *Neutrals*; and partly from *equity*, to extend the *jus postliminii* in favour of the *owner.* No wonder there is so great uncertainty and variety of notions amongst them about fixing a positive boundary by *the mere force of rea-*

(*k*) Goss and another v. Withers, 2 Burrows's Reports, p. 693. In this case reference will be found to some old cases at *common law*, from which it would appear that formerly goods taken from the enemy belonged at once to the captor.

son, where the subject-matter is *arbitrary*, and not the object of *reason alone.*

"Some have said, from the Roman law (which was introduced in favour of the liberty and condition of a Roman citizen taken captive,) 'that the prize must be brought *infra præsidia*;' but '*what* custody *at sea* should be equal to *præsidia at land*,' is a new fund of dispute, and leaves the matter just where it was.

"The writers whom Grotious follows, and many more who follow him, and some nations,(*l*) have made twenty-four hours' quiet possession by the enemy the criterion. But this Bynkershoek,(*m*) and other writers whom he follows, and several nations, absolutely deny.

*"Some have said that the ship must be carried into the enemy's port, condemned there, sail out again, and arrive in a friend's port. All these circumstances are very arbitrary, and therefore this is generally exploded. [*464]

"I have taken the trouble to inform myself of the practice of the Court of Admiralty in England, before any Act of Parliament commanded restitution, or fixed the rate of salvage; and I have talked with Sir George Lee, who has examined the books of the Court of Admiralty, and informs me, that they held the property *not changed*, so as to bar the owner, in favour of a vendee or re-captor, till there had been a sentence of condemnation; and that in the reign of King Charles II., Sir Richard Floyd (father of the late Sir Nathaniel) gave a solemn judgment upon the point, and decreed restitution of a ship retaken by a privateer, after she had been fourteen weeks in the enemy's possession, because *she had not been condemned.* Another case, upon the same principle, against a vendee, is cited at the end of Assievedo v. Cambridge,(*n*) in 1695, after a long possession, two sales, and several voyages."

CCCLIX. With respect to the vesting of the right of capture, according to the law of England, Lord Loughborough remarks, that before the sixth year of the reign of Queen Anne, there were no laws made on this subject. Previous to that time, all prizes taken in war were of right vested in the Crown, and questions concerning the property of such prizes were not the subject of discussion in Courts of Law. But in order to do justice to claimants, from the first year after the restoration of Charles the Second, special commissions were issued to enable the Courts of Admiralty to condemn such captures as appeared to be lawful prizes, to give relief where there was no colour for the taking, and *generally to make satisfaction to parties injured. By the Act of the 13 [*465] Car. II. c. 9,(*o*) indeed, some regulations were made concerning the treatment of ships taken, but no provisions enacted respecting any security to be given on delivery: the sole interest in the thing condemned being in the Crown, it was in public custody, and the disposition of it a mere matter of prerogative; no such provisions therefore was necessary. But in the sixth year of Queen Anne, it was thought proper, for the encouragement of seamen, to vest in them the prizes they should take; and for

(*l*) Vide the Ordonnances of Louis XIV. (*m*) Q. J. Pub. l. i. c. iv.
(*n*) Lucas's Reports, p. 79; 10 Modern Reports, p. 77.
(*o*) Repealed by 22 Geo. II. c. 33.

that purpose the statutes 6 Anne, c. 13, and c. 37, were passed. The first of these Acts only respects proceedings in the Courts of Admiralty in England, but contains no particular directions to them, the practice of those Courts being already settled; the second, 6 Anne, c. 37, is particularly intended for the regulation of the Courts of Vice Admiralty in America, and the operation of it is confined to captures and condemnations there made. One object of that Act was, that the judge should proceed to sentence with all possible expedition. In the fourth section, therefore, this case is provided for; namely, that if, on the preparatory examinations, there should arise a doubt in the breast of the judge whether the capture were prize or not, and further proof should appear to be necessary, the ship and cargo should be appraised by persons named on the part of the captor, and be delivered up to the claimants on their giving *good* and *sufficient security* to pay to the captor the full value thereof according to such appraisement, if the ship should be adjudged lawful prize by the same judge. By this provision, the claimant is entitled to the immediate possession of the subject in dispute, which the captor cannot obtain but on the refusal of the claimant to give security for the appraised value. After a sentence of condemnation, the captor
[*466] has a right to the possession. No appraisement is to *be made in case of an appeal; nor is there any provision for a sale by authority of the Court, in order to ascertain the value. But (by the 8th section of the Act) the appeal is to be allowed in like manner as appeals from the Courts of Admiralty in England, with a special direction that the appellant shall enter into security to prosecute the appeal, answer the condemnation, and pay treble costs, if the sentence shall be affirmed: no direction is given as to any security to be taken from the party appellate, but by reference to the practice of the Court of Admiralty in England on appeals to the Sovereign; and it is added, that the execution of the sentence shall not be suspended by reason of any appeal.(*p*)

CCCLX. Before this part of the subject be dismissed, it should be observed, that in cases where a captured ship has been purchased, under a title invalid indeed, but not notoriously bad, it has been the practice of the English Court of Prize to decree restitution to the original owner, but at the same time to allow the vendor for an amelioration beyond the ordinary repairs, but not for ordinary repairs.(*q*)

CCCLXI. 6. *What must be done by the Captor after capture, and to what ports may the captured property be taken?*

It is incumbent on the captor—as will be seen more at length in a subsequent chapter—to bring his prize as speedily as may be consistent with his other duties within the jurisdiction of the Court which has the power of adjudicating upon it. But he may find it necessary to touch at a neutral port, or to deposit, if permitted, for a while his prize therein: of course, no doubt can arise as to the lawfulness of taking the prize into the port of an ally. According to the law of the English Prize Court, it

(*p*) Brymer v. Atkins, 1 H. Blackstone's Rep., pp. 189-190.

(*q*) The Kierlighett, 3 Rob., p. 96 The Perseverance, 2 Ib., p. 239. See Dig., v. 1. iii. 38, *de hæred petit.*

is not, generally speaking, competent to *captors to carry prizes into a foreign Court, and offer to restore them on bail. It is an [*467] irregularity which can only be justified by the evident necessity of the particular case.(*r*)

CCCLXII. It is perfectly competent to the Neutral State to prohibit(*s*) the ingress into her ports of all prizes made by all Belligerents; such cases of course excepted as belong to the class of urgent necessity, such as arise from distress of weather or the dangerous state of the vessels.(*t*)

CCCLXIII. Upon the subject of permitting prizes to be brought into neutral ports, no uniformity of practice has prevailed. The matter has been sometimes governed (1.) by domestic regulation, sometimes (2.) by Treaties. In the absence of such provisions, it should seem that the presumption is in favour of the permission.(*u*) It is a *primâ facie* presumption, however, only, and capable of being easily rebutted.

CCCLXIV. 1. With respect to domestic regulations upon this subject, Mr. Manning(*x*) refers us to various authorities. By a proclamation of Henry VI. in 1426, it was ordered that all prizes were to be brought into British ports; and a similar regulation was issued by Elizabeth, in 1602. Captors were desired to bring French prizes into the ports of France by various ordinances in 1400, in 1543, in 1674, and in 1689: the Ordinance of 1705 was the first that allowed French prizes to be taken into the ports of an ally. And by the Danish Ordinance of 1710, it was forbidden, on pain *of death, to carry Danish prizes into any but Danish ports.(*y*) But such rules were not univer- [*468] sal; and Loccenius, who wrote in 1651, decided that prizes in Neutral ports could not be interfered with unless special Treaty intervened.(*z*)

By the French *Ordonnance* of 1650, no prizes brought into French ports by foreign cruisers were to be sold there;(*a*) and by subsequent French ordinances, no prize taken by a vessel with a foreign commission was to be allowed to remain more than twenty-four hours in a French port, unless compelled by stress of weather, or unless the prize had been taken from the enemies of the French; and *also* any goods belonging to the French, or to their allies, were to be taken out of any prizes brought into French ports, and restored to the original proprietors.(*b*)

But by the Venetian Edict of 1779, respecting the Neutrality of Venice, the sale of prizes, and even equipment of cruisers, is equally allowed to all Belligerents.(*c*)

(*r*) The Peacock, 4 Rob. Adm. Rep., p. 192.

(*s*) Bynk., Q. J. P., l. i. c. xv. Valin, Ord. de la Marine, t. ii. p. 272. Wheaton's El., (Lawrence) p. 498. De Pist. et Duverd., t. ii. p. 186.

(*t*) Vide antè, vol. i. p. 49, and App., p. 498, as to Treaties relating to what is called *relache forcée*, in time of peace.

(*u*) Wheaton's El., (Lawrence,) p. 498.

(*x*) P. 387. The statements in the text on this subject are principally derived from his accurate and valuable work.

(*y*) Robinson's Collectanea Maritima, p. 30.

(*z*) Loccenius, de Jure Maritimo, l. ii. c. iv. s. 7.

(*a*) Valin, Ord. de la Marine, II. l. iii. t. ix. art. i.

(*b*) Ib., l. iii. tit. ix. arts. xiv. xv.

(*c*) De Martens, Rec., l. iii. p. 85. Manning's Law of Nations, pp. 388, 389.

CCCLXV. 7. *In the Courts of what country must it be adjudicated upon?*

The answer to this question has, with an exception presently to be noticed, been universally the court of the captor or of his ally(*d*)—for, as we have seen, "*unam constituunt civitatem.*(*e*) In such cases there is nothing to prevent the Government from proceeding to that last act of hostility. There is a common interest between them on the subject; [*469] and both Governments may be presumed to authorize *any measures conducing to give effect to their arms, and to consider each others ports as mutually subservient. Such a condemnation is sufficient in regard to property taken in the course of the operations of a common war.(*f*) With respect to the Neutral State itself, the most vehement advocates of neutral rights have holden that it has no power of interfering with prizes brought within its ports; unless, indeed, such power have been conveyed to it by the provisions of special Treaties, of which some notice will be presently taken.(*g*)

CCCLXVI. The exception referred to in the last paragraph is to be found in the practice of the French Government, which took its rise at a period of admitted anomaly with respect to the administration of Prize Law—viz., in the year 1796, during the last war.

No such question can, however, be presented for discussion during the present war by the existing Prize Law of France, for, by the *Décret du* 18 *Julliet*, 1854, of the Emperor Napoleon the Third, all *Commissions Consulaires* are, by implication at least, annulled.(*h*)

In fact, these commissions were never defended at the time of their [*470] *de facto* institution by any eminent French jurists,(*i*) *though a skilful gloss is thrown over their illegality by the authors of the recent *Traité des Prises Maritimes.*(*k*)

They were always open to this dilemma—viz.:

1. Either they sat in the neutral territory without the sanction of the neutral authority, and then they were clearly illegal.

2. Or they sat with the sanction of the neutral authority: and then either the Neutral might be fairly holden, by the accordance of such

(*d*) The Flad Oyen, (leading English case) 1 Rob., p. 136. The doctrine of this case was affirmed by the Court of Appeal. See the Falcon, 6 Rob., p. 198. The Alerta, 9 Cranch's (Amer.) Reports, pp. 359, 364.

(*e*) Vide antè, p. 114, and the Henrick & Maria, 4 Robinson, p. 60.

(*f*) The Christopher, 2 Rob., p. 210.

(*g*) Manning, p. 388, note (1.) Hübner, de la Saisie des Bâtiments Neutres, II. i. c. xi. s. 8. De Martens, l. viii. c. vii. s. 312.

(*h*) Messieurs D'Hauterive and De Cussy state the law correctly: "L'usage moderne a généralement reconnu, pour juger les prises, la juridiction de l'Etat belligérant."—Traités de Commerce, t. ix. p. 375.

(*i*) MM. De Pist. and Duverd., speaking of the Arrété du Germinal An VIII. art. 23, on this subject, are obliged to admit: "La rédaction de cet article est pleine de réserves et de restrictions; on voit qu'elle avait été prise sous l'influence des observations faites au Conseil des Anciens par le rapporteur de la loi du 8 Floréal an IV., lequel avait émis sans contradiction la doctrine que les principes du droit des gens, qui donnent exclusivement à chaque nation le pouvoir juridictionnel sur son territoire, et les traités qui, pour la plupart, répètent ces principes, concourent pour s'opposer à ce que nos consuls exercent une prérogative aussi extraordinaire chez l'étranger."

(*k*) De Pist. et Duverd., t. ii. p. 174.

sanction, to have acted as a Belligerent, or, at all events, the judgments of such Court would not be held binding upon any State but the neutral one which sanctioned so mischievous and unwarrantable an innovation upon the Rights of Nations. The truth is that they were among the worst features of the Revolution, and to them, as well as to other abortive Courts of Prize, were applicable the words of that great jurist M. Merlin, "On ne se rappelle que trop combien furent désastreux les résultats de cette étrange législation—les tribunaux ne tenaient aucun compete dans leurs jugements des rapports de la France avec les puissances étrangères—de les réclamations nombreuses et énergiques."(*l*)

CCCLXVII. The law upon this subject was admirably discussed by Lord Stowell, in a case(*m*) which was adjudicated *upon in the English Prize Court in the early part of the year 1799. [*471]

It was the case of a ship taken by a French Privateer, and carried into the Port of Bergen, in Norway, where it appears she underwent a sort of process, which terminated in a sentence of condemnation pronounced by the French Consul, and under that sentence she was asserted to have been transferred to a neutral proprietor.

"But another question (Lord Stowell observes) has arisen in this case, upon which a great deal of argument has been employed: namely, whether the sentence of condemnation which was pronounced by the French Consul is of such legal authority as to transfer the vessel, supposing the purchase to have been *bonâ fide* made? I directed the counsel for the claimants to begin, because the sentence being of a species altogether new, it lay upon them to prove that it was nevertheless a legal one.

"It has frequently been said, that it is the peculiar doctrine of the law of England to require a sentence of condemnation, as necessary to transfer the property of prize; and that, according to the practice of some nations, twenty-four hours, according to the practice of others, bringing *infra præsidia*, is authority enough to convert the prize. I take that to be not quite correct; for I apprehend that, by the general practice of the Law of Nations, a sentence of condemnation is at present deemed generally necessary; and that a neutral purchaser in Europe, during war, does look to the legal sentence of condemnation as one of the title-deeds of the ship if he buys a prize vessel. I believe there is no

(*l*) Cited De Pist. et Duverd., t. ii. p. 158.

(*m*) The Flad Oyen, 1 Rob., p. 135. The Perseverance, 2 Rob., p. 240. (In this case, the amelioration of a prize ship, purchased by a Neutral, under illegal condemnation, in Norway, allowance made on restitution to original owner.) The Kierlighett, 3 Ib., p. 95. (In this case a condemnation in Norway before a French Consul, holden invalid, not helped by a sentence of a Court of Prize, in the enemy's country, decreeing restitution to the neutral claimant, on the circumstances of a subsequent capture, &c.) Havelock v. Rockwood, 8 Durnford & East, p. 268. Donalson v. Thompson, 1 Campbell's Rep., p. 429. The following decisions in the Prize Courts of the N. A. United States support the judgment of Lord Stowell. The invincible, 2 Gallison's (Amer.) Reports, pp. 28, 36. S. C. 1 Wheaton's (Amer.) Rep. p. 238. Maissionnaire v. Keating, 2 Gallison's (Amer.) Rep., pp. 224-234 The Findlay and the William, 1 Peter's (Amer.) Adm. Rep., p. 12. Wheelwright v. Depeyster, 1 Johnson's (Amer.) Rep., p. 471. Page v. Lenox, 15 Ib., p. 172. 1 Kent's Comm., pp. 103, 104.

[*472] instance in which a man, having purchased a *prize vessel of a Belligerent, has thought himself quite secure in making that purchase, merely because the ship had been in the enemy's possession twenty-four hours, or carried *infra præsidia*. The contrary has been more generally held; and the instrument of condemnation is amongst those documents which are most universally produced by a neutral purchaser, that if she has been taken as prize, it should appear also that she has been, in a proper judicial form, subjected to adjudication.

"Now in what form have these adjudications constantly appeared? They are the sentences of Courts acting and exercising their functions in the belligerent country; and it is for the very first time in the world that, in the year 1799, an attempt is made to impose upon the Court a sentence of a tribunal not existing in the belligerent country, but of a person pretending to be authorized within the dominions of a neutral country. In my opinion, if it could be shown that, regarding mere speculative general principles, such a condemnation ought to be deemed sufficient, that would not be enough; more must be proved; it must be shown that it is conformable to the usage and practice of nations.(*i*)

"A great part of the Law of Nations stands on no other foundation; it is introduced, indeed, by general principles, but it travels with those general principles only to a certain extent; and, if it stops there, you are not at liberty to go farther, and to say that mere general speculations would bear you out in a further progress. Thus, for instance, on mere general principles it is lawful to destroy your enemy, and mere general principles make no great difference as to the manner by which this is to be effected; but the conventional law of mankind, which is evidence in their practice, does make a distinction, and allows some and prohibits other modes of destruction; and a Belligerent is bound to confine himself to those modes which the common practice of mankind has employed, [*473] and to relinquish those *which the same practice has not brought within the ordinary exercise of war, however sanctioned by its principles and purposes.

"Now, it having been the constant usage that the tribunals of the Law of Nations in these matters shall exercise their functions within the belligerent country, if it was proved to me in the clearest manner that on mere general theory such a tribunal might act in the neutral country, I must take my stand on the ancient and universal practice of mankind, and say that, as far as that practice has gone, I am willing to go, and where it has thought proper to stop, there I must stop likewise.

"It is my duty not to admit, that because one nation has thought proper to depart from the common usage of the world, and to meet the notice of mankind in a new and unprecedented manner, that I am on that account under the necessity of acknowledging the efficacy of such a novel institution, merely because general theory might give it a degree of countenance, independent of all practice from the earliest history of mankind. The institution must conform to the text law, and likewise to the constant usage upon the matter; and when I am told that, before

(*i*) Vide antè, vol. i. c. v.

the present war, no sentence of this kind has ever been produced in the annals of mankind, and that it is produced by one nation only in this war, I require nothing more to satisfy me that it is the duty of this Court to reject such a sentence as inadmissible.

"Having thus declared that there must be an antecedent usage upon the subject, I should think myself justified in dismissing this matter without entering into any farther discussion. But even if we look farther, I see no sufficient ground to say, that on mere general principles such a sentence could be sustained: proceedings upon Prize are proceedings *in rem;* and it is presumed that the body and substance of the thing is in the country which has to exercise the jurisdiction."(*k*)

*The learned judge then disposes of an *argumentum ad hominem*, or *ad gentem*, arising from the practice of English [*474] Prize Courts to condemn vessels *lying in neutral ports* at the time of condemnation. To this argument he replies:—

1. That the practice itself was infrequent and irregular.

2. That it did not authorize a bad practice in other States, for "the true mode of correcting the irregular practice of a nation is by protesting against it, and by inducing that country to reform it; it is monstrous to suppose, that because one country has been guilty of an irregularity, every other country is let loose from the Law of Nations, and is at liberty to assume as much as it thinks fit."

3. That this practice had been in use only with respect to vessels lying at Leghorn and Lisbon, where the English had peculiar privileges.(*l*)

4. That Neutrals had no interest in disputing the validity of their sentences.

5. And chiefly, as it should seem in these cases, there was no doubt as to the authority of the tribunal itself, which was acting in the country to which it belonged.

"Here a person, utterly naked of all authority except over the subjects of his own country, and possessing that merely by the indulgence of the country in which he resides, pretends to exercise a jurisdiction in a matter in which the subjects of many other States may be concerned. No such authority was ever conceded by any country to a foreign agent of any description residing within it; and least of all could such an authority be conceded in the matter of Prize of War—a matter over which a neutral country has no cognizance whatever, except in the single case of an infringement of its own territory; and in which such a concession of authority cannot be made without departing from the duties, and losing the benefits of its neutral character.

*"Mark the consequences which must follow from such a pretended concession: observe in the present case how it would affect [*475] the neutral character in the north! If France can station a judge of the Admiralty at Bergen, and can station there its cruisers to carry in prizes for that judge to condemn, who can deny that to every purpose of hostile mischief against the commerce of England, Bergen will differ from Dunkirk in no other respect than this, that it is a port of the enemy to a much

(*k*) The Flad Oyen, 1 Rob., pp, 139-142.
(*l*) See on this point too the Henrick & Maria, 4 Rob., p. 61.

greater extent of practical mischief? To make the ports of Norway the seats of the French tribunals of war, is to make the adjacent sea the theatre of French hostility.

"It gives one Belligerent the unfair advantage of a new station of war which does not properly belong to him, and it gives to the other the unfair disadvantage of an active enemy in a quarter where no enemy would naturally be found. The coasts of Norway could no longer be approached by the British merchant with safety, and a suspension of commerce would soon be followed by a suspension of amity.

"Wisely, therefore, did the American government defeat a similar attempt made on them, at an earlier period of the war: they knew that to permit such an exercise of the rights of war within their cities, would be to make their coasts a station of hostility."(*m*)

CCCLXVIII. But a claimant who has purchased under an originally invalid sentence, may cure the defect of that title, though passed after many changes of property, by the sentence of a proper tribunal.

If the title is impeached before the sentence takes place, it may be vitiated; but when a valid sentence comes, it must be considered as operating retroactively, so as to rehabilitate the former title.(*n*)

[*476] *Where a ship has been captured, and carried into a hostile port, and is afterwards sold to a Neutral, the presumption of law is that she has been regularly condemned, and the burden of proving the contrary rests on the claimant, and not on the purchaser.(*mm*) The case in which this principle was enunciated was decided in the Instance, and not in the Prize Court of Admiralty. It would appear, that if the ship had been carried into a Neutral's port, the burden of proof, if he had been a foreign purchaser, would have laid upon the claimant.(*nn*)

CCCLXIX. It is to be observed that with respect to the interests of parties, not being British subjects, a British Prize Court does not, according to the doctrine of Lord Stowell, inquire into the sufficiency of a sentence passed by a Neutral Court.

This doctrine was laid down in the case of an American ship captured by the French, condemned in Spain, and purchased by a Danish merchant. On a subsequent capture by an English cruiser, a claim was given for the Danish purchaser, and also for the former American proprietor, on the ground that the condemnation, having been in a port neutral towards America, was invalid. The Court declined to judge of the relation of foreign States, and decreed restitution to the Danish purchaser.(*o*)

CCCLXX. It may be remarked here, though perhaps a little out of the proper place, that, a title originally defective, being acquired under the sentence of an incompetent Court, is cured by an intervening peace, for peace has the effect of quieting all titles of possession arising from the war.(*p*)

(*m*) The Flad Oyen, 1 Rob., p. 144. (*n*) The Falcon, 6 Rob., p. 200.
(*mm*) The Countess of Lauderdale, 4 Rob., p. 286.
(*n*) See note, ib. The Constant Mary, referred to in the Kierlighett, 3 Rob., pp. 97-8. S. C., Carthew's Rep., p. 423.
(*o*) The Cosmopolite, 3 Rob., p. 334. (*p*) The Schooner Sophie, 6 Ib., p. 138.

CCCLXXI. These observations may be properly closed *with the opinion of an eminent civilian expressed in the clearest language, and in the most positive tone:— [*477]

"Ut victor intrà propria præsidiæ tutus est, ità si amici fidem elegerit et in ejus præsida se et sua contulerit, etiam illic publico nomine tutus erit. Is verò cui res illæ jure belli adempæ sunt, frustrà eas in communis amici territorio repetitum venit; quod enim belli sors occupanti dedit, in pacato loco apud communem amicum meritò sibi servabit."(q)

CCCLXXII. The rule that the trial of captures made on the high seas, *jure belli*, by a duly commissioned ship of war, whether from an enemy or a Neutral, belongs exclusively to the Courts of the State to which the captor belongs, is undeniable. But it has been truly said that there are two exceptions to this rule equally undeniable: first, if the capture be made within the territorial limits of a neutral country into which the prize is brought; secondly, or by a privateer which had been illegally equipped in such neutral country, the Prize Courts of such neutral country not only possess the power, but it is their duty to restore the property so illegally captured to the owner.(r)

CCCLXXIII. A remarkable instance of the vindication of the rights of neutral jurisdiction grew out of an episode of the Seven Years' War.

In the month of August, 1759, the English Admiral Boscawen fought an action off Cadiz with some French ships under the command of M. De la Clue. The action was unfavourable to the French, and they were compelled to take refuge in the Bay of Lagos; thither they were pursued by the English, who set fire to and destroyed the ships which had sought the protection of the Portuguese ports.

The conduct was a clear and unquestionable violation of the neutral rights of Portugal, and which probably would *not have taken place, but for the very peculiar intimacy of the relations subsisting between England and Portugal. [*478]

It produced, however, a very spirited remonstrance from the then minister of Portugal, the Marquis of Pombal, and the result was that an ambassador extraordinary was sent from England to make a special and public apology for the conduct of the English admiral.(s)

CCCLXXIV. Mr. Lawrence, in his recent and valuable edition of Mr. Wheaton's work, furnishes us(t) with the following case upon this subject:—

It appears that in September, 1814, a case of violation of neutral territory occurred in the destruction, in the harbor of Fayal, of the American privateer *General Armstrong* by an English squadron. Reclamations founded on it were made against the Government of Portugal, which were, by the 2nd article of the Treaty of 26th February, 1851,(u) agreed to be submitted to the arbitration of a sovereign, potentate, or chief of some nation in amity with both the high contracting parties.

(q) Loccenius de jure Maritimo, l. ii. c. iv. s. 6.
(r) The Alerto, 9 Cranch's (Amer.) Rep., p. 364.
(s) Revue de Droit Français et Étranger, (1840) tom. vii. p. 751, LXI.
(t) Wheaton's Elements of International Law, (Lawrence) p. 493, note.
(u) Treaties of the United States, 1854, p. 92.

Under this provision, Louis Napoleon, the President of the French Republic, was selected as arbitrator. There is some discrepancy between the American statement and the summary of facts on which the award proceeds. The Prince President, however, in pronouncing that no indemnity was due from Portugal, does not deny the responsibility of a Neutral to make compensation to a Belligerent whose property has been captured or destroyed within its jurisdictional limits by the opposing Belligerent, but he founds his decision on the assumed fact, that the American commander had not applied, from the beginning, for the intervention of the neutral sovereign; that by having recourse to arms, to [*479] repel an unjust aggression of which he pretended to be the *object, he had himself failed to respect the Neutrality of the territory of the foreign sovereign, and had thereby released that sovereign from the obligation to afford him protection by any other means than that of pacific intervention; and that the Portuguese Government could not be held responsible for the result of the collision which took place in contempt of its rights of sovereignty, and in violation of the Neutrality of its territory, and without the local officers being required in proper time, to grant the necessary aid and protection.(*x*)

CCCLXXV. If a prize, which it is alleged was captured within neutral waters, be brought within the ports of the same Neutral, has the neutral jurisdiction to try *this* question? The answer seems to have been rightly given in the affirmative by the French *Conseil d'Etat.*(*y*)

Does the simple fact that the captured vessel, or cargo, belongs to the Neutral State within whose ports she is brought by the Belligerent as prize, found the jurisdiction of the Neutral over the prize?

This question is sometimes subdivided by jurists into two parts:

1. When the prize has been taken from a Neutral who is not the subject of the State into whose port the captor has brought the prize.

2. When the prize is taken from the Neutral who is the subject of that State.

It appears to the writer of these pages that in both cases the answer must be in the negative; the right of deciding whether a capture made *jure belli* on the high seas(*z*) be lawful or not is a part of the Right of War, and belongs only to a Belligerent. The Neutral may claim justice [*480] *in the Court of the Belligerent, or may refuse altogether, as we have seen, the right of asylum in his ports to any Belligerent bringing a prize.(*a*)

CCCLXXVI. Nevertheless, the affirmative of both these positions has found supporters among jurists of celebrity.

As to the first position—namely, when the prize has been taken from a Neutral who is not the subject of the State into whose port the captor has brought the prize,—it is maintained by Azuni,(*b*) that the captured

(*x*) Cong. Doc. 32nd Cong., 1st Sess., H. Rep. Ex. Doc., No. 53; 32nd Cong., 2nd Sess. Senate, Ex. Doc., No 24.

(*y*) De Pist. et Duver., l. i. p. 191, case of La Satanique contre l'Ary et Maria.

(*z*) That is directly, not incidentally, in a civil case of property, or the like.

(*a*) De Pist. et Duver., t. i. pp. 185-186. The Alerta, 9 Cranch's (Amer.) Rep., pp. 359, 364.

(*b*) T. ii. c. iv. s. 3.

ship may invoke the jurisdiction of the neutral Court; and Hübner(*c*) is, of course, of the same opinion.

On the other hand, Lampredi(*d*) is strongly of opinion that the captured Neutral is to all intents in the same predicament as the captured enemy, and that he is not justiciable in the neutral Court; and he cites a variety of Treaties in which this principle is recognized.

The doctrine and the practice of England, of the North American United States, and of France,(*e*) are in accordance with the opinion of Lampredi.

Spain has recognized it by an express law,(*f*) with the whimsical exception of a case in which one half of the value of the cargo of the captured ship belongs to Spaniards; in which event the prize is to be subject to Spanish Jurisdiction.

CCCLXXVII. With respect to the second position—namely, when the prize is taken from a Neutral who is the subject *of the State into whose port the captor has brought the prize; that in such [*481] a case the neutral Court has jurisdiction over the prize, is maintained in a qualified manner, as has been stated, by the Law of Spain, by Galiani,(*g*) and without any reservation by Azuni,(*h*) who relies upon several judgments of the Sardinian Courts. M. Merlin(*i*) appears to be of the same opinion, and thinks that he is supported in it by the authority of the *Ordonnance de la Marine of* 1681, (Arts. 14, 15.) And, as has been mentioned, the same doctrine is maintained by England and the North American United States.(*k*) On the other hand, Valin(*l*) is of a different opinion, and puts a different construction on the articles of the Ordonnance.

It appears also to be the doctrine upon which the French tribunals of prize intend to act during the present war. "Nous ne pensons pas, en effet" (say MM. De Pistoye and Duverdy,) "que la nationalité du capturé doive être une circonstance suffisante pour attribuer à une puissance neutre le pouvoir de juger de la validité de la prise faite sur un de ses nationaux et amenée dans ses ports. Il y a, en effet, pour donner à la nation neutre pouvoir de relaxer ses nationaux injustement capturés un autre principe qui, indépendamment de la question de validité ou d'invalidité de la prise, lui donne toute latitude. Chaque état est maître dans ses ports, et si l'humanité veut qu'on y admette les corsaires des parties belligérantes et leurs prises, la politique permet qu'on fasse alors payer, pour ainsi dire, le droit d'asile, ainsi que cela existe en France;(*m*) mais *la puissance neutre ne peut pas, parce qu'elle donne asile au capteur et au capturé qui est sien, usurper le droit de juger [*482]

(*c*) T. ii. c. i. s. 7.

(*d*) S. 14.

(*e*) "Quoi que l'on puisse dire contre cette opinion, il est certain qu'elle a été de tout temps celle du gouvernement Français et qu'elle a été constamment pratiquée pour les prises faites sous son pavillon."—Merlin, Rép., t. xiii. p. 143.

(*f*) Cédule Royale of 14 June, 1797, art. 7. Merlin, Rep., t. xiii. p. 145.

(*g*) Merlin, Rép., t. xiii. pp. 143-5. (Prise Maritime.)

(*h*) Ibid.

(*i*) Ibid.

(*k*) The Alerta, 9 Cranch's (Amer.) Rep., p. 359.

(*l*) Merlin, Rép., t. xiii. pp. 143-5. (Prise Maritime.) The Flad Oyen, 1 Rob., p. 135.

(*m*) V. art. 15, de l'Ordonnance de 1681, et ci-après, titre X.

de la validité de la prise; ce droit appartenant exclusivement, en vertu du droit de guerre, au gouvernement au nom duquel la capture a été faite."(n)

CCCLXXVIII. By the convention entered into between France and England during the present war, it is stipulated (Art. 3,) that in case of the capture of a merchant-vessel of one of the two countries, the adjudication of such capture shall always belong to the jurisdiction of the country of the captured vessel; and the cargo shall be dealt with, as to the jurisdiction, in the same manner as the vessel.

CCCLXXIX. 8. *Where must the captured property be at the time of condemnation?*

An attentive review of all the cases decided in the Courts of England and the North American United States, during the last war, leads to the conclusion that the condemnation of a Capture by a regular Prize Court, sitting in the country of the Belligerent, of a prize lying at the time of the sentence in a neutral port, is irregular, but clearly valid.(o) It appears to be the inclination of the English Prize Court, during the present war, to limit to cases of necessity the condemnation of vessels lying in a neutral port.(p) It is scarcely necessary to add, after what has been said as to the former French law on condemnations by Judges of the Belligerent in neutral ports, that such condemnations of vessels lying in neutral ports are holden valid by the French Prize Courts.

[*483] *CCCLXXX. Among the principal Treaties(q) which have altered, as between the contracting parties, the general International Law respecting the non-interference of Neutrals as to prizes brought into their ports, are the following:—

The Treaty of 1654 between England and Portugal, whereby prizes captured by either party, brought into the ports of their ally, are to be restored to their original owners.(r)

A Treaty to the like effect between Portugal and Holland in 1661.(s)

A Treaty between Portugal and France in 1797, whereby no prize of either party was to be sold in the ports of the other, and no privateers, except in cases of imminent peril, received.(t)

A Treaty between France and the North American United States in 1778, whereby no ship of the enemy of either party was allowed to sell her prize, or discharge her cargo, or buy more than provisions immediately indispensable in the ports of either party.(u)

A Treaty between the same parties in 1800, whereby no sale of prizes

(n) De Pistoye et Duverdy, Traité des Prises Maritimei, t. ii. p. 186.

(o) The Henrick and Maria, 4 Rob., p. 43. The Christopher, 2 Ib., p. 207. The Victoria, Edwards, p. 97. Hudson v. Guestier, 4 Cranch's (Amer.) Rep., p. 293. S. C., 6 Cranch's (Amer.) Rep. p. 281. The Arabella & Madeira, 2 Gallison's (Amer.) Rep., p. 368.

(p) The Polka, 1 Spink's Eccles. & Adm. Rep. (1854,) pp. 447-8.

(q) The earlier Treaties between England and the Dukes of Burgundy, and the Treaties between Christian and Algerine and Barbary States on this subject are not referred to in the text. See generally the catalogue of Treaties on this subject between all States. Traités de Commerce de H. et de Cussy, t. ix. p. 375, Prises et Reprises; and Manning, p. 368.

(r) Dumont, VI. t. ii. p. 84.

(s) Ib., p. 369.

(t) De Martens, Rec., t. vi. p. 414.

(u) Ib., t. ii. p. 597.

by either ally is allowed in the ports of the other, and privateers are limited to indispensable provisions.(x)

A Treaty between Holland and the North American *United States in 1782, whereby the sale of prizes brought by either party into the ports of the other was legalized.(y) [*484]

A Treaty between England and the North American United States in 1794, stipulating that prizes made by the enemies of either of the contracting parties shall not be received in their ports.(z)

A Treaty containing similar provisions between the same parties in 1806.(a)

A Treaty in 1829, between Holland and Columbia, allowing the entrance of prizes into their ports.(b)

A Treaty between Spain and Denmark, in 1742, authorizing the reception and sale of prizes in the ports of the respective parties.(c)

A Treaty between England and the Emperor of Germany, in 1795, whereby prizes made from either ally were forbidden to be sold in the ports of the other, and were to remain only twenty-four hours therein, under penalty of confiscation.(d)

CCCLXXXI. 9. *As to the forfeiture by misconduct of the Captor's title to Prize.*

Captors, whether in command of public or private ships of war, may forfeit their rights of prize by misconduct, and this independent of any statutable provision by the old-established law of the Admiralty;(e) and an obstinate neglect *or refusal to comply with the instructions of the Government, or the Regulations of the Prize Act, have been held sufficient to authorize an infliction of the forfeiture; and, in such case, the prize is condemned to the Government;(f) so the unlawful rescue of the prize by the Captors from the custody of the Court.(g) And where the claimant has not affected his property with a hostile character, as by a trade with the enemy, &c., but has been engaged in some other traffic contravening the municipal law of his own country, so that he cannot entitle himself to a restitution of the property, it will be condemned to the Government, and not to the captors.(h) [*485]

(x) Ib., t. vii. p. 108.

(y) De Martens, Rec., t. iii. p. 465. De H. et De C., Tr. de Comm., (2nd Part,) t. iii. p. 270, art. 1. See t. ix. p. 107, of this work, for the mode of reference to the different Volumes and Parts of it.

(z) De H. et De C., (2nd Part,) tom. iii. pp. 204, 5-8, art. 19.

(a) Ib., 228, art. 19. (b) Ib., (2nd Part,) tom. i. p. 369, art. 21.

(c) Ib., (2nd Part,) tom. i. p. 425, art. 3.

(d) De Martens, Rec. VI. lxxxii., art. 7.

(e) La Reine des Anges, Stewart, p. 9. The Cossack, ib., pp. 513-517. The Herkimer, ib., p. 128. S. C., 2 Hall's Am. Law Jour., p. 133. The Clarissa, cited in Stewart, p. 144; and 2 Hall's Am. Law Journ., p. 145. The Der Mohr, 3 Rob., p. 129. The Triton, 4 Ib., p. 78. The Barossa, note to the Woodbridge, 1 Haggard, p. 75. The Nemesis, Edwards, p. 50. With respect to the punishment of the misconduct of Privateers, vide post.

(f) The Bothnea & Janstoff, 2 Gallison's (Amer.) Rep., pp. 78, 92.

(g) The Cossack, Stewart, p. 513.

(h) The Walsingham Packet, 2 Rob. p. 77. The Etrusco, 4 Ib., 262, note (a). The Venus, 8 Cranch's (Amer.) Rep., pp. 277, 287.

[*486]

*CHAPTER V.

1. NON-COMMISSIONED CAPTORS.—2. JOINT CAPTURE.—3. CAPTURES BY TENDERS.

CCCLXXXII. A TREATISE upon International Law does not, perhaps, strictly speaking, require a further investigation of the subject of Maritime Capture than has been given in the preceding chapter; but there are certain outlying and collateral questions of a mixed public and International character, which it is the object of the present and following chapter to consider. In the present chapter it is proposed to consider questions relating to—

1. Non-commissioned Captors.
2. Joint Capture.
3. Captures by Boats and Tenders.

CCCLXXXIII. 1. As to Non-commissioned Captors. In cases of non-commissioned ships, and ships commissioned against one enemy, having no commission against another whose property is captured,(*a*) the Captors are not entitled to any share in the prize, and the property is to be condemned to the Government, or to its special grantee, if any such exist. Bynkershoek, indeed, contends, that if a non-commissioned ship is attacked, and captures the assailant in her defence, the officers and crew are solely entitled to the prize; and this doctrine seems also to be supported by Grotius.(*b*) However, the general Prize Law of France, [*487] Great Britain, and the *United States is as has been above stated.(*c*) If at the time of a Capture by a ship commissioned by letter of marque, the master of the capturing vessel be not on board, the Capture is considered as made without a commission, and it enures to the Government, or its special grantee;(*d*) and if a Capture be made by a cutter fitted out by a captain of a man-of-war as a tender,(*e*) and manned from his ship, but *without any authority or commission*, it is deemed to be made by a non-commissioned vessel, and the Capture will not enure to the benefit of the man-of-war. It would be otherwise if the tender were attached to the ship by public authority, for then, as has been said, the ship would share.(*f*) And if persons in the navy land from their ships and man a fort, and thereby compel a ship to strike as prize, it is considered as a Capture made at sea by a force upon land, which is a Non-commissioned Capture.(*g*) But it would be otherwise if

(*a*) Vide antè, vol. i. c. xx.

(*b*) Bynk., Q. J. Pub., l. i. c. xx. Du Ponceau's ed., pp. 155-161. Grotius, de J. B. et P., l. iii. c. vi. s. 10.

(*c*) Du Ponceau's Bynk., p. 162, note (*d*). 1 Valin sur. l'Ord., tom. i. p. 79. The Haase, 1 Rob., p. 286. The Rebeccah, 1 Ib., p. 227. The Amor Parentum, ib., p. 303. The Twee Gesuster, 2 Ib., p. 284, note (*a*). The Melomane, 5 Ib., p. 41. The Joseph, 1 Gallison's (Amer.) Rep., p. 545.

(*d*) The Charlotte, 5 Rob., p. 280. (*e*) Vide infra as to Tenders.

(*f*) The Melomane, 5 Rob., p. 41. The Charlotte, ib., p. 280. Capture of Curaçoa, 1 Dodson, p. 220, note (*a*). The Dos Hermanos, 2 Wheat. (Amer.) Rep., p. 76.

(*g*) The Rebeccah, 1 Rob., p. 227.

the place on shore were a resort for naval purposes by persons in the navy only, for then it would be deemed a stationary tender, rather attached to and dependent upon the vessels, than having the vessels attached to and dependent upon it.

CCCLXXXIV. In England, by very ancient grants from the Crown, the Lord High Admiral has the benefit of all Captures *made at sea by non-commissioned vessels;* and also of all Captures, by whomsoever made, of all ships and goods *coming, or already come, into ports, creeks, or roads of England and Ireland, by stress of weather or [*488] other accident, or by mistake of port, or by ignorance, not knowing of the war, and also of all derelicts. But the Crown has still reserved to itself all such ships and goods as shall be seized in port before any declaration of war or reprisals; and also all such as shall voluntarily come in, upon revolt from the enemy, and as shall be driven or forced into port by the King's men-of-war.(*i*) The office of the Lord High Admiral has for more than a century past been put in commission; but as the office is still considered to have a legal existence, though now residing in the person of the King, the rights and perquisites of that office are still distinguished as they were anciently, and are ascertained by an observance of the ancient rules, with the same exactness as if the proceeds were carried in the ancient and distinct course.(*k*) Hence arises the well-known distinction of condemnation to the King *jure coronæ*, and the King in his office of Admiralty, as *droits of Admiralty:* the former applying in all cases where the Crown is still entitled to the prize property, in virtue of its sovereignty and inherent prerogatives; the latter applying to all cases where the same belongs to the office of Lord High Admiral. Hence the appointment of an Advocate and Proctor to Her Majesty, in her office of Admiralty, distinct from the appointments of the Queen's Advocate and Queen's Proctor.

CCCLXXXV. In the North American United States, strictly speaking, there are no *droits* of Admiralty; for all prizes *to which no persons can entitle themselves by a public or private commission of [*489] war, are condemnable to the Government itself in its sovereign capacity.(*l*) But the phrase *Droits of Admiralty* is often used in the legal adjudications of the United States, as equivalent to condemnations to the United States, in virtue of their general sovereignty and prerogative, as enforced in the Courts of Admiralty.

But although non-commissioned persons cannot, by making a Capture, entitle themselves to the benefits of prize, yet, in all cases of condemnation as droits of Admiralty, where their conduct has been fair, the Prize Court will, in its discretion, award them a recompense; and even in some cases will award them the whole value of the prize, where there has

(*i*) The Rebeccah, 1 Rob., pp. 227, and 230, note (*a*). The Gertruyda, 2 Ib., p. 211. The Melomane, 5 Ib., p. 22. The Maria Françoise, 6 Ib., p. 282. The Joseph, 1 Gallison's (Amer.) Rep., p. 545. By 1 & 2 Vict. c. ii. s. 2, droits of Admiralty, with other hereditary revenues of the Crown, are transferred to the Consolidated Fund. As to receivers of, see 17 & 18 Vict. c. 120.

(*k*) The Gertruyda, 2 Rob., p. 211. The Maria Françoise, 6 Ib., p. 282.

(*l*) The Joseph, 1 Gallison's (Amer.) Rep., p. 545.

been great personal gallantry and merit.(*m*) It is not necessary to enumerate at large the various cases in which property is deemed a *droit* of Admiralty, or a prize to the Government *jure coronæ.* The preceding authorities will be found to contain almost all the learning on the subject.

CCCLXXXVI. 2. As to Joint Captures.—An accurate examination of the principles of Law applicable to this subject, requires that a distinction should be made between—

1. Private Ships of War, or Privateers.
1. Public Ships of War.

CCCLXXVII. 1. With respect to *Private Ships of War, or Privateers,* it is a general principle, that *no right* to share as Joint Captors accrues merely *by being in sight* at the time when the prize is captured:(*n*) there must be actual intimidation, or actual or constructive assistance.(*o*) And it may *be here observed, that the same
[*490] principle is applied to Captures in sight of fortresses, and of land forces and armies, for they do not share unless there be actual co-operation;(*p*) and in such cases the assistance ought to be material, in order to entitle the parties to share as Joint-Captors.(*q*)

CCCLXXXVIII. The reason of this rule in relation to Privateers is, that the being in sight is not sufficient with respect to them to raise the presumption of co-operation in the Capture. They clothe themselves with commissions of war from views of private advantage only. They are not bound to put their commissions in use on every discovery of an enemy; and, therefore, the court does not presume in their favour, from the mere circumstance of their being in sight, that they were there with a design of contributing assistance, and engaging in the contest. There must be, as to them, the *animûs capiendi* demonstrated by some overt act, by some variation of conduct, which would not have taken place but with reference to that particular object, and if the intention of acting against the enemy had not been entertained.(*r*) Formerly the principle of constructive assistance was carried a great way, but the later inclination of courts has been rather to *restrain than to extend the
[*491] rule;(*s*) and where no actual assistance is alleged, the presump-

(*m*) The Haase, 1 Rob., p. 286. The Amor Parentum, ib., p. 303.

(*n*) Bynk., Q. J. Pub., l. i. c. xviii.

(*o*) Ibid. And see a learned note of M. Du Ponceau, in his translation of Bynkershoek's Q. J. P., p. 144. Talbot v. Three Briggs, 1 Hall's Am. Law Journ., p. 266. S. C., 1 Dallas's (Amer.) Rep., p. 95. De Martens on Capt., sec. 32, p. 91. The Santa Brigada, 3 Rob., p. 52. The Forsigheid, Ib., p. 311. L'Amitié, 6 Ib., p. 261.

"I. Aucun ne pourra être admis au partage d'un vaisseau pris sur les ennemis, s'il n'a contribué à l'arrêter, ou contracté société avec celui qui s'en est rendu maître. II. Celui qui prétend partager un vaisseau ne sera point censé avoir contribué à l'arrêter, *s'il n'a combattu ou s'il n'a fait tel* effort qu'en intimidant l'ennemi par sa présence, ou en lui confrant chemin, et l'empêchant de s'échapper, il l'ait obligé à se rendre, sans qu'il lui suffise d'avoir *été en vue*, d'avoir donné chasse, lorsqu'il sera prouvé que cette chasse aura été inutile."—Règlement du 27 Janvier, 1706.

(*p*) Bynk., Q. J. Pub., l. i. ch. xviii. The Dordrecht, 2 Rob., p. 65.

(*q*) Ibid. (*r*) L'Amitié, 6 Ib., p. 261. La Flora, 5 Ib., p. 268.

(*s*) The Vryheid, 2 Rob., p. 16. The Odin, 4 Ib., p. 318. La Furieuse, Stewart, p. 177.

tion of Law leans in favour of the actual Captors.(*t*) But even with respect to Privateers, it is not necessary that a joint chaser should actually board a prize; it will be enough if there is the *animus persequendi* sufficiently indicated by the conduct of the vessel. The act of chasing, therefore, if continued for any length of time, and not abandoned at the time of Capture, will be sufficient to found a title of Joint-Capture;(*u*) but if the chase be discontinued, it is otherwise.(*x*) And if a ship has actually engaged another, and been beaten off, and yet remains in sight about the enemy, with an evident intention of persisting in the contest, and another vessel then comes up and makes the Capture, the first is entitled to share in the Capture.(*y*)

CCCLXXXIX. 2. With respect to *public* ships of war, public policy has introduced a different rule; and all such ships being in sight are deemed to be constructively assisting, and therefore entitled to share in the Capture.(*z*) The reason *of this distinction is, that public ships are under a constant obligation to attack the enemy wherever seen, and therefore, from the mere circumstance of being in sight, a presumption is sufficiently raised that they are there *animo capiendi*. [*492]

In the case of Privateers, the same obligation does not exist; the law, therefore, does not give them the benefit of the same presumption.(*a*) Where the actual Captor is a public armed ship, the rule is additionally supported by the obvious policy of promoting harmony in the service. But the rule equally applies where the actual Captor is a Privateer;(*b*) though the Privateer, in the converse case, is not entitled to share from merely being in sight.(*c*) There are exceptions, however, to the rule, where the circumstances of the case repel the presumption of the *animus capiendi:* such is the case where a public ship is in sight, but steering an opposite or different course inconsistent with the notion of an intent to capture.(*d*) But the mere sailing on a different course is not sufficient to defeat a title of Joint Capture; for it is not necessary that two ships should pursue the enemy in the same line. If one vessel sail in one direction, and the other in a different direction, with the purpose of capturing, that difference of course would not defeat a unity of purpose, nor destroy the claim of Joint Capture.(*e*) But if the ship

(*t*) The Robert, 3 Rob., p. 194. (*u*) L'Amitié, 6 Ib., p. 261.

(*x*) Ibid. The Waaksamheid, 3 Ib., p. 1. (*y*) La Virginie, 5 Ib., p. 124.

(*z*) The Dordrecht, 2 Ib., p. 55. The Robert, 3 Ib., p. 194. The Forsigheid, 3 Ib., p. 311. La Flore, 5 Ib., p. 268. The Bellona, Edw., p. 63. La Furieuse, Stewart, Vice Adm. Rep., p. 177. The Sparkler, 1 Dodson, p. 359.

"Si plusieurs vaisseaux ont part à une même prise,—*et par vaisseaux preneurs sont entendus ceux qui se seront trouvé ensemble et à vue de la prise lorsqu'elle aura été faite,*—ou faisant partie d'une même escadre, le montant de ce qui reviendra à chaque vaisseau, frégate et autre bâtiment de Sa Majesté, sera constaté sur la proportion du nombre de leur canons en batterie, et de leur calibre, à commencer par celui de quatre livres et au dessus, et du nombre d'équipage étant à bord de chaque vaisseau, et cette proportion ainsi établie, la repartition de ce qui reviendra à chaque vaisseau sera faite sur le pied qui est préscrit dans l'article précédent."—Ordonnance du Roi concernant les prises faites par les vaisseaux, frégates et autres bâtimens de S. M. du 15 Juin, 1757.

(*a*) La Flore, 5 Rob., p. 268. (*b*) Ibid.

(*c*) The Santa Brigada, 3 Ib., p. 52.

(*d*) The Robert, ib., p. 194. The Drie Gebroeders, 5 Ib., p. 339.

(*e*) Le Niemen, 1 Dodson, p. 9.

claiming as Joint Captor has changed her course and discontinued the chase before the Capture, the claim is defeated, unless this conduct be occasioned by the fraud or misconduct of the capturing ship; for then [*493] the Court will let in the claim with a view to punish the *fraud or misconduct.(*f*) So if the persons claiming as Joint Captors have reconnoitered the prize, and abandoned all design of Capture, they are not entitled to share.(*g*)

CCCXC. But even with regard to Public Ships of War,(*h*) cases of constructive assistance in Joint Capture are not to be extended, and therefore the Court requires that the ship should be actually in sight.(*i*) Therefore, being in sight a day or two before the Capture is not sufficient. It must be at the commencement of the engagement or chase, or during its continuance.(*k*) And being in sight when the enemy was first descried, and being detached *before* the chase or preparations, therefore, is not sufficient.(*l*) But it would be otherwise if detached in sight of the enemy at the moment of chase, and under preparation for chase; for there must be some actual contribution of endeavour as well as of general intention.(*m*) And it would seem to be very doubtful, whether the prize being seen from the mast-head would bring the case within the rule of being in sight.(*n*)

CCCXCI. And a like rule is applied to the capitulation of an island; for to entitle a public ship to share in the Capture, she must not be detached upon another service, but must be actually in sight at the time.(*o*)

[*494] CCCXCII. No *antecedent* or *subsequent* services in the expedition *will help the case where the party would not otherwise be entitled to share.(*p*)

CCCXCIII. In respect also to a *joint chase*, if both ships are in chase without any common co-operation, except such as the two parties acting separately, with a common object in view, might produce, and during the chase night comes on, and the enemy is lost sight of, and the ships still are in pursuit, but one of them cruising merely in search, and from conjecture adopts an erroneous course, and in consequence thereof the prize is captured either by the other, or by a third ship on the next day, out of sight, the ship so erroneously cruising is not entitled to share as a Joint Captor, for it is a discontinuance of the chase to change a course upon conjecture.(*q*) Nor will it vary the case that the position or course run by such ship had the effect of throwing the prize into the hands of the other ship, by inducing the prize to alter her course. It would, indeed, be an extravagant position to admit that every fleet or ship which,

(*f*) The Waaksamheid, 3 Rob., p. 1. The Robert, ib., p. 194. La Virginie, 5 Ib., p. 124. The Drie Gebroeders, ib., p. 339.

(*g*) The Lord Middleton, 4 Ib., p. 153. The Drie Gebroeders, 5 Ib., p. 339. L'Amitié, 6 Ib., p. 261.

(*h*) With respect to the mode of procedure in the Prize Courts in cases of joint capture vide post, chapter on the Prize Courts.

(*i*) The Vryheid, 2 Rob. p. 16. The Odin, 4 Ib., p. 318. La Furieuse, Stewart, p. 177.

(*k*) The Vryheid, 2 Rob., p. 16. (*l*) Ibid. (*m*) Ibid.

(*n*) The Robert, 3 Ib., p. 194. (*o*) The Island of Trinidad, 5 Ib., p. 92.

(*p*) The Buenos Ayres, 1 Dodson, p. 28.

(*q*) Le Niemen, ib., p. 9. The Financier, ib., p. 61.

either by accident or design, diverts the course of an enemy, and by so doing occasions her Capture by a totally distinct force, should be considered as a Joint Captor.(*r*)

CCCXCIV. It is certainly true that darkness preventing sight will not universally exclude from a right to share; nor can the rule be laid down universally the other way; for there may not in every case be evidence to show the proximity to the scene of action. Where it can be shown that the asserted Joint Captor was in sight when the darkness came on, and that she continued steering the same course by which she was before nearing the prize, and that the prize itself also continued the same course, it amounts almost to demonstration that the ships would have seen, and been seen by each other, at the time of Capture, if darkness had not *intervened, and, in such case, she ought to be let in to the benefit of Joint Capture.(*s*) [*495]

CCCXCV. But if the ship is lost sight of in the night, and the Capture is afterwards made at such a distance that the asserted Joint Captor would not at the time of Capture have been in sight even if it had been day, the claim of Joint Capture cannot be sustained. Lord Stowell has decided that where a ship is lost sight of in the night, the pursuit of that ship cannot properly be denominated a chase; it is a conjectural pursuit only; it is a feeling about in the dark, a search and inquiry, but no chase.(*t*) And where a ship is herself only a constructive Captor, it is not a sufficient ground to let in another ship that she had joined in a previous chase with the constructive Captor, and lost sight of the prize in the night.(*u*) Therefore, in a case where one or two joint chasers were ordered to pick up the boats of the other, and in consequence of the delay occasioned by her obedience to those orders she lost sight of the prize, which was in the meantime captured by a third ship coming up in the presence of the other, it was held that the ship so out of sight was not entitled to share.(*x*) A revenue cutter, though having a letter of marque, is not considered in England as a public ship of war entitled to the benefit of the rule of constructive assistance from being in sight.(*y*) A convoying ship, notwithstanding her special employment, may be entitled as a Joint Captor, if by chase or intimidation she aid in the Capture, when it does not interfere with convoy duty.(*z*)

CCCXCVI. 3. With respect to Capture made by *Boats*, it is a general rule that the ships to which they belong are entitled *to share.(*a*) But if a boat be detached from the ship to which she belongs, and attached to another, the ship only shares to which she is attached at that time; for she must be taken at that time, and in those operations, to be acting under the authority, and for the benefit of such ship only.(*b*) But constructive assistance by boats will not entitle the ships to which they belong to share in the prize, though actual Capture by the boats [*496]

(*r*) Le Niemen, ib., p. 9. (*s*) The Union, 1 Dodson, p. 346.
(*t*) The Financier, ib., p. 61. (*u*) Ibid. (*x*) Ibid.
(*y*) The Bellona, Edw., p. 63.
(*z*) The Waaksamheid, 3 Rob., p. 1. La Furie, ib., p. 9.
(*a*) The Anna Maria, 3 Rob., p. 211. The Odin, 4 Ib., p. 318.
(*b*) The Melomane, 5 Ib. p. 41.

would be sufficient for this purpose; for they are a part of the force of the ship. And in cases of mere constructive assistance the right of participation must be in proportion to the intimidation caused, and cannot go beyond the force actually seen by the enemy.(*c*) And it is extremely questionable whether a boat of a ship of war could support a title to share on the mere principle of being in sight. In the case of mere constructive Capture, the construction which is laid upon the supposed intimidation of the enemy, and the encouragement of the friend, from a ship of war being seen or in sight, applies very weakly to the case of a boat, an object that attracts very little notice upon the water, and whose character, even if discerned by either of the parties, may be totally unknown to both.(*d*) Nor will the fact that the ship to which the boat belongs is in sight, lying at anchor in a harbour, entitle the ship to share.(*e*)

CCCXCVII. The same principles apply to the case of *Tenders*.

A ship of war is entitled to share in all Captures made by a Tender
[*497] attached to her, however distant she may have been *at the time of Capture.(*f*) In order to support the averment of a ship being attached as a Tender, it must be shown either, (1.) that there had been some express designation of her as of that character by the orders of the Admiralty; or, (2.) that there had been a constant employment and occupation in a manner peculiar to Tenders, equivalent to an express designation, and sufficient to impress that character upon her.(*g*)

CCCXCVIII. In respect to Captures made by *ships which are associated in the same service*, or *engaged in a joint enterprise under the orders of the same superior officer*, it is a general rule that they are entitled to share in each other's prizes, made while in such service or joint enterprise.(*h*) Therefore, if one ship of a squadron takes a prize in the night, unknown to the rest, it will entitle the whole fleet to share, although, possibly, the Capture may have been made at a distance out of sight of most of the ships of war—even if it had been noon-day—for the fleet so associated is considered as one body, unless detached by orders, or entirely separated by accident; and what is done by one, continuing to compose in fact a part of the fleet, enures to the benefit of all.(*i*) Where a fleet is employed in a blockade, the service is considered as joint,
[*498] and all the ships are entitled to share in all Captures, although *all the ships have not joined in the chase, and the Capture has been made after the chase, at a great distance from the blockaded port.(*k*)

(*c*) La Belle Coquette, 1 Dodson, p. 18. The Odin, 4 Rob., p. 318. The Nancy, ib., p. 327, note (*a*).

(*d*) The Odin, ib., p. 318.

(*e*) Ibid. The Nancy, ib., p. 327, note (*a*). La Belle Coquette, 1 Dodson, p. 18.

(*f*) The Carl, (1853,) 2 Spink's Eccl. & Adm. Rep., p. 261.

(*g*) The Charlotte, 5 Rob., p. 580. See also the Melomane, ib., p. 41. The Island of Curaçoa and its Dependencies, (Lords, May 4th, 1805,) ib., p. 282, note (*a*). The Zepherina, 2 Haggard's Adm. Rep., p. 320. The Donna Barbara, ib., p. 373. The Charlotte, 1 Dodson, Adm. Rep., p. 220. The Ville de Varsovie, 2 Ib , p. 313. Two Piratical Gun Boats, 2 Haggard's Adm. Rep., p. 407. The Anna Maria, 3 Rob., p. 211.

(*h*) The Forsigheid, ib., p. 311. The Guillaume Tell, Edw., p. 6. The Empress, 1 Dodson, p. 368.

(*i*) The Forsigheid, 3 Rob., p. 311. S. C., Edw., p. 124.

(*k*) The Guillaume Tell, Edw., p. 6. The Forsigheid, Edw., p. 124.

But if a part of the fleet be detached on a separate service, or if the Capture be not within the purposes for which they were associated, then the rest of the fleet not actually or constructively assisting in the Capture, are not entitled to share.(*l*) And this rule applied to all detachments for some distinct and separate purpose, which, though possibly connected with the main service, carries the detached ships out of the scene of the common operations for the time.(*m*) But if they are only sent to look out, and they preserve their connection with the fleet, and maintain their dependence upon it, and keep within signal distance, this is not a detached service. It is more like stretching one of the arms of the fleet, without dissolving in any manner the connection between them and the main body.(*n*) In respect to transports, mere association in service is not sufficient to entitle them to share as constructive Joint Captors; but for this purpose they must actually acquire a military character, and must be employed in military operations, and there must be an *animus capiendi*, while so employed.(*o*) It is not sufficient that the enemy may have been intimidated by their presence. Mere intimidation may be produced without any co-operation having been given or intended. If a frigate were going to attack an enemy's vessel, and four or five large merchant-ships, unconscious of the transaction, should appear in sight, they might be objects of terror to the enemy, but no one would say that such terror would entitle them to share. *Though the fact of terror were ever so strongly proved, there would not be that co- [*499] operation which the law requires to entitle non-commissioned vessels to be considered as Joint Captors. But if non-commissioned ships chase *animo capiendi*, they are entitled to share if the Capture be made by their contributions in this service.(*p*)

CCCXCIX. 4. With respect to conjunct operation by Land and Sea Forces, how far the former are permitted to share in prizes made by the latter, where no express provision is made by statute, depends upon the circumstances of the case. A mere general co-operation in the same general objects would not be sufficient;(*q*) but an actual co-operation in the particular object is clearly sufficient.(*r*)

CCCC. If the fleet of an ally and our own fleet serve together under a commander, who detatches the squadron of the ally, the latter is not entitled to share in Captures subsequently made; but if an ally actually co-operates in effecting a Capture, he is entitled to a share as a Joint Captor. But the question whether he is a Joint Captor or not, is a question over which Courts of Common Law have no jurisdiction, and which belongs exclusively to the Admiralty.(*s*)

CCCCI. By the convention(*t*) entered into between France and Eng-

(*l*) Ibid., 3 Rob., p. 311. The Nordstern, cited in the Forsigheid, Edw., pp. 124, 126, 127. S. C., 1 Acton, p. 128. The Island of Trinidad, 5 Rob., p. 92. The Stella del Norte, ib., p. 349.

(*m*) The Forsigheid, 3 Ib., p. 311.

(*n*) Ibid.

(*o*) The Cape of Good Hope, 2 Ib., p. 274.

(*p*) The Twee Gesuster, and Le Franc, cited in 2 Rob., pp. 284, 285, notes (*a*) (*b*).

(*q*) The Stella del Norte, 5 Ib., p. 349.

(*r*) Ibid. The Dordrecht, 2 Ib., p. 55.

(*s*) Duckworth v. Tucker, 2 Taunt., p. 7.

(*t*) May 20th, 1854.

land during the present war, it is stipulated (Art. 1,) that when a Joint [*500] Capture shall be made by the *naval forces of the two countries, the adjudication thereof shall belong to the jurisdiction of the country whose flag shall have been borne by the officer having the superior command in the action.

And (Art. 2,) when a Capture shall have been made by a cruiser of either of the two allied nations, in the presence and in the sight of a cruiser of the other, such cruiser having thus contributed to the intimidation of the enemy and the encouragement of the Captor, the adjudication thereof shall belong to the jurisdiction of the actual Captor.

CCCCII. In case of Joint Captures by public ships, the rule as to the proportion in which they are to share is established generally by statute. It is enacted by the present Prize Statute, that "before condemnation no claim on behalf of any asserted Joint Captor shall be admitted until security shall have been given by or on behalf of such asserted Joint Captor to contribute to the actual Captor his proportion of the expenses, costs, and damages that may be incurred by or awarded against the actual Captor on account of the capture and detention of the said ship, vessel, goods, or merchandise; and after final condemnation no such claim shall be admitted until the asserted Joint Captor has paid his proportion of all such expenses as shall have attended the obtaining the final condemnation, and unless he show sufficient cause to the Court why such claim was not asserted at or before the return of the monition: provided always, that nothing herein contained shall extend to the asserted interest of any flag-officer claiming to share in any prize by virtue of his flag."(*u*) In the North American United States the proportion is fixed by the Act of the 22d April, 1800, c. 33, which provides that the capturing ships shall share "according to the number of men and guns on board each ship in sight." In respect to privateers, no statute [*501] regulation exists; and by *the general rule of the Prize Law, they are to share in proportion to their relative strength.(*x*) This relative strength is, by the Law of Great Britain and the United States, ascertained by the number of men on board of such ship assisting in the Capture.(*y*) Such, too, is the rule where an ally co-operates in the Capture.(*z*) And the same rule seems applicable to the case of a Joint Capture by a public ship and a private ship of war, and this whether the latter be commissioned or not.(*a*)

For the Law of France upon this subject, see Merlin, Rep., t. xiii. pp. 156-162. "XIV. Il faut (he says,) sur cette matière, distinguer trois cas: celui où les prises ont été faites par les vaisseaux de l'Etat, agissant avec ou sans le concours de corsaires particuliers; celui où elles ont été faites par des corsaires particuliers agissant isolément; et celui où elles ont été faites, soit par les vaisseaux de l'Etat, soit par des corsaires particuliers, avecle concours des garnisons de forts et batteries de terre ou des préposés des douanes."

(*u*) 17 V., c. 18.

(*x*) Bynk., Q. J., l. i. c. xviii.

(*y*) Roberts v. Hartley, Doug., p. 311. The Dispatch, 2 Gallison's (Amer.) Rep., p. 1.

(*z*) Duckworth v. Tucker, 2 Taunt., p. 7.

(*a*) The Twee Gesuster, 2 Rob., p. 284, note (*a*). Le Franc, ib., p. 285, note (*b*).

*CHAPTER VI. [*502]

POSTLIMINIUM.—RECAPTURE.—RANSOM.

CCCCIII. THE *jus postliminii*(*a*) of the Roman Law related to *persons* and to *things*.

I. With respect to the former, the *person* who was liberated from prison, and who returned to his country, had a right to be replaced in his original legal *status*. It was said of him, "*pristinum jus suum recipit*," or "*postliminium fingit eum qui captus est, in civitate semper fuisse*."(*b*) This *jus postliminii* had a double effect:(*c*) partly of a *passive* character, inasmuch as in some instances it replaced the returned person within the dominion of the right of another person; as, for instance, the returned son fell again under the power of his parent, the returned slave under the power of his master. To produce this *passive* effect, the only requisite was the simple *return* of the individual. But to produce the *active* effect, the *jus postliminii* required that the individual should have returned *for the purpose* of regaining his rights; that he should not have been *abandoned* by his country; that he should not have been the subject of a *deditio*, either during *war*, or at the time of making *peace*. The *jus postliminii* was denied to those who illegally returned to their country during an armistice, to deserters, and to those who had surrendered in battle.

II. With respect to *things*. The Roman Law considered things taken by the enemy as withdrawn from the category of *legal relations during the period of the enemy's possession of them; but they [*503] were restored to this category when they were recovered, either by the State to which the original proprietor belonged, or immediately by the original proprietor himself. In the *former* case, they were considered as booty, or prize of war, and the original right of property was holden to have been extinguished by the intervening hostile possession; with certain exceptions, indeed, which included parcels of territory, horses, mules, and ships used for purposes of war. To these *things* the *jus postliminii* was accorded.(*d*)

CCCCIV. It will be seen, that this maxim of Roman policy has not been engrafted into modern International Law. But, generally speaking, the *jus postliminii* is fully recognized by that law(*e*) as an incident to the state of war; it is a right which, strictly speaking, belongs exclusively to war. The recognition of this right by International Law, has a tendency to mitigate the necessary evils of war; and it is a true general proposition of that law, that property captured by the enemy and recaptured by the fellow-subjects, or allies, of the original owner, does not

(*a*) Dig. 49, 15, 19, De Capt. et Postlim. X. 4 §§ 5–1, Quibus mod. jus. pot. solv.
(*b*) Inst., i. 12, 5.
(*c*) Puchta. Instit., II. 499–500, § 220, (*a*); 324–5, § 223, (*m. q.*) 637, § 241, (2).
(*d*) Puchta. Instit., II. 687, §§ 241, 2.
(*e*) Kent's Comm., vol. i. p. (108,) 115.

become the property of the recaptor, as if it had been a new *booty* or *prize*, but it must be restored *jure postliminii*, upon certain conditions, to the original owner.

It is to be observed, that this right cannot be enforced in Neutral States; because, as we have seen, the Neutral is bound to consider each Belligerent as equally just in his position and demands; and it follows, that he looks upon the acquisitions of both parties as equally lawful; unless, indeed, it has been accompanied by an infringement of neutral territory or neutral rights. It is only, therefore, within the territory or jurisdiction of the Captor or his ally,(*f*) that the *jus postliminii* can accrue.

[*504] *CCCCV. As to *persons*, a different principle is applicable. While, indeed, they remain on board the Captor's ship, or within the Captor's army, they are, by a recognized international custom, *without* the neutral jurisdiction :(*g*) but if they are found on shore, and not within the military lines, then the *jus postliminii* with respect to them may be protected by the Neutral.(*h*)

CCCCVI. We have now to consider the doctrine of the *jus postliminii*, according to the doctrine of International Law,(*i*) and its application to *movable* and *immovable* property captured in war; a distinction, it may be observed, deeply rooted in both branches of International Law, public and private.

With respect to *movable* property or *prize* captured in a war by *sea*, all such property is vested in the Captor. If he part with them to a Neutral, the former proprietor is not entitled to claim them. But such things must be actually and truly in the enemy's power; whether the criterion of their being so be, according to the standard of some authors, twenty-four hours' possession, or, according to the standard of others, the *deductio infra præsidia*, that is, within the army, fleet, towns, or ports of the belligerent Captor.

This latter standard appears to the writer of these pages the best warranted by practice and reason. Vattell, however, inclines to the standard of twenty-four hours.

Upon the question of recaptures of *booty* on *land*, as of recaptures of [*505] *prize* at *sea*, by the *fellow-countryman* of the original proprietor, there may of course be, and in many *instances there are, private or municipal regulations of individual States.

With respect to *immovable* property captured in war, the established doctrine of International Law may now be said to be, that the acquisition of it is not holden to be completed before (1.) either the territory in which it is situated has by submission, and consequent extinction, of its national personality, become incorporated in the possessions of the conqueror; or (2.), what is a much safer title to property so acquired, before

(*f*) Vattel, l. iii. c. 14, ss. 207, 8. L'Amistad de Rues, 5 Wheaton's Amer. Rep., p. 390. (*g*) Vide anté vol. i. pp. 366, 7.

(*h*) 1 Kent, p. (109,) 116. Vattel, l. iii. c. vii. s. 132. Bynk., Q. J. P., l. i. c. xv. See note to M. Duponceau's translation, pp. 116, 117.

The classical reader may consult the provisions on this subject in the commercial Treaty between Rome and Carthage, Polyb. III. c. iii.

(*i*) Vattel, l. iii. cc. xiii–xiv.

a Treaty of Peace has recognized and ratified the possession of the conqueror. Further observations upon the whole subject will be found in the latter part of this volume, where the effect of Peace upon *Prize* and *Booty*, concerning which no provision is made in the Treaty which establishes the Peace, is discussed.

CCCCVII. Having considered the law applicable to the retaking of movable and immovable property captured during the course of hostilities carried on by land, it remains to examine the question of property retaken at sea.

A prize taken from the enemy who had taken it, is called in our language a *Recapture*,(*k*) and the law respecting it requires a particular consideration.

The best mode of dealing with this subject appears to be—First, to consider the general principle of International Law respecting it.

Secondly. The Private or Municipal Laws of States upon this subject.

Thirdly. The decisions of Prize Courts—more especially those of England and the North American United States, *which are [*506] in principle and practice almost identical, and which constitute a complete code upon the subject of Recapture as of Capture.

CCCCVIII. First. As to the general principles of International Law upon the subject.

The sources from which these principles are derived were specified in the beginning of the present work,(*l*) and they are assumed to have been correctly specified in this and in other discussions arising in the course of this work, in which discussions the particular subject requires that these sources should be, and indeed presumes that they are, carefully remembered by the reader,—

" . . . . si prava est regula prima,"
*   *   *   *   *
"Omnia mendosè fieri, atque obstipa necessum est."(*m*)

In the observations which follow as to *Recapture*, it is of course taken for granted that the *first* Capture has been completed according to the mode specified in the former chapter, and up to the time of the *Recapture*, the title of the original proprietor has been entirely divested.

CCCCIX. As to general principles of International Law upon Recapture, it is remarkable, that of all the ancient codes of Maritime Law,—such as the Consolato del Mare, the Rôle des jugements d'Oleron, the laws of Wilsby, the ancient statutes of the cities of Hamburg, Lubeck, Bremen, and the League of the Hanse Towns,—the Consolato del Mare alone deals with the case of Recaptures.

(*k*) In Latin, *Recuperatio;* in French, *Reprise* or *Recousse;* in Italian, *Ripresa;* in Spanish, *Recobro;* in German, *Wiedereroberung* or *Wiedernehmung;* in Dutch, *Hernoomen Schepen.*

The authorities principally relied upon by me on the subject of Recapture, are De Martens, Essai concernant les Armateurs, les Prises, et surtout les Reprises, à Gottingue, 1795. Translation by T. Hartwell Horne, London, 1801. The recent work, already cited, of MM. De Pistoye et Duverdy.

(*l*) Vol. I., chapters iii-viii.

(*m*) Lucretius, de Jure Nat., l. iv. pp. 516—19.

[*507] That venerable authority declares,(*n*) in article *a*, chapter 287, that if a ship and its cargo, taken by an enemy, *are retaken by a friendly ship, the Recaptor ought to restore this property to those who are on board the ship, if there is any person still alive, as a reward for the expenses and trouble of salvage, which shall be estimated according to the expenses and trouble occasioned by the Recapture; that if, on the contrary, the enemy had already conducted it into a place of safety, the ship and merchandise shall belong wholly to the Recaptor.

That if he who has taken the prize abandons it in sight, and for *fear* of an hostile ship, which becomes master of it, it shall be restored to the proprietors in consideration of a similar reward.(*o*)

That if he who has taken the prize abandons it *voluntarily*, and after having taken out of it what pleased him most, and, afterwards, the ship abandoned is recaptured, the Recaptor shall restore it to the first proprietor for a reward; and, if there is no proprietor, it shall be used as a treasure trove,(*p*) which is disposed of by the 157th and 249th articles, or rather chapters.

That if, finally, the ship taken is either ransomed of the enemy, or is ransomed of others, or purchased out of the enemy's hands, we are to distinguish whether the ship was already in a place of safety or not. In the first place, the purchaser shall keep it without restoring it; in the second, the ransomer or purchaser shall be obliged to offer it to the proprietor, in consideration of his restoring him the value or ransom, and a reward, if, at the time of the ransom, the enemy was already master of the ship in such a manner that there were no other means of saving it.(*q*)

[*508] *Lord Stowell remarks(*r*) upon the first of the articles or chapters cited, viz., the 287th, that the doctrine of the *perductio infra prœsidia*, *infra portum tutum*, as constituting a sufficient conversion of property, is expressed therein in terms, indeed, not very intelligible in themselves, but which are satisfactorily explained by Grotius,(*s*) and by his commentator Barbeyrac, in his notes upon that article.(*t*) Bynkershoek lays it down to the same effect in these words: "Sane in libro, quæ inscribitur Consulatus Maris, c. 287, ita, ut modo dicebam, res definita est: nam is, qui navem et onus ab hoste recuperavit, jubetur

(*n*) "*Di nave pigliata e recuperata.* Nave che sarà stato pigliato per suoi nimici, se alcun altra nave d' amici si riscontrerà con i detti nimici, e torrà la detta nave, *quella* e tutto quello che in quella sarà, debba esser ristaurato à quello, ò quelli, di chi sarà, ed essere debbe, *se alcuno vivo ci sarà:* quel imperò dando à quelli, che à i detti nimici solta haveranno, *beveraggio* conveniente secondo la fatica, e secondo il danno, che ne haveranno sofferto. Imperò, se i detti amici torrano, ò haveranno tolta la detta nave, ò navillio à i detti nimici in loco, dove la tenessero à sè, e in loco sicuro, non ne debba esser datto beveraggio, se loro vorranno; anzi debba essere del tutto di loro, senza contrasto," &c.

(*o*) Consolato del Mare, n. 1. (*p*) Ibid., n. 5. (*q*) Ibid., n. 6, 7.

(*r*) The Ceylon, 1 Dodson's Adm. Rep., p. 106.

(*s*) "Cui consequens esse videtur, ut in mari naves, et res aliæ, captæ censeantur tum demum, cum in navalia aut portus, aut ad eum locum ubi tota classis se tenet, perducta sunt: nam tunc desperari incipit recuperatio, sed recentiori jure gentium inter Europæos populos introductum videmus, ut talia capta censeantur ubi *per horas viginti quatuor* in potestate hostium fuerint."—Grotius, de Jure Belli ac Pacis, l. iii. cap. vi. s. 3.

(*t*) Lib. i. cap. 5.

navem et onus restituere pristino domino, salvo tamen servaticio, idque servaticium ut justum sit, constituitur pro modo operæ et impensæ in recuperationem factæ, præteritâ omni distinctione, quamdiu navis onusque in potestate hostium fuerint. Rectè autem ibi additur, eam restitutionem duntaxat obtinere, si navis nondum fuerit deducta in locum tutum, sed si in locum tutum, dominio sic plane et plene in hostem translato, navem mercesque deinde recuperatas, ex asse recuperatori cedere. Quæ apprime conveniunt cum his, quæ hoc capite disputavimus. Vellem omnia, quæ in illâ farragine legum nauticarum reperiuntur, æquè proba recta essent, sed non omnia ibi sunt tam bonæ frugis." Grotius,(*u*) expresses himself very much to the same effect, and Loccenius,(*x*) considers this rule as the general law of Europe.

*CCCCX. The subject of Capture and Recapture is admirably discussed by Bynkershoek.(*y*) The maxim of the Roman Law, [*509] "si quid bello captum est, in *prædâ* est, not *postliminio* redit,"(*z*) was, as we have seen by that law, not applicable to Ships of War. Such retained the privileges of postliminy, others did not.

Bynkershoek, however, agrees with Grotius that *movable* goods are now, without distinction, subjects of Prize, and divested of the privileges of postliminy. As goods captured from the enemy, he argues, vest in the Captor, it follows, when recaptured, they vest in the Recaptor. He then considers when such goods have *pleno jure* become the Captor's property. Clearly, in his opinion, if taken *infra præsidia* of the enemy, the property has been vested in the Captor. But what are *præsidia?* Those of the ally as well as of his ally; though the States General of his country decided, incorrectly, otherwise. In his opinion, too, the bringing the Capture *infra præsidia* of a Neutral suffices to change the property. He does not lay down the doctrine which, we have seen, is now well established in the Prize Courts of England, and of the North American United States, namely, the necessity of a sentence of condemnation by the Captor's tribunal on the Capture, which may be lying in the port of the Captor, the Ally, or the Neutral.

But into one of these ports it must be brought, if recaptured before the property has vested neither in the Captor nor the Recaptor. But has the original owner a right to receive back his property, paying no remuneration to the restorer of it? Certainly not,—on the principles of natural justice, and on the analogies of the Roman Law, into which these principles are so often transcribed, the Recaptor is entitled to a *servaticium,* as salvage reward. What considerations *shall govern the amount of the reward? First. Public policy requires that the award [*510] should be made with a liberal and not a grudging hand. Secondly, The amount of labour, of danger, of time, of cost expended on the Recapture should be duly weighed. Thirdly. The value of the recaptured

(*u*) Lib. iii. cap. 6.

(*x*) "Hodie naves ab hoste captæ, communi inter Christianos et Europæos populos sive jure sive consuetudine postliminio non recipiunter, si hostis eas non eodem die navali pugnâ iterum amisit, sed per viginti quatuor horas in potestate victoris fuerint. Tunc enim verè captæ, et proprii juris factæ censentur."—Loccenius, de Jure Maritimo, lib. ii. c. iv. s. 4.

(*y*) Q. J. P., l. i. cc. iv, v.

(*z*) Dig., 49, 15, 28, De Capt. et Postlim.

property; and in applying these principles of allotment, it matters not whether, according to ancient usage, a part of the recaptured property, or, according to modern usage, a sum of money, be awarded.

No writer has more completely exhausted the general reasoning applicable to this subject than Bynkershoek.

CCCCXI. Secondly. *As to the Private or Municipal Laws of States.*

The Law of France upon the subject of Recapture (*Reprise, Recousse,*)(*a*) is to be found in an Arrêté du 2 Prairial an XI. Article 54, which is a reproduction of the Ordonnances of 1681. It provides different regulations for Recaptures made by (1.) Privateers, and for those made by (2.) Public Ships of War. 1. As to the former, the law is that if a *French* or an *allied* vessel be recaptured from the enemy, after she has been twenty-four hours in the enemy's possession, she shall become the sole property (*en totalité*) of the Privateer; but if the Recapture be made before the twenty-four hours have elapsed, he shall be entitled to only a third of the value of the recaptured ship and cargo.(*b*)

If the Recapture be made by a Public Ship of War (*bâtiment de l'Etat,*) she shall be restored to her original proprietors, on payment to the recapturing crew of the thirtieth part of her value, if the twenty-four hours have not elapsed; and of [*511] *the tenth part if they have elapsed: all the expenses incident to the Recapture to be borne by the recaptured vessel.

The French Law, therefore, makes the profit of the Recaptor depend (1.) partly upon *the time* during which the captured vessel has been taken; (2.) partly on the character of the Recaptors;(*c*) (3.) partly also on the character of the Captors from whom it is recaptured. For instance, if a ship or goods be *recaptured* from a pirate, the Recaptors shall be entitled, as *frais de recousse,* to a third of the value of the ship and cargo, and the remainder shall be resorted to the original proprietor, if he be a subject or an ally.(*d*)

(*a*) "Ces mots *reprise* ou *recousse* sont synonymes: on appelle aller à la recousse d'un navire, courir, après le vaisseau que s'en est emparé, dans l'intention de l'enlever lui-même avec sa prise, ou du moins de l'obliger d'abandonner cette prise pour la lui arracher. La reprise ou recousse doit se faire en observant les mêmes règles qu'une prise directe."—De Pist. et Duverd., II. t. vii. p. 105.

(*b*) A renewal of Art. 61, of the Ordonnance of 1584.

(*c*) The Old law, Art. 61, Ord. 1584, made no difference between public and private ships of war. The omission of the former in the new law was intentional, and before its enactment the French, like the Spanish Crown, had been in the habit of remitting the salvage-profit due to public ships of war.—Ib., p. 107.

(*d*) "2 Prairial an XI., Art. 51. Seront de bonne prise tous bâtiments commandés par des pirates, forbans, ou autres gens courant la mer sans commission spéciale d'aucune puissance.

"Art. 52. Tout bâtiment combattant sous autre pavillon que celui de l'Etat dont il a commission, ou ayant commission de deux puissances différentes, sera aussi de bonne prise; et s'il est armé en guerre, les capitaines et officiers seront punis comme pirates."

"Loi du 10 Avril, 1825, Art. 10. Le produit de la vente des navires et bâtiments de mer capturés pour cause de piraterie sera réparti conformément aux lois et règlements sur les prises maritimes. Lorsque la prise aura été faite par des navires du commerce, ces navires et leurs équipages seront, quant à l'attribution et à la répartition dù produit, assimilés à des bâtiments pourvus de lettres de marque et à leurs équipages."—De Pist. et Duverdy, Traité des Prises Maritimes, pp. 52, 3.

The Law applicable to the Recapture of a French vessel, is equally applicable, as has been shown by the terms of the *Arrêté* of the 2nd Prairial, cited above, to the Recapture of the vessel of an ally.

But a difference subsists between the English Practice and the French Law on this subject. It is said by MM. De Pistoye and Duverdy, that France, during the present war, will apply to Recaptures made by French vessels of English ships taken by Russian Captors (a case which has *not happened at present) the 34th article of the Treaty of Commerce, concluded between France and England on the 26th September, 1786. [*512]

It may well be that the provisions of this Treaty may furnish a reasonable analogy to guide the practice of the French Prize Courts, but it cannot be upon the ground suggested by MM. De Pistoye and Duverdy, viz., that this article of the Treaty is still in force.(*e*) The third article of the Convention, 16th May, 1854, says, "In cases of the Capture of a merchant vessel of one of the two countries, the adjudication of such Capture shall always belong to the jurisdiction of the country of the captured vessel; the cargo shall be dealt with, as to the jurisdiction, in the same manner as the vessel." But it is silent as to Recaptures.

If a ship belonging to the King's allies or subjects is recaptured from a pirate, it shall be restored to the proprietors in consideration of one-third for the recovery of it, independently of the time during which it may have been in the enemy's hands.(*f*)

And if the ship, without being recaptured, is abandoned by the enemy, or if, by tempest or other chance, it returns into the possession of French subjects, previously to having been conducted into an hostile port, it shall be resorted to *the proprietor, although it may have been more than twenty-four hours in the enemy's hands.(*g*) [*513]

CCCCXII. The law of Spain(*h*) agree almost entirely with those of France on the subject of Recaptures belonging to Spanish subjects, made by privateers, so that if a legitimate prize is recaptured before it has been twenty-four hours in the enemy's hands, it shall be restored to the known proprietor, in consideration of one-third for the Recapture,(*i*) but after that period it shall belong wholly to the recaptor. As to Recaptures made by the King's ships, the Ordinance of 1633,(*k*) declares

(*e*) De Pist. et Duverdy, Traités des Prises Maritimes, p. 120. De Martens, Essai, p. 161, § 60. Edit du Roi concernant la Juridiction de l'Amirauté du Mois de Mars, 1584. Art. 61. Ordonnance de la Marine, 1681, tit des Prises. Art. 8. Ordonnance sur les Reprises faites par les Vaisseaux de S. M., June 15, 1779. Ordonnance du 15 Juin, 1779. Ordonnance du 9 Janv., 1780. Valin, Traité des Prises, p. 88. Emerigon, Traité d'Assurances, chap. xii. s. 23, p. 495.

(*f*) Ordonnance de la Marine, 1681, tit. des Prises, art. 10. Cf. De Pist. et Duverd., t. i. p. 51.

(*g*) Ordonnance de la Marine, 1681, tit. des Prises, art. 9. As to whether, in this case, the third part may be demanded for the recovery, compare Valin, Traité des Prises, p. 101, who maintains the affirmative, and Amerigon, l. c. 24, p. 503, who defends the negative.

(*h*) De Martens, Essai, p. 169, § 62, Horne's Translation.

(*i*) Ord. of 1621; Ord. of 1718, art. 10; Ord. of 1779, art. 23. The case, however, of a ship which may have been laden with *contraband commodities*, or which may have sailed for the mere *pleasure* of those who might be on board it, is excepted.

(*k*) Ordinance respecting the Conduct of the Royal Fleet, chap. 397.—Abreu y Bertodano Collecion de los Tratados, Phil. IV. P. II. p. 371.

that property belonging to persons who are known, ought to be restored immediately, unless it has been in the possession of the enemy for twenty-four hours.

If a ship has been abandoned by the enemy,(*l*) or if a tempest, or any other *vis major*, cause it to fall into the hands of the King's subjects before it has been brought into any hostile port, it shall be restored to the first proprietor, even although the enemy should have had it in his power more than twenty-four hours.

But with respect to ships recaptured from pirates, a strange and reprehensible regulation occurs in the Spanish laws; namely, that these Recaptures also shall belong to the privateer, if the pirate has had them in his possession during twenty-four hours.(*m*) With regard to the [*514] rights of *foreign Powers, it must be observed, that though the Ordinances of 1621 and 1718, mention only Recaptures belonging to the King's subjects, and the Ordinance of 1633, for the regulation of the royal fleet, directs only vaguely the restitution of what belongs to persons who are known, the Ordinance of 1st July, 1779, respecting cruising,(*n*) puts foreigners upon the same footing as the King's subjects, directing that the ships of neutral or allied subjects, which the enemy's privateers may have captured, shall be restored to the proprietors, together with their cargoes, if the Recapture has been made before twenty-four hours, in consideration of a *servaticium* of one-third of the value, which shall be given to the recaptor.

CCCCXIII. There have been many and great variations in the laws promulgated by the States-General of the United Provinces of the Low Countries(*o*) on the subject of Recaptures.(*p*) The Ordinance of the States-General of the 14th July, 1625, declares, that if the ship is retaken before it has been twenty-four hours in the enemy's hands, the privateer that makes the Recapture shall have one-eighth; if it be retaken before it has been twice twenty-four hours in the enemy's hands, he shall have one fifth; and if it be recaptured later still, one-third; this has, by another Ordinance of the 22nd July, 1625, been also extended to Recaptures made by *public ships of war*. But the Ordinance of 11th of March, 1632, enacts, that without regard to the time, whether more or less extended, of the Recapture, there shall be two-thirds adjudged to *the privateer* who makes the Recapture. Another Ordinance of the 1st September, 1643, brings the matter back to the Ordinances of 1625; but the Ordinance of 8th February, 1645, introducing anew the regulations of that of 1632, adding, that for want of an amicable arrangement between the first proprietor and the recaptor, concerning the fixing of [*515] the value of the ship and cargo, the Courts of Admiralty *shall decide it. Another Ordinance of 19th April, 1659, without making any distinction between the time and quality of the captor,

(*l*) Ordinance of 1718, art. 2.

(*m*) Ordinance of 1621, art. 10; Declaration of 22nd December, 1624. In the Ordinance of 1718, art. 7 and 12, there is an apparent contradiction on this point, which M. D'Abreu, Traité des Prises, p. 15, endeavours to reconcile; but the Ordinance of 1779 leaves no doubt on this subject.

(*n*) Art. 24. (*o*) De Martens, Essai, p. 197, § 66, Horne's Translation.

(*p*) Bynk., Q. J. Pub., l. i. c. v.

requires him to be content with one-ninth of the vessel and cargo.(*q*) The Ordinance of 13th of April, 1677, directs, with respect to *privateers*, that if the Recapture, the ship or cargo, has not been forty-eight hours in the enemy's hands, there shall be assigned to them, in lieu of all claim to salvage, one-fifth (voor borgloon;) if it has been more than forty-eight hours, and less than ninety-six hours, in the hands of the enemy, one-third; and beyond that, one-half. With respect to Recaptures made by *ships of war*, that Ordinance confirms the ancient laws, without specifying which; it seems, however, that we must understand by these ancient laws the Ordinance of 1659, which had annulled all anterior laws.

The Edict of the States-General, concerning the rewards for privateers, of the 6th June, 1702, Art. 8; that of 1747, Art. 7; that of 1781, Art. 7; and that of 1793, Art. 7, declare together, that if any ship or goods belonging to the inhabitants of those States should be taken by the enemy, and retaken, by any privateer, ship, or other vessel fitted out at the private expense of the inhabitants of those States, the recaptor shall enjoy, if the Recapture be made within forty-eight hours, one-fifth; if it be made within ninety-six hours, one-third; and after that, one-half. These laws are therefore conformable to the regulation of that of 1677, but they make no mention of Recaptures made by ships of war belonging to the State, with respect to which it seems that the Regulation of 1659 is still applicable.(*r*)

All these laws, both ancient and modern, relate only to Recaptures belonging to the State's subjects; they contain no regulation respecting those which may be the Enemy's *property, unless it is that which the Edict of the 28th July, 1705, Art. 18, directs, that as to the Recaptures of allied and neutral ships, privateers shall be content with what has been, or shall be, agreed on with them. This arrangement, however, which in other respects is very insufficient, on account of the very few conventions that subsist concerning it, has not been renewed in the Edicts of 1781 and 1793.(*s*) *[516]

CCCCXIV. With respect to Denmark,(*t*) the code of laws of Christian V. directs, that if a privateer recaptures a Danish ship, he becomes proprietor of it when that ship has been twenty-four hours in the enemy's hands;(*u*) if the Recapture is made before that period, it shall be divided

(*q*) Both De Martens, and his translator Horne, have here mis-translated Bynkershoek. The mis-translation is corrected in the text.

(*r*) Besides, the officers and seamen who are on board the ships of war, have as extensive a claim on their recaptures as privateers.—Edict of 6th June, 1702, art. 7; Edicts of 1747, 1781, 1793, art. 6.

(*s*) Recueil van Zeezaken, D. III., p. 348.

(*t*) De Martens, Essai, p. 204, § 68, Horne's Translation.

(*u*) The ancient maritime law of Denmark of 1561 (See Wesphaliens Monumenta inedita, t. iv. p. 1831) determines nothing on the subject of Recaptures; but in the Maritime Law of Christian V. (Vid. Cod. Legum. Dan. l. iv. c. vii. s. 6,) it is enacted: "Si quis, qui navi præest armatæ, hosti navem Danicam 24 horarum spatio ab eodem possessam eripere possit ac recuperare: unicis ejus lucrum esto prædatorium. Eandem vero si quis intra præfiniti temporis spatium hosti eripuerit, lucrum esto prædatitium inter recuperatorem, ac possessorem æqualiter dividendum."

equally between the privateer and the proprietor.(*x*) The Ordinances, concerning privateers, of the 5th April, 1710,(*y*) and of the 6th April, 1711,(*z*) do not settle the law of Recaptures, any more than the Ordinance of 1756,(*a*) concerning neutral commerce.

This law therefore relates also to the Recaptures of Danish ships only; it leaves the same doubts subsisting with respect to Recaptures belonging to foreign Powers or their subjects.

[*517] *CCCCXV. With respect to Sweden,(*b*) the Ordinance relative to the marine of Charles XI.,(*c*) enacts "that in case a ship belonging to Swedish subjects, after having been taken by the enemy, should be retaken, the recaptor shall have two-thirds of its value, and one-third shall be restored to the proprietor, without respect to the time during which it may have been in the enemy's hands." This law appears to mention only Recaptures made by privateers; but the King's ships have the same claim upon their prizes as privateers.(*d*) The regulations of Sweden concerning privateers,(*e*) of the 8-19th of February, 1715, of the 25th of March, 1719, of the 28th of July, 1741, the Declaration of the 14th August, 1741, do not relate to the subject of Recaptures: it is as little settled by the articles of maritime war (*Sio^e. Articlar*) of the year 1755.

CCCCXVI. The ancient maritime law of the Society of Hanse Towns(*f*) of 1593, revised in 1614, contains no regulation concerning Recaptures; but some of those towns have made laws for themselves relative to that subject. The laws of the city of Lubec(*g*) enact, that [*518] if a ship *be retaken by a *private ship*, the recaptor shall keep the Recapture, and if it be recaptured by a *public ship* belonging to the city, it shall be restored entirely to the proprietor, in consideration of a reward.

This last regulation was observed at Hamburg, at the commencement of the last century; a vessel (Die Drey Bienenkörbe,) bound for Russia,

(*x*) M. de Martens says:—"Cette loi est la seule qui me soit connue au sujet des reprises en Danemarc."—Essai, p. 200.

(*y*) De Martens cites Forord. of Frid. iv. 1710, p. 55; Willenberg, p. 172.

(*z*) Forord. af Frid. iv. 1711, p. 23.

(*a*) Schon. Chron. Reg., D. IV., p. 306. Hübner, de la Saisie, &c., p. 11, Append.

(*b*) De Martens, Essai, p. 207, § 70, Horne's Translation.

(*c*) Ordonnance for the regulation of the Marine of 1667, P. VII. Ammiralskap Balken, cap. viii. § 8.

(*d*) De Martens cites Sio^e. Articlar, 1755, tit. 29; Modee, D. VI. p. 3696.

(*e*) De Martens refers his readers to these regulations:—

For Sweden, the Naval Law of Charles XI., of 1677, P. VII., Ammiralskaps Balk, the Regulation for Privateers of the 8-19th February, 1715, in German, in Willenberg, loc. cit. p. 193; in Swedish, in Modee Utdrag af publique Handlingar, t. i. p. 42. The Regulation of 28th July, 1741, in German, in Hempel Staatslexicon, verb Commissfahrer; in Swedish, in Modee, Utdrag, t. iii. p. 1684.; the Declaration of the Regulation of 14th August, 1741, in Modee, loc. cit. t. lii. p. 1690; the articles for the naval war of 1755, ibid., t. vi. p. 3696. Sweden also gave instructions for privateers, dated 1st July, 1788, (v. Klint, Historia Fed. Belg., P. II. p. 439.) These authorities are cited in a very full and learned note in an earlier part of De Martens, Essai, p. 49, n. *q*. in fine.

(*f*) De Martens, Essai, p. 210, s. 73, Horne's Translation.

(*g*) Stat., l. vi. tit. v. art. 2. Stein, Abhandlungen des Lübrischen Rechts, t. v. p. 209, cited by De Martens.

was taken by a French privateer, and recaptured from him at the mouth of the Elbe by the commander of the city.(*h*)

De Martens observes that the wise policy and laws of these towns prohibited their subjects during war to be concerned with the fitting out of any kind of armaments in their ports, and forbad all participation, direct or indirect, in privateering,(*i*) especially the taking commissions from one of the belligerent Powers.

It is of course not competent to the public or private ship of war of belligerent Powers to make or pursue Captures, or make Recaptures within the maritime jurisdiction of these States, without violating the obligations of Neutrality.

CCCCXVII. Thirdly. *The decisions of the Prize Courts in the North American United States and in England* are to be considered with respect to this subject.(*k*)

CCCCXVIII. In England the right of recovering possession has been by a Prize Statute passed at the beginning of every war, *as between subjects*, preserved for ever, *except where the vessel, after capture, has been fitted out by the enemy for war;* so that the original owner may, in all other cases, claim *restitution upon the payment of a stipulated salvage.(*l*) In cases, however, not governed by municipal regu- [*519]

(*h*) Langenbeck, Anmerkungen, p. 299.

(*i*) Mand. de la Ville de Hamburg, 22nd March, 1672. Langenbeck, p. 307.

(*k*) The following pages on the practice of the English and North American United States Prize Courts, are taken (with some few alterations,) with the permission of Dr. Pratt, from his useful edition of the "Notes on the Principles and Practice of Prize Courts," by Judge Story, originally printed in the Appendix to Wheaton's American Reports, vol. ii.

(*l*) See the present *Prize Act*, 17 Vic. c. 18:—"IX. Any ship, vessel, goods, or merchandise belonging to any of Her Majesty's subjects captured by any of Her Majesty's enemies, and afterwards recaptured from the enemy by any of Her Majesty's ships or vessels of war, shall be adjudged by the decree of the Court of Admiralty to be restored to the owner or proprietor thereof upon payment for and in lieu of salvage of one-eighth part of the true value of the said ship, vessel, goods, or merchandise respectively, and such salvage of one-eighth shall be divided and distributed in such manner and proportion as is hereinbefore directed in cases of prize: provided nevertheless, that if any such ship or vessel captured and recaptured as aforesaid *shall have been by Her Majesty's enemies set forth or used as a ship or vessel of war, it shall not be restored to the former owner or proprietor thereof, but shall be adjudged lawful prize for the benefit of the captors.**

"X. Any ship, or vessel, belonging to any of Her Majesty's subjects, whether in ballast, or laden with any goods or merchandise belonging to the same, which shall have been captured by the enemy and recaptured by any of Her Majesty's ships and vessels of war before the same shall have been carried into an enemy's port, may, with the consent of the recaptors, prosecute her voyage, and it shall not be necessary for the recaptors to proceed to adjudication till the return of the ship or vessel to some port within the United Kingdom: and the master or owner thereof, or his agent, may, with the consent of the recaptor, unlade and dispose of the cargo before adjudication; and in case the ship or vessel shall not within six months return to some port within the United Kingdom, the recaptor may, notwithstanding, institute proceedings against the said ship or vessel, goods or merchandise, in the High Court of Admiralty of England, and the said Court may thereupon award one-eighth part of the value of the said ship, vessel, goods, or merchandise to the recaptor thereof, and may enforce the payment thereof either by warrant of arrest against the said ship or vessel, goods or merchandise respectively, or by monition and attachment against the respective owners thereof."—Marshall on Ins., B. I. ch. xii. s. 8. The Sedulous, 1 Dodson, p. 253.

* Vide post, the Ceylon, 1 Dodson's Ad. Rep., p. 107.

lations, although all nations agree that to change the property by Capture, a firm and secure possession is necessary; yet the practice of nations is so various, that it seems difficult to collect a general rule, as to what constitutes such firm and secure possession, which might properly be asserted to be [*520] *the Law of Nations.(*m*) The rule of bringing *infra præsidia*, or in proper cases, the rule of pernoctation, or twenty-four hours' possession, seems generally recognized by the most eminent jurists on the continent of Europe,(*n*) and it appears to have been anciently the doctrine of the English law. It has been seen, however, that according to the established practice of English Prize Courts, property captured is not deemed to be changed so as to bar the owner in favour of the vendee or recaptor, till there has been a sentence of condemnation; and therefore, until that period, the title of the original owner is not diverted, and he is entitled to restitution, in the hands of whomsoever he may find the property.(*o*) If such sentence of condemnation is passed, it is a sufficient title to a vendee,(*p*) and would also have entitled a recaptor to condemnation of the property, if the statute had not stepped in, and, *as to British subjects*, revived the *jus postliminii* of the original owner, on payment of salvage.

[*521] *CCCCXIX. In the North American United States, cases of Recapture have been the object of several legislative provisions, which, as far as they apply, supersede all discussions upon the principles of general law. The Act of Congress of the 3rd of March, 1800, ch. 14, (new ed.) ch. 168, directs, that in case of recapture of vessels or goods belonging to persons resident within, or under the protection of the United States, the same *not having been condemned as prize by competent authority before the Recapture*, shall be restored on payment of salvage of one-eighth of the value if recaptured by a public ship, and one-sixth if recaptured by a private ship; and if the recaptured vessel shall appear to have been set forth and armed as a vessel of war before such Capture, or afterwards and before the Recapture, then the salvage to be one moiety of the value. If the recaptured vessel belong to the Government, and be *unarmed*, the salvage is to be one-sixth if recaptured by a private ship, and one-twelfth if recaptured by a public ship; if *armed*, then the salvage to be one moiety if recaptured by a public ship.

(*m*) The Santa Cruz, 1 Rob., p. 50. L'Actif, Edw., p. 185. The Ceylon, 1 Dodson, p. 105.

(*n*) The Ceylon, Ib., p. 105. L'Actif, Edw., p. 185. See the Santa Cruz, 1 Rob., p. 50.

"Quoiqu'il en soit, ce délai de vingt-quatre heures adopté par la dite Ordonnance de 1584, et par celle-ci, passé lequel la prise par recousse est bonne, et exclut la réclamation du propriétaire du vaisseau pris et repris, ne peut être regardé que comme un sage réglement, *puisqu'il est du droit commun de l'Europe*, comme Loccenius l'atteste, de Jure maritimo, lib. ii. cap. 4, n. 4, et 8, fol. 157, 162, et 163; où il dit que c'est l'usage observé en France, en Espagne, en Hollande, et chez les autres nations commercantes par mer."—Valin sur l'Ordonnance, l. iii. tit. 9, Des Prises, art. 8.

(*o*) Le Caux v. Eden, Douglas's Rep., pp. 613, 616. Goss v. Withers, 2 Burrow's Rep., p. 694. The Flad Oyen, 1 Rob., p. 135. The Santa Cruz, Ib., p. 50. The Fanny and Elmira, Edwards's Rep., p. 117. The Ceylon, 1 Dodson, p. 105. L'Actif, Edw., p. 185.

(*p*) The Purissima Conception, 6 Rob., p. 45. The Victoria, Edw., p. 97.

In respect to public armed ships, the cargo pays the same rate of salvage as the vessel by the express words of the Act; but in respect to private ships, the rate of salvage (by some probable omission in the Act) is the same on the cargo, whether the vessel be armed or unarmed.(*q*)

CCCCXX. What constitutes a setting forth as a vessel of war within the Act, has not been settled by any adjudications in the United States.

This question has, however, been decided by the English Prize Courts, in cases arising under a similar clause in the English Prize Acts, which are, as Lord Stowell observed, drawn with the intention of expressing the sense and meaning of International Law.(*r*) And it has been there settled that, where a ship was originally armed for the slave trade, and after capture an additional number of men *were put on board, [*522] but where there was no commission of war and no additional arming, it was not a setting forth as a vessel of war under the Prize Act.(*s*) But a commission of war is decisive, if there be guns on board.(*t*) And where the vessel has, after the Capture, been fitted out as a privateer, it is conclusive against her, although when recaptured she is navigating as a mere merchant ship; for where the former character of a captured vessel had been obliterated by her conversion into a ship of war, the Legislature meant to look no farther, but considered the title of the former owner forever extinguished.(*u*) Where it appeared that the vessel had been engaged in the military service of the enemy under the appointment of the Minister of Marine, it was holden a sufficient proof of a setting forth as a vessel of war.(*x*) So, where she is armed, and is employed in the public military service of the enemy by those who have competent authority so to employ her, although she be not regularly commissioned.(*y*) But the mere employment in the military service of the enemy is not a sufficient setting forth for war; but if there be a fair semblance of authority in the person directing the vessel to be so employed, and nothing upon the face of the proceedings to invalidate it, the Court will presume that he is duly authorized, and the commander of a single ship may be presumed to be vested with this authority as commander of a squadron.(*z*) The valuation of the property, when restored under the Acts respecting Recapture, is to be made upon its value at the price of restitution, and not of Recapture.(*a*)

CCCCXXI. In respect *to Recaptures* of the ships and *cargoes [*523] of *allies or co-belligerents*, from the hands of the common enemy, the general rule is to apply the principle of reciprocity; and if they, under like circumstances, restore on salvage or condemn generally, to deal out to them the same measure of reciprocal justice.(*b*) If there should exist a country having no rule on the subject, then the recapturing country applies its own rule, as to its own subjects, to the case, and rests

(*q*) The Adeline, 9 Cranch's (Amer.) Rep., p. 244.
(*r*) The Ceylon, 1 Dodson, pp. 105, 119.
(*s*) The Horatio, 6 Rob., p. 320.
(*t*) The Nostra Signora del Rosario, 3 Ib., p. 10. The Ceylon, 1 Dodson, p. 105.
(*u*) L'Actif, Edw., p. 185.
(*x*) The Santa Brigada, 3 Rob., p. 56.
(*y*) The Ceylon, 1 Dodson, p. 105.
(*z*) The Georgiana, Ib., p. 397.
(*a*) The Progress, Edw., pp. 210, 222.
(*b*) The Santa Cruz, 1 Rob., p. 50.—Vide Valin sur l'Ordonnance, t. ii. p. 262.

on the presumption that the same rule will be administered in the future practice of the other party.(c)

CCCCXXII. Salvage (*servaticium*) is not in general allowed on the Recapture of neutral property, unless there be danger of condemnation, or such unjustifiable conduct on the part of the Government of the captors as to bring the property into jeopardy;(d) but even if, in such case of Recapture, the recaptors have entitled themselves to salvage, they may forfeit the claim by the irregularity of their conduct.(e) But it is
[*524] no objection to an allowance of salvage *on a Recapture, that it was made by a non-commissioned vessel; for no letters of marque are necessary for this purpose, nor is a Recapture at all made under the authority of Prize. It is the duty of every citizen to assist his fellow-citizens in war, and to retake their property out of the possession of the enemy; and no commission is necessary to give a person, so employed, a title to the reward which the law allots to that meritorious act of duty.(*f*) And if a convoying ship actually recapture one of her convoy which has been previously captured by the enemy, it entitles her to salvage.(*g*) But a mere rescue of a ship associated in the same common enterprise, gives no right to salvage.(*h*)

CCCCXXIII. To entitle a party to salvage, as upon a Recapture, there must have been an actual or constructive Capture; for military salvage will not be allowed in any cases where the property has not been actually rescued from the enemy.(*i*) But it is not necessary that the enemy should have actual possession: it is sufficient if the property is completely under the dominion of the enemy.(*k*) If, however, a vessel be captured going in distress into an enemy's port, and is thereby saved, it is merely a case of *civil*, and not of *military*, salvage.(*l*) But to constitute a Recapture it is not necessary that the recaptors should have a bodily and actual possession; it is sufficient if the prize be actually rescued from the grasp of the hostile captor.(*m*)

CCCCXXIV. Where a *hostile* ship is captured, and afterwards is recaptured by the enemy, and is again recaptured from the enemy, the original captors are not entitled to restitution, on paying salvage; but
[*525] the last captors are entitled *to all the rights of Prize, for, by the first Recapture, the whole right of the original captors is divest-

(*c*) Ibid. The San Francisco, Edw., p. 279. The Act of Congress of the 3rd March, 1800, ch. 14, adopts the same regulation. The Adeline, 9 Cranch's (Amer.) Rep., p. 244. Vide Valin sur l'Ordonnance, t. ii. p. 262.

(*d*) The War Onskan, 2 Rob., p. 299. The Eleonora Catharina, 4 Ib., p. 156. The Carlotta, 5 Ib., p. 54. The Huntress, 6 Ib., p. 104. The Acteon, Edw., p. 254. The Sansom, 6 Rob., p. 410. Talbot v. Seeman, 4 Dallas's (Amer.) Rep., p. 34. S. C., 1 Cranch's (Amer.) Rep., p. 1.

"Sa Majesté a jugé pendant la dernière guerre, que la reprise du navire neutre, faite par un corsaire Français (*lorsque le navire n'était pas chargé de marchandises prohibées, ni dans le cas d'être confisqué par l'ennemi*) était nulle."—Code des Prises, ed. 1784, t. ii.

See olso the opinion of M. Portalis in the case of the Statira, 1 Cranch's (Amer.) Rep., p. 102, note *a*.

(*e*) The Barbara, 3 Rob., p. 171.
(*f*) The Helen, 3 Rob., p. 224.
(*g*) The Wight, 5 Ib., p. 315.
(*h*) The Belle, Edw., p. 66.
(*i*) The Franklin, 4 Rob., p. 147.
(*k*) The Edward and Mary, 3 Ib., p. 305. The Pensamento Felix, Edw., p. 116.
(*l*) The Franklin, 4 Bob., p. 147.
(*m*) The Edward and Mary, 3 Ib., p. 305.

ed.(*n*) And where the original captors have abandoned their prize, and she is subsequently captured by other persons, the latter are solely entitled to the property.(*o*) But if the abandonment be involuntary, and produced by the terror of superior force, and especially if produced by the act of the second captors, the rights of the original captors are completely revived.(*p*) And where the enemy has captured a ship, and afterwards deserted her, and she is then recaptured, it is not to be considered as a case of derelict; for the original owner never had the *animus derelinquendi*, and therefore she is to be restored on a payment of salvage; but as it is not strictly a Recapture within the Prize Act, the rate of salvage is discretionary.(*q*) But *if the abandonment by the enemy be produced by the terror of a hostile force, it is a Recapture within the terms of the Prize Act.(*r*) [*526]

CCCCXXV. Where the captors abandon their prize, and she is afterwards brought into port by *neutral salvors*, it has been held that the neutral Court has jurisdiction to decree salvage, but cannot restore the property to the original belligerent owners: for by the Capture, the captors acquired such a right of property as no neutral nation could justly impugn or destroy, and consequently, the proceeds (after deducting salvage) belong to the original captors, and neutral nations ought not to

(*n*) The Polly, 4 Rob., p. 217, note *a*. The Astrea, 1 Wheaton's (Amer.) Rep., p. 125.

"Veut et entend Sa Majesté, que les prises des navires ennemis, faites par ses vaisseaux, ou par ceux de ses sujets armés en course, recousses par les ennemis, et ensuite reprises sur eux, appartiennent en entier au dernier preneur."—Arrêt du Conseil d'Etat du 5 Novembre, 1748. Valin, sur l'Ordonnance, t. ii. pp. 257–9. Traité des Prises, ch. vi. s. 1. Pothier, De Propriété, No. 99.

(*o*) The Lord Nelson, Edw., p. 79. The Diligentia, 1 Dodson, p. 404.

(*p*) The Mary, 2 Wheaton's (Amer.) Rep., p. 123.

(*q*) The John and Jane, 4 Rob., p. 216. The Gage, 6 Ib., p. 273. The Lord Nelson, Edw., p. 79.

"Si le navire, sans être recous, est abandonné par les ennemis, ou si par tempête ou autre cas fortuit il revient en la possession de nos sujets, avant qu'il ait été conduit dans aucun port ennemi, il sera rendu au propriétaire qui le réclamera dans l'an et jour, quoi qu'il ait été plus de vingt-quatre heures entre les mains des ennemis."—Ordonnance de 1681, l. iii. tit. 9, Des Prises, art. 9.

Pothier is of opinion that these words, *avant qu'il soit entré dans aucun port ennemi*, are to be understood not as restricting the right of restitution, on payment of salvage, to the particular case mentioned, of a vessel which is abandoned by the enemy before being carried into port, which case is mentioned merely as an example of what ordinarily happens, *parce que c'est le cas ordinaire auquel un vaisseau échappe à l'ennemi qui l'a pris, ne pouvant plus guere lui échapper lorsqu'il a été conduit dans ses ports.*—De Propriété, No. 99.

But Valin holds that the terms of the Ordinance are to be literally construed, and that the right of the original proprietor is completely divested by the carrying into the enemy's port.—Sur l'Ordonnance, Ib. He is also of opinion that this species of salvage is to be analogized to the case of shipwreck, and that the recaptors are entitled to one-third of the value of the property saved.—Ib.

But Azuni contends, that the rate of salvage, in this case, is not regulated by the Ordinance, but is discretionary, to be proportioned to the nature and extent of the service performed, which can never be equal to the rescue of property from the hands of the enemy by military force, or to the recovery of goods lost by shipwreck.—Part II. ch. iv. ss. 8, 9.

Emerigon is also opposed to Valin on this subject, and cites in support of his own doctrine, the Consolato del Mare, ch. 287, and Targa, ch. 46, n. 10.—Emerigon, Des Assurances, t. i. pp. 504, 505.

(*r*) The Gage, 6 Rob., p. 273.

inquire into the validity of a Capture as between belligerents.(s) But if the captors make a donation of the captured vessel to a neutral crew, the latter are entitled as salvors; but after deducting salvage, the remaining proceeds will be decreed to the original owner.(t)

CCCCXXVI. And it seems to be a general rule, liable to but few exceptions, that the rights of Capture are completely divested by a [*527] *hostile Recapture, escape*, or a *voluntary *discharge* of the captured vessel.(u) And the same principle seems applicable to a *hostile rescue;* but if the rescue be made by a *neutral* crew of a *neutral* ship, it may be doubtful how far such an illegal act, which involves the penalty of confiscation, would be holden in the Courts of the captor's country to divest his original right in case of a subsequent Recapture.

CCCCXXVII. As to recaptors, though their right to salvage is extinguished by a subsequent hostile Recapture, and regular sentence of condemnation carried into execution, divesting the owners of their property, yet if the vessel be restored, upon such Recapture, and resumes her voyage, either upon an acquittal in Court, or a release of the sovereign Power, the recaptors are redintegrated in their right of salvage:(x) and recaptors and salvors have a legal interest in the property, which cannot be divested by other subjects without an adjudication in a competent Court; and it is not for the Government's ships or officers, or for other persons, upon the ground of superior authority, to dispossess them without cause.(y)

CCCCXXVIII. In all cases of salvage, where the rate is not fixed by positive law, it is in the discretion of the Court, as well upon Recaptures as in other cases.(z) And where, upon a Recapture, the parties have entitled themselves to a military salvage under the Prize Acts, the Court may also award them, in addition, a civil salvage, if they have subsequently rendered services by succouring the vessel in distress from perils of the seas.(a)

[*528] *CCCCXXIX. In the construction of the English Prize Acts, it has been held that a revenue-cutter, having a letter of marque, is to be deemed a private ship of war, and entitled to a salvage of one-sixth.(b) But these British revenue-cutters belonged to private individuals, although fitted out, manned, and armed, at the expense of the Government, and it may be thought doubtful whether the authority of this case applied in the United States, where the revenue-cutters are generally built and owned, as well as equipped, manned, and armed, by the Government. A store-ship, however, armed at the public expense, and commanded by commissioned officers, is clearly to be deemed a public armed ship.(c)

(s) The Mary Ford, 3 Dallas's (Amer.) Rep., p. 188.

(t) The Adventure, 8 Cranch's (Amer.) Rep., p. 227. S. C., 1 Wheaton's (Amer.) Rep., p. 128, note *f.*

(u) Hudson v. Guestier, 4 Cranch's (Amer.) Rep., p. 293. S. C., 6 Cranch's (Amer.) Rep., p. 281. The Diligentia, 1 Dodson, p. 404.

(x) The Charlotte Caroline, ib., p. 192. (y) The Blendenhall, ib., p. 414.

(z) Talbot v. Seeman, 1 Cranch's (Amer.) Rep., p. 1. The Apollo, 3 Rob., p. 308. Bynk. Q. J. P., l. i. ch. v. Du Ponceau's ed., pp. 36, 41, 42.

(a) The Louisa, 1 Dodson, p. 317.

(b) The Helen, 3 Rob., p. 224. The Sedulous, 1 Dodson, p. 253. (c) Ibid.

CCCCXXX. M. De Martens considers whether there can be derived from certain expressions and phrases perpetually recurring in Treaties,(*d*) a general concurrence of States as to rules upon this subject, and more especially whether the subject of Recapture can be considered as falling under one or other of two clauses which are most frequently found in Treaties.

1. The clause of being treated as the most favoured nation (*d'être traité comme la nation la plus favorisée.*)(*e*)

2. The clause of being treated as the proper subjects of the State (*d'être traité comme les propres sujets de l'état.*)(*f*)

M. de Martens very wisely decides that Recapture cannot fairly be considered as falling within the purview and intendment of either of these clauses.

CCCCXXXI. So much for two of the sources from which we may in some measure derive the principles of International Law.

And with respect to a third, namely, the opinions of *Jurists, they are summed up by this author in contradiction to his own [*529] opinion(*g*) upon the subject of Recapture, as being agreed upon the two following propositions.

1st. With respect to the Recapture of a vessel, before the original Capture had been completed; that though in such case the captured property ought to be restored to the original proprietor, yet that even in this case the recaptor is entitled to demand a recompense, which, according to the principles of natural justice, cannot be fixed at any certain part of the value of the prize, but which ought to be proportioned to the dangers, expenses, and damages incurred in the effecting of it.

2nd. With respect to the Recapture of property duly vested in the captor, that, upon the same conditions by which it became so vested, it has become by the Recapture vested in the recaptor; and that the rights of the first proprietor lost by the Capture cannot revive, *ipso jure*, by virtue of the seizure effected by the recaptor. And that the first proprietor can no more revindicate his extinguished right of property, than he can exercise a right of redemption, the which always supposes the existence of positive municipal laws, without which no proprietor is bound to sell his property to any person.

CCCCXXXII. By the general Maritime Law, Ransom is allowed, and the master may bind by his contract for Ransom the whole cargo as well as the ship.(*h*) About the middle of George the Third's reign(*i*) Ran-

(*d*) Vide Antè, vol. i., p. 45. For specific Treaties on this subject see De Martens, Essai, and vol. ix. Traités de Comm., De Haut. et de C., p. 374, Prises et Reprises. (*e*) Vide Antè, p. 155. (*f*) Ib., p. 157.

(*g*) He candidly admits that this opinion is at variance with the received opinion of Europe.

"Que toute reprise, faite à une époque quelleconque de la guerre, soit que la prise ait été légitime, soit qu'elle ait été illégitime, soit que la reprise se fasse par le Souverain, soit qu'elle se fasse par un armateur, doit être restituée à l'ancien propriétaire quelconque; moyennant une juste rétribution des frais et dommages du repreneur quelconque; à moins que l'illégitimité de la reprise ne prive le repreneur du droit de demander une réparation."—De Martens, Ess., and vol. ix. Tr. de Com., De Haut. et de C., pp. 130-1., Prises et Reprises.

(*h*) The Gratitudine, 3 Rob., p. 240.

(*i*) Present Prize Act, 17 Vict. c. 18:—"XLII. It shall not be lawful for any of

[*530] soms were, by the policy *of England, forbidden to English subjects.(*k*) But even now under circumstances of necessity they are still allowed.(*l*) Ransoms have never been prohibited by the North American United States; and the Act of Congress of August 2, 1813, interdicting the use of British licenses or passes, was holden not to apply to the contract of Ransom.(*m*)

The general law upon this subject is perspicuously stated in the following extract from a judgment of Lord Justice Story(*n*)—"The second question," he says, "is, whether it be competent for a friendly Belligerent to demand, or take, a ransom for restoring the property of a Neutral after capture. It is argued by the defendant, that every ransom supposes a vested right in the captors; that this does not exist in respect to Neutrals, for the captors have only a right to bring in for adjudication; that neutral property is liable to condemnation, only in case of delinquency; and that captors have no right to remit, in behalf of their Sovereign, a forfeiture for violation of neutral duties.

[*531] It is not true, however, that the right to take a Ransom *is founded in a vested title in the captors to the captured property. For, whether the property vest after twenty-four hours' possession, or after bringing *infra præsidia*, as seems the doctrine of civilians; or after condemnation, as is the doctrine of Great Britain; it is clear that the right to take a Ransom exists from the moment of capture. And, by the general practice of the maritime world, a decree of condemnation is deemed necessary to ascertain and confirm the inchoate title of the captors, at least in respect to the Sovereign and subjects of their own country. Nor is a ransom, strictly speaking, a repurchase of the captured property. It is rather a repurchase of the actual right of the captors at the time, be it what it may; or, more properly, it is a relinquishment of all the interest and benefit, which the captors might acquire or consummate in the property by the regular adjudications of a Prize Tribunal, whether it be an interest *in rem*, a lien, or a mere title to expenses. In this respect there seems to be no legal difference between the case of a Ransom of the property of an enemy, and of a Neutral. For if the property be neutral, and yet there be probable cause of capture, or if the

Her Majesty's subjects to ransom or to enter into any contract or agreement for ransoming any ship, vessel, goods, or merchandise belonging to any of Her Majesty's subjects which shall be captured by any of Her Majesty's enemies; and all contracts and agreements which shall be entered into, and all bills, notes, and other securities, which shall be given by any person for Ransom of any ship, vessel, goods or merchandise, contrary to the provisions of this Act, shall be absolutely null and void.

(*k*) 22 G. III. c. 25, ss. 1, 2. See cases at common law on this subject:—Havelock v. Rockwood, 8 Durnford & East, p. 268. Wilson v. Bird, 1 Lord Raymond's Rep., p. 22. Anthon v. Fisher, 3 Douglas's Rep., p. 166. Same v. Same, 2 Douglas's Rep., p. 649, n. Woodward v. Larkin, 3 Espinasse's Rep., p. 266. Parsons v. Scott, 2 Taunton's Rep., p. 363. Webb v. Brooke, 3 Ib., p. 6. Ricard v. Bettenham, 3 Burrow's Rep., p. 1734. Cornu v. Blackburne, Douglas's Rep., p. 641.

(*l*) The ships taken at Genoa, 4 Rob., p. 403. The Hoop, 1 Ib., p. 169.

(*m*) Goodrich v. Gordon, 15 Johnson's (Amer.) Rep., 6. Kent's Comm. vol. i. pp. (105,) 112.

(*n*) Maisonnaire et al. v. Keating, 2 Gallison's (Amer.) Rep. p. 337, (Story.)

delinquency be such, that the penalty of confiscation might be justly applied; there can be no intrinsic difficulty in supporting a contract, by which the captors agree to waive their rights to a consideration of a sum of money voluntarily paid, or agreed to be paid, by the captured. Indeed, the case stands upon a stronger ground than that of a Ransom between enemies; for the latter have not, in general, a capacity to enter into contracts. The very law of war prohibits all commercial intercourse, and suspends all existing contracts between enemies; and the case of Ransoms is almost the only exception, which has been admitted, from the general rule. If then, neither the subject-matter, nor the nature of the title or consideration, nor the capacity of the parties, presents any serious objection to the contract, as between a friendly Belligerent and a Neutral, it remains to consider, if there be anything in the objection, *that it is a remitter of the right of forfeiture, which belongs exclusively to the sovereign. [*532]

"The Commission of the Sovereign in general authorizes only captures of enemies' property. But, without any express clause, this Commission clearly extends to the capture of all neutral property seized in violating neutral duties; for in such case the property is deemed *quasi* enemies' property. And, for the same reason, it authorizes the bringing in of property, under neutral passports and papers, for adjudication, where there is probable cause to suspect its real character; for, until adjudication, it cannot be ascertained whether it be entitled to the protection of the neutral character. If, therefore, the Commission gives hostile property to the captors, and enables them to deliver it up on ransom, it also enables them to do the same in respect to Neutral property, which has acquired a hostile taint; and the ransom is not, in the one case, any more the exercise of the Sovereign's prerogative to remit a forfeiture, than it is in the other. In both instances, it is considered, by the Law of Nations, as a mere *remitter* of the rights of the captors acquired *jure belli;* and every prohibition of its exercise must expressly depend upon the municipal regulations of the particular country. Upon principle, therefore, the distinction of the counsel for the defendant, as to the incompetency of a Belligerent to deliver neutral property on Ransom is unsupported; and there is not a scintillation of authority in its favour."(*o*)

(*o*) See also:—Miller v. The Resolution, 2 Dallas's (Amer.) Rep., p. 15. Azuni, c. iv. art. 6. 1 Emerigon, c. xii. s. 21. 2 Valin, art. 66, p. 149. Le Guidon, c. vi., art. 2. Pothier, Traité du Droit de Propriété, No. 134, 135, 138, 139, 140, 144. Valin, Ord. des Prises, art. 19. Ib., II. l. iii. t. ix. art. 19. Ib., Comm., t. ix., p. 261.

PART THE ELEVENTH.

[*533] *CHAPTER I.

THE GENERAL CHARACTER AND DUTY OF TRIBUNALS OF PRIZE.

CCCCXXXIII. It has been observed that the tribunal of *maritime* International Law, having cognizance of *Prize*, has, from circumstances sufficiently apparent upon a very slight reflection, assumed a form, consistency, and regularity of procedure which no tribunal of International Law, respecting military operations by land, and having cognizance of *Booty*, has yet attained; and that so far as English legislation and jurisprudence is concerned, there has been a growing tendency to submit both subjects to the same tribunal.(*a*)

It seems to the writer of these pages that, within the whole range of International Jurisprudence, there is no subject of more paramount importance than the character, constitution, and mode of procedure of the Prize Court and of the Appellate Tribunal.(*b*)

It ought to command the respect of nations—it ought to be above, not slander indeed, for then it would not be a human institution, but just and reasonable suspicion. It ought to administer International, not Municipal Law, except, in so far as it might happen that the latter was identical with or declaratory of the former. Its procedure ought to be open
[*534] and exposed to all criticism. It ought to *allow every liberty of speech to the Claimant, or his representative, as well as to the Belligerent, or his representative. It should administer a consistent law upon certain and known principles, impartially applied to all States and to their subjects. The high standard of the great philosopher and jurist of antiquity should be perpetually before its eyes. It should always remember that the law which it has to administer is not of one character at Rome and of another at Athens,(*c*) but one and the same everywhere, founded and applied, so far as human infirmity will permit, upon the principles of immutable right and eternal justice.

CCCCXXXIV. The Prize Courts to whose proceedings the greatest publicity(*d*) has been given, are, it will not be denied by any candid and intelligent person, those of Great Britain and of the United States of North America.

Nor will it be denied by the United States that they have taken, with few and inconsiderable exceptions, the rules, procedure and practice of the English Courts as their approved and recognized model.

(*a*) Vide ante, p. 197.

(*b*) Vide ante, Vol. II., pp. 327, 328, as to International Law administered by the Pope.

(*c*) "Neque erit alia lex Romæ alia Athenis: alia nunc alia posthac, &c."—Cic. de Repub., l. iii. c. 22.

(*d*) The reports are duly published, and in England, during the present war, under the authority of the High Court of Admiralty. These are independent of the daily reports in a great number of newspapers of various political creeds.

In the case of the Ostsee, decided by the highest English tribunal, the Judicial Committee of the Privy Council, during the present war, it was well observed that—

"The law which we are to lay down cannot be confined to the British Navy; the rule must be applied to captors of all nations. No country can be permitted to establish an exceptional rule in its own favour, or in favour of particular classes of its own subjects. On the Law of Nations, foreign decisions are entitled to the same weight as those of the country in which the tribunal sits. America has adopted almost all her principles of prize *law from the decisions of English courts; and whatever may have been the case in former times, no authorities [*535] are now cited in English courts, in cases to which they are applicable, with greater respect than those of the distinguished jurists of France and America. Whatever is held in England to justify or excuse an officer of the British Navy, will be held by the tribunals of every country, both on this and the other side of the Atlantic, to justify or excuse the captors of their own nation."(*e*)

CCCCXXXV. Let us consider, first, whether there has been any *theory* upon this subject—viz. the duty of the Prize Court towards all States—promulgated by the English courts; and next, whether that theory has been in accordance with the premises which have been just laid down; because these facts are of great importance to the civilized world.

States which openly proclaim the standard, by reference to which they assert that international justice ought to be administered in their tribunals, witness, as it were, against themsslves, if they depart from it.

True it is that their *practice* may fall short of their *theory*; but by the joint effect of openly promulgating their theory and openly conducting their practice, they have forever exposed themselves to the severest criticism, and challenged, in some sense, the institution of a constant comparison between the two. Nor, in these days, not only of free but universal discussion through the agency of the press, can it be contended that this exposure and this challenge do not constitute a great check upon the maladministration of justice, and a great safeguard to those States whose interests are necessarily submitted to the decisions of the Belligerent Tribunal.

CCCCXXXVI. It has so happened that, during the long *and general War which ended in 1815, that great magistrate of nations, [*536] Lord Stowell, more than once felt it incumbent upon him to declare from the judgment seat what was in his opinion the duty of the tribunal over which he so long presided.

It has appeared desirable to the writer of these pages to collect these passages, and to place them consecutively before the eyes of the reader.

It has been already observed, that, in time of war, Neutral States have a right to demand, *ex debito justitiæ*,(*f*) that there be courts for the administration of International Law, sitting in the belligerent countries.

(*e*) The Ostsee. Judgment of the Judicial Committee of the Privy Council, delivered March 29th, 1855.

(*f*) The Snipe and others, Edwards's Adm. Rep., p. 381, also published separately. See important remarks of Mably, Droit de Gens, vol. ii. pp. 350, 351; and Wheaton, Hist., p. 171, n.

The duties of these courts are thus faithfully described by Lord Stowell in the case of the Swedish Convoy: "In forming my judgment, I trust that it has not for a moment escaped my anxious recollection what it is that the duty of my station calls for from me; namely, not to deliver occasional and shifting opinions to serve present purposes of particular national interest, but to administer with indifference that justice which the law of nations holds out without distinction to independent States, some happening to be neutral and some belligerent; the seat of judicial authority is indeed locally *here*, in the belligerent country, according to the known law and practice of nations, but the law itself has no locality. It is the duty of the person who sits here to determine this question exactly as he would determine the same question if sitting at Stockholm; to assert no pretensions on the part of Great Britain which he would not allow to Sweden in the same circumstances; and to impose no duties on Sweden, as a neutral country, which he would not admit to belong to Great Britain in the same character."

[*537] *In another case(*g*) he says: "It is to be recollected that this is a Court of the Law of Nations, though sitting here under the authority of the King of Great Britain. It belongs to other nations as well as to our own; and what foreigners have a right to demand from it is the administration of the *Law of Nations* simply, and exclusively of the introduction of principles borrowed from our own municipal jurisprudence, to which, it is well known, they have at all times expressed no inconsiderable reluctance."

In the case of the Fox, decided in 1811, Lord Stowell said:—

"In the course of the discussion a question has been started, What would be the duty of the Court under Orders in Council that were repugnant to the Law of Nations? It has been contended on one side that the Court would at all events be bound to enforce the Orders in Council; on the other, that the Court would be bound to apply the rule of the Law of Nations adapted to the particular case, in disregard of the Orders in Council. I have not observed, however, that these Orders in Council, in their retaliatory character, have been described in the argument as at all repugnant to the Law of Nations, however liable to be so described if merely original and abstract. And, therefore, it is rather to correct possible misapprehension on the subject, than from the sense of any obligation which the present discussion imposes upon me, that I observe that this Court is bound to administer the Law of Nations to the subjects of other countries in the different relations in which they may be placed towards this country and its government. That is what others have a right to demand for their subjects, and to complain if they receive it not. This is its unwritten law, evidenced in the course of its decisions, and collected from the common usage of civilized States. At the same time it is strictly true, that, by the constitution of this country, the King in Council possesses legislative rights over this Court,
[*538] *and has power to issue orders and instructions which it is bound to obey and enforce; and these constitute the written law of

(*g*) The Recovery, 6 Robinson's Adm. Rep., 348, 9.

this Court. These two propositions, that the Court is bound to administer the Law of Nations, and that it is bound to enforce the King's Orders in Council, are not at all inconsistent with each other; because these orders and instructions are presumed to conform themselves, under the given circumstances, to the principles of its unwritten law. They are either directory applications of those principles in the case indicated in them—cases which, with all the facts and circumstances belonging to them, and which constitute their legal character, could be but imperfectly known to the Court itself; or they are positive regulations, consistent with those principles, applying to matters which require more exact and definite rules than those general principles are capable of furnishing.

"The constitution of this Court, relatively to the legislative power of the King in Council, is analogous to that of the Courts of Common Law, relatively to that of the Parliament of this kingdom. Those Courts have their unwritten law, the approved principles of natural reason and justice; they have likewise the written or statute law in Acts of Parliament, which are directory applications of the same principles to particular subjects, or positive regulations consistent with them, upon matters which would remain too much at large if they were left to the imperfect information which the Courts could extract from mere general speculations. What would be the duty of the individuals who presided in those Courts, if required to enforce an Act of Parliament which contradicted those principles, is a question which I presume they would not entertain *à priori*, because they will not entertain *à priori* the supposition that any such will arise. In like manner this Court will not let itself loose into speculations as to what would be its duty under such an emergency; because it cannot, without extreme indecency, presume that any [*539] *such emergency will happen. And it is the less disposed to entertain them, because its own observation and experience attest the general conformity of such orders and instructions to its principles of unwritten law.(*h*) In the particular case of the orders and instructions which give rise to the present question, the Court has not heard it at all maintained in argument that, as retaliatory orders they are not conformable to such principles; for retaliatory orders they are. They are so declared in their own language, and in the uniform language of the Government which has established them. I have no hesitation in saying that they would cease to be just if they ceased to be retaliatory; and they would cease to be retaliatory from the moment the enemy retracts, in a sincere manner, those measures of his which they were intended to retaliate."(*i*)

It is clear from these citations that it never has been the doctrine of the British Prize Courts that, because they sit under the authority of the Crown, the Crown has authority to prescribe to them rules which violate International Law. The Orders in Council of 1807(*k*) did, in

(*h*) "Todos reconocerán espontáneamente y admirarán el perfecto lenguage de esta exposicion," says Pando; but he proceeds to complain of Lord Stowell for not having followed his own rules; while upon his judgments delivered in 1798-9 he passes an unqualified eulogy. Pando (ed. 1852,) p. 536.

(*i*) The Fox and others, Edwards's Adm. Rep., p. 312.

(*k*) Vide ante, p. 250.

the opinion of the writer of these pages, contravene that law; but in the opinion of the Judge of the Prize Court they were, as has been seen, consistent with it: and therefore his decrees carried them into execution.

If he had not so considered them, and nevertheless had executed them, he would have incurred the same guilt and deserved the same reprehension as the judge of a Municipal Court, who executed by his sentence an edict of the Legislature which plainly violated the law written by the finger of the Creator upon the conscience of his creature.

[*540] *There was a case tried before Sir James Mackintosh, when Recorder of Bombay, which illustrates and fortifies this position.

It was that of the Minerva, an American ship taken in a voyage from Providence, in the course of which she had touched at the Isle of France, from which place she sailed to Tegall and Manilla; and on her voyage back from this last place to Batavia she was detained, as trading between enemies' ports, in violation of His Majesty's "Instructions" of June, 1803. Restitution was insisted on by the claimants, on the ground that neither Manilla nor Batavia, nor the Isle of France, were enemies' colonies in such a sense as to render the trading thereto by a Neutral, in time of war, illegal; inasmuch as the trade to these places was open to foreigners in time of peace. For the purpose of ascertaining this last point, commissions had been sent to Calcutta and Madras; and the judge, finding that the trade had been, as alleged, open to foreigners, pronounced for restitution, but without costs.

In pronouncing judgment he observed:—"That the sole point in the case was, whether Manilla and Batavia were colonies, according to the true meaning of His Majesty's 'Instructions' of 1803; or, in other words, whether they were settlements administered, in the time of peace, on principles of colonial monopoly. The word 'colony' was here not a geographical, but a political term. 'His Majesty's Instructions' must be construed so as not to be at variance with the principle of Public Law, maintained by Great Britain, called the Rule of 1756. No settlement could be called a colony under that rule which was open to foreigners in time of peace. As, from the return to the commissions, it appeared that Batavia and Manilla were not such colonies, he did not therefore conceive that trading to them was illegal under the Law of Nations, as relaxed by His Majesty's 'Instructions' of 1803.

[*541] "Something had been said of the obedience due to the **letter* of the 'Instructions.' Undoubtedly the letter of the 'Instructions' was a sufficient warrant for His Majesty's officers for detaining ships which appeared to offend against it; but as to the doctrine that Courts of Prize were bound by *illegal instructions*, he had already in a former case (that of the Erin,) treated it as a groundless charge by an American writer against English Courts. In this case (which had hitherto been, and he trusted ever would continue imaginary) of such illegal instructions he was convinced that English Courts of Admiralty would as much assert their independence of arbitrary mandates as English Courts of Common Law. That happily no judge had ever been called upon to determine, and no writer had distinctly put the case of such a repugnance. He had, therefore, no direct and positive authority;

but he never could hesitate in asserting, that in such an imaginary case, it would be the duty of a judge to disregard the 'Instructions,' and to consult only that universal Law to which all civilized princes and States acknowledge themselves to be subject, and over which none of them can claim any authority."(*l*)

Many years before this judgment was delivered, Lord Mansfield had declared from the Queen's Bench of England that an Act of Parliament would not alter the Law of Nations,(*m*) and that all the world were parties to a sentence in a Court of Admiralty, that is, a Prize Court.(*n*)

---

*CHAPTER II. [*542]

THE CONSTITUTION OF PRIZE TRIBUNALS IN DIFFERENT STATES.

CCCCXXXVII. The tribunals in the United States of North America which take cognizance of maritime capture appear to be the following:—

First. The District Courts.(*a*) These, as well as the Circuit Courts, are derived from the power granted by the Constitution to Congress of constituting tribunals inferior to the Supreme Court.

The United States are at present divided into thirty-five districts, which generally consist of an entire State; but in some States there are more districts than one.

They have exclusive original cognizance of all civil causes of Admiralty and maritime jurisdiction within certain limitations as to the tonnage of vessels. They have also cognizance, concurrently with the Circuit and State Courts, of causes where an alien sues for a tort committed in violation of the Law of Nations or a Treaty of the United States.

They have also cognizance of complaints, by whomsoever instituted, in cases of captures made within the waters of the United States, or within a marine league of the coast.

It is more important to observe that they possess all the powers of a Prize Court.(*b*)

*Secondly. The Circuit or Federal Courts. The United States are now divided into nine great circuits. They have [*543] appellate jurisdiction from all final decrees and judgments of the District Court in matters of Prize, where the matter in dispute, exclusive of costs, exceeds three hundred dollars.(*c*)

Thirdly. The Supreme Court, which is composed of a Chief Justice and eight Associate Justices, of whom five may make a Court. This Court, which is clothed with many attributes and discharges many functions of an international character, receives, as a Court of the last resort, appeals in cases of Prize.(*d*)

(*l*) Life of the Right Honourable Sir James Mackintosh, vol. i. pp. 317-19.

(*m*) Heathfield v. Chilton, 4 Burrow's Reports, p. 2016. "The Act of Parliament (7 Anne, c. 12,) did not intend to alter, *nor can alter the Law of Nations*."

(*n*) Bernardi v. Motteaux, Douglas's Reports, p. 581.

(*a*) 1 Kent's Comm., pp. 332, 3, (303, 4.)

(*b*) Ib., pp. 386, (355.)

(*c*) 1 Kent's Comm., pp. 331, (302.)

(*d*) Ib., pp. 323, (298.)

CCCCXXXVIII. The Prize Tribunal(e) in France has undergone great changes.

Originally the Admiral or his Lieutenant exercised Prize Jurisdiction.

As late as 1624 it appears that Henry de Montmorency exercised this jurisdiction *en vertu du pouvoir attaché à sa charge d'amirauté.*

In the time of Louis XIII. the office of Admiral was suppressed and replaced by that of a Grand-maître who took cognizance of Prizes. This office was filled by Cardinal Richelieu.(f)

During the minority of Louis XIV., Anne of Austria exercised the jurisdiction. She was speedily succeeded by the Duc de Vendôme (1650.) His appointment introduced a great and lasting change in the tribunal. He found himself much embarrassed with the questions of International Law, upon which he was obliged to adjudicate, and appeals were constantly prosecuted from his judgments to the Throne, till at last it became necessary to establish a permanent commission for his assistance, with an [*544] appeal to the Conseil d'Etat *du Roi. Such was the origin of the Conseil des Prises, which, with some interruptions and variations, has continued to the present day.

The office of the Admiral was re-established in favour of M. le Comte de Vermandois; and in 1695 it appears to have been fully revived in the person of M. le Comte de Toulouse. The Admiral continued to adjudicate with his attendant council till 1789. The last Conseil des Prises under the old law was appointed in 1778 to take cognizance of Prizes made from the English during the war between England and her colonies.

This Conseil des Prises was nominated for each war, having no authority during peace. The members were nominated by the King, with a Procureur-général.

The famous treatise of Valin—his Traité des Prises—was supervised and richly instructed with precedents by the Procureur-général of his time.

In 1793, when the war broke out between France and England, a decree of the Convention (14 July, 1793,) gave the jurisdiction over Prizes to the Tribunals of Commerce. Not long afterwards another decree issued, clothing the Conseil executif provisoire with this jurisdiction. The effect of this decree was to restore the jurisdiction to the administrative authority of the State, which the French writers appear,(g) in very direct opposition to the doctrine of the English and North American United States, to consider as the proper repository of International Law. In a short time the Comité du Salut public seized, and abused with shameless ignorance and injustice, the jurisdiction.

Afterwards the Tribunaux de Commerce possessed the jurisdiction,

(e) De Pist. et Duverdy, Traité des Prises, t. ii., P. viii.; cc. i. ii. iii. iv.

(f) Ib., p. 162.

(g) "C'était là rendre la connaissance des prises maritimes à l'autorité administrative, qui devoit naturellement en connoître."—De Pist. et Duverdy, Traité des Prises, t. iii., P. viii., c. iv., p. 149.

and with respect to their discharge of these functions Cambacérès, Minister of Justice, said:—

"Que la course était devenue un brigandage, pour que les lois que lui étaient appliquées étaient insuffisantes ou *mauvaise et que l'on avoit entendu s'élever de toutes parts les plaintes des négociants [*545] et des ministres étrangers, et que, cependant le Gouvernement, pénétré de la justice de ces plaintes, avoit toujours été sans pouvoir pour y faire droit."(*h*)

Under Napoleon the First, a Conseil des Prises was instituted to sit at Paris without any relation to the office of Admiral; and *special tribunals* with a limited jurisdiction were established in the ports, chiefly, it should seem, for the purpose of collecting information as to the facts of the cases submitted to the Conseil des Prises. From this tribunal there was an appeal to the revived Conseil d'Etat.

Besides the Commissions des Ports, there were also Commissions Coloniales to sit in the French Colonies, and Commissions Consulaires, which established, in violation of the soundest principles of International Law, French Tribunals in the ports of Neutrals or Allies.

Napoleon the Third in the present war (1856) re-instituted by decree a Conseil des Prises at Paris. By the fourth article of that decree the sittings of the Council were to be private, a provision which is much to be regretted by all who consider publicity as a great security for the impartial execution of public or international justice.

With respect to Spain, Abreu(*i*) has a chapter upon the necessity of a regular and formal procedure in a Prize Court in order to obtain the condemnation of a capture, the forms of which are, he says, wisely provided for in las Ordonnanzas de Corso,(*k*) with a view to secure the due administration of international justice.

*In Holland(*l*) there are ancient and regular tribunals for the administration of Maritime International Law. [*546]

In fact, no civilized State which has a commercial or an armed navy, is without them.(*m*) There are different forms of procedure in different States, but the principles of the law, and the rules for ascertaining the

(*h*) De Pist. et Duverdy, Tr. des Prises, t. iii. P. viii. c. iv. p. 158.

(*i*) Abreu, cap. xxiii.:—"Sobre el modo de probar el dominio de la Pressa y si la prueba de que se hizo legitimamente incumbe al apressador o el apressado."

(*k*) Ib., p. 251. Ordonnanza para Navegar en Corso, December 4th, 1621, are to be found in Phil. iv. t. i., p. 555, and cedul., pp. 372-430, to be compared with later ordinances of 1718–1779, &c. Cf. Colecion de los Tratados de Paz, Allianza, Neutralidad, &c., por Joseph Antonio De Abreu y Bertodano.—Ed. Madrid, 1740. His collection begins in 1598 (Philip II. and Henry IV.,) consists of eight small folios, ending 1700, and contains Treaties between France and Spain. It has a continuation, published at Madrid in 1796, of Treaties from 1701 to 1736; a work valuable for its accuracy, fulness of detail, and beauty of type and paper.

(*l*) De Martens, His. des Armateurs, s. 7, notes. For the Dutch Laws on the subject he refers to Instructie voor de Collegienter Admiraliteyt in dato d. 13 August, 1597, in the Recueil von Placaarten, C. D. L., P. i., 26.

(*m*) Azuni, Droit Maritime de l'Europe (Paris, 1805,) II. ch. iv. des Tribunaux des Prises. The account is meagre, but useful. The Swedish are to be found in a folio volume, published at Orebro in 1831, by Lindh, entitled Ny Lag. Samling, Första Häftet innehållende de tyra förste Balkarne of 1734 års Lag.

truth of facts ought to be, and, as a general proposition, are, pretty much the same.

The proper constitution of these Courts, and the due administration of justice therein, has not unfrequently been matter of positive stipulation in Treaties.(*n*)

One instance may be cited by way of illustration, taken from Mr. Pitt's Commercial Treaty between France and England in 1787. "Their said Majesties," it is there said, "being willing mutually to treat in their dominions the subjects of each other as favourably as if they were their own subjects, will give such orders as shall be necessary and effectual, that the judgments and decrees, concerning prizes in the Court of Admi-
[*547] ralty, be given *conformably to the rules of justice and equity, and to the stipulations of this treaty, by judges who are above all suspicion, and who have no manner of interest in the cause of dispute."(*o*)

CCCCXXXIX. The constitution of the Prize Court in England is in its origin much the same as that of similar tribunals in other countries.

It is the Court of the Judicial Lieutenant of the Lord High Admiral, which for more than a century it has been the practice of the Legislature(*p*) and the Crown, at the breaking out of every war, to clothe with the authority of a Prize Court, such authority being limited to the continuance of that war.

What amount of international authority it might possess irrespectively of such statutes, is not an uninteresting inquiry, but one of which the discussion would occupy an undue space in the present work.

But there is no reason to doubt that it has such authority exclusive of the Prize Acts.

"It is the common practice" (Lord Stowell observes) "of European States in every war, to issue proclamations and edicts on the subject of Prize; but till they appear, Courts of Admiralty have a law and usage on which they proceed, from ancient habit and practice, as regularly as they afterwards conform to the express regulations of their Prize Acts."(*q*)

Sir L. Jenkins says:—

"A mere routine and common experience will not do the business of a Register of the Admiralty, as it doth in other posts not unlike it. A man must in this place have a stock of Civil law, and endeavour to in-
[*548] crease it, by *searching into the style and practice of Maritime Courts beyond the seas, (which alters and varies considerably in a few years;) and he must be skilled in the neighbour languages, French and Dutch at least, (otherwise he must make use of a deputy, in taking the depositions of foreigners, which hath many great inconveniences in it;) these Mr. Bedford hath perfectly, having sojourned abroad a considerable time in foreign parts, in order to acquire them. . . . .

(*n*) Cf. Traités de Commerce, D'Hauterive et De Cussy, t. ix., p. 374, tit. Prises et Reprises.

(*o*) Chalmer's Collect. of Treaties, vol. i. p. 536, art. xxxii.

(*p*) From the 13 Geo. II. c. iv., A. D. 1740, Prize Acts have been regularly issued.

(*q*) The Santa Cruz, 1 Rob. Rep., p. 63.

"Another thing is, that this Court is one of the King's Courts of Justice, where foreigners almost of all nations are suitors; and 'tis for the reputation of the Government, that such a trust be committed to a person that is to be responsible in his own right; and to one that will have a concern that nothing of mal-administration, either through ignorance or corruption, be charged upon him. For miscarriages in this post have sometimes come at last to public sharpness and resentments between our and other neighbouring nations."(*r*)

The Advocates who practise in the Prize Court constitute, under Royal Charter, a peculiar College,(*s*) and have been for centuries a distinct profession from the Common Law and Equity Bar.

It is the duty of these advocates to be acquainted both with the Civil Law of ancient and, to a certain extent, the Ecclesiastical Law of modern Rome, but especially with International and Maritime Law, many principles of which are to be found in the compilations of Justinian.(*t*)

From these advocates are selected the principal advisers of the Crown(*u*) in matters of International Law; and the *fact has been relied upon in the British House of Peers by a very distinguished person, once Lord High Chancellor of England, as having a most important bearing upon the conduct of the international relations of the Empire.(*x*) [*549]

The appeal from the Prize Court lay formerly to Judges Delegate chosen by the Crown, which sometimes also granted a Commission of Review:(*y*) it now lies to a Judicial Committee,(*z*) composed of the most eminent lawyers of all branches of the profession, who are also Privy Councillors.

This appeal is final. The *form* of the sentence of this Court is a recommendation to the Crown to confirm or reverse the sentence of the Court below; but *in substance and effect* the recommendation operates

(*r*) Life of Sir Leoline Jenkins, vol. ii. pp. 709, 710. Letter to Samuel Pepys, Esq., Secretary to the Lords Commissioners of the Admiralty.

(*s*) Vide ante, Vol. I. Pref. p. xxv., &c.

(*t*) Vide ante, Vol. I. pt. i. ch. iv.

(*u*) The Queen's Advocate is the first law officer of the Crown, and its adviser in all international affairs. The Advocate to the Admiralty advises the Crown only in its office of Admiralty.

(*x*) "He (Lord St. Leonards) had already called the attention of the noble Earl at the head of Her Majesty's Government to the advantage of keeping together a bar for matrimonial causes and testamentary jurisdiction. In the Ecclesiastical Courts the gentlemen who now practised there were disciplined and learned in International Law—men of independence, honour, and high character, whose opinions not only guided the Government in the most difficult cases, but carried a weight with them in Europe; for foreign Governments were satisfied when they found that this Government was acting not merely upon its own will and feelings, but was guided by the learning and opinions of persons who were amenable to the profession and the country for the opinions which they gave."—Hansard, Parl. Deb. vol. cxxxiv. p. 938, June 30th, 1854.

(*y*) Life of Sir Leoline Jenkins, vol. ii. p. 721.

(*z*) 2 & 3 William IV., c. 92, and 3 & 4 William IV., c. 41. 6 & 7 Victoria, c. 38. But it is provided that nothing in the 3 & 4 Will. IV. c. 41 contained shall impeach any Treaty or engagement with a Foreign Power by which it shall be stipulated that the appeal in cases of Prize shall belong to another jurisdiction, but that the judgment of any persons appointed by such Treaty shall be of the same force as if the Act had not been passed.

as a judgment. The Crown never is, and perhaps constitutionally could
[*550] not be, *advised to do otherwise than adopt the recommendation of her Judicial Privy Councillors.

The whole proceedings in the Court of Appeal, as in the High Court of Admiralty, are conducted in an open Court accessible to everybody, and of which the Reports are duly published to the world.

[*551]

*CHAPTER III.

THE PRINCIPLES AND PRACTICE OF THE PRIZE TRIBUNALS.—GENERAL OUTLINE.

CCCCXL. In the year 1794,(*a*) Sir W. Scott and Sir J. Nicholl, the two civilians best acquainted with the jurisprudence and procedure of the Tribunal of Maritime International Law, wrote an answer to a letter of inquiry upon this subject from the American Ambassador, Mr. Jay, which answer contained an outline of the principles and practice of these Courts. Judge Story refers to it as in all respects satisfactory. The North American Prize Courts have seldom if ever departed from the rules contained in it.

It is extremely valuable both on account of the authority of the writers themselves and on account of their unreserved adoption in this letter of the celebrated Memorial of 1753, which has been often referred to in this work.

This remarkable letter(*b*) is in the following terms:—

"Sir,

"We have the honour of transmitting, agreeably to your Excellency's request, a statement of the general principles of proceeding in Prize Causes in British Courts of Admiralty, and of the measures proper to be taken when a ship and cargo are brought in as Prize within their jurisdictions.

"The general principles of proceeding cannot, in our judgment, be stated more correctly or succinctly, than we find them laid down in
[*552] the following extract from a report made *to his late Majesty, in the year 1753, by Sir George Lee, then judge of the Prerogative Court, Dr. Paul, his Majesty's Advocate-General, Sir Dudley Rider, his Majesty's Attorney-General, and Mr. Murray, (afterwards Lord Mansfield,) his Majesty's Solicitor-General:—(*c*)

"'When two powers are at war, they have a right to make prizes of the ships, goods, and effects of each other, upon the high seas. Whatever is the property of the enemy may be acquired by capture at sea; but

(*a*) Pratt's Story, p. 1. Wheaton on Captures, Appendix. 1 Wheaton's (Amer.) Reports, p. 494, Appendix, n. ii.
(*b*) It was enclosed in a civil and formal note to Mr. Jay, the American Minister.
(*c*) Cabinet Library of scarce and celebrated Tracts. Edinb. 1837.

the property of a friend cannot be taken, provided he observes his neutrality.

"'Hence the Law of Nations has established:

"'That the goods of an enemy, on board the ship of a friend, may be taken;

"'That the lawful goods of a friend, on board the ship of an enemy, ought to be restored:

"'That contraband goods, going to the enemy, though the property of a friend, may be taken as Prize; because supplying the enemy with what enables him better to carry on the war, is a departure from neutrality.

"'By the Maritime Law of Nations, universally and immemorially received, there is an established method of determination whether the capture be, or be not, lawful prize.

"'Before the ship, or goods, can be disposed of by the captors, there must be a regular judicial proceeding, wherein both parties may be heard; and condemnation thereupon as Prize, in a Court of Admiralty, judging by the Law of Nations and Treaties.

"'The proper and regular Court, for these condemnations, is the Court of that State to whom the captor belongs.

"'The evidence to acquit or condemn, with or without costs or damages, must, in the first instance, come merely from the ship taken, viz., the papers on board, and the examination on oath of the master and other principal officers; for which purpose there are officers of Admiralty *in all the considerable sea-ports of every maritime power at war, to examine the captains, and other principal officers of every ship brought in as a prize, upon general and impartial interrogatories. [*553]

"'If there do not appear from thence ground to condemn, as enemies' property or contraband goods going to the enemy, there must be an acquittal, unless, from the aforesaid evidence, the property shall appear so doubtful that it is reasonable to go into farther proof thereof.

"'A claim of ship, or goods, must be supported by the oath of somebody, at least as to belief.

"'The law of nations requires good faith. Therefore, every ship must be provided with complete and genuine papers; and the master at least should be privy to the truth of the transaction.

"'To enforce these rules, if there be false or colourable papers; if any papers be thrown overboard; if the master and officers examined *in preparatorio* grossly prevaricate; if proper ship's papers are not on board; or if the master and crew cannot say whether the ship or cargo be the property of a friend or enemy, the Law of Nations allows, according to the different degrees of misbehaviour or suspicion, arising from the fault of the ship taken, and other circumstances of the case, costs to be paid, or not be received by the claimant, in case of acquittal and restitution. On the other hand, if a seizure is made without probable cause, the captor is adjudged to pay costs and damages.

"'For which purpose all privateers are obliged to give security for their good behaviour; and this is referred to and expressly stipulated by many treaties.

"'Though from the ship's papers and the preparatory examinations, the property does not sufficiently appear to be neutral, the claimant is often indulged with time to send over affidavits to supply that defect. If he will not show the property, by sufficient affidavits, to be neutral, it is presumed to belong to the enemy.

[*554] "'Where the property appears from evidence not on board *the ship, the captor is justified in bringing her in, and excused paying costs, because he is not in fault; or, according to the circumstances of the case, may be justly entitled to receive his costs.

"'If the sentence of the Court of Admiralty is thought to be erroneous, there is in every maritime country a Superior Court of Review, consisting of the most considerable persons, to which the parties who think themselves aggrieved may appeal; and this Superior Court judges by the same rule which governs the Court of of Admiralty, viz., the Law of Nations, and the Treaties subsisting with that neutral power whose subject is a party before them.

"'If no appeal is offered, it is an acknowledgment of the justice of the sentence by the parties themselves, and conclusive.

"'This manner of trial and adjudication is supported, alluded to, and enforced, by many Treaties.

"'In this method, all captures at sea were tried, during the last war, by Great Britain, France, and Spain, and submitted to by the neutral powers. In this method, by Courts of Admiralty acting according to the Law of Nations and particular Treaties, all captures at sea have immemorially been judged of in every country in Europe. Any other method of trial would be manifestly unjust, absurd, and impracticable.'

Such are the principles which govern the proceedings of the Prize Courts.

"The following are the measures which ought to be taken by the captor, and by the neutral claimant, upon a ship and cargo being brought in as Prize.

"The captor, immediately upon bringing his Prize into port, sends up, or delivers upon oath, to the Registry of the Court of Admiralty all papers found on board the captured ship. In the course of a few days, the examinations *in preparatorio* of the captain and some of the crew

[*555] of the captured *ship, are taken upon a set of standing interrogatories, before the Commissioners of the port to which the Prize is brought, and which are also forwarded to the Registry of the Admiralty as soon as taken.

A monition is extracted by the captor from the registry, and served upon the Royal Exchange, notifying the capture, and calling upon all persons interested to appear and show cause, why the ship and goods should not be condemned. At the expiration of twenty days, the monition is returned into the registry, with a certificate of its service; and if any claim has been given, the cause is then ready for hearing, upon the evidence arising out of the ship's papers, and preparatory examinations.

"The measures taken on the part of the neutral master or proprietor of the cargo, are as follows:

"Upon being brought into port, the master usually makes a protest, which he forwards to London, as instructions (or with such further directions as he thinks proper) either to the correspondent of his owners, or to the consul of his nation, in order to claim the ship, and such parts of the cargo as belong to his owners, or with which he was particularly entrusted; or the master himself, as soon as he has undergone his examination, goes to London to take the necessary steps.

"The master, correspondent, or consul applies to a proctor, who prepares a claim, supported by an affidavit of the claimant, stating briefly to whom, as he believes, the ship and goods claimed, belong; and that no enemy has any right or interest in them. Security must be given to the amount of sixty pounds to answer costs, if the case should appear so grossly fraudulent on the part of the claimant as to subject him to be condemned therein.

"If the captor has neglected, in the meantime, to take the usual steps (but which seldom happens, as he is strictly enjoined both by his instructions and by the Prize Act to proceed immediately to adjudication,) a process issues *against him on the application of the claimant's proctor, to bring in the ship's papers, and preparatory examinations, and to proceed in the usual way. [*556]

"As soon as the claim is given, copies of the ship's papers and examinations are procured from the registry, and upon the return of the monition, the cause may be heard. It, however, seldom happens (owing to the great pressure of business, especially at the commencement of a war,) that causes can possibly be prepared for hearing immediately upon the expiration of the time for the return of the monition. In that case, each cause must necessarily take its turn; correspondent measures must be taken by the neutral master, if carried within the jurisdiction of a Vice-Admiralty Court, by giving a claim supported by his affidavit, and offering security for costs, if the claim should be pronounced grossly fraudulent.

"If the claimant be dissatisfied with the sentence, his proctor enters an appeal in the registry of the Court where the sentence was given, or before a notary public (which regularly should be entered within fourteen days after the sentence,) and he afterwards applies at the Registry of the Lords of Appeal in Prize Causes (which is held at the same place as the Registry of the High Court of Admiralty) for an instrument called an inhibition, and which should be taken out within three months, if the sentence be in the High Court of Admiralty, and within nine months, if in a Vice-Admiralty Court; but may be taken out at later periods, if a reasonable cause can be assigned for the delay that has intervened. This instrument directs the judge, whose sentence is appealed from, to proceed no further in the cause; it directs the registrar to transmit a copy of all the proceedings of the Inferior Court, and it directs the party who has obtained the sentence, to appear before the superior tribunal, to answer to the appeal. On applying for this inhibition, security is given on the part of the appellant, to the amount *of 200*l.*, to answer costs, in case it should appear to the Court of Appeals that the appeal is merely vexatious. The inhibition is to be served upon the judge, the registrar, and the adverse party and his [*557] proctor, by showing the instrument under seal, and delivering a note or copy of the contents. If the party cannot be found, and the proctor will not accept the service, the instrument is to be served '*viis et modis*;' that is, by fixing it to the door of the last place of residence, or by hanging it upon the pillars of the Royal Exchange. That part of the process above described, which is to be executed abroad, may be performed by any person to whom it is committed, and the formal part at home is executed by the officer of the Court. A certificate of the service is indorsed upon the back of the instrument, sworn before a surrogate of the Superior Court, or before a notary public, if the service is abroad.

"Upon an appeal, fresh evidence may be introduced, if upon hearing the cause the Lords of Appeal shall be of opinion, that the case is of such doubt, as that further proof ought to have been ordered by the Court below.

"If the cause be adjudged in a Vice-Admiralty Court, it is usual, upon entering an appeal there, to procure a copy of the proceedings which the appellant sends over to his correspondent in England, who carries it to a proctor, and the same steps are taken to procure and serve the inhibition as where the cause has been adjudged in the High Court of Admiralty. But if a copy of the proceedings cannot be procured in due time, an inhibition may be obtained, by sending over a copy of the instrument of appeal, or by writing to the correspondent an account only of the time and substance of the sentence.

"Further proof usually consists of affidavits made by the asserted proprietors of the goods, in which they are sometimes joined by their clerks, and others acquainted with the transaction, and with the real property of the goods claimed. In corroboration of these, affidavits may be [*558] annexed, original *correspondence, duplicates of bills of lading, invoices, extracts from books, &c. These papers must be proved by the affidavits of persons who can speak to their authenticity; and if copies or extracts, they should be collated and certified by public notaries. The affidavits are sworn before the magistrates or others competent to administer oaths in the country where they are made, and authenticated by a certificate from the British Consul.

"The degree of proof to be required depends upon the degree of suspicion and doubt, that belongs to the case. In cases of heavy suspicion and great importance, the Court may order what is called 'plea and proof;' that is, instead of admitting affidavits and documents introduced by the claimants only, each party is at liberty to allege, in regular pleadings, such circumstances as may tend to acquit or to condemn the capture, and to examine witnesses in support of the allegations, to whom the adverse party may administer interrogatories. The deposition of the witnesses are taken in writing; if the witnesses are to be examined abroad, a commission issues for that purpose, but in no case is it necessary for them to come to England. These solemn proceedings are not often resorted to.

"Standing commissions may be sent to America,(c) for the general

(c) And of course to all Foreign States not Belligerent.

purpose of receiving examinations of witnesses, in all cases where the Court may find it necessary, for the purposes of justice, to decree an inquiry to be conducted in that manner.

"With respect to captures and condemnations at Martinico, which are the subjects of another inquiry contained in your note, we can only answer in general, that we are not informed of the particulars of such captures and condemnations, but, as we know of no legal Court of Admiralty *established at Martinico, we are clearly of opinion that the legality of any Prizes taken there, must be tried in the High [*559] Court of Admiralty of England, upon claims given, in the manner above described, by such persons as may think themselves aggrieved by the said Captures.

"We have the honour to be, &c.,
"(Signed) "WILLIAM SCOTT,
"JOHN NICHOLL.

"Commons, September 10th, 1794."

---

*CHAPTER IV. [*560]

PRINCIPLES AND PRACTICE OF THE PRIZE TRIBUNALS.—DISTRIBUTION OF THE SUBJECT UNDER DIFFERENT HEADS.

CCCCXLI. THIS important subject of the Principles and Practice of the Tribunal of Maritime International Law generally, but more especially in England and the United States of North America, will be considered under the following heads :—

I. The Custody of the Prize, pending the judicial inquiry as to the legality of the seizure.

II. The Process and the Practice of the Court: which will embrace,—

Generally,

A. The Rights and Duties of Captors, with reference to the conduct of the suit.

B. The Rights and duties of Claimants, with reference to the conduct of the suit.

Particularly,

C. The Pleadings.

D. The Evidence.

E. The question of Further Proof.

α. To Claimants.

β. To Captors.

F. The Sentence, including the Decision.

α. As to the Legality of the Seizure.

β. As to the Subsequent Conduct of Captors and Claimants.

γ. The question of Costs, Expenses, and Freight.

III. The Appellate Tribunal.

[*561] *CCCCXLII. (I.) *Custody of the Property captured.*

The captor's title to his Prize depends upon his obtaining a sentence in his favour from the proper tribunal. It is, therefore, his interest, as well as his duty, to bring in his Prize as speedily as possible for adjudication. But if he neglect to do so, the claimant may himself apply to the Court for restitution.

In either case the property is immediately taken into the custody of the Court; for in all proceedings *in rem* the Court has a right to the custody of the thing in controversy; and as soon as proceeded against, it is always deemed in the custody of the law.(*a*) In the United States, a warrant immediately goes to the Marshal, to take possession of the property; and he is bound to keep it in *salvâ et arctâ custodiâ;* and if any loss happen by his negligence, he is responsible for it to the Court. In England, although the property is now usually put into the hands of the captors, yet it still remains, in contemplation of law, in the custody of the public. Formerly, it actually did remain in its custody, as is still the case in other foreign countries. It is merely for the convenience of the captors, that the English Admiralty permits them to take possession of the property. But it must be remembered, that it is so held by them as agents of the Court, and not in the right of property; and therefore, their possession may be divested by the act of the Court, either *ex officio,* or on the application of the parties interested, showing good cause for taking it out of their hands.(*b*) And the property still remains in the custody of the Court, notwithstanding an unlivery and deposit in public warehouses.(*c*)

[*562] *CCCCXLIII. In fact, in England, where the property is so unlivered, if it has been captured by a public or private commissioned vessel, it is *de facto* under the joint locks of the Government and the captors, although in the legal possession of the Marshal under the tenor of his writ for unlivery; and if captured by a non-commissioned vessel, it is a *droit,* where the king, in his office of Admiralty, being the captor, it is under his locks alone.(*d*) In the United States of North America, the Marshal holds the custody at all times for the Court; and the latter is the guardian of the public rights and revenue, as well as of the rights of the captors and claimants in all cases of Prize. It is, indeed, usual and proper for the collector of the customs to keep an officer on board, for the protection of the revenue, until the duties are duly secured, which the captors may secure if they please; but since it cannot be ascertained until a decree of condemnation, whether the property be good Prize or not, many cases may occur in which it would be highly inconvenient for them to adopt this course. If the property be restored specifically and exported from the country by the claimants, it is held not liable to duties; and if sold under an interlocutory order of

(*a*) Jennings v. Carson, 4 Cranch's (Amer.) Rep., p. 2. Home v. Camden, 2 H. Blackstone's Rep., p. 533.

(*b*) Per Sir W. Scott, arguendo in Smart v. Wolff, 3 Durnford & East's Rep., pp. 323, 329. The Herkimer, Stewart, p. 128. S. C., 2 Hall's (Amer.) Law Journal, p. 133.

(*c*) The Maria, 4 Rob., p. 348.

(*d*) The Rendsberg, 6 Rob., pp. 142, 174.

sale, it is the duty of the Court to reserve, out of the proceeds, the amount of duties which then attach upon it, and direct them to be paid over to the collector.(e) It is true that the American Prize Act of last war,(f) seems to contemplate that the duties may be paid or secured in Prize Cases, in the same manner as goods ordinarily imported. But this clause is *in terms* applied only to goods of British growth, produce, or manufacture, or imported from British ports; and is, at all events, inapplicable to cases where it cannot be ascertained whether the goods are imported or not, until after a judicial decision. And the subsequent act of the 27th *January, 1813, ch. 155, manifestly contemplates, that the payment of the duties is, in cases of condemnation, [*563] to be made by the Marshal, out of the proceeds of Prize Sales. And it has been repeatedly held, in the Circuit Court for the First Circuit, that no forfeiture accrued for not securing the duties upon Prize goods before condemnation; and that the Court might, at any time, direct an unlivery and sale; and upon such sale would deduct the amount of duties, and direct them to be paid to the collector.

CCCCXLIV. It has already been stated, that when the Marshal has possession of the property he is bound for safe and fair custody; and if any loss be sustained, it is at least his duty to be prepared to show that it was not lost by any default of his.(g) If, therefore, property be pillaged while under his care, the Court will hold him responsible for its value, if it arose from his negligence. If, indeed, upon an application to enforce his responsibility, he by his answer deny any negligence and loose custody, the Court may, perhaps, think it no more than a legal and proper confidence in its own officer, to throw the burden of proof of culpable negligence or fraud on the other party;(h) and where the property is lost while actually under the locks of the Government, the Marshal will not be liable, although he may still be considered as constructively having the legal property.(i)

CCCCXLV. (II.) *The Process and the Practice of the Court.*

A. *The Rights and Duties of Captors with reference to the Conduct of the Suit.*(k)

(e) The Concord, 9 Cranch's (Amer.) Rep., p. 387. The Nereide, 1 Wheaton's (Amer.) Rep., p. 171.

(f) Act of the 26th June, 1812, ch. 107, s. 14. (g) The Hoop, 4 Rob., p. 145.

(h) The Rendsberg, 6 Ib., pp. 142, 157. (i) Ibid.

(k) 2 Brown's Civ. and Adm. Law, p. 524. Casaregis Disc., p. 24, No. 24. 2 Wooddeson's Lect., p. 432. Consolato del Mare, ch. cclxxxvii. cclxxxviii. 3 Bulstrode's Rep., p. 27. 4 Inst., (Cooke,) pp. 152, 154. Zouch, Adm. Jurisd., ch. iv. p. 101. Com. Dig. Adm., c. iii. E. p. 3. The Georgianne, 1 Dodson's (Adm.) Rep., p. 397. The Diligentia, Ib., p. 404. The Emulous, 8 Cranch's (Amer.) Rep., p. 131. The Nereide, 9 Cranch's (Amer.) Rep., p. 389. The Dos Hermanos, 2 Wheaton's (Amer.) Rep., p. 76. "Aucun ne pourra armer un vaisseau en guerre, sans commission de l'admiral."—Ordonnance de 1681, l. iii. tit. ix., Des Prises, art. i.

"Il est tellement vrai qu'il n'y a que ceux qui ont commission de l'admiral, qui sont en droit de faire à leur profit des prises sur l'ennemi que si le capitaine d'un vaisseaux marchand a été attaque en mer par un vaisseaux ennemi dont il s'est rendu maître dans le combat, *la prise qu'il a faite du vaisseaux ennemi ne lui appartient pas*, mais appartient à l'admiral, qui est à cet égard aux droits du roi, l'admiral a coutume d'en gratifier pour le tout ou pour partie celui qui a fait la prise,

[*564] *To enable a vessel to make captures which shall insure benefit to the captors, it is necessary that she should have a Commission of Prize. But *non-commissioned* vessels of a belligerent nation may, not only make captures in their own defence, but may, at all times, capture hostile ships and cargoes, without being deemed by the Law of Nations to be pirates, though they can have no interest in Prizes so captured. But every capture, whether made by commissioned or non-commissioned ships, is at the peril of the captors. If they capture property without a reasonable or justifiable cause, they are liable to a suit for restitution, and may also be mulcted in costs and damages.(*l*)

[*565] If the vessel and cargo, or any part thereof, be good *Prize they are completely justified. And although the whole property may, upon a hearing, be restored; yet, if there was *probable cause of capture*, they are not responsible in damages.(*m*) But, on the other hand, they may, under circumstances according to the degree of doubt or suspicion thrown upon the case, either from defects of papers, the nature of the voyage, or the conduct of the captured crew, be entitled to receive their costs and expenses in bringing in the property for adjudication. The circumstances are of course very various, which may constitute *a probable cause of capture*. They were much discussed in the case of the Ostsee decided by the Judicial Committee of the Privy Council in 1855; but it was not the intention of that tribunal to alter the previous practice on this subject.(*n*)

CCCCXLVI. Both in considering what reasons may be sufficient to justify a captor in bringing a vessel into the Prize Court for adjudication, and also in applying the principles to be collected from decided cases upon this subject, it is very necessary to bear in mind the distinction between two cases, viz.:—

1. The case of a vessel seized in the port or harbour of the Belligerent.

2. The case of a vessel seized upon the high seas.

In the (1.) former case the seizor has opportunity and means of obtaining proper legal advice as to the course which he shall pursue. And though even in this case much evidence must, until the examination of witnesses,—that is, of a portion of the crew on board the captured vessel,—remain uncertain, and much allowance must be made for the necessary ignorance of the captor with respect to the possibility of expla-

sans tirer à consequence."—Pothier de propriété, No. 93. Valin sur l'Ordonnance ubi suprà.

(*l*) "Lesdits preneurs empeschans aucuns marchands, navire ou marchandise *sans cause raisonable*, ou qu'ils ne soyent nos adversaires, *nostre dit admiral sera deuement restituer le dommage*, et ne permettra plus l'usage qu'ont à ce contre raison tenué, iceus preneurs, en quoy ils ont fait et donne de grands dommages à aucuns de nos alliez par feinte, ou fausse couleur qu'ils mettoyent de non cognoistre s'ils estoyent nos adversaires, ou non, qui est chose bien damnable, contre raison et justice, que homme soubs telle couleur deust, porter dommage ou destourbier."—Ordonnance de 1400, art. viii. See the opinion of M. Portalis in the case of the Pigou, 2 Cranch's (Amer.) Rep.. p. 98, note (*a*).

(*m*) Opinion of M. Portalis, in the case of the Statira, 2 Cranch's (Amer.) Rep., p. 102, note (*a*), and Traité des Prises Maritimes, ii. p. 121, à De Pist. et Duverd.

(*n*) See Aline and Fanny, July, 1856.

nation being produced by the claimant to do away with the effect of circumstances, *primâ facie*, *fraught with suspicion; still the reason of the thing requires that a rule, in some degree less favourable to the captor, and more favourable to the claimant, should be applied to cases of this description than to cases falling under the latter category, viz. (2.) of captures made upon the high seas. [*566]

The captor in the latter case is, for obvious and various reasons, *inops consilii;* he must act instantly, and without opportunity of prosecuting a minute or careful investigation into all the circumstances of the case.

The reason of the thing therefore prescribes that, in this case, if the captor has acted honestly, a less amount of *probable cause*—to use a phrase now stereotyped in the Prize Court—of suspicion shall avail not only to protect him from the payment of damage to the vessel seized, but to insure to him the payment of costs from her.

During the present war (1856) it will be seen that in the English Prize Courts these principles have certainly not been strained in favour of the captor. It may, perhaps, be questioned whether the decisions have not tended towards a contrary extreme.

But in England, the right to vessels seized in ports or harbours belongs to the Lord High Admiral, or to the Commissioners—usually called Lords of the Admiralty—who execute his office under the authority of the Crown. The Lord High Admiral is furnished with legal advice(*o*) separate and distinct from that which is possessed by the Crown. This is, perhaps, among the reasons why the seizor in ports or harbours of England is obliged to show a greater amount of probable cause than the captor on the high seas.

But in general it may be observed, that if the ship pretend to be neutral, and has not the usual documents of *such a ship on board;(*p*) if the cargo be without any clearance;(*q*) if the destination be untruly stated; if the papers respecting the ship or cargo be false or colourable, or be suppressed or spoliated; or if the neutrality of the cargo does not distinctly and fully appear;(*r*) if the voyage be from, or to a blockaded port,(*s*) or not legal to the parties engaged in the traffic;(*t*) if the cargo be of an ambiguous character as to contraband;(*u*) and generally, if the case be a case of farther proof; all or any of these circumstances furnish a probable cause for capture, and justify the captors in bringing in the ship and cargo for adjudication. [*567]

CCCCXLVII. Whenever the captors are justified in the capture, they are considered as having a *bonâ fide* possession, and are not respon-

(*o*) Advocate and Proctor to Her Majesty in her office of Admiralty. These offices are of high antiquity. See them fully discussed in The Rebeckah, 1 Rob. Adm. Rep., p. 230.

(*p*) The Anna, 5 Rob., p. 382. (*q*) Ibid.

(*r*) Vide ante, p. 552, Report of 1753. Wheaton on Captures, Appendix, p. 320.

(*s*) The Frederick Molke, 1 Rob., p. 86.

(*t*) The Walsingham Packet, 2 Ib., p. 77. The Hoop, 1 Ib., p. 196. The St. Antonius, 1 Acton, p. 113.

(*u*) The Endraught, 1 Rob., p. 22. The Ringende Jacob, Ib., p. 89. The Jonge Margaretha, Ib., p. 189. The Twende Broder, 4 Ib., p. 33. The Frau Margaretha, 9 Ib., p. 92. The Ranger, Ib., p. 125.

sible for any subsequent losses or injuries arising to the property from mere accident or casualty, as from stress of weather, recapture by the enemy, shipwreck, and the like accidents.(*x*)

CCCCXLVIII. They are, however, in all cases bound for fair and safe custody; and if the property be lost from the want of proper care, they are responsible to the amount of the damage; for subsequent mis-
[*568] conduct may forfeit the fair *title of a *bonâ fide* possessor, and make him a trespasser from the beginning.(*y*) Therefore, if the Prize be lost by the misconduct of the Prize Master, or from neglecting to take a pilot, or to put on board a proper Prize Crew, the Court will decree restitution in value against the captors.(*z*) But although in general, irregularity of conduct in captors makes them liable for damages; yet, in case of a *bonâ fide* possession, the irregularity to bind them must be such as produces irreparable loss; as, for instance, such as may prevent restitution from an enemy who recaptures the property.(*a*) And in cases of gross misconduct, the Court will hold the commission of the captors forfeited.(*b*) But if the injured parties lie by for a great length of time, the Court will not issue a monition to the captors to proceed to adjudication, even when misconduct is laid as the ground of the application.(*c*)

CCCCXLIX. When a ship is captured, it is the duty of the captors to send her into some convenient port for adjudication.(*d*) And a con-
[*569] venient port is such a port as the ship *may ride in with safety, without unloading her cargo;(*e*) and the captors are bound to put on board the captured ship a sufficient Prize Crew to navigate the vessel into such a port, unless the captured crew consent to navigate her, which in general they are bound to do; but if they consent, they cannot afterwards impute any fault to the captors.(*f*)

CCCCL. The treatment of the captured crew, especially of a crew belonging to a Neutral State, is a matter of grave importance. The crew ought not to be handcuffed or put in irons, unless in extreme cases; for

(*x*) The Betsey, 1 Ib., p. 93. The Catharine and Anne, 4 Ib., p. 39. The Caroline, Ib., p. 256. Del Col v. Arnold, 3 Dallas's (Amer.) Rep., p. 333.

(*y*) The Betsey, 1 Rob., p. 93. The Catharine and Anne, 4 Ib., p. 39.

(*z*) The Der Mohr, 3 Ib., p. 129. The Speculation, 2 Ib., p. 293. The William, 6 Ib., p. 316. Del Col v. Arnold, 3 Dallas's (Amer.) Rep., p. 333. Wilcocks v. Union Ins. Comp., 2 Binney's (Amer.) Rep., p. 574.

(*a*) The Betsey, 1 Rob., p. 93. (*b*) The Mariamne, 5 Ib., p. 9.

(*c*) The Purissima Conception, 6 Ib., p. 45.

(*d*) The Huldah, 3 Ib., p. 235. The Madonna del Burso, 4 Ib., p. 169. The St. Juan Baptista, 5 Ib., p. 33. The Wilhelmsberg, Ib., p. 143. The Elsebe, 5 Ib., p. 173. The Lively, 1 Gallison's (Amer.) Rep., p. 315.

"Enjoignons aux capitaines qui auront fait quelque prise, de l'amener ou envoyer avec les prisonniers, au port où ils auront armé, à peine de perte de leur droits, et d'amende arbitraire; si ce n'est qu'il fussent forcés par la tempête ou par les ennemis, de relâcher en quelque autre port, auquel cas ils seront tenus d'en donner incessament avis aux interressés à l'armement."—L'Ordonnance de 1681, l. iii. t. ix., Des Prises, art. vii. See also the Ordinance of 1584, art. xliii., Col. Mar., p. 113.

(*e*) The Washington, 6 Rob., p. 275. The Principe, Edwards, p. 70.

(*f*) Wilcocks v. Union Ins. Comp., 2 Binney's (Amer.) Rep., p. 574. The Resolution, 6 Rob., p. 13. The Pennsylvania, 1 Acton, p. 33. The Alexander, 1 Gallison's (Amer.) Rep., p. 532. S. C., 8 Cranch's (Amer.) Rep., p. 169.

if unnecessarily done, the Prize Court will decree damages to the injured parties.(*g*) Captors are not bound to explain the cause of capture, but it is highly proper so to do, as the master may explain it away.(*h*) They may chase under false colours, but the Maritime Law does not permit them to fire under false colours.(*i*)

*CCCCLI. They have no right to make any spoliation or damage to the captured ship, or to embezzle or convert the pro- [*570] perty, or to break bulk, or to remove any of the property from the ship, unless in cases of necessity, or where obvious reasons of policy, or the urgency of the occasion, justify them in so doing.(*k*) And in every case of a removal of property from a captured ship, the Court expects to be satisfied as to the propriety of the removal, before it will proceed to adjudication. But if any of the captured property be shown to be missing, without any default on their part, as where it is lost by robbery or burglary after unlivery, they are not responsible for the loss.(*l*) And if captors, acting *bonâ fide*, and for the benefit of the parties, under peculiar circumstances, land, or even sell, the Prize Goods, this irregularity, if not injurious to the parties, will not be held to deprive them of the effects of a lawful possession.(*m*)

CCCCLII. If the capture is made *without probable cause*, the captors are liable for damages, costs, and expenses to the claimants.(*n*) And the Prize Court has exclusive authority as to *the allowance of freight, damages, expenses, and costs in all cases of captures;(*o*) [*571]

(*g*) The St. Juan Baptista, 5 Rob., p. 33. The Die Fire Damer, Ib., p. 357.

(*h*) The Juffrouw Maria Schroeder, 3 Ib., p. 147.

(*i*) The Peacock, 4 Ib., p. 185. "Sa Majesté a ordonné, et ordonne, que tous les capitaines commandans ses vaisseaux ou ceaux armés en course par ses sujets, seront tenus d'arborer pavillon français avant de tirer le coup d'assurance ou de semonce. Défenses très expresses leur sont faites de tirer sous pavillon étranger, à peine d'être privés eux et leur armateurs, de tous le provenu de la prise, qui sera confisqué au profit de sa Majesté, si le vaisseau est jugé ennemi, et en cas que le vaisseau soit jugé neutre, les capitaines et armateurs seront condamnés aux dépens, dommages, et intérêts des propriétaires.—Ordonnance de 17 Mars, 1696.

(*k*) The Concordia, 2 Rob., p. 102. L'Eole, 6 Ib., p. 220. The Washington, Ib., p. 275. Clerk's Praxis, p. 163. Del Col v. Arnold, 3 Dallas's (Amer.) Rep., p. 333.

(*l*) The Maria, 4 Rob., p. 348. The Rendsberg, 6 Ib., p. 142.

(*m*) The Princessa, 2 Ib., p. 31.

(*n*) Sir W. Scott and Sir J. Nicholl's Letter to Mr. Jay, antè, p. 551. Opinion of M. Portalis in the case of the Pigou, 2 Cranch's (Amer.) Rep., p. 101, note (*a*). Del Col v. Arnold, 3 Dallas's (Amer.) Rep., p. 333. The Charming Betsey, 2 Cranch's (Amer.) Rep., p. 64. Maley v. Shattuck, 3 Cranch's (Amer.) Rep., p. 458. The Triton, 4 Rob., p. 78. Camden v. Home, 4 Durnford & East's Rep., p. 385. Fallijeff v. Elphinstone, 5 Brown's Parl. Cas., p. 343. Clerk's Praxis, p. 162. The Lively, 1 Gallison's (Amer.) Rep., p. 315.

"Si la prise ètoit évidemment mauvaise de manière qu'il n'y eut rien qui fut capable d'excuser le corsaire ; nul doute alors que la main-levée n'en fut ordonnée, non seulment avec exemption de tous frais; mais encore avec tous dépens, dommages, et intérêts contre l'armateur."—2 Valin sur l'Ordonnance, p. 336.

(*o*) Le Caux v. Eden, Doug., p. 594. Lindo v. Rodney, Ib., p. 613. Smart v. Wolff, 3 Durnford & East's Rep., p. 223. The Copenhagen, 1 Rob., p. 289. The St. Juan Baptista, 5 Ib., p. 33. The Die Fire Damer, Ib., p. 357. The Betsey, 1 Ib., p. 93. Duckworth v. Tucker, 2 Taunton's Rep., p. 7. Jennings v. Carson, 4 Cranch's (Amer.) Rep., p. 2. Bingham v. Cabot, 3 Dallas's (Amer.) Rep., p. 19. The United States v. Peters, Ib., p. 121. Talbot v. Johnson, Ib., p. 133. 2 Brown's Civ. and Adm. Law, p. 208.

and though a mere maritime tort unconnected with capture *jure belli* may be cognizable by a Court of Common Law, yet it is clearly established that all captures *jure belli*, and all torts connected therewith, are exclusively cognizable in the Prize Court.

And the Prize Court will not only entertain suits for restitution and damages in case of wrongful capture, and award damages therefor; but it will also allow damages for all personal torts, and that upon a proper case laid before the Court as a mere incident to the possession of the principal cause. And in such a case it will not confine itself to the actual wrong-doer; but will apply the rule of *respondeat superior*, and decree damages against the owners of the offending privateer;(*p*) and where the captured crew have been grossly ill-treated, the Court will award a liberal recompense.(*q*)

As the Prize Court has an unquestionable jurisdiction to apply confiscation by way of penalty for falsity, fraud, and *misconduct of [*572] citizens as well as of Neutrals;(*r*) so it may, in like manner, decree a forfeiture of the rights of Prize against Captors, where they have been guilty of gross irregularity, or criminal neglect, or wanton impropriety and fraud. It is a part of the ancient law of the Admiralty, independent of any statute, that captors may, by their misconduct, forfeit the rights of Prize; and in such cases the property is condemned to the Government generally. And this penalty has been frequently enforced, not only where the captors have been guilty of fraud,(*s*) but also where they have violated the instructions of Government relative to bringing in the Prize Crew, and have proceeded without necessity to dispose of the property before condemnation;(*t*) so where the captors have rescued a Prize Ship from the custody of the Marshal, after a monition duly served.(*u*) In short, the Court is the constitutional guardian of the public interests in relation to matters of Prize; and wherever there is any deviation from the regular course of proceedings, it expects to have a sufficient reason shown for that deviation, before it will give the captors any of the ordinary benefits of Prizes captured by them.(*x*)

(*p*) Del Col v. Arnold, 3 Dallas's (Amer.) Rep., p. 333. The Anna Maria, 2 Wheaton's (Amer.) Rep., p. 327. Bynk. Q. J. Pub., l. i. c. 19. Du Ponceau's Translation, p. 147.

(*q*) The St. Juan Baptista, 5 Rob., p. 33. The Die Fire Damer, Ib., p. 357. The Lively, 1 Gallison's (Amer.) Rep., p. 315.

(*r*) The Johanna Tholen, 6 Rob., p. 75. Oswell v. Vigne, 15 East, p. 70.

(*s*) The Thomas Gibbons, 8 Cranch's (Amer.) Rep., p. 421. The George, 2 Wheaton's (Amer.) Rep., p. 278.

(*t*) La Reine des Anges, Stewart, p. 9. (*u*) The Cossack, Ib., p. 513.

(*x*) "Et si aucuns desdicts preneurs en leur voyage en especial auoient commis faute telle qu'ils fussent attaints d'auoir enfondré aucuns Nauires, ou noyer, les corps des prisonniers descendus à terre un aucune loingtaine coste, pour céler le larrecinet et meffaict, voulons que sans quelque délay, faueur ou déport, nostre dit admiral en face faire punition et iustice selon le cas."—Ordonnance de 1400, art. vii.

"Si aucuns si trouvent avoir commis faute en leur voyage, soit d'avoir mis à fonds aucuns Navires, ou robbé des biens d'iceux ou noyé les corps des Marchands, Maistres, Conducteurs, et autres personnes desdits navires, ou iceux descendus à terre en aucune loingtaine coste, pour céler le larcin et malfait, ou bien quand il adviendroit comme il a fait quelques fois qu'aucuns d'eux se trouvans les plus forts viendront á ranconner à argent les navires de nos subjets, ou d'aucuns nos amis et

*The usual course of the Court is by way of monition; and if that process be disobeyed, an attachment issues against the parties in contempt. But the Court may, in all cases, proceed, in the first instance, by warrant of arrest of the person or property, to compel security to abide its decree. [*573]

CCCCLIII. The three classes of cases(y) affecting this question are: (1.) where *damages* have been given or refused on restitution. (2.) Where *compensation* has been given, or refused, *the Prize being lost in the hands of the captors.* (3.) Where, although restitution was decreed, *the captors have been allowed their costs and expenses.*

I. In the Corier Maritimo(z) demurrage was given for unnecessary detention and unjustifiable delay in proceeding to adjudication. In the Zee Star(a) demurrage was given *to the claimants, and costs and expenses refused to the captors (which are usually allowed even on restitution,) for improper delay in proceeding to adjudication. In the Triton(b) costs and damages were given to the claimant of the goods, and demurrage for the ship, for seizure on an insufficient ground. In the Madonna del Curso (c) all the circumstances concurred of a seizure originally unjustifiable, protracted detention, and improper delay in proceeding to adjudication: costs and damages were given. The Peacock(d) was the case of an unjustifiable detention of the Prize Vessel, carried into Lisbon, and delay in bringing her home to England for adjudication. In the Wilhelmsberg,(e) demurrage was allowed, and the expenses of the application given against the captor, for loss arising from his not bringing the captured vessel to the *most convenient port for adjudication* within the meaning of the Prize Act, In the Zacheman,(f) which was a mistake as to the Law of Contraband under the Swedish Treaty, and the seizure was pronounced perfectly justifiable, demurrage was allowed for unreasonable delay. The Anna(g) was a case of restitution, [*574]

alliez: voulons que sans quelque delay, faveur ou déport, le dit admiral en face ou face faire justice et punition, telle que ce soit exemples á tous autres, deues informations des cas preallablement faites, et selon qu'il sera cy-après ordonné. Et pour ce que souventes fois quand une prise estoit faite sur nos ennemis les preneurs estoyent si coustoumiers de user de leur volentez pour leur profit, qu'ils ne gordoyent l'usage toujours et de toute ancienneté sur ce ordonné et observé, mais sans crainte de Justice, comme innobédiens et pilleurs, eux estans encore sur mer rompent les coffres, balles, boujettes, malles, tonneaux et autres vaisseaux, pour prendre et piller ce qu'ils peuvent des biens de la prise, en quoy ceux qui ont equippé, et mis sur les navires à gros despens sont grandement foullez, dont advient souvent de grandes noises, debats et contentions. Nous prohibons et deffendons à tous chefs, Maistres, contre Maistres, Patrons, Quarteniers, soldats, et compagnons, de ne faire aucune ouverture des coffres, balles, &c., ny autres vaisseaux de quelques prises qu'ils facent, ny aucunes choses des dits prises receler, transporter, vendre, ny eschanger, ou autrement alliener, sins ayent à representer le tout desdites Prises, ensemble les personnes conduisans le navire, audit Admiral ou Vice-Admiral le plustost que faire se pourra, pour en estre fait et dispose selon qu'il appartiendra, et comme contiennent nos presentes ordonnances, et ce sur peine de confiscation de corps et des biens."—Ordonnance de 1584, art. xxxv. xxxvii.

(y) The cases respecting damage for illegal capture and detention will be found collected and classified in 9 Wheaton's (Amer.) Rep., p. 21, note 6.

(z) 1 Rob., p. 287.
(a) 4 Ib., p. 71.
(b) 4 Rob., p. 78.
(c) Ib., p. 169.
(d) Ib., p. 185.
(e) 5 Ib., p. 143.
(f) Ib., p. 152.
(g) Ib., p. 373.

with costs and damages, for a violation of the neutral territory of the United States. The seizure itself was pronounced to be unjustifiable, and costs and damages were given, because the Prize Ship was improperly brought from the mouth of the Mississippi to England for adjudication, instead of being carried into one of the West India Islands. In the Washington,(*h*) damages were given for bringing the vessel to an inconvenient port. The Acteon(*i*) was an American ship sailing under a license, unlawfully seized and burnt. The St. Antonio(*k*) was sailing under a license
[*575] to enter a Port of Holland, but was seized under suspicion of an *intention to go to a French port. On bringing in, the captors offered to liberate on payment of their expenses, but afterwards retracted, and went on to adjudication. There was a decree of restitution, and the claimants appealed to the Lords for costs and damages; the appeal was rejected, and the claimants condemned to pay the costs of the appeal. In the Catharina Elizabeth(*l*) costs and damages were given by the Lords for carrying the captured vessel to an inconvenient port. In the Louis,(*m*) damages were refused by Sir W. Scott, although he held the seizure clearly illegal, it being a case of the first impression.

II. The rule on the subject of compelling the captors to proceed to adjudication, where the property is lost in their hands, is, that where the seizure is unjustifiable, the captor is answerable for every loss or damage. In cases of justifiable seizure, he is responsible for due diligence only, and is held to simple restitution in value.

The Carolina(*n*) was a neutral ship which had been employed in carrying French troops to Egypt, and was taken coming away. Had she been taken in actual *delicto* she would have been liable to condemnation. The captors were held exempt, not only from costs and damages, but from restitution in value, the ship having been lost while in their possession by stress of weather. In the William(*o*) the original seizure was held justifiable, but restitution in value was decreed for a loss occasioned by not taking a pilot on board, but no damages were given. In the Der Mohr(*p*) the original seizure was considered as justifiable, but the captors were held responsible to make restitution in value, (not for costs and damages,) on account of the loss of the vessel by the ignorance and wilfulness of the Prize Master.

[*576] III. In general the Captors are allowed their expenses *and costs on restitution, whenever there is probable cause of capture.(*q*) The only exceptions to this rule are where there has been some negligence or misconduct on the part of the captors. There are a great number of cases decided on this point;(*r*) but all adjudicated upon this principle.

If the captors unjustifiably neglect to proceed to adjudication, the Court will, in case of restitution, decree demurrage against them.(*s*) So,

(*h*) 6 Rob., p. 275. (*i*) 2 Dodson, p. 48. (*k*) Acton's Rep., p. 113.
(*l*) Acton, p. 309. (*m*) 2 Dodson, p. 210. (*n*) 4 Rob., p. 256.
(*o*) 6 Ib., p. 316. (*p*) 3 Ib., p. 129.
(*q*) The Imina, 3 Rob., p. 167. The Principe, Edwards, p. 70.
(*r*) The Marianna Flora, Wheaton's (Amer.) Rep., vol. xi. p. 21, note (*b*).
(*s*) The Corier Maritimo, 1 Rob., p. 287. The Madonna del Burso, 4 Ib., p. 169. The Peacock, Ib., p. 185. The Anna Catharina, 6 Ib., p. 10.

also, if the captors agree to restitution, but unreasonably delay it, demurrage will be allowed against them.(*t*) After an acquittal, a second seizure may be made by other captors; but it is at the peril of damages and costs, in case of failure.(*u*) And although a spoliation of papers be made, yet, if it be produced by the misconduct of captors, as by firing under false colours, it will not protect them from damages and costs.(*x*) Nor is it an objection *in the Prize Court* against awarding damages and costs, that the ship is not navigated by a proper proportion of seamen of her own country, according to its navigation laws; for that is an irregularity which must be referred to another branch of the Admiralty Jurisdiction.(*y*)

CCCCLIV. As to *the time* within which a suit may be brought in the Admiralty for damages for an illegal capture, it may be observed, that as the Statute of Limitations does not apply to Prize Causes, there is no time during the existence of the Prize Commission in which captors may not be legally called on to proceed to adjudication, for the purpose of awarding *damages against them.(*z*) But the Court will extend, by equity, the principles of the Statute of Limitations to Prize [*577] Causes; and therefore, it will not, after a great lapse of time, compel the captors to proceed to adjudication, or entertain a suit for damages for a supposed illegal capture.(*a*)

CCCCLV. In respect to *the measure of damages*, where the vessel and cargo *are actually lost*, it is usual to allow the actual value of the property.(*b*) And where a prize had been illegally condemned by a Vice Admiralty Court, erected by the commanders in the West Indies, under a misapprehension that they possessed an authority to erect such Courts, and afterwards restitution in value was decreed by the High Court of Admiralty in England, the Court allowed the invoice value, 10 per cent. profit, and freight, as well where the ship and cargo belonged to the same persons as where they were separately owned.(*c*) What items may properly form part of the damages, depends upon the nature and circumstances of the case; and for guides to direct his judgment, the reader is referred to the cases mentioned in the note.(*d*) *Where damages and costs are allowed, if, after they are assessed, payment is [*578] delayed, the Court will allow interest upon the principal sum from the time of assessment, although it includes interest as well as principal.(*e*)

(*t*) The Zee Star, 4 Ib., p. 71. (*u*) The Mercurius, 1 Ib., p. 80.
(*x*) The Peacock, 4 Ib., p. 185. (*y*) The Nemesis, Edw., p. 50.
(*z*) The Mentor, 1 Rob., p. 179. The Huldah, 3 Ib., p. 235.
(*a*) The Susannah, 6 Rob., p. 48.
(*b*) Del. Col. v. Arnold, 3 Dallas's (Amer.) Rep., p. 333. Maley v. Shattuck, 3 Cranch's (Amer.) Rep., p. 458. The Anna Maria, 2 Wheaton's (Amer.) Rep., p. 327.
(*c*) The Lucy, 3 Rob., p. 208.
(*d*) Le Caux v. Eden, Doug., pp. 594, 596. Talbot v. Janson, 3 Dallas's (Amer.) Rep., pp. 133, 170. Cotton v. Wallace, Ib., pp. 302, 304. The Charming Betsey, 2 Cranch's (Amer.) Rep., p. 64. Maley v. Shattuck, 3 Ib., p. 458. The Narcissus, 4 Rob., p. 20. The Zee Star, Ib., p. 71. The Corier Maritimo, 1 Ib., p. 287. The St. Juan Baptista, 5 Ib., p. 33. The Die Fire Damei, Ib., p. 357. The Anna Catharina, 6 Ib., p. 10. The Driver, 5 Ib., p. 145. The Lively, 1 Gallison's (Amer.) Rep., p. 315. The Anna Maria, 2 Wheaton's (Amer.) Rep., p. 327.
(*e*) The Driver, 5 Rob., p. 145.

CCCCLVI. As *to the mode of assessing damages,* it is usual for the Court to refer the subject to commissioners, to make inquiry and return a regular report to the Court, of the several items and amount of damages. But in their report, they should state the principles upon which they proceed in making allowances, where the items do not explain themselves, and not report a gross sum without specification or explanation.(*f*)

CCCCLVII. In respect to *the persons who are liable for costs and damages,* it may be observed, that the general rule in respect to public ships is, that the actual wrong-doer, and he alone, is responsible.(*g*) It is not meant by this, that the crew of the capturing ship are responsible for the seizure made in obedience to the commands of their superior; for by the Prize Law the act of the commander is binding upon the interests of all under him, and he alone is responsible for damages and costs.(*h*) The meaning of the rule is, that the person actually ordering the seizure, is liable for the damages, and not his superior in command, (who has not concurred in the particular act,) simply from the fact, that the seizor is acting within the scope of his general orders.(*i*) Therefore a suit cannot be maintained against an admiral upon a station who is not privy to the act of seizure ;(*k*) nor a commodore, who commands the squadron, but gives no orders for the capture.(*l*) In short, the actual wrong-doer [*579] is the person *to answer in judgment, and to him responsibility is attached by the Court. He may have other persons responsible over to him, and that responsibility may be enforced; as, for instance, if a captain make a wrongful seizure under the express orders of his admiral, that admiral may be made answerable in the damages occasioned to the captain by the improper act. But it is the constant and invariable practice of the Prize Court, to have the actual wrong-doer the party before the Court: and the propriety of the practice is manifest; because if the Court was once to open the door to complaints founded on remote and consequential responsibility, it would be difficult to say where it is to stop.(*m*)

CCCCLVIII. In the case of *private armed vessels* the owners, as well as the masters, are responsible for the damages and costs occasioned by illegal captures; and this is to the extent of the actual loss and injury, even if it exceeds the amount of the bond usually given upon the taking out of commissions for Privateers.(*n*) But the sureties to the bond are

(*f*) The Charming Betsey, 2 Cranch's (Amer.) Rep., p. 64. The Lively, 1 Gallison's (Amer.) Rep., p. 315.

(*g*) The Mentor, 1 Rob., p. 179. (*h*) The Diligentia, 1 Dodson, p. 404.

(*i*) The Mentor, 1 Rob., p. 179. (*k*) Ibid., p. 179.

(*l*) The Eleanor, 2 Wheaton's (Amer.) Rep., p. 346.

(*m*) The Mentor, 1 Rob., p. 179. The principles applicable to this class of cases are fully developed in the opinion in the case of The Eleanor, to which the reader is respectfully referred.—2 Wheat. (Amer.) Rep., p. 346.

(*n*) Bynk., Q. J. Pub., l. i. c. xix. Du Ponceau's ed., p. 147. Talbot v. Three Brigs, 1 Dall., (Amer.) Rep., p. 95. S. C., 1 Hall, Am. Law Journ., p. 140. The Die Fire Damer, 5 Rob., p. 357. The Der Mohr, 3 Ib., p. 129. See also:—The Girolamo, 3 Hagg., p. 187. 2 Brown's Civ. and Adm. Law, p. 140. Del Col v. Arnold, 3 Dall. (Amer.) Rep., p. 333. The Anna Maria, 2 Wheat. (Amer.) Rep., p. 327.

Pothier holds, that the owner of the privateer may entirely discharge himself

*responsible only to the extent of the sum in which they are bound.(*o*) [*580]

And if a person appear on behalf of the captain of a private ship of war, and give security in his own name with sureties, instead of the captain, he is liable in the same manner as the captain, as a principal in the stipulation.(*p*) And a part owner of a private armed ship is not exempted from being a party to a suit, on a motion to bring in the prize proceeds and proceed to adjudication, in consequence of having made compensation for his share to the claimant, and *received a release from him; for the claimant has a right to the answer of all parties, [*581] even supposing that the decree ought not to be enforced against such part owner.(*q*) And in a Court of Law of Nations a person may be holden a part owner of a privateer, although his name has never been inserted in the bill of sale or the ship's register.(*r*)

CCCCIX. Where the captors from any cause whatsoever, as from loss of the property, or from fraud or negligence, omit to bring the case before the Court for adjudication, the claimant may apply to the Court for a monition to the captors, to proceed forthwith to adjudication.(*s*) And upon their neglect so to do after service and return of the monition, the Court will, if a proper case is laid before it, proceed to award restitution, with damages and costs.(*t*)

from the responsibility beyond the amount of the penalty in his bond, by abandoning the vessel to the injured party.—De Propriété No. 92; but Valin decides that the Prize Law controls, in this respect the provision of the Municipal Law of France, by which indeed the owners of merchant vessels are discharged from their responsibility by abandoning the ship and freight, in like manner, as they are by the British statute 7 Geo. 2, c. 15. The Girolamo, 3 Haggard's (Adm.) Rep., p. 177.

"En conformité des dits Réglemens de 1704 et 1744 (giving costs and damages to neutrals wrongfully seized) il fait donc tenir aujourd'hui sans égard à la disposition de l'art. 3, du titre des propriétaires, &c., et du present article, en tant qu'il limite le cautionnement à la somme de 15,000 livres que l'armateur repondra indéfiniment de tous les dommages et intérêts résultans des délits et deprédations des gens de son corsaire, et des prises irregulières par eux faites, sans pouvoir même s'en défendre en payant la somme de 15,000 livres pour laquelle il aura donné caution, et en déclarant en même temps qu'il abandonne outre cela son navire avec tons ces agrets, apparaux et autres dépendances, relativement à l'art. 2, du même titre des propriétaires, &c., dont la disposition n'est plus applicable en matière d'armement en course, que celle de l'art. 3, attendu ces mêmes réglemens qui forme une decision particulière à cet égard.—Sur l'Ordonnance, l. iii. t. ix., Des Prises, art. 2.

Such appears to have been the former law of France, but it was changed by the new commercial code:—"Les propriétaires de navires équipés en guerre, ne seront toutefois responsables des délits et déprédations commis en mer, par les gens de guerre qui sont sur leur navires, ou par les équipages, que jusqu'à concurrence de la somme pour laquelle ils auront donné caution, à moins qu'ils n'en soient participans ou complices."—Code de Commerce, art. 217.

But the laws of the United States of North America not only contain no such provision, but have not even adopted the British statute, by which the owners are discharged in ordinary cases by abandoning the vessel and freight to the injured party: there can be no doubt that the responsibility of the owners of privateers is not limited either to the penalty of the bond, or the value of the vessel.

(*o*) Du Ponceau's Bynk., p. 149. 2 Valin, sur l'Ordonnance, p. 228.
(*p*) King v. Ferguson, Edw., p. 84. (*q*) The Karasan, 5 Rob., p. 291.
(*r*) The Nostra Signora de los Dolores, 1 Dodson, p. 290.
(*s*) The William, 4 Rob., p. 214.
(*t*) The Huldah, 3 Ib., p. 205. The Susanna, 6 Ib., p. 48.

It is the usual practice for a party to give in his claim in the first instance, before calling upon the captors to proceed to adjudication; but it will not necessarily vitiate the process, if there has been no claim. If it should in any manner come to the knowledge of the Court that a seizure has been made in the nature of prize, and that no proceedings had been instituted, it would be the duty of the Court to direct proceedings to be commenced.(*u*) The same object is often effected by the claimants by an original suit for restitution, on a petition setting forth all the facts, and praying for a decree of restitution either *in rem* or in value with damages.(*x*)

[*582] *CCCCLX. Whether the proceeding be in the one form or the other, the rights of all parties remain the same. The burden of proving the neutrality of the property rests on the claimants; and when that is shown, the existence of the probable cause of capture is to be established by the other side; and each party has a right to the answer of the other upon all proper interrogatories, supported by oath.(*y*)

CCCCLXI. B. *The Rights and Duties of Claimants with respect to the Conduct of the Suit.*

It is scarcely necessary to observe that the subject of the enemy cannot, except perhaps under very exceptional circumstances, be a claimant. He has no *persona standi,* as civilians say, in the Court of his enemy.

In cases where no claim is made in consequence of this position of law, condemnation passes as a matter of course—to borrow the language of Lord Stowell, "the enemy proprietor is necessarily absent by operation of law, and yet the sentence is completely valid as well against him as against all the world."(*z*) Such an exception giving a *persona standi* to the enemy exists in the case of a ship sailing under a cartel(*a*) agreement, or a flag of truce, and captured by mistake of the captor, or under circumstances of suspicion. The enemy master may appear and claim restitution; and it is the duty of the Prize Court to uphold in a liberal spirit the good faith of any agreement of this kind, and to reject any argument drawn from the *mala fides* of the other party as warranting a reciprocal perfidy.(*b*)

(*u*) The William, 4 Ib., p. 214.

(*x*) Del Col v. Arnold, 3 Dallas's (Amer.) Rep., p. 333. Maley v. Shattuck, 3 Cranch's (Amer.) Rep., p. 458. Jennings v. Carson, 4 Ib., p. 2. The Anna Maria, 2 Wheaton's (Amer.) Rep., p. 327. The Eleanor, 2 Ib., p. 347.

(*y*) Maley v. Shattuck, 3 Cranch's (Amer.) Rep., p. 458.

(*z*) The Falcon, 6 Rob., p. 199.

(*a*) Vide ante, P. 161, p. 2, 3, The Daifjie, 3 Rob., p. 143.

(*b*) "When this case came on before, the Court intimated a disposition to sustain the claim, if it should appear to have been the understanding of the parties, and particularly of the party granting the permission, that a ship sailing on this service, under a flag of truce, should be protected, though not strictly a cartel. Whether the British commander might have exceeded his powers, or have made an improvident concession, would not, I think, supersede the obligation which this Court would feel itself under to support the good faith of the agreement on which the other party had acted with confidence . . . . Something has been said of the bad faith which the Government of France has practised on some similar occasion, in detaining a vessel sent regularly as a cartel ship from this country to a port of France. Such a behaviour would on no account be

*CCCCLXII. The principal duty of the claimants is to resort only to legal means of redress, and to abstain from the use of violence. A lawful force, they are to remember, cannot be lawfully resisted.(*c*) [*583]

CCCCLXIII. The master of the captured vessel, or his correspondent, or his Consul, applies to a Procurator of the Prize Court, who prepares their claim supported by an affidavit which contains an affirmative proposition as to neutral, friendly, or subjects' proprietorship, and a negative proposition as to the absence of any enemy interest.(*d*) In like manner the whole or different parts of the cargo must be claimed. Security for costs may or may not be required of him as of every foreign suitor according to the general principles of International Law upon the subject. He has a right to obtain copies and translations of such papers as he thinks fit to use.

And, as has been emphatically laid down by the English Prize Court during the present war, all presumptions arising from any deficiency in the Belligerent's Tribunal are to be construed in favour of the claimant.(*e*)

CCCCLXIV. A party to be entitled to assert a claim in the Prize Court, must be the general owner of the property; for a person who has a mere lien on the property for a debt due, *whether liquidated or unliquidated, is not so entitled;(*f*) and the same rule has been applied, in America, to a mortgage, where the mortgagor is left in possession.(*g*) The rule that a claimant is not admitted to claim, who is engaged in the traffic prohibited by the Municipal Laws of the country, is applied only to citizens or subjects, and not to foreign neutral proprietors.(*h*) But to citizens or subjects the rule equally applies, whether the transaction is between original contractors or under a sub-contract.(*i*) And an inactive or sleeping partner cannot receive restitution in a transaction in which he could not be lawfully engaged as a sole trader.(*k*) If enemy's property be fraudulently blended in the same claim with neutral property, the latter is liable to share the fate of the former.(*l*) [*584]

CCCCLXV. An appearance by a Proctor for the claimants, duly entered, cures all defects of process, such as the want of a monition or of due notice.(*m*) And even assuming that one partner has no authority to appoint a proctor for all the partners, yet a general appearance for all

resorted to as a precedent, to which this Court would attend, in considering the proper effect of the proceedings of these parties in this transaction."—The Mary, 5 Rob., p. 199.

(*c*) Vide ante, p. 11.

(*d*) The Adeline, 9 Cranch's (Amer.) Rep., p. 244. The Sally, 3 Rob., p. 300, note.

(*e*) The Ottawas, (July 3rd, 1855,) Prize Court.

(*f*) The Eenrom, 2 Rob., pp. 1-5. The Tobago, 5 Rob., p. 218. The Francis, Thompson's Claim, 8 Cranch's (Amer.) Rep., p. 355. Id. Irving's Claim, Ib., p. 418. The Marianna, 6 Rob., p. 24.

(*g*) Bolch v. Darrel, Bee's (Amer.) Rep. p. 74.

(*h*) The Recovery, 6 Rob., p. 341. (*i*) The Cornelis and Maria, 5 Ib., p. 28.

(*k*) The Franklin, 6 Ib., pp. 127-131.

(*l*) The St. Nicholas, 1 Wheaton's (Amer.) Rep., p. 481.

(*m*) Penhallow v. Doane, 3 Dallas's (Amer.) Rep., p. 54.

by a proctor is good and legally binding.(*n*) In cases of captures by Government ships, the proceedings in England are exclusively carried on by the officers of the Government; and no other persons can interfere to support or pursue a suit, where they do not consent.(*o*) Whether the same exclusive authority exists in the North American United States, [*585] has never been *made the subject of question in the Supreme Court(*p*) of that country.

CCCCLXVI. A claimant who wishes to procure the restitution of any property captured as Prize must, after the Prize Libel is filed, and at or before the return of the monition thereon, or time assigned for the trial, enter his claim for such property before the proper Court. And if the captors omit, or unreasonably delay to institute Prize proceedings, any person claiming an interest in the captured property may obtain a monition against them, citing them to proceed to adjudication; which, if they omit to do, or to show cause why the property should be condemned, it will be restored to the claimants proving an interest therein. And the same process is often resorted to where the property is lost or destroyed, through the fault or negligence of the captors, in order to obtain a compensation in damages for the unjust seizure and detention.(*q*) The [*586] claim should be made *by the parties interested, if present, or, in their absence, by the master of the ship, or some agent of the owners. A mere stranger will not be permitted to interpose a claim merely to speculate on the chances of an acquittal.(*r*)

The claim must be accompanied with an affidavit, stating briefly the facts respecting the claim and its verity. This affidavit should be sworn to by the parties themselves, if they are within the jurisdiction; but if they are absent from the country, or at a very great distance from the place where the Court is held, the affidavit may be sworn to by an agent. Before a claim is made, and affidavit put in (which should always be

(*n*) Hills v. Ross, Ib., p. 231. (*o*) The Elsebe, 5 Rob., p. 173.

(*p*) In England it is also held, that the power of the Crown to direct the release of property seized as prize, before adjudication and against the will of the captors, is not taken away by any grant of the prize conferred in the Order of Council, the proclamation, or the Prize Act; (The Elsebe, 5 Rob., p. 155,) and in France the captors cannot, after the prize is brought in for adjudication, terminate the proceedings by a private arrangement with the claimants. Such an arrangement to be valid must be communicated to the Procureur-Général, and approved by the Court; because the rights and interests of the State, of the officers and crew of the capturing vessel, and of the subjects of neutral powers, might be compromitted by such an arrangement.

See the opinion of M. Portalis, on this question, (Code des Prises, par Guichard, t. vii. p. 533.) He distinguishes this case from that of ransoms, which are regulated by peculiar laws, but never favoured; and he cites, in support of his opinion, several ancient *arrêts* of council and rescripts of the admiral.

(*q*) The Betsey, 1 Rob., p. 93. The Mentor, Ib., p. 181. The Huldah, 3 Ib., p. 239. The Der Mohr, Ib., p. 129. The George, Ib., p. 212. The William, 4 Ib., p. 215. The Susanna, 6 Ib., p. 48.

(*r*) "*Il est fait très expresses inhibitions et défences à toutes sortes de personnes de réclamer aucunes des prises faites par ses vaisseaux de guerre ou ceus des armateurs particuliers*, ni faire aucune procédure en l'Amirauté, *sans être au préalable, porteurs de procurations en bonne forme de ceux pour qui ils feront les réclamations*, et les avoir présentées aux officiers de l'Amirauté des ports où les prises auront été conduites à peine de 600 livres d'amende."—Ordonnance du 30 Janvier, 1692. Réglement du 19 Juillet, 1778.

special if the case stands on peculiar grounds,) it is not permitted to the parties to examine the ship's papers, and the preparatory examinations in order to shape their claims; for this might lead to great abuses.

CCCCLXVII. But if it be necessary to ascertain the particulars of a claim, the Court will, upon a special application, suffer so many of the papers to be examined as directly relate to such claim; but a sufficient reason is always expected to be shown on affidavit to sustain such an application.(*s*) It is a general rule that no claim is to be admitted which stands in entire opposition to the ship's papers and to the preparatory examinations.(*t*) But this only applies to cases arising during the war, and not to cases arising before the war;(*u*) and it is not so inflexible as to exclude the interest *of a citizen or subject, where there is an absolute necessity to simulate papers, as in the case of a trade [*587] with the enemy licensed by the State.(*x*) It is also, as has been observed, a general principle that no citizen or subject can be admitted to claim in a Prize Court, where the transaction in which he is engaged is in violation to the municipal laws of his own country.(*y*) Nor can a person be admitted to claim where the trade, in the carrying on of which he is taken, is forbidden by the law of nature, and by the municipal laws of his own country, and that where the Court is sitting.(*z*)

After a claim is once put in, it is not amendable of course; but if an amendment is wanted to correct the generality of the original claim, it will not be allowed, unless a proper case is made out, and sufficient reasons given for the omission in the first instance.(*a*)

CCCCLXVIII. At the return day of the process, if no claim be at that time or previously interposed, and upon proclamation made no person appear to claim, the default is entered on the record; and the Court will then proceed to examine the evidence, and if proof of enemy's property clearly appear, it will immediately decree condemnation; if the case appear doubtful, it will postpone a decision. It is not now usual to condemn the goods for want of a claim, until a year and a day(*b*) have elapsed from the time of the return of the *monition, except in cases where there is a strong presumption, and reasonable proof [*588] that the property actually belongs to an enemy.(*c*) And if no claim be interposed within that period, the property is condemned of course, and

(*s*) The Port Mary, 3 Rob., p. 233.

(*t*) The Vrouw Anna Catharina, 5 Ib., pp. 15-19. La Flora, 6 Ib., p. 1.

(*u*) The Anna Catharina, 5 Ib., p. 15. (*x*) La Flora, 6 Rob., p. 1.

(*y*) The Walshingham Packet, 2 Ib., p. 77. The Etrusco, 4 Ib., p. 262, n. The Cornelis & Maria, 5 Ib., p. 23. The Abby, Ib., p. 251. The Recovery, 6 Ib., p. 341.

(*z*) The Amedie, Edinburgh Review, vol. xvi. no. 21, p. 426.

(*a*) The Graaf Bernstoff, 3 Rob., p. 109. And see the Sally, Ib., p. 179.

(*b*) This term was limited by the Prize Act to three months, 17 Vict. c. 18, s. 37, unadvisedly, as it seems to me. See the Aspasia and the Achilles, before the J. C. of the Privy Council, July, 1856: term extended in both cases.

"*Si par la déposition de l'équipage* et la vente du vaisseau et des marchandises, *on ne peut découvrir sur qui la prise aura été faite, le tout sera inventorié et apprécié et unis sous bonne et sure garde, pour être restitué à qu'il appartiendra, s'il est reclamé dans l'an et jour;* sinon partagé comme épave de la mer, également entre nous, l'amiral, et les armateurs."—Ordonnance de la Marine de 1681, tit. ix. art. xxvi.

(*c*) The Staadt Embden, 1 Rob., pp. 26, 29. And see the Heinrick & Maria, 4 Ib., p. 43. Coll. Ear., p. 88, n.

the question of former ownership is precluded for ever, the owner being deemed, in Law, to have abandoned it.(*d*)

CCCCLXIX. C. *The Pleadings* are of a simple character, formed upon the rules and practice of the Roman law. And so with respect to (D.,) the modes of *Proof* and the reception of *Evidence*, it is the duty of the International Tribunal of Prize to extend any technical rules respecting the admissibility or evidence which may prevail in the country in which it happens to be locally situate. Lord Stowell,(*e*) it will be found, refers to the Roman law, and to the commentators thereon, as great authorities in this matter, and on the general rules, which in all civilized states regulate the question of testimony.

CCCCLXX. In Prize causes, it is not usual to file any *special allegation* of the peculiar circumstances on which the captors found their title to condemnation. The *libel* is and [*589] *always ought to be, the mere general allegation of Prize, such as is used in undoubted cases of hostile property. The act of bringing the vessel in, and proceeding against her, alleges her generally to be a subject of Prize rights; and the captors are not called upon to state, at the commencement of the suit, the particular grounds on which they contend she is so. They have a right to institute the inquiry, and take the chance of the benefit of any fact that may be produced in the course of that inquiry.(*f*) This is an advantage on the side of the captors; but it is controlled by their liability to cost and damages if the inquiry produce nothing; and, to say the very least, is fully balanced by the advantage given to the claimant in this species of proceeding, that no evidence shall be admitted against him, but such as proceeds from himself, from his own documents, and from his own witnesses; the captors not being permitted, except in cases marked by peculiar circumstances, to furnish any evidence whatever.(*g*)

CCCCLXXI. Upon *filing the libel*, the usual practice is immediately to issue a Monition, citing all persons who are interested to appear at a given day and show cause why the property should not be condemned as Prize; and this process, in the Courts of the North American United States, usually includes a warrant to take possession of the property. But where the Prize has been first seized in port, a monition issues, in the first instance, to bring in the papers, if they are in the possession of a subject or citizen.(*h*) The usual monition is directed to the Marshal, and in England is served by posting up a copy at the Royal Exchange, in the City of London. In former times, fourteen [*590] *days were allowed between the service of the monition and the day of hearing the cause; but in most of the later Prize Acts in England, twenty days are allowed after the execution of the Monition.(*i*) In the North

(*d*) The Staadt Embden, 1 Ib., pp. 26-29. The Henrick & Maria, 4 Ib., pp. 43, 44. The Harrison, 1 Wheaton's (Amer.) Rep. p. 298. Robinson's Coll. Mar., p. 98, n. The Avery, 2 Gallison's (Amer.) Rep., p. 308. Ordonn. de la Marine, t. ix. art. 26.

(*e*) The Maria, 1 Rob., p. 363. The Twee Gebrœders, 3 Ib., pp. 338-348, 349.

(*f*) The Adeline, 9 Cranch's (Amer.) Rep., p. 244. The Fortuna, 1 Dodson, p. 81.

(*g*) The Fortuna, 1 Ib., p. 81.

(*h*) The Conqueror, 2 Rob., p. 303.

(*i*) Robinson's Coll. Mar., p. 89, n. Mariot's Formulary, p. 187.

American United States, the return day of the Monition depends upon the discretion of the district judge; but it is usually twenty days at least, after the issuing of the process; and it is served usually by posting up a copy on the mast of the Prize vessel, and at such other public places as the judge may direct; and also by publication in the newspapers printed in or near the principal place or port of the district into which the Prize is brought. This proceeding, by monition and service by public notice, is founded upon the Roman law, by which, when it became impracticable to serve the party with a personal citation, recourse was had to this method, which is called a citation *per edictum.*(k)

CCCCLXXII. As soon as a vessel or other thing captured as Prize arrives in our ports, notice should be given thereof by the captors to the proper officer, whether to the judge or the Commissioners appointed by him,(l) that the examinations of the captured crew, who are brought in, may be regularly taken in writing, upon oath, in answer to the standing interrogatories.

It is also the duty of the Prize Master to deliver up to the Commissioner all the papers and documents found on board, and, at the same time, to make an affidavit that they *are delivered up as taken, without fraud, addition, subduction, or embezzlement.(m) [*591]

In general, the master and principal officers, and some of the crew of the captured vessel, should be brought in for examination. This is a settled rule of the Prize Courts, and was, during the late war, enforced by the express instructions of the American President. The examination must be confined to persons on board at the time of the capture, unless the special permission of the Court is obtained for the examination of others.(n)

(k) Dig. Lib. 5, tit. 1, s. 68. Robinson's Coll. Mar., p. 88, n.

(l) Judge Story observes that "the standing interogatories used in the English High Courts of Admiralty (1 Rob., p. 381,) have been drawn up with great care, precision, and accuracy, and are an excellent model for other Courts. They were generally adopted during the late war by the District Judges in the principal States with a few additions, and scarcely any variations."—Pratt's Story on Prize Courts, p. 15.

(m) "*Aussitôt que la prise aura èté amenée en quelques rades ou ports de Notre royaume, le capitaine qui l'aura faite, s'il y est en personne, si non celui qu'il en aura chargé sera tenu de faire son rapport aux officiers de l'Amirauté; de leur représenter et mettre entre les mains les papiers et prisonniers;* et de leur déclarer le jour et l'heure que le vaisseaux aura été pris; en quel lieu ou à quelle hauteur; si le capitaine a faite refus d'amener les voiles, ou de faire voir sa commission ou son congé, s'il a attaqué ou s'il s'est défendu; quel pavillon il portrait, et les autres circonstances de la prise et de son voyage."—Ordonnance de la Marine, 1681, tit. ix. art. 21. Déclaration du 24 Juin, 1778, art. 42. See also the Swedish Ordinance of 1715, art. 6. Collectanea Maritima, p. 168.

(n) 6 Rob., p. 185. The Eliza and Katy. The Heinrick and Maria, 4 Ib., pp. 43-57.

Thus in a treaty of amity and commerce between Charles VIII., King of France, and Henry VII. of England, concluded at Boulogne, the 15th of May, 1497, and which may be considered as evidence of the Prize Practice of Europe at that period, is contained the following article: "Simili quoque juramento solemniter præstando promittent, quod de qualibet præda, captivia, manubiis, sive spoliis, *adducent duos aut tres viros in capto navi præcipuum locum obtinentes, ut magistrum, submagistrum, patronum, aut hujusmodi conditionis quos Admiraldo, Vice-admiraldo, aut eorum officiariis exhibebunt, ut per eosdem, aut eorum alterum, debite examinetur ubi super quibus, et qualiter navis sive bona capta sint,* nec facient aut fieri permittent

[*592] *In order to guard as much as possible against frauds and misstatements from after contrivances, the examination should take place as soon as possible after the arrival of the vessel, and the witnesses are not allowed to have communication with, or to be instructed by, counsel. The captors should also introduce all their witnesses in succession; for if the Commissioners have taken the depositions of some of the crew, and transmitted them to the Judge, they will not be at liberty, without a special order, to examine others who are afterwards brought by the captors before them.(*o*) On the other hand, an equal strictness is held over the conduct of the claimants. If they keep back any one of the captured crew for two or three days after the vessel comes into port, and then offer him, together with papers in his possession, the Commissioners will be justified in not examining him.(*p*) The ship's papers and other documents found on board, which are not delivered up [*593] to the Commissioners, before, *or at the time of the examinations, will not be admitted as evidence.(*q*)

When the deposition is taken, each sheet is afterwards read over to the witness, and separately signed by him.(*r*) And the Commissioners should be careful that the various answers are taken fully and perfectly, so as to meet the stress of every question, and should not suffer the witness to evade a sifting inquiry by vague and obscure statements. If the witness refuse to answer at all, or to answer fully, the Commissioners are to certify the fact to the Court; and, in addition to the other penal consequences to the owners of the ship and cargo from a suppression of evidence, he will be liable to close imprisonment for the contempt. The witnesses should be examined separately and not in presence of each other, so as to prevent any fraudulent concert between them.

aliquas prædarum, spoliorum mercium, aut bonorum, per eos capiendorum divisiones, partitiones, traditiones, permutationes, alienationesve, priusquam se viros captos, bona et merces, integre Dominis, Admiraldo, Vice-admiraldo, aut eorum vices gerentibus repræsentaverint; qui de illis disponi, si æquum putabunt, permittent, alias nihil hujusmodi permissuri."—Coll. Mar., p. 95.

"De toutes les prisès qui se feront en mer, soit par nos subjects, ou autres tenans nostre party, et tant soubs ombre-et coleur de la guerre q'autrement, *les prisonniers, ou pour les moins deux ou trois de plus apparentes d'iceuse seront amenez à terre, devers nostre dit Admiral, ou son Visadmiral, ou Lieutenant pour* au plustost que faire se pourra *estre par lui examinez et ouys*, avant qu'aucune chose des dits prises soit descendue; *à fin de savoir le pays de là oú ils seront, à qui appartiennent les navires et biens d'iceux*, pour si la prise se trouve avoir esté bien faite, telle la declarer, si non, et on il se trouveroit mal faite, la restituer a qui elle appartiendra." &c.—Ordonnance de 1584, art. 33. Ord. de 1400, art. 4. Ord. de 1543, art. 20. Déclaration du premier Février 1650, art. 9.

"*Les officiers de l'Amirauté entendront sur le fait de la prise, le maître ou commandant du vaisseau pris* même quelques officiers et matelots du vaisseau preneur, s'il est besoin."—Ordonnance de la Marine, 1681, tit. ix. art. 24.

"Si le vaisseau est amené sans prisonniers, charte parties ni connaisemens, les officiers, soldats et équipages de celui qui l'aura pris, seront separement examinés sur les circonstances de la prise, et pourquoi le navire a été amené sans prisonniers, et seront, le vaisseau et les merchandises visites par experts, pour connoitre, s'il se peut, sur qui la prise aura été faite."—Ib., art. 25.

(*o*) The Speculation, 2 Rob., p. 243.

(*p*) 1 Rob., p. 331; and see the William & Mary, 4 Ib., p. 381.

(*q*) The Anna, 1 Rob., p. 331; and see the William & Mary, 4 Ib., p. 381.

(*r*) The Apollo, 5 Ib., p. 286.

As soon as the examinations are completed, they are to be sealed up and directed to the proper Court of Prize, together with all the ship's papers, which have not been already lodged by the captors in the registry of the Court.

CCCCLXXIII. It is upon the ship's papers and depositions thus taken and transmitted, that the cause is, in the first instance, to be heard and tried.(*s*) This is not a mere *matter of practice or form : it is of the very essence of the administration of Prize Law; and it is [*594] a great mistake to admit the Common Law notions, in respect to evidence, to prevail in proceedings which have no analogy to those at Common Law.(*t*)

CCCCLXXIV. The *onus probandi* rests upon the claimants;(*u*) and by the Law of Prize, the evidence to acquit or condemn must, in the first instance, come from the papers and crew of the captured vessel. The captors are not, unless under peculiar circumstances, entitled to adduce any extrinsic testimony. It is of the last importance to preserve the most rigid exactness as to the admission of evidence; since temptations would otherwise be held out to the captured crew, to defeat the just rights of the captors by subsequent contrivances, explanations, and frauds. There can be no honest reason why the whole truth should not be told by the captured persons, at the first examination; and if they then prevaricate, or suppress important facts, it must be from motives which would materially impair the credibility of their subsequent statements.

CCCCLXXV. Although, as has been said, the ship's papers found on board are proper evidence, yet they are so only when properly verified; for papers by themselves prove nothing, and are a mere dead letter, if they are not supported by the oaths of persons in a situation to give them validity.(*x*) *And even upon the original hearing, [*595]

(*s*) The Vigilantia, 1 Ib., p. 1.

"Il est ordonné, &c., *quê pliene et entière foi sera ajoutée aux dépositions des capitaines, matelots, et officiers des vaisseaux pris*, s'il n'y a contre eux aucun reproche valable proposé par les réclamateurs, ou quelque preuve de subornation et de séduction."—Reglement du 26 Octobre, 1692.

"Veut que dans aucun cas, les pièces qui pourraient être rapportées, après la prise des bâtimens, puissent faire aucune foi, ni être d'aucune utilité, tant aux propriétaires des dix bâtimens qu'à ceux des marchandises qui pourraient avoir été chargées. Voulant *qu'en toutes occasions l'on n'ait égard qu'aux seules pièces trouvées abord*."—Réglement du 26 Juillet, 1778. See also the Swedish Ordinance of 1715, art. vii., Coll. Mar., p. 169.

(*t*) Judge Story observes, that "in some few of the District Courts, it was not unusual, during the late war, to allow the witnesses to be examined, *orally*, at the bar of the Court, long after their preparatory examinations had been taken, and full opportunities had been given to enable the parties to shape any new defence, or explain away any asserted facts. This was, unquestionably, a great irregularity, and, in many instances, must have been attended with great public mischiefs."

(*u*) The Rosalie and Betty, 2 Rob., p. 343. The Countess of Lauderdale, 4 Ib., p. 283.

(*x*) The Juno, 2 Ib., pp. 120, 122. "Il y a plus, et parceque les pièces en forme trouvées abord peuvent encore avoir été concertées en fraude, il a été ordonné par arrêt de conseil, du 26 Octobre, 1692, que les dépositions contraires des gens de l'équipage pris, prevau-droit à ces pièces."—Valin sur l'Ordonnance, liv. iii. tit. ix. Des Prises, art. vi.

papers found on board another captured ship, may be invoked into the cause, and used by the captors. But if the papers are taken from a vessel not so captured and carried in, they can only be used upon an order for farther proof.(*y*) But the authenticity of papers thus invoked, must be verified by affidavit and otherwise, to the satisfaction of the Court.(*z*) So, also, the depositions of the claimant in a former case, in which he was owner and master, were permitted to be invoked by the captors to prove his domicil.(*a*) But where nothing appears in the original evidence, which lays a foundation for prosecuting the inquiry farther, it must be under very peculiar circumstances indeed that the Court will be induced to admit extraneous evidence.(*b*) If the instructions found on board of a Prize are transmitted from the department of State for Foreign Affairs to the Prize Court, they are considered as sufficiently authenticated, as having been found on board, without farther proof to that effect.(*c*) A person skilled in nautical affairs, may be called to examine the log-book of the captured ship, and to give his opinion as to the verity of the statement in respect to destination, &c., from the courses, winds, &c.(*d*)

The examinations of the Prize Crew are, as a general rule, to be taken in the manner which has been already alluded to; but if the Prize be [*596] carried into a foreign port where *there is no commission, their affidavits taken in such port have been admitted in evidence.(*e*)

CCCCLXXVI. In the Prize Court, as in every other judicial tribunal, there are certain presumptions which legally affect the parties, and are considered as of general application. Possession is presumptive evidence of property.(*f*) If there be a total defect of evidence to establish the proprietary interest, it is presumed to belong to an enemy.(*g*) So, goods found in an enemy's ship, are presumed to belong to the enemy, unless a distinct neutral character, and documentary proof, accompany them. *Res in hostium navibus præsumuntur esse hostium, donec contrarium probetur.*(*h*)

And in cases where the property falls within the general character of contraband, if the claimant will avail himself of the favourable distinction that it is the produce of his own country, the *onus* of establishing that fact is on him.(*i*)

Primâ facie, a merchant is taken to be acting for himself, and upon his own account; but if a person is not a merchant, that may give a qualified character to his acts.(*k*) If in the ship's papers property in a

(*y*) The Romeo, 6 Rob., p. 351. The Maria, 1 Ib., p. 340.
(*z*) The Romeo, 6 Ib., p. 351.
(*a*) The Vriendschap, 4 Ib., p. 166. (*b*) The Sarah, 3 Ib., p. 330.
(*c*) The Maria, 1 Ib., p. 340. (*d*) The Edward, 4 Ib., p. 68.
(*e*) The Peacock, 4 Rob., p. 185. The Arabella & Madeira, 29 Gallison's (Amer.) Rep., p. 368.
(*f*) Miller v. The Resolution, 2 Dallas's (Amer.) Rep., p. 19.
(*g*) Sir W. Scott and Sir J. Nicholl's Letter to Mr. Jay, ante, p. 551. The Magnus, 1 Rob., p. 31.
(*h*) Loccenius, l. ii. c. iv. n. 11. Grotius, De Jur. Bel. et Pac., l. iii. c. vi. s. 6. See Bynk. Q. J. Pub., l. i. c. xiii.
(*i*) The Twee Juffrouwen, 4 Rob., p. 242.
(*k*) The Jonge Pieter, 4 Ib., p. 79.

voyage from an enemy's port be described "for neutral account," this is such a general mode as points to no designation whatever: and under such a description no person can say that the cargo belongs to him, or can entitle himself to the possession of it as his property. In such a case farther proof is indispensable.(*l*) Where a ship has been captured and carried into an enemy's port, and is *afterwards found in possession of a neutral, the presumption is, that there has been a regular [*597] condemnation, and the proof of the contrary rests on the party claiming the property against the neutral possessor.(*m*) Where a Treaty expressly provides for the removal of persons who happen to be settled in a ceded port, the burden of proof rests on the other party, to show that they did not intend to remove; for the presumption is already to be taken in their favour.(*n*) Where the master of a captured ship is not fairly discredited, his testimony as to destination is generally conclusive on that point.(*o*) So his testimony of the ill-treatment of his crew, if uncontradicted.(*p*) Where the voyage is from the port of one enemy to the port of another enemy, and farther proof is required, the double correspondence of the shipper and consignee should be produced, for there is a double interest to be rebutted; but if the voyage be to a neutral port, the correspondence with the shipper is all that is usually required.(*q*)

CCCCLXXVII. E. We have now to consider the question as to *farther proof.*

α. To Claimants.

β. To Captors.

CCCCLXXVIII. Though it be a cardinal rule that the question of the legality of the capture is to be decided, in the first instance, upon the ship's papers, and upon the depositions of the crew who are examined, it may happen upon the hearing of the case with respect to the facts so put in evidence that it becomes necessary for the ends of justice that *farther* proof should be admitted.

*It is observed by Mr. Justice Story, that in the Supreme Courts of the North American United States, during the whole [*598] of the last maritime war in which that country was engaged, no *farther proof* was ever admitted until the cause had been first heard upon the original evidence; although various applications were made to procure a relaxation of the rule.(*r*)

CCCCLXXIX. Where farther proof is admissible, it may, in the discretion of the Court, be by affidavits and other papers introduced without any formal allegations, or by way of *plea and proof*, where formal allegations are made by each party in the nature of special pleadings; and it may be opened to the *claimants only, or to the captors as well as claimants.* But upon a simple order for farther proof, the captors are not entitled to adduce any new evidence unless by the special direction of the Court; but upon plea and proof, both parties are at liberty to in-

(*l*) The Jonge Pieter, 4 Ib., p. 79.
(*m*) The Countess of Lauderdale, 4 Rob., p. 283. (*n*) The Diana, 5 Rob., p. 60.
(*o*) The Carolina, 3 Ib., p. 75. The Conveníentia, 4 Ib., p. 200.
(*p*) The Die Fire Damer, 5 Ib., p. 357. (*q*) The Vreede, 5 Ib., p. 231.
(*r*) Story on Prize Courts, (by Pratt,) pp. 18, 19.

troduce new evidence to support their respective allegations and the points in issue.(s) During the present war the question of the admissibility of the captors to farther proof has undergone much discussion. The severe construction of the rule as to what is *probable cause* of seizure, pressed against the captors by the Appellate Court in the case of the Ostsee, was urged as a reason for admitting the captors more frequently than Lord Stowell had been inclined to do, to the liberty of farther proof. Nevertheless, the Judge of the Prize Court was of opinion that the *general* rule must be adhered to of refusing the captors the liberty of *farther proof*, and that the concession of it must be a matter of *exception* to that rule.(t)

[*599] The Court is in no case concluded by the original evidence *but may order farther proof on a doubt arising from any course or quarter;(u) and it will sometimes direct it where suspicion is produced by extrinsic evidence.(x) But this is rarely done, unless there be something in the original evidence, which lays a suggestion for prosecuting the inquiry farther;(y) and where the case is perfectly clear, and not liable to any just suspicion, the disposition of the Court leans strongly against the introduction of extraneous matter, and against permitting the captors to enter upon farther inquiry.(z)

The most ordinary cases of farther proof are where the cause appears doubtful upon the original papers, and the answers to the standing interrogatories; and in such cases, if the parties have conducted themselves with good faith, and the error or deficiency may be referred to honest ignorance or mistake, the Court will indulge them with time to supply the defects, by the introduction of new evidence. But farther proof is, in no case, a matter of right, and rests in the sound discretion of the Court. Farther proof is in all cases necessary, where the master does not swear to, or give account of, the property;(a) where the shipment, though stated to be on neutral account, is not stated to be on account of any particular person;(b) where the ship has been purchased in the enemy's country;(c) where there has been any loss or suppression of material papers;(d) and, indeed, in all cases, where the defects of the papers, the conduct of the parties, the nature of the voyage, or the original evidence *in general, induces any doubt of the proprietary interest, [*600] the legality of the trade, or the integrity of the transactions.

CCCCLXXX. But it is not in every case where farther proof is necessary, that the parties will be permitted to introduce it; for the privilege may be forfeited by fraud or gross misconduct. And in cases where farther proof is necessary, if it is not allowed, the penal consequences are as fatal as if the property were originally hostile, since a condemnation

(s) The Adriana, 1 Rob., p. 313.
(t) The Ostsee, Reports of Cases in the Prize Court and Court of Appeal, (1856,) part i. p. 174.
(u) The Romeo, 6 Rob., p. 351. (x) Ibid.
(y) The Sarah, 3 Rob., p. 330. (z) The Romeo, 6 Ib., p. 351.
(a) The Eenrom, 2 Ib., p. 1. The Juno, 2 Ib., p. 121. The Convenientia, 4 Ib., p. 201.
(b) The Jonge Pieter, 4 Ib., p. 79. (c) The Welvaart, 1 Ib., p. 122.
(d) The Polly, 2 Ib., p. 361.

certainly follows the denial.(*e*) Farther proof is never allowed to the claimants where fraudulent papers have been used;(*f*) where there has been a spoliation of papers;(*g*) where there has been a fraudulent covering or suppression of an enemy's interest;(*h*) where there is a false destination and false papers;(*i*) nor in general where the case appears incapable *of fair explanation,(*k*) or where there has been gross prevarication, or an attempt to impose spurious claims upon the Court, or such a want of good faith as shows that the parties cannot safely be trusted with an order for farther proof. [*601]

If, upon farther proof ordered, no proof is adduced, or, the proof be defective, or the parties refuse to swear, or swear evasively, it is deemed conclusive evidence of hostile interests, or of such misconduct as authorizes condemnation.

And it is a general rule of the Prize Court, that the *onus probandi* that the property is neutral rests upon the claimant; and if he fails to show it, condemnation ensues.(*l*)

CCCCLXXXI. In cases where farther proof is admitted on behalf of the captors, they may introduce papers taken on board of another ship, if they are properly verified by affidavit.(*m*) And they may also invoke papers from another Prize Cause.(*n*) It has even been permitted to the captors to invoke the depositions of the claimant given in, in another cause, to prove his domicil at the first hearing, and without an order for farther proof.(*o*) And upon an order for farther proof, the affidavits of the captors, as to the facts within their own knowledge, are admissible evidence.(*p*)

CCCCLXXXII. In respect to *the persons who may be witnesses* in Prize Causes, it is very clear, that an alien enemy, as such, is not in

(*e*) The Welvaart, 1 Ib., p. 122. The Juffrouw Anna, Ib., p. 125. The Graaf Bernstoff, 3 Ib., p. 109. The Eenrom, 2 Ib., p. 1.

(*f*) The Welvaart, 1 Ib., p. 122. The Juffrouw Anna, Ib., p. 125. The Juffrouw Elbrecht, Ib., p. 127.

(*g*) The Rising Sun, 2 Ib., p. 104. (*h*) The Graaf Bernstorff, 3 Ib , p. 109. "*Et pour ce qu'il pourroit advenir, qu'aucuns de nos dits Alliez et Confederez, voudroyent porter plus grande faveur à nos dits ennemis et adversaires, qu'à nous, et à nos dits subjets, et à ceste cause, voudroyent dire et sourstenir contre verité, que les navires pris en mer pas nos dits subjects leur appartiendroyent ensemble la merchandise, pour en frauder nos dits subjets, voulons et ordonnons,* qu'incontinent après la prise et abordement de navire, nos dits subjets facent diligence de recouvrer le charte partie, et autre lettres concernant la charge du navire; et incontinent à leur arrivement à terre, les mettre par devers le lieutenant de nostre dit admiral, à fin de cognoiștre à qui le navire et marchandises appartiennent; et où ne seroit trouvée charte dedans les dits navires, *où que le maistre et campagnons l'eussent jettée en la mer, pour en celer le verité, voulons que les dits navires ainsi pris, avec les dits bien et marchandises estans dedans soyent declarez de bonne prize.*"—Ordonnance de 1584, art. 70, du 5 Septembre, 1708, du 21 Octobre, 1744, art. 6.

(*i*) The Nancy, 3 Rob., p. 122. The Mars, 6 Ib., p. 79.

(*k*) The Vrow Hermina, 1 Rob., p. 163.

(*l*) The Walsingham Packet, 2 Ib., p. 77. The Rosalie and Betty, Ib., p. 343. The Countess of Lauderdale, 4 Ib., p. 283.

(*m*) The Romeo, 6 Ib., p. 351. The Maria, 1 Ib., p. 340.

(*n*) The Romeo, 6 Ib., p. 350. The Sarah, 3 Ib., p. 330. The Vriendschap, 4 Ib., p. 166.

(*o*) Ibid. (*p*) The Maria, 1 Rob., p. 340. The Resolution, 6 Ib., p. 13.

[*602] general disabled to be a witness;(q) and, *indeed, in ordinary cases the prize crew, whether national, neutral, or hostile, are necessary witnesses in the cause.(r) And upon farther proof ordered, the attestations of the claimant and his clerks, and the correspondence between him and his agents, are admissible evidence, and proper proofs of property;(s) and upon farther proof, the affidavits of the captors, even without a release, are good evidence of facts within their own knowledge;(t) but except under peculiar circumstances, the affidavits of captors are not received in our Prize Courts.(u)

Where farther proof is ordered, affidavits taken in foreign countries, before notaries public whose attestations are properly verified, are in general proper evidence. But in the Supreme Court of the United States, it is by a rule of the Court required, that all such evidence shall be taken under a commission from the Court.(x) It is, however, a general rule of the Prize Court not to issue any commission to be executed in the enemy's country.(y)

CCCCLXXXIII. The questions which are most ordinarily discussed in Prize Courts at the hearing of the cause, respect the *national character of the property*; and this depends ordinarily upon the national domicil of the asserted proprietor, or upon the nature of the title which he asserts over the property; but sometimes upon the habits and trade of [*603] the ship, *upon the nature of the voyage or of the cargo, or upon the legal or illegal conduct of the parties themselves. In all these cases where the property is condemned, it is by fiction, or rather by intendment of law, deemed the property of enemies, that is, of persons who are so to be considered in the particular transaction, and is condemned *eo nomine*.(z)

CCCCLXXXIV. With respect to the *Nationality of Persons*, or the question, who are to be considered enemies or not, the general principle is, that every person is to be considered as belonging to that country where he has his domicil, whatever may be his native or adopted country.(a)

(q) The Falcon, 6 Ib., p. 194. (r) The Henrick and Maria, 4 Rob., p. 43.

(s) The Adelaide, 3 Ib., p. 281.

(t) The Maria, 1 Ib., p. 340. The Resolution, 6 Ib., p. 13. The Sally, 1 Gallison's (Amer.) Rep., p. 401.

(u) The Henrick and Maria, 4 Rob., p. 57, note (a). The Grotius, 9 Cranch's (Amer.) Rep., p. 368. The Sally, 1 Gallison's (Amer.) Rep., p. 401. The Haabet, 6 Rob., p. 54. The Glierktigheit, 6 Ib., p. 58, note (a). The Charlotte Caroline, 1 Dodson's Rep., pp. 192, 199.

(x) The London Packet, 2 Wheaton's (Amer.) Rep., p. 371.

(y) The Magnus, 1 Rob., p. 31. The Diana, 2 Gallison's (Amer.) Rep., p. 93.

(z) The Elsebe, 5 Rob., p. 173. The Nelly, 1 Ib., p. 219, note to the Hoop. For American cases, see:—The Alexander, 8 Cranch's (Amer.) Rep., 169. The Julia, Ib., p. 181. The Thomas Gibbons, Ib., p. 421. The St. Lawrence, 1 Gallison's (Amer.) Rep., p. 532. The Joseph, Ib., p. 545.

(a) The Vigilantia, 1 Rob., p. 1. The Endraught, Ib., p. 19. The Sarah Christina, Ib., p. 237. The Indian Chief, 3 Ib., p. 23. The President, 5 Ib., p. 277, The Neptunus, 6 Ib., p. 403. For American cases, see:—The Venus, 9 Cranch's (Amer.) Rep., p. 253. The Frances, Gillespie's Claim, 1 Gallison's (Amer.) Rep., p. 614. The Mary and Susan, Richardson's Claim, 1 Wheaton's (Amer.) Rep. M'Connel v. Hector, 2 Bosanquet & Puller, p. 113. Bynk. Q. J. Pub. ch. iii., Du Ponceau's edition, pp. 19, 25.

And the masters and crews of ships are deemed to possess *the [*604] national character of the ships to which they belong, during the time of their employment;(*b*) and even if a person goes into a belligerent country originally for temporary purposes, he will not preserve his neutral character, if he remain there several years, paying taxes, &c.(*c*) And a neutral consul, resident and trading in a belligerent country, is, as to his mercantile character, deemed a belligerent of that country;(*d*) and the same rule applies to the subject of one belligerent country, resident in the country of its enemy and carrying on trade there:(*e*) but the character acquired by mere domicil ceases upon removal from the country.(*f*) The native character easily reverts, and it requires fewer circumstances to constitute domicil in the case of a native, than to impress the national character on one who is originally of another country;(*g*) and in his favour, a party is deemed to have changed his domicil, and his native character reverts, as soon as he puts himself *in itinere* to return to his native country *animo revertendi*.(*h*)

In general, a neutral merchant trading in the ordinary manner with a belligerent country, does not, by the mere accident of his having a stationed agent there, contract the character of the enemy.(*i*) But it is otherwise, if he be not *engaged in trade upon the ordinary [*605] footing of a neutral merchant, but as a privileged trader of the enemy, for then it is in effect a hostile trade.(*k*) So if the agency carry on a trade from the hostile country, which is not clearly neutral,(*l*) and if a person be a partner in a house of trade in an enemy's country, he is, as to the concerns and trade of that house, deemed an enemy; and his share is liable to confiscation as such, notwithstanding his own residence is in a neutral country, for the domicil of the house is considered in this respect as the domicil of the partners.(*m*) But if he has a house of trade in a neutral country, he has not the benefit of the same principle; for if his own personal residence be in the hostile country, his share in the

"On n'aura aucun égard aux passe-ports accordés par les princes neutres ou alliés, tant au propriétaires qu'aux maîtres des navires sujets des états ennemis, s'ils n'ont été naturalises, et n'ont transferé leure domicile dans les états des dits princes avant la déclaration de la presente guerre. Ne pourront pareillement les dits propriétaires et maîtres des navires ou sujets des états ennemis, qui auront obtenu les dits lettres de naturalité jouir de leur effet si, de puis qu'elle ont été obtenués ils sont retournés dans les états ennemis pour y continuer leur commerce." Réglement du 21 Octobre, 1744, art. 11, Decr. 36, Juillet, 1778, art. 6.

(*b*) The Endraught, 1 Rob., p. 23. The Bernon, Ib., p. 102. Vide the Embden, Ib., p. 17. The Frederick, 5 Ib., p. 8. The Ann, 1 Dodson, p. 221.

(*c*) The Harmony, 2 Rob., p. 322. The Embden, 1 Ib., p. 17.

(*d*) The Indian Chief, 3 Ib., p. 22. The Josephine, 4 Ib., p. 25.

(*e*) The Citto, 3 Ib., p. 38. M'Connel v. Hector, 3 Bosanquet & Puller, p. 113.

(*f* The Indian Chief, 3 Rob., p. 12. (*g*) La Virginie, 5 Ib., p. 98.

(*h*) The Indian Chief, 3 Ib., p. 12. The St. Lawrence, 1 Gallison's (Amer.) Rep., p. 467.

(*i*) The Anna Catharina, 4 Rob., p. 119. The Rendsberg, Ib., p. 139.

(*k*) The Anna Catharina, 4 Rob., p. 119. (*l*) Ibid.

(*m*) The Vigilantia, 1 Rob., pp. 1, 14, 19. The Susa, 2 Ib., p. 255. The Indiana, 3 Ib., p. 44, note (1). The Portland, Ibid. The Vriendschap, 4 Ib., p. 166. The Jonge Klassina, 5 Ib., p. 297. The Antonia Johanna, 1 Wheaton's (Amer.) Rep., p. 159. The St. Joze Indiana, 2 Gallison's (Amer.) Rep., p. 268.

property of the neutral house is liable to condemnation.(*n*) However, where a neutral is engaged *in peace*, in a house of trade in the enemy's country, his property, so engaged in the house, is not, at the commencement of war, confiscated; but if he continues in the house after the knowledge of the war, it is liable, as above stated, to confiscation.(*o*) It is a settled principle, that traffic alone, independent of residence, will, in some cases, confer a hostile character on the individual;(*p*) and if a [*606] neutral be engaged in the enemy's navigation, it not only *affects the peculiar vessel in which he is employed, but all other vessels belonging to him that have no distinct national character impressed upon them.(*q*)

CCCCLXXXV. With respect to the *Nationality of Ships*. Ships are deemed to belong to the country under whose *flag* and *pass* they navigate; and this circumstance is conclusive upon their character.(*r*) So, even if purchased by a neutral, if they are habitually engaged in the trade of the enemy's country,(*s*) even though there be no seaport in the territory of the neutral;(*t*) but, in general, and unless under special circumstances, the national character of ships depends on the residence of the owner.(*u*) When, however, it is said that the flag and pass are conclusive on the character of the ship, the meaning is this: that the party who takes the benefit of them, is himself bound by them; he is not at liberty, when they happen to operate to his disadvantage, to turn round and deny the character which he has worn for his own benefit, and upon the credit of his own oath or solemn declarations; but they do not bind *other parties* as against him; other parties are at liberty to show that these are spurious credentials, assumed for the purpose of disguising the real character of the vessel; and it is no inconsiderable part of the ordinary occupation of a Prize Court, to pull off this mask, and exhibit the vessel so disguised in her true character of an enemy's vessel.(*x*) Ships and cargoes engaged in the privileged and peculiar trade of a nation, under a special contract, and the sanction of the Government, are considered as affected by [*607] *the character of the nation, and if it be hostile, the trade is stamped with the same character;(*y*) and the produce of an estate situated in an hostile colony, is so impressed with the character of the soil, that although the owner of the estate be resident in a neutral country, his interest in the produce is deemed enemy's property.(*z*)

(*n*) Ibid. The Frances, 1 Gallison's (Amer.) Rep., p. 618. S. C. 8 Cranch's (Amer.) Rep., p. 348.

(*o*) The Vigilantia, 1 Rob., pp. 1, 14, 15. The Susa, 2 Ib., pp. 251, 255.

(*p*) Ibid. The Vriendschap, 4 Ib., p. 166.

(*q*) The Vriendschap, 4 Rob., p. 166.

(*r*) The Vigilantia, 1 Rob., pp. 1, 19, 26. The Vrow Anna Catharina, 5 Ib., p. 161. The Success, 1 Dodson, p. 131.

(*s*) The Vigilantia, 1 Rob., pp. 1, 19, 26. The Planter's Wensch, 5 Ib., p. 22.

(*t*) Ibid.

(*u*) Ibid. The Magnus, 1 Rob., p. 31.

(*x*) The Fortuna, 1 Dodson, p. 87. The Success, Ib., p. 131.

(*y*) The Princessa, 2 Rob., p. 49. The Anna Catherina, 4 Ib., p. 107. The Rendsberg, 4 Ib., p. 121. The Vrow Anna Catharina, 5 Ib., p. 161. The Comercen, 1 Wheaton's (Amer.) Rep., p. 382. Vide the Vreede Scholtys, 5 Rob., p. 5, note (*a*).

(*z*) The Phœnix, 5 Rob., p. 20. The Vrow Anna Catharina, Ib., p. 161. The Dree Gebroeders, 4 Ib., p. 232. Bentzou's Claim, 9 Cranch's (Amer.) Rep., p. 191.

CCCCLXXXVI. In respect to the transfers of enemies' ships during war, it is certain that purchases of them by neutrals are not, in general, illegal; but such purchases are liable to great suspicion; and if good proof be not given of their validity by a bill of sale and payment of a reasonable consideration, it will materially impair the validity of the neutral claim;(*a*) and if the purchase be made by an agent, his letters of procuration must be produced and proved;(*b*) and if after such transfer the ship be employed habitually in the enemy's trade, or under the management of a hostile proprietor, the sale will be deemed merely colourable and collusive.(*c*) But the right of purchase by neutrals extends only to merchant *ships of enemies;(*d*) for the purchase [*608] of ships of war belonging to enemies, is held to be invalid;(*e*) and a sale of a merchant ship, made by an enemy to a neutral during war, must be an absolute unconditional sale.(*f*) Anything tending to continue the interest of the enemy in the ship vitiates a contract of this description altogether.(*g*)

CCCCLXXXVII. With respect to the *proprietary interests in cargoes*, though, in general, the rules of the Common Law apply, yet there are many peculiar principles of Prize Law to be considered; it is a general rule that, during hostilities, or imminent and impending danger of hostilities, the property of parties belligerent cannot change its national character during the voyage, or, as is commonly expressed, *in transitu*.(*h*) This rule equally applies to ships and cargoes; and it is so inflexible, that it is not relaxed, even in owners who become subjects by capitulation, after the shipment and before the capture.(*i*) But if the ship sails before hostilities, when there is a *decided state* of amity between the two countries, and before the capture the owner, though circumstances of hostility may have intervened, again becomes a friend, and at the time of the capture, and also at the time of adjudication, he is in a capacity to claim, the Prize Courts will then give him the benefit of the principle, that the national character cannot be altered *in transitu*, and will restore to him.(*k*) The same distinction is applied to purchases made by neutrals of property *in transitu;* if purchased during a state of war existing, or imminent and impending danger of war, the contract is held invalid, and the property is *deemed to continue as it was at the time of shipment until the actual delivery. It is otherwise, how- [*609]

(*a*) The Bernon, 1 Rob., p. 102. The Sechs Geschwistern, 4 Ib., p. 100.
(*b*) The Argo, 1 Ib., p. 158.
"Que tout vaisseau qui sera de fabrique ennemie, ou qui aura eu originairement un propriétaire ennemie, ne pourra être censé neutre, s'il n'eu a été fait une vente parvedant les officiers publics qui doivent passer cette sorte d'actes, et si cette vente ne se trouve aborde, et n'est soutenué d'un pouvoir authentique donné par le premier propriétaire, lorsquil ne vend pas lui-même."—Réglement du 17 Fevrier, 1694; du 12 Mai, 1698.
(*c*) The Jemmy, 4 Rob., p. 31. The Omnibus, 6 Ib., p. 71.
(*d*) The Minerva, 6 Rob., pp. 396, 399. (*e*) Ibid., p. 396.
(*f*) The Packet de Bilboa, 2 Rob., p. 133. The Noydt Gedacht, 2 Ib., p. 137, note (*a*).
(*g*) The Sechs Geschwistern, 4 Ib., p. 100, Prize Rep. (1855).
(*h*) The Danckebaar Africaan, 1 Ib., p. 107. The Herstelder, Ib., p. 114.
(*i*) Ibid. (*k*) Ibid.

ever, if a contract be made during a state of peace, and without contemplation of war; for under such circumstances, the Prize Courts will recognize the contract and enforce the title acquired under it.(*l*) And property is still considered *in transitu*, if it be ultimately destined to the hostile country, notwithstanding it has arrived at a neutral port, and the ship is there changed.(*m*) The reason why Courts of Admiralty have established this rule as to transfers *in transitu* during a state of war, or expected war, is asserted to be, that, if such a rule did not exist, all goods shipped in the enemy's country would be protected by transfers, which it would be impossible to detect.(*n*)

CCCCLXXXVIII. The same public policy has established the rule of the Prize Courts, that property going, *during war*, to be delivered in the enemy's country, and under a contract to become the property of the enemy immediately on arrival, if taken *in transitu*, is to be considered as enemy's property.(*o*) And all contracts of purchase effected on the part of the belligerent, where the payment is executory and contingent on delivery at an ulterior port, at the risk of the neutral vendor or shipper, are considered as contracts in fraud of the Prize Law; and the goods, if captured *in transitu*, are condemned as the absolute property of the enemy.(*p*) But when the contract is made in time of peace, and without any contemplation of war, no such rule exists.(*q*) But the rule is applied where such a contract is originally made between *allies* in the war, if a party to it becomes *neutral* after the [*610] *contract, and before the execution of it, and the shipment is made afterwards.(*r*) A contract by a neutral with a privileged company of the enemy, with a view to the transportation of the whole produce of a colony, or of the company itself, if made during war, or in the contemplation of war, is pronounced illegal, and the property is liable to condemnation as hostile property.(*s*) But if a neutral, during peace, and *without contemplation of war*, purchase goods in a colony from a regular privileged company there, and it is agreed that they shall be transported and sold in the mother country by the company's agents for the benefit of the neutral, the contract is good, and the property remains neutral during its transit, notwithstanding an intervening war of the mother country.(*t*)

In ordinary shipments of goods, unaffected by the foregoing principles, the question of proprietary interest often turns on minute circumstances and distinctions, the general principle being that, if they are going for account of the shipper, or subject to his order or control, the property is not divested *in transitu*. If there be any condition annexed to the delivery of the goods to the consignee, the proprietary interest remains in the shipper, notwithstanding the goods are sent in pursuance of the

(*l*) The Vrow Margaretha, 1 Rob., p. 336. The Jan Frederick, 5 Ib., p. 128.
(*m*) The Carl Walter, 4 Ib., p. 207.
(*n*) The Vrow Margaretha, 1 Ib., p. 336.
(*o*) The Sally, 3 Ib., p. 300, note (*a*).
(*p*) The Atlas, 3 Ib., p. 299. The Anna Catharina, 4 Ib., pp. 107, 113, note.
(*q*) Ibid. (*r*) The Anna Catharina, 4 Rob., pp. 107, 112.
(*s*) The Rendsberg, Ib., p. 121. The Jan Frederick, 5 Ib., p. 128.
(*t*) The Vrow Anna Catharina, 5 Ib., p. 161.

orders of the consignee. Thus, if a merchant in H. sends goods to A. in another country, by order of B. and on account of B., but with directions not to deliver them unless satisfaction could be given for the payment, the property is not divested from the shipper, but remains his *in transitu*.(*u*)

The same principle applies where goods are shipped to the orders of the shippers, but to be delivered by their agents to the consignee, upon the agents being satisfied for the payment.(*x*) So, even if the goods are stated in the invoice to belong to the claimants; yet if [*611] *these papers are inclosed to the consignee* as agent to the shippers, and are to be delivered to the claimants, only upon conditions in the discretion of the agent, the property remains in the shippers.(*y*) But if the goods are consigned to an agent of the shippers, but the invoice, &c., show them to be for the account of the claimants, and the invoice, &c. are, by the shippers, *sent directly to the claimants*, the possession of these documents gives them a title, and establishes the intention of the shipper to vest the property in the claimants at the time of the shipment.(*z*) So, if the goods are shipped to the consignee, unconditionally, for the use of the claimants.(*a*) But if the goods are consigned to the agent of the shippers, and there are discretionary orders given, but no direction for an absolute delivery to the claimants, the property remains in the shippers.(*b*) In all these cases, the goods are supposed to have been purchased in pursuance of the orders of the claimants; for if they are sent by the shippers without orders, or contrary to, or different from orders either in quantity or kind, the proprietary interest remains in the shipper during the transit, notwithstanding they are sent by direct consignment to the consignee.(*c*)

It is certainly competent for an agent abroad, who purchases *goods in pursuance of orders, to vest the proprietary interest in [*612] his principal, immediately on the purchase. This is the case when he purchases exclusively on the credit of the principal, or makes an absolute appropriation and designation of the property for his principal. But where he sells his own goods, or purchases goods on his own credit (and thereby in reality becomes the owner,) no property in such goods vests in his correspondent, until he has done some notorious act to divest himself of his title, or has parted with the possession by an actual and unconditional delivery for the use of such correspondent.(*d*) But such delivery or appropriation to the use of his correspondent, need not be by

(*u*) Cited in the Aurora, 4 Ib., p. 219.

(*x*) The Aurora, 4 Rob., p. 218. The Merrimack, Kimmel and Albert's Claim, 8 Cranch's (Amer.) Rep., p. 317. See the Marianna, 6 Rob., p. 24.

(*y*) The Merrimack, 8 Cranch's (Amer.) Rep., p. 317.

(*z*) Ibid., Messrs. Wilkins' Claim, Ib.

(*a*) Ibid., Messrs. M'Kean and Woodland's Claim. Ib.

(*b*) The St. Joze Indiano, Lizaur's Claim, 2 Gallis. (Amer.) Rep., p. 268. 1 Wheaton's (Amer.) Rep. p. 208.

(*c*) The Venus, 8 Cranch's (Amer.) Rep., p. 253. The Frances, Durham and Randolph's Claim, 1 Gallison's (Amer.) Rep., p. 445. S. C., 8 Cranch's (Amer.) Rep., p. 344; 9 Ib., p. 183. The Frances, French's Claim, 8 Ib., p. 359.

(*d*) The St. Joze Indiano, 2 Gallison's (Amer.) Rep., p. 268. S. C., 1 Wheaton's (Amer.) Rep., p. 208.

a direct act; but it may constructively arise from the circumstances of the case, even where the shipper has made an immediate assignment of the goods.(*e*)

In all these cases, the material question is, whether the shipper retains or possesses any control over the property (independent of the mere right of stoppage *in transitu* in cases of insolvency,) or has parted with the possession and all authority over it. For if an enemy's shipper consign goods or money to his correspondent at H., for the purpose of answering drafts of his correspondent in A., without any letter of advice or document, making it the absolute property of such correspondent, or putting it out of his own control, it still remains the property of the shipper; for he may at any time countermand the order, or give the goods or money a new direction. In substance it is the same transaction as if a person send a sum of money to his private banker, directing him to hold it subject to the order of A.; in which case if, on the next day, and before any such order had been given, or even the fact of lodgment known to the other party, he had changed his purpose, and directed a [*613] conversion *of the money to another object, it is clear that the bankers could not resist with effect.(*f*)

The same penalty is applied to subjects of allies in the war trading with the common enemy(*g*) as to a subject of an enemy. But a citizen of a belligerent country, domiciled in a neutral country, may lawfully trade with the enemy of his native country,(*h*) with the exception of the case of trade in articles contraband of war.(*i*) And if the party intends to trade with the enemy, but, during the voyage, the port becomes neutral, the penalty is saved; for there must be the *act* as well as the intention.(*k*) And even assuming that, after the knowledge of war, a citizen domiciled in the enemy's country may lawfully withdraw his property without a license from his government, which has been denied,(*l*) at all events, it must be done in a reasonable time; and ten months after the war is too late, and the party will then be deemed engaged in a trade with the enemy.(*m*) And if a vessel take on board a cargo from an enemy's ship, under the pretence that it is ransomed, it is an illegal traffic. Even admitting the ransoming of captured property to be legal, it cannot be admitted to be made at any distance of time, and by any new voyages undertaken for this special purpose.(*n*) And sailing under the enemy's license is deemed, *per se*, an efficient cause of condemnation.(*o*)

[*614] *These observations on the subject of proprietary interests, may be concluded with the remark, that to entitle the claimant

(*e*) The Mary and Susan, Ib., p. 25. (*f*) The Josephine, 4 Rob., p. 25.

(*g*) The Naiade, 4 Ib., p. 251. The Neptunus, 6 Ib., p. 403. Bynk. Q. J. Pub., cap. x., Du Ponceau's edition, p. 81.

(*h*) The Danaus, 4 Rob., p. 255, note.

(*i*) The Neptunus, 6 Ib., p. 403. The Ann, 1 Dodson, 221.

(*k*) The Abby, 5 Rob., p. 251.

(*l*) The Mary, 1 Gallison's (Amer.) Rep., p. 620.

(*m*) The St. Lawrence, Ib., p. 467. S. C., 9 Cranch's (Amer.) Rep., p. 120.

(*n*) The Lord Wellington, 2 Gallison's (Amer.) Rep., p. 103.

(*o*) The Julia, 1 Ib., p. 594. S. C., 8 Cranch's (Amer.) Rep., p. 181. The Aurora, 8 Cranch's (Amer.) Rep., p. 203. The Hiram, Ib., p. 444. S. C., 1 Wheaton's (Amer.) Rep., p. 440. The Ariadne, 2 Ib., p. 143.

to sustain his claim in the Prize Court, the property must be proved to be neutral, at all periods from the time of shipment, without intermission, to the arrival and subsequent sale in the port of the enemy.(*p*) And *if it be hostile at the time of shipment*, it is (as has been already stated) a universal rule to condemn it, although the owner has become a friend or subject.(*q*)

CCCCLXXXIX. Before this subject be closed it may be well to consider how far the *illegal acts of the master bind the interests of the owner of the ship or cargo.*

It is a general principle, that the act of the master at all events binds the owner of the ship, as much as if the act were committed by himself.(*r*) If, therefore, the master deviate into a blockaded port, the owner is bound by the act, and is not permitted to aver his ignorance of the act, or that the master acted against his orders.(*s*) And the same principle is applied to the case of carrying goods contraband of war.(*t*) But Grotius,(*u*) Loccenius,(*x*) Pothier,(*y*) and Bynkershoek,(*z*) all contend for a favourable distinction where the owner is ignorant of the fact of unlawful goods being on board. They are, however, contradicted by Valin,(*a*) whose *doctrine is followed in the practice of Prize Courts. The law, indeed, is established, that the principal is [*615] answerable for the acts of his agent (and the master is the accredited agent of the shipowner,) not only civilly but penally, to the amount of the property entrusted to his care.(*b*) It would be impossible for a Court of Prize to affect the proprietor in any other way; and whatever the hardship may be, it is very much softened by recollecting that, if he has sustained any injury by the fraudulent and unauthorized acts of his agent, he will be entitled to his remedy against him.(*c*) But the act of the master does not, in general, bind the owner of the cargo, unless he be owner of the ship, or conusant of the intended violation of law, or the master be his agent.(*d*) In cases of blockade, the deviation into the blockaded port is presumed to be in the service of the cargo, and, therefore, the owner is bound by it, unless where there is no notice of the blockade at the time the ship sailed.(*e*) And if the master at the time of sailing put his ship under convoy, whose instructions he is presumed to know, the act is illegal, and binds both the ship and cargo.(*f*) It is not considered like the case of an unforeseen emergency happening to a ship at sea, where the fact itself proves the owners to be ignorant

(*p*) The Atlas, 3 Rob., p. 299. The Sally, Ib., p. 300, note (*a*).
(*q*) The Boedes Lust, 5 Ib., p. 233.
(*r*) The Vrow Judith, 1 Rob., p. 150.
(*s*) The Adonis, 5 Ib., p. 256. (*t*) The Imina, 3 Ib., p. 167.
(*u*) Jure Belli et Pacis, lib. iii. ch. vi. § 6.
(*x*) De Jur. Mar. lib. ii. ch. iv. no. 12.
(*y*) De Propriété, no. 103. (*z*) Q. J. P. lib. i. ch. xii.
(*a*) Sur l'Ord., tom. ii. p. 253. Emerigon, Des Assurances, tom. i. p. 449.
(*b*) The Mars, 6 Rob., pp. 79, 87. (*c*) Ibid.
(*d*) The Vrow Judith, 1 Rob., p. 150. The Imina, 3 Ib., p. 169. The Rosalie and Betty, 2 Ib., pp. 343, 351. The Alexander, 4 Ib., p. 93. The Elsebe, 5 Ib., p. 173.
(*e*) The Alexander, 4 Ib., p. 93. The Shepherdess, 5 Ib., p. 262.
(*f*) The Elsebe, 5 Ib., p. 173.

and innocent, and where the Court has holden, that being proved innocent by the very circumstances of the case, the owners of the cargo should not be bound by the mere principle of law, which imposes on the employ era responsibility for the acts of his agent. On the contrary, it [*616] is a matter done *antecedently to the voyage*, and must, therefore, be presumed to be done on communication with the owners, and with their consent; the effect of this presumption is such that it cannot be permitted to be averred against, inasmuch as all the evidence must come from the suspected parties themselves, without a possibility of meeting it, however prepared. The Court, therefore, applies the strict principle of law, and holds, as it does in blockade cases of that description, that the master must be taken to be the authorized agent of the cargo; and that if he has exceeded his authority, it is barratry, for which he is personally answerable, and for which the owner must look to him for indemnification.(*g*) Whether a like principle ought not to be applied to the owner of the cargo, in cases where the ship originally sails on the voyage under an enemy's license, has not been decided. The point was made in the Supreme Court in a recent case; but knowledge being brought home to the actual agent of the owners of the cargo, it became unnecessary to decide the more general principle.(*h*) There are many other cases in which the act of the master will bind the owner of the cargo as well as the ship; such are resistance of the right of search, suppressing or fraudulently destroying the ship's papers, rescue by the neutral crew after capture, &c.(*i*) But though the act of a neutral master in resisting search binds both ship and cargo; yet it has been solemnly settled by the Supreme Court, that the resistance of a *belligerent* master does not bind a neutral shipment, unless the proprietor has co-operated in the resistance.(*k*) In a very recent case, however, Sir W. Scott has asserted the contrary doctrine.(*l*)

[*617] *CCCCXC. But the act of the agent or consignee of the cargo, whether he be the master or not, is conclusive upon the owner of the cargo;(*m*) and the act of a *general* agent of the cargo, in covering the enemy's property in the same shipment with his principal's property, affects the whole with condemnation, although the principal had no knowledge of the illegal act.(*n*) And the same principle is applied in the case of simulated papers; for the carrying of simulated papers is an efficient cause of condemnation.(*o*) But in peculiar circumstances, the act of an agent of the cargo will be liberally construed in favour of his principal. As if the agent be a belligerent, and has received orders to purchase goods before the war or before a blockade, his acts in making

(*g*) The Elsebe, 5 Rob., pp. 173, 175.
(*h*) The Hiram, 1 Wheaton's (Amer.) Rep., p. 440.
(*i*) The Elsebe, 5 Rob., p. 173. The Dispatch, 3 Ib., p. 279. The Nereide, 9 Cranch's (Amer.) Rep., pp. 388, 451.
(*k*) Ibid., p. 388.
(*l*) The Fanny, 1 Dodson, p. 443.
(*m*) The Vrow Judith, 1 Rob., p. 150.
(*n*) The St. Nicholas, 1 Wheaton's (Amer.) Rep., p. 417. The Phœnix Ins. Co. v. Pratt, 2 Binney, p. 308.
(*o*) Oswell v. Vigne, 15 East, p. 70.

the shipment during a blockade, are not binding on his principal, unless he had had an opportunity to countermand the orders, and neglected it; for the agent in such cases may have a personal interest in exporting the goods.(*p*) But the act of the master will not bind even the owner of the ship, unless it be in cases within the scope of his ordinary authority. If, therefore, the master of a non-commissioned merchant ship make a capture, the owner is not responsible in damages, if it turns out to be illegal.(*q*)

CCCCXCI. F. We have now to consider *the sentence* in the Prize Court, and the subsidiary questions of *freight*, of *costs*, and *expenses.*

CCCCXCII. Upon the hearing of the proofs, if the case does not require or admit farther proof, the Court proceeds *to pronounce a sentence of *acquittal* or *condemnation*, as the justice of the case requires. [*618] And it may proceed to make a decree as well after as before the death of the parties; for in proceedings *in rem* the suit does not abate by the death or absence of all or any of the parties named in the proceedings.(*r*) It may be proper in many cases, where all the parties on either side are dead, not to proceed to make a decree *in rem* without serving a monition upon the representatives of the deceased party to appear, and pursue or defend his rights. And where the decree is *in personam*, the Court will generally require that the representative should be duly cited to appear to protect his interests, so far as they may be affected by the decree.(*s*) It is, indeed, the duty of the Court to take notice of all interests that result from evidence before it, and not to suffer any persons to be precluded from their just demands from want of notice of any facts that appear in the course of the proceedings.(*t*) And where the parties are not formally before the Court, it acts as a general guardian of all interests which are brought to its notice.(*u*) Indeed, in the common cases of condemnations, the enemy proprietor is necessarily absent by operation of law; and yet the sentence is completely valid, as well against him as against the whole world.(*x*) To give validity, therefore, to decrees *in rem*, it is not necessary that the adverse parties should be before the Court.(*y*)

CCCCXCIII. When a sentence is pronounced in the English Prize Court, either of acquittal or condemnation, it is, in general, by an *interlocutory decree.* An interlocutory *decree is proper in all cases, where anything farther remains to be done by the Court, as in [*619] ascertaining damages in cases of illegal capture, or in deciding who are captors, after deciding that the property is to be condemned. The right to decide *who are captors* entitled to distribution, belongs exclusively to the Prize Court, and its adjudication cannot be examined by a Court of

(*p*) The Neptunas, 1 Robinson, p. 170. Cases cited in the Hoop, Ib., p. 196. The Dankbaarheit, 1 Dodson, p. 183.

(*q*) Bynkershoek, Q. J. P., l. i. c. xix., Du Ponceau's ed., pp. 147, 153.

(*r*) Penhallow v. Doane, 3 Dallas's (Amer.) Rep., pp. 54, 86, 117. The Falcon, 6 Rob., pp. 194, 199.

(*s*) Vide the Nostra Signora de los Dolores, 1 Dodson, p. 290.

(*t*) The Maria François, 6 Rob., p. 282.

(*u*) Ibid.

(*x*) The Falcon, 6 Rob., pp. 194, 199.

(*y*) Ibid.

Common Law.(z) And no title vests in the captors until a final adjudication of the Prize Court.(a) In England the usual practice is to acquit or condemn by interlocutory decree in all cases.(b) And a *definitive sentence* is reserved until all other questions and interests are disposed of.(c) In the North American United States it is more common to reserve a decree until a final decision of all the questions before the Court: but, according to Mr. Justice Story, there can be no doubt of the propriety of an adherence to the English practice, where the circumstances of the case require a suspension of a final sentence, although the propriety of an acquittal or condemnation is perfectly clear; and in case of an acquittal or condemnation by *interlocutory decree* there can be no question that an appeal immediately lies to the proper Appellate Court by the parties affected by that decree; for as to them it is an interlocutory having the effect of a *final decree.*

CCCCXCIV. In respect to cases of *acquittal.* This may be either with or *without damages and costs,* or *upon the terms of paying costs and expenses.* In either case where the damages or expenses are uncertain, and to be ascertained, the Court itself may proceed directly to assess [*620] them.(d) But *the usual practice is, to refer it to commissioners to hear the parties, examine their statements and accounts, and to report to the Court in detail, such allowance as they think equitable or legally due to the parties. Accompanying the report, the reasons of the commissioners for the allowance or disallowance of any particular item are usually given, and the report, when returned to the Court, is heard upon exceptions by the parties.

CCCCXCV. When *restitution* is decreed, if the property remains specifically in the custody of the Court, the warrant issues for the delivery to the claimant; and in such case, unless it is otherwise ordered by the Court, the expenses of the delivery are to be borne by the captors.(e) If the proceeds of the property are in Court, an order for delivery is usually made by the Court; and after a decree of restitution, the captors have no right to arrest the proceeds in the registry of the Court by a *caveat;* that can only be done by an application to the Court itself.(f) If the proceeds are in the hands of the captors or their agents, a monition, and, if necessary, an attachment, issues to them to bring in the proceeds. But where the captors have not conducted themselves unfairly, on restitution decreed, they will not be held answerable for more than the proceeds, although the sale made was less than the original value of the property.(g) The property, upon a decree of restitution, may be delivered to the master as agent of the shipper; for in such case the master is the agent of the shipper, and is answerable to him.(h)

But in such a case, neither the master nor any other Prize Agent can claim the property against his principal, unless so far as to cover his

(z) Home v. Camden, 2 H. Blackstone's Rep., p. 533. 4 Durnford and East's Rep., p. 382. Duckworth v. Tucker, 2 Taunton's Rep., p. 7.

(a) Ibid. (b) Marriott's Form, pp. 194, 196.

(c) Ibid., pp. 198, 203. (d) The Lively, 1 Gallison's (Amer.) Rep., p. 315.

(e) The Rendsberg, 6 Rob., p. 142. (f) The Fortuna, 4 Ib., p. 278.

(g) The Two Susannahs, 2 Ib., p. 132.

(h) Sir W. Scott and Sir J. Nichol's Letter to Mr. Jay, vide ante, p. 551.

expenses, and the Court will thus far protect his rights; but when his expenses and his liens on the *property are discharged, the Court will deliver it directly to the principal upon his own application.(*i*) After a decree for restitution of partnership property to a foreign house *in solidum*, the Court will not sever the property merely because one partner is a bankrupt here; but if the assignees put in a claim for this purpose before a decree it would be otherwise.(*k*) [*621]

CCCCXCVI. *Where damages are decreed*, the decree is either against the parties by name, or by a description of their relation to the ship. Where a decree is against the owners of a privateer generally, a monition issues against them personally to pay the damages assessed; and it may also issue against the sureties to the bond given on taking out the commission. In a Court of International Law, a person may be considered as a part-owner, though his name has not been inserted in the bill of sale or ship's register; and the representative of a person so deemed a part-owner is responsible for costs and damages decreed against the owners generally, though the party of whom he is the representative was not the actual wrong-doer.(*l*) And, as has been already stated, a part-owner is not exempted from being a party to a suit for the proceeds, by having a release from the claimant for his share.(*m*)

CCCCXCVII. In respect to cases of *condemnation*. Where an interlocutory decree of condemnation passes in favour of a privateer, it has been usual in England to deliver that decree, with a proper commission, to the master of the privateer, to make sale of the Prize, and to return an account into Court.(*n*) But in the North American United States, all sales of prizes, before as well as after condemnation, are made by the *Marshal; and in respect to sales after condemnation, this practice is farther enforced by statute.(*o*) [*622]

CCCCXCVIII. With respect to *freight*. It frequently happens that enemies' goods are found on board of neutral ships; and conversely, that neutral goods are found on board of enemies' ships. In these cases, questions often occur as to the right of the parties to freight, expenses, &c.

CCCCXCIX. And first, in respect to neutral ships. In general, where enemies' goods are captured in a neutral ship, the captors take *cum onere;* and if the conduct of the neutral has been perfectly fair and impartial, it is the practice of the Prize Court to allow him his full freight, in the same manner, as if the original voyage had been performed;(*p*) and in like manner to allow him his expenses.(*q*) The freight allowed, is not,

(*i*) The Franklin, 4 Rob., p. 404. The St. Lawrence, 2 Gallison's (Amer.) Rep., p. 19.

(*k*) The Jefferson, 1 Rob., p. 325.

(*l*) The Nostra Signora de los Dolores, 1 Dodson, p. 290.

(*m*) The Karasan, 5 Rob., p. 291. (*n*) Semble, the Venus, 9 Ib., p. 235.

(*o*) January 27th, 1813, c. clv. new ed. c. cccclxxviii.

(*p*) The Hoop, 1 Rob., pp. 196, 219. The Antonia Johanna, 1 Wheaton's (Amer.) Rep., p. 159.

(*q*) The Hoop, 1 Rob., p. 196. The Bremen Flugge, 4 Ib., p. 90. The Der Mohr, Ib., p. 314. Smart v. Wolff, Durnford and East's Rep., p. 323. Vattel, liv. iii. c. vii. s. 115. The Consolato del Mare, ch. cclxxiii. Sir W. Scott and Sir J. Nicholl's Letter to Mr. Jay, ante, p. 551. The Copenhagen, 1 Rob., p. 289. The

however, necessarily the rate agreed on by the parties, if it be inflamed by extraordinary circumstances; but a reasonable freight only will, in such cases, be allowed.(*r*) And where the goods have been once unlivered by order of Court, the whole freight for the voyage is due, and the owner of the goods, even in case of restitution, cannot demand the ship to reload [*623] them, and carry them to the original port of destination, for by the *separation the ship is exonerated;(*s*) but it would be otherwise if there had been no unlivery.(*t*) And the neutral will be allowed his freight where he carries the goods of one belligerent to its enemy; for though such a trade be illegal as to the subjects, it is not so as to neutrals.(*u*) So, on a voyage from the port of one enemy to the port of another enemy.(*x*) But if the neutral has conducted himself fraudulently or unfairly, or in violation of belligerent rights, he will not be allowed freight or expenses, and, in flagrant cases, will be visited with confiscation, even of the ship itself. And he is never allowed freight where he has used false papers;(*y*) nor upon the carriage of contraband goods;(*z*) nor where there has been a spoliation of papers;(*a*) nor where the cause of capture was the ship, and not the cargo.(*b*) But where part of the goods are condemned as contraband, and part restored after unlivery of the cargo, freight may be decreed as a charge upon the part restored.(*c*) If the goods are unlivered under a hostile embargo upon neutral ships, [*624] they are discharged of the lien of the freight; and if freight be *decreed, it can only be against the original consignees or freighters, and not against a prior purchaser, who has received them on bail.(*d*)

When a decree is made that the freight shall be a charge on the cargo, application must be made to the Court for the sale of so much as is necessary for this purpose.(*e*) In general, where a ship and cargo are restored, with a decree that the freight shall be a charge on the cargo, if the proceeds of the cargo are not sufficient to pay the freight, the captors are not responsible for the deficiency.(*f*) But although the capture be right, yet if afterwards the cargo is lost by the negligence of the captors, and the freight be decreed a charge on the cargo, the captors are responsible to pay it.(*g*) Where the freight of the neutral and the expenses of the captors are both decreed to be a charge on the cargo, and

Anna Catharina, 6 Ib., p. 10. The Catharina Elizabeth, Acton's Rep., p. 209. The Fortuna, Edwards's Rep., p. 59.

(*r*) The Twilling Riget, 5 Rob., p. 82.

(*s*) The Hoffnung, 6 Rob., p. 231. The Prosper, Edwards's Rep., p. 72.

(*t*) The Copenhagen, 1 Rob., p. 289. (*u*) The Hoop, Ib., pp. 196, 219.

(*x*) The Wilhelmina, 2 Ib., p. 101, note.

(*y*) The Atlas, 3 Ib., pp. 299, 304, note. Sir W. Scott and Sir J. Nicholl's Letter to Mr. Jay, ante, p. 551.

(*z*) Ibid. Bynk. Q. J. Pub., Du Ponceau's ed., p. 81. The Sarah Christina, 1 Rob., p. 237. The Mercurius, Ib., p. 288. The Emanuel, Ib., p. 296. The Neptunus, 3 Ib., p. 108. The Neutralitet, Ib., p. 295. The Oster Risoer, 4 Ib., p. 199. The Commercea, 1 Wheaton's (Amer.) Rep., p. 382.

(*a*) The Rising Run, 2 Rob., p. 104. The Madonna Del Burso, 4 Ib., pp. 169, 183.

(*b*) The Fortuna, Edwards's Rep., p. 56. (*c*) The Oster Risoer, 4 Rob., p. 199.

(*d*) The Theresa Bonita, 4 Rob., p. 236.

(*e*) The Vrow Margaretha, Ib., p. 304, note.

(*f*) The Haabet, Ib., p. 302. (*g*) The Der Mohr, Ib., p. 315.

the proceeds are insufficient to discharge both, priority of payment of the freight is, in ordinary cases, allowed by the Court, as a lien that takes place of all others.(*h*)

D. In the next place, as to the allowance of freight to the captors.— This may happen when the ship is hostile, and the cargo, or a part thereof, is neutral. The general rule is, that if neutral goods are found on board of a hostile ship, the captors are not entitled to freight therefor, unless they carry the goods to the port of destination.(*i*) And the rule is applied, notwithstanding there may have been a sale of the goods beneficial to the owners.(*k*) But *there are exceptions to the rule itself; for if the captors bring the cargo to the country [*625] where the claimants ultimately designed to send it, but were compelled to take a circuitous route under existing circumstances, the captors are entitled to freight, notwithstanding the ship was actually destined to another country, there to land it.(*l*) So, if brought to the same country, but not to the port of actual destination.(*m*) So, where the goods are brought to the country where the proceeds were ultimately destined, and would have been brought directly, but for a prohibition of municipal law.(*n*) Where freight is decreed to the captors, it will be paid by the Court, out of the cargo or its proceeds, if yet remaining in the Admiralty.(*o*) And under particular circumstances, application may be made to the Court, to decree the sale of so much of the cargo as may be necessary to be sold for the discharge of freight.(*p*) And where freight is allowed to the captors, if they have done any damage to the cargo, the amount may be deducted by way of set-off or compensation.(*q*)

DI. As to *the allowance of costs and expenses.*—In cases when farther proof is directed, costs and expenses are never allowed to the claimant(*r*) nor refused to the captors. Nor where the neutrality of the property does not appear by the papers on board and the preparatory evidence;(*s*) nor where papers are spoliated or thrown overboard, unless the act be produced by the captors' misconduct, as by firing under false colours;(*t*) nor where the master or crew, upon *the preparatory examinations, grossly prevaricate;(*u*) nor where any part of the cargo is [*626] condemned;(*x*) nor where the ship comes from a blockaded port;(*y*) nor

(*h*) The Bremen Flugge, Ib., p. 90.

(*i*) Bynk. Q. J. Pub., lib. i. c. xiii., Du Ponceau's ed., p. 105. The Diana, 5 Rob., p. 67. The Fortuna, Edwards's Rep., p. 56.

(*k*) The Vrow Anna Catharina, 6 Rob., p. 269. The Fortuna, Edwards's Rep., p. 56.

(*l*) The Diana, 5 Rob., p. 67.

(*m*) The Vrouw Henrietta, Ib., p. 75, note. But see the Wilhelmina Eleonora, 3 Ib., p. 234.

(*n*) The Ann Green, 1 Gallison's (Amer.) Rep., p. 274.

(*o*) The Fortuna, 4 Rob., p. 278.

(*p*) 4 Ib., p. 304, note.

(*q*) The Fortuna, Ib., p. 278.

(*r*) The Einigheden, 1 Ib., p. 323.

(*s*) Sir W. Scott and Sir J. Nicholl's Letter to Mr. Jay, ante, p. 551. Opinion of M. Portalis in the Statira, 2 Cranch's (Amer.) Rep., p. 102, note (*a*).

(*t*) The Peacock, 4 Rob., p. 185.

(*u*) The Peacock, 4 Rob., p. 185.

(*x*) The William, 6 Ib., p. 316.

(*y*) The Frederick Molke, 1 Ib., p. 86. The Betsey, Ib., p. 93. The Vrouw Judith, Ib., p. 150.

if the ship be restored by consent, without reserving the question of costs and expenses.(*z*)

DII. But in all these cases it is in the discretion of the Court to allow the captors their costs and expenses;(*a*) and, in general, wherever the captors are justified in the capture, their costs and expenses are decreed to them by the Court, in case of restitution of property.(*b*) Therefore, they are allowed where the original destination was to a blockaded port, although changed on hearing of the blockade;(*c*) where ships, even of our own country, are captured sailing under false papers;(*d*) where the nature of the cargo is ambiguous as to contraband;(*e*) and, generally, in all cases of false papers;(*f*) and in all cases where farther proof is required.(*g*)

DIII. In cases where the captors' expenses are allowed, the expenses [*627] intended are such as are necessarily incurred *in consequence of the act of capture;(*h*) such are the expenses of the captor's agent,(*i*) but not insurance made by the captors,(*k*) nor expenses of transmitting a cargo from a colony to the mother country.(*l*) And property restored to the claimant is not to be charged with any expenses for agency, or for taking care of it, unless made a charge by the Court.(*m*) And the expense of an unlivery or delivery of the property, which is restored, is to be borne by the captors or releasing party, and not by the property, unless it is so directed by the Court.(*n*) In general, where the property is condemned, the expenses of unlivery and warehousing, &c., fall on the captors;(*o*) and where it is restored the Court will apportion them in its discretion on the captors and on the cargo.(*p*)

DIV. In cases of *neutral ships*, it is usual to allow the master his adventure and personal expenses, if his conduct has been fair and unimpeachable;(*q*) but where the master and crew prevaricate in their evidence, their adventures are never restored;(*r*) nor where the ship is engaged in a fraudulent trade.(*s*)

DV. It remains to notice a few miscellaneous and outlying matters.

First, as to the extent of the jurisdiction of the Prize Court.

[*628] The Admiralty Court, according to the law of England *and of the North American United States, merely by its own inherent

(*z*) The Maria Powlona, 6 Ib., p. 236.

(*a*) Sir W. Scott and Sir J. Nicholl's Letter to Mr. Jay, ante, p. 551.

(*b*) The Imina, 3 Rob., p. 167. The Principe, Edw. p. 70. See the case of the Ostsee, decided by the J. C. of the Privy Council. Rep. of Cases in the Prize Court, p. 174, (1854.)

(*c*) The Imina, 3 Rob., p. 167. (*d*) The Sarah, Ib., p. 330.

(*e*) The Twende Brodre, 4 Ib., p. 33. The Gute Gesellschaft, Ib., p. 94. The Christina Maria, Ib., p. 166.

(*f*) The Nostra Signora de Piedade Nova Aurora, 6 Ib., p. 41.

(*g*) See the Frances, 1 Gallison's (Amer.) Rep., p. 445. The Apollo, 4 Rob., p. 158. The Mary, 9 Cranch's (Amer.) Rep. p. 126.

(*h*) The Catharine and Anna, 4 Rob., p. 39.

(*i*) The Asia Grande, Edwards, p. 45.

(*k*) The Catharine and Anna, 4 Rob., p. 39. (*l*) The Narcissus, Ib., p. 17.

(*m*) The Asia Grande, Edwards, p. 45. (*n*) The Rendsberg, 6 Rob., p. 142.

(*o*) The Industrie, 5 Ib., p. 88. (*p*) Ibid.

(*q*) The Calypso, 2 Ib., p. 298. The Anna Catharina, 6 Ib., p. 10.

(*r*) Ibid., 4 Ib., p. 120. (*s*) The Christiansberg, 6 Ib., p. 376.

powers, never exercises jurisdiction as to captures or seizures as Prize made on shore without the co-operation of naval forces, whether made in our own or in a foreign territory;(*t*) whenever such a jurisdiction is exercised, it is by virtue of powers derived *aliunde.* And though when the jurisdiction has once attached, it may be lost by a hostile recapture, escape, or voluntary discharge;(*u*) yet it remains notwithstanding the goods are landed; for it does not depend on their local situation after capture; but the Court will follow the goods or their proceeds with its process, wherever they may be found, or under whatever title acquired.(*x*) Therefore, where the property is carried into a foreign port, and there delivered upon bail by the captors, the Prize Court does not lose its jurisdiction, but may proceed to the adjudication and enforce the stipulation.(*y*) So, if a Prize be lost at sea, the Court may, nevertheless, proceed to adjudication, either at the instance of the captors, or of the claimants;(*z*) so, although the property may be actually lying within a foreign neutral territory, the Court may proceed to adjudication;(*a*) so, [*629] *although the property has been sold by the captors, or has passed into other hands;(*b*) but it rests in the sound discretion of the Court, whether, when property has been sold or converted by the captors, it will proceed to adjudication *in their favour;* for it is only in cases where the same has been justifiably or legally converted by the captors that they can claim its aid. The Court will withhold that aid where there has been a conversion by the captors without necessity or reasonable cause.(*c*) When once the Prize Court has acquired jurisdiction over the principal cause, it will exert its authority over all the incidents.(*d*) It will follow

(*t*) Anthon v. Fisher, Doug., p. 649, note (1). Maisonnaire v. Keating, 2 Gallison's (Amer.) Rep., p. 325.

(*u*) The Two Friends, 1 Rob., pp. 271, 284. The Emulous, 1 Gallison's (Amer.) Rep., p. 563.

(*x*) Hudson v. Guestier, 4 Cranch's (Amer.) Rep., p. 293.

(*y*) Home v. Camden, 2 H. Blackstone's Rep., p. 533. 4 Durnford & East's Rep., p. 383. Willis v. Commissioners of Prize, 5 East, p. 22. The Noysomhed, 7 Vesey, p. 593. The Brig Louis, 5 Rob., p. 146. The Two Friends, 1 Ib., p. 271. The Eliza, 1 Acton, p. 336. Smart v. Wolff, 3 Durnford & East's Rep., p. 223. The Pomona, 1 Dodson, p. 25.

(*z*) The Peacock, 4 Rob., p. 185. The Susanna, 6 Ib., p. 48.

(*a*) Hudson v. Guestier, 4 Cranch's (Amer.) Rep., p. 293. The Christopher, 2 Rob., p. 209. The Henrick and Maria, 4 Rob., p. 43. The Comet, 5 Ib., p. 285. The Victoria, Edwards, p. 97.

(*b*) The Falcon, 6 Rob., p. 194. The Pomona, 1 Dodson, p. 25.

(*c*) L'Eole, 6 Rob., p. 220. La Dame Cecile, Ib., p. 257. The Arabella and Madeira, 2 Gallison's (Amer.) Rep., p. 368.

(*d*) "S'il y a aucun qui rompe coffre, balle ou pippe, ou autre marchandise que nostre dit admiral ne soit présent en sa personne pour luy *il forfera so part du butin* et sa sera par ice luy admiral puny selon le sueffaict."—Ordonnance de 1400, art. 10, Coll. Mar., 76. Ordonnance de 1584, art. 38, id. 111.

"Defendons de faire aucune ouverture des coffres, ballots, sacs, pipes, barriques, tonneaux et armoires, *de transporter ou vendre aucune marchandises de la prise: et à toutes personnes d'en achester ou receler, jusquà ce que la prise ait été jugée* ou qu'il en ait été erdonné par justice; à peine de restitution de quadruple, et de punition corporelle."—Ordonnance de 1681, liv. iii. tit. ix., Des Prises, art. 20, quatre Juin 1783.

"Jugement en dernier resort de l'amirauté de Dunkerque, contre les auteurs du pillage du navire L'Amitié, que les condamne à la restitution du prix des choses pillées, *les prive de leur part aux prises,* et pronounce le banissement contre l'un

[*630] Prize *proceeds into the hands of agents, or other persons holding them for the captors, or by any other title; and in proper cases will decree the parties to pay over the proceeds, with interest upon the same for the time they have been in their hands.(*f*) It may also enforce its decrees against persons having the proceeds of Prizes in their hands, notwithstanding no stipulation, or an insufficient stipulation, has been taken on a delivery on bail; for it may always proceed in *rem* where the *res* can be found, and is not confined to the remedy on the stipulation;(*g*) and in these cases the Court may proceed upon its own authority, *ex officio*, as well as upon the application of parties;(*h*) nor is the Court *functus officio* after sentence pronounced, for it may proceed to enforce all rights and issue process therefor, so long as anything remains to be done touching the subject-matter.(*i*)

The Prize Court has also exclusive jurisdiction as to the question who are the captors and joint captors entitled to share in the distribution; and its decree is conclusive upon all parties.(*k*)

[*631] *DVI. Next as to *unlivery of Cargo.*—It is a settled rule of the Prize Court, not to deliver a cargo on *Bail*, before the cause has been fully heard, unless by the consent of all parties; and if any inconvenience should result from this rule, as if the property be perishable, it may easily be avoided by an interlocutory sale.(*l*) After the hearing, if the claimant obtain a decree in his favour, or an order for farther proof, the Court will listen to an application for a delivery on bail; but if this claim be rejected, or be affected by the imputation of fraudulent or unlawful conduct, the application will not be allowed, notwithstanding an appeal is interposed. Where there is a decree of condemnation, the captors are, in general, entitled to a delivery of the property, or the proceeds thereof, upon bail.

DVII. In the progress of the cause, an unlivery of the cargo often becomes necessary, either to ascertain its nature and quality,(*m*) or more

d'eux avec injonction au capitaine du corsaire capteur, d'être plus circonspect à l'avenir."—Code des Prises, tom. i. p. 118, (Par Guichard.)

"M. l'amiral et les commissaires connoitront aussi *des partages des prises et de tout ce qui leur est incident, même des liquidations, et comptes des dépositaires*, lorsqu'ils le jugeront à propos, comme aussi des échouements des vaisseaux ennemis qui arriveront pendant la guerre, circonstances et dépendances.—Réglement du 23 Avril, 1744, art. 5. 2 Valin sur l'Ordonnance, p. 318.

(*f*) Smart v. Wolff, 3 Durnford & East's Rep., p. 313. Home v. Camden, 2 H. Blackstone, p. 533. 4 Durnford & East's Rep., p. 382. Jennings v. Carson, 4 Cranch's (Amer.) Rep., p. 1. The Two Friends, 1 Rob., p. 273. Willis v. Commissioners of Prizes, 5 East, p. 22. The Noysomhed, 7 Vesey, p. 593. The Princessa, 2 Rob., p. 31. The Brig Louis, 5 Ib., p. 146.

(*g*) Per Buller, J., in 3 Durnford & East's Rep., p. 323. Per Grose, J., in 5 East, p. 22. The Pomona, 1 Dodson, p. 25. The Herkimer, Stewart, p. 128. S. C., 2 Hall's (Amer.) Law Journ., p. 133.

(*h*) The Herkimer, Stewart, p. 128. S. C., 2 Hall's (Amer.) Law Journ., p. 133.

(*i*) Home v. Camden, 2 H. Blackstone's Rep., p. 533. Cases ubi supra.

(*k*) Home v. Camden, 2 H. Blackstone's Rep., p. 533. 4 Durn. & East's Rep., p. 382. The Herkimer, Stewart, p. 128. S. C., 2 Hall's (Amer.) Law Journ., p. 133. Duckworth v. Tucker, 2 Taunton's Rep., p. 7.

(*l*) The Copenhagen, 3 Rob., p. 178.

(*m*) The Liverpool Packet, 1 Gallison's (Amer.) Rep., p. 513. Marriott's Form, p. 229. The Carl Walter, 4 Rob., p. 207. The Richmond, 5 Ib., p. 325. The Jonge Margaretha, 1 Ib., p. 189. The Oster Risoer, 4 Ib., p. 199.

effectually to preserve it from injury and pillage,(*n*) or because the ship stands in a predicament altogether distinct from that of her cargo.(*o*) In all these and other proper cases, the Prize Court will, upon proper application, decree an unlivery. Upon ordering an unlivery, a warrant or commission of unlivery is directed to some competent person, and usually to the Marshal, to unlade the cargo, and to make a true and perfect inventory thereof.(*p*) At the same time, a warrant or commission of *appraisement is usually directed to some competent persons, [*632] who are to reduce into writing a true and perfect inventory of the cargo, and upon oath to appraise the same according to its true value. In England, this commission is sometimes directed to a person who is authorized to choose and swear the appraisers himself.(*q*) But in the North American United States, the general practice is, for the Courts to appoint the appraisers, in the first instance. And where it becomes necessary or proper to unlade the cargo for inspection of its nature or quality, a commission of inspection is issued, directed to some competent persons, in like manner, to return an inventory thereof, with a certificate of the particulars, names, descriptions, and sortments of the goods, together with their several marks and numbers, and the nature, use, quantities, and qualities thereof.(*r*) The Court may also, in its discretion, order the ship, or cargo, or both, to be removed to another place or port; for, having the custody of the things, it is bound to use all reasonable precautions to preserve it, and to consult the best interests of all parties; and in such case a commission of removal is issued, which is *usually* directed to the Marshal; but the Court may direct it to any other person.(*s*)

An unlivery of the cargo is considered as done for the benefit of all parties, and therefore the expense is generally borne by the party ultimately prevailing. If the captors apply for an unlivery, and the property is condemned, the *expense falls on the captors; but if restitution be awarded, the Court, in its discretion, usually makes the [*633] expense a charge on the cargo.(*t*)

After unlivery and appraisement, the Court sometimes decrees a sale,

(*n*) Marriott's Form, p. 323.

(*o*) The Hoffnung, 6 Rob., p. 231. The Prosper, Edwards, p. 72. Marriott's Form, p. 224.

(*p*) Ibid. (*q*) Marriott's Form, p. 227.

(*r*) Ibid., p. 229. "S'il est nécessaire avant le jugement de la prise, de tirer les marchandises du vaisseau, pour en empêcher le dépérissement, il en sera fait inventaire en présence de notre procureur et des parties intéressées, qui le signeront, si elles peuvent signer, pour ensuite être misès sous la garde d'une personne solvable, ou dans des magasins fermans à trois clefs différentes, dont l'une sera delivrée aux armateurs, l'autre au receveur de l'Admiral, et la troisième aux réclamateurs, si aucun se présente, sinon à notre procureur."—L'Ordonnance de 1687, liv. iii. tit. ix., Des Prises, art. 27.

(*s*) Marriott's Form, p. 234. The Rendsberg, 6 Rob., p. 142. The Sacra Familia, 5 Ib., p. 360.

(*t*) The Industrie, Ib., p. 88. "Qu'a l'avenir, *tous les frais faits tants pour la conservation* ou la vente *des marchandises des prises*, dans le cas où elle sera permise, que pour la subsistance du maître et autres officiers mariniers ou matelots qui y seront restés *seront pris sur le bâtiment, et payés par le réclamateur qui en aura obtenu la main levée*, lorsquil en sera remise en possession."—Arrêt du Conseil du 23 Decembre, 1705.

or delivery, on bail, of the property to the captors or the claimants. Where a sale is ordered, which is usually done where the ship and cargo are in a perishing condition, or liable to deterioration pending the process,(*u*) in England a commission of appraisement and sale issues to some competent persons, jointly and severally, to reduce into writing a true inventory of the goods, and to choose appraisers who are to appraise the same on oath; and after appraisement, the commissioners are to expose the same to public sale, and bring the proceeds into the registry of the Court.(*x*) And in England it is the regular practice of the Court, that one of the commissioners should be named by the claimant.(*y*) And in the United States, a sale is sometimes ordered, without a previous appraisement; or if an appraisement be ordered, the appraisers are always named by the Court itself. In case of an appraisement and sale, the expenses of taking out the commission, &c., are, in the first instance, borne [*634] by the party applying for the sale, and ultimately *as the Court may direct;(*z*) and such sale is usually, in England, made by the Marshal; but it seems that the Court may direct it to be made by any other person.(*a*) In the United States, the sale is invariably made by the Marshal: and it would seem highly proper in all cases, to have a previous inventory and appraisement, with a view to check any attempt of fraud, and to establish the proper responsibility of the officers of the Court, in cases of negligent custody. This is the regular practice of the Prize Court; and the most obvious reasons of public policy require a strict adherence to it.

DVIII. The subject of delivery has been already partially discussed; to the observations already made upon the subject may be added the following:(*b*) Sometimes the property is delivered on bail to return the same, or the full value to answer the decree, and in such case, the Court have a right to inquire what is the full value, and to decree accordingly.(*c*) And if the bail security be taken by way of *recognizance* (which is irregular,) and not by way of *stipulation*, still the Court may enforce it as a stipulation.(*d*) Upon such a delivery on bail, the sureties are not responsible beyond the sum in which they become bound;(*e*) but the principal may be made to respond the full value of the property. In ordinary cases, however, the property is delivered on bail at an appraised value; and in such cases, the principal and sureties are bound to the stipulated value but not farther. If, therefore, there be a delivery on bail at an admitted value, the Court will not listen to an application to diminish

(*u*) The St. Lawrence, 1 Gallison's (Amer.) Rep., p. 467. The Frances, Ib., p. 451. Jennings v. Carson, 4 Cranch's (Amer.) Rep., p. 2. Stoddart v. Read, 2 Dallas's (Amer.) Rep., p. 40. Marriott's Form, pp. 237, 318. The Copenhagen, 3 Rob., p. 178.

(*x*) Marriott's Form, pp. 237, 318.

(*y*) The Carl Walter, 4 Rob., pp. 207, 211.

(*z*) The Carl Walter, 4 Rob., p. 207. (*a*) The Rendsberg, 6 Ib., p. 142.

(*b*) The Rendsberg, 6 Rob., pp. 142, 144. The Euphrates, 1 Gallison's (Amer.) Rep., p. 451. The Diana, 2 Ib., p. 93.

(*c*) Brymer v. Atkins, 1 H. Blackstone's Rep., p. 264.

(*d*) Ibid, p. 164. The Alligator, 1 Gallison's (Amer.) Rep., p. 145.

(*e*) Smart v. Wolff, 3 Durnford & East's Rep., p. 323.

the amount *to the proceeds of a subsequent sale, but will hold the parties to the appraised or admitted value.(*f*) In case of a [*635] delivery on bail, the expenses of the delivery are to be borne by the delivering party, unless it is otherwise directed by the Court.(*g*) But generally the Court directs the expenses of the application to be borne by the party who applies for the delivery on bail; and all expenses after the delivery are exclusively borne by the party receiving the property.(*h*) Bail bonds or securities to answer adjudication, are not discharged by lapse of time; but may, at any distance of time, be enforced by the Court; but after a great length of time the Court will, in its discretion, refuse a monition or attachment to enforce the bond, unless some reasonable ground for the delay is established.(*i*) Nor are these bonds considered as mere personal securities given to the individual captors, although taken in their names; they are considered as securities given to the Court, to abide the adjudication of all events at the time impending before it. The Court is not in the habit of considering bonds precisely in the same limited way as they are viewed by the Courts of Common Law. In those Courts they are very properly considered as mere personal securities for the benefit of those parties to whom they are given. In Prize Courts they are subject to more enlarged considerations; they are there regarded as pledges or substitutes for the thing itself, in all points fairly in adjudication before the Court. If, therefore, a bond be given to the actual captors to answer the adjudication of the property, which should, from the locality of the capture, or from other circumstances, be condemned to the government, the bail, would, in such case, be answerable, in the Admiralty, to the government.(*k*) But if the property at the time of capture *was neutral, and delivered on bail pending the proceedings, and hostilities [*636] subsequently intervene with the neutral country, and, in consequence thereof, the property is condemned to the government, it seems that the Court is not in the habit of enforcing the bail bond in such cases; because the event was not originally in the contemplation of the parties, at the time they entered into the security.(*l*) Whether this doctrine would be sustained in the North American United States, is, according to Mr. Justice Story, a question upon which there is no decision to guide the judgment; but he is of opinion that certainly much argument may be used against the asserted exemption; for, the bail bond being a substitute for the property itself, there does not seem any very conclusive reason why it should not be subject to all the events which would have affected the property, if still in the custody of the Court.(*m*)

(*f*) The Betsey, 5 Rob., p. 295, and p. 296, note (*a*).

(*g*) The Rendsberg, 6 Ib., p. 142.

(*h*) 5 Ib., p. 296, note (*a*).

(*i*) The Vreede, 1 Dodson, p. 1.

(*k*) The Nied Elwin, Ib., p. 50.

(*l*) The Nied Elwin, 1 Dodson, p. 50.

(*m*) As to the jurisdiction of the Prize Court over, 1. The Distribution of Prize proceeds, the reader is referred to the following decisions in the English and North American United States Courts:—

ENGLISH.—The Herkimer, Stewart's Rep. p. 128. Home v. Camden, 1 H. Blackstone's Rep. pp. 476, 524. S. C., 2 Ib., p. 633. 4 Durnford & East's Rep., p. 382. Duckworth v. Tucker, 2 Taunton's Rep., p. 7. The Diomede, 1 Acton's Adm. Rep., pp. 63, 239. Gardiner v. Lyne, 13 East's Rep., p. 574. Drury v. Gardiner, 2

PART THE TWELFTH.

[*638] *CHAPTER I.

OF THE MANNER OF ENDING WAR, AND OF RE-ESTABLISHING PEACE.

DIX. "In totâ Belli administratione non potest securus et Deo fidens animus retineri, nisi semper in Pacem prospectet;" and again, "*Bellum pacis causâ suscipitur*," are the maxims of Christianity, justice, and reason, expressed by their noble expounder, the ever illustrious Grotius.(*a*)

When, by use of the legal means of War, the invaded right has been obtained or secured, or the inflicted injury redressed, or the threatened danger averted,—*post juris consecutionem*(*b*)—the *abnormal* state of War *must* cease, the *normal* state of Peace *must* be re-established.(*c*)

We are, indeed, admonished by Grotius, that if a Peace *sufficiently safe* can be had, it is not ill obtained even by the condonation of injuries,

Maule & Selwyn, p. 150. Duncan v. Mitchell, 4 Ib., p. 105. Pill v. Taylor, 11 East's Rep., p. 414. Lumley v. Sutton, 8 Durnford & East's Rep., p. 224. The Nostro Signoro del Carmen, 6 Robinson, p. 302. Wemys v. Linzee, Douglas's Rep. p. 324. The Alert, 1 Dodson, p. 236. Several Dutch Schuyts, 6 Rob., p. 48. L'Alerte, 6 Ib., p. 238. The San Joseph, Ib., p. 331. The Babilion, Edwards's Adm. Rep. p. 39. La Clorinde, 1 Dodson's Adm. Rep., p. 436. L'Elise, 1 Dodson's Adm. Rep., p. 442. The Matilda, Ib., p. 367. The Frederick and Mary Ann, 6 Rob., p. 213. Bynkershoek, Q. J. P., l. i. c. xviii., Du Ponceau's ed., pp. 139, 141.

AMERICAN.—The St. Lawrence, 2 Gallison's (Amer.) Rep., p. 19. Kean v. The Brig Gloucester, 2 Dallas's (Amer.) Rep., p. 36. Penhallow v. Doane, 3 Ib., p. 54. The Herkimer, 2 Hall's (Amer.) Law Journ., p. 133. Bingham v. Cabot, 3 Dallas's (Amer.) Rep., p. 19. Decatur v. Chew, 1 Gallison's (Amer.) Rep., p. 506. Ex parte Giddings, 2 Ib., p. 56.

As to Prize Agents, see the following decisions:—

ENGLISH.—Home v. Camden, 1 H. Blackstone's Rep., pp. 374, 524. S. C., 2 Ib., pp. 5, 33. Willis v. Commissioners, &c., 5 East's Rep., p. 22. The Noysomhed, 7 Vesey's Rep., p. 593. Smart v. Wolff, 3 Durnford & East's Rep., p. 323. The Pomona, 1 Dodson's Adm. Rep., p. 25. The Herkimer, Stewart's Rep., p. 128. The Louis, 5 Robinson, p. 146. The Polly, Ib., p. 147, note. The Printz Henrick von Preussen, 6 Ib., p. 95. The Exeter, 1 Ib., p. 173. The Princessa, 2 Ib., p. 31.

AMERICAN.—The St. Lawrence, 2 Gallison's (Amer.) Rep., p. 19. The Brutus, Ib., p. 526. Bingham v. Cabot, 3 Dallas's (Amer.) Rep., p. 19. Kean v. Brig Gloucester, 2 Ib., p. 36. The Herkimer, 2 Hall's (Amer.) Law Journ., p. 133. Hill v. Ross, 3 Dallas's (Amer.) Rep., p. 331. Penhallow v. Doane, Ib., p. 54.

(*a*) L. iii. c. xxv. s. 2. L. i. c. i. s. 1. (*b*) Vide ante, Vol. I. pp. 11, 12.

(*c*) Albericus Gentilis, l. iii. c. i. Grotius, l. iii. c. vi. viii. ix. xv. xvi. xx. Zouch, pars ii. sect. ix. p. 25, ad finem. Wolff, cap. viii., De Pace et Pactione Pacis. Vattel, l. iv., Du Retablissement de la Paix, &c., ch. i. ii. iii. iv. De Martens, D. des G., l. viii. c. viii. Ompteda, i. 49, 62, 63, ii. 604, continuat, by Carl Albert Von Kamptz, ss. 321, 331, (356, 360.) Klüber, 2 Abschnitt, c. iii., Recht des Friedens, ss. 317, 329. Hefters, ii. B. 4, Abschnitt: "Die Beendigung des Krieges die Usurpation, und das Postliminium." This part of the work, as indeed the work generally, deserves careful study.

damages, and expenses, especially *among Christians,(*d*)—for to them their Lord has bequeathed Peace as his peculiar legacy, [*639] to them the chosen interpreter of their Lord's Testament has made peace the theme of his most earnest exhortations.(*e*) If this admirable doctrine be too excellent for the present condition of the Society of States, it may at least be propounded as an unquestionable proposition of International Jurisprudence that there is a legal as well as moral necessity that, with the ceasing of the causes which justified the inception of the War, the War itself should cease.

Moreover, it is to be remembered that in this cessation every state is interested; because by the conflict between the Belligerents every state, neutral as well as belligerent, is to a certain extent injured; for War, as has been shown,(*f*) necessarily disturbs the relations and affects the condition, in a greater or less degree, of all states.

In the event, therefore, of a War unlawfully continued, though lawfully begun, it would be morally and legally competent to states who have taken no part in the conduct of the contest, to combine for the purpose of compelling the termination of War and the restoration of Peace.(*g*)

The state which continues the evils and horrors of War unrighteously, is but little, if at all, less than an offender against the Society of Societies, against the great Commonwealth of States,(*h*) than the original wrongdoer.

*The duty which Cicero inculcates on the private citizen with respect to Civil War, is equally the duty of a state in a War of [*640] Nations: "Initia belli invitum suscipere extrema libenter non persequi."(*i*)

DX. There appear to be three ways by which War may be concluded and Peace restored.(*k*)

1. By a *de facto* cessation of hostilities on the part of both Belligerents, and a renewal, *de facto*, of the relations of Peace.

2. By the unconditional submission of one Belligerent to another.

3. By the conclusion of a formal Treaty of Peace between the Belligerents.

DXI. A formal declaration on the part of the Belligerents that War

(*d*) Vide ante, Vol. I. pp. 22-7.

(*e*) See this noble passage, l. iii. c. xxv. s. 3: "Pax ergo *tuta satis* haberi si potest, et malefactorum et damnorum et sumtuum condonatione non malè constat: præcipuè inter Christianos quibus pacem suum Dominus legavit. Cujus optimus interpres* nos vult quantum fieri potest quantum in nobis situm est cum omnibus Pacem quærere."

(*f*) P. 47. As to what are causæ belli justificæ.

(*g*) Vide ante, Vol. I. pt. iv. ch. i. On Intervention.

(*h*) Vide ante, Vol. I. pt. ii. s. vi.

"Cæde nocentûm
Se nimis ulciscens, exstitit ipse nocens."
Ovid, De Pont., i. Eleg. viii. 19, 20.

(*i*) "Ostendistique (Cicero writes to Marcellus) sapientem et bonum civem initia belli civilis invitum suscipere, extrema libenter non persequi."—Epist. ad Fam., l. iv. 7.

Grotius (l. iii. c. xxv. s. 3,) misquotes this passage and ascribes it to Sallust.

(*k*) Heffters, p. 311, s. 176.

* St. Paul. Rom. xii. 18.

has ceased, however usual and desirable, cannot be said to be absolutely necessary for the restoration of Peace. War may silently cease and Peace be silently renewed. So ended the War between Sweden and Poland in the year 1716, namely, by a reciprocal intermission of hostilities; it was not till after the lapse of ten years that Peace was formally and *de jure* recognized as subsisting between the two kingdoms.(*l*)

In such a state of things the presumption of law would be, that both parties had agreed that the *status quo ante bellum* should be revived. Yet in the absence of any formal declaration it would not be concluded that the claims which had given occasion to the War, or which had grown out of the War, were abandoned, but they must be considered as
[*641] in abeyance. In fact, it is as difficult to predicate the consequences, *legal and practical, of such a state of things, as it would be to predicate the consequences of a treaty of Peace which contained no clause of amnesty.(*m*)

Since, Grotius observes, it is not usual for Belligerents to make Peace on the basis of a confession from one of them that he is in the wrong, "ea sumenda est in pactis interpretatio quæ partes quoad belli justitiam quam maximè æquet." This end is to be effected by one of two means, viz.:—(1.) Either by an agreement that the possession which has been disturbed by the War, shall be restored, which is expressed by the well-known international *formula* of the *status quo ante bellum*; or (2.) by an agreement that matters shall remain as they were at the period when the War is ended; and this arrangement is expressed by the *formula*, often little understood, though familiar enough in its application of *uti possidetis*, or, as Grotius says, "ut res maneant quo sunt loco; quod Græci dicunt ἔχοντες ἃ ἔχουσι."(*n*) To these two predicaments the learned Samuel Cocceius adds two more,—namely, (3.) where a treaty is made, in which "nihil dictum est de damnis, injuriis et debitis," or (4.) in which "paci clausula generalis amnestiæ adjicitur.(*o*)

[*642] *DXII. Secondly. As to the unconditional submission (*deditio*) of one Belligerent to another.

Instances of such prostration are abundant in the pages of classical history,(*p*) and are not altogether wanting even in very modern times.

(*l*) Ibid. De Steck., Essais sur divers Sujets de Polit. p. 2.

(*m*) Heffters, ubi supra. H. Cocceius, De Postliminio et Amnestiâ.

(*n*) Grot., l. iii. c. xx. ss. 11, § 2. Vide post, Lord Grenville's Remarks on the Treaty of Amiens.

(*o*) Grotius, Illustratus, v. p. 502, (ed. Halæ, 1748.)

The Times, Debate in the House of Commons, Friday, March, 14, 1856.—"The Crimean Tartars.—Mr. Holland asked the First Lord of the Treasury whether the attention of her Majesty's Government had been drawn to the position of the Crimean Tartars in the event of peace being established, and the allied forces, towards whom they had shown themselves favourably disposed, being recalled?—Lord Palmerston: When a year is terminated, in the course of which the armies of one country have occupied the territory of another, it is the invariable practice that there shall be an agreement between the parties to insure a complete amnesty to all subjects of either Power who may have been at all committed in the progress of hostilities; and should peace be now concluded, an arrangement of that kind will, of course, be concluded between the Belligerents."

(*p*) The classical reader will find the formal language of a deditio in Livy: "Itaque populum Campanum urbemque Capuam, agros, delubra Deûm, divina

But the most unconditional submission would be holden according to the principle of International Law to imply a retention of the common rights of humanity,(q) and, between Christian states, of Christian humanity :(r) any infringement of these rights would be beyond the moral competence of the conqueror.

The subject of the *incorporation* and of the *extinction* of a state has been considered in an early part of the present work.(s)

DXIII. Thirdly. We have to consider the termination of War by the conclusion of a formal Treaty of Peace between the Belligerents.

The examination of this part of the subject must embrace the following considerations :—

I. By *whom* the overtures of Peace may be made.

II. *Where*, or within the limits of whose territory, the negotiations may be opened and carried on.

III. *How*, or according to what *forms*.

*IV. *When* the Treaty of Peace takes effect, or the *date* from which the operation of it becomes binding upon the public relations of states, and the private relations of individuals. [*643]

DXIV. I. First, then, to consider by *whom* the overtures of peace may be made.

These overtures may be made by one of the Belligerent States, by a Neutral State acting as the common friend of both litigants, or, by a state which is rather an auxiliary than an ally, or which—to speak as correctly as the nature of the distinction permits—has, as it were, been the *passive* ally of one Belligerent, without positively declaring war against the other Belligerent, without withdrawing its Ambassador from his Court, and indeed while continuing with this Belligerent, formally at least, the relations of amity.

This third kind of *status* is sometimes designated in the books as the *status* of an *auxiliary*,(t) as distinguished from an *ally*.

A Neutral power may also act as a *mediator*, or may merely interpose its *good offices*. Between the two positions there is a marked difference, inasmuch as the former implies the consent of both Belligerents; the latter may be without the consent of either, or with the consent of only one. The good offices of a Neutral State may be accepted and its mediation refused. In the War with Sweden in 1742, Russia accepted the good offices and refused the mediation of France.

The mediator must not be counfounded with the arbitrator, whose character and functions have been discussed in an earlier part of this volume.(u)

DXV. II. Where, or within the limits of whose territory, may the negotiations be carried on?

humanaque omnia in vestram, Patres Conscripti, populique Romani ditionem dedimus; quiquid deinde patiemur *deditícii* vestri passuri."—L. vii. c. xxxi. He will find the *rite* and *manner* in Cæsar, De Bello Civili, l. iii. ss. 97, 98.

(q) Heffters, p. 312, s. 178.

(r) Vide ante, Vol. I.

(s) Vide ante, Vol. I. pp. 147, 157, 158. P. 142, art. vi. of the Constitution of the N. A. United States, on this subject.

(t) De Martens, Essai sur les Armateurs, s. 50.

(u) Vide ante, p. 2.

This question is often adjusted by reference to considerations of local convenience.

[*644] *It ought of course to be the object of all parties to fix upon a spot which may be of the readiest access to the respective Courts of the Belligerents. But this consideration is often overborne by animosities growing out of or connected with the War, which render it desirable either that some Neutral Territory should be selected, and not unfrequently some town of inconsiderable size and character within that territory. These are all considerations belonging rather to Public Policy than to Public International Law.

All that the latter seems to require is, that the place of negotiation shall be clearly and definitively agreed upon before the negotiations themselves are opened. In the case of arbitration, indeed, the Court of the arbiter(*x*) is, for obvious reasons, the proper locality of the tribunal before which states agree to argue their causes.

DXVI. III. How, or according to what forms, are the negotiations to be carried on?

There are no necessarily fixed or unalterable rules upon this subject, apart from those which flow from the respect due to the equality and dignity of states.(*y*) If it should happen that any question would be likely to arise with respect to these forms, they are the subject of agreement before the substance of the Treaty is entered upon. The time has gone by when one ambassador gravely and vigilantly observed, as is said to have been the case at the Treaty of Ryswick, the number of steps backwards or forwards made by the other ambassadors.

DXVII. IV. We have now to consider *when* the Treaty of Peace takes effect, or the date from which the operation of it becomes binding, both upon the public relations of states, and upon the private relations of individual members of states.

[*645] The exact period from which the public Treaty *begins to operate is, as in the case of private contracts, the day upon which it has passed through all the necessary forms and been ratified: from that instant all hostilities ought to cease, unless indeed a particular day has been specified for the beginning of the Peace.(*z*)

Vattel is of opinion that the Treaty does not bind the subjects of states until it has been duly notified to them.(*a*) The extent to which this opinion is adopted by the practice of states will be seen in the following remarks:

DXVIII. According to the doctrine of the best jurists, the effect of

(*x*) Vide ante, pp. 2-7. (*y*) Vide ante, Vol. II. p. 33.

(*z*) "Au surplus les engagemens datent communément du jour de l'échange des ratifications, à moins d'une stipulation contraire."—De Rayneval, ii. p. 113. Vattel, l. iv. c. iii. p. 24. Ib., l. ii. c. xii. p. 156. House of Commons, 31 March, 1856 (Times, April 1, 1856.)—"Lord Palmerston.—The House is perfectly aware, from the 'Gazette,' that yesterday, at 2 o'clock, a Treaty of Peace was signed at Paris. The House will have seen by the announcement in the 'Gazette,' that it was determined by the Congress that the particular conditions of the Treaty should not be made public until the ratifications had been exchanged. And that, indeed, is the usual course, for it is a mark of obvious deference to the Powers who are parties to the Treaty."

(*a*) L. iv. c. iii. p. 24. Heffters, pp. 183, 318.

Peace, once contracted, being to render unlawful every act of force or violence between states, if a capture be made after the stipulation is completed, though by persons ignorant of its completion, it must, *vi pacis*, be restored,(*b*) "*sublatum enim jam erat belli jus.*"(*c*)

For Peace (says the author just cited) is considered to be broken "non modo si *toti corpori* civitatis, sed et si *subditis* vis armata inferatur nimirùm sine novà causâ;" and for this grave and excellent reason, "nam ut omnes subditi *tuti sint pax initur: est enim pax actus civitatis pro toto et pro partibus."(*d*) [*646]

DXIX. Abreu, however, is strongly in favour of the lawfulness of the prize, and maintains stoutly the rights of the captor.(*e*) He was acting under a lawful commission; till that commission was directly or by clear implication revoked, it was his right and duty to act under it. At the time of the capture that commission was not so revoked; the capture was therefore legal. To the argument that the conclusion of the Peace can retrospectively affect the prize, he answers that a *jus superveniens* can never by *retroaction.*(*f*) affect the *jus tertii*, which is the right of the captor in this supposed case.

The answer to the argument of Abreu appears to be that the indemnification of the captor should proceed from the state to which he belongs:(*g*) and that though individuals are not deemed *criminals* for continuing hostilities after their cessation has has been agreed upon, through ignorance of that cessation, yet that they are *civilly* responsible before the tribunals *of International Law.(*h*) When a place is exempted from hostility by articles of Peace it is the duty of Governments to apprise with due diligence their subjects of the fact; and to indemnify them for acts done in ignorance of that Peace.(*i*) [*647]

But it is the actual wrongdoer who is to answer in judgment: the person from whom the injury has been received cannot be passed over in order that it may be fixed upon another person on the ground of a consequential responsibility. So, if a captain, acting under the orders of an

(*b*) "Effectus pacis contractæ est, ut omnis vis tollatur: adeo, ut si post stipulatam pacem ab ignorantibus aliquid captum vel occupatum sit, *vi pacis* id restitui debeat."—S. Cocceius, vol. v. p. 502. (l. vii. c. vii. s. 864.)

(*c*) "Quæ post perfectas pactiones capta sunt reddenda satis constat, sublatum enim jam erat belli jus."—Grot., l. iii. c. xx. s. 20.

(*d*) Grot., l. iii. c. xx. s. 32.

(*e*) "Si la Pressa hecha despues de ajustada la Paz, no haviendo llegado esta á noticia del armador, ó Corsario, que la hizo, ni en la realidad, ni en el concepto del derecho sera legitima, ó nó."—Abreu, c. xxii.

(*f*) The doctrine of the Roman Law, that in certain transactions, *conditio existens retrotrahitur ad initium negotii*, is alluded to by Vinnius in Inst., l. i. tit. De Nuptiis, s. 13, n. 3, "Falsum enim est, quod præsupponunt legitimationis hujus hanc esse vim; ut retrotrahatur tempus nuptiarum ad tempus nativitatis."

(*g*) Grot., l. iii. c. xxi. s. 5: "Illud obiter addam, inducias et si quid est simile ipsos contrahentes statim obligare ex quo contractus absolutus est: at subditos utrinque obligari incipere, ubi induciæ acceperunt forman legis, cui inest exterior quædam publicatio: quâ factâ statim quidem incipit habere vim obligandi subditos, sed ea vis, si publicatio uno tantum loco facta sit, non per omnem ditionem eodem momento se exserit, sed per tempus sufficiens ad perferendam ad singula loca notitiam. *Quare si quid interea a subditis contra inducias factum sit, ipsi a pœnis immunes erunt* neque tamen eo minus contrahentes damnum resarcire debebunt."

(*h*) 1 Kent, Comment., p. 170.

(*i*) The Mentor, 1 Robinson's Rep., p. 171.

admiral, be the seizor, he, and not the admiral, must be called as the immediate wrongdoer, to adjudication.(*k*)

DXX. It may happen that when a period has been fixed by Treaty for the cessation of hostilities, within or at a specified locality, and before this period has arrived, *but with a knowledge of the Peace*, a capture has been made. In such a case is the capture lawful? Jurists have entertained different opinions upon this subject. Mr. Chancellor Kent(*l*) adopts the opinion of Emerigon,(*m*) that it would be unlawful; and his reasoning, viz., that if a *constructive knowledge* of the Peace, after the time limited in different parts of the world, renders the capture void, much more ought *actual knowledge* of the Peace to produce that effect. It appears to the writer of these pages that this reasoning is sound and ought to govern the practice of states.(*n*)

DXXI. The effect of *constructive knowledge* has undergone considerable discussion in the French Prize Courts. It arose on the capture of the British ship Swineherd(*o*) by the French privateer Bellone in 1801. The Swineherd was carried into the Isle of France and condemned as [*648] prize. An *appeal was instituted in the Conseil des Prises at Paris: that tribunal confirmed the judgment of the Court in the Isle of France. We are indebted to M. Merlin(*p*) for the report of the case. Unfortunately we are not indebted to him for the expression of his own opinion, which that learned and laborious jurist expresses his determination to withhold, when he introduces the case to our notice. He reports, however, at length the argument of the Advocate-General, M. Collet Descotils, in favour of the legality of the capture. The case depended in some measure upon the 11th article of the Preliminary Articles of the Peace of Amiens: it was decided, rightly or wrongly, that the French Privateer was entitled to its prize, the Swineherd, upon a variety of grounds, the principal of which appear to have been that the capture was made at a period anterior to the time fixed for restitution; that it was sheltered by the Preliminary Article which has been mentioned; that there was, on the part of the privateer, "le défaut de *connaissance suffisante* de la cessation de toute hostilité."(*q*)

The exposition of the law upon this latter point by the French crown lawyer is sound, whether the application of it to the case before him were correct or not.

"J'en reviens à l'opinion d'Emérigon et de Valin; je pense, comme eux, qu'un corsaire qui a une connaissance positive de la paix avant de rencontrer un bâtiment qui auparavant était ennemi, n'a pas le droit de l'arrêter, hors toutefois le cas d'une legitime défense, encore bien que les délais pour la validité des Prises, ne soient pas encore expirés.

"*Mais qu'entend-on par connaissance positive de la paix?* Ces auteurs en parlent, mais aucun ne la définit. Je vais tâcher de le faire d'après les principes de la raison, et de suppléer par-là au silence qu'ils gardent sur ce point.

(*k*) The Mentor, 1 Robinson's Rep., p. 171.

(*l*) Comment., i. p. 172. (*m*) Traité des Ass., c. xii. s. 19.

(*n*) Valin, Tr. des Prises, c. iv. ss. 4, 5. (*o*) Le Porcher.

(*p*) Rep. tome xxv. (xiii.) tit. Prise Maritime, s. 5, p. 115: "En quel temps peut être exercé le droit de Prise Maritime." (*q*) Ib. p. 130.

"La connaissance dont il s'agit, doit être certaine, assurée, *indubitable; elle doit émaner médiatement ou immédiatement de [*649] la puissance à laquelle appartient l'armateur, et si l'on veut, de l'une ou de l'autre des deux puissances contractantes.

"Cette connaissance doit être telle, qu'elle, prévienne ou dissipe tous les doutes, toutes les incertitudes, toutes les craintes, tous les dangers que pourrait courir le corsaire; elle doit, en même temps qu'elle paralyse les lettres de marque, qu'elle impose au corsaire le devoir de s'abstenir de toutes hostilités, le mettre lui-même á l'abri de la capture; elle doit enfin être transmise par des pièces authentiques et légales qui prémunissent le corsaire contre le danger, en se retirant dans un des ports de sa nation, d'être pris par quelque navire ennemi non encore informé de la conclusion de la paix.

"Il s'en faut donc de beaucoup due je sois de l'opinion qu'une ignorance absolue de la paix soit nécessaire pour qu'une saisse faite avant l'expiration des délais, soit valable: l'admettre, c'est supposer qu'un bruit incertain, qu'une nouvelle douteuse, qu'une rapport dont aucune pièce authentique ne garantil la vérité, sont suffisans pour mettre un corsaire dans l'obligation indispensable de cesser sa croisière, et de rentrer dans le port de son armement, tout en demeurant exposé au danger d'être capturé pendant le temps de sa retraite.

"Je ne saurais convenir, avec le Capitaine Black, que, dans le cas d'une simple annonce de paix, non valablement justifiée, le corsaire n'ait le droit d'arrêter que provisoirement, sauf à relâcher le navire, sans être susceptible de dommages-intérêts, si la nouvelle se trouve vraie, ou à en poursuivre la confiscation, si elle se trouve fausse.

"Au moment même de l'arrestation, la saisie est bonne, ou elle est nulle, selon que le corsaire n'a point ou qu'il a la connaissance *positive* de la paix. S'il l'a, le navire doit être relâché avec dommages-intérêts; s'il ne l'a point, la saisie est valable, et la confiscation doit être prononcée."(r)

*DXXII. Another case different from the foregoing has happened, and been subjected to judicial decision, both in England [*650] and the North American United States,—the case of a *capture* made *before* the period fixed for the cessation of hostilities, and in *ignorance* of the Peace; but not carried into port and condemned. The vessel was *recaptured after* the period fixed for the cessation of hostilities, but in *ignorance* of the Peace. In both countries the possession of the captor was holden lawful, and the divesting him of his possession unlawful.(s) The title of the owner was completely barred by the intervention of Peace, which quiets all titles of possession to property of this kind(t) arising from War.

It is no longer competent to the original proprietor to look back to the enemy's title, either in his own possession or in the hands of neutral purchasers.

(r) Merlin Rep., vol. xxv. (xiii.,) p. 125, see also p. 130.

(s) 1 Kent, p. 173. The Legal Tender, Wheaton's (Amer.) Digest, p. 302. The Schoone Sophie, 6 Rob., p. 138.

(t) Vide ante, p. 504. Vide post, p. 653.

And here it may also be remarked, that if a new War break out after the Treaty of Peace, on account of non-fulfilment of its provisions or for any other reason, though that may change the relation of those who are parties to it, it can, as Lord Stowell observes, have no effect on neutral purchasers, who stand in the same situation as before.(*u*)

DXXIII. Having made the foregoing observations upon the period at which Treaties begin to operate; we have now to examine the effect of Treaties of Peace upon matters of Public Right. In order to do this we must take into our consideration—

(α.) *The rules of interpretation* by which the provisions expressed in a Treaty are to be explained.

(β.) The rules of *legal presumption*, with respect to subjects, upon which the Treaty is *silent*, but which have either been among the matters [*651] of dispute which have caused the War *closed by the Treaty, or have arisen and been debated during the course and progress of the War.

DXXIV. I. (α) With respect to the former the reader must be referred to the rules for *the Interpretation of Treaties* which have been mentioned in the Second Volume of this work.(*x*)

But, both with respect to the rules which govern *the Interpretation of Treaties*, and the *Legal Presumptions* which flow from the *silence* of Treaties, it is expedient to observe that there may be said to be four predicaments of a Treaty to which both are applicable.

The Treaty may adopt as its basis(*y*)—

1. *The state of things existing before the War* (*status quo ante bellum.*)
2. *The state of things existing at the conclusion of the War* (usually, however inaccurately, called *uti possidetis.*)(*z*)
3. *A new state of things*, composed perhaps of both the former.
4. [*652] It may contain a general clause of *amnesty*, the effect *of which is a remission of all public wrongs and obligations.(*a*)
5. It may be *silent* as to all former public wrongs and obligations between the Belligerents.

(*u*) The Schoone Sophie, 6 Rob., p. 143.

(*x*) Vide ante, Vol. II., Part. V. Ch. VIII.

(*y*) "At maximè disceptari solet, *an injuriæ et damna ante bellum data per pacem remissa sint?* Nos quatuor casus distinguimus; *vel* enim paci adjicitur clausula, *quod omnia restitui debeant in statum, quo fuêre ante bellum*, *vel* pactum est, *ut omnia maneant in statu quo nunc sunt*, *vel* plane, *nihil dictum est de damnis injuriis et debitis*, *vel* paci, *clausula generalis amnestiæ* adjicitur."—S. Cocceii Grotius Illustr., vol. v. p. 502, (l. vii. c. vii. s. 1864.)

(*z*) This term is borrowed from the well known interdict of the Roman Prætor. He, finding a litigant in *de facto* possession, forbad his expulsion *by force;* but then it was expressly stated as the foundation of the interdict, that the *possessor* was *not* in this *possession* by *any act of violence.* "Ait Prætor, '*uti* eas ædes, quibus de agitur, *nec vi*, nec clam, nec precariò alter ab altero *possidetis*, quo minus ita possideatis, vim fieri veto;' (4) est igitur hoc interdictum quod vulgo *uti possidetis* appellatur, retinendæ possessionis; nam hujus rei causa redditur, ne vis fiat ei, qui possidet; (5) *perpetuò autem huic interdicto insunt hæc, quod, nec vi*, nec clam, nec precariò ab illo possideas."—Dig. l. xliii. t. xvii. The phrase *uti possidetis* therefore is improperly used to signify the *status quo* of Belligerents at the conclusion of a War.

(*a*) "Remittit enim injuriam, *qui se eam obliturum promittit*, adeoque hactenus quoque omnia in statu, quo nunc sunt manent."—Cocceius, ubi supra, s. 1868.

DXXV. The principal distinction which it is necessary to observe in considering the *legal presumptions* which flow from the *silence* of Treaties, is, whether the property be *movable* or *immovable.*

To the eye of the philosophical jurist this latter division may, as a matter of abstract speculation, appear strange or untenable: but there is no doubt that to the eye of the practical statesman it presents a distinction most deeply and universally rooted in the laws, customs, and practice of all civilized nations. The distinction is indeed of less importance in matters of Public Right, because in practice the necessity for observing it but seldom occurs.(*b*)

DXXVI. It is now pretty generally acknowledged(*c*) that there is both absurdity and iniquity in classing territory obtained by *conquest* under the category of *res nullius;* and of applying, with unreasoning pedantry or sophistical injustice, not the spirit, but the letter, of the Roman law,(*d*) to a subject-matter which, like that of conquest, has necessarily undergone, in all its bearings, a most important change since the time of Justinian.(*e*)

The shameless pretext of Frederic the Second for the invasion of Saxony, in 1756,(*f*) will not be alleged again by the most reckless despiser of International Justice.

*Various and many Treaties of Peace fortify the sound international doctrine that *conquest* and *occupation*(*g*) of territory are [*653] distinct public acts, carrying with them very different consequences, both to the state and to the individual. The language of Treaties which concern the acquisition of conquered territory is that the subdued state *yields* or *concedes* (*cédera*)(*h*) a certain territory to another; not that the conquering state *retains* or *keeps* possession of what it has seized, which would be the proper expression in the Treaty with respect to a State obtaining the recognition of an *occupied* territory.

"Il est incontestable (says Monsieur de Rayneval) que le mot *cêder* suppose essentiellement la propriété, par conséquent ni la guerre ni la conquête ni la détruisent. Ainsi la pratique dément le principe enseigné par le droit Romain et par la plupart des publicistes."

DXXVII. Immovable property, public or private, can, according to the modern understanding of International Law, be acquired under a sure title only in consequence of a Treaty of Peace or the entire subju-

(*b*) Vide ante, p. 504.

(*c*) See pp. 388, 391, tit. Tercero, Seccion Cuarta, s. clix. of the "Elementos del Derecho Internacional obra póstuma, de Don José María de Pando, Ministro de Estado que fué en 1823. Madrid, imprenta de Allegia y Charlain, Cuesta de Santo Domingo, Num. 8, 1843." Pando was born at Lima, 1787; died at Madrid, 1840.

(*d*) Vide ante, Vol. I. p. 34.

(*e*) Inst., l. xi. 1-17. Dig., xli. t. ii. l. i. 1.

(*f*) Pando, p. 616, note 4.

(*g*) Vide ante, vol. I. pp. 237-265.

(*h*) E. g. in the Treaty of Utrecht, 1713, between Louis XIV. and Frederic William of Prussia, it is said, (Art. 7,) "que la partie du quartier de Gueldres que *possede* et *occupe* le Roi de Prusse lui est cédée à la perpetuité."

In the preliminaries of the Peace of 1783, between France and England, it is said, respecting the Isle of Tobago, (Art. 7,) "que le Roi de la Grande-Bretagne *cedéra* à la France l'Ile du Tobago." This island was, at the time of the Treaty, occupied under the title of conquest by the French. De Rayneval, ii. pp. 156, 7, note 35.

gation of the country of the original proprietor. Until one or other of these events the *jus postliminii* remains.(*i*)

[*654] *The question whether, if the people shake off the *subjugation*, the *jus postliminii* would revive, is not without difficulty. Pando(*k*) wisely distinguishes between two predicaments :—

1st. If the subjugation presents the appearance of being a mere temporary and involuntary submission to violence, the state of War continues, and therefore the *jus postliminii* continues.(*l*)

2nd. If the dominion of the conquerors has been confirmed by the consent, express or tacit, of the conquered—a consent which is *presumed in law* after the peaceable possession of some years,(*m*)—then War has ceased, and the *jus postliminii* is for ever extinguished by Peace.

DXXVIII. A striking illustration of the importance generally ascribed to the presumption arising from the *silence* of Treaties is to be found in the recent adjustment effected between Russia and Denmark respecting the succession to the throne of the latter country. The following is a copy of the Protocol of Warsaw relative to the Danish Succession, and of the renewal of that document by Russia in 1852.(*n*)

"(Translation.)

"His Majesty the Emperor of all the Russias and His Majesty the King of Denmark, taking into consideration the engagements entered into between their august predecessors, in the years 1767 and 1773;

"Considering that, as well for *establishing the tranquillity of the North of Europe on a durable footing*, as for removing all that could [*655] then, or for the future, give rise *to misunderstandings or differences in the august House of Oldenburg, the Emperor Paul, of glorious memory, then Grand Duke of Russia, renounced for himself, as also for his heirs and descendants, in favour of His Majesty King Christian VII., of glorious memory, as also of the heirs of his royal crown, all his rights and pretensions to the Duchy of Schleswig in general, and to the heretofore princely portion of that duchy in particular;

"That in the same manner, and from the same motives, His Majesty the Emperor Paul ceded for himself, as also for his descendants, heirs, and successors, all that he possessed in the Duchy of Holstein, whether in common with His Majesty the King of Denmark, or separately;

"Considering that this Act of Cession of the Duchy of Holstein has only been made expressly in favour of His Majesty King Christian VII., and of his male lineage, and also eventually in favour of the late Prince Frederick, the king's brother, and of the male lineage of that prince, and that the eventualities which the terms themselves of this Act of Cession admitted, have already in part been realized by the extinction of

(*i*) Pando, s. clxvii. p. 403: "Con respecto a las *cosas*, hay diferencia: o se trata de bienes-raices, ó de bienes-meubles."

"Asi pues, por lo que respecta à los *bienes-raices*, tanto particulares como publicos, et derecho de postliminio solo expira por et tratado de Paz, o por la completa subjugacion del Estado."—Pando, p. 404: he cites Olmeda, l. ii. c. xii.

(*k*) P. 404. (*l*) Vide ante, Vol. I., p. 275, II. pp. 17-18.

(*m*) Vide ante, Vol. I., Chapter XIII., on Prescription.

(*n*) Return to an Address of the House of Commons, dated 18 February, 1856.

the male lineage of King Christian VII., or may be realized at a period more or less near, without the said transactions having in any manner provided for them;

"*Foreseeing the dangers which this silence in existing Treaties may cause to the Danish monarchy*, if, on the extinction of the male line actually on the throne of Denmark, the *lex regia* should receive its pure and simple application to one part of the monarchy;—

"Have acknowledged the obligation and the right, as successors of the august contracting parties to the engagements of 1767 and 1773, to come to an understanding as to the ulterior arrangements most suited to the double objects which they have had in view.

"In consequence, the undersigned, after mature examination of all the questions connected with this affair, have agreed amongst themselves, under the express reservation of the high approbation of their respective Sovereigns, *and have embodied in the present Protocol the points which follow:— [*656]

"1° The objects proposed in the interest of the peace of the North, as well as that of the internal peace of the august House of Oldenburgh, namely, the maintenance of the integrity of the Danish monarchy, can only be realized by means of an arrangement summoning to the succession of the whole of the states actually united under the sceptre of His Majesty the King of Denmark, the male lineage solely, to the exclusion of women.

"2°. The male lineage of Prince Christian of Sleswig-Holstein Sonderbourg Glücksbourg, and of his consort the Princess Louise of Hesse, unites in itself the rights of inheritance, which, on the extinction of the male line actually reigning in Denmark, devolve upon it in virtue of the renunciations of Her Royal Highness the Landgravine Charlotte of Hesse, of her son Prince Frederick of Hesse, and of her daughter the Princess Mary of Anhalt-Dessau.

"3°. Wishing on his part to complete the titles resulting from these renunciations, and thus to effect an arrangement which would be of such high importance and interest for the maintenance of the Danish monarchy in its integrity, His Majesty the Emperor of all the Russias, as chief of the elder branch of Holstein Gottorp, would be ready to renounce the eventual rights which belong to him in favour of Prince Christian of Glücksbourg, and of his male lineage.

"Nevertheless it is understood:

"That the eventual rights of the two younger branches of Holstein Gottorp should be expressly reserved.

"That those which the august chief of the elder branch should abandon for himself and for his male lineage in favour of Prince Christian of Glücksbourg and of his male lineage, should be revived in the Imperial House of Russia whenever (which God forbid) the male lineage of that prince should become extinct.

"That inasmuch as the renunciation of His Majesty the Emperor would principally have for its object to facilitate *an arrangement called for by the first interests of the monarchy, the offer of such a renunciation would cease to be obligatory if the arrangement itself should fail. [*657]

"4°. In consequence of the considerations which are above pointed out by the above ss. 2 and 3, the Prince Christian of Glücksbourg, conjointly with the Princess, his consort, and in their default, the male lineage of their Highnesses, would have, more than any other branch, claims which qualify them to succeed, if the contingency should arrive, to the states actually united under the sceptre of His Danish Majesty.

"Consequently the two Courts of Copenhagen and St. Petersburgh have agreed,—

"That His Majesty the King of Denmark shall designate the Prince and Princess of Glücksbourg conjointly as heirs presumptive of his Crown, in case the male line of the dynasty actually reigning should become extinct;

"That His Majesty shall make known his high determination to the Powers in amity with Denmark;

"That if, to ensure the complete success of this arrangement, still further renunciations should be deemed useful and desirable, it would be for His Danish Majesty to make himself responsible for the indemnities to which just and equitable claims should be established;

"Finally, that the negotiations necessary to give to the arrangements, in virtue whereof the Prince and Princess of Glücksbourg shall be acknowledged as successors presumptive to the throne of Denmark, the character of an European transaction, shall take place in London.

"The undersigned reserve to themselves to submit the present Protocol to their august Sovereigns, and to solicit their high approbation in favour of the provisions it contains.

"(Signed) NESSELRODE,
"MEYENDORFF,
"REEDTZ.

"Warsaw, this $\frac{24 \text{ May}}{5 \text{ June}}$ 1851."

[*658] *"(Translation.)

"MONSIEUR LE COMTE,

"In accordance with the orders of my Court, it becomes my duty to communicate to your Excellency the accompanying note, which I have this moment given to the Minister of Denmark, upon signing conjointly with him the Treaty of this day's date.

"In requesting you to have the goodness to take cognizance of it,

"I have the honour, &c.

"(signed) BRUNNOW.

"London, $\frac{26 \text{ April}}{8 \text{ May}}$ 1852.

"To His Excellency, the Earl of Malmesbury,
&c., &c., &c."

"Translation of a Note addressed by Baron Brunnow to the Minister for Denmark.

"London, $\frac{26 \text{ April}}{8 \text{ May}}$ 1852.

"The undersigned, Envoy Extraordinary and Minister Plenipotentiary of His Majesty the Emperor of all the Russias to Her Britannic Majesty, having been authorized to sign the Treaty, concluded this day conjointly with His Excellency the Chamberlain de Bille, Envoy Extraordinary and Minister Plenipotentiary of His Majesty the King of Denmark, has been ordered to transmit to him at the same time the present Note, for the purpose of racalling and renewing the reserves contained in the Protocol of Warsaw, of $\frac{24\text{ May}}{5\text{ June}}$ 1851; which, after having received the sanction of His Majesty the Emperor of all the Russias, and of His Majesty the King of Denmark, was conveyed to the knowledge of the Cabinets who have signed the present Treaty.

"The third paragraph of the Protocol above mentioned is worded in these terms:—

*" 'Wishing on his part to complete the titles resulting from these renunciations, and thus to effect an arrangement which [*659] would be of such high importance for the maintenance of the Danish monarchy in its integrity, His Majesty the Emperor of all the Russias, as chief of the elder branch of Holstein Gottorp, would be ready to renounce the eventual rights which belong to him in favour of Prince Christian Glücksbourg and of his male lineage.

" 'Nevertheless, it is understood that the eventual rights of the two younger branches of Holstein Gottorp should be expressly reserved;

" 'That those which the august chief of the elder branch should abandon for himself, and for his male lineage, in favour of Prince Christian of Glücksbourg, and of his male lineage, should be revived in the Imperial House of Russia whenever (which God forbid) the male lineage of that Prince should become extinct;

" 'That inasmuch as the renunciation of his Majesty the Emperor would principally have for its object to facilitate an arrangement called for by the chief interests of the monarchy, the offer of such a renunciation would cease to be obligatory, if the arrangement itself should fail.'

"In renewing, by order of his Government, the reserves above mentioned,

"The undersigned, &c., &c."

---

*CHAPTER II. [*660]

HOW TREATIES ENTERED INTO BEFORE THE WAR ARE AFFECTED WHEN THE WAR IS CONCLUDED AND PEACE RESTORED.

DXXIX. It seems to be a branch of the question, how the public relations of states are affected by a Treaty which concludes a War, to consider what effect the War has upon Treaties existing before the War, but not mentioned or referred to in the new Treaty of Peace.

Many Treaties, especially those relating to leagues for War or for Commerce, are only contracted for a limited period, at the expiration of which they become invalid unless renewed. This renewal is not always *expressly*, but sometimes *tacitly*,(a) effected. M. de Martens observes

(a) G. F. Von Martens, Ueber die Erneuerung der Verträge in den Friedensschlüssen der Europäischen Mächte. Göttingen, 1797.

that more than one Treaty of Commerce entered into in the seventeenth century was in existence towards the end of the eighteenth century.

As, theoretically speaking, a private contract may be tacitly annulled by a total alteration of the circumstances on which it was founded; so it has been made a matter of dispute, with respect to treaties among States, whether a change of circumstances subsequent to the Treaty does not operate to the defeasance of the Treaty itself. For instance, it was a matter of dispute whether Austria, being bound by the Barrier-Treaty of the United Netherlands to admit Dutch garrisons into the fortresses, [*661] which were to serve as a defence *against France, remained under this obligation after the greater part of these fortresses had been demolished during the War of the Austrian Succession. Joseph the Second, in 1781, seems to have had little hesitation in razing(*b*) them to the ground.

With respect to Treaties with a state which has ceased to possess an independent existence,(*c*) it seems evident that the *public* contracts with it cease with the cessation of its distinct personality—as with Poland after its partitions, and the Crimea after its subjugation to Russia in 1783.

But this observation requires an important limitation. Such a loss of personality and independence leaves unimpaired the obligations of what are usually, but somewhat carelessly, termed *transitory* Treaties—that is to say, Treaties relating to cessions of territory, to demarcations of boundary, to that particular class of obligations called *Servitutes Juris Gentium*,(*d*) the nature and character of which have been already discussed in this work.

Certain Genoese families, the Counts of Casati and others, pressed their claims to certain portions of Crimean territory upon the Russians, both in 1779 and in 1783, at which latter period the subjugation of the Crimea was complete. Russia replied on both occasions that she would recognize no claims which did not flow from the provisions of her Treaty with the Porte. This answer, in the opinion of De Martens, was, in 1783, whatever it might have been in 1779, bad in law.(*e*)

DXXX. It was at one time an international custom that the Belligerents should, at the breaking out of War, make a public and solemn [*662] proclamation that the obligations *of Treaties between them had ceased.(*f*) That custom has become obsolete. In the place of it has arisen the general maxim, that War, *ipso facto* (*von selbst*,) abrogates Treaties between the Belligerents. The questions which present themselves for our consideration are: first, whether this proposition be true in all its latitude, or whether it requires any—and if any, what—limitations, before it can be enunciated as one of the admitted and incontrovertible principles of International Jurisprudence?

Secondly, if it be universally, or with certain limitations, true, that

(*b*) See De Martens, Rec. des Tr., t. iv. p. 433, for State Papers on the subject.
(*c*) Vide ante, Vol. I. Pt. II. Ch. VI. VII.
(*d*) Vide ante, Vol. I. Pt. III. Ch. XV.
(*e*) Ueber die Erneuerung der Verträge, p. 7.
(*f*) Leibnitz, Præf. ad Cod. Diplom. Jur. Gentium.

Treaties annulled by War are revived by the return of Peace without express stipulations to that effect?

DXXXI. The general maxim must manifestly be subject to limitation in one case, namely, in the case of Treaties which expressly provide for the contingency of the breaking out of War between the contracting parties: and the Judges of the North American United States were well warranted in saying, "We are not inclined to admit the doctrine urged at the bar, that Treaties become extinguished, *ipso facto*, by War between the two governments, unless they should be revived by an express or implied renewal on the return of Peace. Whatever may be the latitude of doctrine laid down by elementary writers on the law of nations, dealing in general terms in relation to this subject, we are satisfied that the doctrine contended for is not universally true. There may be treaties of such a nature, as to their object and import, as that War will put an end to them; but where Treaties contemplate a permanent arrangement of territorial and other national rights, or which, in their terms are meant to provide for the event of an intervening War, it would be against every principle of just interpretation to hold them extinguished by the event of War. If such were the law, even the Treaty of 1783, so far as it fixed our limits and acknowledged our independence, would *be gone, and we should have had again to struggle for both upon original revolutionary principles. Such a construction was never asserted, and would be so monstrous as to supersede all reasoning."(*g*) [*663]

Some writers on Public and International Law go further and say that War abrogates only those Treaties the existence of which is incompatible with Belligerent relations.(*h*)

Mr. Wildman has expressed his opinion that "all engagements subsisting between Belligerents at the commencement of hostilities are revived by a Treaty of Peace, so far as they are consistent with its provisions."(*i*)

Such an opinion, however, it appears to the writer of these pages, must be considered as at variance with the true doctrines of International Law, and especially with those derived from two of the sources of this jurisprudence, viz., the *conclusions of accredited writers* and the *practice of states*.(*k*)

The opinion(*l*) has arisen partly (1.) from a misapprehension of the

(*g*) The Society, &c. v. New Haven, 5 Curtis's (Amer.) Reports, p. 493.

(*h*) De Martens, in his treatise above referred to, after stating the general maxim, says: "So gilt doch nicht eben dieses von allen übrigen vorhergehenden mit dem jetzigen Kriege nicht in Verbindung stehenden Verträgen: und wenn dieses so allgemein von einzelnen Schriftstellern und wohl gar zuweilen in öffentlichen Staatschriften behauptet worden, so liegt dabei wohl noch mehr eine Verwechselung des Ausdrucks, als eine Irrthum in der Sache selbst zum Grunde."—s. 8. He cites, "Möser, Vermischte Abhandlungen aus dem Europ. Völkerrecht."—s. 3, n. f.

(*i*) Vol. I. p. 176. (*k*) Vide ante, Vol. I. Pt. I. Ch. V. and VII.

(*l*) There is a very able discussion upon this point to be found in the columns of the Morning Chronicle for December, 1853. Heffters, p. 183, s. 99, p. 215, s. 122, p. 317, s. 181, and note 1, in which the author says, "Dieser Punct ist und bleibt einer der schwierigsten:" in the text he says, "Dagegen sind alle Vertragsverpflichtungen deren Erfüllung erst noch in Zukunft geschehen sollte, wo also noch eine Willensänderung in Betreff der übernommenen Verpflichtung möglich

[*664] *meaning of a passage in Vattel, partly (2.) from misapplying judicial *dicta*, uttered with respect to Private Contracts to Public Treaties; partly, (3.) and perhaps chiefly from not discriminating between those parts of a Treaty which contained a *final* adjustment of a particular question, such as the fixing a disputed boundary or ascertaining any contested right or property; or which incorporated by the common consent, express or tacit, of all States concerned in its assertion and maintenance, a great public *principle* into the International Code. That principle once so incorporated, does not require reiteration in subsequent Treaties, and, unless expressly repudiated, revives with Peace, or rather remains unaffected by War waged upon grounds unconnected with it.

(1.) The passage in Vattel is taken from the 42d Section of his Fourth Book. "It is (he says) of great importance to draw a proper distinction between a *new* War and the breach of an *existing* Treaty of Peace; because the rights acquired by *such* a Treaty still subsist notwithstanding the new war: whereas they are *annulled* by the rupture of the Treaty on which they are founded. It is true, indeed, that the party who had granted those rights does not fail to obstruct the exercise of them during the course of the War as far as lies in his power; and he even may, by the right of arms, wholly deprive his enemy of them, as well as he may wrest from him his other possessions. But in that case he withholds those rights as things taken from the enemy, who, on a new Treaty of Peace, may urge the restitution of them. It often happens, when nearly equal success has attended the arms of both parties, that the Belligerents agree mutually to restore their conquests and *to replace everything in its former state. When this is the case, if the War in which they were engaged was a new one, the former Treaties still subsist.*"

But of what is the writer speaking? Not of the effect of War generally upon Treaties,—not whether existing public covenants are dissolved by hostilities,—but whether the dispute between the Belligerents arises [*665] out of an alleged breach *of an existing public covenant, or whether it arises out of a new cause of offence, *e. g.* violation of *general* International Rights, irrespective of any *positive convention* subsisting between the Belligerents.

In the passage under discussion Vattel is not considering Treaties, in which it is agreed that there shall be either an *express* renewal, or a *tacit* revival, of former Treaties, irrespective of the new convention between the parties. He is supposing that the Belligerents have agreed to adopt the *status quo ante bellum* as the adjustment of their quarrel. In order to ascertain what that *status* was, the relations of the parties before the War broke out must be considered, and whether, therefore, independently of *this* War, the former Treaties between the parties were in existence. Now, if the War was a *new War,*—that is a War on account of the violation of some *general right* and not of a *positive convention,*—then, *previously* to the War, the former Treaties were unbroken, and then, by the engagement of both parties to observe the *status quo*

war, durch den Ausbruch des Krieges zweifelhaft und unsicher geworden, so das sie einer Bestätigung durch eine neue deutliche Willenserklarung bedürfen."

ante bellum, these Treaties are considered as still existing. If, on the other hand, former Treaties have been broken, and the War has been waged upon *this account,* then a *specific renewal* of the covenants of these former Treaties would be necessary. In this latter, however, as in the former case, the belligerents would have agreed to adopt the *status quo ante bellum.*

This explanation renders Vattel consistent with himself, and reconciles the passage which has been commented upon with that contained in the 175th Section of his Third Book,(*m*) in which he says that "the conventions made with a nation are *broken* or *annulled* by a War arising between the two contracting parties, either because their compacts are grounded on a tacit supposition of the continuance of Peace, or because each of the parties being authorized to deprive the enemy of what belongs to him, takes from him those *rights which he had conferred on him by Treaty." Vattel, it will be seen, does not speak of Treaties being *suspended,* but of their being *broken* and *annulled,* by War. To give a new occasion for War and to break the Peace, are, as Grotius observes, different things. The difference between the two is important, and has a double bearing; first, as to the penalty incurred by the breaker of the Peace; and secondly, as to how far his act relieves the other party from his engagement. "Peace," he says, "may be broken in three ways; first, by doing what is at variance with the intrinsic character of every Peace (*faciendo contra id quod omni paci inest;*) secondly, by violating the express conditions of the Peace; thirdly, by acting contrary to that which ought to be understood, from the particular nature of each Peace (*contra id quod ex pacis cujusque naturâ intelligi debet.*")(*n*) [*666]

(2.) The misapplication of the doctrine of International Law respecting the revival after Peace of private contracts, the operation of which is suspended during War, to the case of public Treaties, has occasionally led persons into an error on this point.(*o*)

The supposed analogy between the public and the private contract is unsound. It is the State and not the individual who wages War. The contracts between the individuals of *Belligerent States are necessarily suspended during the War of these states, but are not annulled;(*p*) no precedent can therefore be drawn from the tacit renewal of these private relations on the return of Peace, to found the [*667]

(*m*) Chap. x. (*n*) Grot., l. iii. c. xx. s. 27.

(*o*) Grotius furnishes no direct authority on this question. He says: "Quod vero diximus* jus quod ante bellum fuit ademtum facilè censeri non debere, id in *privatorum jure* firmè tenendum est; in jure autem regum et populorum faciliùs est ut condonatio aliqua intelligatur facta, si modo verba aut conjecturæ non improbabiles suppetant; maximè vero si jus de quo agitur non liquidum erat, sed in controversiâ positum. Benignum enim est credere id actum, ut belli semina evellerentur."—L. iii. c. xx. s. 19.

(*p*) Grot., l. iii. c. xx. s. 16. Abbot on Shipping, part. iv. ch. xiii.

* Referring to s. 16: "Jus vero quod ante bellum fuit, quamquam nemini facilè ademtum censeri debet (hanc enim ob causam maximè ut suæ tenerentur res publicæ civitatesque constitutæ sunt, ut rectè ait Cicero) intelligendum id tamen de eo jure quod ex rerum inæqualitate nascitur."

argument for the tacit renewal of public relations. Judicial decisions of Municipal Courts of Law upon the former, are without bearing upon the latter question.

DXXXII. The language of Lord Stowell is strong upon this point, though his opinion is incidentally or parenthetically expressed. He speaks of Treaties being *extinguished* by War.(*q*)

It has been observed with respect to England, that in all her Treaties concluding War she has studiously preserved *silence* upon the disputed questions of Maritime International Law, thereby reserving to herself the right in all future Wars of maintaining her exposition of International Right and Law upon these subjects:(*r*) but she accompanied the last Treaty, which closed her recent War with Russia (March, 1856,) with a Declaration by which she admitted, in concert with the Great Powers of Europe, the doctrine that *free ships make free goods.*(*s*) This Declaration has not yet been embodied in a Treaty.(*t*)

DXXXIII. This point was much discussed between England and the United States of North America during the negotiation at Ghent in 1814, England considering that certain Rights of Fishery accorded by her to the United States by the Treaty of 1783 had been abrogated by subsequent War, and giving notice that she did not intend to renew them.

[*668] *The United States contended, on the other hand, that the Treaty of 1783 was not one of those which by the common consent and understanding of civilized nations is considered as annulled by a subsequent War between the parties.

It is to be observed that England did not wholly traverse this allegation, but denied the application of the principle to the provision relating to Fisheries; the Treaty of 1783, like many others, she said, contained provisions of different character, *some in their own nature irrevocable*, and others merely temporary; that the provision in question was among the latter.(*u*)

DXXXIV. Mr. Wheaton remarks that the reasoning of England seemed to confine the perpetuity of obligation to recognitions and acknowledgments of title, and to consider its perpetual nature as resulting from the subject-matter of the contract, and not from the engagement of the contractor.(*x*)

It appears to the writer of these pages that the doctrine intended to be conveyed in the English note was in harmony with that conveyed in the text, namely, the doctrine that there is a distinction between the

(*q*) The Frau Ilsabe, 4 Robinson's Adm. Rep., p. 64. He is speaking, however, of a War actually existing.

(*r*) De Hautefeuille, i. pp. 160, 161.

(*s*) Vide ante, Ch. X., which was printed before the Declaration mentioned in the text was published.

(*t*) This Declaration will be found in the Appendix to this volume.—See Parliamentary Debates, Hansard, vol. cxlii. (1856,) p. 18, &c.

(*u*) See the whole correspondence, British and Foreign State Papers, (1819-20,) vol. vii. See an analysis of the whole discussion, pp. 334-342, Wheaton's Elem., (by Lawrence.) See, too, a valuable chapter in The Oregon Question, examined by Dr. Twiss, (1846,) chap. x.

(*x*) Wheaton's Elem., (by Lawrence,) p. 341.

parts of a Treaty which recognized a principle and object of permanent policy, and the parts which related to objects of passing and temporary expediency.

DXXXV. Nor is this doctrine at variance with the opinion of Mr. Wheaton himself, who says in one part of his Elements :(*y*)—

"General compacts between nations may be divided into what are called *Transitory Conventions*, and *Treaties* properly so termed. The first are perpetual in their nature, *so that, being once carried into effect, they subsist independent of any change in the sove- [*669] reignty and form of government of the contracting parties; and although their operation may in some cases, be suspended during War, they revive on the return of Peace, without any express stipulation. Such are Treaties of cession, boundary, or exchange of territory, or those which create a permanent servitude in favour of one nation within the territory of another."(*z*)

And in another part of the same treatise :(*a*)—

"Most International Compacts, and especially Treaties of Peace, are of a mixed character, and contain articles of both kinds, which renders it frequently difficult to distinguish between those stipulations which are perpetual in their nature, and such as are extinguished by War between the contracting parties, or by such changes of circumstances as affect the being of either party, and thus render the compact inapplicable to the new condition of things. It is for this reason, and from abundance of caution, that stipulations are frequently inserted in Treaties of Peace, expressly reviving and confirming the Treaties formerly subsisting between the contracting parties, and containing stipulations of a permanent character, or in some other mode excluding the conclusion that the obligation of such antecedent Treaties is meant to be waived by either party. The reiterated confirmations of the Treaties of Westphalia and Utrecht, in almost every subsequent Treaty of Peace or Commerce between the same parties, constituted a sort of written code of conventional law, by which the distribution of power among the principal European States was permanently settled, until violently disturbed by the Partition of Poland and the Wars of the French Revolution."

It must be admitted that a Municipal Court of the United [*670] *States had denied the general doctrine of the abrogation of Treaties by War; but this Court was dealing at the time with a question of *private property*, to which the doctrine was certainly not applicable; and the language of the Court, though certainly going beyond the case, must be considered, in some degree at least, as the *obiter dicta* of judges.(*b*)

But even without these qualifications, the lauguage of the American Court has confined its denial of the general doctrine—that Treaties are

(*y*) Wheaton's Elem., (by Lawrence,) p. 332.

(*z*) Vattel, Droit des Gens, l. ii. c. xii. s. 192. Martens, Précis, &c., l. ii. c. ii. s. 58.

(*a*) Wheaton's Elem., (by Lawrence,) pp. 343, 344.

(*b*) The Society for the Propagation of the Gospel v. The Town of New Haven and William Wheeler, 5 Curtis's (Amer.) Rep., p. 483.

abrogated by War—within limits which are scarcely, if at all, distinguishable from the position which has been maintained in these pages.

The Court expressed its opinion that Treaties stipulating for permanent rights and general arrangements, and professing to aim at perpetuity, and to deal with the case of War as well as of Peace, do not cease on the occurrence of War, but are at most only suspended while it lasts; and that unless they are waived by the parties, or new and repugnant stipulations are made, they revive and come agáin into operation at the return of Peace.(*c*)

In 1830 a question was raised in an English Municipal Court(*d*) whether, by the ninth article of the Treaty of 1794, Between Great Britain and the United States, American citizens who held lands in Great Britain on October 28th, 1795, and their heirs and assigns, are at all times to be considered, as far as regards those lands, not as aliens, but as native subjects of Great Britain. The 28th article of the Treaty declared that the ten first articles should be permanent; but the counsel in support of the objection to the title contended that "it was impossible to suggest that the Treaty was continuing in force in 1813; *it
[*671] necessarily ceased with the commencement of the War. The 37 Geo. III. c. 97, could not continue in operation a moment longer without violating the plainest words of the Act: that the word 'permanent' was used, not as synonymous with 'perpetual,' or 'everlasting,' but in opposition to a period of time expressly limited." On the other hand, the counsel in support of the title maintained that "the Treaty contained articles of two different descriptions; some of them being temporary, others of perpetual obligation. Of those which were temporary, some were to last for a limited period—such as the various regulations concerning trade and navigation; and some were to continue so long as peace subsisted, but, being inconsistent with a state of War, would necessarily expire with the commencement of hostilities. There were other stipulations which were to remain in force in all time to come, unaffected by the contingency of Peace or War. For instance, there are clauses for fixing the boundaries of the United States. Were the boundaries so fixed to cease to be the boundaries the moment that hostilities broke out?"

The Master of the Rolls, in his judgment said:—"The privileges of natives being reciprocally given, not only to the actual possessors of lands, but to their heirs and assigns, it is a reasonable construction that it was the intention of the Treaty that *the operation of the Treaty should be permanent*, and not depend upon the continuance of a state of Peace.

"The Act of the 37 Geo. III. c. 95, gives full effect to this article of the Treaty in the strongest and clearest terms; and if it be, as I consider it, the true construction of this article, that it was to be permanent, and independent of a state of Peace or War, then the Act of Parliament must be held, in the 54th section, to declare this permanency, and when a subsequent section provides that the Act is to continue in force so long

(*c*) The Oregon Question, by Dr. Twiss, p. 180.

(*d*) Sutton v. Sutton, 1 Russell & Mylne's Rep., p. 663, Rolls Court, Sir John Leach.

only as a state of Peace shall subsist, it cannot be construed to be directly repugnant and opposed *to the 24th Section, but is to be understood as referring to such provisions of the Act only as would in their nature depend upon a state of Peace."(*e*) [*672]

After the recent War (1856) Russia and Sardinia, by special Treaty, renewed the obligations of Treaties which had been abrogated by the War.

(3.) The *practice* of states is clear upon this subject. It receives an ample illustration, especially as far as England is concerned, from the debates in both Houses of the English Legislature at the period of the Peace of Amiens (1801.)

DXXXVI. In the House of Lords there were two debates upon the subject of this Peace. Upon a careful perusal and attentive consideration of them(*f*) it will be found that the doctrine of the abrogation of Treaties by the breaking out of War was either expressly, or by implication, admitted by every speaker who had any pretensions to be considered either a jurist or a statesman.

In the first debate Lord Grenville observed that, "In entering into negotiation, every statesman knew that the basis must be one of these two—either to take the *status ante bellum* or the *uti possidetis* at the moment of negotiating. From one of these points every negotiation must set out."(*g*)

He afterwards added, that "he was peculiarly called upon to direct the attention of ministers to the subject of an omission which appeared to him of great consequence, of not stipulating for the renewal of all or most of the Treaties before subsisting between this country and those nations with which we had lately been at war."(*h*) . . . .

*"He next adverted to the non-renewal of ancient Treaties, which he would contend was a principle in the process of negotiation equally novel and injurious; and, in illustrating these propositions, he again referred to the French official papers that he had already quoted, which said, 'the old law is destroyed; a new public law commences;' which principle might be most destructively applied by France in her future projects of aggrandizement; and they might well say to us, that, abiding by the Treaty of Amiens, which in effect ordained a new Law of Nations, we had no right or title to inquire."(*i*) [*673]

In this debate, too, the ex-Lord Chancellor, Lord Thurlow, "insisted that all subsisting Treaties were at an end as soon as a War was commenced with those who were parties to them. It by no means followed as a matter of course that ancient Treaties were necessarily to be revived

(*e*) The Oregon Question, examined by Dr. Twiss, pp. 181, 182.

(*f*) See Appendix to this Volume for extracts from the speeches of the principal speakers in the debate.

(*g*) Debate on the Treaty of Amiens (1802,) Hansard's Parliamentary History, vol. xxxvi. (1801-3,) p. 164. Reported and amplified in second debate on the same Treaty, Ib., p. 690.

(*h*) Ib., pp. 587, 588.

(*i*) Debate on the Treaty of Amiens (1802,) Hansard's Parl. Hist., vol. xxxvi. (1801-3,) p. 593.

and renewed in every Treaty of Peace: that must depend upon the will of the contracting parties."(*k*)

In the second debate Lord Grenville(*l*) moved an address, which in one of its paragraphs adverted to the "immense accessions of territory, influence and power which it (the Treaty) had *tacitly confirmed* to France."

Dr. Lawrence,(*m*) Sir W. Grant,(*n*)—authorities second to none upon a question of International Law,—Mr. Windham, Mr. Pitt, Lord Chancellor Eldon,(*o*) Lord Hawkesbury,(*p*) Lord Carnarvon,(*q*) speakers taking different parts, and maintaining different opinions in the debate
[*674] as to the policy of the Treaty of Amiens, will all be found to *have admitted expressly, or by implication, the doctrine that Treaties are abrogated by War.

DXXXVII. It has been thought that this doctrine respecting the abrogation of Treaties by War, is at variance with the language of the English and French Ministers for Foreign Affairs, Lord Palmerston and M. Guizot, during the painful discussion upon that most discreditable international transaction, *the Spanish Marriages* in 1846.(*r*) It has been said by a modern writer that,(*s*) "in the dispute on the Spanish
[*675] *marriages, the French minister had to defend, and the English foreign secretary to impugn, a transaction which both knew to be too infamous for public discussion; it was for this reason that both parties selected a fictitious issue."(*t*)

(*k*) Ib., p. 596. (*l*) Ib., p. 699. (*m*) Ib., pp. 674, 675, 677-9.
(*n*) Ib., pp. 801, 802, 803. (*o*) Ib., p. 725. (*p*) Ib., pp. 761, 762.
(*q*) Ib., p. 714.

(*r*) Correspondence relating to the Marriages of the Queen and Infanta of Spain. Papers presented to Parliament, 1847.

P. 18, Lord Normanby's account to Lord Palmerston of his (Ld. N.'s) conversation with M. Guizot, who said, as to the union of the crowns of France and Spain, "That need not be feared; it is guarded against by the Treaty of Utrecht."

P. 24, Lord Palmerston. "The decision of the King of the French that the Duke of Montpensier should *not* be a candidate for the hand of the Queen of Spain . . . . was the result of the sense which the King of the French spontaneously entertained of what was due by France *to the faith of the transactions of the Treaty of Utrecht*, and to the just value attached by other states to the maintenance of the balance of power in Furope."

P. 25, "It is perfectly clear that by *virtue of the renunciation made at the Peace of Utrecht* by the Duke of Orleans of that day 'all his descendants, male and female, for that time and for ever, are excluded, disabled, and incapacitated from succeeding to the throne of Spain, in what manner soever the succession might fall to their line:' and therefore the children and descendants of the Duke of Montpensier would, in consequence thereof, be excluded from succeeding to the Spanish crown."

P. 47, M. Guizot says that (1) to secure the throne of Spain to the descendants of Philip V., (2) to prevent the union of the thrones of France and Spain, was the double object of the Treaty of Utrecht, and contends "la double intention du Traité d'Utrecht est donc *toujours* accomplie."

See also pp. 69, 70, 75, 76. The Spanish Minister Xavier de Isturiz admits the validity of the renunciation, and, by implication, the Treaty itself of Utrecht.

"Loque el Gobierno de sue Majestad reconoce como objeto claro y explicito del Tratado de Utrecht, es la estipulacion de que las coronas de España y de Francia no puedan en ningun caso reunirse en una misma persona."—P. 83.

(*s*) Letters in the Morning Chronicle, vide supra, p. 663. n. (*l*).

(*t*) "To which" (the writer adds) "Lord Palmerston might well have demurred, when it was tendered by M. Guizot. On no other theory is it possible to account

But in truth it is hardly necessary to have recourse to this supposition in order to reconcile with the doctrine which has been laid down, the opinion that the Treaty of Utrecht, though not renewed by the later Treaties, was nevertheless a bar to the scheme of uniting France and Spain under one crown.

The Treaty of Utrecht contemplated a *permanent arrangement* of National and International Rights; moreover it contained the assertion of a great *principle* relating to the balance of power and the security of the liberties of Europe; it contained further, a solemn *renunciation* on the part of the Duke of Orleans, for himself and his successors, of any title to the throne of Spain. So far as this *permanent arrangement*, this *principle*, and this *renunciation* are concerned, the Treaty is not abrogated by the omission or the non-renewal of it in later Treaties.(*u*) It would require either an express waiver or repugnant stipulations in these later Treaties to extinguish *these* consequences of the Treaty.(*x*)

for the declaration by a grave statesman, that England would not recognize a Spanish monarch descended from Philip of Orleans, or a French monarch descended from Philip of Spain. Queen Isabella was excluded by one category, and both the Comte de Paris and the Comte de Chambord by the other, from their respective inheritances; but Lord Palmerston was not so much discussing a Treaty as intimating, with diplomatic courtesy, the deep indignation of England and of Europe."

(*u*) Considerations respecting the Marriage of the Duke of Montpensier with reference to the Treaty of Utrecht (London, Ridgway, 1847,) contains a very full and ample discussion of the subject.

(*x*) The suggestion in the text appears to reconcile the language of Lord Palmerston in an earlier debate (1839, upon the Mexican blockade,) as to the Treaty of Utrecht, with the opinion expressed in the case of the Spanish marriages. In the course of this debate, which was brought on by Lord Sandon, as to the legality of the blockade of the Mexican ports, Mr. E Tennent said, "But not only had France thus excluded us from the profitable trade of the La Plata and the Gulf of Mexico, but on another, and, if possible, a still less tenable ground, she had recently taken forcible occupation, and to this hour holds possession of the entire territory of Brazilian Guiana, on no other pretence, and by no other authority, than an alleged inaccuracy in the wording of the Treaty of Utrecht, which, it is asserted, describes inaccurately the relative boundaries of French and Portuguese Guiana. That such an error, that a geographical error, did exist in the wording of the Treaty of Utrecht, on this point, there could be no manner of doubt; but it was also equally certain that it was a matter of easy adjustment; and by the terms of the Treaty of Paris, in 1817, it was expressly determined that Commissioners should be mutually appointed to determine the boundary; and that if at the expiration of one year they should not be able to come to an understanding, 'the two contracting parties should proceed by friendly accord to form another arrangement under the mediation of Great Britain, and conformably to the Treaty of Utrecht, concluded under the guarantee of that power.'"*

To which Lord Palmerston is reported by the historian of Parliamentary Debates to have replied: "By the Treaty of Vienna—for the provisions of the Treaty of Utrecht had long lapsed in the variations of war—and by the 107th article of that Treaty, the Prince Regent of Portugal and the Brazils, to manifest, in the most indisputable manner, his consideration for the King of France, agreed to restore Guiana up to the river Amazon, in the 4th and 5th degrees of northern latitude, being the same limitation as it was considered was imposed on Portugal by the Treaty of Utrecht."†

It would seem also that these expressions with respect to the lapse of the provisions of the Treaty of Utrecht must be confined to those provisions which related

* Hansard's Parl. Deb., vol. xlvi. p. 914.

† Ib., Speech of Viscount Palmerston, p. 939.

[*676] *DXXXVIII. The English minister addressed the following protest to the Spanish Court upon the subject of the Spanish marriages:—

[*677] "Draft of a note to be presented by Mr. BULWER to the Spanish Government. October, 1846.(y)

"The undersigned, &c., has been instructed by his government to refer the government of her Majesty the Queen of Spain to the protest which, on the —— of September of this year, he presented, by the special orders of his government, against the projected marriage of the Infanta Luisa-Fernanda to the Duke of Montpensier.

"On that occasion the undersigned protested, in the name of the British Government, against the conclusion of that marriage, upon the ground that it would be injurious to the political independence of Spain, and detrimental to the balance of power in Europe, and that it would therefore most seriously affect the future relations between Spain and Great Britain. The undersigned is now instructed to declare, on behalf of the British Government, that the issue of such marriage would be held by Great Britain to be disabled, by the stipulations of Treaties and by the Public Law of Europe, from succeeding in any case to the Spanish throne. For, in the first place, on the 19th of November, 1712, the Duke of Orleans, in the act of renunciation then made by him of all eventual right and title to the crown of Spain, declared that his descendants were from that time forward and for ever excluded and disabled from, and incapable of succeeding to the crown of Spain, whatever might be the way in which the succession might devolve upon his line; and this renunciation and declaration on his part having been incorporated in the Treaties signed in 1713 at Utrecht, became thereby part and parcel of the Public Law of Europe. Moreover, the third article of the Treaty concluded in 1725, between Spain and Austria, stipulates that the crowns of France and Spain shall never be united either in the same person or in the same line.

[*678] *"And secondly, Philip the Fifth of Spain declared, on the 8th of July, 1712, that no descendant of any family which might at any time reign in France should be capable of succeeding to the throne of Spain; and in 1713, the same Sovereign issued a Cedula, in which he declared that all the princes of the blood of France, and all their lines, either then in existence, or which might thenceforward exist, should remain excluded from the succession to the Spanish monarchy.

"It is indisputably demonstrable that, in consequence of these public acts, no person being the offspring or the descendant of the Duke of Montpensier, could, under any circumstances, succeed to the throne of Spain; and therefore the offspring or descendants of the marriage of the Duke of Montpensier with the Infanta Luisa-Fernanda, if that marriage

to the Portuguese territory of Guiana, and which had been altered or affected by subsequent Treaties. On the other hand the stipulation respecting the demolition of the fortifications of Dunkirk, which was one of the stipulations of the Treaty of Utrecht, was considered to have been abrogated by the silence of subsequent Treaties respecting it.

(y) P. 28, of Papers presented to Parliament.

should take place, would be for ever excluded from the succession to the Spanish crown, in the event of a failure of succession in the line of her present Majesty, the Queen Isabella; nor could any right or capacity which such offspring or descendants of the marriage of the Duke of Montpensier with the Infanta might inherit from the Infanta prevail against the positive disqualification and exclusion which would attach to them as descendants of the Duke of Orleans of 1712.

"The British Government deems it to be its duty to make this public and solemn declaration of the incapacity, disability, and exclusion, in regard to the succession to the throne of Spain, which would attach to any issue or descendants of the marriage of the Infanta with the Duke of Montpensier, if, in utter disregard of the remonstrance and protest of Great Britain, that marriage should be persisted in; and thus, if at any future time any dispute should in consequence thereof arise as to the succession to the throne of Spain, and if Great Britain should in such case deem it proper to take part in such dispute, in support of the principles which have been set forth in this note, it will not be in the power of any of the parties concerned to allege that *the British Government did not give timely warning of its sentiments and views. [*679]

"The undersigned, &c."

In a recent Message of the President of the N. A. United States, the doctrine in the text is strongly insisted upon: "A state of war" (it says) "abrogates Treaties previously existing between the belligerents, and a Treaty of Peace puts an end to all claims for indemnity for tortious acts committed under the authority of one government against the citizens or subjects of another, unless they are provided for in its stipulations."(z)

---

*CHAPTER III. [*680]

WHERE, HOW, AND UNDER WHAT LIMITATIONS THE DOCTRINE OF POSTLIMINIUM MAY BE APPLIED TO STATES AND THE SUBJECTS OF STATES ON THE RETURN OF PEACE.

DXXXIX. WHERE the Treaty of Peace is *silent*, containing no *express* or *implied* provisions concerning rights or property which have undergone a *de facto* change during the vicissitudes of War, some rules of justice must be applied, when the War is over, to settle the condition of these rights or this property, whether they appertain to a nation or an individual subject.

These rules belong to the category of *Postliminium*,(a) a name which has, ever since its introduction into the Roman Law, obtained universally in Public and International Jurisprudence.

(z) President's Message, Annual Register for 1847, p. 407.

(a) Vide ante, Vol. I. pp. 273, 311. Heffters, s. 187. Dig., xlix. t. xv., De Captivis, et de Postliminio, et Redemptis ab Hostibus. Voet., t. iv. p. 642, upon Dig., xlix. t. xv.

It is true that, strictly speaking, the name itself appertains to a state of War; but the principle, which the doctrine conveys, is applicable to the state of things now under our consideration. For the doctrine of *Postliminium* applies to personal *status*, to property, and to obligations, and says, in its general language, that these, being *de facto* freed from the pressure of the enemy's force, shall return to the channels in which they flowed before they were by the pressure of that force diverted from them. The principle upon which the doctrine rests, is, that rights duly [*681] acquired cannot be permanently *taken away, either by the act of an individual or by the act of an enemy state, without the consent of the state to which the original owner belongs.

It is true that the provisions in the Roman Law upon this subject are applied, almost exclusively, to the question of Private Rights; but, as has been often before observed in the course of this work, the principles of natural justice embodied in the Roman Law are applicable to states, as well as to individuals, in their intercourse with each other.

DXL. Having made these general observations as to the effect of the doctrine of *Postliminium* upon the property of the State after the conclusion of a War, and in the absence of any express stipulations in the Treaty of Peace, it becomes necessary to examine the subject a little further as to its practical application.

It is a subject which has undergone at different periods, both of modern and ancient history, much discussion, and elicited a variety of opinions. An examination of these opinions seems to demonstrate that there has been too often a want of clearness and discrimination upon two cardinal points.

1. As to the distinction which exists between the question considered as a matter of *Public*, and considered as a matter of *International* Law, or, in other words, between the subjects and the government of the *same* state, and between the government of *one* state and the subjects or the government of *another* state.

2. As to the distinction which exists between (α) the effect of a simple *conquest* or the acts of a *conqueror;* and (β) the effect of an *interregnum*(b) or the acts of a *de facto sovereign.*

It is necessary, for the due unravelling of this question, to keep these distinctions continually in mind.

[*682] *It has been already observed in an earlier part of this work, that "Conquest, fortified by subsequent treaty, gives a valid international title to territory."(c)

The distinction between the effect of the doctrine of *Postliminium* upon *movable* and *immovable* property has been already the subject of remark; it is one indeed which has been pretty generally observed by all writers upon the subject.

DXLI. *Conquest* and *occupation* are distinct things, governed as to their legal effects in various respects by different principles and attended with different consequences. Nevertheless there is an analogy between

(b) Pfeiffer, in wiefern sind Regierungshandlungen eines Zwischenherrschers für den rechtmässigen Regenten nach dessen Rückkehr verbindlich, 1819.

(c) Vide ante, Vol. I. p. 300.

the two, and, in some respects, the rules of *occupation* are applicable to the case of *conquest*.

Conquest is often defined as *occupatio bellica;* and it so far partakes of the nature of occupation, that unless the conqueror has *actual possession* of the thing conquered he can exercise no right over it. "Vox ipsa *capta*," Cocceius observes, "indicat rem ita in nostrâ custodiâ et potestate esse ut eximi non potest:"(*d*) and Grotius, speaking of the nature of acquisition by conquest, "non causa aliqua sed *ipsum nudum factum* spectatur, et *ex eo jus nascitur*."(*e*)

DXLII. It has been already seen that, in case of *immovable property, even actual possession* by the conqueror does not confer a right of alienation, which, after the conqueror has departed, will enure to oust the original owner, unless such a result has formed part of the stipulations of a Treaty or been ratified by some public act of the state.

DXLIII. It is upon this principle that the Courts of the United States of North America have determined that grants of territory made by British Governors after the Declaration of Independence by the Americans are invalid.

In the case of a grant of land lying between the *Mississippi and the Chatahouchee rivers, made after the Declaration, by the British Governor of Florida, Justice Johnson said:— [*683]

"Two questions here occur; first, whether this separation had taken effect by any valid act; and secondly, if it had, whether it made any difference in the case upon international principles.

"On both these points we are of opinion that the law is against the validity of this grant. It is true that the power of the Crown was at that time admitted to be very absolute over the limits of the royal provinces; but there is no reason to believe that it had ever been exercised by any means less solemn and notorious than a public proclamation. And although the instrument by which Georgia claimed an extension of her limits to the northern boundary of that territory was of no more authority or solemnity than that by which it was supposed to have been taken from her, it was otherwise with South Carolina. Her territory had been extended to that limit by a solemn grant from the Crown, to the lords proprietors, from whom, in fact, she had wrested it by a revolution, even before the rights of the proprietors had been bought out by the Crown.

"But this is not the material fact in the case; it is this, that this limit was claimed and asserted by both of those states in the Declaration of Independence, and the right to it was established by the most solemn of all International Acts, the Treaty of Peace. It has never been admitted by the United States that they acquired anything by way of *cession* from Great Britain by that Treaty. It has been viewed only as *a recognition of pre-existing rights*, and on that principle, the soil and sovereignty within their acknowledged limits were as much theirs at the Declaration of Independence as at this hour. By reference to the Treaty, it will be found that it amounts to a simple recognition of the independence and the limits of the United States, without any language purporting a cession

(*d*) Grotius, Illustr. iii. p. 308, n. (*m*).

(*e*) L. iii. c. vi. s. 2, n. 4.

[*684] *or relinquishment of right on the part of Great Britain. In the last article of the Treaty of Ghent, will be found a provision respecting grants of land made in the islands then in dispute between the two States, which affords an illustration of this doctrine. By that article, a stipulation is made in favour of grants *before the War*, but none for those which were made *during the War;* and such is unquestionably the Law of Nations. *War is a suit prosecuted by the sword;* and where the question to be decided is one of original claim to territory, grants of soil made *flagrante bello* by the party that fails, can only derive validity from Treaty stipulations. It is not necessary here to consider the rights of the conqueror in the case of *actual conquest*, since the views previously presented put the acquisition of such rights out of this case."(*f*)

DXLIV. This doctrine therefore of the necessity of an *actual possession*, as a foundation for the rights incident to an *occupatio bellica*, finds its principal application with respect to (1.) *movables*, and to (2.) *incorporeal things or rights.* The former may be alienated by the conqueror, who has actual possession of them, and are not subject, as we have seen,(*g*) to *Postliminium.* The latter raises a question as to the power of the conqueror to alienate *incorporeal things or rights*, which is one of no mean difficulty, and which, indeed, ranks among the most remarkable and arduous subjects both of Public and of International Jurisprudence.

It will be necessary to consider the

(I.) *Theory of International Law*, and—

(II.) *The Practice of States*, upon this important subject.

[*685]

*CHAPTER IV.

THE THEORY OF INTERNATIONAL LAW AS TO THE POWER OF THE CONQUEROR, AND OF THE SOVEREIGN DE FACTO, OVER INCORPOREAL THINGS.

DXLVII. As to *the theory of International Law.*

An *occupation* of *Incorporeal* Things or Rights has been truly said(*a*) to be what is technically termed *contradictio in adjecto.* Incorporeal Things or Rights belong to the class described by Seneca "quæ nec visu, nec tactu, nec alio sensu comprehenduntur."(*b*) They cannot in themselves be the subjects of actual possession; they are not external things on which the Conqueror can lay his armed hand. They are Rights which exist in mental apprehension(*c*) as connected with a given subject to which they are attached, and with a material object upon which they

(*f*) Harcourt v. Gaillard, 7 Curtis's (Amer.) Rep., p. 332.

(*g*) Vide ante, Ch. VI. pp. 502-4.

(*a*) Pfeiffer, Das Recht der Kriegseroberung in Beziehung auf Staatscapitalien. Cassel, 1823-41.

(*b*) In Epistolis, n. 58, s. 13.

(*c*) "Quæ non sunt, sed tamen intelliguntur."—Cicero, Topica, c. 5.

can be exercised. Therefore the Roman Law philosophically said, "ipsum *jus obligationis* incorporale est;"(*d*) and again, "nec *possideri* videtur jus incorporale."(*e*)

It is therefore only by the actual possession of the subject to which they adhere that they can be *occupied* by the Conqueror,(*f*) or, as a learned jurist has happily expressed it, "mediantibus corporibus quibus inhærent occupari possunt."(*g*)

*If the conqueror, therefore, possess himself of the *corporeal thing* to which the *incorporeal right* is attached, he possesses himself of both. [*686]

The Roman Law furnishes a strong analogy in the instance of *servitutes.*(*h*)

These *servitutes*, when attached to real property, could only be acquired by the acquisition of the property itself; the *servitus* could not be acquired by *usucapio*(*i*) unless simultaneously with land to which it was attached. Now it has been said that immovable property cannot be permanently alienated by the conqueror without the confirmation of a subsequent treaty, or of some public act of the state.

DXLVI. But a question of greater difficulty presents itself in the case of an *incorporeal thing* attached not to a *corporeal thing* but to a *person.*

Does the capture of the *person* carry with it the possession of his *incorporeal* rights? The language of some great jurists is vague upon this subject: thus Grotius says, "Verum est, incorporalia belli jure, non primò ac per se adquiri, sed, *mediâ personâ*, cujus ea fuerunt;"(*k*) and Cocceius, "Res incorporales sunt, ad quarum substantiam corpus non pertinet, et vel *personis* insunt vel rebus, quibus proinde captis, simul jura illa inhærentia capta censentur."(*l*)

But it is well said by the erudite Pfeiffer,(*m*) whose work may be said to exhaust the learning upon this subject, that neither Grotius nor Cocceius appear to have sufficiently considered the essential distinction between Rights inherent in a *thing* and Rights attached to a *person.* In the latter case there is not the presence of the corporeal medium through which the Right accrues; a free man can neither be himself the subject of possession, nor be the medium through *which a thing, in itself incapable of actual possession, can be acquired. [*687]

Man, as the subject of rights, cannot be compared to a thing;(*n*) his rights do not, so to speak, hang upon him as they hang upon a piece of land; they rather proceed from him; they constitute his intellectual or spiritual property, which cannot by the agency of what Grotius calls a *nudum factum*, be separated, without his consent, from his person.(*o*)

(*d*) Dig., i. t. viii. 1, de Divisione Rerum et Qualitate.

(*e*) Ibid., xli. t. iii. 4, s. 27, de Usurpationibus et Usucapionibus. Ibid., xli. t. ii. 3, *de adquirenda vel amittenda Possessione.*

(*f*) "Incorporalia omnino tenentur *cum re cui cohærent.*"—Grot. Illustr. iii. c. viii. s. 4, n. *v.*

(*g*) Brunleger, Diss. de Occupatione Bellica. Argent, 1702, p. 38; cited by Pfeiffer, p. 44. (*h*) Vide ante, Vol. I. pp. 304-6. (*i*) Ib., pp. 206-8.

(*k*) L. iii. c. vii. s. 4, c. viii. s. 2. (*l*) iii. c. vii. s. 4. (*m*) P. 47.

(*n*) Vide ante, Vol. I. p. 316. Pfeiffer, ubi supra, p. 51.

(*o*) "Jura quæ personæ competunt in aliam personam, cum non nisi hujus consensu

The *jura obilgationis* especially consist in personal relations, binding, so to speak, at one end the obligor, at the other the obligee; they therefore consist in something external, which cannot be taken possession of by the mere seizure of the physical person of the obligor. Therefore, when a person, to whom certain rights belong, is captured by an enemy, such capture gives the captor only the corporeal and actual things in the possession of his prisoner. The case of the capture of a slave might at one time, perhaps, have given rise to different considerations, but that is an *occupatio* not to be recognized by modern International Law.(*p*)

The possession of the creditor's person does not give a *jus exigendi* of his debts. The doctrine on the subject is clearly stated by Burlamaqui: "À l'égard des droits personels sur les choses il ne suffit pas de s'être saisi de la personne de l'ennemi pour avoir acquis tous ces fiers, *à moins qu'on ne j'empare en effet de ces biens mêmes dans l'occasion*:"(*q*) and so Puffendorf, "Si civis ab hoste captus fuerit, bona istius, quæ simul capta non fuerunt, non adquiruntur capienti, sed ad eum perveniunt, quem leges
[*688] *civiles ad successionem vocabant, si iste naturali morte functus est." This latter proposition is, of course, one of Municipal and not International Law.) "Quod si autem," he continues, "*simul cum personâ hostis ipsius quoque bona ceperit,* sufficit ipsi ad dominium rerum captorum titulus captionis bellicæ, nec opus est ut istud dominium demum arcessat ex personâ prioris domini simul capti: adeoque perinde est quantum ad jus captoris in res captos sive dominum simul ceperit sive non."(*r*) The learned Hertius supports, in his commentary on Puffendorf, this position; it is impugned, indeed, by Barbeyrac,(*s*) but upon the ground that the prisoner may be made a slave, and that the possession of a slave is the possession of all that belongs to him,—in fact is the possession of a thing rather than of a person,—a doctrine happily exploded from the code of International Jurisprudence.

DXLVII. It is then the necessary conclusion from the premises which have been laid down, that *Incorporeal* Things, such as debts, do not accrue to the Conqueror as a consequence of his possession of the person who is entitled to them.

DXLVIII. Do they accrue to him from his possession of the instruments or documents which contain the legal statement of the obligation of the obligor, which are, so to speak, the title deeds of the obligee?(*t*) If part of the booty of the Conqueror be a promissory note, can he put

sint quæsita (qui consensus non promiscuè quemlibet spectavit, sed certum duntaxat hominem,) haud quidquam simul adquisita intelligentur, utut persona, cui ista competebant, in hostium manus pervenerit."—Puffendorf, de Jure Nat. et Gent., l. viii. c. vi. s. 22.

(*p*) Pfeiffer, pp. 52, 53.

(*q*) Principe de Droit de la Nat. et des Gens., P. iv. ch. vii. s. 14.

(*r*) De Jure Nat. et Gent., l. viii. c. vi. s. 22.

(*s*) "Car aujourd'hui même dans les pays ou l'on fait des esclaves ceux que l'on prend, on acquiest, comme autrefois, avec la personne, tous ces biens, de quelque nature qu'ils soient, au nombre desquels sont les dettes actives, quelque fondées qu'elles soient sur un contract."—See Barbeyrac's Transl. of Puf., n. 1, to s. xix. l. viii. c. vi.

(*t*) Pfeiffer, p. 55.

himself in the place of the promisee, and exact the debt from the promisor?

Some jurists have answered this question in the affirmative; but in so doing they appear to have been misled by *the analogies of the Roman Law.(*u*) According to that law the testator who bequeathed the promissory note bequeathed the money which it promised. [*689] The person who gave up a promissory note signed by the testator to his heir released the testator's representative from the payment of the money due by the testator. Acting upon this analogy, some jurists have said, "Quod *chirographo* occupato etiam debitum occupatum sit."(*x*) But in the case both of the testator and the creditor the analogy fails.

There is in both cases an intention on the part of the person entitled to the money to transfer his right to another, and the bequest or donation of the instrument is the bequest or donation of the *proof* of his right. No other construction can be put upon the act. In neither case is the *res ipsa* parted with; but it is the possession of the *res ipsa* which is necessary to found the title of the Conqueror. "Regulam (says a learned civilian) quod res ex hostibus captæ capientium fiant, hic applicari non posse, cum *res debita* nondum sit occupata, liquet; nec obstat 1, 59, D. de legat III., nam ab actu benefico ad occupationem hostilem male infertur, si quis enim chirographum tertio vel ipsi debitori leget, tum merito jus suum transtulisse vel *exstinxisse præsumitur, cum alias nihil actum foret, quale interpretandi genus absurdum [*690] est."(*y*)

And another civilian says, "Quæritur, si miles in bello chirographum debitoris occupaverit, an ipsi statim jus, debitum exigendi et solutum accipiendi, adquiratur? Respondetur *negativè*, quia tantum consetur adquisitum, quantum occupatum, chirographo autem occupato, non statim est occupatum jus debitum exigendi, quod *personæ* adhæret et per chirographum tantum *probatur*."(*z*)

In confirmation of these positions it may be observed, that the creditor may recover his debt though these instruments be lost or destroyed;

(*u*) "Eum, qui *chirographum* legat; *debitum* legare, non solum tabulas, argumento est venditio; nam cum *chirographa* veneunt, *nomen* venisse videtur."—Dig. xxx. t. i. s. 44, § 5.

"Qui *chirographum* legat, non tantum de tabulis cogitat, sed etiam de *actionibus*, quarum probatio tabulis continetur. Appellatione enim *chirographi* uti nos pro *ipsis actionibus*, palam est, quum venditis *chirographis* intelligamus *nomen* venisse."—Dig. xxxii. t. i. s. 59.

"Si ita cui legatum esset: "Si tabulas chirographi mei heredi meo reddiderit, *heres meus ei decem dato*, *hujusmodi* conditio hanc vim habet, si heredem meum debito *liberaverit*."—Dig. xxx. t. i. s. 84, § 7.

"Si debitori meo reddiderim *cautionem*, videtur inter nos convenisse, *ne peterem* profuturamque ei conventionis exceptionem placuit."—Dig. ii. t. xiv. s. 2, § 2.

(*x*) Brunleger, in Dissert. cit., v. p. 39, cited by Pfeiffer, p. 57.

(*y*) Titius in Observat. ad Lauterbach, Observat. 1438, cited by Pfeiffer, p. 58.

(*z*) Lauterbach, Colleg. Pandect., lib. xlvi. t. iii. 16, cited by Pfeiffer, p. 60. Lauterbach cites Dig. xx. t. i. § 1. De Pignoribus, &c.: "Conventio generalis in pignore dando bonorum vel postea quæsitorum recepta est; in speciem autem alienæ rei collatâ conventione, si non fuerit ei, qui pignus debat, debita, postea debitori dominio quæsito, difficilius creditori, qui non ignoravit alienum, utilis actio dabitur; sed facilior erit possidenti retentio."

because they are not the debt itself, but one means, and not the only means, under all circumstances, of proving that it exists.

Incorporeal Rights, therefore, do not accrue to the Conqueror from the fact of his having possessed himself of the documents relating to those rights, and it is not competent to him to bestow upon or transfer to another what he has not physically taken possession of himself.

DXLIX. It remains to apply these general principles to the particular case of the seizure and confiscation by the Conqueror of the *public debts* of the conquered country.

In attempting the solution of this vexed question, it is very necessary to bear in mind the distinction already alluded to, between the mere Conqueror and the established Regent of a country.

[*691] *It is the opinion of the best jurists, fortified by reason and practice, that, until a title indicating permanent possession has been superadded to the temporary title of the sword, no valid alienation of *immovable* property can be made by the Conqueror.(*a*)

In effecting the change from conquest to established government, time(*b*) is of course a principal agent; but the recognition of such government by a Treaty of Peace with other States is the most usual and unquestionable evidence. This change, however, may also be effected by the submission of the conquered people to the new government, indicated, either by some public act of the state, or by the fact itself, evidenced by the tranquillity of the people, their obedience to the laws, and, above, all, by the quiet and regular administration of justice in the proper civil tribunals.

It is manifest that the conquest which is to be the foundation of empire must not be the mere conquest of a capital (*victoria particularis,*) but of a country (*victoria universalis.*)

"Quoniam illi," says Wolff,(*c*) "quos gens sua adversus vim hostilem defendere nequit; non amplius eidem obligantur et imperium ejusdem in ipsos extinguitur, jure se subiicere possunt imperio hostis et ejus fieri cives. Victus victoris imperio jure se subiicit, *sive id fiat pacto, sive ipso* [*692] **facto,* quatenus eidem non resistit, seu animum resistendi deponit vel deponere cogitur."

Does the same change—the same establishment of sovereignty (*imperium*) upon the foundation of conquest—which empowers the new Sovereign to alienate immoveable property, empower him also to deal with the public credits and debts?

(*a*) "Il faut bien prendre garde, que la guerre ou la conquête, considerée en elle même, *n'est pas* proprement *la cause* de cet acquisition; elle n'est pas la source ou l'origine immédiate de la souveraineté, c'est toujours le consentement du peuple ou exprès ou tacite; sans ce consentement l'etat de guerre subsiste toujours; la guerre n'est donc, à proprement parler, que *l'occasion* de l'acquisition de la souveraineté."—Burlamaqui, p. iv. ch. viii. s. 2.

"Si les peuples, traités non plus en ennemis, mais *en vrais sujets,* se sont soumis à un gouvernement légitime, ils relevent désormais d'un nouveau souverain, ou ils sont incorporés à l'état conquérant, ils en font partie, ils suivent sa destinée;" but a contrary result follows, "si son vainqueur n'a point quitté l'épée de conquérant, pour prendre la sceptre d'un souverain équitable et pacifique."—Vattel, l. iii. c. xiv. s. 213.

(*b*) Vide ante, Vol. I. p. 272.

(*c*) Jus Gentium, s. 868.

"Potest *imperium victoria adquiri*," Grotius says, "ut est in rege aut imperante, et *tunc ejus jus succeditur*."(d) The conqueror succeeds, according to the commentary of Cocceius, "in *omne id* quod publici juris seu populi est."(e)

Like the lawful heir, he has succeeded to the *universum jus*. And therefore Grotius argues, "Res universitatis eorum fiunt qui sibi subjiciunt universitatem; ergo *et incorporalia jura* quæ universitatis fuerant fient victoris quatenus velit;"(i) or, as it is still more forcibly stated by Conceius, "Si hostis *jure ultimæ victoriæ imperium perpetuum* nactus est, *publica nomina*, ut omnia jura civitatis publica, sibi adquirit quæ proinde aliis donare potest."(g)

This is to be understood, however, of an *imperium* established over the *whole* state, and not over a particular *part* of it. Upon this point the Private Law of the Romans furnishes a striking analogy. By that law the possessor of a *whole* building acquired, by reason of this posession, a *prescriptive* right over the immovable appurtenances of it; but if any of these were separated from the building itself, then the fact of the former possession of the *whole* could not be used in aid of the title to the *part*, but a new *prescription* was invoked, adapted to the character of the severed part.(h)

*"If," says Savigny, in his great work on the Law of Possession,(i) "I possess a carriage, in which is a wheel which has been [*693] *stolen*, and the defect in the original title to which, *therefore*, prescription does not heal, I may nevertheless acquire a valid title to the carriage as a whole, which will include the wheel as a part; but if I separate the wheel from the carriage, the original character of the part returns, and vitiates the title of its possession."

So if the *active debt* (*activum*) of the state be not locally within the *imperium* of the conquering ruler, he does not acquire a title by which he can dispose of it, much less can he do so if he have not an *imperium* over the whole state, and if by the exercise of a simple *jus victoris* he attempt to separate the *active debt*, not in his possession, from the state to which as a whole it is attached.

DL. It becomes necessary, therefore, for the due consideration of the question, whether the debts due to a state are subject to the *imperium* of the conquering ruler, to inquire *in what locality they are situated*.

They may be,

1. In the country which is actually taken possession of.
2. In an unconquered or neutral country.
3. In the country of the Conqueror.

DLI. (1.) If the debts due to a state(k) (*Staatscapitalien*) be actually

(d) L. iii. c. viii. 2, n. 3.

(e) H. Cocceii Grot. Illustr., t. iii. p. 192, prop. iv. S. Cocceii Introd. in Grot. Illustr., Diss. xii. s. 752.

(f) L. iii. c. viii. s. 4.

(g) De Jure Postlimin. in Pace et Amnestiâ, t. i. p. 1113, ss. 15, 16, cited by Pfeiffer, p. 88, n. r.

(h) Dig. xli. t. iii. 23, De Usurp. et Usucap.

(i) Recht des Besitzes, s. 22, (260.)

(k) Vattel says, (l. iii. c. v. s. 77,): "Au nombre des choses appartenantes à

situated in the country of which permanent possession is taken, and over which an *imperium* is exercised, it is clear that if these debts are actually collected from the debtors, they fall within the *imperium* of the Conqueror. [*694] *If they are of the nature of hypothecations (*jura realia, actiones reales*) attached to particular portions of conquered land, and are called in and brought within the possession of the Conqueror, he may make a valid disposition of them.

DLII. (2.) If the debts due to the state be situated not in the conquered country, but either in an unconquered or in a neutral country, there is no doubt that they are not within the *imperium* of the Conqueror. There cannot be a more unquestionable maxim of International Law. "Quodsi ergo," Wolff says, "belligerator in territorio pacato jus quoddam sibi arrogaret in res hostiles, id fieret contra jus domini territorii, consequenter eidem faceret id quod non licet."(*l*)

If, indeed, an actual seizure of enemy's funds did take place in a neutral territory, it must be admitted that these funds would be actually acquired and might be alienated by the Conqueror, because it is the *nudum factum* upon which the *occupatio bellica* is founded. It is said by a civilian(*m*) of great learning upon this point, "Quo autem loco res hostium deprehendantur, nihil interest, etiamsi in territorio tertii vel confœderati. Dominus tamen territorii prohibere potest, ne quid hostiliter ibi fiat, et si contra hanc prohibitionem aliquid factum sit, de eo, tanquam de delicto, poscere potest, ut sibi satisfiat. Ceterum *captum capientis fit*, quia prohibitio conditionem rei hostilis non mutat."(*n*)

DLIII. The general rule, however, remains, that neither *movable* nor *immovable*, *corporeal* nor *incorporeal property* situate within or to [*695] be extracted from a *neutral* or an **unconquered* land, can be considered as among the acquisitions of the Conqueror.

As to enemy's property situate in the territory of an *ally*—it seems difficult to distinguish between this case and the case of property found in the territory of the Conqueror, inasmuch as allies, for the purposes of war, are considered, as has been shown,(*o*) to be one state. No seizure of property in such locality could, however, take place without the full consent of the ally.

DLIV. (3.) If the debts due to the enemy state be situate in the Conqueror's own country, they cannot be acquired upon the principle on which debts in the conquered country are seized; they are not a part of

l'ennemi sont les choses incorporelles, tous ces droits, noms et actions;" and he adds, "La guerre nous donne sur les sommes d'argent que des *nations neutres* pourraient devoir à notre ennemi, les mêmes droits qu'elle peut nous donner sur ses autres biens;" but he does not mean that such money can be lawfully acquired without the consent of the neutral state; in giving which consent she would lose her character of neutrality.

(*l*) Cap. vii. s. 833.

(*m*) Lauterbach, Colleg. Pandect., lib. xlix. t. xv. s. 7, cited by Pfeiffer, p. 109.

(*n*) Founding himself upon this analogy, "Nec interest, quod ad feras bestias et volucres utrum in *suo fundo* quisque capiat, an in *alieno*. Planè, qui in alienum fundum ingreditur venandi aut aucupandi gratiâ, potest a domino, si is præviderit, *prohibere ne ingrediatur*. Quicquid autem eorum *ceperis*, eousque *tuum esse* intelligitur, donec tuâ custodiâ coërcetur."—Inst. l. ii. t. i. s. 12; Dig. xli. t. i. s. 3, § 1.

(*o*) Vide ante, pp. 113, 114.

the *bellica occupatio*, they are not captured simultaneously with the land in which they are situate, but they are acquired on the principle that, when war has broken out, a belligerent has a right to compel his own subjects to pay to their own state the debts due from them to the enemy state. Bynkershoek discusses this subject in one of his celebrated "*Quæstiones Juris Publici*."(*p*) He asks the question, "Hostium actiones et credita quæ *apud nos* invenirentur an exorto bello rectè publicentur?" He answers the question in the affirmative; and though, in the beginning of the chapter, he speaks somewhat loosely, as if the foundation of the right to confiscate them accrued upon the principle that, after the declaration of war, enemy's property in an enemy's country necessarily, and without an act, changed owners, towards the end of the chapter he shows that such was not his meaning, but that there must be an actual possession of the subject of the enemy's obligation before it can be dealt with as Conqueror's booty. No writer has more clearly laid down the true principles of the law upon this question: "Quod dixi," he says, "de actionibus rectè publicandis, *ita demum obtinet*, si, quod subditi nostri hostibus nostris debent, princeps a *subditis suis *reverà exegerit*. Si exegerit, rectè solutum est, si *non exegerit*, [*696] pace factâ reviviscit jus pristinum creditoris, quia occupatio, quæ bello fit, magis in *facto*, quam in potestate juris, consistit. Nomina igitur *non exacta* tempore belli quodammodo intermori videntur, sed per pacem, genere quodam postliminii, ad priorem dominum reverti. Secundum hæc inter gentes ferè convenit, ut, nominibus bello publicatis, pace deinde factâ, exacta censeantur periisse et maneant extincta, *non exacta* autem reviviscant et restituantur veris creditoribus."

DLV. We have seen when and under what circumstances the right of the Conqueror may be so exercised as to acquire a title to *possess* and to *alienate* both *immovable* and *incorporeal* property. Two conditions, we have seen, are requisite—the Conqueror must have become Regent of the country, and he must have reduced into his actual possession the property; in other words, the tide of conquest must not only have overflowed the land and then retreated, but, after its ebb, the fabric of a *de facto* regular government must have been established upon the soil which the inundation has ceased to cover

DLVI. But here another question arises. Assuming that the conquest has subsided into government, the Conqueror been changed into the Regent, and yet that after a lapse of time the former Sovereign and the former Government return, and having returned, claim, at the hands of their debtor, the payment of the debt, which he has discharged, during the interregnum, to the Sovereign or Government *de facto*, does it follow that, if this Sovereign and Government had the right to exact the debt, it was the debtor's duty to pay it? are the two propositions convertible? Or, if so, may not the original creditor demand a second payment?

Bynkershoek, as we have just seen, says that the debt is satisfied and extinct. And such is unquestionably the opinion both of the greater

(*p*) L. i. c. vii.

number and of the most able jurists; such is the conclusion from many analogies of the Roman Law; such is the language of Treaties, which
[*697] latter are about to be *considered under the head of International Practice on this subject.

DLVII. But in order to arrive at this conclusion of law respecting the extinction of the debt paid by the state debtor to the executive authority *de facto* of the state, founded upon conquest, certain conditions are required by reason, justice, practice, and the analogies of positive, especially Roman, Law.

These conditions are as follows :(*q*)—

I. As a general rule, the public authority to which the debt is paid, and from which a receipt is taken, should be that to which the country is actually subject at the time of the payment; it must, as has been said, be the established authority of a Regent grafted upon the bare right of the Conqueror. There can be no doubt, therefore, as to the legality of the payment, if the legitimate sovereign has by a treaty, either before or after the payment, recognized the Government de facto to which the payment is made, or if the legitimate Sovereign has assented, either by a declaration expressed or implied upon the subject, or by treaty with some tnird Power, to any special act of the *de facto* Government.

II. If, however, the payment be made to a mere Conqueror, it may nevertheless be valid; but then a burden of proof lies upon the debtor to show—

1. That the sum was actually paid; for an acquittance or a receipt, without actual payment, is no bar to the demand of the original creditor.

2. That it was due at the very time that it was paid.

[*698] 3. That the payment had not been delayed by a *mora*(*r*) *on the part of the debtor, which had thus operated to defeat the claim of the original creditor.

4. That the payment had been compulsory,—the effect of a *vis major* upon the debtor,—not necessarily extorted by the use of physical force, but paid under an order, the disobedience to which was threatened with punishment.

The debtor, therefore, must either have been a subject of the Conqueror, or a resident within the country subject to his military power. The

(*q*) Pfeiffer, pp. 161-4. Klüber, ss. 258, 259.

(*r*) J. Voet speaks very clearly upon this matter: "Illud circa mercedis præstationem prætermittendum non est, cogendos haud esse prædiorum conductores ad mercedem locatori iterato solvendam, si eam *hostibus*, eâ regione ad tempus potitis, *bonâ fide* ac *sine collusione* solvere *compulsi* sint, nec ante hostilem occupationem *in morâ solvendi* fuerint *ex more regionis*." Nor (he says) does the analogy of the Roman Law respecting the invalidity of payment made to a robber affect the principle, "cum prædo illic accipiatur pro malæ fidei possessore, qui privatus est, ac neque vi coegit ad solvendum, neque, si vi compulisset, ullo id fecisset jure; contrà, quàm est in hostibus, qui belli jure ex jure gentium muniti, et per hoc à prædonibus etiam publicis distincti sunt."—L. xix. t. ii. s. 28.

"Quod te mihi dare oporteat, si id postea perierit, quam per te factum erit, quo minus id mihi dares, tuum fore id detrimentum constat."—Dig. xii. t. i. s. 5, (De Reb. Cred.) "Debitoribus hostium, civibus suis, ut *veniente die solutionis* solvant sibi, imperare potest."—Wolff, c. vii. s. 840. "Le souverain peut donc confisquer les dettes de cette nature (that is, debts due from his subjects to the enemy,) *si le terme du payement tombe au temps de la guerre*."—Vattel, l. iii. c. v. s. 77.

dweller in a land not subject to this powercannot plead compulsion as a justification for paying the debt to a person whom he knew not to be his creditor.

5. That the constitutional law of the state recognized the payment to the conqueror as valid.

It is not a necessary condition, but it is a substantive defence against the original creditor, if the money paid has been applied to his benefit; thus, in the case of a state creditor, if the money has been applied to the benefit of the state, if there has been what civilians term a *versio in rem.*

DLVIII. It is a corollary to this proposition, that any money expended for the benefit of the creditor to preserve property which would otherwise perish (*res alias peritura*) must be deducted from the principal debt. The original *owner is, on the same principle, bound to indemnify the intermediate owner for any improvements which have [*699] been made in the recovered property, according to the maxim of jurisprudence, "Petitor ex alienâ jacturâ lucrum facere non debet."(*s*)

DLIX. There is a means of adjusting all difficulties, and of healing all controversies which might otherwise arise at the return of peace, on the subject of transactions which have taken place more or less under the influence of the enemy during the war: this means is the public declaration of an *amnesty*, which generally does form part of the treaty which concludes the war, and which always ought to do so. It is of course understood that the state against whom the amnesty is to be urged has been a party to the treaty.

The general effect of an amnesty is accurately stated by Cocceius in the following terms: "Post amnestiam nec debitor noster, cujus, cum in hostium potestate esset, debitum publicatum ab hoste vel remissum est, ampliùs conveniri potest; nec vice versâ creditor, cui hostis, cum in ejus potestate esset, nomen abstulit, id post amnestiam repetet, adeo ut, licet ipse debitor, qui ab hostium partibus est, compulerit eum, ut accepto tulerit, non tamen conveniri possit, quia creditor allegare injuriam acceptilationis *propter amnestiam* non potest. At, si creditor sit e gente pacatâ, non obstante ullà amnestiâ is debitum petit, quia pactio amnestiæ hostes tantum, inter quos contrahitur, eorumque subditos, non autem tertium populum, obligat."(*t*)

---

*CHAPTER V. [*700]

INTERNATIONAL PRACTICE AS TO THE POWER OF THE CONQUEROR AND THE SOVEREIGN DE FACTO, OVER INCORPOREAL THINGS.

DLX. Having considered the *theory* of International Jurisprudence, it remains to inquire(*a*) what has been the *practice* of states upon the

(*s*) Dig. v. t. iii. 31, de Hered Petitione.
(*t*) H. Cocceii, Diss. de Postliminio, sect. v. §§ 10, 11.
(*a*) Vide ante, p. 697; and Vol. I. p. 41.

subject which must be evidenced by the (I.) history of their public Acts and (II.) Treaties.(*b*)

DLXI. I. With respect to the former, it is to be observed, that they include acts between states, and acts between a state and the individuals of another state.

The historical event,(*c*) which has furnished the text for almost every commentator upon this subject, happened a very long while ago, and the record of it has been strangely and incidentally preserved.

We learn from the Oratorical Institutes of Quintilian,(*d*) that after the conquest of Thebes, Alexander the Great found documents in which [*701] the Thessalians acknowledged *themselves to have borrowed an hundred talents from the Thebans. The Thessalians had been allies of Alexander, and in return for their aid he *gave* them the documents which contained the acknowledgment of their debt. The Thebans nevertheless being subsequently reinstated in the possession of their state by Cassander, demanded payment of their debt from the Thessalians.

It was admitted on all hands that the hundred talents had been borrowed and not been repaid: the question of law depended upon the validity of the *gift* by Alexander.

The cause was heard before the great International Tribunal of Greece, the Amphictyonic Council. What the decision was we are not told; but it is inferred from Quintilian's silence that it was in favour of the Thessalians.(*e*) He says "Et prima quidem actio facilis ac favorabilis repetentium jure, quod vi sit ablatum, sed hinc aspera et vehemens quæstio exoritur de jure belli; dicentibus Thessalis, hoc regna, populos, fines gentium atque urbium contineri." But, says the great preceptor of oratory, "inveniendum contra est quo distet hæc causa "à ceteris, quæ in potestatem victoris venirent."(*f*) And he observes, that various distinctions may be taken.

(*b*) Vide ante, Vol. I. pp. 43-58. Pfeiffer, p. 165, has some very good remarks on the value of *historical* evidence of International *Practice.*

(*c*) "Sit exempli gratiâ proposita controversia, quæ minimè communes cum aliis quæstiones habet."—Quintil. vide infra.

(*d*) V. 10. (ed. Burman, 1720, p. 431,): "Cum Thebas evertisset Alexander, invenit tabulas, quibus centum talenta mutua Thessalis dedisse Thebanos continebatur. Has, quia usus erat commilitio Thessalorum, donavit his ultro. Postea restituti a Cassandro Thebani reposcunt Thessalos. Apud Amphictyonas agitur. Centum talenta et credidisse eos constat et non recepisse. Lis omnis ex eo, quod Alexander ea Thessalis donasse dicitur, pendet."

(*e*) Ærodius says: "Placuit Thessalos petitione liberari. Ita enim arbitror Amphictyones judicâsse postquam id a Quintiliano est prætermissum."—Rerum Judicatarum Pandectæ, l. ii. tit. ii. c. i., cited by Pfeiffer, p. 172, note *u*.

(*f*) Dicamus in primis, in eo, quod in judicium deduci potest, nihil valere jus belli; nec armis erepta, nisi armis posse retineri. Itaque, ubi illa valeant, *non esse judicem: ubi judex sit, illa nihil valere.* Hoc inveniendum est, ut adhiberi possit argumentum. *Ideo captivos, si in patriam suam redierint, liberos esse, quia bello parta non nisi eadem vi possideantur.* Proprium est ut illud caussæ, quod Amphictyones judicant; ut alia apud centumviros, alia apud privatum judicem in iisdem quæstionibus ratio sit. Tum secundo gradu, non potuisse donari a victore *jus*, quia id demum sit ejus, *quod ipse teneat*, jus autem, quod sit incorporale, apprehendi manu non posse; et aliam esse conditionem *heredis*, aliam *victoris*, quia ad illum *jus* ad hunc *res* transeat."

First, it might have been contended that the *jus belli* in a Court of Law could not be pleaded.

*Secondly, that a *right* (*jus*) could not be the subject of *gift* by a Conqueror; that he could only dispose of what he was actually seised or possessed (*quod ipse teneat.*) *Rights* (*jura*) devolved, indeed, upon a *civil heir*, but only *things themselves* (*res ipsæ,*) upon a *military Conqueror.*(*g*) [*702]

Again, that the title to a national debt (*jus publici crediti*) could not be disposed of while one member of the community survived; and other less important arguments by way of rhetorical exercitation, are suggested. To all of which, it may be observed, Puffendorf(*h*) suggests answers.

DLXII. The great majority of jurists, however, reject the suggestions of Quintilian, and support the supposed decision of the Amphictyons; but it must not be therefore concluded that they contravene the principles which were laid down, when the International Theory was considered, respecting the conditions which are necessary to establish the legality of such a transfer of such Incorporeal Property.

The jurists argue that Alexander had become so entire and absolute a master of Thebes,—the *heir* as it were and *universal successor* to a *defunct* and extinguished state,—that he was possessed of every thing and right appertaining to that city: and on the other hand, those who contend against *the validity of the gift, do so on the ground that the absolute and entire dominion over the universal successorship to Thebes had not accrued to Alexander.(*i*) [*703]

(*g*) Grotius, as has been already observed, is of opinion that possession of the *person* carries with it possession of his *rights*. He says, l. iii. c. viii. s. iv: "Ergo et incorporalia jura, quæ universitatis fuerant, fient victoris quatenus velit. Sic Albâ victâ, quæ Albanorum jura fuerant sibi vindicârunt Romani. Unde sequitur omnino liberatos Thessalos obligatione centum talentorum, qnam summam cum ipsi Thebanis deberent, Alexander Magnus Thebarum dominus factus jure victoriæ ipsis donaverat; neque rerum quod pro Thebanis apud Quintilianum adfertur, id demum victoria esse quod ipse teneat; jus quod sit incorporale apprehendi manu non posse; aliam conditionem esse heredis, aliam victoris, quia ad illum jus, ad hunc res transeat. Nam qui dominus est personarum, idem et rerum est, et juris omnis quod personis competit. Qui possidetur non possidet sibi, nec in potestate habet qui non est suæ potestatis."

(*h*) Jus. Nat. et Gent., l. viii. c. vi. p. 24.

(*i*) "Alexander videri Thebanorum *universalis successor* potuit, quoniam eversæ Thebæ et itaque mortem passæ erant. Fuit Alexander princeps ac dominus non *urbis* modo, sed et *civitatis*, quam redegerat sub se universam."—Alb. Gentilis, de Jure Belli, l. iii. c. v.

"Thebæ interierunt, adeoque et jura ei inhærentia; jure victoriæ *omne jus civitatis* Thebæ in victorem transiit; Thebani non amplius sui juris erant omne eorum jus in victorem transiit; *dissolutâ civitate* eundem populum non censeri, nec postliminio restitui potuit; sed ex novâ gratiâ victoris populus factus est."—Cocceii Grotius Illustratus, t. iii. pp. 202, 236, 237.

"Lorsqu' Alexandre fit présent aux Thessaliens de la somme qu'ils devaient aux Thébains, il étoit *maître absolu* de la republique de Thébes, dont il détruisit la ville et fit vendre les habitants."—Vattel, l. iii. c. xiv. s. 212.

"Quoniam Alexander *non universalis* et juris *successor* est, sicuti *heres* aut *bonorum possessor* sed *particularis* et rerum singularum, ut emtor aut donatarius, quia victores earum demum rerum domini sunt jure belli, quæ manu capi possunt."—Hotman, Quæst. Illustr. Qu. 5, cited by Pfeiffer, p. 180.

"Alle Meinungsverschiedenheit beschränkt sich auf die Vertheilung des historischen Stoffes."—Pfeiffer p. 180.

DLXIII. The next classical example is that furnished, about a hundred years later, by the war of Antiochus, King of Syria, with the Romans. The Rhodians were the allies of the Romans, but the vicinity of their island to the Syrian coast caused a great commercial intercourse between them and Syria; and when the Rhodian was united to the Roman fleet, it might have been supposed that Antiochus would have resorted, as one means of defence, to the confiscation of the Rhodian property, consisting of houses and debts, within the Syrian dominions. But the peace of 189, B. C. provided that the *status quo ante bellum* should be replaced, and especially that the houses of the Rhodians should be restored, what was due to them paid, and what had been confiscated made good to them.(*k*)

[*704] DLXIV. The Macedonian city Dyrrachium was frequently the *scene of the civil war between Cæsar and Pompey. The citizens appear to have inclined to Cæsar. He had remitted to them the payment of a debt which they owed to Caius Flavius, the friend of Decius Brutus. Cicero was the friend both of Dyrrachium(*l*) and Brutus. He appears to have been appealed to on behalf of Flavius.(*m*) The course which he took is, however, uncertain; but it is certain that Brutus, a statesman, and well versed in public law, considered the refusal of Dyrrachium to discharge the debt contrary to law. The jurists who have commented on this transaction have agreed in this opinion, but upon various grounds; partly, because in a civil war there could be no *occupatio*, properly speaking;(*n*) partly, because it was a private and not a public debt,(*o*)—(but this distinction is one of the refinements of modern International Law, and, indeed, rather appertains to comity than strict law,)—partly, for both these reasons together.(*p*) Pfeiffer points out that the *titulus imperii* under which Alexander acted was wanting to Cæsar, especially regard being had to the fact that the Dyrrachian debt was due to a private individual.(*q*)

DLXV. The first example of modern times occurs in the fourteenth century. A Fleming lent a Frenchman a thousand crowns; the time of payment arrived, the money was not paid. The Fleming sued the Frenchman in a French Court of Justice. The Frenchman contrived to protract the litigation until war broke out between Flanders and France.
[*705] The money was then paid by the debtor into *the French Treasury. After the peace the Fleming again demanded his debt: the Frenchman defended himself by alleging the payment to the Royal Treasury. The Fleming replied that the payment had been fraudulently delayed until the breaking out of the war; he was cast in his suit;(*r*)

(*k*) Polybii, Histor. Excerptæ Legationes, c. xxxv.

(*l*) Epist ad Atticum, l. iii. note 22; Ad familiares, l. xiv. note 1.

(*m*) Epist. ad Brutum, note 6.

(*n*) Grotius, l. iii. c. viii. s. 4, § 3: "Imitatus fuit factum Alexandri Cæsar, donato Dyrrachinisære alieno, quod nescio cui adversarum partium debuerant. ed hic objici poterat bellum Cæsaris, non ex eo esse genere de quo jus hoc gentium constitutum est."

(*o*) H. Cocceii, l. c., cited by Pfeiffer, p. 185.

(*p*) Ærodius, l. c., c. ii., cited by Pfeiffer, ib. (*q*) Pfeiffer, p. 185.

(*r*) By an *arrêt* in August, 1349.

but nevertheless, the Frenchman was condemned to pay back so much of the thousand crowns as he should be proved to have expended to his own benefit.

The decision is remarkable, as showing that, even under the circumstance of the debt having been paid to the Sovereign of the debtor, the Court of the same Sovereign considered that the debtor was only relieved to the extent of the sum *actually paid*. The fraudulent *mora* of the debt ought certainly to have been, though it does not appear to have been, the subject of judicial investigation.(*s*)

Cocceius,(*t*) it should be observed, has mistaken the date of this affair, placing it in the year 1554 instead of 1349.

DLXVI. Towards the close of the fifteenth century Pisa and Florence were at war. The Pisan government compelled, by threats of punishment, their subjects, who were debtors to Florentine subjects, to pay their debts into the Pisan Treasury. A Pisan debtor, who had so paid his debt, was nevertheless sued by his Florentine creditor for it; it was admitted that he had paid it under compulsion, having refused to do so as long as he was able.

Philip Decius, a Milanese jurist of the highest reputation, was called in to arbitrate or to adjudicate on the matter. *Decius*, in his *Consilia*, recites the premises, and concludes: "Ex quibus omnibus concludo et indubitanter existimo, quod Ludovicus(*u*) mediante tali solutione fuerit liberatus."(*x*)

*There are two other cases mentioned by Pfeiffer;(*y*) but in one of them the debtor and creditor were both subjects of the [*706] state which made the order for payment into the national treasury, and the creditor had gone over to the enemy. This latter case is narrated by Baldus de Perusio, and it is clearly founded on the doctrine of Public Law that the *Fiscus* is the heir of *confiscated* property: the application of the principle to a matter of International Law is therefore only by way of analogy.(*z*)

DLXVII. In the year 1495, Charles the Eighth of France overran Italy, and replaced for a moment the House of Anjou upon the throne of Naples. During his brief tenure of that kingdom the French King bestowed upon his adherents all that he could lay hands upon. Amongst other devices for enriching the Angevin party, that of calling in debts due to the state from the opposite faction was adopted. Many of these debtors paid honestly the full amount of their debt. Some tried to drive

(*s*) Paponius, Recueil d'Arrêts, notables des Cours Souveraines de France, l. v. t. vi. arr. 2.

(*t*) Diss. des Postlim., s. v. § 10.

(*u*) The Christian name of the debtor.

(*x*) Phil. Decii Consilia, c. xxv.

(*y*) P. 191.

(*z*) Baldus, Consilia, l. ii. c. cxxviii., is cited by Pfeiffer (p. 192,) as saying: "Debitor liberabitur sive coactus solverit sive sponte quia *in jus creditoris* fiscus *successerat*, et ideo fisco solvi debebat quia fiscus habeatur loco hæredis."—L. ii. C. ad l. Jul. de in Publ.

And Pfeiffer remarks that Baldus, in his lecture on Cod. l. xix., De Furtis, observes: "Si debitor est compulsus per viam juris, *priùs confiscato creditore*, tum certum est quod etiam antequam solveret, erat liberatus ab eo, quia *translata* erat in fiscum *obligatio*." See also Hugo Lehrbuch, Des Heutigen Römischen Rechts, s. 68, note 2.

a bargain to their advantage, paying only a portion of their debt, and obtaining a receipt for the whole. Some contrived to pay nothing, and obtain a written discharge from every thing. Four months afterwards, when the French King, with Angevins, was driven out, and Ferdinand, with the Arragonese, was restored, the question as to the validity of these payments and receipts was sharply contested. Among other jurists invoked to adjudicate or arbitrate upon it, was one *summæ auctoritatis*, [*707] named Matthæus *de Afflictis.(*a*) His conclusions on this important subject are here given in his own words:—"*Prima conclusio*, quod illi debitores regum de Arragoniâ, qui fuerunt in morâ solvendi dictis regibus pecuniam debitam in genere, et jussu regis Caroli et suorum officialium solverunt ipsis donatariis, *non sunt liberati*, et tenentur solvere dictis regibus, veris creditoribus. *Secunda conclusio* sit ista, quod illi debitores qui non fuerunt in morâ solvendi dictis creditoribus, sed jussi fuerunt ab officialibus regis Franciæ, quod solvant illis Gallis, virtute largitatis regis, et ipsi fecerunt, quidquid eis fuit possibile, ut non solverent, et realiter eis solverunt propter jussum pœnalem, et isti *sunt liberati*. *Tertia conclusio* sit ista, quod si debitor fuit in morâ, sed erat infra tempus purgandi moram, et infra illud tempus sit exactus ab illis Gallis jussu magistratûs, tunc solvendo Gallis perinde habetur, ac si nonesset in morâ, et sic *erit liberatus*. *Quarta conclusio* sit ista, quod debitor, qui solvit Gallis illam pecuniam debitam regibus de Arragoniâ virtute jussus magistratus, cui non potuit resistere, et pecuniam illam debitam post diem solutionis faciendæ erat solitum, quod ipsi debitores penes se retinebant pro expensis, occurentibus in administratione officii nomine regio, si ipsam pecuniam Gallis solverunt, *sunt liberati*, etiam quod fuerint in morâ. *Quinta conclusio* sit ista, quod illi debitores, qui solutionem probant per confessionem Gallorum publicam vel privatam, ita, quod non probant veram numerationem pecuniæ eis factam, *non sunt liberati*, sed debent solvere veris creditoribus, quantumcunque, ostenderint dictum jussum. *Sexta conclusio*, quod illi debitores, qui se concordaverunt, et non ostendunt veram solutionem in totum vel in partem, *non sunt liberati*. Exitus rei approbavit istas conclusiones."(*b*)

[*708]

*CHAPTER VI.

THE CASE OF THE DEBTS AND DOMAINS OF HESSE-CASSEL CONFISCATED OR ALIENATED BY NAPOLEON THE FIRST.

DLXVIII. The instance of the payments made to the first Napoleon by the debtors of the Prince of Hesse-Cassel furnished the last occasion, upon which these principles of International Law respecting the extinc-

(*a*) Decisiones Neopolitanæ Antiquæ et Novæ, Dec. 150.
(*b*) Matth. de Afflictis, Decisiones Neopolitanæ Antiquæ et Novæ, Dec. 150, Pfeiffer, pp. 196, 197.

tion of public debts by payment of them to a Conqueror were invoked for practical application. The case of the purchasers of the (1.) Debts, and of the (2.) Domains of Hesse-Cassel during the interval between 1807 and 1813 has, from the importance of the principles involved in its discussion, taken its place among the *causes célèbres* of Public and International Law.(*a*)

*DLXIX. First, as to the *Debts*. The war between France and Prussia in 1806 extended its consequences to the Elector of [*709] Hesse-Cassel,(*b*) though he had professedly abstained from interfering in it.

In October 1806 the French troops occupied the Electorate and drove out the Elector, upon the plea that his armed neutrality endangered the security of the French army.

Hesse-Cassel remained under the military government of France until the end of the year 1807, when the greater portion of it, Hanau and Catzenelnbogen alone excepted, was incorporated into the newly-formed kingdom of Westphalia. This result was a consequence of the Peace of Tilsit,(*c*) by which Russia and Prussia recognized Jerome Bonaparte as King of Westphalia, and agreed that the kingdom should be composed of certain provinces then in the *de facto* possession of Napoleon, and of others ceded by Prussia on the left bank of the Elbe. Napoleon retained for his own purposes the half of the *allodial domains* of the Elector, and a compact was entered into at Berlin,(*d*) on the 22nd April, 1808, between Napoleon and Jerome, for the adjustment of the spoils of Hesse-Cassel, namely, with respect to the *active debt* (*active-capitalien*)(*e*) of the Princes and Government of those provinces out of which the Westphalian kingdom was composed.

*The King of Westphalia renounced all claim to the debts which were due from persons who were *not the subjects* of his [*710] kingdom, provided, that these debts were paid to the Emperor of the

(*a*) The reader should consult Pfeiffer's two works—

1. In wiefern sind Regierungshandlungen eines Zwischenherrschers für den rechtmässigen Regenten nach dessen Rückkehr verbindlich (1819);

2. Das Recht der Kriegseroberung in Beziehung auf Staatscapitalien-specialler Theil (Cassel, 1823)—both for the arguments and the accumulation of valuable authorities upon the *general* question; but upon the application to the particular case of Hesse-Cassel, the reader must remember that the author wrote at Cassel, and was "Kurfürstlich Hessischer Oberappellationsrathe." He wrote naturally under a strong, though, very likely, unconscious, bias for the Prince of Hesse-Cassel. See too Zachariah, Ueber die Verpflichtung zur Aufrechtshaltung der Regierung des Königreichs Westphalen. Heidelberg, 1817.

For a list of other writers, see note *, p. 484, vol. iv. of Rotteck and Welcker's Staat's-Lexicon, tit. Domainenkäufer. The authors of this Lexicon remark that no German or Dutch writer or jurist out of the territory of Hesse-Cassel impugned the validity of the transfers and alienations made during the period of the government of the Bonapartes, i. e. Napoleon and Jerome. Schweikart's lesser work. "Napoleon und die Churhessischen Capitalschuldner." Königsberg, 1833. Rotteck und Welcker, Staats-Lexikon, iv. "Domainenkäufer." Conversations-Lexikon, iii. "Domainen." Heffters, p. 326, and note 1.

(*b*) Koch, Hist. des Traités, t. iii. pp. 26, 41, 42. Ed. Bruxelles, 1838, t. ii. pp. 492, 503, 511. Pfeiffer, Das Recht der Kriegseroberung, s. 4, p. 237.

(*c*) De Martens, Suppl. au Rec. des Traités, t. iv. pp. 423, 434, 436, 491.

(*d*) De Martens, Suppl., t. v. p. 34.

(*e*) Pfeiffer, pp. 240, 241.

French, to whom these provinces belonged by right of conquest, and were incorporated in his "*domaine extraordinaire.*" Napoleon, on the other hand, declared that he yielded up all the debts of those debtors, whether of princes or noblemen, who were subjects of the King of Westphalia, or of private persons domiciled in his dominions, to the King of Westphalia, for his full and absolute possession and enjoyment.

DLXX. The legal title of the Emperor was set forth in this way; "Que par suite de la *conquête* de l'Electorat de Hesse, l'Empereur a confisqué au profit de son *domaine extraordinaire* les *créances* appartenantes, soit du ci-devant Electeur de Hesse, soit aux états et provinces, dont il avait été pris possession, et a déclaré, qu'il entendoit, qu'aucun débiteur ne peut se libérer valablement qu'au trésor du dit domaine."

The form of discharge (*bonne et valable quittance*) was : "Au moyen du payement stipulé et par le seul fait de sa réalisation le directeur des domaines *cede, transporte,* et *abandonne* à N. N. tous les droits et actions appartenans à S. M. I. sur l'obligation hypothécaire, consentie primitivement au profit de l'ex-Electeur de Hesse, en vertu du decret impérial du 4 Août, 1807;" or, "Au moyen du dit payement le directeur des domaines assure la garantie la plus formelle et la plus entière à N. N., contre toutes recherches, demandes, et prétentions, *soit de la part de l'ex-Electeur de Hesse,* soit de tout autre détenteur du titre original."(*f*)

DLXXI. Towards the close of the year 1813, after the power of Napoleon was broken by the battle of Leipsic, [*711] *the son of the Elector of Hesse, having borne his part in that great contest, returned to his paternal dominions, and his father was confirmed in the possession of them by a treaty with the Allied Powers of 2nd December, 1813,(*g*) which contained a formal guarantee of his sovereignty; and this was further confirmed by the peace of Paris, 1814.(*h*)

DLXXII. Hesse-Cassel was a very poor country, without foreign commerce, without facility of internal communication, without extraordinary fertility of soil; but the sovereign was a wealthy potentate. Absolute lord over his subjects, he had enriched himself, among other means, by selling their valour and their sinews to aid the wars of foreign nations. The gold of England had at different times largely contributed to the overflowing of his coffers. In the time of Napoleon he was one of the richest of the German princes. His money—for it must be borne in mind that it was his *private property*—was invested in loans and mortgages to the inhabitants of various states of the Continent.

When Napoleon possessed himself of the territories of Hesse-Cassel, he had comparatively little difficulty in compelling the subjects of his newly-acquired dominion to pay their debts to the prince into the exchequer of the Conqueror. This Napoleon could effect *proprio motu.* It was not so easy a task to possess himself of the debts due from foreign subjects to the dethroned prince. He did, however, in great measure, accomplish this object also. One case, the celebrity of which made it the theme of various legal treatises, will serve to illustrate both the fact and the law.

(*f*) Pfeiffer, p. 252. Schweikart, p. 8.
(*g*) Koch, iii. pp. 307, 308. (*h*) Pfeiffer, pp. 246, 247.

A certain Count Von Hahn, the possessor of large landed estates, had borrowed money from the Prince of Hesse-Cassel. The Count was a subject of Mecklenburgh, and his estates were in that duchy. How was Napoleon to obtain *possession of this portion of the Prince of Hesse-Cassel's property, which consisted in the mortgages on the Count's estate? [*712]

The mortgage was duly registered in the proper office in Mecklenburgh. No one but the creditor could cause that mortgage to be crossed out or recorded as extinguished; and by no other procedure could the debtor obtain a valid discharge.

The Duke of Mecklenburgh, at the instance of Napoleon, issued an order (*Circular Rescript*,)(*i*) which, after reciting that Napoleon, being possessed of the Sovereignty of Hesse-Cassel, was possessed, as an accessory to the principal, of the debts due to that sovereignty, directed the Court of Registration to record as extinguished, those mortgages in favour of Hesse-Cassel, for which a particular discharge or receipt had been given by Napoleon, or by his appointee for that purpose.

This Rescript was dated the 15th June, 1810. It appears that it was obeyed, but that a particular minute of the circumstance of the extinguishment of the mortgage was also recorded, so as in some measure to leave open the question of the lawfulness of the discharge.

The affairs of the Count became embarrassed, and after his death creditors claimed his property; among them was the restored Prince of Hesse-Cassel. The *actor communis* or *official assignee* of the creditors (to use the English phrase) brought the question into Court.

The Mecklenburgh Court of Justice(*k*) at Güstrow first entertained the question. The Prince denied both the validity of the discharge, and the legality of the Mecklenburgh order of 1810, and asserted that Napoleon possessed himself of the money in the character of a robber, and not of a Conqueror.

The international character of Universities(*l*) has been *referred to in an earlier part of this work. It is owing, perhaps, in some degree to this character that in Germany these learned institutions possess judicial powers in questions which concern the interests of two or more German States. [*713]

This matter was first remitted to the Prussian University of Breslau. The decision of this tribunal (29 May, 1824) was in substance that the Prince might recover that portion of the debt which had not been *actually* paid in *money* to Napoleon, but no more. It had happened that in many cases Napoleon had remitted—no doubt in order to induce payment—a considerable portion of the original debt, giving, however, a discharge from the whole.

Both parties, being dissatisfied with this judgment, appealed to the Holstein University of Kiel, which, however, confirmed, with some difference as to the costs, the sentence, (24 March, 1831.) But from this

(*i*) Schweikart, pp. 4, 10.
(*k*) Then called Hof and Landgericht; now Justiz-kanzlei.—Schweikart, p. 10.
(*l*) Vol. II. p. 318.

sentence the Court itself(m) sanctioned an appeal "*ad impartiales exteros*," that is, to another German University.(n)

This learned body delivered at great length the reasons of their judgment.

They rightly said that the real question was, whether Napoleon had, or had not, become the true creditor of the Hesse-Cassel funds.(o) They drew a broad distinction between the validity of acts done by a mere transient Conqueror and acts done by him after the kingdom had been wholly subdued, and the subjects had either expressly, or by necessary implication, accepted him as their ruler.

In the former case the Conqueror's right was confined to the effects of his private acts, to the *occupatio bellica*, and required actual seizure and possession for its valid exercise.

In the latter case the rights and title of the Conqueror had been ratified by the Public Act of the State. As [*714] *Napoleon's right and title was of the latter kind, the fact that these funds were the private property of the Prince, and not the public property of the State, became of no importance. There were not, in this respect at least, two questions, (as Pfeiffer has suggested,) one respecting the legal validity of the acts of Napoleon, another respecting those of Jerome, King of Westphalia; for Napoleon had been recognized and had acted as Sovereign of Hesse-Cassel before he delivered that country to his brother.(p) They rejected the consideration of the justice or injustice of the war which Napoleon had waged against the Prince, wisely holding that the presumption of law, upon which they were bound to act, was in favour of its justice.(q) Nor did it matter that the Prince, instead of giving battle to Napoleon, had departed, and resigned his country to the military occupation of the enemy.(r) They pointed out that the Prince had, from the time of his departure or abdication, been an active enemy of the new government established under Napoleon and Jerome, and that, by the laws of all countries, the property of a person, *qui sub publico hoste egit* against the state, was confiscable.

They rejected the doctrine that, because the Prince had retained possession of the instruments containing the written acknowledgments of the debtors, (*schulddocumente*,) he therefore had constructive possession of the debts, the circumstances being considered under which the money had been borrowed,—(s) adopting the principle of the Roman Law, "Dissolutæ quantitatis retentum instrumentum inefficax penes creditorem remanere . . . . non est ambigui juris."(t)

[*715] *They considered how the question was affected by the return of the Prince, and by his reclamation of his former property, and they held that the principle of the decision of the Amphictyons in the

(m) "'Ad impartiales exteros' von Amtswegen verschickt."—Schweikart, p. 12.

(n) The name is not given by Schweikart.

(o) Schweikart, p. 14.

(p) Schweikart, p. 25.

(q) Menochius, de Præsumt., l. vi. præsumt. 96, num. 4, et 17.

(r) Schweikart, pp. 44, 45.

(s) Ib., 55. Cod. de Solut. l. viii. t. xliii. ss. 4, 19. Cod. ad Exhib. l. iii. t. xlii. s. 9. Dig. Cod. l. x. t. iv. s. 18. Cod. Depositi, l. iv. t. xxxiv. s. 5, in fin.

(t) Cod. de Condict. ex Lege, l. iv. t. ix. s. 2.

case of the Thebans and Thessalians was sound law, and that it had been so treated by almost all jurists, ancient and modern.(*u*)

They considered the general question whether, after peace, there did or did not take place a *restitutio in integrum* with respect to those who had been dispossessed by war.(*x*) They held that, even according to the letter of the Roman Law, the restored owner must take the property as he found it, and was entitled to no compensation for the damage which it might have suffered in the interval; that what was actually gone he could not claim to have replaced; and especially that what the public exchequer (*fiscus*) had alienated was not to be restored.(*y*)

That to such alienations the principle of all law, whether private, public, or international, was expressed in the words of the Roman Law, "Non debit quod ritè et secuudum leges ab initio actum est, ex alio eventu resuscitari."(*z*)

It was impossible, these judges observed, to consider the return of the Prince as a continuation of his former government.

He had not been constantly in arms against Napoleon, and at last successful, by force of arms, in recovering his domains. He had been treated by the Peaces of Tilsit and Schönbrunn as politically extinct, and the King of *Westphalia had been recognized by the Continental Powers as Regent of Hesse-Cassel.(*a*) [*716]

They travelled through a variety of Treaties(*b*) to show that the conventional practice of states is in accordance with this view; and especially, that the *non obstante* clause, sometimes found in Treaties—*e. g.*, "non obstante toutes donations, concessions, declarations, confiscations"—(*c*) applied to immovable and not movable property, unless the latter were specially designated.

They remarked that the Prince's own tribunals of Hesse-Cassel had pronounced (27th June, 1818) that those subjects of the King of Westphalia who had paid to him or his exchequer their debts, and received due discharges, could not be legally called upon to pay a second time; and they thought the principle of that decision, as well as the authorities which they had referred to, led them to the judicial conclusion that all the debts, whether the whole sum had been paid or not, for which discharges in full had been given by Napoleon, were validly and effectually paid; and they therefore, so far, reversed the former sentences, leaving, it should seem, both parties to pay their costs.(*d*)

(*u*) "Und so urtheilen fast alle ältere und neuere Rechtgelehrte, welche sich über diesen fall geäussert haben."—Schweikart, pp. 58, 61.

(*x*) Ib., p. 67.

(*y*) "Constitutio autem divæ memoriæ Zenonis benè prospexit iis qui a fisco per venditionem aut donationem, vel alium titulum accipiunt aliquid: ut ipsi quidem securi statim fiant et victores existant sive experiantur sive conveniantur."—Instit., l. ii. t. vi. 14, in Jure.

(*z*) Cod. de Administ. Tutor., l. v. t. xxxvii. s. 25.

(*a*) They refer to Zachariah, Ueber die Verpflichtung zur Aufrechthaltung der Regierung des Königreichs Westphalen. Heidelberg, 1817.

(*b*) Schweikart, pp. 74-79.

(*c*) Ib., p. 79: "Nur an Immobilien und radicirten Renten nicht an bewegliche Sachem wenn dies nicht besonders ausgedrückt war."

(*d*) The judgment was given at Mecklenburgh, and was in the name of the

DLXXIII. (2.) The restored Prince of Hesse-Cassel not only denied the validity of the alienation of the *Debts*, but, as has been said,(*e*) of the *Domains* of his country.

The pretext for this denial was mainly founded upon a misapplication [*717] of the "*lex de captivis et postliminio*," in the *Roman Law. It was manifest, nevertheless, that the analogy(*f*) of this jurisprudence failed in a material point. The law in question applied to propetty found in the land of the enemy or his ally, not to property transferred to a third party, and certainly not to property so transferred, by the deliberate order formally enacted and legally executed of a *de facto* sovereign, acknowledged by the subjects over whom he ruled, and recognized by foreign states.(*g*)

The purchasers of these domains within the territory of Hesse-Cassel were in many instances deprived of their possession, which had been delivered to them with every formality of law. The possessor of the Freienhagen estate, for instance, was driven out of it by a troop of Hesse-Cassel hussars.(*h*) The unfortunate proprietors appealed in vain to the Congress of Vienna. But Prussia, through the mouth of her Chancellor, Prince von Hardenberg, declared in their favour. It was true, he said, that the additional article of the Peace of Paris (30th May, 1814) had declared the Peace of Tilsit (9th July, 1807) null and void; "but it was self-evident," he said, "that this article only applied to the mutual *public* relations of the contracting states, not to *private* relations between individuals, which had legally arisen during the continuance of the Peace of Tilsit. It would he a manifest injustice to declare on that account contracts, had between individuals under the former Westphalian [*718] *Government, invalid, which contracts had been sanctioned by the Government which the Peace of Tilsit had recognized." Nevertheless, the Congress of Vienna gave no aid to those proprietors. The Supreme Court of Appeal in Cassel was stopped by an *inhibitorium*(*i*) from taking cognizance of the matter.

The German Confederation was in vain appealed to; it either could not or would not intervene between a Sovereign and his subjects: though the question appears to have been kept open before this modern Amphictyonic assembly;(*k*) for Rotteck complains in 1837 that, after a lapse of more than twenty years, the fate of many proprietors of Westphalian domains was yet undecided.(*l*)

Grand Duke; but specifies "nach eingeholtern Rathe auswärtiger Rechtsgelehrten für Recht." See the Urtheil itself, Schweikart, pp. 103, 104.

(*e*) Vide ante, p. 708.

(*f*) As to the use of the Roman Law in deciding international questions, vide ante, Vol. I. s. XL.

Indeed the *analogy* of this law is adverse to the position; it recognizes the necessity of the case as validating an act which infringed the rights of a third party; *e. g.* it compelled the father returned from captivity to acknowledge the marriage of his son made, *medio tempore* without his consent,—a great violation of the much prized parental right. "Non mirum (says the law) quia *illius temporis conditio necessitasque* faciebat et *publica* nuptiarum *utilitas* exigebat."—Dig. xlix. t. xv. 12, 3, in fine.

(*g*) Vide ante, Vol. II. c. IV.

(*h*) Rotteck, Staats-Lexikon, pp. 488, 490.

(*i*) Rotteck, Staats-Lexikon, p. 491.

(*k*) Vide ante, Vol. I. c. IV.

(*l*) Staats-Lexikon, iv. p. 521.

DLXXIV. It is a circumstance(*m*) well worthy of the attention of the jurist, the statesman, and the historian, that when the Allied Powers of Europe overthrew the dynasty of Napoleon, and restored to the countries which he had subdued their legitimate sovereigns, there were but two or three inferior states, and those in Germany,(*n*) which attempted to deprive proprietors of domains acquired by them under the authority of their *de facto* rulers. Austria, Prussia, Russia, the Bourbon Sovereigns in France and Italy, Sardinia, and the Pope, respected the law of reason, of justice, and of nations, and left undisturbed titles so acquired.

The discreditable exception of these German States arose, no doubt, in some measure from the habit which their rulers still retained of considering the power which they as sovereigns possessed, as equivalent to that of a father over his children, and of treating the whole country as their patrimony.

On the other hand, the general acquiescence of restored *Sovereigns in the acts of the Conquerors or Usurpers was more remarkable, because the Peace of Paris (Art. 27) had only protected French subjects in their possessions acquired "à titre onéreux" in the departments of Belgium, the left bank of the Rhine, and the Alps beyond the limits of old France. Koch(*o*) actually defends this limitation of the general amnesty on the ground that the Allies would otherwise have recognized the usurpation of Napoleon, and his authority to alienate the domains of countries which he had conquered. Therefore, he says, the Allies did not legalize the alienations in Holland, in the Transrhenish Provinces, in the Tuscan or Papal States. But Koch's reasoning is both inconsistent and unsound:—the former, because, if good at all, it was applicable to *all* the territory acquired by France since the Revolution,—the latter, because it is contrary, as has been attempted to be shown in the preceding pages, to the true principles of International Justice. Moreover, he admits that the restriction of the Amnesty in this particular was solely for the purpose of protecting the restored monarch of France against the reclamations and solicitations of proprietors who had been despoiled during the reign of Napoleon. [*719]

But, as has been seen, the good sense, if no higher motive, of the restored Sovereigns, gave an almost universal application to the principle, and rejected the limitation.

*CHAPTER VII. [*720]

POSTLIMINIUM.—DECISIONS IN ENGLISH COURTS OF JUSTICE.

DLXXV. The question as to the right to confiscate the Public Debts

(*m*) Staats-Lexikon, iv. p. 483.

(*n*) Koch say (Traités de Paix) Hanover and Hesse only, t. iii. p. 364, (Brussels ed. 1838.)

(*o*) Rotteck, Staats-Lexikon, p. 364.

of a State has been already discussed, and, generally speaking, the principles relating to this subject are the same as those which relate to the confiscation of Private Debts.(*a*) It has been stated, in an earlier part of this volume,(*b*) that the right of confiscating the private *debts* of an enemy is a corollary to the right of confiscating his property. That, however rigorous and inexpedient the application of this *summum jus* may be, it is nevertheless competent to an enemy to exercise it. That this position is supported by the reason of the thing, and by the authority of jurists and judges on the Continent of Europe and in the United States of North America.

DLXXVI. Nevertheless, in 1817, the English Court of King's Bench made a decision(*c*) wholly at variance with these authorities. A Dane, who had been for many years naturalized by Act of Parliament, and resided in this country, brought an action in the English Court against a Danish subject, who had been arrested and held to bail in this country. The debt had been contracted in England, at a time when the Danish debtor was resident in Denmark, having a house of trade established there, and when *Denmark and England were at peace with each [*721] other. Proceedings had been instituted in the Court at Denmark for the recovery of this debt: while these were pending, in 1807, a war broke out between England and Denmark, and an ordinance was therefore made by the latter, dated 16th August, 1807, whereby all ships, goods, moneys, and moneys' worth were declared to be sequestrated and detained; and by another ordinance, dated 9th September, 1807, all persons were commanded, within three days after the publication thereof, to transmit an account of the debts due to English subjects, of whatsoever nature or quality they might be, the whole of which were directed to be paid into the Danish Treasury; and in case of concealment, the person so offending was to be proceeded against by the officers of the Exchequer; and Commissioners were appointed to receive the sequestrated debts: to them the debt in this case had been paid, and it was contended, for the defendant, that it was a valid discharge according to International Law. The plaintiff, on the other hand, contended,—(1.) That the ordinance was contrary to International Law; (2.) That it did not appear to have been a *compulsory* payment under the ordinance; (3.) That the defendant, being a Danish subject, paid to himself in paying to the Government, because every subject of a State is deemed to be a party to the laws of his own Government.

The English Court, presided over by Lord Ellenborough, pronounced in favour of the plaintiff, and against the validity of the defence which had been set up. The Court observed, indeed, that the ordinance in question had not been followed up by any practical measure of compulsion upon the subjects of Denmark; that there had been nothing in the nature of process against the defendant to enforce the payment of this particular debt—nothing analogous to the seizure or condemnation of corporeal things taken in the time of war; and that, though the Seques-

(*a*) Vide ante, p. 133. See, too, Story's Conflict of Law, ss. 334, 348, 351.
(*b*) Vide ante, pp. 132-4.
(*c*) Wolff v. Oxholm, 6 Maule and Selwyn's Reports, p. 100.

tration Commissioners were informed of the debt in 1807, the defendant *did not pay the debt till 1812. Yet the Court, in fact, decided upon the broad ground that the Danish Ordinance was a violation of the principles of International Law. The principal grounds of this decision appear to have been:—(1.) The language of Vattel, in which he speaks of the security of enemy's money in the *public* funds, the reason of which, the Court said, extended equally to debts owing to an *individual* in the course of commerce; it was said that Vattel, in laying down that a Sovereign might, at least, prohibit his subjects from paying debts *pendente bello*, intimated a doubt as to the right of confiscating debts; and that the right was properly limited to its operation *in personam*, upon the subject of the state, or upon his property within the reach and control of that state. (2.) That the language of Vattel with respect to the practice of Europe as to not confiscating debts, had become so general that the confiscating state must be holden to violate the public faith. (3.) That, in spite of what is said in Treatises as to the Law of England, there was no case in the books in which debts had been so confiscated. (4.) That even in the time of Grotius(*d*) doubts had been entertained as to the lawfulness of confiscating debts; that he expresses no opinion in favour of such a course, but rather inclined the other way. (5.) That the reasoning of Puffendorf, in the 22nd section of the sixth chapter of the eighth book of his Treatise, "De Jure Naturali et Gentium," was opposed to such a right. [*722]

(6.) Lastly and chiefly, the Court said that it was admitted that, notwithstanding all the violent measures to which recourse had been had during the extraordinary warfare that characterized those times, the Ordinance of the Court of Denmark stood single and alone, not supported by any precedent, nor adopted as an example in any other state. They therefore gave judgment for the plaintiff.

*DLXXVII. The authority both of Bynkershoek and of the Dutch Tribunals is directly opposed to this judgment. "*Quapropter* (he says) si subditus Principi qui credita publicavit, solverit quod hosti debebat liberationem contingere, *optimo jure* responsum est."(*e*) His authority does not appear to have been cited in the argument, and to have been but slightly referred to in the judgment. And it seems to the writer of these pages that the opinion of Grotius *does* countenance the doctrine. The passage, "Incorporalia jura quæ universitatis fuerant, fient victoris quatenus velint," cannot be otherwise interpreted. [*723]

The famous passage in Quintilian(*f*) relating to the remission of the Thessalian debt is, as has been shown, referred to by Grotius, Puffendorf, and Vattel; and it was also discussed in Wolff v. Oxholm.(*g*) The question, it will be remembered, was, did the remission of the debt fall within the *jus victoris?* Quintilian suggests that it did *not* "quia id demum sit ejus quod ipse teneat; jus quod sit *incorporale* apprehendi manu non posse—non *in tabulis* esse jus. These and other arguments

(*d*) L. iii. c. vii. s. 4, c. viii. s. 4.
(*e*) Consil. Holl., t. i., consil. 297, cited by Bynkershoek, Q. J. P., b. i. c. vii.
(*f*) Inst. Orat v. 10. (*g*) 6 Maule & Selwyn's Rep., p. 92.

Grotius *condemns*,(*h*) while mentioning the transaction as exemplifying his position, that *jura incorporalia do* belong to the victor; and yet the judge in Wolff v. Oxholm says that because he does not go on, as Vattel did, to express a conclusion that private debts may be confiscated, "there is nothing in the works of that very learned author (Grotius) which can give a countenance to such a right."(*i*) Surely this is an inaccurate and erroneous statement. Heffters, whose opinion is on the whole in favour of the continuing liability of the creditor, and who there-[*724] fore adopts the argument of *Quintilian, admits that he has to contend against the opinion of a phalanx of International Jurists.(*k*)

In this decision of the English Court, the authority of Vattel appears to have(*l*) been greatly overestimated and not a little overstrained, the inferences from the language of Grotius and Puffendorf to be ingenious rather than sound: while to the high authority of Story and the American Tribunals, no allusion appears to have been made by counsel or judge.

The question for the International Jurists who review this judgment is, really this, whether the *practice* of nations was so rooted and confirmed in opposition to the *strict right* as to have superseded it—whether, to repeat a former passage in this work, this was one of those cases in which a usage, which had its origin in the precarious concession of Comity, had become transferred, through uninterrupted exercise and the lapse of time, into the certain domain of Right.(*m*)

It must be remembered that this was a decision against a foreigner for obeying the law of his own country, and that this law was warranted by the authority of most eminent jurists and judges. There were, no doubt, traces of *mala fides* in this case, which had their effect upon the minds of the English judges; but, as far as the general principal is concerned, the decisions of the American, Dutch, and German Courts (none of which, strange to say, were quoted,) appear much sounder; and perhaps, if the occasion should present itself, the decision of Lord Ellenborough might be reversed in England. It was the decision of a single Court not much accustomed to deal with questions of International Law. [*725] Moreover the argument was not, as in the case of *Potts v. Bell,(*n*) before Lord Kenyon, or in the more recent slave case of the Felicidade, argued with the assistance of Civilians,(*o*) and some of the principal International authorities were not referred to.

DLXXVIII. Where a Treaty has awarded compensation for confiscated property, there have been various decisions in England upon cases alleged to fall under this category: they have been principally decided by the Privy Council, on appeal from Commissioners appointed to inquire into the claims. Among the principal cases the following relate to *In-*

(*h*) L. iii. c. v. s. 77. (*i*) 6 Maule & Selwyn's Rep., p. 103.

(*k*) "Die meisten Publicisten haben sich in lange Reihefolge für ein solches Verfügungsrecht ausgesprochen, u. s. w."—Heffters, p. 131.

(*l*) L. iii. c. viii. s. 4. (*m*) Vol. I. p. 161.

(*n*) 8 Durnford & East's Rep., p. 548.

(*o*) Vide ante, Vol. I. p. 333. Denison's Crown Cases reserved, vol. i. p. 154.

dividuals. It has been decided by the Privy Council that a person who possesses the characters both of a French subject under the Municipal Law of France, and of a British subject under the Statute 13 Geo. 3, c. 26, as the grandson of a natural-born British subject, although both he himself and his father were born in a foreign country, is not entitled to claim compensation for a loss he has sustained from a confiscation of his property by the French Government under a Treaty between Great Britain and France, giving compensation for such a loss to British subjects.(*p*) That an Englishman who has taken out letters of naturalization in France is not entitled to compensation as a British subject under such a Treaty.(*q*) That the foreign wife of a British subject is not entitled to compensation for the loss of her separate property, under a Treaty providing for such a compensation for British subjects, unless she has herself acquired a domicile in Great Britain at the time of her loss.(*r*) That a foreigner domiciled in Great Britain is, *under such a Treaty, [*726] entitled to claim compensation for his losses.(*s*)

The same Judicial body has decided, with respect to *Corporations*, that a corporation of British subjects in a foreign country, existing for objects in opposition to British law, and under the control of a foreign government, is not entitled to claim any compensation from the government of the country in which they existed for the confiscation of their property under a Treaty giving the right to British subjects.(*t*) It has been also decided that the individual members of such a corporation are also equally incapacitated from making any claim, as British subjects, from the loss of their income arising from the funds of such a corporation.(*u*) That a corporation of Irishmen, existing in a foreign country, and under the control of a foreign government, must be considered as a foreign corporation, and is not therefore, entitled to claim compensation for the loss of its property, under a Treaty giving the right of doing so to British subjects.(*x*) That it makes no difference whether the purposes for which such a corporation existed were or were not contrary to the law of Ireland.(*y*)

And *generally* the English Privy Council has decided, that a country re-conquered from an enemy reverts to the same state that it was in before its conquest. The British inhabitants of a part of the French dominions which was conquered by the Dutch, and afterwards re-conquered by the French, ought therefore, the Privy Council decided, to have had, after the re-conquest of that part, the same *protection that they were [*727] entitled to under a Treaty of Commerce of 1786, and they awarded compensation in respect of losses after the re-conquest, incurred by seques-

(*p*) Drummond's Case, 2 Knapp's Privy Council Rep., p. 295.
(*q*) Fanning's Case, Ib., p. 301.
(*r*) Countess de Conway's Case, 2 Knapp's Privy Council Rep., p. 364.
(*s*) Countess de Conway's Case, 2 Knapp's Privy Council Rep., p. 364.
(*t*) Daniel v. Commissioners for Claims in France, 2 Knapp's Privy Council Rep., p. 23.
(*u*) Ibid.
(*x*) Long v. Commissioners for Claims on France, 2 Knapp's Privy Council Rep., p. 51.
(*y*) Ibid.

tration of their property in contravention of that Treaty by the French Government.(z)

[*728]

*CHAPTER VIII.

DOCTRINE OF POSTLIMINIUM AS TO PRIVATE RIGHTS AND PROPERTY WHICH HAVE BEEN DURING THE WAR UNDER THE DOMINION OF THE ENEMY, AND NOT CONFISCATED BY THE STATE.

DLXXIX. We have now inquired into the effect of Peace upon the Public Property and contracts of States; (II.) it remains to consider the effect of Peace, so far as the State is concerned, upon the Private Rights, Property, and Contracts(a) of the subjects of the contracting parties who have been Belligerents, and also partially and incidentally upon the subjects of Neutrals. The General principles which it is important to lay down are these:—First, that a distinction is to be observed between the question of the competency of the State to sacrifice for public domestic purposes the property of the Individual, together with the right of compensation thereby accruing to him, and the question with respect to the competency of the State to surrender property of Individuals to Foreign States. The former question is one of Public if not of Municipal Law, the latter is one of International Jurisprudence; or, as it is clearly stated by Grotius:(b) "*externis* qui cum Rege contrahunt sufficit factum Regis non tantum ob præsumtionem quam secum adfert dignitas personæ, verum etiam ob *Gentium Jus,* quod bona subditorum obligari ex facto regis patitur," it is only necessary, in applying the principle contained in this passage, *to bear in mind that Grotius must be considered [*729] to use the expression Rex as synonymous with the constitutional government, whatever it may be, of the state.

Secondly. The losses of Private Persons, like the losses of the State, inflicted by the war, cannot, unless in the event of a special convention to that effect, be recovered after the peace.(b)

Thirdly. Obligations under which either the State or Private Persons, members of it, lie to Private Persons members of another State, due before the war, are, generally speaking, not cancelled by the war, but sleep during its continuance and awaken at its close.(d)

DLXXX. We have considered the doctrine of *Postliminium* as growing out of *the silence of the Treaty* which concludes the Peace in its application to States and Public Property. We have now to consider the same doctrine in its application to Private Persons, Rights, and Property.

This consideration will relate to the

(z) Gumbe's Case, 2 Knapp's Privy Council Rep., p. 369.
(a) Vide ante, p. 104.
(b) L. iii. c. xx. s. 10.
(c) Grot., l. iii. c. xx. s. 15.
(d) Ib., s. 16.

1. Personal *Status.*
2. Immovable Property (*immobilia.*)
3. Movable Property (*mobilia.*)
4. Obligations such as Contracts, Debts (*jura incorporalia; Forderungsrechte.*)

To all these subdivisions of the subject the general principles mentioned at the beginning of this chapter are of course applicable: and it may be added that it is a proposition equally affecting both kinds of property, that the property of one enemy found within the territory of another at the time of the declaration or breaking out of war, and which has not been confiscated pending the war,(*e*) may be claimed by its owner at the end of the war.(*f*)

DLXXXI. (1.) With respect to Personal *Status*,(*g*) *the doctrines of the Roman Law form a very small part of International [*730] Law. By the latter the right of *Postliminium* and the recovery of Personal *Status* is not always taken away from an individual unless by the municipal law of his own country, or by the express stipulation of the Treaty.

The Roman Law might furnish some analogies for determining, when the captivity of a prisoner of war was at an end, whether if his freedom had been obtained by breach of his parole of honour, or whether, when he had escaped into a neutral territory, he ought or ought not to be delivered back to the enemy. But these are causes not relating to the subject now under consideration. And with respect to those Private Rights which are restored by *Postliminium*, it may be said, generally, that under this category are included all Rights appertaining to Person, or Property, or to Obligation. International Law rejects all distinctions of the Roman Law upon this point.

There are, indeed, two ways by which this *Postliminium* of Rights, so to speak, may take effect.

α. When the prisoner returns during war and re-enters upon the Rights taken from him during the period of his captivity. This is a subject which has been already discussed in the earlier pages of this volume.

β. When the original owner claims, after the restoration of peace, Rights forcibly taken from him by the enemy during war. It is with this predicament that we are now concerned.(*h*)

DLXXXII. As to the Personal *Status*, it unquestionably returns with all its incidents, unless, indeed, it should have been affected by traitorous dealings with the enemy during the war. But this, and also the question as to any claim to a return of the profits of any office from which a person may have been ejected during the war, are matters of public and constitutional, not, strictly speaking, of International Law. But it may be observed that, as to the relation of marriage, *of which the earlier Roman Law appears to have required a *reintegratio*, there [*731]

(*e*) Vide ante, pp. 115, 116, 117, 121.
(*f*) The Adventure, 1 Curtis's (Amer.) Rep., p. 103.
(*g*) Heffters, s. 189. (*h*) Dig., xix. tit. i.

is no doubt that it remains unaffected by the captivity of either party to the contract.(*i*)

DLXXXIII. (2.) With respect to Immovable Private Property, it has been already observed that the laws which relate to the effect of peace upon Public and Private Property are in principle the same, and(*k*) that the rule of International Law is that the Immovable Property returns, on Peace being made, to its original owner, unless there has been an express stipulation to the contrary.(*l*)

The conqueror dethrones the sovereign and assumes the dominion of the conquered territory; but as a general rule he does no more. It has been well laid down by the tribunals of the North American United States that the modern usage of nations, that large and important part of International Law, would be violated—the sense of justice and of right, which is felt and acknowledged by the civilized world, would be outraged, if Private Property were generally confiscated and Private Rights annulled. The people, indeed, change their allegiance, their relation to their ancient sovereign is dissolved; but their relation to each other and their Rights of Property remain undisturbed. And it may be observed that this doctrine applies even more strongly to an *amicable cession* of territory. The cession of a territory by its owner from one [*732] state to another, while it conveys, in intent at least, *both the lands and the people who inhabit them, must be by moral necessity understood to pass the sovereignty only, and not to interfere with the Private Property of individuals.(*m*)

DLXXXIV. It may be observed, with respect to both kinds of property, according to the authority of Vattel, those things, of which the restitution is, without further explanation, simply stipulated in the Treaty of Peace, are to be restored in the same state in which they were when taken; for the word "restitution" naturally implies that everything should be replaced in its former condition. Thus, the restitution of the thing is to be accompanied with that of all the Rights which were annexed to it when taken. But this rule must not be extended to comprise those changes which may have been the natural consequences and effects of the war itself, and of its operations. A town is to be restored in the condition it was in when taken, as far as it still remains in that condition, at the conclusion of the peace. But if the town has been razed or dismantled during the war, that damage was done by the right of arms, and is buried in oblivion by the Act of Amnesty. We are

(*i*) See the provisions in the Roman Law, l. xii. t. xxv. (xxxvi.) s. 1. de Re Milit. Nov. xxii. c. vii.

(*k*) Vide ante, p. 135.

(*l*) Heffters, s. 190. "Integer autem populus si vel propriis viribus, vel sociorum armis jugum hostile excusserit, sine dubio libertatem et statum antiquum recuperat. Quod si autem aliqua pars bonorum, quæ antea ad ipsum pertinuerant, adhuc sub potestate hostis remaneat, ad illam recuperandam prætensionem retinet, quamdiu bellum pace nondum fuit compositum."—S. Puffendorfii de Jure Nat. et Gent., l. viii. c. vi. s. 26.

See Memorandum of Sardinia as to the sequestration by Austria of the property of Lombardo-Venetians who had become Sardinian subjects.—Annuaire des Deux Mondes, (1852-3,) p. 915.

(*m*) C. J. Marshall, in United States v. Percheman, 7 Peters' (Amer.) Rep., pp. 86, 77.

under no obligation to repair the ravages that have been committed in a country which we restore at the peace; we restore it in its existing state. But, as it would be a flagrant perfidy to ravage that country after the conclusion of the peace, the case is the same with respect to a town whose fortifications have escaped the devastation of war: to dismantle it previous to the restoration would be a violation of good faith and honour. If the captor has repaired the breaches, and put the place in the same state it was in before the seige, he is bound to restore it in that state. If he has added any new works, he may indeed demolish these: but if he has razed the ancient fortifications, and constructed others on a new plan, it will be necessary to come to a particular agreement respecting this improvement, or accurately to define in what condition the place shall be *restored. Indeed, Vattel adds, this last precaution should in every case be adopted, in order to obviate all dispute and difficulty.(*n*) [*733]

It is a maxim, however, of universal justice (though Pando complains of its frequent violation in Spain during the recent civil wars of that country,) that if the thing restored have been improved by the temporary owner, the value of the improvement should be defrayed to him before he delivers it back to the original owner.(*o*)

DLXXXV. The English Prize Statute contains the following provisions respecting the authority of the Prize Court after the war is over:—

"This Act shall continue in force during the present war, and no longer, save and except as to all such matters and things as shall then be depending in judgment in the Court of Admiralty, or before the Judicial Committee of the Privy Council, or in any Court of Record within her Majesty's dominions, at the time when the present war shall cease, and also save and except as to the carrying out(*p*) and finally disposing of all such other matters or things as shall arise out of the present war, in reference to the Provisions of this Act; and also save and except as to all offences which may have been committed against, and *all penalties and forfeitures which may have been incurred under the Provisions of this Act, in respect whereof proceedings shall and may be taken as if this Act still continued in force."(*q*) [*734]

DLXXXVI. (3.) With respect to *Movable Property*.

(*n*) Vattel, l. iv. c. iii. s. 31.

(*o*) Pando (tit. tercero, seccion cuarta,) *De las hostilidades contra las cosas del enemigo en la guerra terrestre:* "Antiguamente no se hacia distincion entre las propriedades de los subditos y las de los soberanos: a todos se les miraba como á enemigos y se les trataba con la misma dureza. La politica moderna bajo el influjo de nociones mas sanas y mas analogas á los progressos de la razon humana ha modificado esa rigorosa e injusta jurisprudencia: y en general se respetan las propriedades particulares. . . . Cualquiera que en el dia de otra manera obrara, seria reputado con razon como violador del derecho de gentes, porque haria el mal sin utilidad para el objeto de la guerra."—Pando, p. 392.

"Generalmente fué violado, lo decimos con amargura, varias veces en nuestra España el principio que presente se el adquirente ha hecho *mejoras* reales en la cosa qué á restituir se la obliga, puede exigir que se le indemnice. 'Petitor ex alienâ jacturâ lucrum facere non debit.'—Ib., p. 412.

(*p*) A barbarism meaning carrying into effect, or executing.

(*q*) 17 Vict. c. xviii. s. 57, (Act for Manning the Navy.)

It is a well established rule of International Law that if a Treaty of Peace contains no especial provisions relative to Movable Property captured during the war, that such property remains in the condition in which it exists at the time of the conclusion of the Treaty, and the title of the *de facto* possessor(*r*) is thereby tacitly and by implication confirmed.(*s*)

The intervention of hostilities puts the property of an enemy in such a situation that confiscation may ensue; but unless some step is taken for that purpose, unless there is some legal declaration of the forfeiture, the right of the owner revives on the return of Peace. This, Lord Stowell observes, is an acknowledged principle of the Common Law of England, which it has borrowed from the stores of International Jurisprudence.(*t*)

At the same time due vigilance must be used by the claimant in such cases. No Court of International Law will allow itself to be the depository of slumbering rights and antiquated claims after a lapse of time when it may be impossible to ascend to the whole justice of the case.
[*735] The *maxim "*vigilantibus non dormientibus subveniunt leges*" is a principle of limitation inherent in every sound system of jurisprudence.(*u*)

DLXXXVII. It is a very general modern International usage to consider that the movables *on land*(*x*) of individuals who have taken no part in the war are exempted from hostilities and from consequent capture or confiscation. This is a matter, however, of Comity, not of strict Right.

DLXXXVIII. It remains to say a word upon(*y*) the question of Obligations existing before the war, and more especially upon such as relate to covenants and debts. So far as this subject relates to transactions between states and the individuals of other states, it has been already considered.

DLXXXIX. The sound rule of International Law is that war *suspends* but does not *annul* obligations contracted between individuals of different countries before its existence, or, as it has been happily expressed: "Jus exigendi nobis quæsitum fuit ante bellum, hoc jus non desinit nostrum esse existente bello, utpote quo *non jus tollitur sed juris executio.*"(*z*)

DXC. The principle of this rule covers the case of *penal* damages due

(*r*) Thus, in the case of the Peregrinus who could not acquire property by *mancipatio* or by *in jure cessio*, the Prætor recognized a *de facto* possession as a principle of the *jus gentium*, and indeed of the *jus inter gentes*, for Puchta remarks, Instit. i. p. 360, "Denn so geschiet *die Erwerbung im Krieg* die *unter allen Volken* gilt." Heffters says: "Vermöge eines allgemeinen internationalen Herkommens."—s. 190.

(*s*) 1 Kent's Comm. p. 117, (111.) See too Mably, vol. i. p. 143, some good remarks on the true title of conquest. Güntter, ii. pp. 20, 113, (Erwerbung im Kriege.)

(*t*) Nuestra Señora de Los Dolores, 1 Edwards, (Ad. Rep.,) p. 60.

(*u*) The Rebecca, 5 Robinson's Ad. Rep. p. 105. The Mentor, 1 Robinson, 180, note.

(*x*) "Con excepcion de las buques de guerra y armadores," Pando remarks, p. 407.

(*y*) 1 Curtis's (Amer.) Digest, pp. 484, 485, British Debts.

(*z*) S. Cocceii, l. vii. c. vii. Grotius Illustr., t. v. p. 502, 503.

to a private person: but if the war should happen to have been waged on account of an injury done to a private person, then the payment of his damages should be expressed; for it requires but a slight conjecture to found the remission of a penalty. "Pœnæ," Grotius(*a*) says, "semper aliquid odii habeant; levis verborum conjectura sufficit ut hoc quoque donatum intelligatur."

*The learned Samuel Cocceius expresses his opinion upon this curious and not uninteresting point, as follows:— [*736]

"Quoad *debita pœnalia* certum est, salvam esse actionem non obstante pace, si *privatis* pœna debetur: nam hic quoque valet ratio, quod debita illa non sint belli jure quæsita, sed bello tantum exigi vetita. Adeoque si civis hostium ante cœptum bellum in nostro territorio adulterium commisit, vel homicidium perpetravit, finito bello ideo conveniri et puniri potest. Si *ipsa civitas* pœnam debet, uti si hostis, cum quo pax inita est, extra præsentis belli causam, olim cives nostros violavit, eos occidit, vel res eorum rapuit, nec dum satisfecit, quæritur, an adhuc satisfactio peti possit? Meritò id affirmamus. Tot enim sunt actiones, quot debita, et qui ex unâ causâ bellum gerit, ac de eâ transigit, ideo reliquis debendi causis non renunciat, hæc enim belli causa neque fuit disceptata, adeoque nec pace sopita videri potest; adeoque salvum jus, salvaque actio manet exigendi pœnam ab ipsa civitate, si illa reos vel dedere vel punire nolit.

"Neque *obstat*, quod hac ratione pax non satis pax vidætur, si veteres ad bellum causas relinquat. Resp. 1., hæc ratio æque ad causas civiles pertinet, nam si hostis antiqua debita solvere recusat, itidem pax veteres ad bellum causas relinqueret. Resp. 2., pax satis pax manet, quoad causam, quæ in lite fuit, et jam sopita est: et si pax relinquit veteres ad bellum causas, id ex injuriâ alterius civitatis oritur, quæ, dum jus mihi non tribuit, causam dat bello."(*b*)

The general rule as to the revival of *Obligations* at the close of the War and the restoration of Peace, is thus laid down by Grotius: "Non tamen et quæ privatis deberi cœperunt belli tempore condonata censeri debent, nam hæc non belli jure quæsita sunt, sed bello tantum exigi vetita. Itaque sublato impedimento vim suam retinent."(*c*)

*DXCI. It often happens that the consideration of the effect of conquest upon Private Rights gives rise to a question of the largest magnitude and gravest importance,(*d*) namely, the effect of this event upon the allegiance of the inhabitants of the conquered country. This is a question which requires to be examined with reference to two predicaments; viz.:— [*737]

1. The effect of a foreign conquest upon the allegiance of the conquered.

2. The effect of conquest(*e*) by one of the parties in a civil war upon the allegiance of the adherents of the defeated party.

(*a*) L. iii. c. xx. (*b*) Coccei Grotius Illustratus, v. l. vii. c. vii. p. 503.

(*c*) Grotius de Jure Belli et Pacis, (Whewell,) l. iii. c. xx. s. 16.

(*d*) Inglis v. The Trustees of The Sailors' Snug Harbour, 3 Peters' (Amer.) Rep., p. 100. Judge Story's Remarks, pp. 155, 165, overrule, to a certain extent, M'Ilvaine v. Coxe, 4 Cranch's (Amer.) Rep., p. 209.

(*e*) Johnson and Graham's Lessee v. M'Kintosh, 5 Curtis's (Amer.) Rep., p. 503,

DXCII. As to the effect of a foreign conquest upon the allegiance of the conquered, the following observations in a judgment delivered by Mr. Justice Story are well worthy of observation.

"The second objection," says that learned Judge, "is, that the Court directed the jury that Castine was, under the circumstances, a foreign port. By 'foreign port,' as the terms are here used, may be understood a port within the dominions of a foreign sovereign, and without the dominions of the United States. The port of Castine is the port of entry for the district of Penobscot, and is within the acknowledged territory of the United States. But, at the time referred to in the Bill of Exceptions, it had been captured, and was in the open and exclusive possession of the enemy. [*738] By the conquest and occupation *of Castine, that territory passed under the allegiance and sovereignty of the enemy.(*f*) The sovereignty of the United States over the territory was, of course, suspended, and the laws of the United States could no longer be rightfully enforced, or be obligatory upon the inhabitants who remained and submitted to the Conquerors. Castine, therefore, could not, strictly speaking, be deemed a port of the United States; for its sovereignty no longer extended over the place. Nor, on the other hand, could it strictly speaking, be deemed a port within the dominions of Great Britain, for it had not permanently passed under her sovereignty. The right which existed was the mere right of superior force; the allegiance was temporary, and the possession not that firm possession which gives to the conqueror *plenium dominium et utile*, the complete and perfect ownership of property. It could only be by a renunciation in a Treaty of Peace, or by possession so long and permanent as should afford conclusive proof that the territory was altogether abandoned by its sovereign, or had been irretrievably subdued, that it could be considered as incorporated into the dominions of the British sovereign. Until such incorporation by a recapture or repossession, the territory would be entitled to the full benefit of the law of Postliminy. If then, by the term 'foreign port' were intended a port *absolutely* within the dominions of a foreign sovereign, and incorporated into his realm, it might be very doubtful if the direction of the Court could be sustained. But it seems to me, that taking the whole direction together, in reference to the first and third counts, it meant no more than that Castine, being in the possession of the enemy by right of conquest, it was no longer to be considered as a port of the United States with reference to the non-importation Acts, but that, so far as respected the obligatory force of the laws of the United States, it was to be considered a 'foreign port,' or port [*739] *extra ligeantiam *reipublicœ*. And in this view the direction may well, in point of law, be supported.

"This leads me to the third objection, viz., that the bringing of the goods from Halifax to Castine was sufficient, to all purposes, to entitle

Judgment of C. J. Marshall. The important questions of title derived from Grant, Discovery, and Conquest are much discussed in this case. But I do not assent to the doctrine as to the European grounds of the invalidity of the Indian titles; indeed the Chief Justice (p. 589,) does not assent to them.

(*f*) See The Foltina, Dodson's Adm. Rep., p. 451. It is to be observed, this was a case *prima impressionis*.

the United States to a verdict on the first and third counts, whereas the Court directed the jury to the contrary. Without stopping to examine whether the single fact of bringing the goods from Halifax to Castine was of itself, 'to all the purposes of this libel,' sufficient to entitle the United States to a verdict on these counts, as the opinion guardedly expresses it, let us attend to the substance of the objection. It rests altogether upon the assumption that Castine was to be deemed a port of the United States, in which the laws had their full operation, notwithstanding it was, at the time of the supposed importation, in the actual possession of Great Britain. This position, however, is utterly inadmissible upon every principle of the Law of Nations. By the conquest and occupation, the laws of the United States were necessarily suspended in Castine; and by their surrender the inhabitants became subject to such laws, and such laws only, as the Conquerors chose to impose. No other laws could, in the nature of things, be obligatory upon them, for where there is no protection or sovereignty, there can be no claim to obedience. This objection, therefore, must be also overruled."(*g*)

DXCIII. (2.) We have next to consider the effect of a conquest by one of the parties in a Civil War upon the allegiance of the adherents of the defeated party.

The case supposed is always one of nicety and difficulty.

It would rather seem, as a matter of speculation, that when an old government is so far overthrown that another *government entirely claims, and at least partially exercises, the jurisdiction [*740] which formerly belonged to it, that the individual is left to attach himself to, and to become, by adoption at least, the subject of either government. The analogy under which it is most just to range such cases has been thought to be that which has just been discussed, viz., the rule which applies to cases of foreign conquest, where those only are bound to obedience and allegiance who remain under the protection of the Conqueror.(*h*)

In the cases arising out of the Revolution by which the North American Colonies of Great Britain became an Independent State, it was considered to be an established maxim of Public and International Law that there was vested in an Individual *a right of electing* to remain under the old or of contracting a new allegiance. The choice must be made within a reasonable period of time.(*i*)

DXCIV. In the case of a Civil War, English Law furnishes a good criterion as to whether the country is to be considered as at Peace or at War,—for it does not contemplate a state of transition from the one to the other,—the criterion is that, "wherever the King's Courts are open, it is time of Peace in judgment of law."(*k*)

(*g*) The United States v. Hayward, 2 Gallison's (Amer.) Rep., pp. 500-2. See, too, The United States v. Percheman, 7 Peters' (Amer. Rep., p. 86.

(*h*) Inglis v. The Trustees of the Sailors' Snug Harbour, 3 Peters's (Amer.) Rep., p. 157.

(*i*) Ib. p. 160. Jackson v. White, 20 Johnson's (Amer.) Rep., p. 313.

(*k*) Lord Hale, Pleas of the Crown, pt. i. c. xxvi. p. 344. Coke's Commentary upon Littleton, p. 2496. Elphinstone v. Bedreechund, 1 Knapp's Privy Council

DXCV. The jurisprudence(*l*) of the United States of North America upon this subject is remarkable. The records of their Supreme Court may be said, with few exceptions, to furnish almost the only example of [*741] the disputes of *States submitted to formal trial and decision before judges, in the same manner as the affairs of Private Individuals. This peculiarity is owing to the particular relations in which the executive of the Union stands to the different States which compose that Union, and the now established right of the Supreme Court to decide public disputes arising between State and State, and also those disputes in which the great corporation of the United States has an interest.

It has been truly said, that "a suit in a Court of Justice between such parties and upon such a question, is without example in the jurisprudence of other countries."(*m*)

These decisions will often be found valuable repositories of learning and argument upon questions of International Jurisprudence. They are of course not binding as precedents upon foreign States; and the stream of public justice upon these great topics may sometimes be coloured by the necessities of the peculiar position, actual and historical, in which the North American United States stand, in their relation both to their own territorial acquisitions and to those of other States inhabiting the same continent with themselves. For instance, it has become a cardinal maxim of their public jurisprudence that the system under which the United States were settled has been that of converting the *discovery* of the country into *conquest;* and the property of the great mass of the community originates in this principle, which cannot be rejected by Courts of Justice.(*n*)

With the doctrine of merging the rights of discovery(*o*) into those of conquest, and the denial of rights of property to the native inhabitants, it is certainly not the intention of the writer of these pages to express any concurrence. Though it appears to him perfectly clear that the rights of sovereignty of the United States over their territorial acquisi- [*742] tions are *now placed upon the solid and secure basis of *prescriptive*(*p*) *possession.* It is clear, however, that if the doctrines of Public Law laid down in these decisions of the Supreme Court are adopted by foreign States, they are certainly binding upon the United States themselves, according to one of the principles of International Law laid down at the threshold of this work.(*q*)

DXCVI. This Supreme Court has arrived at the following, among other conclusions, which cannot fail to be interesting to the student of International Law.

Reports, pp. 345, 346. Argument of counsel confirmed by the judgment, pp. 360, 361.

(*l*) The recent edition of Reports of Decisions in the Supreme Court of the United States, by B. R. Curtis, one of the Associate Justices of the Court, is a most valuable contribution to Public and International Jurisprudence.

(*m*) The State of Florida, Complainant v. The State of Georgia, 21 Curtis's (Amer.) Rep., p. 625, (A. D. 1853.)

(*n*) Johnson v. M'Kintosh, 5 Curtis's (Amer.) Rep., pp. 513, 514.

(*o*) Vide ante, Vol. I. Part III. Ch. XII.

(*p*) Vide ante, Vol. I. Part III. Ch. XII.

(*q*) Vide ante, Vol. I. pp. 60, 61.

That by the conquest and military occupation of a portion of the territory of the United States by a public enemy, that portion is to be deemed a foreign country, so far as respects their revenue laws.

That goods imported into it are not imported into the United States; and are subject to such duties only as the Conqueror may impose.

That the subsequent evacuation of the conquered territory by the enemy, and resumption of authority by the United States, cannot change the character of past transactions. That the *jus postliminii* does not apply to such a case; and that goods previously imported do not become liable to pay duties to the United States, by the resumption of their sovereignty over the conquered territory.(*r*)

That the Courts of a conquering power cannot deny the title acquired by conquest.(*s*)

That the people of a conquered territory change their allegiance, but that their relations to each other and their rights of property remain undisturbed.

That it is very unusual, even in cases of conquest, for the Conqueror to do more than to displace the Sovereign and assume dominion over the country. The modern *usage of nations, which has become law, would be violated, that sense of justice and of right which is acknowledged and felt by the whole civilized world would be outraged, if private property should be generally confiscated and private rights annulled. [*743]

That this being the modern rule, even in cases of *conquest*, is yet more applicable to the case of an amicable *cession* of territory.(*t*)

These United States by their Inferior Courts have decided that when a conquered territory is repossessed by its former Sovereign, private individuals acquire a right to all property that belonged to them before it was taken by the Conqueror.(*u*)

---

*CHAPTER IX. [*744]

WHEN PEACE IS BROKEN.—CONCLUDING REMARKS.

DXCVII. It is a frequent question, says one of the learned commentators on Grotius,(*a*) by what acts Peace shall be considered to be broken. It is obvious that this question is closely connected with that which occupied many pages of the earlier part of this volume, viz., what are in any case the causes which justify the original declaration of war?(*b*) Independently of these considerations, the question of the breaking of the particular Peace gives rise to the following observations:—

(*r*) United States v. Rice, 4 Curtis's (Amer.) Rep., p. 391.
(*s*) Johnson v. M'Kintosh, 5 Curtis's (Amer.) Rep., p. 503.
(*t*) United States v. Percheman, 7 Peters's (Amer.) Rep., pp. 86, 87.
(*u*) Wade v. Barnewell, 2 Bay's (Amer.) Rep., p. 299.
(*a*) S. Cocceii Grotius Illustr., v. diii. l. vii. c. vii. pp. 971-4.
(*b*) Vide ante, p. 47, &c.

The particular Peace is broken when what is contrary to it is done by either of the contracting parties, whether by *omitting* to fulfil the stipulations which it contains, or by doing some act which *contravenes* those stipulations.

It is hardly necessary to state that it matters not whether the ally or the principal contracting party be the sufferer by this omission or contravention.(*c*)

The particular Peace may be broken by a palpable evasion of its stipulations, or by a gross violation of its general spirit. The proof, however, of both these latter offences may be very difficult, and they are but too capable of being alleged as pretexts for an unjust war. The violation of the express article of a treaty, however, is a breaking of the Peace, [*745] *which can admit of no doubt; and it is important to observe that the breaking of one article is the dissolution of the whole treaty.(*d*) It is not competent to a State, any more than to an Individual, to reject or neglect one provision of a contract, and to claim the benefit of the others. It may, indeed, happen that an express stipulation to the effect that, though one of the articles be violated, the others shall remain in force, may be a part of the treaty, but in the absence of any such express stipulation, the law is clear that the whole treaty is at an end. Nor can it be allowed as a matter of right to draw distinction between articles of a greater or of less importance, though it may be a matter of wisdom or prudence, according to the circumstances, to make such a distinction; or it may be that a specific penalty is attached to the violation of an article of inferior consequence. It is manifest also that a studied and intentional delay in the fulfilment of the articles of a treaty is equivalent to an express rejection of them, and is, indeed, an artifice which aggravates the offence of breaking faith. Invincible necessity, as we have already seen,(*e*) insurmountable obstacles, must be duly considered in the execution of this, as of every other contract.

Lastly, it is *good faith* which above all things International Law requires, and where that is apparent or demonstrable, the Peace of the world ought never to be broken, in the matter of the construction of a Treaty, upon any inferior consideration.

[*746] *CONCLUSION.

THE writer of these pages has now arrived at the conclusion of the Commentaries upon *Public* International Law (*jus inter gentes.*) Another volume will contain the Commentaries upon *Private* International Law (*jus gentium.*)

(*c*) Vattel, l. iv. c. iv. ss. 38-54, generally as to the manner in which Peace may be broken.

(*d*) Vattel (ubi supra) implicitly follows Grotius, l. iii. c. xix. s. 14, on this matter. Wolff, ss. 1022, 1023, erroneously draws a distinction between articles *connexi* and *diversi*.

(*e*) Vide ante, pp. 60, 61.

Those readers who will take the trouble of comparing the scheme of the work, as sketched out in the early chapters of the First Volume, with the distribution of the subject in that and the following volumes, will see that the original plan has been faithfully adhered to, and the outline, howsoever, filled up.

Whatever defects with respect both to knowledge and to execution the work may have—and that it has many the author is painfully conscious—it will be recollected that this is the first English work published in England in which an attempt has been made to bring the whole subject of the Rights and Duties of States within some approach to the order and arrangement of a regular system. The difficulties of such a task inherent in the nature of the subject can only be fairly appreciated by those who have endeavoured to fulfil it. It has been the object of the writer of these pages to strengthen or add to the previously existing proof that States as well as Individuals of which they are the aggregate, have in their collective capacity a sphere of duty assigned to them by God. He has endeavoured to forward the great argument that there are International Rights, and therefore International Laws, convinced that every work, however humble, which tends to procure the recognition of these laws,—to show, by history, by reason, by authority, that the interest and the duty of States are eventually one,—that the substitution of might for right brings misery, not only on the oppressed but on the oppressor—deserves an indulgent reception from the world to which it is addressed.

*At least he has the consolation of thinking that he has been a fellow-worker with Grotius, and that he has endeavoured, however feebly, to accomplish the wish which Leibnitz expressed, when he said, "Rectè a viris doctis inter desiderata relatum est, jus Naturæ et Gentium, traditum secundum disciplinam Christianorum."(*f*) [*747]

God has so interwoven the interests of individual men, that each, by acting his allotted part, serves himself and benefits his kind.(*g*) The same Divine Author who willed the State, as he willed the Individual, has so interwoven the interests of States that each by the due performance of its duty promotes the welfare of all. "Neque enim" (says St. Augustine) "aliunde beata Civitas aliunde homo: cum aliud Civitas non sit, quam concurs hominum multitudo."(*h*) It was the voice of inspiration, though it borrowed the pen of the heathen, which pronounced that the just State differed in nothing from the just man;(*i*) it was the

(*f*) The whole passage will be found in Leibnitz, xxxii. De Notionibus Juris et Justitiæ (p. 120, ed. Erdman, Berolini, 1840:) "Nam ut Reipublicæ, ita multo magis universi interest ne quis re suâ male utatur. Itaque hinc supremum illud juris præceptum vim accepit quod *honestè* (id est piè) *vivere* jubet. Atque hoc sensu rectè a viris doctis inter desiderata relatum est jus naturæ et gentium, traditum secundum disciplinam Christianorum, id est (ex Christi documentis) *τὰ ἀνώτερα* sublimia divina sapientûm."

(*g*) Light of nature (by Abraham Tucker, under the name of Edward Search.) See Mackintosh's account of this very original writer in his Diss. Ethical Philosophy, p. 268, (ed. Whewell,) vol. v. p. 190.

(*h*) St. Augustin, de Civ. Dei, lib. i. c. xv. 2.

(*i*) *Καὶ δίκαιος ἀρ' ἀνὴρ δικαίας πολέως, κατ' αὐτὸ τὸ τῆς δικαιοσύνης εἶδος οὐδὲν διοίσει, ἀλλ' ὁμοῖς ἔσται.*—Plato, de Republic., l. iv. (443,) ed. Stalbaum, vol. iii. p. 300.

voice and the language of inspiration which has told us that "the work of righteousness shall be peace; and the effect of righteousness, quietness and assurance for ever."(*k*)

(*k*) Isaiah, xxxii. 17.

CONTENTS OF APPENDIX.

The pages referred to are those between brackets [ ].

APPENDIX I.

State Papers.

APPENDIX II.

Causæ Belli Justificæ.

APPENDIX III.

Mediation and Intervention.

APPENDIX IV.

APPENDIX V.

APPENDIX VI.

APPENDIX VII.

APPENDIX VIII.

De Captivis et Postliminio, et Redemptis ab Hostibus.

APPENDIX IX.

APPENDIX X.

APPENDIX XI.

APPENDIX XII.

APPENDIX XIII.

APPENDIX XIV.

APPENDIX XV.

APPENDIX XVI.

APPENDIX XVII.

APPENDIX XVIII.

APPENDIX XIX.

APPENDIX XX.

APPENDIX XXI.

APPENDIX XXII.

TREATIES.—EFFECT OF SILENCE IN.—MEDIATION.—INTERVENTION.

APPENDIX XXIII.

APPENDIX.

*APPENDIX I. [*753]

STATE PAPERS.

Letter of Lord Grenville dismissing French Ambassador, Mons. Chavelin, dated Whitehall, December 31*st*, 1792.—(*From State Papers relating to the War against France. London*, 1794, *p*. 227.)

I HAVE received, Sir, from you a note, in which, styling yourself Minister Plenipotentiary of France, you communicate to me, as the King's Secretary of State, the instructions which you state to have yourself received from the Executive Council of the French Republic. You are not ignorant, that since the unhappy events of the 10th of August, the King has thought proper to suspend all official communication with France. You are yourself no otherwise accredited to the King, than in the name of His Most Christian Majesty. The proposition of receiving a minister accredited by any other authority or power in France would be a new question; which, whenever it should occur, the King would have the right to decide, according to the interests of his subjects, his own dignity, and the regard which he owes to his allies, and to the general system of Europe. I am therefore to inform you, Sir, in express and formal terms, that I acknowledge you in no other public character than that of Minister from His Most Christian Majesty, and that, consequently you cannot be admitted to treat with the King's Ministers, in the quality and under the form stated in your note.

"But observing that you have entered into explanations of some of the circumstances which have given to England strong grounds of uneasiness and jealousy, and that you speak of these explanations as being of a nature to bring our two countries nearer, I have been unwilling to convey to you the notification stated above, without at the same time explaining myself clearly and distinctly on the subject of what you have communicated to me, though under a form which is neither regular nor official.

Your explanations are confined to three points.

The first is, that of the decree of the National Convention, of the 19th of November, in the expressions of which all England saw the formal declaration of a design to extend universally the new principles of government adopted in France, and to encourage disorder and revolt in all countries, even in those which are neutral. If this interpretation which you represent as injurious to the Convention, could admit of any doubt, [*754] it is but *too well justified by the conduct of the Convention itself; and the application of these principles to the King's dominions has been shown unequivocally, by the public reception given to the promoters of sedition in this country, and by the speeches made to them precisely at the time of this decree, and since on several different occasions.

Yet, notwithstanding all these proofs, supported by other circumstances, which are but too notorious, it would have been with pleasure that we should have seen here such explanations and such a conduct as would have satisfied the dignity and honour of England, with respect to what has already passed; and would have offered a sufficient security in future for the maintenance of that respect towards the rights, the government, and the tranquillity of neutral powers, which they have on every account the right to expect.

Neither this satisfaction, nor this security, is found in the terms of an explanation which still declares to the promoters of sedition in every country, what are the cases in which they may count beforehand on the support and succour of France; and which reserves to that country the right of mixing herself in our internal affairs, whenever she shall judge it proper, and on principles incompatible with the political institutions of all the countries of Europe. No one can avoid perceiving how much a declaration like this is calculated to encourage disorder and revolt in every country. No one can be ignorant how contrary it is to the respect which is reciprocally due from independent nations, nor how repugnant to those principles which the King has followed on his part, by abstaining at all times from any interference whatever in the internal affairs of France; and this contrast is alone sufficient to show, not only that England cannot consider such an explanation as satisfactory, but that she must look upon it as a fresh avowal of those dispositions which she sees with so just an uneasiness and jealousy.

I proceed to the two other points of your explanation, which concern the general disposition of France with regard to the allies of Great Britain, and the conduct of the Convention and its officers relative to the Scheldt. The declaration which you there make, that France will not attack Holland so long as that power shall observe an exact neutrality, is conceived nearly in the same terms with that which you was charged to make in the name of His Most Christian Majesty, in the month of June last. Since that first declaration was made, an officer, stating himself to be employed in the service of France, has openly violated both the territory, and the neutrality of the Republic, in going up the Scheldt to attack the citadel of Antwerp, notwithstanding the determination of the Government not to grant this passage, and the formal protest by which [*755] they opposed it. Since the same declaration was made, the Convention has thought itself authorized to *annul the rights of the

Republic exercised within the limits of its own territory, and enjoyed by virtue of the same treaties by which her independence is secured; and at the very moment when, under the name of an amicable explanation, you renew to me in the same terms the promise of respecting the independence and the rights of England and her allies, you announce to me, that those in whose name you speak intend to maintain these open and injurious aggressions.

It is not, certainly, on such a declaration as this that any reliance can be placed for the continuance of public tranquillity.

But I am unwilling to leave, without a more particular reply, what you say on the subject of the Scheldt. If it were true that this question is in itself of little importance, this would only serve to prove more clearly that it was brought forward only for the purpose of insulting the allies of England, by the infraction of their neutrality, and by the violation of their rights, which the faith of treaties obliges us to maintain. But you cannot be ignorant, that here the utmost importance is attached to those principles which France wishes to establish by this proceeding, and to those consequences which would naturally result from them; and that not only those principles and those consequences will never be admitted by England, but that she is, and ever will be, ready to oppose them with all her force.

France can have no right to annul the stipulations relative to the Scheldt, unless she has also the right to set aside equally all the other treaties between all the powers of Europe, and all the other rights of England, or of her allies. She can even have no pretence to interfere in the question of opening the Scheldt, unless she were the sovereign of the Low Countries, or had the right to dictate laws to all Europe.

England never will consent that France shall arrogate the power of annulling at her pleasure, and under the pretence of a pretended natural right of which she makes herself the only judge, the political system of Europe, established by solemn treaties, and guaranteed by the consent of all the Powers. This Government, adhering to the maxims which it has followed for more than a century, will also never see with indifference, that France shall make herself, either directly or indirectly, sovereign of the Low Countries, or general arbitress of the rights and liberties of Europe. If France is really desirous of maintaining friendship and peace with England, she must show herself disposed to renounce her views of aggression and aggrandizement, and to confine herself within her own territory, without insulting other Governments, without disturbing their tranquillity, and without violating their rights.

With respect to that character of ill-will which is endeavoured to be found in the conduct of England towards France, I cannot discuss it, because you speak of it in general terms only, without *alleging a single fact. All Europe has seen the justice and the generosity [*756] which have characterized the conduct of the King. His Majesty has always been desirous of peace: he desires it still; but such as may be real and solid, and consistent with the interests and dignity of his own dominions, and with the general security of Europe.

On the rest of your paper I say nothing. As to what relates to me and my colleagues, the King's Ministers owe to His Majesty the account of their conduct; and I have no answer to give to you on this subject, any more than on that of the appeal which you propose to make to the English Nation. This nation, according to that constitution by which its liberty and its prosperity are secured, and which it will always be able to defend against every attack, direct or indirect, will never have with foreign Powers connection or correspondence, except through the organ of its King; of a King whom it loves and reveres, and who has never for an instant separated his rights, his interests, and his happiness, from the rights, the interests, and the happiness of his people.

I have the honour to be, &c.,

GRENVILLE.

APPENDIX II.

CAUSÆ BELLI JUSTIFICÆ.

Letter of Mr. Canning to Sir Charles Stuart, as to the State of Spain in 1823.—*From State Papers* (*Spain*,) 1822, 1823. Vol. 10. p. 25.

[*Foreign Office, January* 28, 1823.

SIR,—Shortly after I had despatched the messenger yesterday, M. de Marcellus delivered to me the official answer of M. de Chateaubriand to the note addressed by me to M. de Marcellus on the 10th instant.

As it appears from your Excellency's despatch of the 24th, which also reached me yesterday, that M. de Chateaubriand, though he stated to your Excellency the substance of this note, had not furnished you with a copy of it, I think it right to inclose a copy for your information.

Upon a first consideration, I am by no means sure that it will be necessary to reply officially to this note of M. de Chateaubriand; since it, in effect, admits all the material propositions of the note to which it is an answer.

[*757] The questions brought forward by France at Verona are *acknowledged to have been *French* questions, in the sense in which they are in my note described to have been such; that is to say, the interest of France is stated in those questions, not as distinct from the interest of Europe, but as more immediate:—and it is not denied that the refusal of his Majesty's Plenipotentiary to concur in the decisions of Verona was founded on the omission by France to substantiate any specific ground of complaint against the Spanish Government.

In the subsequent part of M. de Chateaubriand's note, while the assertion of my note of the 10th instant—that Great Britain had, in 1820, declined anticipating hypothetical cases in which it might be impossible to remain at peace with Spain—is disputed; the only two cases which are cited in exception of that assertion are cases wholly independent of the principle of interference in the internal concerns of other nations.

It is averred, that we admitted the necessity of war against Spain;

first, if Spain herself should be guilty of aggression against other states; and, secondly and specifically, if she should attempt to possess herself of Portugal.

Unquestionably, with respect to either of those cases, Great Britain would admit, not only prospectively and hypothetically, and as to Spain, but positively and directly as to any Power whatever, that aggression against any of its neighbours would justify war; and that aggression against Portugal would impose upon Great Britain the duty of protecting her ally.

But these admissions leave the question, as to the right of interference in the affairs of Spain, where it was.

With respect to that part of M. de Chateaubriand's note which describes the nature of the demands intended to be made by France upon Spain, and takes credit for the moderation of them; your Excellency will not fail to observe, that our difference with France and the allies throughout, is not as to the arrangements which it might be desirable to obtain from Spain, but as to the principle upon which France and the allies propose to require them.

We disclaim for ourselves, and deny for other Powers, the right of requiring any changes in the internal institutions of independent States, with the menace of hostile attack in case of refusal. The moderation of such demands in no degree justifies in our eyes such a mode of enforcing them; and this distinction it is the more important to keep steadily in view, and to impress upon the French Government at a moment when, for their sake, and at their desire, we are suggesting to Spain, in a tone of friendly counsel, alterations similar to those which France is proposing as the alternative of hostilities.

Your Excellency will speak in this sense to M. de Chateaubriand, when you acknowledge on my part the receipt of his official note; from the general tone of which, and from the friendliness of its expressions towards this country, you will inform M. de *Chateaubriand that [*758] his Majesty's Government derives the liveliest satisfaction; at the same time that it views with deep regret the tendency of that part of the Note which appears to indicate an expectation of hostilities with Spain.

I am, &c.,

George Canning.

H. E. the Rt. Hon. Sir Charles Stuart.

APPENDIX III.

MEDIATION AND INTERVENTION.

Despatch of Mr. Canning on the State of Spain.—From State Papers (Spain.) Vol. 10, *p.* 19.

The undersigned, His Majesty's Principal Secretary of State for

Foreign Affairs, has received from the Duke of Wellington, late His Majesty's Plenipotentiary at the Congress of Verona, and has laid before the King his master, the answer of the Minister for Foreign Affairs of His most Christian Majesty, to the Official Note, in which the Duke of Wellington, on his return from Verona, tendered to the French Government the mediation of the King, for the adjustment of differences between France and Spain.

The undersigned is commanded to address to M. de Marcellus, Chargé d'Affaires of His Most Christian Majesty, the following observations on the Note of His Excellency the Duke de Montmorency, to be transmitted by M. de Marcellus to his Court.

The King has seen with pleasure, that His Most Christian Majesty does justice to the sentiments which dictated the offer of His Majesty's mediation: and although the view which is taken in M. D. Montmorency's Note, of the nature of the differences between the French and Spanish Governments, has induced His Most Christian Majesty to decline that mediation, the King will not the less anxiously employ, in every way that is yet open to him, those "conciliatory dispositions," for which His Most Christian Majesty gives him credit, to bring about a state of things less menacing to the peace of Europe, than that which is exhibited in the present position of those two Governments towards each other.

The British Cabinet had not to learn how fearfully the tranquillity of all Europe must be affected by the hostile collision of France and Spain. Accordingly, in the Duke of Wellington's Official Note, the "adjustment" of the supposed "differences between the French and Spanish Governments," was stated as auxiliary to "the preservation of the peace
[*759] of the world." But *the British Cabinet certainly did not understand the questions brought forward at Verona, by the Plenipotentiary of His Most Christian Majesty, with respect to the actual situation and possible conduct of Spain, to be questions in which the concern of France was so little distinguishable from that of other Powers, as the Duke de Montmorency's Note represents it.

The Plenipotentiary of the King of France solicited from His Most Christian Majesty's allies a Declaration:—1st, Whether, if France should find herself obliged to recall her Minister from Madrid, and to break off all diplomatic relations with Spain, they would be disposed to take the like measure, and to recall their several Legations?

2nd. If war should break out between France and Spain, in what form and by what acts, would they afford to France that moral support which would give to her proceedings the whole force of the alliance, and would inspire a salutary fear into the revolutionists of all countries?

3rd. What were the intentions of the several Powers, both as to the substance and the form of the direct assistance which they would be disposed to give to France, in a case in which, upon her demand, their active intervention should become necessary?

France, therefore, originated the discussions upon Spanish affairs at Verona; and the answers of the three continental members of the Alliance were addressed to the cases supposed, and to the support demanded by France.

In common with the Three Continental Powers, the Plenipotentiary of His majesty considered the question of peace or war with Spain, as a question peculiarly French. In his answer (given in simultaneously with those of the Three Continental Powers) to the queries of the French Plenipotentiary, and in all the discussions which followed thereupon, the Duke of Wellington uniformly alleged, as one of his reasons for not assenting to the propositions of M. de Montmorency, the ignorance of the British Government as to the antecedent transactions and communications (during the last two years) between the Governments of France and Spain.

No objection was stated by the Duke of Wellington, on the part of the King his master, to the precautionary measures of France, within her own frontier; measures which the right of self-defence plainly authorized, not only against the danger of contagious disease (in which they professedly originated, and to which, till the month of September, they were exclusively ascribed,) but against those inconveniences which might possibly arise to France from civil contest in a country separated from France only by a conventional line of demarcation; against the moral infection of political intrigue, and against the violation of French territory by occasional military incursions. But it appeared to His [*760] *Majesty's Plenipotentiary at Verona to be necessary and just, that, before he was called upon to promise eventually the support of his Government to measures on the part of France which were likely to lead to war with Spain, opportunity should have been allowed to his Government to examine the grounds of those measures; that the cause of offence given by Spain to France should have been specifically defined.

It was therefore impossible for His Majesty's Plenipotentiary to "concur" in the decisions of Verona.

It remains for the undersigned to advert to that part of the French Official Note, which appears to insinuate a reproach against this country, as if she had abandoned at Verona opinions which she had formerly declared with respect to the affairs of Spain.

"England," it is said, "partook, in 1820, of the inquietude which the revolution in Spain occasioned to many great Powers; she foresaw cases in which it might be impossible to preserve with Spain the relations of good intelligence and peace."

The undersigned must be permitted to say, that though questions were indeed propounded to England in the year 1820, as to possible future contingencies in the affairs of Spain, so far from "foreseeing cases," and deciding upon the conduct which would be applicable to them, in the manner here described, the British Government positively declined to bind itself, by a contingent opinion, to any conditional course of action.

But there was no indisposition or hesitation to avow the principles upon which the opinion of England would be formed, and her course of action regulated. It was not only declared that the British Government disclaimed any general right of interference in the internal concerns of independent nations; but it was specifically stated that there was, perhaps, no country of equal magnitude with Spain, whose internal disturbances would be so little likely to menace other States with that direct and imminent danger, which could alone, in exception to the general rule, justify foreign interference.

The application of these principles to the cases brought forward by France at Verona, was as direct as it was consistent with the former professions of the British Cabinet. That application was further enforced by other considerations, which, though they had not, perhaps, been distinctly anticipated in a prospective and hypothetical argument, bore nevertheless with undeniable force upon the question to be decided at Verona.

Dangers, not necessarily arising from the existence of the internal agitations of Spain, might nevertheless be created by an uncalled for and injudicious interposition in them. The spirit of revolution, which, shut up within the Pyrenees, might exhaust itself in struggles, trying, indeed, [*761] to Spain, but harmless to her *neighbours, if called forth from within those precincts by the provocation of foreign attack—might find, perhaps, in other countries fresh aliment for its fury; and might renew, throughout Europe, the miseries of the five-and-twenty years which preceded the Peace of 1815.

For these and abundant other reasons, the voice of His Majesty's Plenipotentiary at Verona was for peace. The preservation of general peace is the earnest wish and object of His Majesty: and the undersigned is commanded to repeat, that no means will be left unexhausted by His Majesty's Government, which the impartial employment of good offices can afford, to soothe the irritation at present unhappily subsisting between the Governments of France and Spain, and to prevent, if possible, the commencement of hostilities, the consequences of which no human foresight can calculate.

The undersigned, &c.,
GEORGE CANNING.

The Vicomte de Marcellus.

APPENDIX IV.

Another Despatch from Mr. Canning on the same Subject, dated March 31st, 1823.—From State Papers (Spain,) Vol. 10, pp. 64-70.)

[*Foreign Office, March 31st, 1823.*

SIR,—The hopes of an accommodation between France and Spain, which His Majesty has so long been encouraged to cherish, in despite of all unfavourable appearances, being now unhappily extinguished, I am commanded by His Majesty to address to your Excellency, for the purpose of being communicated to the French Minister, the following explanation of the sentiments of your Government upon the present posture of affairs between those two kingdoms.

The King has exhausted his endeavours to preserve the peace of Europe.

The question of an interference in the internal concerns of Spain, on account of the troubles and distractions which have for some time prevailed in that kingdom, was not one on which His Majesty could, for himself, entertain a moment's hesitation. If His Majesty's Plenipotentiary at Verona did not decline taking *part in the deliberations of the Allied Cabinets upon that question, it was because His [*762] Majesty owed to his Allies, upon that, as upon every other subject, a sincere declaration of his opinions, and because he hoped that a friendly and unreserved communication might tend to the preservation of general peace.

The nature of the apprehensions which had induced the King of France to assemble an army, within his own frontier, upon the borders of Spain, had been indicated, in the first instance, by the designation of the "Cordon Sanitaire." The change of that designation to that of an "Army of Observation" (which took place in the month of September last,) did not appear to His Majesty to imply more than that the defensive system originally opposed to the contagion of physical disease, would be continued against the possible inconveniences, moral or political, which might arise to France, from a civil contest raging in a country separated from the French territory only by a conventional line of demarcation. The dangers naturally incident to an unrestrained intercourse between two countries so situated towards each other, the dangers of political intrigue, or of occasional violation of territory, might sufficiently justify preparations of military defence.

Such was the state of things between France and Spain at the opening of the Congress of Verona. The proposition brought forward by the French Plenipotentiary in the Conferences of the Allied Cabinets were founded on this state of things. Those propositions did not relate to any project of carrying attack into the heart of the Spanish Monarchy, but were in the nature of inquiries:—1st. What countenance France might expect to receive from the Allies, if she should find herself under the necessity of breaking off diplomatic intercourse with the Court of Madrid? and, 2ndly, What assistance, in supposed cases of outrage to be committed, or of violence to be menaced by Spain? These cases were all contingent and precautionary. The answers of the three Continental Powers were of a correspondent character.

The result of the discussions at Verona was a determination of His Majesty's Allies, the Emperors of Austria and Russia and the King of Prussia:—1st. To make known to the Cabinet of Madrid, through their respective Ministers at that Court, their sentiments upon the necessity of a change in the present system of the Spanish Government; and, in the event of an unsatisfactory answer to that communication, to recall their respective Ministers, and to break off all diplomatic intercourse with Spain. 2ndly. To make common cause with France against Spain, in certain specified cases; cases, as has been already observed, altogether contingent and precautionary.

His Majesty's Plenipotentiary declined concurring in these measures; not only because he was unauthorized to pledge the faith of his Government to any hypothetical engagement, but because *his [*763]

Government had, from the month of April, 1820, uniformly recommended to the Powers of the alliance to abstain from all interference in the internal affairs of Spain; and because, having been from the same period entirely unacquainted with whatever transactions might have taken place between France and Spain, his Government could not judge on what grounds the Cabinet of the Tuileries meditated a possible discontinuance of diplomatic relations with the court of Madrid, or on what grounds they apprehended an occurrence, apparently so improbable, as a commencement of hostilities against France by Spain.

No proof was produced to His Majesty's Plenipotentiary of the existence of any design on the part of the Spanish Government to invade the territory of France; of any attempt to introduce disaffection among her soldiery, or of any project to undermine her political institutions; and so long as the struggles and disturbances of Spain should be confined within the circle of her own territory, they could not be admitted by the British Government to afford any plea of foreign interference. If the end of the last and the beginning of the present century saw all Europe combined against France, it was not on account of the internal changes which France thought necessary for her own political and civil reformation, but because she attempted to propagate, first her principles, and afterwards her dominion by the sword.

Impossible as it was for his Majesty to be party to the measures concerted at Verona with respect to Spain, his Majesty's Plenipotentiary declared, that the British Government could only endeavour, through his Majesty's Minister at the Court of the Catholic King, "to allay the ferment which those measures might occasion at Madrid, and to do all the good in his power."

Up to this period no communication had taken place between his Majesty and the Court of Madrid, as to the discussions at Verona. But about the time of the arrival of his Majesty's Plenipotentiary, on his return from Verona, at Paris, Spain expressed a desire for the "friendly interposition" of his Majesty to avert the calamities of war; Spain distinctly limited this desire to the employment of such "good offices," on the part of Great Britain, as would not be inconsistent with "the most strictly conceived system of neutrality." Nor has any period occurred throughout the whole of the intercourse of the British Government with Spain, at which the Spanish Government has been for one moment led, by that of Great Britain, to believe that the policy of his Majesty in a contest between France and Spain, would be other than neutral.

In pursuance of this request, and of his previous declaration at Verona, his Majesty's Plenipotentiary received instructions at Paris, to make to the French Government the offer of his Majesty's mediation. In making this offer the British Government deprecated, from motives of expediency [*764] as well as from considerations *of justice, the employment towards Spain of a language of reproach or intimidation. They represented, as matter of no light moment, the first breach, by whatever Power, of that general pacific settlement which had been so recently established, and at the cost of so many sufferings and sacrifices to all nations. Nor did they disguise from the French Government the anxiety with which they looked forward to all the possible issues of a new war in Europe, if once begun.

In addition to suggestions such as these, the British Government endeavoured to learn from the Cabinet of the Tuileries the nature and amount of the specific grievances of which his Most Christian Majesty complained against Spain; and of such specific measures of redress or conciliation, on the part of Spain, as would arrest the progress of His Most Christian Majesty's warlike preparations.

The French Government declined the formal mediation of His Majesty's alleging, in substance, that the necessity of its warlike preparations was founded, not so much upon any direct cause of complaint against Spain, which might be susceptible of accurate specification and of practical adjustment, as upon the general position in which the two kingdoms found themselves placed towards each other;—upon the effect which all that was passing, and had been for some time passing, in Spain, produced upon the peace and tranquillity of His Most Christian Majesty's dominions; upon the burdensomeness of that defensive armament which France had thought herself obliged to establish on her frontier towards Spain, and which it was alike inconvenient to her to maintain; or, without some change of circumstances which would justify such change of counsel, to withdraw;—upon a state of things, in short, which it was easier to understand than to define; but which, taken altogether, was so intolerable to France, that open hostility would be far preferable to it. War would at least have a tendency to some conclusion; whereas the existing state of the relations between France and Spain might continue for an indefinite time: increasing every day the difficulties of Spain, and propagating disquietude and alarm throughout the French army and nation.

But although His Most Christian Majesty's Government declined, on these grounds, a formal mediation, they professed an earnest desire for peace, and accepted his Majesty's "good offices" with Spain for that object.

Contemplating all the mischiefs which war might inflict upon France, and, through France, ultimately, perhaps, upon all Europe; and which it must inflict more immediately and inevitably, upon Spain,—whose internal animosities and agitations a foreign war could not but exasperate and prolong—the British Government was deeply impressed with the necessity of peace for both kingdoms; and resolved, therefore, whether invested or not with *the formal character of mediator, to make every effort, and to avail itself of every chance for the prevention of [*765] hostilities. The question was now become a question simply and entirely between Spain and France; and the practical point of the inquiry was, not so much how the relations of those two Governments had been brought into their present awkward complication, as how that complication could be solved without recourse to arms, and an amicable adjustment produced, through mutual explanation and concession.

Nothing could have induced his Majesty to suggest to the Spanish nation, a revision of its political institutions as the price of his Majesty's friendship. But Spaniards of all parties and descriptions admitted some modifications of the Constitution of 1812 to be indispensably necessary; and if in such a crisis as that in which Spain now found herself distracted at once by the miseries of civil war and by the apprehension of foreign invasion,—the adoption of modifications, so admitted to be desirable in themselves, might afford a prospect of composing her internal dissensions, and might at the same time furnish to the French Government a motive for withdrawing from the menacing position which it had assumed towards Spain, the British Government felt that no scruple of delicacy, or fear of misconstruction, ought to restrain them from avowing an earnest wish that the Spaniards could prevail upon themselves to consider of such modifications, or at least to declare their disposition to consider them hereafter.

It is useless now to discuss what might have been the result of his Majesty's anxious endeavours to bring about an accommodation between France and Spain, if nothing had occurred to interrupt their progress. Whatever might be the indisposition of the Spanish Government to take the first step towards such an accommodation, it cannot be disguised that the principles avowed, and the pretensions put forward by the French Government, in the Speech from the Throne at the opening of the Chambers at Paris, created new obstacles to the success of friendly intervention. The communication of that speech to the British Government was accompanied, indeed, with renewed assurances of the pacific disposition of France; and the French ministers adopted a construction of the passage most likely to create an unfavourable impression in Spain, which stripped it of part of its objectionable character. But all the attempts of the British Government to give effect at Madrid to such assurances and explanations proved unavailing. The hopes of success became gradually fainter, and have now vanished altogether.

It remains only to describe the conduct which it is his Majesty's desire and intention to observe in a conflict between two nations, to each of whom his Majesty is bound by the ties of amity and alliance.

[*766] *The repeated disavowal by his Most Christian Majesty's Government, of all views of ambition and aggrandizement, forbids the suspicion of any design on the part of France to establish a permanent military occupation of Spain, or to force his Catholic Majesty into any measures derogatory to the independence of his Crown, or to his existing relations with other Powers.

The repeated assurances which his Majesty has received of the determination of France to respect the dominions of his Most Faithful Majesty, relieve his Majesty from any apprehension of being called upon to fulfil the obligations of that intimate defensive connection which has so long subsisted between the Crowns of Great Britain and Portugal.

With respect to the provinces in America, which have thrown off their allegiance to the Crown of Spain, time and the course of events appear to have substantially decided their separation from the mother country; although the formal recognition of those provinces as Independent States, by his Majesty, may be hastened or retarded by various external circumstances, as well as by the more or less satisfactory progress in each State, towards a regular and settled form of government. Spain has long been apprised of his Majesty's opinions upon this subject. Disclaiming in the most solemn manner any intention of appropriating to himself the smallest portion of the late Spanish possessions in America, his Majesty is satisfied that no attempt will be made by France to bring under her dominion any of those possessions, either by conquest or by cession, from Spain.

This frank explanation upon the points on which perhaps alone the possibility of any collision of France with Great Britain can be apprehended in a war between France and Spain, your Excellency will represent to M. de Chateaubriand, as dictated by an earnest desire to be enabled to preserve, in that war, a strict and undeviating neutrality; a neutrality not liable to alteration towards either party, so long as the honour and just interests of Great Britain are equalty respected by both.

I am commanded, in conclusion, to direct your Excellency to declare to the French Minister that his Majesty will be at all times ready to renew the interposition of his good offices, for the purpose of terminating those hostilities which his Majesty has so anxiously, although ineffectually, endeavoured to avert.

I am, &c.,
GEORGE CANNING.

H. E. the Rt. Hon. Sir Charles Stuart.

---

*APPENDIX V. [*767]

Power of the High Court of Admiralty to act as a Court of International Law in time of War, without a Prize Act; and as to Jurisdiction of Prize Court over Freight. Argument of Queen's Advocate (Lord Stowell) in Smart v. Wolff, 3 *Durnford and East's Reports, p.* 329.

THE marginal note is as follows:—

"The Admiralty Court has jurisdiction over the question of freight, claimed by a neutral master against the captor, who has taken the goods as prize. And a monition having issued, after the goods were condemned and decreed to be delivered to the captors, at the suit of such master against the plaintiffs as owners or agents of the prize goods to bring into court *the produce remaining in their hands* to answer the freight, this Court refused a prohibition; though no fidejussory caution had been taken before the goods were delivered to the captor, but *the question of freight had been reserved* by thet erms of the decree *for future consideration.*"

The argument is as follows:—

"The Advocate General (Sir William Scott,) Bearcroft and Bower, showed cause against the rule for prohibition; and submitted two propositions to the court. First, that the Court of Admiralty has power by a monition to order in the proceeds of a prize from any person, in whose hands they are charged (and not denied) to be, for the purpose of adjudication, and to enforce the sentence of adjudication. And 2dly, That this power subsists till the enforcement of a sentence of adjudication on all prize claims arising from the capture. As to the first: although the prize court of the Admiralty acts principally *in rem*, yet it possesses a complete and original power over the *persons of the captors*, and those who by their acts become possessed of the proceeds of a prize. By the capture the thing is acquired not to the individual, but to the State; and though it is now usually put into the hands of the captors, it remains in contemplation of law in the custody of the public. Formerly it actually did remain in their custody, as is still the case in all foreign countries: it is merely for the convenience of the captors that the English admiralty permits them to take possession of the property. But it must be remembered that it is so held by them as *agents of the court*, and not *in right of property*; and therefore their possession may be divested by the act of the court, either *ex officio*, or on the application of the parties interested, showing good cause for taking it out of their hands. Now if [*768] *the captor himself be compellable to bring in the proceeds of the prize, his agent must be equally so, since they are both the agents of the public. It is not necessary here to contend that a case may not exist in which a person charged to be possessed of the proceeds of a prize may not show a sufficient cause why the monition should not be enforced, either by denying the fact of possession, or by giving some satisfactory plea why the possession should not be delivered up. It is sufficient in this case that such a monition may issue, calling on the parties to show why the proceeds should not be brought into court. It may be admitted that no such power as this is to be found in the prize acts; but there are many undoubted privileges of the Court of Admiralty which are not given by them. The prize acts are of a modern date, and form indeed but a very small portion of the law of the Admiralty. They were drawn up principally for the direction of the Vice Admiralty Courts, to which a jurisdiction over questions of prize was thereby for the first time given. But a great part of the Admiralty jurisdiction is founded on the established usage, and (as it were) the common law of the Admiralty. It is not contended that the Admiralty has a jurisdiction inconsistent with those statutes; but being affirmative acts, they leave every other matter, not thereby specially provided for, as it was before. And notwithstanding those statutes require that bail shall be taken in some cases, when the possession of the prize is given up, yet they do not destroy the lien which the Admiralty has *in rem*. When the claimant is a foreigner, or insolvent, it is prudent to take a *personal* security; but the *real* security (the thing itself) still continues so long as it remains within the reach of the process of the Court. The suggestion proceeds on an idea that the Admiralty has only jurisdiction over the thing, and that, when the possession is given up, it has no longer any jurisdiction upon the subject, except to the amount of the stipulation given by the parties. Sureties, indeed, are only answerable to the amount of the stipulation; but the prize court of the Admiralty has also a jurisdiction over every person, who obtains the possession of the proceeds of any prize. And there is a material distinction in this respect between the *instance* and the *prize* court of the Admiralty. The former proceeds originally by arrest, in order to compel bail to be given to submit to its jurisdiction; but that is not done in the prize court, whose jurisdiction is founded on a higher authority than the mere consent of the parties; it is founded on the right to enforce the Law of Nations. That such a power as this now contended for is necessary cannot be disputed. Courts of Admiralty are the only tribunals to which neutral subjects can resort on complaints arising in time of war. It is stipulated between all the maritime powers of Europe, that there shall be a Court of Admiralty in their respective *dominions; and in this country it also subsists on the footing of ancient and estab- [*769] lished usage. Then it would be absurd to allow the existence of such a court, and to deny it the necessary power of enforcing its own decrees. For if it has no power of ordering in the proceeds of a prize which is carried into a neutral port, and sold, and the produce remitted to the agents of the captors here, there must necessarily be a failure of justice. But the constant and regular exercise of this power is a decisive proof of its legality. In the course of the last war several instances of this sort occurred, where the prize court of Admiralty exercised the jurisdiction now contended for, and their proceedings were confirmed by the court of appeals. One of them was in the instance of the Buoen Consago, which was a prize taken by an English ship, and carried into Lisbon, where the proceeds were lodged in an English house under the firm of Mayne and Co.: after condemnation of the cargo there, which was confirmed on appeal here, a claim was set up on the part of the joint captors for their proportion of the prize; and a monition was accordingly issued from the court of appeal (at which court the Lords Camden and Grantley were present,) requiring Mayne and Co. to bring the proceeds into court; for disobeying which monition an attachment issued on the 5th of July, 1786; and in consequence of that the proceeds were brought in. The cases of the Misericordia, the Jean de Theodore, the Vrow Maria, the Nostra Seignora De Saragossa, and the Santa Rita, were also mentioned as similar instances. This power of the Admiralty was also incidentally recognized in Parliament in 1785, when a Bill was brought in for the purpose of compelling the prize agents to deliver the proceeds of the capture at St. Eustatia into the hands of certain commissioners; but that bill was dismissed on the ground that the Admiralty Court had a competent power to compel the production of the proceeds, if a proper case were made out. In consequence of this, a monition has since issued against these agents; some of whom are indeed out of the reach of the process of the court, but the others are made amenable. Then if it be objected that as all events this power of the Admiralty only exists till sentence of condemnation, and that afterwards its jurisdiction is at an end, for that then the parties hold the proceeds of the prize not as agents, but in right of property; it is contended,

"2dly. That that power subsists after a general adjudication, until all claims respecting the prize are determined. Those claims may arise from three different parties; the captor enemy, the captured enemy, or a neutral. The rights of the latter form the most important object of the attention of the prize court; for with regard to enemies, the condemnation puts a

[*770] final end to their claims; but it is otherwise with respect to the *neutrals, *whose claims arise after condemnation;* and the condemnation itself is *subject to such rights as neutrals may have* in the property. The neutral master, who is a mere carrier, has a lien on the cargo for freight and expenses; and this lien still continues, notwithstanding a general condemnation, for the cargo is condemned subject to his right. The master is no party to the suit respecting the question of prize; and a judgment can only conclude those who are parties to the suit. And in this particular case the plaintiffs are bound by their own agreement: for the cargo was put into their hands *with* an *express reservation of the question of freight, to be heard in the regular course of causes.* So that this cargo was only delivered to them *conditionally*, and a part of this cargo sufficient to answer the claim for freight and expenses has not been condemned at all. Neither can it be said that the question of freight is to be determined of course, because the master is, *in general*, entitled to freight and expenses; for his claim is subject to many exceptions, which cannot be determined without involving in it the question of prize; as if the captor plead that the goods were contraband, there a direct question arises whether the freight does not become prize as well as the goods. This is one of the most difficult subjects which are agitated in the Admiralty Court, because it may be affected by particular Treaties, the Law of Nations, Proclamations, or Orders in Council. Or if the captor plead that the neutral refused search, or sailed under convoy of the enemy's ships of war, or conveyed intelligence to the enemy; they also are waivers of the rights of neutrality, and must be discussed before the question of freight can be determined; but of none of them can the common law courts take cognizance. The question of freight must be determined by the same court which determines the principal question of prize; otherwise the courts of common law must be converted into prize courts. It may be said that the freight may be adjudged in the Admiralty, and that a proceeding may be instituted in a common law court to enforce that decree; but it would be in vain for the Admiralty to adjudge the question of prize, if they could not order the proceeds to be brought into their court. If they could not give effect to their own adjudication, they would have a power of adjudging that which they could not execute, and the common law courts would have to execute that decree, the justice of which they could not examine; a species of judicature not only vexatious to the subject, but also degrading to both the courts. This jurisdiction now claimed by the Admiralty was recognized by Lord Mansfield in Livingston and Another v. M'Kenzie, at Nisi Prius in 1766. The ship
[*771] Margaret(*a*) was taken in the war before the last by *a king's ship, but restored by the sentence of the Vice Admiralty Court

(*a*) In 1762, this vessel, being the property of Livingston and Welsh of New York, sailed from thence with a cargo of lumber and provisions bound to Jamaica, where she delivered her cargo; and with the proceeds amounting to 1300*l.* in specie she proceeded on a farther voyage to the Spanish settlement of Monti Christe, in the course of which she was taken by his Majesty's ship the "Defiance," commanded by Captain M'Kensie. He took the specie out of the ship, and put a prize master and mariners on board to conduct her to Jamaica; but before her arrival there she was captured by a French ship of war, and carried into Port au

in Jamaica; that sentence was confirmed on appeal here, and the cause was remitted back to Jamaica. The captured, however, brought an action here at common law, founded on the sentence of reversal; but Lord Mansfield was of opinion that it was not maintainable, as the question arose out of a prize cause, and that the Courts of Admiralty ought to enforce their own decrees; and he nonsuited the plaintiffs. In determining a question of this kind, the situation of neutrals is also entitled to some consideration; they are brought into litigation, without any misconduct on their parts, on account of hostilities between this and some other country; and if they were subject to the vexation and expense of instituting a fresh suit in a common law court, after having gone through all the proceedings in the Court of Admiralty, it would be an inducement to foreign powers in time of war to enter into armed neutralities."

---

*APPENDIX VI. [*772]

Right to Capture Enemy's Goods in Neutral Bottoms. Opinion of Lampredi. (From " Commercio dei Popoli Neutrali in tempo di guerra, Trattato di Gio. M. Lampredi. In Firenze, 1788. *Parte* 1, *pp.* 149-153.)

Del resto non avvi esecuzione di diritto perfetto, che non rechi molestia, e danno a qualche individuo. Io alzo il mio edifizio, e tolgo la luce al mio vicino, circondo di siepe un campo, e impedisco il comodo passo ai confinanti proprietary; vendo le mie grasce, e diminuisco il prezzo di quelle degli altri, perchè scemano i compratori: intraprendo un genere di commercio, e diminuisco il guadagno di un terzo che era solo a sarlo ec: ma per queste molestia, che risente qualche individuo l'esecuzione di quei diritti non si potrebbe impedire, se non nel caso dell' estrema necessità, nella collisione dei diritti, e con le cautela esposte di sopra. Anche il diritto naturale dei neutrali di seguitare con le Nazione Belligeranti il solito. Commercio reca pregiudizio alle medesime; molte Navi neutrali cariche di Merci nemiche eviteranno la vigilanzo degli Armatori, ma per questo quel diritto non è men giusto.

Prince, where she was condemned to the French captors. Captain M'Kenzie soon afterwards instituted a suit in the Vice-Admiralty Court in Jamaica against the specie, which he either kept in his possession or had paid into the hands of his agent there. A claim was then set up by the master for the ship as the property of Livingston and Welch, British subjects, residing at New York, and for the specie, as the property of the said owners and of him the claimant, also a British subject. On the 29th of October, 1762, after hearing the cause, the Judge of the Vice-Admiralty Court at Jamaica decreed the sum of 1300*l.* in the possession of the captor to be restored to the claimant, and the ship and the rest of the effects on board at the time of the capture, or the full value, to be also restored to the claimant. From this decree Captain M'Kenzie appealed to the Lords Commissioners of Appeals in prize causes, who on the 1st of May, 1764, affirmed the sentence below, and decreed the cause to be remitted. About two years after this decree the action was brought here.

Questa riflessione mi fa strada a toglier di mezzo le sopra esposte contradizione. Se è lecito, dicono alcuni, predar la roba del nemico ovunque si trovi, ed anche sopra i Bastimenti pacifici, con lesione evidente della libertà dei Neutrali, e ciò perchè il nemico ha diritto di diminuir le forze dell' altro all' infinito, all' effetto di disporlo alla pace, perchè non è lecito arrestare, e impedire i Neutrali, che portano alle Spiagge nemiche Merci lor proprie? Non traggono da queste i Nemici un rinforzo, che reca all' altra parte un danno irreparabile? Perchè è illecito il primo, e lecito, il secondo? Perchè la necessità, della tua difesa ti permette di attaccar la libertà, ed indipendenza di quelle, che portano le Merci, appartenenti ai nemici, e non ti permette di far lo stesso con i Neutrali che portano le loro proprie Merci? Perche, io rispondo, il danno della preda cade quasi tutto sopra i Nemici, e quel poco che cade sopra gli Amici, e Neutrali, si può, comè si è veduto, facilmente riparare ma il danno che risentirebbero i Neutrali dall' essere impediti di vendere come prima facevano le loro Merci naturali, e industriali alle Nazioni, che ora per accidente sono in Guerra, caderebbe tutto sopra di loro, nè si potrebbe in alcun modo riparare; che se riparar si potesse io non dubito punto che il Guerreggiante non avesse il diritto di arrestare tutte le Navi dei Neutrali che recano
[*773] Merci utili alla Nazione nemica, offerendosi per *esempio di comprarle a contanti, e se si trattasle di permuta, esibendosi a somministrarla esso medesimo all' istesso prezzo, ed alle medesime condizioni; ma siccome il primo esigerebbe una spesa enorme, che nessuna Nazione potrebbe sostenere, l'altro sarebbe moralmente impossibile, giacchè una Nazione non può esser fornita delle cose naturali, ed industriali, che sono proprie dell' altra, così ne viene che tra i due diritti perfetti, che si trovano in collisione si permetta l' esercizio di quello, che impedite arrecherebbe un danno, che non è in modo alcuno riparabile.

Questa ragione fortissima, a cui non mi par che si possa dare nessuna adequata risposta, mi ha persuaso una volta, e mi persuade ancora, che non avvi contradizione alcuna tra le due Leggi delle Nazioni, delle quali l' una permette la preda della roba nemica nei Bastimenti dei Neutrali, l' altra permette ai Neutrali il trasporto, e la vendita della roba loro alle Nazioni nemiche; ambedue devono esser riguardate, come regole inviolabili per le Nazioni Belligeranti, e per i Popoli pacifici in tempo di guerra, ed ambedue son fondate in ragione, perchè salvano ad un tempo medesimo e i Diritti dei Guerreggianti, e quelli dei Neutrali, tra i quali se i Locatori dell' Opere, e delle Navi loro risentono qualche danno, debbono piuttosto che dei Guerreggianti, dolersi dell' infortunio della Guerra, di cui gli effetti dannosi e funesti sono risentiti più, ò meno non solamente da loro, ma ancora da tutte le altre Nazioni Commercianti, e particolarmente da quelle, che erano usate ad avere un commercio ordinario con le Nazioni in Guerra.(*a*)

(*a*) Dell' Commercio dei Popoli Neutrali in Tempo di Guerra. Trattato di Gio. M. Lampredi (in Firenze, 1788,) Parte I. pp. 149-153.

APPENDIX VII.

D'Abreu.—Collecion de los Tratados de Paz, Allianza, Neutralidad, &c.—Conspectus Capitum, in this Work.

Indice de los Capitulos de este Tratado.

Capitulo I. De la Pressa, su Ethimologia, y definicion; lo que debe preceder para hacerse legitimamente el Corso y utilidades, que de él resultan. Pag. 1.

Cap. II. Si serán de buena Pressa los Navios Mercantiles, que navegaren sin Passaporte, y demás Despachos necessarios, y quales deban ser estos. Pag. 16.

Cap. III. Si los Navios Apressados deben ser conducidos á los [*774] *Puertos, ó basta haverlos posseído por espacio de veinte y quatro horas, para que se adquiera el dominio irrevocable de ellos, y de sus efectos al Apressador. Pag. 40.

Cap. IV. Si las Pressas hechas á los Enemigos en los Puertos de los Soberanos, se adquieren plena, é irrevocablemente el Apressador. Pag. 53.

Cap. V. Si la Prohibicion de Apressar dentro de los Puertos del Soberano Amigo comun, debe extenderse â sus Mares adjacentes. Pag. 68.

Cap. VI. Si la Pressa llevada á Puertos de Amigos Comunes, debe restituírse á sus antiguos Dueños, ó nó. Pag. 81.

Cap. VII. Si pueden ser licitamente Apressadas las Naves, que no abatieren al Estandarte Real, amaynaren sus Velas, ni hizieren el Saludo correspondiente. Pag. 88.

Cap. VIII. Si las Mercaderias, y demás Efectos pertenecientes á Confederados, y Amigos, que vienen embarcados en Navios de Enemigos, pueden ser licitamente Apressados. Pag. 104.

Cap. IX. Si las Mercaderias, y otros Efectos pertenecientes á Enemigos, que vienen embarcados en Naves de Amigos, y Confederados, pueden ser licitamente Apressados, igualmente que la Nave Conductora. Pag. 111.

Cap. X. Si pueden ser licitamente Apressados los Bienes de los Moros, y Judios, aunque vengan al abrigo de Navios de Amigos, Aliados, ó Confederados. Pag. 129.

Cap. XI. Si se puede passar licitamente al Apressamiento de los Navios de Amigos, ó Aliados, que conduxeren á nuestros Enemigos, Mercaderias de Contravando, como son Armas, y Municiones: y en qué casos se podrán Apressar los Bastimentos, que se conducen por Navios Amigos, y Aliados á Plazas de Enemigos; y quales se entiendan Sitiadas, y Bloqueadas, para observarse en este particular los Tratados de Pazes. Pag. 141.

Cap. XII. Si debe estimarse por buena Pressa el Navio, que Navegare con Patentes de dos diferentes Principes. Pag. 151.

Cap. XIII. Si los Armadores estarán obligados á conducir las Pressas al Puerto en donde Armaron, ó podrán llevarlas á otro qualquiera, dentro, o fuera del Reyno. Pag. 155.

Cap. XIV. Del Juez Competente en prîmera, y segunda instancia, par el conocimiento de la legitimidad de las Pressas. Pag. 169.

la Real Hazicnda los Armadores, assi Naturales como Estrangeros, que las trageren al Reyno. Y con motivo de una *duda, que se suscito en la Junta del Almirantazgo de Inglaterra, se trata de la [*776] parte, que debentener en la reparticion de las Pressas los que ayudaron â su Rendicion. Pag. 272.

Articulos de Tratados de Pazes, desde la pagina 291 hasta la 308.

Patente de Corso. Pag. 309.

Ordenanza de Corso. Pag. 315.

APPENDIX VIII.

DE CAPTIVIS ET POSTLIMINIO, ET REDEMPTIS AB HOSTIBUS.

(Extract from Voet, Commentarius ad Pandectas. Tom. IV. lib. xlix. tit. xv. p. 642.)

SUMMARIA.

I. Quales res captæ per hostes, et recuperatæ, postliminio ad dominos priores redeant? Quales capti ac reversi gaudeant jure postliminii? An et dediti? An et redempti, licèt lutro necdum reddito, et an quasi pignori sint pro lutro? An et, qui sponte aliquandiu apud hostes remanserunt, et post redierunt; vel redierunt, sed animo remeandi ad hotes? An transfugæ?

II. Quid sit jus postliminii? An, et quo respectu in pace postliminium sit? An, et quandò postliminio gaudeant, qui per pacis conditiones reversi sunt? An tempore induciarum? An jus postliminii pertineat ad ea, quæ apud hostes fiant? An ad ea, quæ facti sunt? ad possessionem?

III. Quid moribus obtineat de captis in bello rebus et personis, ac variis circa ea dubiis? *remiss.* An capta statim cedant hostibus jure dominii, an demùm postquàm intra præsidia eorum delata sunt?

IV. De jure postliminii circa naves per hostes captas cum mercibus, et post recuperatas, ex jure medio et recentissimo Fœderati Belgii, ac pactionibus publicis.

V. De captâ nave hostili, in quâ sunt merces eorum, qui hostes non sunt; et quid, si hostes in eas merces jus aliquod habeant? An in dubio nave hostili vectæ res præsumantur hostiles? Et quid circa hæc pactionibus publicis Ordinum Generalium cum aliis populis definitum sit?

VI. An navis eorum, qui extra belli causam erant, per nostros capta hostes, et per nos iisdem erepta, pristinis dominis reddi debeat?

*VII. Quid juris, si navis non vi recepta, sed per aliquem redempta sit, verùm pretio viliore? [*777]

I. In bello justo (quòd nempe populus liber alteri populo libero indixit,) capta cedunt hostibus capientibus, sed recuperata gaudent jure postliminii et ad pristinos dominos revertuntur, si quidem immobilia sint, non item, si mobilia, nisi sit navis longa oneraria propter belli usum, vel equus freni patiens, quia sine culpâ equitis proripere sese potuit. L. navibus 2, pr. et § seqq.; l. 3, ff., h. t. Sed et ipsi cives capti aut dediti capientium quidem servi fiunt, verùm iterum reversi ex hoc postliminii jure statum pristinum juraque omnia per captivitatem amissa recuperant, non modo si capti, sed etiam, si ex vis majoris necessitate dediti sint, l. eos qui 4, l. retro 16, et passim, ff., h. t.; l. si quos forte 19, C. h. t.; vel publico decreto hostibus quidem dediti, sed ab iis non recepti, l. ult. in fine, ff., de legation.; non tamen, si armis positis sese turpiter hostibus dederint; quo de casu accipienda l. postliminio 17, ff., h. t.; nec, si, cùm ex pacis conditionibus reverti possent, suâ voluntate apud hostes manserint, ac post revertantur, l. si captivus 20, ff., h. t.; nec reversi, sed cum animo ad hostes remeandi, l. postliminii jus 5, § ult., ff., h. t.; nec illi, qui priùs malo consilio et proditoris animo ad hostes transfugerunt. L. postliminium 19, § transfugæ 4, ff., h. t. Nec interest, quantùm ad jus postliminii attinet, utrùm lutro dato, redempti ab hostibus, an aliter dimissi, aut vi aut fallaciâ potestatem hostium evadentes reversi sint, l. nihil interest 26, ff., h. t.; cùm et redempti eodem jure gaudeant, non modo postquàm lutrum redemptori suo restituerint, sed et ante, quàm primum scilicèt in pristinum limen imperii reversi fuerint; arg. l. cum et 6 et 7, C. h. t.; de postliminio; l. ab hostibus 2, C. h. t.; l. qui testamento 20, potestatis 1, ff., qui testam. fac. poss.; ubi ante lutrum redditum ingenuitas restituta supponitur. Undè et tanquàm ingenui hæreditatem sibi delatam vindicare possunt, l. is qui liber 15, C. h. t.; de postliminio; licèt quodam quasi pignoris jure devincti maneant redemptori suo, donec lutrum ab ipsis, vel ab alio quocumque pro ipsis, restitutum fuerit, ut dictum tit. quæ res pign. dari, num. 1; vel juris interpretatione pro restitutâ habeatur, dum redemptor illud remisit, l. si liber. 11, C. h. t., de postlim.; vel mulierem redemptam prostituit, l. fædissimæ 7, C. h. t.; vel eam sibi duxit uxorem, L. si quis ingenuam 21, ff., h. t.; l. si is, qui 13, C. h. t.

II. Est autem postliminium jus amissæ rei recipiendæ ab extraneo, et in statum pristinum restituendæ inter nos ac liberos populos Regesque moribus ac legibus constitutum: nam quod bello amisimus, *aut etiam circa bellum*, hoc si rursus recipiamus, dicimur postliminio recipere. L. postliminium 19, ff. h. t. Non enim in bello tantùm, sed et in pace postliminium aliquo respectu esse, manifestum est ex Pomponio in l. postliminii jus 5, pr. et § 1, 2, ff., h. t. Quemadmodum et pace redintegratâ postliminio locus esse potest in his, qui eò usque captivi apud hostes manserunt; [*778] *sed tamen non aliter, quàm si id per pacis conditiones cautum fuerit, ut ad suos revertantur: quod ideò placuisse Servius scribit, quia spem revertendi civibus in virtute bellicâ magìs, quàm in pace esse, Romani voluerunt, l. in bello 12, ff., h. t. (in cujus legis principio pro eo, *de quibus nihil in pactis*, legendum esse, *de de quibus id in pactis*, monet ex Petro Fabro ac Cujacio Gothofredus *in notis*, et Hugo Grotius, *de jure belli et pacis*, lib. 3, cap. 9, num. 4;) nisi si qui essent, qui pacis tempore venerant ad alteros, et bello subito exardescente facti erant belli jure servi eorum, apud quos, jam hostes, suo *facto*, vel magìs *fato* (ut quosdam legere scribit Simon van Leeuwen, *in notis*,) adeòque sine culpâ suâ, deprehendebantur: hos enim postliminii jure in pace gaudere comprobatum fuit, si non fœdere cautum fuerit, ne his esset postliminii jus. D. l. in bello 12, in fine princip., ff., h. t. Planè induciarum tempore cùm in breve et præsens tempus convenit, ne invicem se lacessant, postliminium non esse Paulus auctor est. D. l. postliminium 19, § induciæ 1, ff., h. t. Neque etiam jus postliminii ad ea pertinet, quæ apud hostes fiunt, non magìs quàm fictio legis Corneliæ : nisi fictione juris intelligantur retrò in urbe facta esse, § ult. Inst. quib. non est permiss. fac. testam.; l. ejus, qui apud 8, ff., qui testam. fac. poss.; arg. l. in bello 12, § codicilli 5, ff., h. t.; l. 1, C. h. t.; nec per hoc jus redintegrantur ea, quæ facti, sed tantùm ea, quæ juris sunt, sive illa jura reverso commoda, sive gravia sint; quale est inter alia onus tutelæ, l. quamvis jure 8, ff., de tutelæ et ration. distrahend. § ab hostibus 2, Inst. de *Attiliano* tutore; ac proindè non possessio, quæ in se spectata tantùm facti est, si ea per captivitatem amissa sit. L. denique 19, ff., ex quibus caus. majores 25 annis; l. si is, qui 15, ff., de usurpat. et usucap.; junct. l. 1, § furiosus 3, ff., de acquirend. vel amitt. possess.

III. Quid moribus nostris circa res bello captas obtineat, quid circa personas ipsas hostiles, quid juris sit, si res hostium captæ, per hostes receptæ, iterumque mox per alios hosti extortæ sint, petendum unà cum aliis similibus ex iis, quæ scripsi in titul. de acquirend, rerum domin., numer. 8. Et quamvis Hugoni Grotio, de jure belli, libr. 3, cap. 9, num. 16; aliisque, placeat, prædam per hostes captam tum demum eorum fieri propriam naturali ratione, cùm intra præsidia hostium delata fuit, arg. l. Pomponius tractat. 44, ff., de acquir. rerum domin.; l. Pomponius scribit, 8, § ult., ff., familæ ercisc.; l. postliminii 5, § in bello 1, ff., h. t.; verius tamen, etiam antè per solam occupationem dominium prædæ hostibus acquiri; cùm naturali ratione dominia rerum à possessione cœperint, et utì cœlo, mari, terrâ capta statim capienti cedunt, ità quoque bello capta, quæ superioribus in eo comparantur à Paulo in l. 1, § 1, ff., de acquir. vel amitt. possess. Adest certè in hoste capiente naturalis apprehensio, adest animus acquirendi, adest justa acquirendi causa in belli jure, adeòque concurrunt ea omnia, quæ ad dominium acquirendum sunt necessaria, *etiam antequàm res captæ intra præsidia deductæ fuerint. Et sanè, ni ità statuas, dominiumque hostibus neges, [*779] donec intra præsidia res delatæ fuerint, dicendum foret, id, quod unus militum manipulus occupavit, per alium manipulum socium et amicum, sed numerosiorem posse iterum auferri, quasi id nondum manipuli primò capientis, sed adhuc hostium res esset: quod utique absurdum est. Nec repugnat d. l. 5, § 1, ff., hoc titul.; cùm tantùm dicat, civem per hostes captum liberum manere, quandiu intra præsidia delatus non est, quod ità favore libertatis, ut multa alia, inductum, ad res trahendum non est. Alterum verò argumentum ex d. libr. 8, § ultim., et d. libr. 44; petitum à bestiis per lupum ereptis, debilius est; quia talis lupus non hosti, cum quo jus belli, sed prædoni, dominium per rapinam haud auferenti, similis est.

IV. Porrò quid itidem anteà apud nos obtinuerit circa naves nostras per hostes captas, iterumque receptas, expositum à me secundùm jura tunc servata in tractatu de jure militari, c. 5., numer. 23. Sed hæc rursùs posteriori jure mutata, dum Placito Ordinum Generalium 13 aprilis, 1677, vol. 3, placit. Holl., pag. 340; constitutum, naves cum mercibus impositis per hostes captas, iterumque per nostrates, proprio sumptu navigantes, recuperatas, jure postliminii ad suos debere dominos reverti, sed ità, ut recuperatori cedat in præmium salvationis pars quinta omnium recuperatorum, si intra horas quadraginta octo navis recepta sit; pars tertia, si posteà, sed intra duplicatum tempus, seu quatuor dies, ex quo hostes occupaverant; dimidia verò, si demùm post quatuor dierum lapsum quantocumque tempore interjecto rursùs hostibus erepta sit. Quòd et anno præcedente per specialem conventionem inter Regem Hispaniæ et Ordines Generales inductum fuerat, sine distinctione, an per naves bellicas, an per alias privatim instructas recuperatio facta esset; quoties vel Belgæ navem Hispanicam, vel Hispani navem Belgicam sic hostis communis potestati iterum subduxissent. Déclaration sur le Traité de la Marine, 25 novembr. 1676, artic. 3, d. vol. 3, pag. 390. Cùm alioquin extra pactionem res sociorum nostrorum per hostes captæ, perque nostros iisdem rursùs ereptæ, nulli subessent restitutioni, secundùm ea, quæ habet Grotius, de jure belli ac pacis, lib. 3, cap. 6, numer. 7; quemadmodum etiam non restituendæ forent, si semel in hostiles portus deductæ fuerint; atque ità plenissimo jure hostium factæ. Groenewegen, ad l. 2, ff., hoc titul.; d. tract. de jure militari, cap. 5, numer. 23. Cæterùm si navis ad subjectos Belgas pertinens, non per privato sumptu instructas naves Belgicas, sed per bellicas Fœderati Belgii recuperata fuisset, placuit Ordinibus Generalibus, in d. placito 12 aprilis, 1677, rata manere ea, quæ anteà fuerant de eo disposita. Tandem novissimè cautum Placito Ordinum Generalium 31 maii 1697, artic. 8, dimidiam partem navis recuperatæ cedere recuperantibus, si illi privato sumptu navigent, [*780] quartam verò, si per *navem bellicam recuperatio facta sit, si modò recepta navis non fuerit sub tutelâ ejus, qui eam recepit, *onder des selfs Convoy*, nullâ ampliùs adhibitâ distinctione, quanto temporis spatio navis per hostes detenta seu possessa fuerit. Sed post hæc scripta, rursùs placuit Ordinibus Generalibus comprobare ea, quæ anno 1677, 13 aprilis, definita fuerant, distinctione scilicet adhibitâ, utrùm recuperatio intra 48, horas, an demum posteà intra duplicatas horas quadraginta octo ab occupatione computandas, an deniquè post duplicatas 48 horas, quandòcumque facta esset; ut primo quidem casu quinta, secundo tertia, ultimo autem dimidia pars recuperantibus, qui suo sumptu naves instruxerunt, cedat. Placit. Ordinum Generalium 6 junii, 1702.

V. Quòd si in navi hostili captâ inveniantur res quædam ad eos pertinentes, qui hostes non sunt; naturali ratione non possunt jure belli acquiri capientibus, quibus cum rerum talium dominis bellum non est, ut dixi d. tract. de jure milit., cap. 5, numer. 21; et auctor est Grotius, de jure belli et pacis, d. lib. 3, cap. 6, numer. 5, 6; nisi hostes in rebus illis aliquod jus habeant. Confer Responsa Juriscons. Holland., part. 3, vol. 2, consil. 1. Sed cùm experientia docuerit, clandestinis fraudibus fingi facilè posse, ut res navibus captis contentæ non ad hostes, sed alios pertinere videantur, præsumptio in dubio hæc concipi potest, hostiles credi res, quæ navibus hostilibus vehuntur; si non aliud pactionibus publicis inter populos constitutum fuerit. Hugo Grotius, d. libr., 3, de jure belli, cap. 6, num. 6. In quam sententiam etiam conceptæ apud nos inveniuntur conventiones inter Ordines Generales Belgii Fœderati, et Reges Galliæ, Sueciæ, Lusitaniæ, dictantes, merces eorum, qui extra partes sunt, in navibus hostilibus captis inventas unà cum navi cedere capienti; contrà verò merces hostium vectas navibus eorum, qui bello impliciti non sunt, jure belli non posse ex istis navibus educi et occupari, nisi sint merces belli usibus inservientes, vulgò, waren van contrabande, vide Tractaat van Vrede met Portugal, 6 aug. 1661, artic. 24, vol. 2, placit. Holland., pag. 2862; Tractaat met Vrankrijk, 27 aprilis, 1662, artic. 35, d. vol. 2, pag. 2915, et 10 augusti, 1678, artic. 22, vol. 3, pag. 372; item Tractaat van Commercie met Vrankrijk, 20 septembr., 1697, art. 26, 27; met Sweden, 1 octobr., 1679, artic. 22, vol. 3, placit. pag. 1399.

VI. Quod si navis eorum, qui bello non erant impliciti, quæque ideò jure belli capi non poterat; à nostris tamen hostibus capta sit, et iisdem deinceps per nostros erepta, pristinis, dominis reddenda videtur, quia nullo justo titulo dominium ejus à vero domino recessisse dici potest, adeòque, ùti hostium nunquàm fuit, itá nec jure belli nostrum fieri potest. Responsa Jurisc. Holl., part. 2, consil. 95, et cons. 151, pag. 305. Contrà, quàm respondendum foret, si id obtineat; ut naves eorum, qui neutri student parti, jure belli possint occupari, quoties ad hostiles portus *tendunt aut ex iis solvunt. Responsa Jurisc. Holland., [*781] part. 5, consil. 161.

VII. Quid juris sit, si navis per hostes capta, per tertium non vi armatâ recuperetur, sed redimatur, verum redempta sit pretio viliore, exposui in d. tract. de jure milil., cap. 5, num. 24. Et de prohibitâ conventione cum hostibus, ut dimissâ nave captâ solus magister navis pro pretio redemptionis retineatur, vide placitum Ordinum Generalium 2 julii, 1689, et, 12 julii, 1690, vol. 4. placit, pag. 210.

APPENDIX IX.

MEMOIRE RAISONNE, BY THE PRINCE DE TALLEYRAND, ON THE TREATMENT OF THE KING OF SAXONY, BY THE EUROPEAN POWERS, IN 1814.

(From the "Traité Complet de Diplomatie par Mons. le Comte de Garden," t. III. p. 146.)

LA question sur le sort de la Saxe et de son souverain, peut être envisagée sous le double rapport du *droit* et de *l'utilité*. On parle du royaume comme d'un pays vacant, du roi comme d'un criminel qui n'a plus rien à attendre, si ce n'est peut-être de la clémence.

Le roi n'a point abdiqué; si donc il a perdu ses droits, il faut nécessairement de deux choses l'une: ou que la conquête seule ait pu les lui faire pedre, ou qu'un jugement l'en ait privé.

Quand l'oppresseur de l'Europe disposa du Hanovre, qu'il avait conquis, loin de reconnaître qu'il avait pu en disposer, l'Angleterre déclara la guerre à la puissance qui avait consenti à le recevoir de lui.

Quand, par représailles, celle-ci donna la Guadeloupe à la Suède, le même oppresseur de l'Europe réprouva, à son tour, sa doctrine que la conquête seule peut ôter la souveraineté. L'Angleterre et son ennemi ont donc également rejeté cette doctrine; la conquête n'a donc pas pu rendre le royaume de Saxe vacant.

Le roi de Saxe n'a certainement pas été jugé, car il n'a été, ni cité ni entendu; il est donc tout au plus dans le simple état d'accusé, c'est-à-dire, dans un état où celui qui s'y trouve ne [*782] *perd pas même le droit d'être tenu pour innocent jusqu'à ce qu'il ait été condamné.

Si le roi de Saxe devait être jugé, par qui le serait-il? Serait-ce par ses accusateurs? Serait-ce par ceux qui veulent profiter de ses dépouilles? Serait-ce par ceux dont la politique a seule créé cette nécessité qui l'absout de toutes les fautes qu'elle aurait pu lui faire commettre?

Serait-il jugé par la Saxe? La Saxe le rappelle de tous ses vœux. Par l'Allemagne? L'Allemagne désire, avant toutes choses, qu'il soit rétabli dans ses droits. Par le congrès? Quel est celui d'entre les ministres qui doivent le former, qui a reçu une telle mission?

Mais à quoi bon ces questions? Est-ce aux souverains de l'Europe qu'il faut dire que les rois n'ont d'autre juge que celui qui juge les justices? Et doit-on craindre d'entendre les maximes contraires, de la bouche des ministres de ces souverains?

Le roi n'a point été jugé, il ne pouvait pas l'être. Comment donc serait-il condamné?

Admettons, pour un moment, qu'il puisse l'être et qu'il le soit: d'après quel principe de justice la peine portée contre lui serait-elle étendue aux princes de sa ligne, et à ceux de la ligne ducale qui ont combattu dans les rangs des alliés, qui ont versé leur sang, qui ont tout sacrifié pour la cause commune? La confiscation que les nations éclairées ont bannie de leurs codes, serait-elle introduite au dix-neuviéme siécle dans le droit général de l'Europe? Ou la confiscation d'un royaume seraitelle moins odieuse, que celle d'une simple chaumière?

Quand Charles-Quint, chef de l'empire, dont Jean-Frédéric n'était que vassal, et dont, conséquemment, il était justiciable, transféra l'electorat de Saxe, il ne le transféra point à une autre maison.

L'Europe réunie, si elle pouvait juger le roi de Saxe, serait-elle moins juste que ne le fut Charles-Quint? Les puissances alliées qui ont voulu restaurer l'Europe, veulent-elles, d'ailleurs, imiter les exemples que leur offre le règne de Charles-Quint?

En toute chose, considérons les suites. Agir comme si la conquête seule donnait la soveraineté, c'est anéantir le droit public de l'Europe, et la placer sous l'empire exécutif de l'arbitraire et de la force. Se constituer juge d'un souverain, c'est sanctionner toutes les révolutions; le tenir pour condamné, lorsqu'il n'est pas et qu'il ne peut pas même être jugé, c'est fouler aux pieds les premiers principes de la justice naturelle et de la raison même.

Maintenant, à qui la disposition que l'on prétend faire de la Saxe serait-elle utile?

A la Prusse? Deux millions de sujets qui, d'ici à plus d'un [*783] *siècle, peut-être, ne s'affectionneraient point à la dynastie nouvelle, qui se sentiraient opprimés, et croiraient légitime tout moyen de sortir d'oppression, seraient pour elle une cause permanente d'embarras, d'inquiétude et de danger. On veut fortifier la Prusse, on l'aura réellement affaibli. Est-ce, d'ailleurs, la Prusse qui a droit de s'approprier les biens de ses voisins ? Oublie-t-on la protection qu'elle a donnée à l'Allemagne par les négociations à Bâle, à Rastadt, à Ratisbonne, en 1805, à Vienne.

A l'Allemagne ? Pour savoir quels sont ses intérêts, il n'y a qu'à consulter son vœu. Les princes n'ignorent assurément pas ce qu'ils doivent désirer ou craindre ; or tous, à l'exception d'un seul, disent que c'en est fait de l'Allemagne, si la Saxe est sacrifiée.

La situation de l'Allemagne est un des obstacles les plus forts à la réunion de la Saxe à la Prusse ; mille feux y couvent la cendre. Cette réunion serait peut-être l'étincelle qui embraserait tout ! Si cela arrivait, la France resterait-elle spectatrice tranquille de ces discordes civiles ? Il est plutôt à croire qu'elle en profiterait, et peut-être ferait-elle sagement d'en profiter.

A l'Angleterre ? Elle, à qui il faut surtout des marchés, que gagnerait-elle, si l'une des plus grandes villes de commerce de l'Allemagne, théâtre d'une des plus grandes foires du pays et de l'Europe, et jusqu'ici sous la domination d'un prince avec lequel l'Angleterre ne pourrait jamais avoir des démêlés, passait sous la domination d'une puissance avec laquelle elle ne peut être sûre de conserver une éternelle paix ?

Un autre prétexte allégué en faveur de la réunion de la Saxe à la Prusse, c'est qu'on veut faire de cette dernière une barrière contre la Russie. Mais les souverains des deux pays sont unis par des liens, qui font, que tant qu'ils vivront tous deux, l'un n'aura rien à craindre de l'autre ; cette précaution ne pourrait donc regarder qu'un avenir fort éloigné ; mais que diraient ceux qui appuient avec tant de chaleur le projet de réunion, si, témoins de cet avenir, ils voyaient la Prusse s'appuyer de la Russie, pour obtenir en Allemagne une extension qu'ils lui auraient facilitée, et appuyer à son tour la Russie dans des entreprises sur l'empire ottoman ? Non-seulement la chose est possible, elle est encore probable, parce qu'elle est dans l'ordre naturel.

L'union de l'Autriche et de la Prusse est nécessaire au repos et à la sûreté de l'Allemagne ; mais la disposition qu'on prétend faire de la Saxe, serait la chose du monde la plus propre à rallumer une rivalité qui a duré jusqu'aux désastres de la Prusse, et que ces désastres ont suspendue, mais n'ont pas peut-être éteinte.

Ainsi, ces dispositions iraient contre le but même qui les *aurait fait faire, et d'un premier mal naîtraient une foule de [*784] maux. Reconnaissons donc que l'injustice est un mauvais fondement, sur lequel le monde politique ne saurait bâtir que pour sa ruine.

APPPENDIX X.

Protest of the King of Saxony, 4th November, 1814, on the Subject.

(From the same Work, p. 203.)

Frederick-Auguste, par la grâce de Dieu, roi de Saxe, duc de Varsovie, etc.

Nous venons d'apprendre avec une vive douleur que notre royaume de Saxe va être occupé provisoirement par les troupes de S. M. prussienne. Cunstamment décidés à ne point séparer notre sort de celui de nos peuples; remplis de confiance en la justice et la magnanimité des monarques alliés, et intentionnés d'accéder à leur alliance aussitôt que nous en aurions les moyens, nous résolûmes, après la bataille de Leipzig, d'y attendre les vainqueurs; mais les souverains refusèrent de nous écouter. On nous obligea de sortir de nos États et de nous rendre à Berlin. S. M. l'empereur de Russie nous fit néanmoins connâitre que notre éloignement de la Saxe n'était commandé que par les intérêts militaires; S. M. nous invita en même temps à lui vouer une confiance entiére. Nous reçumes aussi de LL. MM. l'empereur d'Autriche et le roi de Prusse, des preuves touchantes d'intérêt et de sensibilité. Il nous était permis en conséquence, de nous abandonner à l'espoir qu'aussitôt que les considérations militaires auraient cessé, nous serions réintégrés dans nos droits et rendus à nos sujets chéris. Nous étions d'autant plus autorisés à attendre un prompt et heureux changement dans notre situation, que nous avions fait connaître aux souverains alliés notre désir sincère de coopérer au rétablissement du repos et de la liberté, et que nous avions manifesté de toutes les manières, dont on nous avait laissé le pouvoir, notre dévouement véritable pour leurs personnes et pour la cause qui fut l'objet de leurs efforts.

La paix conclue avec la France, il nous fut infiniment douloureux [*785] d'apprendre que nos instances réitérées pour notre *prompte réintégration n'avaient point été accueillies, que nos justes esperances se trouvaient encore déçues, et que la décision de nos plus chers intérêts et de ceux de nos peuples avait été adjournée au congrès de Vienne. Loin cependant d'adjouter foi aux bruits répandus sur le sort de nos états depuis l'époque de la paix de Paris, nous mettons une confiance entière dans la justice des monarques alliés, quoiqu'il nous soit impossible de pénétrer les motifs des procédés qu'on a observés envers nous.

Conserver et consolider les dynasties légitimes, tel a été le grand but d'une guerre qui vient d'être terminée si heureusement; les puissances réunies pour cet effet ont proclamé, à différentes reprises, de la maniére la plus solennelle, qu'éloignées de tout projet de conquête ou d'agrandissement, elles, n'avaient en vue que le rétablissement du droit et de la liberté de l'Europe. La Saxe, en particulier, a reçu l'assurance la plus positive que son intégrité sera maintenue. Cette intégrité comprend essentiellement la conservation de la dynastie pour laquelle la nation a manifesté publiquement son constant attachement, et le vœu unanime d'être réunie à son souverain.

Nous avons communiqué aux principales cours de l'Europe un exposé franc et complet des motifs qui avaient dirigé notre marche politique pendant ces derniers temps; et fidèles à la confiance inébranlable que nous mettons dans leurs lumières et leur justice, nous nous persuadons qu'elles auront reconnu nonseulement la pureté de nos intentions, mais aussi que la position particulière de nos états et l'empire des circonstances nous ont seuls empêchés de prendre part à la lutte entreprise pour l'Allemagne.

L'inviolabilité de nos droits et de ceux de notre maison sur l'héritage de nos ancêtres, bien et justement acquis, est reconnue. Notre prompte réintégration doit en être la suite.

Nous manquerions à des devoirs sacrés envers notre maison royale et envers notre peuple, en gardant le silence sur les mesures nouvelles projetées contre nos états au moment où nous sommes en droit d'en attendre la restitution. L'intention manifestée par la cour royale de Prusse, d'occuper provisoirement nous états de Saxe, nous oblige de prémunir, contre une démarche pareille, nos droits bien fondés, et de protester solennellement contre les conséquences qui pourraient être tirées de cette mesure.

C'est auprès du congrès de Vienne, et en face de toute l'Europe, que nous nous acquittons de ce devoir, en signant de notre main les présentes, et en même temps en réitérant publiquement la déclaration communiquée il y a quelque temps aux cours alliées, que nous ne consentirons jamais à la cession *des états hérités de nos ancêtres, et que nous n'acc- [*786]
cepterons aucun dédommagement ou équivalant qui nous serait offert.

Donné à Friederichsfeld, le 4 novembre 1814.

FREDERIC-AUGUSTE.

APPENDIX XI.

As to the Right of Austria to incorporate her Non-German Territories into the German Confederation. Memorandum of France on the subject, 5*th March* 1851. (*Extract from Annuaire des deux Mondes* (1851, 2,) *pp.* 753-7. (*Appendice.*)

Memorandum addressé par le gouvernement français aux Puissances signataires des traités de Vienne, au sujet du projet d'incorporation des provinces non-allemandes de l'Autriche dans la Confédération germanique.

5 Mars, 1851.

LA Confédération germanique a été constituée par le pacte fédéral conclu à Vienne, le 8 juin, 1815, entre tous les gouvernements allemands, et dont le premier article est ainsi conçu :

"Les princes souverains et les villes libres d'Allemagne, en comprenant dans cette transaction leurs majestés l'empereur d'Autriche, les rois de Prusse, de Danemark, et des Pays-Bas, et nommément l'empereur d'Autriche, et le roi de Prusse, pour toutes celles de leurs possessions qui ont anciennement appartenu à l'empire germanique, le roi de Danémark pour le duché de Holstein, le roi des Pays-Bas pour le grand-duché de Luxembourg, établissent entre eux une confédération perpétuelle qui portera le nom de Confédération germanique."

Cet article et les dix autres articles du pacte fédéral qui contiennent les bases principales de la Confédération, furent reproduits textuellement sous les Nos. 53-63, dans l'acte général de Vienne, signé le lendemain, 9 juin, par les représentants des principales puissances européennes. Quant aux arts. 12-20, du pacte fédéral, compris collectivement sous le nom de dispositions particulières, et qui s'appliquent à des questions moins importantes, ils ne furent pas, comme les précédents, formellement reproduits dans l'acte général du congrès, mais, ce qui revient au même, l'art. 64, de cet acte, auquel on les annexa, déclara qu'ils auraient la même force et valeur que s'ils y étaient textuellement insérés.

Ainsi donc le pacte constitutif de la Confédération, y compris ses clauses les moins essentielles, fait partie intégrante de l'acte général du [*787] congrés, et, dans la rigueur du principe, il ne pourrait *être apporté la moindre altération à la moindre de ces clauses sans le concours de tous les gouvernements qui ont signé ce dernier acte.

A plus forte raison, ce principe s'applique-t-il à l'article cité plus haut (le 1er du pacte fédéral, le 53me de l'acte général,) qui crée la Confédération, lui donne place dans l'ordre européen, et en détermine les limites.

On a voulu inférer des déclarations faites par l'Autriche et la Prusse, en 1818, au moment où, en exécution de la clause qui les concerne dans l'art. 1er de l'acte fédéral du 8 juin, 1815 (art. 53, du traité du 9 du même mois,) elles désignèrent comme devant faire partie de la Confédération germanique *celles de leurs possessions qui ont anciennement appartenu à l'empire;* on a voulu inférer que cette clause était considérée comme facultative plutôt que comme strictement obligatoire, d'où il suivrait que si l'Autriche particulièrement ne comprit pas la Lombardie parmi ses provinces appelées à entrer dans la Confédération, comme elle prétendit alors pouvoir le faire, à raison des rapports qui avaient existé entre cette possession italienne et l'empire romain, c'est parcequ'elle voulut bien, ainsi qu'elle le déclara, ne pas donner *cette extension à l'article.*

L'Autriche n'avait ni à interpréter ni à *étendre* cet article. Pour elle, comme pour la Prusse, il s'agissait simplement de l'exécuter, en indiquant celles de leurs possessions allemandes qui devaient entrer dans la circonscription territoriale de la Confédération. La Lombardie ne pouvait assurément être considérée comme devant figurer dans une telle nomenclature, pour avoir eu des rapports féodaux avec l'empire d'Allemagne. C'est ce que le cabinet de Vienne comprit très-bien lui-même en l'excluant, dans la séance de la diète du 6 avril, 1818, de la liste des provinces autrichiennes qui devaient faire partie de la *Confédération.* L'Autriche tenait alors à prouver à l'Allemagne *combien peu il entrait dans ses vues d'étendre au-delà des Alpes la ligne de défense de la Confédération.*

L'Autriche n'avait aucun droit en dehors de celui que le traité du 9 juin, 1815, lui a créé par rapport à cette circonscription territoriale de la Confédération germanique.

Il serait tout aussi difficile d'admettre cette autre supposition que la Prusse, en 1818, "aurait voulu donner à entendre qu'à la rigueur elle ne serait pas tenue d'entrer dans la Confédération avec toutes celles de ses provinces qui avaient été autrefois des dépendances de l'empire."

Qu'on en juge par les termes mêmes du vote émis, au nom du roi de Prusse, dans la séance de la diète du 4 mai:

"Sa majesté ne croit pas pouvoir mieux constater la part sincère qu'elle continue de prendre à tout ce qui promet d'assurer le repos futur de l'Allemagne, et le développement le plus parfait de sa force intérieure qu'en s'associant dans ce but à la Confédération *germanique avec toutes les provinces allemandes de la monarchie déjà ancien- [*788] nement attachées à l'Allemagne par la langue, par les mœurs, par les lois, et en général par la nationalité." (*Suit la désignation de ces provinces.*)

Une telle déclaration n'implique aucune espèce de réserve, ne suppose aucune arrière-pensée : elle montre au contraire combien la Prusse entrait alors dans l'esprit *d'homogénéité germanique qui* présidait à la formation et à la composition de la Confédération.

La Prusse se conformait purement et simplement à la clause de l'art. 1er de l'acte fédéral du 6 juin, 1815, et mieux encore à l'art. 53, du traité européen du 9 du même mois.

Le seul argument que l'on ait produit jusqu'à présent pour contester aux puissances européennes signataires de l'acte de Vienne le droit d'intervenir dans les modifications à apporter aux limites territoriales de la Confédération, repose sur l'art. 6, de l'acte final conclu à Vienne en 1820, entre les plénipotentiaires des gouvernements germaniques, pour compléter et développer les dispositions de l'acte fédéral.

Il y est dit "que l'admission d'un nouveau membre dans la Confédération ne peut avoir lieu que lorsqu'elle est unanimement jugée compatible avec les rapports existants et avec l'intérêt général des états confédérés."

Il est difficile de comprendre en quoi cet article pouraait infirmer le droit des puissances européennes de prendre part aux altérations que l'on croirait devoir faire subir aux arrangements de 1815.

D'abord il parle de l'admission d'un *nouveau membre,* et il ne s'agit aujourd' hui de rien de tel. L'Autriche fait partie de la Confédération, et elle ne demande qu'à y figurer désormais avec toutes ses provinces, au lieu d'y figurer seulement avec ses provinces germaniques.

Dut-on admettre, au surplus, qu'à défaut du sens textuel, l'esprit de cette stipulation, s'applique au cas de l'incorporation de nouveaux territoires dans la Confédération, elle n'aurait pas encore la portée qu'on semble supposer? De ce qu'elle exige pour ce cas le consentement unanime de tous les gouvernements germaniques, il ne s'ensuit nullement qu'elle déclare ce consentement suffisant, et qu'elle conteste aux signataires des traités de 1815 le droit d'intervenir pour légitimer ce changement, ou pour s'y opposer. Elle dit qu'il faut, pour régulariser une telle mesure, le consentement de tous les gouvernements germaniques; elle ne dit pas que ce consentement dispense de celui des autres puissances, et elle ne peut pas le dire, puisque le contraire résulte positivement du traité de Vienne. On comprend en effet qu'il n'a pas dépendu des seuls gouvernements allemands d'altérer des stipulations que l'Europe avait réglées en commun.

Il est donc évident que l'art. 6, de l'acte final n'a, sous aucun rapport, dérogé, ni pu déroger, à l'art. 53, de l'acte général qu'il a laissé les choses dans l'état où ce dernier article les avait mises, et que par conséquent, [*789] pour les modifier, il faudrait recourir à l'autorité *qui les aurait ainsi réglées, c'est-à-dire, obtenir le consentement des principaux gouvernements européens.

On objecte qu'en 1848 la diète de Francfort a, sans ce consentement, fait entrer dans la Confédération plusieurs provinces de la Prusse qui y avaient été jusqu'alors étrangères. Il est facile de répondre que, l'Europe n'ayant pas sanctionné cette décision, elle est en droit non avenue, et que les circonstances générales qui ebranlaient l'édifice européen tout entier expliquent assez l'absence de protestations formelles. Personne, ce semble, n'a intérêt à soutenir que tout ce qui s'est passé alors en Europe, sans devenir l'objet d'une protestation, a été légitimé par ce seul fait. La France a d'ailleurs fait connaître son opinion.

Il reste à examiner s'il y a des raisons suffisantes pour déterminer les puissances européennes à donner le consentement dont on vient d'établir la nécessité.

L'Autriche, dit-on, ayant établi dans son administration intérieure le système d'unité, ne peut rester dans la Confédération qu'avec la totalité de son territoire. Si on ne lui permettait pas, elle cesserait d'en faire partie plutôt que de scinder ses possessions, en les soumettant à deux régimes différents.

Il y a ici une question de fait. Examinons d'abord la première.

Lorsque la Confédération s'est formée, le système intérieur de l'Autriche lui a permis de s'y associer aux conditions prescrites par l'acte fédéral et par l'acte général du congrès. Elle ne pourrait arguer aujourd'hui des modifications qu'il lui a plu d'apporter à sa constitution particulière, pour exiger qu'on change en conséquence la nature même de la Confédération. Elle ne peut davantage menacer de se retirer de la Confédération si l'on n'accède à sa demande. Il est dit, en effet, dans l'art. 53, de l'acte général, déjà si souvent cité, que les gouvernements allemands établissent entre eux une *confédération perpétuelle*, et l'acte final de 1820, interprétant cette clause, porte expressément dans son art. 5, "que la Confédération est indissoluble par le principe même de son institution, en sorte qu'aucun de ses membres n'a la liberté de s'en détacher."

Voilà pour le droit; quant au fait, dont il faut sans doute tenir grand compte lorsqu'il s'agit d'un état aussi puissant que l'Autriche, on peut affirmer sans hésiter que le Cabinet de Vienne, qu'il obtienne ou qu'il n'obtienne pas l'incorporation de la totalité de ses provinces, ne renoncera jamais volontairement à faire partie d'une confédération sur laquelle il exerce une influence qui est un des éléments principaux de sa force politique. On peut ajouter que l'existence unitaire de l'empire autrichien n'a pas encore un caractère tellement absolu, n'est pas un fait tellement accompli, qu'on ne puisse trouver moyen de la concilier avec le maintien d'une portion de cet empire en dehors de la Confédération, dont le reste continuerait à en faire partie.

*Pour rassurer l'Europe contre les conséquences de l'innovation proposée, et pour l'amener même à y trouver des avantages, [*790] on a recours à des arguments de natures bien diverses.

En réponse á ceux qui allèguent que la France et la Russie, en cas de lutte contre l'Autriche, soit en Italie, soit du côté de l'Orient, se verraient nécessairement, par l'effet de cette innovation, réduites à la nécessité de combattre la Confédération tout entière, que par conséquent leur condition en serait empirée, et qu'elles ont le droit de s'y opposer, on donne à entendre que cela ne changerait·rien aux changes actuelles, la force des choses devant nécessairement entraîner tôt ou tard la Confédération dans tout conflit un peu sérieux où pourront se trouver engagés ses membres les plus puissants.

Cette allégation, et par conséquent les inductions qu'on en veut tirer, ne sont pas parfaitement exactes. Dans le passé, alors même que l'Autriche, par la dignité impériale dont son souverain était habituellement revêtu, se trouvait placée à la tête de l'Allemagne, on ne voit pas qu'elle ait toujours réussi à l'entraîner dans les guerres d'Italie et de Hongrie. Rien ne prouve donc d'une manière absolue que, sous l'empire du pacte fédéral de 1815, elle dût y réussir davantage. En supposant même que ce résultat fût probable, il ne s'agirait encore que d'une vraisemblance, tandis qu'après l'incorporation projetée, lefait deviendrait certain. C'est assez dire que cette incorporation n'est pas, comme on essaie de le faire croire, une circonstance indifférente au point de vue de l'équilibre européen, et dont les autres gouvernements n'aient pas à se préoccuper sous ce rapport.

Le Cabinet de Vienne prétend aussi qu'au fond il n'y aurait rien de changé dans les principes du droit fédéral allemand par l'agrégation explicite et effective à la Confédération germanique des provinces non-allemandes de l'Autriche, attendu qu'en cas de guerre défensive, dans laquelle l'Autriche ou la Prusse se trouveraient engagées, l'une ou l'autre, avant comme après une telle annexion, apporterait dans la lutte toutes ses forces disponibles, sans distinction entre celles que fourniraient les provinces allemandes et celles qui proviendraient de ses provinces non-germaniques. On ajoute que, dans l'état actuel des choses, pour peu que la guerre eût pris de vastes proportions, la Confédération tout entière aurait été inévitablement amenée à s'y associer en vertu de l'article 47 de l'acte final du 15 mai, 1820. Cet article stipule que si un état confédéré "se trouvait menacé ou attaqué dans ses possessions non comprises dans la Confédération, celle-ci n'est obligée de prendre des mesures de défense ou une part active à la guerre qu'après que la diète aurait reconnu en conseil permanent, à la pluralité des voix, l'existence d'un danger pour le territoire de la Confédération." On voit clairement, par les termes mêmes de cet article, qu'un état de la confédération germanique, ayant à combattre pour ses possessions non allemandes, ne peut entraîner *_ipso facto_ l'Allemagne dans sa querelle, mais qu'il faut avant tout que l'Allemagne juge nécessaire à sa propre sûreté d'y [*791] prendre une part active, tandis que, dans la situation nouvelle et anormale que lui ferait l'incorporation de toutes les provinces de la monarchie autrichienne, la Confédération se trouverait engagé *à priori*, par l'effet d'une solidarité militaire complète, à prendre fait et cause pour l'Autriche dans une guerre que celle-ci pourrait avoir à soutenir hors de l'Allemagne. En l'état présent des choses, la Confédération doit examiner, discuter, consentir ou refuser, selon qu'elle le croit à propos. Dans la combinaison dont-il s'agit, elle n'aurait plus qu'à obéir son libre arbitrer disparaîtrait. Certes, cette situation serait bien différente.

On suppose, il est vrai, que l'Autriche tout entière faisant partie de la Confédération, la diète, usant de son droit sur un état soumis en entier à sa juridiction, empêcherait le gouvernement autrichien de s'engager trop facilement dans des luttes dont elle aurait à subir les conséquences. Cet argument se lie à la supposition que l'Autriche, bien que figurant dans la Confédération pour un territoire et une population trois fois aussi considérable qu'aujourd'hui, n'y exercerait pas la prépondérance absolue que semblerait devoir lui assurer un tel accroissement, et n'y prétendrait pas à plus d'influence que par le passé.

Les apologistes du projet d'incorporation prétendent en effet que cette mesure, exigée par les nécessités intérieures de l'empire, ne doit d'ailleurs lui apporter aucun accroissement de puissance, ni en Europe, ni dans le sein même de la Confédération.

Cette assertion paraît assez difficile à concilier avec le raisonnement auquel on a recours, lorsqu'on veut démontrer les avantages que l'incorporation aurait pour la cause de l'ordre et de la paix. On dit alors que l'Autriche, devenue plus puissante dans les conseils fédéraux, y serait mieux en mesure de contenir en Allemagne l'esprit révolutionnaire et les influences ambitieuses qui ont trop souvent cherché à s'en faire un moyen d'aggrandissement et d'usurpation.

Sans doute, en s'exprimant ainsi, le cabinet impérial n'a pas entendu agiter, pour le besoin de sa cause, un vain fantôme de terreur. La réalité révolutionnaire, telle qu'il la voit, le presse, l'oblige à sortir de la légalité. A ses yeux, le danger est imminent, et le faisceau de l'Allemagne n'est pas trop puissant pour le prévenir. Mais qu'il soit permis de le dire, il y a une exagération évidente dans cette manière de poser la question. Les faits n'autorisent pas l'Autriche à tenir un tel langage. Son armée est forte, l'a révolte l'a trouvée inébranlable; les détestables doctrines de la démagogie ne l'ont point atteinte; elle présente 400,000 hommes aguerris par une épreuve qui démoralise quelquefois les troupes les plus braves: le contact avec les idées révolutionnaires et les populations insurgées. Rien n'a affaibli cette puissante armée, et ce serait en vain
[*792] que l'on voudrait représenter comme *débile et comme dépourvue de moyens suffisants de répression une puissance qui se trouve si forte après avoir traversé les dangers, des guerres et des revolutions.

Il faut opter entre ces deux thèmes. Ou le changement proposé accroîtra démesurément la puissance autrichienne, et alors l'Europe, la France particulièrement, sont en droit de se préoccuper du maintien de l'équilibre politique; ou il n'aura sous ce rapport aucun effet sensible, et dans cette hypothèse encore, comme il n'en résulterait aucun avantage, il faudrait repousser une innovation qui inquiéterait l'opinion publique, en changeant le droit public européen.

La Confédération germanique est une des bases de ce droit public. Interposée entre les grandes puissances dont elle a surtout intérêt à arrêter les impiètements, elle contribue puissamment par sa masse, et si l'on peut ainsi parler, par sa force passive, à la conservation de la paix générale. L'homogénéité de races qui, au milieu de nombreuses diversités, lui constitue une unité véritable, la rend merveilleusement propre à ce grand et noble rôle. Renfermée dans les limites qui lui assigne cette homogénéité, tant que la Confédération s'imposera tout à la fois la loi de ne pas les dépasser, et celle de ne pas souffrir qu'on les restreigne, elle sera la plus sûre sauvegarde de l'ordre et de la paix européens. Une politique contraire aurait naturellement des conséquences tout opposées. Etendre arbitrairement ces limites naturelles ou consacrées par le temps, adjoindre aux populations allemandes des populations slaves, hongroises, illyriennes, italiennes, au milieu desquelles elles seraient noyées, ce serait dénaturer la Confédération, dont il faudrait changer même le nom, pour le pas être en contradiction avec la réalité. Cette masse, absorbant dans son sein vingt peuples et vingt états différents, se présenterait à l'esprit, non plus comme une garantie de paix et d'equilibre, mais comme une menace, comme un symbole de confusion et d'envahissement. Dans l'intérieur même des territoires qu'elle réunirait, il est douteux que, malgré sa force apparente, elle réussit mieux, ou même aussi bien que la Confédération actuelle, à maintenir l'ordre et l'autorité. On conçoit qu'on fond de nationalité commune permette de faire intervenir, sans trop choquer le sentiment public, les forces de l'Autriche, de la Prusse, de la Bavière, pour soutenir ou pour relever en Saxe, dans le grand-duché de Bade, dans l'électorat de Hesse, dans le duché de Holstein, le pouvoir ébranlé ou renversé des gouvernements; mais se rend-on bien compte de l'effet que produirait à la longue, ou dans un moment de crise violente, l'emploi des troupes hongroises ou polonaises pour rétablir l'ordre sur les bords du Rhin, celui des troupes bavaroises ou prussiennes pour soumettre la Hongrie insurgée? Un tel régime proclamé, non plus à titre de mesure exceptionnelle et dans une circonstance donnée, mais comme un état de choses normal, constitutionnel, ne soulèverait-il pas tôt ou tard des répugnances, des irritations qui compromettraient le repos de l'Europe? N'eston *pas effrayé d'ailleurs de la difficulté que l'on éprouverait, à mettre en mouvement, une machine aussi énorme, aussi compli- [*793]
quée? L'organisation fédérale, sincèrement appliquée, et respectant par conséquent l'indépendance des gouvernements particuliers, y serait évidemment impuissante. Un homme de génie, un despote favorisé par les circonstances, tel que Charles-Quint ou Ferdinand II, y réussirait peut-être pour un moment; mais alors l'instrument remis entre ses mains deviendrait trop redoutable à l'Allemagne et à l'Europe entière. Ce moment passé le prétendu pouvoir fédéral, épuisé par cet excès même tomberait dans une véritable atonie, et la Confédération, pour avoir trop voulu s'étendre, pour avoir forcé res ressorts de son existence, finirait peut-être par se dissoudre, livrant l'Allemagne à une anarchie qui laisserait l'Europe sans contre-poids.

Il faut donc écarter des combinaisons auxquelles se lient, sans aucune chance avantageuse, tant de chances dangereuses et funestes.*

APPENDIX XII.

Memorandum of England on the Subject. (*From Ib., pp.* 959, 60.)

ANGLETERRE.

Note addressée par Lord Cowley, ministre plénipotentiaire de la Grande-Bretagne près la Confédération germanique, au président de la diète de Francfort.

LE soussigné, envoyé extraordinaire et ministre plénipotentiaire de sa majesté britannique près la Confédération germanique, a été chargé par son gouvernement de faire la communication suivante à M. le comte de Thun, président de la diète germanique.

Il a été porté à la connaissance du gouvernement de sa majesté que les gouvernements d'Autriche et de Prusse avaient l'intention de présenter à la diète germanique une motion tendant à incorporer dans la Confédération tous les pas parties de leur territoire qu'en exceptait le traité de Vienne de 1815. Le gouvernement de sa majesté est d'avis qu'une pareille mesure, si on veut la concilier avec le respect dû au droit public en Europe, ne peut recevoir son exécution qu'avec le consentement de toutes les puissances qui ont concouru au traité de Vienne, par lequel la Confédération germanique a été créée, et qui a fixé les territoires dont elle devait se composer. Il ne faut pas oublier que la Confédération germanique n'est pas uniquement une association libre de certains états qui n'a été formée que par leur volonté, et qui puisse par [*794] *conséquent être changée ou transformée seulement par une résolution de leur part : la Confédération germanique est le résultat d'un traité européen, et forme un élément de l'organization générale de l'Europe fixée et reglée par ce traité ; aussi le gouvernement de sa majesté croit-il qu'on ne peut apporter de changements essentiels au caractère national et à l'étendue du territoire de la Confédération germanique qu'avec le consentement et le concours formel de toutes les puissances qui ont pris part au traité général de Vienne du 8 juin, 1815.

L'art. 53, de ce traité spécifie les souverains et les états qui doivent former la Confédération germanique, et cet article contient la disposition expresse que sa majesté l'empereur d'Autriche et sa majesté le roi de Prusse seront membres de la Confédération germanique, avec toutes celles de leurs possessions qui auparavant avaient fait partie de l'empire germanique. La même restriction a été stipulée au No. 9, de l'acte séparé, qui forme une des annexes du traité général auxquelles on a attribué, à l'art. 118, dudit traité, la même force obligatoire que si elles étaient textuellement reproduites dans le traité général. Il faut faire remarquer en

*Extracted from Annuaire des deux Mondes (1851-52,) pp. 953-7. (Appendice.)

outre que l'art. 54, du traité général et l'art. 2, de l'annexe No. 9, établissent comme but de la Confédération germanique le maintien de la sécurité interieure et extérieure de l'Allemagne : ce serait donc agir contrairement à la lettre, ainsi qu'à l'esprit du traité, que de faire servir l'organization de la Confédération à un autre but quelconque qu'au but allemand qui lui est assigné par la Confédération même.

Le gouvernement de sa majesté n'ignore pas que plusieurs cherchent à faire valoir l'opinion que l'art. 6, de l'acte final de la constitution de la Confédération germanique autorise l'incorporation dans cette derniére d'autres états et d'autres territoires que ceux auxquels la Confédération a été limitée par la traité de 1815.

Le soussigné est chargé de faire observer à ce sujet que, quand même on pourrait fort bien interpréter dans ce sens l'art. 6, de l'acte final de 1820, cet acte final de 1820, n'a été rédigé et sanctionné que par les membres de la Confédération, qu'il n'est point un traité européen, que des états allemands seuls y ont participé, et qu'une pareille résolution de la part de ces derniers ne peut ni abroger ni changer les dispositions d'un traité dont d'autres puissances ont été les parties contractantes. Le soussigné est chargé de faire observer que, quand, même l'art. 6, de l'acte final de 1820, serait une disposition reconnue par les puissances qui ont concouru au traité de Vienne de l'année 1815, et obligatoire pour elles, ledit article n'a ni ne peut avoir le sens qu'on voudrait lui attribuer, ainsi qu'il a été dit plus haut, car cet article ne contient point une disposition facultative, mais au contraire une disposition restrictive.

Il ne dit pas qu'il suffiit du consentement unanime de tous les membres de la Confédération, sans le concours d'autres puissances [*795]
*quelconques, pour sanctionner et valider l'admission d'un nouveau membre dans la Confédération ; il dit toute autre chose : il déclare uniquement qu'aucun nouveau membre ne peut être admis dans la Confédération sans le consentement unanime de tous les membres de celle-ci. Cette disposition provenait de l'intention de veiller à sa propre défense ; elle avait pour but, comme on sait fort bien, d'empêcher qu'on n'admit dans la Confédération, ce qu'on redoutait alors, quelques princes allemands médiatisés. Le sens clair et unique de cet art. 6, de l'acte final de 1820 est que, attendu que la Confédération a été fondée originairement par le traité de Vienne, auquel n'avaient concouru qu'un certain nombre de grands états européens, et attendu que beaucoup de membres de la Confédération n'avaient pas signé ce traité, ladite Confédération, fondée de cette manière, ne voulait pas consentir qu'un nouveau membre quelconque fût admis dans son sein par la seule volonté des puissances qui avaient signé le traité de Vienne, et qu'une pareille admission ne pouvait avoir lieu sans le consentement unanime de tous les membres de la Confédération.

Il n'est que juste et raisonnable que la Confédération, bien qu'elle ait été fondée en vertu d'un traité auquel n'ont pas pris part tous ses membres, revendique cependant, comme toute autre association, le droit d'empêcher l'admission d'un nouveau membre sans le vœu unanime de ses membres. Toutefois il faut faire observer en outre que l'art. 6, de l'acte final ne fait mention que de l'admission de nouveaux membres : or, d'après l'esprit et la tendance, du traité de Vienne, il faut supposer que de pareils nouveaux membres seraient nécessairement des membres allemands; mais cet art. 6, de l'acte final ne parle pas de l'incorporation de parties de territoire exclues qui appartiennent à des membres déjà existants de la Confédération. Le soussigné a encore à faire observer que le principe qui doit être établi par l'adoption de la motion que l'Autriche et la Prusse se proposent, dit-on, de soumettre à la diète germanique ôterait à la Confédération germanique son caractère allemand, attendu que celle-ci s'adjoindrait des pays qui géographiquement sont séparés de l'Allemagne, et qui ont une population tout-à-fait différente de celle de l'Allemagne tant sous le rapport de la langue que de l'origine. Un pareil précédent, une fois établi, pourrait engager la Confédération à s'écarter encore davantage de son caractère national, que le traité de Vienne a voulu maintenir à l'égard des pays qui doivent former la Confédération germanique.

En conséquence, comme le gouvernement de sa majesté britannique est convaincu que la mesure que l'Autriche et la Prusse ont, à ce qu'on apprend, l'intention de proposer à la diète germanique altérerait essentiellement le caractère assigné à la Confédération germanique par les traités de 1815, et qu'il prévoit en même temps qu'un pareil changement dérangerait l'équilibre général, et entraînerait, selon toutes les probabili-
[*796] tés, des conséquences *si graves, que les intérêts généraux de l'Europe pourraient en être compromis, il a chargé le soussigné de protester contre une pareille mesure, et d'exprimer le ferme espoir que la diète germanique n'adoptera pas une proposition de ce genre, mais qu'elle maintiendra les limites du territoire fédéral telles qu'elles ont été fixées par le traité de Vienne du 8 juin, 1815, et qu'elle maintiendra en outre à la Confédération le caractère national que lui a été assigné conformément aux intentions dudit traité.

Le soussigné prie M. le président de saisir le plus tôt possible l'occasion de porter la présente communication à la connaissance de la diète germanique.*

APPENDIX XIII.

Papers relative to the Succession to the Throne of Denmark, laid before Parliament, 1853.

M. DE BLUME to M. DE BILLE.

Copenhagen, May 9, 1853.

MONSIEUR,

BY the despatch which I had the honour to address to your Excellency on the 20th ultimo, announcing to you the dissolution of the Diet, I limited myself to conveying to you some explanations as to the views of

*Extracted from Annuaire des deux Mondes (1851-52) (Appendix, pp. 959, 960.)

the King's Government on those of the Opposition, as regards the Royal Message of the 4th of last October.

I consider it my duty, both towards the King's Government and towards the Diet, to contribute, as far as lies in my power, towards placing the signing Powers of the Treaty at London in a position correctly to judge not only of the line of conduct which the King has taken in submitting to the Diet the above-mentioned message, in its form and actual wording, but also of the motives on account of which this proposition of His Majesty could not obtain the assent required by the constitution of the kingdom.

I shall commence by stating, that the choice made by the King of the person of Prince Christian of Glücksbourg has met with unanimous approbation in the united Houses of the Diet, as well as in the whole nation; the discussions of the said Assembly give testimony of the most sincere gratitude towards the Powers who have confirmed, by a public act, the measure taken by the king for eventually establishing the dynasty of this Prince on the throne of Denmark.

*I informed you at the time, M. le Ministre, of the report of the Committee charged by the last Diet but one, to submit the Royal Message to preliminary consideration; and you have therefore, no need of a more positive assurance to be convinced that even the members of the Diet, who have made the most decided opposition to the Government, have for a long time received with the greatest joy the prospect of seeing in the future the Prince Christian and his descendants occupying the throne. [*797]

But while declaring itself ready to give the consent, desired by the fundamental law, for Prince Christian and his descendants male and agnate of his marriage to succeed eventually, the Opposition nevertheless maintains that the Royal Message, in proposing the abolition of the succession etablished by the *Lex Regia*, goes further than the Treaty of London requires.

The King announces in the message the intention to establish for all the countries subject to his sceptre, such a form of succession that, in the case of the extinction of the male descendants in the male line of King Frederick the Third, who, in virtue of the Royal Law made by that Sovereign on the 14th of November, 1665, have the right of succession to the throne of Denmark; *all succession according to the Articles* XXVII.—XL. *of that Royal Law shall thenceforth be suppressed:* and the succession to the throne, for all the countries united under the sceptre of His Majesty, shall devolve on the Prince Christian of Glücksbourg, and to the descendants male of this Prince, the issue of his marriage with the Princess Louise, born Princess of Hesse.

It is the passage above underlined that has given birth to the division in the united Chambers. The opponents of the message find in this document two distinct propositions: one having for its object the transfer of the succession to the Prince Christian and his male descendants, and another suppressing the order of succession established by the *Lex Regia*. The first of these propositions has been considered sufficient to carry out all the intentions of the Treaty of London, and unanimously approved: but the second has met the opposition of a minority, which has been strong enough to reject the message, the fourth section of the fundamental law of the Kingdom of Denmark requiring, for changes in the order of succession of the *Lex Regia*, a majority of three-fourths of the voters.

In taking for a point of departure the acts and negotiations anterior to the Treaty of London, the opponents of the message cause it to be remarked that the abrogation of the order of succession of the Royal Law would be found in contradiction to the said acts and negotiations; and thence they conclude that the Treaty of London cannot have in view the suppression of this order of succession. They strive to place the expressed tenor of the Treaty in harmony with their ideas, in making a distinction
[*798] between the whole (totalité) of the States united under the sceptre *of the King and the different portions of the monarchy taken separately. They maintain that the Treaty of London bears reference only to the succession to the whole (totalité) of the States of the King: they admit that, as regards this whole, the Treaty introduces the agnate succession (succession agnatique,) but add that no stipulation has been made as regards the different countries composing the Monarchy, and thence they infer that it is not contrary to the Treaty in question that the order of succession of the Royal Law, and especially the cognate order of succession, should be preserved, together with the order of succession arising from the express tenor of the Treaty, with the object of being applied subsidiarily (subsidiairement) in all parts of the Monarchy where it can be legally applied, in default of any agnate descendants of the Prince Christian, or, in fact, in case that the pretensions of the House of Gottorp should revive, in conformity with the reservations made by His Majesty the Emperor of Russia.

The Government of the King cannot adopt this view. It considers the abrogation of the Royal Law which calls women and the descendants of women to the succession, as the logical consequence of the Treaty of London, which expressly excludes women. It cannot, therefore, admit that the message can be divided into two distinct parts, of which the one would be superfluous or rather excessive (de trop;) for, as it apprehends, all measures tending to put the said Treaty into execution, and not at the same time stipulating for the suppression of every other law of succession established in favour of women, or of their descendants, would be incomplete, obscure, and dangerous. The transactions which preceded the Treaty of London by no means change the express tenor of this act; in the first place, because it is of a date more recent; in the second, because there exists no connection between the engagements taken by the Powers with whom the King's Government has made a contract, and the special provisions of the said transactions.

There is a great difference between the Royal Message and the arrangement desired by the Opposition, and although it may not be evident at the first glance, although actually it has no practical effect so long as the male and agnate descendants of Prince Christian and the Princess Louise succeed each other on the throne, as during all this time there would be no question of cognate succession, this difference is nevertheless not less real.

According to the message, the abrogation of all the dispositions of the *Lex Regia*, relative to the succession, would take place on the extinction of the agnate and male descendants of King Frederic III., and the new dynasty would then succeed, not in virtue of the Royal Law, but solely in virtue of the act by which the King, free to dispose of his crown by the Protocol of Warsaw and the acts by which his nearest cognates (cognats) have abandoned *their rights, carries out the engagement taken by Article I. of the Treaty of London in definitively [*799] regulating the order of succession. This Treaty would serve also exclusively as a base for the new arrangement. The opponents of the message, on the contrary, while they admit that the Royal Law should be temporarily modified in Article XXXVII., so that Prince Christian might take his place amongst the legitimate heirs, maintain that this Prince should succeed solely in virtue of the Royal Law in all the parts of the Monarchy where this law may be applied, and if they do not deny that a special Act is necessary for the new dynasty to succeed to the whole (totalité) of the Monarchy, especially to the territories where the succession could be contested, they pretend at the same time that this Act, having for its object a combination based for the most part on the Royal Law, should also be principally founded on the said law.

According to the message, on the extinction of the male descendants of the Prince Christian, the succession to the Danish Monarchy would be open; while, according to the views of the Opposition, the rights of succession to all parts of the Monarchy where the provisions of the Royal Law can be applied, would be, on the same eventuality transferred, following the order prescribed in the aforesaid law, to the cognate descendants of the Prince Christian, or rather of the Princess Louise.

In comparing the advantages which would be the consequence of the adoption of the message, with those which would result from the arrangement desired by the Opposition, it cannot be overlooked that the message affords to the King very great liberty in putting into execution Article II. of the Treaty of London, in so much that to take the initiative mentioned in this Article, His Majesty need not seek at once the successive renunciations of those possessing rights, annulled by the Treaty, or rendered impossible by other reasons. If, on the contrary, the provisions of the Royal Law were preserved, the result would be that, on the extinction of the male line of Prince Christian, the subject of the Danish succession would be reduced exactly to the same state it is in at present, or rather in which it was before the King entered into preliminary consultation with his nearest cognates. If the order of succession be regulated according to the message, the King will be thenceforward in a position to decide (constater) which are the pretensions that can be put forward with respect to the succession. His Majesty will then be able from that moment to endeavour to set them aside. In fact, in allowing the old order of things to remain, there would be the chance of seeing revived at some future time, more or less near, doubts, hopes, and heart-burnings, like those, the effects of which we have just undergone; whilst in adopting the message and in substituting thus the clear and strict interpretation of the Treaty of London, for the provisions hitherto regulating the order of succession to the Danish [*800] *Monarchy, all pretensions not founded on this Treaty would be removed.

In a political point of view, the greatest advantage which would result from the adoption of the Royal Message, would undoubtedly be that of seeing a solemn compact, entered into by almost the whole of Europe, exclusively take the place of old regulations which may have a claim to bear weight with us ourselves, but the import of which, if it be not misunderstood, has nevertheless, up to our days at least, remained generally unknown. In what I have just stated, I have not lost sight of the reservations made in favour of the house of Gottorp: I proceed to mention them; and it will be acknowledged, I hope, that essentially they make no change in my view.

The opponents of the message, in wishing to preserve the order of succession established by the *Lex Regia*, have it principally in view to prevent that at the extinction of the agnate descendants of Prince Christian, not only the whole (totalité) of the Monarchy, but especially the portions of the Monarchy subjected to the provisions of the above-mentioned law, should be placed under a legitimate heir, in opposition to the pretensions that it might be wished to put forward with respect to the portions of Monarchy where the application of the Royal Law is contested. They fear a preponderating influence on the part of Russia in the application of Article II. of the Treaty of London, it being in the power of His Majesty the Emperor, by the means of the reservations made by the Protocol of Warsaw, and renewed at the conclusion of the Treaty of May 8, of last year, to support a claimant which all the Monarchy would be forced to accept, because the cognate succession established by the Royal Law abolished once for all through all parts of the Monarchy open to this succession, would have no claimant to oppose to him.

As to the King's Government, it by no means partakes of these apprehensions. The dangers which, in the opinion of the Opposition, might menace Denmark on the part of Russia appear to it in part exaggerated, in part null. If the Emperor had wished to take advantage of his position, as chief of the elder branch of Holstein-Gottorp, to render the arrangement of the succession, present or future, a family matter, to be regulated exclusively between himself and the King of Denmark, the fear of Russian preponderance might have been explained; but had such been his intention, His Imperial Majesty could never have consented to Article II. of the Treaty of London, which Article leaves, in case of the extinction of the agnate descendants of the Prince and of the Princess of Glücksbourg, the initiative in new propositions to the King of Denmark, and expressly stipulates that the propositions must be submitted to all the Powers who have signed the Treaty. This stipulation, which renders European any future question of the Danish succession, is, for the incredulous and untrusting, [*801] *the best and only possible guarantee against all arbitrary influence.

In this exposition I have scrupulously endeavoured to place the views of the Opposition, and the arguments brought forward in support of those views, in the most impartial light possible. But as I have not been able to dwell upon all the special details of the discussions which preceded the rejection of the Message, as I have been obliged to limit myself to showing the characteristic points of the opinions that have arisen, it is not superfluous for me to state expressly, with a view to prevent and remove any sort of annoying prejudice, opposed to the object of this communication, that the opinions defended by the Opposition are founded on Conservative principles, and arise principally from a laudable feeling of respect and natural predilection for the ancient law, that for centuries has regulated the succession to the throne of Denmark.

You are aware, M. le Ministre, that the King's Government sincerely participates in this feeling, as well as the whole Danish nation. Nevertheless it will never join in the views of the Opposition. It is convinced that the provisions of the Royal Message are much more advantageous for the future prospects of the country than the arrangement desired by the opponents of this Act; and it will perseveringly exert itself for the realization of the end which it proposes, even could it admit that a different line of conduct were compatible with the Treaty of London. But this Treaty, interpreted in a natural manner, does not admit the maintenance of an order of succession other than that which is expressly mentioned therein. If the intention of the High Contracting Powers had been to preserve the cognate succession, the Treaty of London, and especially its preamble, would have been otherwise drawn up.

In concluding this despatch, I beg you, M. le Ministre, again to peruse both the report cited at the beginning, and the journal of the Diet, which I have caused to be forwarded to you, and in which you will find an exact recapitulation of all the discussions which have taken place in the United Chambers on the subject of the Message. After you have thus formed a correct idea of the question therein treated, you will have the goodness, Monsieur, to communicate to the Earl of Clarendon, not only the views and arguments of the King's Government, but also the motives and reasons alleged by the Opposition in support of their idea. The Government to which you have the honour to be accredited may with reason wish to receive, through our own organ, authentic explanations on the motives which, to our great regret, have retarded the application of the Treaty of London, and I hope that with the information of which you are now in possession, you will find yourself able to furnish a faithful and impartial picture of the matter in question. I have, &c.

(Signed) BLUHME.

*No. 3. [*802]

THE EARL OF CLARENDON TO SIR H. W. WILLIAMS WYNN.

Foreign Office, June 7, 1853.

SIR,—M. de Bille has communicated to me the despatch addressed by the Danish Government to the Danish Ministers at the Courts, parties to the Treaty of the 8th of May, a copy of which was inclosed in your despatch of the 11th ultimo, and which contains an explanation of the reasons which induced the Danish Government not to confine themselves to a simple communication of that Treaty to the Danish Chambers, but to accompany it by a proposition for the abolition of the *Lex Regia.*

Although the course which the Danish Government has deemed it expedient to pursue in this respect would not appear to call for the expression of an opinion on the part of a foreign Government, I have yet to instruct you, as the expression of such opinion appears from your despatch to be desired, to assure the Danish Minister that Her Majesty's Government do full justice to the motives by which the Danish Government have been actuated, and that they see no reason for changing the opinion already on various occasions expressed by Viscount Palmerston that the abolition of the law in question would afford a simple, safe, and apparently unobjectionable method of hereafter preventing renewed complications, such as those to which the Treaty of the 8th May so happily put an end.

I am, &c.,
(Signed) CLARENDON.

APPENDIX XIV.

Treaty between Her Majesty and the United States of America relative to Fisheries and to Commerce and Navigation.

RATIFICATIONS EXCHANGED AT WASHINGTON, SEPT. 9, 1854. SIGNED AT WASHINGTON, JUNE, 5, 1854.

HER Majesty the Queen of Great Britain, being equally desirous with the Government of the United States to avoid further misunderstanding between their respective subjects and citizens in regard to the extent of the right of fishing on the coasts of British North America, secured to each by Article I. of a convention between Great Britain and the United [*803] States, signed at London on *the 28th day of October, 1818, and being also desirous to regulate the commerce and navigation between their respective territories and people, and more especially between Her Majesty's possessions in North America and the United States, in such a manner as to render the same reciprocally beneficial and satisfactory, have respectively named plenipotentiaries to confer and agree thereupon; that is to say—

Her Majesty the Queen of the United Kingdom of Great Britain and Ireland, James, Earl of Elgin and Kincardine, Lord Bruce and Elgin, a peer of the United Kingdom, Knight of the most Ancient and most Noble Order of the Thistle, and Governor-General in and over all Her Britannic Majesty's provinces on the continent of North America, and in and over the island of Prince Edward;

And the President of the United States of America, William L. Marcy, Secretary of State of the United States;

Who, after having communicated to each other their respective full powers, found in good and due form, have agreed to the following articles:—

Article I.

It is agreed by the high contracting parties, that, in addition to the liberty secured to the United States' fishermen by the above mentioned Convention of October 20, 1818, of taking, curing, and drying fish on certain coasts of the British North American colonies therein defined, the inhabitants of the United States shall have, in common with the subjects of Her Britannic Majesty, the liberty to take fish of every kind, except shell-fish, on the sea-coasts and shores, and in the bays, harbours, and creeks of Canada, New Brunswick, Nova Scotia, Prince Edward's Island, and of the several islands thereunto adjacent, without being restricted to any distance from the shore; with permission to land upon the coasts and shores of those colonies and the islands thereof, and also upon the Magdalen Islands, for the purpose of drying their nets and curing their fish; provided that in so doing they do not interfere with the rights of private property, or with British fishermen, in the peaceable use of any part of the said coast in their occupancy for the same purpose.

It is understood that the above-mentioned liberty applies solely to the sea fishery, and that the salmon and shad fisheries, and all fisheries in the rivers and the mouths of rivers, are hereby reserved exclusively to British fishermen.

And it is further agreed that in order to prevent or settle disputes as to the places to which the reservation of exclusive right to British fishermen contained in this article, and that of fishermen of the United States contained in the next succeeding article, apply, each of the high contracting parties, on the application *of either to the other, shall within six months thereafter, appoint a commissioner. The said [*804] commissioners before proceeding to any business, shall make and subscribe a solemn declaration that they will impartially and carefully examine and decide, to the best of their judgment, and according to justice and equity, without fear, favour, or affection to their own country, upon all such places as are intended to be reserved and excluded from the common liberty of fishing under this and the next succeeding article; and such declaration shall be entered on the record of their proceedings. The commissioners shall name some third person to act as an arbitrator or umpire in any case or cases on which they may themselves differ in opinion. If they should not be able to agree upon the name of such third person, they shall each name a person, and it shall be determined by lot which of the two persons so named shall be the arbitrator or umpire in cases of difference or disagreement between the commissioners. The person so to be chosen to be arbitrator or umpire shall, before proceeding to act as such in any case, make and subscribe a solemn declaration in a form similar to that which shall have been already made and subscribed by the commissioners, which shall be entered on the record of their proceedings. In the event of the death, absence, or incapacity of either of the commissioners or of the arbitrator or umpire, or of their or his omitting, declining, or ceasing to act as such commissioner, arbitrator, or umpire, another and different person shall be appointed or named as aforesaid, to act as such commissioner, arbitrator, or umpire, in the place and stead of the person so originally appointed or named as aforesaid, and shall make and subscribe such declaration as aforesaid.

Such commissioners shall proceed to examine the coasts of the North American provinces and of the United States embraced within the provisions of the first and second articles of this Treaty, and shall designate the places reserved by the said articles from the common right of fishing therein.

The decision of the commissioners and of the arbitrator or umpire shall be given in writing in each case, and shall be signed by them respectively.

The high contracting parties hereby solemnly engage to consider the decision of the commissioners conjointly, or of the arbitrator or umpire, as the case may be, as absolutely final and conclusive in each case decided upon by them or him respectively.

Art. II.

It is agreed by the high contracting parties, that British subjects shall have in common with the citizens of the United States, the liberty to take fish of every kind, except shell-fish, on the eastern sea-coasts and shores of the United States north of the 36th parallel of north latitude, [*805] and on the shores of the several *islands thereunto adjacent, and in the bays, harbours, and creeks of the said sea-coasts and shores of the United States, and of the said islands, without being restricted to any distance from the shore; with permission to land upon the said coasts of the United States and of the islands aforesaid, for the purpose of drying their nets and curing their fish, provided that in so doing they do not interfere with the rights of private property or with the fishermen of the United States in the peaceable use of any part of the said coasts in their occupancy for the same purpose.

It is understood that the above-mentioned liberty applies solely to the sea-fishery, and that salmon and shad fisheries, and all fisheries in rivers and mouths of rivers, are hereby reserved exclusively for fishermen of the United States.

Art. III.

It is agreed that the articles enumerated in the schedule hereunto annexed, being the growth and produce of the aforesaid British colonies, or of the United States, shall be admitted into each country respectively free of duty:—

Schedule.

Grain, flour, and bread stuffs of all kinds; animals of all kinds; fresh, smoked, and salted meats; cotton, wool, seeds, and vegetables; undried fruits; dried fruits; fish of all kinds; products of fish and of all other creatures living in the water; poultry; eggs; hides, furs, skins or tails undressed; stone or marble in its crude or unwrought state; slate, butter, cheese, tallow; lard, horns, manures; ores of metals of all kinds; coal; pitch, tar, turpentine, ashes; timber and lumber of all kinds, round, hewed, and sawed; unmanufactured in whole or in part; firewood; plants, shrubs, and trees, pelts, wool; fish-oil; rice, broom-corn, and bark; gypsum, ground or unground; hewn, or wrought, or unwrought, burr or grindstones; dye stuffs; flax, hemp, and tow, unmanufactured; unmanufactured tobacco; rags.

Art. IV.

It is agreed that the citizens and inhabitants of the United States shall have the right to navigate the river St. Lawrence and the canals in Canada used as the means of communicating between the Great Lakes and the Atlantic Ocean, with their vessels, boats, and crafts, as fully and freely as the subjects of Her Britannic Majesty, subject only to the same tolls, and other assessments as now are or may hereafter be exacted of Her Majesty's said subjects; it being understood, however, that the British Government retains the right of suspending this privilege, on giving due notice thereof to the Government of the United States.

*It is further agreed, that if at any time the British Government should exercise the said reserved right, the Government of [*806] the United States shall have the right of suspending, if it think fit, the operation of Art. 3, of the present Treaty, in so far as the province of Canada is affected thereby, for so long as the suspension of the free navigation of the river St. Lawrence or the canals may continue.

It is further agreed that British subjects shall have the right freely to navigate Lake Michigan with their vessels, boats, and crafts, so long as the privilege of navigating the river St. Lawrence, secured to American citizens by the above clause of the present article, shall continue; and the Government of the United States further engages to urge upon the State Governments to secure to the subjects of Her Britannic Majesty the use of several state canals on terms of equality with the inhabitants of the United States.

And it is further agreed, that no export duty or other duty shall be levied on lumber or timber of any kind cut in that portion of the American territory in the State of Maine, watered by the river St. John and its tributaries, and floated down that river to the sea, when the same is shipped to the United States from the province of New Brunswick.

Art. V.

The present Treaty shall take effect as soon as the laws required to carry it into operation shall have been passed by the Imperial Parliament of Great Britain and by the Provincial Parliaments of those of the British North American Colonies which are affected by this Treaty on the one hand, and by the Congress of the United States on the other. Such assent having been given, the Treaty shall remain in force for ten years from the date at which it may come into operation, and further, until the expiration of twelve months after either of the high contracting parties shall give notice to the other of its wish to terminate the same; each of the high contracting parties being at liberty to give such notice to the other at the end of the said term of ten years, or at any time afterwards.

It is clearly understood, however, that this stipulation is not intended to affect the reservation made by Art. 4, of the present Treaty with regard to the right of temporarily suspending the operation of Arts. 3, and 4, thereof.

Art. VI.

And it is hereby further agreed, that the provisions and stipulations of the foregoing articles shall extend to the island of Newfoundland, so far as they are applicable to that colony. But if [*807] *the Imperial Parliament, the Provincial Parliament of Newfoundland, or the Congress, of the United States, shall not embrace, in their laws enacted for carrying this Treaty into effect, the colony of Newfoundland, then this article shall be of no effect; but the omission to make provision by law to give it effect, by either of the legislative bodies aforesaid, shall not in any way impair the remaining articles of this Treaty.

Art. VII.

The present Treaty shall be duly ratified, and the mutual exchange of ratifications shall take place at Washington, within six months from the date hereof, or earlier if possible.

In faith whereof, we, the respective Plenipotentiaries, have signed this Treaty, and have hereunto affixed our seals.

Done, in triplicate, at Washington, the 5th day of June, A. D. 1854.

Elgin and Kincardine. W. L. Marcy.

APPENDIX XV.

Convention with Honduras.

"Her Majesty the Queen of the United Kingdom of Great Britain and Ireland, and the Republic of Honduras, being desirous to settle by means of a convention certain points resulting from the territorial arrangements which form the subject of another convention concluded between them on this day, have named as their plenipotentiaries for that purpose, that is to say,

"Her Majesty the Queen of the United Kingdom of Great Britain and Ireland, the Right Hon. George William Frederick, Earl of Clarendon, Baron Hyde of Hindon, a peer of the United Kingdom, a member of Her Britannic Majesty's most Hon. Privy Council, Knight of the Most Noble Order of the Garter, Knight Grand Cross of the Most Hon.

Order of the Bath, Her Britannic Majesty's Principal Secretary of State for Foreign Affairs;

"And his Excellency the President of the Republic of Honduras, Señor Dr. Juan Victor Herran, Minister Plenipotentiary of the Republic to Her Britannic Majesty;

"Who, after having communicated to each other their respective full powers, found in good and due form, have agreed upon and concluded the following articles:—

*ARTICLE I. [*808]

"The Republic of Honduras engages not to disturb the subjects of Her Britannic Majesty in the enjoyment of any property of which they may be in possession in the islands of Ruatan, Bonaca, Elena, Utile, Barbarete, and Morat, situated in the Bay of Honduras.

ART. II.

"Her Britannic Majesty agrees to recognize the mid channel of the river Wanx or Segovia, which falls into the Caribbean Sea at Gracias à Dios, as the boundary between the Republic of Honduras and the territory of the Mosquito Indians, without prejudice, however, to any question of boundary between the Republics of Honduras and of Nicaragua.

"And whereas the Mosquito Indians have heretofore possessed and exercised rights in and over the territories lying between the river Wanx or Segovia and the Roman river, Her Britannic Majesty agreed to recommend to the Mosquito Indians to renounce any such rights in favour of the Republic of Honduras, on condition of receiving from the Republic some reasonable sum by way of annuity for a limited period, to be paid half-yearly, as an indemnity and compensation for the loss and extinction of their interest in the said territory. When such an arrangement shall have been acceded to by the Mosquito Indians, Her Britannic Majesty engages to recognize the sovereignty over the said territory as belonging to the Republic of Honduras; and Her Britannic Majesty and the Republic will, within twelve months thereafter, appoint two commissioners, one to be named by each party, for the purpose of determining the amount, the period of duration, and the time, place, and mode of payment of the annuity so to be paid to the Mosquito Indians as indemnity and compensation.

"And whereas British subjects have, by grant, lease, or otherwise, heretofore obtained from the Mosquito Indians interests in various lands situated within the territory above described, lying between the river Wanx or Segovia and the river Roman, the Republic of Honduras engages to respect and maintain such interests. And it is further agreed that the commissioners mentioned in the present article shall investigate the claims of British subjects arising out of such grants or leases, or otherwise; and all British subjects whose claims shall by the commissioners be pronounced well founded and valid shall be quieted in the possession of their respective interests in the said lands.

ART. III.

"The Republic of Honduras further engages to carry into effect any [*809] agreements already made and now in course of being *carried out for the satisfaction of British claims; and it is agreed between the contracting parties that the commissioners mentioned in the preceding article shall also examine and decide upon any British claims upon the Government of Honduras that may be submitted to them other than those specified in the preceding article; and not already in train of settlement.

ART. IV.

"The commissioners mentioned in the preceding articles shall meet at Truxillo, at the earliest convenient period after they shall have been respectively named, and shall, before proceeding to any business, make and subscribe a solemn declaration that they will impartially and carefully examine and decide, to the best of their judgment, and according to justice and equity, without fear, favour, or affection to their own country, upon all the matters referred to them for their decision; and such declaration shall be entered on the record of their proceedings.

"The commissioners shall then, and before proceeding to any other business, name some third person to act as arbitrator or umpire in any case or cases in which they may themselves differ in opinion. The person so to be chosen as arbitrator or umpire shall, before proceeding to act as such, make and subscribe a solemn declaration, in a form similar to that which shall already have been made and subscribed by the commissioners, and which shall also be entered on the record of the proceedings. In the event of the death, absence, or incapacity of such person, or of his omitting or declining, or ceasing to act as such arbitrator or umpire, another person shall be named as aforesaid to act as arbitrator or umpire in his place, and shall make and subscribe such declaration aforesaid.

"Her Britannic Majesty and the Republic of Honduras hereby engage to consider the decision of the commissioners conjointly, or of the arbitrator or umpire, as the case may be, as final and conclusive on the matters hereby referred to their decision; and they further engage forthwith to give full effect to the same.

ART. V.

"The commissioners and the arbitrator or umpires shall keep an accurate record and correct minutes or notes of all their proceedings, with the dates thereof, and shall appoint and employ a clerk or other persons to assist them in the transaction of the business which may come before them. The salaries of the commissioners shall be paid by their respective Governments. The contingent expenses of the commission, including the salary of the arbitrator or umpire, and of the clerk or clerks, shall be defrayed in equal moieties by the two Governments.

*ART. VI. [*810]

"The present convention shall be ratified, and the ratifications shall be exchanged at London, as soon as possible within twelve months from this date.

"In witness whereof the respective Plenipotentiaries have signed the same, and have affixed thereto their respective seals.

"Done at London, the 27th day of August, in the year of our Lord, 1856.

"CLARENDON.
"VR. HERRAN."

APPENDIX XVI.

Treaty between Her Majesty, the Emperor of Austria, and the Emperor of the French, guaranteeing the Independence and integrity of the Ottoman Empire. Signed at Paris, April 15, 1856.—[*Ratifications exchanged at Paris, April* 29, 1856.]

SA Majesté la Reine du Royaume Uni de la Grande Bretagne et d'Irlande, Sa Majesté l'Empereur d'Autriche, et Sa Majesté l'Empereur des Français, voulant régler entre Elles l'action combinée qu'entraînerait, de leur part, toute infraction aux stipulations de la Paix de Paris, ont nommé, à cet effet, pour leurs Plénipotentiaires, savoir:

Sa Majesté la Reine du Royaume Uni de la Grande Bretagne et d'Irlande, le Très Honorable George Guillaume Frédéric Comte de Clarendon, Baron Hyde de Hindon, Pair du Royaume Uni, Conseiller de Sa Majesté Britannique en Son Conseil Privé, Chevalier du Très Noble Ordre de la Jarretière, Chevalier Grand-Croix du Très Honorable Ordre du Bain, Principal Secrétaire d'Etat de Sa Majesté pour les Affaires Etrangères; et le Très Honorable Henri Richard Charles Baron Cowley, Pair du Royaume Uni, Conseiller de Sa Majesté en Son Conseil Privé, Chevalier Grand-Croix du Très Honorable Ordre du Bain, Ambassadeur Extraordinaire et Plénipotentiaire de Sa Majesté près Sa Majesté l'Empereur des Français;

Sa Majesté l'Empereur d'Autriche, le Sieur Charles Ferdinand Comte de Buol-Schauenstein, Grand-Croix des Ordres Impériaux de Saint-Etienne et de Léopold d' Autriche, Chevalier de l'Ordre de la Couronne de Fer de première classe, Grand-Croix de l'Ordre Impérial de la Légion d'Honneur, Grand-Croix de l'Ordre de Saint-Jean *de Jérusalem, &c., &c., &c., Son Chambellan et Conseiller Intime Actuel, [*811] Son Ministre de la Maison et des Affaires Etrangères, Président de la Conférence des Ministres; et le Sieur Joseph Alexandre Baron de Hübner, Chevalier de l'Ordre Impérial de la Couronne de Fer de première classe, Grand Officier de l'Ordre Impérial de la Légion d'Honneur, &c., &c., &c., Son Conseiller Intime Actuel, et Son Envoyé Extraordinaire et Ministre Plénipotentiaire à la Cour de France;

Et sa Majesté l'Empereur des Français, le Sieur Alexandre Comte Colonna Walewski, Sénateur de l'Empire, Grand-Croix de l'Ordre Impérial de la Légion d'Honneur, &c., &c., &c., Son Ministre et Secrétaire d'Etat au Département des Affaires Etrangères; et le Sieur François Adolphe Baron de Bourqueney, Sénateur de l'Empire, Grand-Croix de l'Ordre Impérial de la Légion d'Honneur et de l'Ordre de Léopold d'Autriche, &c., &c., &c., Son Envoyé Extraordinaire et Ministre Plénipotentiaire près Sa Majesté Impériale et Royale Apostolique;

Lesquels, après avoir échangé leurs pleins pouvoirs, trouvés en bonne et due forme, sont convenus des Articles suivants:—

Article I.

Les Hautes Parties Contractantes garantissent solidairement entre Elles l'indépendance et l'intégrité de l'Empire Ottoman, consacrées par le Traité conclu à Paris, le trente Mars, mil huit cent cinquante-six.

Art. II.

Toute infraction aux stipulations du dit Traité sera considérée par les Puissances signataires du présent Traité comme *casus belli*. Elles s'entendront avec la Sublime Porte sur les mesures devenues nécessaires, et détermineront sans retard entre Elles l'emploi de leurs forces militaires et navales.

Art. III.

Le présent Traité sera ratifié, et les ratifications en seront échangées dans l'espace de quinze jours, ou plus tôt si faire se peut.

En foi de quoi les Plénipotentiaires respectifs l'ont signé, et y ont apposé le sceau de leurs armes.

Fait à Paris, le quinzième jour du mois d'Avril, de l'an mil huit cent cinquante-six.

(L.S.) Clarendon.
(L.S.) Cowley.
(L.S.) Buol-Schauenstein.
(L.S.) Hubner.
(L.S.) A. Walewski.
(L.S.) Bourqueney.

[*812] *(Translation.)

Her Majesty the Queen of the United Kingdom of Great Britain and Ireland, His Majesty the Emperor of Austria, and His Majesty the Emperor of the French, wishing to settle between themselves the combined action which any infraction of the stipulations of the Peace of Paris would involve on their part, have named for that purpose as their Plenipotentiaries, that is to say, &c.,

Who, after having exchanged their full powers, found in good and due form, have agreed upon the following Articles:—

Article I.

The High Contracting Parties guarantee, jointly and severally, the independence and the integrity of the Ottoman Empire, recorded in the Treaty concluded at Paris on the thirtieth of March, one thousand eight hundred and fifty-six.

Art. II.

Any infraction of the stipulations of the said Treaty will be considered by the Powers signing the present Treaty as *casus belli*. They will come to an understanding with the Sublime Porte as to the measures which have become necessary, and will without delay determine among themselves as to the employment of their military and naval forces.

Art. III.

The present Treaty shall be ratified, and the ratifications shall be exchanged in a fortnight or sooner if possible.

In witness whereof the respective Plenipotentiaries have signed the same, and have affixed thereto the seal of their arms.

Done at Paris, the fifteenth day of the month of April, in the year one thousand eight hundred and fifty-six.

(L.S.) Clarendon.
(L.S.) Cowley.
(L.S.) Buol-Schauenstein.
(L.S.) Hubner.
(L.S.) A. Walewski.
(L.S.) Bourqueney.

APPENDIX XVII. [*813]

Treaty between Great Britain, Austria, France, Prussia, Russia, Sardinia, and Turkey, for the Re-establishment of Peace. Signed at Paris, March, 30, 1856.

Au Nom de Dieu Tout-Puissant.

Leurs Majestés la Reine du Royaume Uni de la Grande Bretagne et d'Irlande, l'Empereur des Français, l'Empereur de toutes les Russies, le Roi de Sardaigne, et l'Empereur des Ottomans, animées du désir de mettre un terme aux calamités de la guerre, et voulant prévenir le retour des complications qui l'ont fait naître, ont résolu de s'entendre avec Sa Majesté l'Empereur d'Autriche sur les bases à donner au rétablissement et à la consolidation de la paix, en assurant, par des garanties efficaces et réciproques, l'indépendance et l'intégrité de l'Empire Ottoman.

A cet effet, Leurs dites Majestés ont nommé pour leurs Plénipotentiaires, savoir, &c.

* * * * * * *

Les Plénipotentiaires, après avoir échangé, leurs pleins pouvoirs, trouvés en bonne et due forme, sont convenus des Articles suivants :—

ARTICLE I.

Il y aura, à dater du jour de l'échange des ratifications du présent Traité, Paix et Amitié entre Sa Majesté la Reine du Royaume Uni de la Grande Bretagne et d'Irlande, Sa Majesté l'Empereur des Français, Sa Majesté le Roi de Sardaigne, Sa Majesté Impériale le Sultan, d'une part; et Sa Majesté l'Empereur de toutes les Russies, de l'autre part; ainsi qu'entre leurs héritiers et successeurs, leurs états et sujets respectifs, à perpétuité.

ART. II.

La paix étant heureusement rétablie entre Leurs dites Majestés, les territoires conquis ou occupés par leurs armées pendant la guerre seront réciproquement évacués.

Des arrangements spéciaux régleront le mode de l'évacuation, qui devra être aussi prompte que faire se pourra.

ART. III.

Sa Majesté l'Empereur de toutes les Russies s'engage à restituer à Sa Majesté le Sultan la ville et citadelle de Kars, aussi bien que les autres parties du territoire Ottoman dont les troupes Russes se trouvent en possession.

[*814] ART. IV.

Leurs Majestés la Reine du Royaume Uni de la Grande Bretagne et d'Irlande, l'Empereur des Français, le Roi de Sardaigne, et le Sultan, s'engagent à restituer à Sa Majesté l'Empereur de toutes les Russies les villes et ports de Sébastopol, Balaklava, Kamiesch, Eupatoria, Kertch, Jenikale, Kinburn, ainsi que tous autres territoires occupées par les troupes alliées.

ART. V.

Leurs Majestés la Reine du Royaume Uni de la Grande Bretagne et d'Irlande, l'Empereur des Français, l'Empereur de toutes les Russies, le Roi de Sardaigne, et le Sultan, accordent une amnistie pleine et entière à ceux de leurs sujets qui auraient été compromis par une participation quelconque aux évènements de la guerre en faveur de la cause ennemie.

Il est expressément entendu que cette amnistie s'étendra aux sujets de chacune des Parties belligérantes qui auraient continué, pendant la guerre, à être employés dans le service de l'un des autres belligérants.

ART VI.

Les prisonniers de guerre seront immédiatement rendus de part et d'autre.

Art. VII.

Sa Majesté la Reine du Royaume Uni de la Grande Bretagne et d'Irlande, Sa Majesté l'Empereur d'Autriche, Sa Majesté l'Empereur des Français, Sa Majesté le Roi de Prusse, Sa Majesté l'Empereur de toutes les Russies, et Sa Majesté le Roi de Sardaigne, déclarent la Sublime Porte admise à participer aux avantages du droit public et du concert Européens. Leurs Majestés s'engagent, chacune de son côté, à respecter l'indépendance et l'intégrité territoriale de l'Empire Ottoman; garantissent en commun la stricte observation de cet engagement; et considéreront, en conséquence, tout acte de nature à y porter atteinte comme une question d'intérêt général.

Art. VIII.

S'il survenait, entre la Sublime Porte et l'une ou plusieurs des autres Puissances signataires, un dissentiment qui menaçât le maintien de leurs relations, la Sublime Porte et chacune de ces Puissances, avant de recourir à l'emploi de la force, mettront les autres Parties Contractantes en mesure de prévenir cette extrémité par leur action médiatrice.

*Art. IX. [*815]

Sa Majesté Impériale le Sultau, dans sa constante sollicitude pour le bien-être de ses sujets, ayant octroyé un firman qui, en améliorant leur sort, sans distinction de religion ni de race, consacre ses généreuses intentions envers les populations Chrétiennes de son Empire, et voulant donner un nouveau témoignage de ses sentiments à cet égard, a résolu de communiquer aux Puissances Contractantes le dit firman spontanément émané de sa volonté souveraine.

Les Puissances Contractantes constatent la haute valeur de cette communication. Il est bien entendu qu'elle ne saurait, en aucun cas, donner le droit aux dites Puissances de s'immiscer, soit collectivement, soit séparément, dans les rapports de sa Majesté le Sultan avec ses sujets, ni dans l'administration intérieure de son Empire.

Art. X.

La Convention du treize Juillet, mil huit cent quarante-un, qui maintient l'antique règle de l'Empire Ottoman relative à la clôture des Détroits du Bosphore et des Dardanelles, a été revisée d'un commun accord.

L'Acte conclu à cet effet et conformément à ce principe entre les Hautes Parties Contractantes, est et demeure annexé au présent Traité, et aura même force et valeur que s'il en faisait partie intégrante.

Art. XI.

La Mer Noire est neutralisée: ouverts à la marine marchande de toutes les nations, ses eaux et ses ports sont formellement et à perpétuité interdits au pavillon de guerre, soit des Puissances riveraines, soit de toute autre Puissance, sauf les exceptions mentionnées aux Articles XIV et XIX du présent Traité.

ART. XII.

Libre de tout entrave, le commerce dans les ports, et dans les eaux de la Mer Noire ne sera assujetti qu'à des réglements de santé, de douane, de police, conçus dans un esprit favorable au développement des transactions commerciales.

Pour donner aux intérêts commerciaux et maritimes de toutes les nations la sécurité désirable, la Russie et la Sublime Porte admettront des Consuls dans leurs ports situés sur le littoral de la Mer Noire, conformément aux principes du droit international.

[*816] *ART. XIII.

La Mer Noire etant neutralisée aux termes de l'Article XI, le maintien ou l'établissement sur son littoral d'arsenaux militaires-maritimes devient sans nécessité comme sans objet; en conséquence, Sa Majesté l'Empereur de toutes les Russies et Sa Majesté Impériale le Sultan s'engagent à n'élever et à ne conserver, sur ce littoral, aucun arsenal militaire-maritime.

ART. XIV.

Leurs Majestés l'Empereur de toutes les Russies et le Sultan ayant conclu une Convention à l'effet de déterminer la force et le nombre des bâtiments légers, nécessaires au service de leurs côtes, qu'elles se réservent d'éntretenir dans la Mer Noire, cette Convention est annexée au présent Traité, et aura même force et valeur que si elle en faisait partie intégrante. Elle ne pourra être ni annulée ni modifiée sans l'assentiment des Puissances signataires du présent Traité.

ART. XV.

L'Acte du Congrès de Vienne ayant établi les principes destinés à régler la navigation des fleuves qui séparent ou traversent plusieurs Etats, les Puissances Contractantes stipulent entre elles qu'à l'avenir ces principes seront également appliqués au Danube et à ses embouchures. Elles déclarent que cette disposition fait désormais partie du droit public de l'Europe, et la prennent sous leur garantie.

La navigation du Danube ne pourra être assujettie à aucune entrave ni redevance qui ne serait pas expressément prévue par les stipulations contenues dans les Articles suivants. En conséquence, il ne sera perçu aucun péage basé uniquement sur le fait de la navigation du fleuve, ni aucun droit sur les marchandises qui se trouvent à bord des navires. Les réglements de police et de quarantaine à établir, pour la sûreté des Etats séparés ou traversés par ce fleuve, seront conçus de manière à favoriser, autant que faire se pourra, la circulation des navires. Sauf ces réglements, il ne sera apporté aucun obstacle, quel qu'il soit, à la libre navigation.

ART. XVI.

Dans le but de réaliser les dispositions de l'Article précédent, une Commission dans laquelle la Grande Bretagne, l'Autriche, la France, la Prusse, La Russie, la Sardaigne, et la Turquie seront, chacune, représentées par un Délégué, sera chargée de désigner et de faire exécuter les travaux nécessaires, depuis Isatcha, pour dégager *les embouchures du Danube, ainsi que les parties de la mer y avoisinantes, des sables et autres obstacles qui les obstruent, affin de mettre cette partie du fleuve et les dites parties de la mer dans les meilleures conditions possibles de navigabilité. [*817]

Pour couvrir les frais de ces travaux, ainsi que des établissements ayant pour objet d'assurer et de faciliter la navigation aux bouches du Danube, des droits fixes d'un taux convenable, arrêtés par la Commission à la majorité des voix, pourront être prélvées, à la condition expresse que, sous ce rapport comme sous tous les autres, les pavillons de toutes les nations seront traités sur le pied d'une parfaite égalité.

Art. XVII.

Une Commission sera établie et se composera des Délégués de l'Autriche, de la Bavière, de la Sublime Porte, et du Wurtemberg (un pour chacune de ces Puissances,) auxquels se réuniront les Commissaires des trois Principautés Danubiennes, dont la nomination aura été approuvée par la Porte. Cette Commission, qui sera permanente : 1, élaborera les réglements de navigation et de police fluviale; 2, fera disparaître les entraves, de quelque nature qu'elles puissent être, qui s'opposent encore à l'application au Danube des dispositions du Traité de Vienne; 3, ordonnera et fera exécuter les travaux nécessaires sur tout le parcours du fleuve; et, 4, veillera, après la dissolution de la Commission Européenne, au maintien de la navigablité des embouchures du Danube et des parties de la mer y avoisinantes.

Art. XVIII.

Il est entendu que la Commission Européenne, aura rempli sa tâche, et que la Commission Riveraine aura terminé les travaux désignés dans l'Article précédent sous les Nos. 1 et 2, dans l'espace de deux ans. Les Puissances signataires réunies en conférence, informées de ce fait, prononceront, après en avoir pris acte, la dissolution de la Commission Européenne; et, dès lors, la Commission Riveraine permanente jouira des mêmes pouvoirs que ceux dont la Commission Européenne, aura été investie jusqu'alors.

Art. XIX.

Afin d'assurer l'exécution des réglements qui auront été arrêtés d'un commun accord, d'après les principes ci-dessus énoncés, chacune des Puissances Contractantes aura le droit de faire stationner, en tout temps, deux bâtiments légers aux embouchures du Danube.

Art. XX.

En échange des villes, ports, et territoires énumérés dans l'Article IV

[*818] du présent Traité, et pour mieux assurer la liberté de *la navigation du Danube, Sa Majesté l'Empereur de toutes les Russies consent à la rectification de sa frontière en Bessarabie.

La nouvelle frontière partira de la Mer Noire, à un kilomètre à l'est du Lac Bourna Sola, rejoindra perpendiculairement la route d'Akerman, suivra cette route jusqu'au Val de Trajan, passera au sud de Bolgrad, remontera le long de la Rivière de Yalpuck jusqu'à la Hauteur de Saratsika, et ira aboutir à Katamori sur le Pruth. En amont de ce point, l'ancienne frontière entre les deux Empires ne subira aucune modification.

Des Délégués des Puissances Contractantes fixeront dans ses détails le tracé de la nouvelle frontière.

Art. XXI.

Le territoire cédé par la Russie sera annexé à la Principauté de Moldavie sous la suzeraineté de la Sublime Porte.

Les habitants de ce territoire jouiront des droits et privilèges assurés aux Principautés; et, pendant l'espace de trois années, il leur sera permis de transporter ailleurs leur domicile, en disposant librement de leurs propriétés.

Art. XXII.

Les Principautés de Valachie et de Moldavie continueront à jouir, sous la suzeraineté de la Porte et sous la garantie des Puissances Contractantes, des privilèges et des immunités dont elles sont en possession. Aucune protection exclusive ne sera exercée sur elles par une des Puissances garantes. Il n'y aura aucun droit particulier d'ingérence dans leurs affaires intérieures.

Art. XXIII.

La Sublime Porte s'engage à conserver aux dites Principautés une administration indépendante et nationale; ainsi que la pleine liberté de culte, de législation, de commerce, et de navigation.

Les lois et statuts aujourd'hui en viguer seront revisés, Pour établir un complet accord sur cette révision, une Commission Spéciale, sur la composition de laquelle les Hautes Puissances Contractantes s'entendront, se réunira sans délai à Bucharest, avec un Commissaire de la Sublime Porte.

Cette Commission aura pour tâche de s'enquérir de l'état actuel des Principautés, et de proposer les bases de leur future organization.

Art. XXIV.

Sa Majesté le Sultan promet de convoquer immédiatement dans chacune [*819] des deux Provinces un Divan *ad hoc*, composé de *manière à constituer la représentation la plus exacte des intérêts de toutes les classes de la société. Ces Divans seront appelés à exprimer les vœux des populations relativement à l'organisation définitive des Principautés.

Une instruction du Congrès réglera les rapports de la Commission avec ces Divans.

Art. XXV.

Prenant en considération l'opinion émise par les deux Divans, la Commission transmettra sans retard, au siège actuel des Conférences, le résultat de son propre travail.

L'entente finale avec la Puissance Suzeraine sera consacrée par une Convention conclue à Paris entre les Hautes Parties Contractantes; et un hatti-schériff, conforme aux stipulations de la Convention, constituera définitivement l'organisation de ces provinces, placée, désormais, sous la garantie collective de toutes les Puissances signataires.

Art. XXVI.

Il est convenu qu'il y aura dans les Principautés une force armée nationale, organisée dans le but de maintenir la sûreté de l'intérieure et d'assurer celle des frontières. Aucune entrave ne pourra être apportée aux mesures extraordinaires de défense que, d'accord avec la Sublime Porte, elles seraient appelées à prendre pour repousser toute agression étrangère.

Art. XXVII.

Si le repos intérieur des Principautés se trouvait menacé ou compromis, la Sublime Porte s'entendra avec les autres Puissances Contractantes sur les mesures à prendre pour maintenir ou rétablir l'ordre légal. Une intervention armée ne pourra avoir lieu sans un accord préalable entre ces Puissances.

Art. XXVIII.

La Principauté de Servie continuera à relever de la Sublime Porte, conformément aux Hats Impériaux qui fixent et déterminent ses droits et immunités, placés, désormais, sous la garantie collective des Puissances Contractantes.

En conséquence, la dite Principauté conservera son administration indépendante et nationale, ainsi que la pleine liberté de culte, de législation, de commerce, et de navigation.

Art. XXIX.

Le droit de garnison de la Sublime Porte, tel qu'il se trouve stipulé par les réglements antérieurs, et maintenu. Aucune intervention armée ne pourra avoir lieu en Servie sans un accord préalable entre les Hautes Puissances Contractantes.

*Art. XXX. [*820]

Sa Majesté l'Empereur de toutes les Russies et Sa Majesté le Sultan maintiennent, dans son intégrité, l'état de leurs possessions en Asie, tel qu'il existait légalement avant la rupture.

Pour prévenir toute contestation locale, le tracé de la frontière sera vérifié, et s'il y a lieu, rectifié, sans qu'il puisse en résulter un préjudice territorial pour l'une ou l'autre des deux Parties.

A cet effet, une Commission Mixte, composée de deux Commissaires Russes, de deux Commissaires Ottomans, d'un Commissaire Anglais, et d'un Commissaire Français, sera envoyée sur les lieux immédiatement après le rétablissement des relations diplomatiques entre la Cour de Russie et la Sublime Porte. Son travail devra être terminée dans l'espace de huit mois à dater de l'échange des ratifications du présent Traité.

Art. XXXI.

Les territoires occupés pendant la guerre par les troupes de Leurs Majestés la Reine du Royaume Uni de la Grande Bretagne et d'Irlande, l'Empereur d'Autriche, l'Empereur des Français, et le Roi de Sardaigne, aux termes des Conventions signées à Constantinople le douze Mars, mil huit cent cinquante-quatre, entre la Grande Bretagne, la France, et la Sublime Porte; le quatorze Juin de la même année, entre l'Autriche et la Sublime Porte; et le quinze Mars, mil huit cent cinquante-cinq, entre la Sardaigne et la Sublime Porte; seront évacués après l'échange des ratifications du présent Traité, aussitôt que faire se pourra. Les délais et les moyens d'exécutions feront l'objet d'un arrangement entre la Sublime Porte et les Puissances dont les troupes ont occupé son territoire.

Art. XXXII.

Jusqu'à ce que les Traités ou Conventions qui existaient avant la guerre entre les Puissances belligérantes aient été ou renouvelés ou remplacés par des Actes nouveaux, le commerce d'importation ou d'exportation aura lieu réciproquement sur le pied des réglements en vigueur avant la guerre; et leurs sujets en toute autre matière seront respectivement traités sur le pied de la nation la plus favorisée.

Art. XXXIII.

La Convention conclue en ce jour entre Leurs Majestés la Reine du Royaume Uni de la Grande Bretagne et d'Irlande, l'Empereur des Français, d'une part, et Sa Majesté l'Empereur de toutes les Russies, de l'autre part, relativement aux Iles de Aland, est et demeure annexée au présent Traité, et aura même force et valeur que si elle en faisait partie.

[*821]

Art. XXXIV.

Le présent Traité sera ratifié, et les ratifications en seront échangées à Paris dans l'espace de quatre semaines, ou plus tôt si faire se peut.

En foi de quoi les Plénipotentiaires respectifs l'ont signé, et y ont apposé le sceau de leurs armes.

Fait à Paris, le trentième jour du mois de Mars, de l'an mil huit cent cinquante-six.

(L.S.) CLARENDON.
(L.S.) COWLEY.
(L.S.) BUOL-SCHAUENSTEIN.
(L.S.) HUBNER.
(L.S.) A. WALEWSKI.
(L.S.) BOURQUENEY.
(L.S.) MANTEUFFEL.
(L.S.) C. M. D'HATZFELDT.
(L.S.) ORLOFF.
(L.S.) BRUNNOW.
(L.S.) C. CAVOUR.
(L.S.) DE VILLAMARINA.
(L.S.) AALI.
(L.S.) MHEMMED DJEMIL.

ARTICLE ADDITIONAL ET TRANSITOIRE.

Les stipulations de la Convention des Détroits signée en ce jour, ne seront pas applicables aux bâtiments de guerre employés par les Puissances belligérentes pour l'évacuation, par mer, des territories occupés par leurs armées ; mais les dites stipulations reprendront leur entier effet aussitôt que l'évacuation sera terminée.

Fait à Paris, le trentième jour du mois de Mars, de l'an mil huit cent cinquante-six.

(L.S.) CLARENDON.
(L.S.) COWLEY.
(L.S.) BUOL-SCHAUENSTEIN.
(L.S.) HUBNER.
(L.S.) A. WALEWSKI.
(L.S.) BOURQUENEY.
(L.S.) MANTEUFFEL.
(L.S.) C. M. D'HATZFELDT.
(L.S.) ORLOFF.
(L.S.) BRUNNOW.
(L.S.) C. CAVOUR.
(L.S.) DE VILLAMARINA.
(L.S.) AALI.
(L.S.) MEHEMMED DJEMIL.

*CONVENTIONS ANNEXED TO THE PRECEDING TREATY. [*822]

1.—*Convention between Her Majesty, the Emperor of Austria, the Emperor of the French, the King of Prussia, the Emperor of Russia, and the King of Sardinia, on the one part, and the Sultan, on the other part, respecting the Straits of the Dardanelles and of the Bosphorus.*

Signed at Paris, March 30, 1856.

[*Ratifications exchanged at Paris, April*, 27, 1856.]

Au Nom Dieu Tout-Puissant.

Leurs Majestés la Reine du Royaume Uni de la Grande Bretagne et d'Irlande, l'Empereur d'Autriche, l'Empereur des Français, le Roi de Prusse, l'Empereur de toutes les Russies, signataires de la Convention du treize Julliet, mil huit cent quarante-un; et Sa Majesté le Roi de Sardaigne; voulant constater en commun leür détermination unanime de se conformer à l'ancienne règle de l'Empire Ottoman, d'après laquelle les Détroits des Dardanelles et du Bosphore sont fermés aux bâtiments de guerre étrangers tant que la Porte se trouve en paix;

Les dites Majestés, d'une part, et Sa Majesté le Sultan, de l'autre ont résolu de renouveler la Convention conclue à Londres la Treize Juillet, mil huit cent quarante-un, sauf quelques modifications de détail qui ne portent aucune atteinte au principe sur lequel elle repose.

En conséquence, Leurs dites Majestés ont nommé à cet effet pour leurs Plénipotentiaires, savoir, &c.

* * * * * * * *

Lequels, après avoir échangé leurs pleins pouvoirs, trouvés en bonne et due forme, sont-convenus des Articles suivants :—

ARTICLE I.

Sa Majesté le Sultan, d'une part, déclare qu'il a la ferme résolution de maintenir à l'avenir le principe invariablement établi comme ancienne règle de son Empire, et en vertu duquel il a été de tout temps défendu aux bâtiments de guerre des Puissances étrangères d'entrer dans les Détroits des Dardanelles et du Bosphore; et que, tant que la Porte se trouve en paix, Sa Majesté n'admettra aucun bâtiment de guerre étranger dans les dits Détroits.

Et Leurs Majestés la Reine du Royaume Uni de la Grande Bretagne et d'Irlande, l'Empereur d'Autriche, l'Empereur des Français, le Roi de Prusse, l'Empereur de toutes les Russies, et le Roi de Sardaigne, de l'autre part, s'engagent à respecter cette détermination du Sultan, et à se conformer au principe ci dessus énoncé.

[*823] *ART. II.

Le Sultan se réserve, comme par le passé, de délivrer des firmans de passage aux bâtiments légers sous pavillon de guerre, lesquels seront employés, comme il est d'usage, au service des Légations des Puissances amies.

ART. III.

La même exception s'applique aux bâtiments légers sous pavillon de guerre que chacune des Puissances Contractantes est autorisée à faire stationner aux embouchures du Danube, pour assurer l'exécution des réglements relatifs, à la liberté du fleuve, et dont le nombre ne devra pas excéder deux pour chaque Puissance.

ART. IV.

La présente Convention, annexée au Traité Général signé à Paris en ce jour, sera ratifiée, et les ratifications en seront échangées dans l'espace de quatre semaines, ou plus tôt si faire se peut.

En foi de quoi, les Plénipotentiaires respectifs l'ont signée, et y ont apposé le sceau de leurs armes.

Fait à Paris, le trentième jour du mois de Mars, de l'an mil huit cent cinquante-six.

(L.S.) CLARENDON.
(L.S.) COWLEY.
(L.S.) BUOL SCHAUENSTEIN.
(L.S.) HUBNER.
(L.S.) A. WALEWSKI.
(L.S.) BOURQUENEY.
(L.S.) MANTEUFFEL.
(L.S.) C. M. D'HATZFELDT.
(L.S.) ORLOEF.
(L.S.) BRUNNOW.
(L.S.) C. CAVOUR.
(L.S.) DE VILLAMARINA.
(L.S.) AALI.
(L.S.) MEHEMMED DJEMIL.

*2.—*Convention between the Emperor of Russia and the Sultan, limiting their Naval Force in the Black Sea.* [*824]

Signed at Paris, March 30, 1856.

[*Ratifications exchanged at Paris, April* 27, 1856.]

Au Nom de Dieu Tout-Puissant.

Sa Majesté l'Empereur de toutes les Russies, et Sa Majesté Impériale le Sultan, prenant en considération le principe de la neutralisation de la Mer Noire etabli par les Préliminaires consignés au Protocole No. 1, signé à Paris le 25 Février de la présente année, et voulant, en conséquence, régler d'un commun accord le nombre et la force des bâtiments légers qu'elles se sont réservé d'entretenir dans la Mer Noire pour le service de leurs côtes, ont résolu de signer, dans ce but, une Convention Spéciale, et ont nommé à cet effet, &c.

Lesquels, après avoir échangé leurs pleins pouvoirs, trouvés en bonne et due forme, sont convenus des Articles suivants :—

ARTICLE I.

Les Hautes Parties Contractantes s'engagent mutuellement à n'avoir dans la Mer Noire d'autres bâtiments de guerre que ceux dont le nombre, la force, et les dimensions sont stipulés ci-après.

ART. II.

Les Hautes Parties Contractantes se réservent d'entretenir chacune dans cette mer, six bâtiments-à-vapeur de cinquante mètres de longueur à la flottaison, d'un tonnage de huit cents tonneaux *au maximum*, et quatre bâtiments légers à vapeur ou à voile d'un tonnage qui ne dépassera pas deux cents tonneaux chacun.

ART. III.

La présente Convention, annexée au Traité Général signé à Paris en ce jour, sera ratifié, et les ratifications en seront échangées dans l'espace de quatre semaines, ou plus tôt si faire se peut.

En foi de quoi les Plénipotentiaires respectifs l'ont signée, et y ont apposé le sceau de leurs armes.

Fait à Paris, le trentième jour du mois de Mars, de l'an mil huit cent cinquante-six.

(L.S.) ORLOFF.
(L.S.) BRUNNOW.
(L.S.) AALI.
(L.S.) MEHEMMED DJEMIL.

[*825] *3.—*Convention between Her Majesty, the Emperor of the French, and the Emperor of Russia, respecting the Aland Islands.*

Signed at Paris, March 30, 1856.

[*Ratifications exchanged at Paris, April* 27, 1856.]

Au Nom de Dieu Tout-Puissant.

Sa Majesté la Reine du Royaume Uni de la Grande Bretagne et d'Irlande, Sa Majesté l'Empereur des Français, et Sa Majesté l'Empereur de toutes les Russies, voulant étendre à la Mer Baltique l'accord si heureusement rétabli entre Elles en Orient, et consolider par là les bienfaits de la paix générale, ont résolu de conclure une Convention, et nommé à cet effet, &c.

* * * * * *

Lesquels, après avoir échangé leurs pleins pouvoirs, trouvés en bonne et du forme, sont convenus des Articles suivants :—

ARTICLE I.

Sa Majesté l'Empereur de toutes les Russies, pour répondre au désir qui lui a été exprimé par Leurs Majestés la Reine du Royaume Uni de la Grande Bretagne et d'Irlande et l'Empereur des Francais, déclare que les Iles d'Aland ne seront pas fortifiées, et qu'il n'y sera maintenu ni créé aucun établissement militaire ou naval.

ART. II.

La présente Convention, annexée au Traité Général signé à Paris en ce jour, sera ratifiée, et les ratifications en seront échangées dans l'espace de quatre semaines, ou plus tôt si faire se peut.

En foi de quoi les Plénipotentiaires respectifs l'ont signée, et y ont apposé le sceau de leurs armes.

Fait à Paris, le trentième jour du mois de Mars, de l'an mil huit cent cinquante-six.

(L.S.) CLARENDON.
(L.S.) COWLEY.
(L.S.) A. WALEWSKI.
(L.S.) BOURQUENEY.
(L.S.) ORLOFF.
(L.S.) BRUNNOW.

*(*Translation.*) [*826]

General Treaty between Her Majesty, the Emperor of Austria, the Emperor of the French, the King of Prussia, the Emperor of Russia, the King of Sardinia, and the Sultan.

Signed at Paris, March 30, 1856.

[*Ratifications exchanged at Paris, April* 27, 1856.]

In the Name of Almighty God.

Their Majesties the Queen of the United Kingdom of Great Britain and Ireland, the Emperor of the French, the Emperor of all the Russias, the King of Sardinia, and the Emperor of the Ottomans, animated by the desire of putting an end to the calamities of war, and wishing to prevent the return of the complications which occasioned it, resolved to come to an understanding with His Majesty the Emperor of Austria as to the bases on which peace might be re-established and consolidated, by securing, through effectual and reciprocal guarantees, the independence and integrity of the Ottoman Empire.

For this purpose, their said Majesties named as their Plenipotentiaries, that is to say, &c., &c.

The Plenipotentiaries, after having exchanged their full powers, found in good and due form, have agreed upon the following articles:—

ARTICLE I.

From the day of the exchange of the ratifications of the present Treaty, there shall be peace and friendship between Her Majesty the Queen of the United Kingdom of Great Britain and Ireland, His Majesty the Emperor of the French, His Majesty the King of Sardinia, His Imperial Majesty the Sultan, on the one part, and His Majesty the Emperor of all the Russias, on the other part; as well as between their heirs and successors, their respective dominions and subjects, in perpetuity.

ART. II.

Peace being happily re-established between their said Majesties, the territories conquered or occupied by their armies during the war shall be reciprocally evacuated.

Special arrangements shall regulate the mode of the evacuation, which shall be as prompt as possible.

[*827] *ART. III.

His Majesty the Emperor of all the Russias engages to restore to His Majesty the Sultan the town and citadel of Kars, as well as the other parts of the Ottoman territory of which the Russian troops are in possession.

ART. IV.

Their Majesties the Queen of the United Kingdom of Great Britain and Ireland, the Emperor of the French, the King of Sardinia, and the Sultan, engage to restore to His Majesty the Emperor of all the Russias, the towns and ports of Sebastopol, Balaklava, Kamiesch, Eupatoria, Kertch, Jenikale, Kinburn, as well as all other territories occupied by the allied troops.

ART. V.

Their Majesties the Queen of the United Kingdom of Great Britain and Ireland, the Emperor of the French, the Emperor of all the Russias, the King of Sardinia, and the Sultan, grant a full and entire amnesty to those of their subjects who may have been compromised by any participation whatsoever in the events of the war in favour of the cause of the enemy.

It is expressly understood that such amnesty shall extend to the subjects of each of the belligerent parties who may have continued, during the war, to be employed in the service of one of the other belligerents.

ART. VI.

Prisoners of war shall be immediately given up on either side.

ART. VII.

Her Majesty the Queen of the United Kingdom of Great Britain and Ireland, His Majesty the Emperor of Austria, His Majesty the Emperor of the French, His Majesty the King of Prussia, His Majesty the Emperor of all the Russias, and His Majesty the King of Sardinia, declare the Sublime Porte admitted to participate in the advantages of the public law and system (*concert*) of Europe. Their Majesties engage, each on his part, to respect the independence and the territorial integrity of the Ottoman Empire; guarantee in common the strict observance of that engagement, and will, in consequence, consider any act tending to its violation as a question of general interest.

*Art. VIII. [*828]

If there should arise between the Sublime Porte and one or more of the other signing Powers, any misunderstanding which might endanger the maintenance of their relations, the Sublime Porte, and each of such Powers, before having recourse to the use of force, shall afford the other Contracting Parties the opportunity of preventing such an extremity by means of their mediation.

Art. IX.

His Imperial Majesty the Sultan, having, in his constant solicitude for the welfare of his subjects, issued a firman which, while ameliorating their condition without distinction of religion or of race, records his generous intentions towards the Christian population of his empire, and wishing to give a further proof of his sentiments in that respect, has resolved to communicate to the contracting parties the said firman, emanating spontaneously from his sovereign will.

The contracting Powers recognize the high value of this communication. It is clearly understood that it cannot, in any case, give to the said Powers the right to interfere, either collectively or separately, in the relations of His Majesty the Sultan with his subjects, nor in the internal administration of his Empire.

Art. X.

The Convention of the 13th of July, 1841, which maintains the ancient rule of the Ottoman Empire relative to the closing of the Straits of the Bosphorus and of the Dardanelles, has been revised by common consent.

The Act concluded for that purpose, and in conformity with that principle, between the high contracting parties, is and remains annexed to the present Treaty, and shall have the same force and validity as if it formed an integral part thereof.

Art. XI.

The Black Sea is neutralized: its waters and its ports thrown open to the mercantile marine of every nation, are formally and in perpetuity interdicted to the flag of war, either of the Powers possessing its coasts, or of any other Power, with the exceptions mentioned in Articles XIV. and XIX. of the present Treaty.

Art. XII.

Free from any impediment, the commerce in the ports and waters of the Black Sea shall be subject only to regulations of *health, customs, and police, framed in a spirit favourable to the development of commercial transactions. [*829]

In order to afford to the commercial and maritime interests of every nation the security which is desired, Russia and the Sublime Porte will admit Consuls into their ports situated upon the coast of the Black Sea, in conformity with the principles of international law.

ART. XIII.

The Black Sea being neutralized according to the terms of Article XI., the maintenance or establishment upon its coast of military-maritime arsenals becomes alike unnecessary and purposeless; in consequence, His Majesty the Emperor of all the Russias and His Imperial Majesty the Sultan engage not to establish or to maintain upon that coast any military-maritime arsenal.

ART. XIV.

Their Majesties the Emperor of all the Russias and the Sultan having concluded a Convention for the purpose of settling the force, and the number of light vessels necessary for the service of their coasts, which they reserve to themselves to maintain in the Black Sea, that Convention is annexed to the present Treaty, and shall have the same force and validity as if it formed an integral part thereof. It cannot be either annulled or modified without the assent of the Powers signing the present Treaty.

ART. XV.

The Act of the Congress of Vienna having established the principles intended to regulate the navigation of rivers which separate or traverse different States, the contracting Powers stipulate among themselves that those principles shall in future be equally applied to the Danube and its mouths. They declare that this arrangement henceforth forms a part of the public law of Europe, and take it under their guarantee.

The navigation of the Danube cannot be subjected to any impediment or charge not expressly provided for by the stipulations contained in the following articles: in consequence, there shall not be levied any toll founded solely upon the fact of the navigation of the river, nor any duty upon the goods which may be on board of vessels. The regulations of police and of quarantine to be established for the safety of the States separated or traversed by that river, shall be so framed as to facilitate, as much as possible, the passage of vessels. With the exception of such regulations, no obstacle whatever shall be opposed to free navigation.

[*830] *ART. XVI.

With the view to carry out the arrangements of the preceding Article, a Commission, in which Great Britain, Austria, France, Prussia, Russia, Sardinia, and Turkey, shall each be represented by one delegate, shall be charged to designate and to cause to be executed the works necessary below Isatcha, to clear the mouths of the Danube, as well as the neighbouring parts of the sea, from the sands and other impediments which obstruct them, in order to put that part of the river and the said parts of the sea in the best possible state for navigation.

In order to cover the expenses of such works, as well as of the establishments intended to secure and to facilitate the navigation at the mouths of the Danube, fixed duties, of a suitable rate, settled by the Commission by a majority of votes, may be levied, on the express condition that, in this respect as in every other, the flags of all nations shall be treated on the footing of perfect equality.

Art. XVII.

A Commission shall be established, and shall be composed of delegates of Austria, Bavaria, the Sublime Porte, and Wurtemberg (one for each of those Powers,) to whom shall be added Commissioners from the three Danubian Principalities, whose nomination shall have been approved by the Porte. This Commission, which shall be permanent: 1. Shall prepare regulations of navigation and river police: 2. Shall remove the impediments, of whatever nature they may be, which still prevent the application to the Danubē of the arrangements of the Treaty of Vienna; 3. Shall order and cause to be executed the necessary works throughout the whole course of the river; and 4. Shall, after the dissolution of the European Commission, see to maintaining the mouths of the Danube and the neighbouring parts of the sea in a navigable state.

Art. XVIII.

It is understood that the European Commission shall have completed its task, and that the River Commission shall have finished the works described in the preceding Article, under Nos. 1 and 2, within the period of two years. The signing Powers assembled in Conference having been informed of that fact, shall, after having placed it on record, pronounce the dissolution of the European Commission, and from that time the permanent River Commission shall enjoy the same powers as those with which the European Commission shall have until then been invested.

*Art. XIX. [*831]

In order to insure the execution of the regulations which shall have been established by common agreement, in conformity with the principles above declared, each of the Contracting Powers shall have the right to station, at all times, two light vessels at the mouths of the Danube.

Art. XX.

In exchange for the towns, ports, and territories enumerated in Article IV. of the present Treaty, and in order more fully to secure the freedom of the navigation of the Danube, His Majesty the Emperor of all the Russias consents to the rectification of his frontier in Bessarabia.

The new frontier shall begin from the Black Sea, one kilometre to the east of the Lake Bourna Sola, shall run perpendicularly to the Akerman road, shall follow that road to the *Val de Trajan,* pass to the south of Bolgrad, ascend the course of the River Yalpuck to the Height of Saratsika, and terminate at Katamori on the Pruth. Above that point the old frontier between the two Empires shall not undergo any modification.

Delegates of the Contracting Powers shall fix, in its details, the line of the new frontier.

Art XXI.

The territory ceded by Russia shall be annexed to the Principality of Moldavia under the suzerainty of the Sublime Porte.

The inhabitants of that territory shall enjoy the rights and privileges secured to the Principalities; and, during the space of three years, they shall be permitted to transfer their domicile elsewhere, disposing freely of their property.

Art. XXII.

The Principalities of Wallachia and Moldavia shall continue to enjoy under the suzerainty of the Porte, and under the guarantee of the Contracting Powers, the privileges and immunities of which they are in possession. No exclusive protection shall be exercised over them by any of the guaranteeing Powers. There shall be no separate right of interference in their internal affairs.

Art. XXIII.

The Sublime Porte engages to preserve to the said Principalities an independent and national administration, as well as full liberty of worship, of legislation, of commerce, and of navigation.

[*832] The laws and statutes at present in force shall be revised. In *order to establish a complete agreement in regard to such revision, a Special Commission, as to the composition of which the High Contracting Powers will come to an understanding among themselves, shall assemble, without delay, at Bucharest, together with a commissioner of the Sublime Porte.

The business of this Commission shall be to investigate the present state of the Principalities, and to propose bases for their future organization.

Art. XXIV.

His Majesty the Sultan promises to convoke immediately in each of the two Provinces a Divan *ad hoc*, composed in such a manner as to represent most closely the interests of all classes of society. These Divans shall be called upon to express the wishes of the people in regard to the definite organization of the Principalities.

An instruction from the congress shall regulate the relations between the Commission and these Divans.

Art. XXV.

Taking into consideration the opinion expressed by the two Divans, the Commission shall transmit, without delay, to the present seat of the Conferences, the result of its own labours.

The final agreement with the Suzerain Power shall be recorded in a Convention to be concluded at Paris between the High Contracting Parties; and a hatti-sherif, in conformity with the stipulations of the Convention, shall constitute definitively the organization of those Provinces, placed thenceforward under the collective guarantee of all the signing Powers.

ART. XXVI.

It is agreed that there shall be in the Principalities a national armed force, organized with the view to maintain the security of the interior, and to ensure that of the frontiers. No impediment shall be opposed to the extraordinary measures of defence which, by agreement with the Sublime Porte, they may be called upon to take in order to repel any external aggression.

ART. XXVII.

If the internal tranquillity of the Principalities should be menaced or compromised, the Sublime Porte shall come to an understanding with the other Contracting Powers in regard to the measures to be taken for maintaining or re-establishing legal order. No armed intervention can take place without previous agreement between those Powers.

*ART. XXVIII. [*833]

The Principality of Servia shall continue to hold of the Sublime Porte, in conformity with the Imperial Hats which fix and determine its rights and immunities, placed henceforward under the collective guarantee of the Contracting Powers.

In consequence, the said Principality shall preserve its independent and national administration, as well as full liberty of worship, of legislation, of commerce, and of navigation.

ART. XXIX.

The right of garrison of the Sublime Porte, as stipulated by anterior regulations, is maintained. No armed intervention can take place in Servia without previous agreement between the High Contracting Powers.

ART. XXX.

His Majesty the Emperor of all the Russias and His Majesty the Sultan maintain, in its integrity, the state of their possessions in Asia, such as it legally existed before the rupture.

In order to prevent all local dispute, the line of frontier shall be verified, and, if necessary, rectified, without any prejudice as regards territory being sustained by either Party.

For this purpose a mixed Commission, composed of two Russian Commissioners, two Ottoman Commissioners, one English Commissioner, and one French Commissioner, shall be sent to the spot immediately after the re-establishment of diplomatic relations between the Court of Russia and the Sublime Porte. Its labours shall be completed within the period of eight months after the exchange of the ratifications of the present Treaty.

ART. XXXI.

The territories occupied during the war by the troops of their Majesties the Queen of the United Kingdom of Great Britain and Ireland, the Emperor of Austria, the Emperor of the French, and the King of Sardinia, according to the terms of the Conventions signed at Constantinople on the twelfth of March, one thousand eight hundred and fifty-four, between Great Britain, France, and the Sublime Porte; on the fourteenth of June of the same year, between Austria and the Sublime Porte; and on the fifteenth of March, one thousand eight hundred and fifty-five, between Sardinia and the Sublime Porte; shall be evacuated as soon as possible
[*834] after the exchange of the ratifications of the present Treaty. The *periods and the means of execution shall form the object of an arrangement between the Sublime Porte and the Powers whose troops have occupied its territory.

ART. XXXII.

Until the Treaties or Conventions which existed before the war between the belligerent Powers have been either renewed or replaced by new Acts, commerce of importation or of exportation shall take place reciprocally on the footing of the regulations in force before the war; and in all other matters their subjects shall be respectively treated upon the footing of the most favoured nation.

ART. XXXIII.

The Convention concluded this day between their Majesties the Queen of the United Kingdom of Great Britain and Ireland, the Emperor of the French, on the one part, and His Majesty the Emperor of all the Russias, on the other part, respecting the Aland Islands, is and remains annexed to the present Treaty, and shall have the same force and validity as if it formed a part thereof.

ART. XXXIV.

The present Treaty shall be ratified, and the ratifications shall be exchanged at Paris in the space of four weeks, or sooner if possible.

In witness whereof the respective Plenipotentiaries have signed the same, and have affixed thereto the seal of their arms.

Done at Paris, the thirtieth day of the month of March, in the year one thousand eight hundred and fifty-six.

(L.S.) CLARENDON.
(L.S.) COWLEY.
(L.S.) BUOL-SCHAUENSTEIN.
(L.S.) HUBNER.
(L.S.) A. WALEWSKI.
(L.S.) BOURQUENEY.
(L.S.) MANTEUFFEL.
(L.S.) C. M. D'HATZFELDT.
(L.S.) ORLOFF.
(L.S.) BRUNNOW.
(L.S.) C. CAVOUR.
(L.S.) DE VILLAMARINA.
(L.S.) AALI.
(L.S.) MEHEMMED DJEMIL.

*ADDITIONAL AND TRANSITORY ARTICLE. [*835]

The stipulations of the Convention respecting the Straits, signed this day, shall not be applicable to the vessels of war employed by the belligerent Powers, for the evacuation, by sea, of the territories occupied by their armies; but the said stipulations shall resume their entire effect as soon as the evacuation shall be terminated.

Done at Paris, the thirtieth day of the month of March, in the year one thousand eight hundred and fifty-six.

(L.S.) CLARENDON.
(L.S.) COWLEY.
(L.S.) BUOL-SCHAUENSTEIN.
(L.S.) HUBNER.
(L.S.) A. WALEWSKI.
(L.S.) BOURQUENEY.
(L.S.) MANTEUFFEL.
(L.S.) C. M. D'HATZFELDT.
(L.S.) ORLOFF.
(L.S.) BRUNNOW.
(L.S.) C. CAVOUR.
(L.S.) DE VILLAMARINA.
(L.S.) AALI.
(L.S.) MEHEMMED DJEMIL.

CONVENTIONS ANNEXED TO THE PRECEDING TREATY.

1.—*Convention between Her Majesty, the Emperor of Austria, the Emperor of the French, the King of Prussia, the Emperor of Russia, and the King of Sardinia, on the one part, respecting the Straits of the Dardanelles and of the Bosphorus.*

Signed at Paris, March 30, 1856.

[*Ratifications exchanged at Paris, April* 27, 1856.]

In the Name of Almighty God.

Their Majesties the Queen of the United Kingdom of Great Britain and Ireland, the Emperor of Austria, the Emperor of the French, the King of Prussia, the Emperor of all the Russias, signing Parties to the Convention of the thirteenth day of July, one thousand eight hundred and forty-one, and His Majesty the King of Sardinia, wishing to record in common their unanimous determination to conform to the ancient rule of the Ottoman Empire, according to which the Straits of the Dardanelles and of the Bosphorus are closed to foreign ships of war, so long as the Porte is at Peace;

[*836] *Their said Majesties on the one part, and His Majesty the Sultan, on the other, have resolved to renew the Convention concluded at London on the thirteenth day of July, one thousand eight hundred and forty-one, with the exception of some modifications of detail which do not affect the principle upon which it rests.

In consequence their said Majesties have named for that purpose as their Plenipotentiaries, that is to say, &c.

Who, after having exchanged their full powers, found in good and due form, have agreed upon the following Articles:—

ARTICLE I.

His Majesty the Sultan, on the one part, declares that he is firmly resolved to maintain for the future the principle invariably established as the ancient rule of his Empire, and in virtue of which it has, at all times, been prohibited for the ships of war of foreign Powers to enter the Straits of the Dardanelles and of the Bosphorus; and that, so long as the Porte is at peace, His Majesty will admit no foreign ship of war into the said Straits.

And their Majesties the Queen of the United Kingdom of Great Britain, and Ireland, the Empereor of Austria, the Emperor of the French, the King of Prussia, the Emperor of all the Russias, and the King of Sardinia, on the other part, engage to respect this determination of the Sultan, and to conform themselves to the principle above declared.

ART. II.

The Sultan reserves to himself, as in past times, to deliver firmans of passage for light vessels under flag of war, which shall be employed, as is usual, in the service of the Missions of Foreign Powers.

ART. III.

The same exception applies to the light vessels under flag of war, which each of the Contracting Powers is authorized to station at the mouths of the Danube, in order to secure the execution of the regulations relative to the liberty of that river, and the number of which is not to exceed two for each Power.

ART. IV.

The present Convention annexed to the General Treaty signed at Paris this day, shall be ratified, and the ratifications shall be exchanged in the space of four weeks, or sooner if possible.

*In witness whereof the respective Plenipotentiaries have signed the same, and have affixed thereto the seal of their arms. [*837]

Done at Paris, the thirtieth day of the month of March, in the year one thousand eight hundred and fifty-six.

(L.S.) CLARENDON.
(L.S.) COWLEY.
(L.S.) BUOL-SCHAUENSTEIN.
(L.S.) HUBNER.
(L.S.) A. WALEWSKI.
(L.S.) BOURQUENEY.
(L.S.) MANTEUFFEL.
(L.S.) C. M. D'HATZFELDT.
(L.S.) ORLOFF.
(L.S.) BRUNNOW.
(L.S.) C. CAVOUR.
(L.S.) DE VILLAMARINA.
(L.S.) AALI.
(L.S.) MEHEMMED DJEMIL.

2.—*Convention between the Emperor of Russia and the Sultan, limiting their Naval Force in the Black Sea.*

Signed at Paris, March 30, 1856.

[*Ratifications exchanged at Paris, April* 27, 1856.]

In the Name of Almighty God.

His Majesty the Emperor of all the Russias, and His Imperial Majesty the Sultan, taking into consideration the principle of the neutralization of the Black Sea, established by the preliminaries contained in the Protocol No. 1, signed at Paris on the twenty-fifth of February, of the present year, and wishing, in consequence, to regulate by common agreement the number and the force of the light vessels which they have reserved to themselves to maintain in the Black Sea for the service of their coasts, have resolved to sign, with that view, a special Convention, and have named for that purpose, &c.

Who, after having exchanged their full powers, found in good and due form, have agreed upon the following Articles:—

ARTICLE I.

The High Contracting Parties mutually engage not to have in the Black Sea any other vessels of war than those of which the number, the force, and the dimensions are hereinafter stipulated.

[*838] *ART. II.

The High Contracting Parties reserve to themselves each to maintain in that sea six steam vessels of fifty mètres in length at the line of floatation, of a tonnage of eight hundred tons at the maximum, and four light steam or sailing vessels of a tonnage which shall not exceed two hundred tons each.

ART. III.

The present Convention annexed to the General Treaty signed at Paris this day, shall be ratified, and the ratifications shall be exchanged in the space of four weeks, or sooner if possible.

In witness whereof the respective Plenipotentiaries have signed the same, and affixed thereto the seal of their arms.

Done at Paris the thirtieth day of the month of March, in the year one thousand eight hundred and fifty-six.

(L.S.) ORLOFF.
(L.S.) BRUNNOW.
(L.S.) AALI.
(L.S.) MEHEMMED DJEMIL.

3.—*Convention between Her Majesty, the Emperor of the French, and the Emperor of Russia, respecting the Aland Islands.*

Signed at Paris, March 30, 1856.

[*Ratifications exchanged at Paris, April* 27, 1856.]

In the Name of Almighty God.

Her Majesty the Queen of the United Kingdom of Great Britain and Ireland, His Majesty the Emperor of the French, and His Majesty the Emperor of all the Russias, wishing to extend to the Baltic Sea the harmony so happily re-established between them in the East, and thereby to consolidate the benefits of the general peace, have resolved to conclude a Convention, and have named for that purpose, &c.

Who, after having exchanged their full powers, found in good and due form, have agreed upon the following Articles :—

ARTICLE I.

His Majesty the Emperor of all the Russias, in order to respond to the desire which has been expressed to him by their Majesties the Queen of the United Kingdom of Great Britain and Ireland, and the Emperor of the French, declares that the Aland Islands shall not be fortified, and that no military or naval establishment shall be maintained or created there.

*Art. II. [*839]

The present Convention annexed to the General Treaty signed at Paris this day, shall be ratified, and the ratifications shall be exchanged in the space of four weeks, or sooner if possible.

In witness whereof, the respective Plenipotentiaries have signed the same, and have affixed thereto the seal of their arms.

Done at Paris, the thirtieth day of the month of March, in the year one thousand eight hundred and fifty-six.

(L.S.) Clarendon.
(L.S.) Cowley.
(L.S.) A. Walewski.
(L.S.) Bourqueney.
(L.S.) Orloff.
(L.S.) Brunnow.

APPENDIX XVIII.

Firman and Hatti-Sherif by the Sultan, relative to Privileges and Reforms in Turkey.

Lord Stratford de Redcliffe to the Earl of Clarendon.
(*Received March* 5.)

(Extract.) *Constantinople, February* 21, 1856.

Inclosed herewith in Turkish and French are printed copies of the Sultan's firman, and hatti-sheriff, on the subject of privileges and reforms.

The French publication is considered as official, and I received the copies in that language from Fuad Pasha.

Inclosure.

Firman.

Qu'il soit fait en conformité du contenu.	Let it be done as herein set forth.
A vous, mon Grand Vizir, Mehemed Emin Aali Pacha, décoré de mon Ordre Impérial du Medjidiyé de la première classe et de l'Ordre du Mérite Personnel; que Dieu vous accorde la grandeur et double votre pouvoir!	To you, my Grand Vizier, Mehemed Emin Aali Pasha, decorated with my Imperial Order of the Medjidiyé, of the first class, and with the Order of Personal Merit; may God grant to you greatness and increase your power!

[*840] *Mon désir le plus cher a toujours été d'assurer le bonheur de toutes les classes des sujets que la Divine Providence a placés sous mon sceptre Impérial, et, depuis mon avènement au Trône, je n'ai cessé de faire tous mes efforts dans ce but.

It has always been my most earnest desire to insure the happiness of all classes of the subjects whom Divine Providence has placed under my Imperial sceptre, and since my accession to the Throne I have not ceased to direct all my efforts to the attainment of that end.

Grâces en soient rendues au Tout-Puissant, ces efforts incessants ont déjà porté des fruits utiles et nombreux. De jour en jour le bonheur de la nation et la richesse de mes Etats vont en augmentant.

Thanks to the Almighty, these unceasing efforts have already been productive of numerous useful results. From day to day the happiness of the nation and the wealth of my dominions go on augmenting.

Désirant aujourd'hui renouveler et élargir encore les réglements nouveaux institués dans le but d'arriver à obtenir un état de choses conforme à la dignité de mon Empire et à la position qu'il occupe parmi les nations civilisées, et les droits de mon Empire ayant aujourd'hui, par la fidélité et les louables efforts de tous mes sujets et par le concours bienveillant et amical des Grandes Puissances, mes nobles alliées, reçu de l'extérieur une consécration qui doit être le commencement d'une ère nouvelle, je veux en augmenter le bien-être et la prospérité intérieure, obtenir le bonheur de tous mes sujets, qui, à mes yeux, sont tous égaux et me sont également chers, et qui sont unis entre eux par des rapports cordiaux de patriotisme, et assurer les moyens de faire de jour en jour croître la prospérité de mon Empire.

It being now my desire to renew and enlarge still more the new institutions ordained with the view of establishing a state of things conformable with the dignity of my Empire and the position which it occupies among civilized nations, and the rights of my Empire having, by the fidelity and praiseworthy efforts of all my subjects, and by the kind and friendly assistance of the great Powers, my noble allies, received from abroad a confirmation which will be the commencement of a new era, it is my desire to augment its well-being and prosperity, to effect the happiness of all my subjects, who in my sight are all equal, and equally dear to me, and who are united to each other by the cordial ties of patriotism, and to insure the means of daily increasing the prosperity of my Empire.

J'ai donc résolu et j'ordonne la mise à exécution des mesures suivantes :

I have therefore resolved upon and I order the execution of the following measures :

Les garanties promises de notre part à tous les sujets de mon Empire [*841] *par le Hatt-i-Humaïoun de Gul-Hané et en conformité du Tanzimat, sans distinction de classes ni de culte, pour la sécurité de leurs personnes et de leurs biens, et pour la conservation de leur hon-

The guarantees promised on our part by the Hatt-i-Humaïoun of Gul-Hané, and in conformity with the Tanzimat, to all the subjects of my Empire, without distinction of classes or of religion, for the security of their persons and property and the preservation of

neur, sont aujourd'hui confirmées et consolidées; et, pour qu'elles reçoivent leur plein et entier effet, des mesures efficaces seront prises.

their honour, are to-day confirmed and consolidated, and efficacious measures shall be taken in order that they may have their full and entire effect.

Tous les priviléges et immunités spirituels accordés *ab antiquo* de la part de mes ancêtres, et à des dates postérieures, à toutes les communautés Chrétiennes ou d'autres rites non Musulmans établis dans mon Empire sous mon égide protectrice, seront confirmés et maintenus.

All the privileges and spiritual immunities granted by my ancestors *ab antiquo*, and at subsequent dates, to all Christian communities or other non-Mussulman persuasions established in my Empire under my protection, shall be confirmed and maintained.

Chaque communauté Chrétienne ou d'autre rite non-Musulman, sera tenue, dans un délai fixé et avec le concours d'une Commission formée *ad hoc* dans son sein, de procéder, avec ma haute approbation et sous la surveillance de ma Sublime Porte, à l'examen de ses immunités et priviléges actuels, et d'y discuter et soumettre à ma Sublime Porte les réformes exigées par le progrès des lumières et du temps. Les pouvoirs concédés aux Patriarches et aux Evêques des rites Chrétiens par le Sultan Mahomet II et ses successeurs, seront mis en harmonie avec la position nouvelle que mes intentions généreuses et bienveillantes assurent à ces communautés.

Every Christian or other non-Mussulman community shall be bound, within a fixed period, and with the concurrence of a Commission, composed *ad hoc* of members of its own body, to proceed, with my high approbation and under the inspection of my Sublime Porte, to examine into its actual immunities and privileges, and to discuss and submit to my Sublime Porte the reforms required by the progress of civilization and of the age. The powers conceded to the Christian Patriarchs and Bishops by the Sultan Mahomet II. and his successors, shall be made to harmonize with the new position which my generous and beneficent intentions insure to these communities.

Le principe de la nomination à vie des Partriarches, après la révision des réglements d'élection aujourd'hui en vigueur, sera exactement appliqué *conformément à la teneur de leurs firmans d'investiture.

The principle of nominating the Patriarchs for life, after the revision of the rules of election now in force, shall be exactly carried out, conformably to the tenor of their firmans of investiture. [*842]

Les Patriarches, les Métropolitans, Archevêques. Evêques, et Rabins seront assermentés à leur entrée en fonctions, d'après une formule concertée en commun entre ma Sublime Porte et les chefs spirituels des diverses communautés. Les redevances ecclésiastiques, de quelque forme et nature qu'elles soient,

The Patriarchs, Metropolitans, Archbishops, Bishops, and Rabbins shall take an oath on their entrance into office according to a form agreed upon in common by my Sublime Porte and the spiritual heads of the different religious communities. The ecclesiastical dues, of whatever sort or nature they be, shall be abo-

seront supprimées et remplacées par la fixation des revenus des Patriarches et chefs des communautés et par l'allocation de traitements et de salaires équitablement proportionnés à l'importance, au rang et à la dignité des divers membres du clergé.

Il ne sera porté aucune atteinte aux propriétés mobilières et immobilières des divers clergés Chrétiens; toutefois, l'administration temporelle des communautés Chrétiennes ou d'autres rites non-Musulmans, sera placée sous la sauvegarde d'une Assemblée, choisie dans le sein de chacune des dites communautés, parmi les membres du clergé et les laïcs.

Dans les villes, bourgades et villages où la population appartiendra en totalité au même culte, il ne sera apporté aucune entrave à la réparation, d'après leur plan primitif, des édifices destinés au culte, aux écoles, aux hôpitaux et aux cimitières.

Les plans de ces divers édifices, en cas d'érection nouvelle, approuvés par les Patriarches ou chefs de communautés, devront être soumis à ma Sublime Porte, qui les [*843] *approuvera par mon ordre Impérial, ou fera ses observations dans un délai déterminé.

Chaque culte, dans les localités où ne se trouveront pas d'autres confessions religieuses, ne sera soumis à aucune espèce de restriction dans la manifestation publique de sa religion.

Dans les villes, bourgades et villages où les cultes sont mélangés, chaque communauté, habitant un quartier distinct, pourra également, en se conformant aux préscriptions ci-dessus indiquées réparer et consolider ses églises, ses hôpitaux,

lished and replaced by fixed revenues for the Patriarchs and heads of communities, and by the allocation of allowances and salaries equitably proportioned to the importance of the rank and the dignity of the different members of the clergy.

The property, real or personal, of the different Christian ecclesiastics shall remain intact; the temporal administration of the Christian or other non-Mussulman communities shall, however, be placed under the safeguard of an Assembly to be chosen from among the members, both ecclesiastics and laymen, of the said communities.

In the towns, small boroughs, and villages, where the whole population is of the same religion, no obstacle shall be offered to the repair, according to their original plan, of buildings set apart for religious worship, for schools, for hospitals, and for cemeteries.

The plans of these different buildings, in case of their new erection, must, after having been approved by the Patriarchs or heads of communities, be submitted to my Sublime Porte, which will approve of them by my Imperial order, or make known its observations upon them within a certain time.

Each sect, in localities where there are no other religious denominations, shall be free from every species of restraint as regards the public exercise of its religion.

In the towns, small boroughs, and villages where different sects are mingled together, each community, inhabiting a distinct quarter, shall, by conforming to the abovementioned ordinances, have equal power to repair and improve its

ses écoles et ses cimitières. Lorsqu'il s'agira de la construction d'édifices nouveaux, l'autorisation nécessaire sera demandée par l'organe des Patriarches ou chefs des communautés à ma Sublime Porte, qui prendra une décision souveraine, en accordant cette autorisation, à moins d'obstacles administratifs. L'intervention de l'autorité administrative dans tous les actes de cette nature sera entièrement gratuite. Ma Sublime Porte prendra des mesures énergiques pour assurer à chaque culte, quel que soit le nombre de ses adhérens, la pleine liberté de son exercice.

churches, its hospitals, its schools, and its cemeteries. When there is question of the erection of new buildings, the necessary authority must be asked for through the medium of the Patriarchs and heads of communities from my Sublime Porte, which will pronounce a sovereign decision according that authority, except in the case of administrative obstacles. The intervention of the administrative authority in all measures of this nature will be entirely gratuitous. My Sublime Porte will take energetic measures to insure to each sect, whatever be the number of its adherents, entire freedom in the exercise of its religion.

Toute distinction ou appellation tendant à rendre une classe quelconque des sujets de mon Empire inférieure à une autre classe, à raison du culte, de la langue ou de la race, sera à jamais effacée du Protocole Administratif. Les lois séviront contre *l'usage, entre particuliers ou de la part des autorités, de toute qualification injurieuse ou blessante.

Every distinction or designation tending to make any class whatever of the subjects of my Empire inferior to another class, on account of their religion, language, or race, shall be for ever effaced from the Administrative Protocol. The laws shall be put in force against the use of any injurious or [*844] offensive term, either among private individuals or on the part of the authorities.

Vu que tous les cultes sont et seront librement pratiqués dans mes Etats, aucun sujet de mon Empire ne sera gêné dans l'exercice de la religion qu'il professe et ne sera d'aucune manière inquiété à cet égard. Personne ne pourra être contraint à changer de religion.

As all forms of religion are and shall be freely professed in my dominions, no subject of my Empire shall be hindered in the exercise of the religion that he professes, nor shall be in any way annoyed on this account. No one shall be compelled to change their religion.

La nomination et le choix de tous les fonctionnaires et autres employés de mon Empire, étant entièrement dépendante de ma volonté souveraine, tous les sujets de mon Empire, sans distinction de nationalité, seront admissibles aux emplois publics et aptes à les occuper, selon leurs capacités et leurs

The nomination and choice of all functionaries and other *employés* of my Empire being wholly dependent upon my sovereign will, all the subjects of my Empire, without distinction of nationality, shall be admissible to public employments, and qualified to fill them according to their capacity

mérites, et conformément à des règles d'une application générale.

and merit, and conformably with rules to be generally applied.

Tous les sujets de mon Empire seront indistinctement reçus dans les Ecoles Civiles et Militaires du Gouvernement, s'ils remplissent d'ailleurs les conditions d'âge et d'examen spécifiées dans les Réglements Organiques des dites Ecoles. De plus, chaque communauté est autorisée à établir des Ecoles Publiques de Sciences, d'Arts et l'Industrie. Seulement le mode d'enseignement et le choix des professeurs dans les écoles de cette catégorie, seront sous le contrôle d'un Conseil Mixte d'Instruction Publique, dont les membres seront nommés par un ordre souverain de ma part.

All the subjects of my Empire, without distinction, shall be received into the Civil and Military Schools of the Government, if they otherwise satisfy the conditions as to age and examination which are specified in the Organic Regulations of the said schools. Moreover, every community is authorized to establish Public Schools of Science, Art, and Industry. Only the method of instruction and the choice of professors in schools of this class shall be under the control of a Mixed Council of Public Instruction, the members of which shall be named by my sovereign command.

Toutes les affaires commerciales, [*845] correctionnelles et *criminelles entre des Musulmans et des sujets Chrétiens ou autres non-Musulmans, ou bien des Chrétiens ou autres de rites différents non-Musulmans, seront déférées à des Tribunaux Mixtes.

All commercial, correctional, and criminal suits between Mussulmans and Christian or other non-Mussulman subjects, or between Christians or other non-Mussulmans of different sects, shall be referred to Mixed Tribunals.

L'audience de ces tribunaux sera publique; les parties seront mises en présence et produiront leurs témoins, dont les dépositions seront reçues indistinctement, sous un serment prêté selon la loi religieuse de chaque culte.

The proceedings of these tribunals shall be public; the parties shall be confronted, and shall produce their witnesses, whose testimony shall be received, without distinction, upon an oath taken according to the religious law of each sect.

Les procés ayant trait aux affaires civiles continueront d'être publiquement jugés, d'après les lois et les réglements, par devant les Conseils Mixtes des Provinces, en présence du Gouverneur et du Juge du lieu. Les procès civils spéciaux, comme ceux de succession ou autres de ce genre, entre les sujets d'un même rite Chrétien ou autre non-Musulman, pourront, à leur demande, être envoyés par

Suits relating to civil affairs shall continue to be publicly tried, according to the laws and regulations, before the Mixed Provincial Councils, in the presence of the governor and judge of the place. Special civil proceedings, such as those relating to successions or others of that kind, between subjects of the same Christian or other non-Mussulman faith, may, at the request of the parties, be sent before the

devant les Conseils des Patriarches ou des communautés.

Les lois pénales, correctionnelles, commerciales et les règles de procédure à appliquer dans les Tribunaux Mixtes seront complétées le plus tôt possible et codifiées. Il en sera publié des traductions dans toutes les langues en usage dans l'Empire.

Il sera procédé dans le plus bref délai possible, à la réforme du système pénitentiaire, dans son application aux maisons de détention, de punition ou de correction, et autres établissements de même nature, afin de concilier les droits de *l'humanité avec ceux de la justice. Aucune peine corporelle, même dans les prisons, ne pourra être appliquée que conformément à des réglements disciplinaires émanés de ma Sublime Porte, et tout ce qui resemblerait à la torture sera radicalement aboli.

Les infractions à ce sujet seront sévèrement réprimées, et entraîneront en outre, de plein droit, la punition, en conformité du Code Criminel, des autorités qui les auraient ordonnées et des agents qui les auraient commises.

L'organisation de la police dans la capitale, dans les villes de province et dans les campagnes, sera révisée de façon à donner à tous les sujets paisibles de mon Empire, les garanties les plus fortes de sécurité quant à leurs personnes et à leurs biens.

L'égalité des impôts entraînant l'égalité des charges, comme celle des devoirs entraîne celle des droits, les sujets Chrétiens et des autres rites non-Musulmans devront, ainsi qu'il a été antérieurement résolu, aussi bien que les Musulmans, satisfaire aux obligations de la Loi

Councils of the Patriarchs or of the communities.

Penal, correctional, and commercial laws, and rules of procedure for the Mixed Tribunals, shall be drawn up as soon as possible, and formed into a code. Translations of them shall be published in all the languages current in the Empire.

Proceedings shall be taken, with as little delay as possible, for the reform of the penitentiary system as applied to houses of detention, punishment or correction, and other establishments of like nature, so as to reconcile the rights of humanity with those of justice. Corporal punishment shall not [*846] be administered, even in the prisons, except in conformity with the disciplinary regulations established by my Sublime Porte, and everything that resembles torture shall be entirely abolished.

Infractions of the law in this particular shall be severely repressed, and shall besides entail, as of right, the punishment, in conformity with the Civil Code, of the authorities who may order and of the agents who may commit them.

The organization of the police in the capital, in the provincial towns, and in the rural districts, shall be revised in such a manner as to give to all the peaceable subjects of my Empire the strongest guarantees for the safety both of their persons and property.

The equality of taxes entailing equality of burdens, as equality of duties entails that of rights, Christian subjects, and those of other non-Mussulman sects, as it has been already decided, shall, as well as Mussulmans, be subject to the obligations of the Law of Recrutement.

de Recrutement. Le principe du remplacement ou du rachat sera admis. Il sera publié, dans le plus bref délai possible, une loi compléte sur le mode d'admission et de service des sujets Chrétiens et d'autres rites non-Musulmans dans l'armée.

The principle of obtaining substitutes, or of purchasing exemption, shall be admitted. A complete law shall be published, with as little delay as possible, respecting the admission into and service in the army of Christian and other non-Mussulman subjects.

Il sera procédé à une réforme dans la composition des Conseils Provinciaux et Communaux pour [*847] garantir la *sincérité des choix des Délégués des communautés Musulmans, Chrétiennes et autres, et la liberté des votes dans les Conseils. Ma Sublime Porte avisera à l'emploi des moyens les plus efficaces de connaître éxactement et de contrôler le résultat des délibérations et des décisions prises.

Proceedings shall be taken for a reform in the constitution of the Provincial and Communal Councils, in order to ensure fairness in the choice of the Deputies of the Mussulman, Christian, and other communities, and freedom of voting in the Councils. My Sublime Porte will take into consideration the adoption of the most effectual means for ascertaining exactly and for controlling the result of the deliberations and of the decisions arrived at.

Comme les lois qui régissent l'achat, la vente et la disposition des propriétés immobilières sont communes à tous les sujets de mon Empire, il pourra être permis aux étrangers de posséder des propriétés foncières dans mes Etats, en se conformant aux lois et aux réglements de police, en acquittant les mêmes charges que les indigènes et après que des arrangements auront eu lieu avec les Puissances étrangères.

As the laws regulating the purchase, sale, and disposal of real property are common to all the subjects of my Empire, it shall be lawful for foreigners to possess landed property in my dominions, conforming themselves to the laws and police regulations, and bearing the same charges as the native inhabitants, and after arrangements have been come to with foreign Powers.

Les impôts sont exigibles au même titre de tous les sujets de mon Empire, sans distinction de classe ni de culte. On avisera aux moyens les plus prompts et les plus énergiques de corriger les abus dans la perception des impôts et notamment des dîmes. Le système de la perception directe sera, successivement et aussitôt que faire se pourra, substitué au régime des fermes dans toutes les branches des revenus de l'Etat. Tant que ce système demeurera en vigueur, il sera interdit, sous les peines les plus sévères, à

The taxes are to be levied under the same denomination from all the subjects of my Empire, without distinction of class or of religion. The most prompt and energetic means for remedying the abuses in collecting the taxes, and especially the tithes, shall be considered. The system of direct collection shall gradually, and as soon as possible, be substituted for the plan of farming, in all the branches of the revenues of the State. As long as the present system remains in force, all agents of the Government

tous les agents de l'autorité et à tous les membres des Medjlis de se rendre adjudicataires des fermes, qui seront annoncées avec publicité et concurrence, ou d'avoir une *part quelconque d'intérêt dans leur exploitation. Les impositions locales seront, autant que possible, calculées de façon à ne pas affecter les sources de la production, ni à entraver le mouvement du commerce intérieur.

Les travaux d'utilité publique recevront une dotation convenable, à laquelle concourront les impositions particulières et spéciales des Provinces appelées à jouir de l'établissement des voies de communication par terre et par mer.

Une loi spéciale ayant déjà été rendue, qui ordonne que le Budget des recettes et des dépenses de l'Etat sera fixé et communiqué chaque année, cette loi sera observée de la manière la plus scrupuleuse. On procédera à la révision des traitements affectés à chaque emploi.

Les chefs et un délégué de chaque communauté, désigné par ma Sublime Porte, seront appelés à prendre part aux délibérations du Conseil Suprême de Justice dans toutes les circonstances qui intéresseraient la généralité des sujets de mon Empire. Ils seront spécialement convoquée à cet effet par mon Grand Vizir. Le mandat des délégués sera annuel; ils prêteront serment en entrant en charge. Tous les membres du Conseil, dans les réunions ordinaires et extraordinaires, émettront librement leurs avis et leurs votes sans qu'on puisse jamais les inquiéter à ce sujet.

*Les lois contre la corruption, la concussion ou la malversation seront

and all members of the Medjlis shall be forbidden, under the severest penalties, to become lessees of any farming contracts which are announced for public competition, or to have any [*848] beneficial interest in carrying them out. The local taxes shall, as far as possible, be so imposed as not to affect the sources of production, or to hinder the progress of internal commerce.

Works of public utility shall receive a suitable endowment, part of which shall be raised from private and special taxes levied in the Provinces which shall have the benefit of the advantages arising from the establishment of ways of communication by land and sea.

A special law having been already passed, which declares that the Budget of the revenue and expenditure of the State shall be drawn up and made known every year, the said law shall be most scrupulously observed. Proceedings shall be taken for revising the emoluments attached to each office.

The heads of each community and a delegate, designated by my Sublime Porte, shall be summoned to take part in the deliberations of the Supreme Council of Justice on all occasions which might interest the generality of the subjects of my Empire. They shall be summoned specially for this purpose by my Grand Vizier. The delegates shall hold office for one year; they shall be sworn on entering upon their duties. All the members of the Council, at the ordinary and extraordinary meetings, shall freely give their opinions and their votes, and no one shall ever annoy them on this account.

The laws against corruption, extortion or malversa- [*849]

appliquées, d'après les formes légales, à tous les sujets de mon Empire, quelle que soit leur classe et la nature de leurs fonctions.

On s'occupera de la création de banques et d'autres institutions semblables pour arriver à la réforme du système monétaire et financier, ainsi que de la création de fonds destinés à augmenter les sources de la richesse matérielle de mon Empire.

On s'occupera également de la création de routes et de canaux qui rendront les communications plus faciles et augmenteront les sources de la richesse du pays. On abolira tout ce que peut entraver le commerce et l'agriculture. Pour arriver à ces buts, on recherchera les moyens de mettre à profit les sciences, les arts et les capitaux de l'Europe et de les mettre ainsi successivement en exécution.

Tels étant mes volontés et mes ordres, vous qui êtes mon Grand Vizir, vous ferez, suivant l'usage, publier, soit dans ma capitale, soit dans toutes les parties de mon Empire, ce firman Impérial, et vous veillerez avec attention et prendrez toutes les mesures nécessaires, afin que tous les ordres qu'il contient soient dorénavant exécutés avec la plus rigoureuse ponctualité.

tion shall apply, according to the legal forms, to all the subjects of my Empire, whatever may be their class and the nature of their duties.

Steps shall be taken for the formation of banks and other similar institutions, so as to effect a reform in the monetary and financial system, as well as to create funds to be employed in augmenting the sources of the material wealth of my Empire.

Steps shall also be taken for the formation of roads and canals to increase the facilities of communication and increase the sources of the wealth of the country. Everything that can impede commerce or agriculture shall be abolished. To accomplish these objects means shall be sought to profit by the science, the art, and the funds of Europe, and thus gradually to execute them.

Such being my wishes and my commands, you, who are my Grand Vizier, will, according to custom, cause this Imperial firman to be published in my capital, and in all parts of my Empire; and you will watch attentively and take all the necessary measures that all the orders which it contains be henceforth carried out with the most rigorous punctuality.

[*850]

*APPENDIX XIX.

Declaration respecting Maritime Law, signed by the Plenipotentiaries of Great Britain, Austria, France, Prussia, Russia, Sardinia, and Turkey, assembled in Congress at Paris, April 16, 1856.

Les Plénipotentiaires qui ont signé le Traité de Paris du trente Mars, mil huit cent cinquante-six, réunis en Conférence,—

The Plenipotentiaries who signed the Treaty of Paris of the thirtieth of March, one thousand eight hundred and fifty-six, assembled in Conference,—

Considérant :

Que le droit maritime, en temps de guerre, a été pendant longtemps l'objet de contestations regrettables ;

Que l'incertitude du droit et des devoirs en pareille matière, donne lieu, entre les neutres et les belligérants, à des divergences d'opinion qui peuvent faire naître des difficultés sérieuses et même des conflits ;

Qu'il y a avantage, par conséquent, à établir une doctrine uniforme sur un point aussi important ;

Que les Plénipotentiaires assemblés au Congrès de Paris ne sauraient mieux répondre aux intentions dont leurs Gouvernements sont animés, qu'en cherchant à introduire dans les rapports internationaux des principes fixes à cet égard ;

Dûment autorisés, les susdits Plénipotentiaires sont convenus de se concerter sur les moyens d'atteindre ce but ; et étant tombés d'accord ont arrêté la Déclaration solennelle ci-après :

1. La course est et demeure abolie ;

2. Le pavillon neutre couvre la marchandise ennemie, à l'exception de la contrebande de guerre ;

*3. La marchandise neutre, à l'exception de la contrebande de guerre, n'est pas saisissable sous pavillon ennemi ;

4. Les blocus, pour être obligatoires, doivent être effectifs, c'est-à-dire, maintenus par une force suffisante pour interdire réellement l'accès du littoral de l'ennemi.

Les Gouvernements des Plénipotentiaires soussignés s'engagent à porter cette Déclaration a la connaissance des Etats qui n'ont pas été appelés à participer au Congrès

Considering

That maritime law, in time of war, has long been the subject of deplorable disputes ;

That the uncertainty of the law and of the duties in such a matter, gives rise to differences of opinion between neutrals and belligerents which may occasion serious difficulties, and even conflicts ;

That it is consequently advantageous to establish a uniform doctrine on so important a point ;

That the Plenipotentiaries assembled in Congress at Paris cannot better respond to the intentions by which their Governments are animated, than by seeking to introduce into international relations fixed principles in this respect ;

The above-mentioned Plenipotentiaries, being duly authorized, resolved to concert among themselves as to the means of attaining this object ; and, having come to an agreement, have adopted the following solemn Declaration :

1. Privateering is, and remains abolished ;

2. The neutral flag covers enemy's goods, with the exception of contraband of war ;

3. Neutral goods, with the exception of contra- [*851] band of war, are not liable to capture under enemy's flag ;

4. Blockades, in order to be binding, must be effective, that is to say, maintained by a force sufficient really to prevent access to the coast of the enemy.

The Governments of the undersigned Plenipotentiaries engage to bring the present Declaration to the knowledge of the States which have not taken part in the Congress

de Paris, et à les inviter à y acceder.

Convaincus que les maximes qu'ils viennent de proclamer ne sauraient être accueillies qu'avec gratitude par le monde entier, les Plénipotentiaires soussignés ne doutent pas que les efforts de leurs Gouvernements pour en généraliser l'adoption ne soient couronnés d'un plein succès.

La présente Déclaration n'est et ne sera obligatoire qu'entre les Puissances qui y ont ou qui y auront accédé.

Fait à Paris, le seize Avril, mil huit cent cinquante-six.

(Signé) Buol-Schauenstein.
Hubner.
Walewski.
Bourqueney.
Clarendon.
Cowley.
Manteuffel.
Hatzfeldt.
Orloff.
Brunnow.
Cavour.
De Villamarina.
Aali.
Mhemmed Djemil.

of Paris, and to invite them to accede to it.

Convinced that the maxims which they now proclaim cannot but be received with gratitude by the whole world, the undersigned Plenipotentiaries doubt not that the efforts of their Governments to obtain the general adoption thereof, will be crowned with full success.

The present Declaration is not and shall not be binding, except between those Powers who have acceded, or shall accede, to it.

Done at Paris, the sixteenth of April, one thousand eight hundred and fifty-six.

(Signed) Buol-Schauenstein.
Hubner.
Walewski.
Bourqueney.
Clarendon.
Cowley.
Manteuffel.
Hatzfeldt.
Orloff.
Brunnow.
Cavour.
De Villamarina.
Aali.
Mehemmed Djemil.

[*852]

*APPENDIX XX.

Treaty between Her Majesty, the Emperor of the French, and the King of Sweden and Norway. Signed at Stockholm, November 21, 1855.

[*Ratifications exchanged at Stockholm, December* 17, 1855.]

Sa Majesté la Reine du Royaume Uni de la Grande Bretagne et d'Irlande, Sa Majesté l'Empereur des Français, et Sa Majesté le Roi de Suède et de Norvège désirant prévenir toute complication de nature

Her Majesty the Queen of the United Kingdom of Great Britain and Ireland, His Majesty the Emperor of the French, and His Majesty the King of Sweden and Norway, being anxious to avert any

à troubler léquilibre Européen, ont résolu de s'entendre dans le but d'assurer l'intégrité des Royaumes Unis de Suède et de Norvège, et ont nommé Plénipotentiaires pour conclure un Traité à cet effet, savoir:

Sa Majesté la Reine du Royaume Uni de la Grande Bretagne et d'Irlande, le Sieur Arthur Charles Magenis, Ecuyer, Son Envoyé Extraordinaire et Ministre Plénipotentiaire près Sa Majesté le Roi de Suède et de Norvège;

Sa Majesté l'Empereur des Français, le Sieur Charles Victor Lobstein, Officier de l'Ordre Imperial de la Légion d'Honneur, Grand-Croix de l'Ordre Royal de l'Etoile Polaire de Suède, Commander de l'Ordre du Christ et Chevalier de celui de la Conception de Portugal, Son Envoyé Extraordinaire et Ministre Plénipotentiaire près Sa Majesté le Roi de Suède et de Norvège;

*Et Sa Majesté le Roi de Suède et de Norvège, le Sieur Gustave Nicholas Algernon Adolphe Baron von Stierneld, Son Ministre d'Etatet des Affaires Etrangères, Chevalier et Commandeur de Ses Ordres, Grand-Croix de Son Ordre de Saint Olaf de Norvège, &c., &c., &c.

Lesquels, après s'être communiqué leurs pleins pouvoirs respectifs, trouvés en bonne et due forme, sont convenus de ce qui suit:—

ARTICLE I.

Sa Majesté le Roi de Suède et de Norvège s'engage à ne céder à la Russie, ni à échanger avec elle, ni à lui permettre d'occuper, aucune partie des territoires appartenant aux Couronnes de Suède et de Nor-

complication which might disturb the existing balance of power in Europe, have resolved to come to an understanding with a view to secure the integrity of the United Kingdoms of Sweden and Norway, and have named as their Plenipotentiaries to conclude a Treaty for that purpose, that is to say:

Her Majesty the Queen of the United Kingdom of Great Britain and Ireland, Arthur Charles Magenis, Esquire, Her Envoy Extraordinary and Minister Plenipotentiary to His Majesty the King of Sweden and Norway;

His Majesty the Emperor of the French, the Sieur Charles Victor Lobstein, Officer of the Imperial Order of the Legion of Honour, Grand Cross of the Royal Order of the Polar Star of Sweden, Commander of the Order of Christ, and Knight of that of the Conception of Portugal, His Envoy Extraordinary and Minister Plenipotentiary to His Majesty the King of Sweden and Norway.

[*853] And His Majesty the King of Sweden and Norway, the Sieur Gustavus Nicholas Algernon Adolphus Baron de Stierneld, His Minister of State and for Foreign Affairs, Knight and Commander of His Orders, Grand Cross of His Order of St. Olaf, of Norway, &c., &c., &c.

Who, after having communicated to each other their respective full powers, found in good and due form, have agreed as follows:—

ARTICLE I.

His Majesty the King of Sweden and Norway engages not to cede to nor to exchange with Russia, nor to permit her to occupy, any part of the territories belonging to the Crowns of Sweden and Norway.

vège. Sa Majesté le Roi de Suède et de Norvège s'engage, en outre, à ne céder à la Russie aucun droit de pâturage, de pêche, ou de quelque autre nature que ce soit, tant sur les dits territoires que sur les côtes de Suède et de Norvège, et à repousser toute prétention que pourrait élever la Russie à établir l'existence d'aucun des droits précités.

His Majesty the King of Sweden and Norway engages, further, not to cede to Russia any right of pasturage, of fishery, or of any other nature whatsoever, either on the said territories or upon the coasts of Sweden and Norway, and to resist any pretension which may be put forward by Russia with a view to establish the existence of any of the rights aforesaid.

ART. II.

Dans le cas où la Russie ferait à Sa Majesté le Roi de Suède et de Norvège quelque proposition ou demande ayant pour objet d'obtenir soit la cession ou l'échange d'une partie quelconque des territoires appartenant aux Couronnes de Suède et de Norvège, soit la faculté d'occuper certains points [*854] *des dits territoires, soit la cession de droits de pêche, de pâturage, ou tout autre sur ces mêmes territoires et sur les côtes de Suède et de Norvège, Sa Majesté le Roi de Suède et de Norvège s'engage à communiquer immédiatement cette proposition ou demande à Sa Majesté Britannique et à Sa Majesté l'Empereur des Français; et leurs dites Majestés prennent, de leur côté, l'engagement de fournir à Sa Majesté le Roi de Suède et de Norvège, des forces navales et militaires suffisantes pour coopérer avec les forces navales et militaires de Sa dite Majesté, dans le but de résister aux prétentions ou aux agressions de la Russie. La nature, l'importance, et la destination des forces dont il s'agit, seront, le cas échéant, arrêtées d'un commun accord entre les trois Puissances.

ART. II.

In case Russia should make to His Majesty the King of Sweden and Norway any proposal or demand having for its object to obtain either the cession or the exchange of any part whatsoever of the territories belonging to the Crowns of Sweden and Norway, or the power of occupying certain points of the said territories, or the cession of rights of fishery, of pasturage, or of any other right upon the said territories and upon the coasts of Sweden and Norway, His Majesty the King of Sweden and Norway engages forthwith to communicate such proposal or demand to Her Britannic Majesty and His Majesty the Emperor of the French; and their said Majesties, on their part, engage to furnish to His Majesty the King of Sweden and Norway sufficient naval and military forces to co-operate with the naval and military forces of His said Majesty, for the purpose of resisting the pretensions or aggressions of Russia. The description, number, and destination of such forces shall, if occasion should arise, be determined by common agreement between the three Powers.

ART. III.

Le présent traité sera ratifié, et

ART. III.

The present Treaty shall be rati-les ratifications seront échangées à Stockholm le plus tôt que faire se pourra.

En foi de quoi les Plénipotentiaires respectifs l'ont signé, et y ont apposé le cachet de leurs armes.

Fait à Stockholm, le vingtun Novembre, l'an de grâce mil huit cent cinquante-cinq.

(L.S.) ARTHUR C. MAGENIS.
(L.S.) VOR. LOBSTEIN.
(L.S.) STIERNELD.

fied, and the ratifications shall be exchanged at Stockholm as soon as possible.

In witness whereof the respective Plenipotentiaires have signed the same, and have affixed thereto the seal of their arms.

Done at Stockholm, the twenty-first of November, in the year of our Lord one thousand eight hundred and fifty-five.

(L.S.) ARTHUR C. MAGENIS.
(L.S.) VOR. LOBSTEIN.
(L.S.) STIERNELD.

---

*APPENDIX XXI. [*855]

Extract from debates in both Houses on Motions for Papers relative to the Treaty of Peace with France. [*Hansard's Parliamentary Debates* (1802,) vol. xxxvi. pp. 674–5.] [*Speech of Dr. Lawrence.*]

"May 12th.

"DR. LAWRENCE said that nothing had passed that could induce him to abandon the opinion he entertained, that the Treaty of Peace lately signed was, in many respects, most fatal to the country. Let any person consider of what importance to this country were its possessions in the East; and let him at the same time consider how the security and well-being of those possessions were endangered by the non-renewal of the Treaties by which they were heretofore protected. Let it be considered what advantages were given to the enemy by this neglect, or omission, or by whatever other name it was to be called—advantages which the enemy himself already exaggerated."

"The Convention of 1787 granted a general exemption to all factories, and a general jurisdiction over all persons within certain limits. The omission of any regulation to this effect in the present Treaty, might renew the ancient jealousies." (Ib., p. 677.)

"It might be urged, he said, in defence of the non-revival of former Treaties, that we did not give up our rights, but were prepared to defend them to the utmost. But though they had not been revived generally, it was surely worth while to revive specifically that part which protected our commerce in the East Indies. (Ib., p. 679.)

Speech of Lord Grenville. Debate in the Lords on the Definitive Treaty of Paris. Ibid., pp. 688–9.

"It was asked what was the use of discussion now, when peace was concluded? Was it wished to overthrow the Treaty? If not, what benefit could arise from debating upon the subject of it? He should be sorry to bring forward any motion, if he had it not in his power to meet such an argument. Whatever disadvantages might arise to the country from this unfortunate Treaty, he would be one of the first to say, it was concluded by the power which had the right, by the constitution of the country, to conclude it; and, therefore, whatever were its terms, Parliament was bound to accede to it. It was ratified by His Majesty, and the Great Seal of the Kingdom affixed to it; consequently it was irrevocable; and not to carry it into effect would be to add dishonour to the loss occasioned by the Treaty, and to impeach the national integrity. The first proposition he should make to the House was, to declare to His Majesty their opinion, that the public faith was pledged to the observance of the Peace; that it was an obligation binding upon the country to maintain it inviolable."

[*856] *He had already stated to the House his objections to the preliminary Treaty: if the definitive Treaty had been conformable to the preliminary articles, and the relative situation of France and Spain had not altered by intervening circumstances, however he might have been disposed to have protested against the definitive Treaty, he should not have thought it necessary to have proposed to the House the adoption of any new measure; but he found that all the grounds of the pretensions on the part of France, as contained in the preliminary Treaty, had not only been confirmed by the definitive Treaty, but exceeded. The terms of the latter were therefore infinitely more prejudicial than the former. He could not avoid calling the attention of the House to what had been the arguments used against the preliminary articles. It had been stated that in all negotiations for peace there are two grounds or bases necessary to be adhered to; when after a long contest between two nations, the respective Governments were considering how they might restore the blessings of peace and tranquillity, the basis on which the negotiation proceeded was, either the *status ante bellum*, the actual situation in which the parties stood before the war, or the situation in which they stood at the time of the negotiation, which was called the *uti possidetis*. Instead of the negotiators of the definitive Treaty proceeding distinctly upon one of these grounds, they had applied both in the most prejudicial manner possible to this country. They had referred to the *status ante bellum* with regard to England, by giving up all she had taken during the war to France; and they had adopted the *uti possidetis* as to France, by leaving her in possession of all that she had acquired. It was obvious that at the commencement of the negotiation each country was in possession of some advantage which operated to the disadvantage of the other. It was to our disadvantage that France possessed so much power on the Continent; and it was to the disadvantage of France that we, by the superior skill and valour of our navy, were possessed of the colonies of France and Spain. The arrangement to have been desired was, that we should have diminished the power of France upon the Continent in proportion to our sacrifices with respect to the colonies that we had taken. If France could not have been persuaded to that, then it was

our duty to have extended our maritime power for the purpose of compelling her. As far as appeared by the Treaty, ministers had made no attempt whatever to reduce the power of France on the Continent, but had, by concessions abroad, given her the means of weakening our colonial strength. This was not acting upon the principle adopted by Lord Chatham at the Peace of 1763. That enlightened statesman had always considered that every preliminary Treaty should be as definitive as possible. If the preliminary articles of 1763 were compared with the definitive, it would appear that there was scarcely any difference between them; while the direct contrary was the case with regard to the present Treaty." (Ibid, pp. 689—691.)

*"That it is impossible for us to have seen, without the utmost anxiety and alarm, all the unexampled circumstances [*857] which have attended the final conclusion of the present peace;—the extensive and important sacrifices which, without any corresponding concession, this Treaty has added to those already made on our part by the preliminary articles; the unlooked-for and immense accessions of territory, influence, and power, which it has tacitly confirmed to France." (Ibid., p. 697.)

Speech of the Lord Chancellor. Ibid., p. 725.

"And here he must differ a little from his learned friend in respect to the importance of Treaties solemnly executed between nation and nation. He had, during twenty years of his professional life, witnessed the growth and improvement of the distinguished talents of his learned brother, with whom he had lived in habits of uninterrupted friendship; he could not, however, agree with him in thinking, that Treaties deserved to be treated in the light manner he had treated them. He would, however, assert, with his learned friend, that most of the conditions of the Treaties, the omission of the revival of which were complained of by the noble mover, were from the violent change that the circumstances of Europe, and more especially of France, had undergone within the last twenty years, wholly inapplicable to the present Treaty; and at the same time, all the great and important rights which his noble friend thought lost and abandoned, because they were not recognized in the definitive Treaty, stood secured on a much stronger basis than any recognition of them by any Treaty whatsoever."

Speech of Lord Hawkesbury. Ibid., pp. 761, 762.

"With respect to the definitive Treaty, gentlemen complain of it on two grounds; namely, for faults of omission and commission. Under the first class the principal is the non-revival of the several commercial and political Treaties, and two particular conventions. As to the first, I should suppose, if gentlemen would look into those Treaties, they would not be so very solicitous for their revival. From the Treaty of Westphalia, up to that of 1763, it was the practice, as the system of Europe was perpetually changing, to renew former Treaties, with such alterations and additions as suited existing circumstancess, until at length these Treaties became so confused, inconsistent, and contradictory, as to contribute more to augment litigation, than to produce the adjustment of any difference. If we made any engagements, they should be precise and explicit—not such as those Treaties; besides, we ought to be cautious how we consented to multiply our engagements. Another objection that I have to the renewal of those Treaties is, that we should bind ourselves too much.

[*858] *"I shall state the former practice as to such renewal of Treaties. In 1748, when we guaranteed the pragmatic sanction, we also guaranteed Silesia to Russia. What, then, if agreeable to such a precedent, we should have to guarantee the Netherlands and Sardinia to France? I would ask my right honourable friend, whether this was not a sufficiently strong objection to the renewal of former Treaties? The situation of ministers in this case was one of extreme difficulty; they were rather willing to sacrifice some advantages than place themselves in the dilemma that I have described; and they determined if they could not get Europe to do right, they would not be a party to her wrong. I would ask my right honourable friend, whether the renewal of political Treaties, accompanied by such consequences, was so desirable? As to commercial Treaties, if any person looked into them, they would be found not less objectionable than the former. Our Treaty with Holland gave the Dutch the power of carrying warlike stores over in the time of war to an enemy's ports. Would it be advisable, after the experience of the last war, to renew such a Treaty as that? Objections equally strong would be found to operate against the renewal of our former Treaties with France. From these considerations, I think it will scarcely be disputed that it was better to leave commercial arrangements to be hereafter adjusted, than to postpone the conclusion of the definitive Treaty, even if the country was to be left in the state it was in before the preliminaries were signed."

Debate in the Commons on the Definitive Treaty of Peace.—Speech of the Master of the Rolls. [*Hansard's Parliamentary Debates* (1802,) vol. xxxvi. pp. 801-3.]

"With respect to the non-revival of Treaties, he was of opinion that those gentlemen who had brought forward arguments against this omission in the definite Treaty, had argued against themselves. They had brought forward claims on the part of France, which they admitted were utterly destitute of foundation. They had assumed an injustice on the part of France, and proved that former Treaties ought to have been revived by the very same arguments which would render those Treaties absolutely nugatory; for, if France disregarded Treaties for the purpose of reviving former claims, which had been settled by those Treaties, then all Treaties with her would be useless. If this was the character of the French Government, we ought to be constantly at war with her, and publicly to state the reason of it. Confidence begot confidence; and if we entertained these opinions of France, we should be acting in the same manner as the French Directory, who received every declaration of ours with a declaration on their side that they doubted our sincerity. It was certainly not fair to put into the mouth of France claims and pretensions which we ourselves reprobated and condemned. With respect to [*859] *the general ground of the revival of former Treaties, he was not disposed to admit the propriety of it; but he supposed that some motive which he had not been able to discover, had induced the renewal of former Treaties in other negotiations. There were some instances, at least, in which, as in the present case, if former Treaties were renewed, they would be renewed without an object to refer to. France had generally begun in former Treaties with the renewal of the Treaty of Westphalia, and proceeded forward from thence. It was asserted, that we had in this instance departed from the established law of nations; but respecting the practice, it was not so uniform as it seemed to be supposed. Treaties had been before made with France, in which no mention was made of former Treaties; in the Treaties of Ryswick and Utrecht, for instance, no mention was made of former Treaties; yet Europe stood as before. There were several Treaties between this country and France, which, if now renewed, would not only have no object to refer to, but would be absolutely contrary in their operation to the present situation of affairs. In adverting to the renewal of former Treaties, it should have been stated for what purpose they ought to be renewed; for unless gentlemen could show him some benefit to be derived from that renewal, he should see no reason for it. One effect was stated to be the consequence of this omission, which was, that all Treaties not renewed fell to the ground. There were some which he thought it was of little consequence whether they fell to the ground or not. For instance, if a cession was made, it became absolutely part of the dominion of the country to which it was ceded; it was of no consequence that the Treaty was not renewed in the event of a war and a subsequent peace, as the territory ceded could not revert back to the party ceding. Thus, with respect to the Bay of Honduras, which had been alluded to, it was said to be doubtful; our right to cut log-wood there was not done away by the non-renewal of former Treaties. In the first place, however, it was not very clear that we derived our title to it from a Treaty; and in the next, we were in possession of the right of property at the commencement of the war, which we had retained, and still held at the conclusion of the war. The right of property, therefore, still remained in this country, and there could not be a clause inserted in the Treaty to give us that which we had never lost; we merely restored what we had taken possession of; what we had before possessed in our own right must remain vested in the same manner, without any necessity for its being so stipulated by Treaty."

Speech of Dr. Lawrence. Ibid., p. 806.

"He would not plead for the indiscriminate renewal of all our political and commercial Treaties, but there were some which *he thought [*860] it would have been wise to renew, and not to rely solely upon the Treaty before the House, in which nothing definitive was to be found, and yet it was to form the basis of the future system of Europe; the principles and practice of all former statesmen being totally rejected.

The vessel of the State was to be thrown afloat on the ocean of politics and commerce, with no rudder but the very distinct and comprehensive Treaty on the table."

APPENDIX XXII.

Treaties.—Effect of Silence in.—Mediation.—Intervention.—Treaty relating to the Succession to the Throne of Greece (1852). [*From the Annuaire des Deux Mondes*, 1852–3, p. 918.]

SUCCESSION AU TRONE HELLENIQUE.

Protocole d'une Conférence tenue au Foreign Office le 20 *Novembre*, 1852.

PRESENS : les plénipotentiaires de Bavière, de France, de la-Grande-Bretagne, de Grèce, et de Russie.

Les plénipotentiaires s'étant réunis au jour fixé dans la dernière conférence pour la signature du traité, dont le texte paraphé est annexé au protocole du 12 Novembre, ont procédé, séance tenante, à ladite signature.

Le Ministre de Bavière, en signant *sub spe rati*, a présenté, d'ordre de sa cour, la déclaration ci-jointe pour être annexée au présent protocole (*sub lit.* A.)

En conséquence, le Ministre de Grèce a cru devoir déposer également aux actes de la conférence la déclaration ci-annexée (*sub lit.* B.)

Considérant leur tâche, toute de conciliation, comme entièrement accomplie par les dispositions du traité signé en ce jour, les plénipotentiaires de France, de la Grande-Bretagne et de Russie, n'admettant point l'opportunité d'une discussion déjà épuisée, ont cru devoir se borner à s'en référer simplement au texte du traité et aux explications contenues dans les précédens protocoles.

Signé : A. DE CETTO, A. WALEWSKI, MALMESBURY, S. TRICOUPI, BRUNNOW.

Traité relatif à la Succession au Trône de Grèce, signé à Londres, le 20 *Novembre*, 1852.

Au nom de la très-sainte et indivisible Trinité.

Sa Majesté la Reine du Royaume Uni de la Grande-Bretagne et d'Irlande, le Prince President de la République Française, et Sa [*861] *Majesté l'Empereur de toutes les Russies, en vue de consolider l'ordre de succession au trône de Grèce, placée sous leur commune garantie ; reconnaissant la nécessité, dans ce but, de mettre les stipulations dé l'article 8, de la Convention du 7 Mai, 1832, en harmonie avec la condition établie par l'article 40, de la Constitution Hellénique, ont résolu de conclure à cet effet un traité avec le concours de Sa Majesté le

Roi de Bavière, comme signataire de la Convention de 1832, et de Sa Majesté Hellénique, comme directement intéressée à prendre part à une transaction destinée à assurer le repos à venir de la Grèce.

Leurs Majestés le Roi de Bavière et le Roi de Grèce ayant répondu à cette invitation, les hautes parties contractantes ont nommé pour leurs plénipotentiaires (suivent les noms des plénipotentiaires.)

Lesquels, après s'être communiqué leurs pleins pouvoirs, trouvés en bonne et due forme, ont arrêté et signé les articles suivans :

Art. 1er. Les princes de la maison de Bavière, appelés par la Convention de 1832 et par la Constitution Hellénique, à succéder à la couronne de Grèce dans les cas où le Roi Othon viendrait à décéder sans postérité directe et légitime, ne pourront monter sur le trône de Grèce qu'on se conformant à l'article 40, de la Constitution Hellénique ainsi conçu :

"Tout successeur de la couronne de Grèce doit professor la religion de l'église orthodoxe orientale."

Art. 2. Conformément au troisième décret de l'Assemblée Hellénique, Sa Majesté la Reine Amélie est appelée de droit à la régence, en cas de minorité ou d'absence de successeur au trône, d'après les conditions de l'article 40, de la constitution.

Art. 3. Le présent traité sera ratifié, et les ratifications en seront échangées à Londres dans l'espace de six semaines ou plus tôt, si faire se peut.

En foi de quoi les plénipotentiaires respectifs l'ont signé et y ont apposé le cachet de leurs armes.

Fait à Londres, le 20 Novembre, l'an de grâce mil huit cent cinquante-deux.

(L.S.) MALMESBURY.
(L.S.) A. DE CETTO (sauf approbation de son Gouvernement.)
(L.S.) A. WALEWSKI.
(L.S.) S. TRICOUPI.
(L.S.) BRUNNOW.

Annexe (A) *au Protocole de la Conférence du* 20 *Novembre*, 1852.

Au moment de donner, sauf approbation, le concours de son Gouvernement à la convention qui a pour objet de mettre l'art. *40, de la Constitution Hellénique en harmonie avec les stipulations du [*862] traité du 7 Mai, 1832, le soussigné, plénipotentiaire de Sa Majesté le Roi de Bavière, se tient pour obligé de réserver à sadite Majesté la faculté de donner suite plus tard à l'arrangement de famille dont communication a été faite aux cabinets de France, de Grande-Bretagne et de Russie, en comptant pour cela sur leur assistance bienveillante.

Il se tient aussi pour obligé de constater d'une manière positive que l'obligation de remplir la condition de l'art. 40, de la Constitution Hellénique, ainsi que le veut l'article 1er de la convention, n'incombe aux princes de la maison de Bavière qu'après le décès du Roi Othon, non avant ; et qu'alors celui des princes de Bavière qui remplira cette condition montera de droit sur le trône de Grèce.

Il doit enfin exprimer la conviction que l'art. 2, de la convention, dans lequel le décret 3, de l'Assemblée Hellénique est cité, ne saurait être entendu comme devant ou pouvant préjudicier, en aucun cas, aux droits de succession que les princes de Bavière ont acquis par les traités.

Le soussigné a encore un devoir à remplir. L'art. 1er de la convention, en nommant le traité du 7 Mai, 1832, conjointement avec la Constitution Hellénique, ne fait nulle mention de l'article explicatif et complémentaire du 30 Avril, 1833. Toutefois, MM. les Plénipotentiaires de France, de la Grande-Bretagne, et de Russie ont bien voulu, de vive voix, donner l'assurance au soussigné que, dans leur pensée comme dans leur intention, l'article explicatif et complémentaire de 1833, bien que non expressément mentionné, est compris implicitement dans la citation du traité de 1832, vu qu'aux termes dudit article, celui-ci fait partie intégrante du traité comme s'il y était inséré mot à mot. Ayant transmis cette assurance à Munich, le soussigné a reçu l'ordre de déclarer, ainsi qu'il le déclare par la présente, que le Gouvernement Bavarois l'accepte, et, qu'en procédant à la signature de la convention, il regarde comme expressément entendu entre les cabinets de France, de la Grande-Bretagne, et de Russie, et le cabinet de Bavière, que *le silence* de l'article 1er de cette convention, par rapport à l'article explicatif et complémentaire de 1833, 30 Avril, est sans préjudice aucun pour les stipulations contenues dans celui-ci, stipulations en vertu desquelles les femmes ne sont appelées à monter sur le trône de Grèce qu'à l'extinction totale des mâles dans toutes les trois branches de la maison de Bavière désignées pour succéder en Grèce.

Le soussigné a l'honneur de demander que la présente soit jointe comme annexe au protocole de ce jour, et se déterminerait pour lors à signer la convention, sauf l'approbation de son Gouvernement.

Londres, le 20 Novembre, 1852.

(Signé) A. de Cetto.

[*863] **Annexe* (B) *au Protocole de la Conférence du* 20 *Novembre,* 1852.

A la suite de la déclaration du plénipotentiaire de Bavière, le soussigné, plénipotentiaire de Grèce, après avoir fait observer que la Constitution Grecque ne renferme que les conditions de l'article 8, de la Convention du 7 Mai, 1832, et ne fait nullement mention de l'article dont il est question dans la déclaration du plénipotentiaire Bavarois, a remarqué qu'il n'est autorisé par son Gouvernement que d'accepter, et par conséquent il n'accepte, que ce qui a été déjà inséré d'un commun accord au traité paraphé, le 12 de ce mois, par les plénipotentiaires de France, de la Grande-Bretagne, de Grèce et de Russie.

(Signé) S. Tricoupi.

APPENDIX XXIII.

Memorandum of the Sardinian Government as to the Sequestration of the Property of Lombardo-Venetian Emigrants having become Sardinian Subjects. [*From Annuaire des Deux Mondes*, 1852–3, pp. 914–18.]

DANS la dernière guerre d'Italie, le Piémont fut vaincu, mais non humilié. Lorsqu'il fut question de signer la paix, le Piemont déclara qu'il ne pouvait abandonner à la sévérité des lois les citoyens du royaume Lombardo-Vénitien qui s'étaient compromis dans les derniers événemens, et qui, faisant cause commune avec nous, avaient arboré nos drapeaux.

Ce sentiment, inspiré par l'honneur, fut apprécié par l'homme d'etat distingué qui présidait alors aux conseils de l'empire Autrichien. L'Autriche promit qu'une amniste suivrait immédiatement la signature du traité de paix.

L'amnistie fut en effet promulguée avec la ratification du traité.

L'Autriche régla de son plein gré le sort des citoyens Lombards-Vénitiens qui s'etaient expatriés à la suite des derniers événemens, et qui, dans des délais fixés, ne rentrèrent pas dans leurs foyers, soit parce qu'ils étaient exclus de l'amniste, soit pour toute autre cause independante.

La liberté de se choisir une nouvelle patrie, lorsq'un intérêt puissant nous engage à quitter les lieux qui nous ont vus naître, étant un des droits les moins contestés, aucune législation n'a mis un obstacle absolu à la faculté d'émigrer.

Dans l'Empire Autrichien, la loi du 24 Mars, 1832, promulguée *le 15 Juin en Lombardie, reconnâit aux sujets de l'empe- [*864]
reur le droit à l'émigration légale, à la charge d'en demander l'autorisation préalable en remplissant les conditions prescrites. Elle déclare à l'art 9, "que les émigrés avec autorisation perdront la qualité de sujets Autrichiens et seront traités comme étrangers pour tous les effets de droit civil et politique."

L'art. 10, frappe de peines sévères la délit d'émigration non autorisée.

L'art. 11, ordonne le séquestre des biens des coupables.

Le maréchal comte Radetzky, investi des pouvoirs souverains dans le royaume Lombardo-Vénitien, se conforma aux principes clairement établis par la loi précitée, dans les différentes notifications qu'il publia après le traité de paix du 6 Août, 1849.

La première notification du 12 du même mois accorde l'amnistie; elle exclut cependant de cette faveur quatre-vingt-six individus qui sont désignés nominativement.

Le maréchal déclare que ceux qui ne rentreront pas dans le délai fixé ne pourront plus profiter de l'amnistie; que ceux qui ne rentreront pas, soit par un effet de la présente proclamation (*les citoyens exclus de l'amnistie,*) soit par un effet de leur volonté (*per fatto proprio,*) pourront demander l'autorisation d'émigrer en conformité des lois.

Une autre notification du 12 Mars, 1850 :

« Considérant que tous les amnistiés n'ont pas profité de l'alternative qu'on leur avait laissé de rentrer dans les états Autrichiens, ou de demander, dans la voie légale, leur émigration ;

« Attendu qu'il ne peut être indifférent au Gouvernement de laisser la jouissance des droits de citoyen à ceux qui prolongent volontairement une absence non autorisée, déclare qu'on les poursuivra comme coupables d'émigration illégale."

Mais, par une proclamation en date du 29 Décembre de la même année, Sa Majesté l'Empereur révoqua ces dispositions du gouverneur-général :

« En considération, y-est-il dit, de l'option qu'on a laissée à mes sujets compromis dans les événemens rèvolutionnaires de la Lombardie et de la Vénétie de rentrer dans leur patrie ou de demander leur émigration légale, et par un effet de ma grâce, je veux que ceux qui n'ont pas profité de cette faculté, quoiqu'ils ne soient pas exclus de l'amnistie, soient nèanmoins considérés et traités comme étant déliés des droits et devoirs de sujets Autrichiens (*come sciolti dal vincolo della sudditanza Austriaca*), et je permets qu'ils soient assimilés aux sujets qui ont obtenu l'auotrisation d'émigrer.

Nous voyons donc une loi de l'empire qui permet aux sujets Autrichiens d'émigrer avec l'autorisation préalable du Gouvernement, loi qui a trait aux rapports internationaux, et qui fait par conséquent partie du droit public, tant qu'elle n'est pas révoquée. Nous voyons le Gouvernement Autrichien, après la guerre de *1848-9, engager à demander l'émigration, en conformité de cette loi, ceux de ses sujets compromis qui ne pourraient pas (*les exclus de l'amnistie*) ou qui n'entendraient pas rentrer dans leurs foyers.

[*865]

Enfin, nous voyons l'Autriche, impatiente des lenteurs d'une partie des amnistiés à se prononcer, leur donner en masse l'autorisation d'émigrer qu'ils hésitaient à demander, et déclarer qu'ils seront considérés comme déliés des devoirs de sujets Autrichiens et comme émigrés légalement.

L'Autriche ayant défini d'une manière nette, précise, large, la position légale des émigrés, elle avait accordé à plusieurs d'entre eux, soit amnistiés, soit exclus de l'amnistie, sur leur demande, et à teneur de la loi de 1832, la permission d'émigrer.

Un grand nombre, placé dans ces conditions, demanda la naturalization Sarde, qui fut accordée aux uns, refusée aux autres.

Ceux qui furent naturalisés sont devenus légitimement, d'après les lois de l'Autriche, comme d'après les nôtres, *citoyens Sardes*, et ne sont plus, pour l'Autriche, que des étrangers sur lesquels elle ne peut revendiquer aucun droit de souveraineté, et dont les biens sont placés sous la protection de l'art. 33, du Code Civil Autrichien.

Si cette position des émigrés *naturalisés Sardes* avait eu besoin d'être améliorée ou raffermie, nous n'aurions qu'à citer l'art. 1er du traité de commerce stipulé entre la Sardaigne et l'Autriche, le 18 Octobre, 1851, que déclare que « les sujets de chacune des hautes parties contractantes pourront disposer librement, par testament, donation, échange, vente, ou de toute autre manière, de tous les biens qu'ils pourraient acquérir ou posséder légalement dans les états de l'autre puissance, etc. . . ., en payant seulement les impôts, taxes et autres droits auxquels sont assujettis les autres habitans du pays où la propriété existe."

Le 6 Février dernier ont eu lieu les déplorables événemens dont la ville de Milan a été le théâtre.

Sept jours après, au moment même où l'Autriche déclarait apprécier la conduite ferme et légale que le gouvernement du roi avait tenue à son égard, on signait une proclamation, par laquelle, en déclarant évidente (*manifesta*) la complicté des émigrés politiques du royaume Lombardo-Vénitien dans ces derniers événemens, on frappait de séquestre tous leurs biens meubles et immeubles situés dans les états Autrichiens; on ne faisait aucune distinction entre les émigrés exclus ou non de l'amnistie; entre ceux qui avaient obtenu un décret particulier d'émigration ou qui avaient été autorisés en masse à émigrer.

La proclamation finissait par ces mots: "J'attends des propositions ultérieures relativement à la destination à donner aux biens séquestrés; c'est-à-dire qu'avec le séquestre, il y avait menace de confiscation."

L'Europe apprit avec une surprise douloureuse une mesure qui [*866] *violait tous les droits, qu'aucune raison ne pouvait justifier, qui n'avait pas d'exemple dans l'histoire. On s'étonnait de la voir émaner d'une monarchie éminemment conservatrice, d'un gouvernement régulier. On se demanda comment on pouvait affirmer à Vienne, sept jours après les troubles de Milan, et quand les enquêtes, étaient à peine commencées, que tous les émigrés politiques étaient complices de ces attentats; s'il était possible que cette complicité universelle, qu'aucun fait ne venait confirmer, n'admit aucune exception; si une insurrection organisée par Mazzini pouvait être imputée à ceux qui s'étaient toujours posés en adversaires de ses théories et de ses actes, et qui en auraient été les premières victimes s'il avait triomphé; on se demandait enfin pourquoi, s'il y avait trace de complicité, on ne laissait point à l'action juridique des tribunaux le soin de la constater et de la punir, sans intervertir tous les rôles, sans usurper les fonctions judiciaires, condamner les prétendus coupables, en masse, non-seulement sans les entendre et presque sans les nommer, et commencer une procédure par l'exécution de l'arrêt rendu d'avance, non sur des preuves, mais sur des suppositions.

Le gouvernement du roi, qui venait de prouver à l'Autriche par des faits irrécusables qu'il avait la volonté et le pouvoir de réprimer et de contenir tout élément révolutionnaire, et qui, par des mesures promptes et énergiques, avait éloigné de la frontière Lombarde et ensuite expulsé de ses états le petit nombre d'émigrés turbulens (ils ne montaient pas à cent) qui suivaient les inspirations de Mazzini, fut très-péniblement affecté de la manière dont le gouvernement Autrichien répondait à cet acte de loyauté et de bon voisinage. Néammoins, voyant que la proclamation ne faisait aucune mention des émigrés qui, après avoir été déliés régulièrement de leurs devoirs de sujets Autrichiens, avaient obtenu des lettres de naturalisation dans un autre état, il se borna à demander des explications à ce sujet au cabinet de Vienne; car, tout en déplorant pour les autres la mesure adoptée par l'Autriche, il ne jugeait pas devoir s'ériger en censeur des actes du gouvernement impérial, en tant qu'ils ne touchaient point aux droits du Piémont et aux stipulations internationales. La réponse fut que l'Autriche ne faisait aucune distinction entre les émigrés politiques; que tous étaient frappés également, les naturalisés comme les non naturalisés.

Le gouvernement Sarde, pressé par l'impérieux devoir de ne pas permettre la spoliation violente de ceux qui, selon les lois des deux pays, les traités et le droit public, de l'aveu de l'Autriche et par un effet des facilités qu'elle a accordées, étaient devenus sujets du roi, adressa, en termes modérés, ses réclamations au comte de Buol.

Il s'attacha à lui démontrer que la proclamation, en tant qu'elle frappait les anciens sujets de l'Autriche, réfugiés politiques, qui, après avoir [*867] obtenu l'autorisation d'émigrer, avaient acquis la *naturalisation Sarde, était contraire à la loi de l'empire Autrichien du 24 Mars, 1832, aux notifications impériales du 12 Août, 1849, 12 Mars et 1er Décembre, 1850; au traité de commerce du 18 Octobre, 1851, ainsi qu'à l'art. 33, du Code Civil Autrichien. Il annonçait l'espoir que le cabinet de Vienne, revenu de ses premières impressions, et appréciant mieux l'atteinte profonde que l'application, aux sujets du roi, de la mesure en question portait aux principes du droit public et aux stipulations solennelles des traités existans entre la Sardaigne et l'Autriche, consentirait à en modifier l'exécution.

Le cabinet Sarde était bien loin de s'attendre à la réponse dont M. le comte de Buol chargea le ministre impérial à Turin de lui donner communication.

Cette réponse est si extraordinaire par le fond et par la forme, elle est si peu conforme aux bons rapports qui existent entre l'Autriche et le Piémont, que le gouvernement du roi s'est trouvé dans le pénible devoir de protester, et contre l'acte de spoliation qu'on entend consommer au préjudice de sujets Sardes non atteints ni convaincus légalement d'aucun crime, et contre les théories subversives de tout principe d'ordre et de légalité par lesquélles on aurait la prétention de les justifier.

Cependant, avant de s'acquitter de cette obligation, et voulant laisser à l'Autriche le temps de revenir à des sentimens plus équitables et plus conformes aux bons rapports qui ont existé jusqu'à présent entre les deux états le cabinet de Turin répondit en termes empreints d'un vif désir de conciliation à la dépêche de M. le comte de Buol, et s'attacha à réfuter les argumens à l'aide desquels ce ministre s efforçait de démontrer la nécessité d'une mesure que rien ne peut justifier. Malheureusement, les nouvelles démarches du gouvernement du roi n'ont abouti à aucun résultat. D'après les réponses faites au comte de Revel, le Piémont n'a pu concevoir la moindre espérance que le séquestre serait, en tout ou en partie, révoqué ou modifié.

En conséquence, il a cru que sa conscience et sa dignité ne pouvaient lui permettre de différer plus longtemps l'accomplissement du devoir positif et sacré de protester de nouveau solennellement.

M. le comte de Buol laisse de côté la question de l'égalité, terrain sur lequel il ne pourrait soutenir la discussion, et déclare hautement que la mesure contre laquelle nous réclamons a été prise dans un intérêt de sûreté publique.

Qu'il nous soit permis, à notre tour, de faire observer que l'intérêt de la sûreté publique peut autoriser des mesures extraordinaires et *extra légales*, telles que l'état de siége avec toutes ses rigueurs.

L'Autriche en a usé largement, et aucun gouvernement ne s'est avisé d'intervenir dans une question de politique intérieure, ni d'examiner jusqu'à quel point elle peut être justifiée.

*Mais l'intérêt de la sûreté de l'état ne peut jamais autoriser l'emploi de mesures illégales; it ne peut jamais autoriser l'Autriche à porter atteinte aux droits des gens, à déchirer une page de son code civil, à revenir sur ses propres actes et sur ses promesses les plus solennelles, à méconnaître les droits acquis, à annuler un traité stipulé tout récemment et observé par la Sardaigne avec une scrupuleuse fidélité, à violer le droit de propriété des citoyens Sardes, à mettre en pratique, sans qu'elle en ait l'intention, ces principes révolutionnaires et socialistes qu'elle réprouve si hautement, que tout gouvernement régulier est appelé à combattre et à paralyser, parce qu'ils minent la base de l'édifice social. [*868]

M. de Buol n'hésite pas à affirmer que les émigrés Lombards-Vénitiens, réfugiés en Piémont, ont employé une partie des revenus qu'ils tiraient de la Lombardie à subventionner la presse démagogique, à seconder activement des machinations criminelles, telles que l'emprunt Mazzini. Mais ce sont là des allégations tout à fait gratuites, n'ayant aucune preuve à l'appui; le manque de fondement en serait même démontré par les injures et les menaces auxquelles les émigrés riches ont toujours été et sont encore en butte, particulièrement depuis l'échauffourée de Milan, de la part des journaux démagogiques et du parti Mazzinien. D'ailleurs, si, malgré la réprobation dont les émigrés ont frappé cet attentat, il existe quelques faits qui prouvent que quelqu'un d'entre eux, naturalisé Sarde ou non, ait pris part à ce mouvement ou à des conspirations contre l'Autriche, elle a des lois et des juges; dès que la justice aura prononcé, le Piémont n'élévera pas la voix pour défendre le coupable. Mais tant que l'autorité politique, mettant de côté les lois et les tribunaux, procédera, sur des suppositions, à des actes de spoliation envers des sujets Sardes, le sentiment de l'honneur et du devoir imposera au Piémont l'obligation d'intervenir en leur faveur, de protester contre l'abus de la force, d'épuiser tous les moyens qui sont en son pouvoir pour faire modifier un état de choses si peu en harmonie avec les principes les plus sacrés du droit des gens. L'Autriche n'a certainement pas le droit de s'en étonner ni de dire que nous faisons cause commune avec les émigrés. Nous protégeons nos concitoyens, et l'Autriche, dans un cas semblable, ne tiendrait pas une autre ligne de conduite.

M. de Buol, récriminant, nous demande ce que nous avons fait pour mettre un frein à cette presse abominable, qui n'est au fond qu'un appel incessant à la révolte.

Quoique cette interpellation tende évidemment à déplacer la question, nous répondrons en remarquant d'abord que ce ministre prête une influence bien funeste à des journaux qui ne sont les un Autriche que par les hauts fonctionnaires, et dont l'introduction est défendue en Lombardie sous des peines tellement rigoureuses qu'elle suffit pour donner lieu au *giudizio statario.* Mais disons ensuite qu'il y a chez nous des [*869] lois répressives de la licence de la *presse; que les tribunaux ont été appelés bien souvent à les appliquer; que nous avons souvent, et dans le journal officiel et devant les chambres, repoussé hautement ses écarts, les infamies de certains journaux et surtout les attaques contre les princes étrangers; que nous avons même présenté et fait agréer une loi tendant à faciliter les poursuites judiciaires contre les auteurs, de ces excès, lois que la Belgique a imitées, dont on lui a su gré, et dont l'Autriche n'a pas voulu nous tenir compte.

D'ailleurs, il ne faut pas oublier que chez nous la presse est libre, que le gouvernement lui-même est en butte à des attaques incessantes, que la liberté de la presse est une condition des gouvernemens constitutionnels, qu'on ne peut y toucher qu'en touchant aux statuts que nous avons juré d'observer, et que ni le pouvoir exécutif ni les chambres ne seront disposés à y laisser porter atteinte; car la liberté pour nous, c'est l'independance, et nous l'acceptons avec ses avantages et ses inconvéniens.

M. de Buol nous reproche aussi d'avoir violé le traité d'extradition. L'extradition appliquée aux délits politiques n'est plus dans les mœurs actuelles; elle serait moins possible encore si on avait voulu l'appliquer à la révolution de 1848. Le traité de paix ayant gardé le silence sur ce point et fait revivre en masse les traités antérieurs, le chevalier d'Azéglio, interpellé à ce sujet dans la chambre élective, n'hésita pas à répondre que les prévenus de délits politiques devaient s'entendre exceptés. Il est bien vrai que l'Autriche, en demandant en 1050 l'extradition d'un compromis de ce genre, a soutenu que son gouvernement n'etait pas lié par la déclaration du chevalier d'Azéglio; mais elle n'a jamais protesté formellement. Elle n'a jamais dit que cette déclaration la mettait dans le cas de se refuser é l'exécution du traité. Bien plus, elle a cessé d'insister pour l'extradition des prévenus politiques du moment où le gouvernement du roi a laissé entrevoir qu'il ne serait pas éloigné de dénoncer, comme on lui en reconnaissait le droit, la convention de 1838, si l'on persistait à vouloir en appliquer les effets aux délinquans politiques. Comment peutelle maintenant nous accuser d'une omission qu'elle a acceptée au moins implicitement et sanctionnée par l'exécution donnée au traité?

En dernier lieu, M. de Buol établit trois catégories d'émigrés réfugiés en Piémont: la première, composée d'instrumens actifs qui savent manier le poignard; la seconde, de ceux qui les dirigent et les soudient; la troisième, *de ceux qui se tiennent sur une prudent réserve, et attendent avec calme si les tentatives des enfans perdus de la révolution aboutissent ou non à un événement favorable.*

Le gouvernement impérial déclare qu'ils sont tous solidaires. Nous n'avons pas besoin de réfuter cette nouvelle et étrange espèce de solidarité.

[*870] En admettant pour un moment l'hypothèse des trois catégories, *ce sont spécialement les prudens et les calmes qui ne soudoient pas, qui ne dirigent pas les révolutionnaires, que l'Autriche a frappés. Comment M. le comte de Buol peut-il leur imputer à crime cette conduite?

Parmi ces hommes prudens et calmes, plusieurs sont à présent des étrangers pour l'Autriche et ont acquis une autre patrie.

L'acte de séquestre et de confiscation dont il s'agit a éte dernièrement qualifié par l'Autriche de mesure de précaution et d'acte provisoire; mais d'abord cette manière de l'envisager est en opposition directe avec la lettre et l'esprit de la proclamation du séquestre, et surtout des dispositions administratives subséquentes, qui, bien loin d'en atténuer les effets, les ont, au contraire, aggravés. Que dirons-nous, au reste, d'une mesure dé précaution qui enlève les moyens d'existence à toute une catégorie, non d'accusés, mais de suspects, d'une mesure provisoire dont le terme est indéfini, dont ceux qui en sont les victimes, sans que leur culpabilité soit, nous ne dirons pas établie, mais au moins spécifiquement indiquée, ne pourront être délivrés qu'en prouvant leur innocence? Et comment prouveront-ils leur innocence, puisque l'acte d'accusation et les argumens dont on l'étaie ne leur sont pas signifiés? . . . .

Cette nouvelle manière d'envisager la question peut être polie, mais elle n'est certes pas sérieuse. Nous nous bornerons donc à répéter que, s'il résulte, par enquête judiciaire, pour l'Autriche, que quelque citoyen Piémontais, ancien ou nouveau, se soit rendu complice d'un crime public ou privé au préjudice de cette puissance, que les tribunaux le jugent selon la rigueur des lois; nous n'interviendrons pas en sa faveur.

Ce que nous ne pouvons tolérer sans forfaire à l'honneur, sans manquer au devoir le plus sacré, c'est que, sur de simples suppositions, l'autorité politique Autrichienne se permette de violer les droits les mieux établis et les plus incontestables, en frappant de séquestre les biens de tant de familles qui ont cessé d'être émigrées et dont les membres sont devenus, d'après les dois des deux pays, sujets Sardes.

C'est un grave attentat, sur lequel mous faisons appel à la conscience mieux informée du cabinet de Vienne, sur lequel nous invoquons les bons offices des souverains alliés et amis.

INDEX.

The pages referred to are those between brackets [ ].

B.

D.

F.

G.

H.

I.

N.

O.

P.

S.

T.

W.

Z.

END OF THE THIRD VOLUME.

I. Form and obligation generally.

(a) What is a Bill of Exchange.

Instrument drawn payable on a contingency, not a bill. Palmer *v.* Pratt, ix. 538; 2 Bing. 185. Ralli *v.* Sarell, xvi. 422; 1 D. & R. 33.

Instrument treated as a bill, where an obviously supplied omission is made. Phipps *v.* Tanner, xxiv. 669; 5 C. & P. 488.

An order to pay money "provided certain terms are complied with," not available as a bill. Kingston *v.* Long, xxvi. 308; 4 Doug. 9.

The order of time in which the names of the drawer and acceptor of a bill are placed upon it is immaterial. Molloy *v.* Delves, xix. 617; 4 C. & P. 492. S. C. xx. 194; 7 Bing. 428.

Bill may be accepted and indorsed, before drawn. Schultz *v.* Astley, xxix. 655; 2 B. N. C. 544.

But a blank acceptance for a certain sum, altered by the drawer before drawing into a smaller sum, is not a drawing of the bill for the sum expressed in the acceptance. Baker *v.* Jubber, xxxix. 724; 1 M. & G. 212.

Words "value received" not essential to constitute a bill of exchange. White *v.* Ledwick, xxvi. 454; 4 Doug. 247.

A paper containing a request for the payment of money, but not purporting to be made by one having a right to call on the other to pay, is not a bill of exchange. Little *v.* Slackford, xxii. 498; 1 M. & M. 171.

There must be a drawer to a bill. Vyse *v.* Clarke, xxiv. 626; 5 C. & P. 403.

Instrument drawn, payable to drawer or order at a particular place, without being addressed to any person by name, if afterwards accepted by one at the place where made payable, may be declared upon as a bill of exchange. Gray *v.* Milner, iv. 361; 8 Taun. 739.

Bill at sight is not a bill payable on demand, within exception in stat. 22 G. 3, c. 49. Janson *v.* Thomas, xxvi. 276; 3 Doug. 421.

Drawn payable ninety days after sight or when realized is not a bill within custom of merchants. Alexander *v.* Thomas, lxxi. 332; 16 Q. B. 333.

Acceptance in blank for drawer and payee's name not a bill. Stoessiger *v.* Railway, lxxvii. 548; 3 E. & B. 549.

"Fifty-three days after date credit A. or order 500*l.* in cash on account of," signed by managing director of company, is a bill of exchange. Ellison *v.* Collingridge, lxvii.; 9 C. B. 570.

Dividend warrant not negotiable. Partridge *v.* Bank, lviii. 396; 9 Q. B. 396.

Exchequer bills are negotiable passing by delivery. Brandao *v.* Barnett, liv. 518; 3 C. B. 519.

Statement of deposit of leases as security in the body of the note does not affect its negotiability. Fancourt *v.* Thorne, lviii. 310; 9 Q. B. 311.

Instrument in form of note with address in the corner and accepted by that party, may be treated as his acceptance or the note of the drawer. Lloyd *v.* Oliver, lxxxiii.; 18 Q. B. 471.

(b) What is a Promissory Note.

Not necessary that a promissory note should be in itself negotiable. Rex *v.* Box, i. 635; 6 Taun. 325.

It is sufficient that it is a note for the certain payment of a sum of money, whether negotiable or not. Ibid.

www.ingramcontent.com/pod-product-compliance
Lightning Source LLC
LaVergne TN
LVHW021054110826
845150LV00001B/69

* 9 7 8 1 4 2 5 5 6 7 2 5 5 *